Mathematica®

A System for Doing Mathematics by Computer

Second Edition

Stephen Wolfram

Mathematica®

A System for Doing Mathematics by Computer

Second Edition

Addison-Wesley Publishing Company, Inc.

The Advanced Book Program

Redwood City, California • Menlo Park, California • Reading, Massachusetts • New York • Don Mills, Ontario •
Wokingham, United Kingdom • Amsterdam • Bonn • Sydney • Singapore • Tokyo • Madrid • San Juan

Library of Congress Cataloging-in-Publication Data

Wolfram, Stephen, 1959–
    Mathematica: a system for doing mathematics by computer / Stephen Wolfram
    2nd ed.
    p.   cm.
    Includes index.
    ISBN 0-201-51502-4; 0-201-51507-5 (pbk).
    1. Mathematica (Computer program) 2. Mathematics–Data processing.
  I. Title.
  QA76.95.W65 1991
  510'.285'53—dc20

91-46832
CIP

For information on *Mathematica*, contact:

Wolfram Research, Inc.
100 Trade Center Drive
Champaign, Illinois 61820-7237, USA
telephone: 217-398-0700
fax: 217-398-0747
email: `info@wri.com`

ABCDEFGHIJ-DO-943210

About the Author

Stephen Wolfram is president and founder of Wolfram Research, Inc., the company that developed *Mathematica*. Wolfram was the principal architect of the *Mathematica* system, and was responsible for a significant part of its implementation.

Born in London in 1959, Wolfram was educated at Eton, Oxford and Caltech. He received a Ph.D. in theoretical physics from Caltech in 1979. After two years on the faculty at Caltech and four years at the Institute for Advanced Study in Princeton, Wolfram moved to the University of Illinois, to become Director of the Center for Complex Systems Research, and Professor of Physics, Mathematics and Computer Science. He founded Wolfram Research in 1987. Wolfram received a MacArthur Prize Fellowship in 1981.

Wolfram's scientific contributions have spanned a number of areas. His early research (1976–1980) was primarily in high-energy physics, quantum field theory and cosmology. In 1980–1981, Wolfram led the development of the SMP computer algebra system, a forerunner of some elements of *Mathematica*.

In 1982, Wolfram started work on the major project of understanding the mechanisms by which complex behavior arises in a wide variety of natural and artificial systems. Wolfram pioneered the use of computational models known as cellular automata to study the origins of complexity in systems whose component parts are simple. His research has found applications in many areas, from physical and biological pattern formation, to chaos theory and massively parallel computation. In 1984, Wolfram invented a fast encryption scheme based on cellular automata, and in 1985, he was co-inventor of a new approach to computational fluid dynamics. Wolfram's work laid an important part of the groundwork for the burgeoning new field of complex systems research. In 1986, Wolfram founded *Complex Systems*, the primary journal in the field.

Wolfram continues his work on the development of *Mathematica*, as well as on the science of complex systems.

About *Mathematica*

Mathematica is a general software system for mathematical and other applications. It is currently used by many tens of thousands of researchers, engineers and analysts, as well as students from high school to graduate school. The applications of *Mathematica* span all areas of science, technology and business where quantitative methods are used.

Mathematica Version 1 was announced on June 23, 1988, and was immediately acclaimed as a major advance in the technology of mathematics. *Mathematica* has received many industry awards. It was ranked among the 10 best new products of 1988 in all categories by *Business Week* magazine.

A version of *Mathematica* for the Apple Macintosh was first released in June 1988. Versions for various workstations followed, and in January 1989 a version for 386-based IBM PC compatibles was released. As of the end of 1990, versions of *Mathematica* are available for a wide variety of computer systems, including: Apple Macintosh, CONVEX, DEC VAX (Ultrix and VMS) and RISC, Hewlett-Packard/Apollo, IBM 386-based PC compatibles (MS-DOS and Microsoft Windows) and IBM RISC, MIPS, NeXT, Silicon Graphics, Sony and Sun (and SPARC compatibles). *Mathematica* Version 2, as described in this book, was first released in January 1991.

Mathematica is available both directly from Wolfram Research, and from dealers and distributors worldwide. *Mathematica* is also included as standard software on certain computer systems. Wolfram Research, Inc. is a privately held company based in Champaign, Illinois. As of 1990, it has approximately 100 employees.

Table of Contents

Tour of *Mathematica*

Part 1. A Practical Introduction to *Mathematica*

Part 2. Principles of *Mathematica*

Part 3. Advanced Mathematics in *Mathematica*

Appendix. *Mathematica* Reference Guide

What Is *Mathematica*?

Mathematica is a general computer software system and language intended for mathematical and other applications.

You can use *Mathematica* as:

- A **numerical** and **symbolic calculator** where you type in questions, and *Mathematica* prints out answers.

- A **visualization system** for functions and data.

- A high-level **programming language** in which you can create programs, large and small.

- A **modeling** and **data analysis** environment.

- A system for **representing knowledge** in scientific and technical fields.

- A **software platform** on which you can run packages built for specific applications.

- A way to create **interactive documents** that mix text, animated graphics and sound with active formulas.

- A **control language** for external programs and processes.

- An **embedded system** called from within other programs.

Mathematical computations can be divided into three main classes: **numerical**, **symbolic** and **graphical**. *Mathematica* handles these three classes in a unified way.

Mathematica uses symbolic expressions to provide a very general representation of mathematical and other structures. The generality of symbolic expressions allows *Mathematica* to cover a wide variety of applications with a fairly small number of methods from mathematics and computer science.

The simplest way to use *Mathematica* is like a calculator. You type in a calculation, and *Mathematica* prints back the answer. The range of calculations that you can do with *Mathematica* is however far greater than with a traditional electronic calculator, or, for that matter, with a traditional programming language such as Fortran or BASIC. Thus, for example, while a traditional system might support perhaps 30 mathematical operations, *Mathematica* has over 750 built in. In addition, while traditional systems handle only numerical computations, *Mathematica* also handles symbolic and graphical computations.

Here are some simple examples. Each one consists of a short "dialog" with *Mathematica*. The text on the lines labeled *In[n]:=* is what you type in; the lines labeled *Out[n]=* are what *Mathematica* prints back. The "Tour of *Mathematica*" on page 1 gives more examples.

■ Numerical Computation

Example: Find the numerical value of $\log(4\pi)$.

Log[4 Pi] is the *Mathematica* version of $\log(4\pi)$. The N tells *Mathematica* that you want a numerical result.

```
In[1]:= N[ Log[ 4 Pi ] ]
Out[1]= 2.53102
```

Here is $\log(4\pi)$ to 40 decimal places.

```
In[2]:= N[ Log[ 4 Pi ], 40 ]
Out[2]= 2.531024246969290792977891594269411847798
```

Whereas a traditional calculator or numerical computation system handles numbers only to fixed degree of precision, *Mathematica* can handle numbers of any precision. In addition, *Mathematica* includes a full range of higher mathematical functions, from elliptic integrals and complex Bessel functions to hypergeometric functions and integer factorization.

Mathematica can do numerical computations not only with individual numbers, but also with objects such as matrices. It supports linear algebra operations such as matrix inversion and eigensystem computation. *Mathematica* can handle numerical data, allowing you to do statistical and other analysis, as well as performing operations such as Fourier transforms, interpolation and least-square fitting.

Mathematica can do numerical operations on functions, such as numerical integration, numerical minimization, and linear programming. It can also generate numerical solutions to both algebraic equations and ordinary differential equations.

■ Symbolic Computation

Example: Find a formula for the integral $\int x^4/(x^2-1)\,dx$.

Here is the expression $x^4/(x^2-1)$ in *Mathematica*.

```
In[1]:= x^4 / (x^2 - 1)
```

$$Out[1]= \frac{x^4}{-1 + x^2}$$

This tells *Mathematica* to integrate the previous expression. *Mathematica* finds an explicit formula for the integral.

```
In[2]:= Integrate[%, x]
```

$$Out[2]= x + \frac{x^3}{3} + \frac{\text{Log}[-1 + x]}{2} - \frac{\text{Log}[1 + x]}{2}$$

One major class of calculations made possible by *Mathematica*'s symbolic computation capabilities is those involving the manipulation of algebraic formulas. *Mathematica* can do many kinds of algebraic operations. It can expand, factor and simplify polynomials and rational expressions. It can find algebraic solutions to polynomial equations and systems of equations.

Mathematica can also do calculus. It can evaluate derivatives and integrals symbolically and find symbolic solutions to ordinary differential equations. It can derive and manipulate power series approximations, and find limits. Standard *Mathematica* packages cover areas such as vector analysis and Laplace transforms.

■ Graphics

Example: Plot the function sin(xy) *for* x *and* y *between* 0 *and* π.

This generates a three-dimensional plot of sin(xy) as a function of x and y. There are many options for controlling graphics in *Mathematica*.

`In[1]:= Plot3D[ Sin[x y], {x, 0, Pi}, {y, 0, Pi} ]`

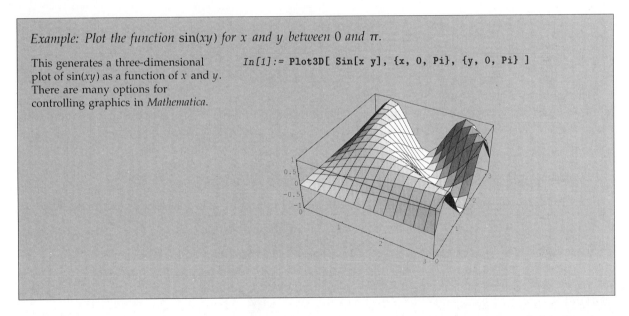

Mathematica produces both two- and three-dimensional graphics, as well as contour and density plots. You can plot both functions and lists of data. *Mathematica* provides many options for controlling the details of graphics output. In three dimensions, for example, you can control shading, color, lighting, surface shininess and other parameters. Many versions of *Mathematica* also support animated graphics.

Mathematica incorporates a graphics language, in which you can give symbolic representations of geometrical objects using primitives such as polygons, then render the objects graphically. All graphics produced by *Mathematica* are in standard PostScript, and can be transferred to a wide variety of other programs.

■ The *Mathematica* Language

In addition to having a large number of built-in functions, *Mathematica* also includes a full programming language, which allows you to add your own extensions to the system.

Mathematica is a high-level programming language, in which you can write programs, both large and small. The fact that *Mathematica* is an interactive system means that you can run your programs as soon as you have typed them in.

Example: Define a function to generate a list of primes.

This defines a function **f** which makes a table of the first *n* prime numbers.

```
In[1]:= f[n_] := Table[Prime[i], {i, n}]
```

You can use the definition of *f* immediately. Here is a table of the first 10 prime numbers.

```
In[2]:= f[10]

Out[2]= {2, 3, 5, 7, 11, 13, 17, 19, 23, 29}
```

Mathematica programs can make use of the symbolic aspects of *Mathematica*. They can create and manipulate arbitrary symbolic data structures. *Mathematica* programs themselves are also symbolic expressions, and can be combined and manipulated using standard *Mathematica* operations.

Mathematica supports several programming styles, including:

- *Procedural programming*, with block structure, conditionals, iteration and recursion.

- *Functional programming*, with pure functions, functional operators and program-structure operations.

- *Rule-based programming*, with pattern matching and object orientation.

Fundamental to much of *Mathematica* is the notion of transformation rules, which specify how symbolic expressions of one form should be transformed into expressions of another form. Transformations are a very general and natural way to represent many kinds of information, particularly mathematical relations.

Using transformation rules you can, for example, transcribe almost directly into *Mathematica* the kind of material that appears in tables of mathematical formulas.

Example: Define your own logarithm function in Mathematica.

Mathematical form	Mathematica form
$\log(1) = 0$	`log[1] = 0`
$\log(e) = 1$	`log[E] = 1`
$\log(xy) = \log(x) + \log(y)$	`log[x_ y_] := log[x] + log[y]`
$\log(x^n) = n\log(x)$	`log[x_^n_] := n log[x]`

■ *Mathematica* Interfaces

Many *Mathematica* systems are divided into two parts: the kernel, which actually performs computations, and the front end, which handles interaction with the user. The kernel works the same on all computers that run *Mathematica*. The front end, on the other hand, is optimized for particular computers and graphical user interfaces.

On many computers, the front end for *Mathematica* supports sophisticated interactive documents called *notebooks*. These consist of text arranged in a hierarchical way, together with graphics that can be animated, and *Mathematica* expressions that can be used for actual *Mathematica* computations. With notebooks, you can create pedagogical and other material that both explains and performs computations.

Mathematica follows many software standards that allow it to exchange material with other programs. Thus, for example, *Mathematica* graphics are represented in PostScript, so that they can be exchanged with desktop publishing and other programs. In addition, *Mathematica* can read data in various formats, and can generate output for systems such as C, Fortran and TEX.

Mathematica can communicate at a high level with other programs using the *MathLink* communication standard. Many kinds of programs can be adapted to be *MathLink* compatible, so that they can exchange data and commands with *Mathematica*. The standard *Mathematica* front end, for example, can use *MathLink* to communicate with the kernel. The communication can be done both within a single computer, and across a network between different computers.

With *MathLink*, you can use *Mathematica* to control external programs. You can prepare input and commands using the *Mathematica* language, then send these to an external program via *MathLink*. You can then get results back into *Mathematica* for analysis or display.

You can also use *MathLink* to create programs that call *Mathematica* as if it were a subroutine. In this way, you can set up your own complete front end or control system for *Mathematica*.

About This Book

■ The Scope of This Book

This book is intended to be a complete introduction to *Mathematica*. The book describes essentially all the capabilities of *Mathematica*, and assumes no prior knowledge of the system.

In most uses of *Mathematica*, you will need to know only a small part of the system. This book is organized to make it easy for you to learn the part you need for a particular calculation. In many cases, for example, you may be able to set up your calculation simply by adapting some appropriate examples from the book.

You should understand, however, that the examples in this book are chosen primarily for their simplicity, rather than to correspond to realistic calculations in particular application areas.

There are other publications, some mentioned below, that discuss *Mathematica* from the viewpoint of particular classes of applications. In some cases, you may find it better to read one of those publications first, and read this book only when you need a more general perspective on *Mathematica*.

Mathematica is a system built on a fairly small set of very powerful principles. This book describes those principles, but by no means spells out all of their implications. In particular, while the book describes the elements that go into *Mathematica* programs, it does not give detailed examples of complete programs. For those, you should look at other publications.

■ The *Mathematica* System Described in This Book

This book describes the standard *Mathematica* kernel, as it exists on all computers that run *Mathematica*. All supported features of the kernel in *Mathematica* Version 2 are covered in this book.

This book does not describe in detail aspects of *Mathematica* that differ from one computer system to another. To find out about these, you should read the documentation that came with your computer, or with your copy of *Mathematica*.

This book does not discuss issues such as how to install *Mathematica*, how to edit input for *Mathematica*, how to print your output, and other matters specific to particular computer systems.

Versions of *Mathematica* for systems such as the Macintosh and PC have special "front ends" which handle interaction with the user. These front ends allow you to prepare input for the *Mathematica* kernel. This book describes what the content of that input should be. It does not describe in detail how to prepare the input using the features of the front end.

Mathematica is an open software system that can be customized in a wide variety of ways. It is important to realize that this book covers only the basic *Mathematica* system. If your system is customized in some way, then it may behave differently from what is described in the book.

The most common form of customization is the addition of various *Mathematica* function definitions. These may come, for example, from loading a *Mathematica* package. Sometimes the definitions may actually modify the behavior of functions described in this book. In other cases, the definitions may simply add a collection of new functions that are not described in the book. In certain applications, it may be primarily these new functions that you use, rather than the standard ones described in the book.

This book describes what to do when you interact directly with the *Mathematica* kernel. Sometimes, however, you may not be using *Mathematica* directly. Instead, *Mathematica* may be an embedded component of another system that you are using. This system may for example call on *Mathematica* only for certain computations, and may hide the details of those computations from you. Most of what is in this book will only be useful if you can give explicit input to *Mathematica*. If all of your input is substantially modified by the system you are using, then you must rely on the documentation for that system.

This book covers user-level interaction with *Mathematica*. It does not go into the details of how programs can communicate with *Mathematica* using the *MathLink* communication standard.

■ The Parts of This Book

This book has several sections, which are intended to be used in somewhat different ways.

- **This Introduction**: A superficial sketch of *Mathematica*.

- **Tour of *Mathematica***: Sample sessions illustrating features of *Mathematica*.

- ***Mathematica* Graphics Gallery**: Examples of color graphics produced by *Mathematica*.

- **Part 1. A Practical Introduction to *Mathematica***: A tutorial treatment of the features of *Mathematica* needed in most calculations.

- **Part 2. The Principles of *Mathematica***: An exposition of the structure and principles of *Mathematica*, and its use as a language.

- **Part 3. Advanced Mathematics in *Mathematica***: A more complete discussion of the mathematical capabilities of *Mathematica*.

- **Appendix. *Mathematica* Reference Guide**: The definitive reference on *Mathematica*, including a list of all built-in *Mathematica* functions.

Most of Part 1 should be accessible to anyone with a high-school level knowledge of mathematics. It does not assume any prior experience with computers.

Part 2 assumes general familiarity with the concepts of computing, but requires almost no mathematical knowledge.

Part 3 is intended for those interested in using the more advanced mathematical features of *Mathematica*. Parts of it assume a knowledge of mathematics at an advanced college level.

The Appendix is intended for those who are already familiar with *Mathematica*. Even if you have used many other computer systems, you should probably start by looking at Parts 1 and 2, not at the Appendix.

■ How to Read This Book

If at all possible, you should read this book in conjunction with using an actual *Mathematica* system. When you see examples in the book, you should try them out on your computer.

You can get a basic feeling of what *Mathematica* does by looking at the "Tour of *Mathematica*" on page 1, and the "Graphics Gallery" that follows. You may find it useful to try out examples from the Tour with your own copy of *Mathematica*.

Whatever your background, you should make sure to look at the first three or four sections in Part 1 before you start to use *Mathematica* on your own. These sections describe the basics that you need to know in order to use *Mathematica* at any level.

The remainder of Part 1 shows you how to do many different kinds of computations with *Mathematica*. If you are trying to do a specific calculation, you will often find it sufficient just to look at the parts of Part 1 that discuss the features of *Mathematica* you need to use. A good approach is to try and find examples in the book which are close to what you want to do.

The emphasis in Part 1 is on using the basic functions that are built into *Mathematica* to carry out various different kinds of computations.

Part 2, on the other hand, discusses the basic structure and principles that underlie all of *Mathematica*. Rather than describing a sequence of specific features, Part 2 takes a more global approach. If you want to learn how to create your own *Mathematica* functions, you should read Part 2.

Part 3 is intended for those with more sophisticated mathematical interests and knowledge. It covers the more advanced mathematical features of *Mathematica*, as well as describing some features already mentioned in Part 1 in greater mathematical detail.

Each part of the book is divided into sections and subsections. There are two special kinds of subsections, indicated by the following headings:

- **Advanced Topic**: Advanced material which can be omitted on a first reading.

- **Special Topic**: Material which applies only to certain computer systems.

The main parts in this book are intended to be pedagogical, and can meaningfully be read in a sequential fashion. The Appendix, however, is intended solely for reference purposes. Once you are familiar with *Mathematica*, you will probably find the list of functions in the Appendix the best place to look up details you need.

■ About the Examples in This Book

All the examples given in this book were generated by running an actual copy of *Mathematica* Version 2. If you have a copy of this version, you should be able to reproduce the examples on your computer as they appear in the book.

There are, however, a few points to watch:

■ Until you are familiar with *Mathematica*, make sure to type the input *exactly* as it appears in the book. Do not change any of the capital letters or brackets. Later, you will learn what things you can change. When you start out, however, it is important that you do not make any changes; otherwise you may not get the same results as in the book.

■ Never type the prompt `In[n]:=` that begins each input line. Type only the text that follows this prompt.

■ You will see that the lines in each dialog are numbered in sequence. Most subsections in the book contain separate dialogs. To make sure you get exactly what the book says, you should start a new *Mathematica* session each time the book does.

■ "Special Topic" subsections give examples that may be specific to particular computer systems.

■ On computer systems where memory is scarce, *Mathematica* may be set up to ask you to load necessary files when you try to use certain functions.

■ Any examples that involve random numbers will generally give different results than in the book, since the sequence of random numbers produced by *Mathematica* is different in every session.

■ Some examples that use machine-precision arithmetic may come out differently on different computer systems. This is a result of differences in floating-point hardware. If you use arbitrary-precision *Mathematica* numbers, you should not see differences.

■ Almost all of the examples in this book assume that your computer or terminal uses a standard U.S. ASCII character set. If you cannot find some of the characters you need on your keyboard, or if *Mathematica* prints out different characters than you see in the book, you will need to look at your computer documentation to find the correspondence with the character set you are using. The most common problem is that the dollar sign character (SHIFT-4) may come out as your local currency character.

■ If the version of *Mathematica* is more recent than the one used to produce this book, then it is possible that some results you get may be different.

■ Most of the examples in the "Tour of *Mathematica*", as well as Parts 1 and 2, are chosen so as to be fairly quick to execute. Assuming you have a machine with a clock speed of over about 16 MHz (and most machines produced in 1989 or later do), then few of the examples should take more than a minute or so. If they do, there is probably something wrong. Section 1.3.7 describes how to stop the calculation.

■ Suggestions about Learning *Mathematica*

As with any other computer system, there are a few points that you need to get straight before you can even start using *Mathematica*. For example, you absolutely must know how to type your input to *Mathematica*. To find out these kinds of basic points, you should read at least the first section of Part 1 in this book.

Once you know the basics, you can begin to get a feeling for *Mathematica* by typing in some examples from this book. Always be sure that you type in exactly what appears in the book – do not change any capitalization, bracketing, etc.

After you have tried a few examples from the book, you should start experimenting for yourself. Change the examples slightly, and see what happens. You should look at each piece of output carefully, and try to understand why it came out as it did.

After you have run through some simple examples, you should be ready to take the next step: learning to go through what is needed to solve a complete problem with *Mathematica*.

You will probably find it best to start by picking a specific problem to work on. Pick a problem that you understand well – preferably one whose solution you could easily reproduce by hand. Then go through each step in solving the problem, learning what you need to know about *Mathematica* to do it. Always be ready to experiment with simple cases, and understand the results you get with these, before going back to your original problem.

In going through the steps to solve your problem, you will learn about various specific features of *Mathematica*, typically from parts of Part 1. After you have done a few problems with *Mathematica*, you should get a feeling for many of the basic features of the system.

When you have built up a reasonable knowledge of the features of *Mathematica*, you should go back and learn about the overall structure of the *Mathematica* system. You can do this by systematically reading Part 2 of this book. What you will discover is that many of the features that seemed unrelated actually fit together into a coherent overall structure. Knowing this structure will make it much easier for you to understand and remember the specific features you have already learned.

You should not try to learn the overall structure of *Mathematica* too early. Unless you have had broad experience with advanced computer languages or pure mathematics, you will probably find Part 2 difficult to understand at first. You will find the structure and principles it describes difficult to remember, and you will always be wondering why particular aspects of them might be useful. However, if you first get some practical experience with *Mathematica*, you will find the overall structure much easier to grasp. You should realize that the principles on which *Mathematica* is built are very general, and it is usually difficult to understand such general principles before you have seen specific examples.

One of the most important aspects of *Mathematica* is that it applies a fairly small number of principles as widely as possible. This means that even though you have used a particular feature only in a specific situation, the principle on which that feature is based can probably be applied in many other situations. One reason it is so important to understand the underlying principles of *Mathematica* is that by doing so you can leverage your knowledge of specific features into a more general context. As an example, you may first learn about transformation rules in the context of algebraic expressions. But the basic principle of transformation rules applies to any symbolic expression. Thus you can also use such rules to modify the structure of, say, an expression that represents a *Mathematica* graphics object.

Learning to use *Mathematica* well involves changing the way you solve problems. The balance of what aspects of problem solving are difficult changes when you move from pencil and paper to *Mathematica*. With pencil and paper, you can often get by with a fairly imprecise initial formulation of your problem. Then when you actually do calculations in solving the problem, you can usually fix up the formulation as you go along. However, the calculations you do have to be fairly simple, and you cannot afford to try out many different cases.

When you use *Mathematica*, on the other hand, the initial formulation of your problem has to be quite precise. However, once you have the formulation, you can easily do many different calculations with it. This means that you can effectively carry out many mathematical experiments on your problem. By looking at the results you get, you can then refine the original formulation of your problem.

There are typically many different ways to formulate a given problem in *Mathematica*. In almost all cases, however, the most direct and simple formulations will be best. The more you can formulate your problem in *Mathematica* from the beginning, the better. Often, in fact, you will find that formulating your problem directly in *Mathematica* is better than first trying to set up a traditional mathematical formulation, say an algebraic one. The main point is that *Mathematica* allows you to express not only traditional mathematical operations, but also algorithmic and structural ones. This greater range of possibilities gives you a better chance of being able to find a direct way to represent your original problem.

For most of the more sophisticated problems that you want to solve with *Mathematica*, you will have to create *Mathematica* programs. *Mathematica* supports several types of programming, and you have to choose which one to use in each case. It turns out that no single type of programming suits all cases well. As a result, it is very important that you learn several different types of programming.

If you already know a traditional programming language such as BASIC, C, Fortran or Pascal, you will probably find it easiest to learn procedural programming in *Mathematica*, using Do, For and so on. But while almost any *Mathematica* program can, in principle, be written in a procedural way, this is rarely the best approach. In a symbolic system like *Mathematica*, functional and rule-based programming typically yield programs that are more efficient, and easier to understand.

If you find yourself using procedural programming a lot, you should make an active effort to convert at least some of your programs to other types. At first, you may find functional and rule-based programs difficult to understand. But after a while, you will find that their global structure is usually much easier to grasp than procedural programs. And as your experience with *Mathematica* grows over a period of months or years, you will probably find that you write more and more of your programs in non-procedural ways.

As you proceed in using and learning *Mathematica*, it is important to remember that *Mathematica* is a large system. Although after a while you should know all of its basic principles, you may never learn the details of all its features. As a result, even after you have had a great deal of experience with *Mathematica*, you will undoubtedly still find it useful to look through this book. When you do so, you are quite likely to notice features that you never noticed before, but that with your experience, you can now see how to use.

■ What Else to Read

There is much to be said about *Mathematica*, and only a very small part of it is said in this book.

Every copy of *Mathematica* should come with some additional material, particularly information on setting up and using *Mathematica* on your particular computer system.

Beyond what comes with each copy of *Mathematica*, there are now many other publications related to *Mathematica* available.

Some of the books about *Mathematica* that have appeared so far are:

■ Roman Maeder: *Programming in Mathematica* (Addison-Wesley, 1989). A general introduction to *Mathematica* programming.

■ Wade Ellis and Ed Lodi: *A Tutorial Introduction to Mathematica* (Brooks/Cole, 1990). An elementary introduction to *Mathematica*.

■ Richard Crandall: *Mathematica for the Sciences* (Addison-Wesley, 1990). Examples of using *Mathematica* in many areas of science.

■ Stan Wagon: *Mathematica in Action* (W.H. Freeman, 1990). Examples of using *Mathematica* in mathematics.

■ Theodore Gray and Jerry Glynn: *Exploring Mathematics with Mathematica* (Addison-Wesley, 1990). Examples of using *Mathematica* in mathematics.

■ Cameron Smith: *The Mathematica Graphics Guidebook* (Addison-Wesley, 1990). A guide to creating graphics in *Mathematica*.

■ Ilan Vardi: *Mathematica Recreations* (Addison-Wesley, 1990). Examples of using *Mathematica* in recreational mathematics.

■ Steven Skiena: *Implementing Discrete Mathematics: Combinatorics and Graph Theory with Mathematica* (Addison-Wesley, 1990). *Mathematica* programs for discrete mathematics.

■ Donald Brown, Horacio Porta and Jerry Uhl: *Calculus&Mathematica* (Preliminary edition: Addison-Wesley, 1990). A calculus course based on *Mathematica*.

Important ongoing sources of information about *Mathematica* include:

■ *The Mathematica Journal*, published by Addison-Wesley. The journal includes news and articles about uses of *Mathematica*, and an electronic supplement containing actual *Mathematica* packages and notebooks.

■ The *Mathematica Conference*. An annual conference with lectures, tutorials, exhibits and other events.

■ *Mathematica* User Groups. A variety of groups exist to serve the needs of users in particular geographical and subject areas.

■ Changes since the First Edition

While the basic structure of this book is the same as in the first edition, almost all of it has been rewritten.

The most important change in content is the addition of a large amount of material associated with Version 2 of *Mathematica*.

Functions that were added in Version 2 are indicated by ■ in the listing of built-in objects given in the Appendix. Of the 843 objects listed in the Appendix, 284 of them are new.

For the most part, the changes made in Version 2 are purely additions. There are, however, a number of objects from Version 1 which are considered obsolete in Version 2. These include:

■ Accumulate (superseded by FoldList).

■ Alias (essentially superseded by $PreRead).

■ CellArray (superseded by Raster and RasterArray).

■ Compose (superseded by Composition).

■ Debug (superseded by Trace and related functions).

■ ContourLevels and ContourSpacing (superseded by Contours).

■ Framed (superseded by Frame and related options).

■ FromASCII (superseded by FromCharacterCode).

■ Plot3Matrix (superseded by ViewCenter and ViewVertical).

■ Release (split into Evaluate and ReleaseHold).

■ ResetMedium (folded into SetOptions).

■ StartProcess (superseded by Install).

■ ToASCII (superseded by ToCharacterCode).

■ $$Media (superseded by Streams).

The scoping construct Block, while still supported in Version 2, is less appropriate than the new construct Module for most applications.

Among the functions which existed in Version 1 but whose operation has changed significantly in Version 2 are:

■ Condition (/;) (now used in patterns as well as rules).

■ FontForm (now takes a different form of font specification).

- `Limit` (now remains unevaluated if it encounters an unknown function).

- `Mod` (now handles only numbers; `PolynomialMod` handles polynomials).

- `PostScript` (now represents raw PostScript code).

- `Power` (no longer automatically simplifies, *e.g.*, `Sqrt[x^2]`).

More detailed information on changes made between Versions 1 and 2 of *Mathematica* is given in the Wolfram Research technical report "Major New Features in Version 2.0".

To keep this book to a manageable size, some elements present in the first edition are not included in this edition. In particular, the chapter on *Mathematica* as a programming language has been dropped, as well as the appendix giving examples of *Mathematica* packages. There are now other publications which adequately cover these areas.

■ About the Production of This Book

The production of this book, from textual source to printed film, was handled entirely by computer. The original source form of the book contained text, together with *Mathematica* input for each sample session. The first step in producing the book was to run the *Mathematica* input through an actual *Mathematica* system, thereby generating the *Mathematica* output that is given.

The book was typeset using the TEX typesetting system, with approximately 5000 lines of special macros. The fonts used in the book include Palatino, Univers, Computer Modern Typewriter (with modifications) and Lucida Math, as well as the JTEX Kanji font.

The output from TEX was converted into the PostScript page description language, where graphics were added directly from *Mathematica* in PostScript form. The resulting material was then output on a phototypesetter at a resolution of 2750 dots per inch.

Color graphics were produced directly from color PostScript generated by *Mathematica*. Final color-separated images were output on a Scitex pre-press system.

Acknowledgments

The kernel of *Mathematica* Version 2 is approximately one-third of a million lines of source code.

The main individuals responsible for this code were:

- Arkady Borkovsky: Text manipulation and streams.
- Henry Cejtin: *MathLink*.
- Matthew Cook: Sound and various system functions.
- Jerry Keiper: Numerical functions.
- Roman Maeder: Polynomial manipulation, including factoring and GCD.
- Igor Rivin: 3D graphics, symbolic differential equations, etc.
- Kelly Roach: Symbolic integration and trigonometric simplification.
- Bruce K. Smith: Language features such as `Trace` and scoping constructs.
- Hon Wah Tam: Numerical differential equations.
- Tom Wickham-Jones: Graphics.
- David Withoff: System messages, statistical functions, etc.
- Stephen Wolfram: Overall system design and implementation of various features.

Version 1.0 of *Mathematica* contained code by David Ballman, Henry Cejtin, Daniel Grayson, Jerry Keiper, Roman Maeder, Stephen Omohundro and Stephen Wolfram.

Contributors of packages for Version 2 included: Paul Abbott, Michael Chan, Kevin McIsaac, Cameron Smith, Ilan Vardi and Eran Yehudai, as well as the individuals responsible for the code of Version 2.

The notebook front end for *Mathematica* on the Macintosh and NeXT computer was created by Theodore Gray, with help from Doug Stein.

The notebook front end under Microsoft Windows was written by Tom Sherlock, with help from Harold Barker, Paul Katula and Bo Liu.

Ports of *Mathematica* to other systems were done by Kate Ebneter (VMS) and Rory Murtagh (Unix), with Al Chang, Simon Damberger, Scott Midler and Monte Seyer.

In-house testers for *Mathematica* Version 2 included: Paul Abbott, Peter Altenberg, Rob Brewer, Martin Buchholz, Larry Calmer, Ben Cox, Janet Downen, Kate Ebneter, Mike Evans, Jack Gidding, Jeffrey Lanter, Matthew Markert, Emily Martin, Scott May, Kevin McIsaac, John Novak, Greg Seibel, Shawn Sheridan and Erik Winfree.

Beyond code development, a host of other activities were needed to create *Mathematica* Version 2. In fact, nearly all of the 100 or so current employees of Wolfram Research, Inc. have been involved in one way or another in the creation of *Mathematica* Version 2.

The creation of this book involved many people from Wolfram Research and Addison-Wesley. At Wolfram Research, John Bonadies was responsible for the design of the book. Sue Ann Kendall supervised the editorial and typesetting work. Frances Brodt and Peter Altenberg did layout; Joe Kaiping developed TEX macros. Jan Progen and Jerry Walsh did copyediting. Images for the graphics gallery were rendered by Peter Altenberg and Arun Chandra; color separations were done by John Herzig of Barcode Graphics (Toronto). At Addison-Wesley, Allan Wylde was the publisher responsible for the project, Jan Benes was in charge of production, and Laura Likely coordinated marketing.

The continued development of *Mathematica* owes most to the support of the users of *Mathematica*. Many users have contributed comments and suggestions which helped to shape *Mathematica* Version 2. Almost as important in the continued development of *Mathematica* has been the involvement of many computer companies, including: Apple Computer, CONVEX, Data General, Digital Equipment Corporation, Hewlett-Packard/Apollo, IBM, MIPS, NeXT Computer, Silicon Graphics, Sony and Sun Microsystems.

The original idea of developing *Mathematica* came from a suggestion by Debra Lewis. The name "*Mathematica*" was proposed by Steven Jobs.

The algorithms used in *Mathematica* are based on work done by a great many mathematicians and computer scientists. Beyond their published work, many of these individuals have contributed specific suggestions for *Mathematica*.

Tour of *Mathematica*

1. Numerical Calculations

You can do arithmetic with *Mathematica* just as you would on a calculator. You type the input 5 + 7; *Mathematica* prints the result 12.

```
In[1]:= 5 + 7
Out[1]= 12
```

Unlike a calculator, however, *Mathematica* can give you *exact* results. Here is the exact result for 3^{100}. The ^ is the *Mathematica* notation for raising to a power.

```
In[2]:= 3 ^ 100
Out[2]= 515377520732011331036461129765621272702107522001
```

You can use the *Mathematica* function N to get approximate numerical results. The % stands for the last result. The answer is given in scientific notation.

```
In[3]:= N[%]
Out[3]= 5.15378 10
```
$$Out[3]= 5.15378 \times 10^{47}$$

You can find numerical results to any degree of precision. This calculates $\sqrt{10}$ to 50 digits of precision.

```
In[4]:= N[ Sqrt[10], 50 ]
Out[4]= 3.1622776601683793319988935444327185337195551393252
```

Mathematica can also handle complex numbers. Here is $(3 + 4i)^{10}$. In *Mathematica*, I stands for the imaginary number $\sqrt{-1}$.

```
In[5]:= (3 + 4 I) ^ 10
Out[5]= -9653287 + 1476984 I
```

Mathematica can evaluate all standard mathematical functions. Here is the value of the Bessel function $J_0(14.5)$.

```
In[6]:= BesselJ[0, 14.5]
Out[6]= 0.0875449
```

Here is a root of $J_0(x)$ near $x = 14.5$.

```
In[7]:= FindRoot[BesselJ[0, x], {x, 14.5}]
Out[7]= {x -> 14.9309}
```

You can calculate mathematical functions to any precision. This gives the Riemann zeta function $\zeta(\frac{1}{2} + 13i)$ to 40 digits of precision.

```
In[8]:= N[ Zeta[ 1/2 + 13 I ], 40 ]
Out[8]= 0.4430047825053681891978974413328491262 6 -
    0.6554830983211689430513696491913355062 2 I
```

You can do numerical integrals. Here is the numerical value of $\int_0^\pi \sin(\sin(x))dx$.

```
In[9]:= NIntegrate[ Sin[Sin[x]], {x, 0, Pi} ]
Out[9]= 1.78649
```

Mathematica can do many kinds of exact computations with integers. FactorInteger gives the factors of an integer.

```
In[10]:= FactorInteger[ 70612139395722186 ]
Out[10]= {{2, 1}, {3, 2}, {43, 5}, {26684839, 1}}
```

2. Graphics

Here is a plot of the function sin(exp(x)), with x ranging from 0 to π.

In[1]:= **Plot[Sin[Exp[x]], {x, 0, Pi}]**

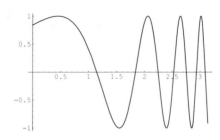

Mathematica provides many options that you can set to determine exactly how your plots will look.

In[2]:= **Show[%, Frame -> True,**
FrameLabel -> {"Time", "Signal"},
GridLines -> Automatic]

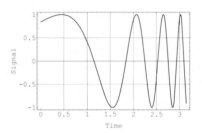

This makes a contour plot of the function sin(x + sin(y)). The lighter areas are higher.

Mathematica generates all its graphics in PostScript, which can be interpreted for many kinds of displays and printers.

In[3]:= **ContourPlot[Sin[x + Sin[y]], {x, -2, 2}, {y, -2, 2}]**

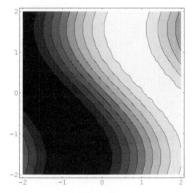

Here is a three-dimensional surface plot
of the same function.

`In[4]:= Plot3D[ Sin[x + Sin[y]], {x, -3, 3}, {y, -3, 3} ]`

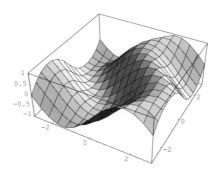

This generates a three-dimensional
parametric surface. The x, y and z
coordinates of points on the surface are
specified as a function of the parameters
t and u. The space in `u Sin[t]` denotes
multiplication.

`In[5]:= ParametricPlot3D[ {u Sin[t], u Cos[t], t/3},`
`              {t, 0, 15}, {u, -1, 1}, Ticks -> None ]`

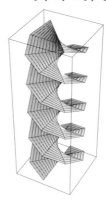

Here is a more complicated parametric
surface.

`In[6]:= ParametricPlot3D[`
`              {Sin[t], Sin[2t] Sin[u], Sin[2t] Cos[u]},`
`                {t, -Pi/2, Pi/2}, {u, 0, 2 Pi}, Ticks -> None ]`

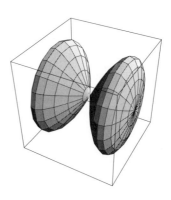

Mathematica allows you to combine different pieces of graphics together. The % stands for the last result; the %% for the last but one result.

In[7]:= **Show[%, %%]**

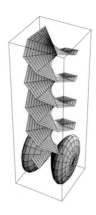

Mathematica serves as a graphics language in which you can build up graphics from components. In this case, a three-dimensional graphic is built up from a collection of cubes placed at different points.

In[8]:= **Show[Graphics3D[**
{Cuboid[{0, 0, 0}], Cuboid[{2, 2, 2}],
Cuboid[{2, 1, 3}], Cuboid[{3, 2, 1}],
Cuboid[{2, 1, 1}]}]]

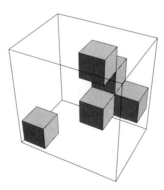

On computer systems with sound output, this generates an 8-second long sound with the specified amplitude as a function of time.

In[9]:= **Play[Sin[10000 / t], {t, -4, 4}]**

Out[9]= -Sound-

3. Algebra and Calculus

Mathematica can work not only with numbers, but also with algebraic formulas. Here is the formula $9(2 + x)(x + y) + (x + y)^2$.

$In[1] := $ **9 (2 + x) (x + y) + (x + y)^2**

$Out[1] = $ 9 (2 + x) (x + y) + (x + y)^2

This takes the previous expression, represented by %, raises it to the third power, and expands out products and powers. The result is fairly complicated.

$In[2] := $ **Expand[%^3]**

$Out[2] = $ 5832 x^3 + 9720 x^4 + 5400 x^5 + 1000 x^6 + 17496 x^2 y +

30132 x^3 y + 17280 x^4 y + 3300 x^5 y + 17496 x y^2 +

32076 x^2 y^2 + 19494 x^3 y^2 + 3930 x^4 y^2 + 5832 y^3 +

12636 x y^3 + 8802 x^2 y^3 + 1991 x^3 y^3 + 972 y^4 + 1242 x y^4 +

393 x^2 y^4 + 54 y^5 + 33 x y^5 + y^6

Factoring this expression yields a much simpler form.

$In[3] := $ **Factor[%]**

$Out[3] = $ (x + y)^3 (18 + 10 x + y)^3

Mathematica can do calculus as well as algebra. Here is the integral of $\int x^2 \sin(x)^2 \, dx$.

$In[4] := $ **Integrate[x^2 Sin[x]^2, x]**

$Out[4] = $ $\dfrac{x^3}{6}$ - $\dfrac{x \ Cos[2 \ x]}{4}$ + $\dfrac{(1 - 2 \ x^2) \ Sin[2 \ x]}{8}$

Differentiating the result gives the original integrand, but in a somewhat different form.

$In[5] := $ **D[%, x]**

$Out[5] = $ $\dfrac{x^2}{2}$ - $\dfrac{Cos[2 \ x]}{4}$ + $\dfrac{(1 - 2 \ x^2) \ Cos[2 \ x]}{4}$

The *Mathematica* function Simplify uses algebraic and trigonometric identities to simplify the expression, in this case recovering the original form.

$In[6] := $ **Simplify[%]**

$Out[6] = $ x^2 Sin[x]^2

This finds the power-series expansion of the previous result about the point $x = 0$.

$In[7] := $ **Series[%, {x, 0, 14}]**

$Out[7] = $ x^4 - $\dfrac{x^6}{3}$ + $\dfrac{2 \ x^8}{45}$ - $\dfrac{x^{10}}{315}$ + $\dfrac{2 \ x^{12}}{14175}$ - $\dfrac{2 \ x^{14}}{467775}$ + O[x]^{15}

Series can also handle purely symbolic functions such as **f**.

$In[8] := $ **Series[(f[x + h] - f[x - h])/(2h), {h, 0, 6}]**

$Out[8] = $ f'[x] + $\dfrac{f^{(3)}[x] \ h^2}{6}$ + $\dfrac{f^{(5)}[x] \ h^4}{120}$ + $\dfrac{f^{(7)}[x] \ h^6}{5040}$ + O[h]^7

4. Solving Equations

Here is the algebraic equation $x^3 - 7x^2 + 3ax = 0$ in *Mathematica*.

```
In[1]:= x^3 - 7 x^2 + 3 a x == 0
                 2     3
Out[1]= 3 a x - 7 x  + x  == 0
```

This solves the equation on the previous line, represented by %, and gives the solutions in terms of the parameter a.

```
In[2]:= Solve[ %, x ]
                           7 + Sqrt[49 - 12 a]
Out[2]= {{x -> 0}, {x ->  ───────────────────},
                                    2

            7 - Sqrt[49 - 12 a]
      {x -> ───────────────────}}
                     2
```

Here is the solution to a simple set of simultaneous equations.

```
In[3]:= Solve[ { a x + b y == 0, x + y == c } , {x, y} ]
                         b c          a c
Out[3]= {{x -> -(─────), y -> ─────}}
                   a - b          a - b
```

NSolve finds numerically the 5 complex solutions to this fifth-order algebraic equation.

```
In[4]:= NSolve[ x^5 + 2 x + 1 == 0, x ]
Out[4]= {{x -> -0.701874 - 0.879697 I},
    {x -> -0.701874 + 0.879697 I}, {x -> -0.486389},
    {x -> 0.945068 - 0.854518 I}, {x -> 0.945068 + 0.854518 I}}
```

FindRoot allows you to solve transcendental equations numerically. This gives the solution to a pair of simultaneous equations near $x = 1$, $y = 0$.

```
In[5]:= FindRoot[ { Sin[x] == x - y, Cos[y] == x + y },
                                    {x, 1}, {y, 0} ]
Out[5]= {x -> 0.883401, y -> 0.1105}
```

Mathematica can also solve differential equations. Here is the closed-form solution for $y''(x) - ky(x) = 1$.

```
In[6]:= DSolve[y''[x] - k y[x] == 1, y[x], x]
                     1      C[1]          Sqrt[k] x
Out[6]= {{y[x] -> -(-) + ───────── + E              C[2]}}
                     k    Sqrt[k] x
                        E
```

NDSolve finds numerical solutions to differential equations. This solves for the function y with x in the range 0 to 20.

```
In[7]:= NDSolve[ { y''[x] + Sin[x]^2 y'[x] + y[x] == Cos[x]^2 ,
                 y[0] == 1, y'[0] == 0 }, y, {x, 0, 20} ]
Out[7]= {{y -> InterpolatingFunction[{0., 20.}, <>]}}
```

This takes the solution found by NDSolve, and plots it as a function of x. The solution is given as an "interpolating function", which allows values of $y(x)$ to be found when specific values of x are supplied.

```
In[8]:= Plot[ Evaluate[ y[x] /. % ], {x, 0, 20} ]
```

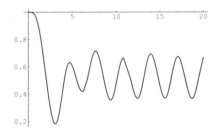

5. Lists

This makes a list of the first 15 factorials.

```
In[1]:= Table[ n!, {n, 1, 15} ]
Out[1]= {1, 2, 6, 24, 120, 720, 5040, 40320, 362880, 3628800,
    39916800, 479001600, 6227020800, 87178291200, 1307674368000}
```

This takes the logarithm of each entry in the list, and evaluates the result numerically. Functions like Log have the property of being "listable", so that they apply separately to each element in a list.

```
In[2]:= N[ Log[ % ] ]
Out[2]= {0, 0.693147, 1.79176, 3.17805, 4.78749, 6.57925,
    8.52516, 10.6046, 12.8018, 15.1044, 17.5023, 19.9872,
    22.5522, 25.1912, 27.8993}
```

Here is a plot of the entries in the list. The fact that the points lie close to a straight line is a consequence of the mathematical result that $\log n! \sim n \log n$ for large n.

```
In[3]:= ListPlot[ % ]
```

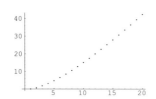

Fit finds least-squares fits to data. This finds the quadratic formula which gives the best fit to the list of numbers.

```
In[4]:= Fit[ %2, {1, x, x^2}, x ]
                                          2
Out[4]= -1.48508 + 0.963131 x + 0.06766 x
```

This creates a two-dimensional array in which the i, j element is 1 if i and j are relatively prime, and is 0 otherwise. Ending with a semicolon stops *Mathematica* from printing the rather large array.

```
In[5]:= array = Table[ If[GCD[i, j] == 1, 1, 0],
                               {i, 30}, {j, 30} ] ;
```

This makes a plot of the array.

```
In[6]:= ListDensityPlot[array]
```

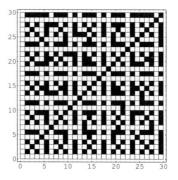

This finds the largest absolute value in the Fourier transform of the array.

```
In[7]:= Max[ Abs[Fourier[array]] ]
Out[7]= 18.5
```

6. Matrices

This generates a matrix whose i,j^{th} element is $1/(i+j+1)$. *Mathematica* represents the matrix as a list of lists.

In[1]:= m = Table[1 / (i + j + 1), {i, 3}, {j, 3}]

Out[1]= {{$\frac{1}{3}$, $\frac{1}{4}$, $\frac{1}{5}$}, {$\frac{1}{4}$, $\frac{1}{5}$, $\frac{1}{6}$}, {$\frac{1}{5}$, $\frac{1}{6}$, $\frac{1}{7}$}}

Here is the inverse of the matrix.

In[2]:= Inverse[m]

Out[2]= {{300, -900, 630}, {-900, 2880, -2100},

{630, -2100, 1575}}

Multiplying the inverse by the original matrix gives an identity matrix.

In[3]:= % . m

Out[3]= {{1, 0, 0}, {0, 1, 0}, {0, 0, 1}}

This gives a new matrix, with a modified leading diagonal.

In[4]:= m - x IdentityMatrix[3]

Out[4]= {{$\frac{1}{3}$ - x, $\frac{1}{4}$, $\frac{1}{5}$}, {$\frac{1}{4}$, $\frac{1}{5}$ - x, $\frac{1}{6}$}, {$\frac{1}{5}$, $\frac{1}{6}$, $\frac{1}{7}$ - x}}

The determinant of the new matrix gives the characteristic polynomial for the original matrix.

In[5]:= Det[%]

Out[5]= $\frac{1}{378000}$ - $\frac{317\ x}{25200}$ + $\frac{71\ x^2}{105}$ - x^3

Using the function Eigenvalues, you can find the numerical eigenvalues of m directly.

In[6]:= Eigenvalues[N[m]]

Out[6]= {0.657051, 0.0189263, 0.000212737}

This finds the eigenvalues of a 100×100 matrix of random real numbers. The semicolon suppresses printing.

In[7]:= Eigenvalues[Table[Random[ ], {100}, {100}]] ;

This plots the eigenvalues as points in the complex plane.

In[8]:= ListPlot[Transpose[{Re[%], Im[%]}]]

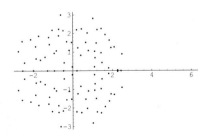

Mathematica can also manipulate symbolic matrices. This finds the eigenvectors of a matrix, then simplifies the algebraic result.

In[9]:= Simplify[Eigenvectors[{{a, b}, {-b, 2a}}]]

Out[9]= {{$\frac{a + Sqrt[a^2 - 4\ b^2]}{2\ b}$, 1}, {$\frac{a - Sqrt[a^2 - 4\ b^2]}{2\ b}$, 1}}

7. Transformation Rules and Definitions

This uses the rule $x \to 1 + a$ on the algebraic expression $1 + x^2 + 3x^3$.

```
In[1]:= 1 + x^2 + 3 x^3  /.  x -> 1 + a
                      2              3
Out[1]= 1 + (1 + a)  + 3 (1 + a)
```

You can give transformation rules for any expression. This uses a rule for `f[2]`.

```
In[2]:= {f[1], f[2], f[3]}  /.  f[2] -> b
Out[2]= {f[1], b, f[3]}
```

This replaces `f[`*anything*`]`, where *anything* is named `n`, by `n^2`.

```
In[3]:= {f[1], f[2], f[3]}  /.  f[n_] -> n^2
Out[3]= {1, 4, 9}
```

Here is a *Mathematica* function definition. It specifies that `f[`*n*`]` is *always* to be transformed to *n*`^2`.

```
In[4]:= f[n_] := n^2
```

The definition for `f` is automatically used whenever it applies.

```
In[5]:= f[3] + f[a + b]
                       2
Out[5]= 9 + (a + b)
```

Here is the recursive rule for the factorial function.

```
In[6]:= fac[n_] := n fac[n-1]
```

This gives a rule for the end condition of the factorial function.

```
In[7]:= fac[1] := 1
```

Here are the two rules you have defined for `fac`.

```
In[8]:= ?fac
Global`fac
fac[1] := 1
fac[n_] := n*fac[n - 1]
```

Mathematica can now apply these rules to find values for factorials.

```
In[8]:= fac[20]
Out[8]= 2432902008176640000
```

Mathematica lets you give rules for transforming any expression. This defines `log` of a product to be a sum of `log` functions.

```
In[9]:= log[x_ y_] := log[x] + log[y]
```

Mathematica uses the definition you have given to expand out this expression.

```
In[10]:= log[a b c d]
Out[10]= log[a] + log[b] + log[c] + log[d]
```

You can set up rules to specify the behavior of any kind of object. This defines a rule associated with `g` for sums of "g objects".

```
In[11]:= g/: g[i_] + g[j_] := g[i + j]
```

Mathematica now automatically uses the rule for g objects.

```
In[12]:= g[x] + g[y] + g[z]
Out[12]= g[x + y + z]
```

8. Advanced Topic: Symbolic Computation

Here are the 6 possible permutations of the elements a, b and c.

```
In[1]:= Permutations[{a, b, c}]
Out[1]= {{a, b, c}, {a, c, b}, {b, a, c}, {b, c, a}, {c, a, b},
    {c, b, a}}
```

Flatten "unravels" lists.

```
In[2]:= Flatten[ % ]
Out[2]= {a, b, c, a, c, b, b, a, c, b, c, a, c, a, b, c, b, a}
```

This gives the positions at which b appears in the list.

```
In[3]:= Position[ %, b ]
Out[3]= {{2}, {6}, {7}, {10}, {15}, {17}}
```

Here are cumulative products of the positions.

```
In[4]:= FoldList[Times, {1}, %]
Out[4]= {{1}, {2}, {12}, {84}, {840}, {12600}, {214200}}
```

This produces a list of successively nested cosine functions.

```
In[5]:= NestList[ Cos, x, 3 ]
Out[5]= {x, Cos[x], Cos[Cos[x]], Cos[Cos[Cos[x]]]}
```

Here are plots of the nested cosine functions. The curves meet at the point where $\cos(x) = x$.

```
In[6]:= Plot[ Evaluate[%], {x, 0, 1} ]
```

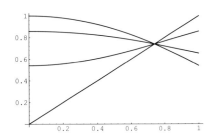

The Map operator allows you to "wrap" a function around each element in a list.

```
In[7]:= Map[f, {a, b, c, d}]
Out[7]= {f[a], f[b], f[c], f[d]}
```

With Function you can create "pure functions" that do not have explicit names.

```
In[8]:= Map[ Function[x, 1 + x^2], {a, b, c, d} ]
Out[8]= {1 + a , 1 + b , 1 + c , 1 + d }
                2       2       2       2
```

This sets up a Fibonacci function using a recursive definition.

```
In[9]:= f[0] = f[1] = 1;   f[n_] := f[n-1] + f[n-2]
```

Trace creates a symbolic data structure which represents the execution history of a *Mathematica* program. This shows the instances of the pattern f[_] which occur in the evaluation of f[4].

```
In[10]:= Trace[ f[4], f[_] ]
Out[10]= {f[4], {f[3], {f[2], {f[1]}, {f[0]}}, {f[1]}},
    {f[2], {f[1]}, {f[0]}}}
```

9. Programming

Here is a simple *Mathematica* program which generates an $n \times n$ Hilbert matrix.

```
Hilbert[n_] := Table[1/(i + j - 1), {i, n}, {j, n}]
```

This program finds the characteristic polynomial for a matrix. The /; clause at the end checks that m is indeed a matrix.

```
CharPoly[m_, x_] :=
        Det[m - x IdentityMatrix[Length[m]]] /; MatrixQ[m]
```

Here is a procedural program in *Mathematica* for finding the next prime after a given integer. The pattern n_Integer matches only integers.

```
NextPrime[n_Integer] :=
        Module[{k = n}, While[!PrimeQ[k], k++]; Return[k]]
```

You can often avoid using loops in *Mathematica* by operating directly on complete lists. The resulting programs are usually more elegant and more efficient. Here are programs for computing the mean, variance and quantiles of a list.

```
Mean[list_List] := Apply[Plus, list] / Length[list]

Variance[list_List] := Mean[ (list - Mean[list])^2 ]

Quantile[list_List, q_] :=
    Part[ Sort[list], -Floor[-q Length[list]] ] /; 0 < q < 1
```

This function takes a list of random numbers, and forms a succession of cumulative sums, thereby producing a sequence of points in a one-dimensional random walk.

```
RandomWalk[n_Integer] :=
        FoldList[Plus, 0, Table[Random[ ] - 1/2, {n}]]
```

Here is an elegant program, written in a functional programming style, which finds the first *n* terms in the continued fraction decomposition of a number *x*.

```
ContinuedFraction[x_Real, n_Integer] :=
 Floor[ NestList [ Function[{u}, 1/(u - Floor[u])], x, n - 1 ] ]
```

You can mix symbolic programming constructs with mathematical operations. Outer yields a matrix in which D is applied to all possible pairs of elements from funs and vars.

```
Jacobian[funs_List, vars_List] := Outer[D, funs, vars]
```

It is common to use transformation rules to build up programs in *Mathematica*. Here are some rules for Laplace transforms.

```
Laplace[c_, t_, s_] := c/s /; FreeQ[c, t]

Laplace[a_ + b_, t_, s_] := Laplace[a, t, s] + Laplace[b, t, s]

Laplace[c_ a_, t_, s_] := c Laplace[a, t, s] /; FreeQ[c, t]

Laplace[t_^n_., t_, s_] := n!/s^(n+1) /; (FreeQ[n, t] && n > 0)

Laplace[a_. Exp[b_. + c_. t_], t_, s_] :=
              Laplace[a Exp[b],  t,  s - c] /; FreeQ[{b, c}, t]
```

You can write elegant and efficient programs using pattern matching. This rather short program produces a run-length-encoded form of a list of integers.

```
RunEncode[{rest___Integer, same:(n_Integer)..}] :=
        Append[ RunEncode[{rest}], {n, Length[{same}]} ]

RunEncode[{ }] := { }
```

Mathematica programs can create graphics. This program makes polar plots.

```
PolarPlot[r_, {t_, tmin_, tmax_}] :=
        ParametricPlot[{r Cos[t], r Sin[t]}, {t, tmin, tmax},
                                    AspectRatio->Automatic]
```

Here is a program which plots the solutions to a polynomial equation as points in the complex plane.

```
RootPlot[poly_, z_] :=
        ListPlot[{Re[z], Im[z]} /. NSolve[poly == 0, z]] /;
                                    PolynomialQ[poly, z]
```

This program makes a 3D plot of a matrix of numbers read from a data file.

```
FilePlot3D[file_String] :=
        ListPlot3D[ ReadList[file, Number, RecordLists -> True] ]
```

You can write programs which manipulate external data. This program gives a list of the files in your current directory which contain a particular string.

```
Where[s_String] :=
        Select[ FileNames[ ], (Length[FindList[#, s, 1]] > 0)& ]
```

10. *Mathematica* Packages

Mathematica comes with various packages for specialized applications. This loads the Laplace transform package.

```
In[1]:= <<Calculus`LaplaceTransform`
```

Here is the Laplace transform of $t^n \exp(-c/t)$.

```
In[2]:= LaplaceTransform[t^n Exp[-c/t], t, s]
```

$$Out[2]= 2\ \left(\frac{c}{s}\right)^{(1 + n)/2} BesselK[1 + n, 2\ Sqrt[c\ s]]$$

This loads a package for constructing Padé approximants.

```
In[3]:= <<Calculus`Pade`
```

Here is the (2, 3) Padé approximant for $\exp(\sin(x))$.

```
In[4]:= Pade[ Exp[Sin[x]], {x, 0, 2, 3} ]
```

$$Out[4]= \frac{1 + \dfrac{8\ x}{15} + \dfrac{x^2}{4}}{1 - \dfrac{7\ x}{15} + \dfrac{13\ x^2}{60} + \dfrac{x^3}{60}}$$

This loads part of the standard *Mathematica* data analysis system.

```
In[5]:= <<Statistics`DescriptiveStatistics`;
```

Here is a report of location statistics for a table of 20 random numbers.

```
In[6]:= LocationReport[ Table[Random[ ], {20}] ]
Out[6]= {Mean -> 0.436778, HarmonicMean -> 0.278483,
    Median -> 0.374784}
```

This loads a package for manipulating permutations.

```
In[7]:= <<DiscreteMath`Permutations`
```

Here is a randomly chosen permutation of 10 elements.

```
In[8]:= RandomPermutation[10]
Out[8]= {3, 1, 2, 6, 5, 7, 8, 10, 4, 9}
```

And here is its cycle decomposition.

```
In[9]:= ToCycles[%]
Out[9]= {{3, 2, 1}, {6, 7, 8, 10, 9, 4}, {5}}
```

This loads a package that contains data on the chemical elements.

In[10]:= **<<Miscellaneous`ChemicalElements`**

This finds the atomic weight of tungsten from the data in the package.

In[11]:= **AtomicWeight[Tungsten]**

Out[11]= 183.85

If you ask for the atomic weight of an unstable element, *Mathematica* prints a warning message.

In[12]:= **AtomicWeight[Plutonium]**

AtomicWeight::unstable: No stable isotope of Plutonium exists

Out[12]= 244

This switches off the warning message.

In[13]:= **Off[AtomicWeight::unstable]**

This plots the ratio of atomic weight to atomic number for all the elements.

In[14]:= **ListPlot[AtomicWeight[Elements] /**
AtomicNumber[Elements], PlotJoined -> True]

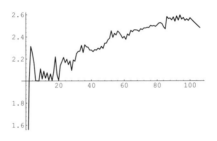

This loads a package which defines the geometry of various polyhedra.

In[15]:= **<<Graphics`Polyhedra`**

This generates a picture of the so-called "great icosahedron".

In[16]:= **Show[Polyhedron[GreatIcosahedron]]**

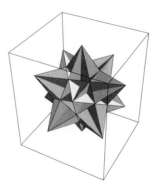

11. Interfacing with *Mathematica*

Mathematica usually prints out expressions in an approximation to standard mathematical notation.

```
In[1]:= (a^2 + b^2)/(x + y)^3

           2    2
          a  + b
Out[1]= ----------
                 3
          (x + y)
```

InputForm prints out expressions in a form that you can use as input to *Mathematica*. You can use a standard text editor to modify expressions in this form.

```
In[2]:= InputForm[ % ]
Out[2]//InputForm= (a^2 + b^2)/(x + y)^3
```

If you need to typeset the formulas you get from *Mathematica*, you can convert them into TEX input form using TeXForm.

```
In[3]:= TeXForm[ % ]
Out[3]//TeXForm=
  {{{a^2} + {b^2}}\over {{{\left( x + y \right) }^3}}}
```

FortranForm allows you to put *Mathematica* expressions in a form that you can include in Fortran programs.

```
In[4]:= FortranForm[ % ]
Out[4]//FortranForm= (a**2 + b**2)/(x + y)**3
```

You can use **ReadList** to read in data from files. This returns a list of the numbers in the file `tour.dat`.

```
In[5]:= ReadList["tour.dat", Number]
Out[5]= {15.6, 23.4, 1.77, 18.9, 20.7}
```

This executes an external command called `square5`, then uses a pipe to read the list of numbers that it produces.

```
In[6]:= ReadList["!square5", Number]
Out[6]= {1, 4, 9, 16, 25}
```

This creates a link to the external program `extdata`, and installs *Mathematica* functions for communicating with the program.

```
In[7]:= Install["extdata"]
Out[7]= LinkObject[extdata, 1]
```

This calls one of the *Mathematica* functions which has been set up to communicate with the external program.

```
In[8]:= getdata["probe 1", 5]
Out[8]= {1.54144, 11.2447, 6.40071, 2.28119, 2.9387}
```

Mathematica can also do various kinds of text manipulation. This searches for lines containing the string `Transform` in the file `packages`.

```
In[9]:= FindList["packages", "Transform"]
Out[9]= {FourierTransform.m, LaplaceTransform.m,
   MellinTransform.m}
```

You can use **StringReplace** to modify the strings.

```
In[10]:= StringReplace[%, ".m" -> "`"]
Out[10]= {FourierTransform`, LaplaceTransform`, MellinTransform`}
```

12. Front Ends and Notebooks

On some computer systems, there is a "front end" for *Mathematica* which allows you to take advantage of graphical user interface features.

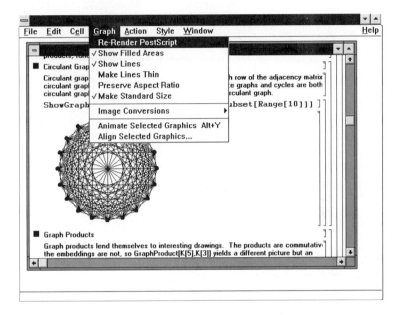

The *Mathematica* front end supports "notebooks", in which you can mix text, animated graphics, and actual *Mathematica* input.

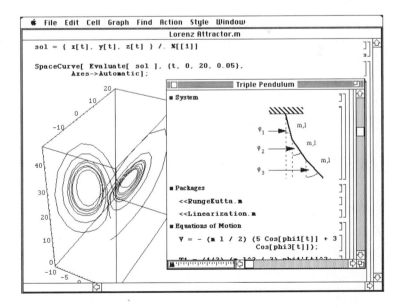

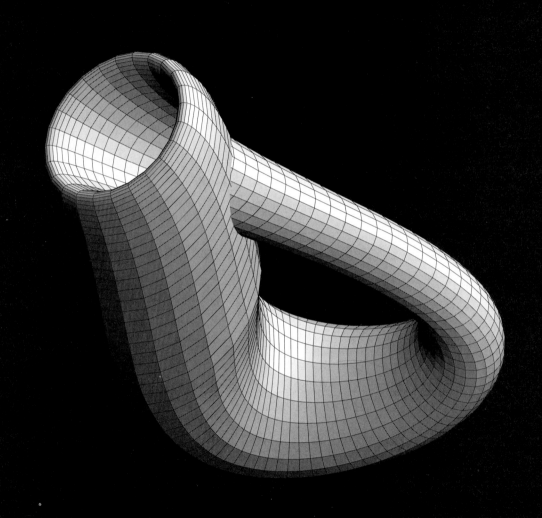

Mathematica
Graphics Gallery

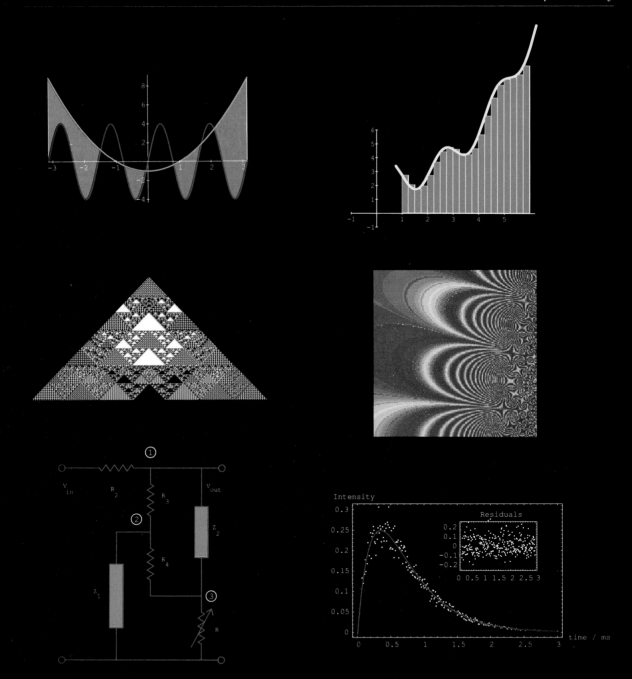

Two-Dimensional Graphics

From top left: Region satisfied by a non-linear inequality (T. Gray, J. Glynn); Approximation of an area by rectangles (D. Brown, H. Porta, J. Uhl); History of a one-dimensional cellular automaton (M. Cook); Density plot of $\sin(\text{Re}(\Gamma(x + iy)))$ (P. Abbott); Bridge T-type filter circuit (A. Riddle); Experimental data points, a fit, and the residuals (T. Wickham-Jones).

From top left: Recursively constructed tree (T. Gray, J. Glynn); Generation of a hypocycloid (C. Smith); Complex polynomial vector field (C. Smith, P. Boyland); Subgraphs which cannot appear in a linegraph (S. Skiena); Hyperbolic tiling of the Poincaré disk (I. Rivin); Robinson projection world map (J. Novak).

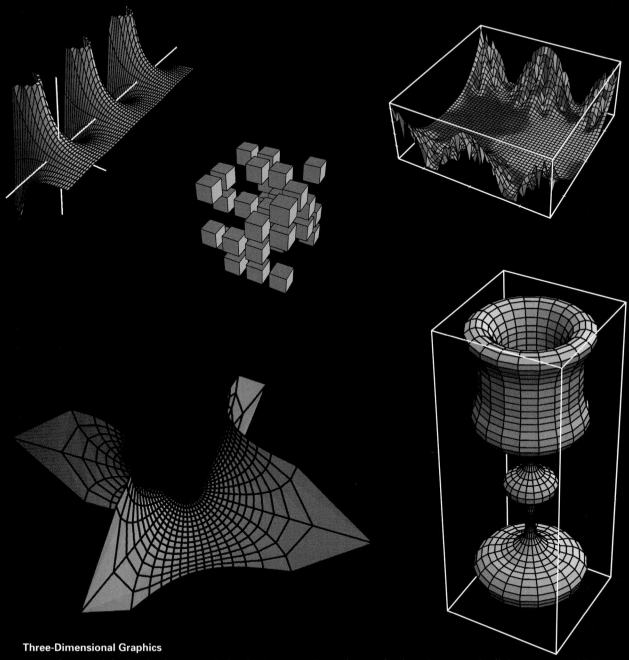

Three-Dimensional Graphics

Across from top left: Graph of $e^{-y}\cos x$ (C. Smith); A state in the evolution of a three-dimensional cellular automaton (C. Bays, C. Smith); Graph of an iterated transcendental function (T. Gray, J. Glynn); Three-dimensional bar chart (M. Chan); Five tetrahedra making a stellated icosahedron (S. Kim); Crystal structure of a high-temperature superconductor in the $YBa_2Cu_3O_7$ family (S. Ryu); Part of Scherk's second minimal surface (S. Dickson); Surface of revolution (T. Gray, J. Glynn); Three-dimensional plot of the Mandelbrot set (P. Abbott); Strange attractor in the equations for an electric circuit (P. Boyland).

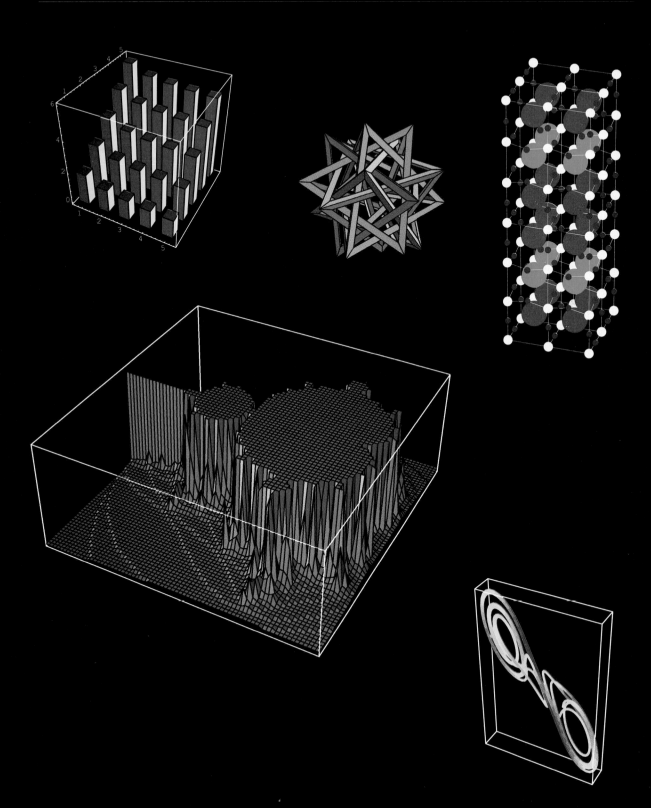

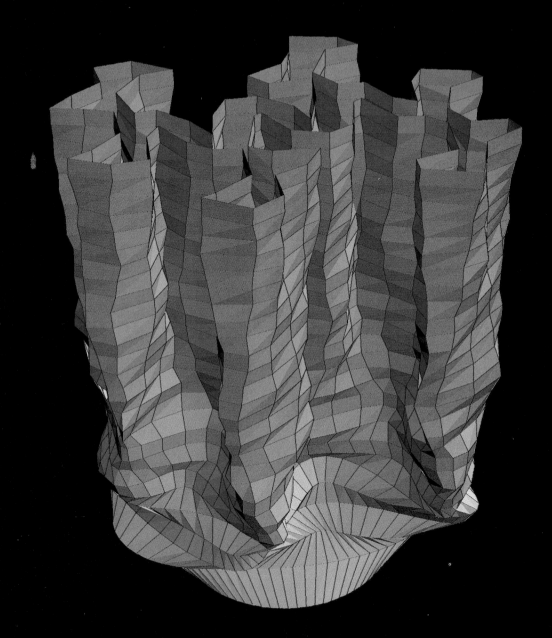

Evolution towards Fractals

Above: A one-parameter family of curves generated using the Fourier polynomials approximating a fractal curve (R. W. Gosper); Facing page: Third step in the construction of a Sierpinski sponge (R. Maeder).

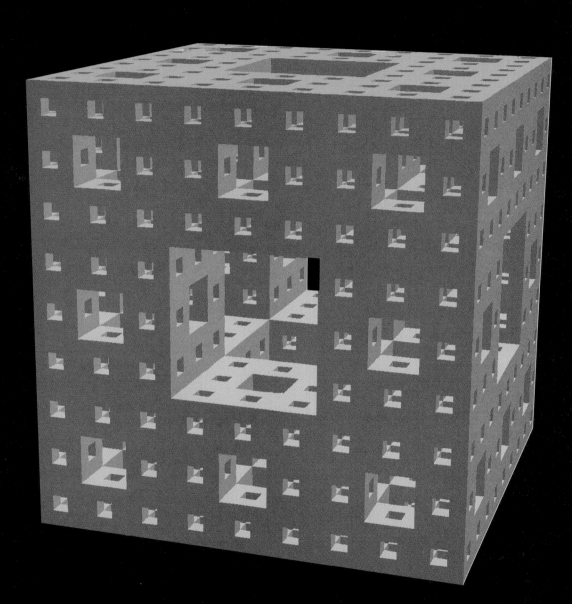

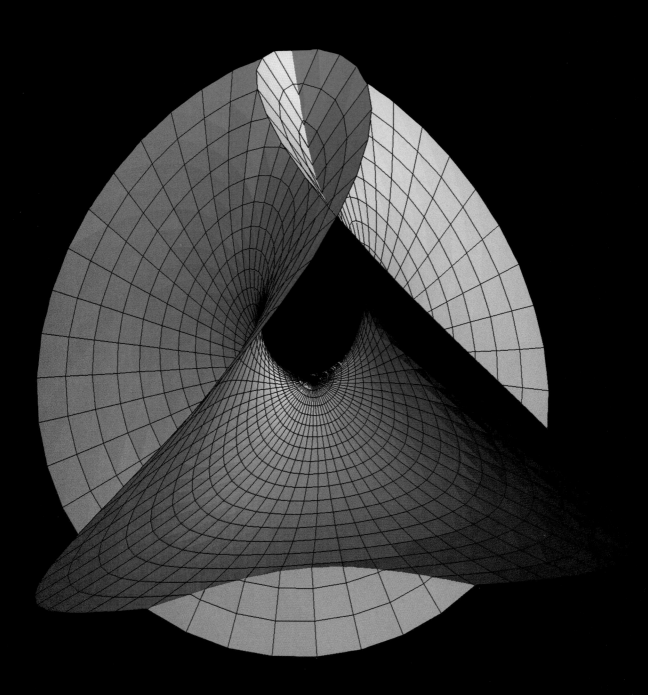

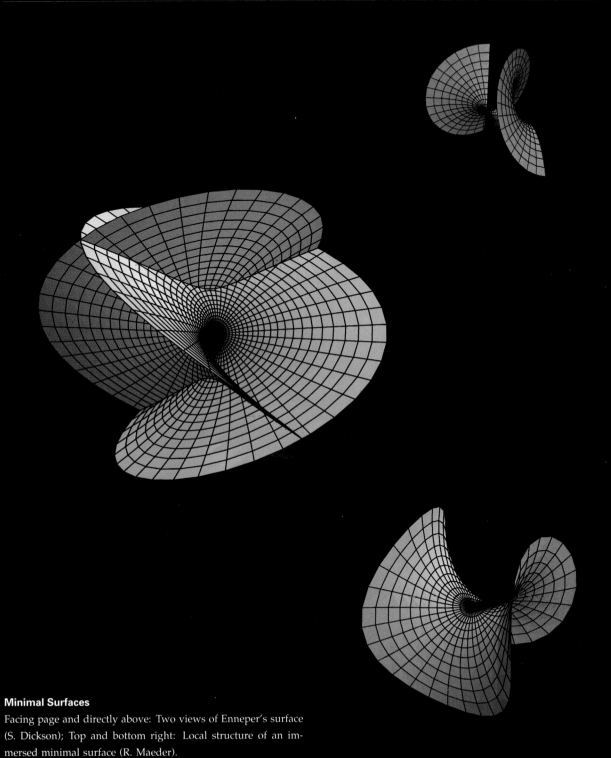

Minimal Surfaces

Facing page and directly above: Two views of Enneper's surface
(S. Dickson); Top and bottom right: Local structure of an im-
mersed minimal surface (R. Maeder).

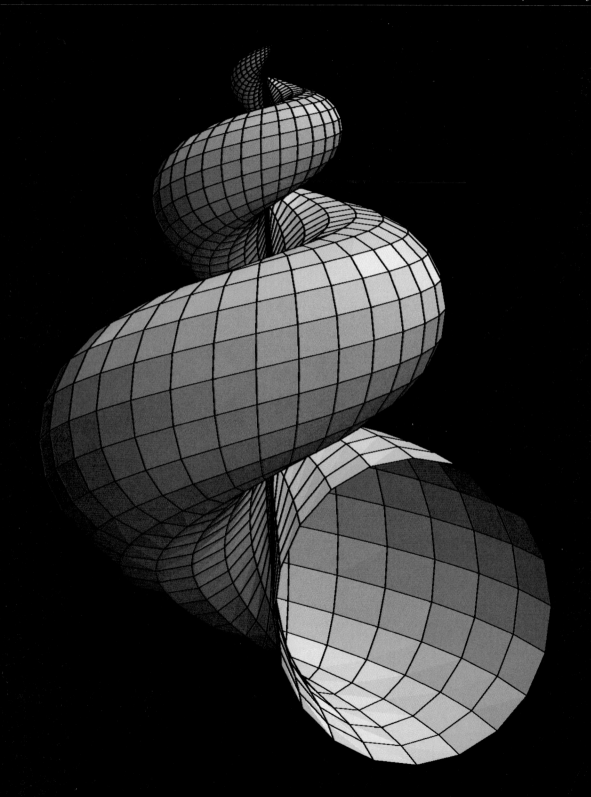

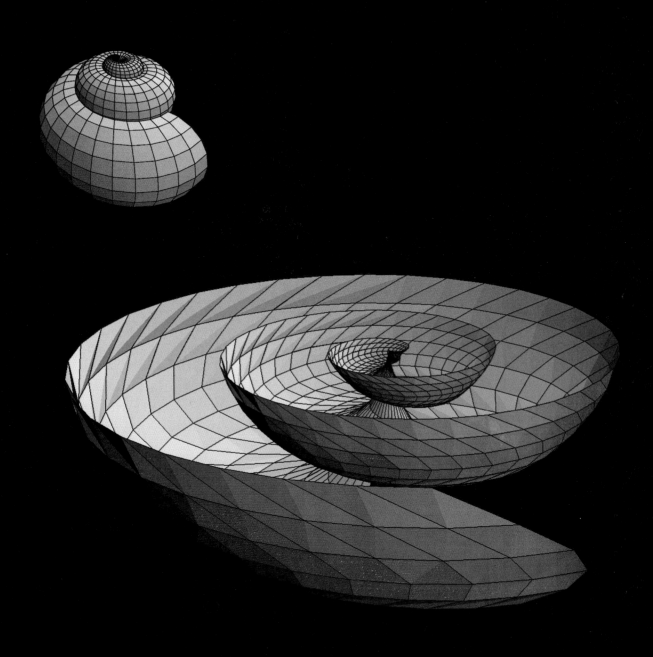

Conchoid Surfaces

Mathematical models of seashell geometry. Facing page: Upright conical spiral; Above: Upright conical spiral with gradual slope and cross section of flat conical spiral (S. Dickson).

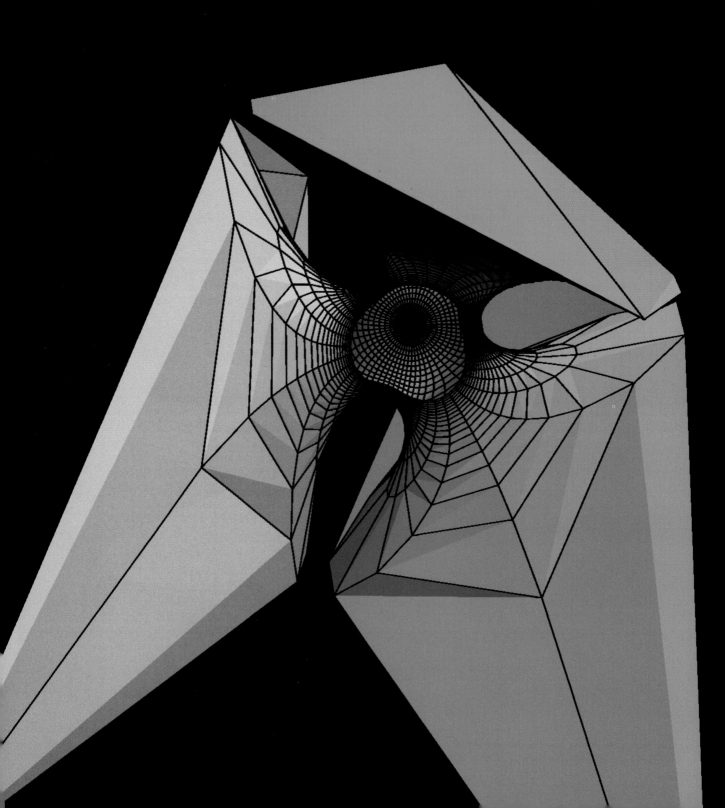

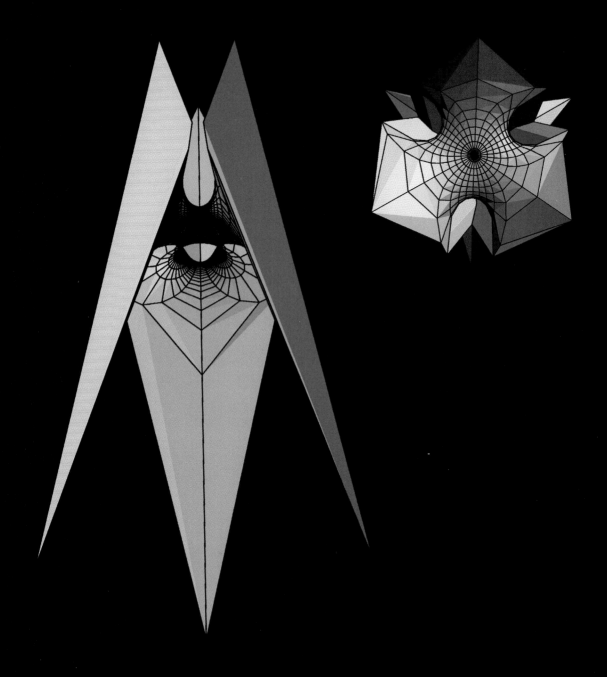

Trinoids

Three views of a trinoid minimal surface (S. Dickson).

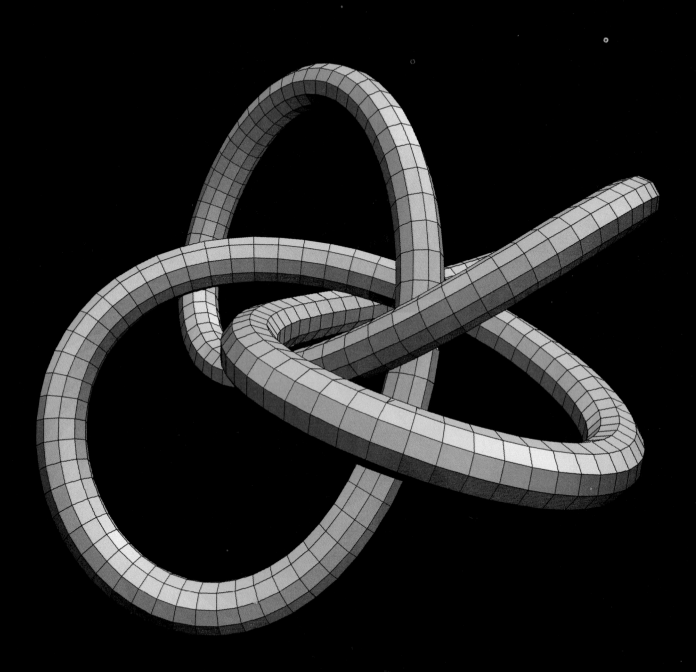

Knots

Counterclockwise from top left: Trefoil knot (H. Cejtin after R. W. Gosper); Figure-eight knot, the closed three braid $\sigma_1^2\sigma_2^2\sigma_1^{-2}\sigma_2^{-2}(\sigma_1\sigma_2^{-1})^2$ and a $(3, 4)$-torus knot (S. Dickson).

Ideal Hyperbolic Polyhedra

From left: Hyperbolic cube, hyperbolic octahedron, hyperbolic icosahedron, hyperbolic dodecahedron (H. Cejtin, I. Rivin).

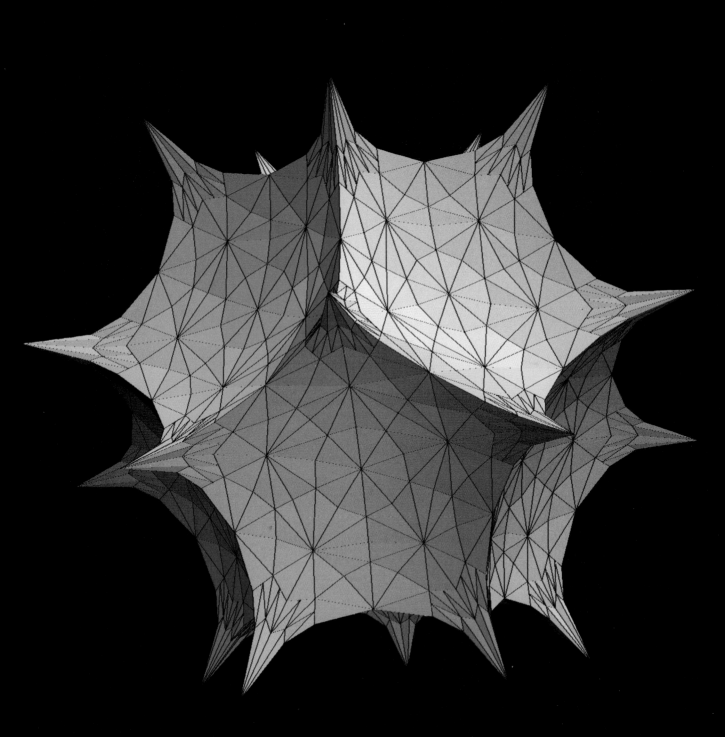

Symmetric Quasitilings
Recursively defined partial tilings of the plane (R. W. Gosper).

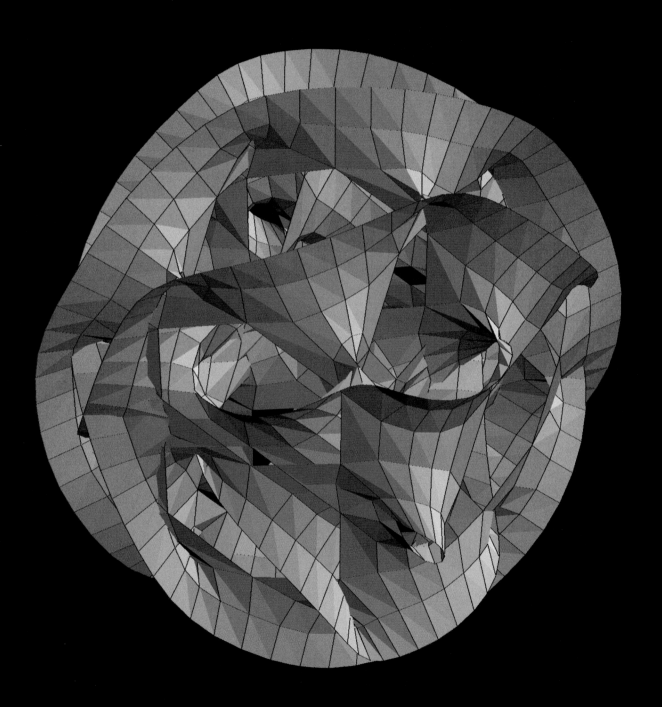

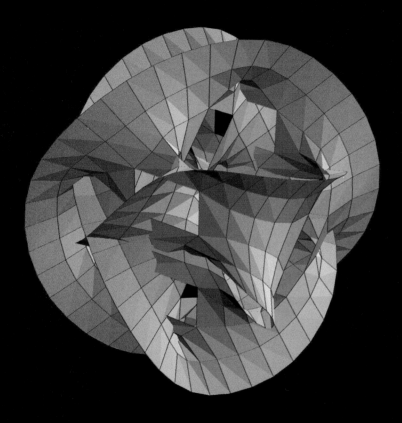

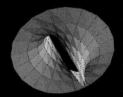

Visualization of Fermat's Last Theorem

Complex projective varieties determined by $x^n + y^n = z^n$, projected into three space. From left: Surfaces for $n = 6$, $n = 5$ and $n = 2$ (A. J. Hanson, S. Dickson).

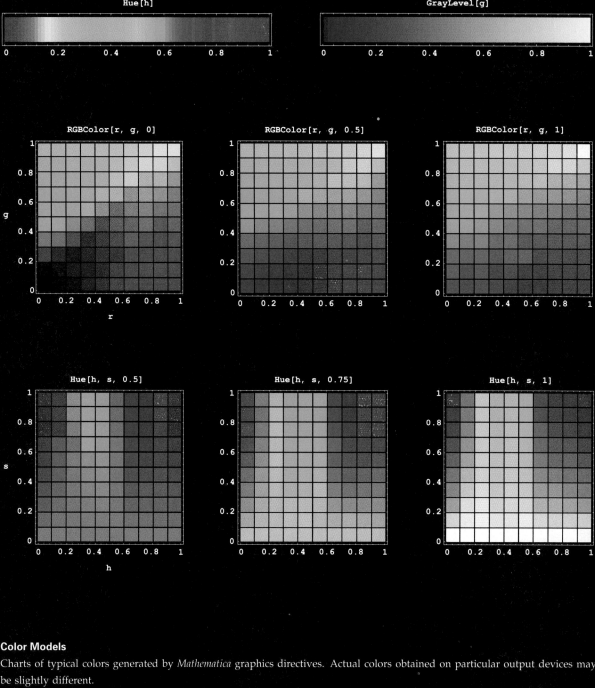

Color Models

Charts of typical colors generated by *Mathematica* graphics directives. Actual colors obtained on particular output devices may be slightly different.

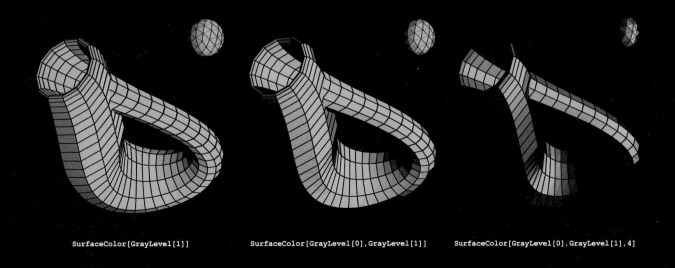

SurfaceColor[GrayLevel[1]]   SurfaceColor[GrayLevel[0],GrayLevel[1]]   SurfaceColor[GrayLevel[0],GrayLevel[1],4]

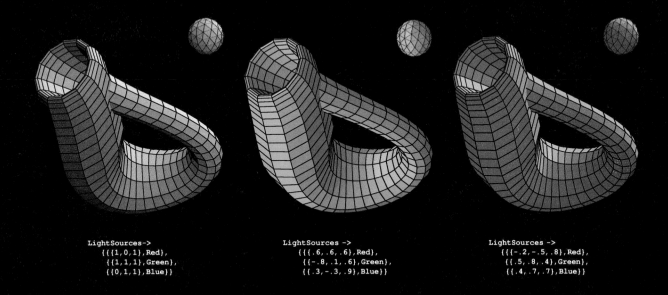

```
LightSources->
   {{{1,0,1},Red},
    {{1,1,1},Green},
    {{0,1,1},Blue}}
```

```
LightSources ->
   {{{.6,.6,.6},Red},
    {{-.8,.1,.6},Green},
    {{.3,-.3,.9},Blue}}
```

```
LightSources ->
   {{{-.2,-.5,.8},Red},
    {{.5,.8,.4},Green},
    {{.4,.7,.7},Blue}}
```

Lighting and Reflection Models

A Klein bottle and a geodesic sphere rendered with various choices of *Mathematica* lighting and reflection. Top row: Three choices of surface reflection properties, with a single light source at position $(1, 0, 1)$; Bottom row: Three arrangements of light sources, with the default arrangement on the left.

Part 1.

A Practical Introduction to *Mathematica*

1.0 Running *Mathematica*

To find out how to install and run *Mathematica* you should read the documentation that came with your copy of *Mathematica*. The details differ from one computer system to another, and are affected by various kinds of customization that can be done on *Mathematica*. Nevertheless, this section outlines two common cases.

Note that although the details of running *Mathematica* differ from one computer system to another, the structure of *Mathematica* calculations is the same in all cases. You enter input, then *Mathematica* processes it, and returns a result.

■ 1.0.1 Text-Based Interfaces

`math`	the operating system command to start *Mathematica*
text RETURN	input for *Mathematica*
CONTROL-D or `Quit[ ]`	exiting *Mathematica*

Running *Mathematica* with a text-based interface.

With a text-based interface, you interact with the computer primarily by typing text on the keyboard. This kind of interface is available for *Mathematica* on many computer systems, for example those running the Unix or VMS operating systems.

On such systems, *Mathematica* is typically started by typing the command `math` at an operating system prompt.

When *Mathematica* has started, it will print the prompt `In[1]:=`, signifying that it is ready for your input. You can then type your input. Ending a line (usually by pressing RETURN or ENTER) tells *Mathematica* that you have finished giving your input.

Mathematica will then process the input, and generate a result. If it prints the result out, it will label it with `Out[1]`.

Throughout this book, dialogs with *Mathematica* are shown in the following way:

The computer prints `In[1]:=`. You just type in 2 + 2. The line that starts with `Out[1]=` is the result from *Mathematica*.

```
In[1]:= 2 + 2
Out[1]= 4
```

Page xv discusses some important details about reproducing the dialogs on your computer system. Note that you do not explicitly type the `In[n]:=` prompt; only type the text that follows this prompt.

Section 1.3.1 gives more details on running *Mathematica* with a text-based interface. To exit *Mathematica*, either type CONTROL-D or Quit[ ] at an input prompt.

■ 1.0.2 Notebook Interfaces

double-click the *Mathematica* icon	the typical action for starting *Mathematica*
text SHIFT-RETURN	input for *Mathematica*
choose the **Quit** menu item	exiting *Mathematica*

Running *Mathematica* with a notebook interface.

Mathematica supports a special "notebook" interface on certain computers with graphical user interfaces.

To start *Mathematica* on such a system, you typically double-click the *Mathematica* icon.

When *Mathematica* starts up, it usually gives you a blank notebook. You enter *Mathematica* input into the notebook, then press SHIFT-RETURN (or certain other keys) to make *Mathematica* process your input. You can use the standard editing features of your graphical interface to prepare your input, which may go on for several lines. SHIFT-RETURN (or certain other keys) tells *Mathematica* that you have finished your input.

After you send input from your notebook to *Mathematica*, *Mathematica* will label your input with In[*n*]:=. It labels the corresponding output Out[*n*]=.

You type 2 + 2, then end your input with SHIFT-RETURN. *Mathematica* processes the input, then adds the input label In[1]:=, and gives the output.

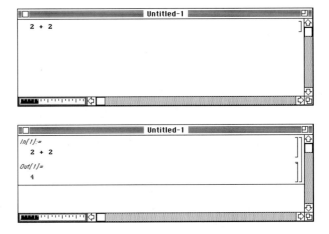

Throughout this book, "dialogs" with *Mathematica* are shown in the following way:

With a notebook interface, you just type   *In[1]:=* **2 + 2**
in 2 + 2. *Mathematica* then adds the
label *In[1]:=*, and prints the result.   *Out[1]=* 4

Page xv discusses some important details about reproducing the dialogs on your computer system. Section 1.3 gives more information on notebook interfaces to *Mathematica*.

You should realize that notebook interfaces are part of the "front end" for *Mathematica*. The *Mathematica* kernel which actually performs computations may be run either on the same computer as the front end, or on another computer connected via some kind of network or serial line. In most cases, the kernel is not even started until you actually do a calculation with *Mathematica*.

To exit *Mathematica*, you typically choose the **Quit** menu item in the notebook interface.

1.1 Numerical Calculations

■ 1.1.1 Arithmetic

You can do arithmetic with *Mathematica* just as you would on an electronic calculator.

This is the sum of two numbers.	*In[1]:=* **2.3 + 5.63**
	Out[1]= 7.93
Here the / stands for division, and the ∧ stands for power.	*In[2]:=* **2.4 / 8.9 ∧ 2**
	Out[2]= 0.0302992
Spaces denote multiplication in *Mathematica*. You can use a * for multiplication if you want to.	*In[3]:=* **2 3 4**
	Out[3]= 24
You can type arithmetic expressions with parentheses.	*In[4]:=* **(3 + 4) ∧ 2 - 2 (3 + 1)**
	Out[4]= 41
Spaces are not needed, though they often make your input easier to read.	*In[5]:=* **(3+4)∧2-2(3+1)**
	Out[5]= 41

x∧y	power
$-x$	minus
x/y	divide
$x\ y\ z$ or $x*y*z$	multiply
$x+y+z$	add

Arithmetic operations in *Mathematica*.

Arithmetic operations in *Mathematica* are grouped according to the standard mathematical conventions. As usual, 2 ∧ 3 + 4, for example, means (2 ∧ 3) + 4, and not 2 ∧ (3 + 4). You can always control grouping by explicitly using parentheses.

This result is given in scientific notation.	*In[6]:=* **2.4 ∧ 45**
	Out[6]= $1.28678\ 10^{17}$
You can enter numbers in scientific notation like this.	*In[7]:=* **2.3 10∧-70**
	Out[7]= $2.3\ 10^{-70}$

■ 1.1.2 Exact and Approximate Results

A standard electronic calculator does all your calculations to a particular accuracy, say ten decimal digits. With *Mathematica*, however, you can often get *exact* results.

Mathematica gives an *exact* result for 2^{100}, even though it has 31 decimal digits.	$In[1]:= \textbf{2 ^ 100}$ $Out[1]= 1267650600228229401496703205376$

You can tell *Mathematica* to give you an approximate numerical result, just as a calculator would, by ending your input with //N. The N stands for "numerical". It must be a capital letter. Section 2.1.3 will explain what the // means.

This gives an approximate numerical result.	$In[2]:= \textbf{2 ^ 100 //N}$ $Out[2]= 1.26765 \; 10^{30}$
Mathematica can give results in terms of rational numbers.	$In[3]:= \textbf{1/3 + 2/7}$ $Out[3]= \dfrac{13}{21}$
//N always gives the approximate numerical result.	$In[4]:= \textbf{1/3 + 2/7 //N}$ $Out[4]= 0.619048$

---

expr //N	give an approximate numerical value for *expr*

Getting numerical approximations.

When you type in an integer like 7, *Mathematica* assumes that it is exact. If you type in a number like 4.5, with an explicit decimal point, *Mathematica* assumes that it is accurate only to a fixed number of decimal places.

This is taken to be an exact rational number, and reduced to its lowest terms.	$In[5]:= \textbf{452/62}$ $Out[5]= \dfrac{226}{31}$
Whenever you give a number with an explicit decimal point, *Mathematica* produces an approximate numerical result.	$In[6]:= \textbf{452.3/62}$ $Out[6]= 7.29516$
Here again, the presence of the decimal point makes *Mathematica* give you an approximate numerical result.	$In[7]:= \textbf{452./62}$ $Out[7]= 7.29032$

When any number in an arithmetic expression is given with an explicit decimal point, you get an approximate numerical result for the whole expression.

```
In[8]:= 1. + 452/62
Out[8]= 8.29032
```

■ 1.1.3 Some Mathematical Functions

Mathematica includes a very large collection of mathematical functions. Section 3.2 gives the complete list. Here are a few of the common ones.

Sqrt[x]	square root ($\sqrt{x}$)
Exp[x]	exponential (e^x)
Log[x]	natural logarithm ($\log_e x$)
Log[b, x]	logarithm to base b ($\log_b x$)
Sin[x], Cos[x], Tan[x]	trigonometric functions (with arguments in radians)
ArcSin[x], ArcCos[x], ArcTan[x]	
	inverse trigonometric functions
n!	factorial (product of integers $1, 2, \ldots, n$)
Abs[x]	absolute value
Round[x]	closest integer to x
Mod[n, m]	n modulo m (remainder on division of n by m)
Random[ ]	pseudorandom number between 0 and 1
Max[x, y, ...], Min[x, y, ...]	maximum, minimum of $x, y, \ldots$
FactorInteger[n]	prime factors of n (see page 554)

Some common mathematical functions.

■ The arguments of all *Mathematica* functions are enclosed in *square brackets*.

■ The names of built-in *Mathematica* functions begin with *capital letters*.

Two important points about functions in *Mathematica*.

It is important to remember that all function arguments in *Mathematica* are enclosed in *square brackets*, not parentheses. Parentheses in *Mathematica* are used only to indicate the grouping of terms, and never to give function arguments.

This gives $\log_e(8.4)$. Notice the capital letter for **Log**, and the *square brackets* for the argument.	`In[1]:= Log[8.4]` `Out[1]= 2.12823`

Just as with arithmetic operations, *Mathematica* tries to give exact values for mathematical functions when you give it exact input.

This gives $\sqrt{16}$ as an exact integer.	`In[2]:= Sqrt[16]` `Out[2]= 4`
This gives an approximate numerical result for $\sqrt{2}$.	`In[3]:= Sqrt[2] //N` `Out[3]= 1.41421`
The presence of an explicit decimal point tells *Mathematica* to give an approximate numerical result.	`In[4]:= Sqrt[2.]` `Out[4]= 1.41421`
Mathematica cannot work out an exact result for $\sqrt{2}$, so it leaves the original form. This kind of "symbolic" result is discussed in Section 1.4.1.	`In[5]:= Sqrt[2]` `Out[5]= Sqrt[2]`
Here is the exact integer result for $30 \times 29 \times ... \times 1$. Computing factorials like this can give you very large numbers. You should be able to calculate up to at least 1000! in a reasonable amount of time.	`In[6]:= 30!` `Out[6]= 265252859812191058636308480000000`
This gives the approximate numerical value of the factorial.	`In[7]:= 30! //N` `Out[7]= 2.65253 10`³²

Pi	$\pi \simeq 3.14159$
E	$e \simeq 2.71828$
Degree	$\pi/180$: degrees-to-radians conversion factor
I	$i = \sqrt{-1}$
Infinity	∞

Some common mathematical constants.

Notice that the names of these built-in constants all begin with capital letters.

This gives the numerical value of π^2.

```
In[8]:= Pi ^ 2 //N
Out[8]= 9.8696
```

This gives the exact result for $\sin(\pi/2)$. Notice that the arguments to trigonometric functions are always in radians.

```
In[9]:= Sin[Pi/2]
Out[9]= 1
```

This gives the numerical value of $\sin(20°)$. Multiplying by the constant **Degree** converts the argument to radians.

```
In[10]:= Sin[20 Degree] //N
Out[10]= 0.34202
```

Log[x] gives logarithms to base e.

```
In[11]:= Log[E ^ 5]
Out[11]= 5
```

You can get logarithms in any base b using Log[b, x]. As in standard mathematical notation, the b is optional.

```
In[12]:= Log[2, 256]
Out[12]= 8
```

■ 1.1.4 Arbitrary-Precision Calculations

When you use //N to get a numerical result, *Mathematica* does what a standard calculator would do: it gives you a result to a fixed number of significant figures. You can also tell *Mathematica* exactly how many significant figures to keep in a particular calculation. This allows you to get numerical results in *Mathematica* to any degree of precision.

expr//N or N[*expr*]	approximate numerical value of *expr*
N[*expr*, *n*]	numerical value of *expr* calculated with *n*-digit precision

Numerical evaluation functions.

This gives the numerical value of π to a fixed number of significant digits. Typing N[Pi] is exactly equivalent to Pi //N.

```
In[1]:= N[Pi]
Out[1]= 3.14159
```

This gives π to 40 digits.

```
In[2]:= N[Pi, 40]
Out[2]= 3.141592653589793238462643383279502884197
```

Here is $\sqrt{7}$ to 30 digits.

```
In[3]:= N[Sqrt[7], 30]
Out[3]= 2.64575131106459059050161575364
```

Doing any kind of numerical calculation can introduce small roundoff errors into your results. When you increase the numerical precision, these errors typically become correspondingly smaller. Making sure that you get the same answer when you increase numerical precision is often a good way to check your results.

The quantity $e^{\pi\sqrt{163}}$ turns out to be very close to an integer. To check that the result is not, in fact, an integer, you have to use sufficient numerical precision.

```
In[4]:= N[Exp[Pi Sqrt[163]], 50]
```
$$Out[4]= 2.6253741264076874399999999999992500725971981856890\ 10^{17}$$

■ 1.1.5 Complex Numbers

You can enter complex numbers in *Mathematica* just by including the constant I, equal to $\sqrt{-1}$. Make sure that you type a capital I.

This gives the imaginary number result $2i$.

```
In[1]:= Sqrt[-4]
Out[1]= 2 I
```

This gives the ratio of two complex numbers.

```
In[2]:= (4 + 3 I) / (2 - I)
Out[2]= 1 + 2 I
```

Here is the numerical value of a complex exponential.

```
In[3]:= Exp[2 + 9 I] //N
Out[3]= -6.73239 + 3.04517 I
```

x + I y	the complex number $x + i\,y$
Re[z]	real part
Im[z]	imaginary part
Conjugate[z]	complex conjugate z^* or $\bar{z}$
Abs[z]	absolute value $|z|$
Arg[z]	the argument ϕ in $|z|e^{i\phi}$

Complex number operations.

■ 1.1.6 Getting Used to *Mathematica*

- Arguments of functions are given in *square brackets*.
- Names of built-in functions have their first letters capitalized.
- Multiplication can be represented by a space.
- Powers are denoted by ∧.
- Numbers in scientific notation are entered, for example, as 2.5 10∧−4.

Important points to remember in *Mathematica*.

This section has given you a first glimpse of *Mathematica*. If you have used other computer systems before, you will probably have noticed some similarities and some differences. Often you will find the differences the most difficult parts to remember. It may help you, however, to understand a little about *why Mathematica* is set up the way it is, and why such differences exist.

One important feature of *Mathematica* that differs from other computer languages, and from conventional mathematical notation, is that function arguments are enclosed in square brackets, not parentheses. Parentheses in *Mathematica* are reserved specifically for indicating grouping of terms. There is obviously a conceptual distinction between giving arguments to a function and grouping terms together; the fact that the same notation has often been used for both is largely a consequence of typography and of early computer keyboards. In *Mathematica*, the concepts are distinguished by different notation.

This distinction has several advantages. In parenthesis notation, it is not clear whether $c(1+x)$ means c[1 + x] or c*(1 + x). Using square brackets for function arguments removes this ambiguity. It also allows multiplication to be indicated without an explicit * or other character. As a result, *Mathematica* can handle expressions like 2x and a x or a (1 + x), treating them just as in standard mathematical notation.

You will have seen in this section that built-in *Mathematica* functions often have quite long names. You may wonder why, for example, the pseudorandom number function is called Random, rather than, say, Rand. The answer, which pervades much of the design of *Mathematica*, is consistency. There is a general convention in *Mathematica* that all function names are spelled out as full English words, unless there is a standard mathematical abbreviation for them. The great advantage of this scheme is that it is *predictable*. Once you know what a function does, you will usually be able to guess exactly what its name is. If the names were abbreviated, you would always have to remember which shortening of the standard English words was used.

Another feature of built-in *Mathematica* names is that they all start with capital letters. In later sections, you will see how to define variables and functions of your own. The capital letter convention makes it easy to distinguish built-in objects. If *Mathematica* used i to represent $\sqrt{-1}$, then you would never be able to use i as the name of one of your variables. In addition, when you read programs written in *Mathematica*, the capitalization of built-in names makes them easier to pick out.

1.2 Building Up Calculations

■ 1.2.1 Using Previous Results

In doing calculations, you will often need to use previous results that you have got. In *Mathematica*, % always stands for your last result.

%	the last result generated
%%	the next-to-last result
%%... % (*k* times)	the *k*th previous result
%*n*	the result on output line Out [*n*] (to be used with care)

Ways to refer to your previous results.

Here is the first result.

```
In[1]:= 77 ^ 2
Out[1]= 5929
```

This adds 1 to the last result.

```
In[2]:= % + 1
Out[2]= 5930
```

This uses both the last result, and the result before that.

```
In[3]:= 3 % + % ^ 2 + %%
Out[3]= 35188619
```

You will have noticed that all the input and output lines in *Mathematica* are numbered. You can use these numbers to refer to previous results.

This adds the results on lines 2 and 3 above.

```
In[4]:= %2 + %3
Out[4]= 35194549
```

If you use a text-based interface to *Mathematica*, then successive input and output lines will always appear in order, as they do in the dialogs in this book. However, if you use a notebook interface to *Mathematica*, as discussed in Section 1.3.1, then successive input and output lines need not appear in order. You can for example "scroll back" and insert your next calculation wherever you want in the notebook. You should realize that % is always defined to be the last result that *Mathematica* generated. This may or may not be the result that appears immediately above your present position in the notebook. With a notebook interface, the only way to tell when a particular result was generated is to look at the Out[*n*] label that it has. Because you can insert and delete anywhere in a notebook, the textual ordering of results in a notebook need have no relation to the order in which the results were generated.

■ 1.2.2 Defining Variables

When you do long calculations, it is often convenient to give *names* to your intermediate results. Just as in standard mathematics, or in other computer languages, you can do this by introducing named *variables*.

This sets the value of the *variable* x to be 5.	`In[1]:= x = 5` `Out[1]= 5`
Whenever x appears, *Mathematica* now replaces it with the value 5.	`In[2]:= x ^ 2` `Out[2]= 25`
This assigns a new value to x.	`In[3]:= x = 7 + 4` `Out[3]= 11`
pi is set to be the numerical value of π to 40-digit accuracy.	`In[4]:= pi = N[Pi, 40]` `Out[4]= 3.141592653589793238462643383279502884197`
Here is the value you defined for pi.	`In[5]:= pi` `Out[5]= 3.141592653589793238462643383279502884197`
This gives the numerical value of π^2, to the same accuracy as pi.	`In[6]:= pi ^ 2` `Out[6]= 9.869604401089358618834490099987615113531`

x = *value*	assign a value to the variable x
x = y = *value*	assign a value to both x and y
x =. or Clear[x]	remove any value assigned to x

Assigning values to variables.

It is very important to realize that values you assign to variables are *permanent*. Once you have assigned a value to a particular variable, the value will be kept until you explicitly remove it. The value will, of course, disappear if you start a whole new *Mathematica* session.

Forgetting about definitions you made earlier is the single most common cause of mistakes when using *Mathematica*. If you set x = 5, *Mathematica* assumes that you *always* want x to have the value 5, until or unless you explicitly tell it otherwise. To avoid mistakes, you should remove values you have defined as soon as you have finished using them.

■ Remove values you assign to variables as soon as you finish using them.

A useful principle in using *Mathematica*.

The variables you define can have almost any names. There is no limit on the length of their names. One constraint, however, is that variable names can never *start* with numbers. For example, x2 could be a variable, but 2x means 2*x. (See Section A.2 for information on international character sets.)

Mathematica uses both upper- and lower-case letters. There is a convention that built-in *Mathematica* objects always have names starting with upper-case (capital) letters. To avoid confusion, you should always choose names for your own variables that start with lower-case letters.

aaaaa	a variable name containing only lower-case letters
Aaaaa	a built-in object whose name begins with a capital letter

Naming conventions.

You can type formulas involving variables in *Mathematica* almost exactly as you would in mathematics. There are a few important points to watch, however.

- x y means x times y.

- xy with no space is the variable with name xy.

- 5x means 5 times x.

- x∧2y means (x∧2) y, not x∧(2y).

Some points to watch when using variables in *Mathematica*.

■ 1.2.3 Making Lists of Objects

In doing calculations, it is often convenient to collect together several objects, and treat them as a single entity. *Lists* give you a way to make collections of objects in *Mathematica*. As you will see later, lists are very important and general structures in *Mathematica*.

A list such as {3, 5, 1} is a collection of three objects. But in many ways, you can treat the whole list as a single object. You can, for example, do arithmetic on the whole list at once, or assign the whole list to be the value of a variable.

Here is a list of three numbers.

```
In[1]:= {3, 5, 1}
Out[1]= {3, 5, 1}
```

This squares each number in the list, and adds 1 to it.

```
In[2]:= {3, 5, 1}∧2 + 1
Out[2]= {10, 26, 2}
```

This takes differences between corresponding elements in the two lists. The lists must be the same length.	$In[3] := $ **{6, 7, 8} - {3.5, 4, 2.5}** $Out[3] = $ {2.5, 3, 5.5}
The value of % is the whole list.	$In[4] := $ **%** $Out[4] = $ {2.5, 3, 5.5}
You can apply any of the mathematical functions in Section 1.1.3 to whole lists.	$In[5] := $ **Exp[%] // N** $Out[5] = $ {12.1825, 20.0855, 244.692}

Just as you can set variables to be numbers, so also you can set them to be lists.

This assigns v to be a list.	$In[6] := $ **v = {2, 4, 3.1}** $Out[6] = $ {2, 4, 3.1}
Wherever v appears, it is replaced by the list.	$In[7] := $ **v / (v - 1)** $Out[7] = $ {2, $\frac{4}{3}$, 1.47619}

■ 1.2.4 Manipulating Elements of Lists

Many of the most powerful list manipulation operations in *Mathematica* treat whole lists as single objects. Sometimes, however, you need to pick out or set individual elements in a list.

You can refer to an element of a *Mathematica* list by giving its "index". The elements are numbered in order, starting at 1.

$\{a,\ b,\ c\}$	a list
Part[*list*, *i*] or *list*[[*i*]]	the ith element of *list* (the first element is *list*[[1]])
Part[*list*, {*i*, *j*, ... }] or *list*[[{*i*, *j*, ... }]]	a list of the ith, j^{th}, ... elements of *list*

Operations on list elements.

This extracts the second element of the list.	$In[1] := $ **{5, 8, 6, 9}[[2]]** $Out[1] = $ 8
This extracts a list of elements.	$In[2] := $ **{5, 8, 6, 9}[[{3, 1, 3, 2, 4}]]** $Out[2] = $ {6, 5, 6, 8, 9}
This assigns the value of v to be a list.	$In[3] := $ **v = {2, 4, 7}** $Out[3] = $ {2, 4, 7}

You can extract elements of v. $In[4]:=$ **v[[2]]**

                                                  $Out[4]=$ 4

By assigning a variable to be a list, you can use *Mathematica* lists much like "arrays" in other computer languages. Thus, for example, you can reset an element of a list by assigning a value to $v[[i]]$.

Part[v, i] or $v[[i]]$	extract the ith element of a list
Part[v, i] = *value* or $v[[i]]$ = *value*	
	reset the ith element of a list

Array-like operations on lists.

Here is a list. $In[5]:=$ **v = {4, -1, 8, 7}**

                                                  $Out[5]=$ {4, -1, 8, 7}

This resets the third element of the list. $In[6]:=$ **v[[3]] = 0**

                                                  $Out[6]=$ 0

Now the list assigned to v has been $In[7]:=$ **v**
modified.
                                                  $Out[7]=$ {4, -1, 0, 7}

■ 1.2.5 The Four Kinds of Bracketing in *Mathematica*

Over the course of the last few sections, we have introduced each of the four kinds of bracketing used in *Mathematica*. Each kind of bracketing has a very different meaning. It is important that you remember all of them.

(*term*)	parentheses for grouping
$f[x]$	square brackets for functions
{a, b, c}	curly braces for lists
$v[[i]]$	double brackets for indexing (Part[v, i])

The four kinds of bracketing in *Mathematica*.

When the expressions you type in are complicated, it is often a good idea to put extra space inside each set of brackets. This makes it somewhat easier for you to see matching pairs of brackets. $v[[\{a, b\}]]$ is, for example, easier to recognize than $v[[\{a, b\}]]$.

■ 1.2.6 Sequences of Operations

In doing a calculation with *Mathematica*, you usually go through a sequence of steps. If you want to, you can do each step on a separate line. Often, however, you will find it convenient to put several steps on the same line. You can do this simply by separating the pieces of input you want to give with semicolons.

$expr_1$; $expr_2$; $expr_3$	do several operations, giving the result of the last one
$expr_1$; $expr_2$;	do the operations, but print no output

Ways to do sequences of operations in *Mathematica*.

This does three operations on the same line. The result is the result from the last operation.

```
In[1]:= x = 4; y = 6; z = y + 6

Out[1]= 12
```

If you end your input with a semicolon, it is as if you are giving a sequence of operations, with an "empty" one at the end. This has the effect of making *Mathematica* perform the operations you specify, but display no output.

expr ;	do an operation, but display no output

Inhibiting output.

Putting a semicolon at the end of the line tells *Mathematica* to produce no output.

```
In[2]:= x = 67 - 5 ;
```

You can still use % to get the output that would have been produced.

```
In[3]:= %

Out[3]= 62
```

1.3 Using the *Mathematica* System

■ 1.3.1 Interfaces to *Mathematica*

Mathematica is built to be both exactly the same and yet quite different on different computer systems. It is exactly the same in the sense that the input you give and the output you get are the same. It is different in that the ways you give input and get output are typically customized to your particular kind of computer system.

This section describes the two kinds of interface to *Mathematica* that are currently most common: text based and notebook based. Page 44 describes the basic modes of interaction with these two kinds of interface. If your system uses another kind of interface, then you will need to look at the specific documentation for it.

With a text-based interface, you interact with the computer primarily by typing successive lines of input at the keyboard, and getting back successive lines of output on the screen. Many versions of *Mathematica*, for example those running under the Unix operating system, support this kind of interface.

On certain computers with graphical user interfaces, *Mathematica* supports a special "notebook" interface. Notebooks are interactive documents, into which you can insert *Mathematica* input as well as ordinary text and graphics. You typically interact with notebooks not only by typing text, but also by using a pointing device such as a mouse to indicate actions or choices graphically.

The fundamental computational part of *Mathematica* is called the *kernel*. Most of what is in this book is concerned with the operation of the kernel. The kernel is set up to work the same on all computers that run *Mathematica*. When you use *Mathematica* with a text-based interface, you are interacting almost directly with the kernel. But it is also possible to have a *front end* which lies between you and the *Mathematica* kernel. The front end is usually a separate program which handles various aspects of user interaction. Front ends typically allow you to prepare input in various ways, then send the input to the kernel, and then get results back for display. The notebook interface for *Mathematica* is an example of a *Mathematica* front end.

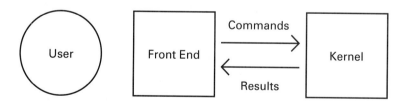

The kernel and front end can operate quite separately. They do not, for example, need to be running on the same computer. Instead, they can be on separate computers, connected, say, via a network. The *Mathematica* kernel can communicate with the front end by means of a high-level communication standard called *MathLink*.

The notebook interface is currently a standard type of *Mathematica* front end, although it is by no means the only possible type. It is intended to provide easy and fairly direct access to all of the capabilities of the *Mathematica* kernel. There are other front ends for other purposes. Some front ends, for example, are active programs in their own right, which access *Mathematica* only for specific calculations, often in a way that is hidden from the user.

■ 1.3.2 Entering Input

Text-Based Interfaces

With a text-based interface, your whole *Mathematica* session looks much like the dialogs in this book. When *Mathematica* is ready for input, it prints a prompt of the form *In[n]:=*. When you have entered your input, *Mathematica* processes it, and, if appropriate, prints out the result, with a label of the form *Out[n]=*. Then *Mathematica* prints a new input prompt, and the cycle begins again.

If your input is short, then you can give it on a single line, ending the line by pressing RETURN or ENTER. If your input is longer, it may continue for several lines. *Mathematica* will not start processing your input until it has received a complete expression. It will instead go on reading lines of input until all open parentheses are closed, and so on. If you enter a completely blank line, *Mathematica* will throw away the lines you have typed so far, and issue a new input prompt.

When you have input that you know will continue for several lines, a useful trick is to open parentheses on the first line, and close them only when you get to the very end of your input.

Mathematica knows that the first line cannot be your whole expression, so it waits for you to give more input on the next line.	*In[1]:= 3 + 4 +* 5 *Out[1]= 12*

Mathematica will wait for as long as is needed to get a complete expression.	*In[2]:= (3*
	
	        + 4
	
	        + 5
	
	        )
	
	Out[2]= 12

Mathematica requires that the input you give follow a definite syntax. Input like 4 +/ 5 does not follow the syntax, and cannot be processed by *Mathematica*. If you give input like this, *Mathematica* will reject it, and tell you to re-enter it. Usually, *Mathematica* will give you an indication of where on your input line it first encountered a problem.

With text-based interfaces, *Mathematica* has no built-in editing capabilities. Instead, it allows you to use whatever standard editor exists on your computer system. Several editing functions which call your standard editor are nevertheless typically provided in versions of *Mathematica* with text-based interfaces.

Edit[ ]	start your editor with an empty buffer; read in the expression you write out from your editor
Edit[*expr*]	start your editor with a version of *expr* suitable for input in the buffer
EditIn[ ]	start your editor with the text of your latest input in the buffer
EditIn[*n*]	start your editor with the text of In[*n*] in the buffer
EditDefinition[*f*]	start your editor with the definition of *f* in the buffer

Typical editing functions provided with text-based interfaces.

What all the editing functions do is to start your standard external editor with certain text in a buffer or temporary file. After you finish your editing, you should write out the buffer or temporary file, then exit your editor. The final form of your text will be used as input to *Mathematica*.

With a text-based interface, each line of *Mathematica* input and output appears sequentially. Often your computer system will allow you to scroll backwards to review previous work.

%*n* or Out[*n*]	the value of the nth output
InString[*n*]	the text of the nth input
In[*n*]	the nth input, for re-evaluation

Retrieving and re-evaluating previous input and output.

Whatever kind of computer system you have, you can always use *Mathematica* to retrieve or re-evaluate previous input and output. In general, re-evaluating a particular piece of input or output may give you a different result than when you evaluated it in the first place. The reason is that in between you may have reset the values of variables that are used in that piece of input or output. If you ask for Out[*n*], then *Mathematica* will give you the final form of your n^{th} output. On the other hand, if you ask for In[*n*], then *Mathematica* will take the nth input you gave, and re-evaluate it using whatever current assignments you have given for variables.

Notebook Interfaces

In a notebook interface, your *Mathematica* input and output appear as elements in the notebook document, potentially mixed with text and graphics. A complete notebook can look much like this book. It can contain specific pieces of *Mathematica* input and output, analogous to the dialogs in this book, together with explanatory text, graphics, and so on.

All the material in a notebook is organized into a sequence of *cells*. Each cell contains text or other material that is to be treated as some kind of unit. Thus, for example, each complete piece of *Mathematica* input occupies its own cell. When you evaluate the input, *Mathematica* automatically generates a new cell to be used for the output.

Within a particular cell, you can typically use any of the standard positioning and editing capabilities of the graphical user interface for your computer system. A piece of *Mathematica* input within a single cell may go on for several lines. Thus, for example, pressing the RETURN key when you are typing input into a particular cell simply goes to the next line in the cell. It does not tell the *Mathematica* front end that you have finished giving input in that cell.

In most notebook interfaces, you tell *Mathematica* that you have finished preparing input for it in a particular cell by pressing SHIFT-RETURN or ENTER. When you do this, all the text in your current cell is given as input to the *Mathematica* kernel.

■ Press SHIFT-RETURN or ENTER to send input to *Mathematica*.

Terminating your input with a notebook interface.

Mathematica requires that the input you give follow a definite syntax. Input like 4 +/ 5 does not follow the syntax, and cannot be processed by *Mathematica*. If you give input like this, *Mathematica* will reject it. Typically it will make your computer beep, then put you at the point in your current input cell where it first encountered a problem. You can then edit the material in the cell, and press SHIFT-RETURN or ENTER to resend it to *Mathematica*.

When you are first entering text in a particular notebook cell, the *Mathematica* front end does not yet know whether the text you give is intended to be actual *Mathematica* input. It is only when you press SHIFT-RETURN or ENTER that it can tell. As a result, it is only at this point that the front end labels your input with `In[n]:=`. In addition, if you ever go back and edit the cell, the label automatically disappears.

In general, notebook interfaces allow you to move around in, edit and annotate the "history" of your *Mathematica* session. As a result, the sequence of input and output lines that you gave to *Mathematica* may not appear in your notebook in the order in which they were given. In this case, only the `In[n]:=` and `Out[n]=` labels tell you the actual sequence that was used.

Notebook interfaces typically provide various features to reduce the amount of typing involved in entering *Mathematica* input. One standard feature is command completion. If you type part of a name known to *Mathematica*, you can ask your notebook interface to complete the name. If there is a unique completion, it is done. Otherwise, you get a menu of possible completions.

There are also various parameters, particularly graphical ones, that notebook interfaces typically allow you to choose using graphical tools. For example, many notebook interfaces allow you to choose the view point for a three-dimensional plot by interactively rotating a three-dimensional box. When you have found the view point you want, the front end generates the appropriate text to specify this view point in *Mathematica*.

By rotating the box, you can specify a view point, which is then fed to *Mathematica* in textual form.

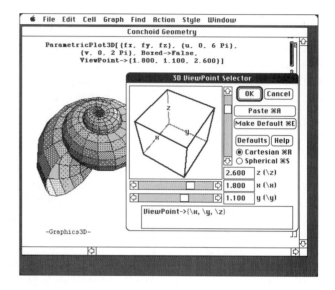

■ 1.3.3 Special Topic: Notebooks

Notebooks are interactive documents that consist of a hierarchy of cells. Each cell contains a particular kind of material: text, graphics, *Mathematica* input or output, and so on. Sequences of cells can be arranged in groups representing related material. A group of cells might, for example, correspond to a section or chapter in your document.

Notebooks consist of cells, which can be arranged hierarchically in groups.

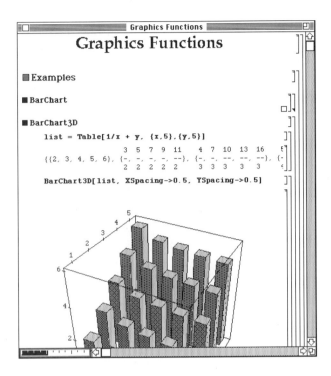

The extent of each cell in a notebook is typically indicated by a bracket to its right. When you have a group of cells, another bracket shows the extent of the group. By looking at these brackets, you can see how a particular notebook is organized.

When a group of cells corresponds to a section or chapter of your document, the first cell in the group typically gives some kind of heading for the section or chapter. Notebook interfaces allow you to "close" groups of cells so that only their first cells are visible. If the first cells contain headings, you can get an outline of your document in this way.

Double-clicking the bracket that spans a group of cells closes the group, leaving only the first cell visible.

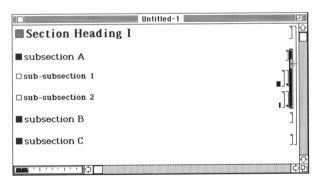

When a group is closed, the bracket for it has an arrow at the bottom. Double-clicking this arrow opens the group again.

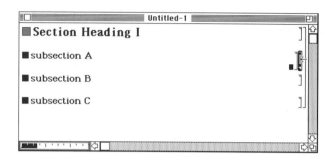

An important feature of notebook interfaces is that they allow you to manipulate your document at several levels. At the lowest level, you can modify text or other material within a single cell. At a higher level, you can do the same kinds of operations on a whole cell at a time. And beyond that, you can manipulate whole groups of cells.

Notebook interfaces can typically take advantage of the typographical capabilities of your computer system's graphical user interface. Thus, for example, cells containing text can have a variety of "styles". The styles can involve various fonts, sizes, and so on. In addition, even within a single cell, you can often mix several styles, allowing you to produce typographically complex text.

Notebook interfaces support many styles of text, allowing you to produce typographically complex documents.

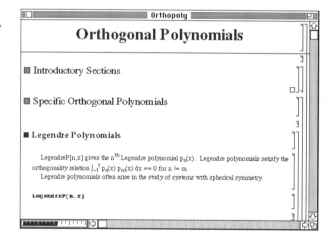

Notebook interfaces typically provide many options for displaying and importing graphics. One important feature is that you can take sequences of graphics cells, and "animate" them, treating each cell like a frame in a movie. The notebook interface typically allows you to set various parameters, such as speed and direction of your "movie".

Another graphical feature common in notebook interfaces is the ability to read coordinates from graphs using a pointing device such as a mouse. You can also usually enter new points, whose coordinates you can get in textual form as *Mathematica* input.

Notebook interfaces typically allow you to find and specify coordinates graphically.

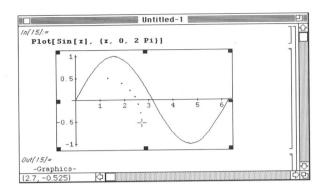

■ 1.3.4 *Mathematica* Packages

One of the most important features of *Mathematica* is that it is an extensible system. There is a certain amount of mathematical and other functionality that is built into *Mathematica*. But by using the *Mathematica* language, it is always possible to add more functionality.

For many kinds of calculations, what is built into the standard version of *Mathematica* will be quite sufficient. However, if you work in a particular specialized area, you may find that you often need to use certain functions that are not built into *Mathematica*.

In such cases, you may well be able to find a *Mathematica* package that contains the functions you need. *Mathematica* packages are files written in the *Mathematica* language. They consist of collections of *Mathematica* definitions which "teach" *Mathematica* about particular application areas.

<<*name*	read in a *Mathematica* package

Reading in *Mathematica* packages.

If you want to use functions from a particular package, you must first read the package into *Mathematica*. The details of how to do this are discussed in Section 1.10. There are various conventions that govern the names you should use to refer to packages.

This command reads in a particular
Mathematica package.

```
In[1]:= << DiscreteMath`CombinatorialFunctions`
```

The Subfactorial function is defined
in the package.

```
In[2]:= Subfactorial[10]
Out[2]= 1334961
```

There are a number of subtleties associated with such issues as conflicts between names of functions in different packages. These are discussed in Section 2.6.9. One point to note, however, is that you must not refer to a function that you will read from a package before actually reading in the package. If you do this by mistake, you will have to execute the command Remove["*name*"] to get rid of the function before you read in the package which defines it. If you do not call `Remove`, *Mathematica* will use "your" version of the function, rather than the one from the package.

The fact that *Mathematica* can be extended using packages means that the boundary of exactly what is "part of *Mathematica*" is quite blurred. As far as usage is concerned, there is actually no difference between functions defined in packages and functions that are fundamentally built into *Mathematica*.

In fact, a fair number of the functions described in this book are actually implemented as *Mathematica* packages. However, on most *Mathematica* systems, the necessary packages have been preloaded, so that the functions they define are always present. (On some systems with severe memory limitations, even these packages may be loaded only on request.)

To blur the boundary of what is part of *Mathematica* even further, Section 2.8.7 describes how you can tell *Mathematica* automatically to load a particular package if you ever try to use a certain function. If you never use that function, then it will not be present. But as soon as you try to use it, its definition will be read in from a *Mathematica* package.

As a practical matter, the functions that should be considered "part of *Mathematica*" are probably those that are present in all *Mathematica* systems. It is these functions that are primarily discussed in this book.

Nevertheless, most versions of *Mathematica* come with a standard set of *Mathematica* packages, which contain definitions for many more functions. Some of these functions are mentioned in this book. But to get them, you must usually read in the necessary packages explicitly.

Of course, it is possible to set your *Mathematica* system up so that particular packages are pre-loaded, or are automatically loaded when needed. If you do this, then there may be many functions that appear as standard in your version of *Mathematica*, but which are not documented in this book.

One point that should be mentioned is the relationship between packages and notebooks. Both are stored as files on your computer system, and both can be read into *Mathematica*. However, a notebook is intended to be displayed, typically with a notebook interface, while a package is intended only to be used as *Mathematica* input. Many notebooks in fact contain sections that can be considered as packages, and which contain sequences of definitions intended for input to *Mathematica*.

■ 1.3.5 Getting Information from *Mathematica*

Notebook interfaces typically provide various graphical mechanisms for getting help and information on *Mathematica* objects. These are based on the general mechanism for getting information which is built into the *Mathematica* kernel, and which is available on all versions of *Mathematica*.

?Name	show information on *Name*
??Name	show extra information on *Name*
?Aaaa*	show information on all objects whose names begin with *Aaaa*

Ways to get information on *Mathematica* objects.

This gives information on the built-in function Log.

```
In[1]:= ?Log

Log[z] gives the natural logarithm of z (logarithm to base E).
    Log[b, z] gives the logarithm to base b.
```

You can ask for information about any object, whether it is built into *Mathematica*, has been read in from a *Mathematica* package, or has been introduced by you.

When you use ? to get information, you must make sure that the question mark appears as the first character in your input line. You need to do this so that *Mathematica* can tell when you are requesting information rather than giving ordinary input for evaluation.

You can get extra information by using ??. **Attributes** will be discussed in Section 2.5.3.

```
In[1]:= ??Log

Log[z] gives the natural logarithm of z (logarithm to base E).
    Log[b, z] gives the logarithm to base b.

Attributes[Log] = {Listable, Protected}
```

This gives information on all *Mathematica* objects whose names begin with L. When there is more than one object, *Mathematica* just lists their names.

```
In[1]:= ?L*

Label              LessEqual           ListContourPlot
LaguerreL          LetterQ             ListDensityPlot
Last               Level               ListPlay
LatticeReduce      Lighting            ListPlot
LCM                LightSources        ListPlot3D
LeafCount          Limit               ListQ
Left               Line                Literal
LegendreP          LinearProgramming   Locked
LegendreQ          LinearSolve         Log
LegendreType       LineBreak           LogGamma
Length             LineForm            LogicalExpand
LerchPhi           List                LogIntegral
Less               Listable            LowerCaseQ
```

?Aaaa will give you information on the particular object whose name you specify. Using the "metacharacter" *, however, you can get information on collections of objects with similar names. The rule is that * is a "wild card" that can stand for any sequence of ordinary characters. So, for example, ?L* gets information on all objects whose names consist of the letter L, followed by any sequence of characters.

You can put a * anywhere in the string you ask ? about. For example, ?*Expand would give you all objects whose names *end* with Expand. Similarly, ?x*0 would give you objects whose names start with x, and end with 0, and have any sequence of characters in between. (You may notice that the way you use * to specify names in *Mathematica* is similar to the way you use * in Unix and other operating systems to specify file names.)

You can ask for information on most of
the special input forms that *Mathematica*
uses. This asks for information about
the := operator.

```
In[1]:= ?:=
```

```
lhs := rhs or SetDelayed[lhs, rhs] assigns rhs to be the delayed
    value of lhs. rhs is maintained in an unevaluated form. When
    lhs appears, it is replaced by rhs, evaluated afresh each
    time.
```

■ 1.3.6 Warnings and Messages

Mathematica usually goes about its work silently, giving output only when it has finished doing the calculations you asked for.

However, if it looks as if *Mathematica* is doing something you definitely did not intend, *Mathematica*
will usually print a message to warn you. There is a list of standard *Mathematica* messages available as
a Wolfram Research technical report.

The square root function should have
only one argument. *Mathematica* prints a
message to warn you that you have
given two arguments here.

```
In[1]:= Sqrt[4, 5]
```

```
Sqrt::argx: Sqrt called with 2
    arguments; 1 argument is expected.
```

```
Out[1]= Sqrt[4, 5]
```

Each message has a name. You can
switch off messages using Off.

```
In[2]:= Off[Sqrt::argx]
```

The message Sqrt::argx has now been
switched off, and will no longer appear.

```
In[3]:= Sqrt[4, 5]
```

```
Out[3]= Sqrt[4, 5]
```

This switches Sqrt::argx back on
again.

```
In[4]:= On[Sqrt::argx]
```

Off[*Function*::*tag*]	switch off (suppress) a message
On[*Function*::*tag*]	switch on a message

Functions for controlling message output.

■ 1.3.7 Interrupting Calculations

There will probably be times when you want to stop *Mathematica* in the middle of a calculation. Perhaps you realize that you asked *Mathematica* to do the wrong thing. Or perhaps the calculation is just
taking a long time, and you want to find out what is going on.

The way that you interrupt a *Mathematica* calculation depends on what front end you are using.

CONTROL-C	text-based interfaces
COMMAND-.	notebook interfaces

Typical keys to interrupt calculations in *Mathematica*.

On some computer systems, it may take *Mathematica* some time to respond to your interrupt. When *Mathematica* does respond, it will typically give you a menu of possible things to do.

continue	continue the calculation
show	show what *Mathematica* is doing
inspect	inspect the current state of your calculation
abort	abort this particular calculation
exit	exit *Mathematica* completely

Some typical options available when you interrupt a calculation in *Mathematica*.

1.4 Algebraic Calculations

■ 1.4.1 Symbolic Computation

One of the most important features of *Mathematica* is that it can do *symbolic*, as well as *numerical* calculations. This means that it can handle algebraic formulas as well as numbers.

Here is a typical numerical computation.

$In[1]:= $ **3 + 62 - 1**

$Out[1]= $ 64

This is a symbolic computation.

$In[2]:= $ **3x - x + 2**

$Out[2]= $ 2 + 2 x

numerical computation	3 + 62 − 1 ⟶ 64
symbolic computation	3x − x + 2 ⟶ 2 + 2 x

Numerical and symbolic computations.

You can type any algebraic expression into *Mathematica*. The expression is printed out in an approximation to standard mathematical notation.

$In[3]:= $ **-1 + 2x + x∧3**

$Out[3]= $ $-1 + 2 x + x^3$

Mathematica automatically carries out standard algebraic simplifications. Here it combines x^2 and $-4x^2$ to get $-3x^2$.

$In[4]:= $ **x∧2 + x - 4 x∧2**

$Out[4]= $ $x - 3 x^2$

You can type in any algebraic expression, using the operators listed on page 47. You can use spaces to denote multiplication. Be careful not to forget the space in x y. If you type in xy with no space, *Mathematica* will interpret this as a single symbol, with the name xy, not as a product of the two symbols x and y.

Mathematica rearranges and combines terms using the standard rules of algebra.

$In[5]:= $ **x y + 2 x∧2 y + y∧2 x∧2 - 2 y x**

$Out[5]= $ $-(x\ y) + 2 x^2 y + x^2 y^2$

Here is another algebraic expression.

$In[6]:= $ **(x + 2y + 1)(x - 2)∧2**

$Out[6]= $ $(-2 + x)^2 (1 + x + 2 y)$

The function **Expand** multiplies out products and powers.

$In[7]:= $ **Expand[%]**

$Out[7]= $ $4 - 3 x^2 + x^3 + 8 y - 8 x y + 2 x^2 y$

Factor does essentially the inverse of Expand.

$In[8]:=$ **Factor[%]**

$Out[8]= (-2 + x)^2 (1 + x + 2 y)$

When you type in more complicated expressions, it is important that you put parentheses in the right places. Thus, for example, you have to give the expression x^{4y} in the form x^(4y). If you leave out the parentheses, you get x^4y instead. It never hurts to put in too many parentheses, but to find out exactly when you need to use parentheses, look at Section A.2.

Here is a more complicated formula, requiring several parentheses.

$In[9]:=$ **Sqrt[8]/9801 (4n)! (1103 + 26390 n) /**
$\qquad$ **(n!^4 396^(4n))**

$$Out[9]= \frac{2 \; Sqrt[2] \; (1103 + 26390 \; n) \; (4 \; n)!}{9801 \; 396^{4 \, n} \; n!^4}$$

When you type in an expression, *Mathematica* automatically applies its large repertoire of rules for transforming expressions. These rules include the standard rules of algebra, such as $x - x = 0$, together with much more sophisticated rules involving higher mathematical functions.

Mathematica uses standard rules of algebra to replace $(\sqrt{1+x})^4$ by $(1+x)^2$.

$In[10]:=$ **Sqrt[1 + x]^4**

$Out[10]= (1 + x)^2$

Mathematica knows no rules for this expression, so it leaves the expression in the original form you gave.

$In[11]:=$ **Sqrt[1 + Cos[x]]**

$Out[11]= Sqrt[1 + Cos[x]]$

The notion of transformation rules is a very general one. In fact, you can think of the whole of *Mathematica* as simply a system for applying a collection of transformation rules to many different kinds of expressions.

The general principle that *Mathematica* follows is simple to state. It takes any expression you input, and gets results by applying a succession of transformation rules, stopping when it knows no more transformation rules that can be applied.

■ Take any expression, and apply transformation rules until the result no longer changes.

The fundamental principle of *Mathematica*.

■ 1.4.2 Values for Symbols

When *Mathematica* transforms an expression such as x + x into 2x, it is treating the variable x in a purely symbolic or formal fashion. In such cases, x is a symbol which can stand for any expression.

Often, however, you need to replace a symbol like x with a definite "value". Sometimes this value will be a number; often it will be another expression.

To take an expression such as 1 + 2x and replace the symbol x that appears in it with a definite value, you can create a *Mathematica* transformation rule, and then apply this rule to the expression. To replace x with the value 3, you would create the transformation rule x -> 3. You must type -> as a pair of characters, with no space in between. You can think of x -> 3 as being a rule in which "x goes to 3".

To apply a transformation rule to a particular *Mathematica* expression, you type *expr /. rule*. The "replacement operator" /. is typed as a pair of characters, with no space in between.

This uses the transformation rule x->3 in the expression 1 + 2x.	$In[1]:= $ **1 + 2x /. x -> 3** $Out[1]= $ 7
You can replace x with any expression. Here every occurrence of x is replaced by 2 - y.	$In[2]:= $ **1 + x + x^2 /. x -> 2 - y** $Out[2]= $ 3 + (2 - y)^2 - y
Here is a transformation rule. *Mathematica* treats it like any other symbolic expression.	$In[3]:= $ **x -> 3 + y** $Out[3]= $ x -> 3 + y
This applies the transformation rule on the previous line to the expression x^2 - 9.	$In[4]:= $ **x^2 - 9 /. %** $Out[4]= $ -9 + (3 + y)^2

expr /. x -> value	replace *x* by *value* in the expression *expr*
expr /. {x -> xval, y -> yval}	perform several replacements

Replacing symbols by values in expressions.

You can apply rules together by putting the rules in a list.	$In[5]:= $ **(x + y) (x - y)^2 /. {x -> 3, y -> 1 - a}** $Out[5]= $ (3 - (1 - a))^2 (4 - a)

The replacement operator /. allows you to apply transformation rules to a particular expression. Sometimes, however, you will want to define transformation rules that should *always* be applied. For example, you might want to replace x with 3 whenever x occurs.

As discussed in Section 1.2.2, you can do this by *assigning* the value 3 to x using x = 3. Once you have made the assignment x = 3, x will always be replaced by 3, whenever it appears.

This assigns the value 3 to x.	$In[6]:= $ **x = 3** $Out[6]= $ 3
Now x will automatically be replaced by 3 wherever it appears.	$In[7]:= $ **x^2 - 1** $Out[7]= $ 8
This assigns the expression 1 + a to be the value of x.	$In[8]:= $ **x = 1 + a** $Out[8]= $ 1 + a

Now x is replaced by 1 + a.

$In[9]:=$ x^2 - 1

$Out[9]=$ -1 + $(1 + a)^2$

You can define the value of a symbol to be any expression, not just a number. You should realize that once you have given such a definition, the definition will continue to be used whenever the symbol appears, until you explicitly change or remove the definition. For most people, forgetting to remove values you have assigned to symbols is the single most common source of mistakes in using *Mathematica*.

x = *value*	define a value for x which will always be used
x =.	remove any value defined for x

Assigning values to symbols.

The symbol x still has the value you assigned to it above.

$In[10]:=$ x + 5 - 2x

$Out[10]=$ 6 + a - 2 (1 + a)

This removes the value you assigned to x.

$In[11]:=$ x =.

Now x has no value defined, so it can be used as a purely symbolic variable.

$In[12]:=$ x + 5 - 2x

$Out[12]=$ 5 - x

A symbol such as x can serve many different purposes in *Mathematica*, and in fact, much of the flexibility of *Mathematica* comes from being able to mix these purposes at will. However, you need to keep some of the different uses of x straight in order to avoid making mistakes. The most important distinction is between the use of x as a name for another expression, and as a symbolic variable that stands only for itself.

Traditional programming languages that do not support symbolic computation allow variables to be used only as names for objects, typically numbers, that have been assigned as values for them. In *Mathematica*, however, x can also be treated as a purely formal variable, to which various transformation rules can be applied. Of course, if you explicitly give a definition, such as x = 3, then x will always be replaced by 3, and can no longer serve as a formal variable.

You should understand that explicit definitions such as x = 3 have a global effect. On the other hand, a replacement such as *expr* /. x->3 affects only the specific expression *expr*. It is usually much easier to keep things straight if you avoid using explicit definitions except when absolutely necessary.

You can always mix replacements with assignments. With assignments, you can give names to expressions in which you want to do replacements, or to rules that you want to use to do the replacements.

This assigns a value to the symbol t.

$In[13]:=$ t = 1 + x^2

$Out[13]=$ 1 + x^2

This finds the value of t, and then replaces x by 2 in it.	$In[14]:= \mathbf{t \ /. \ x \ -> \ 2}$ $Out[14]= 5$
This finds the value of t for a different value of x.	$In[15]:= \mathbf{t \ /. \ x \ -> \ 5a}$ $Out[15]= 1 + 25 \ a^2$
This finds the value of t when x is replaced by Pi, and then evaluates the result numerically.	$In[16]:= \mathbf{t \ /. \ x \ -> \ Pi \ //N}$ $Out[16]= 10.8696$

■ 1.4.3 Transforming Algebraic Expressions

There are often many different ways to write the same algebraic expression. As one example, the expression $(1 + x)^2$ can be written as $1 + 2x + x^2$. *Mathematica* provides a large collection of functions for converting between different forms of algebraic expressions.

Expand[*expr*]	multiply out products and powers, writing the result as a sum of terms
Factor[*expr*]	write *expr* as a minimal product of factors

Two common functions for transforming algebraic expressions.

Expand gives the "expanded form", with products and powers multiplied out.	$In[1]:= \mathbf{Expand[\ (1 \ + \ x)\wedge2 \ ]}$ $Out[1]= 1 + 2 \ x + x^2$
Factor recovers the original form.	$In[2]:= \mathbf{Factor[\ \% \ ]}$ $Out[2]= (1 + x)^2$
It is easy to generate complicated expressions with Expand.	$In[3]:= \mathbf{Expand[\ (1 \ + \ x \ + \ 3 \ y)\wedge4 \ ]}$ $Out[3]= 1 + 4 \ x + 6 \ x^2 + 4 \ x^3 + x^4 + 12 \ y + 36 \ x \ y + 36 \ x^2 \ y +$ $\quad 12 \ x^3 \ y + 54 \ y^2 + 108 \ x \ y^2 + 54 \ x^2 \ y^2 + 108 \ y^3 + 108 \ x \ y^3 +$ $\quad 81 \ y^4$
Factor often gives you simpler expressions.	$In[4]:= \mathbf{Factor[\ \% \ ]}$ $Out[4]= (1 + x + 3 \ y)^4$

There are some cases, though, where
Factor can give you more complicated
expressions.

$In[5]:=$ **Factor[x^10 - 1]**

$Out[5]=$ $(-1 + x) (1 + x) (1 - x + x^2 - x^3 + x^4)$
$(1 + x + x^2 + x^3 + x^4)$

In this case, **Expand** gives the "simpler"
form.

$In[6]:=$ **Expand[%]**

$Out[6]=$ $-1 + x^{10}$

■ 1.4.4 Simplifying Algebraic Expressions

There are many situations where you want to write a particular algebraic expression in the simplest possible form. Although it is difficult to know exactly what one means in all cases by the "simplest form", a worthwhile practical procedure is to look at many different forms of an expression, and pick out the one that involves the smallest number of parts.

Simplify[*expr*]	try to find the form of *expr* with the smallest number of parts, by applying a variety of algebraic transformations

Simplifying algebraic expressions.

Simplify writes $x^2 + 2x + 1$ in factored
form.

$In[1]:=$ **Simplify[x^2 + 2x + 1]**

$Out[1]=$ $(1 + x)^2$

Simplify leaves $x^{10} - 1$ in expanded
form, since for this expression, the
factored form is larger.

$In[2]:=$ **Simplify[x^10 - 1]**

$Out[2]=$ $-1 + x^{10}$

You can often use **Simplify** to "clean up" complicated expressions that you get as the results of computations.

Here is the integral of $1/(x^4 - 1)$.
Integrals are discussed in more detail in
Section 1.5.3.

$In[3]:=$ **Integrate[1/(x^4-1), x]**

$Out[3]=$ $\dfrac{-ArcTan[x]}{2} + \dfrac{Log[-1 + x]}{4} - \dfrac{Log[1 + x]}{4}$

Differentiating the result from
Integrate should give back your
original expression. In this case, as is
common, you get a more complicated
version of the expression.

$In[4]:=$ **D[%, x]**

$Out[4]=$ $\dfrac{1}{4 (-1 + x)} - \dfrac{1}{4 (1 + x)} - \dfrac{1}{2 (1 + x^2)}$

Simplify succeeds in getting back the original, more simple, form of the expression.

$$In[5] := \mathtt{Simplify[\%]}$$

$$Out[5] = \frac{1}{-1 + x^4}$$

For many simple algebraic calculations, you may find it convenient to use Simplify routinely on your results.

In more complicated calculations, however, you often need to exercise more control over the exact form of answer that you get. In addition, when your expressions are complicated, Simplify may spend a long time testing a large number of possible forms in its attempt to find the simplest one.

■ 1.4.5 Advanced Topic: Putting Expressions into Different Forms

Complicated algebraic expressions can usually be written in many different ways. *Mathematica* provides a variety of functions for converting expressions from one form to another.

In most applications, the commonest of these functions are Expand, Factor and Simplify. However, particularly when you have rational expressions that contain quotients, you may need to use other functions.

Expand[*expr*]	multiply out products and powers
ExpandAll[*expr*]	apply Expand everywhere
Factor[*expr*]	reduce to a product of factors
Together[*expr*]	put all terms over a common denominator
Apart[*expr*]	separate into terms with simple denominators
Cancel[*expr*]	cancel common factors between numerators and denominators
Simplify[*expr*]	try a sequence of algebraic transformations and give the smallest form of *expr* found

Functions for transforming algebraic expressions.

Here is a rational expression that can be written in many different forms.

$$In[1] := \mathtt{e = (x - 1)^2 (2 + x) / ((1 + x) (x - 3)^2)}$$

$$Out[1] = \frac{(-1 + x)^2 (2 + x)}{(-3 + x)^2 (1 + x)}$$

Expand expands out the numerator, but
leaves the denominator in factored form.

$$In[2] := \texttt{Expand[e]}$$

$$Out[2] = \frac{2}{(-3 + x)^2 \ (1 + x)} - \frac{3 \ x}{(-3 + x)^2 \ (1 + x)} + \frac{x^3}{(-3 + x)^2 \ (1 + x)}$$

ExpandAll expands out everything,
including the denominator.

$$In[3] := \texttt{ExpandAll[e]}$$

$$Out[3] = \frac{2}{9 + 3 \ x - 5 \ x^2 + x^3} - \frac{3 \ x}{9 + 3 \ x - 5 \ x^2 + x^3} + \frac{x^3}{9 + 3 \ x - 5 \ x^2 + x^3}$$

Together collects all the terms together
over a common denominator.

$$In[4] := \texttt{Together[\%]}$$

$$Out[4] = \frac{2 - 3 \ x + x^3}{9 + 3 \ x - 5 \ x^2 + x^3}$$

Apart breaks the expression apart into
terms with simple denominators.

$$In[5] := \texttt{Apart[\%]}$$

$$Out[5] = 1 + \frac{5}{(-3 + x)^2} + \frac{19}{4 \ (-3 + x)} + \frac{1}{4 \ (1 + x)}$$

Factor factors everything, in this case
reproducing the original form.

$$In[6] := \texttt{Factor[\%]}$$

$$Out[6] = \frac{(-1 + x)^2 \ (2 + x)}{(-3 + x)^2 \ (1 + x)}$$

According to Simplify, the original
form is the simplest way to write the
expression.

$$In[7] := \texttt{Simplify[e]}$$

$$Out[7] = \frac{(-1 + x)^2 \ (2 + x)}{(-3 + x)^2 \ (1 + x)}$$

Getting expressions into the form you want is something of an art. In most cases, it is best simply
to experiment, trying different transformations until you get what you want.

When you have an expression with a single variable, you can choose to write it as a sum of terms,
a product, and so on. If you have an expression with several variables, there is an even wider selection of possible forms. You can, for example, choose to group terms in the expression so that one or
another of the variables is "dominant".

Collect[*expr*, *x*]	group together powers of *x*
FactorTerms[*expr*, *x*]	pull out factors that do not depend on *x*

Rearranging expressions in several variables.

Here is an algebraic expression in two variables.

$In[8] := $ **v = Expand[(3 + 2 x)∧2 (x + 2 y)∧2]**

$Out[8] = 9 x^2 + 12 x^3 + 4 x^4 + 36 x y + 48 x^2 y + 16 x^3 y +$

$36 y^2 + 48 x y^2 + 16 x^2 y^2$

This groups together terms in v that involve the same power of x.

$In[9] := $ **Collect[v, x]**

$Out[9] = 4 x^4 + 36 y^2 + x^3 (12 + 16 y) + x^2 (9 + 48 y + 16 y^2) +$

$x (36 y + 48 y^2)$

This groups together powers of y.

$In[10] := $ **Collect[v, y]**

$Out[10] = 9 x^2 + 12 x^3 + 4 x^4 + (36 x + 48 x^2 + 16 x^3) y +$

$(36 + 48 x + 16 x^2) y^2$

This factors out the piece that does not depend on y.

$In[11] := $ **FactorTerms[v, y]**

$Out[11] = (9 + 12 x + 4 x^2) (x^2 + 4 x y + 4 y^2)$

As we have seen, even when you restrict yourself to polynomials and rational expressions, there are many different ways to write any particular expression. If you consider more complicated expressions, involving, for example, higher mathematical functions, the variety of possible forms becomes still greater. As a result, it is totally infeasible to have a specific function built into *Mathematica* to produce each possible form. Rather, *Mathematica* allows you to construct arbitrary sets of transformation rules for converting between different forms. Many *Mathematica* packages include such rules; the details of how to construct them for yourself are given in Section 2.4.

There are nevertheless a few additional built-in *Mathematica* functions for transforming expressions.

Expand[*expr*, Trig -> True]	expand out trigonometric functions, writing sin(x)² in terms of sin(2x), etc.
Factor[*expr*, Trig -> True]	factor trigonometric functions, writing sin(2x) in terms of sin(x)², etc.
ComplexExpand[*expr*]	perform expansions assuming that all variables are real
PowerExpand[*expr*]	transform (xy)^p into x^p y^p, etc.

Some other functions for transforming expressions.

This generates a multiple angle form for the trigonometric expression.
Trig->True is an option specification, explained in Section 1.9.3.

In[12]:= **Expand[Cos[x]^3 Sin[x]^2, Trig->True]**

$$Out[12]= \frac{Cos[x]}{8} - \frac{Cos[3\ x]}{16} - \frac{Cos[5\ x]}{16}$$

This gets back the original form.

In[13]:= **Factor[%, Trig->True]**

$$Out[13]= Cos[x]^3\ Sin[x]^2$$

This expands the cosine assuming that x and y are both real.

In[14]:= **ComplexExpand[Sin[x + I y]]**

$$Out[14]= Cosh[y]\ Sin[x] + I\ Cos[x]\ Sinh[y]$$

This does the expansion allowing x and y to be complex.

In[15]:= **ComplexExpand[Sin[x + I y], {x, y}]**

$$Out[15]= -(Cosh[Im[x] + Re[y]]\ Sin[Im[y] - Re[x]]) +$$
$$I\ Cos[Im[y] - Re[x]]\ Sinh[Im[x] + Re[y]]$$

The transformations on expressions done by functions like Expand and Factor are always correct, whatever values the symbolic variables in the expressions may have. Sometimes, however, it is useful to perform transformations which are correct only if certain assumptions are made about the possible values of symbolic variables. One such transformation is performed by PowerExpand.

Mathematica does not automatically expand out non-integer powers of products.

In[16]:= **Sqrt[x y]**

$$Out[16]= Sqrt[x\ y]$$

PowerExpand does the expansion.

In[17]:= **PowerExpand[%]**

$$Out[17]= Sqrt[x]\ Sqrt[y]$$

The expansion is guaranteed to be correct only if x and y are both non-negative.

In[18]:= **{Sqrt[x y], Sqrt[x] Sqrt[y]} /. {x -> -1, y -> -1}**

$$Out[18]= \{1, -1\}$$

■ 1.4.6 Picking Out Pieces of Algebraic Expressions

Coefficient[*expr*, *form*]	coefficient of *form* in *expr*
Exponent[*expr*, *form*]	maximum power of *form* in *expr*
Part[*expr*, *n*] or *expr*[[*n*]]	n^{th} term of *expr*

Functions to pick out pieces of polynomials.

Here is an algebraic expression.

$$In[1]:= \textbf{e = Expand[(1 + 3x + 4y}\textasciicircum\textbf{2)}\textasciicircum\textbf{2]}$$

$$Out[1]= 1 + 6\ x + 9\ x^2 + 8\ y^2 + 24\ x\ y^2 + 16\ y^4$$

This gives the coefficient of x in e.

$$In[2]:= \textbf{Coefficient[e, x]}$$

$$Out[2]= 6 + 24\ y^2$$

Exponent[*expr*, *y*] gives the highest power of *y* that appears in *expr*.

$$In[3]:= \textbf{Exponent[e, y]}$$

$$Out[3]= 4$$

This gives the fourth term in e.

$$In[4]:= \textbf{Part[e, 4]}$$

$$Out[4]= 8\ y^2$$

You may notice that the function Part[*expr*, *n*] used to pick out the nth term in a sum is the same as the function described in Section 1.2.4 for picking out elements in lists. This is no coincidence. In fact, as discussed in Section 2.1.5, every *Mathematica* expression can be manipulated structurally much like a list. However, as discussed in Section 2.1.5, you must be careful, because *Mathematica* often shows algebraic expressions in a form that is different from the way it treats them internally.

Numerator[*expr*]	numerator of *expr*
Denominator[*expr*]	denominator of *expr*

Functions to pick out pieces of rational expressions.

Coefficient and Exponent are functions for working with *polynomials*. They work only on expressions that are explicitly written out as sums of terms, in the form you get from Expand.

Numerator and Denominator work on rational expressions.

Here is a rational expression.

$$In[5]:= \textbf{r = (1 + x)/(2 (2 - y))}$$

$$Out[5]= \frac{1 + x}{2\ (2 - y)}$$

Denominator picks out the denominator.	$In[6] := $ **Denominator[%]** $Out[6] = 2 \ (2 - y)$
Denominator gives 1 for expressions that are not quotients.	$In[7] := $ **Denominator[1/x + 2/y]** $Out[7] = 1$

■ 1.4.7 Controlling the Display of Large Expressions

When you do symbolic calculations, it is quite easy to end up with extremely complicated expressions. Often, you will not even want to *see* the complete result of a computation.

If you end your input with a semicolon, *Mathematica* will do the computation you asked for, but will not display the result. You can nevertheless use % or Out[*n*] to refer to the result.

Even though you may not want to see the *whole* result from a computation, you often do need to see its basic form. You can use Short to display the *outline* of an expression, omitting some of the terms.

Ending your input with ; stops *Mathematica* from displaying the complicated result of the computation.	$In[1] := $ **Expand[(x + 5 y + 10)^4]** ;
You can still refer to the result as %. //Short displays a one-line outline of the result. The <<*n*>> stands for *n* terms that have been left out.	$In[2] := $ **% //Short** $Out[2]//Short = 10000 + 4000 \ x + \ \text{<<12>>} + 625 \ y^4$
This shows a three-line version of the expression. More parts are now visible.	$In[3] := $ **Short[%, 3]** $Out[3]//Short =$ $$10000 + 4000 \ x + 600 \ x^2 + 40 \ x^3 + x^4 + 20000 \ y + 6000 \ x \ y +$$ $$\text{<<4>>} + 150 \ x^2 \ y^2 + 5000 \ y^3 + 500 \ x \ y^3 + 625 \ y^4$$
This gives the total number of terms in the sum.	$In[4] := $ **Length[%]** $Out[4] = 15$

command ;	execute *command*, but do not print the result
expr // Short	show a one-line outline form of *expr*
Short[*expr*, *n*]	show an *n*-line outline of *expr*

Some ways to shorten your output.

■ 1.4.8 The Limits of *Mathematica*

In just one *Mathematica* command, you can easily specify a calculation that is far too complicated for any computer to do. For example, you could ask for Expand[(1+x)^(10^100)]. The result of this calculation would have $10^{100} + 1$ terms — more than the total number of particles in the universe.

You should have no trouble working out Expand[(1+x)^100] on any computer that can run *Mathematica*. But as you increase the exponent of (1+x), the results you get will eventually become too big for your computer's memory to hold. Exactly at what point this happens depends not only on the total amount of memory your computer has, but often also on such details as what other jobs happen to be running on your computer when you try to do your calculation.

If your computer does run out of memory in the middle of a calculation, most versions of *Mathematica* have no choice but to stop immediately. As a result, it is important to plan your calculations so that they never need more memory than your computer has.

Even if the result of an algebraic calculation is quite simple, the intermediate expressions that you generate in the course of the calculation can be very complicated. This means that even if the final result is small, the intermediate parts of a calculation can be too big for your computer to handle. If this happens, you can usually break your calculation into pieces, and succeed in doing each piece on its own. You should know that the internal scheme which *Mathematica* uses for memory management is such that once part of a calculation is finished, the memory used to store intermediate expressions that arose is immediately made available for new expressions.

Memory space is the most common limiting factor in *Mathematica* calculations. Time can also, however, be a limiting factor. You will usually be prepared to wait a second, or even a minute, for the result of a calculation. But you will less often be prepared to wait an hour or a day, and you will almost never be able to wait a year.

One class of calculations where time is often the limiting factor is those that effectively involve searching or testing a large number of possibilities. Integer factorization is a classic example. At some level, the problem of factoring an integer always seems to boil down to something related to testing a large number of candidate factors. As far as one knows now, the number of cases to test can increase almost as fast as the exponential of the number of digits in the integer we are trying to factor. As a result, the time needed to factor integers can increase very rapidly with the size of the integers you try to factor. In practice, you will find that FactorInteger[*k*] will give a result almost immediately when *k* has fewer than about 25 digits. But when *k* has 50 digits, FactorInteger[*k*] will often take an unmanageably long time.

In the field of computational complexity theory, an important distinction is drawn between algorithms which are "polynomial time", and those which are not. A polynomial time algorithm can always be executed in a time that increases only like a polynomial in the length of the input. Non-polynomial time algorithms may take times that increase exponentially with the length of their input.

The internal code of *Mathematica* typically uses polynomial time algorithms whenever it is feasible. There are some problems, however, for which no polynomial time algorithms are known. In such cases, *Mathematica* has no choice but to use non-polynomial time algorithms, which may take times that increase exponentially with the length of their input. Integer factorization is one such case. Other cases include factoring polynomials and solving equations when the number of variables involved becomes large.

Even when the time needed to do a computation does not increase exponentially, there will always come a point where the computation is too large or time-consuming to do on your particular computer system. As you work with *Mathematica*, you should develop some feeling for the limits on the kinds of calculations you can do in your particular application area.

- Doing arithmetic with numbers containing ten thousand digits.

- Expanding out a polynomial that gives a thousand terms.

- Factoring a polynomial in three variables with a few hundred terms.

- Applying a recursive rule ten thousand times.

- Finding the numerical inverse of a 100×100 matrix.

- Formatting ten pages of output.

Some operations that typically take a few seconds on a 1990 vintage workstation.

■ 1.4.9 Using Symbols to Tag Objects

There are many ways to use symbols in *Mathematica*. So far, we have concentrated on using symbols to store values and to represent mathematical variables. This section describes another way to use symbols in *Mathematica*.

The idea is to use symbols as "tags" for different types of objects.

Working with physical units gives one simple example. When you specify the length of an object, you want to give not only a number, but also the units in which the length is measured. In standard notation, you might write a length as 12 meters.

You can imitate this notation almost directly in *Mathematica*. You can for example simply use a symbol `meters` to indicate the units of our measurement.

The symbol `meters` here acts as a tag, which indicates the units used.	`In[1]:= 12 meters`
	
	`Out[1]= 12 meters`

You can add lengths like this.	`In[2]:= % + 5.3 meters`
	
	`Out[2]= 17.3 meters`

This gives a speed.	`In[3]:= % / (25 seconds)` `Out[3]=` $\dfrac{0.692 \text{ meters}}{\text{seconds}}$

This converts to a speed in feet per
second.

In[4]:= **% /. meters -> 3.28084 feet**

$$Out[4]= \frac{2.27034 \text{ feet}}{\text{seconds}}$$

There is in fact a standard *Mathematica* package that allows you to work with units. The package
defines many symbols that represent standard types of units.

Load the *Mathematica* package for
handling units.

In[5]:= **<<Miscellaneous`Units`**

The package uses standardized names
for units.

In[6]:= **12 Meter/Second**

$$Out[6]= \frac{12 \text{ Meter}}{\text{Second}}$$

The function Convert[*expr*, *units*]
converts to the specified units.

In[7]:= **Convert[%, Mile/Hour]**

$$Out[7]= \frac{26.8432 \text{ Mile}}{\text{Hour}}$$

You have to give prefixes for units as
separate words.

In[8]:= **Convert[3 Kilo Meter / Hour, Inch / Minute]**

$$Out[8]= \frac{1968.5 \text{ Inch}}{\text{Minute}}$$

1.5 Symbolic Mathematics

■ 1.5.1 Basic Operations

Mathematica's ability to deal with symbolic expressions, as well as numbers, allows you to use it for many kinds of mathematics.

Calculus is one example. With *Mathematica*, you can differentiate an expression *symbolically*, and get a formula for the result.

This finds the derivative of x^n.

```
In[1]:= D[ x^n , x ]
             -1 + n
Out[1]= n x
```

Here is a slightly more complicated example.

```
In[2]:= D[x^2 Log[x + a], x]
             2
            x
Out[2]= ------- + 2 x Log[a + x]
         a + x
```

D[f, x]	the (partial) derivative $\frac{\partial f}{\partial x}$
Integrate[f, x]	the indefinite integral $\int f \, dx$
Sum[f, {i, *imin*, *imax*}]	the sum $\sum_{i=imin}^{imax} f$
Solve[*lhs*==*rhs*, x]	solution to an equation for x
Series[f, {x, x_0, *order*}]	a power series expansion of f about the point $x = x_0$
Limit[f, x->x_0]	the limit $\lim_{x \to x_0} f$

Some symbolic mathematical operations.

Getting formulas as the results of computations is usually desirable when it is possible. There are however many circumstances where it is mathematically impossible to get an explicit formula as the result of a computation. This happens, for example, when you try to solve an equation for which there is no "closed form" solution. In such cases, you must resort to numerical methods and approximations. These are discussed in Section 1.6.

■ 1.5.2 Differentiation

Here is the derivative of x^n with respect to x.

```
In[1]:= D[ x^n , x ]
             -1 + n
Out[1]= n x
```

Mathematica knows the derivatives of all the standard mathematical functions.

$In[2]:=$ **D[ArcTan[x] , x]**

$$Out[2]= \frac{1}{1 + x^2}$$

This differentiates three times with respect to **x**.

$In[3]:=$ **D[x^n, {x, 3}]**

$$Out[3]= (-2 + n) \ (-1 + n) \ n \ x^{-3 + n}$$

The function D[x^n, x] really gives a *partial* derivative, in which n is assumed not to depend on x. *Mathematica* has another function, called Dt, which finds *total* derivatives, in which all variables are assumed to be related. In mathematical notation, D[*f*, *x*] is like $\frac{\partial f}{\partial x}$, while Dt[*f*, *x*] is like $\frac{df}{dx}$. You can think of Dt as standing for "derivative total".

Dt gives a *total derivative*, which assumes that n can depend on x. Dt[n, x] stands for $\frac{dn}{dx}$.

$In[4]:=$ **Dt[x^n , x]**

$$Out[4]= n \ x^{-1 + n} + x^n \ Dt[n, x] \ Log[x]$$

This gives the total differential $d(x^n)$. Dt[x] is the differential dx.

$In[5]:=$ **Dt[x^n]**

$$Out[5]= n \ x^{-1 + n} \ Dt[x] + x^n \ Dt[n] \ Log[x]$$

D[*f*, *x*]	partial derivative $\frac{\partial}{\partial x} f$
D[*f*, x_1, x_2, ...]	multiple derivative $\frac{\partial}{\partial x_1} \frac{\partial}{\partial x_2} ... f$
D[*f*, {*x*, *n*}]	repeated derivative $\frac{\partial^n f}{\partial x^n}$
Dt[*f*]	total differential df
Dt[*f*, *x*]	total derivative $\frac{d}{dx} f$

Some differentiation functions.

As well as treating variables like *x* symbolically, you can also treat functions in *Mathematica* symbolically. Thus, for example, you can find formulas for derivatives of f[x], without specifying any explicit form for the function f.

Mathematica does not know how to differentiate **f**, so it gives you back a symbolic result in terms of **f'**.

$In[6]:=$ **D[f[x], x]**

$Out[6]=$ f'[x]

Mathematica uses the chain rule to simplify derivatives.

$In[7]:=$ **D[2 x f[x^2], x]**

$$Out[7]= 2 \ f[x^2] + 4 \ x^2 \ f'[x^2]$$

■ 1.5.3 Integration

Here is the integral $\int x^n\, dx$ in *Mathematica*.

```
In[1]:= Integrate[x^n, x]

           1 + n
          x
Out[1]= -------
         1 + n
```

Here is a slightly more complicated example.

```
In[2]:= Integrate[1/(x^4 - a^4), x]

                    x
          -ArcTan[-------]
                        2
                   Sqrt[a ]     Log[-a + x]   Log[a + x]
Out[2]= ------------------- + ----------- - ----------
               2       2           3            3
            2 a  Sqrt[a ]        4 a          4 a
```

Mathematica knows how to do many kinds of integrals. It can integrate any rational expression (ratio of polynomials), at least as long as the denominator does not involve too high a power of x. *Mathematica* can also integrate expressions that include exponential, logarithmic and trigonometric functions, as long as the resulting integrals can be given in terms of this same set of functions.

There are however many integrals for which no explicit formulas can be given, at least in terms of standard mathematical functions. Even a seemingly innocuous integral like $\int \frac{\log(1+2x)}{x}\, dx$ can only be evaluated in terms of the dilogarithm function `PolyLog[2, x]`. And an integral like $\int \sin(\sin(x))\, dx$ simply cannot be done in terms of any of the functions that are defined in standard mathematical handbooks. Section 3.5.7 discusses how *Mathematica* treats different kinds of integrals.

Mathematica can do integrals like this.

```
In[3]:= Integrate[ Log[x]^2 (1 + x^2)/x , x ]

            2      2           2       2          3
         3 x  - 6 x  Log[x] + 6 x  Log[x]  + 4 Log[x]
Out[3]= --------------------------------------------------
                            12
```

This integral simply cannot be done in terms of standard mathematical functions. As a result, *Mathematica* just leaves it undone.

```
In[4]:= Integrate[ Sin[Sin[x]], x ]

Out[4]= Integrate[Sin[Sin[x]], x]
```

Here is the definite integral $\int_a^b \log(x)\, dx$.

```
In[5]:= Integrate[ Log[x], {x, a, b} ]

Out[5]= a - b - a Log[a] + b Log[b]
```

Mathematica cannot give you a formula for this definite integral.

```
In[6]:= Integrate[ Sin[Sin[x]], {x, 0, 1} ]

Out[6]= Integrate[Sin[Sin[x]], {x, 0, 1}]
```

You can still get a numerical result, though.

```
In[7]:= N[ % ]

Out[7]= 0.430606
```

When you evaluate definite integrals symbolically with *Mathematica*, there are a number of subtle points, discussed in Section 3.5. You should realize that if your integrand contains certain kinds of singularities, then it is possible that *Mathematica* may give results, which, while formally correct, will lead to incorrect answers when you substitute particular values for variables.

$$\text{Integrate}[f, \ x] \qquad \text{the indefinite integral } \int f \ dx$$

$$\text{Integrate}[f, \ \{x, \ xmin, \ xmax\}]$$

$$\text{the definite integral } \int_{xmin}^{xmax} f \ dx$$

$$\text{Integrate}[f, \ \{x, \ xmin, \ xmax\}, \ \{y, \ ymin, \ ymax\}]$$

$$\text{the multiple integral } \int_{xmin}^{xmax} dx \int_{ymin}^{ymax} dy \ f$$

Integration.

This evaluates the multiple integral $\int_0^1 dx \int_0^x dy \ (x^2 + y^2)$. The range of the outermost integration variable appears first.

```
In[8]:= Integrate[ x^2 + y^2, {x, 0, 1}, {y, 0, x} ]
```

$$Out[8]= \frac{1}{3}$$

■ 1.5.4 Sums and Products

This constructs the sum $\sum_{i=1}^{7} \frac{x^i}{i}$.

```
In[1]:= Sum[x^i/i, {i, 1, 7}]
```

$$Out[1]= x + \frac{x^2}{2} + \frac{x^3}{3} + \frac{x^4}{4} + \frac{x^5}{5} + \frac{x^6}{6} + \frac{x^7}{7}$$

You can leave out the lower limit if it is equal to 1.

```
In[2]:= Sum[x^i/i, {i, 7}]
```

$$Out[2]= x + \frac{x^2}{2} + \frac{x^3}{3} + \frac{x^4}{4} + \frac{x^5}{5} + \frac{x^6}{6} + \frac{x^7}{7}$$

This makes i increase in steps of 2, so that only odd-numbered values are included.

```
In[3]:= Sum[x^i/i, {i, 1, 5, 2}]
```

$$Out[3]= x + \frac{x^3}{3} + \frac{x^5}{5}$$

Products work just like sums.

```
In[4]:= Product[x + i, {i, 1, 4}]
```

$$Out[4]= (1 + x) \ (2 + x) \ (3 + x) \ (4 + x)$$

Sum[f, {i, $imin$, $imax$}]	the sum $\sum_{i=imin}^{imax} f$
Sum[f, {i, $imin$, $imax$, di}]	the sum with i increasing in steps of di
Sum[f, {i, $imin$, $imax$}, {j, $jmin$, $jmax$}]	
	the nested sum $\sum_{i=imin}^{imax} \sum_{j=jmin}^{jmax} f$
Product[f, {i, $imin$, $imax$}]	the product $\prod_{i=imin}^{imax} f$

Sums and products.

Mathematica gives an exact result for this sum.	In[5]:= **Sum[1/i^3, {i, 1, 20}]**
	Out[5]= $\dfrac{33665881463886437653838323}{280346265322438720204800}$
Here is the numerical value.	In[6]:= **N[%]**
	Out[6]= 1.20087
Mathematica cannot give you an exact result for this infinite sum.	In[7]:= **Sum[1/i^3, {i, 1, Infinity}]**
	Out[7]= Sum[i^{-3}, {i, 1, Infinity}]
You can still get a numerical result.	In[8]:= **N[%]**
	Out[8]= 1.20206

Mathematica also has a notation for multiple sums and products.

Sum[f, {i, $imin$, $imax$}, {j, $jmin$, $jmax$}] represents a sum over i and j, which would be written in standard mathematical notation as $\sum_{i=imin}^{imax} \sum_{j=jmin}^{jmax} f$. Notice that in *Mathematica* notation, as in standard mathematical notation, the range of the *outermost* variable is given *first*.

This is the multiple sum $\sum_{i=1}^{3} \sum_{j=1}^{i} x^i y^j$. Notice that the outermost sum over **i** is given first, just as in the mathematical notation.	In[9]:= **Sum[x^i y^j, {i, 1, 3}, {j, 1, i}]**
	Out[9]= x y + x^2 y + x^3 y + x^2 y^2 + x^3 y^2 + x^3 y^3

The way the ranges of variables are specified in Sum and Product is an example of the rather general *iterator notation* that *Mathematica* uses. You will see this notation again when we discuss generating tables and lists using Table (Section 1.8.2), and when we describe Do loops (Section 1.7.3).

{imax}	iterate *imax* times, without incrementing any variables
{i, imax}	*i* goes from 1 to *imax* in steps of 1
{i, imin, imax}	*i* goes from *imin* to *imax* in steps of 1
{i, imin, imax, di}	*i* goes from *imin* to *imax* in steps of *di*
{i, imin, imax}, *{j, jmin, jmax}*, ...	
	i goes from *imin* to *imax*, and for each value of *i*, *j* goes from *jmin* to *jmax*, etc.

Mathematica iterator notation.

■ 1.5.5 Equations

Section 1.2.2 discussed *assignments* such as $x = y$ which *set* x equal to y. This section discusses *equations*, which *test* equality. The equation $x == y$ tests whether x is equal to y.

This *tests* whether 2 + 2 and 4 are
equal. The result is the symbol **True**.

```
In[1]:= 2 + 2 == 4

Out[1]= True
```

It is very important that you do not confuse $x = y$ with $x == y$. While $x = y$ is an *imperative* statement that actually causes an assignment to be done, $x == y$ merely *tests* whether x and y are equal, and causes no explicit action. If you have used the C programming language, you will recognize that the notation for assignment and testing in *Mathematica* is the same as in C.

$x = y$	assigns x to have value y
$x == y$	tests whether x and y are equal

Assignments and tests.

This *assigns* **x** to have value 4.

```
In[2]:= x = 4

Out[2]= 4
```

If you ask for **x**, you now get 4.

```
In[3]:= x

Out[3]= 4
```

This *tests* whether **x** is equal to 4. In
this case, it is.

```
In[4]:= x == 4

Out[4]= True
```

x is equal to 4, not 6.

```
In[5]:= x == 6

Out[5]= False
```

This removes the value assigned to x.   *In[6]:= x =.*

The tests we have used so far involve only numbers, and always give a definite answer, either True or False. You can also do tests on symbolic expressions.

Mathematica cannot get a definite result for this test unless you give x a specific numerical value.	*In[7]:= x == 5*
	Out[7]= x == 5

If you replace x by the specific numerical value 4, the test gives False.	*In[8]:= % /. x -> 4*
	Out[8]= False

Even when you do tests on symbolic expressions, there are some cases where you can get definite results. An important one is when you test the equality of two expressions that are *identical*. Whatever the numerical values of the variables in these expressions may be, *Mathematica* knows that the expressions must always be equal.

The two expressions are *identical*, so the result is True, whatever the value of x may be.	*In[9]:= 2 x + x^2 == 2 x + x^2*
	Out[9]= True

Mathematica does not try to tell whether these expressions are equal. In this case, using Expand would make them have the same form.	*In[10]:= 2 x + x^2 == x (2 + x)*
	Out[10]= 2 x + x^2 == x (2 + x)

Expressions like x == 4 represent *equations* in *Mathematica*. There are many functions in *Mathematica* for manipulating and solving equations.

This is an *equation* in *Mathematica*. Subsection 1.5.7 will discuss how to solve it for x.	*In[11]:= x^2 + 2 x - 7 == 0*
	Out[11]= -7 + 2 x + x^2 == 0

You can assign a name to the equation.	*In[12]:= eqn = %*
	Out[12]= -7 + 2 x + x^2 == 0

If you ask for eqn, you now get the equation.	*In[13]:= eqn*
	Out[13]= -7 + 2 x + x^2 == 0

■ 1.5.6 Relational and Logical Operators

x == y	equal
x != y	unequal
x > y	greater than
x >= y	greater than or equal to
x < y	less than
x <= y	less than or equal to
x == y == z	all equal
x != y != z	all unequal (distinct)
x > y > z, etc.	strictly decreasing, etc.

Relational operators.

This tests whether 10 is less than 7. The result is **False**.

```
In[1]:= 10 < 7
Out[1]= False
```

Not all of these numbers are unequal, so this gives **False**.

```
In[2]:= 3 != 2 != 3
Out[2]= False
```

You can mix < and <=.

```
In[3]:= 3 < 5 <= 6
Out[3]= True
```

Mathematica does not know whether this is true or false.

```
In[4]:= x > y
Out[4]= x > y
```

!p	not
p && q && ...	and
p || q || ...	or
Xor[p, q, ...]	exclusive or
If[p, *then*, *else*]	give *then* if p is **True**, and *else* if p is **False**
LogicalExpand[*expr*]	expand out logical expressions

Logical operations.

| Both tests give **True**, so the result is **True**. | $In[5]:=$ **7 > 4 && 2 != 3** |
| | $Out[5]=$ True |

You should remember that the logical operations ==, && and || are all *double characters* in *Mathematica*. (If you have used the C programming language, you will recognize this notation as being the same as in C.)

| *Mathematica* does not know whether this is true or false. | $In[6]:=$ **p && q** |
| | $Out[6]=$ p && q |

| *Mathematica* leaves this expression unchanged. | $In[7]:=$ **(p || q) && !(r || s)** |
| | $Out[7]=$ (p || q) && !(r || s) |

| You can use **LogicalExpand** to expand out the terms. | $In[8]:=$ **LogicalExpand[%]** |
| | $Out[8]=$ p && !r && !s || q && !r && !s |

■ 1.5.7 Solving Equations

An expression like x^2 + 2 x - 7 == 0 represents an *equation* in *Mathematica*. You will often need to *solve* equations like this, to find out for what values of x they are true.

| This gives the two solutions to the quadratic equation $x^2 + 2x - 7 = 0$. The solutions are given as replacements for x. | $In[1]:=$ **Solve[x^2 + 2x - 7 == 0, x]** |
| | $Out[1]=$ $\{\{x \to \dfrac{-2 + 4\,\mathrm{Sqrt}[2]}{2}\}, \{x \to \dfrac{-2 - 4\,\mathrm{Sqrt}[2]}{2}\}\}$ |

| Here are the numerical values of the solutions. | $In[2]:=$ **N[%]** |
| | $Out[2]=$ {{x -> 1.82843}, {x -> -3.82843}} |

| You can get a list of the actual solutions for x by applying the rules generated by **Solve** to x using the replacement operator. | $In[3]:=$ **x /. %** |
| | $Out[3]=$ {1.82843, -3.82843} |

| You can equally well apply the rules to any other expression involving x. | $In[4]:=$ **x^2 + 3 x /. %%** |
| | $Out[4]=$ {8.82843, 3.17157} |

Solve[*lhs* == *rhs*, *x*]	solve an equation, giving a list of rules for *x*
x /. *solution*	use the list of rules to get values for *x*
expr /. *solution*	use the list of rules to get values for an expression

Finding and using solutions to equations.

Solve always tries to give you explicit *formulas* for the solutions to equations. However, it is a basic mathematical result that, for sufficiently complicated equations, explicit algebraic formulas cannot be given. If you have an algebraic equation in one variable, and the highest power of the variable is at most four, then *Mathematica* can always give you formulas for the solutions. However, if the highest power is five or more, it may be mathematically impossible to give explicit algebraic formulas for all the solutions.

Mathematica can always solve algebraic equations in one variable when the highest power is less than five.

$In[5]:=$ **Solve[x^4 - 5 x^2 - 3 == 0, x]**

$Out[5]=$ $\{\{x \to \mathrm{Sqrt}[\dfrac{5 + \mathrm{Sqrt}[37]}{2}]\}, \{x \to -\mathrm{Sqrt}[\dfrac{5 + \mathrm{Sqrt}[37]}{2}]\},$

$\{x \to \mathrm{Sqrt}[\dfrac{5 - \mathrm{Sqrt}[37]}{2}]\}, \{x \to -\mathrm{Sqrt}[\dfrac{5 - \mathrm{Sqrt}[37]}{2}]\}\}$

It can solve some equations that involve higher powers.

$In[6]:=$ **Solve[x^6 == 1, x]**

$Out[6]=$ $\{\{x \to 1\}, \{x \to E^{I/3\ \mathrm{Pi}}\}, \{x \to E^{(2\ I)/3\ \mathrm{Pi}}\},$

$\{x \to -1\}, \{x \to E^{(4\ I)/3\ \mathrm{Pi}}\}, \{x \to E^{(5\ I)/3\ \mathrm{Pi}}\}\}$

There are some equations, however, for which it is mathematically impossible to find explicit formulas for the solutions. *Mathematica* uses the function **Roots** to represent the solutions in this case.

$In[7]:=$ **Solve[2 - 4 x + x^5 == 0, x]**

$Out[7]=$ $\{\mathrm{ToRules}[\mathrm{Roots}[-4\ x + x^5 == -2, x]]\}$

Even though you cannot get explicit formulas, you can still find the solutions numerically.

$In[8]:=$ **N[%]**

$Out[8]=$ $\{\{x \to -1.51851\}, \{x \to -0.116792 - 1.43845\ I\},$

$\{x \to -0.116792 + 1.43845\ I\}, \{x \to 0.508499\}, \{x \to 1.2436\}\}$

In addition to being able to solve purely algebraic equations, *Mathematica* can also solve some equations involving other functions.

After printing a warning, *Mathematica* returns one solution to this equation.

$In[9]:=$ **Solve[Sin[x] == a, x]**

Solve::ifun:
   Warning: inverse functions are being used by Solve, so some
      solutions may not be found.

$Out[9]=$ $\{\{x \to \mathrm{ArcSin}[a]\}\}$

It is important to realize that an equation such as $\sin(x) = a$ actually has an infinite number of possible solutions, in this case differing by multiples of 2π. However, Solve by default returns just one solution, but prints a message telling you that other solutions may exist. Section 3.4.4 discusses this in more detail.

There is no explicit "closed form" solution for a transcendental equation like this.

$In[10]:=$ **Solve[Cos[x] == x, x]**

Solve::ifun:
   Warning: inverse functions are being used by Solve, so some
      solutions may not be found.

$Out[10]=$ $\mathrm{Solve}[\mathrm{Cos}[x] == x, x]$

You can find an approximate numerical solution using **FindRoot**, and giving a starting value for **x**.

$In[11]:=$ **FindRoot[Cos[x] == x, {x, 1}]**

$Out[11]=$ $\{x \to 0.739085\}$

Solve can also handle equations involving symbolic functions. In such cases, it again prints a warning, then gives results in terms of formal inverse functions.

Mathematica returns a result in terms of the formal inverse function of f.

$In[12]:=$ **Solve[f[x^2] == a, x]**

Solve::ifun:
   Warning: inverse functions are being used by Solve, so some
      solutions may not be found.

$Out[12]= \{\{x \to Sqrt[f^{(-1)}[a]]\}, \{x \to -Sqrt[f^{(-1)}[a]]\}\}$

Solve[{lhs_1==rhs_1, lhs_2==rhs_2, ... }, {x, y, ... }]
                                            solve a set of simultaneous equations for x, y, ...

Solving sets of simultaneous equations.

You can also use *Mathematica* to solve sets of simultaneous equations. You simply give the list of equations, and specify the list of variables to solve for.

Here is a list of two simultaneous equations, to be solved for the variables x and y.

$In[13]:=$ **Solve[{a x + y == 0, 2 x + (1-a) y == 1}, {x, y}]**

$$Out[13]= \{\{x \to -(\frac{1}{-2 + a - a^2}), y \to \frac{a}{-2 + a - a^2}\}\}$$

Here are some more complicated simultaneous equations. The two solutions are given as two lists of replacements for x and y.

$In[14]:=$ **Solve[{x^2 + y^2 == 1, x + 3 y == 0}, {x, y}]**

$$Out[14]= \{\{x \to \frac{-3}{Sqrt[10]}, y \to \frac{1}{Sqrt[10]}\},$$

$$\{x \to \frac{3}{Sqrt[10]}, y \to -(\frac{1}{Sqrt[10]})\}\}$$

This uses the solutions to evaluate the expression x + y.

$In[15]:=$ **x + y /. %**

$$Out[15]= \{\frac{-2}{Sqrt[10]}, \frac{2}{Sqrt[10]}\}$$

Mathematica can solve any set of simultaneous *linear* equations. It can also solve a large class of simultaneous polynomial equations. Even when it does not manage to solve the equations explicitly, *Mathematica* will still usually reduce them to a much simpler form.

When you are working with sets of equations in several variables, it is often convenient to reorganize the equations by eliminating some variables between them.

This eliminates y between the two equations, giving a single equation for x.

$In[16]:=$ **Eliminate[{a x + y == 0, 2 x + (1-a) y == 1}, y]**

$$Out[16]= -(a x) + a^2 x == 1 - 2 x$$

If you have several equations, there is no guarantee that there exists *any* consistent solution for a particular variable.

There is no consistent solution to these equations, so *Mathematica* returns {}, indicating that the set of solutions is empty.

```
In[17]:= Solve[{x==1, x==2}, x]
Out[17]= {}
```

There is also no consistent solution to these equations for almost all values of a.

```
In[18]:= Solve[{x==1, x==a}, x]
Out[18]= {}
```

The general question of whether a set of equations has any consistent solution is quite a subtle one. For example, for most values of a, the equations {x==1, x==a} are inconsistent, so there is no possible solution for x. However, if a is equal to 1, then the equations *do* have a solution. Solve is set up to give you *generic* solutions to equations. It discards any solutions that exist only when special constraints between parameters are satisfied.

If you use Reduce instead of Solve, *Mathematica* will however keep *all* the possible solutions to a set of equations, including those that require special conditions on parameters.

This shows that the equations have a solution only when a == 1. The notation x==1 && x==a represents the requirement that *both* x==1 *and* x==a should be True.

```
In[19]:= Reduce[{x==1, x==a}, x]
Out[19]= a == 1 && x == 1
```

This gives the complete set of possible solutions to the equation. The answer is stated in terms of a combination of simpler equations. && indicates equations that must simultaneously be true; || indicates alternatives.

```
In[20]:= Reduce[a x + b == 0, x]
```

$$Out[20]= a \;!=\; 0 \;\&\&\; x == -(\frac{b}{a}) \;||\; a == 0 \;\&\&\; b == 0$$

This gives a more complicated combination of equations.

```
In[21]:= Reduce[a x^2 + b == 0, x]
```

$$Out[21]= a \;!=\; 0 \;\&\&\; (x == Sqrt[-(\frac{b}{a})] \;||\; x == -Sqrt[-(\frac{b}{a})]) \;||$$

$$a == 0 \;\&\&\; b == 0$$

You can use LogicalExpand to manipulate the set of equations.

```
In[22]:= LogicalExpand[%]
```

$$Out[22]= a \;!=\; 0 \;\&\&\; x == Sqrt[-(\frac{b}{a})] \;||$$

$$a \;!=\; 0 \;\&\&\; x == -Sqrt[-(\frac{b}{a})] \;||\; a == 0 \;\&\&\; b == 0$$

Solve[*lhs*==*rhs*, *x*]	solve an equation for *x*
Solve[{*lhs₁*==*rhs₁*, *lhs₂*==*rhs₂*, ... }, {*x*, *y*, ... }]	
	solve a set of simultaneous equations for *x*, *y*, ...
Eliminate[{*lhs₁*==*rhs₁*, *lhs₂*==*rhs₂*, ... }, {*x*, ... }]	
	eliminate *x*, ... in a set of simultaneous equations
Reduce[{*lhs₁*==*rhs₁*, *lhs₂*==*rhs₂*, ... }, {*x*, *y*, ... }]	
	give a set of simplified equations, including all possible solutions

Functions for solving and manipulating equations.

■ 1.5.8 Differential Equations

DSolve[*eqns*, *y*[*x*], *x*]	solve a differential equation for *y*[*x*], taking *x* as the independent variable
DSolve[*eqns*, *y*, *x*]	give a solution for *y* in pure function form

Solving an ordinary differential equation.

Here is the solution to the differential equation $y'(x) = ay(x)$. C[1] is a coefficient which must be determined from boundary conditions.

```
In[1]:= DSolve[ y'[x] == a y[x], y[x], x ]

Out[1]= {{y[x] -> E  C[1]}}
```

If you include appropriate boundary conditions, there are no undetermined coefficients in the solution.

```
In[2]:= DSolve[ {y'[x] == a y[x], y[0] == 1}, y[x], x ]

Out[2]= {{y[x] -> E  }}
```

Whereas algebraic equations such as $x^2 + x = 1$ are equations for *variables*, differential equations such as $y''(x) + y'(x) = y(x)$ are equations for *functions*. In *Mathematica*, you must always give differential equations explicitly in terms of functions such as $y[x]$, and you must specify the variables such as x on which the functions depend. As a result, you must write an equation such as $y''(x) + y'(x) == y(x)$ in the form y''[x] + y'[x] == y[x]. You cannot write it as y'' + y' == y.

Mathematica can solve both linear and non-linear ordinary differential equations, as well as lists of simultaneous equations. In many cases, the solutions you get will involve undetermined coefficients. Each time you use DSolve, it names the undetermined coefficients C[1], C[2], etc.

Here is a pair of simultaneous differential equations. The solution you get involves two undetermined coefficients.

$In[3]:=$ `DSolve[ {x'[t] == y[t], y'[t] == x[t]},`
                                            `{x[t], y[t]}, t ]`

$Out[3]=$ $\left\{ \left\{ x[t] \rightarrow \dfrac{C[1] + E^{2t} C[1] - C[2] + E^{2t} C[2]}{2 E^{t}}, \right. \right.$

$\left. y[t] \rightarrow \dfrac{-C[1] + E^{2t} C[1] + C[2] + E^{2t} C[2]}{2 E^{t}} \right\} \right\}$

When you ask `DSolve` to get you a solution for `y[x]`, the rules it returns specify how to replace `y[x]` in any expression. However, these rules do not specify how to replace objects such as `y'[x]`. If you want to manipulate solutions that you get from `DSolve`, you will often find it better to ask for solutions for `y`, rather than for `y[x]`.

This gives the solution for `y` as a "pure function".

$In[4]:=$ `DSolve[ y'[x] == x + y[x], y, x ]`

$Out[4]=$ `{{y -> (-1 + E`$^{\#1}$` C[1] - #1 & )}}`

You can now use the replacement operator to apply this solution to expressions involving `y`.

$In[5]:=$ `y''[x] + y[x] /. %`

$Out[5]=$ `{-1 - x + 2 E`^{x}` C[1]}`

Section 2.2.5 explains how the "pure function" `Function` object returned by `DSolve` works.

■ 1.5.9 Power Series

The mathematical operations we have discussed so far are *exact*. Given precise input, their results are exact formulas.

In many situations, however, you do not need an exact result. It may be quite sufficient, for example, to find an *approximate* formula that is valid, say, when the quantity x is small.

This gives a power series approximation to $(1+x)^n$ for x close to 0, up to terms of order x^3.

$In[1]:=$ `Series[(1 + x)^n, {x, 0, 3}]`

$Out[1]=$ $1 + n\ x + \dfrac{(-1 + n)\ n\ x^2}{2} + \dfrac{(-2 + n)\ (-1 + n)\ n\ x^3}{6} + O[x]^4$

Mathematica knows the power series expansions for many mathematical functions.

$In[2]:=$ `Series[Exp[-a t] (1 + Sin[2 t]), {t, 0, 4}]`

$Out[2]=$ $1 + (2 - a)\ t + (-2\ a + \dfrac{a^2}{2})\ t^2 + (-(\dfrac{4}{3}) + a^2 - \dfrac{a^3}{6})\ t^3 +$

$(\dfrac{4\ a}{3} - \dfrac{a^3}{3} + \dfrac{a^4}{24})\ t^4 + O[t]^5$

If you give it a function that it does not know, **Series** writes out the power series in terms of derivatives.

$In[3]:=$ **Series[1 + f[t], {t, 0, 3}]**

$Out[3]= (1 + f[0]) + f'[0] \ t + \dfrac{f''[0] \ t^2}{2} + \dfrac{f^{(3)}[0] \ t^3}{6} + O[t]^4$

Power series are approximate formulas that play much the same role with respect to algebraic expressions as approximate numbers play with respect to numerical expressions. *Mathematica* allows you to perform operations on power series, in all cases maintaining the appropriate order or "degree of precision" for the resulting power series.

Here is a simple power series, accurate to order x^5.

$In[4]:=$ **Series[Exp[x], {x, 0, 5}]**

$Out[4]= 1 + x + \dfrac{x^2}{2} + \dfrac{x^3}{6} + \dfrac{x^4}{24} + \dfrac{x^5}{120} + O[x]^6$

When you do operations on a power series, the result is computed only to the appropriate order in **x**.

$In[5]:=$ **%^2 (1 + %)**

$Out[5]= 2 + 5 \ x + \dfrac{13 \ x^2}{2} + \dfrac{35 \ x^3}{6} + \dfrac{97 \ x^4}{24} + \dfrac{55 \ x^5}{24} + O[x]^6$

This turns the power series back into an ordinary expression.

$In[6]:=$ **Normal[%]**

$Out[6]= 2 + 5 \ x + \dfrac{13 \ x^2}{2} + \dfrac{35 \ x^3}{6} + \dfrac{97 \ x^4}{24} + \dfrac{55 \ x^5}{24}$

Now the square is computed *exactly*.

$In[7]:=$ **%^2**

$Out[7]= (2 + 5 \ x + \dfrac{13 \ x^2}{2} + \dfrac{35 \ x^3}{6} + \dfrac{97 \ x^4}{24} + \dfrac{55 \ x^5}{24})^2$

Applying **Expand** gives a result with ten terms.

$In[8]:=$ **Expand[%]**

$Out[8]= 4 + 20 \ x + 51 \ x^2 + \dfrac{265 \ x^3}{3} + \dfrac{467 \ x^4}{4} + \dfrac{1505 \ x^5}{12} +$

$\dfrac{7883 \ x^6}{72} + \dfrac{1385 \ x^7}{18} + \dfrac{24809 \ x^8}{576} + \dfrac{5335 \ x^9}{288} + \dfrac{3025 \ x^{10}}{576}$

Series[*expr*, {*x*, x_0, *n*}]	find the power series expansion of *expr* about the point $x = x_0$ to at most *n* terms
Normal[*series*]	truncate a power series to give an ordinary expression

Power series operations.

■ 1.5.10 Limits

Here is the expression $\sin(x)/x$.

```
In[1]:= t = Sin[x]/x
```

$$Out[1]= \frac{\text{Sin}[x]}{x}$$

If you replace x by 0, the expression becomes 0/0, and you get an indeterminate result.

```
In[2]:= t /. x->0
```

```
                                       1
Power::infy: Infinite expression  -  encountered.
                                       0
```

```
Infinity::indet:
     Indeterminate expression 0 ComplexInfinity encountered.
```

```
Out[2]= Indeterminate
```

If you find the numerical value of $\sin(x)/x$ for x close to 0, however, you get a result that is close to 1.

```
In[3]:= t /. x->0.01
```

```
Out[3]= 0.999983
```

This finds the *limit* of $\sin(x)/x$ as x approaches 0. The result is indeed 1.

```
In[4]:= Limit[t, x->0]
```

```
Out[4]= 1
```

`Limit[`*expr*`, `*x*`->`*x₀*`]`	the limit of *expr* as x approaches x_0

Limits.

■ 1.5.11 Packages for Symbolic Mathematics

There are many *Mathematica* packages which implement symbolic mathematical operations. This section describes a few examples drawn from the standard set of packages distributed with *Mathematica*. As discussed in Section 1.3.4, some copies of *Mathematica* may be set up so that the functions described here are automatically loaded into *Mathematica* if they are ever needed.

Laplace Transforms

`<<Calculus`LaplaceTransform``	load the Laplace transform package
`LaplaceTransform[`*expr*`, `*t*`, `*s*`]`	find the Laplace transform of *expr*
`InverseLaplaceTransform[`*expr*`, `*s*`, `*t*`]`	
	find the inverse Laplace transform of *expr*

Laplace transforms.

This loads the Laplace transform package. In some versions of *Mathematica*, you may not need to load this package explicitly.

In[1]:= **<<Calculus`LaplaceTransform`**

This evaluates a Laplace transform.

In[2]:= **LaplaceTransform[t^3 Exp[a t], t, s]**

$$Out[2]= \frac{6}{(-a + s)^4}$$

Here is the inverse transform.

In[3]:= **InverseLaplaceTransform[%, s, t]**

$$Out[3]= E^{a t} t^3$$

Vector Analysis

<<Calculus`VectorAnalysis`	load the vector analysis package
SetCoordinates[*system* **[***names***]]**	specify the coordinate system to be used (**Cartesian**, **Cylindrical**, **Spherical**, etc.), giving the names of the coordinates in that system
Grad[*f***]**	evaluate the gradient ∇f of f in the coordinate system chosen
Div[*f***]**	evaluate the divergence $\nabla \cdot f$ of the list f
Curl[*f***]**	evaluate the curl $\nabla \times f$ of the list f
Laplacian[*f***]**	evaluate the Laplacian $\nabla^2 f$ of f
CrossProduct[*v₁*** , *v₂***]**	find the cross product of two vectors

Vector analysis.

This loads the vector analysis package. In some versions of *Mathematica*, you may not need to load the package explicitly.

In[1]:= **<<Calculus`VectorAnalysis`**

This specifies that a spherical coordinate system with coordinate names **r**, **theta** and **phi** should be used.

In[2]:= **SetCoordinates[Spherical[r, theta, phi]]**

Out[2]= Spherical

This evaluates the gradient of $r^2 \sin(\theta)$ in the spherical coordinate system.

In[3]:= **Grad[r^2 Sin[theta]]**

Out[3]= {2 r Sin[theta], r Cos[theta], 0}

Symbolic Summation of Series

`<<Algebra`SymbolicSum``	load the symbolic summation package
`SymbolicSum[f, {i, n}]`	find the symbolic sum of *f* with *i* running up to *n*

Symbolic summation.

This loads the symbolic summation package. In some versions of *Mathematica*, you may not need to load the package explicitly.

```
In[1]:= <<Algebra`SymbolicSum`
```

This evaluates a symbolic sum.

```
In[2]:= Simplify[ SymbolicSum[i^5 - 2/i^2, {i, n}] ]
```

$$Out[2]= \frac{-n^2 + 5 n^4 + 6 n^5 + 2 n^6 - 4 Pi^2 + 24\ PolyGamma[1, 1 + n]}{12}$$

1.6 Numerical Mathematics

■ 1.6.1 Basic Operations

Exact symbolic results are usually very desirable when they can be found. In many calculations, however, it is not possible to get symbolic results. In such cases, you must resort to numerical methods.

N[*expr*]	numerical value of an expression (see Section 1.1)
NIntegrate[*f*, {*x*, *xmin*, *xmax*}]	numerical approximation to $\int_{xmin}^{xmax} f\, dx$
NSum[*f*, {*i*, *imin*, Infinity}]	numerical approximation to $\sum_{imin}^{\infty} f$
NSolve[*lhs==rhs*, *x*]	numerical approximation to the solutions of a polynomial equation
FindRoot[*lhs==rhs*, {*x*, x_0}]	search for a numerical solution to an equation, starting with $x=x_0$
FindMinimum[*f*, {*x*, x_0}]	search for a minimum of *f*, starting with $x=x_0$

Basic numerical operations.

Mathematica maintains this expression in an exact, symbolic, form.

```
In[1]:= (3 + Sqrt[2])^3
```
$$Out[1]= (3 + Sqrt[2])^3$$

You can even use standard symbolic operations on it.

```
In[2]:= Expand[ % ]
```
$$Out[2]= 45 + 27 \, Sqrt[2] + 2^{3/2}$$

N[*expr*] gives you a numerical approximation.

```
In[3]:= N[ % ]
```
$$Out[3]= 86.0122$$

Functions such as Integrate always try to get exact results for computations. When they cannot get exact results, they typically return unevaluated. You can then find numerical approximations by explicitly applying N. Functions such as NIntegrate do the calculations numerically from the start, without first trying to get an exact result.

Mathematica cannot get an exact formula for this integral, so it returns the integral unevaluated.

```
In[4]:= Integrate[Sin[Sin[x]], {x, 1, 2}]
```
$$Out[4]= Integrate[Sin[Sin[x]], \{x, 1, 2\}]$$

You can use N to get an approximate numerical result.

```
In[5]:= N[ % ]
```
$$Out[5]= 0.81645$$

NIntegrate does the integral
numerically from the start.

```
In[6]:= NIntegrate[Sin[Sin[x]], {x, 1, 2}]
Out[6]= 0.81645
```

■ 1.6.2 Numerical Sums, Products and Integrals

NSum[*f*, {*i*, *imin*, Infinity}]	numerical approximation to $\sum_{imin}^{\infty} f$
NProduct[*f*, {*i*, *imin*, Infinity}]	
	numerical approximation to $\prod_{imin}^{\infty} f$
NIntegrate[*f*, {*x*, *xmin*, *xmax*}]	
	numerical approximation to $\int_{xmin}^{xmax} f \, dx$
NIntegrate[*f*, {*x*, *xmin*, *xmax*}, {*y*, *ymin*, *ymax*}]	
	the multiple integral $\int_{xmin}^{xmax} dx \int_{ymin}^{ymax} dy \, f$

Numerical sums, products and integrals.

Here is a numerical approximation to
$\sum_{i=1}^{\infty} \frac{1}{i^3}$.

```
In[1]:= NSum[1/i^3, {i, 1, Infinity}]
Out[1]= 1.20206
```

NIntegrate can handle singularities at
the end points of the integration region.

```
In[2]:= NIntegrate[1/Sqrt[x], {x, 0, 1}]
Out[2]= 2.
```

You can do numerical integrals over
infinite regions.

```
In[3]:= NIntegrate[Exp[-x^2], {x, -Infinity, Infinity}]
Out[3]= 1.77245
```

Here is a double integral over a
triangular domain. Note the order in
which the variables are given.

```
In[4]:= NIntegrate[ Sin[x y], {x, 0, 1}, {y, 0, x} ]
Out[4]= 0.119906
```

■ 1.6.3 Numerical Equation Solving

NSolve[*lhs*==*rhs*, *x*]	solve a polynomial equation numerically
NSolve[{*lhs₁*==*rhs₁*, *lhs₂*==*rhs₂*, ... }, {*x*, *y*, ... }]	
	solve a system of polynomial equations numerically
FindRoot[*lhs*==*rhs*, {*x*, *x₀*}]	search for a numerical solution to an equation, starting at $x=x_0$
FindRoot[{*lhs₁*==*rhs₁*, *lhs₂*==*rhs₂*, ... }, {*x*, *x₀*}, {*y*, *y₀*}, ...]	
	search for numerical solutions to simultaneous equations

Numerical root finding and minimization.

NSolve gives you numerical approximations to all the roots of a polynomial equation.

```
In[1]:= NSolve[ x^5 + x + 1 == 0, x ]
Out[1]= {{x -> -0.754878}, {x -> -0.5 - 0.866025 I},
    {x -> -0.5 + 0.866025 I}, {x -> 0.877439 - 0.744862 I},
    {x -> 0.877439 + 0.744862 I}}
```

You can also use NSolve to solve sets of simultaneous equations numerically.

```
In[2]:= NSolve[{x + y == 2, x - 3 y + z == 3, x - y + z == 0},
            {x, y, z}]
             7        3
Out[2]= {{x -> -, y -> -(-), z -> -5}}
             2        2
```

If your equations involve only linear functions or polynomials, then you can use NSolve to get numerical approximations to all the solutions. However, when your equations involve more complicated functions, there is in general no systematic procedure for finding all solutions, even numerically. In such cases, you can use FindRoot to search for solutions. You have to give FindRoot a place to start its search.

This searches for a numerical solution, starting at $x = 1$.

```
In[3]:= FindRoot[ 3 Cos[x] == Log[x], {x, 1} ]
Out[3]= {x -> 1.44726}
```

The equation has several solutions. If you start at a different x, FindRoot may return a different solution.

```
In[4]:= FindRoot[ 3 Cos[x] == Log[x], {x, 10} ]
Out[4]= {x -> 13.1064}
```

You can search for solutions to sets of equations. Here the solution involves complex numbers.

```
In[5]:= FindRoot[{x==Log[y], y==Log[x]}, {x, 1}, {y, 2}]
Out[5]= {x -> 0.318132 + 1.33724 I, y -> 0.318132 + 1.33724 I}
```

■ 1.6.4 Numerical Differential Equations

NDSolve[*eqns*, *y*, {*x*, *xmin*, *xmax*}]

                          solve numerically for the function *y*, with the independent
                          variable *x* in the range *xmin* to *xmax*

NDSolve[*eqns*, {y_1, y_2, ... }, {*x*, *xmin*, *xmax*}]

                          solve a system of equations for the y_i

---

Numerical solution of ordinary differential equations.

This generates a numerical solution to the equation $y'(x) = y(x)$ with $0 < x < 2$. The result is given in terms of an InterpolatingFunction.	`In[1]:= NDSolve[{y'[x] == y[x], y[0] == 1}, y, {x, 0, 2}]`
	
	`Out[1]= {{y -> InterpolatingFunction[{0., 2.}, <>]}}`

Here is the value of $y(1.5)$.	`In[2]:= y[1.5] /. %`
	
	`Out[2]= {4.48191}`

With an algebraic equation such as $x^2 + 3x + 1 = 0$, each solution for x is simply a single number. For a differential equation, however, the solution is a *function*, rather than a single number. For example, in the equation $y'(x) = y(x)$, you want to get an approximation to the function $y(x)$ as the independent variable x varies over some range.

Mathematica represents numerical approximations to functions as InterpolatingFunction objects. These objects are functions which, when applied to a particular x, return the approximate value of $y(x)$ at that point. The InterpolatingFunction effectively stores a table of values for $y(x_i)$, then interpolates this table to find an approximation to $y(x)$ at the particular x you request.

---

           y[*x*] /. *solution*   use the list of rules for the function *y* to get values for *y*[*x*]

InterpolatingFunction[*data*][*x*]

                       evaluate an interpolated function at the point *x*

Plot[Evaluate[*y*[*x*] /. *solution*]], {*x*, *xmin*, *xmax*}]

                       plot the solution to a differential equation

---

Using results from NDSolve.

This solves a system of two coupled differential equations.	`In[3]:= NDSolve[ {y'[x] == z[x], z'[x] == -y[x], y[0] == 0,`
	`                              z[0] == 1}, {y, z}, {x, 0, Pi} ]`
	
	`Out[3]= {{y -> InterpolatingFunction[{0., 3.14159}, <>],`
	`          z -> InterpolatingFunction[{0., 3.14159}, <>]}}`

Here is the value of z[2] found from the solution.

```
In[4]:= z[2] /. %
Out[4]= {-0.416167}
```

Here is a plot of the solution for y[x] found on line 1. Plot is discussed in Section 1.9.1.

```
In[5]:= Plot[Evaluate[y[x] /. %1], {x, 0, 2}]
```

■ 1.6.5 Numerical Optimization

ConstrainedMin[*f*, *ineqs*, {*x*, *y*, ... }]	minimize the linear function *f* subject to the linear constraints *ineqs*
FindMinimum[*f*, {*x*, x_0}]	search for a local minimum of the arbitrary function *f*, starting at $x=x_0$
FindMinimum[*f*, {*x*, x_0}, {*y*, y_0}, ...]	search for a local minimum in several variables

Numerical minimization functions.

The function ConstrainedMin allows you to solve linear programming problems in which you give a linear function *f*, then find its minimum over a domain specified by a list of linear inequalities. ConstrainedMin assumes that all the variables you give are constrained to be non-negative.

This gives the minimum value of $x - y - z$ in the specified domain, followed by the values of x, y and z at which the value is attained.

```
In[1]:= ConstrainedMin[x - y - z, {y + z < 3, x > 7},
                                              {x, y, z}]
Out[1]= {4, {x -> 7, y -> 3, z -> 0}}
```

When the function you want to minimize is linear, you can always use ConstrainedMin to find its global minimum. For more complicated functions, however, there is usually no systematic way to find a global minimum. Instead, you can use FindMinimum to search for local minima.

This searches for a local minimum of $x \cos(x)$, starting at $x = 1$.

```
In[2]:= FindMinimum[x Cos[x], {x, 1}]
Out[2]= {-3.28837, {x -> 3.42562}}
```

With a different starting point, you may reach a different local minimum.

```
In[3]:= FindMinimum[x Cos[x], {x, 10}]
Out[3]= {-9.47729, {x -> 9.52933}}
```

This finds a minimum of sin(*xy*).

```
In[4]:= FindMinimum[Sin[x y], {x, 2}, {y, 2}]
Out[4]= {-1., {x -> 2.1708, y -> 2.1708}}
```

■ 1.6.6 Manipulating Numerical Data

When you have numerical data, it is often convenient to find a simple formula that approximates it. For example, you can try to "fit" a line or curve through the points in your data.

$\texttt{Fit}[\{y_1, y_2, \ldots\}, \{f_1, f_2, \ldots\}, x]$

fit the values y_n to a linear combination of functions f_i

$\texttt{Fit}[\{\{x_1, y_1\}, \{x_2, y_2\}, \ldots\}, \{f_1, f_2, \ldots\}, x]$

fit the points (x_n, y_n) to a linear combination of the f_i

Functions for fitting curves.

This generates a table of the numerical values of the exponential function. **Table** will be discussed in Section 1.8.2.

```
In[1]:= data = Table[ Exp[x/5.] , {x, 7}]
Out[1]= {1.2214, 1.49182, 1.82212, 2.22554, 2.71828, 3.32012,
   4.0552}
```

This finds a least-squares fit to **data** of the form $c_1 + c_2 x + c_3 x^2$. The elements of **data** are assumed to correspond to values 1, 2, ... of x.

```
In[2]:= Fit[data, {1, x, x^2}, x]
                                                     2
Out[2]= 1.09428 + 0.0986337 x + 0.0459482 x
```

This finds a fit of the form $c_1 + c_2 x + c_3 x^3 + c_4 x^5$.

```
In[3]:= Fit[data, {1, x, x^3, x^5}, x]
                                         3            -6  5
Out[3]= 0.96806 + 0.246829 x ÷ 0.00428281 x  - 6.57948 10   x
```

This gives a table of x, y pairs.

```
In[4]:= data = Table[ {x, Exp[Sin[x]]} , {x, 0., 1., 0.2}]
Out[4]= {{0., 1.}, {0.2, 1.21978}, {0.4, 1.47612},
   {0.6, 1.75882}, {0.8, 2.04901}, {1., 2.31978}}
```

This finds a fit to the new data, of the form $c_1 + c_2 \sin(x) + c_3 \sin(2x)$.

```
In[5]:= Fit[%, {1, Sin[x], Sin[2x]}, x]
Out[5]= 0.989559 + 2.04199 Sin[x] - 0.418176 Sin[2 x]
```

One common way of picking out "signals" in numerical data is to find the *Fourier transform*, or frequency spectrum, of the data.

Fourier[*data*]	numerical Fourier transform
InverseFourier[*data*]	inverse Fourier transform

Fourier transforms.

Here is a simple square pulse.

```
In[6]:= data = {1, 1, 1, 1, -1, -1, -1, -1}
Out[6]= {1, 1, 1, 1, -1, -1, -1, -1}
```

This takes the Fourier transform of the pulse.

```
In[7]:= Fourier[data]
Out[7]= {0., 0.707107 + 1.70711 I, 0., 0.707107 + 0.292893 I,
         0., 0.707107 - 0.292893 I, 0., 0.707107 - 1.70711 I}
```

Note that the Fourier function in *Mathematica* is defined with the sign convention typically used in the physical sciences – opposite to the one often used in electrical engineering. Section 3.8.3 gives more details.

■ 1.6.7 Statistics Packages

The standard set of packages distributed with *Mathematica* includes several for doing statistical analyses of data.

Statistics`DescriptiveStatistics`	
	descriptive statistics functions
Statistics`ContinuousDistributions`	
	properties of continuous statistical distributions
Statistics`DiscreteDistributions`	
	properties of discrete statistical distributions
Statistics`HypothesisTests`	hypothesis tests based on the normal distribution
Statistics`ConfidenceIntervals`	
	confidence intervals derived from the normal distribution
Statistics`LinearRegression`	linear regression analysis

Some standard statistical analysis packages.

```
<<Statistics`DescriptiveStatistics`
```
        load the descriptive statistics package

        `Mean[`*data*`]`   mean (average value)

      `Median[`*data*`]`   median (central value)

    `Variance[`*data*`]`   variance

`StandardDeviation[`*data*`]`   standard deviation

`LocationReport[`*data*`]`, `DispersionReport[`*data*`]`, `ShapeReport[`*data*`]`
        give lists of quantities characterizing the statistical
        distribution of data

Basic descriptive statistics.

This loads the descriptive statistics package. In some versions of *Mathematica*, you may not need to load this package explicitly.

```
In[1]:= <<Statistics`DescriptiveStatistics`
```

Here is some "data".

```
In[2]:= data = {4.3, 7.2, 8.4, 5.8, 9.2, 3.9}
Out[2]= {4.3, 7.2, 8.4, 5.8, 9.2, 3.9}
```

This gives the mean of your data.

```
In[3]:= Mean[data]
Out[3]= 6.46667
```

Here is the variance.

```
In[4]:= Variance[data]
Out[4]= 4.69467
```

This gives a list of rules for various quantities that characterize the dispersion of your data.

```
In[5]:= DispersionReport[data]
Out[5]= {Variance -> 4.69467, StandardDeviation -> 2.16672,
   SampleRange -> 5.3, MeanDeviation -> 1.8,
   MedianDeviation -> 2.05, QuartileDeviation -> 2.05}
```

1.7 Functions and Programs

■ 1.7.1 Defining Functions

In this part of the book, we have seen many examples of functions that are built into *Mathematica*. In this section, we discuss how you can add your own simple functions to *Mathematica*. Part 2 will describe in much greater detail the mechanisms for adding functions to *Mathematica*.

As a first example, consider adding a function called f which squares its argument. The *Mathematica* command to define this function is f[x_] := x^2. The _ (referred to as "blank") on the left-hand side is very important; what it means will be discussed below. For now, just remember to put a _ on the left-hand side, but not on the right-hand side, of your definition.

This defines the function f. Notice the _ on the left-hand side.	In[1]:= **f[x_] := x^2**
f squares its argument.	In[2]:= **f[a+1]** Out[2]= $(1 + a)^2$
The argument can be a number.	In[3]:= **f[4]** Out[3]= 16
Or it can be a more complicated expression.	In[4]:= **f[3x + x^2]** Out[4]= $(3\ x + x^2)^2$
You can use f in a calculation.	In[5]:= **Expand[f[(x+1+y)]]** Out[5]= $1 + 2\ x + x^2 + 2\ y + 2\ x\ y + y^2$
This shows the definition you made for f.	In[6]:= **?f** Global`f f[x_] := x^2

f[x_] := x^2	define the function f
?f	show the definition of *f*
Clear[*f*]	clear all definitions for *f*

Defining a function in *Mathematica*.

The names like f that you use for functions in *Mathematica* are just symbols. Because of this, you should make sure to avoid using names that begin with capital letters, to prevent confusion with built-in *Mathematica* functions. You should also make sure that you have not used the names for anything else earlier in your session.

Mathematica functions can have any number of arguments.	`In[6]:= hump[x_, xmax_] := (x - xmax)^2 / xmax`

You can use the `hump` function just as you would any of the built-in functions.

`In[7]:= 2 + hump[x, 3.5]`

`Out[7]= 2 + 0.285714 (-3.5 + x)`^{2}

This gives a new definition for `hump`, which overwrites the previous one.

`In[8]:= hump[x_, xmax_] := (x - xmax)^4`

The new definition is displayed.

`In[9]:= ?hump`

`Global`hump`

`hump[x_, xmax_] := (x - xmax)^4`

This clears all definitions for `hump`.

`In[9]:= Clear[hump]`

When you have finished with a particular function, it is always a good idea to clear definitions you have made for it. If you do not do this, then you will run into trouble if you try to use the same function for a different purpose later in your *Mathematica* session. You can clear all definitions you have made for a function or symbol f by using `Clear[f]`.

■ 1.7.2 Functions as Procedures

In many kinds of calculations, you may find yourself typing the same input to *Mathematica* over and over again. You can save yourself a lot of typing by defining a *function* that contains your input commands.

This constructs a product of three terms, and expands out the result.

`In[1]:= Expand[ Product[x + i, {i, 3}] ]`

`Out[1]= 6 + 11 x + 6 x`^{2}` + x`^{3}

This does the same thing, but with four terms.

`In[2]:= Expand[ Product[x + i, {i, 4}] ]`

`Out[2]= 24 + 50 x + 35 x`^{2}` + 10 x`^{3}` + x`^{4}

This defines a function `exprod` which constructs a product of n terms, then expands it out.

`In[3]:= exprod[n_] := Expand[ Product[ x + i, {i, 1, n} ] ]`

Every time you use the function, it will execute the `Product` and `Expand` operations.

`In[4]:= exprod[5]`

`Out[4]= 120 + 274 x + 225 x`^{2}` + 85 x`^{3}` + 15 x`^{4}` + x`^{5}

The functions you define in *Mathematica* are essentially procedures that execute the commands you give. You can have several steps in your procedures, separated by semicolons.

The result you get from the whole function is simply the last expression in the procedure. Notice that you have to put parentheses around the procedure when you define it like this.

```
In[5]:= cex[n_, i_] := ( t = exprod[n]; Coefficient[t, x^i] )
```

This "runs" the procedure.

```
In[6]:= cex[5, 3]
Out[6]= 85
```

$expr_1$; $expr_2$; ...	a sequence of expressions to evaluate
Module[{a, b, ... }, proc]	a procedure with local variables a, b, ...

Constructing procedures.

When you write procedures in *Mathematica*, it is usually a good idea to make variables you use inside the procedures *local*, so that they do not interfere with things outside the procedures. You can do this by setting up your procedures as *modules*, in which you give a list of variables to be treated as local.

The function cex defined above is not a module, so the value of t "escapes", and exists even after the function returns.

```
In[7]:= t
Out[7]= 120 + 274 x + 225 x^2 + 85 x^3 + 15 x^4 + x^5
```

This function is defined as a module with local variable u.

```
In[8]:= ncex[n_, i_] :=
            Module[{u}, u = exprod[n]; Coefficient[u, x^i]]
```

The function gives the same result as before.

```
In[9]:= ncex[5, 3]
Out[9]= 85
```

Now, however, the value of u does not escape from the function.

```
In[10]:= u
Out[10]= u
```

■ 1.7.3 Repetitive Operations

In using *Mathematica*, you sometimes need to repeat an operation many times. There are many ways to do this. Often the most natural is in fact to set up a structure such as a list with many elements, and then apply your operation to each of the elements.

Another approach is to use the *Mathematica* function Do, which works much like the iteration constructs in languages such as C and Fortran. Do uses the standard *Mathematica* iterator notation introduced for Sum and Product in Section 1.5.4.

Do[*expr*, {*i*, *imax*}]	evaluate *expr* with *i* running from 1 to *imax*
Do[*expr*, {*i*, *imin*, *imax*, *di*}]	evaluate *expr* with *i* running from *imin* to *imax* in steps of *di*
Print[*expr*]	print *expr*
Table[*expr*, {*i*, *imax*}]	make a list of the values of *expr* with *i* running from 1 to *imax*

Implementing repetitive operations.

This prints out the values of the first five factorials.

```
In[1]:= Do[ Print[i!], {i, 5} ]
1
2
6
24
120
```

It is often more useful to have a list of results, which you can then manipulate further.

```
In[2]:= Table[ i!, {i, 5} ]
Out[2]= {1, 2, 6, 24, 120}
```

If you do not give an iteration variable, *Mathematica* simply repeats the operation you have specified, without changing anything.

```
In[3]:= r = 1; Do[ r = 1/(1 + r), {100} ]; r
```

$$Out[3]= \frac{573147844013817084101}{927372692193078999176}$$

■ 1.7.4 Transformation Rules for Functions

Section 1.4.2 discussed how you can use transformation rules of the form *x* -> *value* to replace symbols by values. The notion of transformation rules in *Mathematica* is, however, quite general. You can set up transformation rules not only for symbols, but for any *Mathematica* expression.

Applying the transformation rule x -> 3 replaces x by 3.

```
In[1]:= 1 + f[x] + f[y] /. x -> 3
Out[1]= 1 + f[3] + f[y]
```

You can also use a transformation rule for f[x]. This rule does not affect f[y].

```
In[2]:= 1 + f[x] + f[y] /. f[x] -> p
Out[2]= 1 + p + f[y]
```

f[t_] is a *pattern* that stands for f with any argument.

```
In[3]:= 1 + f[x] + f[y] /. f[t_] -> t^2
```

$$Out[3]= 1 + x^2 + y^2$$

Probably the most powerful aspect of transformation rules in *Mathematica* is that they can involve not only literal expressions, but also *patterns*. A pattern is an expression such as f[t_] which contains a blank (underscore). The blank can stand for any expression. Thus, a transformation rule for f[t_] specifies how the function f with *any* argument should be transformed. Notice that, in contrast, a transformation rule for f[x] without a blank, specifies only how the literal expression f[x] should be transformed, and does not, for example, say anything about the transformation of f[y].

When you give a function definition such as f[t_] := t^2, all you are doing is telling *Mathematica* to automatically apply the transformation rule f[t_] -> t^2 whenever possible.

You can set up transformation rules for expressions of any form.	*In[4]:=* **f[a b] + f[c d] /. f[x_ y_] -> f[x] + f[y]**
	Out[4]= **f[a] + f[b] + f[c] + f[d]**
This uses a transformation rule for x^p_.	*In[5]:=* **1 + x^2 + x^4 /. x^p_ -> f[p]**
	Out[5]= **1 + f[2] + f[4]**

Sections 2.3 and 2.4 will explain in detail how to set up patterns and transformation rules for any kind of expression. Suffice it to say here that in *Mathematica* all expressions have a definite symbolic structure; transformation rules allow you to transform parts of that structure.

1.8 Lists

■ 1.8.1 Collecting Objects Together

We first encountered lists in Section1.2.3 as a way of collecting numbers together. In this section, we shall see many different ways to use lists. You will find that lists are some of the most flexible and powerful objects in *Mathematica*. You will see that lists in *Mathematica* represent generalizations of several standard concepts in mathematics and computer science.

At a basic level, what a *Mathematica* list essentially does is to provide a way for you to collect together several expressions of any kind.

Here is a list of numbers.

```
In[1]:= {2, 3, 4}
Out[1]= {2, 3, 4}
```

This gives a list of symbolic expressions.

```
In[2]:= x^% - 1
Out[2]= {-1 + x , -1 + x , -1 + x }
                  2        3        4
```

You can differentiate these expressions.

```
In[3]:= D[%, x]
Out[3]= {2 x, 3 x , 4 x }
                 2     3
```

Or you can find their values when x is replaced with 3.

```
In[4]:= % /. x -> 3
Out[4]= {6, 27, 108}
```

The mathematical functions that are built into *Mathematica* are mostly set up so that they act separately on each element of a list. This is, however, not true of all functions in *Mathematica*. Unless you set it up specially, a new function f that you introduce will treat lists just as single objects. Sections 2.2.4 and 2.2.10 will describe how you can use Map and Thread to apply a function like this separately to each element in a list.

■ 1.8.2 Making Tables of Values

You can use lists as tables of values. You can generate the tables, for example, by evaluating an expression for a sequence of different parameter values.

This gives a table of the values of i^2, with i running from 1 to 6.

```
In[1]:= Table[i^2, {i, 6}]
Out[1]= {1, 4, 9, 16, 25, 36}
```

Here is a table of $\sin(n\pi/5)$ for n from 0 to 4.

```
In[2]:= Table[Sin[n Pi/5], {n, 0, 4}]
                 Pi        2 Pi        3 Pi        4 Pi
Out[2]= {0, Sin[--],  Sin[----],  Sin[----],  Sin[----]}
                 5          5           5           5
```

This gives the numerical values.

```
In[3]:= N[%]
Out[3]= {0, 0.587785, 0.951057, 0.951057, 0.587785}
```

You can also make tables of formulas.

$In[4]:=$ **Table[x^i + 2i, {i, 5}]**

$Out[4]=$ {2 + x, 4 + x^2, 6 + x^3, 8 + x^4, 10 + x^5}

Table uses exactly the same iterator notation as the functions **Sum** and **Product**, which were discussed in Section 1.5.4.

$In[5]:=$ **Product[x^i + 2i, {i, 5}]**

$Out[5]=$ (2 + x) (4 + x^2) (6 + x^3) (8 + x^4) (10 + x^5)

This makes a table with values of **x** running from 0 to 1 in steps of 0.25.

$In[6]:=$ **Table[Sqrt[x], {x, 0, 1, 0.25}]**

$Out[6]=$ {0, 0.5, 0.707107, 0.866025, 1.}

You can perform other operations on the lists you get from **Table**.

$In[7]:=$ **%^2 + 3**

$Out[7]=$ {3, 3.25, 3.5, 3.75, 4.}

TableForm displays lists in a "tabular" format. Notice that both words in the name **TableForm** begin with capital letters.

$In[8]:=$ **% // TableForm**

$Out[8]//TableForm=$ 3

3.25

3.5

3.75

4.

All the examples so far have been of tables obtained by varying a single parameter. You can also make tables that involve several parameters. These multidimensional tables are specified using the standard *Mathematica* iterator notation, discussed in Section 1.5.4.

This makes a table of $x^i + y^j$ with *i* running from 1 to 3 and *j* running from 1 to 2.

$In[9]:=$ **Table[x^i + y^j, {i, 3}, {j, 2}]**

$Out[9]=$ {{x + y, x + y^2}, {x^2 + y, x^2 + y^2}, {x^3 + y, x^3 + y^2}}

The table in this example is a *list of lists*. The elements of the outer list correspond to successive values of *i*. The elements of each inner list correspond to successive values of *j*, with *i* fixed.

Sometimes you may want to generate a table by evaluating a particular expression many times, without incrementing any variables.

This creates a list containing four copies of the symbol **x**.

$In[10]:=$ **Table[x, {4}]**

$Out[10]=$ {x, x, x, x}

This gives a list of four pseudorandom numbers. **Table** re-evaluates **Random[ ]** for each element in the list, so that you get a different pseudorandom number.

$In[11]:=$ **Table[Random[ ], {4}]**

$Out[11]=$ {0.104826, 0.767415, 0.216417, 0.519263}

Table[*f*, {*imax*}]	give a list of *imax* values of *f*
Table[*f*, {*i*, *imax*}]	give a list of the values of *f* as *i* runs from 1 to *imax*
Table[*f*, {*i*, *imin*, *imax*}]	give a list of values with *i* running from *imin* to *imax*
Table[*f*, {*i*, *imin*, *imax*, *di*}]	use steps of *di*
Table[*f*, {*i*, *imin*, *imax*}, {*j*, *jmin*, *jmax*}, ...]	
	generate a multidimensional table
TableForm[*list*]	display a list in tabular form

Functions for generating tables.

You can use the operations discussed in Section 1.2.4 to extract elements of the table.

This creates a 2×2 table, and gives it the name m.

```
In[12]:= m = Table[i - j, {i, 2}, {j, 2}]
Out[12]= {{0, -1}, {1, 0}}
```

This extracts the first sublist from the list of lists that makes up the table.

```
In[13]:= m[[1]]
Out[13]= {0, -1}
```

This extracts the second element of that sublist.

```
In[14]:= %[[2]]
Out[14]= -1
```

This does the two operations together.

```
In[15]:= m[[1,2]]
Out[15]= -1
```

This displays m in a "tabular" form.

```
In[16]:= TableForm[m]
Out[16]//TableForm= 0    -1
                    1     0
```

t[[*i*]] or Part[*t*, *i*]	give the ith sublist in *t*
t[[{*i₁*, *i₂*, ... }]] or Part[*t*, {*i₁*, *i₂*, ... }]	
	give a list of the $i_1{}^{th}$, $i_2{}^{th}$, ... parts of *t*
t[[*i*, *j*, ...]] or Part[*t*, *i*, *j*, ...]	
	give the part of *t* corresponding to *t*[[*i*]][[*j*]]...

Ways to extract parts of tables.

As we mentioned in Section 1.2.4, you can think of lists in *Mathematica* as being analogous to "arrays". Lists of lists are then like two-dimensional arrays. When you lay them out in a tabular form, the two indices of each element are like its x and y coordinates.

You can use `Table` to generate arrays with any number of dimensions.

This generates a three-dimensional $2 \times 2 \times 2$ array. It is a list of lists of lists.	`In[17]:= Table[i j^2 k^3, {i, 2}, {j, 2}, {k, 2}]` `Out[17]= {{{1, 8}, {4, 32}}, {{2, 16}, {8, 64}}}`

■ 1.8.3 Vectors and Matrices

Vectors and matrices in *Mathematica* are simply represented by lists and by lists of lists, respectively.

$$\{a,\ b,\ c\} \qquad \text{vector } (a,b,c)$$

$$\{\{a,\ b\},\ \{c,\ d\}\} \qquad \text{matrix } \begin{pmatrix} a & b \\ c & d \end{pmatrix}$$

The representation of vectors and matrices by lists.

This is a 2×2 matrix.	`In[1]:= m = {{a, b}, {c, d}}` `Out[1]= {{a, b}, {c, d}}`
Here is the first row.	`In[2]:= m[[1]]` `Out[2]= {a, b}`
Here is the element m_{12}.	`In[3]:= m[[1,2]]` `Out[3]= b`
This is a two-component vector.	`In[4]:= v = {x, y}` `Out[4]= {x, y}`
The objects p and q are treated as scalars.	`In[5]:= p v + q` `Out[5]= {q + p x, q + p y}`
Vectors are added component by component.	`In[6]:= v + {xp, yp} + {xpp, ypp}` `Out[6]= {x + xp + xpp, y + yp + ypp}`
This takes the dot ("scalar") product of two vectors.	`In[7]:= {x, y} . {xp, yp}` `Out[7]= x xp + y yp`
You can also multiply a matrix by a vector.	`In[8]:= m . v` `Out[8]= {a x + b y, c x + d y}`

Or a matrix by a matrix.	$In[9]:=$ **m . m**
	$Out[9]=$ {{a^2 + b c, a b + b d}, {a c + c d, b c + d^2}}
Or a vector by a matrix.	$In[10]:=$ **v . m**
	$Out[10]=$ {a x + c y, b x + d y}
This combination makes a scalar.	$In[11]:=$ **v . m . v**
	$Out[11]=$ x (a x + c y) + y (b x + d y)

Because of the way *Mathematica* uses lists to represent vectors and matrices, you never have to distinguish between "row" and "column" vectors.

Table[f, {i, n}]	build a length-n vector by evaluating f with i=1, i=2, ... , i=n
Array[a, n]	build a length-n vector of the form {a[1], a[2], ... }
Range[n]	create the list {1, 2, 3, ... , n}
Range[n_1, n_2]	create the list {n_1, n_1+1, ... , n_2}
Range[n_1, n_2, dn]	create the list {n_1, n_1+dn, ... , n_2}
list[[i]] or Part[*list*, i]	give the ith element in the vector *list*
Length[*list*]	give the number of elements in *list*
ColumnForm[*list*]	display the elements of *list* in a column

Functions for vectors.

Table[f, {i, m}, {j, n}]	build an $m \times n$ matrix by evaluating f with i ranging from 1 to m and j ranging from 1 to n
Array[a, {m, n}]	build an $m \times n$ matrix with i,j^{th} element a[i, j]
IdentityMatrix[n]	generate an $n \times n$ identity matrix
DiagonalMatrix[*list*]	generate a square matrix with the elements in *list* on the diagonal
list[[i]] or Part[*list*, i]	give the ith row in the matrix *list*
list[[i, j]] or Part[*list*, i, j]	give the i,j^{th} element in matrix *list*
Dimensions[*list*]	give the dimensions of a matrix represented by *list*
MatrixForm[*list*]	display *list* in matrix form

Functions for matrices.

This builds a 3×3 matrix *s* with elements $s_{ij} = i + j$.

```
In[12]:= s = Table[i+j, {i, 3}, {j, 3}]
Out[12]= {{2, 3, 4}, {3, 4, 5}, {4, 5, 6}}
```

This displays **s** in standard two-dimensional matrix format.

```
In[13]:= MatrixForm[s]
                         2   3   4
                         3   4   5
Out[13]//MatrixForm= 4   5   6
```

This gives a vector with symbolic elements. You can use this in deriving general formulas that are valid with any choice of vector components.

```
In[14]:= Array[a, 4]
Out[14]= {a[1], a[2], a[3], a[4]}
```

This gives a 3×2 matrix with symbolic elements. Section 2.2.6 will discuss how you can produce other kinds of elements with **Array**.

```
In[15]:= Array[p, {3, 2}]
Out[15]= {{p[1, 1], p[1, 2]}, {p[2, 1], p[2, 2]},
    {p[3, 1], p[3, 2]}}
```

Here are the dimensions of the matrix on the previous line.

```
In[16]:= Dimensions[%]
Out[16]= {3, 2}
```

This generates a 3×3 diagonal matrix.

```
In[17]:= DiagonalMatrix[{a, b, c}]
Out[17]= {{a, 0, 0}, {0, b, 0}, {0, 0, c}}
```

c m	multiply by a scalar
a . b	matrix product
Inverse[*m*]	matrix inverse
MatrixPower[*m*, *n*]	n^{th} power of a matrix
Det[*m*]	determinant
Transpose[*m*]	transpose
Eigenvalues[*m*]	eigenvalues
Eigenvectors[*m*]	eigenvectors
Eigenvalues[N[*m*]], Eigenvectors[N[*m*]]	numerical eigenvalues and eigenvectors

Some mathematical operations on matrices.

Here is the 2×2 matrix of symbolic variables that was defined above.

```
In[18]:= m
Out[18]= {{a, b}, {c, d}}
```

This gives its determinant.

```
In[19]:= Det[m]
Out[19]= -(b c) + a d
```

Here is the transpose of m.

```
In[20]:= Transpose[m]
Out[20]= {{a, c}, {b, d}}
```

This gives the inverse of m in symbolic form.

```
In[21]:= Inverse[m]
```

$$Out[21]= \{\{\frac{d}{-(b\ c)\ +\ a\ d},\ -(\frac{b}{-(b\ c)\ +\ a\ d})\},$$

$$\{-(\frac{c}{-(b\ c)\ +\ a\ d}),\ \frac{a}{-(b\ c)\ +\ a\ d}\}\}$$

Here is a particular 3×3 rational matrix known as a "Hilbert matrix".

```
In[22]:= h = Table[1/(i+j-1), {i, 3}, {j, 3}]
```

$$Out[22]= \{\{1,\ \frac{1}{2},\ \frac{1}{3}\},\ \{\frac{1}{2},\ \frac{1}{3},\ \frac{1}{4}\},\ \{\frac{1}{3},\ \frac{1}{4},\ \frac{1}{5}\}\}$$

This gives its inverse.

```
In[23]:= Inverse[h]
Out[23]= {{9, -36, 30}, {-36, 192, -180}, {30, -180, 180}}
```

Taking the dot product of the inverse with the original matrix gives the identity matrix.

```
In[24]:= % . h
Out[24]= {{1, 0, 0}, {0, 1, 0}, {0, 0, 1}}
```

Here is a 3×3 matrix.

```
In[25]:= r = Table[i+j+1, {i, 3}, {j, 3}]
Out[25]= {{3, 4, 5}, {4, 5, 6}, {5, 6, 7}}
```

Eigenvalues gives the eigenvalues of the matrix.

```
In[26]:= Eigenvalues[r]
```

$$Out[26]= \{0,\ \frac{15\ +\ Sqrt[249]}{2},\ \frac{15\ -\ Sqrt[249]}{2}\}$$

This gives a numerical approximation to the matrix.

```
In[27]:= rn = N[r]
Out[27]= {{3., 4., 5.}, {4., 5., 6.}, {5., 6., 7.}}
```

Here are numerical approximations to the eigenvalues.

```
In[28]:= Eigenvalues[rn]
```

$$Out[28]= \{15.3899,\ -0.389867,\ 8.84733\ 10^{-16}\}$$

Section 3.7 discusses other matrix operations that are built into *Mathematica*.

■ **1.8.4 Getting Pieces of Lists**

First [*list*]	the first element in *list*
Last [*list*]	the last element
Part [*list*, *n*] or *list* [[*n*]]	the nth element
Part [*list*, −*n*] or *list* [[−*n*]]	the nth element from the end
Part [*list*, {n_1, n_2, ... }] or *list* [[{n_1, n_2, ... }]]	the list of elements n_1, n_2, ...

Picking out elements of lists.

We will use this list for the examples.	*In[1]:=* **t = {a,b,c,d,e,f,g}**
	Out[1]= {a, b, c, d, e, f, g}
Here is the last element of t.	*In[2]:=* **Last[t]**
	Out[2]= g
This gives the third element.	*In[3]:=* **t[[3]]**
	Out[3]= c
This gives a list of the first and fourth elements.	*In[4]:=* **t[[{1, 4}]]**
	Out[4]= {a, d}

Take [*list*, *n*]	the first *n* elements in *list*
Take [*list*, −*n*]	the last *n* elements
Take [*list*, {*m*, *n*}]	elements *m* through *n* (inclusive)
Rest [*list*]	*list* with its first element dropped
Drop [*list*, *n*]	*list* with its first *n* elements dropped
Drop [*list*, −*n*]	*list* with its last *n* elements dropped
Drop [*list*, {*m*, *n*}]	*list* with elements *m* through *n* dropped

Picking out sequences in lists.

This gives the first three elements of the list t defined above.	*In[5]:=* **Take[t, 3]**
	Out[5]= {a, b, c}

This gives the last three elements.

```
In[6]:= Take[t, -3]
Out[6]= {e, f, g}
```

This gives elements 2 through 5 inclusive.

```
In[7]:= Take[t, {2, 5}]
Out[7]= {b, c, d, e}
```

This gives t with the first element dropped.

```
In[8]:= Rest[t]
Out[8]= {b, c, d, e, f, g}
```

This gives t with its first three elements dropped.

```
In[9]:= Drop[t, 3]
Out[9]= {d, e, f, g}
```

This gives t with only its third element dropped.

```
In[10]:= Drop[t, {3, 3}]
Out[10]= {a, b, d, e, f, g}
```

Part[*list*, *i*, *j*, ...]   or   *list*[[*i*, *j*, ...]]
    the element *list*[[*i*]][[*j*]]...

Part[*list*, {*i₁*, *i₂*, ... }, {*j₁*, *j₂*, ... }, ...]   or   *list*[[{*i₁*, *i₂*, ... }, {*j₁*, *j₂*, ... }, ...]]
    the list of elements obtained by picking out parts $i_1, i_2, ...$ at the first level, etc.

Extracting parts of nested lists.

Here is a list of lists.

```
In[11]:= t = {{a, b, c}, {d, e, f}}
Out[11]= {{a, b, c}, {d, e, f}}
```

This picks out the first sublist.

```
In[12]:= t[[1]]
Out[12]= {a, b, c}
```

This picks out the second element in the first sublist.

```
In[13]:= t[[1, 2]]
Out[13]= b
```

This is equivalent to t[[1, 2]], but is clumsier to write.

```
In[14]:= t[[1]][[2]]
Out[14]= b
```

This gives a list containing two copies of the second part of t, followed by one copy of the first part.

```
In[15]:= t[[{2, 2, 1}]]
Out[15]= {{d, e, f}, {d, e, f}, {a, b, c}}
```

For each of the parts picked out on the previous line, this gives a list of their second and third parts.

```
In[16]:= t[[{2, 2, 1}, {2, 3}]]
Out[16]= {{e, f}, {e, f}, {b, c}}
```

Section 2.1.5 will show how all the functions in this section can be generalized to work not only on lists, but on any *Mathematica* expressions.

The functions in this section allow you to pick out pieces that occur at particular positions in lists. Section 2.3.2 will show how you can use functions like Select and Cases to pick out elements of lists based not on their positions, but instead on their properties.

■ 1.8.5 Testing and Searching List Elements

Position[*list*, *form*]	the positions at which *form* occurs in *list*
Count[*list*, *form*]	the number of times *form* appears as an element of *list*
MemberQ[*list*, *form*]	test whether *form* is an element of *list*
FreeQ[*list*, *form*]	test whether *form* occurs nowhere in *list*

Testing and searching for elements of lists.

The previous section discussed how to extract pieces of lists based on their positions or indices. *Mathematica* also has functions that search and test for elements of lists, based on the values of those elements.

This gives a list of the positions at which a appears in the list.

```
In[1]:= Position[{a, b, c, a, b}, a]
Out[1]= {{1}, {4}}
```

Count counts the number of occurrences of a.

```
In[2]:= Count[{a, b, c, a, b}, a]
Out[2]= 2
```

This shows that a is an element of {a, b, c}.

```
In[3]:= MemberQ[{a, b, c}, a]
Out[3]= True
```

On the other hand, d is not.

```
In[4]:= MemberQ[{a, b, c}, d]
Out[4]= False
```

This assigns m to be the 3×3 identity matrix.

```
In[5]:= m = IdentityMatrix[3]
Out[5]= {{1, 0, 0}, {0, 1, 0}, {0, 0, 1}}
```

This shows that 0 does occur *somewhere* in m.

```
In[6]:= FreeQ[m, 0]
Out[6]= False
```

This gives a list of the positions at which 0 occurs in m.

```
In[7]:= Position[m, 0]
Out[7]= {{1, 2}, {1, 3}, {2, 1}, {2, 3}, {3, 1}, {3, 2}}
```

As discussed in Section 2.3.2, the functions Count and Position, as well as MemberQ and FreeQ, can be used not only to search for *particular* list elements, but also to search for classes of elements which match specific "patterns".

■ 1.8.6 Adding, Removing and Modifying List Elements

Prepend[*list*, *element*]	add *element* at the beginning of *list*
Append[*list*, *element*]	add *element* at the end of *list*
Insert[*list*, *element*, *i*]	insert *element* at position *i* in *list*
Insert[*list*, *element*, -*i*]	insert at position *i* counting from the end of *list*
Insert[*list*, *element*, {*i*, *j*, ... }]	
	insert at position *i*, *j*, ... in *list*
Delete[*list*, *i*]	delete the element at position *i* in *list*
Delete[*list*, {*i*, *j*, ... }]	delete at position *i*, *j*, ... in *list*

Functions for adding and deleting elements in lists.

This gives a list with **x** prepended.

```
In[1]:= Prepend[{a, b, c}, x]
Out[1]= {x, a, b, c}
```

This adds **x** at the end.

```
In[2]:= Append[{a, b, c}, x]
Out[2]= {a, b, c, x}
```

This inserts **x** so that it becomes element number 2.

```
In[3]:= Insert[{a, b, c}, x, 2]
Out[3]= {a, x, b, c}
```

Negative numbers count from the end of the list.

```
In[4]:= Insert[{a, b, c}, x, -2]
Out[4]= {a, b, x, c}
```

Delete removes an element from the list.

```
In[5]:= Delete[{a, b, c, d}, 3]
Out[5]= {a, b, d}
```

ReplacePart[*list*, *element*, *i*]	replace the element at position *i* in *list*
ReplacePart[*list*, *element*, -*i*]	replace at position *i* counting from the end
ReplacePart[*list*, *element*, {*i*, *j*, ... }]	
	replace *list*[[*i*, *j*, ...]]
ReplacePart[*list*, *element*, {{i_1, j_1, ... }, {i_2, ... }, ... }]	
	replace all parts *list*[[i_k, j_k, ...]] with the same element

Modifying parts of lists.

This replaces the third element in the list with x.

```
In[6]:= ReplacePart[{a, b, c, d}, x, 3]
Out[6]= {a, b, x, d}
```

This replaces the first and fourth parts of the list. Notice the need for double lists in specifying multiple parts to replace.

```
In[7]:= ReplacePart[{a, b, c, d}, x, {{1}, {4}}]
Out[7]= {x, b, c, x}
```

Here is a 3×3 identity matrix.

```
In[8]:= IdentityMatrix[3]
Out[8]= {{1, 0, 0}, {0, 1, 0}, {0, 0, 1}}
```

This replaces the $(2, 2)$ component of the matrix by x.

```
In[9]:= ReplacePart[%, x, {2, 2}]
Out[9]= {{1, 0, 0}, {0, x, 0}, {0, 0, 1}}
```

■ 1.8.7 Combining Lists

Join[$list_1$, $list_2$, ...]	concatenate lists together
Union[$list_1$, $list_2$, ...]	combine lists, removing repeated elements and sorting the result

Functions for combining lists.

Join concatenates any number of lists together.

```
In[1]:= Join[{a, b, c}, {x, y}, {c, {d, e}, a}]
Out[1]= {a, b, c, x, y, c, {d, e}, a}
```

Union combines lists, keeping only distinct elements.

```
In[2]:= Union[{a, b, c}, {c, a, d}, {a, d}]
Out[2]= {a, b, c, d}
```

■ 1.8.8 Advanced Topic: Lists as Sets

Mathematica usually keeps the elements of a list in exactly the order you originally entered them. If you want to treat a *Mathematica* list like a mathematical *set*, however, you may want to ignore the order of elements in the list.

Union[$list_1$, $list_2$, ...]	give a list of the distinct elements in the $list_i$
Intersection[$list_1$, $list_2$, ...]	give a list of the elements that are common to all the $list_i$
Complement[$universal$, $list_1$, ...]	give a list of the elements that are in $universal$, but not in any of the $list_i$

Set theoretical functions.

Union gives the elements that occur in *any* of the lists.

```
In[1]:= Union[{c, a, b}, {d, a, c}, {a, e}]
Out[1]= {a, b, c, d, e}
```

Intersection gives only elements that occur in *all* the lists.

```
In[2]:= Intersection[{a, c, b}, {b, a, d, a}]
Out[2]= {a, b}
```

Complement gives elements that occur in the first list, but not in any of the others.

```
In[3]:= Complement[{a, b, c, d}, {a, d}]
Out[3]= {b, c}
```

■ 1.8.9 Rearranging Lists

Sort [*list*]	sort the elements of *list* into a standard order
Union [*list*]	sort elements, removing any duplicates
Reverse [*list*]	reverse the order of elements in *list*
RotateLeft [*list*, *n*]	rotate the elements of *list* *n* places to the left
RotateRight [*list*, *n*]	rotate *n* places to the right
RotateLeft [*list*], RotateRight [*list*]	
	rotate by one position

Functions for rearranging lists.

This sorts the elements of a list into a standard order. In simple cases like this, the order is alphabetical or numerical.

```
In[1]:= Sort[{b, a, c, a, b}]
Out[1]= {a, a, b, b, c}
```

This sorts the elements, removing any duplicates.

```
In[2]:= Union[{b, a, c, a, b}]
Out[2]= {a, b, c}
```

This reverses the list.

```
In[3]:= Reverse[{a, b, c, d}]
Out[3]= {d, c, b, a}
```

This rotates ("shifts") the elements in the list two places to the left.

```
In[4]:= RotateLeft[{a, b, c, d, e}, 2]
Out[4]= {c, d, e, a, b}
```

You can rotate to the right by giving a negative displacement, or by using RotateRight.

```
In[5]:= RotateLeft[{a, b, c, d, e}, -2]
Out[5]= {d, e, a, b, c}
```

■ 1.8.10 Grouping Together Elements of Lists

Partition[*list*, *n*]	partition *list* into *n* element pieces
Partition[*list*, *n*, *d*]	use offset *d* for successive pieces

Functions for grouping together elements of lists.

Here is a list.

$In[1]:=$ **t = {a, b, c, d, e, f, g}**

$Out[1]=$ {a, b, c, d, e, f, g}

This groups the elements of the list in pairs, and in this case throws away the single element which is left at the end.

$In[2]:=$ **Partition[t, 2]**

$Out[2]=$ {{a, b}, {c, d}, {e, f}}

This groups elements in triples. There is no overlap between the triples.

$In[3]:=$ **Partition[t, 3]**

$Out[3]=$ {{a, b, c}, {d, e, f}}

This makes triples of elements, with each successive triple offset by just one element.

$In[4]:=$ **Partition[t, 3, 1]**

$Out[4]=$ {{a, b, c}, {b, c, d}, {c, d, e}, {d, e, f}, {e, f, g}}

■ 1.8.11 Mathematical Operations on Lists

Section 2.2.3 will discuss in detail how to do mathematical operations on lists. Here are a couple of cases that often occur in practice; Section 2.2.3 will give many generalizations.

Apply[Plus, *list*] or Plus @@ *list*	
	add together all the elements in *list*
Apply[Times, *list*] or Times @@ *list*	
	multiply together all the elements in *list*

Simple mathematical operations on lists.

This adds all the elements in a list.

$In[1]:=$ **Apply[Plus, {a, b, c, d}]**

$Out[1]=$ a + b + c + d

■ 1.8.12 Advanced Topic: Rearranging Nested Lists

You will encounter nested lists if you use matrices or generate multidimensional arrays and tables. Rearranging nested lists can be a complicated affair, and you will often have to experiment to get the right combination of commands.

Transpose[*list*]	interchange the top two levels of lists
Transpose[*list*, *n*]	interchange the top level with the nth level
Flatten[*list*]	flatten out all levels in *list*
Flatten[*list*, *n*]	flatten out the top *n* levels in *list*
FlattenAt[*list*, *i*]	flatten out a sublist that appears at position *i*
FlattenAt[*list*, {*i*, *j*, ... }]	flatten out a sublist at position *i*, *j*, ...
FlattenAt[*list*, {{*i_1*, *j_1*, ... }, {*i_2*, ... }, ... }]	
	flatten out several sublists
RotateLeft[*list*, {*n_1*, *n_2*, ... }]	
	rotate successive levels by n_i places
Partition[*list*, {*n_1*, *n_2*, ... }, {*d_1*, *d_2*, ... }]	
	partition successive levels into n_i element pieces with offsets d_i

Functions for rearranging nested lists.

Here is a 3×2 array.

```
In[1]:= t = {{a, b}, {c, d}, {e, f}}
Out[1]= {{a, b}, {c, d}, {e, f}}
```

You can rearrange it to get a 2×3 array.

```
In[2]:= Transpose[t]
Out[2]= {{a, c, e}, {b, d, f}}
```

This "flattens out" sublists. You can think of it as effectively just removing the inner sets of braces.

```
In[3]:= Flatten[t]
Out[3]= {a, b, c, d, e, f}
```

Here is a 2×2×2 array.

```
In[4]:= t = Table[i^2 +j^2 +k^2, {i, 2}, {j, 2}, {k, 2}]
Out[4]= {{{3, 6}, {6, 9}}, {{6, 9}, {9, 12}}}
```

This flattens out all the levels.

```
In[5]:= Flatten[t]
Out[5]= {3, 6, 6, 9, 6, 9, 9, 12}
```

This flattens only the first level of sublists.

```
In[6]:= Flatten[t, 1]
Out[6]= {{3, 6}, {6, 9}, {6, 9}, {9, 12}}
```

This flattens out only the sublist that appears at position 2.

```
In[7]:= FlattenAt[{{a, b}, {c, d}}, 2]
Out[7]= {{a, b}, c, d}
```

There are many other operations you can perform on nested lists. We will discuss some more of them when we look at Map, Apply, Scan and Level in Part 2.

■ 1.8.13 Advanced Topic: Combinatorial Operations

You can use lists to set up many kinds of combinatorial calculations. Here are a few examples.

Permutations[*list*]	give all possible orderings of *list*
Outer[List, *list₁*, *list₂*, ...]	give lists of elements in the *listᵢ* combined in all possible ways
OrderedQ[*list*]	give True if the elements of *list* are in order
Signature[*list*]	give the signature of the permutation needed to put *list* into standard order

Some combinatorial operations on lists.

This gives the 3! = 6 possible permutations of three elements.

```
In[1]:= Permutations[{a,b,c}]
Out[1]= {{a, b, c}, {a, c, b}, {b, a, c}, {b, c, a}, {c, a, b},
    {c, b, a}}
```

This combines the list elements in all possible ways. This operation is analogous to a mathematical "outer product" (see Section 3.7.12).

```
In[2]:= Outer[List, {a, b}, {c, d}]
Out[2]= {{{a, c}, {a, d}}, {{b, c}, {b, d}}}
```

1.9 Graphics and Sound

■ 1.9.1 Basic Plotting

> Plot[*f*, {*x*, *xmin*, *xmax*}]   plot *f* as a function of *x* from *xmin* to *xmax*
>
> Plot[{*f₁*, *f₂*, ... }, {*x*, *xmin*, *xmax*}]
>
>   plot several functions together

Basic plotting functions.

This plots a graph of sin(*x*) as a function of *x* from 0 to 2π.

In[1]:= **Plot[Sin[x], {x, 0, 2Pi}]**

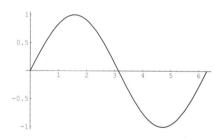

You can plot functions that have singularities. *Mathematica* will try to choose appropriate scales.

In[2]:= **Plot[Tan[x], {x, -3, 3}]**

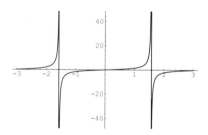

You can give a list of functions to plot.   *In[3]:=* **Plot[{Sin[x], Sin[2x], Sin[3x]}, {x, 0, 2Pi}]**

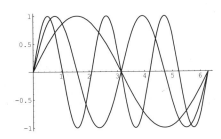

To get smooth curves, *Mathematica* has to evaluate functions you plot at a large number of points. As a result, it is important that you set things up so that each function evaluation is as quick as possible.

When you ask *Mathematica* to plot an object, say *f*, as a function of *x*, there are two possible approaches it can take. One approach is first to try and evaluate *f*, presumably getting a symbolic expression in terms of *x*, and then subsequently evaluate this expression numerically for the specific values of *x* needed in the plot. The second approach is first to work out what values of *x* are needed, and only subsequently to evaluate *f* with those values of *x*.

If you type Plot[*f*, {*x*, *xmin*, *xmax*}] it is the second of these approaches that is used. This has the advantage that *Mathematica* only tries to evaluate *f* for specific numerical values of *x*; it does not matter whether sensible values are defined for *f* when *x* is symbolic.

There are, however, some cases in which it is much better to have *Mathematica* evaluate *f* before it starts to make the plot. A typical case is when *f* is actually a command that generates a table of functions. You want to have *Mathematica* first produce the table, and then evaluate the functions, rather than trying to produce the table afresh for each value of *x*. You can do this by typing Plot[Evaluate[*f*], {*x*, *xmin*, *xmax*}].

This makes a plot of the Bessel functions $J_n(x)$ with *n* running from 1 to 4. The **Evaluate** tells *Mathematica first* to make the table of functions, and only *then* to evaluate them for particular values of **x**.

In[4]:= **Plot[Evaluate[Table[BesselJ[n, x], {n, 4}]],**
{x, 0, 10}]

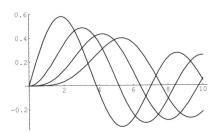

This finds the numerical solution to a differential equation, as discussed in Section 1.6.4.

```
In[5]:= NDSolve[{y'[x] == Sin[y[x]], y[0] == 1}, y, {x, 0, 4}]
Out[5]= {{y -> InterpolatingFunction[{0., 4.}, <>]}}
```

Here is a plot of the solution. The `Evaluate` tells *Mathematica* to first set up an `InterpolatingFunction` object, then evaluate this at a sequence of `x` values.

```
In[6]:= Plot[Evaluate[ y[x] /. % ], {x, 0, 4}]
```

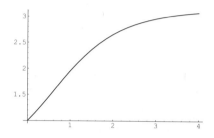

`Plot[f, {x, xmin, xmax}]`	*first* choose specific numerical values for x, then evaluate f for each value of x
`Plot[Evaluate[f], {x, xmin, xmax}]`	*first* evaluate f, then choose specific numerical values of x
`Plot[Evaluate[Table[f, ... ]], {x, xmin, xmax}]`	generate a list of functions, and then plot them
`Plot[Evaluate[y[x] /. solution], {x, xmin, xmax}]`	plot a numerical solution to a differential equation obtained from `NDSolve`

Methods for setting up objects to plot.

■ 1.9.2 Special Topic: How Graphics Are Output

The details of how *Mathematica* outputs graphics vary between different computer systems and different *Mathematica* interfaces. The documentation that came with your copy of *Mathematica* should tell you what is relevant in your case.

With text-based *Mathematica* interfaces, each piece of graphics output typically fills your complete screen, or causes a new window to be created which is then filled with graphics. The details of how you get rid of the graphics vary from one system to another. Note that when you start *Mathematica* with a text-based interface, you may have to load a *Mathematica* package to tell *Mathematica* how you want graphics output to be done. The details of this should be described in the documentation that came with your copy of *Mathematica*.

With a notebook-based *Mathematica* interface, each piece of graphics is placed in a cell in your notebook. The *Mathematica* front end allows you to manipulate the graphics in several ways, for example by resizing them, or redisplaying them with different options.

Many *Mathematica* systems allow you to collect together sequences of graphic images and display them in quick succession to produce an animated "movie". Notebook-based interfaces typically allow you to select a sequence of cells to serve as the frames in your animation. Many text-based interfaces also provide animation capabilities; typically the function ShowAnimation[{g_1, g_2, ... }], where the g_i are pieces of graphics output, generates a movie.

You should understand that when *Mathematica* produces any kind of graphics output, it does so in three stages. The first stage is to execute commands like Plot to produce a sequence of *Mathematica* graphics primitives. These primitives, to be discussed in Section 2.9, represent objects such as lines, points and polygons as *Mathematica* expressions. The second stage of producing graphics output is to convert these graphics primitives to a standardized device-independent representation of your graphical image. *Mathematica* generates this representation in the PostScript page description language.

The final stage of graphics output is to take the PostScript description of a graphical image, and render it on the particular device you want. In a notebook-based interface, the *Mathematica* front end performs this rendering. On other systems, the rendering is usually done by an external program which is automatically called from within *Mathematica*.

The importance of using PostScript as a graphics description language is that it can be rendered on many different kinds of devices, including both displays and printers, and it can be imported into many kinds of programs. Specific versions of *Mathematica* come with various conversion utilities to produce Encapsulated PostScript form, and other standard graphics formats.

With text-based *Mathematica* interfaces, the command PSPrint[*graphics*] is typically set up to print a piece of graphics. The command Display["*file*", *graphics*] saves the raw PostScript representation of the graphics in a file. This file typically requires some processing before it can be printed or used in other programs.

Although most graphics from *Mathematica* are first converted to PostScript, and then rendered on particular devices, there are some cases where it is more convenient to render directly from the original *Mathematica* form. One example is on systems that manipulate images of three-dimensional objects in real time. On such systems, the function Live[*graphics*] is typically set up to produce a "live" version of a piece of *Mathematica* graphics, which can then be manipulated directly using the various tools available on the particular computer system.

■ 1.9.3 Options

When *Mathematica* plots a graph for you, it has to make many choices. It has to work out what the scales should be, where the function should be sampled, how the axes should be drawn, and so on. Most of the time, *Mathematica* will probably make pretty good choices. However, if you want to get the very best possible pictures for your particular purposes, you may have to help *Mathematica* in making some of its choices.

There is a general mechanism for specifying "options" in *Mathematica* functions. Each option has a definite name. As the last arguments to a function like Plot, you can include a sequence of rules of the form *name->value*, to specify the values for various options. Any option for which you do not give an explicit rule is taken to have its "default" value.

Plot[*f*, {*x*, *xmin*, *xmax*}, *option->value*]

　　　　　　　　　　　　　　make a plot, specifying a particular value for an option

Choosing an option for a plot.

A function like Plot has many options that you can set. Usually you will need to use at most a few of them at a time. If you want to optimize a particular plot, you will probably do best to experiment, trying a sequence of different settings for various options.

Each time you produce a plot, you can specify options for it. Section 1.9.4 will also discuss how you can change some of the options, even after you have produced the plot.

option name	default value	
AspectRatio	1/GoldenRatio	the height-to-width ratio for the plot; Automatic sets it from the absolute x and y coordinates
Axes	True	whether to include axes
AxesLabel	None	labels to be put on the axes: *ylabel* specifies a label for the y axis, {*xlabel*, *ylabel*} for both axes
AxesOrigin	Automatic	the point at which axes cross
DefaultFont	$DefaultFont	the default font to use for text in the plot
DisplayFunction	$DisplayFunction	how to display graphics; Identity causes no display
Frame	False	whether to draw a frame around the plot
FrameLabel	None	labels to be put around the frame; give a list in clockwise order starting with the lower x axis
FrameTicks	Automatic	what tick marks to draw if there is a frame; None gives no tick marks
GridLines	None	what grid lines to include: Automatic includes a grid line for every major tick mark
PlotLabel	None	an expression to be printed as a label for the plot
PlotRange	Automatic	the range of coordinates to include in the plot: All includes all points
Ticks	Automatic	what tick marks to draw if there are axes; None gives no tick marks

Some of the options for **Plot**. These can also be used in **Show**.

Here is a plot with all options having their default values.

In[1]:= **Plot[Sin[x^2], {x, 0, 3}]**

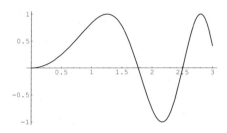

This draws axes on a frame around the plot.

In[2]:= **Plot[Sin[x^2], {x, 0, 3}, Frame->True]**

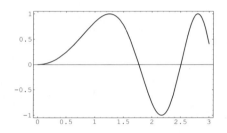

This specifies labels for the x and y axes. The expressions you give as labels are printed just as they would be if they appeared as *Mathematica* output. You can give any piece of text by putting it inside a pair of double quotes.

In[3]:= **Plot[Sin[x^2], {x, 0, 3},**
            AxesLabel -> {"x value", "Sin[x^2]"}]

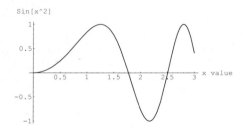

You can give several options at the same time, in any order.

In[4]:= **Plot[Sin[x∧2], {x, 0, 3}, Frame -> True,**
                                  GridLines -> Automatic]

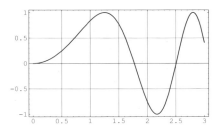

Setting the **AspectRatio** option changes the whole shape of your plot.
AspectRatio gives the ratio of width to height. Its default value is the inverse of the Golden Ratio – supposedly the most pleasing shape for a rectangle.

In[5]:= **Plot[Sin[x∧2], {x, 0, 3}, AspectRatio -> 1]**

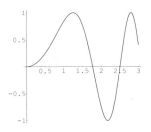

Automatic	use internal algorithms
None	do not include this
All	include everything
True	do this
False	do not do this

Some common settings for various options.

When *Mathematica* makes a plot, it tries to set the x and y scales to include only the "interesting" parts of the plot. If your function increases very rapidly, or has singularities, the parts where it gets too large will be cut off. By specifying the option PlotRange, you can control exactly what ranges of x and y coordinates are included in your plot.

Automatic	show at least a large fraction of the points, including the "interesting" region (the default setting)
All	show all points
{*ymin*, *ymax*}	show a specific range of *y* values
{*xrange*, *yrange*}	show the specified ranges of *x* and *y* values

Settings for the option `PlotRange`.

The setting for the option `PlotRange` gives explicit *y* limits for the graph. With the *y* limits specified here, the bottom of the curve is cut off.

In[6]:= **Plot[Sin[x^2], {x, 0, 3}, PlotRange -> {0, 1.2}]**

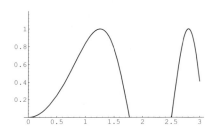

Mathematica always tries to plot functions as smooth curves. As a result, in places where your function wiggles a lot, *Mathematica* will use more points. In general, *Mathematica* tries to *adapt* its sampling of your function to the form of the function. There is, however, a limit, which you can set, to how finely *Mathematica* will ever sample a function.

The function $\sin(\frac{1}{x})$ wiggles infinitely often when $x \simeq 0$. *Mathematica* tries to sample more points in the region where the function wiggles a lot, but it can never sample the infinite number that you would need to reproduce the function exactly. As a result, there are slight glitches in the plot.

In[7]:= **Plot[Sin[1/x], {x, -1, 1}]**

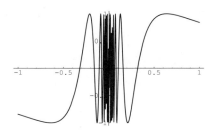

option name	default value	
PlotStyle	Automatic	a list of lists of graphics primitives to use for each curve (see Section 2.9.3)
PlotPoints	25	the minimum number of points at which to sample the function
MaxBend	10.	the maximum kink angle between successive segments of a curve
PlotDivision	20.	the maximum factor by which to subdivide in sampling the function
Compiled	True	whether to compile the function being plotted

More options for **Plot**. These cannot be used in **Show**.

It is important to realize that since *Mathematica* can only sample your function at a limited number of points, it can always miss features of the function. By increasing PlotPoints, you can make *Mathematica* sample your function at a larger number of points. Of course, the larger you set PlotPoints to be, the longer it will take *Mathematica* to plot *any* function, even a smooth one.

Since Plot needs to evaluate your function many times, it is important to make each evaluation as quick as possible. As a result, *Mathematica* usually *compiles* your function into a low-level pseudocode that can be executed very efficiently. One potential problem with this, however, is that the pseudocode allows only machine-precision numerical operations. If the function you are plotting requires higher precision operations, you may have to switch off compilation in Plot. You can do this by setting the option Compiled -> False. Note that *Mathematica* can only compile "in-line code"; it cannot for example compile functions that you have defined. As a result, you should, when possible, use Evaluate as described on page 135 to evaluate any such definitions and get a form that the *Mathematica* compiler can handle.

■ 1.9.4 Redrawing and Combining Plots

Mathematica saves information about every plot you produce, so that you can later redraw it. When you redraw plots, you can change some of the options you use.

Show[*plot*]	redraw a plot
Show[*plot*, *option->value*]	redraw with options changed
Show[*plot₁*, *plot₂*, ...]	combine several plots
Show[GraphicsArray[{{*plot₁*, *plot₂*, ... }, ... }]]	
	draw an array of plots
InputForm[*plot*]	show the information that is saved about a plot

Functions for manipulating plots.

Here is a simple plot. -Graphics- is usually printed on the output line to stand for the information that *Mathematica* saves about the plot.

In[1]:= **Plot[ChebyshevT[7, x], {x, -1, 1}]**

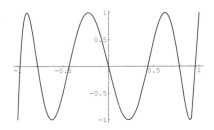

This redraws the plot from the previous line.

In[2]:= **Show[%]**

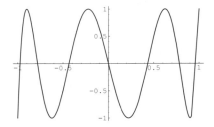

When you redraw the plot, you can change some of the options. This changes the choice of *y* scale.

In[3]:= **Show[%, PlotRange -> {-1, 2}]**

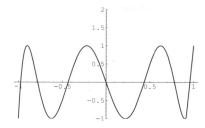

This takes the plot from the previous line, and changes another option in it.

In[4]:= **Show[%, PlotLabel -> "A Chebyshev Polynomial"]**

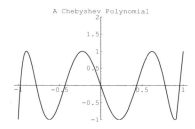

By using Show with a sequence of different options, you can look at the same plot in many different ways. You may want to do this, for example, if you are trying to find the best possible setting of options.

You can also use Show to combine plots. It does not matter whether the plots have the same scales: *Mathematica* will always choose new scales to include the points you want.

This sets gj0 to be a plot of $J_0(x)$ from *x* = 0 to 10.

In[5]:= **gj0 = Plot[BesselJ[0, x], {x, 0, 10}]**

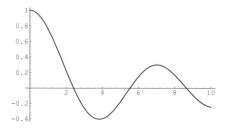

Here is a plot of $Y_1(x)$ from $x = 1$ to 10.   *In[6]:=* **gy1 = Plot[BesselY[1, x], {x, 1, 10}]**

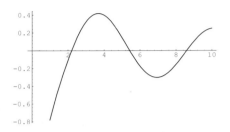

This shows the previous two plots   *In[7]:=* **gjy = Show[gj0, gy1]**
combined into one. Notice that the scale
is adjusted appropriately.

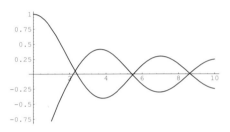

Using Show[*plot₁*, *plot₂*, ...] you can combine several plots into one. GraphicsArray allows you to draw several plots in an array.

Show[GraphicsArray[{*plot₁*, *plot₂*, ... }]]
                        draw several plots side by side

Show[GraphicsArray[{{*plot₁*}, {*plot₂*}, ... }]]
                        draw a column of plots

Show[GraphicsArray[{{*plot₁₁*, *plot₁₂*, ... }, ... }]]
                        draw a rectangular array of plots

Show[GraphicsArray[*plots*, GraphicsSpacing -> {*h*, *v*}]]
                        put the specified horizontal and vertical spacing between
                        the plots

Drawing arrays of plots.

This shows the plots given above in an array.

In[8]:= **Show[GraphicsArray[{{gj0, gjy}, {gy1, gjy}}]]**

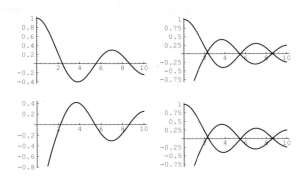

If you redisplay an array of plots using **Show**, any options you specify will be used for whole array, rather than for individual plots.

In[9]:= **Show[%, Frame->True, FrameTicks->None]**

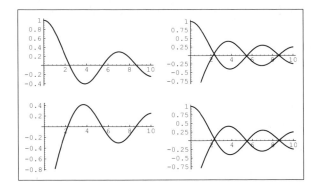

Here is a way to change options for all the plots in the array.

In[10]:= `Show[ % /. (Ticks -> Automatic) -> (Ticks -> None) ]`

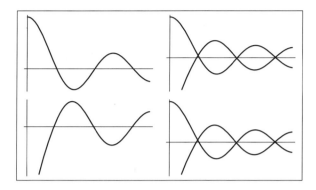

GraphicsArray by default puts a narrow border around each of the plots in the array it gives. You can change the size of this border by setting the option **GraphicsSpacing -> {*h*, *v*}**. The parameters *h* and *v* give the horizontal and vertical spacings to be used, as fractions of the width and height of the plots.

This increases the horizontal spacing, but decreases the vertical spacing between the plots in the array.

In[11]:= `Show[%, GraphicsSpacing -> {0.3, 0}]`

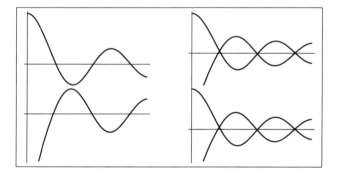

When you make a plot, *Mathematica* saves the list of points it used, together with some other information. Using what is saved, you can redraw plots in many different ways with **Show**. However, you should realize that no matter what options you specify, **Show** still has the same basic set of points to work with. So, for example, if you set the options so that *Mathematica* displays a small portion of your original plot magnified, you will probably be able to see the individual sample points that **Plot** used. Options like **PlotPoints** can only be set in the original **Plot** command itself. (*Mathematica* always plots the actual points it has; it avoids using smoothed or splined curves, which can give misleading results in mathematical graphics.)

Here is a simple plot.

$In[12]:=$ **Plot[Cos[x], {x, -Pi, Pi}]**

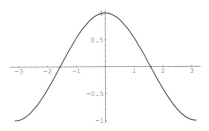

This shows a small region of the plot in a magnified form. At this resolution, you can see the individual line segments that were produced by the original **Plot** command.

$In[13]:=$ **Show[%, PlotRange -> {{0, .3}, {.92, 1}}]**

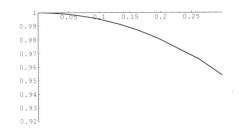

■ 1.9.5 Advanced Topic: Manipulating Options

There are a number of functions built into *Mathematica* which, like **Plot**, have various options you can set. *Mathematica* provides some general mechanisms for handling such options.

If you do not give a specific setting for an option to a function like **Plot**, then *Mathematica* will automatically use a default value for the option. The function **Options**[*function*, *option*] allows you to find out the default value for a particular option. You can reset the default using **SetOptions**[*function*, *option->value*]. Note that if you do this, the default value you have given will stay until you explicitly change it.

Options[*function*]	give a list of the current default settings for all options
Options[*function*, *option*]	give the default setting for a particular option
SetOptions[*function*, *option->value*, ...]	reset defaults

Manipulating default settings for options.

Here is the default setting for the PlotRange option of Plot.

```
In[1]:= Options[Plot, PlotRange]
Out[1]= {PlotRange -> Automatic}
```

This resets the default for the PlotRange option. The semicolon stops *Mathematica* from printing out the rather long list of options for Plot.

```
In[2]:= SetOptions[Plot, PlotRange->All] ;
```

Until you explicitly reset it, the default for the PlotRange option will now be All.

```
In[3]:= Options[Plot, PlotRange]
Out[3]= {PlotRange -> All}
```

The graphics objects that you get from Plot or Show store information on the options they use. You can get this information by applying the Options function to these graphics objects.

Options[*plot*]	show all the options used for a particular plot
Options[*plot*, *option*]	show the setting for a specific option
FullOptions[*plot*, *option*]	show the actual form used for a specific option, even if the setting for the option is Automatic or All

Getting information on options used in plots.

Here is a plot, with default settings for all options.

```
In[4]:= g = Plot[SinIntegral[x], {x, 0, 20}]
```

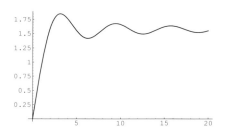

The setting used for the PlotRange option was All.

```
In[5]:= Options[g, PlotRange]
Out[5]= {PlotRange -> All}
```

FullOptions gives the *actual* automatically chosen values used for PlotRange.

```
In[6]:= FullOptions[g, PlotRange]
Out[6]= {{-0.5, 20.5}, {-0.0462981, 1.89822}}
```

■ 1.9.6 Contour and Density Plots

ContourPlot[*f*, {*x*, *xmin*, *xmax*}, {*y*, *ymin*, *ymax*}]
>   make a contour plot of *f* as a function of *x* and *y*

DensityPlot[*f*, {*x*, *xmin*, *xmax*}, {*y*, *ymin*, *ymax*}]
>   make a density plot of *f*

Contour and density plots.

This gives a contour plot of the function $\sin(x)\sin(y)$.

In[1]:= **ContourPlot[Sin[x] Sin[y], {x, -2, 2}, {y, -2, 2}]**

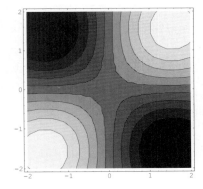

A contour plot gives you essentially a "topographic map" of a function. The contours join points on the surface that have the same height. The default is to have contours corresponding to a sequence of equally spaced *z* values. Contour plots produced by *Mathematica* are by default shaded, in such a way that regions with higher *z* values are lighter.

option name	default value	
ColorFunction	Automatic	what colors to use for shading; Hue uses a sequence of hues
Contours	10	the total number of contours, or the list of z values for contours
PlotRange	Automatic	the range of values to be included; you can specify $\{zmin, zmax\}$, All or Automatic
ContourShading	True	whether to use shading
ContourSmoothing	None	what smoothing to use for contour lines
PlotPoints	15	number of evaluation points in each direction
Compiled	True	whether to compile the function being plotted

Some options for **ContourPlot**. The first set can also be used in **Show**.

Particularly if you use a display or printer that does not handle gray levels well, you may find it better to switch off shading in contour plots.

In[2]:= **Show[%, ContourShading -> False]**

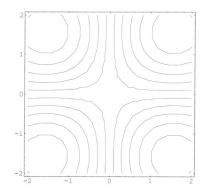

This increases the density of contours, and tells *Mathematica* to apply a smoothing algorithm to each contour.

In[3]:= **Show[%, Contours -> 30, ContourSmoothing -> Automatic]**

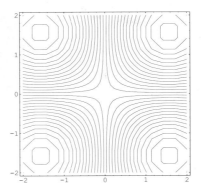

You should realize that if you do not evaluate your function on a fine enough grid, there may be inaccuracies in your contour plot. One point to notice is that whereas a curve generated by `Plot` may be inaccurate if your function varies too quickly in a particular region, the shape of contours can be inaccurate if your function varies too slowly. A rapidly varying function gives a regular pattern of contours, but a function that is almost flat can give irregular contours. You can often use the `ContourSmoothing` option to `ContourPlot` to reduce the visual impact of these irregularities.

Density plots show the values of your function at a regular array of points. Lighter regions are higher.

In[4]:= **DensityPlot[Sin[x] Sin[y], {x, -2, 2}, {y, -2, 2}]**

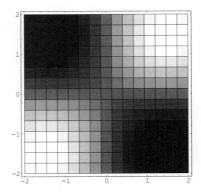

You can get rid of the mesh like this. But unless you have a very large number of regions, plots usually look better when you include the mesh.

In[5]:= **Show[%, Mesh -> False]**

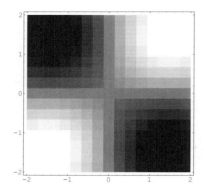

option name	default value	
ColorFunction	Automatic	what colors to use for shading; Hue uses a sequence of hues
Mesh	True	whether to draw a mesh
PlotPoints	15	number of evaluation points in each direction
Compiled	True	whether to compile the function being plotted

Some options for **DensityPlot**. The first set can also be used in **Show**.

■ 1.9.7 Three-Dimensional Surface Plots

Plot3D[*f*, {*x*, *xmin*, *xmax*}, {*y*, *ymin*, *ymax*}]
               make a three-dimensional plot of *f* as a function of the variables *x* and *y*

Basic 3D plotting function.

This makes a three-dimensional plot of the function sin(*xy*).

In[1]:= **Plot3D[Sin[x y], {x, 0, 3}, {y, 0, 3}]**

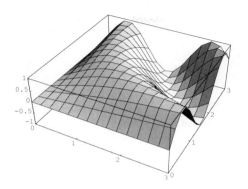

There are many options for three-dimensional plots in *Mathematica*. Some will be discussed in this section; others will be described in Section 2.9.

The first set of options for three-dimensional plots is largely analogous to those provided in the two-dimensional case.

option name	default value	
Axes	True	whether to include axes
AxesLabel	None	labels to be put on the axes: *zlabel* specifies a label for the *z* axis, {*xlabel*, *ylabel*, *zlabel*} for all axes
Boxed	True	whether to draw a three-dimensional box around the surface
ColorFunction	Automatic	what colors to use for shading; Hue uses a sequence of hues
DefaultFont	$DefaultFont	the default font to use for text in the plot
DisplayFunction	$DisplayFunction	how to display graphics; Identity causes no display
FaceGrids	None	how to draw grids on faces of the bounding box; All draws a grid on every face
HiddenSurface	True	whether to draw the surface as solid
Lighting	True	whether to color the surface using simulated lighting
Mesh	True	whether an *xy* mesh should be drawn on the surface
PlotRange	Automatic	the range of coordinates to include in the plot: you can specify All, {*zmin*, *zmax*} or {{*xmin*,*xmax*}, {*ymin*,*ymax*}, {*zmin*,*zmax*}}
Shading	True	whether the surface should be shaded or left white
ViewPoint	{1.3, -2.4, 2}	the point in space from which to look at the surface
PlotPoints	15	the number of points in each direction at which to sample the function; {n_x, n_y} specifies different numbers in the *x* and *y* directions
Compiled	True	whether to compile the function being plotted

Some options for **Plot3D**. The first set can also be used in **Show**.

This redraws the plot on the previous line, with options changed. With this setting for **PlotRange**, only the part of the surface in the range $-0.5 \leq z \leq 0.5$ is shown.

In[2]:= **Show[%, PlotRange -> {-0.5, 0.5}]**

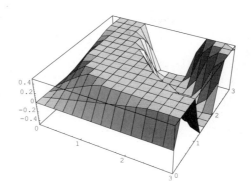

When you make the original plot, you can choose to sample more points. You will need to do this to get good pictures of functions that wiggle a lot.

In[3]:= **Plot3D[10 Sin[x + Sin[y]], {x, -10, 10}, {y, -10, 10},**
PlotPoints -> 40]

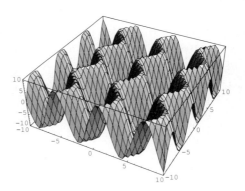

Here is the same plot, with labels for the axes, and grids added to each face.

In[4]:= **Show[%, AxesLabel -> {"Time", "Depth", "Value"},**

FaceGrids -> All]

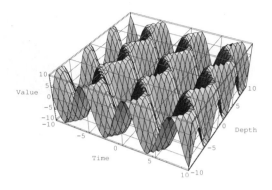

   Probably the single most important issue in plotting a three-dimensional surface is specifying where you want to look at the surface from. The `ViewPoint` option for `Plot3D` and `Show` allows you to specify the point {*x*, *y*, *z*} in space from which you view a surface. The details of how the coordinates for this point are defined will be discussed in Section 2.9.10. In many versions of *Mathematica*, there are ways to choose three-dimensional view points interactively, then get the coordinates to give as settings for the `ViewPoint` option.

Here is a surface, viewed from the default view point {1.3, -2.4, 2}. This view point is chosen to be "generic", so that visually-confusing coincidental alignments between different parts of your object are unlikely.

In[5]:= **Plot3D[Sin[x y], {x, 0, 3}, {y, 0, 3}]**

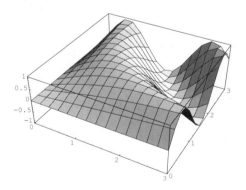

This redraws the picture, with the view point directly in front. Notice the perspective effect that makes the back of the box look much smaller than the front.

In[6]:= **Show[%, ViewPoint -> {0, -2, 0}]**

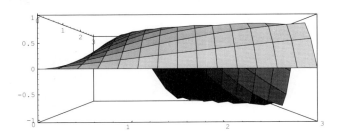

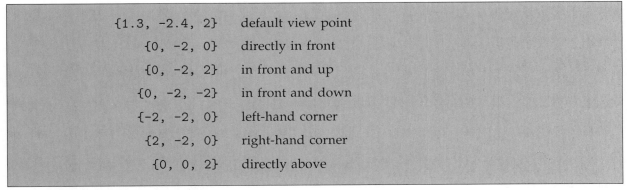

{1.3, -2.4, 2}	default view point
{0, -2, 0}	directly in front
{0, -2, 2}	in front and up
{0, -2, -2}	in front and down
{-2, -2, 0}	left-hand corner
{2, -2, 0}	right-hand corner
{0, 0, 2}	directly above

Typical choices for the **ViewPoint** option.

The human visual system is not particularly good at understanding complicated mathematical surfaces. As a result, you need to generate pictures that contain as many clues as possible about the form of the surface.

View points slightly above the surface usually work best. It is generally a good idea to keep the view point close enough to the surface that there is some perspective effect. Having a box explicitly drawn around the surface is helpful in recognizing the orientation of the surface.

Here is a plot with the default settings for surface rendering options.

`In[7]:= g = Plot3D[Exp[-(x^2+y^2)], {x, -2, 2}, {y, -2, 2}]`

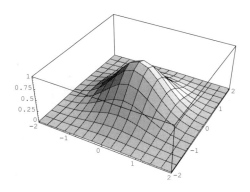

This shows the surface without the mesh drawn. It is usually much harder to see the form of the surface if the mesh is not there.

`In[8]:= Show[g, Mesh -> False]`

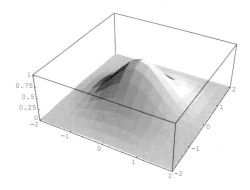

This shows the surface with no shading. Some display devices may not be able to show shading.

`In[9]:= Show[g, Shading -> False]`

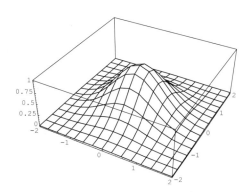

The inclusion of shading and a mesh are usually great assets in understanding the form of a surface. On some vector graphics output devices, however, you may not be able to get shading. You should also realize that when shading is included, it may take a long time to render the surface on your output device.

To add an extra element of realism to three-dimensional graphics, *Mathematica* by default colors three-dimensional surfaces using a simulated lighting model. In the default case, *Mathematica* assumes that there are three light sources shining on the object from the upper right of the picture. Section 2.9.12 describes how you can set up other light sources, and how you can specify the reflection properties of an object.

While in most cases, particularly with color output devices, simulated lighting is an asset, it can sometimes be confusing. If you set the option Lighting -> False, then *Mathematica* will not use simulated lighting, but will instead shade all surfaces with gray levels determined by their height.

Plot3D usually colors surfaces using a simulated lighting model.

In[10]:= **Plot3D[Sin[x y], {x, 0, 3}, {y, 0, 3}]**

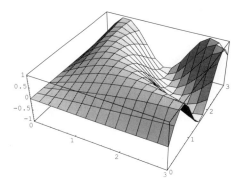

Lighting -> False switches off the simulated lighting, and instead shades surfaces with gray levels determined by height.

In[11]:= **Show[%, Lighting -> False]**

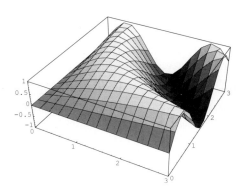

With `Lighting -> False`, *Mathematica* shades surfaces according to height. You can also tell *Mathematica* explicitly how to shade each element of a surface. This allows you effectively to use shading to display an extra coordinate at each point on your surface.

`Plot3D[{f, GrayLevel[s]}, {x, xmin, xmax}, {y, ymin, ymax}]`
    plot a surface corresponding to *f*, shaded in gray according to the function *s*

`Plot3D[{f, Hue[s]}, {x, xmin, xmax}, {y, ymin, ymax}]`
    shade by varying color hue rather than gray level

Specifying shading functions for surfaces.

This shows a surface whose height is determined by the function `Sin[x y]`, but whose shading is determined by `GrayLevel[x/3]`.

`In[12]:= Plot3D[{Sin[x y], GrayLevel[x/3]},`
                    `{x, 0, 3}, {y, 0, 3}]`

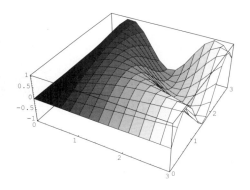

■ 1.9.8 Converting between Types of Graphics

Contour, density and surface plots are three different ways to display essentially the same information about a function. In all cases, you need the values of a function at a grid of points.

The *Mathematica* functions `ContourPlot`, `DensityPlot` and `Plot3D` all produce *Mathematica* graphics objects that include a list of the values of your function on a grid. As a result, having used any one of these functions, *Mathematica* can easily take its output and use it to produce another type of graphics.

Here is a surface plot.

In[1]:= **Plot3D[BesselJ[nu, 3x], {nu, 0, 3}, {x, 0, 3}]**

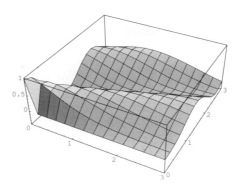

This converts the object produced by **Plot3D** into a contour plot.

In[2]:= **Show[ContourGraphics[%]]**

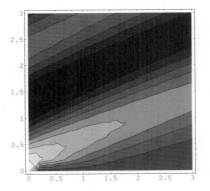

Show[ContourGraphics[g]]	convert to a contour plot
Show[DensityGraphics[g]]	convert to a density plot
Show[SurfaceGraphics[g]]	convert to a surface plot
Show[Graphics[g]]	convert to a two-dimensional image

Conversions between types of graphics.

You can use `GraphicsArray` to show different types of graphics together.

$In[3]:=$ `Show[ GraphicsArray[ {%, %%} ] ]`

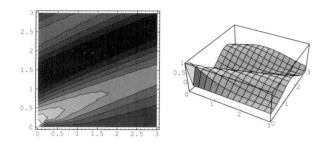

■ 1.9.9 Plotting Lists of Data

So far, we have discussed how you can use *Mathematica* to make plots of *functions*. You give *Mathematica* a function, and it builds up a curve or surface by evaluating the function at many different points.

This section describes how you can make plots from lists of data, instead of functions. (Section 1.10.3 discusses how to read data from external files and programs.) The *Mathematica* commands for plotting lists of data are direct analogs of the ones discussed above for plotting functions.

`ListPlot[{`y_1`, `y_2`, ... }]`	plot $y_1, y_2, ...$ at x values 1, 2, ...
`ListPlot[{{`x_1`, `y_1`}, {`x_2`, `y_2`}, ... }]`	
	plot points $(x_1, y_1), ...$
`ListPlot[`*list*`, PlotJoined -> True]`	
	join the points with lines
`ListPlot3D[{{`z_{11}`, `z_{12}`, ... }, {`z_{21}`, `z_{22}`, ... }, ... }]`	
	make a three-dimensional plot of the array of heights z_{xy}
`ListContourPlot[`*array*`]`	make a contour plot from an array of heights
`ListDensityPlot[`*array*`]`	make a density plot

Functions for plotting lists of data.

Here is a list of values.

$In[1]:=$ `t = Table[i^2, {i, 10}]`

$Out[1]=$ `{1, 4, 9, 16, 25, 36, 49, 64, 81, 100}`

This plots the values.

In[2]:= **ListPlot[t]**

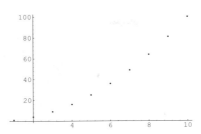

This joins the points with lines.

In[3]:= **ListPlot[t, PlotJoined -> True]**

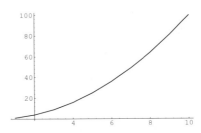

This gives a list of x, y pairs.

In[4]:= **Table[{i^2, 4 i^2 + i^3}, {i, 10}]**

Out[4]= {{1, 5}, {4, 24}, {9, 63}, {16, 128}, {25, 225}, {36, 360}, {49, 539}, {64, 768}, {81, 1053}, {100, 1400}}

This plots the points.

In[5]:= **ListPlot[%]**

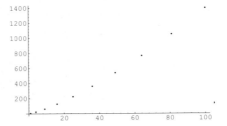

This gives a rectangular array of values. The array is quite large, so we end the input with a semicolon to stop the result from being printed out.

In[6]:= **t3 = Table[Mod[y, x], {x, 20}, {y, 20}] ;**

This makes a three-dimensional plot of the array of values.

In[7]:= **ListPlot3D[t3]**

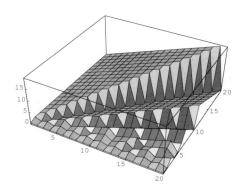

You can redraw the plot using Show, as usual.

In[8]:= **Show[%, ViewPoint -> {1.5, -0.5, 0}]**

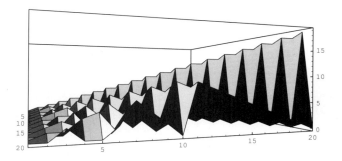

This gives a density plot of the array of values.

In[9]:= **ListDensityPlot[t3]**

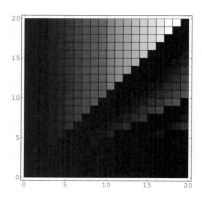

■ 1.9.10 Parametric Plots

Section 1.9.1 described how to plot curves in *Mathematica* in which you give the y coordinate of each point as a function of the x coordinate. You can also use *Mathematica* to make *parametric* plots. In a parametric plot, you give both the x and y coordinates of each point as a function of a third parameter, say t.

ParametricPlot[{f_x, f_y}, {t, *tmin*, *tmax*}]

                       make a parametric plot

ParametricPlot[{{f_x, f_y}, {g_x, g_y}, ... }, {t, *tmin*, *tmax*}]

                      plot several parametric curves together

ParametricPlot[{f_x, f_y}, {t, *tmin*, *tmax*}, AspectRatio -> Automatic]

                   attempt to preserve the shapes of curves

Functions for generating parametric plots.

Here is the curve made by taking the x coordinate of each point to be Sin[t] and the y coordinate to be Sin[2t].

In[1]:= **ParametricPlot[{Sin[t], Sin[2t]}, {t, 0, 2Pi}]**

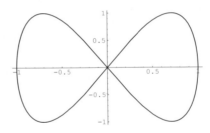

The "shape" of the curve produced depends on the ratio of height to width for the whole plot.

In[2]:= **ParametricPlot[{Sin[t], Cos[t]}, {t, 0, 2Pi}]**

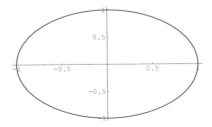

Setting the option **AspectRatio** to **Automatic** makes *Mathematica* preserve the "true shape" of the curve, as defined by the actual coordinate values it involves.

In[3]:= **Show[%, AspectRatio -> Automatic]**

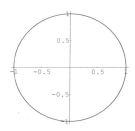

ParametricPlot3D[{f_x, f_y, f_z}, {t, $tmin$, $tmax$}]
                    make a parametric plot of a three-dimensional curve

ParametricPlot3D[{f_x, f_y, f_z}, {t, $tmin$, $tmax$}, {u, $umin$, $umax$}]
                    make a parametric plot of a three-dimensional surface

ParametricPlot3D[{f_x, f_y, f_z, s}, ...]
                    shade the parts of the parametric plot according to the function s

ParametricPlot3D[{{f_x, f_y, f_z}, {g_x, g_y, g_z}, ... }, ...]
                    plot several objects together

Three-dimensional parametric plots.

ParametricPlot3D[{f_x, f_y, f_z}, {t, $tmin$, $tmax$}] is the direct analog in three dimensions of ParametricPlot[{f_x, f_y}, {t, $tmin$, $tmax$}] in two dimensions. In both cases, *Mathematica* effectively generates a sequence of points by varying the parameter t, then forms a curve by joining these points. With ParametricPlot, the curve is in two dimensions; with ParametricPlot3D, it is in three dimensions.

This makes a parametric plot of a helical curve. Varying t produces circular motion in the x, y plane, and linear motion in the z direction.

In[4]:= **ParametricPlot3D[{Sin[t], Cos[t], t/3}, {t, 0, 15}]**

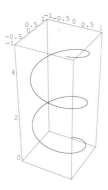

ParametricPlot3D[$\{f_x$, f_y, $f_z\}$, $\{t$, *tmin*, *tmax*$\}$, $\{u$, *umin*, *umax*$\}$] creates a surface, rather than a curve. The surface is formed from a collection of quadrilaterals. The corners of the quadrilaterals have coordinates corresponding to the values of the f_i when t and u take on values in a regular grid.

Here the x and y coordinates for the quadrilaterals are given simply by t and u. The result is a surface plot of the kind that can be produced by Plot3D.

In[5]:= **ParametricPlot3D[{t, u, Sin[t u]},**
{t, 0, 3}, {u, 0, 3}]

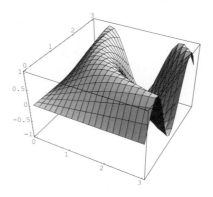

This shows the same surface as before, but with the *y* coordinates distorted by a quadratic transformation.

In[6]:= **ParametricPlot3D[{t, u∧2, Sin[t u]},**
{t, 0, 3}, {u, 0, 3}]

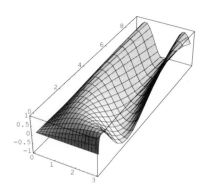

This produces a helicoid surface by taking the helical curve shown above, and at each section of the curve drawing a quadrilateral.

In[7]:= **ParametricPlot3D[{u Sin[t], u Cos[t], t/3},**
{t, 0, 15}, {u, -1, 1}]

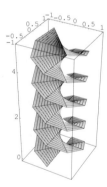

In general, it is possible to construct many complicated surfaces using **ParametricPlot3D**. In each case, you can think of the surfaces as being formed by "distorting" or "rolling up" the *t*, *u* coordinate grid in a certain way.

This produces a cylinder. Varying the t parameter yields a circle in the *x*, *y* plane, while varying u moves the circles in the *z* direction.

In[8]:= **ParametricPlot3D[{Sin[t], Cos[t], u},**
{t, 0, 2Pi}, {u, 0, 4}]

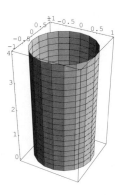

This produces a torus. Varying t yields a circle, while varying u rotates the circle around the *z* axis to form the torus.

In[9]:= **ParametricPlot3D[**
{Cos[t] (3 + Cos[u]), Sin[t] (3 + Cos[u]), Sin[u]},
{t, 0, 2Pi}, {u, 0, 2Pi}]

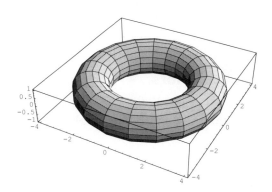

This produces a sphere.

In[10]:= **ParametricPlot3D[**
{Cos[t] Cos[u], Sin[t] Cos[u], Sin[u]},
{t, 0, 2Pi}, {u, -Pi/2, Pi/2}]

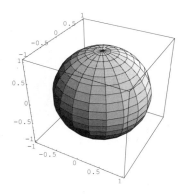

You should realize that when you draw surfaces with `ParametricPlot3D`, the exact choice of parametrization is often crucial. You should be careful, for example, to avoid parametrizations in which all or part of your surface is covered more than once. Such multiple coverings often lead to discontinuities in the mesh drawn on the surface, and may make `ParametricPlot3D` take much longer to render the surface.

■ 1.9.11 Some Special Plots

As discussed in Section 2.9, *Mathematica* includes a full graphics programming language. In this language, you can set up many different kinds of plots. A few of the common ones are included in standard *Mathematica* packages.

`<<Graphics`Graphics``	load a package with additional graphics functions
`LogPlot[f, {x, xmin, xmax}]`	generate a log-linear plot
`LogLogPlot[f, {x, xmin, xmax}]`	
	generate a log-log plot
`LogListPlot[list]`	generate a log-linear plot from a list of data
`LogLogListPlot[list]`	generate a log-log plot from a list of data
`PolarPlot[r, {t, tmin, tmax}]`	generate a polar plot of the radius r as a function of angle t
`ErrorListPlot[{{x_1, y_1, dy_1}, ... }]`	
	generate a plot of data with error bars
`TextListPlot[{{x_1, y_1, "s_1"}, ... }]`	
	plot a list of data with each point given by the text string s_i
`BarChart[list]`	plot a list of data as a bar chart
`PieChart[list]`	plot a list of data as a pie chart
`PlotVectorField[{f_x, f_y, f_z}, {x, xmin, xmax}, {y, ymin, ymax}]`	
	plot the vector field corresponding to the vector function f
`ListPlotVectorField[list]`	plot the vector field corresponding the two-dimensional array of vectors in *list*
`SphericalPlot[r, {theta, min, max}, {phi, min, max}]`	
	generate a three-dimensional spherical plot

Some special plotting functions defined in standard *Mathematica* packages.

This loads the standard *Mathematica* package of additional graphics functions.

`In[1]:= <<Graphics`Graphics``

This generates a log-linear plot.

`In[2]:= LogPlot[ Exp[-x] + 4 Exp[-2x], {x, 0, 6} ]`

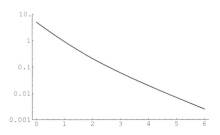

Here is a list of the first ten primes.

In[3]:= **p = Table[Prime[n], {n, 10}]**

Out[3]= {2, 3, 5, 7, 11, 13, 17, 19, 23, 29}

This plots the primes using the integers 1, 2, 3, ... as plotting symbols.

In[4]:= **TextListPlot[p]**

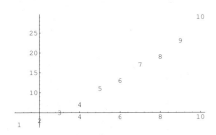

Here is a bar chart of the primes.

In[5]:= **BarChart[p]**

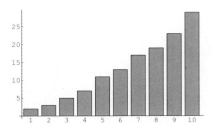

This gives a pie chart.

In[6]:= **PieChart[p]**

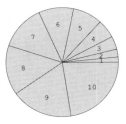

■ 1.9.12 Special Topic: Animated Graphics

On many computer systems, *Mathematica* can produce not only static images, but also animated graphics or "movies".

The basic idea in all cases is to generate a sequence of "frames" which can be displayed in rapid succession. You can use the standard *Mathematica* graphics functions described above to produce each frame. The mechanism for displaying the frames as a movie depends on the *Mathematica* interface you are using. With a notebook-based interface, you typically put the frames in a sequence of cells, then select the cells and choose a command to animate them. With text-based interfaces, there is often an external program provided for displaying animated graphics. The program can typically be accessed from inside *Mathematica* using the function `Animate`.

`<<Graphics`Animation``	load the animation package (if necessary)
`Animate[plot, {t, tmin, tmax}]`	execute the graphics command *plot* for a sequence of values of *t*, and animate the resulting sequence of frames
`ShowAnimation[{g_1, g_2, ... }]`	produce an animation from a sequence of graphics objects

Typical ways to produce animated graphics.

When you produce a sequence of frames for a movie, it is important that different frames be consistent. Thus, for example, you should typically give an explicit setting for the `PlotRange` option, rather than using the default `Automatic` setting, in order to ensure that the scales used in different frames are the same. If you have three-dimensional graphics with different view points, you should similarly set `SphericalRegion -> True` in order to ensure that the scaling of different plots is the same.

This generates a list of graphics objects. Setting `DisplayFunction -> Identity` stops `Plot3D` from rendering the graphics it produces. Explicitly setting `PlotRange` ensures that the scale is the same in each piece of graphics.

```
In[1]:= Table[ Plot3D[ BesselJ[0, Sqrt[x^2 + y^2] + t],
            {x, -10, 10}, {y, -10, 10}, Axes -> False,
            PlotRange -> {-0.5, 1.0},
            DisplayFunction -> Identity ],
        {t, 0, 8} ] // Short
Out[1]//Short= {-SurfaceGraphics-, <<7>>, -SurfaceGraphics-}
```

On an appropriate computer system, `ShowAnimation[%]` would animate the graphics. This partitions the graphics into three rows, and shows the resulting array of images.

```
In[2]:= Show[ GraphicsArray[ Partition[%, 3] ] ]
```

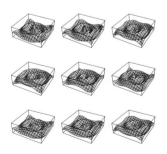

■ 1.9.13 Special Topic: Sound

On some computer systems, *Mathematica* can produce not only graphics but also sound. *Mathematica* treats graphics and sound in a closely analogous way.

For example, just as you can use Plot[f, {x, $xmin$, $xmax$}] to plot a function, so also you can use Play[f, {t, 0, $tmax$}] to "play" a function. Play takes the function to define the waveform for a sound: the values of the function give the amplitude of the sound as a function of time.

Play[f, {t, 0, $tmax$}]	play a sound with amplitude f as a function of time t in seconds

Playing a function.

On a suitable computer system, this plays a pure tone with a frequency of 440 hertz for one second.

```
In[1]:= Play[Sin[2Pi 440 t], {t, 0, 1}]
Out[1]= -Sound-
```

Sounds produced by Play can have any waveform. They do not, for example, have to consist of a collection of harmonic pieces. In general, the amplitude function you give to Play specifies the instantaneous signal associated with the sound. This signal is typically converted to a voltage, and ultimately to a displacement. Note that *amplitude* is sometimes defined to be the *peak* signal associated with a sound; in *Mathematica*, it is always the *instantaneous* signal as a function of time.

This plays a more complex sound.

```
In[2]:= Play[ Sin[700 t + 25 t Sin[350 t]], {t, 0, 4} ]
Out[2]= -Sound-
```

Play is set up so that the time variable that appears in it is always measured in absolute seconds. When a sound is actually played, its amplitude is sampled a certain number of times every second. You can specify the sample rate by setting the option SampleRate.

Play[f, {t, 0, $tmax$}, SampleRate -> r]	play a sound, sampling it r times a second

Specifying the sample rate for a sound.

In general, the higher the sample rate, the better high-frequency components in the sound will be rendered. A sample rate of r typically allows frequencies up to $r/2$ hertz. The human auditory system can typically perceive sounds in the frequency range 20 to 22000 hertz (depending somewhat on age and sex). The fundamental frequencies for the 88 notes on a piano range from 27.5 to 4096 hertz.

The standard sample rate used for compact disk players is 44100. The effective sample rate in a typical telephone system is around 8000. On most computer systems, the default sample rate used by *Mathematica* is around 8000.

You can use Play[{f_1, f_2}, ...] to produce stereo sound. In general, *Mathematica* supports any number of sound channels.

ListPlay[{a_1, a_2, ... }, SampleRate -> r]
play a sound with a sequence of amplitude levels

Playing sampled sounds.

The function ListPlay allows you simply to give a list of values which are taken to be sound amplitudes sampled at a certain rate.

When sounds are actually rendered by *Mathematica*, only a certain range of amplitudes is allowed. The option PlayRange in Play and ListPlay specifies how the amplitudes you give should be scaled to fit in the allowed range. The settings for this option are analogous to those for the PlotRange graphics option discussed on page 142.

PlayRange -> Automatic (default)	
	use an internal procedure to scale amplitudes
PlayRange -> All	scale so that all amplitudes fit in the allowed range
PlayRange -> {*amin*, *amax*}	make amplitudes between *amin* and *amax* fit in the allowed range, and clip others

Specifying the scaling of sound amplitudes.

While it is often convenient to use the default setting PlayRange -> Automatic, you should realize that Play may run significantly faster if you give an explicit PlayRange specification, so it does not have to derive one.

Show[*sound*]	replay a sound object

Replaying a sound object.

Both Play and ListPlay return Sound objects which contain procedures for synthesizing sounds. You can replay a particular Sound object using the function Show that is also used for redisplaying graphics.

The internal structure of Sound objects is discussed in Section 2.9.18.

1.10 Files and External Operations

■ 1.10.1 Reading and Writing *Mathematica* Files

You can use files on your computer system to store definitions and results from *Mathematica*. The most general approach is to store everything as plain text that is appropriate for input to *Mathematica*. With this approach, a version of *Mathematica* running on one computer system produces files that can be read by a version running on any computer system. In addition, such files can be manipulated by other standard programs, such as text editors.

`<<`*name*	read in a plain text file of *Mathematica* input
expr `>>` *name*	output *expr* to a file as plain text
expr `>>>` *name*	append *expr* to a file
`!!`*name*	display the contents of a plain text file

Reading and writing files.

This expands $(x + y)^3$, and outputs the result to a file called `tmp`.	`In[1]:= Expand[ (x + y)^3 ]  >> tmp`
Here are the contents of `tmp`. They can be used directly as input for *Mathematica*.	`In[2]:= !!tmp` `x^3 + 3*x^2*y + 3*x*y^2 + y^3`
This reads in `tmp`, evaluating the *Mathematica* input it contains.	`In[2]:= <<tmp` $Out[2]= x^3 + 3 x^2 y + 3 x y^2 + y^3$

If you are familiar with the Unix operating system, you will recognize the *Mathematica* redirection operators `>>`, `>>>` and `<<` as being analogous to the Unix shell operators `>`, `>>` and `<`.

The redirection operators `>>` and `>>>` are convenient for storing results you get from *Mathematica*. The function `Save["`*name*`", `f`, `g`, ... ]` allows you to save definitions for variables and functions.

`Save["`*name*`", `f`, `g`, ... ]`	save definitions for variables or functions in a file

Saving definitions in plain text files.

Here is a definition for a function `f`.	`In[3]:= f[x_] := x^2 + c`
This gives `c` the value 17.	`In[4]:= c = 17` `Out[4]= 17`

This saves the definition of **f** in the file **ftmp**.	*In[5]:=* **Save["ftmp", f]**
Mathematica automatically saves both the actual definition of **f**, and the definition of **c** on which it depends.	*In[6]:=* **!!ftmp** **f[x_] := x^2 + c** **c = 17**
This clears the definitions of **f** and **c**.	*In[6]:=* **Clear[f, c]**
You can reinstate the definitions you saved simply by reading in the file **ftmp**.	*In[7]:=* **<<ftmp** *Out[7]=* **17**

The methods for reading and writing files that we have discussed so far work in versions of *Mathematica* on all computer systems. On some systems, however, you can also use other methods.

On systems with notebook-based interfaces, you will usually find it easier to save whole notebooks, rather than saving specific *Mathematica* expressions and definitions. The standard notebook interface for *Mathematica* allows you to specify certain cells of *Mathematica* input as being "initialization cells". These cells can contain definitions and results that are automatically set up again whenever you open the notebook.

Although systems without notebook-based interfaces cannot make use of the full structure of *Mathematica* notebooks, all versions of *Mathematica* are set up to be able to read notebooks as input. If you read a notebook using <<*name*, *Mathematica* will ignore all the material in the notebook except those pieces that are in initialization cells. The pieces in initialization cells *Mathematica* will execute as input.

Mathematica expression files	save specific results and definitions – available on all systems
Notebooks	save text, graphics and expressions – available with notebook-based interfaces
Dump files	save complete state of *Mathematica* – available only on specific computer systems

Ways to save *Mathematica* material.

As you go through a *Mathematica* session, you typically build up a complicated "state", including various definitions, values of variables, and results. When you terminate the session, any part of this state that you have not explicitly saved is lost. On some computer systems, particularly those based on the Unix and VMS operating systems, it is possible to "dump" the complete state of *Mathematica* into a file. Then when you restart from the dump file, your *Mathematica* will be in exactly the state it was when you dumped it.

Dump["*name*"]	dump the complete state of *Mathematica* to a file
math -x *name*	typical operating system command to restart from a dump file

Dumping the complete state of *Mathematica* on certain computer systems.

You should realize that in most cases, specifying the complete state of *Mathematica* requires a very large amount of data. As a result, the files generated by Dump are usually many megabytes in size. Nevertheless, if you always want to start *Mathematica* with the same set of definitions loaded up, dump files are a convenient mechanism.

■ 1.10.2 Advanced Topic: Finding and Manipulating Files

Although the details of how files are named and organized differ from one computer system to another, *Mathematica* provides some fairly general mechanisms for finding and handling files.

Mathematica assumes that files on your computer system are organized in a collection of *directories*. At any point, you have a *current working directory*. You can always refer to files in this directory just by giving their names.

Directory[ ]	give your current working directory
SetDirectory["*dir*"]	set your current working directory
FileNames[ ]	list the files in your current working directory
FileNames["*form*"]	list the files whose names match a certain form
<<*name*	read in a file with the specified name
<<*context*`	read in a file corresponding to the specified context
CopyFile["*file₁*", "*file₂*"]	copy *file₁* to *file₂*
DeleteFile["*file*"]	delete a file

Functions for finding and manipulating files.

This is the current working directory. The form it has differs from one computer system to another.

```
In[1]:= Directory[ ]
Out[1]= /users/swolf
```

This resets the current working directory.

```
In[2]:= SetDirectory["Examples"]
Out[2]= /users/swolf/Examples
```

This gives a list of all files on your search path whose names match the form Test*.m.	*In[3]:=* **FileNames["Test*.m"]** *Out[3]=* {Test1.m, Test2.m, TestFinal.m}

Although you usually want to create files only in your current working directory, you often need to read in files from other directories. As a result, when you ask *Mathematica* to read in a file with a particular name, *Mathematica* automatically searches a list of directories (specified by the value of the search path variable $Path) to try and find a file with that name.

One issue in handling files in *Mathematica* is that the form of file and directory names varies between computer systems. This means for example that names of files which contain standard *Mathematica* packages may be quite different on different systems. Through a sequence of conventions, it is however possible to read in a standard *Mathematica* package with the same command on all systems. The way this works is that each package defines a so-called *Mathematica* context, of the form *name`name`*. On each system, all files are named in correspondence with the contexts they define. Then when you use the command <<*name`name`* *Mathematica* automatically translates the context name into the file name appropriate for your particular computer system.

FindList["*file*", "*text*"]	give a list of all lines in a file that contain the specified text
FindList[FileNames[ ], "*text*"]	search in all files in your current directory

Searching for text in files.

This searches all lines in the file index containing Laplace.	*In[4]:=* **FindList["index", "Laplace"]** *Out[4]=* {Laplace transforms: Calculus`LaplaceTransform`, Inverse Laplace transforms: Calculus`LaplaceTransform`}

■ 1.10.3 Reading Data Files

ReadList["*file*", Number]	read numbers from a file, and return a *Mathematica* list of them
ReadList["*file*", Number, RecordLists->True]	read numbers from a file, making a separate list for each line in the file

Reading numerical data files.

If you have a table of numbers in a file, generated for example by an external program, you can read them into *Mathematica* using ReadList. The numbers in your file can be given in C or Fortran-like form, as 2.3E5 and so on. ReadList converts all numbers to the appropriate *Mathematica* form.

This shows the contents of the file rand.dat.

```
In[1]:= !!rand.dat

3.4     -5.7E-2     8.4E+2
4.5     -7.8E-2     1.9E+3
6.4     -0.1        4.7E+4
```

This reads the file rand.dat, and returns a list of the numbers in the file.

```
In[1]:= ReadList["rand.dat", Number]

Out[1]= {3.4, -0.057, 840., 4.5, -0.078, 1900., 6.4, -0.1,
   47000.}
```

This reads the numbers making a separate list for each line in the file.

```
In[2]:= ReadList["rand.dat", Number, RecordLists -> True]

Out[2]= {{3.4, -0.057, 840.}, {4.5, -0.078, 1900.},
   {6.4, -0.1, 47000.}}
```

Mathematica allows you to read files in many different ways. For example, instead of reading numbers, you can read strings or "words". In addition, you can use Find to search for particular parts of files to read. These possibilities are discussed in Section 2.10.6.

■ 1.10.4 Generating C and Fortran Expressions

If you have special-purpose programs written in C or Fortran, you may want to take formulas you have generated in *Mathematica* and insert them into the source code of your programs. *Mathematica* allows you to convert mathematical expressions into C and Fortran expressions.

CForm[*expr*]	write out *expr* so it can be used in a C program
FortranForm[*expr*]	write out *expr* for Fortran

Mathematica output for programming languages.

Here is an expression, written out in standard mathematical form.

```
In[1]:= Expand[(1 + x + y)^2]

Out[1]= 1 + 2 x + x  + 2 y + 2 x y + y
                    2                   2
```

Here is the expression in Fortran form.

```
In[2]:= FortranForm[%]

Out[2]//FortranForm= 1 + 2*x + x**2 + 2*y + 2*x*y + y**2
```

Here is the same expression in C form. Macros for objects like Power are defined in the C header file mdefs.h that comes with most versions of *Mathematica*.

```
In[3]:= CForm[%]

Out[3]//CForm= 1 + 2*x + Power(x,2) + 2*y + 2*x*y + Power(y,2)
```

You should realize that there are many differences between *Mathematica* and C or Fortran. As a result, expressions you translate may not work exactly the same as they do in *Mathematica*. In addition, there are so many differences in programming constructs that no attempt is made to translate these automatically.

■ 1.10.5 Generating TeX Input

When you are preparing documents for publication, you may need to use a full-function formatting system, such as TeX. You can use `TeXForm` to write out results from *Mathematica* in a form suitable for input to TeX.

`TeXForm[`*expr*`]`	write out *expr* in TeX input form

Mathematica output for formatting systems.

Here is an expression, written out in
standard *Mathematica* form.

```
In[1]:= (x + y)^2 / (x y)
```

$$Out[1]= \frac{(x + y)^2}{x\ y}$$

Here is the expression in TeX input
form.

```
In[2]:= TeXForm[%]
```

```
Out[2]//TeXForm= {{{{\left( x + y \right) }^2}}\over {x\,y}}
```

Here is a more complicated example.

This is the standard *Mathematica* form of
an expression.

```
In[3]:= Sum[ 2 Sqrt[2]/9801 (4n)! (1103 + 26390 n) /
                    (n!^4 396^(4n)), {n, 1, Infinity} ]
```

$$Out[3]= Sum[\frac{2\ Sqrt[2]\ (1103 + 26390\ n)\ (4\ n)!}{9801\ 396^{4\ n}\ n!^4}, \{n, 1, Infinity\}]$$

Here is the expression in TeX input
form.

```
In[4]:= TeXForm[%]
```

```
Out[4]//TeXForm=
  \sum_{n = 1}^{\infty}{{2\,{\sqrt{2}}\,
       \left( 1103 + 26390\,n \right) \,\left( 4\,n \right) !}
       \over {9801\,{{396}^{4\,n}}\,{{n!}^4}}}
```

Here is the result of running the TeX input through TeX:

$$\sum_{n=1}^{\infty} \frac{2\sqrt{2}\left(1103+26390\,n\right)\left(4\,n\right)!}{9801\,396^{4\,n}\,n!^4}$$

`TeXForm` automatically converts a number of *Mathematica* symbol names to TeX forms.

Mathematica form	TEX output form
alpha, beta, gamma, etc.	α, β, γ, etc.
ALPHA, BETA, GAMMA, etc.	A, B, Γ, etc.
I, E, Pi, Infinity	i, e, π, ∞

Some transformations made by `TeXForm`.

■ 1.10.6 Splicing *Mathematica* Output into External Files

If you want to make use of *Mathematica* output in an external file such as a program or document, you will often find it useful to "splice" the output automatically into the file.

Splice["*file.mx*"]	splice *Mathematica* output into an external file named *file*.m*x*, putting the results in the file *file*.*x*
Splice["*infile*", "*outfile*"]	splice *Mathematica* output into *infile*, sending the output to *outfile*

Splicing *Mathematica* output into files.

The basic idea is to set up the definitions you need in a particular *Mathematica* session, then run `Splice` to use the definitions you have made to produce the appropriate output to insert into the external files.

```
#include "mdefs.h"

double f(x)
double x;
{
double y;

y = <* Integrate[Sin[x]^5, x] *> ;

return(2*y - 1) ;
}
```

A simple C program containing a *Mathematica* formula.

```
#include "mdefs.h"

double f(x)
double x;
{
double y;
```

```
y = -5*Cos(x)/8 + 5*Cos(3*x)/48 - Cos(5*x)/80 ;

return(2*y - 1) ;
}
```

The C program after processing with `Splice`.

■ 1.10.7 Running External Programs

Although *Mathematica* does many things well, there are some things that are inevitably better done by external programs. You can use *Mathematica* to control the external programs, or to analyze output they generate.

On most computer systems, it is possible to run external programs directly from within *Mathematica*. *Mathematica* communicates with the external programs through interprocess communication mechanisms such as Unix pipes.

In the simplest cases, the only communication you need is to send and receive plain text. You can prepare input in *Mathematica*, then give it as the standard input for the external program. Or you can take the standard output of the external program, and use it as input to *Mathematica*.

In general, *Mathematica* allows you to treat streams of data exchanged with external programs just like files. In place of a file name, you give the external command to run, prefaced by an exclamation point.

`<<`*file*	read in a file
`<<"!`*command*`"`	run an external command, and read in the output it produces
expr `>> "!`*command*`"`	feed the textual form of *expr* to an external command
`ReadList["!`*command*`", Number]`	run an external command, and read in a list of the numbers it produces

Some ways to communicate with external programs.

This feeds the expression `x^2 + y^2` as input to the external command `lpr`, which, on a typical Berkeley Unix system, sends output to a printer.

```
In[1]:= x^2 + y^2 >> "!lpr"
```

Putting a ! at the beginning of a line causes the remainder of the line to be executed as an external command. `squares` is an external program which prints numbers and their squares.

```
In[2]:= !squares 4
1    1
2    4
3    9
4    16
```

This runs the external command `squares 4`, then reads numbers from the output it produces.	`In[2]:= ReadList["!squares 4", Number, RecordLists->True]` `Out[2]= {{1, 1}, {2, 4}, {3, 9}, {4, 16}}`

■ 1.10.8 *MathLink*

The previous section discussed how to exchange plain text with external programs. In many cases, however, you will find it convenient to communicate with external programs at a higher level, and to exchange more structured data with them.

On most computer systems, *Mathematica* supports the *MathLink* communication standard, which allows higher-level communication between *Mathematica* and external programs. In order to use *Math-Link*, an external program has to include some special source code, which is usually distributed with *Mathematica*.

MathLink allows external programs both to call *Mathematica*, and to be called by *Mathematica*. Section 2.10.10 discusses some of the details of *MathLink*. By using *MathLink*, you can, for example, treat *Mathematica* essentially like a subroutine embedded inside an external program. Or you can create a front end that implements your own user interface, and communicates with the *Mathematica* kernel via *MathLink*.

You can also use *MathLink* to let *Mathematica* call individual functions inside an external program. As described in Section 2.10.10, you can set up a *MathLink* template file to specify how particular functions in *Mathematica* should call functions inside your external program. From the *MathLink* template file, you can generate source code to include in your program. Then when you start your program, the appropriate *Mathematica* definitions are automatically made, and when you call a particular *Mathematica* function, code in your external program is executed.

`Install["`*command*`"]`	start an external program and install *Mathematica* definitions to call functions it contains
`Uninstall[`*link*`]`	terminate an external program and uninstall definitions for functions in it

Calling functions in external programs.

This starts the external program `simul`, and installs *Mathematica* definitions to call various functions in it.	`In[1]:= Install["simul"]` `Out[1]= LinkObject[simul, 1]`
Here is a usage message for a function that was installed in *Mathematica* to call a function in the external program.	`In[2]:= ?srun` `srun[{a, r, gamma}, x] performs a simulation with the specified parameters.`
When you call this function, it executes code in the external program.	`In[3]:= srun[{3, 0, 7}, 5]` `Out[3]= 6.781241`
This terminates the `simul` program.	`In[4]:= Uninstall["simul"]`

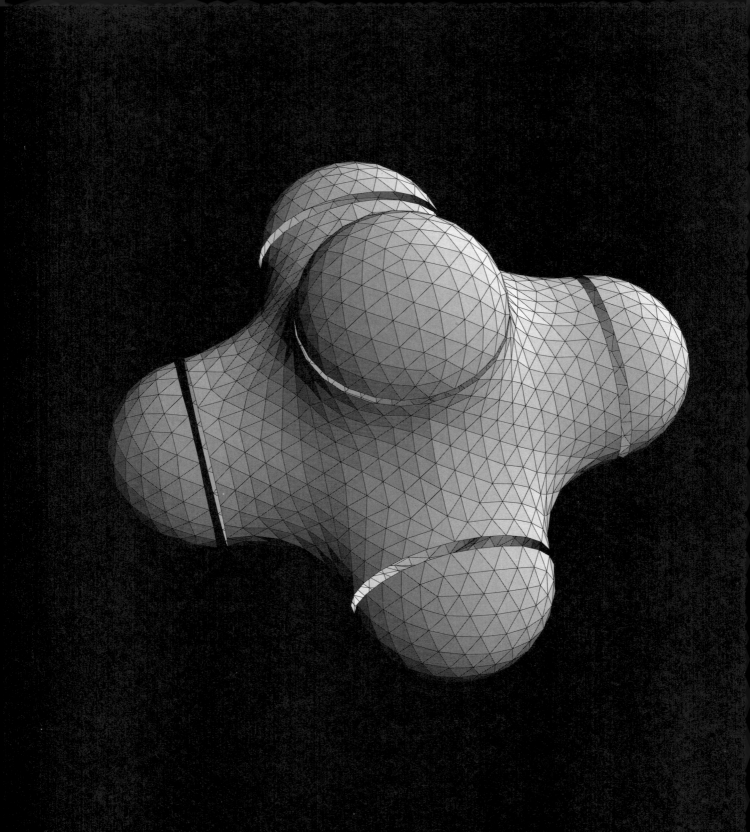

Part 2.

Principles of *Mathematica*

2.1 Expressions

■ 2.1.1 Everything Is an Expression

Mathematica handles many different kinds of things: mathematical formulas, lists and graphics, to name a few. Although they often look very different, *Mathematica* represents all of these things in one uniform way. They are all *expressions*.

A prototypical example of a *Mathematica* expression is f[x, y]. You might use f[x, y] to represent a mathematical function $f(x, y)$. The function is named f, and it has two arguments, x and y.

You do not always have to write expressions in the form $f[x,y,\ldots]$. For example, x + y is also an expression. When you type in x + y, *Mathematica* converts it to the standard form Plus[x, y]. Then, when it prints it out again, it gives it as x + y.

The same is true of other "operators", such as ∧ (Power) and / (Divide).

In fact, everything you type into *Mathematica* is treated as an expression.

x + y + z	Plus[x, y, z]
x y z	Times[x, y, z]
x∧n	Power[x, n]
{a, b, c}	List[a, b, c]
a -> b	Rule[a, b]
a = b	Set[a, b]

Some examples of *Mathematica* expressions.

You can see the full form of any expression by using FullForm[*expr*].

Here is an expression.
```
In[1]:= x + y + z
Out[1]= x + y + z
```

This is the full form of the expression.
```
In[2]:= FullForm[%]
Out[2]//FullForm= Plus[x, y, z]
```

Here is another expression.
```
In[3]:= 1 + x∧2 + (y + z)∧2
Out[3]= 1 + x  + (y + z)
```
$$Out[3]= 1 + x^2 + (y + z)^2$$

Its full form has several nested pieces.
```
In[4]:= FullForm[%]
Out[4]//FullForm= Plus[1, Power[x, 2], Power[Plus[y, z], 2]]
```

The object *f* in an expression *f*[*x*, *y*, ...] is known as the *head* of the expression. You can extract it using `Head`[*expr*]. Particularly when you write programs in *Mathematica*, you will often want to test the head of an expression to find out what kind of thing the expression is.

`Head` gives the "function name" f.	*In[5]:=* **Head[f[x, y]]**
	Out[5]= f
Here `Head` gives the name of the "operator".	*In[6]:=* **Head[a + b + c]**
	Out[6]= Plus
Everything has a head.	*In[7]:=* **Head[{a, b, c}]**
	Out[7]= List
Numbers also have heads.	*In[8]:=* **Head[23432]**
	Out[8]= Integer
You can distinguish different kinds of numbers by their heads.	*In[9]:=* **Head[345.6]**
	Out[9]= Real

`Head`[*expr*]	give the head of an expression: the *f* in *f*[*x*, *y*]
`FullForm`[*expr*]	display an expression in the full form used by *Mathematica*

Functions for manipulating expressions.

■ 2.1.2 The Meaning of Expressions

The notion of expressions is a crucial unifying principle in *Mathematica*. It is the fact that every object in *Mathematica* has the same underlying structure that makes it possible for *Mathematica* to cover so many areas with a comparatively small number of basic operations.

Although all expressions have the same basic structure, there are many different ways that expressions can be used. Here are a few of the interpretations you can give to the parts of an expression.

meaning of f	*meaning of x, y, ...*	*examples*
Function	arguments or parameters	`Sin[x]`, `f[x, y]`
Command	arguments or parameters	`Expand[(x + 1)∧2]`
Operator	operands	`x + y`, `a = b`
Head	elements	`{a, b, c}`
Object type	contents	`RGBColor[r, g, b]`

Some interpretations of parts of expressions.

Expressions in *Mathematica* are often used to specify operations. So, for example, typing in 2 + 3 causes 2 and 3 to be added together, while `Factor[x∧6 - 1]` performs factorization.

Perhaps an even more important use of expressions in *Mathematica*, however, is to maintain a structure, which can then be acted on by other functions. An expression like `{a, b, c}` does not specify an operation. It merely maintains a list structure, which contains a collection of three elements. Other functions, such as `Reverse` or `Dot`, can act on this structure.

The full form of the expression `{a, b, c}` is `List[a, b, c]`. The head `List` performs no operations. Instead, its purpose is to serve as a "tag" to specify the "type" of the structure.

You can use expressions in *Mathematica* to create your own structures. For example, you might want to represent points in three-dimensional space, specified by three coordinates. You could give each point as `point[x, y, z]`. The "function" `point` again performs no operation. It serves merely to collect the three coordinates together, and to label the resulting object as a `point`.

You can think of expressions like `point[x, y, z]` as being "packets of data", tagged with a particular head. Even though all expressions have the same basic structure, you can distinguish different "types" of expressions by giving them different heads. You can then set up transformation rules and programs which treat different types of expressions in different ways.

■ 2.1.3 Special Ways to Input Expressions

Mathematica allows you to use special notation for many common operators. For example, although internally *Mathematica* represents a sum of two terms as `Plus[x, y]`, you can enter this expression in the much more convenient form *x* + *y*.

The *Mathematica* language has a definite grammar which specifies how your input should be converted to internal form. One aspect of the grammar is that it specifies how pieces of your input should be grouped. For example, if you enter an expression such as a + b ∧ c, the *Mathematica* grammar specifies that this should be considered, following standard mathematical notation, as a + (b ∧ c) rather than (a + b) ∧ c. *Mathematica* chooses this grouping because it treats the operator ∧ as having a higher *precedence* than +. In general, the arguments of operators with higher precedence are grouped before those of operators with lower precedence.

You should realize that absolutely every special input form in *Mathematica* is assigned a definite precedence. This includes not only the traditional mathematical operators, but also forms such as ->, := or the semicolons used to separate expressions in a *Mathematica* program.

The table on pages 716–718 gives all the operators of *Mathematica* in order of decreasing precedence. The precedence is arranged, where possible, to follow standard mathematical usage, and to minimize the number of parentheses that are usually needed.

You will find, for example, that relational operators such as < have lower precedence than arithmetic operators such as +. This means that you can write expressions such as x + y > 7 without using parentheses.

There are nevertheless many cases where you do have to use parentheses. For example, since ; has a lower precedence than =, you need to use parentheses to write x = (a ; b). *Mathematica* interprets the expression x = a ; b as (x = a) ; b. In general, it can never hurt to include extra parentheses, but it can cause a great deal of trouble if you leave parentheses out, and *Mathematica* interprets your input in a way you do not expect.

$f[x, y]$	standard form for $f[x, y]$
$f @ x$	prefix form for $f[x]$
$x // f$	postfix form for $f[x]$
$x \sim f \sim y$	infix form for $f[x, y]$

Four ways to write expressions in *Mathematica*.

There are several common types of operators in *Mathematica*. The + in $x + y$ is an "infix" operator. The − in $-p$ is a "prefix" operator. Even when you enter an expression such as $f[x, y, ...]$ *Mathematica* allows you to do it in ways that mimic infix, prefix and postfix forms.

This "postfix form" is exactly equivalent to f[x + y].

```
In[1]:= x + y //f
Out[1]= f[x + y]
```

You will often want to add functions like N as "afterthoughts", and give them in postfix form.

```
In[2]:= 3^(1/4) + 1  //N
Out[2]= 2.31607
```

It is sometimes easier to understand what a function is doing when you write it in infix form.

```
In[3]:= {a, b, c} ~Join~ {d, e}
Out[3]= {a, b, c, d, e}
```

You should notice that // has very low precedence. If you put //*f* at the end of any expression containing arithmetic or logical operators, the *f* is applied to the *whole expression*. So, for example, x+y //f means f[x+y], not x+f[y].

The prefix form @ has a much higher precedence. f @ x + y is equivalent to f[x] + y, not f[x + y]. You can write f[x + y] in prefix form as f @ (x + y).

■ 2.1.4 Parts of Expressions

Since lists are just a particular kind of expression, it will come as no surprise that you can refer to parts of any expression much as you refer to parts of a list.

This gets the second element in the list {a, b, c}.	*In[1]:=* **{a, b, c}[[2]]** *Out[1]=* b
You can use the same method to get the second element in the sum x + y + z.	*In[2]:=* **(x + y + z)[[2]]** *Out[2]=* y
This gives the last element in the sum.	*In[3]:=* **(x + y + z)[[-1]]** *Out[3]=* z
Part 0 is the head.	*In[4]:=* **(x + y + z)[[0]]** *Out[4]=* Plus

You can refer to parts of an expression such as *f[g[a], g[b]]* just as you refer to parts of nested lists.

This is part 1.	*In[5]:=* **f[g[a], g[b]] [[1]]** *Out[5]=* g[a]
This is part {1,1}.	*In[6]:=* **f[g[a], g[b]] [[1, 1]]** *Out[6]=* a
This extracts part {2,1} of the expression 1 + x^2.	*In[7]:=* **(1 + x^2) [[2, 1]]** *Out[7]=* x
To see what part is {2,1}, you can look at the full form of the expression.	*In[8]:=* **FullForm[1 + x^2]** *Out[8]//FullForm=* Plus[1, Power[x, 2]]

You should realize that the assignment of indices to parts of expressions is done on the basis of the internal *Mathematica* forms of the expression, as shown by FullForm. These forms do not always correspond directly with what you see printed out. This is particularly true for algebraic expressions, where *Mathematica* uses a standard internal form, but prints the expressions in special ways.

Here is the internal form of x / y.	*In[9]:=* **FullForm[x / y]** *Out[9]//FullForm=* Times[x, Power[y, -1]]

It is the internal form that is used in specifying parts.

In[10]:= **(x / y)[[2]]**

$$Out[10]= \frac{1}{y}$$

You can manipulate parts of expressions just as you manipulate parts of lists.

This replaces the third part of a + b + c + d by x^2. Note that the sum is automatically rearranged when the replacement is done.

In[11]:= **ReplacePart[a + b + c + d, x^2, 3]**

$$Out[11]= a + b + d + x^2$$

Here is an expression.

In[12]:= **t = 1 + (3 + x)^2 / y**

$$Out[12]= 1 + \frac{(3 + x)^2}{y}$$

This is the full form of t.

In[13]:= **FullForm[t]**

Out[13]//FullForm=

Plus[1, Times[Power[Plus[3, x], 2], Power[y, -1]]]

This resets a part of the expression t.

In[14]:= **t[[2, 1, 1]] = x**

Out[14]= x

Now the form of t has been changed.

In[15]:= **t**

$$Out[15]= 1 + \frac{x^2}{y}$$

> Part[*expr*, *n*] or *expr*[[*n*]] the nth part of *expr*
>
> Part[*expr*, {n_1, n_2, ... }] or *expr*[[{n_1, n_2, ... }]]
>   a combination of parts of an expression
>
> ReplacePart[*expr*, *elem*, *n*] replace the nth part of *expr* by *elem*

Functions for manipulating parts of expressions.

Section 1.2.4 discussed how you can use lists of indices to pick out several elements of a list at a time. You can use the same procedure to pick out several parts in an expression at a time.

This picks out elements 2 and 4 in the list, and gives a list of these elements.

In[16]:= **{a, b, c, d, e}[[{2, 4}]]**

Out[16]= {b, d}

This picks out parts 2 and 4 of the sum, and gives a *sum* of these elements.

In[17]:= **(a + b + c + d + e)[[{2, 4}]]**

Out[17]= b + d

Any part in an expression can be viewed as being an argument of some function. When you pick out several parts by giving a list of indices, the parts are combined using the same function as in the expression.

■ 2.1.5 Manipulating Expressions Like Lists

You can use most of the list operations discussed in Section 1.8 on any kind of *Mathematica* expression. By using these operations, you can manipulate the structure of expressions in many ways.

Here is an expression that corresponds to a sum of terms.	*In[1]:=* `t = 1 + x + x^2 + y^2`
	Out[1]= $1 + x + x^2 + y^2$
`Take[t, 2]` takes the first two elements from t, just as if t were a list.	*In[2]:=* `Take[t, 2]`
	Out[2]= `1 + x`
`Length` gives the number of elements in t.	*In[3]:=* `Length[t]`
	Out[3]= `4`
You can use `FreeQ[`*expr*`, `*form*`]` to test whether *form* appears nowhere in *expr*.	*In[4]:=* `FreeQ[t, x]`
	Out[4]= `False`
This gives a list of the positions at which x appears in t.	*In[5]:=* `Position[t, x]`
	Out[5]= `{{2}, {3, 1}}`

You should remember that all functions which manipulate the structure of expressions act on the internal forms of these expressions. You can see these forms using `FullForm[`*expr*`]`. They may not be what you would expect from the printed versions of the expressions.

Here is a function with four arguments.	*In[6]:=* `f[a, b, c, d]`
	Out[6]= `f[a, b, c, d]`
You can add an argument using `Append`.	*In[7]:=* `Append[%, e]`
	Out[7]= `f[a, b, c, d, e]`
This reverses the arguments.	*In[8]:=* `Reverse[%]`
	Out[8]= `f[e, d, c, b, a]`

There are a few extra functions that can be used with expressions, as discussed in Section 2.2.10.

■ 2.1.6 Expressions as Trees

Here is an expression in full form.	*In[1]:=* `FullForm[x^3 + (1 + x)^2]`
	Out[1]//FullForm= `Plus[Power[x, 3], Power[Plus[1, x], 2]]`

`TreeForm` prints out expressions to show their "tree" structure.	`In[2]:= TreeForm[x^3 + (1 + x)^2]`

```
Out[2]//TreeForm= Plus[|                 , |                        ]
                       Power[x, 3]  Power[|            , 2]
                                          Plus[1, x]
```

You can think of any *Mathematica* expression as a tree. In the expression above, the top node in the tree consists of a Plus. From this node come two "branches", x^3 and (1 + x)^2. From the x^3 node, there are then two branches, x and 3, which can be viewed as "leaves" of the tree.

This matrix is a simple tree with just two levels.	`In[3]:= TreeForm[{{a, b}, {c, d}}]`

```
Out[3]//TreeForm= List[|            , |            ]
                       List[a, b]  List[c, d]
```

Here is a more complicated expression.	`In[4]:= {{a b, c d^2}, {x^3 y^4}}`

$$Out[4]= \{\{a\ b,\ c\ d^2\}, \{x^3\ y^4\}\}$$

The tree for this expression has several levels. The representation of the tree here was too long to fit on a single line, so it had to be broken onto two lines.	`In[5]:= TreeForm[%]`

```
Out[5]//TreeForm=
   List[|                                            ,
        List[|            , |                       ]
             Times[a, b]  Times[c, |            ]
                                   Power[d, 2]

   |                                      ]
   List[|                               ]
        Times[|            , |            ]
              Power[x, 3]  Power[y, 4]
```

The indices that label each part of an expression have a simple interpretation in terms of trees. Descending from the top node of the tree, each index specifies which branch to take in order to reach the part you want.

■ 2.1.7 Advanced Topic: Levels in Expressions

The Part function allows you to access specific parts of *Mathematica* expressions. But particularly when your expressions have fairly uniform structure, it is often convenient to be able to refer to a whole collection of parts at the same time.

Levels provide a general way of specifying collections of parts in *Mathematica* expressions. Many *Mathematica* functions allow you to specify the levels in an expression on which they should act.

Here is a simple expression, displayed in tree form.	`In[1]:= (t = {x, {x, y}, y}) // TreeForm`

```
Out[1]//TreeForm= List[x, |            , y]
                          List[x, y]
```

This searches for x in the expression t down to level 1. It finds only one occurrence.	`In[2]:= Position[t, x, 1]`
	`Out[2]= {{1}}`

This searches down to level 2. Now it finds both occurrences of **x**.	*In[3]:=* **Position[t, x, 2]**
	Out[3]= **{{1}, {2, 1}}**
This searches only at level 2. It finds just one occurrence of **x**.	*In[4]:=* **Position[t, x, {2}]**
	Out[4]= **{{2, 1}}**

Position[*expr*, *form*, *n*]	give the positions at which *form* occurs in *expr* down to level *n*
Position[*expr*, *form*, {*n*}]	give the positions exactly at level *n*

Controlling **Position** using levels.

You can think of levels in expressions in terms of trees. The level of a particular part in an expression is simply the distance down the tree at which that part appears, with the top of the tree considered as level 0.

It is equivalent to say that the parts which appear at level *n* are those that can be specified by a sequence of exactly *n* indices.

n	levels 1 through *n*
Infinity	all levels
{*n*}	level *n* only
{*n₁*, *n₂*}	levels n_1 through n_2
Heads -> True	include heads
Heads -> False	exclude heads

Level specifications.

Here is an expression, displayed in tree form.	*In[5]:=* **(u = f[f[g[a], a], a, h[a], f]) // TreeForm**

	Out[5]//TreeForm= f[| , a, | , f]
	      f[| , a] h[a]
	        g[a]

This searches for **a** at levels from 2 downwards.	*In[6]:=* **Position[u, a, {2, Infinity}]**
	Out[6]= **{{1, 1, 1}, {1, 2}, {3, 1}}**
This shows where **f** appears other than in the head of an expression.	*In[7]:=* **Position[u, f, Heads->False]**
	Out[7]= **{{4}}**

This includes occurrences of **f** in heads of expressions.

In[8]:= **Position[u, f, Heads->True]**

Out[8]= {{0}, {1, 0}, {4}}

Level[*expr*, *lev*]	a list of the parts of *expr* at the levels specified by *lev*
Depth[*expr*]	the total number of levels in *expr*

Testing and extracting levels.

This gives a list of all parts of **u** that occur down to level 2.

In[9]:= **Level[u, 2]**

Out[9]= {g[a], a, f[g[a], a], a, a, h[a], f}

Here are the parts specifically at level 2.

In[10]:= **Level[u, {2}]**

Out[10]= {g[a], a, a}

When you have got the hang of ordinary levels, you can try thinking about *negative levels*. Negative levels label parts of expressions starting at the *bottom* of the tree. Level −1 contains all the leaves of the tree: objects like symbols and numbers.

This shows the parts of **u** at level -1.

In[11]:= **Level[u, {-1}]**

Out[11]= {a, a, a, a, f}

You can think of expressions as having a "depth", which is equal to the maximum number of levels shown by **TreeForm**. In general, level −*n* in an expression is defined to consist of all subexpressions whose depth is *n*.

The depth of **g[a]** is 2.

In[12]:= **Depth[g[a]]**

Out[12]= 2

The parts of **u** at level -2 are those that have depth exactly 2.

In[13]:= **Level[u, {-2}]**

Out[13]= {g[a], h[a]}

2.2 Functional Operations

■ 2.2.1 Function Names as Expressions

In an expression like $f[x]$, the "function name" f is itself an expression, and you can treat it as you would any other expression.

You can replace names of functions using transformation rules.	In[1]:= **f[x] + f[1 - x] /. f -> g** Out[1]= g[1 - x] + g[x]
Any assignments you have made are used on function names.	In[2]:= **p1 = p2; p1[x, y]** Out[2]= p2[x, y]
This defines a function which takes a function name as an argument.	In[3]:= **pf[f_, x_] := f[x] + f[1 - x]**
This gives Log as the function name to use.	In[4]:= **pf[Log, q]** Out[4]= Log[1 - q] + Log[q]

The ability to treat the names of functions just like other kinds of expressions is an important consequence of the symbolic nature of the *Mathematica* language. It makes possible the whole range of *functional operations* discussed in the sections that follow.

Ordinary *Mathematica* functions such as Log or Integrate typically operate on data such as numbers and algebraic expressions. *Mathematica* functions that represent functional operations, however, can operate not only on ordinary data, but also on functions themselves. Thus, for example, the functional operation InverseFunction takes a *Mathematica* function name as an argument, and represents the inverse of that function.

InverseFunction is a functional operation: it takes a *Mathematica* function as an argument, and returns another function which represents its inverse.	In[5]:= **InverseFunction[ArcSin]** Out[5]= Sin
The result obtained from InverseFunction is a function which you can apply to data.	In[6]:= **%[x]** Out[6]= Sin[x]
You can also use InverseFunction in a purely symbolic way.	In[7]:= **InverseFunction[f] [x]** Out[7]= f$^{(-1)}$[x]

There are many kinds of functional operations in *Mathematica*. Some represent mathematical operations; others represent various kinds of procedures and algorithms.

Unless you are familiar with advanced symbolic languages, you will probably not recognize most of the functional operations discussed in the sections that follow. At first, the operations may seem difficult to understand. But it is worth persisting. Functional operations provide one of the most conceptually and practically efficient ways to use *Mathematica*.

■ 2.2.2 Applying Functions Repeatedly

Nest[*f*, *x*, *n*]	apply the function *f* nested *n* times to *x*
NestList[*f*, *x*, *n*]	generate the list {*x*, *f*[*x*], *f*[*f*[*x*]], ... }, where *f* is nested up to *n* deep
FixedPoint[*f*, *x*]	apply the function *f* repeatedly until the result no longer changes
FixedPointList[*f*, *x*]	generate the list {*x*, *f*[*x*], *f*[*f*[*x*]], ... }, stopping when the elements no longer change
FixedPoint[*f*, *x*, SameTest -> *comp*]	
	stop when the function *comp* applied to two successive results yields True

Ways to apply functions of one argument repeatedly.

Nest[*f*, *x*, *n*] takes the "name" *f* of a function, and applies the function *n* times to *x*.

```
In[1]:= Nest[f, x, 4]
Out[1]= f[f[f[f[x]]]]
```

This makes a list of each successive nesting.

```
In[2]:= NestList[f, x, 4]
Out[2]= {x, f[x], f[f[x]], f[f[f[x]]], f[f[f[f[x]]]]}
```

Here is a simple function.

```
In[3]:= recip[x_] := 1/(1 + x)
```

You can iterate the function using Nest.

```
In[4]:= Nest[recip, x, 3]
```

$$Out[4]= \cfrac{1}{1 + \cfrac{1}{1 + \cfrac{1}{1 + x}}}$$

Many programs you write will involve operations that need to be iterated several times. Nest and NestList are powerful constructs for doing this.

Here is a function that takes one step in Newton's approximation to $\sqrt{3}$.

```
In[5]:= newton3[x_] := N[ 1/2 ( x + 3/x ) ]
```

Here are five successive iterates of the function, starting at $x = 1$.

```
In[6]:= NestList[newton3, 1.0, 5]
Out[6]= {1., 2., 1.75, 1.73214, 1.73205, 1.73205}
```

Using the function `FixedPoint`, you can automatically continue applying `newton3` until the result no longer changes.

```
In[7]:= FixedPoint[newton3, 1.0]
Out[7]= 1.73205
```

Here is the sequence of results.

```
In[8]:= FixedPointList[newton3, 1.0]
Out[8]= {1., 2., 1.75, 1.73214, 1.73205, 1.73205, 1.73205}
```

You control when `FixedPointList` stops by giving a function with which to compare successive results.

```
In[9]:= FixedPointList[newton3, 1.0,
            SameTest -> (Abs[#1 - #2] < 10.^-4 &)]
Out[9]= {1., 2., 1.75, 1.73214, 1.73205}
```

The functional operations `Nest` and `NestList` take a function *f* of one argument, and apply it repeatedly. At each step, they use the result of the previous step as the new argument of *f*.

It is important to generalize this notion to functions of two arguments. You can again apply the function repeatedly, but now each result you get supplies only one of the new arguments you need. A convenient approach is to get the other argument at each step from the successive elements of a list.

`FoldList[f, x, {a, b, ... }]`	create the list $\{x, f[x, a], f[f[x, a], b], ... \}$
`Fold[f, x, {a, b, ... }]`	give the last element of the list produced by `FoldList[f, x, {a, b, ... }]`

Ways to repeatedly apply functions of two arguments.

Here is an example of what `FoldList` does.

```
In[10]:= FoldList[f, x, {a, b, c}]
Out[10]= {x, f[x, a], f[f[x, a], b], f[f[f[x, a], b], c]}
```

`Fold` gives the last element of the list produced by `FoldList`.

```
In[11]:= Fold[f, x, {a, b, c}]
Out[11]= f[f[f[x, a], b], c]
```

This gives a list of cumulative sums.

```
In[12]:= FoldList[Plus, 0, {a, b, c}]
Out[12]= {0, a, a + b, a + b + c}
```

Using `Fold` and `FoldList` you can write many elegant and efficient programs in *Mathematica*. In some cases, you may find it helpful to think of `Fold` and `FoldList` as producing a simple nesting of a family of functions indexed by their first argument.

This defines a function `nextdigit`.

```
In[13]:= nextdigit[a_, b_] := 10 a + b
```

Here is a rather elegant definition of a function that gives the number corresponding to a list of digits in base 10.

```
In[14]:= tonumber[digits_] := Fold[nextdigit, 0, digits]
```

Here is an example of `tonumber` in action.

```
In[15]:= tonumber[{1, 3, 7, 2, 9, 1}]
Out[15]= 137291
```

■ 2.2.3 Applying Functions to Lists and Other Expressions

In an expression like `f[{a, b, c}]` you are giving a list as the argument to a function. Often you need instead to apply a function directly to the elements of a list, rather than to the list as a whole. You can do this in *Mathematica* using `Apply`.

This makes each element of the list an argument of the function `f`.

```
In[1]:= Apply[f, {a, b, c}]
Out[1]= f[a, b, c]
```

This gives `Plus[a, b, c]` which yields the sum of the elements in the list.

```
In[2]:= Apply[Plus, {a, b, c}]
Out[2]= a + b + c
```

Here is the definition of the statistical mean, written using `Apply`.

```
In[3]:= mean[list_] := Apply[Plus, list] / Length[list]
```

`Apply[f, {a, b, ... }]`	apply *f* to a list, giving *f*[*a*, *b*, ...]
`Apply[f, expr]` or *f* `@@` *expr*	apply *f* to the top level of an expression
`Apply[f, expr, lev]`	apply *f* at the specified levels in an expression

Applying functions to lists and other expressions.

What `Apply` does in general is to replace the head of an expression with the function you specify. Here it replaces `Plus` by `List`.

```
In[4]:= Apply[List, a + b + c]
Out[4]= {a, b, c}
```

Here is a matrix.

```
In[5]:= m = {{a, b, c}, {b, c, d}}
Out[5]= {{a, b, c}, {b, c, d}}
```

Using `Apply` without an explicit level specification replaces the top-level list with `f`.

```
In[6]:= Apply[f, m]
Out[6]= f[{a, b, c}, {b, c, d}]
```

This applies `f` only to parts of `m` at level 1.

```
In[7]:= Apply[f, m, {1}]
Out[7]= {f[a, b, c], f[b, c, d]}
```

This applies `f` at levels 0 through 1.

```
In[8]:= Apply[f, m, {0, 1}]
Out[8]= f[f[a, b, c], f[b, c, d]]
```

■ 2.2.4 Applying Functions to Parts of Expressions

If you have a list of elements, it is often important to be able to apply a function separately to each of the elements. You can do this in *Mathematica* using Map.

This applies f separately to each element in a list.	`In[1]:= Map[f, {a, b, c}]` `Out[1]= {f[a], f[b], f[c]}`
This defines a function which takes the first two elements from a list.	`In[2]:= take2[list_] := Take[list, 2]`
You can use Map to apply take2 to each element of a list.	`In[3]:= Map[take2, {{1, 3, 4}, {5, 6, 7}, {2, 1, 6, 6}}]` `Out[3]= {{1, 3}, {5, 6}, {2, 1}}`

Map[*f*, {*a*, *b*, ... }]   apply *f* to each element in a list, giving {*f*[*a*], *f*[*b*], ... }

Applying a function to each element in a list.

What `Map[f, expr]` effectively does is to "wrap" the function *f* around each element of the expression *expr*. You can use Map on any expression, not just a list.

This applies f to each element in the sum.	`In[4]:= Map[f, a + b + c]` `Out[4]= f[a] + f[b] + f[c]`
This applies Sqrt to each argument of g.	`In[5]:= Map[Sqrt, g[x^2, x^3]]` `Out[5]= g[Sqrt[x^2], Sqrt[x^3]]`

`Map[f, expr]` applies *f* to the first level of parts in *expr*. You can use `MapAll[f, expr]` to apply *f* to *all* the parts of *expr*.

This defines a 2×2 matrix m.	`In[6]:= m = {{a, b}, {c, d}}` `Out[6]= {{a, b}, {c, d}}`
Map applies f to the first level of m, in this case the rows of the matrix.	`In[7]:= Map[f, m]` `Out[7]= {f[{a, b}], f[{c, d}]}`
MapAll applies f at *all* levels in m. If you look carefully at this expression, you will see an f wrapped around every part.	`In[8]:= MapAll[f, m]` `Out[8]= f[{f[{f[f[a], f[b]}], f[{f[c], f[d]}]}]]`

In general, you can use level specifications as described on page 198 to tell Map to which parts of an expression to apply your function.

This applies f only to the parts of m at level 2.	`In[9]:= Map[f, m, {2}]` `Out[9]= {{f[a], f[b]}, {f[c], f[d]}}`

Setting the option **Heads->True** wraps **f** around the head of each part, as well as its elements.

```
In[10]:= Map[f, m, Heads->True]
Out[10]= f[List][f[{a, b}], f[{c, d}]]
```

Map[*f, expr*] or *f* /@ *expr*	apply *f* to the first-level parts of *expr*
MapAll[*f, expr*] or *f* //@ *expr*	apply *f* to all parts of *expr*
Map[*f, expr, lev*]	apply *f* to each part of *expr* at levels specified by *lev*

Ways to apply a function to different parts of expressions.

Level specifications allow you to tell Map to which levels of parts in an expression you want a function applied. With MapAt, however, you can instead give an explicit list of parts where you want a function applied. You specify each part by giving its indices, as discussed in Section 2.1.4.

Here is a 3×2 matrix.

```
In[11]:= mm = {{a, b, c}, {b, c, d}}
Out[11]= {{a, b, c}, {b, c, d}}
```

This applies **f** to parts {1, 2} and {2, 3}.

```
In[12]:= MapAt[f, mm, {{1, 2}, {2, 3}}]
Out[12]= {{a, f[b], c}, {b, c, f[d]}}
```

This gives a list of the positions at which **b** occurs in **mm**.

```
In[13]:= Position[mm, b]
Out[13]= {{1, 2}, {2, 1}}
```

You can feed the list of positions you get from **Position** directly into MapAt.

```
In[14]:= MapAt[f, mm, %]
Out[14]= {{a, f[b], c}, {f[b], c, d}}
```

To avoid ambiguity, you must put each part specification in a list, even when it involves only one index.

```
In[15]:= MapAt[f, {a, b, c, d}, {{2}, {3}}]
Out[15]= {a, f[b], f[c], d}
```

MapAt[*f, expr*, {*part$_1$*, *part$_2$*, ... }] apply *f* to specified parts of *expr*

Applying a function to specific parts of an expression.

Here is an expression.

```
In[16]:= t = 1 + (3 + x)^2 / x
```

$$Out[16]= 1 + \frac{(3 + x)^2}{x}$$

This is the full form of **t**.

```
In[17]:= FullForm[ t ]
Out[17]//FullForm=
    Plus[1, Times[Power[x, -1], Power[Plus[3, x], 2]]]
```

You can use **MapAt** on any expression. Remember that parts are numbered on the basis of the full forms of expressions.

In[18]:= **MapAt[f, t, {{2, 1, 1}, {2, 2}}]**

$$Out[18]= 1 + \frac{f[(3 + x)^2]}{f[x]}$$

MapIndexed[*f***,** *expr***]**	apply *f* to the elements of an expression, giving the part specification of each element as a second argument to *f*
MapIndexed[*f***,** *expr***,** *lev***]**	apply *f* to parts at specified levels, giving the list of indices for each part as successive arguments to *f*

Applying a function to parts and their indices.

This applies **f** to each element in a list, giving the index of the element as a second argument to **f**.

In[19]:= **MapIndexed[f, {a, b, c}]**
Out[19]= {f[a, {1}], f[b, {2}], f[c, {3}]}

This applies **f** to both levels in a matrix.

In[20]:= **MapIndexed[f, {{a, b}, {c, d}}, 2]**
Out[20]= {f[{f[a, {1, 1}], f[b, {1, 2}]}, {1}],
    f[{f[c, {2, 1}], f[d, {2, 2}]}, {2}]}

Map allows you to apply a function of one argument to parts of an expression. Sometimes, however, you may instead want to apply a function of several arguments to corresponding parts of several different expressions. You can do this using **MapThread**.

MapThread[*f***, {***expr₁***,** *expr₂***, ... }]**	apply *f* to corresponding elements in each of the *expr_i*
MapThread[*f***, {***expr₁***,** *expr₂***, ... },** *lev***]**	apply *f* to parts of the *expr_i* at the specified levels

Applying a function to several expressions at once.

This applies **f** to corresponding pairs of list elements.

In[21]:= **MapThread[f, {{a, b, c}, {ap, bp, cp}}]**
Out[21]= {f[a, ap], f[b, bp], f[c, cp]}

MapThread works with any number of expressions, so long as they have the same structure.

In[22]:= **MapThread[f, {{a, b}, {ap, bp}, {app, bpp}}]**
Out[22]= {f[a, ap, app], f[b, bp, bpp]}

Functions like **Map** allow you to create expressions with parts modified. Sometimes you simply want to go through an expression, and apply a particular function to some parts of it, without building a new expression. A typical case is when the function you apply has certain "side effects", such as making assignments, or generating output.

| Scan[f, *expr*] | evaluate *f* applied to each element of *expr* in turn |
| Scan[f, *expr*, *lev*] | evaluate *f* applied to parts of *expr* on levels specified by *lev* |

Evaluating functions on parts of expressions.

Map constructs a new list in which f has been applied to each element of the list.

```
In[23]:= Map[f, {a, b, c}]
Out[23]= {f[a], f[b], f[c]}
```

Scan evaluates the result of applying a function to each element, but does not construct a new expression.

```
In[24]:= Scan[Print, {a, b, c}]
a
b
c
```

Scan visits the parts of an expression in a depth-first walk, with the leaves visited first.

```
In[25]:= Scan[Print, 1 + x^2, Infinity]
1
x
2
 2
x
```

■ 2.2.5 Pure Functions

Function[*x*, *body*]	a pure function in which *x* is replaced by any argument you provide
Function[{x_1, x_2, ... }, *body*]	a pure function that takes several arguments
body &	a pure function in which arguments are specified as # or #1, #2, #3, etc.

Pure functions.

When you use functional operations such as Nest and Map, you always have to specify a function to apply. In all the examples above, we have used the "name" of a function to specify the function. Pure functions allow you to give functions which can be applied to arguments, without having to define explicit names for the functions.

This defines a function h.

```
In[1]:= h[x_] := f[x] + g[x]
```

Having defined h, you can now use its name in Map.

```
In[2]:= Map[h, {a, b, c}]
Out[2]= {f[a] + g[a], f[b] + g[b], f[c] + g[c]}
```

Here is a way to get the same result using a pure function.

```
In[3]:= Map[ f[#] + g[#] &, {a, b, c} ]
Out[3]= {f[a] + g[a], f[b] + g[b], f[c] + g[c]}
```

There are several equivalent ways to write pure functions in *Mathematica*. The idea in all cases is to construct an object which, when supplied with appropriate arguments, computes a particular function. Thus, for example, if *fun* is a pure function, then *fun*[*a*] evaluates the function with argument *a*.

Here is a pure function which represents the operation of squaring.	*In[4]:=* **Function[x, x^2]** *Out[4]=* Function[x, x^2]
Supplying the argument n to the pure function yields the square of n.	*In[5]:=* **%[n]** *Out[5]=* n^2

You can use a pure function wherever you would usually give the name of a function.

You can use a pure function in Map.	*In[6]:=* **Map[Function[x, x^2], a + b + c]** *Out[6]=* $a^2 + b^2 + c^2$
Or in Nest.	*In[7]:=* **Nest[Function[q, 1/(1+q)], x, 3]** *Out[7]=* $\cfrac{1}{1 + \cfrac{1}{1 + \cfrac{1}{1 + x}}}$

If you are going to use a particular function repeatedly, then you can define the function using $f[x\_] := body$, and refer to the function by its name *f*. On the other hand, if you only intend to use a function once, you will probably find it better to give the function in pure function form, without ever naming it.

If you are familiar with formal logic or the LISP programming language, you will recognize *Mathematica* pure functions as being like λ expressions or anonymous functions. Pure functions are also close to the pure mathematical notion of operators.

#	the first variable in a pure function
#*n*	the nth variable in a pure function
##	the sequence of all variables in a pure function
##*n*	the sequence of variables starting with the nth one

Short forms for pure functions.

Just as the name of a function is irrelevant if you do not intend to refer to the function again, so also the names of arguments in a pure function are irrelevant. *Mathematica* allows you to avoid using explicit names for the arguments of pure functions, and instead to specify the arguments by giving "slot numbers" #*n*. In a *Mathematica* pure function, #*n* stands for the nth argument you supply. # stands for the first argument.

#^2 & is a short form for a pure function that squares its argument.	$In[8]:=$ **Map[#^2 &, a + b + c]** $Out[8]=$ $a^2 + b^2 + c^2$
This applies a function that takes the first two elements from each list. By using a pure function, you avoid having to define the function separately.	$In[9]:=$ **Map[Take[#, 2]&, {{2, 1, 7}, {4, 1, 5}, {3, 1, 2}}]** $Out[9]=$ {{2, 1}, {4, 1}, {3, 1}}
Using short forms for pure functions, you can simplify the definition of **tonumber** given on page 202.	$In[10]:=$ **tonumber[digits_] := Fold[(10 #1 + #2)&, 0, digits]**

When you use short forms for pure functions, it is very important that you do not forget the ampersand. If you leave the ampersand out, *Mathematica* will not know that the expression you give is to be used as a pure function.

When you use the ampersand notation for pure functions, you must be careful about the grouping of pieces in your input. As shown on page A.2.3 the ampersand notation has fairly low precedence, which means that you can type expressions like #1 + #2 & without parentheses. On the other hand, if you want, for example, to set an option to be a pure function, you need to use parentheses, as in *option* -> (*fun* &).

Pure functions in *Mathematica* can take any number of arguments. You can use ## to stand for all the arguments that are given, and ##*n* to stand for the nth and subsequent arguments.

## stands for all arguments.	$In[11]:=$ **f[##, ##]& [x, y]** $Out[11]=$ f[x, y, x, y]
##2 stands for all arguments except the first one.	$In[12]:=$ **Apply[f[##2, #1]&, {{a, b, c}, {ap, bp}}, {1}]** $Out[12]=$ {f[b, c, a], f[bp, ap]}

■ 2.2.6 Building Lists from Functions

Array[f, n]	generate a length n list of the form $\{f[1], f[2], \ldots\}$
Array[f, {n_1, n_2, ... }]	generate an $n_1 \times n_2 \times \ldots$ nested list, each of whose entries consists of f applied to its indices
NestList[f, x, n]	generate a list of the form $\{x, f[x], f[f[x]], \ldots\}$, where f is nested up to n deep
FoldList[f, x, {a, b, ... }]	generate a list of the form $\{x, f[x, a], f[f[x, a], b], \ldots\}$
ComposeList[{f_1, f_2, ... }, x]	generate a list of the form $\{x, f_1[x], f_2[f_1[x]], \ldots\}$

Making lists from functions.

This makes a list of 5 elements, each of the form p[i].

```
In[1]:= Array[p, 5]
Out[1]= {p[1], p[2], p[3], p[4], p[5]}
```

Here is another way to produce the same list.

```
In[2]:= Table[p[i], {i, 5}]
Out[2]= {p[1], p[2], p[3], p[4], p[5]}
```

This produces a list whose elements are $i + i^2$.

```
In[3]:= Array[ # + #^2 &, 5]
Out[3]= {2, 6, 12, 20, 30}
```

This generates a 2×3 matrix whose entries are m[i, j].

```
In[4]:= Array[m, {2, 3}]
Out[4]= {{m[1, 1], m[1, 2], m[1, 3]},
         {m[2, 1], m[2, 2], m[2, 3]}}
```

This generates a 3×3 matrix whose elements are the squares of the sums of their indices.

```
In[5]:= Array[Plus[##]^2 &, {3, 3}]
Out[5]= {{4, 9, 16}, {9, 16, 25}, {16, 25, 36}}
```

NestList and FoldList were discussed in Section 2.2.2. Particularly by using them with pure functions, you can construct some very elegant and efficient *Mathematica* programs.

This gives a list of results obtained by successively differentiating x^n with respect to x.

```
In[6]:= NestList[ D[#, x]&, x^n, 3 ]
Out[6]= {x , n x        , (-1 + n) n x        ,
         n     -1 + n                  -2 + n

         (-2 + n) (-1 + n) n x        }
                              -3 + n
```

■ 2.2.7 Selecting Parts of Expressions with Functions

Section 1.2.4 showed how you can pick out elements of lists based on their *positions*. Often, however, you will need to select elements based not on *where* they are, but rather on *what* they are.

Select[*list*, *f*] selects elements of *list* using the function *f* as a criterion. Select applies *f* to each element of *list* in turn, and keeps only those for which the result is True.

This selects the elements of the list for which the pure function yields True, *i.e.*, those numerically greater than 4.

In[1]:= **Select[{2, 15, 1, a, 16, 17}, # > 4 &]**

Out[1]= {15, 16, 17}

You can use Select to pick out pieces of any expression, not just elements of a list.

This gives a sum of terms involving x, y and z.

In[2]:= **t = Expand[(x + y + z)^2]**

$$Out[2]= x^2 + 2\ x\ y + y^2 + 2\ x\ z + 2\ y\ z + z^2$$

You can use Select to pick out only those terms in the sum that do not involve the symbol x.

In[3]:= **Select[t, FreeQ[#, x]&]**

$$Out[3]= y^2 + 2\ y\ z + z^2$$

Select[*expr*, *f*]	select the elements in *expr* for which the function *f* gives True
Select[*expr*, *f*, *n*]	select the first *n* elements in *expr* for which the function *f* gives True

Selecting pieces of expressions.

Section 2.3.5 discusses some "predicates" that are often used as criteria in Select.

This gives the first element which satisfies the criterion you specify.

In[4]:= **Select[{-1, 3, 10, 12, 14}, # > 3 &, 1]**

Out[4]= {10}

■ 2.2.8 Expressions with Heads That Are Not Symbols

In most cases, you want the head *f* of a *Mathematica* expression like *f*[*x*] to be a single symbol. There are, however, some important applications of heads that are not symbols.

This expression has f[3] as a head. You can use heads like this to represent "indexed functions".

In[1]:= **f[3][x, y]**

Out[1]= f[3][x, y]

You can use any expression as a head. Remember to put in the necessary parentheses.

In[2]:= **(a + b)[x]**

Out[2]= (a + b)[x]

One case where we have already encountered the use of complicated expressions as heads is in working with pure functions in Section 2.2.5. By giving Function[*vars*, *body*] as the head of an expression, you specify a function of the arguments to be evaluated.

With the head `Function[x, x^2]`, the value of the expression is the square of the argument.

```
In[3]:= Function[x, x^2] [a + b]

Out[3]= (a + b)
                 2
```

There are several constructs in *Mathematica* which work much like pure functions, but which represent specific kinds of functions, typically numerical ones. In all cases, the basic mechanism involves giving a head which contains complete information about the function you want to use.

`Function[`*vars*, *body*`] [`*args*`]`	pure function
`InterpolatingFunction[`*data*`] [`*args*`]`	
	approximate numerical function (generated by `Interpolation` and `NDSolve`)
`CompiledFunction[`*data*`] [`*args*`]`	compiled numerical function (generated by `Compile`)

Some expressions which have heads that are not symbols.

`NDSolve` returns a list of rules that give `y` as an `InterpolatingFunction` object.

```
In[4]:= NDSolve[{y''[x] == y[x], y[0]==y'[0]==1}, y, {x, 0, 5}]
Out[4]= {{y -> InterpolatingFunction[{0., 5.}, <>]}}
```

Here is the `InterpolatingFunction` object.

```
In[5]:= y /. First[%]
Out[5]= InterpolatingFunction[{0., 5.}, <>]
```

You can use the `InterpolatingFunction` object as a head to get numerical approximations to values of the function `y`.

```
In[6]:= % [3.8]
Out[6]= 44.7048
```

Another important use of more complicated expressions as heads is in implementing *functionals* and *functional operators* in mathematics.

As one example, consider the operation of differentiation. As will be discussed in Section 3.5.4, an expression like `f'` represents a *derivative function*, obtained from `f` by applying a functional operator to it. In *Mathematica*, `f'` is represented as `Derivative[1][f]`: the "functional operator" `Derivative[1]` is applied to `f` to give another function, represented as `f'`.

This expression has a head which represents the application of the "functional operator" `Derivative[1]` to the "function" `f`.

```
In[7]:= f'[x] // FullForm
Out[7]//FullForm= Derivative[1][f][x]
```

You can replace the head `f'` with another head, such as `fp`. This effectively takes `fp` to be a "derivative function" obtained from `f`.

```
In[8]:= % /. f' -> fp
Out[8]= fp[x]
```

■ 2.2.9 Advanced Topic: Working with Operators

You can think of an expression like $f[x]$ as being formed by applying an *operator* f to the expression x. You can think of an expression like $f[g[x]]$ as the result of *composing* the operators f and g, and applying the result to x.

Composition[*f*, *g*, ...]	the composition of functions $f, g, \ldots$
InverseFunction[*f*]	the inverse of a function f
Identity	the identity function

Some functional operations.

This represents the composition of the functions **f**, **g** and **h**.

```
In[1]:= Composition[f, g, h]
Out[1]= Composition[f, g, h]
```

You can manipulate compositions of functions symbolically.

```
In[2]:= InverseFunction[Composition[%, q]]
Out[2]= Composition[q^(-1), h^(-1), g^(-1), f^(-1)]
```

The composition is evaluated explicitly when you supply a specific argument.

```
In[3]:= %[x]
Out[3]= q^(-1)[h^(-1)[g^(-1)[f^(-1)[x]]]]
```

You can get the sum of two expressions in *Mathematica* just by typing $x + y$. Sometimes it is also worthwhile to consider performing operations like addition on *operators*.

You can think of this as containing a sum of two operators **f** and **g**.

```
In[4]:= (f + g)[x]
Out[4]= (f + g)[x]
```

Using **Through**, you can convert the expression to a more explicit form.

```
In[5]:= Through[%, Plus]
Out[5]= f[x] + g[x]
```

This corresponds to the mathematical operator $1 + \frac{\partial}{\partial x}$.

```
In[6]:= Identity + (D[#, x]&)
Out[6]= Identity + (D[#1, x] & )
```

Mathematica does not automatically apply the separate pieces of the operator to an expression.

```
In[7]:= % [x^2]
Out[7]= (Identity + (D[#1, x] & ))[x^2]
```

You can use **Through** to apply the operator.

```
In[8]:= Through[%, Plus]
Out[8]= 2 x + x^2
```

Identity[*expr*]	the identity function
Through[*p*[f_1, f_2][*x*], *q*]	give *p*[f_1[*x*], f_2[*x*]] if *p* is the same as *q*
Operate[*p*, *f*[*x*]]	give *p*[*f*][*x*]
Operate[*p*, *f*[*x*], *n*]	apply *p* at level *n* in *f*
MapAll[*p*, *expr*, Heads->True]	apply *p* to all parts of *expr*, including heads

Operations for working with operators.

This has a complicated expression as a head.

```
In[9]:= t = ((1 + a)(1 + b))[x]
Out[9]= ((1 + a) (1 + b))[x]
```

Functions like Expand do not automatically go inside heads of expressions.

```
In[10]:= Expand[%]
Out[10]= ((1 + a) (1 + b))[x]
```

With the Heads option set to True, MapAll goes inside heads.

```
In[11]:= MapAll[Expand, t, Heads->True]
Out[11]= (1 + a + b + a b)[x]
```

The replacement operator /. does go inside heads of expressions.

```
In[12]:= t /. a->1
Out[12]= (2 (1 + b))[x]
```

You can use Operate to apply a function specifically to the head of an expression.

```
In[13]:= Operate[p, t]
Out[13]= p[(1 + a) (1 + b)][x]
```

■ 2.2.10 Structural Operations

Mathematica contains some powerful primitives for making structural changes to expressions. You can use these primitives both to implement mathematical properties such as associativity and distributivity, and to provide the basis for some succinct and efficient programs.

This section describes various operations that you can explicitly perform on expressions. Section 2.5.3 will describe how some of these operations can be performed automatically on all expressions with a particular head by assigning appropriate attributes to that head.

You can use the *Mathematica* function Sort[*expr*] to sort elements not only of lists, but of expressions with any head. In this way, you can implement the mathematical properties of commutativity or symmetry for arbitrary functions.

You can use Sort to put the arguments of any function into a standard order.

```
In[1]:= Sort[ f[c, a, b] ]
Out[1]= f[a, b, c]
```

Sort [*expr*]	sort the elements of a list or other expression into a standard order
Sort [*expr*, *pred*]	sort using the function *pred* to determine whether pairs are in order
OrderedQ [*expr*]	give True if the elements of *expr* are in standard order, and False otherwise
Order [*expr₁*, *expr₂*]	give 1 if $expr_1$ comes before $expr_2$ in standard order, and −1 if it comes after

Sorting into order.

The second argument to Sort is a function used to determine whether pairs are in order. This sorts numbers into descending order.

```
In[2]:= Sort[ {5, 1, 8, 2}, (#2 < #1)& ]
Out[2]= {8, 5, 2, 1}
```

This sorting criterion puts elements that do not depend on x before those that do.

```
In[3]:= Sort[ {x^2, y, x+y, y-2}, FreeQ[#1, x]& ]
                           2
Out[3]= {y, -2 + y, x + y, x }
```

Flatten [*expr*]	flatten out all nested functions with the same head as *expr*
Flatten [*expr*, *n*]	flatten at most *n* levels of nesting
Flatten [*expr*, *n*, *h*]	flatten functions with head *h*
FlattenAt [*expr*, *i*]	flatten only the ith element of *expr*

Flattening out expressions.

Flatten removes nested occurrences of a function.

```
In[4]:= Flatten[ f[a, f[b, c], f[f[d]]] ]
Out[4]= f[a, b, c, d]
```

You can use Flatten to "splice" sequences of elements into lists or other expressions.

```
In[5]:= Flatten[ {a, f[b, c], f[a, b, d]}, 1, f ]
Out[5]= {a, b, c, a, b, d}
```

You can use Flatten to implement the mathematical property of associativity. The function Distribute allows you to implement properties such as distributivity and linearity.

`Distribute[f[a + b + ... , ... ]]`	
	distribute f over sums to give $f[a, ...] + f[b, ...] + ...$
`Distribute[f[args], g]`	distribute f over any arguments which have head g
`Distribute[expr, g, f]`	distribute only when the head is f
`Distribute[expr, g, f, gp, fp]`	distribute f over g, replacing them with fp and gp, respectively

Applying distributive laws.

This "distributes" f over a + b.

```
In[6]:= Distribute[ f[a + b] ]
Out[6]= f[a] + f[b]
```

Here is a more complicated example.

```
In[7]:= Distribute[ f[a + b, c + d] ]
Out[7]= f[a, c] + f[a, d] + f[b, c] + f[b, d]
```

In general, if f is distributive over Plus, then an expression like $f[a + b]$ can be "expanded" to give $f[a] + f[b]$. The function Expand does this kind of expansion for standard algebraic operators such as Times. Distribute allows you to perform the same kind of expansion for arbitrary operators.

Expand uses the distributivity of Times over Plus to perform algebraic expansions.

```
In[8]:= Expand[ (a + b) (c + d) ]
Out[8]= a c + b c + a d + b d
```

This applies distributivity over lists, rather than sums. The result contains all possible pairs of arguments.

```
In[9]:= Distribute[ f[{a, b}, {c, d}], List ]
Out[9]= {f[a, c], f[a, d], f[b, c], f[b, d]}
```

This distributes over lists, but does so only if the head of the whole expression is f.

```
In[10]:= Distribute[ f[{a, b}, {c, d}], List, f ]
Out[10]= {f[a, c], f[a, d], f[b, c], f[b, d]}
```

This distributes over lists, making sure that the head of the whole expression is f. In the result, it uses gp in place of List, and fp in place of f.

```
In[11]:= Distribute[ f[{a, b}, {c, d}], List, f, gp, fp ]
Out[11]= gp[fp[a, c], fp[a, d], fp[b, c], fp[b, d]]
```

Related to Distribute is the function Thread. What Thread effectively does is to apply a function in parallel to all the elements of a list or other expression.

`Thread[f[{a_1, a_2}, {b_1, b_2}]]`	thread f over lists to give $\{f[a_1, b_1], f[a_2, b_2]\}$
`Thread[f[args], g]`	thread f over objects with head g in *args*

Functions for threading expressions.

Here is a function whose arguments are lists.	*In[12]:=* **f[{a1, a2}, {b1, b2}]**
	Out[12]= f[{a1, a2}, {b1, b2}]
Thread applies the function "in parallel" to each element of the lists.	*In[13]:=* **Thread[%]**
	Out[13]= {f[a1, b1], f[a2, b2]}
Arguments that are not lists get repeated.	*In[14]:=* **Thread[f[{a1, a2}, {b1, b2}, c, d]]**
	Out[14]= {f[a1, b1, c, d], f[a2, b2, c, d]}

As mentioned in Section 1.8.1, and discussed in more detail in Section 2.5.3, many built-in *Mathematica* functions have the property of being "listable", so that they are automatically threaded over any lists that appear as arguments.

Built-in mathematical functions such as Log are listable, so that they are automatically threaded over lists.	*In[15]:=* **Log[{a, b, c}]**
	Out[15]= {Log[a], Log[b], Log[c]}
Log is, however, not automatically threaded over equations.	*In[16]:=* **Log[x == y]**
	Out[16]= Log[x == y]
You can use Thread to get functions applied to both sides of an equation.	*In[17]:=* **Thread[%, Equal]**
	Out[17]= Log[x] == Log[y]

Outer[f, $list_1$, $list_2$, ...]	generalized outer product
Inner[f, $list_1$, $list_2$, g]	generalized inner product

Generalized inner and outer products.

Outer[f, $list_1$, $list_2$, ...] takes all possible combinations of elements from the $list_i$, and combines them with f. Outer can be viewed as a generalization of a Cartesian product for tensors, as discussed in Section 3.7.12.

Outer forms all possible combinations of elements, and applies f to them.	*In[18]:=* **Outer[f, {a, b}, {1, 2, 3}]**
	Out[18]= {{f[a, 1], f[a, 2], f[a, 3]},
	{f[b, 1], f[b, 2], f[b, 3]}}
Here Outer produces a lower-triangular Boolean matrix.	*In[19]:=* **Outer[Greater, {1, 2, 3}, {1, 2, 3}]**
	Out[19]= {{False, False, False}, {True, False, False},
	{True, True, False}}
You can use Outer on any sequence of expressions with the same head.	*In[20]:=* **Outer[g, f[a, b], f[c, d]]**
	Out[20]= f[f[g[a, c], g[a, d]], f[g[b, c], g[b, d]]]

Outer, like Distribute, constructs all possible combinations of elements. On the other hand, Inner, like Thread, constructs only combinations of elements that have corresponding positions in the expressions it acts on.

Here is a structure built by Inner.	In[21]:= **Inner[f, {a, b}, {c, d}, g]** Out[21]= g[f[a, c], f[b, d]]
Inner is a generalization of Dot.	In[22]:= **Inner[Times, {a, b}, {c, d}, Plus]** Out[22]= a c + b d

2.3 Patterns

■ 2.3.1 Introduction

Patterns are used throughout *Mathematica* to represent classes of expressions. A simple example of a pattern is the expression f[x_]. This pattern represents the class of expressions with the form f[*anything*].

The main power of patterns comes from the fact that many operations in *Mathematica* can be done not only with single expressions, but also with patterns that represent whole classes of expressions.

You can use patterns in transformation rules to specify how classes of expressions should be transformed.

```
In[1]:= f[a] + f[b] /. f[x_] -> x^2
           2    2
Out[1]= a  + b
```

You can use patterns to find the positions of all expressions in a particular class.

```
In[2]:= Position[{f[a], g[b], f[c]}, f[x_]]
Out[2]= {{1}, {3}}
```

The basic object that appears in almost all *Mathematica* patterns is _ (pronounced "blank"). The fundamental rule is simply that _ *stands for any expression*.

Thus, for example, the pattern f[_] stands for any expression of the form f[*anything*]. The pattern f[x_] also stands for any expression of the form f[*anything*], but gives the name x to the expression *anything*, allowing you to refer to it on the right-hand side of a transformation rule.

You can put blanks anywhere in an expression. What you get is a pattern which matches all expressions that can be made by "filling in the blanks" in any way.

f[n_]	f with any argument, named n
f[n_, m_]	f with two arguments, named n and m
x^n_	x to any power, with the power named n
x_^n_	any expression to any power
a_ + b_	a sum of two expressions
{a1_, a2_}	a list of two expressions
f[n_, n_]	f with two *identical* arguments

Some examples of patterns.

You can construct patterns for expressions with any structure.

```
In[3]:= f[{a, b}] + f[c] /. f[{x_, y_}] -> p[x + y]
Out[3]= f[c] + p[a + b]
```

One of the most common uses of patterns is for "destructuring" function arguments. If you make a definition for f[list_], then you need to use functions like Part explicitly in order to pick out elements of the list. But if you know for example that the list will always have two elements, then it is usually much more convenient instead to give a definition instead for f[{x_, y_}]. Then you can refer to the elements of the list directly as x and y. In addition, *Mathematica* will not use the definition you have given unless the argument of f really is of the required form of a list of two expressions.

Here is one way to define a function which takes a list of two elements, and evaluates the first element raised to the power of the second element.	*In[4]:=* **g[list_] := Part[list, 1] ^ Part[list, 2]**

Here is a much more elegant way to make the definition, using a pattern.	*In[5]:=* **h[{x_, y_}] := x ^ y**

A crucial point to understand is that *Mathematica* patterns represent classes of expressions with a given *structure*. One pattern will match a particular expression if the structure of the pattern is the same as the structure of the expression, in the sense that by filling in blanks in the pattern you can get the expression. Even though two expressions may be *mathematically equal*, they cannot be represented by the same *Mathematica* pattern unless they have the same structure.

Thus, for example, the pattern (1 + x_)^2 can stand for expressions like (1 + a)^2 or (1 + b^3)^2 that have the same *structure*. However, it cannot stand for the expression 1 + 2 a + a^2. Although this expression is *mathematically equal* to (1 + a)^2, it does not have the same *structure* as the pattern (1 + x_)^2.

The fact that patterns in *Mathematica* specify the *structure* of expressions is crucial in making it possible to set up transformation rules which change the *structure* of expressions, while leaving them mathematically equal.

It is worth realizing that in general it would be quite impossible for *Mathematica* to match patterns by mathematical, rather than structural, equivalence. In the case of expressions like (1 + a)^2 and 1 + 2 a + a^2, you can determine equivalence just by using functions like Expand and Factor. But, as discussed on page 270 there is no general way to find out whether an arbitrary pair of mathematical expressions are equal.

As another example, the pattern x^_ will match the expression x^2. It will not, however, match the expression 1, even though this could be considered as x^0. Section 2.3.9 will discuss how to construct a pattern for which this particular case will match. But you should understand that in all cases pattern matching in *Mathematica* is fundamentally structural.

The x^n_ matches only x^2 and x^3. 1 and x can mathematically be written as x^n, but do not have the same structure.	*In[6]:=* **{1, x, x^2, x^3} /. x^n_ -> r[n]** *Out[6]=* **{1, x, r[2], r[3]}**

Another point to realize is that the structure *Mathematica* uses in pattern matching is the full form of expressions printed by FullForm. Thus, for example, an object such as 1/x, whose full form is Power[x, -1] will be matched by the pattern x_^n_, but not by the pattern x_/y_, whose full form is Times[x_, Power[y_, -1]]. Again, Section 2.3.9 will discuss how you can construct patterns which can match all these cases.

The full form of the expressions in the list contains explicit powers of b, so the transformation rule can be applied.

`In[7]:= {a/b, 1/b^2, 2/b^2} /. b^n_ -> d[n]`

`Out[7]= {a d[-1], d[-2], 2 d[-2]}`

Although *Mathematica* does not use mathematical equivalences such as $x^1 = x$ when matching patterns, it does use certain structural equivalences. Thus, for example, *Mathematica* takes account of properties such as commutativity and associativity in pattern matching.

To apply this transformation rule, *Mathematica* makes use of the commutativity and associativity of addition.

`In[8]:= f[a + b] + f[a + c] + f[b + d] /.`
`                    f[a + x_] + f[c + y_] -> p[x, y]`

`Out[8]= f[b + d] + p[b, a]`

The discussion so far has considered only pattern objects such as x_ which can stand for any single expression. In later subsections, we discuss the constructs that *Mathematica* uses to extend and restrict the classes of expressions represented by patterns.

■ 2.3.2 Finding Expressions That Match a Pattern

Cases[*list*, *form*]	give the elements of *list* that match *form*
Count[*list*, *form*]	give the number of elements in *list* that match *form*
Position[*list*, *form*, {1}]	give the positions of elements in *list* that match *form*
Select[*list*, *test*]	give the elements of *list* on which *test* gives True

Picking out elements that match a pattern.

This gives the elements of the list which match the pattern x^_.

`In[1]:= Cases[ {3, 4, x, x^2, x^3}, x^_ ]`

`Out[1]= {x , x }`
       $\{x^2, x^3\}$

Here is the total number of elements which match the pattern.

`In[2]:= Count[ {3, 4, x, x^2, x^3}, x^_ ]`

`Out[2]= 2`

You can apply functions like Cases not only to lists, but to expressions of any kind. In addition, you can specify the level of parts at which you want to look.

Cases[*expr*, *lhs->rhs*]	find elements of *expr* that match *lhs*, and give a list of the results of applying the transformation rule to them
Cases[*expr*, *lhs->rhs*, *lev*]	test parts of *expr* at levels specified by *lev*
Count[*expr*, *form*, *lev*]	give the total number of parts that match *form* at levels specified by *lev*
Position[*expr*, *form*, *lev*]	give the positions of parts that match *form* at levels specified by *lev*

Searching for parts of expressions that match a pattern.

This returns a list of the exponents n.

In[3]:= `Cases[ {3, 4, x, x^2, x^3}, x^n_ -> n]`

Out[3]= `{2, 3}`

The pattern _Integer matches any integer. This gives a list of integers appearing at any level.

In[4]:= `Cases[ {3, 4, x, x^2, x^3}, _Integer, Infinity]`

Out[4]= `{3, 4, 2, 3}`

| DeleteCases[*expr*, *form*] | delete elements of *expr* that match *form* |
| DeleteCases[*expr*, *form*, *lev*] | delete parts of *expr* that match *form* at levels specified by *lev* |

Deleting parts of expressions that match a pattern.

This deletes the elements which match x^n_.

In[5]:= `DeleteCases[ {3, 4, x, x^2, x^3}, x^n_ ]`

Out[5]= `{3, 4, x}`

This deletes all integers appearing at any level.

In[6]:= `DeleteCases[ {3, 4, x, 2+x, 3+x}, _Integer, Infinity ]`

Out[6]= `{x, x, x}`

■ 2.3.3 Naming Pieces of Patterns

Particularly when you use transformation rules, you often need to name pieces of patterns. An object like x_- stands for any expression, but gives the expression the name x. You can then, for example, use this name on the right-hand side of a transformation rule.

An important point is that when you use x_-, *Mathematica* requires that all occurrences of blanks with the same name x in a particular expression must stand for the same expression.

Thus f[x_, x_] can only stand for expressions in which the two arguments of f are exactly the same. f[_, _], on the other hand, can stand for any expression of the form f[x, y], where x and y need not be the same.

The transformation rule applies only to cases where the two arguments of f are identical.	*In[1]:=* **{f[a, a], f[a, b]} /. f[x_, x_] -> p[x]**
	Out[1]= **{p[a], f[a, b]}**

Mathematica allows you to give names not just to single blanks, but to any piece of a pattern. The object *x*:*pattern* in general represents a pattern which is assigned the name *x*. In transformation rules, you can use this mechanism to name exactly those pieces of a pattern that you need to refer to on the right-hand side of the rule.

_	any expression
*x*_	any expression, to be named *x*
x:*pattern*	an expression to be named *x*, matching *pattern*

Patterns with names.

This gives a name to the complete form _^_ so you can refer to it as a whole on the right-hand side of the transformation rule.	*In[2]:=* **f[a^b] /. f[x:_^_] -> p[x]**
	Out[2]= **p[a^b]**
Here the exponent is named n, while the whole object is x.	*In[3]:=* **f[a^b] /. f[x:_^n_] -> p[x, n]**
	Out[3]= **p[a^b, b]**

When you give the same name to two pieces of a pattern, you constrain the pattern to match only those expressions in which the corresponding pieces are identical.

Here the pattern matches both cases.	*In[4]:=* **{f[h[4], h[4]], f[h[4], h[5]]} /. f[h[_], h[_]] -> q**
	Out[4]= **{q, q}**
Now both arguments of f are constrained to be the same, and only the first case matches.	*In[5]:=* **{f[h[4], h[4]], f[h[4], h[5]]} /. f[x:h[_], x_] -> r[x]**
	Out[5]= **{r[h[4]], f[h[4], h[5]]}**

■ 2.3.4 Specifying Types of Expression in Patterns

You can tell a lot about what "type" of expression something is by looking at its head. Thus, for example, an integer has head Integer, while a list has head List.

In a pattern, _*h* and *x*_*h* represent expressions that are constrained to have head *h*. Thus, for example, _Integer represents any integer, while _List represents any list.

*x*_*h*	an expression with head *h*
*x*_Integer	an integer
*x*_Real	an approximate real number
*x*_Complex	a complex number
*x*_List	a list
*x*_Symbol	a symbol

Patterns for objects with specified heads.

This replaces just those elements that are integers.

```
In[1]:= {a, 4, 5, b} /. x_Integer -> p[x]
Out[1]= {a, p[4], p[5], b}
```

You can think of making an assignment for f[x_Integer] as like defining a function f that must take an argument of "type" Integer.

This defines a value for the function gamma when its argument is an integer.

```
In[2]:= gamma[n_Integer] := (n - 1)!
```

The definition applies only when the argument of gamma is an integer.

```
In[3]:= gamma[4] + gamma[x]
Out[3]= 6 + gamma[x]
```

The object 4. has head Real, so the definition does not apply.

```
In[4]:= gamma[4.]
Out[4]= gamma[4.]
```

This defines values for expressions with integer exponents.

```
In[5]:= d[x_^n_Integer] := n x^(n-1)
```

The definition is used only when the exponent is an integer.

```
In[6]:= d[x^4] + d[(a+b)^3] + d[x^(1/2)]

Out[6]= 3 (a + b)^2 + 4 x^3 + d[Sqrt[x]]
```

■ 2.3.5 Putting Constraints on Patterns

Mathematica provides a general mechanism for specifying constraints on patterns. All you need do is to put /; *condition* at the end of a pattern to signify that it applies only when the specified condition is True. You can read the operator /; as "slash-semi", "whenever" or "provided that".

pattern /; *condition*	a pattern that matches only when a condition is satisfied
lhs :> *rhs* /; *condition*	a rule that applies only when a condition is satisfied
lhs := *rhs* /; *condition*	a definition that applies only when a condition is satisfied

Putting conditions on patterns and transformation rules.

This gives a definition for `fac` that applies only when its argument `n` is positive.

```
In[1]:= fac[n_ /; n > 0] := n!
```

The definition for `fac` is used only when the argument is positive.

```
In[2]:= fac[6] + fac[-4]

Out[2]= 720 + fac[-4]
```

This gives the negative elements in the list.

```
In[3]:= Cases[{3, -4, 5, -2}, x_ /; x < 0]

Out[3]= {-4, -2}
```

You can use /; on whole definitions and transformation rules, as well as on individual patterns. In general, you can put /; *condition* at the end of any := definition or :> rule to tell *Mathematica* that the definition or rule applies only when the specified condition holds. Note that /; conditions should not usually be put at the end of = definitions or -> rules, since they will then be evaluated immediately, as discussed in Section 2.4.8.

Here is another way to give a definition for `fac` which applies only when its argument `n` is positive.

```
In[4]:= fac[n_] := n! /; n > 0
```

Once again, `fac` evaluates only when its argument is positive.

```
In[5]:= fac[6] + fac[-4]

Out[5]= 720 + fac[-4]
```

You can use the /; operator to implement arbitrary mathematical constraints on the applicability of rules. In typical cases, you give patterns which *structurally* match a wide range of expressions, but then use *mathematical* constraints to reduce the range of expressions to a much smaller set.

This rule applies only to expressions that have the structure `v[x_, 1 - x_]`.

```
In[6]:= v[x_, 1 - x_] := p[x]
```

This expression has the appropriate structure, so the rule applies.

```
In[7]:= v[a^2, 1 - a^2]

Out[7]= p[a ]
        2
```

This expression, while mathematically of the correct form, does not have the appropriate structure, so the rule does not apply.

```
In[8]:= v[4, -3]

Out[8]= v[4, -3]
```

This rule applies to any expression of the form `w[x_, y_]`, with the added restriction that `y == 1 - x`.

```
In[9]:= w[x_, y_] := p[x] /; y == 1 - x
```

The new rule does apply to this expression.	*In[10]:=* **w[4, -3]**
	Out[10]= p[4]

In setting up patterns and transformation rules, there is often a choice of where to put /; conditions. For example, you can put a /; condition on the right-hand side of a rule in the form *lhs* :> *rhs* /; *condition*, or you can put it on the left-hand side in the form *lhs* /; *condition* -> *rhs*. You may also be able to insert the condition inside the expression *lhs*. The only constraint is that all the names of patterns that you use in a particular condition must appear in the pattern to which the condition is attached. If this is not the case, then some of the names needed to evaluate the condition may not yet have been "bound" in the pattern-matching process. If this happens, then *Mathematica* uses the global values for the corresponding variables, rather than the values determined by pattern matching.

Thus, for example, the condition in f[x_, y_] /; (x + y < 2) will use values for x and y that are found by matching f[x_, y_], but the condition in f[x_ /; x + y < 2, y_] will use the global value for y, rather than the one found by matching the pattern.

As long as you make sure that the appropriate names are defined, it is usually most efficient to put /; conditions on the smallest possible parts of patterns. The reason for this is that *Mathematica* matches pieces of patterns sequentially, and the sooner it finds a /; condition which fails, the sooner it can reject a match.

Putting the /; condition around the x_ is slightly more efficient than putting it around the whole pattern.	*In[11]:=* **Cases[{z[1, 1], z[-1, 1], z[-2, 2]}, z[x_ /; x < 0, y_]]**
	Out[11]= {z[-1, 1], z[-2, 2]}

You need to put parentheses around the /; piece in a case like this.	*In[12]:=* **{1 + a, 2 + a, -3 + a} /. (x_ /; x < 0) + a -> p[x]**
	Out[12]= {1 + a, 2 + a, p[-3]}

It is common to use /; to set up patterns and transformation rules that apply only to expressions with certain properties. There is a collection of functions built into *Mathematica* for testing the properties of expressions. It is a convention that functions of this kind have names that end with the letter Q, indicating that they "ask a question".

NumberQ[*expr*]	number
IntegerQ[*expr*]	integer
EvenQ[*expr*]	even number
OddQ[*expr*]	odd number
PrimeQ[*expr*]	prime number
PolynomialQ[*expr*, {x_1, x_2, ... }]	
	polynomial in x_1, x_2, ...
VectorQ[*expr*]	a list representing a vector
MatrixQ[*expr*]	a list of lists representing a matrix
VectorQ[*expr*, NumberQ], MatrixQ[*expr*, NumberQ]	
	vectors and matrices where all elements are numbers
VectorQ[*expr*, *test*], MatrixQ[*expr*, *test*]	
	vectors and matrices for which the function *test* yields True when applied to any element

Some functions for testing mathematical properties of expressions.

The rule applies to all elements of the list that are numbers.

```
In[13]:= {2.3, 4, 7/8, a, b} /. (x_ /; NumberQ[x]) -> x^2
```

$$Out[13]= \{5.29,\ 16,\ \frac{49}{64},\ a,\ b\}$$

This definition applies only to vectors of integers.

```
In[14]:= mi[list_] := list^2 /; VectorQ[list, IntegerQ]
```

An important feature of all the *Mathematica* property-testing functions whose names end in Q is that they always return False if they cannot determine whether the expression you give has a particular property.

4561 is an integer, so this returns True.

```
In[15]:= IntegerQ[4561]
Out[15]= True
```

This returns False, since x is not known to be an integer.

```
In[16]:= IntegerQ[x]
Out[16]= False
```

In some cases, you can explicitly specify the results that property-testing functions should give. Thus, for example, with the definition x /: IntegerQ[x] = True, *Mathematica* will assume that x is an integer. This means that if you explicitly ask for IntegerQ[x], you will now get True, rather than False. However, *Mathematica* does not automatically propagate assertions, so it cannot determine for example that IntegerQ[x^2] is True. You must load an appropriate *Mathematica* package to make this possible.

SameQ[x, y] or x === y	x and y are identical
UnsameQ[x, y] or x =!= y	x and y are not identical
OrderedQ[{a, b, ... }]	a, b, ... are in standard order
MemberQ[*expr*, *form*]	*form* matches an element of *expr*
FreeQ[*expr*, *form*]	*form* matches nothing in *expr*
MatchQ[*expr*, *form*]	*expr* matches the pattern *form*
ValueQ[*expr*]	a value has been defined for *expr*
AtomQ[*expr*]	*expr* has no subexpressions

Some functions for testing structural properties of expressions.

With ==, the equation remains in symbolic form; === yields **False** unless the expressions are manifestly equal.

```
In[17]:= {x == y, x === y}
Out[17]= {x == y, False}
```

The expression n is not a *member* of the list {x, x^n}.

```
In[18]:= MemberQ[{x, x^n}, n]
Out[18]= False
```

The expression n does however appear *somewhere* in {x, x^n}.

```
In[19]:= FreeQ[{x, x^n}, n]
Out[19]= False
```

You can use **FreeQ** to define a "linearity" rule for h.

```
In[20]:= h[a_ b_, x_] := a h[b, x] /; FreeQ[a, x]
```

Terms free of x are pulled out of each h.

```
In[21]:= h[a b x, x] + h[2 (1+x) x^2, x]

Out[21]= a b h[x, x] + 2 h[x^2 (1 + x), x]
```

pattern ? *test*	a pattern which matches an expression only if *test* yields **True** when applied to the expression

Another way to constrain patterns.

The construction *pattern* /; *condition* allows you to evaluate a condition involving pattern names to determine whether there is a match. The construction *pattern* ? *test* instead applies a function *test* to the whole expression matched by *pattern* to determine whether there is a match. Using ? instead of /; sometimes leads to more succinct definitions.

With this definition matches for x_ are tested with the function **NumberQ**.

```
In[22]:= p[x_?NumberQ] := x^2
```

The definition applies only when p has a numerical argument.

```
In[23]:= p[4.5] + p[3/2] + p[u]
Out[23]= 22.5 + p[u]
```

Here is a more complicated definition. Do not forget the parentheses around the pure function.

```
In[24]:= q[{x_Integer, y_Integer} ?
                (Function[v, v.v > 4])] := qp[x + y]
```

The definition applies only in certain cases.

```
In[25]:= {q[{3, 4}], q[{1, 1}], q[{-5, -7}]}
Out[25]= {qp[7], q[{1, 1}], qp[-12]}
```

■ 2.3.6 Patterns Involving Alternatives

$patt_1$	$patt_2$	...	a pattern that can have one of several forms

Specifying patterns that involve alternatives.

This defines h to give p when its argument is either a or b.

```
In[1]:= h[a | b] := p
```

The first two cases give p.

```
In[2]:= {h[a], h[b], h[c], h[d]}
Out[2]= {p, p, h[c], h[d]}
```

You can also use alternatives in transformation rules.

```
In[3]:= {a, b, c, d} /. (a | b) -> p
Out[3]= {p, p, c, d}
```

Here is another example, in which one of the alternatives is itself a pattern.

```
In[4]:= {1, x, x^2, x^3, y^2} /. (x | x^_) -> q
                                             2
Out[4]= {1, q, q, q, y }
```

When you use alternatives in patterns, you should make sure that the same set of names appear in each alternative. When a pattern like (a[x_] | b[x_]) matches an expression, there will always be a definite expression that corresponds to the object x. On the other hand, if you try to match a pattern like (a[x_] | b[y_]), then there will be a definite expression corresponding either to x, or to y, but not to both. As a result, you cannot use x and y to refer to definite expressions, for example on the right-hand side of a transformation rule.

Here f is used to name the head, which can be either a or b.

```
In[5]:= {a[2], b[3], c[4], a[5]} /. (f:(a|b))[x_] -> r[f, x]
Out[5]= {r[a, 2], r[b, 3], c[4], r[a, 5]}
```

■ 2.3.7 Flat and Orderless Functions

Although *Mathematica* matches patterns in a purely structural fashion, its notion of structural equivalence is quite sophisticated. In particular, it takes account of properties such as commutativity and associativity in functions like Plus and Times.

This means, for example, that *Mathematica* considers the expressions $x + y$ and $y + x$ equivalent for the purposes of pattern matching. As a result, a pattern like g[x_ + y_, x_] can match not only g[a + b, a], but also g[a + b, b].

This expression has exactly the same form as the pattern.	*In[1]:=* **g[a + b, a] /. g[x_ + y_, x_] -> p[x, y]** *Out[1]=* p[a, b]
In this case, the expression has to be put in the form g[b + a, b] in order to have the same structure as the pattern.	*In[2]:=* **g[a + b, b] /. g[x_ + y_, x_] -> p[x, y]** *Out[2]=* p[b, a]

Whenever *Mathematica* encounters an *orderless* or *commutative* function such as Plus or Times in a pattern, it effectively tests all the possible orders of arguments to try and find a match. Sometimes, there may be several orderings that lead to matches. In such cases, *Mathematica* just uses the first ordering it finds. For example, h[x_ + y_, x_ + z_] could match h[a + b, a + b] with x→a, y→b, z→b or with x→b, y→a, z→a. *Mathematica* tries the case x→a, y→b, z→b first, and so uses this match.

This can match either with x → a or with x → b. *Mathematica* tries x → a first, and so uses this match.	*In[3]:=* **h[a + b, a + b] /. h[x_ + y_, x_ + z_] -> p[x, y, z]** *Out[3]=* p[a, b, b]
By the trick of adding a Print condition which never evaluates to True, you can see both the matches *Mathematica* tries.	*In[4]:=* **h[a + b, a + b] /.** 　　　　**h[x_ + y_, x_ + z_] :> p[x, y, z] /; Print[{x, y, z}]** {a, b, b} {b, a, a} *Out[4]=* h[a + b, a + b]

As discussed in Section 2.5.3, *Mathematica* allows you to assign certain attributes to functions, which specify how those functions should be treated in evaluation and pattern matching. Functions can for example be assigned the attribute Orderless, which specifies that they should be treated as commutative or symmetric, and allows their arguments to be rearranged in trying to match patterns.

Orderless	commutative function: $f[b, c, a]$, etc. are equivalent to $f[a, b, c]$
Flat	associative function: $f[f[a], b]$, etc. are equivalent to $f[a, b]$
OneIdentity	$f[f[a]]$, etc. are equivalent to a
Attributes[*f*]	give the attributes assigned to f
SetAttributes[*f*, *attr*]	add *attr* to the attributes of f
ClearAttributes[*f*, *attr*]	remove *attr* from the attributes of f

Some attributes that can be assigned to functions.

Plus has attributes `Orderless` and `Flat`, as well as others.

```
In[5]:= Attributes[Plus]
Out[5]= {Flat, Listable, OneIdentity, Orderless, Protected}
```

This defines q to be an orderless or commutative function.

```
In[6]:= SetAttributes[q, Orderless]
```

The arguments of q are automatically sorted into order.

```
In[7]:= q[b, a, c]
Out[7]= q[a, b, c]
```

Mathematica rearranges the arguments of q functions to find a match.

```
In[8]:= f[q[a, b], q[b, c]] /.
            f[q[x_, y_], q[x_, z_]] -> p[x, y, z]
Out[8]= p[b, a, c]
```

In addition to being orderless, functions like `Plus` and `Times` also have the property of being *flat* or *associative*. This means that you can effectively "parenthesize" their arguments in any way, so that, for example, x + (y + z) is equivalent to x + y + z, and so on.

Mathematica takes account of flatness in matching patterns. As a result, a pattern like g[x_ + y_] can match g[a + b + c], with x → a and y → (b + c).

The argument of g is written as a + (b + c) so as to match the pattern.

```
In[9]:= g[a + b + c] /. g[x_ + y_] -> p[x, y]
Out[9]= p[a, b + c]
```

If there are no other constraints, *Mathematica* will match x_ to the first element of the sum.

```
In[10]:= g[a + b + c + d] /. g[x_ + y_] -> p[x, y]
Out[10]= p[a, b + c + d]
```

If necessary, however, it will try all the possible arrangements.

```
In[11]:= g[a + b + c] /. g[x_ + y_] :> p[x, y] /; Print[{x, y}]
{a, b + c}
{b, a + c}
{c, a + b}
{a + b, c}
{a + c, b}
{b + c, a}
Out[11]= g[a + b + c]
```

Here x_ is forced to match b + d.

```
In[12]:= g[a + b + c + d, b + d] /. g[x_ + y_, x_] -> p[x, y]
Out[12]= p[b + d, a + c]
```

Mathematica can usually apply a transformation rule to a function only if the pattern in the rule covers all the arguments in the function. However, if you have a flat function, it is sometimes possible to apply transformation rules even though not all the arguments are covered.

This rule applies even though it does not cover all the terms in the sum.

```
In[13]:= a + b + c /. a + c -> p
Out[13]= b + p
```

This combines two of the terms in the sum.

```
In[14]:= u[a] + u[b] + v[c] + v[d] /. u[x_] + u[y_] -> u[x + y]
Out[14]= u[a + b] + v[c] + v[d]
```

Functions like `Plus` and `Times` are both flat and orderless. There are, however, some functions, such as `Dot`, which are flat, but not orderless.

Both `x_` and `y_` can match any sequence of terms in the dot product.	`In[15]:= a . b . c . d . a . b /. x_ . y_ . x_ -> p[x, y]`
	
	`Out[15]= p[a . b, c . d]`

This assigns the attribute `Flat` to the function `r`.	`In[16]:= SetAttributes[r, Flat]`

Mathematica writes the expression in the form `r[r[a, b], r[a, b]]` to match the pattern.	`In[17]:= r[a, b, a, b] /. r[x_, x_] -> rp[x]`
	
	`Out[17]= rp[r[a, b]]`

Mathematica writes this expression in the form `r[a, r[r[b], r[b]], c]` to match the pattern.	`In[18]:= r[a, b, b, c] /. r[x_, x_] -> rp[x]`
	
	`Out[18]= r[a, rp[r[b]], c]`

In an ordinary function that is not flat, a pattern such as `x_` matches an individual argument of the function. But in a function $f[a, b, c, \dots]$ that is flat, `x_` can match objects such as $f[b, c]$ which effectively correspond to a sequence of arguments. However, in the case where `x_` matches a single argument in a flat function, the question comes up as to whether the object it matches is really just the argument *a* itself, or $f[a]$. *Mathematica* chooses the first of these cases if the function carries the attribute `OneIdentity`, and chooses the second case otherwise.

This adds the attribute `OneIdentity` to the function `r`.	`In[19]:= SetAttributes[r, OneIdentity]`

Now `x_` matches individual arguments, without `r` wrapped around them.	`In[20]:= r[a, b, b, c] /. r[x_, x_] -> rp[x]`
	
	`Out[20]= r[a, rp[b], c]`

The functions `Plus`, `Times` and `Dot` all have the attribute `OneIdentity`, reflecting the fact that `Plus[x]` is equivalent to *x*, and so on. However, in representing mathematical objects, it is often convenient to deal with flat functions that do not have the attribute `OneIdentity`.

■ 2.3.8 Functions with Variable Numbers of Arguments

Unless *f* is a flat function, a pattern like $f[x_, y_]$ stands only for instances of the function with exactly two arguments. Sometimes you need to set up patterns that can allow any number of arguments.

You can do this using *multiple blanks*. While a single blank such as `x_` stands for a single *Mathematica* expression, a double blank such as `x__` stands for a sequence of one or more expressions.

Here `x__` stands for the sequence of expressions (a, b, c).	`In[1]:= f[a, b, c] /. f[x__] -> p[x, x, x]`
	
	`Out[1]= p[a, b, c, a, b, c, a, b, c]`

Here is a more complicated definition, which picks out pairs of duplicated elements in `h`.	`In[2]:= h[a___, x_, b___, x_, c___] := hh[x] h[a, b, c]`

The definition is applied twice, picking
out the two paired elements.

In[3]:= **h[2, 3, 2, 4, 5, 3]**

Out[3]= h[4, 5] hh[2] hh[3]

"Double blanks" __ stand for sequences of one or more expressions. "Triple blanks" ___ stand for
sequences of zero or more expressions. You should be very careful whenever you use triple blank
patterns. It is easy to make a mistake that can lead to an infinite loop. For example, if you define
p[x_, y___] := p[x] q[y], then typing in p[a] will lead to an infinite loop, with y repeatedly matching a sequence with zero elements. Unless you are sure you want to include the case of zero elements,
you should always use double blanks rather than triple blanks.

_	any single expression
*x*_	any single expression, to be named *x*
__	any sequence of one or more expressions
*x*__	sequence named *x*
*x*_*h*	sequence of expressions, all of whose heads are *h*
*x*___	sequence of zero or more expressions
*x*___*h*	sequence of zero or more expressions, all of whose heads are *h*

More kinds of pattern objects.

Notice that with flat functions such as Plus and Times, *Mathematica* automatically handles variable
numbers of arguments, so you do not explicitly need to use double or triple blanks, as discussed in
Section 2.3.7.

When you use multiple blanks, there are often several matches that are possible for a particular expression. In general, *Mathematica* tries first those matches that assign the shortest sequences of arguments to the first multiple blanks that appear in the pattern.

Using the trick of adding a condition
which prints but always fails, you can
see the sequence of matches that
Mathematica tries.

In[4]:= **f[a, b, c, d, e] /. f[x__, y__] :> q /; Print[{x}, {y}]**

{a}{b, c, d, e}
{a, b}{c, d, e}
{a, b, c}{d, e}
{a, b, c, d}{e}

Out[4]= f[a, b, c, d, e]

■ 2.3.9 Optional and Default Arguments

Sometimes you may want to set up functions where certain arguments, if omitted, are given "default
values". The pattern *x*_:*v* stands for an object that can be omitted, and if so, will be replaced by the
default value *v*.

This defines a function j with a required argument x, and optional arguments y and z, with default values 1 and 2, respectively.

```
In[1]:= j[x_, y_:1, z_:2] := jp[x, y, z]
```

The default value of z is used here.

```
In[2]:= j[a, b]

Out[2]= jp[a, b, 2]
```

Now the default values of both y and z are used.

```
In[3]:= j[a]

Out[3]= jp[a, 1, 2]
```

$x\_:v$	an expression which, if omitted, is taken to have default value v
$x\_h:v$	an expression with head h and default value v
$x\_.$	an expression with a built-in default value

Pattern objects with default values.

Some common *Mathematica* functions have built-in default values for their arguments. In such cases, you need not explicitly give the default value in $x\_:v$, but instead you can use the more convenient notation $x\_.$ in which a built-in default value is assumed.

x_ + y_.	default for y is 0
x_ y_.	default for y is 1
x_^y_.	default for y is 1

Some patterns with optional pieces.

Here a matches the pattern x_ + y_. with y taken to have the default value 0.

```
In[4]:= {f[a], f[a + b]} /. f[x_ + y_.] -> p[x, y]

Out[4]= {p[a, 0], p[b, a]}
```

Because Plus is a flat function, a pattern such as x_ + y_ can match a sum with any number of terms. This pattern cannot, however, match a single term such as a. However, the pattern x_ + y_. contains an optional piece, and can match either an explicit sum of terms in which both x_ and y_ appear, or a single term x_, with y taken to be 0.

Using constructs such as $x\_.$, you can easily construct single patterns that match expressions with several different structures. This is particularly useful when you want to match several mathematically equal forms that do not have the same structure.

The pattern matches g[a^2], but not g[a + b].

```
In[5]:= {g[a^2], g[a + b]} /. g[x_^n_] -> p[x, n]

Out[5]= {p[a, 2], g[a + b]}
```

By giving a pattern in which the exponent is optional, you can match both cases.

`In[6]:= {g[a^2], g[a + b]} /. g[x_^n_.] -> p[x, n]`

`Out[6]= {p[a, 2], p[a + b, 1]}`

The pattern a_. + b_. x_ matches any linear function of x_.

`In[7]:= lin[a_. + b_. x_, x_] := p[a, b]`

In this case, b → 1.

`In[8]:= lin[1 + x, x]`

`Out[8]= p[1, 1]`

Here b → 1 and a → 0.

`In[9]:= lin[y, y]`

`Out[9]= p[0, 1]`

Standard *Mathematica* functions such as Plus and Times have built-in default values for their arguments. You can also set up defaults for your own functions, as described in Section A.5.1.

■ 2.3.10 Setting Up Functions with Optional Arguments

When you define a complicated function, you will often want to let some of the arguments of the function be "optional". If you do not give those arguments explicitly, you want them to take on certain "default" values.

Built-in *Mathematica* functions use two basic methods for dealing with optional arguments. You can choose between the same two methods when you define your own functions in *Mathematica*.

The first method is to have the meaning of each argument determined by its position, and then to allow one to drop arguments, replacing them by default values. Almost all built-in *Mathematica* functions that use this method drop arguments from the end. For example, the built-in function Flatten[*list*, *n*] allows you to drop the second argument, which is taken to have a default value of Infinity.

You can implement this kind of "positional" argument using _: patterns.

f[*x*_, *k*_:*kdef*] := *value*	a typical definition for a function whose second argument is optional

Defining a function with positional arguments.

This defines a function with an optional second argument. When the second argument is omitted, it is taken to have the default value Infinity.

`In[1]:= f[list_, n_:Infinity] := f0[list, n]`

Here is a function with two optional arguments.

`In[2]:= fx[list_, n1_:1, n2_:2] := fx0[list, n1, n2]`

Mathematica assumes that arguments are dropped from the end. As a result m here gives the value of n1, while n2 has its default value of 2.

```
In[3] := fx[k, m]
Out[3]= fx0[k, m, 2]
```

The second method that built-in *Mathematica* functions use for dealing with optional arguments is to give explicit names to the optional arguments, and then to allow their values to be given using transformation rules. This method is particularly convenient for functions like Plot which have a very large number of optional parameters, only a few of which usually need to be set in any particular instance.

The typical arrangement is that values for "named" optional arguments can be specified by including the appropriate transformation rules at the end of the arguments to a particular function. Thus, for example, the rule PlotJoined->True, which specifies the setting for the named optional argument PlotJoined, could appear as ListPlot[*list*, PlotJoined->True].

When you set up named optional arguments for a function *f*, it is conventional to store the default values of these arguments as a list of transformation rules assigned to Options[*f*].

f[*x*_, *opts*___] := *value*	a typical definition for a function with named optional arguments
name /. {*opts*} /. Options[*f*]	replacements used to get the value of a named optional argument in the body of the function

Named arguments.

This sets up default values for two named optional arguments opt1 and opt2 in the function fn.

```
In[4] := Options[fn] = { opt1 -> 1, opt2 -> 2 }
Out[4]= {opt1 -> 1, opt2 -> 2}
```

This gives the default value for opt1.

```
In[5] := opt1 /. Options[fn]
Out[5]= 1
```

The rule opt1->3 is applied first, so the default rule for opt1 in Options[fn] is not used.

```
In[6] := opt1 /. opt1->3 /. Options[fn]
Out[6]= 3
```

Here is the definition for a function fn which allows zero or more named optional arguments to be specified.

```
In[7] := fn[x_, opts___] := k[x, opt2/.{opts}/.Options[fn]]
```

With no optional arguments specified, the default rule for opt2 is used.

```
In[8] := fn[4]
Out[8]= k[4, 2]
```

If you explicitly give a rule for opt2, it will be used before the default rules stored in Options[fn] are tried.

```
In[9] := fn[4, opt2->7]
Out[9]= k[4, 7]
```

■ 2.3.11 Repeated Patterns

expr . .	a pattern or other expression repeated one or more times
expr . . .	a pattern or other expression repeated zero or more times

Repeated patterns.

Multiple blanks such as $x\_\_$ allow you to give patterns in which sequences of arbitrary expressions can occur. The *Mathematica pattern repetition operators* . . and . . . allow you to construct patterns in which particular forms can be repeated any number of times. Thus, for example, f[a..] represents any expression of the form f[a], f[a, a], f[a, a, a] and so on.

The pattern f[a..] allows the argument a to be repeated any number of times.

```
In[1]:= Cases[{ f[a], f[a, b, a], f[a, a, a] }, f[a..]]
Out[1]= {f[a], f[a, a, a]}
```

This pattern allows any number of a arguments, followed by any number of b arguments.

```
In[2]:= Cases[{ f[a], f[a, a, b], f[a, b, a], f[a, b, b] },
                                                       f[a.., b..]]
Out[2]= {f[a, a, b], f[a, b, b]}
```

Here each argument can be either a or b.

```
In[3]:= Cases[{ f[a], f[a, b, a], f[a, c, a] }, f[(a | b)..]]
Out[3]= {f[a], f[a, b, a]}
```

You can use . . and . . . to represent repetitions of any pattern. If the pattern contains named parts, then each instance of these parts must be identical.

This defines a function whose argument must consist of a list of pairs.

```
In[4]:= v[x:{{_, _}..}] := Transpose[x]
```

The definition applies in this case.

```
In[5]:= v[{{a1, b1}, {a2, b2}, {a3, b3}}]
Out[5]= {{a1, a2, a3}, {b1, b2, b3}}
```

With this definition, the second elements of all the pairs must be the same.

```
In[6]:= vn[x:{{_, n_}..}] := Transpose[x]
```

The definition applies in this case.

```
In[7]:= vn[{{a, 2}, {b, 2}, {c, 2}}]
Out[7]= {{a, b, c}, {2, 2, 2}}
```

■ 2.3.12 Patterns for Some Common Types of Expression

Using the objects described above, you can set up patterns for many kinds of expressions. In all cases, you must remember that the patterns must represent the structure of the expressions in *Mathematica* internal form, as shown by FullForm.

Especially for some common kinds of expressions, the standard output format used by *Mathematica* is not particularly close to the full internal form. But it is the internal form that you must use in setting up patterns.

n_Integer	an integer n
x_Real	an approximate real number x
z_Complex	a complex number z
Complex[x_, y_]	a complex number $x + iy$
Complex[x_Integer, y_Integer]	
	a complex number where both real and imaginary parts are integers
(r_Rational | r_Integer)	rational number or integer r
Rational[n_, d_]	a rational number $\frac{n}{d}$
(x_ /; NumberQ[x] && Im[x]==0)	
	a real number of any kind
(x_ /; NumberQ[x])	a number of any kind

Some typical patterns for numbers.

Here are the full forms of some numbers.

```
In[1]:= {2, 2.5, 2.5 + I, 2/7} // FullForm

Out[1]//FullForm= List[2, 2.5, Complex[2.5, 1.], Rational[2, 7]]
```

The rule picks out each piece of the complex numbers.

```
In[2]:= {2.5 - I, 3 + I} /. Complex[x_, y_] -> p[x, y]

Out[2]= {p[2.5, -1.], p[3, 1]}
```

The fact that these expressions have different full forms means that you cannot use x_ + I y_ to match a complex number.

```
In[3]:= {2.5 - I, x + I y} // FullForm

Out[3]//FullForm=
 List[Complex[2.5, -1.], Plus[x, Times[Complex[0, 1], y]]]
```

The pattern here matches both ordinary integers, and complex numbers where both the real and imaginary parts are integers.

```
In[4]:= Cases[ {2.5 - I, 2, 3 + I, 2 - 0.5 I, 2 + 2 I},
               _Integer | Complex[_Integer, _Integer] ]

Out[4]= {2, 3 + I, 2 + 2 I}
```

As discussed in Section 1.4.1, *Mathematica* puts all algebraic expressions into a standard form, in which they are written essentially as a sum of products of powers. In addition, ratios are converted into products of powers, with denominator terms having negative exponents, and differences are converted into sums with negated terms. To construct patterns for algebraic expressions, you must use this standard form. This form often differs from the way *Mathematica* prints out the algebraic expressions. But in all cases, you can find the full internal form using FullForm[*expr*].

Here is a typical algebraic expression.

In[5]:= **-1/z^2 - z/y + 2 (x z)^2 y**

Out[5]= $-z^{-2} - \dfrac{z}{y} + 2 x^2 y z^2$

This is the full internal form of the expression.

In[6]:= **FullForm[%]**

Out[6]//FullForm=

  Plus[Times[-1, Power[z, -2]], Times[-1, Power[y, -1], z],

    Times[2, Power[x, 2], y, Power[z, 2]]]

This is what you get by applying a transformation rule to all powers in the expression.

In[7]:= **% /. x_^n_ -> e[x, n]**

Out[7]= -(z e[y, -1]) - e[z, -2] + 2 y e[x, 2] e[z, 2]

$x\_ + y\_$	a sum of two or more terms
$x\_ + y\_.$	a single term or a sum of terms
$n\_Integer \; x\_$	an expression multiplied by an integer other than 1
$n\_Integer:1 \; x\_$	an expression with or without an explicit integer multiplier
$a\_. + b\_. \; x\_$	a linear expression $a + bx$
$x\_ \wedge n\_$	x^n with $n \neq 0, 1$
$x\_ \wedge n\_.$	x^n with $n \neq 0$
$a\_. + b\_. \; x\_ + c\_. \; x\_\wedge 2$	a quadratic expression

Some typical patterns for algebraic expressions.

This pattern picks out linear functions of x.

In[8]:= **{1, a, x, 2 x, 2 x + 1} /. a_. + b_. x -> p[a, b]**

Out[8]= {1, a, p[0, 1], p[0, 2], p[1, 2]}

x_List or $x{:}\{\_\_\_\}$	a list
x_List /; VectorQ[x]	a vector containing no sublists
x_List /; VectorQ[x, NumberQ]	
	a vector of numbers
$x{:}\{\_\_\_\text{List}\}$ or $x{:}\{\{\_\_\_\}...\}$	a list of lists
x_List /; MatrixQ[x]	a matrix containing no sublists
x_List /; MatrixQ[x, NumberQ]	
	a matrix of numbers
$x{:}\{\{\_,\ \_\}...\}$	a list of pairs

Some typical patterns for lists.

This defines a function whose argument must be a list containing lists with either one or two elements.	`In[9]:= h[x:{ ({_} | {_, _})... }] := q`
The definition applies in the second and third cases.	`In[10]:= {h[{a, b}], h[{{a}, {b}}], h[{{a}, {b, c}}]}` `Out[10]= {h[{a, b}], q, q}`

■ 2.3.13 An Example: Defining Your Own Integration Function

Now that we have introduced the basic features of patterns in *Mathematica*, we can use them to give a more or less complete example. We will show how you could define your own simple integration function in *Mathematica*.

From a mathematical point of view, the integration function is defined by a sequence of mathematical relations. By setting up transformation rules for patterns, you can implement these mathematical relations quite directly in *Mathematica*.

mathematical form	*Mathematica definition*
$\int (y+z)\,dx = \int y\,dx + \int z\,dx$	`integrate[y_ + z_, x_] :=` `    integrate[y, x] + integrate[z, x]`
$\int c\,y\,dx = c \int y\,dx$ (*c* independent of *x*)	
	`integrate[c_ y_, x_] :=` `    c integrate[y, x] /; FreeQ[c, x]`
$\int c\,dx = c\,x$	`integrate[c_, x_] := c x /; FreeQ[c, x]`
$\int x^n\,dx = \frac{x^{(n+1)}}{n+1},\ n \neq -1$	`integrate[x_^n_., x_] := x^(n+1)/(n+1) /;` `    FreeQ[n, x] && n != -1`
$\int \frac{1}{ax+b}\,dx = \frac{\log(ax+b)}{a}$	`integrate[1/(a_. x_ + b_.), x_] :=` `    Log[a x + b]/a /; FreeQ[{a,b}, x]`
$\int e^{ax+b}\,dx = \frac{1}{a}e^{ax+b}$	`integrate[Exp[a_. x_ + b_.], x_] :=` `    Exp[a x + b]/a /; FreeQ[{a,b}, x]`

Definitions for an integration function.

This implements the linearity relation for integrals: $\int (y+z)\,dx = \int y\,dx + \int z\,dx$.

```
In[1]:= integrate[y_ + z_, x_] :=
                integrate[y, x] + integrate[z, x]
```

The associativity of Plus makes the linearity relation work with any number of terms in the sum.

```
In[2]:= integrate[a x + b x^2 + 3, x]
                                                2
Out[2]= integrate[3, x] + integrate[a x, x] + integrate[b x , x]
```

This makes integrate pull out factors that are independent of the integration variable x.

```
In[3]:= integrate[c_ y_, x_] := c integrate[y, x] /; FreeQ[c, x]
```

Mathematica tests each term in each product to see whether it satisfies the FreeQ condition, and so can be pulled out.

```
In[4]:= integrate[a x + b x^2 + 3, x]
                                                    2
Out[4]= integrate[3, x] + a integrate[x, x] + b integrate[x , x]
```

This gives the integral $\int c\,dx = c\,x$ of a constant.

```
In[5]:= integrate[c_, x_] := c x /; FreeQ[c, x]
```

Now the constant term in the sum can be integrated.

```
In[6]:= integrate[a x + b x^2 + 3, x]
                                            2
Out[6]= 3 x + a integrate[x, x] + b integrate[x , x]
```

This gives the standard formula for the integral of x^n. By using the pattern x_^n_., rather than x_^n_, we include the case of $x^1 = x$.

```
In[7]:= integrate[x_^n_., x_] :=
                        x^(n+1)/(n+1) /; FreeQ[n, x] && n != -1
```

Now this integral can be done completely.

```
In[8]:= integrate[a x + b x^2 + 3, x]
                       2      3
                    a x    b x
Out[8]= 3 x + ---- + ----
                     2      3
```

Of course, the built-in integration function **Integrate** (with a capital I) could have done the integral anyway.

```
In[9]:= Integrate[a x + b x^2 + 3, x]
                       2      3
                    a x    b x
Out[9]= 3 x + ---- + ----
                     2      3
```

Here is the rule for integrating the reciprocal of a linear function. The pattern a_. x_ + b_. stands for any linear function of x.

```
In[10]:= integrate[1/(a_. x_ + b_.), x_] :=
                        Log[a x + b]/a /; FreeQ[{a,b}, x]
```

Here both a and b take on their default values.

```
In[11]:= integrate[1/x, x]
Out[11]= Log[x]
```

Here is a more complicated case. The symbol a now matches 2 p.

```
In[12]:= integrate[1/(2 p x - 1), x]
            Log[-1 + 2 p x]
Out[12]= ---------------
                 2 p
```

You can go on and add many more rules for integration. Here is a rule for integrating exponentials.

```
In[13]:= integrate[Exp[a_. x_ + b_.], x_] :=
                        Exp[a x + b]/a /; FreeQ[{a,b}, x]
```

2.4 Transformation Rules and Definitions

■ 2.4.1 Applying Transformation Rules

expr /. *lhs* -> *rhs*	apply a transformation rule to *expr*
expr /. {*lhs$_1$* -> *rhs$_1$*, *lhs$_2$* -> *rhs$_2$*, ... }	try a sequence of rules on each part of *expr*

Applying transformation rules.

The replacement operator /.
(pronounced "slash-dot") applies rules
to expressions.

```
In[1]:= x + y /. x -> 3
Out[1]= 3 + y
```

You can give a list of rules to apply.
Each rule will be tried once on each part
of the expression.

```
In[2]:= x + y /. {x -> a, y -> b}
Out[2]= a + b
```

expr /. {*rules$_1$*, *rules$_2$*, ... }	give a list of the results from applying each of the *rules$_i$* to *expr*

Applying lists of transformation rules.

If you give a list of lists of rules, you get
a list of results.

```
In[3]:= x + y /. {{x -> 1, y -> 2}, {x -> 4, y -> 2}}
Out[3]= {3, 6}
```

Functions such as Solve and NSolve
return lists whose elements are lists of
rules, each representing a solution.

```
In[4]:= Solve[x^3 - 5x^2 +2x + 8 == 0, x]
Out[4]= {{x -> -1}, {x -> 4}, {x -> 2}}
```

When you apply these rules, you get a
list of results, one corresponding to each
solution.

```
In[5]:= x^2 + 6 /. %
Out[5]= {7, 22, 10}
```

When you use *expr* /. *rules*, each rule is tried in turn on each part of *expr*. As soon as a rule applies,
the appropriate transformation is made, and the resulting part is returned.

The rule for x^3 is tried first; if it does
not apply, the rule for x^n_ is used.

```
In[6]:= {x^2, x^3, x^4} /. {x^3 -> u, x^n_ -> p[n]}
Out[6]= {p[2], u, p[4]}
```

A result is returned as soon as the rule
has been applied, so the inner instance
of h is not replaced.

```
In[7]:= h[x + h[y]] /. h[u_] -> u^2
Out[7]= (x + h[y])^2
```

The replacement *expr* /. *rules* tries each rule just once on each part of *expr*.

Since each rule is tried just once, this serves to swap x and y.	*In[8]:=* `{x^2, y^3} /. {x -> y, y -> x}` *Out[8]=* $\{y^2, x^3\}$
You can use this notation to apply one set of rules, followed by another.	*In[9]:=* `x^2 /. x -> (1 + y) /. y -> b` *Out[9]=* $(1 + b)^2$

Sometimes you may need to go on applying rules over and over again, until the expression you are working on no longer changes. You can do this using the repeated replacement operation *expr* //. *rules* (or `ReplaceRepeated[`*expr*, *rules*`]`).

expr /. *rules*	try rules once on each part of *expr*
expr //. *rules*	try rules repeatedly until the result no longer changes

Single and repeated rule application.

With the single replacement operator /. each rule is tried only once on each part of the expression.	*In[10]:=* `x^2 + y^6 /. {x -> 2 + a, a -> 3}` *Out[10]=* $(2 + a)^2 + y^6$
With the repeated replacement operator //. the rules are tried repeatedly until the expression no longer changes.	*In[11]:=* `x^2 + y^6 //. {x -> 2 + a, a -> 3}` *Out[11]=* $25 + y^6$
Here the rule is applied only once.	*In[12]:=* `log[a b c d] /. log[x_ y_] -> log[x] + log[y]` *Out[12]=* `log[a] + log[b c d]`
With the repeated replacement operator, the rule is applied repeatedly, until the result no longer changes.	*In[13]:=* `log[a b c d] //. log[x_ y_] -> log[x] + log[y]` *Out[13]=* `log[a] + log[b] + log[c] + log[d]`

When you use //. (pronounced "slash-slash-dot"), *Mathematica* repeatedly passes through your expression, trying each of the rules given. It goes on doing this until it gets the same result on two successive passes.

If you give a set of rules that is circular, then //. can keep on getting different results forever. In practice, the maximum number of passes that //. makes on a particular expression is determined by the setting for the option MaxIterations. If you want to keep going for as long as possible, you can use `ReplaceRepeated[`*expr*, *rules*, `MaxIterations -> Infinity]`. You can always stop by explicitly interrupting *Mathematica*.

By setting the option MaxIterations, you can explicitly tell ReplaceRepeated how many times to try the rules you give.	*In[14]:=* `ReplaceRepeated[x, x -> x + 1, MaxIterations -> 1000]` `ReplaceRepeated::rrlim: Exiting after x scanned 1000 times.` *Out[14]=* `1000 + x`

The replacement operators /. and //. share the feature that they try each rule on every subpart of your expression. On the other hand, Replace[*expr*, *rules*] tries the rules only on the whole of *expr*, and not on any of its subparts.

You can use Replace, together with functions like Map and MapAt, to control exactly which parts of an expression a replacement is applied to. Remember that you can use the function ReplacePart[*expr*, *new*, *pos*] to replace part of an expression with a specific object.

The operator /. applies rules to all subparts of an expression.	In[15]:= x∧2 /. x -> a Out[15]= a^2
Replace applies rules only to the whole expression.	In[16]:= Replace[x∧2, x∧2 -> b] Out[16]= b
No replacement is done here.	In[17]:= Replace[x∧2, x -> a] Out[17]= x^2

expr /. *rules*	apply rules to all subparts of *expr*
Replace[*expr*, *rules*]	apply rules to the whole of *expr* only

Applying rules to whole expressions.

■ 2.4.2 Manipulating Sets of Transformation Rules

You can manipulate lists of transformation rules in *Mathematica* just like other symbolic expressions. It is common to assign a name to a rule or set of rules.

This assigns the "name" sinexp to the trigonometric expansion rule.	In[1]:= sinexp = Sin[2 x_] -> 2 Sin[x] Cos[x] Out[1]= Sin[2 (x_)] -> 2 Cos[x] Sin[x]
You can now request the rule "by name".	In[2]:= Sin[2 (1 + x)∧2] /. sinexp Out[2]= 2 Cos[(1 + x)^2] Sin[(1 + x)^2]

You can use lists of rules to represent mathematical and other relations. Typically you will find it convenient to give names to the lists, so that you can easily specify the list you want in a particular case.

In most situations, it is only one rule from any given list that actually applies to a particular expression. Nevertheless, the /. operator tests each of the rules in the list in turn. If the list is very long, this process can take a long time.

Mathematica allows you to preprocess lists of rules so that /. can operate more quickly on them. You can take any list of rules and apply the function Dispatch to them. The result is a representation of the original list of rules, but including dispatch tables which allow /. to "dispatch" to potentially applicable rules immediately, rather than testing all the rules in turn.

Here is a list of rules for the first five factorials.	`In[3]:= facs = Table[f[i] -> i!, {i, 5}]`
	`Out[3]= {f[1] -> 1, f[2] -> 2, f[3] -> 6, f[4] -> 24,`
	`  f[5] -> 120}`

This sets up dispatch tables that make the rules faster to use.	`In[4]:= dfacs = Dispatch[facs]`
	`Out[4]= Dispatch[{f[1] -> 1, f[2] -> 2, f[3] -> 6, f[4] -> 24,`
	`  f[5] -> 120}, -DispatchTables-]`

You can apply the rules using the /. operator.	`In[5]:= f[4] /. dfacs` `Out[5]= 24`

Dispatch[*rules*]	create a representation of a list of rules that includes dispatch tables
expr /. *drules*	apply rules that include dispatch tables

Creating and using dispatch tables.

For long lists of rules, you will find that setting up dispatch tables makes replacement operations much faster. This is particularly true when your rules are for individual symbols or other expressions that do not involve pattern objects. Once you have built dispatch tables in such cases, you will find that the /. operator takes a time that is more or less independent of the number of rules you have. Without dispatch tables, however, /. will take a time directly proportional to the total number of rules.

■ 2.4.3 Making Definitions

The replacement operator /. allows you to apply transformation rules to a specific expression. Often, however, you want to have transformation rules automatically applied whenever possible.

You can do this by assigning explicit values to *Mathematica* expressions and patterns. Each assignment specifies a transformation rule to be applied whenever an expression of the appropriate form occurs.

expr /. *lhs* -> *rhs*	apply a transformation rule to a specific expression
lhs = *rhs*	assign a value which defines a transformation rule to be used whenever possible

Manual and automatic application of transformation rules.

This applies a transformation rule for x
to a specific expression.

$In[1]:=$ `(1 + x)^6 /. x -> 3 - a`

$Out[1]= (4 - a)^6$

By assigning a value to x, you tell
Mathematica to apply a transformation
rule for x whenever possible.

$In[2]:=$ `x = 3 - a`

$Out[2]= 3 - a$

Now x is transformed automatically.

$In[3]:=$ `(1 + x)^7`

$Out[3]= (4 - a)^7$

You should realize that except inside constructs like `Module` and `Block`, all assignments you make in a *Mathematica* session are *permanent*. They continue to be used for the duration of the session, unless you explicitly clear or overwrite them.

The fact that assignments are permanent means that they must be made with care. Probably the single most common mistake in using *Mathematica* is to make an assignment for a variable like x at one point in your session, and then later to use x having forgotten about the assignment you made.

There are several ways to avoid this kind of mistake. First, you should avoid using assignments whenever possible, and instead use more controlled constructs such as the `/.` replacement operator. Second, you should explicitly use the deassignment operator `=.` or the function `Clear` to remove values you have assigned when you have finished with them.

Another important way to avoid mistakes is to think particularly carefully before assigning values to variables with common or simple names. You will often want to use a variable such as x as a symbolic parameter. But if you make an assignment such as x = 3, then x will be replaced by 3 whenever it occurs, and you can no longer use x as a symbolic parameter.

In general, you should be sure not to assign permanent values to any variables that you might want to use for more than one purpose. If at one point in your session you wanted the variable c to stand for the speed of light, you might assign it a value such as `3.*10^8`. But then you cannot use c later in your session to stand, say, for an undetermined coefficient. One way to avoid this kind of problem is to make assignments only for variables with more explicit names, such as `SpeedOfLight`.

x `=.`	remove the value assigned to the object x
`Clear[`x, y, ... `]`	clear all the values of $x, y, \ldots$

Removing assignments.

This does not give what you might
expect, because x still has the value you
assigned it above.

$In[4]:=$ `Factor[ x^2 - 1 ]`

$Out[4]= (-4 + a) (-2 + a)$

This removes any value assigned to x.

$In[5]:=$ `Clear[x]`

Now this gives the result you expect.

$In[6]:=$ **Factor[x^2 - 1]**

$Out[6]=$ (-1 + x) (1 + x)

■ 2.4.4 Special Forms of Assignment

Particularly when you write procedural programs in *Mathematica*, you will often need to modify the value of a particular variable repeatedly. You can always do this by constructing the new value and explicitly performing an assignment such as *x = value*. *Mathematica*, however, provides special notations for incrementing the values of variables, and for some other common cases.

i++	increment the value of *i* by 1
i--	decrement *i*
++i	pre-increment *i*
--i	pre-decrement *i*
i += di	add *di* to the value of *i*
i -= di	subtract *di* from *i*
*x *= c*	multiply *x* by *c*
x /= c	divide *x* by *c*

Modifying values of variables.

This assigns the value 7x to the variable t.

$In[1]:=$ **t = 7x**

$Out[1]=$ 7 x

This increments the value of t by 18x.

$In[2]:=$ **t += 18x**

$Out[2]=$ 25 x

The value of t has been modified.

$In[3]:=$ **t**

$Out[3]=$ 25 x

This sets t to 8, multiplies its value by 7, then gives the final value of t.

$In[4]:=$ **t = 8; t *= 7; t**

$Out[4]=$ 56

The value of i++ is the value of i *before* the increment is done.

$In[5]:=$ **i=5; Print[i++]; Print[i]**

5
6

The value of ++i is the value of i *after* the increment.

$In[6]:=$ **i=5; Print[++i]; Print[i]**

6
6

$x = y = value$	assign the same value to both x and y
$\{x,\ y\} = \{value_1,\ value_2\}$	assign different values to x and y
$\{x,\ y\} = \{y,\ x\}$	interchange the values of x and y

Assigning values to several variables at a time.

This assigns the value 5 to x and 8 to y.	`In[7]:= {x, y} = {5, 8}`
	`Out[7]= {5, 8}`

This interchanges the values of x and y.	`In[8]:= {x, y} = {y, x}`
	`Out[8]= {8, 5}`

Now x has value 8.	`In[9]:= x`
	`Out[9]= 8`

And y has value 5.	`In[10]:= y`
	`Out[10]= 5`

You can use assignments to lists to permute values of variables in any way.	`In[11]:= {a, b, c} = {1, 2, 3}; {b, a, c} = {a, c, b}; {a, b, c}`
	`Out[11]= {3, 1, 2}`

When you write programs in *Mathematica*, you will sometimes find it convenient to take a list, and successively add elements to it. You can do this using the functions `PrependTo` and `AppendTo`.

`PrependTo[`$v,$ *elem*`]`	prepend *elem* to the value of v
`AppendTo[`$v,$ *elem*`]`	append *elem*
$v = \{v,\ elem\}$	make a nested list containing *elem*

Assignments for modifying lists.

This assigns the value of v to be the list {5, 7, 9}.	`In[12]:= v = {5, 7, 9}`
	`Out[12]= {5, 7, 9}`

This appends the element 11 to the value of v.	`In[13]:= AppendTo[v, 11]`
	`Out[13]= {5, 7, 9, 11}`

Now the value of v has been modified.	`In[14]:= v`
	`Out[14]= {5, 7, 9, 11}`

Although `AppendTo[`$v,$ *elem*`]` is always equivalent to v = `Append[`$v,$ *elem*`]`, it is often a convenient notation. However, you should realize that because of the way *Mathematica* stores lists, it is usually less efficient to add a sequence of elements to a particular list than to create a nested structure that consists, for example, of lists of length 2 at each level. When you have built up such a structure, you can always reduce it to a single list using `Flatten`.

This sets up a nested list structure for `w`.	`In[15]:= w = {1}; Do[ w = {w, k^2}, {k, 1, 4} ]; w` `Out[15]= {{{{{1}, 1}, 4}, 9}, 16}`
You can use `Flatten` to unravel the structure.	`In[16]:= Flatten[w]` `Out[16]= {1, 1, 4, 9, 16}`

■ 2.4.5 Making Definitions for Indexed Objects

In many kinds of calculations, you need to set up "arrays" which contain sequences of expressions, each specified by a certain index. One way to implement arrays in *Mathematica* is by using lists. You can define a list, say $a = \{x, y, z, \dots\}$, then access its elements using $a[[i]]$, or modify them using $a[[i]]$ = *value*. This approach has a drawback, however, in that it requires you to fill in all the elements when you first create the list.

Often, it is more convenient to set up arrays in which you can fill in only those elements that you need at a particular time. You can do this by making definitions for expressions such as $a[i]$.

This defines a value for `a[1]`.	`In[1]:= a[1] = 9` `Out[1]= 9`
This defines a value for `a[2]`.	`In[2]:= a[2] = 7` `Out[2]= 7`
This shows all the values you have defined for expressions associated with `a` so far.	`In[3]:= ?a` `Global`a` `a[1] = 9` `a[2] = 7`
You can define a value for `a[5]`, even though you have not yet given values to `a[3]` and `a[4]`.	`In[3]:= a[5] = 0` `Out[3]= 0`
This generates a list of the values of the `a[i]`.	`In[4]:= Table[a[i], {i, 5}]` `Out[4]= {9, 7, a[3], a[4], 0}`

You can think of the expression `a[i]` as being like an "indexed" or "subscripted" variable. (Section 2.7.8 describes how to make i actually print as a subscript.)

a [*i*] = *value*	add or overwrite a value
a [*i*]	access a value
a [*i*] =.	remove a value
?*a*	show all defined values
Clear[*a*]	clear all defined values
Table[*a*[i], {i, 1, *n*}] or Array[*a*, *n*]	
	convert to an explicit List

Manipulating indexed variables.

When you have an expression of the form *a* [*i*], there is no requirement that the "index" *i* be a number. In fact, *Mathematica* allows the index to be any expression whatsoever. By using indices that are symbols, you can for example build up simple databases in *Mathematica*.

This defines the "object" **area** with "index" **square** to have value 1.	*In[5]:=* **area[square] = 1**
	Out[5]= 1
This adds another result to the **area** "database".	*In[6]:=* **area[triangle] = 1/2**
	Out[6]= $\frac{1}{2}$
Here are the entries in the **area** database so far.	*In[7]:=* **?area**
	Global`area
	area[square] = 1
	area[triangle] = 1/2
You can use these definitions wherever you want. You have not yet assigned a value for **area[pentagon]**.	*In[7]:=* **4 area[square] + area[pentagon]**
	Out[7]= 4 + area[pentagon]

■ 2.4.6 Making Definitions for Functions

Section 1.7.1 discussed how you can define functions in *Mathematica*. In a typical case, you would type in f [x_] = x^2 to define a function f. (Actually, the definitions in Section 1.7.1 used the := operator, rather than the = one. Section 2.4.8 will explain exactly when to use := and =.)

The definition f [x_] = x^2 specifies that whenever *Mathematica* encounters an expression which matches the pattern f [x_], it should replace the expression by x^2. Since the pattern f [x_] matches all expressions of the form f [*anything*], the definition applies to functions f with any "argument".

Function definitions like f [x_] = x^2 can be compared with definitions like f [a] = b for indexed variables discussed in the previous subsection. The definition f [a] = b specifies that whenever the *particular* expression f[a] occurs, it is to be replaced by b. But the definition says nothing about expressions such as f[y], where f appears with another "index".

To define a "function", you need to specify values for expressions of the form f[x], where the argument x can be anything. You can do this by giving a definition for the pattern f[x_], where the pattern object x_ stands for any expression.

f[x] = *value*	definition for a *specific expression x*
f[x_] = *value*	definition for *any expression*, referred to as x

The difference between defining an indexed variable and a function.

Making definitions for f[2] or f[a] can be thought of as being like giving values to various elements of an "array" named f. Making a definition for f[x_] is like giving a value for a set of "array elements" with arbitrary "indices". In fact, you can actually think of any function as being like an array with an arbitrarily variable index.

In mathematical terms, you can think of f as a *mapping*. When you define values for, say, f[1] and f[2], you specify the image of this mapping for various discrete points in its domain. Defining a value for f[x_] specifies the image of f on a continuum of points.

This defines a transformation rule for the *specific expression* f[x].	*In[1]:=* **f[x] = u** *Out[1]=* u
When the specific expression f[x] appears, it is replaced by u. Other expressions of the form f[*argument*] are, however, not modified.	*In[2]:=* **f[x] + f[y]** *Out[2]=* u + f[y]
This defines a value for f with *any expression* as an "argument".	*In[3]:=* **f[x_] = x^2** *Out[3]=* x^2
The old definition for the *specific expression* f[x] is still used, but the new general definition for f[x_] is now used to find a value for f[y].	*In[4]:=* **f[x] + f[y]** *Out[4]=* u + y^2
This removes all definitions for f.	*In[5]:=* **Clear[f]**

Mathematica allows you to define transformation rules for any expression or pattern. You can mix definitions for specific expressions such as f[1] or f[a] with definitions for patterns such as f[x_].

Many kinds of mathematical functions can be set up by mixing specific and general definitions in *Mathematica*. As an example, consider the factorial function. This particular function is in fact built into *Mathematica* (it is written n!). But you can use *Mathematica* definitions to set up the function for yourself.

The standard mathematical definition for the factorial function can be entered almost directly into *Mathematica*, in the form: `f[n_] := n f[n-1]; f[1] = 1`. This definition specifies that for any *n*, `f[n]` should be replaced by *n* `f[n-1]`, except that when *n* is 1, `f[1]` should simply be replaced by 1.

Here is the value of the factorial function with argument 1.	*In[6]:=* **f[1] = 1** *Out[6]=* 1
Here is the general recursion relation for the factorial function.	*In[7]:=* **f[n_] := n f[n-1]**
Now you can use these definitions to find values for the factorial function.	*In[8]:=* **f[10]** *Out[8]=* 3628800
The results are the same as you get from the built-in version of factorial.	*In[9]:=* **10!** *Out[9]=* 3628800

■ 2.4.7 The Ordering of Definitions

When you make a sequence of definitions in *Mathematica*, some may be more general than others. *Mathematica* follows the principle of trying to put more general definitions after more specific ones. This means that special cases of rules are typically tried before more general cases.

This behavior is crucial to the factorial function example given in the previous section. Regardless of the order in which you entered them, *Mathematica* will always put the rule for the special case `f[1]` ahead of the rule for the general case `f[n_]`. This means that when *Mathematica* looks for the value of an expression of the form `f[n]`, it tries the special case `f[1]` first, and only if this does not apply, it tries the general case `f[n_]`. As a result, when you ask for `f[5]`, *Mathematica* will keep on using the general rule until the "end condition" rule for `f[1]` applies.

- *Mathematica* tries to put specific definitions before more general definitions.

Treatment of definitions in *Mathematica*.

If *Mathematica* did not follow the principle of putting special rules before more general ones, then the special rules would always be "shadowed" by more general ones. In the factorial example, if the rule for `f[n_]` was ahead of the rule for `f[1]`, then even when *Mathematica* tried to evaluate `f[1]`, it would use the general `f[n_]` rule, and it would never find the special `f[1]` rule.

Here is a general definition for `f[n_]`.	*In[1]:=* **f[n_] := n f[n-1]**
Here is a definition for the special case `f[1]`.	*In[2]:=* **f[1] = 1** *Out[2]=* 1

Mathematica puts the special case before
the general one.

```
In[3]:= ?f

Global`f

f[1] = 1

f[n_] := n*f[n - 1]
```

In the factorial function example used above, it is clear which rule is more general. Often, however, there is no definite ordering in generality of the rules you give. In such cases, *Mathematica* simply tries the rules in the order you give them.

These rules have no definite ordering in
generality.

```
In[3]:= log[x_ y_] := log[x] + log[y] ; log[x_^n_] := n log[x]
```

Mathematica stores the rules in the order
you gave them.

```
In[4]:= ?log

Global`log

log[(x_)*(y_)] := log[x] + log[y]

log[(x_)^(n_)] := n*log[x]
```

This rule is a special case of the rule for
log[x_ y_].

```
In[4]:= log[2 x_] := log[x] + log2
```

Mathematica puts the special rule before
the more general one.

```
In[5]:= ?log

Global`log

log[2*(x_)] := log[x] + log2

log[(x_)*(y_)] := log[x] + log[y]

log[(x_)^(n_)] := n*log[x]
```

Although in many practical cases, *Mathematica* can recognize when one rule is more general than another, you should realize that this is not always possible. For example, if two rules both contain complicated /; conditions, it may not be possible to work out which is more general, and, in fact, there may not be a definite ordering. Whenever the appropriate ordering is not clear, *Mathematica* stores rules in the order you give them.

■ 2.4.8 Immediate and Delayed Definitions

You may have noticed that there are two different ways to make assignments in *Mathematica*: *lhs* = *rhs* and *lhs* := *rhs*. The basic difference between these forms is *when* the expression *rhs* is evaluated. *lhs* = *rhs* is an *immediate assignment*, in which *rhs* is evaluated at the time when the assignment is made. *lhs* := *rhs*, on the other hand, is a *delayed assignment*, in which *rhs* is not evaluated when the assignment is made, but is instead evaluated each time the value of *lhs* is requested.

lhs = *rhs* (immediate assignment)	*rhs* is evaluated when the assignment is made
lhs := *rhs* (delayed assignment)	*rhs* is evaluated each time the value of *lhs* is requested

The two types of assignments in *Mathematica*.

This uses the := operator to define the function **ex**.

```
In[1]:= ex[x_] := Expand[(1 + x)^2]
```

Because := was used, the definition is maintained in an unevaluated form.

```
In[2]:= ?ex
Global`ex
ex[x_] := Expand[(1 + x)^2]
```

When you make an assignment with the = operator, the right-hand side is evaluated immediately.

```
In[2]:= iex[x_] = Expand[(1 + x)^2]
```

$$Out[2]= 1 + 2 x + x^2$$

The definition now stored is the result of the **Expand** command.

```
In[3]:= ?iex
Global`iex
iex[x_] = 1 + 2*x + x^2
```

When you execute **ex**, the **Expand** is performed.

```
In[3]:= ex[y + 2]
```

$$Out[3]= 9 + 6 y + y^2$$

iex simply substitutes its argument into the already expanded form, giving a different answer.

```
In[4]:= iex[y + 2]
```

$$Out[4]= 1 + 2 (2 + y) + (2 + y)^2$$

As you can see from the example above, both = and := can be useful in defining functions, but they have different meanings, and you must be careful about which one to use in a particular case.

One rule of thumb is the following. If you think of an assignment as giving the final "value" of an expression, use the = operator. If instead you think of the assignment as specifying a "command" for finding the value, use the := operator. If in doubt, it is usually better to use := than =.

lhs = *rhs*	*rhs* is intended to be the "final value" of *lhs* (*e.g.*, f[x_] = 1 - x^2)
lhs := *rhs*	*rhs* gives a "command" or "program" to be executed whenever you ask for the value of *lhs* (*e.g.*, f[x_] := Expand[1 - x^2])

Interpretations of assignments with the = and := operators.

Although := is probably used more often than = in defining functions, there is one important case in which you must use = to define a function.

If you do a calculation, and get an answer in terms of a symbolic parameter x, you often want to go on and find results for various specific values of x. One way to do this is to use the /. operator to apply appropriate rules for x in each case. It is usually more convenient however, to use = to define a function whose argument is x.

Here is an expression involving x.	`In[5]:= D[Log[Sin[x]]^2, x]`
	`Out[5]= 2 Cot[x] Log[Sin[x]]`
This defines a function whose argument is the value to be taken for x.	`In[6]:= dlog[x_] = %`
	`Out[6]= 2 Cot[x] Log[Sin[x]]`
Here is the result when x is taken to be 1 + a.	`In[7]:= dlog[1 + a]`
	`Out[7]= 2 Cot[1 + a] Log[Sin[1 + a]]`

An important point to notice in the example above is that there is nothing special about the name x that appears in the x_ pattern. It is just a symbol, indistinguishable from an x that appears in any other expression.

$f[x\_]$ = $expr$	define a function which gives the value $expr$ for any particular value of x

Defining functions for evaluating expressions.

You can use = and := not only to define functions, but also to assign values to variables. If you type x = $value$, then $value$ is immediately evaluated, and the result is assigned to x. On the other hand, if you type x := $value$, then $value$ is not immediately evaluated. Instead, it is maintained in an unevaluated form, and is evaluated afresh each time x is used.

This evaluates Random[ ] to find a pseudorandom number, then assigns this number to r1.	`In[8]:= r1 = Random[ ]`
	`Out[8]= 0.104826`
Here Random[ ] is maintained in an unevaluated form, to be evaluated afresh each time r2 is used.	`In[9]:= r2 := Random[ ]`
Here are values for r1 and r2.	`In[10]:= {r1, r2}`
	`Out[10]= {0.104826, 0.767415}`
The value of r1 never changes. Every time r2 is used, however, a new pseudorandom number is generated.	`In[11]:= {r1, r2}`
	`Out[11]= {0.104826, 0.216417}`

The distinction between immediate and delayed assignments is particularly important when you set up chains of assignments.

This defines a to be 1.

In[12]:= **a = 1**

Out[12]= 1

Here a + 2 is evaluated to give 3, and the result is assigned to be the value of ri.

In[13]:= **ri = a + 2**

Out[13]= 3

Here a + 2 is maintained in an unevaluated form, to be evaluated every time the value of rd is requested.

In[14]:= **rd := a + 2**

In this case, ri and rd give the same values.

In[15]:= **{ri, rd}**

Out[15]= {3, 3}

Now the value of a is changed.

In[16]:= **a = 2**

Out[16]= 2

Now rd uses the new value for a, while ri keeps its original value.

In[17]:= **{ri, rd}**

Out[17]= {3, 4}

You can use delayed assignments such as *t := rhs* to set up variables whose values you can find in a variety of different "environments". Every time you ask for *t*, the expression *rhs* is evaluated using the current values of the objects on which it depends.

The right-hand side of the delayed assignment is maintained in an unevaluated form.

In[18]:= **t := {a, Factor[x^a - 1]}**

This sets a to 4, then finds the value of t.

In[19]:= **a = 4; t**

Out[19]= {4, (-1 + x) (1 + x) (1 + x^2)}

Here a is 6.

In[20]:= **a = 6; t**

Out[20]= {6, (-1 + x) (1 + x) (1 - x + x^2) (1 + x + x^2)}

In the example above, the symbol a acts as a "global variable", whose value affects the value of t. When you have a large number of parameters, many of which change only occasionally, you may find this kind of setup convenient. However, you should realize that implicit or hidden dependence of one variable on others can often become quite confusing. When possible, you should make all dependencies explicit, by defining functions which take all necessary parameters as arguments.

lhs -> *rhs*	*rhs* is evaluated when the rule is given
lhs :> *rhs*	*rhs* is evaluated when the rule is used

Two types of transformation rules in *Mathematica*.

Just as you can make immediate and delayed assignments in *Mathematica*, so you can also set up immediate and delayed transformation rules.

The right-hand side of this rule is evaluated when you give the rule.

```
In[21]:= f[x_] -> Expand[(1 + x)^2]

Out[21]= f[x_] -> 1 + 2 x + x^2
```

A rule like this is probably not particularly useful.

```
In[22]:= f[x_] -> Expand[x]

Out[22]= f[x_] -> x
```

Here the right-hand side of the rule is maintained in an unevaluated form, to be evaluated every time the rule is used.

```
In[23]:= f[x_] :> Expand[x]

Out[23]= f[x_] :> Expand[x]
```

Applying the rule causes the expansion to be done.

```
In[24]:= f[(1 + p)^2] /. f[x_] :> Expand[x]

Out[24]= 1 + 2 p + p^2
```

In analogy with assignments, you should typically use -> when you want to replace an expression with a definite value, and you should use :> when you want to give a command for finding the value.

■ 2.4.9 Functions That Remember Values They Have Found

When you make a function definition using :=, the value of the function is recomputed every time you ask for it. In some kinds of calculations, you may end up asking for the same function value many times. You can save time in these cases by having *Mathematica* remember all the function values it finds. Here is an "idiom" for defining a function that does this.

$f[x\_]$:= $f[x]$ = *rhs*	define a function which remembers values that it finds

Defining a function that remembers values it finds.

This defines a function f which stores all values that it finds.

```
In[1]:= f[x_] := f[x] = f[x - 1] + f[x - 2]
```

Here are the end conditions for the recursive function f.

```
In[2]:= f[0] = f[1] = 1

Out[2]= 1
```

Here is the original definition of **f**.	*In[3]:=* **?f**
	Global`f
	f[0] = 1
	f[1] = 1
	f[x_] := f[x] = f[x - 1] + f[x - 2]
This computes **f[5]**. The computation involves finding the sequence of values **f[5]**, **f[4]**, ... **f[2]**.	*In[3]:=* **f[5]**
	Out[3]= 8
All the values of **f** found so far are explicitly stored.	*In[4]:=* **?f**
	Global`f
	f[0] = 1
	f[1] = 1
	f[2] = 2
	f[3] = 3
	f[4] = 5
	f[5] = 8
	f[x_] := f[x] = f[x - 1] + f[x - 2]
If you ask for **f[5]** again, *Mathematica* can just look up the value immediately; it does not have to recompute it.	*In[4]:=* **f[5]**
	Out[4]= 8

You can see how a definition like f[x_] := f[x] = f[x-1] + f[x-2] works. The function f[x_] is defined to be the "program" f[x] = f[x-1] + f[x-2]. When you ask for a value of the function f, the "program" is executed. The program first calculates the value of f[x-1] + f[x-2], then saves the result as f[x].

It is often a good idea to use functions that remember values when you implement mathematical *recursion relations* in *Mathematica*. In a typical case, a recursion relation gives the value of a function f with an integer argument x in terms of values of the same function with arguments $x-1$, $x-2$, etc. The Fibonacci function definition $f(x) = f(x - 1) + f(x - 2)$ used above is an example of this kind of recursion relation. The point is that if you calculate say $f(10)$ by just applying the recursion relation over and over again, you end up having to recalculate quantities like $f(5)$ many times. In a case like this, it is therefore better just to *remember* the value of $f(5)$, and look it up when you need it, rather than having to recalculate it.

There is of course a trade-off involved in remembering values. It is faster to find a particular value, but it takes more memory space to store all of them. You should usually define functions to remember values only if the total number of different values that will be produced is comparatively small, or the expense of recomputing them is very great.

■ 2.4.10 Associating Definitions with Different Symbols

When you make a definition in the form *f[args]* = *rhs* or *f[args]* := *rhs*, *Mathematica* associates your definition with the object *f*. This means, for example, that such definitions are displayed when you type ?*f*. In general, definitions for expressions in which the symbol *f* appears as the head are termed *downvalues* of *f*.

Mathematica however also supports *upvalues*, which allow definitions to be associated with symbols that do not appear directly as their head.

Consider for example a definition like Exp[g[x_]] := *rhs*. One possibility is that this definition could be associated with the symbol Exp, and considered as a downvalue of Exp. This is however probably not the best thing either from the point of view of organization or efficiency.

Better is to consider Exp[g[x_]] := *rhs* to be associated with g, and to correspond to an upvalue of g.

f[args] := *rhs*	define a downvalue for *f*
f[g[args], ...] ^:= *rhs*	define an upvalue for *g*

Associating definitions with different symbols.

This is taken to define a downvalue for **f**.

```
In[1]:= f[g[x_]] := fg[x]
```

You can see the definition when you ask about **f**.

```
In[2]:= ?f
Global`f
f[g[x_]] := fg[x]
```

This defines an upvalue for g.

```
In[2]:= g/: Exp[g[x_]] := expg[x]
```

The definition is associated with g.

```
In[3]:= ?g
Global`g
Exp[g[x_]] ^:= expg[x]
```

It is not associated with Exp.

```
In[3]:= ?Exp
Exp[z] is the exponential function.
```

The definition is used to evaluate this expression.

```
In[3]:= Exp[g[5]]
Out[3]= expg[5]
```

In simple cases, you will get the same answers to calculations whether you give a definition for *f[g[x]]* as a downvalue for *f* or an upvalue for *g*. However, one of the two choices is usually much more natural and efficient than the other.

A good rule of thumb is that a definition for *f[g[x]]* should be given as an upvalue for *g* in cases where the function *f* is more common than *g*. Thus, for example, in the case of Exp[g[x]], Exp is a built-in *Mathematica* function, while *g* is presumably a function you have added. In such a case, you will typically think of definitions for Exp[*g*[*x*]] as giving relations satisfied by *g*. As a result, it is more natural to treat the definitions as upvalues for *g* than as downvalues for Exp.

This gives the definition as an upvalue for g.	`In[4]:= g/: g[x_] + g[y_] := gplus[x, y]`

Here are the definitions for g so far.	`In[5]:= ?g` `Global`g`  `Exp[g[x_]] ^:= expg[x]`  `g[x_] + g[y_] ^:= gplus[x, y]`

The definition for a sum of g's is used whenever possible.	`In[5]:= g[5] + g[7]`
	
	`Out[5]= gplus[5, 7]`

Since the full form of the pattern g[x_] + g[y_] is Plus[g[x_], g[y_]], a definition for this pattern could be given as a downvalue for Plus. It is almost always better, however, to give the definition as an upvalue for g.

In general, whenever *Mathematica* encounters a particular function, it tries all the definitions you have given for that function. If you had made the definition for g[x_] + g[y_] a downvalue for Plus, then *Mathematica* would have tried this definition whenever Plus occurs. The definition would thus be tested every time *Mathematica* added expressions together, making this very common operation slower in all cases.

However, by giving a definition for g[x_] + g[y_] as an upvalue for g, you associate the definition with g. In this case, *Mathematica* only tries the definition when it finds a g inside a function such as Plus. Since g presumably occurs much less frequently than Plus, this is a much more efficient procedure.

$f[g]$ ^=*value* or $f[g[args]]$ ^=*value*	make assignments to be associated with *g*, rather than *f*
$f[g]$ ^:=*value* or $f[g[args]]$ ^:=*value*	make delayed assignments associated with *g*
$f[arg_1, arg_2, \ldots]$ ^=*value*	make assignments associated with the heads of *all* the arg_i

Shorter ways to define upvalues.

A typical use of upvalues is in setting up a "database" of properties of a particular object. With upvalues, you can associate each definition you make with the object that it concerns, rather than with the property you are specifying.

This defines an upvalue for square which gives its area.	`In[6]:= area[square] ^= 1`
	
	`Out[6]= 1`

This adds a definition for the perimeter.	*In[7]:=* **perimeter[square] ^= 4**
	Out[7]= 4
Both definitions are now associated with the object **square**.	*In[8]:=* **?square**
	Global`square
	area[square] ^= 1
	perimeter[square] ^= 4

In general, you can associate definitions for an expression with any symbol that occurs at a sufficiently high level in the expression. With an expression of the form $f[args]$, you can define an upvalue for a symbol g so long as either g itself, or an object with head g, occurs in $args$. Similarly, you can give an upvalue for g with an expression of the form $g[par][args]$, where g effectively appears as the head of the head of the whole expression. If g occurs at a lower level in an expression, you cannot associate definitions with it.

g occurs as the head of an argument, so you can associate a definition with it.	*In[8]:=* **g/: h[w[x_], g[y_]] := hwg[x, y]**
Here g appears too deep in the left-hand side for you to associate a definition with it.	*In[9]:=* **g/: h[w[g[x_]], y_] := hw[x, y]**
	TagSetDelayed::tagpos:
	Tag g in h[w[g[x_]], y_]
	is not in a valid position for assignment.
	Out[9]= $Failed

$f[\dots\,]\ :=\ rhs$	downvalue for f
$f/:\ f[g[\dots\,]][\dots\,]\ :=\ rhs$	downvalue for f
$g/:\ f[\dots\,,\ g,\ \dots\,]\ :=\ rhs$	upvalue for g
$g/:\ f[\dots\,,\ g[\dots\,],\ \dots\,]\ :=\ rhs$	upvalue for g

Possible positions for symbols in definitions.

As discussed in Section 2.1.2, you can use *Mathematica* symbols as "tags", to indicate the "type" of an expression. For example, complex numbers in *Mathematica* are represented internally in the form Complex[*x*, *y*], where the symbol Complex serves as a tag to indicate that the object is a complex number.

Upvalues provide a convenient mechanism for specifying how operations act on objects that are tagged to have a certain type. For example, you might want to introduce a class of abstract mathematical objects of type quat. You can represent each object of this type by a *Mathematica* expression of the form quat[*data*].

In a typical case, you might want quat objects to have special properties with respect to arithmetic operations such as addition and multiplication. You can set up such properties by defining upvalues for quat with respect to Plus and Times.

This defines an upvalue for quat with respect to Plus.	`In[10]:= quat[x_] + quat[y_] ^:= quat[x + y]`

The upvalue you have defined is used to simplify this expression.	`In[11]:= quat[a] + quat[b] + quat[c]`
	`Out[11]= quat[a + b + c]`

When you define an upvalue for quat with respect to an operation like Plus, what you are effectively doing is to extend the domain of the Plus operation to include quat objects. You are telling *Mathematica* to use special rules for addition in the case where the things to be added together are quat objects.

In defining addition for quat objects, you could always have a special addition operation, say quatPlus, to which you assign an appropriate downvalue. It is usually much more convenient, however, to use the standard *Mathematica* Plus operation to represent addition, but then to "overload" this operation by specifying special behavior when quat objects are encountered.

You can think of upvalues as a way to implement certain aspects of object-oriented programming. A symbol like quat represents a particular type of object. Then the various upvalues for quat specify "methods" that define how quat objects should behave under certain operations, or on receipt of certain "messages".

■ 2.4.11 Defining Numerical Values

If you make a definition such as f[x_] := *value*, *Mathematica* will use the value you give for any f function it encounters. In some cases, however, you may want to define a value that is to be used specifically when you ask for numerical values.

expr = *value*	define a value to be used whenever possible
N[*expr*] = *value*	define a value to be used for numerical approximation

Defining ordinary and numerical values.

This defines a numerical value for the function f.	`In[1]:= N[f[x_]] := Sum[x^-i/i^2, {i, 20}]`

Defining the numerical value does not tell *Mathematica* anything about the ordinary value of f.	`In[2]:= f[2] + f[5]`
	`Out[2]= f[2] + f[5]`

If you ask for a numerical approximation, however, *Mathematica* uses the numerical values you have defined.	`In[3]:= N[%]`
	`Out[3]= 0.793244`

You can define numerical values for both functions and symbols. The numerical values are used by all numerical *Mathematica* functions, including `NIntegrate`, `FindRoot` and so on.

N[*expr*] = *value*	define a numerical value to be used when default numerical precision is requested
N[*expr*, *n*] = *value*	define a numerical value to be used when *n*-digit precision is requested

Defining numerical values that depend on numerical precision.

This defines a numerical value for the symbol `const`, using 4n + 5 terms in the product for n-digit precision.

```
In[4]:= N[const, n_] := Product[1 - 2^-i, {i, 2, 4n + 5}]
```

Here is the value of `const`, computed to 30-digit precision using the value you specified.

```
In[5]:= N[const, 30]

Out[5]= 0.577576190173204842557799443858
```

Mathematica treats numerical values essentially like upvalues. When you define a numerical value for *f*, *Mathematica* effectively enters your definition as an upvalue for *f* with respect to the numerical evaluation operation N.

■ 2.4.12 Modifying Built-in Functions

Mathematica allows you to define transformation rules for any expression. You can define such rules not only for functions that you add to *Mathematica*, but also for intrinsic functions that are already built into *Mathematica*. As a result, you can enhance, or modify, the features of built-in *Mathematica* functions.

This capability is powerful, but potentially dangerous. *Mathematica* will always follow the rules you give it. This means that if the rules you give are incorrect, then *Mathematica* will give you incorrect answers.

To avoid the possibility of changing built-in functions by mistake, *Mathematica* "protects" all built-in functions from redefinition. If you want to give a definition for a built-in function, you have to remove the protection first. After you give the definition, you should usually restore the protection, to prevent future mistakes.

Unprotect[*f*]	remove protection
Protect[*f*]	add protection

Protection for functions.

Built-in functions are usually "protected", so you cannot redefine them.

```
In[1]:= Log[7] = 2
Set::write: Tag Log in Log[7] is Protected.
Out[1]= 2
```

This removes protection for Log.

```
In[2]:= Unprotect[Log]
Out[2]= {Log}
```

Now you can give your own definitions for Log. This particular definition is not mathematically correct, but *Mathematica* will still allow you to give it.

```
In[3]:= Log[7] = 2
Out[3]= 2
```

Mathematica will use your definitions whenever it can, whether they are mathematically correct or not.

```
In[4]:= Log[7] + Log[3]
Out[4]= 2 + Log[3]
```

This removes the incorrect definition for Log.

```
In[5]:= Log[7] =.
```

This restores the protection for Log.

```
In[6]:= Protect[Log]
Out[6]= {Log}
```

Definitions you give can override built-in features of *Mathematica*. In general, *Mathematica* tries to use your definitions before it uses built-in definitions.

The rules that are built into *Mathematica* are intended to be appropriate for the broadest range of calculations. In specific cases, however, you may not like what the built-in rules do. In such cases, you can give your own rules to override the ones that are built in.

There is a built-in rule for simplifying Exp[Log[*expr*]].

```
In[7]:= Exp[Log[y]]
Out[7]= y
```

You can give your own rule for Exp[Log[*expr*]], overriding the built-in rule.

```
In[8]:= (
        Unprotect[Exp] ;
        Exp[Log[expr_]] := explog[expr] ;
        Protect[Exp] ;
      )
```

Now your rule is used, rather than the built-in one.

```
In[9]:= Exp[Log[y]]
Out[9]= explog[y]
```

■ 2.4.13 Advanced Topic: Manipulating Value Lists

DownValues[*f*]	give the list of downvalues of *f*
UpValues[*f*]	give the list of upvalues of *f*
DownValues[*f*] = *rules*	set the downvalues of *f*
UpValues[*f*] = *rules*	set the upvalues of *f*

Finding and setting values of symbols.

Mathematica effectively stores all definitions you give as lists of transformation rules. When a particular symbol is encountered, the lists of rules associated with it are tried.

Under most circumstances, you do not need direct access to the actual transformation rules associated with definitions you have given. Instead, you can simply use *lhs* = *rhs* and *lhs* =. to add and remove rules. In some cases, however, you may find it useful to have direct access to the actual rules.

Here is a definition for f.

$$In[1]:= \text{f[x\_]} := \text{x}^2$$

This gives the explicit rule corresponding to the definition you made for f.

$$In[2]:= \text{DownValues[f]}$$

$$Out[2]= \{\text{Literal[f[x\_]]} :> \text{x}^2\}$$

Notice that the rules returned by DownValues and UpValues are set up so that neither their left- nor right-hand sides get evaluated. The left-hand sides are wrapped in Literal, and the rules are delayed, so that the right-hand sides are not immediately evaluated.

As discussed in Section 2.4.6, *Mathematica* tries to order definitions so that more specific ones appear before more general ones. In general, however, there is no unique way to make this ordering, and you may want to choose a different ordering from the one that *Mathematica* chooses by default. You can do this by reordering the list of rules obtained from DownValues or UpValues.

Here are some definitions for the object g.

$$In[3]:= \text{g[x\_ + y\_]} := \text{gp[x, y]} ; \quad \text{g[x\_ y\_]} := \text{gm[x, y]}$$

This shows the default ordering used for the definitions.

$$In[4]:= \text{DownValues[g]}$$

$$Out[4]= \{\text{Literal[g[(x\_) + (y\_)]]} :> \text{gp[x, y]},$$
$$\text{Literal[g[(x\_) (y\_)]]} :> \text{gm[x, y]}\}$$

This reverses the order of the definitions for g.

$$In[5]:= \text{DownValues[g]} = \text{Reverse[DownValues[g]]}$$

$$Out[5]= \{\text{Literal[g[(x\_) (y\_)]]} :> \text{gm[x, y]},$$
$$\text{Literal[g[(x\_) + (y\_)]]} :> \text{gp[x, y]}\}$$

2.5 Evaluation of Expressions

■ 2.5.1 Principles of Evaluation

The fundamental operation that *Mathematica* performs is *evaluation*. Whenever you enter an expression, *Mathematica* evaluates the expression, then returns the result.

Evaluation in *Mathematica* works by applying a sequence of definitions. The definitions can either be ones you explicitly entered, or ones that are built into *Mathematica*.

Thus, for example, *Mathematica* evaluates the expression 6 + 7 using a built-in procedure for adding integers. Similarly, *Mathematica* evaluates the algebraic expression x - 3x + 1 using a built-in simplification procedure. If you had made the definition x = 5, then *Mathematica* would use this definition to reduce x - 3x + 1 to -9.

The two most central concepts in *Mathematica* are probably *expressions* and *evaluation*. Section 2.1 discussed how all the different kinds of objects that *Mathematica* handles are represented in a uniform way using expressions. This section describes how all the operations that *Mathematica* can perform can also be viewed in a uniform way as examples of evaluation.

Computation	5 + 6	$\longrightarrow$ 13
Simplification	x - 3x + 1	$\longrightarrow$ 1 - 2x
Execution	x = 5	$\longrightarrow$ 5

Some interpretations of evaluation.

Mathematica is an *infinite evaluation* system. When you enter an expression, *Mathematica* will keep on using definitions it knows until it gets a result to which no definitions apply.

This defines x1 in terms of x2, and then defines x2.	*In[1]:=* **x1 = x2 + 2 ; x2 = 7** *Out[1]=* 7
If you ask for x1, *Mathematica* uses all the definitions it knows to give you a result.	*In[2]:=* **x1** *Out[2]=* 9
Here is a recursive definition in which the factorial function is defined in terms of itself.	*In[3]:=* **fac[1] = 1 ; fac[n_] := n fac[n-1]**
If you ask for fac[10], *Mathematica* will keep on applying the definitions you have given until the result it gets no longer changes.	*In[4]:=* **fac[10]** *Out[4]=* 3628800

When *Mathematica* has used all the definitions it knows, it gives whatever expression it has obtained as the result. Sometimes the result may be an object such as a number. But usually the result is an expression in which some objects are represented in a symbolic form.

Mathematica uses its built-in definitions for simplifying sums, but knows no definitions for `f[3]`, so leaves this in symbolic form.	`In[5]:= f[3] + 4f[3] + 1`
	
	`Out[5]= 1 + 5 f[3]`

Mathematica follows the principle of applying definitions until the result it gets no longer changes. This means that if you take the final result that *Mathematica* gives, and enter it as *Mathematica* input, you will get back the same result again. (There are some subtle cases discussed in Section 2.5.12 in which this does not occur.)

If you type in a result from *Mathematica*, you get back the same expression again.	`In[6]:= 1 + 5 f[3]`
	
	`Out[6]= 1 + 5 f[3]`

At any given time, *Mathematica* can only use those definitions that it knows at that time. If you add more definitions later, however, *Mathematica* will be able to use these. The results you get from *Mathematica* may change in this case.

Here is a new definition for the function `f`.	`In[7]:= f[x_] = x^2`
	
	`Out[7]= x^2`

With the new definition, the results you get can change.	`In[8]:= 1 + 5 f[3]`
	
	`Out[8]= 46`

The simplest examples of evaluation involve using definitions such as `f[x_] = x^2` which transform one expression directly into another. But evaluation is also the process used to execute programs written in *Mathematica*. Thus, for example, if you have a procedure consisting of a sequence of *Mathematica* expressions, some perhaps representing conditionals and loops, the execution of this procedure corresponds to the evaluation of these expressions. Sometimes the evaluation process may involve evaluating a particular expression several times, as in a loop.

The expression `Print[zzzz]` is evaluated three times during the evaluation of the Do expression.	`In[9]:= Do[Print[zzzz], {3}]`
	
	`zzzz`
	`zzzz`
	`zzzz`

■ 2.5.2 Reducing Expressions to Standard Form

The built-in functions in *Mathematica* operate in a wide variety of ways. But many of the mathematical functions share an important approach: they are set up so as to reduce classes of mathematical expressions to standard forms.

The built-in definitions for the `Plus` function, for example, are set up to write any sum of terms in a standard, unparenthesized, form. The associativity of addition means that expressions like (a + b) + c, a + (b + c) and a + b + c are all equivalent. But for many purposes it is convenient for all these forms to be reduced to the single standard form a + b + c. The built-in definitions for Plus are set up to do this.

Through the built-in definitions for Plus, this expression is reduced to a standard unparenthesized form.

$In[1]:= (a + b) + c$

$Out[1]= a + b + c$

Whenever *Mathematica* knows that a function is associative, it tries to remove parentheses (or nested invocations of the function) to get the function into a standard "flattened" form.

A function like addition is not only associative, but also commutative, which means that expressions like a + c + b and a + b + c with terms in different orders are equal. Once again, *Mathematica* tries to put all such expressions into a "standard" form. The standard form it chooses is the one in which all the terms are in a definite order, corresponding roughly to alphabetical order.

Mathematica sorts the terms in this sum into a standard order.

$In[2]:= c + a + b$

$Out[2]= a + b + c$

flat (associative)	$f[f[a, b], c]$ is equivalent to $f[a, b, c]$, etc.
orderless (commutative)	$f[b, a]$ is equivalent to $f[a, b]$, etc.

Two important properties that *Mathematica* uses in reducing certain functions to standard form.

There are several reasons to try and put expressions into standard forms. The most important is that if two expressions are really in standard form, it is obvious whether or not they are equal.

When the two sums are put into standard order, they are immediately seen to be equal, so that two f's cancel, leaving the result 0.

$In[3]:= f[a + c + b] - f[c + a + b]$

$Out[3]= 0$

You could imagine finding out whether a + c + b was equal to c + a + b by testing all possible orderings of each sum. It is clear that simply reducing both sums to standard form is a much more efficient procedure.

One might think that *Mathematica* should somehow automatically reduce *all* mathematical expressions to a single standard canonical form. With all but the simplest kinds of expressions, however, it is quite easy to see that you do not want the *same* standard form for all purposes.

For polynomials, for example, there are two obvious standard forms, which are good for different purposes. The first standard form for a polynomial is a simple sum of terms, as would be generated in *Mathematica* by applying the function Expand. This standard form is most appropriate if you need to add and subtract polynomials.

There is, however, another possible standard form that you can use for polynomials. By applying Factor, you can write any polynomial as a product of irreducible factors. This canonical form is useful if you want to do operations like division.

Expanded and factored form are in a sense both equally good standard forms for polynomials. Which one you decide to use simply depends on what you want to use it for. As a result, *Mathematica* does not automatically put polynomials into one of these two forms. Instead, it gives you functions like Expand and Factor that allow you explicitly to put polynomials in whatever form you want.

Here is a list of two polynomials that are mathematically equal.

```
In[4]:= t = {x^2 - 1, (x + 1)(x - 1)}

Out[4]= {-1 + x , (-1 + x) (1 + x)}
                2
```

You can write both of them in expanded form just by applying Expand. In this form, the equality of the polynomials is obvious.

```
In[5]:= Expand[t]

Out[5]= {-1 + x , -1 + x }
                2        2
```

You can also see that the polynomials are equal by writing them both in factored form.

```
In[6]:= Factor[t]

Out[6]= {(-1 + x) (1 + x), (-1 + x) (1 + x)}
```

Although it is clear that you do not always want expressions reduced to the *same* standard form, you may wonder whether it is at least *possible* to reduce all expressions to *some* standard form.

There is a basic result in the mathematical theory of computation which shows that this is, in fact, not always possible. You cannot guarantee that any finite sequence of transformations will take any two arbitrarily chosen expressions to a standard form.

In a sense, this is not particularly surprising. If you could in fact reduce all mathematical expressions to a standard form, then it would be quite easy to tell whether any two expressions were equal. The fact that so many of the difficult problems of mathematics can be stated as questions about the equality of expressions suggests that this can in fact be difficult.

■ 2.5.3 Attributes

Definitions such as f[x_] = x^2 specify *values* for functions. Sometimes, however, you need to specify general properties of functions, without necessarily giving explicit values.

Mathematica provides a selection of *attributes* that you can use to specify various properties of functions. For example, you can use the attribute Flat to specify that a particular function is "flat", so that nested invocations are automatically flattened, and it behaves as if it were associative.

This assigns the attribute Flat to the function f.

```
In[1]:= SetAttributes[f, Flat]
```

Now f behaves as a flat, or associative, function, so that nested invocations are automatically flattened.

```
In[2]:= f[f[a, b], c]

Out[2]= f[a, b, c]
```

Attributes like `Flat` can affect not only evaluation, but also operations such as pattern matching. If you give definitions or transformation rules for a function, you must be sure to have specified the attributes of the function first.

Here is a definition for the flat function f.

In[3]:= **f[x_, x_] := f[x]**

Because f is flat, the definition is automatically applied to every subsequence of arguments.

In[4]:= **f[a, a, a, b, b, b, c, c]**

Out[4]= f[a, b, c]

`Attributes[`*f*`]`	give the attributes of *f*
`Attributes[`*f*`] = {`*attr₁* , *attr₂* , ... `}`	set the attributes of *f*
`Attributes[`*f*`] = {}`	set *f* to have no attributes
`SetAttributes[`*f, attr*`]`	add *attr* to the attributes of *f*
`ClearAttributes[`*f, attr*`]`	remove *attr* from the attributes of *f*

Manipulating attributes of symbols.

This shows the attributes assigned to f.

In[5]:= **Attributes[f]**

Out[5]= {Flat}

This removes the attributes assigned to f.

In[6]:= **Attributes[f] = { }**

Out[6]= {}

Orderless	orderless, commutative, function (arguments are sorted into standard order)
Flat	flat, associative, function (arguments are "flattened out")
OneIdentity	$f[f[a]]$, etc. are equivalent to a for pattern matching
Listable	f is automatically "threaded" over lists that appear as arguments (*e.g.*, $f[\{a,b\}]$ becomes $\{f[a], f[b]\}$)
Constant	all derivatives of f are zero
Protected	values of f cannot be changed
Locked	attributes of f cannot be changed
ReadProtected	values of f cannot be read
HoldFirst	the first argument of f is not evaluated
HoldRest	all but the first argument of f is not evaluated
HoldAll	all the arguments of f are not evaluated
Temporary	f is a local variable, removed when no longer used
Stub	Needs is automatically called if f is ever explicitly input

The complete list of attributes for symbols in *Mathematica*.

Here are the attributes for the built-in function Plus.

```
In[7]:= Attributes[Plus]

Out[7]= {Flat, Listable, OneIdentity, Orderless, Protected}
```

An important attribute assigned to all built-in mathematical functions in *Mathematica* is the attribute Listable. This attribute specifies that a function should automatically be distributed or "threaded" over lists that appear as its arguments. This means that the function effectively gets applied separately to each element in any lists that appear as its arguments.

The built-in Sqrt function is Listable.

```
In[8]:= Sqrt[{5, 8, 11}]

Out[8]= {Sqrt[5], 2 Sqrt[2], Sqrt[11]}
```

This defines the function p to be listable.

```
In[9]:= SetAttributes[p, Listable]
```

Now p is automatically threaded over lists that appear as its arguments.

```
In[10]:= p[{a, b, c}, d]

Out[10]= {p[a, d], p[b, d], p[c, d]}
```

Many of the attributes you can assign to functions in *Mathematica* directly affect the evaluation of those functions. Some attributes, however, affect only other aspects of the treatment of functions. For example, the attribute OneIdentity affects only pattern matching, as discussed in Section 2.3.7. Similarly, the attribute Constant is only relevant in differentiation, and operations that rely on differentiation.

The Protected attribute affects assignments. *Mathematica* does not allow you to make any definition associated with a symbol that carries this attribute. The functions Protect and Unprotect discussed in Section 2.4.12 can be used as alternatives to SetAttributes and ClearAttributes to set and clear this attribute. As discussed in Section 2.4.12 most built-in *Mathematica* objects are initially protected so that you do not make definitions for them by mistake.

Here is a definition for the function g.	`In[11]:= g[x_] = x + 1`
	`Out[11]= 1 + x`
This sets the Protected attribute for g.	`In[12]:= Protect[g]`
	`Out[12]= {g}`
Now you cannot modify the definition of g.	`In[13]:= g[x_] = x`
	`Set::write: Tag g in g[x_] is Protected.`
	`Out[13]= x`

You can usually see the definitions you have made for a particular symbol by typing ?*f*, or by using a variety of built-in *Mathematica* functions. However, if you set the attribute ReadProtected, *Mathematica* will not allow you to look at the definition of a particular symbol. It will nevertheless continue to use the definitions in performing evaluation.

Although you cannot modify it, you can still look at the definition of g.	`In[14]:= ?g`
	`Global`g`
	`Attributes[g] = {Protected}`
	`g[x_] = 1 + x`
This sets the ReadProtected attribute for g.	`In[14]:= SetAttributes[g, ReadProtected]`
Now you can no longer read the definition of g.	`In[15]:= ?g`
	`Global`g`
	`Attributes[g] = {Protected, ReadProtected}`

Functions like SetAttributes and ClearAttributes usually allow you to modify the attributes of a symbol in any way. However, if you once set the Locked attribute on a symbol, then *Mathematica* will not allow you to modify the attributes of that symbol for the remainder of your *Mathematica* session. Using the Locked attribute in addition to Protected or ReadProtected, you can arrange for it to be impossible for users to modify or read definitions.

Clear[*f*]	remove values for *f*, but not attributes
ClearAll[*f*]	remove both values and attributes of *f*

Clearing values and attributes.

This clears values and attributes of p which was given attribute Listable above.

In[15]:= **ClearAll[p]**

Now p is no longer listable.

In[16]:= **p[{a, b, c}, d]**

Out[16]= p[{a, b, c}, d]

By defining attributes for a function you specify properties that *Mathematica* should assume whenever that function appears. Often, however, you want to assume the properties only in a particular instance. In such cases, you will be better off not to use attributes, but instead to call a particular function to implement the transformation associated with the attributes.

By explicitly calling Thread, you can implement the transformation that would be done automatically if p were listable.

In[17]:= **Thread[p[{a, b, c}, d]]**

Out[17]= {p[a, d], p[b, d], p[c, d]}

Orderless	Sort[*f*[*args*]]
Flat	Flatten[*f*[*args*]]
Listable	Thread[*f*[*args*]]
Constant	Dt[*expr*, Constants->*f*]

Functions that perform transformations associated with some attributes.

Attributes in *Mathematica* can only be permanently defined for single symbols. However, *Mathematica* also allows you to set up pure functions which behave as if they carry attributes.

Function[*vars*, *body*, {*attr₁*, ... }]   a pure function with attributes *attr₁*, ...

Function[*vars*, *body*, {*attr*$_1$, ... }]

a pure function with attributes *attr*$_1$, ...

Pure functions with attributes.

This pure function applies p to the whole list.

In[18]:= **Function[{x}, p[x]] [{a, b, c}]**

Out[18]= p[{a, b, c}]

By adding the attribute Listable, the function gets distributed over the elements of the list before applying p.

In[19]:= **Function[{x}, p[x], {Listable}] [{a, b, c}]**

Out[19]= {p[a], p[b], p[c]}

■ 2.5.4 The Standard Evaluation Procedure

This section describes the standard procedure used by *Mathematica* to evaluate expressions. This procedure is the one followed for most kinds of expressions. There are however some kinds of expressions, such as those used to represent *Mathematica* programs and control structures, which are evaluated in a non-standard way. The treatment of such expressions is discussed in the sections that follow this one.

In the standard evaluation procedure, *Mathematica* first evaluates the head of an expression, and then evaluates each element of the expressions. These elements are in general themselves expressions, to which the same evaluation procedure is recursively applied.

The three `Print` functions are evaluated in turn, each printing its argument, then returning the value `Null`.	`In[1]:= {Print[1], Print[2], Print[3]}`
	
	1
	2
	3
	
	`Out[1]= {Null, Null, Null}`

This assigns the symbol ps to be Plus.	`In[2]:= ps = Plus` `Out[2]= Plus`
The head `ps` is evaluated first, so this expression behaves just like a sum of terms.	`In[3]:= ps[ps[a, b], c]` `Out[3]= a + b + c`

As soon as *Mathematica* has evaluated the head of an expression, it sees whether the head is a symbol that has attributes. If the symbol has the attributes `Orderless`, `Flat` or `Listable`, then immediately after evaluating the elements of the expression *Mathematica* performs the transformations associated with these attributes.

The next step in the standard evaluation procedure is to use definitions that *Mathematica* knows for the expression it is evaluating. *Mathematica* first tries to use definitions that you have made, and if there are none that apply, it tries built-in definitions.

If *Mathematica* finds a definition that applies, it performs the corresponding transformation on the expression. The result is another expression, which must then in turn be evaluated according to the standard evaluation procedure.

- Evaluate the head of the expression.
- Evaluate each element in turn.
- Apply transformations associated with the attributes `Orderless`, `Listable` and `Flat`.
- Apply any definitions that you have given.
- Apply any built-in definitions.
- Evaluate the result.

The standard evaluation procedure.

As discussed in Section 2.5.1, *Mathematica* follows the principle that each expression is evaluated until no further definitions apply. This means that *Mathematica* must continue re-evaluating results until it gets an expression which remains unchanged through the evaluation procedure.

Here is an example that shows how the standard evaluation procedure works on a simple expression. We assume that a = 7.

`2 a x + a^2 + 1`	here is the original expression
`Plus[Times[2, a, x], Power[a, 2], 1]`	
	this is the internal form
`Times[2, a, x]`	this is evaluated first
`Times[2, 7, x]`	a is evaluated to give 7
`Times[14, x]`	built-in definitions for Times give this result
`Power[a, 2]`	this is evaluated next
`Power[7, 2]`	here is the result after evaluating a
`49`	built-in definitions for Power give this result
`Plus[Times[14, x], 49, 1]`	here is the result after the arguments of Plus have been evaluated
`Plus[50, Times[14, x]]`	built-in definitions for Plus give this result
`50 + 14 x`	the result is printed like this

A simple example of evaluation in *Mathematica*.

Mathematica provides various ways to "trace" the evaluation process, as discussed in Section 2.5.10. The function Trace[*expr*] gives a nested list showing each subexpression generated during evaluation. (Note that the standard evaluation traverses the expression tree in a depth-first way, so that the smallest subparts of the expression appear first in the results of Trace.)

First set a to 7.

```
In[4]:= a = 7
Out[4]= 7
```

This gives a nested list of all the subexpressions generated during the evaluation of the expression.

```
In[5]:= Trace[2 a x + a^2 + 1]

Out[5]= {{a, 7}, 2 7 x, 14 x}, {{a, 7}, 7 , 49},
         14 x + 49 + 1, 1 + 49 + 14 x, 50 + 14 x}
```

The order in which *Mathematica* applies different kinds of definitions is important. The fact that *Mathematica* applies definitions you have given before it applies built-in definitions means that you can give definitions which override the built-in ones, as discussed in Section 2.4.12.

This expression is evaluated using the built-in definition for ArcSin.	*In[6]:=* **ArcSin[1]**
	Out[6]= $\dfrac{Pi}{2}$
You can give your own definitions for ArcSin. You need to remove the protection attribute first.	*In[7]:=* **Unprotect[ArcSin]; ArcSin[1] = 5Pi/2;**
Your definition is used before the one that is built in.	*In[8]:=* **ArcSin[1]**
	Out[8]= $\dfrac{5\ Pi}{2}$

As discussed in Section 2.4.10, you can associate definitions with symbols either as upvalues or downvalues. *Mathematica* always tries upvalue definitions before downvalue ones.

If you have an expression like $f[g[x]]$, there are in general two sets of definitions that could apply: downvalues associated with f, and upvalues associated with g. *Mathematica* tries the definitions associated with g before those associated with f.

This ordering follows the general strategy of trying specific definitions before more general ones. By applying upvalues associated with arguments before applying downvalues associated with a function, *Mathematica* allows you to make definitions for special arguments which override the general definitions for the function with any arguments.

This defines a rule for f[g[x_]], to be associated with f.	*In[9]:=* **f/: f[g[x_]] := frule[x]**
This defines a rule for f[g[x_]], to be associated with g.	*In[10]:=* **g/: f[g[x_]] := grule[x]**
The rule associated with g is tried before the rule associated with f.	*In[11]:=* **f[g[2]]**
	Out[11]= grule[2]
If you remove rules associated with g, the rule associated with f is used.	*In[12]:=* **Clear[g] ; f[g[1]]**
	Out[12]= frule[1]

■ Definitions associated with g are applied before definitions associated with f in the expression $f[g[x]]$.

The order in which definitions are applied.

Most functions such as `Plus` that are built into *Mathematica* have downvalues. There are, however, some objects in *Mathematica* which have built-in upvalues. For example, `SeriesData` objects, which represent power series, have built-in upvalues with respect to various mathematical operations.

For an expression like $f[g[x]]$, the complete sequence of definitions that are tried in the standard evaluation procedure is:

- Definitions you have given associated with g;

- Built-in definitions associated with g;

- Definitions you have given associated with f;

- Built-in definitions associated with f.

The fact that upvalues are used before downvalues is important in many situations. In a typical case, you might want to define an operation such as composition. If you give upvalues for various objects with respect to composition, these upvalues will be used whenever such objects appear. However, you can also give a general procedure for composition, to be used if no special objects are present. You can give this procedure as a downvalue for composition. Since downvalues are tried after upvalues, the general procedure will be used only if no objects with upvalues are present.

Here is a definition associated with q for composition of "q objects".	`In[13]:= q/: comp[q[x_], q[y_]] := qcomp[x, y]`
Here is a general rule for composition, associated with `comp`.	`In[14]:= comp[f_[x_], f_[y_]] := gencomp[f, x, y]`
If you compose two q objects, the rule associated with q is used.	`In[15]:= comp[q[1], q[2]]` `Out[15]= qcomp[1, 2]`
If you compose r objects, the general rule associated with `comp` is used.	`In[16]:= comp[r[1], r[2]]` `Out[16]= gencomp[r, 1, 2]`

In general, there can be several objects that have upvalues in a particular expression. *Mathematica* first looks at the head of the expression, and tries any upvalues associated with it. Then it successively looks at each element of the expression, trying any upvalues that exist. *Mathematica* performs this procedure first for upvalues that you have explicitly defined, and then for upvalues that are built in. The procedure means that in a sequence of elements, upvalues associated with earlier elements take precedence over those associated with later elements.

This defines an upvalue for p with respect to c.	`In[17]:= p/: c[l___, p[x_], r___] := cp[x, {l, r}]`
This defines an upvalue for q.	`In[18]:= q/: c[l___, q[x_], r___] := cq[x, {l, r}]`
Which upvalue is used depends on which occurs first in the sequence of arguments to c.	`In[19]:= {c[p[1], q[2]], c[q[1], p[2]]}` `Out[19]= {cp[1, {q[2]}], cq[1, {p[2]}]}`

■ 2.5.5 Non-Standard Evaluation

While most built-in *Mathematica* functions follow the standard evaluation procedure, some important ones do not. For example, most of the *Mathematica* functions associated with the construction and execution of programs use non-standard evaluation procedures. In typical cases, the functions either never evaluate some of their arguments, or do so in a special way under their own control.

$x = y$	do not evaluate the left-hand side
If[p, a, b]	evaluate a if p is True, and b if it is false
Do[$expr$, {n}]	evaluate $expr$ n times
Plot[f, {x, ... }]	evaluate f with a sequence of numerical values for x
Function[{x}, $body$]	do not evaluate until the function is applied

Some functions that use non-standard evaluation procedures.

When you give a definition such as a = 1, *Mathematica* does not evaluate the a that appears on the left-hand side. You can see that there would be trouble if the a was evaluated. The reason is that if you had previously set a = 7, then evaluating a in the definition a = 1 would put the definition into the nonsensical form 7 = 1.

In the standard evaluation procedure, each argument of a function is evaluated in turn. This is prevented by setting the attributes HoldFirst, HoldRest and HoldAll. These attributes make *Mathematica* "hold" particular arguments in an unevaluated form.

HoldFirst	do not evaluate the first argument
HoldRest	evaluate only the first argument
HoldAll	evaluate none of the arguments

Attributes for holding function arguments in unevaluated form.

With the standard evaluation procedure, all arguments to a function are evaluated.	*In[1]:=* **f[1 + 1, 2 + 4]** *Out[1]=* f[2, 6]
This assigns the attribute HoldFirst to h.	*In[2]:=* **SetAttributes[h, HoldFirst]**
The first argument to h is now held in an unevaluated form.	*In[3]:=* **h[1 + 1, 2 + 4]** *Out[3]=* h[1 + 1, 6]

When you use the first argument to h   *In[4]:=* **h[1 + 1, 2 + 4] /. h[x_, y_] -> x^y**
like this, it will get evaluated.
                                             Out[4]= 64

Built-in functions like Set carry   *In[5]:=* **Attributes[Set]**
attributes such as HoldFirst.
                                             Out[5]= {HoldFirst, Protected}

Even though a function may have attributes which specify that it should hold certain arguments un-evaluated, you can always explicitly tell *Mathematica* to evaluate those arguments by giving the arguments in the form Evaluate[*arg*].

Evaluate effectively overrides the   *In[6]:=* **h[Evaluate[1 + 1], 2 + 4]**
HoldFirst attribute, and causes the first
argument to be evaluated.   *Out[6]=* h[2, 6]

f[Evaluate[*arg*]]	evaluate *arg* immediately, even though attributes of *f* may specify that it should be held

Forcing the evaluation of function arguments.

By holding its arguments, a function can control when those arguments are evaluated. By using Evaluate, you can force the arguments to be evaluated immediately, rather than being evaluated under the control of the function. This capability is useful in a number of circumstances.

One example discussed on page 135 occurs when plotting graphs of expressions. The *Mathematica* Plot function holds unevaluated the expression you are going to plot, then evaluates it at a sequence of numerical positions. In some cases, you may instead want to evaluate the expression immediately, and have Plot work with the evaluated form. For example, if you want to plot a list of functions generated by Table, then you will want the Table operation done immediately, rather than being done every time a point is to be plotted.

Evaluate causes the list of functions to   *In[7]:=* **Plot[**
be constructed immediately, rather than   **Evaluate[Table[Sin[n x], {n, 1, 3}]],**
being constructed at each value of x
chosen by Plot.   **{x, 0, 2Pi}]**

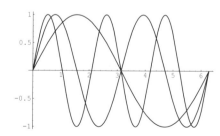

There are a number of built-in *Mathematica* functions which, like Plot, are set up to hold some of their arguments. You can always override this behavior using Evaluate.

The *Mathematica* Set function holds its first argument, so the symbol a is not evaluated in this case.	*In[8]* := **a = b** *Out[8]* = b
You can make Set evaluate its first argument using Evaluate. In this case, the result is the object which is the *value* of a, namely b is set to 6.	*In[9]* := **Evaluate[a] = 6** *Out[9]* = 6
b has now been set to 6.	*In[10]* := **b** *Out[10]* = 6

In most cases, you want all expressions you give to *Mathematica* to be evaluated. Sometimes, however, you may want to prevent the evaluation of certain expressions. For example, if you want to manipulate pieces of a *Mathematica* program symbolically, then you must prevent those pieces from being evaluated while you are manipulating them.

You can use the functions Hold and HoldForm to keep expressions unevaluated. These functions work simply by carrying the attribute HoldFirst, which prevents their argument from being evaluated. The functions provide "wrappers" inside which expressions remain unevaluated.

The difference between Hold[*expr*] and HoldForm[*expr*] is that in standard *Mathematica* output format, Hold is printed explicitly, while HoldForm is not. If you look at the full internal *Mathematica* form, you can however see both functions.

Hold maintains expressions in an unevaluated form.	*In[11]* := **Hold[1 + 1]** *Out[11]* = Hold[1 + 1]
HoldForm also keep expressions unevaluated, but is invisible in standard *Mathematica* output format.	*In[12]* := **HoldForm[1 + 1]** *Out[12]* = 1 + 1
HoldForm is still present internally.	*In[13]* := **FullForm[%]** *Out[13]//FullForm* = HoldForm[Plus[1, 1]]
The function ReleaseHold removes Hold and HoldForm, so the expressions they contain get evaluated.	*In[14]* := **ReleaseHold[%]** *Out[14]* = 2

Hold[*expr*]	keep *expr* unevaluated
HoldForm[*expr*]	keep *expr* unevaluated, and print without HoldForm
ReleaseHold[*expr*]	remove Hold and HoldForm in *expr*
HeldPart[*expr*, *index*]	get a part of *expr*, wrapping it with Hold to prevent evaluation
ReplaceHeldPart[*expr*, *value*, *index*]	replace part of *expr*, without evaluating the part

Functions for handling unevaluated expressions.

Parts of expressions are usually evaluated as soon as you extract them.

```
In[15]:= Part[ Hold[1 + 1, 2 + 3], 1]
Out[15]= 2
```

Using HeldPart, however, you can extract a part, and immediately have it wrapped with Hold, so it does not get evaluated.

```
In[16]:= HeldPart[ Hold[1 + 1, 2 + 3], 1]
Out[16]= Hold[1 + 1]
```

ReplaceHeldPart allows you to replace parts without evaluation.

```
In[17]:= ReplaceHeldPart[ Hold[1 + 1, 2 + 3], 7 + 8, 1]
Out[17]= Hold[15, 2 + 3]
```

f[... , Unevaluated[*expr*] , ...]	give *expr* unevaluated as an argument to *f*

Temporary prevention of argument evaluation.

1 + 1 evaluates to 2, and Length[2] gives 0.

```
In[18]:= Length[1 + 1]
Out[18]= 0
```

This gives the unevaluated form 1 + 1 as the argument of Length.

```
In[19]:= Length[Unevaluated[1 + 1]]
Out[19]= 2
```

Unevaluated[*expr*] effectively works by temporarily giving a function an attribute like HoldFirst, and then supplying *expr* as an argument to the function.

■ 2.5.6 Evaluation in Patterns, Rules and Definitions

There are a number of important interactions in *Mathematica* between evaluation and pattern matching. The first observation is that pattern matching is usually done on expressions that have already been at least partly evaluated. As a result, it is usually appropriate that the patterns to which these expressions are matched should themselves be evaluated.

The fact that the pattern is evaluated means that it matches the expression given.	*In[1]:=* **f[k^2] /. f[x_^(1 + 1)] -> p[x]** *Out[1]=* p[k]
The right-hand side of the /; condition is not evaluated until it is used during pattern matching.	*In[2]:=* **f[{a, b}] /. f[list_ /; Length[list] > 1] -> list^2** *Out[2]=* {a^2, b^2}

There are some cases, however, where you may want to keep all or part of a pattern unevaluated. You can do this by wrapping the parts you do not want to evaluate with Literal. In general, when Literal[*patt*] appears in a pattern, it is equivalent for the purpose of pattern matching to *patt*, but it maintains *patt* in an unevaluated form.

Literal[*patt*]	equivalent to *patt* for pattern matching, with *patt* kept unevaluated

Preventing evaluation in patterns.

One application for Literal is in specifying patterns which can apply to unevaluated expressions, or expressions held in an unevaluated form.

Literal keeps the 1 + 1 from being evaluated, and allows it to match the 1 + 1 on the left-hand side of the /. operator.	*In[3]:=* **Hold[u[1 + 1]] /. Literal[1 + 1] -> x** *Out[3]=* Hold[u[x]]

Notice that while functions like Hold prevent evaluation of expressions, they do not affect the manipulation of parts of those expressions with /. and other operators.

This defines values for r whenever its argument is not an atomic object.	*In[4]:=* **r[x_] := x^2 /; !AtomQ[x]**
According to the definition, expressions like r[3] are left unchanged.	*In[5]:=* **r[3]** *Out[5]=* r[3]
However, the pattern r[x_] is transformed according to the definition for r.	*In[6]:=* **r[x_]** *Out[6]=* (x_)^2
You need to wrap Literal around r[x_] to prevent it from being evaluated.	*In[7]:=* **{r[3], r[5]} /. Literal[r[x_]] -> x** *Out[7]=* {3, 5}

As illustrated above, the left-hand sides of transformation rules such as *lhs* -> *rhs* are usually evaluated immediately, since the rules are usually applied to expressions which have already been evaluated. The right-hand side of *lhs* -> *rhs* is also evaluated immediately. With the delayed rule *lhs* :> *rhs*, however, the expression *rhs* is not evaluated.

The right-hand side is evaluated immediately in -> but not :> rules.

```
In[8]:= {{x -> 1 + 1}, {x :> 1 + 1}}

Out[8]= {{x -> 2}, {x :> 1 + 1}}
```

Here are the results of applying the rules. The right-hand side of the :> rule gets inserted inside the Hold without evaluation.

```
In[9]:= {x^2, Hold[x]} /. %

Out[9]= {{4, Hold[2]}, {4, Hold[1 + 1]}}
```

lhs -> *rhs*	evaluate both *lhs* and *rhs*
lhs :> *rhs*	evaluate *lhs* but not *rhs*

Evaluation in transformation rules.

While the left-hand sides of transformation rules are usually evaluated, the left-hand sides of definitions are usually not. The reason for the difference is as follows. Transformation rules are typically applied using /. to expressions that have already been evaluated. Definitions, however, are used during the evaluation of expressions, and are applied to expressions that have not yet been completely evaluated. To work on such expressions, the left-hand sides of definitions must be maintained in a form that is at least partially unevaluated.

Definitions for symbols are the simplest case. As discussed in the previous section, a symbol on the left-hand side of a definition such as x = *value* is not evaluated. If x had previously been assigned a value y, then if the left-hand side of x = *value* were evaluated, it would turn into the quite unrelated definition y = *value*.

Here is a definition. The symbol on the left-hand side is not evaluated.

```
In[10]:= k = w[3]

Out[10]= w[3]
```

This redefines the symbol.

```
In[11]:= k = w[4]

Out[11]= w[4]
```

If you evaluate the left-hand side, then you define not the symbol k, but the *value* w[4] of the symbol k.

```
In[12]:= Evaluate[k] = w[5]

Out[12]= w[5]
```

Now w[4] has value w[5].

```
In[13]:= w[4]

Out[13]= w[5]
```

Although individual symbols that appear on the left-hand sides of definitions are not evaluated, more complicated expressions are partially evaluated. In an expression such as *f*[*args*] on the left-hand side of a definition, the *args* are evaluated.

The 1 + 1 is evaluated, so that a value is defined for g[2].

```
In[14]:= g[1 + 1] = 5

Out[14]= 5
```

This shows the value defined for g.

```
In[15]:= ?g
Global`g
g[2] = 5
```

You can see why the arguments of a function that appears on the left-hand side of a definition must be evaluated by considering how the definition is used during the evaluation of an expression. As discussed in Section 2.5.1, when *Mathematica* evaluates a function, it first evaluates each of the arguments, then tries to find definitions for the function. As a result, by the time *Mathematica* applies any definition you have given for a function, the arguments of the function must already have been evaluated. An exception to this occurs when the function in question has attributes which specify that it should hold some of its arguments unevaluated.

symbol = *value*	*symbol* is not evaluated; *value* is evaluated
symbol := *value*	neither *symbol* nor *value* is evaluated
f[*args*] = *value*	*args* are evaluated; left-hand side as a whole is not
f[`Literal`[*arg*]] = *value*	*f*[*arg*] is assigned, without evaluating *arg*
`Evaluate`[*lhs*] = *value*	left-hand side is evaluated completely

Evaluation in definitions.

While in most cases it is appropriate for the arguments of a function that appears on the left-hand side of a definition to be evaluated, there are some situations in which you do not want this to happen. In such cases, you can wrap `Literal` around the parts that you do not want to be evaluated.

■ 2.5.7 Evaluation in Iteration Functions

The built-in *Mathematica* iteration functions such as `Table` and `Sum`, as well as `Plot` and `Plot3D`, evaluate their arguments in a slightly special way.

When evaluating an expression like `Table[`*f*`, {`*i*`, `*imax*`}]`, the first step, as discussed on page 330 is to make the value of *i* local. Next, the limit *imax* in the iterator specification is evaluated. The expression *f* is maintained in an unevaluated form, but is repeatedly evaluated as a succession of values are assigned to *i*. When this is finished, the global value of *i* is restored.

The function `Random[ ]` is evaluated four separate times here, so four different pseudorandom numbers are generated.

```
In[1]:= Table[Random[ ], {4}]
Out[1]= {0.104826, 0.767415, 0.216417, 0.519263}
```

This evaluates `Random[ ]` before feeding it to `Table`. The result is a list of four identical numbers.

```
In[2]:= Table[ Evaluate[Random[ ]], {4} ]
Out[2]= {0.81383, 0.81383, 0.81383, 0.81383}
```

In most cases, it is convenient for the function *f* in an expression like Table[*f*, {*i*, *imax*}] to be maintained in an unevaluated form until specific values have been assigned to *i*. This is true in particular if a complete symbolic form for *f* valid for any *i* cannot be found.

This defines fac to give the factorial when it has an integer argument, and to give NaN (standing for "Not a Number") otherwise.	*In[3]:=* **fac[n_Integer] := n! ; fac[x_] := NaN**

In this form, fac[i] is not evaluated until an explicit integer value has been assigned to i.	*In[4]:=* **Table[fac[i], {i, 5}]** *Out[4]=* {1, 2, 6, 24, 120}

Using Evaluate forces fac[i] to be evaluated with i left as a symbolic object.	*In[5]:=* **Table[Evaluate[fac[i]], {i, 5}]** *Out[5]=* {NaN, NaN, NaN, NaN, NaN}

In cases where a complete symbolic form for *f* with arbitrary *i* in expressions such as Table[*f*, {*i*, *imax*}] *can* be found, it is often more efficient to compute this form first, and then feed it to Table. You can do this using Table[Evaluate[*f*], {*i*, *imax*}].

The Sum in this case is evaluated separately for each value of i.	*In[6]:=* **Table[Sum[i^k, {k, 4}], {i, 8}]** *Out[6]=* {4, 30, 120, 340, 780, 1554, 2800, 4680}

It is however possible to get a symbolic formula for the sum, valid for any value of i.	*In[7]:=* **Sum[i^k, {k, 4}]** *Out[7]=* $i + i^2 + i^3 + i^4$

By inserting Evaluate, you tell *Mathematica* first to evaluate the sum symbolically, then to iterate over i.	*In[8]:=* **Table[Evaluate[Sum[i^k, {k, 4}]], {i, 8}]** *Out[8]=* {4, 30, 120, 340, 780, 1554, 2800, 4680}

Table[*f*, {*i*, *imax*}]	keep *f* unevaluated until specific values are assigned to *i*
Table[Evaluate[*f*], {*i*, *imax*}]	evaluate *f* first with *i* left symbolic

Evaluation in iteration functions.

As discussed on page 135, it is convenient to use Evaluate when you plot a graph of a function or a list of functions. This causes the symbolic form of the function or list to be found first, before the iteration begins.

■ 2.5.8 Conditionals

Mathematica provides various ways to set up *conditionals*, which specify that particular expressions should be evaluated only if certain conditions hold.

lhs := *rhs* /; *test*	use the definition only if *test* evaluates to True
If [*test*, *then*, *else*]	evaluate *then* if *test* is True, and *else* if it is False
Which[*test₁*, *value₁*, *test₂*, ...]	evaluate the *testᵢ* in turn, giving the value associated with the first one that is True
Switch[*expr*, *form₁*, *value₁*, *form₂*, ...]	compare *expr* with each of the *formᵢ*, giving the value associated with the first form it matches
Switch[*expr*, *form₁*, *value₁*, *form₂*, ... , _, *def*]	use *def* as a default value

Conditional constructs.

The test gives **False**, so the *"else"* expression **y** is returned.

```
In[1]:= If[7 > 8, x, y]
Out[1]= y
```

Only the *"else"* expression is evaluated in this case.

```
In[2]:= If[7 > 8, Print[x], Print[y]]
y
```

When you write programs in *Mathematica*, you will often have a choice between making a single definition whose right-hand side involves several branches controlled by If functions, or making several definitions, each controlled by an appropriate /; condition. By using several definitions, you can often produce programs that are both clearer, and easier to modify.

This defines a step function, with value 1 for $x > 0$, and −1 otherwise.

```
In[3]:= f[x_] := If[x > 0, 1, -1]
```

This defines the positive part of the step function using a /; condition.

```
In[4]:= g[x_] := 1 /; x > 0
```

Here is the negative part of the step function.

```
In[5]:= g[x_] := -1 /; x <= 0
```

This shows the complete definition using /; conditions.

```
In[6]:= ?g
Global`g
g[x_] := 1 /; x > 0
g[x_] := -1 /; x <= 0
```

The function If provides a way to choose between two alternatives. Often, however, there will be more than two alternatives. One way to handle this is to use a nested set of If functions. Usually, however, it is instead better to use functions like Which and Switch.

This defines a function with three regions. Using **True** as the third test makes this the default case.

```
In[6]:= h[x_] := Which[x < 0, x^2, x > 5, x^3, True, 0]
```

This uses the first case in the Which.

In[7]:= **h[-5]**

Out[7]= 25

This uses the third case.

In[8]:= **h[2]**

Out[8]= 0

This defines a function that depends on the values of its argument modulo 3.

In[9]:= **r[x_] := Switch[Mod[x, 3], 0, a, 1, b, 2, c]**

Mod[7, 3] is 1, so this uses the second case in the Switch.

In[10]:= **r[7]**

Out[10]= b

17 matches neither 0 or 1, but does match _.

In[11]:= **Switch[17, 0, a, 1, b, _, q]**

Out[11]= q

An important point about symbolic systems such as *Mathematica* is that the conditions you give may yield neither True nor False. Thus, for example, the condition x == y does not yield True or False unless x and y have specific values, such as numerical ones.

In this case, the test gives neither True nor False, so both branches in the If remain unevaluated.

In[12]:= **If[x == y, a, b]**

Out[12]= If[x == y, a, b]

You can add a special fourth argument to If, which is used if the test does not yield True or False.

In[13]:= **If[x == y, a, b, c]**

Out[13]= c

If[*test*, *then*, *else*, *unknown*]	a form of If which includes the expression to use if *test* is neither True nor False
TrueQ[*expr*]	give True if *expr* is True, and False otherwise
lhs === *rhs* or SameQ[*lhs*, *rhs*]	give True if *lhs* and *rhs* are identical, and False otherwise
lhs =!= *rhs* or UnsameQ[*lhs*, *rhs*]	give True if *lhs* and *rhs* are not identical, and False otherwise
MatchQ[*expr*, *form*]	give True if the pattern *form* matches *expr*, and give False otherwise

Functions for dealing with symbolic conditions.

Mathematica leaves this as a symbolic equation.

In[14]:= **x == y**

Out[14]= x == y

Unless *expr* is manifestly **True**, **TrueQ**[*expr*] effectively assumes that *expr* is **False**.	`In[15]:= TrueQ[x == y]`
	
	`Out[15]= False`

Unlike **==**, **===** tests whether two expressions are manifestly identical. In this case, they are not.	`In[16]:= x === y`
	
	`Out[16]= False`

The main difference between *lhs* **===** *rhs* and *lhs* **==** *rhs* is that **===** always returns **True** or **False**, whereas **==** can leave its input in symbolic form, representing a symbolic equation, as discussed in Section 1.5.5. You should typically use **===** when you want to test the *structure* of an expression, and **==** if you want to test mathematical equality. The *Mathematica* pattern matcher effectively uses **===** to determine when one literal expression matches another.

You can use **===** to test the structure of expressions.	`In[17]:= Head[a + b + c] === Times`
	
	`Out[17]= False`

The **==** operator gives a less useful result.	`In[18]:= Head[a + b + c] == Times`
	
	`Out[18]= Plus == Times`

In setting up conditionals, you will often need to use combinations of tests, such as *test₁* **&&** *test₂* **&&** ... . An important point is that the result from this combination of tests will be **False** if *any* of the *testᵢ* yield **False**. *Mathematica* always evaluates the *testᵢ* in turn, stopping if any of the *testᵢ* yield **False**.

expr₁ **&&** *expr₂* **&&** *expr₃*	evaluate until one of the *exprᵢ* is found to be **False**
expr₁ **||** *expr₂* **||** *expr₃*	evaluate until one of the *exprᵢ* is found to be **True**

Evaluation of logical expressions.

This function involves a combination of two tests.	`In[19]:= t[x_] := (x != 0 && 1/x < 3)`

Here both tests are evaluated.	`In[20]:= t[2]`
	
	`Out[20]= True`

Here the first test yields **False**, so the second test is not tried. The second test would involve 1/0, and would generate an error.	`In[21]:= t[0]`
	
	`Out[21]= False`

The way that *Mathematica* evaluates logical expressions allows you to combine sequences of tests where later tests may make sense only if the earlier ones are satisfied. The behavior, which is analogous to that found in languages such as C, is convenient in constructing many kinds of *Mathematica* programs.

■ 2.5.9 Loops and Control Structures

The execution of a *Mathematica* program involves the evaluation of a sequence of *Mathematica* expressions. In simple programs, the expressions to be evaluated may be separated by semicolons, and evaluated one after another. Often, however, you need to evaluate expressions several times, in some kind of "loop".

Do[*expr*, {*i*, *imax*}]	evaluate *expr* repetitively, with *i* varying from 1 to *imax* in steps of 1
Do[*expr*, {*i*, *imin*, *imax*, *di*}]	evaluate *expr* with *i* varying from *imin* to *imax* in steps of *di*
Do[*expr*, {*n*}]	evaluate *expr* *n* times

Simple looping constructs.

This evaluates `Print[i^2]`, with `i` running from 1 to 4.

```
In[1]:= Do[Print[i^2], {i, 4}]

1
4
9
16
```

This executes an assignment for `t` in a loop with `k` running from 2 to 6 in steps of 2.

```
In[2]:= t = x; Do[t = 1/(1 + k t), {k, 2, 6, 2}]; t
```

$$Out[2]= \cfrac{1}{1 + \cfrac{6}{1 + \cfrac{4}{1 + 2 x}}}$$

The way iteration is specified in Do is exactly the same as in functions like `Table` and `Sum`. Just as in those functions, you can set up several nested loops by giving a sequence of iteration specifications to Do.

This loops over values of `i` from 1 to 4, and for each value of `i`, loops over `j` from 1 to `i-1`.

```
In[3]:= Do[Print[{i,j}], {i, 4}, {j, i-1}]

{2, 1}
{3, 1}
{3, 2}
{4, 1}
{4, 2}
{4, 3}
```

Sometimes you may want to repeat a particular operation a certain number of times, without changing the value of an iteration variable. You can specify this kind of repetition in Do just as you can in `Table` and other iteration functions.

This repeats the assignment t = 1/(1+t) three times.

In[4]:= **t = x; Do[t = 1/(1+t), {3}]; t**

$$Out[4]= \cfrac{1}{1 + \cfrac{1}{1 + \cfrac{1}{1 + x}}}$$

You can put a procedure inside Do.

In[5]:= **t = 67; Do[Print[t]; t = Floor[t/2], {3}]**

```
67
33
16
```

Nest[*f*, *expr*, *n*]	apply *f* to *expr* *n* times
FixedPoint[*f*, *expr*]	start with *expr*, and apply *f* repeatedly until the result no longer changes
FixedPoint[*f*, *expr*, SameTest -> *comp*]	stop when the function *comp* applied to two successive results yields True

Applying functions repetitively.

Do allows you to repeat operations by evaluating a particular expression many times with different values for iteration variables. Often, however, you can make more elegant and efficient programs using the functional programming constructs discussed in Section 2.2.2. Nest[*f*, *x*, *n*], for example, allows you to apply a function repeatedly to an expression.

This nests f three times.

In[6]:= **Nest[f, x, 3]**

Out[6]= **f[f[f[x]]]**

By nesting a pure function, you can get the same result as in the example with Do above.

In[7]:= **Nest[Function[t, 1/(1+t)], x, 3]**

$$Out[7]= \cfrac{1}{1 + \cfrac{1}{1 + \cfrac{1}{1 + x}}}$$

Nest allows you to apply a function a specified number of times. Sometimes, however, you may simply want to go on applying a function until the results you get no longer change. You can do this using FixedPoint[*f*, *x*].

FixedPoint goes on applying a function until the result no longer changes.

```
In[8]:= FixedPoint[Function[t, Print[t]; Floor[t/2]], 67]
67
33
16
8
4
2
1
0

Out[8]= 0
```

You can use FixedPoint to imitate the evaluation process in *Mathematica*, or the operation of functions such as *expr //. rules*. In general, FixedPoint goes on until two successive results it gets are the same. By default, FixedPoint uses SameQ to test whether results are the same. You can specify an alternative function to use by setting the SameTest option.

While[*test*, *body*]	evaluate *body* repetitively, so long as *test* is True
For[*start*, *test*, *incr*, *body*]	evaluate *start*, then repetitively evaluate *body* and *incr*, until *test* fails

General loop constructs.

Functions like Do, Nest and FixedPoint provide rather structured ways to make loops in *Mathematica* programs. Sometimes, however, you need to create loops with less structure. In such cases, you may find it convenient to use the functions While and For, which perform operations repeatedly, stopping when a specified condition fails to be true.

The While loop continues until the condition fails.

```
In[9]:= n = 17; While[(n = Floor[n/2]) != 0, Print[n]]
8
4
2
1
```

The functions While and For in *Mathematica* are similar to the control structures while and for in languages such as C. Notice, however, that there are a number of important differences. For example, the roles of comma and semicolon are reversed in *Mathematica* For loops relative to C language ones.

This is a very common form for a For loop. i++ increments the value of i.

```
In[10]:= For[i=1, i < 4, i++, Print[i]]
1
2
3
```

Here is a more complicated For loop. Notice that the loop terminates as soon as the test i∧2 < 10 fails.

```
In[11]:= For[i=1; t=x, i∧2 < 10, i++, t = t∧2 + i;
                        Print[t]]
```

$$1 + x^2$$
$$2 + (1 + x^2)^2$$
$$3 + (2 + (1 + x^2)^2)^2$$

In *Mathematica*, both While and For always evaluate the loop test before evaluating the body of the loop. As soon as the loop test fails to be True, While and For terminate. The body of the loop is thus only evaluated in situations where the loop test is True.

The loop test fails immediately, so the body of the loop is never evaluated.

`In[12]:= While[False, Print[x]]`

In a While or For loop, or in general in any *Mathematica* procedure, the *Mathematica* expressions you give are evaluated in a definite sequence. You can think of this sequence as defining the "flow of control" in the execution of a *Mathematica* program.

In most cases, you should try to keep the flow of control in your *Mathematica* programs as simple as possible. The more the flow of control depends for example on specific values generated during the execution of the program, the more difficult you will typically find it to understand the structure and operation of the program.

Functional programming constructs typically involve very simple flow of control. While and For loops are always more complicated, since they are set up to make the flow of control depend on the values of the expressions given as tests. Nevertheless, even in such loops, the flow of control does not usually depend on the values of expressions given in the body of the loop.

In some cases, however, you may need to construct *Mathematica* programs in which the flow of control is affected by values generated during the execution of a procedure or of the body of a loop. *Mathematica* provides various functions for modifying the flow of control. The functions work somewhat as they do in languages such as C.

Break[ ]	exit the nearest enclosing loop
Continue[ ]	go to the next step in the current loop
Return[*expr*]	return the value *expr*, exiting all procedures and loops in a function
Goto[*name*]	go to the element Label[*name*] in the current procedure
Throw[*expr*]	return *expr* as the value of the nearest enclosing Catch (non-local return)

Control flow functions.

The Break[ ] causes the loop to terminate as soon as t exceeds 19.

```
In[13]:= t = 1; Do[t *= k; Print[t];
                    If[t > 19, Break[]], {k, 10}]
```

```
1
2
6
24
```

When k < 3, the Continue[ ] causes
the loop to be continued, without
executing t += 2.

```
In[14]:= t = 1; Do[t *= k; Print[t];
                If[k < 3, Continue[]]; t += 2, {k, 10}]
1
2
6
32
170
1032
7238
57920
521298
5213000
```

- Control flow functions are recognized only when they are generated directly as elements of a procedure or values of loop bodies.

An important principle about control flow.

Mathematica determines control flow by evaluating expressions, then seeing whether the results are control flow functions such as Break[ ] and Continue[ ]. It is crucial that such functions appear directly as results of evaluation. If the results have forms like f[Break[ ]], they will not be recognized as control flow directives.

The examples above work because If[*test*, *then*] yields the expression *then* when *test* is True. This means that the control flow functions are generated directly as elements of a *Mathematica* procedure, where they are recognized, and used to determine the sequence of expressions evaluated.

The fact that constructs such as f[Break[ ]] can ever occur in *Mathematica* is a consequence of the uniform representation of symbolic expressions in the system. In a language such as C, such constructs cannot occur because the analog of Break[ ] is viewed as a "statement" rather than an expression.

Here is an example of the use of
Return. This particular procedure could
equally well have been written without
using Return.

```
In[15]:= f[x_] :=
            (If[x > 5, Return[big]]; t = x^3; Return[t - 7])
```

When the argument is greater than 5, the
first Return in the procedure is used.

```
In[16]:= f[10]
Out[16]= big
```

Return[*expr*] allows you to exit a particular function, returning a value. *Mathematica* also provides a capability for non-local returns with which you can exit a sequence of nested functions. Non-local returns can be convenient for handling certain error conditions.

This function "throws" overflow if its
argument is greater than 10.

```
In[17]:= g[x_] := If[x > 10, Throw[overflow], x!]
```

g[20] throws overflow, which is
returned as the value of the enclosing
Catch.

```
In[18]:= Catch[ 2 + g[20] ]
Out[18]= overflow
```

In this case, `overflow` is not generated, and the `Catch` has no effect.

```
In[19]:= Catch[ 2 + g[5] ]
Out[19]= 122
```

Functions like `Continue[ ]` and `Break[ ]` allow you to "transfer control" to the beginning or end of a loop in a *Mathematica* program. Sometimes you may instead need to transfer control to a particular element in a *Mathematica* procedure. If you give a `Label` as an element in a procedure, you can use `Goto` to transfer control to this element.

This goes on looping until q exceeds 6.

```
In[20]:= (q = 2; Label[begin]; Print[q]; q += 3;
                                 If[q < 6, Goto[begin]])

2
5
```

Note that you can use `Goto` in a particular *Mathematica* procedure only when the `Label` it specifies occurs as an element of the same *Mathematica* procedure. In general, use of `Goto` reduces the degree of structure that can readily be perceived in a program, and therefore makes the operation of the program more difficult to understand.

■ 2.5.10 Tracing Evaluation

The standard way in which *Mathematica* works is to take any expression you give as input, evaluate the expression completely, and then return the result. When you are trying to understand what *Mathematica* is doing, however, it is often worthwhile to look not just at the final result of evaluation, but also at intermediate steps in the evaluation process.

Trace[*expr*]	generate a list of all expressions used in the evaluation of *expr*
Trace[*expr*, *form*]	include only expressions which match the pattern *form*

Tracing the evaluation of expressions.

The expression 1 + 1 is evaluated immediately to 2.

```
In[1]:= Trace[1 + 1]
Out[1]= {1 + 1, 2}
```

Since the `Plus` operation is orderless, the 2 and 3 are sorted before the addition is done.

```
In[2]:= Trace[3 + 2]
Out[2]= {3 + 2, 2 + 3, 5}
```

The 2^3 is evaluated before the addition is done.

```
In[3]:= Trace[2^3 + 4]
Out[3]= {{2 , 8}, 8 + 4, 4 + 8, 12}
```

The evaluation of each subexpression is shown in a separate sublist.

```
In[4]:= Trace[2^3 + 4^2 + 1]
Out[4]= {{2 , 8}, {4 , 16}, 8 + 16 + 1, 1 + 8 + 16, 25}
```

Trace[*expr*] gives a list which includes *all* the intermediate expressions involved in the evaluation of *expr*. Except in rather simple cases, however, the number of intermediate expressions generated in this way is typically very large, and the list returned by Trace is difficult to understand.

Trace[*expr*, *form*] allows you to "filter" the expressions that Trace records, keeping only those which match the pattern *form*.

Here is a recursive definition of a factorial function.

```
In[5]:= fac[n_] := n fac[n-1]; fac[1] = 1
Out[5]= 1
```

This gives *all* the intermediate expressions generated in the evaluation of fac[3]. The result is quite complicated.

```
In[6]:= Trace[fac[3]]
Out[6]= {fac[3], 3 fac[3 - 1],
   {{3 - 1, -1 + 3, 2}, fac[2], 2 fac[2 - 1],
     {{2 - 1, -1 + 2, 1}, fac[1], 1}, 2 1, 1 2, 2}, 3 2, 2 3, 6}
```

This shows only intermediate expressions of the form fac[n_].

```
In[7]:= Trace[fac[3], fac[n_]]
Out[7]= {fac[3], {fac[2], {fac[1]}}}
```

You can specify any pattern in Trace.

```
In[8]:= Trace[fac[10], fac[n_/;n > 5]]
Out[8]= {fac[10], {fac[9], {fac[8], {fac[7], {fac[6]}}}}}
```

Trace[*expr*, *form*] effectively works by intercepting every expression that is about to be evaluated during the evaluation of *expr*, and picking out those that match the pattern *form*.

If you want to trace "calls" to a function like fac, you can do so simply by telling Trace to pick out expressions of the form fac[n_]. You can also use patterns like f[n_, 2] to pick out calls with particular argument structure.

A typical *Mathematica* program, however, consists not only of "function calls" like fac[n], but also of other elements, such as assignments to variables, control structures, and so on. All of these elements are represented as expressions. As a result, you can use patterns in Trace to pick out any kind of *Mathematica* program element. Thus, for example, you can use a pattern like k = _ to pick out all assignments to the symbol k.

This shows the sequence of assignments made for k.

```
In[9]:= Trace[(k=2; Do[k = i/k, {i, 4}]; k), k=_]
```
$$Out[9]= \{\{k = 2\}, \{\{k = \frac{1}{2}\}, \{k = 4\}, \{k = \frac{3}{4}\}, \{k = \frac{16}{3}\}\}\}$$

Trace[*expr*, *form*] can pick out expressions that occur at any time in the evaluation of *expr*. The expressions need not, for example, appear directly in the form of *expr* that you give. They may instead occur, say, during the evaluation of functions that are called as part of the evaluation of *expr*.

Here is a function definition.

```
In[10]:= h[n_] := (k=n/2; Do[k = i/k, {i, n}]; k)
```

You can look for expressions generated during the evaluation of h.

```
In[11]:= Trace[h[3], k=_]
```
$$Out[11]= \{\{k = \frac{3}{2}\}, \{\{k = \frac{2}{3}\}, \{k = 3\}, \{k = 1\}\}\}$$

Trace allows you to monitor intermediate steps in the evaluation not only of functions that you define, but also of some functions that are built into *Mathematica*. Thus, for example, you can use Trace to record the sequence of values assigned to an iteration variable by a built-in *Mathematica* function such as Do. You should realize, however, that the specific sequence of intermediate steps followed by built-in *Mathematica* functions depends in detail on their implementation and optimization in a particular version of *Mathematica*.

Do performs a sequence of assignments for i, which you can see using Trace.

In[12]:= **Trace[Do[i∧2, {i, 5}], i=_]**

Out[12]= {{i = 1}, {i = 2}, {i = 3}, {i = 4}, {i = 5}}

This shows assignments for either i or k during the evaluation of h[3].

In[13]:= **Trace[h[3], (i=_)|(k=_)]**

Out[13]= {{k = $\frac{3}{2}$}, {{i = 1}, {k = $\frac{2}{3}$}, {i = 2}, {k = 3},

{i = 3}, {k = 1}}}

This shows assignments for i only when the values assigned are larger than 3.

In[14]:= **Trace[h[5], (i=n_/;n>3)|(k=_)]**

Out[14]= {{k = $\frac{5}{2}$}, {{k = $\frac{2}{5}$}, {k = 5}, {k = $\frac{3}{5}$}, {i = 4},

{k = $\frac{20}{3}$}, {i = 5}, {k = $\frac{3}{4}$}}}

Trace[*expr*, *f*[___]]	show all calls to the function *f*
Trace[*expr*, *i* = _]	show assignments to *i*
Trace[*expr*, _ = _]	show all assignments
Trace[*expr*, Message[___]]	show messages generated

Some ways to use Trace.

The function Trace returns a list that represents the "history" of a *Mathematica* computation. The expressions in the list are given in the order that they were generated during the computation. In most cases, the list returned by Trace has a nested structure, which represents the "structure" of the computation.

The basic idea is that each sublist in the list returned by Trace represents the "evaluation chain" for a particular *Mathematica* expression. The elements of this chain correspond to different forms of the same expression. Usually, however, the evaluation of one expression requires the evaluation of a number of other expressions, often subexpressions. Each subsidiary evaluation is represented by a sublist in the structure returned by Trace.

Here is a sequence of assignments.

In[15]:= **a[1] = a[2]; a[2] = a[3]; a[3] = a[4]**

Out[15]= a[4]

| This yields an evaluation chain reflecting the sequence of transformations for a[*i*] used. | *In[16]*:= **Trace[a[1]]** |
| | *Out[16]*= {a[1], a[2], a[3], a[4]} |

The successive forms generated in the simplification of y + x + y show up as successive elements in its evaluation chain.

In[17]:= **Trace[y + x + y]**

Out[17]= {y + x + y, x + y + y, x + 2 y}

Each argument of the function f has a separate evaluation chain, given in a sublist.

In[18]:= **Trace[f[1 + 1, 2 + 3, 4 + 5]]**

Out[18]= {{1 + 1, 2}, {2 + 3, 5}, {4 + 5, 9}, f[2, 5, 9]}

The evaluation chain for each subexpression is given in a separate sublist.

In[19]:= **Trace[x x + y y]**

Out[19]= {{x x, x^2}, {y y, y^2}, $x^2 + y^2$}

Tracing the evaluation of a nested expression yields a nested list.

In[20]:= **Trace[f[f[f[1 + 1]]]]**

Out[20]= {{{{1 + 1, 2}, f[2]}, f[f[2]]}, f[f[f[2]]]}

There are two basic ways that subsidiary evaluations can be required during the evaluation of a *Mathematica* expression. The first way is that the expression may contain subexpressions, each of which has to be evaluated. The second way is that there may be rules for the evaluation of the expression that involve other expressions which themselves must be evaluated. Both kinds of subsidiary evaluations are represented by sublists in the structure returned by Trace.

The subsidiary evaluations here come from evaluation of the arguments of f and g.

In[21]:= **Trace[f[g[1 + 1], 2 + 3]]**

Out[21]= {{{1 + 1, 2}, g[2]}, {2 + 3, 5}, f[g[2], 5]}

Here is a function with a condition attached.

In[22]:= **fe[n_] := n + 1 /; EvenQ[n]**

The evaluation of fe[6] involves a subsidiary evaluation associated with the condition.

In[23]:= **Trace[fe[6]]**

Out[23]= {fe[6], {{EvenQ[6], True}, RuleCondition[6 + 1, True], 6 + 1}, 6 + 1, 1 + 6, 7}

You often get nested lists when you trace the evaluation of functions that are defined "recursively" in terms of other instances of themselves. The reason is typically that each new instance of the function appears as a subexpression in the expressions obtained by evaluating previous instances of the function.

Thus, for example, with the definition fac[n_] := n fac[n-1], the evaluation of fac[6] yields the expression 6 fac[5], which contains fac[5] as a subexpression.

The successive instances of fac generated appear in successively nested sublists.

In[24]:= **Trace[fac[6], fac[_]]**

Out[24]= {fac[6], {fac[5], {fac[4], {fac[3], {fac[2], {fac[1]}}}}}}

With this definition, fp[*n*-1] is obtained directly as the value of fp[*n*].

In[25]:= **fp[n_] := fp[n - 1] /; n > 1**

fp[*n*] never appears in a subexpression, so no sublists are generated.

In[26]:= **Trace[fp[6], fp[_]]**

Out[26]= {fp[6], fp[6 - 1], fp[5], fp[5 - 1], fp[4], fp[4 - 1],

    fp[3], fp[3 - 1], fp[2], fp[2 - 1], fp[1]}

Here is the recursive definition of the Fibonacci numbers.

In[27]:= **fib[n_] := fib[n - 1] + fib[n - 2]**

Here are the end conditions for the recursion.

In[28]:= **fib[0] = fib[1] = 1**

Out[28]= 1

This shows all the steps in the recursive evaluation of **fib[5]**.

In[29]:= **Trace[fib[5], fib[_]]**

Out[29]= {fib[5], {fib[4],

    {fib[3], {fib[2], {fib[1]}, {fib[0]}}, {fib[1]}},

    {fib[2], {fib[1]}, {fib[0]}}},

    {fib[3], {fib[2], {fib[1]}, {fib[0]}}, {fib[1]}}}

Each step in the evaluation of any *Mathematica* expression can be thought of as the result of applying a particular transformation rule. As discussed in Section 2.4.10, all the rules that *Mathematica* knows are associated with specific symbols or "tags". You can use Trace[*expr*, *f*] to see all the steps in the evaluation of *expr* that are performed using transformation rules associated with the symbol *f*. In this case, Trace gives not only the expressions to which each rule is applied, but also the results of applying the rules.

In general, Trace[*expr*, *form*] picks out all the steps in the evaluation of *expr* where *form* matches *either* the expression about to be evaluated, *or* the tag associated with the rule used.

Trace[*expr*, *f*]	show all evaluations which use transformation rules associated with the symbol *f*
Trace[*expr*, *f* | *g*]	show all evaluations associated with either *f* or *g*

Tracing evaluations associated with particular tags.

This shows only intermediate expressions that match **fac[_]**.

In[30]:= **Trace[fac[3], fac[_]]**

Out[30]= {fac[3], {fac[2], {fac[1]}}}

This shows all evaluations that use transformation rules associated with the symbol **fac**.

In[31]:= **Trace[fac[3], fac]**

Out[31]= {fac[3], 3 fac[3 - 1],

    {fac[2], 2 fac[2 - 1], {fac[1], 1}}}

Here is a rule for the **log** function.

In[32]:= **log[x_ y_] := log[x] + log[y]**

This traces the evaluation of **log[a b c d]**, showing all transformations associated with **log**.

In[33]:= **Trace[log[a b c d], log]**

Out[33]= {log[a b c d], log[a] + log[b c d],

    {log[b c d], log[b] + log[c d], {log[c d], log[c] + log[d]}}}

Trace[*expr*, *form*, TraceOn -> *oform*]

> switch on tracing only within forms matching *oform*

Trace[*expr*, *form*, TraceOff -> *oform*]

> switch off tracing within any form matching *oform*

Switching off tracing inside certain forms.

Trace[*expr*, *form*] allows you to trace expressions matching *form* generated at any point in the evaluation of *expr*. Sometimes, you may want to trace only expressions generated during certain parts of the evaluation of *expr*.

By setting the option TraceOn -> *oform*, you can specify that tracing should be done only during the evaluation of forms which match *oform*. Similarly, by setting TraceOff -> *oform*, you can specify that tracing should be switched off during the evaluation of forms which match *oform*.

This shows all steps in the evaluation.

```
In[34]:= Trace[log[fac[2] x]]
Out[34]= {{{fac[2], 2 fac[2 - 1],
    {{2 - 1, -1 + 2, 1}, fac[1], 1}, 2 1, 1 2, 2}, 2 x},
   log[2 x], log[2] + log[x]}
```

This shows only those steps that occur during the evaluation of fac.

```
In[35]:= Trace[log[fac[2] x], TraceOn -> fac]
Out[35]= {{{fac[2], 2 fac[2 - 1],
    {{2 - 1, -1 + 2, 1}, fac[1], 1}, 2 1, 1 2, 2}}}
```

This shows only those steps that do not occur during the evaluation of fac.

```
In[36]:= Trace[log[fac[2] x], TraceOff -> fac]
Out[36]= {{{fac[2], 2}, 2 x}, log[2 x], log[2] + log[x]}
```

Trace[*expr*, *lhs* -> *rhs*]   find all expressions matching *lhs* that arise during the evaluation of *expr*, and replace them with *rhs*

Applying rules to expressions encountered during evaluation.

This tells Trace to return only the arguments of fib used in the evaluation of fib[5].

```
In[37]:= Trace[fib[5], fib[n_] -> n]
Out[37]= {5, {4, {3, {2, {1}, {0}}, {1}}, {2, {1}, {0}}},
   {3, {2, {1}, {0}}, {1}}}
```

A powerful aspect of the *Mathematica* Trace function is that the object it returns is basically a standard *Mathematica* expression which you can manipulate using other *Mathematica* functions. One important point to realize, however, is that Trace wraps all expressions that appear in the list it produces with HoldForm to prevent them from being evaluated. The HoldForm is not displayed in standard *Mathematica* output format, but it is still present in the internal structure of the expression.

This shows the expressions generated at intermediate stages in the evaluation process.

```
In[38]:= Trace[1 + 3^2]
                 2
Out[38]= {{3 , 9}, 1 + 9, 10}
```

The expressions are wrapped with HoldForm to prevent them from evaluating.

```
In[39]:= Trace[1 + 3^2] // InputForm
Out[39]//InputForm=
   {{HoldForm[3^2], HoldForm[9]}, HoldForm[1 + 9], HoldForm[10]}
```

In standard *Mathematica* output format, it is sometimes difficult to tell which lists are associated with the structure returned by Trace, and which are expressions being evaluated.

```
In[40]:= Trace[{1 + 1, 2 + 3}]
Out[40]= {{1 + 1, 2}, {2 + 3, 5}, {2, 5}}
```

Looking at the input form resolves any ambiguities.

```
In[41]:= InputForm[%]
Out[41]//InputForm=
   {{HoldForm[1 + 1], HoldForm[2]},
    {HoldForm[2 + 3], HoldForm[5]}, HoldForm[{2, 5}]}
```

When you use a transformation rule in Trace, the result is evaluated before being wrapped with HoldForm.

```
In[42]:= Trace[fac[4], fac[n_] -> n + 1]
Out[42]= {5, {4, {3, {2}}}}
```

For sophisticated computations, the list structures returned by Trace can be quite complicated. When you use Trace[*expr*, *form*], Trace will include as elements in the lists only those expressions which match the pattern *form*. But whatever pattern you give, the nesting structure of the lists remains the same.

This shows all occurrences of fib[_] in the evaluation of fib[3].

```
In[43]:= Trace[fib[3], fib[_]]
Out[43]= {fib[3], {fib[2], {fib[1]}, {fib[0]}}, {fib[1]}}
```

This shows only occurrences of fib[1], but the nesting of the lists is the same as for fib[_].

```
In[44]:= Trace[fib[3], fib[1]]
Out[44]= {{{fib[1]}}, {fib[1]}}
```

You can set the option TraceDepth -> *n* to tell Trace to include only lists nested at most *n* levels deep. In this way, you can often pick out the "big steps" in a computation, without seeing the details. Note that by setting TraceDepth or TraceOff you can avoid looking at many of the steps in a computation, and thereby significantly speed up the operation of Trace for that computation.

This shows only steps that appear in lists nested at most two levels deep.

```
In[45]:= Trace[fib[3], fib[_], TraceDepth->2]
Out[45]= {fib[3], {fib[2]}, {fib[1]}}
```

Trace[*expr*, *form*, TraceDepth -> *n*]	
	trace the evaluation of *expr*, ignoring steps that lead to lists nested more than *n* levels deep

Restricting the depth of tracing.

When you use Trace[*expr*, *form*], you get a list of all the expressions which match *form* produced during the evaluation of *expr*. Sometimes it is useful to see not only these expressions, but also the results that were obtained by evaluating them. You can do this by setting the option TraceForward -> True in Trace.

This shows not only expressions which match fac[_], but also the results of evaluating those expressions.	*In[46]:=* **Trace[fac[4], fac[_], TraceForward->True]**
	Out[46]= {fac[4], {fac[3], {fac[2], {fac[1], 1}, 2}, 6}, 24}

Expressions picked out using Trace[*expr*, *form*] typically lie in the middle of an evaluation chain. By setting TraceForward -> True, you tell Trace to include also the expression obtained at the end of the evaluation chain. If you set TraceForward -> All, Trace will include *all* the expressions that occur after the expression matching *form* on the evaluation chain.

With TraceForward->All, all elements on the evaluation chain after the one that matches fac[_] are included.	*In[47]:=* **Trace[fac[4], fac[_], TraceForward->All]**
	Out[47]= {fac[4], 4 fac[4 - 1],
	{fac[3], 3 fac[3 - 1], {fac[2], 2 fac[2 - 1], {fac[1], 1},
	2 1, 1 2, 2}, 3 2, 2 3, 6}, 4 6, 24}

By setting the option TraceForward, you can effectively see what happens to a particular form of expression during an evaluation. Sometimes, however, you want to find out not what happens to a particular expression, but instead how that expression was generated. You can do this by setting the option TraceBackward. What TraceBackward does is to show you what *preceded* a particular form of expression on an evaluation chain.

This shows that the number 120 came from the evaluation of fac[5] during the evaluation of fac[10].	*In[48]:=* **Trace[fac[10], 120, TraceBackward->True]**
	Out[48]= {{{{{{fac[5], 120}}}}}}

Here is the whole evaluation chain associated with the generation of the number 120.	*In[49]:=* **Trace[fac[10], 120, TraceBackward->All]**
	Out[49]= {{{{{{fac[5], 5 fac[5 - 1], 5 24, 120}}}}}}

TraceForward and TraceBackward allow you to look forward and backward in a particular evaluation chain. Sometimes, you may also want to look at the evaluation chains within which the particular evaluation chain occurs. You can do this using TraceAbove. If you set the option TraceAbove -> True, then Trace will include the initial and final expressions in all the relevant evaluation chains. With TraceAbove -> All, Trace includes all the expressions in all these evaluation chains.

This includes the initial and final expressions in all evaluation chains which contain the chain that contains 120.	*In[50]:=* **Trace[fac[7], 120, TraceAbove->True]**
	Out[50]= {fac[7], {fac[6], {fac[5], 120}, 720}, 5040}

This shows all the ways that fib[2] is generated during the evaluation of fib[5].	*In[51]:=* **Trace[fib[5], fib[2], TraceAbove->True]**
	Out[51]= {fib[5], {fib[4], {fib[3], {fib[2], 2}, 3},
	{fib[2], 2}, 5}, {fib[3], {fib[2], 2}, 3}, 8}

`TraceForward -> True`	include the final expression in the evaluation chain containing *form*
`TraceForward -> All`	include all expressions following *form* in the evaluation chain
`TraceBackward -> True`	include the first expression in the evaluation chain containing *form*
`TraceBackward -> All`	include all expressions preceding *form* in the evaluation chain
`TraceAbove -> True`	include the first and last expressions in all evaluation chains which contain the chain containing *form*
`TraceAbove -> All`	include all expressions in all evaluation chains which contain the chain containing *form*

Option settings for including extra steps in trace lists.

The basic way that Trace [*expr*, …] works is to intercept each expression encountered during the evaluation of *expr*, and then to use various criteria to determine whether this expression should be recorded. Normally, however, Trace intercepts expressions only *after* function arguments have been evaluated. By setting TraceOriginal -> True, you can get Trace also to look at expressions *before* function arguments have been evaluated.

This includes expressions which match
fac[_] both before and after argument
evaluation.

In[52]:= **Trace[fac[3], fac[_], TraceOriginal -> True]**

Out[52]= {fac[3], {fac[3 - 1], fac[2], {fac[2 - 1], fac[1]}}}

The list structure produced by Trace normally includes only expressions that constitute steps in non-trivial evaluation chains. Thus, for example, individual symbols that evaluate to themselves are not normally included. Nevertheless, if you set TraceOriginal -> True, then Trace looks at absolutely every expression involved in the evaluation process, including those that have trivial evaluation chains.

In this case, Trace includes absolutely
all expressions, even those with trivial
evaluation chains.

In[53]:= **Trace[fac[1], TraceOriginal -> True]**

Out[53]= {fac[1], {fac}, {1}, fac[1], 1}

option name	default value	
TraceForward	False	whether to show expressions following *form* in the evaluation chain
TraceBackward	False	whether to show expressions preceding *form* in the evaluation chain
TraceAbove	False	whether to show evaluation chains leading to the evaluation chain containing *form*
TraceOriginal	False	whether to look at expressions before their heads and arguments are evaluated

Additional options for Trace.

When you use Trace to study the execution of a program, there is an issue about how local variables in the program should be treated. As discussed in Section 2.6.3, *Mathematica* scoping constructs such as Module create symbols with new names to represent local variables. Thus, even if you called a variable x in the original code for your program, the variable may effectively be renamed x$*nnn* when the program is executed.

Trace[*expr*, *form*] is set up so that by default a symbol *x* that appears in *form* will match all symbols with names of the form *x*$*nnn* that arise in the execution of *expr*. As a result, you can for example use Trace[*expr*, x = _] to trace assignment to all variables, local and global, that were named *x* in your original program.

Trace[*expr*, *form*, MatchLocalNames -> False]   include all steps in the execution of *expr* that match *form*, with no replacements for local variable names allowed

Preventing the matching of local variables.

In some cases, you may want to trace only the global variable *x*, and not any local variables that were originally named *x*. You can do this by setting the option MatchLocalNames -> False.

This traces assignments to all variables with names of the form x$*nnn*.

```
In[54]:= Trace[Module[{x}, x = 5], x = _]

Out[54]= {x$1 = 5}
```

This traces assignments only to the specific global variable *x*.

```
In[55]:= Trace[Module[{x}, x = 5], x = _,
                                  MatchLocalNames -> False]

Out[55]= {}
```

The function `Trace` performs a complete computation, then returns a structure which represents the history of the computation. Particularly in very long computations, it is however sometimes useful to see traces of the computation as it proceeds. The function `TracePrint` works essentially like `Trace`, except that it prints expressions when it encounters them, rather than saving all of the expressions up to create a list structure.

This prints expressions encountered in the evaluation of `fib[3]`.	*In[56]:=* `TracePrint[fib[3], fib[_]]`
	
	`fib[3]`
	  `fib[3 - 1]`
	  `fib[2]`
	    `fib[2 - 1]`
	    `fib[1]`
	    `fib[2 - 2]`
	    `fib[0]`
	  `fib[3 - 2]`
	  `fib[1]`
	Out[56]= 3

The sequence of expressions printed by `TracePrint` corresponds to the sequence of expressions given in the list structure returned by `Trace`. Indentation in the output from `TracePrint` corresponds to nesting in the list structure from `Trace`. You can use the `Trace` options `TraceOn`, `TraceOff` and `TraceForward` in `TracePrint`. However, since `TracePrint` produces output as it goes, it cannot support the option `TraceBackward`. In addition, `TracePrint` is set up so that `TraceOriginal` is effectively always set to True.

`Trace[`*expr*`, ... ]`	trace the evaluation of *expr*, returning a list structure containing the expressions encountered
`TracePrint[`*expr*`, ... ]`	trace the evaluation of *expr*, printing the expressions encountered
`TraceDialog[`*expr*`, ... ]`	trace the evaluation of *expr*, initiating a dialog when each specified expression is encountered
`TraceScan[`*f*`, `*expr*`, ... ]`	trace the evaluation of *expr*, applying *f* to `HoldForm` of each expression encountered

Functions for tracing evaluation.

This enters a dialog when `fac[5]` is encountered during the evaluation of `fac[10]`.	*In[57]:=* `TraceDialog[fac[10], fac[5]]` `TraceDialog::dgbgn: Entering Dialog; use Return[ ] to exit.` *Out[58]=* `fac[5]`

Inside the dialog you can for example find out where you are by looking at the "stack".

```
In[59]:= Stack[ ]
Out[59]= {TraceDialog, Times, Times, Times, Times, Times, fac}
```

This returns from the dialog, and gives the final result from the evaluation of `fac[10]`.

```
In[60]:= Return[ ]
TraceDialog::dgend: Exiting Dialog.
Out[57]= 3628800
```

The function `TraceDialog` effectively allows you to stop in the middle of a computation, and interact with the *Mathematica* environment that exists at that time. You can for example find values of intermediate variables in the computation, and even reset those values. There are however a number of subtleties, mostly associated with pattern and module variables.

What `TraceDialog` does is to call the function `Dialog` on a sequence of expressions. The `Dialog` function is discussed in detail in Section 2.11.2. When you call `Dialog`, you are effectively starting a subsidiary *Mathematica* session with its own sequence of input and output lines.

In general, you may need to apply arbitrary functions to the expressions you get while tracing an evaluation. `TraceScan[f, expr, ... ]` applies *f* to each expression that arises. The expression is wrapped with `HoldForm` to prevent it from evaluating.

In `TraceScan[f, expr, ... ]`, the function *f* is applied to expressions before they are evaluated. `TraceScan[f, expr, patt, fp]` applies *f* before evaluation, and *fp* after evaluation.

■ 2.5.11 Advanced Topic: The Evaluation Stack

Throughout any computation, *Mathematica* maintains an *evaluation stack* containing the expressions it is currently evaluating. You can use the function `Stack` to look at the stack. This means, for example, that if you interrupt *Mathematica* in the middle of a computation, you can use `Stack` to find out what *Mathematica* is doing.

The expression that *Mathematica* most recently started to evaluate always appears as the last element of the evaluation stack. The previous elements of the stack are the other expressions whose evaluation is currently in progress.

Thus at the point when *x* is being evaluated, the stack associated with the evaluation of an expression like $f[g[x]]$ will have the form $\{f[g[x]], g[x], x\}$.

`Stack[_]` gives the expressions that are being evaluated at the time when it is called, in this case including the `Print` function.

```
In[1]:= f[g[ Print[Stack[_]] ]] ;
{f[g[Print[Stack[_]]]]; , f[g[Print[Stack[_]]]],
 g[Print[Stack[_]]], Print[Stack[_]]}
```

`Stack[ ]` gives the tags associated with the evaluations that are being done when it is called.

```
In[2]:= f[g[ Print[Stack[ ]] ]] ;
{CompoundExpression, f, g, Print}
```

In general, you can think of the evaluation stack as showing what functions called what other functions to get to the point *Mathematica* is at in your computation. The sequence of expressions corresponds to the first elements in the successively nested lists returned by Trace with the option TraceAbove set to True.

Stack[ ]	give a list of the tags associated with evaluations that are currently being done
Stack[_]	give a list of all expressions currently being evaluated
Stack[*form*]	include only expressions which match *form*

Looking at the evaluation stack.

It is rather rare to call Stack directly in your main *Mathematica* session. More often, you will want to call Stack in the middle of a computation. Typically, you can do this from within a dialog, or subsidiary session, as discussed in Section 2.11.2.

Here is the standard recursive definition of the factorial function.

```
In[3]:= fac[1] = 1; fac[n_] := n fac[n-1]
```

This evaluates fac[10], starting a dialog when it encounters fac[4].

```
In[4]:= TraceDialog[fac[10], fac[4]]

TraceDialog::dgbgn: Entering Dialog; use Return[ ] to exit.

Out[5]= fac[4]
```

This shows what objects were being evaluated when the dialog was started.

```
In[6]:= Stack[ ]

Out[6]= {TraceDialog, Times, Times, Times, Times, Times,
   Times, fac}
```

This ends the dialog.

```
In[7]:= Return[ ]

TraceDialog::dgend: Exiting Dialog.

Out[4]= 3628800
```

In the simplest cases, the *Mathematica* evaluation stack is set up to record *all* expressions currently being evaluated. Under some circumstances, however, this may be inconvenient. For example, executing Print[Stack[ ]] will always show a stack with Print as the last function.

The function StackInhibit allows you to avoid this kind of problem. StackInhibit[*expr*] evaluates *expr* without modifying the stack.

StackInhibit prevents Print from being included on the stack.

```
In[5]:= f[g[ StackInhibit[Print[Stack[ ]]] ]] ;

{CompoundExpression, f, g}
```

Functions like TraceDialog automatically call StackInhibit each time they start a dialog. This means that Stack does not show functions that are called within the dialog, only those outside.

`StackInhibit[`*expr*`]`	evaluate *expr* without modifying the stack
`StackBegin[`*expr*`]`	evaluate *expr* with a fresh stack
`StackComplete[`*expr*`]`	evaluate *expr* with intermediate expressions in evaluation chains included on the stack

Controlling the evaluation stack.

By using `StackInhibit` and `StackBegin`, you can control which parts of the evaluation process are recorded on the stack. `StackBegin[`*expr*`]` evaluates *expr*, starting a fresh stack. This means that during the evaluation of *expr*, the stack does not include anything outside the `StackBegin`. Functions like `TraceDialog[`*expr*`, ... ]` call `StackBegin` before they begin evaluating *expr*, so that the stack shows how *expr* is evaluated, but not how `TraceDialog` was called.

StackBegin[*expr*] uses a fresh stack in the evaluation of *expr*.

```
In[6]:= f[ StackBegin[ g[h[ StackInhibit[Print[Stack[ ]]] ]] ] ]
{g, h}
Out[6]= f[g[h[Null]]]
```

`Stack` normally shows you only those expressions that are currently being evaluated. As a result, it includes only the latest form of each expression. Sometimes, however, you may find it useful also to see earlier forms of the expressions. You can do this using `StackComplete`.

What `StackComplete[`*expr*`]` effectively does is to keep on the stack the complete evaluation chain for each expression that is currently being evaluated. In this case, the stack corresponds to the sequence of expressions obtained from `Trace` with the option `TraceBackward -> All` as well as `TraceAbove -> True`.

■ 2.5.12 Advanced Topic: Controlling Infinite Evaluation

The general principle that *Mathematica* follows in evaluating expressions is to go on applying transformation rules until the expressions no longer change. This means, for example, that if you make an assignment like x = x + 1, *Mathematica* should go into an infinite loop. In fact, *Mathematica* stops after a definite number of steps, determined by the value of the global variable `$RecursionLimit`. You can always stop *Mathematica* earlier by explicitly interrupting it.

This assignment could cause an infinite loop. *Mathematica* stops after a number of steps determined by `$RecursionLimit`.

```
In[1]:= x = x + 1
$RecursionLimit::reclim: Recursion depth of 256 exceeded.
Out[1]= 250 + Hold[1 + x]
```

When *Mathematica* stops without finishing evaluation, it returns a held result. You can continue the evaluation by explicitly calling `ReleaseHold`.

```
In[2]:= ReleaseHold[%]
$RecursionLimit::reclim: Recursion depth of 256 exceeded.
Out[2]= 499 + Hold[1 + x]
```

`$RecursionLimit`	maximum depth of the evaluation stack
`$IterationLimit`	maximum length of an evaluation chain

Global variables that limit infinite evaluation.

Here is a circular definition, whose evaluation is stopped by `$IterationLimit`.

```
In[3]:= {a, b} = {b, a}
$IterationLimit::itlim: Iteration limit of 4096 exceeded.
$IterationLimit::itlim: Iteration limit of 4096 exceeded.
Out[3]= {Hold[b], Hold[a]}
```

The variables `$RecursionLimit` and `$IterationLimit` control the two basic ways that an evaluation can become infinite in *Mathematica*. `$RecursionLimit` limits the maximum depth of the evaluation stack, or equivalently, the maximum nesting depth that would occur in the list structure produced by `Trace`. `$IterationLimit` limits the maximum length of any particular evaluation chain, or the maximum length of any single list in the structure produced by `Trace`.

Functions such as `FixedPoint`, `Do` and `ReplaceRepeated` (the `//.` operator) use the global value of `$IterationLimit` as the default setting for their own `IterationLimit` option, which determines the maximum number of iterations they will allow.

`$RecursionLimit` and `$IterationLimit` are by default set to values that are appropriate for most computations, and most computer systems. You can, however, reset these variables to any integer (above a lower limit), or to `Infinity`. Note that on most computer systems, you should never set `$RecursionLimit = Infinity`, as discussed on page 528.

This resets `$RecursionLimit` and `$IterationLimit` to 20.

```
In[4]:= $RecursionLimit = $IterationLimit = 20
Out[4]= 20
```

Now infinite definitions like this are stopped after just 20 steps.

```
In[5]:= t = {t}
$RecursionLimit::reclim: Recursion depth of 20 exceeded.
Out[5]= {{{{{{{{{{{{{{{{Hold[{t}]}}}}}}}}}}}}}}}}
```

Without an end condition, this recursive definition leads to infinite computations.

```
In[6]:= fn[n_] := {fn[n-1], n}
```

A fairly large structure is built up before the computation is stopped.

```
In[7]:= fn[10]
```

$RecursionLimit::reclim: Recursion depth of 20 exceeded.

$RecursionLimit::reclim: Recursion depth of 20 exceeded.

$RecursionLimit::reclim: Recursion depth of 20 exceeded.

```
General::stop:
   Further output of $RecursionLimit::reclim
     will be suppressed during this calculation.
```

```
Out[7]= {{{{{{{{{{{{{{{Hold[fn[Hold[-2 - 1] - 1]],
               Hold[Hold[-2 - 1]]}, -2}, -1}, 0}, 1}, 2}, 3}, 4},
          5}, 6}, 7}, 8}, 9}, 10}
```

Here is another recursive definition.

```
In[8]:= fm[n_] := fm[n - 1]
```

In this case, no complicated structure is built up, and the computation is stopped by $IterationLimit.

```
In[9]:= fm[0]
```

$IterationLimit::itlim: Iteration limit of 20 exceeded.

```
Out[9]= Hold[fm[-19 - 1]]
```

It is important to realize that infinite loops can take up not only time but also computer memory. Computations limited by $IterationLimit do not normally build up large intermediate structures. But those limited by $RecursionLimit often do. In many cases, the size of the structures produced is a linear function of the value of $RecursionLimit. But in some cases, the size can grow exponentially, or worse, with $RecursionLimit.

An assignment like x = x + 1 is obviously circular. When you set up more complicated recursive definitions, however, it can be much more difficult to be sure that the recursion terminates, and that you will not end up in an infinite loop. The main thing to check is that the right-hand sides of your transformation rules will always be different from the left-hand sides. This ensures that evaluation will always "make progress", and *Mathematica* will not simply end up applying the same transformation rule to the same expression over and over again.

Some of the trickiest cases occur when you have rules that depend on complicated /; conditions (see Section 2.3.5). One particularly awkward case is when the condition involves a "global variable". *Mathematica* may think that the evaluation is finished because the expression did not change. However, a side effect of some other operation could change the value of the global variable, and so should lead to a new result in the evaluation. The best way to avoid this kind of difficulty is not to use global variables in /; conditions. If all else fails, you can type Update[s] to tell *Mathematica* to update all expressions involving s. Update[ ] tells *Mathematica* to update absolutely all expressions.

■ 2.5.13 Advanced Topic: Interrupts and Aborts

Section 1.3.7 described how you can interrupt a *Mathematica* computation by pressing appropriate keys on your keyboard.

In some cases, you may want to simulate such interrupts from within a *Mathematica* program. In general, executing `Interrupt[ ]` has the same effect as pressing interrupt keys. On a typical system, a menu of options is displayed, as discussed in Section 1.3.7.

`Interrupt[ ]`	interrupt a computation
`Abort[ ]`	abort a computation
`CheckAbort[`*expr*`, `*failexpr*`]`	evaluate *expr*, returning *failexpr* if an abort occurs
`AbortProtect[`*expr*`]`	evaluate *expr*, masking the effect of aborts until the evaluation is complete

Interrupts and aborts.

The function `Abort[ ]` has the same effect as interrupting a computation, and selecting the `abort` option in the interrupt menu.

You can use `Abort[ ]` to implement an "emergency stop" in a program. In almost all cases, however, you should try to use functions like `Return` and `Throw`, which lead to more controlled behavior.

Abort terminates the computation, so only the first Print is executed.	`In[1]:= Print[a]; Abort[ ]; Print[b]`
	a
	`Out[1]= $Aborted`

If you abort at any point during the evaluation of a *Mathematica* expression, *Mathematica* normally abandons the evaluation of the whole expression, and returns the value `$Aborted`.

You can, however, "catch" aborts using the function `CheckAbort`. If an abort occurs during the evaluation of *expr* in `CheckAbort[`*expr*`, `*failexpr*`]`, then `CheckAbort` returns *failexpr*, but the abort propagates no further. Functions like `Dialog` use `CheckAbort` in this way to contain the effect of aborts.

CheckAbort catches the abort, and returns the value aborted.	`In[2]:= CheckAbort[Print[a]; Abort[ ]; Print[b], aborted]`
	a
	`Out[2]= aborted`
The effect of the Abort is contained by CheckAbort, so the second Print is executed.	`In[3]:= CheckAbort[Print[a]; Abort[ ], aborted]; Print[b]`
	a
	b

When you construct sophisticated programs in *Mathematica*, you may sometimes want to guarantee that a particular section of code in a program cannot be aborted, either interactively or by calling `Abort`. The function `AbortProtect` allows you to evaluate an expression, saving up any aborts until after the evaluation of the expression is complete.

The `Abort` is saved up until `AbortProtect` is finished.	`In[4]:= AbortProtect[Abort[ ]; Print[a]]; Print[b]`
	`a`
	`Out[4]= $Aborted`
The `CheckAbort` sees the abort, but does not propagate it further.	`In[5]:= AbortProtect[Abort[ ]; CheckAbort[Print[a], x]]; Print[b]`
	`b`

Even inside `AbortProtect`, `CheckAbort` will see any aborts that occur, and will return the appropriate *failexpr*. Unless this *failexpr* itself contains `Abort[ ]`, the aborts will be "absorbed" by the `CheckAbort`.

■ 2.5.14 Compiling *Mathematica* Expressions

If you make a definition like `f[x_] := x Sin[x]`, *Mathematica* will store the expression `x Sin[x]` in a form that can be evaluated for any x. Then when you give a particular value for x, *Mathematica* substitutes this value into `x Sin[x]`, and evaluates the result. The internal code that *Mathematica* uses to perform this evaluation is set up to work equally well whether the value you give for x is a number, a list, an algebraic object, or any other kind of expression.

Having to take account of all these possibilities inevitably makes the evaluation process slower. However, if *Mathematica* could *assume* that x will be a machine number, then it could avoid many steps, and potentially evaluate an expression like `x Sin[x]` much more quickly.

Using `Compile`, you can construct *compiled functions* in *Mathematica*, which evaluate *Mathematica* expressions assuming that all the parameters which appear are numbers (or logical variables). `Compile[{`x_1`, `x_2`, ... }, `*expr*`]` takes an expression *expr* and returns a "compiled function" which evaluates this expression when given arguments x_1, x_2, ...

In general, `Compile` creates a `CompiledFunction` object which contains a sequence of simple instructions for evaluating the compiled function. The instructions are chosen to be close to those found in the machine code of a typical computer, and can thus be executed quickly.

`Compile[{`x_1`, `x_2`, ... }, `*expr*`]`	create a compiled function which evaluates *expr* for numerical values of the x_i

Creating compiled functions.

This defines `f` to be a pure function which evaluates `x Sin[x]` for any x.	`In[1]:= f = Function[{x}, x Sin[x]]`
	`Out[1]= Function[{x}, x Sin[x]]`
This creates a compiled function for evaluating `x Sin[x]`.	`In[2]:= fc = Compile[{x}, x Sin[x]]`
	`Out[2]= CompiledFunction[<>]`

f and fc yield the same results, but fc runs faster when the argument you give is a number.

```
In[3]:= {f[2.5], fc[2.5]}
Out[3]= {1.49618, 1.49618}
```

Compile is useful in situations where you have to evaluate a particular numerical or logical expression many times. By taking the time to call Compile, you can get a compiled function which can be executed more quickly than an ordinary *Mathematica* function.

For simple expressions such as x Sin[x], there is usually little difference between the execution speed for ordinary and compiled functions. However, as the size of the expressions involved increases, the advantage of compilation also increases. For large expressions, compilation can speed up execution by a factor as large as 20.

Compilation makes the biggest difference for expressions containing a large number of simple, say arithmetic, functions. For more complicated functions, such as BesselK or Eigenvalues, most of the computation time is spent executing internal *Mathematica* algorithms, on which compilation has no effect.

This creates a compiled function for finding values of the tenth Legendre polynomial.

```
In[4]:= pc = Compile[{x}, Evaluate[LegendreP[10, x]]]
Out[4]= CompiledFunction[<>]
```

This finds the value of the tenth Legendre polynomial with argument 0.4.

```
In[5]:= pc[0.4]
Out[5]= 0.0968391
```

This uses built-in numerical code.

```
In[6]:= LegendreP[10, 0.4]
Out[6]= 0.0968391
```

Even though you can use compilation to speed up numerical functions that you write, you should still try to use built-in *Mathematica* functions whenever possible. Built-in functions will usually run faster than any compiled *Mathematica* programs you can create. In addition, they typically use more extensive algorithms, with more complete control over numerical precision and so on.

You should realize that built-in *Mathematica* functions quite often themselves use Compile. Thus, for example, NIntegrate by default automatically uses Compile on the expression you tell it to integrate. Similarly, functions like Plot and Plot3D use Compile on the expressions you ask them to plot. Built-in functions that use Compile typically have the option Compiled. Setting Compiled -> False tells the functions not to use Compile.

Compile[{{x_1, t_1}, {x_2, t_2}, ... }, *expr*]

compile *expr* assuming that x_i is of type t_i

Compile[*vars*, *expr*, {{p_1, pt_1}, ... }]

compile *expr*, assuming that subexpressions which match p_i are of type pt_i

_Integer	machine-size integer
_Real	machine-precision approximate real number
_Complex	machine-precision approximate complex number
True | False	logical variable

Specifying types for compilation.

Compile works by making assumptions about the types of objects that occur in evaluating the expression you give. The default assumption is that all variables in the expression are approximate real numbers.

Compile nevertheless also allows integers, complex numbers and logical variables (True or False). You can specify the type of a particular variable by giving a pattern which matches only values that have that type. Thus, for example, you can use the pattern _Integer to specify the integer type. Similarly, you can use True | False to specify a logical variable that must be either True or False.

This compiles the expression 5 i + j with the assumption that i and j are integers.

In[7]:= Compile[{{i, _Integer}, {j, _Integer}}, 5 i + j]

Out[7]= CompiledFunction[<>]

This yields an integer result.

In[8]:= %[8, 7]

Out[8]= 47

The types that Compile handles correspond essentially to the types that computers typically handle at a machine-code level. Thus, for example, Compile can handle approximate real numbers that have machine precision, but it cannot handle arbitrary-precision numbers. In addition, if you specify that a particular variable is an integer, Compile generates code only for the case when the integer is of "machine size", typically between $\pm 2^{31}$.

When the expression you ask to compile involves only standard arithmetic and logical operations, Compile can deduce the types of objects generated at every step simply from the types of the input variables. However, if you call other functions, Compile will typically not know what type of value they return. If you do not specify otherwise, Compile assumes that any other function yields an approximate real number value. You can, however, also give an explicit list of patterns, specifying what type to assume for an expression that matches a particular pattern.

This defines a function which yields an integer result when given an integer argument.

```
In[9]:= com[i_] := Binomial[2i, i]
```

This compiles x^com[i] using the assumption that com[_] is always an integer.

```
In[10]:= Compile[{x, {i, _Integer}}, x^com[i],
                                    {{com[_], _Integer}}]
Out[10]= CompiledFunction[<>]
```

This evaluates the compiled function.

```
In[11]:= %[5.6, 1]
Out[11]= 31.36
```

The idea of Compile is to create a function which is optimized for certain types of arguments. Compile is nevertheless set up so that the functions it creates work with whatever types of arguments they are given. When the optimization cannot be used, a standard *Mathematica* expression is evaluated to find the value of the function.

Here is a compiled function for taking the square root of a variable.

```
In[12]:= sq = Compile[{x}, Sqrt[x]]
Out[12]= CompiledFunction[<>]
```

If you give a real number argument, optimized code is used.

```
In[13]:= sq[4.5]
Out[13]= 2.12132
```

In this case, a standard *Mathematica* expression is evaluated to get the result.

```
In[14]:= sq[1 + u]
Out[14]= Sqrt[1 + u]
```

The compiled code generated by Compile must make assumptions not only about the types of arguments you will supply, but also about the types of all objects that arise during the execution of the code. Sometimes these types depend on the actual *values* of the arguments you specify. Thus, for example, Sqrt[x] yields a real number result for real x if x is not negative, but yields a complex number if x is negative.

Compile always makes a definite assumption about the type returned by a particular function. If this assumption turns out to be invalid in a particular case when the code generated by Compile is executed, then *Mathematica* simply abandons the compiled code in this case, and evaluates an ordinary *Mathematica* expression to get the result.

The optimized code cannot be used in this case, so a standard *Mathematica* expression is evaluated to get the result.

```
In[15]:= sq[-4.5]
Out[15]= 2.12132 I
```

An important feature of Compile is that it can handle not only mathematical expressions, but also various simple *Mathematica* programs. Thus, for example, Compile can handle conditionals and control flow structures.

In all cases, Compile[*vars*, *expr*] holds its arguments unevaluated. This means that you can explicitly give a "program" as the expression to compile.

This creates a compiled version of a *Mathematica* program which implements Newton's approximation to square roots.

```
In[16]:= newt = Compile[ {x, {n, _Integer}},
               Module[{t}, t = x; Do[t = (t + x/t)/2, {n}]; t]
           ]
Out[16]= CompiledFunction[<>]
```

This executes the compiled code.

```
In[17]:= newt[2.4, 6]
Out[17]= 1.54919
```

■ 2.5.15 Advanced Topic: Manipulating Compiled Code

If you use compiled code created by Compile only within *Mathematica* itself, then you should never need to know the details of its internal form. Nevertheless, the compiled code can be represented by an ordinary *Mathematica* expression, and it is sometimes useful to manipulate it.

For example, you can take compiled code generated by Compile, and feed it to external programs or devices. You can also create CompiledFunction objects yourself, then execute them in *Mathematica*.

In all of these cases, you need to know the internal form of CompiledFunction objects. The first element of a CompiledFunction object is always a list of patterns which specifies the types of arguments accepted by the object. The fourth element of a CompiledFunction object is a *Mathematica* pure function that is used if the compiled code instruction stream fails for any reason to give a result.

CompiledFunction[{arg_1, arg_2, ... }, {n_i, n_r, n_c, n_l}, *instr*, *func*]
                                 compiled code taking arguments of type arg_i and executing
                                 the instruction stream *instr* using n_k registers of type k

The structure of a compiled code object.

This shows the explicit form of the compiled code generated by Compile.

```
In[1]:= Compile[{x}, x^2] // InputForm
Out[1]//InputForm=
    CompiledFunction[{_Real}, {1, 2, 0, 0},
      {{1, 1}, {3, 1, 0}, {10, 2, 0}, {40, 0, 0, 1}, {7, 1}},
      #1^2 & ]
```

The instruction stream in a CompiledFunction object consists of a list of instructions for a simple idealized computer. The computer is assumed to have numbered "registers", on which operations can be performed. There are four types of registers: integer, real, complex and logical. A list of the total number of registers of each type required to evaluate a particular CompiledFunction object is given as the second element of the object.

The actual instructions in the compiled code object are given as lists. The first element is an integer "opcode" which specifies what operation should be performed. Subsequent elements are either the numbers of registers of particular types, or literal constants. Typically the last element of the list is the number of a "destination register", into which the result of the operation should be put.

Full details of compiled code objects are given in the Wolfram Research technical report "The *Mathematica* Compiler".

2.6 Modularity and the Naming of Things

■ 2.6.1 Modules and Local Variables

Mathematica normally assumes that all your variables are *global*. This means that every time you use a name like x, *Mathematica* normally assumes that you are referring to the *same* object.

Particularly when you write programs, however, you may not want all your variables to be global. You may, for example, want to use the name x to refer to two quite different variables in two different programs. In this case, you need the x in each program to be treated as a *local* variable.

You can set up local variables in *Mathematica* using *modules*. Within each module, you can give a list of variables which are to be treated as local to the module.

Module[{x, y, ... }, *body*]	a module with local variables *x, y, ...*

Creating modules in *Mathematica*.

This defines the global variable t to have value 17.

In[1]:= **t = 17**

Out[1]= 17

The t inside the module is local, so it can be treated independently of the global t.

In[2]:= **Module[{t}, t=8; Print[t]]**

8

The global t still has value 17.

In[3]:= **t**

Out[3]= 17

The most common way that modules are used is to set up temporary or intermediate variables inside functions you define. It is important to make sure that such variables are kept local. If they are not, then you will run into trouble whenever their names happen to coincide with the names of other variables.

The intermediate variable t is specified to be local to the module.

In[4]:= **f[v_] := Module[{t}, t = (1 + v)^2; t = Expand[t]]**

This runs the function f.

In[5]:= **f[a + b]**

Out[5]= $1 + 2 a + a^2 + 2 b + 2 a b + b^2$

The global t still has value 17.

In[6]:= **t**

Out[6]= 17

You can treat local variables in modules just like other symbols. Thus, for example, you can use them as names for local functions, you can assign attributes to them, and so on.

This sets up a module which defines a local function f.	*In[7]:=* **gfac10[k_] :=** **Module[{f, n}, f[1] = 1; f[n_] := k + n f[n-1]; f[10]]**
In this case, the local function f is just an ordinary factorial.	*In[8]:=* **gfac10[0]** *Out[8]=* 3628800
In this case, f is set up as a generalized factorial.	*In[9]:=* **gfac10[2]** *Out[9]=* 8841802

When you set up a local variable in a module, *Mathematica* initially assigns no value to the variable. This means that you can use the variable in a purely symbolic way, even if there was a global value defined for the variable outside the module.

This uses the global value of t defined above, and so yields a number.	*In[10]:=* **Expand[(1 + t)^3]** *Out[10]=* 5832
Here **Length** simply receives a number as its argument.	*In[11]:=* **Length[Expand[(1 + t)^3]]** *Out[11]=* 0
The local variable t has no value, so it acts as a symbol, and **Expand** produces the anticipated algebraic result.	*In[12]:=* **Module[{t}, Length[Expand[(1 + t)^3]]]** *Out[12]=* 4

Module[{x = x_0, y = y_0, ... }, *body*]
          a module with initial values for local variables

Assigning initial values to local variables.

This specifies t to be a local variable, with initial value u.	*In[13]:=* **g[u_] := Module[{ t = u }, t += t/(1 + u)]**
This uses the definition of g.	*In[14]:=* **g[a]** *Out[14]=* $a + \dfrac{a}{1 + a}$

You can define initial values for any of the local variables in a module. The initial values are always evaluated before the module is executed. As a result, even if a variable x is defined as local to the module, the global x will be used if it appears in an expression for an initial value.

The initial value of u is taken to be the global value of t.	*In[15]:=* **Module[{t = 6, u = t}, u^2]** *Out[15]=* 289

> *lhs* := Module[*vars*, *rhs* /; *cond*]
>
>   share local variables between *rhs* and *cond*

Using local variables in definitions with conditions.

When you set up /; conditions for definitions, you often need to introduce temporary variables. In many cases, you may want to share these temporary variables with the body of the right-hand side of the definition. *Mathematica* allows you to enclose the whole right-hand side of your definition in a module, including the condition.

This defines a function with a condition attached.	`In[16]:= h[x_] := Module[{t}, t^2 - 1 /; (t = x - 4) > 1]`

Mathematica shares the value of the local variable t between the condition and the body of the right-hand side.	`In[17]:= h[10]`
	
	`Out[17]= 35`

■ 2.6.2 Local Constants

> With[{*x* = x_0, *y* = y_0, ... }, *body*]
>
>   define local constants *x*, *y*, ...

Defining local constants.

Module allows you to set up local *variables*, to which you can assign any sequence of values. Often, however, all you really need are local *constants*, to which you assign a value only once. The *Mathematica* With construct allows you to set up such local constants.

This defines a global value for t.	`In[1]:= t = 17`
	
	`Out[1]= 17`

This defines a function using t as a local constant.	`In[2]:= w[x_] := With[{t = x + 1}, t + t^3]`
This uses the definition of w.	`In[3]:= w[a]` `Out[3]= 1 + a + (1 + a)`^{3}

t still has its global value.	`In[4]:= t`
	
	`Out[4]= 17`

Just as in Module, the initial values you define in With are evaluated before the With is executed.

The expression t + 1 which gives the value of the local constant t is evaluated using the global t.

```
In[5]:= With[{t = t + 1}, t^2]

Out[5]= 324
```

The way With[{x = x_0, ... }, *body*] works is to take *body*, and replace every occurrence of x, etc. in it by x_0, etc. You can think of With as a generalization of the / . operator, suitable for application to *Mathematica* code instead of other expressions.

This replaces x with a.

```
In[6]:= With[{x = a}, x = 5]

Out[6]= 5
```

After the replacement, the body of the With is a = 5, so a gets the global value 5.

```
In[7]:= a

Out[7]= 5
```

This clears the value of a.

```
In[8]:= Clear[a]
```

In some respects, With is like a special case of Module, in which each local variable is assigned a value exactly once.

One of the main reasons for using With rather than Module is that it typically makes the *Mathematica* programs you write easier to understand. In a module, if you see a local variable x at a particular point, you potentially have to trace through all of the code in the module to work out the value of x at that point. In a With construct, however, you can always find out the value of a local constant simply by looking at the initial list of values, without having to trace through specific code.

If you have several With constructs, it is always the innermost one for a particular variable that is in effect. You can mix Module and With. The general rule is that the innermost one for a particular variable is the one that is in effect.

With nested With constructs, the innermost one is always the one in effect.

```
In[9]:= With[{t = 8}, With[{t = 9}, t^2]]

Out[9]= 81
```

You can mix Module and With constructs.

```
In[10]:= Module[{t = 8}, With[{t = 9}, t^2]]

Out[10]= 81
```

Local variables in inner constructs do not mask ones outside unless the names conflict.

```
In[11]:= With[{t = a}, With[{u = b}, t + u]]

Out[11]= a + b
```

Except for the question of when x and *body* are evaluated, With[{x = x_0}, *body*] works essentially like *body* / . x -> x_0. However, With behaves in a special way when the expression *body* itself contains With or Module constructs. The main issue is to prevent the local constants in the various With constructs from conflicting with each other, or with global objects. The details of how this is done are discussed in Section 2.6.3 below.

The y in the inner With is renamed to prevent it from conflicting with the global y.

```
In[12]:= With[{x = 2 + y}, Hold[With[{y = 4}, x + y]]]

Out[12]= Hold[With[{y$ = 4}, 2 + y + y$]]
```

■ 2.6.3 How Modules Work

The way modules work in *Mathematica* is basically very simple. Every time any module is used, a new symbol is created to represent each of its local variables. The new symbol is given a unique name which cannot conflict with any other names. The name is formed by taking the name you specify for the local variable, followed by $, with a unique "serial number" appended.

The serial number is found from the value of the global variable $ModuleNumber. This variable counts the total number of times any Module of any form has been used.

> ■ Module generates symbols with names of the form $x\$nnn$ to represent each local variable.

The basic principle of modules in *Mathematica*.

This shows the symbol generated for t within the module.

```
In[1]:= Module[{t}, Print[t]]

t$1
```

The symbols are different every time any module is used.

```
In[2]:= Module[{t, u}, Print[t]; Print[u]]

t$2
u$2
```

For most purposes, you will never have to deal directly with the actual symbols generated inside modules. However, if for example you start up a dialog while a module is being executed, then you will see these symbols. The same is true whenever you use functions like Trace to watch the evaluation of modules.

You see the symbols that are generated inside modules when you use Trace.

```
In[3]:= Trace[ Module[{t}, t = 3] ]

Out[3]= {Module[{t}, t = 3], t$3 = 3, 3}
```

This starts a dialog inside a module.

```
In[4]:= Module[{t}, t = 6; Dialog[ ]]
```

Inside the dialog, you see the symbols generated for local variables such as t.

```
In[5]:= Stack[_]

Out[5]= {t$4 = 6; Dialog[], Dialog[]}
```

You can work with these symbols as you would with any other symbols.

```
In[6]:= t$4 + 1

Out[6]= 7
```

This returns from the dialog.

```
In[7]:= Return[t$4 ^ 2]

Out[4]= 36
```

Under some circumstances, it is convenient explicitly to return symbols that are generated inside modules.

You can explicitly return symbols that are generated inside modules.

```
In[5]:= Module[{t}, t]

Out[5]= t$5
```

You can treat these symbols as you
would any others.

```
In[6]:= %^2 + 1
```

$$Out[6]= 1 + t\$5^2$$

Unique[*x*]	generate a new symbol with a unique name of the form *x$nnn*
Unique[{*x*, *y*, ... }]	generate a list of new symbols

Generating new symbols with unique names.

The function Unique allows you to generate new symbols in the same way as Module does. Each time you call Unique, $ModuleNumber is incremented, so that the names of new symbols are guaranteed to be unique.

This generates a unique new symbol
whose name starts with x.

```
In[7]:= Unique[x]
```

```
Out[7]= x$6
```

Each time you call Unique you get a
symbol with a larger serial number.

```
In[8]:= {Unique[x], Unique[x], Unique[x]}
```

```
Out[8]= {x$7, x$8, x$9}
```

If you call Unique with a list of names,
you get the same serial number for each
of the symbols.

```
In[9]:= Unique[{x, xa, xb}]
```

```
Out[9]= {x$10, xa$10, xb$10}
```

You can use the standard *Mathematica ?name* mechanism to get information on symbols that were generated inside modules or by the function Unique.

Executing this module generates the
symbol q$*nnn*.

```
In[10]:= Module[{q}, q^2 + 1]
```

$$Out[10]= 1 + q\$11^2$$

You can see the generated symbol here.

```
In[11]:= ?q*
```

```
q      q$11
```

Symbols generated by Module and Unique behave in exactly the same way as other symbols for the purposes of evaluation. However, these symbols carry the attribute Temporary, which specifies that they should be removed completely from the system when they are no longer used. Thus most symbols that are generated inside modules are removed when the execution of those modules is finished. The symbols survive only if they are explicitly returned.

This shows a new q variable generated
inside a module.

```
In[11]:= Module[{q}, Print[q]]
```

```
q$12
```

The new variable is removed when the
execution of the module is finished, so it
does not show up here.

```
In[12]:= ?q*
```

```
q      q$11
```

You should realize that the use of names such as *x$nnn* for generated symbols is purely a convention. You can in principle give any symbol a name of this form. But if you do, the symbol may collide with one that is produced by Module or Unique.

An important point to note is that symbols generated by Module and Unique are in general unique only within a particular *Mathematica* session. The variable $ModuleNumber which determines the serial numbers for these symbols is always reset at the beginning of each session.

This means in particular that if you save expressions containing generated symbols in a file, and then read them into another session, there is no guarantee that conflicts will not occur.

One way to avoid such conflicts is explicitly to set $ModuleNumber differently at the beginning of each session. In particular, if you set $ModuleNumber = 10^10 $SessionID, you should avoid any conflicts. The global variable $SessionID should give a unique number which characterizes a particular *Mathematica* session on a particular computer. The value of this variable is determined from such quantities as the absolute date and time, the ID of your computer, and, if appropriate, the ID of the particular *Mathematica* process.

$ModuleNumber	the serial number for symbols generated by Module and Unique
$SessionID	a number that should be different for every *Mathematica* session

Variables to be used in determining serial numbers for generated symbols.

Having generated appropriate symbols to represent the local variables you have specified, Module[*vars*, *body*] then has to evaluate *body* using these symbols. The first step is to take the actual expression *body* as it appears inside the module, and effectively to use With to replace all occurrences of each local variable name with the appropriate generated symbol. After this is done, Module actually performs the evaluation of the resulting expression.

An important point to note is that Module[*vars*, *body*] inserts generated symbols only into the actual expression *body*. It does not, for example, insert such symbols into code that is called from *body*, but does not explicitly appear in *body*.

Section 2.6.6 below will discuss how you can use Block to set up "local values" which work in a different way.

Since x does not appear explicitly in the body of the module, the local value is not used.

```
In[12]:= tmp = x^2 + 1; Module[{x = 4}, tmp]

Out[12]= 1 + x^2
```

Most of the time, you will probably set up modules by giving explicit *Mathematica* input of the form Module[*vars*, *body*]. Since the function Module has the attribute HoldAll, the form of *body* will usually be kept unevaluated until the module is executed.

It is, however, possible to build modules dynamically in *Mathematica*. The generation of new symbols, and their insertion into *body* are always done only when a module is actually executed, not when the module is first given as *Mathematica* input.

This evaluates the body of the module immediately, making x appear explicitly.	`In[13]:= tmp = x^2 + 1; Module[{x = 4}, Evaluate[tmp]]`
	
	`Out[13]= 17`

■ 2.6.4 Advanced Topic: Variables in Pure Functions and Rules

`Module` and `With` allow you to give a specific list of symbols whose names you want to treat as local. In some situations, however, you want to automatically treat certain symbol names as local.

For example, if you use a pure function such as `Function[{x}, x + a]`, you want x to be treated as a "formal parameter", whose specific name is local. The same is true of the x that appears in a rule like `f[x_] -> x^2`, or a definition like `f[x_] := x^2`.

Mathematica uses a uniform scheme to make sure that the names of formal parameters which appear in constructs like pure functions and rules are kept local, and are never confused with global names. The basic idea is to replace formal parameters when necessary by symbols with names of the form *x*$. By convention, *x*$ is never used as a global name.

Here is a nested pure function.	`In[1]:= Function[{x}, Function[{y}, x + y]]`
	
	`Out[1]= Function[{x}, Function[{y}, x + y]]`

Mathematica renames the formal parameter y in the inner function to avoid conflict with the global object y.	`In[2]:= %[2y]`
	
	`Out[2]= Function[{y$}, 2 y + y$]`

The resulting pure function behaves as it should.	`In[3]:= %[a]`
	
	`Out[3]= a + 2 y`

In general, *Mathematica* renames the formal parameters in an object like `Function[`*vars*`, `*body*`]` whenever *body* is modified in any way by the action of another pure function.

The formal parameter y is renamed because the body of the inner pure function was changed.	`In[4]:= Function[{x}, Function[{y}, x + y]] [a]`
	
	`Out[4]= Function[{y$}, a + y$]`

Since the body of the inner function does not change, the formal parameter is not renamed.	`In[5]:= Function[{x}, x + Function[{y}, y^2]] [a]`
	
	`Out[5]= a + Function[{y}, y^2]`

Mathematica renames formal parameters in pure functions more liberally than is strictly necessary. In principle, renaming could be avoided if the names of the formal parameters in a particular function do not actually conflict with parts of expressions substituted into the body of the pure function. For uniformity, however, *Mathematica* still renames formal parameters even in such cases.

In this case, the formal parameter x in the inner function shields the body of the function, so no renaming is needed.	`In[6]:= Function[{x}, Function[{x}, x + y]] [a]` `Out[6]= Function[{x}, x + y]`

Here are three nested functions.	`In[7]:= p = Function[{x},`
	`            Function[{y}, Function[{z}, x + y + z]]]`
	`Out[7]= Function[{x}, Function[{y}, Function[{z}, x + y + z]]]`

Both inner functions are renamed in this case.	`In[8]:= %[a]` `Out[8]= Function[{y$}, Function[{z$}, a + y$ + z$]]`

As mentioned on page 208, pure functions in *Mathematica* are like λ expressions in formal logic. The renaming of formal parameters allows *Mathematica* pure functions to reproduce all the semantics of standard λ expressions faithfully.

`Function[{`*x*`, ... }, `*body*`]`	local parameters
lhs `-> ` *rhs* and *lhs* `:> ` *rhs*	local pattern names
lhs `= ` *rhs* and *lhs* `:= ` *rhs*	local pattern names
`With[{`*x* `= ` x_0`, ... }, `*body*`]`	local constants
`Module[{`*x*`, ... }, `*body*`]`	local variables

Scoping constructs in *Mathematica*.

Mathematica has several "scoping constructs" in which certain names are treated as local. When you mix these constructs in any way, *Mathematica* does appropriate renamings to avoid conflicts.

Mathematica renames the formal parameter of the pure function to avoid a conflict.	`In[9]:= With[{x = a}, Function[{a}, a + x]]` `Out[9]= Function[{a$}, a$ + a]`
Here the local constant in the inner With is renamed to avoid a conflict.	`In[10]:= With[{x = y}, Hold[With[{y = 4}, x + y]]]` `Out[10]= Hold[With[{y$ = 4}, y + y$]]`
There is no conflict between names in this case, so no renaming is done.	`In[11]:= With[{x = y}, Hold[With[{z = x + 2}, z + 2]]]` `Out[11]= Hold[With[{z = y + 2}, z + 2]]`
The local variable y in the module is renamed to avoid a conflict.	`In[12]:= With[{x = y}, Hold[Module[{y}, x + y]]]` `Out[12]= Hold[Module[{y$}, y + y$]]`
If you execute the module, however, the local variable is renamed again to make its name unique.	`In[13]:= ReleaseHold[%]` `Out[13]= y + y$1`

Mathematica treats transformation rules as scoping constructs, in which the names you give to patterns are local. You can set up named patterns either using *x_*, *x__* and so on, or using *x:patt*.

The x in the h goes with the x_, and is considered local to the rule.

In[14]:= **With[{x = 5}, g[x_, x] -> h[x]]**

Out[14]= g[x_, 5] -> h[x]

In a rule like f[x_] -> x + y, the x which appears on the right-hand side goes with the name of the x_ pattern. As a result, this x is treated as a variable local to the rule, and cannot be modified by other scoping constructs.

The y, on the other hand, is not local to the rule, and *can* be modified by other scoping constructs. When this happens, *Mathematica* renames the patterns in the rule to prevent the possibility of a conflict.

Mathematica renames the x in the rule to prevent a conflict.

In[15]:= **With[{w = x}, f[x_] -> w + x]**

Out[15]= f[x$_] -> x + x$

When you use With on a scoping construct, *Mathematica* automatically performs appropriate renamings. In some cases, however, you may want to make substitutions inside scoping constructs, without any renaming. You can do this using the /. operator.

When you substitute for y using With, the x in the pure function is renamed to prevent a conflict.

In[16]:= **With[{y = x + a}, Function[{x}, x + y]]**

Out[16]= Function[{x$}, x$ + (a + x)]

If you use /. rather than With, no such renaming is done.

In[17]:= **Function[{x}, x + y] /. y -> a + x**

Out[17]= Function[{x}, x + (a + x)]

When you apply a rule such as *f*[*x*_] -> *rhs*, or use a definition such as *f*[*x*_] := *rhs*, *Mathematica* implicitly has to substitute for *x* everywhere in the expression *rhs*. It effectively does this using the /. operator. As a result, such substitution does not respect scoping constructs. However, when the insides of a scoping construct are modified by the substitution, the other variables in the scoping construct are renamed.

This defines a function for creating pure functions.

In[18]:= **mkfun[var_, body_] := Function[{var}, body]**

The x and x^2 are explicitly inserted into the pure function, effectively by using the /. operator.

In[19]:= **mkfun[x, x^2]**

Out[19]= Function[{x}, x^2]

The pure function created by this definition takes an additional argument.

In[20]:= **mkfun2[var_, body_] := Function[{var, x}, body + x]**

The x already inside the pure function is renamed in this case.

In[21]:= **mkfun2[x, x^2]**

Out[21]= Function[{x, x$}, x^2 + x$]

■ 2.6.5 Dummy Variables in Mathematics

When you set up mathematical formulas, you often have to introduce various kinds of local objects or "dummy variables". You can treat such dummy variables using modules and other *Mathematica* scoping constructs.

Integration variables are a common example of dummy variables in mathematics. When you write down a formal integral, conventional notation requires you to introduce an integration variable with a definite name. This variable is essentially "local" to the integral, and its name, while arbitrary, must not conflict with any other names in your mathematical expression.

Here is a function for evaluating an integral.	`In[1]:= p[n_] := Integrate[f[s] s^n, {s, 0, 1}]`

The s here conflicts with the integration variable.

`In[2]:= p[s + 1]`

$$Out[2]= \text{Integrate}[s^{1 + s}\ f[s], \{s, 0, 1\}]$$

Here is a definition with the integration variable specified as local to a module.

`In[3]:= pm[n_] := Module[{s}, Integrate[f[s] s^n, {s, 0, 1}]]`

Since you have used a module, *Mathematica* automatically renames the integration variable to avoid a conflict.

`In[4]:= pm[s + 1]`

$$Out[4]= \text{Integrate}[s\$1^{1 + s}\ f[s\$1], \{s\$1, 0, 1\}]$$

In many cases, the most important issue is that dummy variables should be kept local, and should not interfere with other variables in your mathematical expression. In some cases, however, what is instead important is that different uses of the *same* dummy variable should not conflict.

Repeated dummy variables often appear in products of vectors and tensors. With the "summation convention", any vector or tensor index that appears exactly twice is summed over all its possible values. The actual name of the repeated index never matters, but if there are two separate repeated indices, it is essential that their names do not conflict.

This sets up the repeated index j as a dummy variable.

`In[5]:= q[i_] := Module[{j}, a[i, j] b[j]]`

The module gives different instances of the dummy variable different names.

`In[6]:= q[i1] q[i2]`

`Out[6]= a[i1, j$2] a[i2, j$3] b[j$2] b[j$3]`

There are many situations in mathematics where you need to have variables with unique names. One example is in representing solutions to equations. With an equation like $\sin(x) = 0$, there are an infinite number of solutions, each of the form $x = n\pi$, where n is a dummy variable that can be equal to any integer. If you generate solutions to the equation on two separate occasions, there is no guarantee that the value of n should be same in both cases. As a result, you must set up the solution so that the object n is different every time.

This defines a value for `sinsol`, with n as a dummy variable.

`In[7]:= sinsol := Module[{n}, n Pi]`

Different occurrences of the dummy variable are distinguished.	*In[8]:=* **sinsol - sinsol**
	Out[8]= **n$4 Pi - n$5 Pi**

Another place where unique objects are needed is in representing "constants of integration". When you do an integral, you are effectively solving an equation for a derivative. In general, there are many possible solutions to the equation, differing by additive "constants of integration". The standard *Mathematica* **Integrate** function always returns a solution with no constant of integration. But if you were to introduce constants of integration, you would need to use modules to make sure that they are always unique.

■ 2.6.6 Blocks and Local Values

Modules in *Mathematica* allow you to treat the *names* of variables as local. Sometimes, however, you want the names to be global, but *values* to be local. You can do this in *Mathematica* using **Block**.

Block[{x, y, ... }, *body*]	evaluate *body* using local values for $x, y, ...$
Block[{x = x_0, y = y_0, ... }, *body*]	assign initial values to $x, y, ...$

Setting up local values.

Here is an expression involving **x**.	*In[1]:=* **x^2 + 3**
	Out[1]= $3 + x^2$
This evaluates the previous expression, using a local value for **x**.	*In[2]:=* **Block[{x = a + 1}, %]**
	Out[2]= $3 + (1 + a)^2$
There is no global value for **x**.	*In[3]:=* **x**
	Out[3]= **x**

As described in the sections above, the variable x in a module such as **Module[{x}, *body*]** is always set up to refer to a unique symbol, different each time the module is used, and distinct from the global symbol x. The x in a block such as **Block[{x}, *body*]** is, however, taken to be the global symbol x. What the block does is to make the *value* of x local. The value x had when you entered the block is always restored when you exit the block. And during the execution of the block, x can take on any value.

This sets the symbol **t** to have value 17.	*In[4]:=* **t = 17**
	Out[4]= **17**
Variables in modules have unique local names.	*In[5]:=* **Module[{t}, Print[t]]**
	t$1

In blocks, variables retain their global names, but can have local values.	*In[6]:=* `Block[{t}, Print[t]]` t
t is given a local value inside the block.	*In[7]:=* `Block[{t}, t = 6; t^4 + 1]` *Out[7]=* 1297
When the execution of the block is over, the previous value of t is restored.	*In[8]:=* t *Out[8]=* 17

Blocks in *Mathematica* effectively allow you to set up "environments" in which you can temporarily change the values of variables. Expressions you evaluate at any point during the execution of a block will use the values currently defined for variables in the block. This is true whether the expressions appear directly as part of the body of the block, or are produced at any point in its evaluation.

This defines a delayed value for the symbol u.	*In[9]:=* `u := x^2 + t^2`
If you evaluate u outside a block, the global value for t is used.	*In[10]:=* `u` *Out[10]=* $289 + x^2$
You can specify a temporary value for t to use inside the block.	*In[11]:=* `Block[{t = 5}, u + 7]` *Out[11]=* $32 + x^2$

An important implicit use of `Block` in *Mathematica* is for iteration constructs such as `Do`, `Sum` and `Table`. *Mathematica* effectively uses `Block` to set up local values for the iteration variables in all of these constructs.

`Sum` automatically makes the value of the iterator t local.	*In[12]:=* `Sum[t^2, {t, 10}]` *Out[12]=* 385
The local values in iteration constructs are slightly more general than in `Block`. They handle variables such as a[1], as well as pure symbols.	*In[13]:=* `Sum[a[1]^2, {a[1], 10}]` *Out[13]=* 385

When you set up functions in *Mathematica*, it is sometimes convenient to have "global variables" which can affect the functions without being given explicitly as arguments. Thus, for example, *Mathematica* itself has a global variable `$RecursionLimit` which affects the evaluation of all functions, but is never explicitly given as an argument.

Mathematica will usually keep any value you define for a global variable until you explicitly change it. Often, however, you want to set up values which last only for the duration of a particular computation, or part of a computation. You can do this by making the values local to a *Mathematica* block.

This defines a function which depends on the "global variable" t.	*In[14]:=* `f[x_] := x^2 + t`

In this case, the global value of t is used.	*In[15]:=* **f[a]** *Out[15]=* $17 + a^2$
Inside a block, you can set up a local value for t.	*In[16]:=* **Block[{t = 2}, f[b]]** *Out[16]=* $2 + b^2$

You can use global variables not only to set parameters in functions, but also to accumulate results from functions. By setting up such variables to be local to a block, you can arrange to accumulate results only from functions called during the execution of the block.

This function increments the global variable t, and returns its current value.	*In[17]:=* **h[x_] := (t += x^2)**
If you do not use a block, evaluating h[a] changes the global value of t.	*In[18]:=* **h[a]** *Out[18]=* $17 + a^2$
With a block, only the local value of t is affected.	*In[19]:=* **Block[{t = 0}, h[c]]** *Out[19]=* c^2
The global value of t remains unchanged.	*In[20]:=* **t** *Out[20]=* $17 + a^2$

When you enter a block such as Block[{x}, *body*], any value for x is removed. This means that you can in principle treat x as a "symbolic variable" inside the block. However, if you explicitly return x from the block, it will be replaced by its value outside the block as soon as it is evaluated.

The value of t is removed when you enter the block.	*In[21]:=* **Block[{t}, Print[Expand[(t + 1)^2]]]** $1 + 2 t + t^2$
If you return an expression involving t, however, it is evaluated using the global value for t.	*In[22]:=* **Block[{t}, t^2 - 3]** *Out[22]=* $-3 + (17 + a^2)^2$

■ 2.6.7 Blocks Compared with Modules

When you write a program in *Mathematica*, you should always try to set it up so that its parts are as independent as possible. In this way, the program will be easier for you to understand, maintain and add to.

One of the main ways to ensure that different parts of a program do not interfere is to give their variables only a certain "scope". *Mathematica* provides two basic mechanisms for limiting the scope of variables: modules and blocks.

In writing actual programs, modules are far more common than blocks. When scoping is needed in interactive calculations, however, blocks are often convenient.

`Module[`*vars*`, `*body*`]`	lexical scoping
`Block[`*vars*`, `*body*`]`	dynamic scoping

Mathematica variable scoping mechanisms.

Most traditional computer languages use a so-called "lexical scoping" mechanism for variables, which is analogous to the module mechanism in *Mathematica*. Some symbolic computer languages such as LISP also allow "dynamic scoping", analogous to *Mathematica* blocks.

When lexical scoping is used, variables are treated as local to a particular section of the *code* in a program. In dynamic scoping, the values of variables are local to a part of the *execution history* of the program.

In compiled languages like C, there is a very clear distinction between "code" and "execution history". The symbolic nature of *Mathematica* makes this distinction slightly less clear, since "code" can in principle be built up dynamically during the execution of a program.

What `Module[`*vars*`, `*body*`]` does is to treat the form of the expression *body* at the time when the module is executed as the "code" of a *Mathematica* program. Then when any of the *vars* explicitly appears in this "code", they are considered to be local.

`Block[`*vars*`, `*body*`]` does not look at the *form* of the expression *body*. Instead, throughout the evaluation of *body*, the block uses local values for the *vars*.

This defines m in terms of i.	`In[1]:= m = i^2`
	`Out[1]= i`^{2}
The local value for i in the block is used throughout the evaluation of i + m.	`In[2]:= Block[{i = a}, i + m]`
	`Out[2]= a + a`^{2}
Here only the i that appears explicitly in i + m is treated as a local variable.	`In[3]:= Module[{i = a}, i + m]`
	`Out[3]= a + i`^{2}

■ 2.6.8 Contexts

It is always a good idea to give variables and functions names that are as explicit as possible. Sometimes, however, such names may get inconveniently long.

In *Mathematica*, you can use the notion of "contexts" to organize the names of symbols. Contexts are particularly important in *Mathematica* packages which introduce symbols whose names must not conflict with those of any other symbols. If you write *Mathematica* packages, or make sophisticated use of packages that others have written, then you will need to know about contexts.

The basic idea is that the *full name* of any symbol is broken into two parts: a *context* and a *short name*. The full name is written as *context‘short*, where the ‘ is the backquote or grave accent character (ASCII decimal code 96), called a "context mark" in *Mathematica*.

Here is a symbol with short name x, and context aaaa.	*In[1]:=* **aaaa‘x**
	Out[1]= aaaa‘x
You can use this symbol just like any other symbol.	*In[2]:=* **%^2 - %**
	Out[2]= -aaaa‘x + aaaa‘x^2
You can for example define a value for the symbol.	*In[3]:=* **aaaa‘x = 78**
	Out[3]= 78
Mathematica treats a‘x and b‘x as completely different symbols.	*In[4]:=* **a‘x == b‘x**
	Out[4]= a‘x == b‘x

It is typical to have all the symbols that relate a particular topic in a particular context. Thus, for example, symbols that represent physical units might have a context PhysicalUnits‘. Such symbols might have full names like PhysicalUnits‘Joule or PhysicalUnits‘Mole.

Although you can always refer to a symbol by its full name, it is often convenient to use a shorter name.

At any given point in a *Mathematica* session, there is always a *current context* $Context. You can refer to symbols that are in this context simply by giving their short names.

The default context for *Mathematica* sessions is Global‘.	*In[5]:=* **$Context**
	Out[5]= Global‘
Short names are sufficient for symbols that are in the current context.	*In[6]:=* **{x, Global‘x}**
	Out[6]= {x, x}

Contexts in *Mathematica* work somewhat like file directories in many operating systems. You can always specify a particular file by giving its complete name, including its directory. But at any given point, there is usually a current working directory, analogous to the current *Mathematica* context. Files that are in this directory can then be specified just by giving their short names.

Like directories in many operating systems, contexts in *Mathematica* can be hierarchical. Thus, for example, the full name of a symbol can involve a sequence of context names, as in $c_1‘c_2‘c_3‘name$.

context`*name*  or  $c_1$`c_2`... `*name*	a symbol in an explicitly specified context
`*name*	a symbol in the current context
`*context*`*name* or `$c_1$`c_2`... `*name*	
	a symbol in a specific context relative to the current context
name	a symbol in the current context, or found on the context search path

Specifying symbols in various contexts.

Here is a symbol in the context a`b`.

In[7]:= a`b`x

Out[7]= a`b`x

When you start a *Mathematica* session, the default current context is Global`. Symbols that you introduce will usually be in this context. However, built-in symbols such as Pi are in the context System`.

In order to let you easily access not only symbols in the context Global`, but also in contexts such as System`, *Mathematica* supports the notion of a *context search path*. At any point in a *Mathematica* session, there is both a current context $Context, and also a current context search path $ContextPath. The idea of the search path is to allow you to type in the short name of a symbol, then have *Mathematica* search in a sequence of contexts to find a symbol with that short name.

The context search path for symbols in *Mathematica* is analogous to the "search path" for program files provided in operating systems such as Unix and MS-DOS.

The default context path includes the contexts for system-defined symbols.

In[8]:= $ContextPath

Out[8]= {Global`, System`}

When you type in Pi, *Mathematica* interprets it as the symbol with full name System`Pi.

In[9]:= Context[Pi]

Out[9]= System`

Context[*s*]	the context of a symbol
$Context	the current context in a *Mathematica* session
$ContextPath	the current context search path
Contexts[ ]	a list of all contexts

Finding contexts and context search paths.

When you use contexts in *Mathematica*, there is no reason that two symbols which are in different contexts cannot have the same short name. Thus, for example, you can have symbols with the short name Mole both in the context PhysicalUnits` and in the context BiologicalOrganisms`.

There is, however, then the question of which symbol you actually get when you type in only the short name `Mole`. The answer to this question is determined by which of the contexts comes first in the sequence of contexts listed in the context search path.

This introduces two symbols, both with short name `Mole`.

In[10]:= `{PhysicalUnits`Mole, BiologicalOrganisms`Mole}`

Out[10]= {PhysicalUnits`Mole, BiologicalOrganisms`Mole}

This adds two additional contexts to $ContextPath.

In[11]:= `$ContextPath =`
         `Join[$ContextPath,`
             `{"PhysicalUnits`", "BiologicalOrganisms`"}]`

Out[11]= {Global`, System`, PhysicalUnits`,
  BiologicalOrganisms`}

Now if you type in `Mole`, you get the symbol in the context `PhysicalUnits`.

In[12]:= `Context[Mole]`

Out[12]= PhysicalUnits`

In general, when you type in a short name for a symbol, *Mathematica* assumes that you want the symbol with that name whose context appears earliest in the context search path. As a result, symbols with the same short name whose contexts appear later in the context search path are effectively "shadowed". To refer to these symbols, you need to use their full names.

Mathematica always warns you when you introduce new symbols that "shadow" existing symbols with your current choice for $ContextPath.

This introduces a symbol with short name `Mole` in the context `Global`. *Mathematica* warns you that the new symbol shadows existing symbols with short name `Mole`.

In[13]:= `Global`Mole`

Mole::shdw: Warning: Symbol Mole appears in multiple contexts
    {Global`, PhysicalUnits`, BiologicalOrganisms`};
    definitions in context Global`
    may shadow other definitions.

Out[13]= Mole

Now when you type in `Mole`, you get the symbol in context `Global`.

In[14]:= `Context[Mole]`

Out[14]= Global`

If you once introduce a symbol which shadows existing symbols, it will continue to do so until you either rearrange $ContextPath, or explicitly remove the symbol. You should realize that it is not sufficient to clear the *value* of the symbol; you need to actually remove the symbol completely from *Mathematica*. You can do this using the function `Remove[s]`.

`Clear[s]`	clear the values of a symbol
`Remove[s]`	remove a symbol completely from the system

Clearing and removing symbols in *Mathematica*.

This removes the symbol `Global`Mole`.

In[15]:= `Remove[Mole]`

Now if you type in Mole, you get the   *In[16]:=* **Context[Mole]**
symbol PhysicalUnits`Mole.

                                         Out[16]= PhysicalUnits`

When *Mathematica* prints out the name of a symbol, it has to choose whether to give the full name, or just the short name. What it does is to give whatever version of the name you would have to type in to get the particular symbol, given your current settings for $Context and $ContextPath.

The short name is printed for the first   *In[17]:=* **{PhysicalUnits`Mole, BiologicalOrganisms`Mole}**
symbol, so this would give that symbol
if you typed it in.   *Out[17]=* {Mole, BiologicalOrganisms`Mole}

If you type in a short name for which there is no symbol either in the current context, or in any context on the context search path, then *Mathematica* has to *create* a new symbol with this name. It always puts new symbols of this kind in the current context, as specified by $Context.

This introduces the new symbol with   *In[18]:=* **tree**
short name tree.

                                         Out[18]= tree

Mathematica puts tree in the current   *In[19]:=* **Context[tree]**
context Global`.

                                         Out[19]= Global`

■ 2.6.9 Contexts and Packages

A typical package written in *Mathematica* introduces several new symbols intended for use outside the package. These symbols may correspond for example to new functions or new objects defined in the package.

There is a general convention that all new symbols introduced in a particular package are put into a context whose name is related to the name of the package. When you read in the package, it adds this context at the beginning of your context search path $ContextPath.

This reads in a package for doing   *In[1]:=* **<<Calculus`LaplaceTransform`**
Laplace transforms.

The package prepends its context to   *In[2]:=* **$ContextPath**
$ContextPath.

                                         Out[2]= {Calculus`LaplaceTransform`,

                                              Calculus`Common`LaplaceFunctions`, Global`, System`}

The symbol LaplaceTransform is in the   *In[3]:=* **Context[LaplaceTransform]**
context set up by the package.

                                         Out[3]= Calculus`LaplaceTransform`

You can refer to the symbol using its   *In[4]:=* **LaplaceTransform[t^3, t, s]**
short name.

$$Out[4]= \frac{6}{s^4}$$

The full names of symbols defined in packages are often quite long. In most cases, however, you will only need to use their short names. The reason for this is that after you have read in a package, its context is added to $ContextPath, so the context is automatically searched whenever you type in a short name.

There is a complication, however, when two symbols with the same short name appear in two different packages. In such a case, *Mathematica* will warn you when you read in the second package. It will tell you which symbols will be "shadowed" by the new symbols that are being introduced.

The symbol `LaplaceTransform` in the context `Calculus`LaplaceTransform`` is shadowed by the symbol with the same short name in the new package.	`In[5]:= <<NewLaplace`` `LaplaceTransform::shdw:` `Warning: Symbol LaplaceTransform` `appears in multiple contexts {NewLaplace`,`     `Calculus`LaplaceTransform`}; definitions in context`     `NewLaplace` may shadow other definitions.`
You can access the shadowed symbol by giving its full name.	`In[6]:= Calculus`LaplaceTransform`LaplaceTransform[t^3, t, s]` `Out[6]=` $\dfrac{6}{s^4}$

Conflicts can occur not only between symbols in different packages, but also between symbols in packages and symbols that you introduce directly in your *Mathematica* session. If you define a symbol in your current context, then this symbol will shadow any other symbol with the same short name in packages that you read in. The reason for this is that *Mathematica* always searches for symbols in the current context before looking in contexts on the context search path.

This defines a function in the current context.	`In[7]:= Div[f_] = 1/f` `Out[7]=` $\dfrac{1}{f}$
Any other functions with short name `Div` will be shadowed by the one in your current context.	`In[8]:= <<Calculus`VectorAnalysis`` `Div::shdw: Warning: Symbol Div appears in multiple contexts` `{Calculus`VectorAnalysis`, Global`}; definitions in context`     `Global` may shadow other definitions.`

This sets up the coordinate system for vector analysis.	`In[9]:= SetCoordinates[Cartesian[x, y, z]]`
	
	`Out[9]= Cartesian`

This removes `Div` completely from the current context.	`In[10]:= Clear[Div]; Remove[Div]`

Now the `Div` from the package is used.	`In[11]:= Div[{x, y^2, x}]`
	
	`Out[11]= 1 + 2 y`

If you get into the situation where unwanted symbols are shadowing the symbols you want, the best thing to do is usually to get rid of the unwanted symbols using `Remove[s]`. An alternative that is sometimes appropriate is to rearrange the entries in `$ContextPath` and the value of `$Context` so as to make the contexts containing symbols you want be searched first.

`$Packages`	a list of the contexts corresponding to all packages loaded into your *Mathematica* session

Getting a list of packages.

■ 2.6.10 Setting Up *Mathematica* Packages

In a typical *Mathematica* package, there are generally two kinds of new symbols that are introduced. The first kind are ones that you want to "export" for use outside the package. The second kind are ones that you want to use only internally within the package. You can distinguish these two kinds of symbols by putting them in different contexts.

The usual convention is to put symbols intended for export in a context with a name *Package`* that corresponds to the name of the package. Whenever the package is read in, it adds this context to the context search path, so that the symbols in this context can be referred to by their short names.

Symbols that are not intended for export, but are instead intended only for internal use within the package, are conventionally put into a context with the name *Package*`Private`. This context is *not* added to the context search path. As a result, the symbols in this context cannot be accessed except by giving their full names.

Package`	symbols for export
Package`Private`	symbols for internal use only
`System``	built-in *Mathematica* symbols
Needed$_1$`, *Needed$_2$*`, ...	other contexts needed in the package

Contexts conventionally used in *Mathematica* packages.

There is a standard sequence of *Mathematica* commands that is typically used to set up the contexts in a package. These commands set the values of `$Context` and `$ContextPath` so that the new symbols which are introduced are created in the appropriate contexts.

BeginPackage["*Package*`"]	set *Package*` to be the current context, and put only System` on the context search path
f::usage = "*text*", ...	introduce the objects intended for export (and no others)
Begin["`Private`"]	set the current context to *Package*`Private`
f[*args*] = *value*, ...	give the main body of definitions in the package
End[ ]	revert to the previous context (here *Package*`)
EndPackage[ ]	end the package, prepending the *Package*` to the context search path

The standard sequence of context control commands in a package.

```
BeginPackage["Collatz`"]

Collatz::usage =
        "Collatz[n] gives a list of the iterates in the 3n+1 problem,
        starting from n. The conjecture is that this sequence always
        terminates."

Begin["`Private`"]

Collatz[1] := {1}

Collatz[n_Integer]  := Prepend[Collatz[3 n + 1], n] /; OddQ[n] && n > 0

Collatz[n_Integer]  := Prepend[Collatz[n/2], n] /; EvenQ[n] && n > 0

End[ ]

EndPackage[ ]
```

The sample package `Collatz.m`.

The convention of defining usage messages at the beginning of a package is essentially a trick for creating symbols you want to export in the appropriate context. The point is that in defining these messages, the only symbols you mention are exactly the ones you want to export. These symbols are then created in the context *Package*`, which is then current.

In the actual definitions of the functions in a package, there are typically many new symbols, introduced as parameters, temporary variables, and so on. The convention is to put all these symbols in the context *Package*`Private`, which is not put on the context search path when the package is read in.

This reads in the sample package given above.

In[1]:= <<Collatz.m

The `EndPackage` command in the package adds the context associated with the package to the context search path.	`In[2]:= $ContextPath` `Out[2]= {Collatz`, Global`, System`}`
The `Collatz` function was created in the context `Collatz`.	`In[3]:= Context[Collatz]` `Out[3]= Collatz``
The parameter `n` is put in the private context `Collatz`Private`.	`In[4]:= ?Collatz`Private`*` `Collatz`Private`n`

In the `Collatz` package, the functions that are defined depend only on built-in *Mathematica* functions. Often, however, the functions defined in one package may depend on functions defined in another package.

Two things are needed to make this work. First, the other package must be read in, so that the functions needed are defined. And second, the context search path must include the context that these functions are in.

You can explicitly tell *Mathematica* to read in a package at any point using the command `<<context`. (Section 2.10.4 discusses the tricky issue of translation from system-independent context names to system-dependent file names.) Often, however, you want to set it up so that a particular package is read in only if it is needed. The command `Needs["context`"]` tells *Mathematica* to read in a package if the context associated with that package is not already in the list `$Packages`.

`Get["context`"]`  or  `<<context``	read in the package corresponding to the specified context
`Needs["context`"]`	read in the package if the specified context is not already in `$Packages`
`BeginPackage["Package`", {"Needed₁`", ... }]`	begin a package, specifying that certain contexts in addition to `System`` are needed

Functions for specifying interdependence of packages.

If you use `BeginPackage["Package`"]` with a single argument, *Mathematica* puts on the context search path only the *Package*` context and the contexts for built-in *Mathematica* symbols. If the definitions you give in your package involve functions from other packages, you must make sure that the contexts for these packages are also included in your context search path. You can do this by giving the additional contexts as arguments to `BeginPackage`. `BeginPackage` automatically calls `Needs` on these contexts, reading in the corresponding packages if necessary, and then making sure that the contexts are on the context search path.

Begin["*context*`"]	switch to a new current context
End[ ]	revert to the previous context

Context manipulation functions.

Executing a function like Begin which manipulates contexts changes the way that *Mathematica* interprets names you type in. However, you should realize that the change is effective only in subsequent expressions that you type in. The point is that *Mathematica* always reads in a complete input expression, and interprets the names in it, before it executes any part of the expression. As a result, by the time Begin is executed in a particular expression, the names in the expression have already been interpreted, and it is too late for Begin to have an effect.

The fact that context manipulation functions do not have an effect until the *next* complete expression is read in means that you must be sure to give those functions as separate expressions, typically on separate lines, when you write *Mathematica* packages.

The name x is interpreted before this expression is executed, so the Begin has no effect.

In[4]:= **Begin["a`"]; Print[Context[x]]; End[ ]**

Global`

Out[4]= a`

Context manipulation functions are used primarily as part of packages intended to be read into *Mathematica*. Sometimes, however, you may find it convenient to use such functions interactively.

This can happen, for example, if you go into a dialog, say using TraceDialog, while executing a function defined in a package. The parameters and temporary variables in the function are typically in a private context associated with the package. Since this context is not on your context search path, *Mathematica* will print out the full names of the symbols, and will require you to type in these full names in order to refer to the symbols. You can however use Begin["*Package*`Private`"] to make the private context of the package your current context. This will make *Mathematica* print out short names for the symbols, and allow you to refer to the symbols by their short names.

■ 2.6.11 Automatic Loading of Packages

Previous sections have discussed explicit loading of *Mathematica* packages using <<*package* and Needs[*package*]. Sometimes, however, you may want to set *Mathematica* up so that it automatically loads a particular package when the package is needed.

You can use DeclarePackage to give the names of symbols which are defined in a particular package. Then, when one of these symbols is actually used, *Mathematica* will automatically load the package where the symbol is defined.

> **DeclarePackage["*context*`", {"*name₁*", "*name₂*", ... }]**
> declare that a package should automatically be loaded if a symbol with any of the names *nameᵢ* is used

Arranging for automatic loading of packages.

This specifies that the symbols Div, Grad and Curl are defined in Calculus`VectorAnalysis`.

```
In[1]:= DeclarePackage["Calculus`VectorAnalysis`",
                                    {"Div", "Grad", "Curl"}]

Out[1]= Calculus`VectorAnalysis`
```

When you first use Grad, *Mathematica* automatically loads the package that defines it.

```
In[2]:= Grad[x^2 + y^2]

Out[2]= {2 x, 2 y, 0}
```

When you set up a large collection of *Mathematica* packages, it is often a good idea to create an additional "names file" which contains a sequence of DeclarePackage commands, specifying packages to load when particular names are used. Within a particular *Mathematica* session, you then need to load explicitly only the names file. When you have done this, all the other packages will automatically be loaded if and when they are needed.

DeclarePackage works by immediately creating symbols with the names you specify, but giving each of these symbols the special attribute Stub. Whenever *Mathematica* finds a symbol with the Stub attribute, it automatically loads the package corresponding to the context of the symbol, in an attempt to find the definition of the symbol.

2.7 Textual Output

■ 2.7.1 Output Formats

When you have finished a computation, you typically need to output the result. *Mathematica* provides a variety of *output formats* in which you can give your results.

The standard format that *Mathematica* uses in a typical session is set up to approximate traditional mathematical notation. In this format, expressions are laid out in a two-dimensional fashion, with exponents raised, fractions built up, and so on.

While two-dimensional format is convenient for output, it cannot be used for subsequent input to *Mathematica*. Any input given to *Mathematica* must consist of lines of text with an effectively one-dimensional structure. You can use InputForm[*expr*] to format an expression in a form suitable for input to *Mathematica*.

OutputForm[*expr*]	standard two-dimensional mathematical form
InputForm[*expr*]	one-dimensional form suitable for input to *Mathematica*

Two basic output formats.

Here is an expression printed in standard *Mathematica* output form. It involves superscripts and built-up fractions.

```
In[1]:= x^4/4 + 1/y^2

         4
        x      -2
Out[1]= -- + y
        4
```

Here is the same expression in a one-dimensional form suitable for input to *Mathematica*.

```
In[2]:= InputForm[%]

Out[2]//InputForm= x^4/4 + y^(-2)
```

InputForm allows you to generate a textual form for any *Mathematica* expression, suitable for editing, or other kinds of textual manipulation.

When you use a text-based interface to *Mathematica*, functions like Edit automatically call InputForm to write the expressions you want to edit in a suitable form. When you use a notebook interface to *Mathematica*, the front end usually requests an input form version of *every* result you generate, as well as an output form version. You can typically switch between the output form and input form versions of a particular cell in a *Mathematica* notebook by choosing the "formatted" and "unformatted" options for it. In unformatted form, you can usually modify the contents of a cell using standard text editing tools.

TeXForm[*expr*]	TEX input form
CForm[*expr*]	C language input form
FortranForm[*expr*]	Fortran input form

Mathematica output suitable for input to other systems.

By using `InputForm`, you can write a *Mathematica* expression in a form suitable for input to *Mathematica* itself. In some cases, however, you want to take an expression generated by *Mathematica*, and feed it as input to *another* system. *Mathematica* includes functions for writing expressions in forms suitable for input to the TEX typesetting system, and the C and Fortran programming languages. Some details of these functions are discussed in Sections 1.10.5 and 1.10.4.

Here is an expression in standard *Mathematica* output form.	`In[3]:= x^5/7 + y^3 - Log[y]` $$Out[3]= \frac{x^5}{7} + y^3 - Log[y]$$
Here is the same expression in a form suitable for input to the TEX typesetting system.	`In[4]:= TeXForm[%]` `Out[4]//TeXForm= {{{x^5}}\over 7} + {y^3} - \log (y)`
Here is the expression in C language form. C macros for objects like `Power` are defined in the header file `mdefs.h`.	`In[5]:= CForm[%]` `Out[5]//CForm= Power(x,5)/7 + Power(y,3) - Log(y)`
Here is the Fortran form.	`In[6]:= FortranForm[%]` `Out[6]//FortranForm= x**5/7 + y**3 - Log(y)`

In most output formats, the way *Mathematica* prints a particular expression often bears little relation to the way in which it stores that expression internally. For most purposes, you never need to know exactly how an expression is stored. But if you want to manipulate the *structure* of the expression, particularly as part of a program, you may need to see what its internal form is. You can do this using an output format such as `FullForm`.

FullForm[*expr*]	the explicit form of *expr* in functional notation
TreeForm[*expr*]	a representation of the expression tree for *expr*
PrintForm[*expr*]	the internal representation of the print form for *expr*

Output forms that reveal internal representation.

Here is an expression in standard *Mathematica* output form.

```
In[7]:= x^2/3 + 1/y^2

         2
        x     -2
Out[7]= ─── + y
         3
```

Here is the same expression in an explicit functional notation that mirrors the internal representation of the expression.

```
In[8]:= FullForm[%]

Out[8]//FullForm=
  Plus[Times[Rational[1, 3], Power[x, 2]], Power[y, -2]]
```

Here is a representation of the expression as a tree structure.

```
In[9]:= TreeForm[%]

Out[9]//TreeForm=
  Plus[|                                      ,  |            ]
       Times[|              ,  |          ]    Power[y, -2]
              Rational[1, 3]    Power[x, 2]
```

■ 2.7.2 How Output Formats Work

In every *Mathematica* calculation, there are at least two basic steps. The first step is to perform the actual computation, taking your input, and evaluating it to get a result. The second step is to take the result, and format it for output.

It is important to understand that the output formatting functions such as TeXForm discussed in the previous section affect only the formatting step.

What TeXForm and so on do is to act as "wrappers", which tell *Mathematica* to format the expressions they contain in a special way. The TeXForm function has no effect on evaluation; it merely serves as a way of labeling expressions which should be formatted in a special way.

The TeXForm tells *Mathematica* to format a/b in a special way.

```
In[1]:= t = TeXForm[a/b]

Out[1]//TeXForm= {a\over b}
```

InputForm shows that t contains the TeXForm "wrapper".

```
In[2]:= InputForm[t]

Out[2]//InputForm= {a\over b}
```

Since t contains TeXForm, it will always be printed in TEX form.

```
In[3]:= t

Out[3]//TeXForm= {a\over b}
```

Here the t is printed in TEX form, but the exponent is in standard output form.

```
In[4]:= t^5

                        5
Out[4]= {a\over b}
```

It is very common to want to see an expression you are working with in various different output forms. Usually, when you apply a function like TeXForm to an expression, the function remains "wrapped" around your expression, and to recover your expression, you have to "dig" inside the function. In the particular case when your expression is the current output line %, *Mathematica* has a special mechanism which allows you to avoid "digging" inside functions like TeXForm to get your expression.

Mathematica recognizes when the outermost function in an output expression is the name of an output form (InputForm, TeXForm, etc., or in general any symbol in the list $OutputForms). In this case, *Mathematica* sets the value of Out[*n*] to be not the whole output expression, but instead the expression inside the output form function. This behavior is reflected in the special output label that *Mathematica* uses in this case. Instead of writing just Out[*n*]= at the beginning of your output, *Mathematica* writes something like Out[*n*]//TeXForm=. This label represents the fact that TeXForm[Out[*n*]] is the expression you have generated. As a result, Out[*n*] is the part *inside* the TeXForm function. This means that when you ask for %, or when you refer to the output line later on, you get your expression *without* TeXForm wrapped around it.

The current output line is set to be the expression a^2/b^2, without FortranForm wrapped around it.	*In[5]:=* **FortranForm[(a/b)^2]** *Out[5]//FortranForm=* a**2/b**2
% refers to the expression, without the FortranForm wrapped around it.	*In[6]:=* **%^2** $$Out[6]= \frac{a^4}{b^4}$$

■ 2.7.3 Short and Shallow Output

When you generate a very large output expression in *Mathematica*, you often do not want to see the whole expression at once. Rather, you would first like to get an idea of the general structure of the expression, and then, perhaps, go in and look at particular parts in more detail.

The functions Short and Shallow allow you to see "outlines" of large *Mathematica* expressions.

Short[*expr*]	show a one-line outline of *expr*
Short[*expr*, *n*]	show an *n*-line outline of *expr*
Shallow[*expr*]	show the "top parts" of *expr*
Shallow[*expr*, {*depth*, *length*}]	show the parts of *expr* to the specified depth and length

Showing outlines of expressions.

This generates a long expression. If the whole expression were printed out here, it would go on for 23 lines.	*In[1]:=* **t = Expand[(1 + x + y)^12] ;**
This gives a one-line "outline" of t. The <<87>> indicates that 87 terms are omitted.	*In[2]:=* **Short[t]** *Out[2]//Short=* $1 + 12\ x + 66\ x^2 + <<87>> + y^{12}$

When *Mathematica* generates output, it first effectively writes the output in one long row. Then it looks at the width of text you have asked for, and it chops the row of output into a sequence of separate "lines". Each of the "lines" may of course contain superscripts and built-up fractions, and so may take up more than one actual line on your output device. When you specify a particular number of lines in Short, *Mathematica* takes this to be the number of "logical lines" that you want, not the number of actual physical lines on your particular output device.

Here is a four-line version of t. More terms are shown in this case.

$In[3]:=$ **Short[t, 4]**

$Out[3]//Short=$

$1 + 12\,x + 66\,x^2 + 220\,x^3 + 495\,x^4 + 792\,x^5 + 924\,x^6 +$

$792\,x^7 + 495\,x^8 + 220\,x^9 + 66\,x^{10} + <<75>> + 132\,x\,y^{10} +$

$66\,x^2\,y^{10} + 12\,y^{11} + 12\,x\,y^{11} + y^{12}$

You can use Short with other output forms, such as InputForm.

$In[4]:=$ **Short[InputForm[t]]**

$Out[4]//Short=$ 1 + 12*x + 66*x^2 + <<87>> + y^12

Short works by removing a sequence of parts from an expression until the output form of the result fits on the number of lines you specify. Sometimes, however, you may find it better to specify not how many final output lines you want, but which parts of the expression to drop. Shallow[*expr*, {*depth*, *length*}] includes only *length* arguments to any function, and drops all subexpressions that are below the specified depth.

Shallow shows a different outline of t.

$In[5]:=$ **Shallow[t]**

$Out[5]=$ 1 + 12 x + 66 Power[<<2>>] + 220 Power[<<2>>] + <<87>>

This includes only 10 arguments to each function, but allows any depth.

$In[6]:=$ **Shallow[t, {Infinity, 10}]**

$Out[6]=$ $1 + 12\,x + 66\,x^2 + 220\,x^3 + 495\,x^4 + 792\,x^5 + 924\,x^6 +$

$792\,x^7 + 495\,x^8 + 220\,x^9 + <<81>>$

Shallow is particularly useful when you want to drop parts in a uniform way throughout a highly nested expression, such as a large list structure returned by Trace.

Here is the recursive definition of the Fibonacci function.

$In[7]:=$ **fib[n_] := fib[n-1] + fib[n-2] ; fib[0] = fib[1] = 1**

$Out[7]=$ 1

This generates a large list structure.

$In[8]:=$ **tr = Trace[fib[8]] ;**

You can use Shallow to see an outline of the structure.

$In[9]:=$ **Shallow[tr]**

$Out[9]=$ {fib[<<1>>], Plus[<<2>>],

{{<<3>>}, <<1>>, <<1>>, {<<8>>}, <<4>>},

{{<<3>>}, <<1>>, <<1>>, {<<8>>}, <<4>>}, <<3>>}

Short gives you a less uniform outline, which is more difficult to understand.

```
In[10]:= Short[tr, 3]
Out[10]//Short= {fib[8], fib[8 - 1] + fib[8 - 2], <<4>>, 34}
```

■ 2.7.4 Textual Output Formats

"text"	a string containing arbitrary text

Text strings.

The quotes are not included in standard *Mathematica* output form.

```
In[1]:= "This is a string."
Out[1]= This is a string.
```

In input form, the quotes are included.

```
In[2]:= InputForm[%]
Out[2]//InputForm= "This is a string."
```

You can put any kind of text into a *Mathematica* string. This includes non-English characters, as well as newlines and other control information. Section 2.8.1 discusses in more detail how strings work.

StringForm["cccc``cccc", x_1, x_2, ...]	
	output a string in which successive `` are replaced by successive x_i
StringForm["cccc`i`cccc", x_1, x_2, ...]	
	output a string in which each `i` is replaced by the corresponding x_i

Using format strings.

In many situations, you may want to generate output using a string as a "template", but "splicing" in various *Mathematica* expressions. You can do this using StringForm.

This generates output with each successive `` replaced by an expression.

```
In[3]:= StringForm["x = ``, y = ``", 3, (1 + u)^2]
Out[3]= x = 3, y = (1 + u)^2
```

You can use numbers to pick out expressions in any order.

```
In[4]:= StringForm["{`1`, `2`, `1`}", a, b]
Out[4]= {a, b, a}
```

The string in StringForm acts somewhat like a "format directive" in the formatted output statements of languages such as C and Fortran. You can determine how the expressions in StringForm will be formatted by wrapping them with standard output format functions.

You can specify how the expressions in StringForm are formatted using standard output format functions.

```
In[5]:= StringForm["The `` of `` is ``.",
                        TeXForm, a/b, TeXForm[a/b]]

                             a
Out[5]= The TeXForm of - is {a\over b}.
                             b
```

You should realize that StringForm is only an output format. It does not evaluate in any way. You can use the function StringInsert discussed in Section 2.8.3 to actually splice expressions into strings.

StringForm generates formatted output in standard *Mathematica* output form.

```
In[6]:= StringForm["Q: `` -> ``", a, b]

Out[6]= Q: a -> b
```

In input form, you can see the actual StringForm object.

```
In[7]:= InputForm[%]

Out[7]//InputForm= StringForm["Q: `` -> ``", a, b]
```

StringForm allows you to specify a "template string", then fill in various expressions. Sometimes all you want to do is to concatenate together the output forms for a sequence of expressions. You can do this using SequenceForm.

SequenceForm[*expr*$_1$, *expr*$_2$, ...]	give the output forms of the *expr*$_i$ concatenated together

Output of sequences of expressions.

SequenceForm prints as a sequence of expressions concatenated together.

```
In[8]:= SequenceForm["[x = ", 56, "]"]

Out[8]= [x = 56]
```

HoldForm[*expr*]	give the output form of *expr*, with *expr* maintained unevaluated

Output of unevaluated expressions.

Using text strings and functions like StringForm, you can generate pieces of output that do not necessarily correspond to valid *Mathematica* expressions. Sometimes, however, you want to generate output that corresponds to a valid *Mathematica* expression, but only so long as the expression is not evaluated. The function HoldForm maintains its argument unevaluated, but allows it to be formatted in the standard *Mathematica* output form.

HoldForm maintains 1 + 1 unevaluated.

```
In[9]:= HoldForm[1 + 1]

Out[9]= 1 + 1
```

The HoldForm prevents the actual assignment from being done.

```
In[10]:= HoldForm[x = 3]

Out[10]= x = 3
```

If it was not for the HoldForm, the power would be evaluated.

```
In[11]:= HoldForm[34^78]
```

$$Out[11]= 34^{78}$$

■ 2.7.5 Output Formats for Numbers

ScientificForm[*expr*]	print all numbers in scientific notation
EngineeringForm[*expr*]	print all numbers in engineering notation (exponents divisible by 3)
AccountingForm[*expr*]	print all numbers in standard accounting format

Output formats for numbers.

These numbers are given in the default output format. Large numbers are given in scientific notation.

```
In[1]:= {6.7^-4, 6.7^6, 6.7^8}
```

$$Out[1]= \{0.00049625,\ 90458.4,\ 4.06068\ 10^{6}\}$$

This gives all numbers in scientific notation.

```
In[2]:= ScientificForm[%]
```

$$Out[2]//ScientificForm= \{4.9625\ 10^{-4},\ 9.04584\ 10^{4},\ 4.06068\ 10^{6}\}$$

This gives the numbers in engineering notation, with exponents arranged to be multiples of three.

```
In[3]:= EngineeringForm[%]
```

$$Out[3]//EngineeringForm= \{496.25\ 10^{-6},\ 90.4584\ 10^{3},\ 4.06068\ 10^{6}\}$$

In accounting form, negative numbers are given in parentheses, and scientific notation is never used.

```
In[4]:= AccountingForm[{5.6, -6.7, 10.^7}]
```

$$Out[4]//AccountingForm= \{5.6,\ (6.7),\ 10000000.\}$$

NumberForm[*expr*, *tot*]	print at most *tot* digits of all approximate real numbers in *expr*
ScientificForm[*expr*, *tot*]	use scientific notation with at most *tot* digits
EngineeringForm[*expr*, *tot*]	use engineering notation with at most *tot* digits

Controlling the printed precision of real numbers.

Here is π^9 to 30 decimal places.

```
In[5]:= N[Pi^9, 30]
```

$$Out[5]= 29809.0993334462116665094024401$$

This prints just 10 digits of π^9.

```
In[6]:= NumberForm[%, 10]
```

$$Out[6]//NumberForm= 29809.09933$$

This gives 12 digits, in engineering notation.

$In[7]:=$ **EngineeringForm[%, 12]**

$Out[7]//EngineeringForm=$ 29.8090993334 10^3

option name	default value	
DigitBlock	Infinity	maximum length of blocks of digits between breaks
NumberSeparator	{",", " "}	strings to insert at breaks between blocks of digits to the left and right of a decimal point
NumberPoint	"."	string to use for a decimal point
NumberSigns	{"-", ""}	strings to use for signs of negative and positive numbers
NumberPadding	{"", ""}	strings to use for padding on the left and right
SignPadding	False	whether to insert padding after the sign
NumberFormat	Automatic	function to generate final format of number
ExponentFunction	Automatic	function to determine the exponent to use

Options for number formatting.

All the options in the table except the last one apply to both integers and approximate real numbers.

All the options can be used in any of the functions NumberForm, ScientificForm, EngineeringForm and AccountingForm. In fact, you can in principle reproduce the behavior of any one of these functions simply by giving appropriate options settings in one of the others. The default option settings listed in the table are those for NumberForm.

Setting DigitBlock->n breaks digits into blocks of length n.

$In[8]:=$ **NumberForm[30!, DigitBlock->3]**

$Out[8]//NumberForm=$ 265,252,859,812,191,058,636,308,480,000,000

You can specify any string to use as a separator between blocks of digits.

$In[9]:=$ **NumberForm[30!, DigitBlock->5, NumberSeparator->" "]**

$Out[9]//NumberForm=$ 265 25285 98121 91058 63630 84800 00000

This gives an explicit plus sign for positive numbers, and uses | in place of a decimal point.

$In[10]:=$ **NumberForm[{4.5, -6.8}, NumberSigns->{"-", "+"},**
            NumberPoint->"|"]

$Out[10]//NumberForm=$ {+4|5, -6|8}

When *Mathematica* prints an approximate real number, it has to choose whether scientific notation should be used, and if so, how many digits should appear to the left of the decimal point. What *Mathematica* does is first to find out what the exponent would be if scientific notation were used, and one digit were given to the left of the decimal point. Then it takes this exponent, and applies any function given as the setting for the option ExponentFunction. This function should return the actual exponent to be used, or Null if scientific notation should not be used.

The default is to use scientific notation for all numbers with exponents outside the range -5 to 5.

```
In[11]:= {8.^5, 11.^7, 13.^9}
```

$$Out[11]= \{32768., 1.94872\ 10^7, 1.06045\ 10^{10}\}$$

This uses scientific notation only for numbers with exponents of 10 or more.

```
In[12]:= NumberForm[%,
              ExponentFunction -> (If[-10 < # < 10, Null, #]&)]
```

$$Out[12]//NumberForm= \{32768., 19487171., 1.06045\ 10^{10}\}$$

This forces all exponents to be multiples of 3.

```
In[13]:= NumberForm[%, ExponentFunction -> (3 Quotient[#, 3]&)]
```

$$Out[13]//NumberForm= \{32.768\ 10^3, 19.4872\ 10^6, 10.6045\ 10^9\}$$

Having determined what the mantissa and exponent for a number should be, the final step is to assemble these into the object to print. The option NumberFormat allows you to give an arbitrary function which specifies the print form for the number. The function takes as arguments three strings: the mantissa, the base, and the exponent for the number. If there is no exponent, it is given as "".

This gives the exponents in Fortran-like "e" format.

```
In[14]:= NumberForm[{5.6^10, 7.8^20},
              NumberFormat -> (SequenceForm[#1, "e", #3]&) ]
```

$$Out[14]//NumberForm= \{3.03305e7, 6.94852e17\}$$

You can use FortranForm to print individual numbers in Fortran format.

```
In[15]:= FortranForm[7.8^20]
```

$$Out[15]//FortranForm= 6.94852e17$$

PaddedForm[*expr*, *tot*]	print with all numbers having room for *tot* digits, padding with leading spaces if necessary
PaddedForm[*expr*, {*tot*, *frac*}]	print with all numbers having room for *tot* digits, with exactly *frac* digits to the right of the decimal point
NumberForm[*expr*, {*tot*, *frac*}]	print with all numbers having at most *tot* digits, exactly *frac* of them to the right of the decimal point
ColumnForm[{*expr_1*, *expr_2*, ... }]	print with the *expr_i* in a column

Controlling the alignment of numbers in output.

Whenever you print a collection of numbers in a column or some other definite arrangement, you typically need to be able to align the numbers in a definite way. Usually you want all the numbers to be set up so that the digit corresponding to a particular power of 10 always appears at the same position within the region used to print a number.

You can change the positions of digits in the printed form of a number by "padding" it in various ways. You can pad on the right, typically adding zeros somewhere after the decimal. Or you can pad on the left, typically inserting spaces, in place of leading zeros.

This pads with spaces to make room for up to 7 digits in each integer.

```
In[16]:= PaddedForm[{456, 12345, 12}, 7]

Out[16]//PaddedForm= {     456,     12345,        12}
```

This creates a column of integers.

```
In[17]:= PaddedForm[ColumnForm[{456, 12345, 12}], 7]

Out[17]//PaddedForm=        456
                          12345
                             12
```

This prints each number with room for a total of 7 digits, and with 4 digits to the right of the decimal point.

```
In[18]:= PaddedForm[{-6.7, 6.888, 6.99999}, {7, 4}]

Out[18]//PaddedForm= {  -6.7000,    6.8880,    7.0000}
```

In `NumberForm`, the 7 specifies the maximum precision, but does not make *Mathematica* pad with spaces.

```
In[19]:= NumberForm[{-6.7, 6.888, 6.99999}, {7, 4}]

Out[19]//NumberForm= {-6.7, 6.888, 7.}
```

If you set the option `SignPadding->True`, *Mathematica* will insert leading spaces *after* the sign.

```
In[20]:= PaddedForm[{-6.7, 6.888, 6.99999}, {7, 4},
                               SignPadding->True]

Out[20]//PaddedForm= {-  6.7000,    6.8880,    7.0000}
```

Only the mantissa portion is aligned when scientific notation is used.

```
In[21]:= PaddedForm[
             ColumnForm[{6.7 10^8, 48.7, -2.3 10^-16}], {4, 2}]

                                8
Out[21]//PaddedForm=    6.70 10
                       48.70
                                -16
                       -2.30 10
```

With the default setting for the option `NumberPadding`, both `NumberForm` and `PaddedForm` insert trailing zeros when they pad a number on the right. You can use spaces for padding on both the left and the right by setting `NumberPadding -> {" ", " "}`.

This uses spaces instead of zeros for padding on the right.

```
In[22]:= PaddedForm[{-6.7, 6.888, 6.99999}, {7, 4},
                            NumberPadding -> {" ", " "}]

Out[22]//PaddedForm= {  -6.7  ,    6.888 ,    7.    }
```

`BaseForm[`*expr, b*`]`	print with all numbers given in base *b*

Printing numbers in other bases.

This prints a number in base 2.

```
In[23]:= BaseForm[2342424, 2]

Out[23]//BaseForm= 1000111011111000011000
                                          2
```

In bases higher than 10, letters are used for the extra digits.

```
In[24]:= BaseForm[242345341, 16]
Out[24]//BaseForm= e71e57d
                          16
```

BaseForm also works with approximate real numbers.

```
In[25]:= BaseForm[2.3, 2]
Out[25]//BaseForm= 10.0101
                          2
```

You can even use BaseForm for numbers printed in scientific notation.

```
In[26]:= BaseForm[2.3 10^8, 2]
                              27
Out[26]//BaseForm= 1.10111 2
                          2
```

Section 3.1.2 discusses how to enter numbers in arbitrary bases, and also how to get lists of the digits in a number.

■ 2.7.6 Tables and Matrices

TableForm[*list*]	print in tabular form
MatrixForm[*list*]	print in matrix form

Formatting lists as tables and matrices.

Here is a list.

```
In[1]:= Table[(i + 45)^j, {i, 3}, {j, 3}]
Out[1]= {{46, 2116, 97336}, {47, 2209, 103823},
  {48, 2304, 110592}}
```

TableForm displays the list in a tabular format.

```
In[2]:= TableForm[%]
Out[2]//TableForm= 46    2116    97336
                   47    2209    103823
                   48    2304    110592
```

MatrixForm displays the list as a matrix, in which each "cell" has the same size.

```
In[3]:= MatrixForm[%]
Out[3]//MatrixForm= 46      2116      97336
                    47      2209      103823
                    48      2304      110592
```

This displays an array of algebraic expressions as a matrix.

```
In[4]:= MatrixForm[Table[x^i - y^j, {i, 3}, {j, 3}] ]
                                2        3
Out[4]//MatrixForm= x - y    x - y    x - y
                     2        2    2    2    3
                    x  - y   x  - y   x  - y
                     3        3    2    3    3
                    x  - y   x  - y   x  - y
```

> PaddedForm[TableForm[*list*], *tot*]
>
> print a table with all numbers padded to have room for *tot* digits
>
> PaddedForm[TableForm[*list*], {*tot*, *frac*}]
>
> put *frac* digits to the right of the decimal point in all approximate real numbers

Printing tables of numbers.

Here is a list of numbers.

```
In[5]:= fac = {10!, 15!, 20!}
Out[5]= {3628800, 1307674368000, 2432902008176640000}
```

TableForm displays the list in a column.

```
In[6]:= TableForm[fac]
Out[6]//TableForm= 3628800
                   1307674368000
                   2432902008176640000
```

This aligns the numbers by padding each one to leave room for up to 20 digits.

```
In[7]:= PaddedForm[TableForm[fac], 20]
Out[7]//PaddedForm=                3628800
                         1307674368000
                   2432902008176640000
```

In this particular case, you could also align the numbers using the TableAlignments option.

```
In[8]:= TableForm[fac, TableAlignments -> {Right}]
Out[8]//TableForm=             3628800
                        1307674368000
                  2432902008176640000
```

This lines up the numbers, padding each one to have room for 8 digits, with 5 digits to the right of the decimal point.

```
In[9]:= PaddedForm[TableForm[{6.7, 6.888, 6.99999}], {8, 5}]
Out[9]//PaddedForm=    6.70000
                       6.88800
                       6.99999
```

You can use TableForm and MatrixForm to format lists that are nested to any depth, corresponding to arrays with any number of dimensions.

Here is the format for a 2×2 array of elements $a[i, j]$.

```
In[10]:= TableForm[ Array[a, {2, 2}] ]
Out[10]//TableForm= a[1, 1]   a[1, 2]
                    a[2, 1]   a[2, 2]
```

Here is a $2 \times 2 \times 2$ array.

```
In[11]:= TableForm[ { Array[a, {2, 2}], Array[b, {2, 2}] } ]
Out[11]//TableForm= a[1, 1]   a[2, 1]
                    a[1, 2]   a[2, 2]

                    b[1, 1]   b[2, 1]
                    b[1, 2]   b[2, 2]
```

And here is a $2 \times 2 \times 2 \times 2$ array.

```
In[12]:= TableForm[ { {Array[a, {2, 2}], Array[b, {2, 2}]},
                      {Array[c, {2, 2}], Array[d, {2, 2}]} } ]

Out[12]//TableForm= a[1, 1] a[1, 2]   b[1, 1] b[1, 2]
                    a[2, 1] a[2, 2]   b[2, 1] b[2, 2]

                    c[1, 1] c[1, 2]   d[1, 1] d[1, 2]
                    c[2, 1] c[2, 2]   d[2, 1] d[2, 2]
```

In general, when you print an *n*-dimensional table, successive dimensions are alternately given as columns and rows. By setting the option `TableDirections -> {`dir_1`, `dir_2`, ... }`, where the dir_i are `Column` or `Row`, you can specify explicitly which way each dimension should be given. By default, the option is effectively set to `{Column, Row, Column, Row, ... }`.

The option `TableDirections` allows you to specify explicitly how each dimension in a multi-dimensional table should be given.

```
In[13]:= TableForm[ { Array[a, {2, 2}], Array[b, {2, 2} ] },
                     TableDirections -> {Row, Row, Column} ]

Out[13]//MatrixForm= a[1, 1]   a[2, 1]   b[1, 1]   b[2, 1]
                     a[1, 2]   a[2, 2]   b[1, 2]   b[2, 2]
```

Whenever you make a table from a nested list such as {$list_1$, $list_2$, ... }, there is a question of whether it should be the $list_i$ or their elements which appear as the basic entries in the table. The default behavior is slightly different for `MatrixForm` and `TableForm`.

`MatrixForm` handles only arrays that are "rectangular". Thus, for example, to consider an array as two-dimensional, all the rows must have the same length. If they do not, `MatrixForm` treats the array as one-dimensional, with elements that are lists.

`MatrixForm` treats this as a one-dimensional array, since the rows are of differing lengths.

```
In[14]:= MatrixForm[{{a, a, a}, {b, b}}]

Out[14]//MatrixForm= {a, a, a}

                     {b, b}
```

While `MatrixForm` can handle only "rectangular arrays", `TableForm` can handle arbitrary "ragged" arrays. It leaves blanks wherever there are no elements supplied.

`TableForm` can handle "ragged" arrays.

```
In[15]:= TableForm[{{a, a, a}, {b, b}}]

Out[15]//TableForm= a    a    a

                    b    b
```

You can include objects that behave as "subtables".

```
In[16]:= TableForm[{{a, {{p, q}, {r, s}}, a, a}, {{x, y}, b, b}}]

Out[16]//TableForm=        p q
                    a      r s    a    a

                           x
                           y    b    b
```

You can control the number of levels in a nested list to which both `TableForm` and `MatrixForm` go by setting the option `TableDepth`.

This tells `TableForm` only to go down to depth 2. As a result {x, y} is treated as a single table entry.

```
In[17]:= TableForm[{{a, {x, y}}, {c, d}}, TableDepth -> 2]

Out[17]//TableForm= a    {x, y}

                    c    d
```

option name	*default value*	
TableDepth	Infinity	maximum number of levels to include in the table
TableDirections	{Column, Row, Column, ... }	whether to arrange dimensions as rows or columns
TableAlignments	{Left, Bottom, Left, ... }	how to align the entries in each dimension
TableSpacing	{1, 3, 0, 1, 0, ... }	how many spaces to put between entries in each dimension
TableHeadings	{None, None, ... }	how to label the entries in each dimension

Options for `TableForm`.

With the option TableAlignments, you can specify how each entry in the table should be aligned with its row or column. For columns, you can specify Left, Center or Right. For rows, you can specify Bottom, Center or Top. If you set TableAlignments -> Center, all entries will be centered both horizontally and vertically. TableAlignments -> Automatic uses the default choice of alignments.

Entries in columns are by default aligned on the left.

```
In[18]:= TableForm[{a, bbbb, ccccccc}]
Out[18]//TableForm= a
                    bbbb
                    ccccccc
```

This centers all entries.

```
In[19]:= TableForm[{a, bbbb, ccccccc},
                   TableAlignments->Center]
Out[19]//TableForm=    a
                     bbbb
                    ccccccc
```

You can use the option TableSpacing to specify how much horizontal space there should be between successive columns, or how much vertical space there should be between successive rows. A setting of 0 specifies that successive objects should abut.

This leaves 6 spaces between the entries in each row, and no space between successive rows.

```
In[20]:= TableForm[{{a, b}, {ccc, d}}, TableSpacing -> {0, 6}]
Out[20]//TableForm= a        b
                    ccc      d
```

None	no labels in any dimension
Automatic	successive integer labels in each dimension
$\{\{lab_{11},\ lab_{12},\ ...\ \},\ ...\ \}$	explicit labels

Settings for the option `TableHeadings`.

This puts integer labels in a $2\times2\times2$ array.

```
In[21]:= TableForm[Array[a, {2, 2, 2}],
                               TableHeadings -> Automatic]
Out[21]//TableForm=                 1                2

                        1    a[1, 1, 1]    a[1, 2, 1]
                   1    2    a[1, 1, 2]    a[1, 2, 2]

                        1    a[2, 1, 1]    a[2, 2, 1]
                   2    2    a[2, 1, 2]    a[2, 2, 2]
```

This gives a table in which the rows are labeled by integers, and the columns by a list of strings.

```
In[22]:= TableForm[{{a, b, c}, {ap, bp, cp}},
              TableHeadings ->
                  {Automatic, {"first", "middle", "last"}}]
Out[22]//TableForm=      first    middle    last

              1      a        b        c

              2      ap       bp       cp
```

This labels the rows but not the columns. `TableForm` automatically inserts a blank row to go with the third label.

```
In[23]:= TableForm[{{2, 3, 4}, {5, 6, 1}},
              TableHeadings ->
                  {{"row a", "row b", "row c"}, None}]
Out[23]//TableForm= row a    2    3    4

              row b    5    6    1

              row c
```

■ 2.7.7 Defining Your Own Output Forms

Just as *Mathematica* allows you to specify *values* that are produced when expressions are evaluated, so also *Mathematica* allows you to specify *output forms* that are produced when expressions are formatted.

Mathematica effectively formats an expression *expr* by evaluating Format [*expr*]. As a result, you can specify the output form for an expression *expr* by defining a value for Format [*expr*].

Format[*expr*] := *form*	define the standard output form for *expr*
Format[*expr*, *type*] := *form*	define the output form in output format *type*
InputForm[*expr*]	give the input form of *expr*, ignoring special output forms

Defining output forms.

This defines pair with two arguments to print like a list.	*In[1]:=* **Format[pair[x_, y_]] := {x, y}**
Now pair prints as a list.	*In[2]:=* **pair[a+b, c]**
	Out[2]= {a + b, c}
The list form was used only for output. Internally, this is still a pair function.	*In[3]:=* **InputForm[%]**
	Out[3]//InputForm= pair[a + b, c]

It is important to understand the difference between defining the *value* of an object, and defining its *output form*. If you make a definition like f[x_] := *value*, then every time the function f appears in a calculation, *Mathematica* will automatically replace it with the value you have defined. Making a definition like Format[f[x_]] := *form*, however, has no effect on the *value* of f used in calculations. A definition like this affects only the formatting of f after the calculations are finished.

pair is treated as list for formatting, but not for evaluation.	*In[4]:=* **pair[1, 2] + pair[3, 4]**
	Out[4]= {1, 2} + {3, 4}

When you define an output form using Format[*expr*] := *form*, *Mathematica* allows *form* to be any expression. *Mathematica* evaluates this expression when it formats *expr*. The expression can, for example, correspond to a computation that must be done to work out the output form for *expr*.

This defines the output form of rep to be the result of replicating x n times.	*In[5]:=* **Format[rep[n_]] := Table[x, {n}]**
The list of four elements is created when rep[4] is formatted.	*In[6]:=* **rep[4]**
	Out[6]= {x, x, x, x}
rep[4] only *prints* as a list. Internally, it is still just rep[4].	*In[7]:=* **1 + %**
	Out[7]= 1 + {x, x, x, x}

What a definition like Format[*expr*] := *form* effectively does is to tell *Mathematica* to make the output form of *expr* be whatever the output form of *form* is. When *Mathematica* formats *expr*, it evaluates *form*, then gets the output form of *form*, and uses this as the output form of *expr*.

This defines the function pow to have the printed form of a power, but with the power remaining unevaluated.	*In[8]:=* **Format[pow[x_,y_]] := HoldForm[x^y]**

This prints just like 2∧3, but without
evaluating 2∧3.

$In[9]:=$ **pow[2, 3]**

$Out[9]=$ 2^3

You can use definitions like Format [*expr*] := *form* to specify output forms not only for functions,
but also for symbols.

This specifies that the output form of
the symbol catalan should be the
string "G".

$In[10]:=$ **Format[catalan] := "G"**

Whenever catalan appears, it is now
printed out as G. Notice that in standard
Mathematica output form, the double
quotes around strings are not included.

$In[11]:=$ **catalan∧2/4**

$Out[11]=$ $\dfrac{G^2}{4}$

When you make an assignment for Format [*expr*], you are defining the output form for *expr* in the
standard *Mathematica* output format (OutputForm). By making definitions for Format [*expr*, *type*], you
can specify output forms in other types of output format.

This specifies the TeXForm for the
symbol x.

$In[12]:=$ **Format[x, TeXForm] := "{\\bf x}"**

The output form for x that you specified
is now used whenever the TEX form is
needed.

$In[13]:=$ **TeXForm[1 + x∧2]**

$Out[13]//TeXForm=$ 1 + {{{\bf x}}∧2}

■ 2.7.8 Mimicking Mathematical Notation

In creating your own output forms, the goal is often to mimic standard mathematical notation. One
of the most common elements of standard notation is the use of subscripts and superscripts. Output
forms for these are built in to *Mathematica*.

Subscripted[$f[x_1,\ x_2,\ \ldots\ ]$]	a function with arguments given as subscripts
Subscripted[$f[args]$, n]	a function with the first n arguments as subscripts
Subscripted[$f[args]$, $\{d_0,\ d_1\}$, $\{u_0,\ u_1\}$]	
	arguments d_0 through d_1 as subscripts; u_0 through u_1 as superscripts

Output forms that give subscripts and superscripts.

This gives an output form with both
arguments of a as subscripts.

$In[1]:=$ **Subscripted[a[1, 2]]**

$Out[1]=$ $a_{1,2}$

This defines a with any number of arguments to be output with the arguments as subscripts.	*In[2]:=* **Format[a[x__]] := Subscripted[a[x]]**

The subscripts can themselves contain superscripts.	*In[3]:=* **a[x^2, y^2]** *Out[3]=* a_{x^2, y^2}

You can specify what sequences of arguments to a function should be subscripts or superscripts. The notation for each sequence is the same as in Take and Drop. Any arguments that you do not explicitly specify as subscripts or superscripts are output in standard functional notation.

This outputs the first two arguments as subscripts, and the remainder in standard functional notation.	*In[4]:=* **Subscripted[f[a, b, c, d], 2]** *Out[4]=* $f_{a,b}[c,d]$

This gives the last argument as a subscript.	*In[5]:=* **Subscripted[f[a, b, c, d], -1]** *Out[5]=* $f_d[a,b,c]$

Here the first two arguments of f are printed as subscripts, and the last one is a superscript. The remaining argument is given in standard functional notation.	*In[6]:=* **Subscripted[f[a, b, c, d], 2, -1]** *Out[6]=* $f_{a,b}^d[c]$

Mathematica allows you to go beyond just having subscripts and superscripts, and to define any kind of two-dimensional output form. In a typical case, you can build up a complicated two-dimensional form from a combination of horizontal (SequenceForm) and vertical (ColumnForm) "boxes".

SequenceForm[f_1, f_2, ...]	a sequence of objects, arranged horizontally
ColumnForm[{f_1, f_2, ... }]	a column of objects
ColumnForm[*list*, *h*, *v*]	a column with horizontal alignment *h* (Left, Center or Right), and vertical alignment *v* (Below, Center or Above)
Subscript[*x*]	a subscript
Superscript[*x*]	a superscript

Objects for building up two-dimensional output forms.

SequenceForm concatenates the output forms of expressions, with no spaces in between.	*In[7]:=* **SequenceForm["-+-", 1/x, "-+-"]** *Out[7]=* $-+-\dfrac{1}{x}-+-$

ColumnForm arranges lists of expressions in vertical columns.

```
In[8]:= ColumnForm[{"-+-", x + y, "-+-"}]

Out[8]= -+-
        x + y
        -+-
```

You can build up more complicated two-dimensional structures by nesting SequenceForm and ColumnForm.

```
In[9]:= SequenceForm[%, "***", %]

Out[9]= -+-    ***-+-
        x + y     x + y
        -+-       -+-
```

Subscript and Superscript are output as subscripts and superscripts.

```
In[10]:= f[Subscript[x], y, Superscript[z^2]]

                       2
                      z
Out[10]= f[ , y,      ]
          x
```

Many common *Mathematica* functions, such as Plus, can be input using "operators" such as +. *Mathematica* provides output forms which allow you to mimic these kinds of operators.

Prefix[$f[x]$, h]	prefix form h x
Postfix[$f[x]$, h]	postfix form x h
Infix[$f[x, y, \ldots]$, h]	infix form x h y h ...
Prefix[$f[x]$]	standard prefix form $f@x$
Postfix[$f[x]$]	standard postfix form $x//f$
Infix[$f[x, y, \ldots]$]	standard infix form $x\sim f\sim y\sim f\sim$...
PrecedenceForm[*expr*, n]	an object to be parenthesized with a precedence level n

Output forms for operators.

This prints with f represented by the "prefix operator" <>.

```
In[11]:= Prefix[f[x], "<>"]

Out[11]= <>x
```

Here is output with the "infix operator" =*=.

```
In[12]:= s = Infix[{a, b, a/b, b/a}, " =*= "]

                          a          b
Out[12]= a =*= b =*= (-) =*= (-)
                          b          a
```

By default, the "infix operator" =*= is assumed to have "higher precedence" than Power, so no parentheses are inserted.

```
In[13]:= s^2

                          a          b  2
Out[13]= a =*= b =*= (-) =*= (-)
                          b          a
```

When you have an output form involving operators, the question arises of whether the arguments of some of them should be parenthesized. As discussed in Section 2.1.3, this depends on the "precedence" of the operators. When you set up output forms involving operators, you can use PrecedenceForm to specify the precedence to assign to each operator. *Mathematica* uses integers from 1 to 1000 to represent "precedence levels". The higher the precedence level for an operator, the less it needs to be parenthesized.

Here =*= is treated as an operator with precedence 100. This precedence turns out to be low enough that parentheses are inserted.	$In[14]:=$ **PrecedenceForm[s, 100]^2** $Out[14]=$ (a =*= b =*= $(\frac{a}{b})$ =*= $(\frac{b}{a})$)^2

■ 2.7.9 Generating Output

The functions described so far in this section determine *how* expressions should be formatted when they are printed, but they do not actually cause anything to be printed.

In the most common way of using *Mathematica* you never in fact explicitly have to issue a command to generate output. Usually, *Mathematica* automatically prints out the final result that it gets from processing input you gave. Sometimes, however, you may want to get *Mathematica* to print out expressions at intermediate stages in its operation. You can do this using the function Print.

Print[*expr$_1$* , *expr$_2$* , ...]	print the *expr$_i$*, with no spaces in between, but with a newline (line feed) at the end

Printing expressions.

Print prints its arguments, with no spaces in between, but with a newline (line feed) at the end.	$In[1]:=$ **Print[a, b]; Print[c]** ab c
This prints a table of the first five integers and their squares.	$In[2]:=$ **Do[Print[i, " ", i^2], {i, 5}]** 1 1 2 4 3 9 4 16 5 25

Print simply takes the arguments you give, and prints them out one after the other, with no spaces in between. In many cases, you will need to print output in a more complicated format. You can do this by giving an output form as an argument to Print.

This prints the matrix in the form of a table.	$In[3]:=$ **Print[TableForm[{{1, 2}, {3, 4}}]]** 1 2 3 4
Here the output format is specified using StringForm.	$In[4]:=$ **Print[StringForm["x = ``, y = ``", a^2, b^2]]** x = a^2, y = b^2

The output generated by `Print` is usually given in the standard *Mathematica* output format. You can however explicitly specify that some other output format should be used.

This prints output in *Mathematica* input form.	`In[5]:= Print[InputForm[a^2 + b^2]]`
	a^2 + b^2

You should realize that `Print` is only one of several mechanisms available in *Mathematica* for generating output. Another is the function `Message` described in Section 2.8.8, used for generating named messages. There are also a variety of lower-level functions described in Section 2.10.3 which allow you to produce output in various formats both as part of an interactive session, and for files and external programs.

2.8 Strings, Names and Messages

■ 2.8.1 Text Strings

While much of what *Mathematica* does involves the structure and meaning of expressions, you can also use *Mathematica* to handle pure strings of text. You can give any string of text in the form "*text*".

"*text*"	a string containing arbitrary text

Text strings.

In the standard output format, *Mathematica* does not explicitly show the quotation marks around text strings. These are included, however, if you ask for the input form.

In the standard *Mathematica* output form, the quotation marks are not included.

```
In[1]:= "Here is some text."
Out[1]= Here is some text.
```

The quotation marks are included in input form.

```
In[2]:= InputForm[%]
Out[2]//InputForm= "Here is some text."
```

The fact that quotation marks around strings are not shown in the standard *Mathematica* output format is important in being able to use strings to create output forms. However, it does have the consequence that a symbol x and a string "x" look the same in the standard output format. You can always see the difference by asking for the input form.

The symbol x and the string "x" are quite different objects, even though they look the same in the standard output format.

```
In[3]:= x != "x"
Out[3]= x != x
```

You can test whether an object is a string by looking at its head. All strings have the head String.

All strings have head String.

```
In[4]:= Head["x"]
Out[4]= String
```

You can use strings in transformation rules. The pattern _String matches any string.

This gives a definition involving a string.

```
In[5]:= z["gold"] = 79
Out[5]= 79
```

You can use strings in transformation rules.

```
In[6]:= {"aaa", "aa", "bb", "aa"} /. "aa" -> p
Out[6]= {aaa, p, bb, p}
```

Mathematica allows you to include various special characters in strings. Sometimes these are useful in creating various special output formats. The next section discusses in more detail how to specify special and international characters in strings and elsewhere.

a	an ordinary character
\"	a " to be included in a string
\\	a \ to be included in a string
\n	a newline (line feed)
\t	a tab

Special characters in strings.

You can include quotation marks in a string using \".

```
In[7]:= "You can give \"quotes\" in a string."
Out[7]= You can give "quotes" in a string.
```

The \n represents a newline character.

```
In[8]:= "First line.\nSecond line."
Out[8]= First line.
        Second line.
```

In standard *Mathematica* output format, strings with newlines are printed as columns.

```
In[9]:= {%, %, %}
Out[9]= {First line. , First line. , First line. }
         Second line.  Second line.  Second line.
```

Newlines and tabs are often useful in producing output from *Mathematica* intended for other programs. However, you should try to avoid using these characters in producing ordinary *Mathematica* output. The problem with them is that their effect cannot necessarily be accounted for by the formatting procedures in *Mathematica*, since it can depend on the details of the final output device you use. For example, the position of tab stops may vary, making it impossible for *Mathematica* to assign a definite width to the tab character.

Characters["*string*"]	give a list of the characters in a string
ToCharacterCode["*string*"]	give a list of the integer codes for the characters in a string
FromCharacterCode[*n*]	construct a character from an integer code
FromCharacterCode[{n_1, n_2, ... }]	construct a string from a list of integer codes

Conversions between strings, characters and character codes.

Any string in *Mathematica* can be viewed as consisting of a sequence of *characters*. The function **Characters** breaks a string up into a list of characters. Each character is itself represented as a string.

This gives a list of the characters in the string.

```
In[10]:= Characters["A string."]
Out[10]= {A,  , s, t, r, i, n, g, .}
```

Here are the first three characters in the list.

In[11]:= **Take[%, 3]**

Out[11]= {A, , s}

Associated with every possible character in a string, there is a definite integer "character code". The codes can vary from one computer system to another. For a certain standard set of printable characters, however, ASCII codes are always used.

This gives the character code for the letter **a**.

In[12]:= **ToCharacterCode["a"]**

Out[12]= {97}

This makes the character **"a"** from its code.

In[13]:= **FromCharacterCode[%]**

Out[13]= a

This produces a list of characters.

In[14]:= **Map[FromCharacterCode, Range[97, 110]]**

Out[14]= {a, b, c, d, e, f, g, h, i, j, k, l, m, n}

■ 2.8.2 Advanced Topic: Special and International Characters

All text that *Mathematica* gets as input consists of a sequence of characters. The exact set of characters that you can type in may vary from one computer system to another.

For example, computer systems available in a particular country typically provide special characters necessary to support the language used in that country. Thus in continental Europe, you can typically type in accented characters such as é and ö. In Japan, you can enter ideographic characters such as 数.

Mathematica can handle any character that you can type in. The basic principle it uses is simple: it stores any character it receives, and produces the character unchanged as output when appropriate.

operator characters	characters that appear in the operators of the *Mathematica* language
text characters	all other characters

The two kinds of characters in *Mathematica*.

Mathematica distinguishes two kinds of characters: those that are grammatically significant for the *Mathematica* language, and those that are not. Within the *Mathematica* language, there are certain "operators", such as + and =. The set of characters that appear in these operators are called *operator characters*. All characters that are not in this set are called *text characters*.

Mathematica follows the principle that *any text character* can appear in a string, symbol name, or comment. This is true not only for standard alphabetic characters, but also for special characters.

alphabetic characters	upper- and lower-case English letters
printable ASCII characters	English letters and *Mathematica* operators
7-bit ASCII characters	printable ASCII characters and control characters
8-bit characters	character sets for alphabetic writing systems (*e.g.*, ISO Latin standards)
16-bit characters	character sets for ideographic writing systems (*e.g.*, JIS and Shift-JIS)

Some typical character sets.

On any computer system, characters are ultimately represented as binary bit patterns. A particular terminal or input program typically allows you to generate a certain definite set of bit patterns, representing a certain set of characters. As discussed below, you should realize, however, that on different computer systems a particular bit pattern may represent completely different characters.

Nevertheless, virtually all current computer systems do deal in the same way with the limited set of characters that are essential to *Mathematica*. This set of characters consists of the *Mathematica* operators, together with upper- and lower-case English letters. These characters make up the "printable ASCII character set".

In general, each character in the standard ASCII character set has a definite bit pattern, corresponding to a definite integer character code. The printable ASCII characters have codes in the range 32 through 126.

Here is a list of the characters with codes at the beginning and end of the range used for printable ASCII.

```
In[1]:= Map[ FromCharacterCode,
             {32, 33, 34, 35, 123, 124, 125, 126} ]
Out[1]= { , !, ", #, {, |, }, ~}
```

Here are various character codes in binary.

```
In[2]:= BaseForm[{32, 33, 125, 126}, 2]
Out[2]//BaseForm= {100000 , 100001 , 1111101 , 1111110 }
                         2         2          2          2
```

On most computer systems, you will be able to type in all the printable ASCII characters using single keys on your keyboard. In any case, to use *Mathematica* effectively, you will have to find some way to enter all of these characters. Notice that in most cases, the characters will appear on your computer screen just as they are shown in this book. These are some computer systems, however, on which even the standard printable ASCII characters are displayed in a different way. The most common problem is that $ (Shift-4) is shown as a local currency symbol, such as £.

An important feature of the printable ASCII characters is that they can all be represented by bit patterns that contain only 7 bits. There are however only 95 printable ASCII characters. There are therefore 33 other bit patterns out of the $2^7 = 128$ possible with 7 bits.

Exactly what these other bit patterns mean may depend on the computer system you are using. Nevertheless, on most computers, with the notable exception of the Macintosh and PC, these bit patterns correspond to the non-printable characters in the ASCII character set.

The non-printable ASCII characters with codes between 1 and 26 can typically be typed as CONTROL-A, where *A* is any of the 26 letters of the alphabet. The remaining non-printable ASCII characters are usually typed using combinations of the CONTROL key with other keys, or by keys such as ESCAPE (code 27). A few of the "control characters" have standard meanings. For example, CONTROL-J is a newline (line feed), CONTROL-I is a tab and CONTROL-G is a bell (beep).

On most computer systems, certain non-printable ASCII characters are intercepted by the operating system. Thus, for example, CONTROL-C is typically interpreted by the operating system as an interrupt. Similarly, CONTROL-S and CONTROL-Q are often used for "flow control", allowing communication devices to tell your computer when they are ready to receive more data.

In *Mathematica*, you should usually avoid using any non-printable ASCII characters that could interfere with your operating system. However, since commands for terminals and display devices are often given as non-printable ASCII characters, you may sometimes want to generate these characters.

The main issue with all special characters in *Mathematica* is how to enter them. Sometimes you will be able to enter special characters directly. But in all cases, you can enter special characters by giving various ordinary character sequences beginning with the backslash character \. Once inside *Mathematica*, there is no difference between special characters that were entered directly, and ones that were entered using sequences of ordinary characters.

\\	single backslash (decimal code 92)
\b	backspace or CONTROL-H (code 8)
\t	tab or CONTROL-I (code 9)
\n	newline or CONTROL-J (code 10)
\f	form feed or CONTROL-L (code 12)
\r	carriage return or CONTROL-M (code 13)

\^A through \^Z or \^a through \^z

CONTROL-A (code 1) through CONTROL-Z (code 26)

\0	null byte (code 0)
nnn	an 8-bit character with octal code *nnn*
\.*nn*	an 8-bit character with hexadecimal code *nn*

\:*nnnn*	a 16-bit character with hexadecimal form *nnnn*
\!*c*	a 16-bit character *c*
\+*cccccc*	a sequence of 16-bit characters, terminated by a double null byte

Sequences for entering special characters.

This gives the octal codes for the characters in f[x].

In[3]:= **BaseForm[ToCharacterCode["f[x]"], 8]**

Out[3]//BaseForm= {146_8 , 133_8 , 170_8 , 135_8 }

You can enter any character using its character code in octal.

In[4]:= **\146\133\170\135 + g[x]**

Out[4]= f[x] + g[x]

You can use \ sequences to create *Mathematica* strings that contain any sequence of characters or bit patterns. Note that *Mathematica* strings can contain null bytes, specified as \0, at any position.

Once you produce a special character in *Mathematica*, the next issue is how it should be printed out. You should realize that the fact that *Mathematica* can generate a particular character in no way means that your computer system can necessarily handle the character in a reasonable way.

Typically, you will either want special characters to be printed directly, or to be given as \ sequences.

FullForm always gives special characters as \ sequences.

FullForm prints the ordinary character \100 directly, but prints the special characters using \ sequences.

In[5]:= **FullForm["\100\210\007"]**

Out[5]//FullForm= "@\210\007"

In general, the special character conversions that *Mathematica* does for output are determined by the value you assign to $StringConversion. $StringConversion = None specifies that no conversion should be done, and all special characters should be printed directly. $StringConversion = Automatic specifies that all special characters should be converted to \ sequences. Finally, you can assign $StringConversion to be a function which is then used to get the output form for every string that is generated.

None	output all special characters directly
Automatic	convert all special characters to \ sequences
f	apply the function *f* to each complete string, and give the output form of the result

Settings for $StringConversion.

When you start up *Mathematica*, $StringConversion is usually set to have the value None, so that special characters are printed without any conversion.

This specifies that special characters should always be converted to \ sequences.

```
In[6]:= $StringConversion = Automatic
Out[6]= Automatic
```

Special characters are now printed using \ sequences.

```
In[7]:= "\210\211\212"
Out[7]= \210\211\212
```

You can override the character conversion specified by $StringConversion by explicitly setting the option StringConversion in the various *Mathematica* printing and output functions.

InputForm[*expr*, StringConversion -> *f*]	give the input form of *expr* using character conversion function *f*
Put[*expr*, "*file*", StringConversion -> *f*]	put an expression in a file using character conversion function *f*
OpenWrite["*file*", StringConversion -> *f*]	open a stream, specifying a character conversion function
SetOptions["*file*", StringConversion -> *f*]	reset the character conversion function for a stream

Overriding the global specification for character conversion.

When you set character conversion to None, *Mathematica* prints out all special characters directly. It is then up to your computer system to interpret the special characters.

The most common case in which you will want to use special characters extensively is in handling characters in languages other than English.

Written languages can be divided into two broad classes: those based on alphabets, and those based on ideograms.

English is an example of written language based on an alphabet. The other European written languages are similarly based on alphabets. Some languages, such as French and German, use essentially the same alphabet as English, with a few additions. Other languages, such as Greek and Russian, use completely different alphabets. In no case, however, does a specific European language need more than about 70 additional upper and lower-case characters, beyond those in the standard English alphabet.

There is a sequence of standards for introducing the additional characters that are needed in particular groups of European languages. These standards work by taking the usual 7-bit ASCII English character set, and adding a new set of "8-bit characters" whose bit patterns have the eighth bit set.

It should be said immediately that unless your computer system has specifically been set up to handle 8-bit characters, this may cause considerable trouble. The basic problem is that in many communication systems, the eighth bit has traditionally been used to provide a "parity check" on the other seven bits. In such cases, you cannot use the eighth bit to specify additional characters.

Nevertheless, assuming your computer system can handle 8-bit characters, there are standards for what the characters mean. Different groups of European languages require different meanings for each particular character. However, the possible meanings are codified in nine standards, labeled ISO 8859-1 through 8859-9.

The most common of these standards is ISO 8859-1, the "ISO Latin-1 standard". This standard includes the additional characters needed for the most common European languages whose alphabets are based on the Latin one. The additional characters include standard English characters, with accents or other diacritical marks added, such as é or ö, as well as non-English characters such as ø or ß.

Here is a string that uses ISO Latin-1 characters. Since $StringConversion was set to Automatic above, the special characters are shown here as \ sequences.	`In[8]:= str = "à gauche"`
	
	`Out[8]= \340 gauche`

This specifies that all special characters should be output directly.	`In[9]:= $StringConversion = None`
	
	`Out[9]= None`

Now the special characters are printed out just as you typed them in.	`In[10]:= str`
	
	`Out[10]= à gauche`

You can use special characters in symbol names as well as strings.

$In[11]:=$ **Vitesse[Lumière] = 3. 10^8 Mètres/Seconde**

$$Out[11]= \frac{3.\ 10^8\ \text{Mètres}}{\text{Seconde}}$$

Although the ISO Latin-1 standard covers the vast majority of Latin-based alphabets, including all the Romance and Germanic languages, there are other cases, covered by the ISO Latin-2 through Latin-4 standards. Thus, for example, the Latin-2 standard contains the character æ used in Czech, while the Latin-4 contains the character ǫ used in Lappish.

It is very important to realize that different standards use exactly the same bit patterns to represent different characters. As a result, if you enter text in *Mathematica* according to one standard, you must use the same standard whenever you read the text. If you use a different standard, the text will be quite meaningless.

The point is that *Mathematica* never knows the *meaning* of the text you type in. All that it does is to store the bit patterns it receives. It is up to you and your computer system to interpret these bit patterns as characters according to some standard.

Here is the string given above, now interpreted using the ISO Latin-2 standard. The result is quite meaningless.

$In[12]:=$ **str**

$Out[12]=$ ŕ gauche

Some European languages have alphabets quite different from English. There are ISO standards for Greek, Cyrillic (Russian), Hebrew and Arabic. In all cases, the characters are encoded as bit patterns involving 8 bits.

Here is a string given and interpreted using the ISO Latin/Greek standard.

$In[13]:=$ **"The Ψ function"**

$Out[13]=$ The Ψ function

So long as you use this standard, you can include Greek letters in symbol names and other objects.

$In[14]:=$ **Expand[(Γ + Δ)^2]**

$$Out[14]= \Gamma^2 + 2\ \Gamma\ \Delta + \Delta^2$$

The number of characters required for languages based on alphabets is usually small enough that all the characters can be represented by bit patterns containing just 8 bits. This is not true, however, for ideographic languages.

In ideographic languages, complete words or parts of words can be represented by individual characters. As a result, the total number of characters required for such languages can be in the several tens of thousands.

Written Japanese is an example of an ideographic language. While the katakana and hiragana phonetic syllabaries can be used for some purposes, standard Japanese text includes Chinese or kanji ideographic characters. The number of kanji characters in common use is around 3,000.

In order to represent all the characters needed in a language like Japanese, it is necessary to use not 8 but 16 bits per character.

The basic *Mathematica* system requires that *whenever* you enter 16-bit characters, they are preceded by special \ sequences. In some cases, *Mathematica* front ends may automatically insert the necessary \ sequences, so you may not explicitly see them.

Nevertheless, if you interact directly with the *Mathematica* kernel, you need to use \ sequences whenever you enter 16-bit characters. If you enter a single 16-bit character, you must preface it with the sequence \!. If you enter several 16-bit characters together, you can instead preface the sequence of characters by \+, then insert a special null character with all 16 bits zero at the end of your sequence of 16-bit characters.

Here is a string containing 16-bit Japanese characters.	`In[15]:= "\!数\!学"`
	
	`Out[15]= 数学`

In input form, the \! sequence which precedes each character is explicitly given.	`In[9]:= InputForm[%]`
	
	`Out[9]//InputForm= "\!数\!学"`

FullForm shows the character codes corresponding to the 16-bit characters.	`In[10]:= FullForm[%]`
	
	`Out[10]//FullForm= "\:a0fd\:a079"`

Since \ sequences are required *whenever* you enter 16-bit characters, these sequences are always included when you ask for the input form of text that contains 16-bit characters.

Several issues make it essential for *Mathematica* always to be able to distinguish individual 16-bit characters from pairs of 8-bit characters. The most important is that in a 16-bit character, the second set of 8 bits might erroneously be interpreted as a character such as + or = which has a definite meaning in *Mathematica*.

`StringLength["`*string*`"]`	the number of characters in a string
`StringByteCount["`*string*`"]`	the total number of bytes in a string
`Characters["`*string*`"]`	a list of the 8- or 16-bit characters in a string
`ToCharacterCode["`*string*`"]`	the integer character codes for 8- or 16-bit characters in a string
`FromCharacterCode[`*n*`]`	the 8- or 16-bit character with integer code *n*
`FromCharacterCode[{`n_1`, `n_2`, ... }]`	the string constructed from 8- or 16-bit characters with codes n_i

Operations on strings containing 16-bit characters.

Here is a string containing both English and Japanese characters.	`In[18]:= jps = "math is \!数\!学"`
	
	`Out[18]= math is 数学`

StringLength gives the number of characters in the string.

```
In[19]:= StringLength[jps]
Out[19]= 10
```

StringByteCount gives the number of bytes in the string; each Japanese character takes two bytes.

```
In[20]:= StringByteCount[jps]
Out[20]= 12
```

In *Mathematica*, the number of bits in a character can always be recognized by looking at its integer code. All 8-bit characters have integer codes in the range 0 to 255, while 16-bit characters have codes ranging from 256 to 65791. For 8-bit characters, the codes are always obtained directly by interpreting bits as binary digits. For 16-bit characters, on the other hand, this procedure is used only when the top 8 bits are not all zero. When the top 8 bits are all zero, $2^{16} = 65536$ is added to the integer code derived by treating the bits directly as binary digits. As a result, you can always tell whether a particular character has 16 bits simply by testing whether its integer code is larger than 255. Notice that if you enter a 16-bit character in the form \:*nnnn*, you can enter characters whose top 8 bits are all zero simply by using \:00*nn*.

All 16-bit characters have codes larger than 255.

```
In[21]:= ToCharacterCode[jps]
Out[21]= {77, 97, 116, 104, 128, 105, 115, 41213, 41081}
```

This tells *Mathematica* to convert all special characters to \ sequences.

```
In[22]:= $StringConversion = Automatic
Out[22]= Automatic
```

Now the Japanese characters are given using \: sequences with hexadecimal codes.

```
In[23]:= jps
Out[23]= math is \:a0fd\:a079
```

■ 2.8.3 Operations on Strings

Mathematica provides various functions for manipulating strings. These functions work by treating strings as sequences of characters. Many of the functions are analogous to the functions for manipulating lists discussed in Sections 1.8.4 and 1.8.6.

StringLength[s]	give the number of characters in a string
s_1 <> s_2 <> ... or StringJoin[s_1, s_2, ...]	
	join several strings together
StringReverse[s]	reverse the characters in a string
StringTake[s, n]	make a string by taking the first n characters from s
StringTake[s, {n}]	take the nth character from s
StringTake[s, {n_1, n_2}]	take characters n_1 through n_2
StringDrop[s, n]	make a string by dropping the first n characters in s
StringDrop[s, {n_1, n_2}]	drop characters n_1 through n_2
StringInsert[s, $snew$, n]	insert the string *snew* at the nth position in s
StringPosition[s, sub]	give a list of the starting and ending positions at which *sub* appears as a substring of s
StringPosition[s, sub, k]	include only the first k occurrences of *sub* in s
StringPosition[s, {sub_1, sub_2, ... }]	
	include occurrences of any of the sub_i
StringReplace[s, {s_1 -> sp_1, s_2 -> sp_2, ... }]	
	replace the s_i by the corresponding sp_i whenever they appear as substrings of s
s_1 == s_2	test whether two strings are the same
StringToStream[s]	convert a string to an input stream so that it can be searched and read (see Section 2.10.8)

String manipulation operations.

You can join together any number of strings using <>.

```
In[1]:= "aaaaaaa" <> "bbb" <> "cccccccccc"
Out[1]= aaaaaaabbbcccccccccc
```

StringLength gives the number of characters in a string.

```
In[2]:= StringLength[%]
Out[2]= 20
```

StringReverse reverses the characters in a string.

```
In[3]:= StringReverse["A string."]
Out[3]= .gnirts A
```

StringTake and StringDrop are the analogs for strings of Take and Drop for lists. They use standard *Mathematica* sequence specifications. Thus, for example, by using negative numbers, you can count character positions from the end of a string.

Here is a sample string.	`In[4]:= alpha = "ABCDEFGHIJKLMNOPQRSTUVWXYZ"`
	
	`Out[4]= ABCDEFGHIJKLMNOPQRSTUVWXYZ`

This takes the first five characters from `alpha`.	`In[5]:= StringTake[alpha, 5]`
	
	`Out[5]= ABCDE`

Here is the fifth character in `alpha`.	`In[6]:= StringTake[alpha, {5}]`
	
	`Out[6]= E`

This drops the characters 10 through 2, counting from the end of the string.	`In[7]:= StringDrop[alpha, {-10, -2}]`
	
	`Out[7]= ABCDEFGHIJKLMNOPZ`

`StringInsert` allows you to "splice" a new substring into a string at a particular position. In general, `StringInsert[s, snew, n]` produces a string whose n^{th} character is the first character of *snew*.

This produces a new string whose fourth character is the first character of the string `"XX"`.	`In[8]:= StringInsert["abcdefgh", "XX", 4]`
	
	`Out[8]= abcXXdefgh`

Negative positions are counted from the end of the string.	`In[9]:= StringInsert["abcdefgh", "XXX", -1]`
	
	`Out[9]= abcdefghXXX`

You can use `StringPosition` to find where a particular substring appears within a given string. `StringPosition` returns a list, each of whose elements corresponds to an occurrence of the substring. The elements consist of lists giving the starting and ending character positions for the substring. These lists are in the form used as sequence specifications in `StringTake` and `StringDrop`.

This gives a list of the positions of the substring `"abc"`.	`In[10]:= StringPosition["abcdabcdaabcabcd", "abc"]`
	
	`Out[10]= {{1, 3}, {5, 7}, {10, 12}, {13, 15}}`

This gives only the first occurrence of `"abc"`.	`In[11]:= StringPosition["abcdabcdaabcabcd", "abc", 1]`
	
	`Out[11]= {{1, 3}}`

This shows where both `"abc"` and `"cd"` appear. Overlaps between these strings are taken into account.	`In[12]:= StringPosition["abcdabcdaabcabcd", {"abc", "cd"}]`
	
	`Out[12]= {{1, 3}, {3, 4}, {5, 7}, {7, 8}, {10, 12}, {13, 15}, {15, 16}}`

`StringReplace` allows you to perform replacements for substrings within a string. `StringReplace` sequentially goes through a string, testing substrings that start at each successive character position. To each substring, it tries in turn each of the transformation rules you have specified. If any of the rules apply, it replaces the substring, then continues to go through the string, starting at the character position after the end of the substring.

This replaces all occurrences of the character `a` by the string `XX`.	`In[13]:= StringReplace["abcdabcdaabcabcd", "a" -> "XX"]`
	
	`Out[13]= XXbcdXXbcdXXXXbcXXbcd`

This replaces abc by Y, and d by XXX.

```
In[14]:= StringReplace["abcdabcdaabcabcd",
                            {"abc" -> "Y", "d" -> "XXX"}]
Out[14]= YXXXYXXXaYYXXX
```

The first occurrence of cde is not replaced because it overlaps with abc.

```
In[15]:= StringReplace["abcde abacde",
                            {"abc" -> "X", "cde" -> "Y"}]
Out[15]= Xde abaY
```

Characters[*string*]	give a list of the characters in a string
StringJoin[*list*]	construct a string from a list of characters

Converting between strings and lists of characters.

In doing some kinds of string manipulation, you may find it useful to convert strings into lists of characters, and then to perform operations on these lists.

This turns a string into a list of characters.

```
In[16]:= Characters["abcdef"]
Out[16]= {a, b, c, d, e, f}
```

You can apply standard list manipulation operations to this list.

```
In[17]:= RotateLeft[%, 3]
Out[17]= {d, e, f, a, b, c}
```

You can build a string by applying StringJoin to the list of individual characters.

```
In[18]:= StringJoin[%]
Out[18]= defabc
```

DigitQ[*string*]	test whether all characters in a string are digits
LetterQ[*string*]	test whether all characters in a string are letters
UpperCaseQ[*string*]	test whether all characters in a string are upper-case letters
LowerCaseQ[*string*]	test whether all characters in a string are lower-case letters
ToUpperCase[*string*]	generate a string in which all letters are upper case
ToLowerCase[*string*]	generate a string in which all letters are lower case

Operations on letters and digits.

All characters in the string given are letters.

```
In[19]:= LetterQ["Fish"]
Out[19]= True
```

This converts all letters to upper case.

```
In[20]:= ToUpperCase["The Fish"]
Out[20]= THE FISH
```

Particularly when you use international or extended character sets, it may not be clear exactly which characters should be counted as letters, or what their lower- and upper-case forms should be. In general, `$Letters` gives a list of all characters to be counted as letters. If two characters appear as $\{"c_1", "c_2"\}$ in this list, they are taken to be the lower- and upper-case forms of a particular letter.

`StringPosition[s, sub, IgnoreCase -> True]`	find where *sub* occurs in *s*, treating lower- and upper-case letters as equivalent
`StringReplace[s, {s₁ -> sp₁, ... }, IgnoreCase -> True]`	replace s_i by sp_i in *s*, treating lower- and upper-case letters as equivalent

Case-independent operations.

This replaces all occurrences of `"the"`, independent of case.

```
In[21]:= StringReplace["The cat in the hat.", "the" -> "a",
                                        IgnoreCase -> True]

Out[21]= a cat in a hat.
```

`Sort[{s₁, s₂, ... }]`	sort a list of strings

Sorting strings.

`Sort` sorts strings into standard "dictionary" order.

```
In[22]:= Sort[{"cat", "fish", "catfish", "Cat"}]
Out[22]= {cat, Cat, catfish, fish}
```

By default, `Sort` puts strings into essentially the standard order used for English-language indices and dictionaries. In general, however, the order is determined by the value of the global variable `$StringOrder`. If you use international or extended character sets, you may have to modify this value.

The default value for `$StringOrder` is `{{"a", "A"}, {"b", "B"}, ... , {"z", "Z"}, "0", "1", ... , "9"}`. The reason for the sublists is as follows. With a purely linear ordering in which upper-case letters come directly after their lower-case forms, the example above would give `"cat"`, `"catfish"`, `"Cat"` rather than `"cat"`, `"Cat"`, `"catfish"`.

To get the correct result, there must be several levels of ordering for characters. The first step in comparing two strings uses the first-level ordering. Characters not in the list `$StringOrder` are ignored, and those that appear in sublists of `$StringOrder` are treated as equivalent. In most cases, this first step will give a definite ordering for the strings. If it fails to, however, then the second-level ordering given by the order of characters in the sublists of `$StringOrder` is used. If this still fails to give a definite ordering for the strings, then the characters which do not appear at all in `$StringOrder` are considered. These characters are taken be ordered in terms of the integer codes. Note that by setting `$StringOrder = {}`, you can make all ordering be done simply according to these integer codes.

`ToCharacterCode[`*string*`]`	give a list of the integer codes for each character in a string
`FromCharacterCode[`*list*`]`	construct a string from a list of character codes

Converting between strings and lists of character codes.

As discussed in the previous section, every character in a *Mathematica* string can be represented by an integer code. There are some kinds of operations that can conveniently be performed by converting strings into lists of such codes.

This gives a list of the integer codes for each character in the string.

```
In[23]:= ToCharacterCode["mathematics"]
Out[23]= {109, 97, 116, 104, 101, 109, 97, 116, 105, 99, 115}
```

Here is a modified string.

```
In[24]:= FromCharacterCode[ % + 2 ]
Out[24]= ocvjgocvkeu
```

All the string manipulation functions discussed in this section work on strings that contain any kind of characters, including 16-bit ones. It is common to set the `$StringConversion` variables discussed in the previous section to a function that uses `StringReplace` to replace special characters by sequences of ordinary characters.

This defines `$StringConversion` to make replacements for certain accented characters.

```
In[25]:= $StringConversion = (StringReplace[#,
              {"é" -> "e'", "è" -> "e`"}]&)
Out[25]= StringReplace[#1, {é -> e', è -> e`}] &
```

If you now type in a string that contains accented characters, they will be replaced when the string is printed out.

```
In[26]:= "programmé"
Out[26]= programme'
```

■ 2.8.4 Converting between Strings and Expressions

`ToString[`*expr*`]`	give the textual form of an expression as a string
`ToExpression["`*string*`"]`	convert a string to an expression, if possible

Converting between strings and expressions.

This generates a string corresponding to the textual form of the expression.

```
In[1]:= ToString[x + 2 y + z]
Out[1]= x + 2 y + z
```

This converts the string back to an expression.

```
In[2]:= ToExpression[%]
Out[2]= x + 2 y + z
```

By default, `ToString[`*expr*`]` generates a string which corresponds to the expression *expr* formatted in output form. You can however explicitly tell `ToString` to use other formats.

This generates a string corresponding to the standard output form of the expression.

```
In[3]:= ToString[x^2 + a/b]

Out[3]= a    2
        - + x
        b
```

The string contains explicit spaces and newlines.

```
In[4]:= InputForm[%]

Out[4]//InputForm= "a     2\n- + x\nb"
```

You can use InputForm to generate a string suitable to be used as input to *Mathematica*.

```
In[5]:= ToString[InputForm[x^2 + a/b]]

Out[5]= a/b + x^2
```

This creates a string corresponding to the TEX form of the expression.

```
In[6]:= ToString[TeXForm[x^2 + a/b]]

Out[6]= {a\over b} + {x^2}
```

ToString[*expr*] takes a variety of options for specifying details of formatting. These options correspond exactly to those you can give when you open a file or other output stream, as discussed on page 488.

This formats the expression assuming a page width of 20 characters.

```
In[7]:= ToString[Expand[(1 + x)^4], PageWidth->20] // InputForm

Out[7]//InputForm=
       "                 2\n1 + 4 x + 6 x  + \n \n    3     4\n 4 x  + x"
```

By setting StringConversion -> Automatic, you make ToString use \ sequences for all special characters.

```
In[8]:= ToString["Gröbner", StringConversion->Automatic]

Out[8]= Gr\366bner
```

By applying ToString to constructs like StringForm, you can effectively perform various kinds of string manipulation.

You can use StringForm with ToString to splice expressions into strings.

```
In[9]:= ToString[StringForm["x = ``, y = ``", 4, 4^7]]

Out[9]= x = 4, y = 16384
```

ToExpression["*string*"]	convert a string to an expression
ToExpression[{"s_1", "s_2", ... }]	convert a list of strings to expressions
ToHeldExpression["*string*"]	convert a string to a held expression
SyntaxQ["*string*"]	determine whether a whole string corresponds to syntactically correct *Mathematica* input
SyntaxLength["*string*"]	find out how long a sequence of characters starting at the beginning of a string is syntactically correct

Converting strings to expressions.

ToExpression converts a string to an
expression, then immediately evaluates
the expression.

```
In[10]:= ToExpression["1 + 1"]

Out[10]= 2
```

ToHeldExpression yields an expression
with Hold wrapped around it.

```
In[11]:= ToHeldExpression["1 + 1"]

Out[11]= Hold[1 + 1]
```

You can get rid of the Hold using
ReleaseHold.

```
In[12]:= ReleaseHold[%]

Out[12]= 2
```

ToExpression takes any string, and attempts to interpret it as *Mathematica* input. If you give a string that does not correspond to syntactically correct *Mathematica* input, then ToExpression will print a message, and return $Failed.

This is not syntactically correct input, so
ToExpression does not convert it to an
expression.

```
In[13]:= ToExpression["1 +/+ 2"]

ToExpression::esntx:
    Could not parse 1 +/+ 2 as Mathematica input.

Out[13]= $Failed
```

ToExpression requires that the string
correspond to a *complete Mathematica*
expression.

```
In[14]:= ToExpression["1 + 2 + "]

ToExpression::esntx:
    Could not parse 1 + 2 +  as Mathematica input.

Out[14]= $Failed
```

You can use the function SyntaxQ to test whether a particular string corresponds to syntactically correct *Mathematica* input. If SyntaxQ returns False, you can find out where the error occurred using SyntaxLength. SyntaxLength returns the number of characters which were successfully processed before a syntax error was detected.

SyntaxQ shows that this string does not
correspond to syntactically correct
Mathematica input.

```
In[15]:= SyntaxQ["1 +/+ 2"]

Out[15]= False
```

SyntaxLength reveals that an error was
detected after the third character in the
string.

```
In[16]:= SyntaxLength["1 +/+ 2"]

Out[16]= 3
```

Here SyntaxLength returns a value
greater than the length of the string, indicating that the input was correct so far
as it went, but needs to be continued.

```
In[17]:= SyntaxLength["1 + 2 + "]

Out[17]= 9
```

StringToStream["*string*"]	create an input stream corresponding to a string

Setting up a string to act like a file.

As mentioned in Section 1.10.3 and discussed in detail in Sections 2.10.6 and 2.10.7 *Mathematica* has various functions for processing textual input from files and other input streams. It is sometimes convenient to use these same functions for processing strings. You can do this by treating strings as special forms of input streams.

This converts a string to an input stream object.

In[18]:= **str1 = StringToStream["567 12 67923"]**

Out[18]= InputStream[String, 3]

This reads the first number from the stream object.

In[19]:= **Read[str1, Number]**

Out[19]= 567

This reads the remaining numbers from the stream object.

In[20]:= **ReadList[str1, Number]**

Out[20]= {12, 67923}

Note that by using Read[*str*, Expression] and Read[*str*, Hold[Expression]] you can read *Mathematica* expressions from strings that are being treated as streams. If what you try to read does not correspond to a syntactically correct expression, then Read will return $Failed.

■ 2.8.5 String Patterns

You can use the standard *Mathematica* equality test s_1 == s_2 to test whether two strings are identical. Sometimes, however, you may want to find out whether a particular string matches a certain *string pattern*.

Mathematica allows you to define *string patterns* which consist of ordinary strings in which certain characters are interpreted as special "metacharacters". You can then use the function StringMatchQ to find out whether a particular string matches a string pattern you have defined. You should realize however that string patterns have nothing to do with the ordinary *Mathematica* patterns for expressions that were discussed in Section 2.3.

"*string₁*" == "*string₂*"	test whether two strings are identical
StringMatchQ["*string*", "*pattern*"]	
	test whether a string matches a particular string pattern

Matching strings.

The character * can be used in a string pattern as a metacharacter to stand for any sequence of alphanumeric characters. Thus, for example, the string pattern "a*b" would match any string which begins with an a, ends with a b, and has any number of alphanumeric characters in between. Similarly, "a*b*" would match any string that starts with a, and has any number of other characters, including at least one b.

The string matches the string pattern you have given.

In[1]:= **StringMatchQ["aaaaabbbbcccbbb", "a*b*"]**

Out[1]= True

The way * is used in *Mathematica* string patterns is analogous to the way it is used for filename patterns in many operating systems. *Mathematica* however provides some other string pattern metacharacters that are tailored to matching different classes of *Mathematica* symbol names.

*		zero or more characters
@		one or more characters which are not upper-case letters
* etc.		literal * etc.

Metacharacters used in string patterns.

In *Mathematica* there is a general convention that only built-in names should contain upper-case characters. Assuming that you follow this convention, you can use @ as a metacharacter to set up string patterns which match names you have defined, but avoid matching built-in names.

StringMatchQ["*string*", "*pattern*", SpellingCorrection -> True]
　　　　　　　　　test whether *pattern* matches *string*, allowing a small
　　　　　　　　　fraction of characters to differ

StringMatchQ["*string*", "*pattern*", IgnoreCase -> True]
　　　　　　　　　test whether *pattern* matches *string*, treating lower- and
　　　　　　　　　upper-case letters as equivalent

Options for matching strings.

These strings do not match.

```
In[2]:= StringMatchQ["platypus", "paltypus"]
Out[2]= False
```

Allowing for spelling correction, these strings are considered to match.

```
In[3]:= StringMatchQ["platypus", "paltypus",
                            SpellingCorrection -> True]
Out[3]= True
```

These strings match when lower- and upper-case letters are treated as equivalent.

```
In[4]:= StringMatchQ["AAaaBBbb", "a*b*", IgnoreCase -> True]
Out[4]= True
```

■ 2.8.6 Symbol Names

?*nameform*	give information on all objects with names of a particular form
Names["*nameform*"]	give a list of symbols with names of a particular form
Names["*nameform*", SpellingCorrection -> Automatic]	
	include symbols whose names have the form given after spelling correction
NameQ["*nameform*"]	give True if symbols with names of the specified form exist
Contexts["*nameform*`"]	give a list of contexts with names of a particular form
Clear["*nameform*"]	clear the values of all symbols with names of a particular form
Remove["*nameform*"]	remove completely all symbols with names of a particular form

Functions that work with symbol names.

This lists all objects whose names begin with W.	*In[1]:= ?W**		
	WeierstrassP	With	WorkingPrecision
	WeierstrassPPrime	Word	Write
	Which	WordSearch	WriteString
	While	WordSeparators	WynnDegree

Here is a list of the names of symbols which match the string pattern Qu*.	*In[1]:=* **Names["Qu*"]**
	Out[1]= {Quartics, Quit, Quotient}
The names are given as strings.	*In[2]:=* **InputForm[%]**
	Out[2]//InputForm= {"Quartics", "Quit", "Quotient"}
You can turn the strings into symbols using ToExpression.	*In[3]:=* **ToExpression[%] // InputForm**
	Out[3]//InputForm= {Quartics, Quit, Quotient}

You can use Names to get lists of symbols that have similar names. By asking for Names["*context*`*"], for example, you can get a list of all symbols in a particular context. With the option SpellingCorrection -> Automatic, you can get all symbols whose names are "close" to a given form. Typically, names are considered "close" if a small fraction of the letters in them differ.

The functions Clear and Remove allow you to specify not only explicit symbols, but also strings or string patterns that represent collections of symbols with similar names. Thus, for example, Clear["x*"] clears the values of all symbols whose names start with x. Clear[Global`*] would remove the values of all symbols in the Global context.

■ 2.8.7 Advanced Topic: Intercepting the Creation of New Symbols

Mathematica creates a new symbol when you first type in a particular name. Sometimes it is useful to "intercept" the process of creating a new symbol. *Mathematica* provides several ways to do this.

`On[General::newsym]`	print a message whenever a new symbol is created
`Off[General::newsym]`	switch off the message printed when new symbols are created

Printing a message when new symbols are created.

This tells *Mathematica* to print a message whenever a new symbol is created.	`In[1]:= On[General::newsym]`

Mathematica now prints a message about each new symbol that it creates.

```
In[2]:= sin[k]

General::newsym: Symbol sin is new.

General::newsym: Symbol k is new.

Out[2]= sin[k]
```

This switches off the message.

`In[3]:= Off[General::newsym]`

Generating a message when *Mathematica* creates a new symbol is often a good way to catch typing mistakes. *Mathematica* itself cannot tell the difference between an intentionally new name, and a misspelling of a name it already knows. But by reporting all new names it encounters, *Mathematica* allows you to see whether any of them are mistakes.

`$NewSymbol`	a function to be applied to the name and context of new symbols which are created

Performing operations when new symbols are created.

When *Mathematica* creates a new symbol, you may want it not just to print a message, but instead to perform some other action. Any function you specify as the value of the global variable `$NewSymbol` will automatically be applied to strings giving the name and context of each new symbol that *Mathematica* creates.

This defines a function to be applied to each new symbol which is created.

```
In[4]:= $NewSymbol = Print["Name: ", #1, "  Context: ", #2]&

Out[4]= Print[Name: , #1,   Context: , #2] &
```

The function is applied once to `v` and once to `w`.

```
In[5]:= v + w

Name: v  Context: Global`
Name: w  Context: Global`

Out[5]= v + w
```

■ 2.8.8 Messages

Mathematica has a general mechanism for handling messages generated during computations. Many built-in *Mathematica* functions use this mechanism to produce error and warning messages. You can also use the mechanism for messages associated with functions you write.

The basic idea is that every message has a definite name, of the form *symbol*::*tag*. You can use this name to refer to the message. (The object *symbol*::*tag* has head `MessageName`.)

Off[*s*::*tag*]	switch off a message, so it is not printed
On[*s*::*tag*]	switch on a message

Controlling the printing of messages.

As discussed in Section 1.3.6, you can use `On` and `Off` to control the printing of particular messages. Most messages associated with built-in functions are switched on by default. You can use `Off` to switch them off if you do not want to see them.

This prints a warning message.	*In[1]:=* **Log[a, b, c]**
	Log::argt: Log called with 3 arguments; 1 or 2 arguments are expected.
	Out[1]= Log[a, b, c]
You can switch off the message like this.	*In[2]:=* **Off[Log::argt]**
Now no warning message is produced.	*In[3]:=* **Log[a, b, c]**
	Out[3]= Log[a, b, c]

Although most messages associated with built-in functions are switched on by default, there are some which are switched off by default, and which you will see only if you explicitly switch them on. An example is the message `General::newsym`, discussed in Section 1.1.6, which tells you every time a new symbol is created.

s::*tag*	give the text of a message
s::*tag* = *string*	set the text of a message
Messages[*s*]	show all messages associated with *s*

Manipulating messages.

The text of a message with the name *s*::*tag* is stored simply as the value of *s*::*tag*, associated with the symbol *s*. You can therefore see the text of a message simply by asking for *s*::*tag*. You can set the text by assigning a value to *s*::*tag*.

If you give **Inverse** a singular matrix, it prints a warning message.	*In[4]:=* **Inverse[{{1, 1}, {2, 2}}]** Inverse::sing: Matrix {{1, 1}, {2, 2}} is singular. *Out[4]=* Inverse[{{1, 1}, {2, 2}}]
Here is the text of the message.	*In[5]:=* **Inverse::sing** *Out[5]=* Matrix `1` is singular.
This redefines the message.	*In[6]:=* **Inverse::sing = "Matrix `1` is not invertible."** *Out[6]=* Matrix `1` is not invertible.
Now the new form will be used.	*In[7]:=* **Inverse[{{1, 1}, {2, 2}}]** Inverse::sing: Matrix {{1, 1}, {2, 2}} is not invertible. *Out[7]=* Inverse[{{1, 1}, {2, 2}}]

Messages are always stored as strings suitable for use with **StringForm**. When the message is printed, the appropriate expressions are "spliced" into it. The expressions are wrapped with **HoldForm** to prevent evaluation. In addition, any function that is assigned as the value of the global variable **$MessagePrePrint** is applied to the resulting expressions before they are given to **StringForm**. The default for **$MessagePrePrint** is **Short**.

Most messages are associated directly with the functions that generate them. There are, however, some "general" messages, which can be produced by a variety of functions.

If you give the wrong number of arguments to a function *F*, *Mathematica* will warn you by printing a message such as *F*::argx. If *Mathematica* cannot find a message named *F*::argx, it will use the text of the "general" message General::argx instead. You can use Off[*F*::argx] to switch off the argument count message specifically for the function *F*. You can also use Off[General::argx] to switch off all messages that use the text of the general message.

Mathematica prints a message if you give the wrong number of arguments to a built-in function.	*In[8]:=* **Sqrt[a, b]** Sqrt::argx: Sqrt called with 2 arguments; 1 argument is expected. *Out[8]=* Sqrt[a, b]
This argument count message is a general one, used by many different functions.	*In[9]:=* **General::argx** *Out[9]=* `1` called with `2` arguments; 1 argument is expected.

If something goes very wrong with a calculation you are doing, it is common to find that the same warning message is generated over and over again. This is usually more confusing than useful. As a result, *Mathematica* keeps track of all messages that are produced during a particular calculation, and stops printing a particular message if it comes up more than three times. Whenever this happens, *Mathematica* prints the message General::stop to let you know. If you really want to see all the messages that *Mathematica* tries to print, you can do this by switching off General::stop.

$MessageList	a list of the messages produced during a particular computation
MessageList[*n*]	a list of the messages produced during the processing of the nth input line in a *Mathematica* session

Finding out what messages were produced during a computation.

In every computation you do, *Mathematica* maintains a list $MessageList of all the messages that are produced. In a standard *Mathematica* session, this list is cleared after each line of output is generated. However, during a computation, you can access the list. In addition, when the nth output line in a session is generated, the value of $MessageList is assigned to MessageList[*n*].

This returns $MessageList, which gives a list of the messages produced.

```
In[10]:= Sqrt[a, b, c]; Exp[a, b]; $MessageList

Sqrt::argx: Sqrt called with 3
       arguments; 1 argument is expected.

Exp::argx: Exp called with 2 arguments; 1 argument is expected.

Out[10]= {Sqrt::argx, Exp::argx}
```

The message names are wrapped in HoldForm to stop them from evaluating.

```
In[11]:= InputForm[%]

Out[11]//InputForm= {HoldForm[Sqrt::argx], HoldForm[Exp::argx]}
```

In writing programs, it is often important to be able to check automatically whether any messages were generated during a particular calculation. If messages were generated, say as a consequence of producing indeterminate numerical results, then the result of the calculation may be meaningless.

Check[*expr*, *failexpr*]	if no messages are generated during the evaluation of *expr*, then return *expr*, otherwise return *failexpr*
Check[*expr*, *failexpr*, s_1::t_1, s_2::t_2, ...]	check only for the messages s_i::t_i

Checking for warning messages.

Evaluating 1^0 produces no messages, so the result of the evaluation is returned.

```
In[12]:= Check[1^0, err]

Out[12]= 1
```

Evaluating 0^0 produces a message, so the second argument of Check is returned.

```
In[13]:= Check[0^0, err]

Power::indet: Indeterminate expression 0$^0$ encountered.

Out[13]= err
```

Check[*expr*, *failexpr*] tests for all messages that are actually printed out. It does not test for messages whose output has been suppressed using Off.

In some cases you may want to test only for a specific set of messages, say ones associated with numerical overflow. You can do this by explicitly telling Check the names of the messages you want to look for.

The message generated by
Log[1, 2, 3] is ignored by Check,
since it is not the one specified.

```
In[14]:= Check[Log[1, 2, 3], err, General::ind]
Out[14]= Log[1, 2, 3]
```

Message[*s*::*tag*]	print a message
Message[*s*::*tag*, *expr₁*, ...]	print a message, splicing the *exprᵢ* into its string form

Generating messages.

By using the function Message, you can mimic all aspects of the way in which built-in *Mathematica* functions generate messages. You can for example switch on and off messages using On and Off, and Message will automatically look for General::*tag* if it does not find the specific message *s*::*tag*.

This defines the text of a message
associated with f.

```
In[15]:= f::overflow = "Factorial argument `1` too large."
Out[15]= Factorial argument `1` too large.
```

Here is the function f.

```
In[16]:= f[x_] :=
            If[x > 10,
                (Message[f::overflow, x]; Infinity), x!]
```

When the argument of f is greater than
10, the message is generated.

```
In[17]:= f[20]
f::overflow: Factorial argument 20 too large.
Out[17]= Infinity
```

This switches off the message.

```
In[18]:= Off[f::overflow]
```

Now the message is no longer
generated.

```
In[19]:= f[20]
Out[19]= Infinity
```

When you call Message, it first tries to find a message with the explicit name you have specified. If this fails, it tries to find a message with the appropriate tag associated with the symbol General. If this too fails, then *Mathematica* takes any function you have defined as the value of the global variable $NewMessage, and applies this function to the symbol and tag of the message you have requested.

By setting up the value of $NewMessage appropriately, you can for example, get *Mathematica* to read in the text of a message from a file when that message is first needed.

■ 2.8.9 International Messages

The standard set of messages for built-in *Mathematica* functions are written in American English. In some versions of *Mathematica*, messages are also available in other languages. In addition, if you set up messages yourself, you can give ones in other languages.

Languages in *Mathematica* are conventionally specified by strings. The languages are given in English, in order to avoid the possibility of needing special characters. Thus, for example, the French language is specified in *Mathematica* as "French".

$Language = "*lang*"	set the language to use
$Language = {"*lang₁*", "*lang₂*", ... }	
	set a sequence of languages to try

Setting the language to use for messages.

This tells *Mathematica* to use French language versions of messages.

```
In[1]:= $Language = "French"
Out[1]= French
```

If your version of *Mathematica* has French language messages, the message generated here will be in French.

```
In[2]:= Sqrt[a, b, c]

Sqrt::argx: Sqrt est demandé avec 3 arguments;
    il faut y avoir 1.

Out[2]= Sqrt[a, b, c]
```

symbol::*tag*	the default form of a message
symbol::*tag*::*Language*	a message in a particular language

Messages in different languages.

When built-in *Mathematica* functions generate messages, they look first for messages of the form $s::t::Language$, in the language specified by $Language. If they fail to find any such messages, then they use instead the form $s::t$ without an explicit language specification.

The procedure used by built-in functions will also be followed by functions you define if you call `Message` with message names of the form $s::t$. If you give explicit languages in message names, however, only those languages will be used.

■ 2.8.10 Documentation Constructs

When you write programs in *Mathematica*, there are various ways to document your code. As always, by far the best thing is to write clear code, and to name the objects you define as explicitly as possible.

Sometimes, however, you may want to add some "commentary text" to your code, to make it easier to understand. You can add such text at any point in your code simply by enclosing it in matching (* and *). Notice that in *Mathematica*, "comments" enclosed in (* and *) can be nested in any way.

You can use comments anywhere in the *Mathematica* code you write.	`In[1]:= If[a > b, (* then *) p, (* else *) q]`
	`          (* This is a conditional. *)`
	
	`Out[1]= If[a > b, p, q]`

(* *text* *)	a comment that can be inserted anywhere in *Mathematica* code

Comments in *Mathematica*.

There is a convention in *Mathematica* that all functions intended for later use should be given a definite "usage message", which documents their basic usage. This message is defined as the value of *f*::usage, and is retrieved when you type ?*f*.

f::usage = "*text*"	define the usage message for a function
?*f*	get information about a function
??*f*	get more information about a function

Usage messages for functions.

Here is the definition of a function f.	`In[2]:= f[x_] := x^2`

Here is a "usage message" for f.	`In[3]:= f::usage = "f[x] gives the square of x."`
	
	`Out[3]= f[x] gives the square of x.`

This gives the usage message for f.	`In[4]:= ?f`
	
	`f[x] gives the square of x.`

??f gives all the information *Mathematica* has about f, including the actual definition.	`In[5]:= ??f`
	
	`f[x] gives the square of x.`
	
	`f[x_] := x^2`

When you define a function f, you can usually display its value using $?f$. However, if you give a usage message for f, then $?f$ just gives the usage message. Only when you type $??f$ do you get all the details about f, including its actual definition.

If you ask for information using ? about just one function, *Mathematica* will print out the complete usage messages for the function. If you ask for information on several functions at the same time, however, *Mathematica* will just give you the name of each function.

f::usage	main usage message
f::notes	notes about the function
f::qv	related functions
f::usage::*Language*, etc.	messages in a particular language

Some typical documentation messages.

In addition to the usage message, there are some messages such as notes and qv that are often defined to document functions.

If you use *Mathematica* with a text-based interface, then messages and comments are the primary mechanisms for documenting your definitions. However, if you use *Mathematica* with a notebook interface, then you will be able to give much more extensive documentation in text cells in the notebook.

2.9 The Structure of Graphics and Sound

■ 2.9.1 The Structure of Graphics

Section 1.9 discussed how to use functions like `Plot` and `ListPlot` to plot graphs of functions and data. In this section, we discuss how *Mathematica* represents such graphics, and how you can program *Mathematica* to create more complicated images.

The basic idea is that *Mathematica* represents all graphics in terms of a collection of *graphics primitives*. The primitives are objects like `Point`, `Line` and `Polygon`, that represent elements of a graphical image, as well as directives such as `RGBColor`, `Thickness` and `SurfaceColor`.

This generates a plot of a list of points.   *In[1]:=* `ListPlot[ Table[Prime[n], {n, 20}] ]`

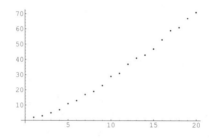

`InputForm` shows how *Mathematica* represents the graphics. Each point is represented as a `Point` graphics primitive. All the various graphics options used in this case are also given.

In[2]:= `InputForm[%]`

```
Out[2]//InputForm=
  Graphics[{Point[{1, 2}], Point[{2, 3}], Point[{3, 5}],
    Point[{4, 7}], Point[{5, 11}], Point[{6, 13}],
    Point[{7, 17}], Point[{8, 19}], Point[{9, 23}],
    Point[{10, 29}], Point[{11, 31}], Point[{12, 37}],
    Point[{13, 41}], Point[{14, 43}], Point[{15, 47}],
    Point[{16, 53}], Point[{17, 59}], Point[{18, 61}],
    Point[{19, 67}], Point[{20, 71}]},
    {PlotRange -> Automatic, AspectRatio -> GoldenRatio^(-1),
    DisplayFunction :> $DisplayFunction,
    ColorOutput -> Automatic, Axes -> Automatic,
    AxesOrigin -> Automatic, PlotLabel -> None,
    AxesLabel -> None, Ticks -> Automatic, GridLines -> None,
    Prolog -> {}, Epilog -> {}, AxesStyle -> Automatic,
    Background -> Automatic, DefaultColor -> Automatic,
    DefaultFont :> $DefaultFont, RotateLabel -> True,
    Frame -> False, FrameStyle -> Automatic,
    FrameTicks -> Automatic, FrameLabel -> None,
    PlotRegion -> Automatic}]
```

Each complete piece of graphics in *Mathematica* is represented as a *graphics object*. There are several different kinds of graphics object, corresponding to different types of graphics. Each kind of graphics object has a definite head which identifies its type.

Graphics [*list*]	general two-dimensional graphics
DensityGraphics [*list*]	density plot
ContourGraphics [*list*]	contour plot
SurfaceGraphics [*list*]	three-dimensional surface
Graphics3D [*list*]	general three-dimensional graphics
GraphicsArray [*list*]	array of other graphics objects

Graphics objects in *Mathematica*.

The functions like Plot and ListPlot discussed in Section 1.9 all work by building up *Mathematica* graphics objects, and then displaying them.

Graphics	Plot, ListPlot, ParametricPlot
DensityGraphics	DensityPlot, ListDensityPlot
ContourGraphics	ContourPlot, ListContourPlot
SurfaceGraphics	Plot3D, ListPlot3D
Graphics3D	ParametricPlot3D

Generating graphics objects by plotting functions and data.

You can create other kinds of graphical images in *Mathematica* by building up your own graphics objects. Since graphics objects in *Mathematica* are just symbolic expressions, you can use all the standard *Mathematica* functions to manipulate them.

Once you have created a graphics object, you must then display it. The function Show allows you to display any *Mathematica* graphics object.

Show [*g*]	display a graphics object
Show [g_1, g_2, ...]	display several graphics objects combined
Show [GraphicsArray [{{g_{11}, g_{12}, ... }, ... }]]	
	display an array of graphics objects

Displaying graphics objects.

This uses **Table** to generate a polygon graphics primitive.

```
In[3]:= poly = Polygon[
               Table[N[{Cos[n Pi/5], Sin[n Pi/5]}], {n, 0, 5}] ]
Out[3]= Polygon[{{1., 0}, {0.809017, 0.587785},
        {0.309017, 0.951057}, {-0.309017, 0.951057},
        {-0.809017, 0.587785}, {-1., 0}}]
```

This creates a two-dimensional graphics object that contains the polygon graphics primitive. In standard output format, the graphics object is given simply as **-Graphics-**.

```
In[4]:= Graphics[ poly ]
Out[4]= -Graphics-
```

InputForm shows the complete graphics object.

```
In[5]:= InputForm[%]
Out[5]//InputForm=
  Graphics[Polygon[{{1., 0},
      {0.809016994374947, 0.5877852522924732},
      {0.3090169943749474, 0.951056516295153},
      {-0.3090169943749474, 0.951056516295154},
      {-0.809016994374947, 0.5877852522924733}, {-1., 0}}]]
```

This displays the graphics object you have created.

```
In[6]:= Show[%]
```

Graphics directives	Examples: RGBColor, Thickness, SurfaceColor
Graphics options	Examples: PlotRange, Ticks, AspectRatio, ViewPoint

Local and global ways to modify graphics.

Given a particular list of graphics primitives, *Mathematica* provides two basic mechanisms for modifying the final form of graphics you get. First, you can insert into the list of graphics primitives certain *graphics directives*, such as RGBColor, which modify the subsequent graphical elements in the list. In this way, you can specify how a particular set of graphical elements should be rendered.

This takes the list of graphics primitives created above, and adds the graphics directive GrayLevel[0.3].

```
In[7]:= Graphics[ {GrayLevel[0.3], poly} ]
Out[7]= -Graphics-
```

Now the polygon is rendered in gray.   *In[8]:=* **Show[%]**

By inserting graphics directives, you can specify how particular graphical elements should be rendered. Often, however, you want to make global modifications to the way a whole graphics object is rendered. You can do this using *graphics options*.

By adding the graphics option **Frame**   *In[9]:=* **Show[%, Frame -> True]**
you can modify the overall appearance
of the graphics.

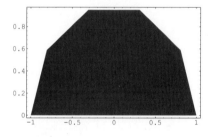

Show returns a graphics object with the   *In[10]:=* **InputForm[%]**
options in it.

Out[10]//InputForm=
    Graphics[{GrayLevel[0.3],
        Polygon[{{1., 0}, {0.809016994374947, 0.5877852522924732},
            {0.3090169943749474, 0.951056516295153},
            {-0.3090169943749474, 0.951056516295154},
            {-0.809016994374947, 0.5877852522924733}, {-1., 0}}]},
        Frame -> True]

You can specify graphics options in Show. As a result, it is straightforward to take a single graphics object, and show it with many different choices of graphics options.

Notice however that Show always returns the graphics objects it has displayed. If you specify graphics options in Show, then these options are automatically inserted into the graphics objects that Show returns. As a result, if you call Show again on the same objects, the same graphics options will be used, unless you explicitly specify other ones. Note that in all cases new options you specify will overwrite ones already there.

Options[*g*]	give a list of all graphics options for a graphics object
Options[*g*, *opt*]	give the setting for a particular option
FullOptions[*g*, *opt*]	give the actual value used for a particular option, even if the setting is Automatic

Finding the options for a graphics object.

Some graphics options work by requiring you to specify a particular value for a parameter related to a piece of graphics. Other options allow you to give the setting Automatic, which makes *Mathematica* use internal algorithms to choose appropriate values for parameters. In such cases, you can find out the values that *Mathematica* actually used by applying the function FullOptions.

Here is a plot.   *In[11]:=* **zplot = Plot[Abs[Zeta[1/2 + I x]], {x, 0, 10}]**

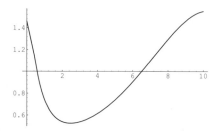

The option PlotRange is set to its default value of Automatic, specifying that *Mathematica* should use internal algorithms to determine the actual plot range.

In[12]:= **Options[zplot, PlotRange]**

Out[12]= {PlotRange -> Automatic}

FullOptions gives the actual plot range determined by *Mathematica* in this case.

In[13]:= **FullOptions[zplot, PlotRange]**

Out[13]= {{-0.25, 10.25}, {0.50068, 1.57477}}

FullGraphics[*g*]	translate objects specified by graphics options into lists of explicit graphics primitives

Finding the complete form of a piece of graphics.

When you use a graphics option such as Axes, *Mathematica* effectively has to construct a list of graphics elements to represent the objects such as axes that you have requested. Usually *Mathematica* does not explicitly return the list it constructs in this way. Sometimes, however, you may find it useful to get this list. The function FullGraphics gives the complete list of graphics primitives needed to generate a particular plot, without any options being used.

This plots a list of values.

In[14]:= **ListPlot[Table[EulerPhi[n], {n, 10}]]**

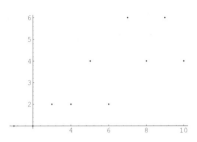

FullGraphics yields a graphics object that includes graphics primitives representing axes and so on.

In[15]:= **Short[InputForm[FullGraphics[%]], 6]**

Out[15]//Short=

Graphics[{{Point[{1, 1}], Point[{2, 1}], Point[{3, 2}],

 Point[{4, 2}], Point[{5, 4}], Point[{6, 2}], Point[{7, 6}],

 Point[{8, 4}], Point[{9, 6}], Point[{10, 4}]},

 {{{{GrayLevel[0.], Thickness[0.002],

 Line[{{0.775, 1.}, {10.225, 1.}}]}, None}}, <<2>>,

 {{<<2>>}, <<24>>}}}]

With their default option settings, functions like Plot and Show actually cause *Mathematica* to generate graphical output. In general, the actual generation of graphical output is controlled by the graphics option DisplayFunction. The default setting for this option is the value of the global variable $DisplayFunction.

In most cases, $DisplayFunction and the DisplayFunction option are set to use the lower-level rendering function Display to produce output, perhaps after some preprocessing. Sometimes, however, you may want to get a function like Plot to produce a graphics object, but you may not immediately want that graphics object actually rendered as output. You can tell *Mathematica* to generate the object, but not render it, by setting the option DisplayFunction -> Identity. Section 2.9.14 will explain exactly how this works.

Plot[*f*, ... , DisplayFunction -> Identity], etc.
  generate a graphics object for a plot, but do not actually display it

Show[*g*, DisplayFunction -> $DisplayFunction]
  show a graphics object using the default display function

Generating and displaying graphics objects.

This generates a graphics object, but does not actually display it.

In[16]:= **Plot[BesselJ[0, x], {x, 0, 10},**
                                    DisplayFunction -> Identity]

Out[16]= -Graphics-

This modifies the graphics object, but still does not actually display it.

In[17]:= **Show[%, Frame -> True]**

Out[17]= -Graphics-

To display the graphic, you explicitly have to tell *Mathematica* to use the default display function.

In[18]:= **Show[%, DisplayFunction -> $DisplayFunction]**

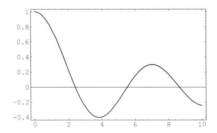

■ 2.9.2 Two-Dimensional Graphics Elements

Point[{x, y}]	point at position x, y
Line[{{x_1, y_1}, {x_2, y_2}, ... }]	line through the points {x_1, y_1}, {x_2, y_2}, ...
Rectangle[{$xmin$, $ymin$}, {$xmax$, $ymax$}]	filled rectangle
Polygon[{{x_1, y_1}, {x_2, y_2}, ... }]	filled polygon with the specified list of corners
Circle[{x, y}, r]	circle with radius r centered at x, y
Disk[{x, y}, r]	filled disk with radius r centered at x, y
Raster[{{a_{11}, a_{12}, ... }, {a_{21}, ... }, ... }]	rectangular array of gray levels between 0 and 1
Text[$expr$, {x, y}]	the text of $expr$, centered at x, y (see Section 2.9.16)

Basic two-dimensional graphics elements.

Here is a line primitive.

In[1]:= **sawline = Line[Table[{n, (-1)^n}, {n, 6}]]**

Out[1]= Line[{{1, -1}, {2, 1}, {3, -1}, {4, 1}, {5, -1},
    {6, 1}}]

This shows the line as a
two-dimensional graphics object.

In[2]:= **sawgraph = Show[Graphics[sawline]]**

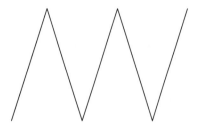

This redisplays the line, with axes
added.

In[3]:= **Show[%, Axes -> True]**

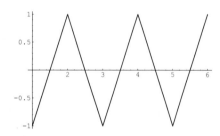

You can combine graphics objects that you have created explicitly from graphics primitives with ones
that are produced by functions like Plot.

This produces an ordinary *Mathematica*
plot.

In[4]:= **Plot[Sin[Pi x], {x, 0, 6}]**

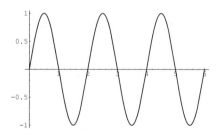

This combines the plot with the sawtooth picture made above.

In[5]:= **Show[%, sawgraph]**

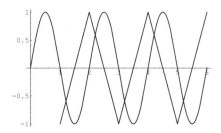

You can combine different graphical elements simply by giving them in a list. In two-dimensional graphics, *Mathematica* will render the elements in exactly the order you give them. Later elements are therefore effectively drawn on top of earlier ones.

Here is a list of two Rectangle graphics elements.

In[6]:= **{Rectangle[{1, -1}, {2, -0.6}],**
                          Rectangle[{4, .3}, {5, .8}]}

Out[6]= {Rectangle[{1, -1}, {2, -0.6}],

  Rectangle[{4, 0.3}, {5, 0.8}]}

This draws the rectangles on top of the line that was defined above.

In[7]:= **Show[Graphics[{sawline, %}]]**

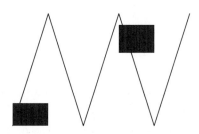

The Polygon graphics primitive takes a list of *x, y* coordinates, corresponding to the corners of a polygon. *Mathematica* joins the last corner with the first one, and then fills the resulting area.

Here are the coordinates of the corners of a regular pentagon.

In[8]:= **pentagon = Table[{Sin[2 Pi n/5], Cos[2 Pi n/5]}, {n, 5}]**

Out[8]= $\{\{Sin[\frac{2\ Pi}{5}],\ Cos[\frac{2\ Pi}{5}]\},\ \{Sin[\frac{4\ Pi}{5}],\ Cos[\frac{4\ Pi}{5}]\},$

  $\{Sin[\frac{6\ Pi}{5}],\ Cos[\frac{6\ Pi}{5}]\},\ \{Sin[\frac{8\ Pi}{5}],\ Cos[\frac{8\ Pi}{5}]\},\ \{0,\ 1\}\}$

This displays the pentagon. With the default choice of aspect ratio, the pentagon looks somewhat squashed.

In[9]:= **Show[Graphics[Polygon[pentagon]]]**

This chooses the aspect ratio so that the shape of the pentagon is preserved.

In[10]:= **Show[%, AspectRatio -> Automatic]**

Mathematica can handle polygons which fold over themselves.

In[11]:= **Show[Graphics[**
 Polygon[{{-1, -1}, {1, 1}, {1, -1}, {-1, 1}}]]]

Circle[{x, y}, r]	a circle with radius r centered at the point {x, y}
Circle[{x, y}, {r_x, r_y}]	an ellipse with semi-axes r_x and r_y
Circle[{x, y}, r, {*theta$_1$*, *theta$_2$*}]	
	a circular arc
Circle[{x, y}, {r_x, r_y}, {*theta$_1$*, *theta$_2$*}]	
	an elliptical arc
Disk[{x, y}, r], etc.	filled disks

Circles and disks.

This shows two circles with radius 2. Setting the option
AspectRatio -> Automatic makes the circles come out with their natural aspect ratio.

```
In[12]:= Show[ Graphics[
            {Circle[{0, 0}, 2], Circle[{1, 1}, 2]} ],
                    AspectRatio -> Automatic ]
```

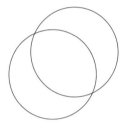

This shows a sequence of disks with progressively larger semi-axes in the x direction, and progressively smaller ones in the y direction.

```
In[13]:= Show[ Graphics[
            Table[Disk[{3n, 0}, {n/4, 2-n/4}], {n, 4}] ],
                    AspectRatio -> Automatic ]
```

Mathematica allows you to generate arcs of circles, and segments of ellipses. In both cases, the objects are specified by starting and finishing angles. The angles are measured counterclockwise in radians with zero corresponding to the positive x direction.

This draws a 140° wedge centered at the origin.

`In[14]:= Show[ Graphics[ Disk[{0, 0}, 1, {0, 140 Degree}] ],`
`          AspectRatio -> Automatic ]`

`Raster[{{`a_{11}`, `a_{12}`, ... }, {`a_{21}`, ... }, ... }]`
    array of gray levels between 0 and 1

`Raster[`*array*`, {{`*xmin*`, `*ymin*`}, {`*xmax*`, `*ymax*`}}, {`*zmin*`, `*zmax*`}]`
    array of gray levels between *zmin* and *zmax* drawn in the
    rectangle defined by {*xmin*, *ymin*} and {*xmax*, *ymax*}

`RasterArray[{{`g_{11}`, `g_{12}`, ... }, {`g_{21}`, ... }, ... }]`
    rectangular array of cells colored according to the graphics
    directives g_{ij}

Raster-based graphics elements.

Here is a 4×4 array of values between 0 and 1.

`In[15]:= modtab = Table[Mod[i, j]/3, {i, 4}, {j, 4}] // N`
`Out[15]= {{0, 0.333333, 0.333333, 0.333333},`
`  {0, 0, 0.666667, 0.666667}, {0, 0.333333, 0, 1.},`
`  {0, 0, 0.333333, 0}}`

This uses the array of values as gray levels in a raster.

In[16]:= **Show[Graphics[Raster[%]]]**

This shows two overlapping copies of the raster.

In[17]:= **Show[Graphics[{Raster[modtab, {{0, 0}, {2, 2}}],**
Raster[modtab, {{1.5, 1.5}, {3, 2}}]}]]

In the default case, Raster always generates an array of gray cells. As described on page 425, you can use the option ColorFunction to apply a "coloring function" to all the cells.

You can also use the graphics primitive RasterArray. While Raster takes an array of *values*, RasterArray takes an array of *Mathematica graphics directives*. The directives associated with each cell are taken to determine the color of that cell. Typically the directives are chosen from the set GrayLevel, RGBColor or Hue. By using RGBColor and Hue directives, you can create color rasters using RasterArray.

■ 2.9.3 Graphics Directives and Options

When you set up a graphics object in *Mathematica*, you typically give a list of graphical elements. You can include in that list *graphics directives* which specify how subsequent elements in the list should be rendered.

In general, the graphical elements in a particular graphics object can be given in a collection of nested lists. When you insert graphics directives in this kind of structure, the rule is that a particular graphics directive affects all subsequent elements of the list it is in, together with all elements of sublists that may occur. The graphics directive does not, however, have any effect outside the list it is in.

The first sublist contains the graphics directive GrayLevel.

```
In[1]:= {{GrayLevel[0.5], Rectangle[{0, 0}, {1, 1}]},
                        Rectangle[{1, 1}, {2, 2}]}

Out[1]= {{GrayLevel[0.5], Rectangle[{0, 0}, {1, 1}]},
         Rectangle[{1, 1}, {2, 2}]}
```

Only the rectangle in the first sublist is affected by the GrayLevel directive.

```
In[2]:= Show[Graphics[ % ]]
```

Mathematica provides various kinds of graphics directives. One important set is those for specifying the colors of graphical elements. Even if you have a black-and-white display device, you can still give color graphics directives. The colors you specify will be converted to gray levels at the last step in the graphics rendering process. Note that you can get black-and-white display even on a color device by setting the option ColorOutput -> GrayLevel.

GrayLevel[*i*]	gray level between 0 (black) and 1 (white)
RGBColor[*r*, *g*, *b*]	color with specified red, green and blue components, each between 0 and 1
Hue[*h*]	color with hue *h* between 0 and 1
Hue[*h*, *s*, *b*]	color with specified hue, saturation and brightness, each between 0 and 1

Basic *Mathematica* color specifications.

On a color display, the two curves
would be shown in color. Here they are
shown in gray.

```
In[3]:= Plot[{BesselI[1, x], BesselI[2, x]}, {x, 0, 5},
            PlotStyle ->
                {{RGBColor[1, 0, 0]}, {RGBColor[0, 1, 0]}}]
```

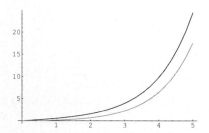

The function Hue[*h*] provides a convenient way to specify a range of colors using just one parameter. As *h* varies from 0 to 1, Hue[*h*] runs through red, yellow, green, cyan, blue, magenta, and back to red again. Hue[*h*, *s*, *b*] allows you to specify not only the "hue", but also the "saturation" and "brightness" of a color. Taking the saturation to be equal to one gives the deepest colors; decreasing the saturation towards zero leads to progressively more "washed out" colors.

Page 40 shows examples of colors generated with various color specifications.

For most purposes, you will be able to specify the colors you need simply by giving appropriate RGBColor or Hue directives. However, if you need very precise or repeatable colors, particularly for color printing, there are a number of subtleties which arise, as discussed in Section 2.9.17 below.

When you give a graphics directive such as RGBColor, it affects *all* subsequent graphical elements that appear in a particular list. *Mathematica* also supports various graphics directives which affect only specific types of graphical elements.

The graphics directive PointSize[*r*] specifies that all Point elements which appear in a graphics object should be drawn as circles with a radius *r*. In PointSize, the radius *r* is measured as a fraction of the width of your whole plot.

Mathematica also provides the graphics directive AbsolutePointSize[*d*], which allows you to specify the "absolute" radii of points, measured in fixed units. The units are approximately printer's points, equal to $\frac{1}{72}$ of an inch.

PointSize[*r*]	give all points a radius *r* as a fraction of the width of the whole plot
AbsolutePointSize[*d*]	give all point a radius *d* measured in absolute units

Graphics directives for points.

Here is a list of points.

```
In[4]:= Table[Point[{n, Prime[n]}], {n, 6}]
Out[4]= {Point[{1, 2}], Point[{2, 3}], Point[{3, 5}],
   Point[{4, 7}], Point[{5, 11}], Point[{6, 13}]}
```

This makes each point have a radius equal to one-tenth of the width of the plot.

```
In[5]:= Show[Graphics[{PointSize[0.1], %}], PlotRange -> All]
```

Here each point has size 3 in absolute units.

```
In[6]:= ListPlot[Table[Prime[n], {n, 20}],
          Prolog -> AbsolutePointSize[3]]
```

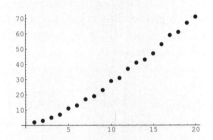

Thickness[r]	give all lines a thickness r as a fraction of the width of the whole plot
AbsoluteThickness[d]	give all lines a thickness d measured in absolute units
Dashing[{r_1, r_2, ... }]	show all lines as a sequence of dashed segments, with lengths r_1, r_2, ...
AbsoluteDashing[{d_1, d_2, ... }]	use absolute units to measure dashed segments

Graphics directives for lines.

This generates a list of lines with
different absolute thicknesses.

```
In[7]:= Table[
            {AbsoluteThickness[n], Line[{{0, 0}, {n, 1}}]}, {n, 4}]
Out[7]= {{AbsoluteThickness[1], Line[{{0, 0}, {1, 1}}]},
    {AbsoluteThickness[2], Line[{{0, 0}, {2, 1}}]},
    {AbsoluteThickness[3], Line[{{0, 0}, {3, 1}}]},
    {AbsoluteThickness[4], Line[{{0, 0}, {4, 1}}]}}
```

Here is a picture of the lines.

```
In[8]:= Show[Graphics[%]]
```

The Dashing graphics directive allows you to create lines with various kinds of dashing. The basic idea is to break lines into segments which are alternately drawn and omitted. By changing the lengths of the segments, you can get different line styles. Dashing allows you to specify a sequence of segment lengths. This sequence is repeated as many times as necessary in drawing the whole line.

This gives a dashed line with a
succession of equal-length segments.

```
In[9]:= Show[Graphics[ {Dashing[{0.05, 0.05}],
                Line[{{-1, -1}, {1, 1}}]} ]]
```

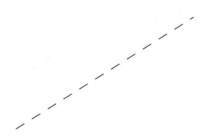

This gives a dot-dashed line.

`In[10]:= Show[Graphics[{Dashing[{0.01, 0.05, 0.05, 0.05}],`
`Line[{{-1, -1}, {1, 1}}]}]]`

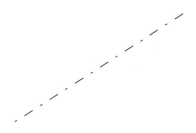

One way to use *Mathematica* graphics directives is to insert them directly into the lists of graphics primitives used by graphics objects. Sometimes, however, you want the graphics directives to be applied more globally, and for example to determine the overall "style" with which a particular type of graphical element should be rendered. There are typically graphics options which can be set to specify such styles in terms of lists of graphics directives.

PlotStyle -> *style*	specify a style to be used for all curves in Plot
PlotStyle -> {{*style₁*}, {*style₂*}, ... }	
	specify styles to be used (cyclically) for a sequence of curves in Plot
MeshStyle -> *style*	specify a style to be used for a mesh in density and surface graphics
BoxStyle -> *style*	specify a style to be used for the bounding box in three-dimensional graphics

Some graphics options for specifying styles.

This generates a plot in which the curve is given in a style specified by graphics directives.

`In[11]:= Plot[BesselJ[2, x], {x, 0, 10},`
`PlotStyle -> {{Thickness[0.02], GrayLevel[0.5]}}]`

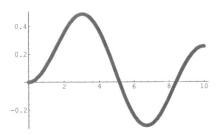

GrayLevel[0.5]	gray
RGBColor[1, 0, 0], etc.	red, etc.
Thickness[0.05]	thick
Dashing[{0.05, 0.05}]	dashed
Dashing[{0.01, 0.05, 0.05, 0.05}]	
	dot-dashed

Some typical styles.

The various "style options" allow you to specify how particular graphical elements in a plot should be rendered. *Mathematica* also provides options that affect the rendering of the whole plot.

Background -> *color*	specify the background color for a plot
DefaultColor -> *color*	specify the default color for a plot
Prolog -> *g*	give graphics directives to use before a plot is started
Epilog -> *g*	give graphics directives to use after a plot is finished

Graphics options that affect whole plots.

This draws the whole plot on a gray background.

```
In[12]:= Plot[Sin[Sin[x]], {x, 0, 10},
            Background -> GrayLevel[0.6]]
```

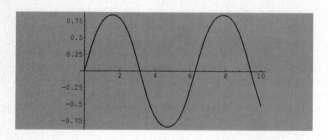

This makes the default color white. $In[13]:=$ **Show[%, DefaultColor -> GrayLevel[1]]**

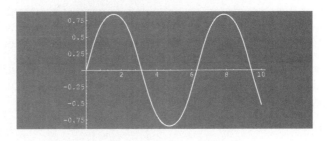

■ 2.9.4 Coordinate Systems for Two-Dimensional Graphics

When you set up a graphics object in *Mathematica*, you give coordinates for the various graphical elements that appear. When *Mathematica* renders the graphics object, it has to translate the original coordinates you gave into "display coordinates" which specify where each element should be placed in the final display area.

Sometimes, you may find it convenient to specify the display coordinates for a graphical element directly. You can do this by using "scaled coordinates" Scaled[{*sx*, *sy*}] rather than {*x*, *y*}. The scaled coordinates are defined to run from 0 to 1 in *x* and *y*, with the origin taken to be at the lower-left corner of the display area.

{*x*, *y*}	original coordinates
Scaled[{*sx*, *sy*}]	scaled coordinates

Coordinate systems for two-dimensional graphics.

The rectangle is drawn at a fixed position relative to the display area, independent of the original coordinates used for the plot.

$In[1]:=$ **Plot[Tan[x], {x, 0, 2Pi},**
        Prolog ->
            Rectangle[Scaled[{0.7, 0.7}], Scaled[{1, 1}]]]

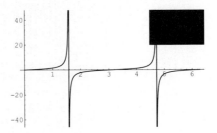

When you use {*x*, *y*} or Scaled[{*sx*, *sy*}], you are specifying position either completely in orig-inal coordinates, or completely in scaled coordinates. Sometimes, however, you may need to use a combination of these coordinate systems. For example, if you want to draw a line at a particular point whose length is a definite fraction of the width of the plot, you will have to use original coordinates to specify the basic position of the line, and scaled coordinates to specify its length.

You can use Scaled[{*dsx*, *dsy*}, {*x*, *y*}] to specify a position using a mixture of original and scaled coordinates. In this case, {*x*, *y*} gives a position in original coordinates, and {*dsx*, *dsy*} gives the offset from the position in scaled coordinates.

Note that you can use Scaled with either one or two arguments to specify radii in Disk and Circle graphics elements.

PlotRange -> {{*xmin*, *xmax*}, {*ymin*, *ymax*}}
> the range of original coordinates to include in the plot

PlotRegion -> {{*sxmin*, *sxmax*}, {*symin*, *symax*}}
> the region of the display specified in scaled coordinates which the plot fills

Options which determine translation from original to display coordinates.

When *Mathematica* renders a graphics object, one of the first things it has to do is to work out what range of original *x* and *y* coordinates it should actually display. Any graphical elements that are out-side this range will be "clipped", and not shown.

The option PlotRange specifies the range of original coordinates to include. As discussed on page 141, the default setting is PlotRange -> Automatic, which makes *Mathematica* try to choose a range which includes all "interesting" parts of a plot, while dropping "outliers". By setting PlotRange -> All, you can tell *Mathematica* to include everything. You can also give explicit ranges of coordinates to include.

This sets up a polygonal object whose corners have coordinates between roughly ±1.

```
In[2]:= obj = Polygon[
            Table[{Sin[n Pi/10], Cos[n Pi/10]} + 0.05 (-1)^n,
                  {n, 20}]] ;
```

In this case, the polygonal object fills almost the whole display area.

$In[3]:=$ **Show[Graphics[obj]]**

With the default
`PlotRange -> Automatic`, the outlying point is not included, but does affect the range of coordinates chosen.

$In[4]:=$ **Show[Graphics[{obj, Point[{20, 20}]}]]**

With `PlotRange -> All`, the outlying point is included, and the coordinate system is correspondingly modified.

$In[5]:=$ **Show[%, PlotRange -> All]**

The option `PlotRange` allows you to specify a rectangular region in the original coordinate system, and to drop any graphical elements that lie outside this region. In order to render the remaining elements, however, *Mathematica* then has to determine how to position this rectangular region with respect to the final display area.

The option `PlotRegion` allows you to specify where the corners of the rectangular region lie within the final display area. The positions of the corners are specified in scaled coordinates, which are defined to run from 0 to 1 across the display area. The default is `PlotRegion -> {{0, 1}, {0, 1}}`, which specifies that the rectangular region should fill the whole display area.

By specifying PlotRegion, you can effectively add "margins" around your plot.

```
In[6]:= Plot[ArcTan[x], {x, 0, 10},
              PlotRegion -> {{0.2, 0.8}, {0.3, 0.7}}]
```

AspectRatio -> *r*	make the ratio of height to width for the display area equal to *r*
AspectRatio -> Automatic	determine the shape of the display area from the original coordinate system

Specifying the shape of the display area.

What we have discussed so far is how *Mathematica* translates the original coordinates you specify into positions in the final display area. What remains to discuss, however, is what the final display area is like.

On most computer systems, there is a certain fixed region of screen or paper into which the *Mathematica* display area must fit. How it fits into this region is determined by its "shape" or aspect ratio. In general, the option AspectRatio specifies the ratio of height to width for the final display area.

It is important to note that the setting of AspectRatio does not affect the meaning of the scaled or display coordinates. These coordinates always run from 0 to 1 across the display area. What AspectRatio does is to change the shape of this display area.

This generates a graphic object corresponding to a hexagon.

```
In[7]:= hex = Graphics[Polygon[
              Table[{Sin[n Pi/3], Cos[n Pi/3]}, {n, 6}] ]] ;
```

This renders the hexagon in a display area whose height is three times its width.

In[8]:= **Show[hex, AspectRatio -> 3]**

For two-dimensional graphics, AspectRatio is set by default to the fixed value of 1/GoldenRatio. Sometimes, however, you may want to determine the aspect ratio for a plot from the original coordinate system used in the plot. Typically what you want is for one unit in the x direction in the original coordinate system to correspond to the same distance in the final display as one unit in the y direction. In this way, objects that you define in the original coordinate system are displayed with their "natural shape". You can make this happen by setting the option AspectRatio -> Automatic.

With AspectRatio -> Automatic, the aspect ratio of the final display area is determined from the original coordinate system, and the hexagon is shown with its "natural shape".

In[9]:= **Show[hex, AspectRatio -> Automatic]**

Using scaled coordinates, you can specify the sizes of graphical elements as fractions of the size of the display area. You cannot, however, tell *Mathematica* the actual physical size at which a particular graphical element should be rendered. Of course, this size ultimately depends on the details of your graphics output device, and cannot be determined for certain within *Mathematica*. Nevertheless, graphics directives such as AbsoluteThickness discussed on page 409 do allow you to indicate "absolute sizes" to use for particular graphical elements. The sizes you request in this way will be respected by most, but not all, output devices. (For example, if you optically project an image, it is neither possible nor desirable to maintain the same absolute size for a graphical element within it.)

■ 2.9.5 Labeling Two-Dimensional Graphics

Axes -> True	give a pair of axes
GridLines -> Automatic	draw grid lines on the plot
Frame -> True	put axes on a frame around the plot
PlotLabel -> "*text*"	give an overall label for the plot

Ways to label two-dimensional plots.

Here is a plot, using the default
Axes -> True.

*In[1]:= * bp = Plot[BesselJ[2, x], {x, 0, 10}]

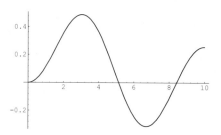

Setting Frame -> True generates a
frame with axes, and removes tick
marks from the ordinary axes.

*In[2]:= * Show[bp, Frame -> True]

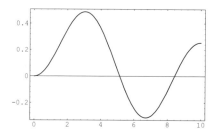

This includes grid lines, which are shown in light blue on color displays.

In[3]:= **Show[%, GridLines -> Automatic]**

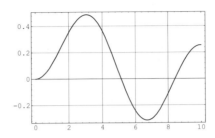

Axes -> False	draw no axes
Axes -> True	draw both *x* and *y* axes
Axes -> {False, True}	draw a *y* axis but no *x* axis
AxesOrigin -> Automatic	choose the crossing point for the axes automatically
AxesOrigin -> {*x*, *y*}	specify the crossing point
AxesStyle -> *style*	specify the style for axes
AxesStyle -> {{*xstyle*}, {*ystyle*}}	
	specify individual styles for axes
AxesLabel -> None	give no axis labels
AxesLabel -> *ylabel*	put a label on the *y* axes
AxesLabel -> {*xlabel*, *ylabel*}	put labels on both *x* and *y* axes

Options for axes.

This makes the axes cross at the point {5, 0}, and puts a label on each axis.

In[4]:= **Show[bp, AxesOrigin->{5, 0}, AxesLabel->{"x", "y"}]**

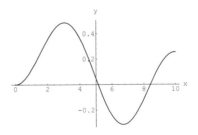

`Ticks -> None`	draw no tick marks
`Ticks -> Automatic`	place tick marks automatically
`Ticks -> {xticks, yticks}`	tick mark specifications for each axis

Settings for the `Ticks` option.

With the default setting `Ticks -> Automatic`, *Mathematica* creates a certain number of major and minor tick marks, and places them on axes at positions which yield the minimum number of decimal digits in the tick labels. In some cases, however, you may want to specify the positions and properties of tick marks explicitly. You will need to do this, for example, if you want to have tick marks at multiples of π, or if you want to put a non-linear scale on an axis.

`None`	draw no tick marks
`Automatic`	place tick marks automatically
$\{x_1, x_2, \dots\}$	draw tick marks at the specified positions
$\{\{x_1, label_1\}, \{x_2, label_2\}, \dots\}$	draw tick marks with the specified labels
$\{\{x_1, label_1, len_1\}, \dots\}$	draw tick marks with the specified scaled lengths
$\{\{x_1, label_1, \{plen_1, mlen_1\}\}, \dots\}$	
	draw tick marks with the specified lengths in the positive and negative directions
$\{\{x_1, label_1, len_1, style_1\}, \dots\}$	draw tick marks with the specified styles
func	a function to be applied to *xmin*, *xmax* to get the tick mark option

Tick mark options for each axis.

This gives tick marks at specified positions on the *x* axis, and chooses the tick marks automatically on the *y* axis.

`In[5]:= Show[bp, Ticks -> {{0, Pi, 2Pi, 3Pi}, Automatic}]`

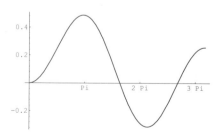

This adds tick marks with no labels at multiples of $\pi/2$.

```
In[6]:= Show[bp,
            Ticks -> {{0, {Pi/2, ""}, Pi, {3Pi/2, ""},
                      2Pi, {5Pi/2, ""}, 3Pi}, Automatic}]
```

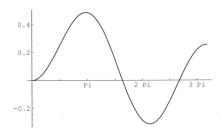

Particularly when you want to create complicated tick mark specifications, it is often convenient to define a "tick mark function" which creates the appropriate tick mark specification given the minimum and maximum values on a particular axis.

This defines a function which gives a list of tick mark positions with a spacing of 1.

```
In[7]:= units[xmin_, xmax_] :=
            Range[Floor[xmin], Floor[xmax], 1]
```

This uses the **units** function to specify tick marks for the *x* axis.

```
In[8]:= Show[bp, Ticks -> {units, Automatic}]
```

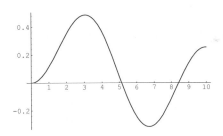

Sometimes you may want to generate tick marks which differ only slightly from those produced automatically with the setting Ticks -> Automatic. You can get the complete specification for tick marks that were generated automatically in a particular plot by using FullOptions[*g*, Ticks], as discussed on page 398.

Frame -> False	draw no frame
Frame -> True	draw a frame around the plot
FrameStyle -> *style*	specify a style for the frame
FrameStyle -> {{*xmstyle*}, {*ymstyle*}, ... }	
	specify styles for each edge of the frame
FrameLabel -> None	give no frame labels
FrameLabel -> {*xmlabel*, *ymlabel*, ... }	
	put labels on edges of the frame
RotateLabel -> False	do not rotate text in labels
FrameTicks -> None	draw no tick marks on frame edges
FrameTicks -> Automatic	position tick marks automatically
FrameTicks -> {{*xmticks*, *ymticks*, ... }}	
	specify tick marks for frame edges

Options for frame axes.

The **Axes** option allows you to draw a single pair of axes in a plot. Sometimes, however, you may instead want to show the scales for a plot on a frame, typically drawn around the whole plot. The option **Frame** allows you effectively to draw four axes, corresponding to the four edges of the frame around a plot. These four axes are ordered clockwise, starting from the one at the bottom.

This draws frame axes, and labels each of them.

```
In[9]:= Show[bp, Frame -> True,
           FrameLabel -> {"label 1", "label 2",
                          "label 3", "label 4"}]
```

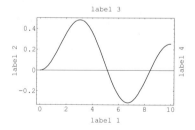

GridLines -> None	draw no grid lines
GridLines -> Automatic	position grid lines automatically
GridLines -> {*xgrid*, *ygrid*}	specify grid lines in analogy with tick marks

Options for grid lines.

Grid lines in *Mathematica* work very much like tick marks. As with tick marks, you can specify explicit positions for grid lines. There is no label or length to specify for grid lines. However, you can specify a style.

This generates *x* but not *y* grid lines.   *In[10]:=* **Show[bp, GridLines -> {Automatic, None}]**

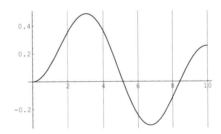

■ 2.9.6 Making Plots within Plots

Section 1.9.4 described how you can make regular arrays of plots using `GraphicsArray`. Using the `Rectangle` graphics primitive, however, you can combine and superimpose plots in any way.

Rectangle[{*xmin*, *ymin*}, {*xmax*, *ymax*}, *graphics*]
render a graphics object within the specified rectangle

Creating a subplot.

Here is a three-dimensional plot.

In[1]:= **p3 = Plot3D[Sin[x] Exp[y], {x, -5, 5}, {y, -2, 2}]**

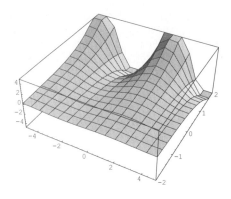

This creates a two-dimensional graphics object which contains two copies of the three-dimensional plot.

In[2]:= **Show[Graphics[{Rectangle[{0, 0}, {1, 1}, p3],**
Rectangle[{0.8, 0.8}, {1.2, 1.4}, p3]}]]

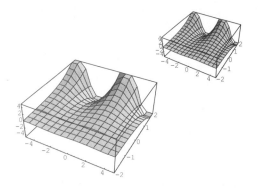

Mathematica can render any graphics object within a `Rectangle`. In all cases, what it puts in the rectangle is a scaled down version of what would be obtained if you displayed the graphics object on its own. Notice that in general the display area for the graphics object will be sized so as to touch at least one pair of edges of the rectangle.

■ 2.9.7 Density and Contour Plots

DensityGraphics [*array*]	density plot
ContourGraphics [*array*]	contour plot

Graphics objects that represent density and contour plots.

The functions DensityPlot and ContourPlot discussed in Section 1.9.6 work by creating ContourGraphics and DensityGraphics objects containing arrays of values.

Most of the options for density and contour plots are the same as those for ordinary two-dimensional plots. There are, however, a few additional options.

option name	default value	
ColorFunction	Automatic	how to assign colors to each cell
Mesh	True	whether to draw a mesh
MeshStyle	Automatic	a style for the mesh

Additional options for density plots.

In a density plot, the color of each cell represents its value. By default, each cell is assigned a gray level, running from black to white as the value of the cell increases. In general, however, you can specify other "color maps" for the relation between the value of a cell and its color. The option ColorFunction allows you to specify a function which is applied to each cell value to find the color of the cell. The cell values are scaled so as to run between 0 and 1 in a particular density plot. The function you give as the setting for ColorFunction may return any *Mathematica* color directive, such as GrayLevel, Hue or RGBColor. A common setting to use is ColorFunction -> Hue.

Here is a density plot with the default
ColorFunction.

In[1]:= **DensityPlot[Sin[x y], {x, -1, 1}, {y, -1, 1}]**

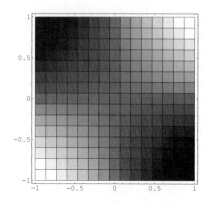

This gives a density plot with a different
"color map".

In[2]:= **Show[%, ColorFunction -> (GrayLevel[#^3]&)]**

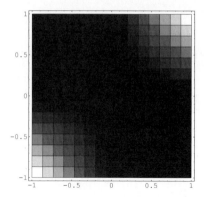

option name	default value	
Contours	10	what contours to use
ContourLines	True	whether to draw contour lines
ContourStyle	Automatic	style to use for contour lines
ContourSmoothing	None	how to smooth contour lines
ContourShading	True	whether to shade regions in the plot
ColorFunction	Automatic	how to assign colors to contour levels

Options for contour plots.

In constructing a contour plot, the first issue is what contours to use. With the default setting Contours -> Automatic, *Mathematica* uses a sequence of contours levels equally spaced between the minimum and maximum values defined by the PlotRange option.

Contours -> n	use a sequence of n equally spaced contours
Contours -> {z_1, z_2, ... }	use contours with values z_1, z_2, ...

Specifying contours.

This creates a contour plot with two contours.

$In[3]:=$ **ContourPlot[Sin[x y], {x, -1, 1}, {y, -1, 1},**
                    Contours -> {-.5, .5}]

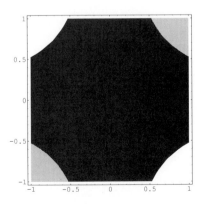

To find the contour associated with a particular z value, *Mathematica* effectively has to solve an implicit equation. Given the value of the contour, the goal is to find those values of x and y for which $f(x,y)=z$, where f is the function you are plotting.

In a `ContourGraphics` object, however, the exact function f is not given. Instead, what is given is an array of values of f at a grid of x, y points. To find the positions of contours, it is necessary to interpolate these values in some way.

The simplest approach is to assume that the function varies linearly between each adjacent pair of grid points. With this assumption, it is straightforward to work out where each contour crosses each of the lines joining adjacent grid points.

This is essentially the approach used by *Mathematica* with the option setting `ContourSmoothing -> None`. Particularly when shading is included in the contour plot, this approach is often satisfactory. However, it can lead to contours that appear quite jagged.

With `ContourSmoothing -> Automatic`, *Mathematica* attempts to smooth contours. To do this, it assumes that the function you are plotting is fairly smooth, and then effectively breaks each grid square into a number of smaller squares, and finds the path of the contour through each square.

Here is a contour plot with some fairly jagged contours.

`In[4]:= ContourPlot[Sin[x y], {x, -2, 2}, {y, -2, 2}, ContourShading -> False]`

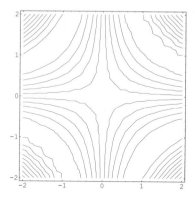

This tells *Mathematica* to try and smooth the contours.

`In[5]:= Show[%, ContourSmoothing -> Automatic]`

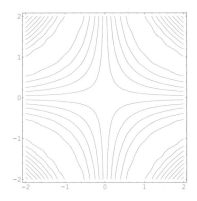

`ContourSmoothing -> None`	use no smoothing on contours
`ContourSmoothing -> Automatic`	smooth contours
`ContourSmoothing -> n`	smooth contours by subdividing n times in each direction

Options for smoothing contour plots.

There are some slight subtleties associated with labeling density and contour plots. Both the **Axes** and **Frame** options from ordinary two-dimensional graphics can be used. But setting **AxesOrigin -> Automatic** keeps the axes outside the plot in both cases.

■ 2.9.8 Three-Dimensional Graphics Primitives

One of the most powerful aspects of graphics in *Mathematica* is the availability of three-dimensional as well as two-dimensional graphics primitives. By combining three-dimensional graphics primitives, you can represent and render three-dimensional objects in *Mathematica*.

Point[{x, y, z}]	point with coordinates x, y, z
Line[{{x_1, y_1, z_1}, {x_2, y_2, z_2}, ... }]	
	line through the points {x_1, y_1, z_1}, {x_2, y_2, z_2}, ...
Polygon[{{x_1, y_1, z_1}, {x_2, y_2, z_2}, ... }]	
	filled polygon with the specified list of corners
Cuboid[{$xmin$, $ymin$, $zmin$}, {$xmax$, $ymax$, $zmax$}]	
	cuboid
Text[$expr$, {x, y, z}]	text at position {x, y, z} (see Section 2.9.16)

Three-dimensional graphics elements.

Every time you evaluate rcoord, it generates a random coordinate in three dimensions.

`In[1]:= rcoord := {Random[ ], Random[ ], Random[ ]}`

This generates a list of 20 random points in three-dimensional space.

`In[2]:= pts = Table[Point[rcoord], {20}] ;`

Here is a plot of the points.

`In[3]:= Show[ Graphics3D[ pts ] ]`

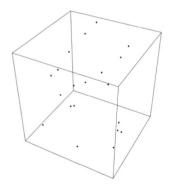

This gives a plot showing a line through 10 random points in three dimensions.

$In[4]:=$ `Show[ Graphics3D[ Line[ Table[rcoord, {10}] ] ] ]`

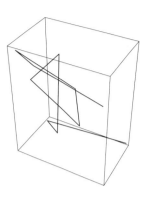

If you give a list of graphics elements in two dimensions, *Mathematica* simply draws each element in turn, with later elements obscuring earlier ones. In three dimensions, however, *Mathematica* collects together all the graphics elements you specify, then displays them as three-dimensional objects, with the ones in front in three-dimensional space obscuring those behind.

Every time you evaluate rantri, it generates a random triangle in three-dimensional space.

$In[5]:=$ `rantri := Polygon[ Table[ rcoord, {3} ] ]`

This draws a single random triangle.

$In[6]:=$ `Show[ Graphics3D[ rantri ] ]`

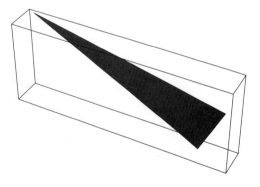

This draws a collection of 5 random triangles. The triangles in front obscure those behind.

In[7]:= **Show[Graphics3D[Table[rantri, {5}]]]**

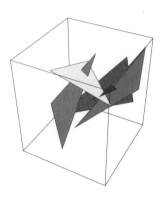

By creating an appropriate list of polygons, you can build up any three-dimensional object in *Mathematica*. Thus, for example, all the surfaces produced by `ParametricPlot3D` are represented simply as lists of polygons.

The package `Graphics`Polyhedra`` contains examples of lists of polygons which correspond to polyhedra in three dimensions.

This loads a package which defines various polyhedra.

In[8]:= **<<Graphics`Polyhedra`;**

Here is the list of polygons corresponding to a tetrahedron centered at the origin.

In[9]:= **Tetrahedron[ ]**

Out[9]= {Polygon[{{0., 0., 1.73205}, {0., 1.63299, -0.57735},
     {-1.41421, -0.816497, -0.57735}}],
  Polygon[{{0., 0., 1.73205}, {-1.41421, -0.816497, -0.57735},
     {1.41421, -0.816497, -0.57735}}],
  Polygon[{{0., 0., 1.73205}, {1.41421, -0.816497, -0.57735},
     {0., 1.63299, -0.57735}}],
  Polygon[{{0., 1.63299, -0.57735},
     {1.41421, -0.816497, -0.57735},
     {-1.41421, -0.816497, -0.57735}}]}

This displays the tetrahedron as a three-dimensional object.

In[10]:= **Show[Graphics3D[%]]**

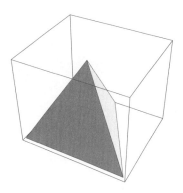

Dodecahedron[ ] is another three-dimensional object defined in the polyhedra package.

In[11]:= **Show[Graphics3D[Dodecahedron[ ]]]**

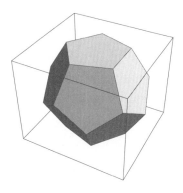

This shows four intersecting dodecahedra.

In[12]:= **Show[Graphics3D[**
        Table[Dodecahedron[0.8 {k, k, k}], {k, 0, 3}]]]

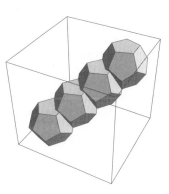

Mathematica allows polygons in three dimensions to have any number of vertices. However, these vertices should lie in a plane, and should form a convex figure. If they do not, then *Mathematica* will break the polygon into triangles, which are planar by definition, before rendering it.

Cuboid[{*x*, *y*, *z*}]	a unit cube with opposite corners having coordinates {*x*, *y*, *z*} and {*x*+1, *y*+1, *z*+1}
Cuboid[{*xmin*, *ymin*, *zmin*}, {*xmax*, *ymax*, *zmax*}]	
	a cuboid (rectangular parallelepiped) with opposite corners having the specified coordinates

Cuboid graphics elements.

This draws 20 random unit cubes in three-dimensional space.

In[13]:= **Show[Graphics3D[Table[Cuboid[10 rcoord], {20}]]]**

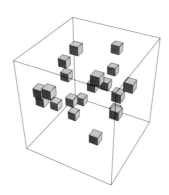

■ 2.9.9 Three-Dimensional Graphics Directives

In three dimensions, just as in two dimensions, you can give various graphics directives to specify how the different elements in a graphics object should be rendered.

All the graphics directives for two dimensions also work in three dimensions. There are however some additional directives in three dimensions.

Just as in two dimensions, you can use the directives PointSize, Thickness and Dashing to tell *Mathematica* how to render Point and Line elements. Note that in three dimensions, the lengths that appear in these directives are measured as fractions of the total width of the display area for your plot.

This generates a list of 20 random points in three dimensions.

In[1]:= **pts = Table[Point[Table[Random[ ], {3}]], {20}];**

This displays the points, with each one being a circle whose radius is 5% of the display area width.

`In[2]:= Show[Graphics3D[ { PointSize[0.05], pts } ]]`

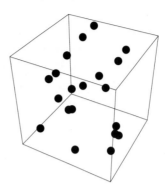

As in two dimensions, you can use `AbsolutePointSize`, `AbsoluteThickness` and `AbsoluteDashing` if you want to measure length in absolute units.

This generates a line through 10 random points in three dimensions.

`In[3]:= line = Line[Table[Random[ ], {10}, {3}]] ;`

This shows the line dashed, with a thickness of 2 printer's points.

`In[4]:= Show[Graphics3D[ { AbsoluteThickness[2],`
`                            AbsoluteDashing[{5, 5}], line } ]]`

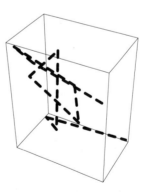

For `Point` and `Line` objects, the color specification directives also work the same in three dimensions as in two dimensions. For `Polygon` objects, however, they can work differently.

In two dimensions, polygons are always assumed to have an intrinsic color, specified directly by graphics directives such as `RGBColor`. In three dimensions, however, *Mathematica* also provides the option of generating colors for polygons using a more physical approach based on simulated illumination. With the default option setting `Lighting -> True` for `Graphics3D` objects, *Mathematica* ignores explicit colors specified for polygons, and instead determines all polygon colors using the simulated illumination model. Even in this case, however, explicit colors are used for points and lines.

Lighting -> False	intrinsic colors
Lighting -> True	colors based on simulated illumination (default)

The two schemes for coloring polygons in three dimensions.

This loads a package which defines various polyhedra.

`In[5]:= <<Graphics`Polyhedra` ;`

This draws an icosahedron, using the same gray level for all faces and all edges. Only a silhouette is left.

`In[6]:= Show[Graphics3D[{GrayLevel[0.7], Icosahedron[ ]}],`
`                                        Lighting -> False]`

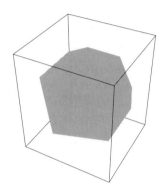

With the default setting Lighting -> True, the colors of polygons are determined by the simulated illumination model, and explicit color specifications are ignored.

`In[7]:= Show[%, Lighting -> True]`

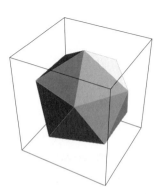

Explicit color directives are, however, always followed for points and lines.

In[8]:= **Show[{%, Graphics3D[{GrayLevel[0.5], Thickness[0.05],**
Line[{{0, 0, -2}, {0, 0, 2}}]}]}]

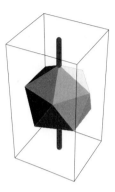

EdgeForm[ ]	draw no lines at the edges of polygons
EdgeForm[*g*]	use the graphics directives *g* to determine how to draw lines at the edges of polygons

Giving graphics directives for the edges of polygons.

When you render a three-dimensional graphics object in *Mathematica*, there are two kinds of lines that can appear. The first kind are lines from explicit Line primitives that you included in the graphics object. The second kind are lines that were generated as the edges of polygons.

You can tell *Mathematica* how to render lines of the second kind by giving a list of graphics directives inside EdgeForm.

This renders a dodecahedron with its edges shown as thick gray lines.

```
In[9]:= Show[Graphics3D[
           {EdgeForm[{GrayLevel[0.5], Thickness[0.02]}],
           Dodecahedron[ ]}]]
```

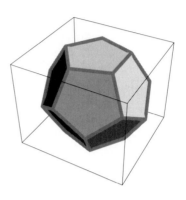

FaceForm[*gfront*, *gback*]	use *gfront* graphics directives for the front face of each polygon, and *gback* for the back

Rendering the fronts and backs of polygons differently.

An important aspect of polygons in three dimensions is that they have both front and back faces. *Mathematica* uses the following convention to define the "front face" of a polygon: if you look at a polygon from the front, then the corners of the polygon will appear counter-clockwise, when taken in the order that you specified them.

This defines a dodecahedron with one face removed.

```
In[10]:= d = Drop[Dodecahedron[ ], {6}] ;
```

You can now see inside the dodecahedron.

```
In[11]:= Show[Graphics3D[d]]
```

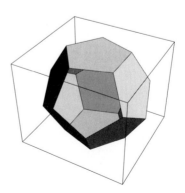

This makes the front (outside) face of each polygon light gray, and the back (inside) face dark gray.

```
In[12]:= Show[Graphics3D[
                {FaceForm[GrayLevel[0.8], GrayLevel[0.3]], d}],
             Lighting -> False]
```

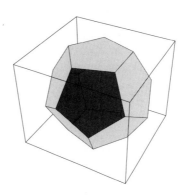

■ 2.9.10 Coordinate Systems for Three-Dimensional Graphics

Whenever *Mathematica* draws a three-dimensional object, it always effectively puts a cuboidal box around the object. With the default option setting Boxed -> True, *Mathematica* in fact draws the edges of this box explicitly. But in general, *Mathematica* automatically "clips" any parts of your object that extend outside of the cuboidal box.

The option PlotRange specifies the range of x, y and z coordinates that *Mathematica* should include in the box. As in two dimensions the default setting is PlotRange -> Automatic, which makes *Mathematica* use an internal algorithm to try and include the "interesting parts" of a plot, but drop outlying parts. With PlotRange -> All, *Mathematica* will include all parts.

This loads a package defining various polyhedra.

```
In[1]:= <<Graphics`Polyhedra` ;
```

This creates a stellated icosahedron.

```
In[2]:= stel = Stellate[Icosahedron[ ]] ;
```

Here is the stellated icosahedron, drawn   *In[3]:=* **Show[Graphics3D[stel], Axes -> True]**
in a box.

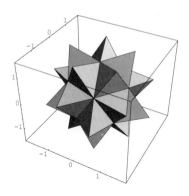

With this setting for **PlotRange**, many   *In[4]:=* **Show[%, PlotRange -> {-1, 1}]**
parts of the stellated icosahedron lie
outside the box, and are clipped.

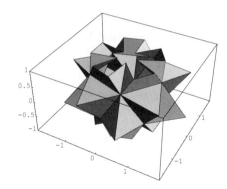

Much as in two dimensions, you can use either "original" or "scaled" coordinates to specify the positions of elements in three-dimensional objects. Scaled coordinates, specified as **Scaled[{**sx**,** sy**,** sz**}]** are taken to run from 0 to 1 in each dimension. The coordinates are set up to define a right-handed coordinate system on the box.

{x**,** y**,** z**}**	original coordinates
Scaled[{sx**,** sy**,** sz**}]**	scaled coordinates, running from 0 to 1 in each dimension

Coordinate systems for three-dimensional objects.

This puts a cuboid in one corner of the box.

```
In[5]:= Show[Graphics3D[{stel,
              Cuboid[Scaled[{0, 0, 0}],
                 Scaled[{0.2, 0.2, 0.2}]]}]]
```

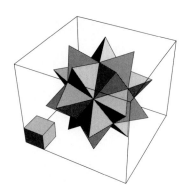

Once you have specified where various graphical elements go inside a three-dimensional box, you must then tell *Mathematica* how to draw the box. The first step is to specify what shape the box should be. This is analogous to specifying the aspect ratio of a two-dimensional plot. In three dimensions, you can use the option BoxRatios to specify the ratio of side lengths for the box. For Graphics3D objects, the default is BoxRatios -> Automatic, specifying that the shape of the box should be determined from the ranges of actual coordinates for its contents.

BoxRatios -> {*xr*, *yr*, *zr*}	specify the ratio of side lengths for the box
BoxRatios -> Automatic	determine the ratio of side length from the range of actual coordinates (default for Graphics3D)
BoxRatios -> {1, 1, 0.4}	specify a fixed shape of box (default for SurfaceGraphics)

Specifying the shape of the bounding box for three-dimensional objects.

This displays the stellated icosahedron in a tall box.

In[6]:= **Show[Graphics3D[stel], BoxRatios -> {1, 1, 5}]**

To produce an image of a three-dimensional object, you have to tell *Mathematica* from what view point you want to look at the object. You can do this using the option **ViewPoint**.

Some common settings for this option were given on page 159. In general, however, you can tell *Mathematica* to use any view point, so long as it lies outside the box.

View points are specified in the form **ViewPoint -> {sx, sy, sz}**. The values *si* are given in a special coordinate system, in which the center of the box is {0, 0, 0}. The special coordinates are scaled so that the longest side of the box corresponds to one unit. The lengths of the other sides of the box in this coordinate system are determined by the setting for the **BoxRatios** option. For a cubical box, therefore, each of the special coordinates runs from –1/2 to 1/2 across the box. Note that the view point must always lie outside the box.

This generates a picture using the default view point {1.3, –2.4, 2}.

In[7]:= **surf = Plot3D[(2 + Sin[x]) Cos[2 y],**
{x, -2, 2}, {y, -3, 3},
AxesLabel -> {"x", "y", "z"}]

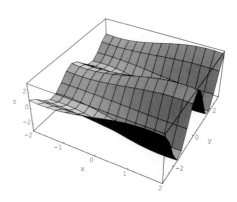

This is what you get with a view point close to one of the corners of the box.

`In[8]:= Show[%, ViewPoint -> {1.2, 1.2, 1.2}]`

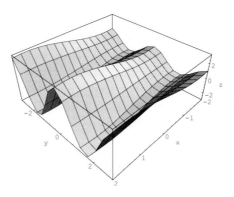

As you move away from the box, the perspective effect gets smaller.

`In[9]:= Show[%, ViewPoint -> {5, 5, 5}]`

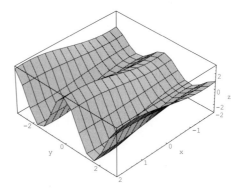

option name	default value	
ViewPoint	{1.3, -2.4, 2}	the point in a special scaled coordinate system from which to view the object
ViewCenter	Automatic	the point in the scaled coordinate system which appears at the center of the final image
ViewVertical	{0, 0, 1}	the direction in the scaled coordinate system which appears as vertical in the final image

Specifying the position and orientation of three-dimensional objects.

In making a picture of a three-dimensional object you have to specify more than just *where* you want to look at the object from. You also have to specify how you want to "frame" the object in your final image. You can do this using the additional options `ViewCenter` and `ViewVertical`.

`ViewCenter` allows you to tell *Mathematica* what point in the object should appear at the center of your final image. The point is specified by giving its scaled coordinates, running from 0 to 1 in each direction across the box. With the setting `ViewCenter -> {1/2, 1/2, 1/2}`, the center of the box will therefore appear at the center of your final image. With many choices of view point, however, the box will not appear symmetrical, so this setting for `ViewCenter` will not center the whole box in the final image area. You can do this by setting `ViewCenter -> Automatic`.

`ViewVertical` specifies which way up the object should appear in your final image. The setting for `ViewVertical` gives the direction in scaled coordinates which ends up vertical in the final image. With the default setting `ViewVertical -> {0, 0, 1}`, the *z* direction in your original coordinate system always ends up vertical in the final image.

With this setting for `ViewCenter`, a corner of the box appears in the center of your image.	`In[10]:= Show[surf, ViewCenter -> {1, 1, 1}]`

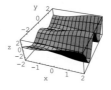

This setting for `ViewVertical` makes the *x* axis of the box appear vertical in your image.	`In[11]:= Show[surf, ViewVertical -> {1, 0, 0}]`

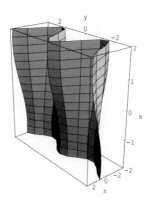

When you set the options `ViewPoint`, `ViewCenter` and `ViewVertical`, you can think about it as specifying how you would look at a physical object. `ViewPoint` specifies where your head is relative to the object. `ViewCenter` specifies where you are looking (the center of your gaze). And `ViewVertical` specifies which way up your head is.

In terms of coordinate systems, settings for `ViewPoint`, `ViewCenter` and `ViewVertical` specify how coordinates in the three-dimensional box should be transformed into coordinates for your image in the final display area.

For some purposes, it is useful to think of the coordinates in the final display area as three dimensional. The x and y axes run horizontally and vertically, respectively, while the z axis points into the page. Positions specified in this "display coordinate system" remain fixed when you change `ViewPoint` and so on. The positions of light sources discussed in the next section are defined in this display coordinate system.

Box coordinate system	measured relative to the box around your object
Display coordinate system	measured relative to your final display area

Coordinate systems for three-dimensional graphics.

Once you have obtained a two-dimensional image of a three-dimensional object, there are still some issues about how this image should be rendered. The issues however are identical to those that occur for two-dimensional graphics. Thus, for example, you can modify the final shape of your image by changing the `AspectRatio` option. And you specify what region of your whole display area your image should take up by setting the `PlotRegion` option.

This modifies the aspect ratio of the final image.

In[12]:= `Show[surf, Axes -> False, AspectRatio -> 0.3]`

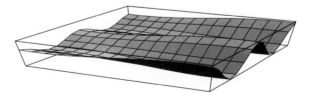

Mathematica usually scales the images of three-dimensional objects to be as large as possible, given the display area you specify. Although in most cases this scaling is what you want, it does have the consequence that the size at which a particular three-dimensional object is drawn may vary with the orientation of the object. You can set the option `SphericalRegion -> True` to avoid such variation. With this option setting, *Mathematica* effectively puts a sphere around the three-dimensional bounding box, and scales the final image so that the whole of this sphere fits inside the display area you specify. The sphere has its center at the center of the bounding box, and is drawn so that the bounding box just fits inside it.

This draws a rather elongated version of the plot.

`In[13]:= Show[surf, BoxRatios -> {1, 5, 1}]`

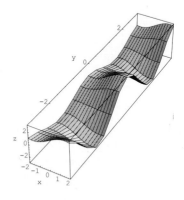

With `SphericalRegion -> True`, the final image is scaled so that a sphere placed around the bounding box would fit in the display area.

`In[14]:= Show[%, SphericalRegion -> True]`

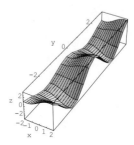

By setting `SphericalRegion -> True`, you can make the scaling of an object consistent for all orientations of the object. This is useful if you create animated sequences which show a particular object in several different orientations.

| SphericalRegion -> False | scale three-dimensional images to be as large as possible |
| SphericalRegion -> True | scale images so that a sphere drawn around the three-dimensional bounding box would fit in the final display area |

Changing the magnification of three-dimensional images.

■ 2.9.11 Plotting Three-Dimensional Surfaces

By giving an appropriate list of graphics primitives, you can represent essentially any three-dimensional object in *Mathematica* with Graphics3D. You can represent three-dimensional surfaces with Graphics3D by giving explicit lists of polygons with adjacent edges.

If you need to represent arbitrary surfaces which can fold over and perhaps intersect themselves, there is no choice but to use explicit lists of polygons with Graphics3D, as ParametricPlot3D does.

However, there are many cases in which you get simpler surfaces. For example, Plot3D and ListPlot3D yield surfaces which never fold over, and have a definite height at every x, y point. You can represent simple surfaces like these in *Mathematica* without giving an explicit list of polygons. Instead, all you need do is to give an array which specifies the z height at every point in an x, y grid. The graphics object SurfaceGraphics[*array*] represents a surface constructed in this way.

| Graphics3D[*primitives*] | arbitrary three-dimensional objects, including folded surfaces |
| SurfaceGraphics[*array*] | simple three-dimensional surfaces |

Three-dimensional graphics objects.

Here is a 4×4 array of values.

```
In[1]:= moda = Table[Mod[i, j], {i, 4}, {j, 4}]

Out[1]= {{0, 1, 1, 1}, {0, 0, 2, 2}, {0, 1, 0, 3}, {0, 0, 1, 0}}
```

This uses the array to give the height of each point on the surface.

In[2]:= **Show[SurfaceGraphics[moda]]**

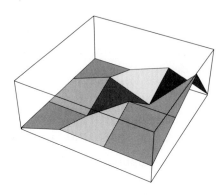

Both `Plot3D` and `ListPlot3D` work by creating `SurfaceGraphics` objects.

Graphics3D[*surface*]   convert SurfaceGraphics to Graphics3D

Converting between representations of surfaces.

If you apply `Graphics3D` to a `SurfaceGraphics` object, *Mathematica* will generate a `Graphics3D` object containing an explicit list of polygons representing the surface in the `SurfaceGraphics` object. Whenever you ask *Mathematica* to combine two `SurfaceGraphics` objects together, it automatically converts them both to `Graphics3D` objects.

Here is a surface represented by a SurfaceGraphics object.

In[3]:= **Plot3D[(1 - Sin[x]) (2 - Cos[2 y]),**
                    {x, -2, 2}, {y, -2, 2}]

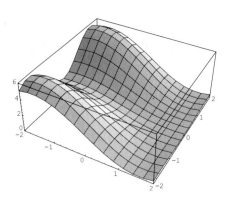

Here is another surface.

In[4]:= **Plot3D[(2 + Sin[x]) (1 + Cos[2 y]),**
                          {x, -2, 2}, {y, -2, 2}]

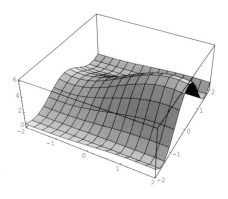

Mathematica shows the two surfaces together by converting each of them to a **Graphics3D** object containing an explicit list of polygons.

In[5]:= **Show[%, %%]**

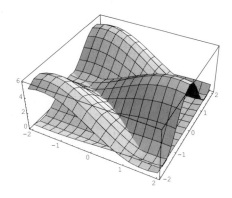

option name	default value	
Mesh	True	whether to draw a mesh on the surface
MeshStyle	Automatic	graphics directives specifying how to render the mesh
MeshRange	Automatic	the original range of coordinates corresponding to the mesh

Mesh options in **SurfaceGraphics**.

When you create a surface using `SurfaceGraphics`, the default is to draw a rectangular mesh on the surface. As discussed on page 160, including this mesh typically makes it easier for one to see the shape of the surface. You can nevertheless get rid of the mesh by setting the option `Mesh -> False`. You can also set the option `MeshStyle` to a list of graphics directives which specify thickness, color or other properties of the mesh lines.

A `SurfaceGraphics` object contains an array of values which specify the height of a surface at points in an x, y grid. By setting the option `MeshRange`, you can give the range of original x and y coordinates that correspond to the points in this grid. When you use `Plot3D[f, {x, xmin, xmax}, {y, ymin, ymax}]` to generate a `SurfaceGraphics` object, the setting `MeshRange -> {{xmin, xmax}, {ymin, ymax}}` is automatically generated. The setting for `MeshRange` is used in labeling the x and y axes in surface plots, and in working out polygon coordinates if you convert a `SurfaceGraphics` object to an explicit list of polygons in a `Graphics3D` object.

`None`	leave out clipped parts of the surface, so that you can see through
`Automatic`	show the clipped part of the surface with the same shading as an actual surface in the same position would have (default setting)
`GrayLevel[i]`, `RGBColor[r, g, b]`, etc.	
	show the clipped part of the surface with a particular gray level, color, etc.
`{bottom, top}`	give different specifications for parts that are clipped at the bottom and top

Settings for the `ClipFill` option.

The option `PlotRange` works for `SurfaceGraphics` as it does for other *Mathematica* graphics objects. Any parts of a surface that lie outside the range of coordinates defined by `PlotRange` will be "clipped". The option `ClipFill` allows you to specify what should happen to the parts of a surface that are clipped.

Here is a three-dimensional plot in which the top and bottom of the surface are clipped. With the default setting for ClipFill, the clipped parts are shown as they would be if they were part of the actual surface.

In[6]:= **Plot3D[Sin[x y], {x, 0, 3}, {y, 0, 3},
                PlotRange -> {-.5, .5}]**

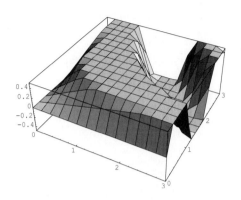

With ClipFill->None, parts of the surface which are clipped are left out, so that you can "see through" the surface there. *Mathematica* always leaves out parts of the surface that correspond to places where the value of the function you are plotting is not a real number.

In[7]:= **Show[%, ClipFill -> None]**

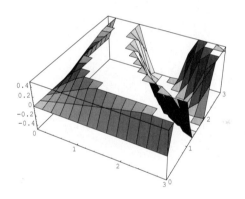

This makes the bottom clipped face white (gray level 1), and the top one black.

In[8]:= **Show[%, ClipFill -> {GrayLevel[1], GrayLevel[0]}]**

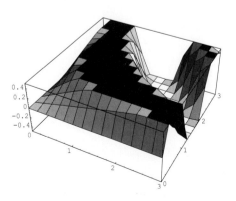

Whenever *Mathematica* draws a surface, it has to know not only the height, but also the color of the surface at each point. With the default setting Lighting -> True, *Mathematica* colors the surface using a simulated lighted model. However, with Lighting -> False, *Mathematica* uses a "color function" to determine how to color the surface.

The default color function takes the height of the surface, normalized to run from 0 to 1, and colors each part of the surface with a gray level corresponding to this height. There are two ways to change the default.

First, if you set the option ColorFunction -> c, then *Mathematica* will apply the function c to each height value to determine the color to use at that point. With ColorFunction -> Hue, *Mathematica* will for example color the surface with a range of hues.

Plot3D[f, ... , ColorFunction -> c]

            apply c to the normalized values of f to determine the color of each point on a surface

ListPlot3D[array, ColorFunction -> c]

            apply c to the elements of array to determine color

SurfaceGraphics[array, ColorFunction -> c]

            apply c to the elements of array to determine color

Specifying functions for coloring surfaces.

With Lighting -> False, the default is to color surfaces with gray scales determined by height.

```
In[9]:= exp = Plot3D[Exp[-Sqrt[x^2 + y^2]],
              {x, -2, 2}, {y, -2, 2}, Lighting -> False,
                     PlotPoints -> 25]
```

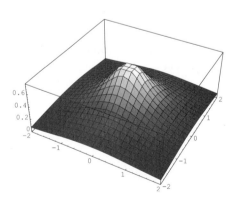

This defines a function which maps alternating ranges of values into black and white.

```
In[10]:= stripes[f_] :=
            If[Mod[f, 1] > 0.5, GrayLevel[1], GrayLevel[0]]
```

This shows the surface colored with black and white stripes.

```
In[11]:= Show[exp, ColorFunction :> (stripes[5 #]&)]
```

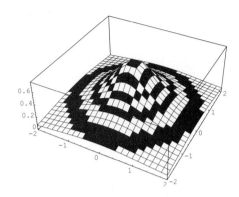

The second way to change the default coloring of surfaces is to supply an explicit second array along with the array of heights. ColorFunction is then applied to the elements of this second array, rather than the array of heights, to find the color directives to use. In the second array, you can effectively specify the value of another coordinate for each point on the surface. This coordinate will be plotted using color, rather than position.

You can generate an array of color values automatically using Plot3D[{f, s}, ...]. If you give the array explicitly in ListPlot3D or SurfaceGraphics, you should realize that with an $n \times n$ array of heights, you need an $(n-1) \times (n-1)$ array to specify colors. The reason is that the heights are specified for *points* on a grid, whereas the colors are specified for *squares* on the grid.

When you supply a second function or array to Plot3D, ListPlot3D, and so on, the default setting for the ColorFunction option is Automatic. This means that the function or array should contain explicit *Mathematica* color directives, such as GrayLevel or RGBColor. However, if you give another setting, such as ColorFunction -> Hue, then the function or array can yield pure numbers or other data which are converted to color directives when the function specified by ColorFunction is applied.

`Plot3D[{f, s}, {x, xmin, xmax}, {y, ymin, ymax}]`	plot a surface whose height is determined by *f* and whose color is determined by *s*
`ListPlot3D[`*height*`, `*color*`]`	generate a colored surface plot from an array of heights and colors
`SurfaceGraphics[`*height*`, `*color*`]`	a graphics object representing a surface with a specified array of heights and colors

Specifying arrays of colors for surfaces.

This plots a surface with gray level determined by the *y* coordinate.

In[12]:= `Plot3D[{Sin[x] Sin[y]^2, GrayLevel[y/3]},`
                                    `{x, 0, 3}, {y, 0, 3}]`

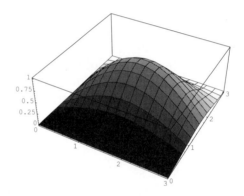

This puts a random gray level in each grid square. Notice that the array of grid squares is 9×9, whereas the array of grid points is 10×10.

In[13]:= `ListPlot3D[ Table[i/j, {i, 10}, {j, 10}],`
                      `Table[GrayLevel[Random[ ]], {i, 9}, {j, 9}] ]`

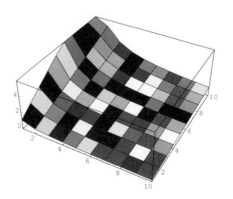

■ 2.9.12 Lighting and Surface Properties

With the default option setting Lighting -> True, *Mathematica* uses a simulated lighting model to determine how to color polygons in three-dimensional graphics.

Mathematica allows you to specify two components to the illumination of an object. The first is "ambient lighting", which produces uniform shading all over the object. The second is light from a collection of point sources, each with a particular position and color. *Mathematica* adds together the light from all of these sources in determining the total illumination of a particular polygon.

AmbientLight -> *color*	diffuse isotropic lighting
LightSources -> {{*pos₁* , *col₁*}, {*pos₂* , *col₂*}, ... }	
	point light sources with specified positions and colors

Options for simulated illumination.

The default lighting used by *Mathematica* involves three point light sources, and no ambient component. The light sources are colored respectively red, green and blue, and are placed at 45° angles on the right-hand side of the object.

Here is a surface, shaded using simulated lighting using the default set of lights.

```
In[1]:= Plot3D[Sin[x + Sin[y]], {x, -3, 3}, {y, -3, 3},
                                      Lighting -> True]
```

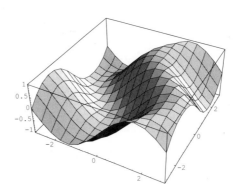

This shows the result of adding ambient
light, and removing all point light
sources.

In[2]:= **Show[%, AmbientLight -> GrayLevel[0.5],**

                           LightSources -> {}]

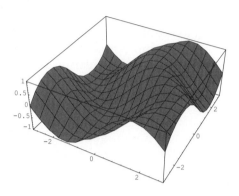

This adds a single point light source at
the left-hand side of the image.

In[3]:= **Show[%,**

           LightSources -> {{{-1, 0, 0.5}, GrayLevel[0.5]}}]

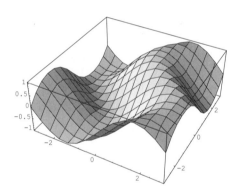

The positions of light sources in *Mathematica* are specified in the *display* coordinate system. The *x*
and *y* coordinates are in the plane of the final display, and the *z* coordinate goes into the plane. Using this coordinate system ensures that the light sources remain fixed with respect to the viewer, even
when the relative positions of the viewer and object change.

Page 41 shows some examples of results obtained with various different arrangements of light sources.

Even though the view point is changed, the light source is kept fixed on the left-hand side of the image.

`In[4]:= Show[%, ViewPoint -> {2, 2, 6}]`

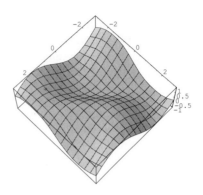

The perceived color of a polygon depends not only on the light which falls on the polygon, but also on how the polygon reflects that light. You can use the graphics directive `SurfaceColor` to specify the way that polygons reflect light.

If you do not explicitly use `SurfaceColor` directives, *Mathematica* effectively assumes that all polygons have matte white surfaces. Thus the polygons reflect light of any color incident on them, and do so equally in all directions. This is an appropriate model for materials such as uncoated white paper.

Using `SurfaceColor`, however, you can specify more complicated models. The basic idea is to distinguish two kinds of reflection: *diffuse* and *specular*.

In diffuse reflection, light incident on a surface is scattered equally in all directions. When this kind of reflection occurs, a surface has a "dull" or "matte" appearance. Diffuse reflectors obey Lambert's Law of light reflection, which states that the intensity of reflected light is $\cos(\alpha)$ times the intensity of the incident light, where α is the angle between the incident light direction and the surface normal vector. Note that when $\alpha > 90°$, there is no reflected light.

In specular reflection, a surface reflects light in a mirror-like way. As a result, the surface has a "shiny" or "gloss" appearance. With a perfect mirror, light incident at a particular angle is reflected at exactly the same angle. Most materials, however, scatter light to some extent, and so lead to reflected light that is distributed over a range of angles. *Mathematica* allows you to specify how broad the distribution is by giving a *specular exponent*, defined according to the Phong lighting model. With specular exponent n, the intensity of light at an angle θ away from the mirror reflection direction is assumed to vary like $\cos(\theta)^n$. As $n \to \infty$, therefore, the surface behaves like a perfect mirror. As n decreases, however, the surface becomes less "shiny", and for $n = 0$, the surface is a completely diffuse reflector. Typical values of n for actual materials range from about 1 to several hundred.

Most actual materials show a mixture of diffuse and specular reflection. In addition, they typically behave as if they have a certain intrinsic color. When the incident light is white, the reflected light has the color of the material. When the incident light is not white, each color component in the reflected light is a product of the corresponding component in the incident light and and in the intrinsic color of the material.

In *Mathematica*, you can specify reflection properties by giving an intrinsic color associated with diffuse reflection, and another one associated with specular reflection. To get no reflection of a particular kind, you must give the corresponding intrinsic color as black, or `GrayLevel[0]`. For materials that are effectively "white", you can specify intrinsic colors of the form `GrayLevel[a]`, where *a* is the reflectance or albedo of the surface.

Page 41 shows examples of results obtained with various choices of reflection parameters.

`SurfaceColor[GrayLevel[a]]`	matte surface with albedo *a*
`SurfaceColor[RGBColor[r, g, b]]`	
	matte surface with intrinsic color
`SurfaceColor[diff, spec]`	surface with diffuse intrinsic color *diff* and specular intrinsic color *spec*
`SurfaceColor[diff, spec, n]`	surface with specular exponent *n*

Specifying surface properties of lighted polygons.

This loads a package containing various graphics objects.	`In[5]:= <<Graphics`Shapes` ;`
Sphere creates a graphics object which represents a sphere.	`In[6]:= s = Sphere[ ] ;`
This shows the sphere with the default matte white surface.	`In[7]:= Show[Graphics3D[s]]`

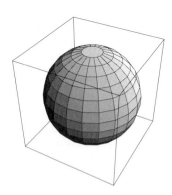

This makes the sphere have low diffuse reflectance, but high specular reflectance. As a result, the sphere has a "specular highlight" near the light sources, and is quite dark elsewhere.

```
In[8]:= Show[Graphics3D[{
                SurfaceColor[GrayLevel[0.2],
                    GrayLevel[0.8], 5], s}]]
```

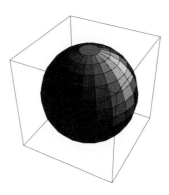

When you set up light sources and surface colors, it is important to make sure that the total intensity of light reflected from a particular polygon is never larger than 1. You will get strange effects if the intensity is larger than 1.

■ 2.9.13 Labeling Three-Dimensional Graphics

Mathematica provides various options for labeling three-dimensional graphics. Some of these options are directly analogous to those for two-dimensional graphics, discussed in Section 2.9.5. Others are different.

Boxed -> True	draw a cuboidal bounding box around the graphics (default)
Axes -> True	draw x, y and z axes on the edges of the box (default for SurfaceGraphics)
Axes -> {False, False, True}	draw the z axis only
FaceGrids -> All	draw grid lines on the faces of the box
PlotLabel -> *text*	give an overall label for the plot

Some options for labeling three-dimensional graphics.

This loads a package containing various polyhedra.

```
In[1]:= <<Graphics`Polyhedra` ;
```

The default for `Graphics3D` is to include a box, but no other forms of labeling.

In[2]:= **Show[Graphics3D[Dodecahedron[ ]]]**

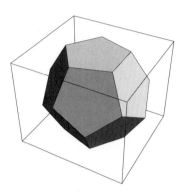

Setting **Axes -> True** adds x, y and z axes.

In[3]:= **Show[%, Axes -> True]**

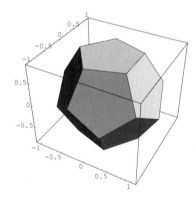

This adds grid lines to each face of the box.

In[4]:= **Show[%, FaceGrids -> All]**

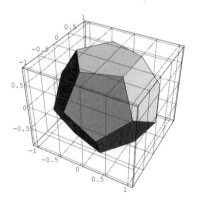

BoxStyle -> *style*	specify the style for the box
AxesStyle -> *style*	specify the style for axes
AxesStyle -> {{*xstyle*}, {*ystyle*}, {*zstyle*}}	
	specify separate styles for each axis

Style options.

This makes the box dashed, and draws axes which are thicker than normal.

```
In[5]:= Show[Graphics3D[Dodecahedron[ ]],
            BoxStyle -> Dashing[{0.02, 0.02}],
            Axes -> True, AxesStyle -> Thickness[0.01]]
```

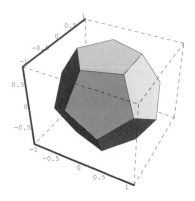

By setting the option Axes -> True, you tell *Mathematica* to draw axes on the edges of the three-dimensional box. However, for each axis, there are in principle four possible edges on which it can be drawn. The option AxesEdge allows you to specify on which edge to draw each of the axes.

AxesEdge -> Automatic	use an internal algorithm to choose where to draw all axes
AxesEdge -> {*xspec*, *yspec*, *zspec*}	
	give separate specifications for each of the *x*, *y* and *z* axes
None	do not draw this axis
Automatic	decide automatically where to draw this axis
{*dir_i*, *dir_j*}	specify on which of the four possible edges to draw this axis

Specifying where to draw three-dimensional axes.

This draws the x on the edge with larger y and z coordinates, draws no y axis, and chooses automatically where to draw the z axis.

In[6]:= `Show[Graphics3D[Dodecahedron[ ]], Axes -> True,`
`            AxesEdge -> {{1, 1}, None, Automatic}]`

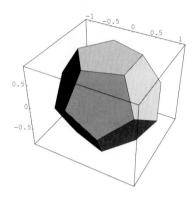

When you draw the x axis on a three-dimensional box, there are four possible edges on which the axis can be drawn. These edges are distinguished by having larger or smaller y and z coordinates. When you use the specification {dir_y, dir_z} for where to draw the x axis, you can set the dir_i to be +1 or −1 to represent larger or smaller values for the y and z coordinates.

AxesLabel -> None	give no axis labels
AxesLabel -> *zlabel*	put a label on the z axis
AxesLabel -> {*xlabel*, *ylabel*, *zlabel*}	
	put labels on all three axes

Axis labels in three-dimensional graphics.

You can use **AxesLabel** to label edges of the box, without necessarily drawing scales on them.

In[7]:= `Show[Graphics3D[Dodecahedron[ ]], Axes -> True,`
`            AxesLabel -> {"x", "y", "z"}, Ticks -> None]`

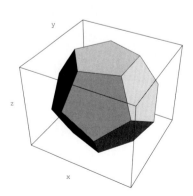

Ticks -> None	draw no tick marks
Ticks -> Automatic	place tick marks automatically
Ticks -> {*xticks*, *yticks*, *zticks*}	tick mark specifications for each axis

Settings for the `Ticks` option.

You can give the same kind of tick mark specifications in three dimensions as were described for two-dimensional graphics in Section 2.9.5 above.

FaceGrids -> None	draw no grid lines on faces
FaceGrids -> All	draw grid lines on all faces
FaceGrids -> {*face₁*, *face₂*, ... }	
	draw grid lines on the faces specified by the *face_i*
FaceGrids -> {{*face₁*, {*xgrid₁*, *ygrid₁*}}, ... }	
	use *xgrid_i*, *ygrid_i* to determine where and how to draw grid lines on each face

Drawing grid lines in three dimensions.

Mathematica allows you to draw grid lines on the faces of the box that surrounds a three-dimensional object. If you set FaceGrids -> All, grid lines are drawn in gray on every face. By setting FaceGrids -> {*face₁*, *face₂*, ... } you can tell *Mathematica* to draw grid lines only on specific faces. Each face is specified by a list {dir_x, dir_y, dir_z}, where two of the dir_i must be 0, and the third one is +1 or −1. For each face, you can also explicitly tell *Mathematica* where and how to draw the grid lines, using the same kind of specifications as you give for the GridLines option in two-dimensional graphics.

This draws grid lines only on the top and bottom faces of the box.

In[8]:= **Show[Graphics3D[Dodecahedron[ ]],**
                FaceGrids -> {{0, 0, 1}, {0, 0, -1}}]

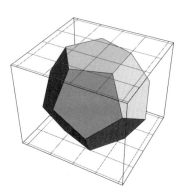

■ 2.9.14 Advanced Topic: Low-Level Graphics Rendering

All *Mathematica* graphics functions such as Show and Plot have an option DisplayFunction, which specifies how the *Mathematica* graphics objects they produce should actually be displayed. The way this works is that the setting you give for DisplayFunction is automatically applied to each graphics object that is produced.

DisplayFunction -> $DisplayFunction	
	default setting
DisplayFunction -> Identity	generate no display
DisplayFunction -> *f*	apply *f* to graphics objects to produce display

Settings for the DisplayFunction option.

Within the *Mathematica* kernel, graphics are always represented by graphics objects involving graphics primitives. When you actually render graphics, however, they must be converted to a lower-level form which can be processed by a *Mathematica* front end, such as a notebook interface, or by other external programs.

The standard low-level form that *Mathematica* uses for graphics is *PostScript*. The *Mathematica* function Display takes any *Mathematica* graphics object, and converts it into a block of PostScript code. It can then send this code to a file, an external program, or in general any output stream.

`Display["`*file*`", `*graphics*`]`	store the PostScript for a piece of *Mathematica* graphics in a file
`Display["!`*program*`", `*graphics*`]`	send the PostScript to an external program
`Display[`*stream*`, `*graphics*`]`	send the PostScript to an arbitrary stream

Converting *Mathematica* graphics to PostScript.

The default value of the global variable `$DisplayFunction` is
`Function[ Display[$Display, #] ]`. With this default, graphics objects produced by functions like
`Show` and `Plot` are automatically converted to PostScript, and sent to whatever stream is specified by
the value of the global variable `$Display`. The variable `$Display` is typically set during the initialization of a particular *Mathematica* session.

| `PostScript["`*string$_1$*`", "`*string$_2$*`", ... ]` | |
| | a two-dimensional graphics primitive giving PostScript code to include verbatim |

Inserting verbatim PostScript code.

With the standard two-dimensional graphics primitives in *Mathematica* you can produce most of
the effects that can be obtained with PostScript. Sometimes, however, you may find it necessary to
give PostScript code directly. You can do this using the special two-dimensional graphics primitive
`PostScript`.

The strings you specify in the `PostScript` primitive will be inserted verbatim into the final PostScript
code generated by `Display`. You should use the `PostScript` primitive with care. For example, it is
crucial that the code you give restores the PostScript stack to exactly its original state when it is finished. In addition, to specify positions of objects, you will have to understand the coordinate scaling
that *Mathematica* does in its PostScript output. Finally, any PostScript primitives that you insert can
only work if they are supported in the final PostScript interpreter that you use to display your graphics.

The PostScript primitive gives raw
PostScript code which draws a Bézier
curve.

```
In[1]:= Show[Graphics[ {
            PostScript[".008 setlinewidth"],
            PostScript[".1 .1 moveto"],
            PostScript["1.1 .6 -.1 .6 .9 .1 curveto stroke"] },
                Frame -> True]]
```

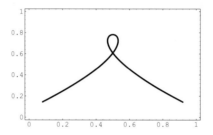

In most cases, a particular *Mathematica* graphics object always generates PostScript of a particular form. For Graphics3D objects, the option RenderAll allows you to choose between two different forms.

The main issue is how the polygons which make up three-dimensional objects should be rendered. With the default setting RenderAll -> True, all polygons you specify are drawn in full, but those behind are drawn first. When all the polygons are drawn, only those in front are visible. However, while an object is being drawn on a display, you can typically see the polygons inside it.

The problem with this approach is that for an object with many layers, you may generate a large amount of spurious PostScript code associated with polygons that are not visible in the final image. You can potentially avoid this by setting RenderAll -> False. In this case, *Mathematica* works out exactly which polygons or parts of polygons will actually be visible in your final image, and renders only these. So long as there are fairly few intersections between polygons, this approach will typically yield less PostScript code, though it may be much slower.

RenderAll -> True	draw all polygons, starting from the back (default)
RenderAll -> False	draw only those polygons or parts of polygons that are visible in the final image

An option for rendering three-dimensional pictures.

When you generate a PostScript representation of a three-dimensional object, you lose all information about the depths of the parts of the object. Sometimes, you may want to send to external programs a representation which includes depth information. Often, the original Graphics3D object in *Mathematica* form is then the appropriate representation. But some external programs cannot handle intersecting polygons. To deal with this, Graphics3D includes the option PolygonIntersections. If you set `PolygonIntersections -> False`, then `Show` will return not your original `Graphics3D` object, but rather one in which intersecting polygons have been broken into disjoint pieces, at least with the setting for `ViewPoint` and so on that you have given.

■ 2.9.15 Fonts for Text in Graphics

`$DefaultFont`	the default font to use in graphics
`{"name", size}`	a font with specified name and size

Font specifications in *Mathematica*.

All text that is included in *Mathematica* graphics must be in a definite *font*. The default font to use is typically specified by the value of the global variable `$DefaultFont`.

Every font in *Mathematica* has a *name*, and a *size*. The size gives the basic height of characters in the font. It is specified in absolute units of printer's points, with one point being $\frac{1}{72}$ inches. (The main text of this book, for example, is set in 10-point type.)

Since font sizes are specified in absolute units, the size of pieces of text in *Mathematica* plots always remain fixed whatever size the whole plots are. The only way to change the size of the text is explicitly to change the font size.

Here is the default font used in producing graphics in this book.

```
In[1]:= $DefaultFont
Out[1]= {Courier, 5.5}
```

This changes the default font to use in graphics.

```
In[2]:= $DefaultFont = {"Courier-Oblique", 7}
Out[2]= {Courier-Oblique, 7}
```

Now all text in the plot is slightly larger than normal, and italic.

```
In[3]:= Plot[Sin[Sin[x]], {x, 0, Pi}]
```

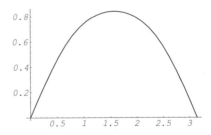

If you reset the global variable `$DefaultFont`, you change the default font to use in all graphics. Often you may want to specify a different default font only for a particular *Mathematica* plot. You can do this using the `DefaultFont` option that exists for `Show`, `Plot` and other *Mathematica* graphics functions.

In other cases, you may want to specify a font only for a specific piece of text. In such cases, you can wrap the text with a FontForm directive.

DefaultFont -> *font*	an option to change the default font in a particular plot
FontForm["*text*", *font*]	a piece of text in a specific font

More local ways to specify fonts.

This uses an italic font for labeling the axes, and a larger bold font for the overall plot label.

```
In[4]:= Show[%, DefaultFont -> {"Times-Italic", 6},
            PlotLabel ->
                FontForm["The label", {"Helvetica-Bold", 12}]]
```

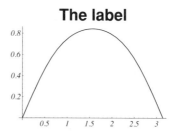

The most complicated aspect of using fonts in *Mathematica* graphics is their naming. When you tell *Mathematica* to use a font with a particular name, all that *Mathematica* actually does is to pass that request through to your final rendering device. It is then up to this device to find the appropriate font, and render it.

The problem is that not all devices support the same set of fonts. In all cases, *Mathematica* specifies fonts by inserting their names in the PostScript code it sends to your rendering device. Rendering devices that have built-in PostScript interpreters typically support at least some minimal set of standard fonts. Usually these fonts include "Courier", "Helvetica" and "Times", and their "*Name*-Bold", "*Name*-Oblique" and "*Name*-BoldOblique" variants. ("Times" has Italic in place of Oblique.) If you ask for a font that your rendering device does not have, it will typically substitute another font.

Although *Mathematica* can in principle produce text in any font that your rendering device supports, you should realize that with some fonts, the text you get may not be properly aligned when it occurs on several lines. Only with fonts such as Courier that are monospaced so that every character is given the same horizontal space can you be sure that text will always be aligned correctly.

Display[*stream*, *graphics*, StringConversion -> *f*]

specify a function to convert strings containing special characters

Special character conversion.

A final complication associated with rendering text in graphics concerns the treatment of special characters in text strings. Just as discussed in Section 2.8.2 for standard text output, *Mathematica* allows you to give a function to replace special characters that appear in strings used in graphics. You can specify this function by setting the option StringConversion when you call Display for final output of your graphics.

You should realize that when you use international character sets, you will almost always find that the way the characters are encoded for graphics output needs to be different from the way they are usually entered in *Mathematica*. In addition, the appropriate encoding may even differ from one font to another.

■ 2.9.16 Graphics Primitives for Text

With the Text graphics primitive, you can insert text at any position in two- or three-dimensional *Mathematica* graphics. Unless you explicitly specify a font using FontForm, the text will be given in your current default font.

Text[*expr*, {*x*, *y*}]	text centered at the point {*x*, *y*}
Text[*expr*, {*x*, *y*}, {-1, 0}]	text with its left-hand end at {*x*, *y*}
Text[*expr*, {*x*, *y*}, {1, 0}]	right-hand end at {*x*, *y*}
Text[*expr*, {*x*, *y*}, {0, -1}]	centered above {*x*, *y*}
Text[*expr*, {*x*, *y*}, {0, 1}]	centered below {*x*, *y*}
Text[*expr*, {*x*, *y*}, {*dx*, *dy*}]	text positioned so that {*x*, *y*} is at relative coordinates {*dx*, *dy*} within the box that bounds the text
Text[*expr*, {*x*, *y*}, {*dx*, *dy*}, {0, 1}]	text oriented vertically to read from bottom to top
Text[*expr*, {*x*, *y*}, {*dx*, *dy*}, {0, -1}]	text that reads from top to bottom
Text[*expr*, {*x*, *y*}, {*dx*, *dy*}, {-1, 0}]	text that is upside-down

Two-dimensional text.

This generates five pieces of text, and displays them in a plot.

```
In[1]:= Show[Graphics[
            Table[ Text[Expand[(1 + x)^n], {n, n}], {n, 5} ] ],
            PlotRange -> All]
```

$$1 + 5\,x + 10\,x^2 + 10\,x^3 + 5\,x^4 + x^5$$

$$1 + 4\,x + 6\,x^2 + 4\,x^3 + x^4$$

$$1 + 3\,x + 3\,x^2 + x^3$$

$$1 + 2\,x + x^2$$

$$1 + x$$

Here is some vertically oriented text with its left-hand side at the point {2, 2}.

```
In[2]:= Show[Graphics[
            Text[FontForm["Some text", {"Courier-Bold", 14}],
                {2, 2}, {-1, 0}, {0, 1}]], Frame -> True]
```

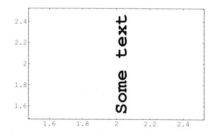

When you specify an offset for text, the relative coordinates that are used are taken to run from -1 to 1 in each direction across the box that bounds the text. The point {0, 0} in this coordinate system is defined to be center of the text. Note that the offsets you specify need not lie in the range -1 to 1.

Note that you can specify the color of a piece of text by preceding the Text graphics primitive with an appropriate RGBColor or other graphics directive.

Text[*expr*, {*x, y, z*}]	text centered at the point {*x, y, z*}
Text[*expr*, {*x, y, z*}, {*sdx, sdy*}]	
	text with a two-dimensional offset

Three-dimensional text.

This loads a package containing definitions of polyhedra.

```
In[3]:= <<Graphics`Polyhedra` ;
```

This puts text at the specified position in three dimensions.

```
In[4]:= Show[Graphics3D[{Dodecahedron[ ],
                        Text["a point", {2, 2, 2}, {1, 1}]}]]
```

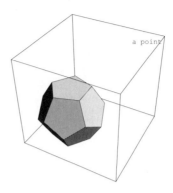

Note that when you use text in three-dimensional graphics, *Mathematica* assumes that the text is never hidden by any polygons or other objects.

■ 2.9.17 Advanced Topic: Color Output

Monochrome displays	gray levels
Color displays	red, green and blue mixtures
Color printing	cyan, magenta, yellow and black mixtures

Specifications of color for different kinds of output devices.

When you generate graphics output in *Mathematica*, there are different specifications of color which are natural for different kinds of output devices. Sometimes output devices may automatically convert from one form of color specification to another. But *Mathematica* provides graphics directives which allow you directly to produce color specifications appropriate for particular devices.

GrayLevel[*i*]	gray level (setgray in PostScript)
RGBColor[*r*, *g*, *b*]	red, green and blue components for a display (setrgbcolor)
Hue[*h*, *s*, *b*]	hue, saturation and brightness components for a display (setrgbcolor)
CMYKColor[*c*, *m*, *y*, *k*]	cyan, magenta, yellow and black components for four-color process printing (setcmykcolor)

Color directives in *Mathematica*.

Each color directive in *Mathematica* yields a definite color directive in the PostScript code that *Mathematica* sends to your output device. Thus, for example, the RGBColor directive in *Mathematica* yields setrgbcolor in PostScript. The final treatment of the PostScript color directives is determined by your output device, and the PostScript interpreter that is used.

Nevertheless, in most cases, the parameters specified in the *Mathematica* color directives will be used fairly directly to set the intensities or densities of the components of the color output.

When this is done, it is important to realize that a given set of parameters in a *Mathematica* color directive may yield different perceived colors on different output devices. For example, the actual intensities of red, green and blue components will often differ between different color displays even when the settings for these components are the same. Such differences also occur when the brightness or contrast of a particular color display is changed.

In addition, you should realize that the complete "gamut" of colors that you can produce by varying parameters on a particular output device is smaller, often substantially so, than the gamut of colors which can be perceived by the human visual system. Even though the space of colors that we can perceive can be described with three parameters, it is not possible to reach all parts of this space with mixtures of a fixed number of "primary colors".

Different choices of primary colors are typically made for different types of output devices. Color displays, which work with emitted or transmitted light, typically use red, green and blue primary colors. However, color printing, which works with reflected light, typically uses cyan, magenta, yellow and black as primary colors. When a color image is printed, four separate passes are typically made, each time laying down one of these primary colors.

Thus, while RGBColor and Hue are natural color specifications for color displays, CMYKColor is the natural specification for color printing.

By default, *Mathematica* takes whatever color specifications you give, and uses them directly. The option ColorOutput, however, allows you to make *Mathematica* always convert the color specifications you give to ones appropriate for a particular kind of output device.

ColorOutput -> Automatic	use color specifications as given (default)
ColorOutput -> GrayLevel	convert all color specifications to gray levels
ColorOutput -> RGBColor	convert to RGBColor form
ColorOutput -> CMYKColor	convert to CMYKColor form
ColorOutput -> f	apply f to each color directive

Color output conversions.

One of the most complicated issues in color output is performing the "color separation" necessary to take a color specified using red, green and blue primaries, and render the color using cyan, magenta, yellow and black printing inks. *Mathematica* has a built-in algorithm for doing this conversion. The algorithm is based on an approximation to typical monitor colors and the standard set of four-color process printing inks. Note that the colors of these printing inks are not even close to complementary to typical monitor colors, and the actual transformation is quite non-linear.

While *Mathematica* has built-in capabilities for various color conversions, you can also specify your own color conversions using ColorOutput -> f. With this option setting, the function f is automatically applied to each color directive generated by *Mathematica*.

Note that while any of the color directives given above can be used in setting up graphics objects, simulated lighting calculations in *Mathematica* are always done using RGBColor, and so all color directives are automatically converted to this form when simulated lighting is used.

This defines a transformation on RGBColor objects, which extracts the red component, and squares it.

```
In[1]:= red[RGBColor[r_, g_, b_]] = GrayLevel[r^2]

Out[1]= GrayLevel[r^2]
```

This specifies that red should simply square any GrayLevel specification.

```
In[2]:= red[GrayLevel[g_]] = GrayLevel[g^2]

Out[2]= GrayLevel[g^2]
```

This plots the squared red component, rather than using the usual transformation from color to black and white.

$In[3]:=$ **Plot3D[Sin[x + y], {x, -3, 3}, {y, -3, 3},**
                                           ColorOutput -> red]

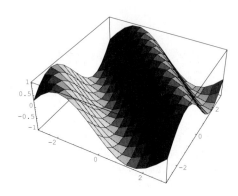

Note that if you give your own ColorOutput transformation, you must specify how the transformation acts on every color directive that arises in the image you are producing. For three-dimensional plots shaded with simulated lighting, you must typically specify the transformation at least for RGBColor and GrayLevel.

■ 2.9.18 The Representation of Sound

Section 1.9.13 described how you can take functions and lists of data and produce sounds from them. This subsection discusses how sounds are represented in *Mathematica*.

Mathematica treats sounds much like graphics. In fact, *Mathematica* allows you to combine graphics with sound to create pictures with "sound tracks".

In analogy with graphics, sounds in *Mathematica* are represented by symbolic sound objects. The sound objects have head Sound, and contain a list of sound primitives, which represent sounds to be played in sequence.

Sound[{s_1, s_2, ... }]   a sound object containing a list of sound primitives

The structure of a sound object.

The functions Play and ListPlay discussed in Section 1.9.13 return Sound objects.

Play returns a Sound object. On appropriate computer systems, it also produces sound.

$In[1]:=$ **Play[Sin[300 t + 2 Sin[400 t]], {t, 0, 2}]**

$Out[1]=$ -Sound-

The Sound object contains a `SampledSoundFunction` primitive which uses a compiled function to generate amplitude samples for the sound.

```
In[2]:= Short[ InputForm[%] ]

Out[2]//Short= Sound[SampledSoundFunction[<<3>>]]
```

`SampledSoundList[{`a_1`,` a_2`, ... },` r`]`

        a sound with a sequence of amplitude levels, sampled at rate r

`SampledSoundFunction[`f`,` n`,` r`]`

        a sound whose amplitude levels sampled at rate r are found by applying the function f to n successive integers

Mathematica sound primitives.

At the lowest level, all sounds in *Mathematica* are represented as a sequence of amplitude samples. In `SampledSoundList`, these amplitude samples are given explicitly in a list. In `SampledSoundFunction`, however, they are generated when the sound is output, by applying the specified function to a sequence of integer arguments. In both cases, all amplitude values obtained must be between -1 and 1.

`ListPlay` generates `SampledSoundList` primitives, while `Play` generates `SampledSoundFunction` primitives. With the default option setting `Compiled -> True`, `Play` will produce a `SampledSoundFunction` object containing a `CompiledFunction`.

Once you have generated a Sound object containing various sound primitives, you must then output it as a sound. Much as with graphics, the basic scheme is to take the *Mathematica* representation of the sound, and convert it to a lower-level form that can be handled by an external program, such as a *Mathematica* front end.

The low-level representation of sound used by *Mathematica* consists of a sequence of hexadecimal numbers specifying amplitude levels. Within *Mathematica*, amplitude levels are given as approximate real numbers between -1 and 1. In producing the low-level form, the amplitude levels are "quantized". You can use the option `SampleDepth` to specify how many bits should be used for each sample. The default is `SampleDepth -> 8`, which yields 256 possible amplitude levels, sufficient for most purposes.

You can use the option `SampleDepth` in either of the functions `Play` and `ListPlay`. In sound primitives, you can specify the sample depth by replacing the sample rate argument by the list {*rate*, *depth*}.

Since graphics and sound can be combined in *Mathematica*, their low-level representations must not conflict. As discussed in Section 2.9.14, all graphics in *Mathematica* are generated in the PostScript language. Sounds are also generated as a special PostScript function, which can be ignored by PostScript interpreters on devices which do not support sound output.

> Display[*stream*, *sound*]   output sound to a stream
>
> Display[*stream*, {*graphics*, *sound*}]
>
> output graphics and sound to a stream

Sending sound to a stream.

Mathematica uses the same function Display to output sound, graphics, and combinations of the two.

In Play and ListPlay, the option DisplayFunction specifies how the sound should ultimately be output. The default for this option is the global variable $SoundDisplayFunction. Typically, this is set to an appropriate call to Display.

2.10 Input and Output

■ 2.10.1 Reading and Writing *Mathematica* Files

Particularly if you use a text-based *Mathematica* interface, you will often need to read and write files containing definitions and results from *Mathematica*. Section 1.10.1 gave a general discussion of how to do this. This section gives some more details.

`<<`*file* or `Get["`*file*`"]`	read in a file of *Mathematica* input, and return the last expression in the file
`!!`*file*	display the contents of a file

Reading files.

This shows the contents of the file factors.

```
In[1]:= !!factors
(* Factors of x^20 - 1 *)
  (-1 + x)*(1 + x)*(1 + x^2)*(1 - x + x^2 - x^3 + x^4)*
    (1 + x + x^2 + x^3 + x^4)*(1 - x^2 + x^4 - x^6 + x^8)
```

This reads in the file, and returns the last expression in it.

$$In[1]:= \verb|<<factors|$$

$$Out[1]= (-1 + x) (1 + x) (1 + x^2) (1 - x + x^2 - x^3 + x^4)$$

$$(1 + x + x^2 + x^3 + x^4) (1 - x^2 + x^4 - x^6 + x^8)$$

If *Mathematica* cannot find the file you ask it to read, it prints a message, then returns the symbol $Failed.

```
In[2]:= <<faxors

General::noopen: Cannot open faxors.

Out[2]= $Failed
```

Mathematica input files can contain any number of expressions. Each expression, however, must start on a new line. The expressions may however continue for as many lines as necessary. Just as in a standard interactive *Mathematica* session, the expressions are processed as soon as they are complete. Note, however, that in a file, unlike an interactive session, you can insert a blank line at any point without effect.

When you read in a file with `<<`*file*, *Mathematica* returns the last expression it evaluates in the file. You can avoid getting any visible result from reading a file by the trick of making `Null` be the last expression in the file.

If *Mathematica* encounters a syntax error while reading a file, it reports the error, skips the remainder of the file, then returns $Failed. If the syntax error occurs in the middle of a package which uses `BeginPackage` and other context manipulation functions, then *Mathematica* tries to restore the context to what it was before the package was read.

> *expr* >> *file*   or   Put[*expr*, "*file*"]
>
>   write an expression to a file
>
> *expr* >>> *file*   or   PutAppend[*expr*, "*file*"]
>
>   append an expression to a file

Writing expressions to files.

This writes an expression to the file tmp.	*In[3]*:= **Factor[x∧6 - 1] >> tmp**
Here are the contents of the file.	*In[4]*:= **!!tmp**
	(-1 + x)*(1 + x)*(1 - x + x∧2)*(1 + x + x∧2)
This appends another expression to the same file.	*In[4]*:= **Factor[x∧8 - 1] >>> tmp**
Both expressions are now in the file.	*In[5]*:= **!!tmp**
	(-1 + x)*(1 + x)*(1 - x + x∧2)*(1 + x + x∧2)
	(-1 + x)*(1 + x)*(1 + x∧2)*(1 + x∧4)

When you use *expr* >>> *file*, *Mathematica* appends each new expression you give to the end of your file. If you use *expr* >> *file*, however, then *Mathematica* instead wipes out anything that was in the file before, and then puts *expr* into the file.

When you use either >> or >>> to write expressions to files, the expressions are usually given in *Mathematica* input format, so that you can read them back into *Mathematica*. Sometimes, however, you may want to save expressions in other formats. You can do this by explicitly wrapping a format directive such as OutputForm around the expression you write out.

This writes an expression to the file tmp in output format.	*In[5]*:= **OutputForm[Factor[x∧6 - 1]] >> tmp**
The expression in tmp is now in output format.	*In[6]*:= **!!tmp**
	$(-1 + x) \ (1 + x) \ (1 - x + x^2) \ (1 + x + x^2)$

One of the most common reasons for using files is to save definitions of *Mathematica* objects, to be able to read them in again in a subsequent *Mathematica* session. The operators >> and >>> allow you to save *Mathematica* expressions in files. You can use the function Save to save complete definitions of *Mathematica* objects, in a form suitable for execution in subsequent *Mathematica* sessions.

Save["*file*", s_1, s_2, ...]	save the complete definitions of the symbols s_i in a file
Definition[*s*] >> *file*	write the definition of *s* to a file
FullDefinition[*s*] >> *file*	write the complete definition of *s* to a file, including definitions of any objects on which *s* depends

Writing out definitions.

This assigns a value to the symbol a.

In[6]:= **a = 2 - x^2**

Out[6]= $2 - x^2$

You can use **Save** to write the definition of a to a file.

In[7]:= **Save["afile", a]**

Here is the definition of a that was saved in the file.

In[8]:= **!!afile**

a = 2 - x^2

When you define a new object in *Mathematica*, your definition will often depend on other objects that you defined before. If you are going to be able to reconstruct the definition of your new object in a subsequent *Mathematica* session, it is important that you store not only its own definition, but also the definitions of other objects on which it depends. The function Save looks through the definitions of the objects you ask it to save, and automatically also saves all definitions of other objects on which it can see that these depend. However, in order to avoid saving a large amount of unnecessary material, Save never includes definitions for symbols that have the attribute Protected. It assumes that the definitions for these symbols are also built in. Nevertheless, with such definitions taken care of, it should always be the case that reading the output generated by Save back into a new *Mathematica* session will set up the definitions of your objects exactly as you had them before.

This defines a function f which depends on the symbol a defined above.

In[8]:= **f[z_] := a^2 - 2**

This saves the complete definition of f in a file.

In[9]:= **Save["ffile", f]**

The file contains not only the definition of f itself, but also the definition of the symbol a on which f depends.

In[10]:= **!!ffile**

f[z_] := a^2 - 2

a = 2 - x^2

The function Save makes use of the output forms Definition and FullDefinition, which print as definitions of *Mathematica* symbols. In some cases, you may find it convenient to use these output forms directly.

The output form Definition[*f*] prints as the sequence of definitions that have been made for *f*.

In[10]:= **Definition[f]**

Out[10]= $f[z\_] := a^2 - 2$

FullDefinition[*f*] includes definitions
of the objects on which *f* depends.

$In[11]:=$ **FullDefinition[f]**

$Out[11]=$ $\text{f}[\text{z\_}] := \text{a}^2 - 2$

$\text{a} = 2 - \text{x}^2$

When you create files for input to *Mathematica*, you usually want them to contain only "plain text", which can be read or modified directly. Sometimes, however, you may want the contents of a file to be "encoded" so that they cannot be read or modified directly as plain text, but can be loaded into *Mathematica*. You can create encoded files using the *Mathematica* function Encode.

Encode["*source*", "*dest*"]	write an encoded version of the file *source* to the file *dest*
<<*dest*	read in an encoded file
Encode["*source*", "*dest*", "*key*"]	encode with the specified key
Get["*dest*", "*key*"]	read in a file that was encoded with a key
Encode["*source*", "*dest*", MachineID -> "*ID*"]	create an encoded file which can only be read on a machine with a particular ID

Creating and reading encoded files.

This writes an expression in plain text to
the file tmp.

$In[12]:=$ **Factor[x^2 - 1] >> tmp**

This writes an encoded version of the
file tmp to the file tmp.x.

$In[13]:=$ **Encode["tmp", "tmp.x"]**

$Out[13]=$ tmp.x

Here are the contents of the encoded file.
The only recognizable part is the special
Mathematica comment at the beginning.

$In[14]:=$ **!!tmp.x**

(*!1N!*)mcm
_QZ9tcI1cfre*Wo8:) P

Even though the file is encoded, you can
still read it into *Mathematica* using the
<< operator.

$In[14]:=$ **<<tmp.x**

$Out[14]=$ (-1 + x) (1 + x)

■ 2.10.2 External Programs

On most computer systems, you can execute external programs or commands from within *Mathematica*. Often you will want to take expressions you have generated in *Mathematica*, and send them to an external program, or take results from external programs, and read them into *Mathematica*.

Mathematica supports two basic forms of communication with external programs: *structured* and *unstructured*.

Structured communication	use *MathLink* to exchange expressions with *MathLink*-compatible external programs
Unstructured communication	use file reading and writing operations to exchange ordinary text

Two kinds of communication with external programs in *Mathematica*.

The idea of structured communication is to exchange complete *Mathematica* expressions to external programs which are specially set up to handle such objects. The basis for structured communication is the *MathLink* system, discussed in Section 2.10.10.

Unstructured communication consists in sending and receiving ordinary text from external programs. The basic idea is to treat an external program very much like a file, and to support the same kinds of reading and writing operations.

expr >> "!*command*"	send the text of an expression to an external program
<< "!*command*"	read in text from an external program as *Mathematica* input

Reading and writing to external programs.

In general, wherever you might use an ordinary file name, *Mathematica* allows you instead to give a *pipe*, written as an external command, prefaced by an exclamation point. When you use the pipe, *Mathematica* will execute the external command, and send or receive text from it.

This sends the result from `FactorInteger` to the external program `lpr`. On many Unix systems, this program generates a printout.	`In[1]:= FactorInteger[2^31 - 1] >> !lpr`
This executes the external command `echo $TERM`, then reads the result as *Mathematica* input.	`In[2]:= <<"!echo $TERM"` `Out[2]= sun`

One point to notice is that you can get away with dropping the double quotes around the name of a pipe on the right-hand side of << or >> if the name does not contain any spaces or other special characters.

Pipes in *Mathematica* provide a very general mechanism for unstructured communication with external programs. On many computer systems, *Mathematica* pipes are implemented using pipe mechanisms in the underlying operating system; in some cases, however, other interprocess communication mechanisms are used. One restriction of unstructured communication in *Mathematica* is that a given pipe can only be used for input or for output, and not for both at the same time. In order to do genuine two-way communication, you need to use *MathLink*.

Even with unstructured communication, you can nevertheless set up somewhat more complicated arrangements by using temporary files. The basic idea is to write data to a file, then to read it as needed.

OpenTemporary[ ]	open a temporary file with a unique name

Opening a temporary file.

Particularly when you work with temporary files, you may find it useful to be able to execute external commands which do not explicitly send or receive data from *Mathematica*. You can do this using the *Mathematica* function Run.

Run["*command*", arg_1, ...]	run an external command from within *Mathematica*

Running external commands without input or output.

This executes the external Unix command date. The returned value is an "exit code" from the operating system.

```
In[3]:= Run["date"]

Wed Oct 17 12:01:14 CDT 1990

Out[3]= 0
```

Note that when you use Run, you must not preface commands with exclamation points. Run simply takes the textual forms of the arguments you specify, then joins them together with spaces in between, and executes the resulting string as an external command.

It is important to realize that Run never "captures" any of the output from an external command. As a result, where this output goes is purely determined by your operating system. Similarly, Run, does not supply input to external commands. This means that the commands can get input through any mechanism provided by your operating system. Sometimes external commands may be able to access the same input and output streams that are used by *Mathematica* itself. In some cases, this may be what you want. But particularly if you are using *Mathematica* with a front end, this can cause considerable trouble.

!*command*	intercept a line of *Mathematica* input, and run it as an external command

Shell escapes in *Mathematica*.

If you use *Mathematica* with a text-based interface, there is usually a special mechanism for executing external commands. With such an interface, *Mathematica* takes any line of input that starts with an exclamation point, and executes the text on the remainder of the line as an external command.

The way *Mathematica* uses !*command* is typical of the way "shell escapes" work in programs running under the Unix operating system. In most versions of *Mathematica*, you will be able to start an interactive shell from *Mathematica* simply by typing a single exclamation point on its own on a line.

This line is taken as a "shell escape", and executes the Unix command date.

In[4]:= **!date**

Wed Oct 17 12:01:16 CDT 1990

RunThrough["*command*", *expr*]	run *command*, using *expr* as input, and reading the output back into *Mathematica*

Running *Mathematica* expressions through external programs.

As discussed above, << and >> cannot be used to both send and receive data from an external program at the same time. Nevertheless, by using temporary files, you can effectively both send and receive data from an external program while still using unstructured communication.

The function RunThrough writes the text of an expression to a temporary file, then feeds this file as input to an external program, and captures the output as input to *Mathematica*. Note that in RunThrough, like Run, you should not preface the names of external commands with exclamation points.

This feeds the expression 789 to the external program cat, which in this case simply echoes the text of the expression. The output from cat is then read back into *Mathematica*.

In[4]:= **RunThrough["cat", 789]**

Out[4]= 789

■ 2.10.3 Advanced Topic: Streams and Low-Level Input and Output

Files and pipes are both examples of general *Mathematica* objects known as *streams*. A stream in *Mathematica* is a source of input or output. There are many operations that you can perform on streams.

You can think of >> and << as "high-level" *Mathematica* input-output functions. They are based on a set of lower-level input-output primitives that work directly with streams. By using these primitives, you can exercise more control over exactly how *Mathematica* does input and output. You will often need to do this, for example, if you write *Mathematica* programs which store and retrieve intermediate data from files or pipes.

The basic low-level scheme for writing output to a stream in *Mathematica* is as follows. First, you call OpenWrite or OpenAppend to "open the stream", telling *Mathematica* that you want to write output to a particular file or external program, and in what form the output should be written. Having opened a stream, you can then call Write or WriteString to write a sequence of expressions or strings to the stream. When you have finished, you call Close to "close the stream".

"*name*"	a file, specified by name
"!*name*"	a command, specified by name
InputStream["*name*", *n*]	an input stream
OutputStream["*name*", *n*]	an output stream

Streams in *Mathematica*.

When you open a file or a pipe, *Mathematica* creates a "stream object" that specifies the open stream associated with the file or pipe. In general, the stream object contains the name of the file or the external command used in a pipe, together with a unique number.

The reason that the stream object needs to include a unique number is that in general you can have several streams connected to the same file or external program at the same time. For example, you may start several different instances of the same external program, each connected to a different stream.

Nevertheless, when you have opened a stream, you can still refer to it using a simple file name or external command name so long as there is only one stream associated with this object.

This opens an output stream to the file tmp.

```
In[1]:= stmp = OpenWrite["tmp"]

Out[1]= OutputStream[tmp, 3]
```

This writes a sequence of expressions to the file.

```
In[2]:= Write[stmp, a, b, c]
```

Since you only have one stream associated with file tmp, you can refer to it simply by giving the name of the file.

```
In[3]:= Write["tmp", x]
```

This closes the stream.

```
In[4]:= Close[stmp]

Out[4]= tmp
```

Here is what was written to the file.

```
In[5]:= !!tmp

abc
x
```

OpenWrite["*file*"]	open an output stream to a file, wiping out the previous contents of the file
OpenAppend["*file*"]	open an output stream to a file, appending to what was already in the file
OpenWrite["!*command*"]	open an output stream to an external command
Write[*stream*, *expr₁*, *expr₂*, ...]	write a sequence of expressions to a stream, ending the output with a newline (line feed)
WriteString[*stream*, *str₁*, *str₂*, ...]	write a sequence of character strings to a stream, with no extra newlines
Display[*stream*, *graphics*]	write graphics or sound output to a stream, in PostScript form
Close[*stream*]	tell *Mathematica* that you are finished with a stream

Low-level output functions.

When you call Write[*stream*, *expr*], it writes an expression to the specified stream. The default is to write the expression in *Mathematica* input form. If you call Write with a sequence of expressions, it will write these expressions one after another to the stream. In general, it leaves no space between the successive expressions. However, when it has finished writing all the expressions, Write always ends its output with a newline.

This re-opens the file tmp.	In[5]:= stmp = OpenWrite["tmp"]
	Out[5]= OutputStream[tmp, 4]
This writes a sequence of expressions to the file, then closes the file.	In[6]:= Write[stmp, a^2, 1 + b^2]; Write[stmp, c^3]; Close[stmp]
	Out[6]= tmp
All the expressions are written in input form. The expressions from a single Write are put on the same line.	In[7]:= !!tmp
	a^21 + b^2
	c^3

Write provides a way of writing out complete *Mathematica* expressions. Sometimes, however, you may want to write out less structured data. WriteString allows you to write out any character string. Unlike Write, WriteString adds no newlines or other characters.

This opens the stream.	In[7]:= stmp = OpenWrite["tmp"]
	Out[7]= OutputStream[tmp, 5]
This writes two strings to the stream.	In[8]:= WriteString[stmp, "Arbitrary output.\n", "More output."]

This writes another string, then closes the stream.

```
In[9]:= WriteString[stmp, "  Second line.\n"]; Close[stmp]

Out[9]= tmp
```

Here are the contents of the file. The strings were written exactly as specified, including only the newlines that were explicitly given.

```
In[10]:= !!tmp

Arbitrary output.
More output.  Second line.
```

Write[{*stream₁* , *stream₂* , ... }, *expr₁* , ...]
      write expressions to a list of streams

WriteString[{*stream₁* , *stream₂* , ... }, *str₁* , ...]
      write strings to a list of streams

Writing output to lists of streams.

An important feature of the functions Write and WriteString is that they allow you to write output not just to a single stream, but also to a list of streams.

In using *Mathematica*, it is often convenient to define a *channel* which consists of a list of streams. You can then simply tell *Mathematica* to write to the channel, and have it automatically write the same object to several streams.

In a standard interactive *Mathematica* session, there are several output channels that are usually defined. These specify where particular kinds of output should be sent. Thus, for example, $Output specifies where standard output should go, while $Messages specifies where messages should go. The function Print then works essentially by calling Write with the $Output channel. Message works in the same way by calling Write with the $Messages channel. Page 518 lists the channels used in a typical *Mathematica* session.

Note that when you run *Mathematica* through *MathLink*, a different approach is usually used. All output is typically written to a single *MathLink* link, but each piece of output appears in a "packet" which indicates what type it is.

In most cases, the names of files or external commands that you use in *Mathematica* correspond exactly with those used by your computer's operating system. On some systems, however, *Mathematica* supports various streams with special names.

"stdout"	standard output
"stderr"	standard error

Special streams used on some computer systems.

The special stream "stdout" allows you to give output to the "standard output" provided by the operating system. Note however that you can use this stream only with simple text-based interfaces to *Mathematica*. If your interaction with *Mathematica* is more complicated, then this stream will not work, and trying to use it may cause considerable trouble.

option name	default value	
FormatType	InputForm	the default output format to use
PageWidth	78	the width of the page in characters
StringConversion	Identity	conversion function to be applied to strings containing special characters

Some options for output streams.

You can associate a number of options with output streams. You can specify these options when you first open a stream using OpenWrite or OpenAppend.

This opens a stream, specifying that the default output format used should the standard *Mathematica* two-dimensional output format.

```
In[10]:= stmp = OpenWrite["tmp", FormatType -> OutputForm]

Out[10]= OutputStream[tmp, 6]
```

This writes expressions to the stream, then closes the stream.

```
In[11]:= Write[stmp, x^2 + y^2, "      ", z^2]; Close[stmp]

Out[11]= tmp
```

The expressions were written to the stream in standard *Mathematica* output format.

```
In[12]:= !!tmp
 2    2       2
x  + y       z
```

Note that you can always override the output format specified for a particular stream by wrapping a particular expression you write to the stream with an explicit *Mathematica* format directive, such as OutputForm or TeXForm.

The option PageWidth gives the width of the page available for textual output from *Mathematica*. All lines of output are broken so that they fit in this width. If you do not want any lines to be broken, you can set PageWidth -> Infinity. Usually, however, you will want to set PageWidth to the value appropriate for your particular output device. On many systems, you will have to run an external program to find out what this value is. Using SetOptions, you can make the default rule for PageWidth be, for example, PageWidth :> <<"!devicewidth", so that an external program is run automatically to find the value of the option.

This opens a stream, specifying that the page width is 20 characters.

```
In[12]:= stmp = OpenWrite["tmp", PageWidth -> 20]

Out[12]= OutputStream[tmp, 7]
```

This writes out an expression, then closes the stream.

```
In[13]:= Write[stmp, Expand[(1 + x)^5]]; Close[stmp]
Out[13]= tmp
```

The lines in the expression written out are all broken so as to be at most 20 characters long.

```
In[14]:= !!tmp

1 + 5*x + 10*x^2 +
    10*x^3 + 5*x^4 +
    x^5
```

The option `StringConversion` allows you to give a function that will be applied to all strings containing special characters which are sent to a particular output stream, whether by `Write` or `WriteString`. You will typically need to use `StringConversion` if you want to modify an international character set, or prevent a particular output device from receiving characters that it cannot handle.

`Options[`*stream*`]`	find the options that have been set for a stream
`SetOptions[`*stream*`, ` *opt₁* `-> ` *val₁*`, ... ]`	
	reset options for an open stream

Manipulating options of streams.

This opens a stream with the default settings for options.

```
In[14]:= stmp = OpenWrite["tmp"]
Out[14]= OutputStream[tmp, 8]
```

This changes the `FormatType` option for the open stream.

```
In[15]:= SetOptions[stmp, FormatType -> TeXForm]
Out[15]= {FormatType -> TeXForm, PageWidth -> 78,
    PageHeight -> 22, TotalWidth -> Infinity,
    TotalHeight -> Infinity, StringConversion -> None}
```

`Options` shows the options you have set for the open stream.

```
In[16]:= Options[stmp]
Out[16]= {FormatType -> TeXForm, PageWidth -> 78,
    PageHeight -> 22, TotalWidth -> Infinity,
    TotalHeight -> Infinity, StringConversion -> None}
```

This closes the stream again.

```
In[17]:= Close[stmp]
Out[17]= tmp
```

`Options[$Output]`	find the options set for all streams in the channel `$Output`
`SetOptions[$Output, ` *opt₁* `-> ` *val₁*`, ... ]`	
	set options for all streams in the channel `$Output`

Manipulating options for the standard output channel.

At every point in your session, *Mathematica* maintains a list Streams[ ] of all the input and output streams that are currently open, together with their options. In some cases, you may find it useful to look at this list directly. *Mathematica* will not, however, allow you to modify the list, except indirectly through OpenRead and so on.

■ 2.10.4 Naming and Finding Files

The precise details of the naming of files differ from one computer system to another. Nevertheless, *Mathematica* provides some fairly general mechanisms that work on all systems.

As mentioned in Section 1.10.2, *Mathematica* assumes that all your files are arranged in a hierarchy of *directories*. To find a particular file, *Mathematica* must know both what the name of the file is, and what sequence of directories it is in.

At any given time, however, you have a *current working directory*, and you can refer to files or other directories by specifying where they are relative to this directory. Typically you can refer to files or directories that are actually *in* this directory simply by giving their names, with no directory information.

Directory[ ]	give your current working directory
SetDirectory["*dir*"]	set your current working directory
ResetDirectory[ ]	revert to your previous working directory

Manipulating directories.

This gives a string representing your current working directory.

```
In[1]:= Directory[ ]

Out[1]= /users/swolf
```

This sets your current working directory to be the **Packages** subdirectory of your current working directory.

```
In[2]:= SetDirectory["Packages"]

Out[2]= /users/swolf/Packages
```

Now your current working directory is different.

```
In[3]:= Directory[ ]

Out[3]= /users/swolf/Packages
```

This reverts to your previous working directory.

```
In[4]:= ResetDirectory[ ]

Out[4]= /users/swolf
```

When you call SetDirectory, you can give any directory name that is recognized by your operating system. Thus, for example, on Unix-based systems, you can specify a directory one level up in the directory hierarchy using the notation .., and you can specify your "home" directory as ~.

Whenever you go to a new directory using SetDirectory, *Mathematica* always remembers what the previous directory was. You can return to this previous directory using ResetDirectory. In general, *Mathematica* maintains a stack of directories, given by DirectoryStack[ ]. Every time you call

SetDirectory, it adds a new directory to the stack, and every time you call ResetDirectory it removes a directory from the stack.

ParentDirectory[ ]	give the parent of your current working directory
HomeDirectory[ ]	give your "home" directory, if defined

Special directories.

Whenever you ask for a particular file, *Mathematica* in general goes through several steps to try and find the file you want. The first step is to use whatever standard mechanisms exist in your operating system or shell.

Mathematica scans the full name you give for a file, and looks to see whether it contains any of the "metacharacters" *, $, ~, ?, [, ", \ and '. If it finds such characters, then it passes the full name to your operating system or shell for interpretation. This means that if you are using a Unix-based system, then constructions like *name** and $*VAR* will be expanded at this point. But in general, *Mathematica* takes whatever was returned by your operating system or shell, and treats this as the full file name.

For output files, this is the end of the processing that *Mathematica* does. If *Mathematica* cannot find a unique file with the name you specified, then it will proceed to create the file.

If you are trying to get input from a file, however, then there is another round of processing that *Mathematica* does. What happens is that *Mathematica* looks at the value of the global variable $Path to find the names of directories relative to which it should search for the file.

$Path	a list of directories relative to which to search for input files

Search path for files.

In general, the global variable $Path is defined to be a list of strings, with each string representing a directory. Every time you ask for an input file, what *Mathematica* effectively does is temporarily to make each of these directories in turn your current working directory, and then from that directory to try and find the file you have requested.

Here is a typical setting for $Path. The current directory (.), and your home directory (~) are listed first.

```
In[5]:= $Path

Out[5]= {., ~, /users/math/bin, /users/math/Packages}
```

You should realize that all the mechanisms just described apply only to *file names*, and not, for example, to the names of external programs. *Mathematica* always passes any external commands you give directly to your operating system, without any processing. Thus, for example, the *Mathematica* $Path mechanism is not used for external programs that you call from within *Mathematica*. Nevertheless, particularly in Unix-based systems, there is usually a path mechanism built directly into operating system for finding programs, that you can use independent of *Mathematica*.

FileNames[ ]	list all files in your current working directory
FileNames["*form*"]	list all files in your current working directory whose names match the string pattern *form*
FileNames[{"*form₁*", "*form₂*", ... }]	list all files whose names match any of the *form*ᵢ
FileNames[*forms*, {"*dir₁*", "*dir₂*", ... }]	give the full names of all files whose names match *forms* in any of the directories *dir*ᵢ
FileNames[*forms*, *dirs*, *n*]	include files that are in subdirectories up to *n* levels down
FileNames[*forms*, *dirs*, Infinity]	include files in all subdirectories
FileNames[*forms*, $Path, Infinity]	give all files whose names match *forms* in any subdirectory of the directories in $Path

Getting lists of files in particular directories.

Here is a list of all files in the current working directory whose names end with .m.

```
In[6]:= FileNames["*.m"]
Out[6]= {alpha.m, control.m, signals.m, test.m}
```

This lists files whose names start with a in the current directory, and in subdirectories with names that start with P.

```
In[7]:= FileNames["a*", {".", "P*"}]
Out[7]= {alpha.m, Packages/astrodata, Packages/astro.m,
   Previous/atmp}
```

FileNames returns a list of strings corresponding to file names. When it returns a file that is not in your current directory, it gives the name of the file relative to the current directory. Note that all names are given in the format appropriate for the particular computer system on which they were generated.

You should realize that different computer systems may give file names in different ways. Thus, for example, Unix systems typically give names in the form *dir/dir/name*, Macintosh systems in the form :*dir*:*dir*:*name*, and VMS systems in the form [*dir*]*name*. Particularly when you create or use *Mathematica* packages, you will often need to refer to a file in a system-independent way.

Mathematica allows you to use contexts to refer to files in a system-independent way. The basic idea is that on every computer system there is a convention about how files corresponding to *Mathematica* contexts should be named. Then, when you refer to a file using a context, the particular version of *Mathematica* you are using converts the context name to the file name appropriate for the computer system you are on.

| ContextToFilename ["*context*`"] | convert a context name to the associated file name on your current computer system |
| <<*context*` | read in the file corresponding to the specified context |

Using contexts to specify files.

The documentation that came with your particular computer system should tell you how the correspondence between contexts and file names work on your system. On Unix-based systems, for example, the file corresponding to the context *ccc*`*ccc*` is typically *ccc*/*ccc*.m.

This gives the file name corresponding to the context **aaa`bbb`** on the particular computer system where it is run.

In[8]:= **ContextToFilename["aaa`bbb`"]**

Out[8]= aaa/bbb.m

■ 2.10.5 Manipulating Files and Directories

CopyFile ["*file₁*", "*file₂*"]	copy *file₁* to *file₂*
RenameFile ["*file₁*", "*file₂*"]	give *file₁* the name *file₂*
DeleteFile ["*file*"]	delete a file
FileByteCount ["*file*"]	give the number of bytes in a file
FileDate ["*file*"]	give the modification date for a file
SetFileDate ["*file*"]	set the modification date for a file to be the current date
FileType ["*file*"]	give the type of a file as File, Directory or None

Functions for manipulating files.

Different operating systems have different commands for manipulating files. *Mathematica* provides a simple set of file manipulation functions, intended to work in the same way under all operating systems.

Notice that CopyFile and RenameFile give the final file the same modification date as the original one. FileDate returns modification dates in the {*year*, *month*, *day*, *hour*, *minute*, *second*} format used by Date.

CreateDirectory["*name*"]   create a new directory

DeleteDirectory["*name*"]   delete an empty directory

DeleteDirectory["*name*", DeleteContents -> True]
     delete a directory and all files and directories it contains

RenameDirectory["*name₁*", "*name₂*"]
     rename a directory

CopyDirectory["*name₁*", "*name₂*"]
     copy a directory and all the files in it

Functions for manipulating directories.

■ 2.10.6 Reading Data

With <<, you can read files which contain *Mathematica* expressions given in input form. Sometimes, however, you may instead need to read files of *data* in other formats. For example, you may have data generated by an external program which consists of a sequence of numbers separated by spaces. This data cannot be read directly as *Mathematica* input. However, the function ReadList can take such data from a file or input stream, and convert it to a *Mathematica* list.

ReadList["*file*", Number]   read a sequence of numbers from a file, and put them in a *Mathematica* list

Reading numbers from a file.

Here is a file of numbers.	`In[1]:= !!numbers`
	
	`56.5   -23   14`
	`23     78    12.78`

This reads all the numbers in the file, and returns a list of them.	`In[1]:= ReadList["numbers", Number]`
	
	`Out[1]= {56.5, -23, 14, 23, 78, 12.78}`

ReadList["*file*", {Number, Number}]	
	read numbers from a file, putting each successive pair into a separate list
ReadList["*file*", Table[Number, {*n*}]]	
	put each successive block of *n* numbers in a separate list
ReadList["*file*", Number, RecordLists -> True]	
	put all the numbers on each line of the file into a separate list

Reading blocks of numbers.

This puts each successive pair of numbers from the file into a separate list.

```
In[2]:= ReadList["numbers", {Number, Number}]
Out[2]= {{56.5, -23}, {14, 23}, {78, 12.78}}
```

This makes each line in the file into a separate list.

```
In[3]:= ReadList["numbers", Number, RecordLists -> True]
Out[3]= {{56.5, -23, 14}, {23, 78, 12.78}}
```

ReadList can handle numbers which are given in Fortran-like "E" notation. Thus, for example, ReadList will read 2.5E+5 as 2.5×10^5. Note that ReadList can handle numbers with any number of digits of precision.

Here is a file containing numbers in Fortran-like "E" notation.

```
In[4]:= !!bignum
4.5E-5       7.8E4
2.5E2       -8.9
```

ReadList can handle numbers in this form.

```
In[4]:= ReadList["bignum", Number]
Out[4]= {0.000045, 78000., 250., -8.9}
```

ReadList["*file*", *type*]	read a sequence of objects of a particular type
ReadList["*file*", *type*, *n*]	read at most *n* objects

Reading objects of various types.

ReadList can read not only numbers, but also a variety of other types of object. Each type of object is specified by a symbol such as Number.

Here is a file containing text.

```
In[5]:= !!strings
Here is text.
And more text.
```

This produces a list of the characters in the file, each given as a one-character string.

```
In[5]:= ReadList["strings", Character]
Out[5]= {H, e, r, e,  , i, s,  , t, e, x, t, .,  , , A, n, d,
          , m, o, r, e,  , t, e, x, t, ., }
```

Here are the integer codes corresponding to each of the bytes in the file.

```
In[6]:= ReadList["strings", Byte]
Out[6]= {72, 101, 114, 101, 32, 105, 115, 32, 116, 101, 120,
          116, 46, 32, 10, 65, 110, 100, 32, 109, 111, 114, 101, 32,
          116, 101, 120, 116, 46, 10}
```

This puts the data from each line in the file into a separate list.

```
In[7]:= ReadList["strings", Byte, RecordLists -> True]
Out[7]= {{72, 101, 114, 101, 32, 105, 115, 32, 116, 101, 120,
           116, 46, 32}, {65, 110, 100, 32, 109, 111, 114, 101, 32,
           116, 101, 120, 116, 46}}
```

Byte	single byte of data, returned as an integer
Character	single character, returned as a one-character string
Real	approximate number in Fortran-like notation
Number	exact or approximate number in Fortran-like notation
Word	sequence of characters delimited by word separators
Record	sequence of characters delimited by record separators
String	string terminated by a newline
Expression	complete *Mathematica* expression
Hold[Expression]	complete *Mathematica* expression, returned inside Hold

Types of objects to read.

This returns a list of the "words" in the file **strings**.

```
In[8]:= ReadList["strings", Word]
Out[8]= {Here, is, text., And, more, text.}
```

ReadList allows you to read "words" from a file. It considers a "word" to be any sequence of characters delimited by word separators. You can set the option WordSeparators to specify the strings you want to treat as word separators. The default is to include spaces and tabs, but not to include, for example, standard punctuation characters. Note that in all cases successive words can be separated by any number of word separators. These separators are never taken to be part of the actual words returned by ReadList.

option name	default value	
RecordLists	False	whether to make a separate list for the objects in each record
RecordSeparators	{"\n"}	separators for records
WordSeparators	{" ", "\t"}	separators for words
NullRecords	False	whether to keep zero-length records
NullWords	False	whether to keep zero-length words
TokenWords	{}	words to take as tokens

Options for `ReadList`.

This reads the text in the file `strings` as a sequence of words, using the letter `e` and `.` as word separators.

```
In[9]:= ReadList["strings", Word, WordSeparators -> {"e", "."}]

Out[9]= {H, r,  is t, xt,  , And mor,  t, xt}
```

Mathematica considers any data file to consist of a sequence of *records*. By default, each line is considered to be a separate record. In general, you can set the option `RecordSeparators` to give a list of separators for records. Note that words can never cross record separators. As with word separators, any number of record separators can exist between successive records, and these separators are not considered to be part of the records themselves.

By default, each line of the file is considered to be a record.

```
In[10]:= ReadList["strings", Record] // InputForm

Out[10]//InputForm= {"Here is text.", "And more text."}
```

Here is a file containing three "sentences" ending with periods.

```
In[11]:= !!sentences

Here is text. And more.
And a second line.
```

This allows both periods and newlines as record separators.

```
In[11]:= ReadList["sentences", Record,
                          RecordSeparators -> {".", "\n"}]

Out[11]= {Here is text,  And more, And a second line}
```

This puts the words in each "sentence" into a separate list.

```
In[12]:= ReadList["sentences", Word, RecordLists -> True,
                          RecordSeparators -> {".", "\n"}]

Out[12]= {{Here, is, text}, {And, more},

  {And, a, second, line}}
```

ReadList ["*file*", Record, RecordSeparators -> { }]
> read the whole of a file as a single string

ReadList ["*file*", Record, RecordSeparators -> {{"*lsep₁*", ... }, {"*rsep₁*", ... }}]
> make a list of those parts of a file which lie between the
> *lsep₁* and the *rsep₁*

Settings for the `RecordSeparators` option.

Here is a file containing some text.	`In[13]:= !!source`
	
	`f[x] (: function f :)`
	`g[x] (: function g :)`

This reads all the text in the file source, and returns it as a single string.	`In[13]:= InputForm[`
	`            ReadList["source", Record, RecordSeparators -> { }]`
	`          ]`
	
	`Out[13]//InputForm=`
	`  {"f[x] (: function f :)\ng[x] (: function g :)\n"}`

This gives a list of the parts of the file that lie between (: and :) separators.	`In[14]:= ReadList["source", Record,`
	`                    RecordSeparators -> {{"(: "}, {" :)"}}]`
	
	`Out[14]= {function f, function g}`

By choosing appropriate separators, you can pick out specific parts of files.	`In[15]:= ReadList[ "source", Record,`
	`            RecordSeparators ->`
	`                    {{"(: function ", "["}, {" :)", "]"}} ]`
	
	`Out[15]= {x, f, x, g}`

Mathematica usually allows any number of appropriate separators to appear between successive records or words. Sometimes, however, when several separators are present, you may want to assume that a "null record" or "null word" appears between each pair of adjacent separators. You can do this by setting the options `NullRecords -> True` or `NullWords -> True`.

Here is a file containing "words" separated by colons.	`In[16]:= !!words`
	
	`first:second::fourth:::seventh`

Here the repeated colons are treated as single separators.	`In[16]:= ReadList["words", Word, WordSeparators -> {":"}]`
	
	`Out[16]= {first, second, fourth, seventh}`

Now repeated colons are taken to have null words in between.	`In[17]:= ReadList["words", Word, WordSeparators -> {":"},`
	`                                    NullWords -> True]`
	
	`Out[17]= {first, second, , fourth, , , seventh}`

In most cases, you want words to be delimited by separators which are not themselves considered as words. Sometimes, however, it is convenient to allow words to be delimited by special "token words", which are themselves words. You can give a list of such token words as a setting for the option `TokenWords`.

Here is some text.	*In[18]:=* `!!language` `22*a*b+56*c+13*a*d`
This reads the text, using the specified token words to delimit words in the text.	*In[18]:=* `ReadList["language", Word, TokenWords -> {"+", "*"}]` *Out[18]=* `{22, *, a, *, b, +, 56, *, c, +, 13, *, a, *, d}`

You can use `ReadList` to read *Mathematica* expressions from files. In general, each expression must end with a newline, although a single expression may go on for several lines.

Here is a file containing text that can be used as *Mathematica* input.	*In[19]:=* `!!exprs`
	
	`x + y +`
	`z`
	`2^8`

This reads the text in `exprs` as *Mathematica* expressions.	*In[19]:=* `ReadList["exprs", Expression]` *Out[19]=* `{x + y + z, 256}`
This prevents the expressions from being evaluated.	*In[20]:=* `ReadList["exprs", Hold[Expression]]` *Out[20]=* `{Hold[x + y + z], Hold[2^8]}`

`ReadList` can insert the objects it reads into any *Mathematica* expression. The second argument to `ReadList` can consist of any expression containing symbols such as `Number` and `Word` specifying objects to read. Thus, for example, `ReadList["`*file*`", {Number, Number}]` inserts successive pairs of numbers that it reads into lists. Similarly, `ReadList["`*file*`", Hold[Expression]]` puts expressions that it reads inside `Hold`.

If `ReadList` reaches the end of your file before it has finished reading a particular set of objects you have asked for, then it inserts the special symbol `EndOfFile` in place of the objects it has not yet read.

Here is a file of numbers.	*In[21]:=* `!!numbers`
	
	`56.5    -23    14`
	`23       78    12.78`

The symbol `EndOfFile` appears in place of numbers that were needed after the end of the file was reached.	*In[21]:=* `ReadList["numbers", {Number, Number, Number, Number}]` *Out[21]=* `{{56.5, -23, 14, 23},` `   {78, 12.78, EndOfFile, EndOfFile}}`

`ReadList["!`*command*`", `*type*`]`	execute a command, and read its output
`ReadList[`*stream*`, `*type*`]`	read any input stream

Reading from commands and streams.

This executes the Unix command date, and reads its output as a string.

In[22]:= **ReadList["!date", String]**

Out[22]= {Wed Oct 17 12:03:09 CDT 1990}

OpenRead["*file*"]	open a file for reading
OpenRead["!*command*"]	open a pipe for reading
Read[*stream*, *type*]	read an object of the specified type from a stream
Skip[*stream*, *type*]	skip over an object of the specified type in an input stream
Skip[*stream*, *type*, *n*]	skip over *n* objects of the specified type in an input stream
Close[*stream*]	close an input stream

Functions for reading from input streams.

ReadList allows you to read *all* the data in a particular file or input stream. Sometimes, however, you want to get data a piece at a time, perhaps doing tests to find out what kind of data to expect next.

When you read individual pieces of data from a file, *Mathematica* always remembers the "current point" that you are at in the file. When you call OpenRead, *Mathematica* sets up an input stream from a file, and makes your current point the beginning of the file. Every time you read an object from the file using Read, *Mathematica* sets your current point to be just after the object you have read. Using Skip, you can advance the current point past a sequence of objects without actually reading the objects.

Here is a file of numbers.

In[23]:= **!!numbers**

```
56.5    -23    14
23       78    12.78
```

This opens an input stream from the file.

In[23]:= **snum = OpenRead["numbers"]**

Out[23]= InputStream[numbers, 20]

This reads the first number from the file.

In[24]:= **Read[snum, Number]**

Out[24]= 56.5

This reads the second pair of numbers.

In[25]:= **Read[snum, {Number, Number}]**

Out[25]= {-23, 14}

This skips the next number.

In[26]:= **Skip[snum, Number]**

And this reads the remaining numbers.

In[27]:= **ReadList[snum, Number]**

Out[27]= {78, 12.78}

This closes the input stream.

In[28]:= **Close[snum]**

Out[28]= numbers

You can use the options WordSeparators and RecordSeparators in Read and Skip just as you do in ReadList.

Note that if you try to read past the end of file, Read returns the symbol EndOfFile.

■ 2.10.7 Searching Files

FindList ["*file*", "*text*"]	get a list of all the lines in the file that contain the specified text
FindList ["*file*", "*text*", *n*]	get a list of the first *n* lines that contain the specified text
FindList ["*file*", {"*text₁*", "*text₂*", ... }]	get lines that contain any of the *text_i*

Finding lines that contain specified text.

Here is a file containing some text.	`In[1]:= !!textfile`
	
	`Here is the first line of text.`
	`And the second.`
	`And the third. Here is the end.`

This returns a list of all the lines in the file containing the text is.	`In[1]:= FindList["textfile", "is"]`
	
	`Out[1]= {Here is the first line of text.,`
	
	`  And the third. Here is the end.}`

The text fourth appears nowhere in the file.	`In[2]:= FindList["textfile", "fourth"]`
	
	`Out[2]= {}`

By default, FindList scans successive lines of a file, and return those lines which contain the text you specify. In general, however, you can get FindList to scan successive *records*, and return complete records which contain specified text. As in ReadList, the option RecordSeparators allows you to tell *Mathematica* what strings you want to consider as record separators. Note that by giving a pair of lists as the setting for RecordSeparators, you can specify different left and right separators. By doing this, you can make FindList search only for text which is between specific pairs of separators.

This finds all "sentences" ending with a period which contain And.	`In[3]:= FindList["textfile", "And", RecordSeparators -> {"."}]`
	
	`Out[3]= {And the second, And the third}`

option name	default value	
RecordSeparators	{"\n"}	separators for records
AnchoredSearch	False	whether to require the text searched for to be at the beginning of a record
WordSeparators	{" ", "\t"}	separators for words
WordSearch	False	whether to require that the text searched for appear as a word
IgnoreCase	False	whether to treat lower- and upper-case letters as equivalent

Options for `FindList`.

This finds only the occurrence of Here which is at the beginning of a line in the file.

```
In[4]:= FindList["textfile", "Here", AnchoredSearch -> True]
Out[4]= {Here is the first line of text.}
```

In general, FindList finds text that appears anywhere inside a record. By setting the option WordSearch -> True, however, you can tell FindList to require that the text they are looking for appears as a separate *word* in the record. The option WordSeparators specifies the list of separators for words.

The text th does appear in the file, but not as a word. As a result, the FindList fails.

```
In[5]:= FindList["textfile", "th", WordSearch -> True]
Out[5]= {}
```

FindList[{"*file₁*", "*file₂*", ... }, "*text*"]	
	search for occurrences of the text in any of the *fileᵢ*

Searching in multiple files.

This searches for third in two copies of textfile.

```
In[6]:= FindList[{"textfile", "textfile"}, "third"]
Out[6]= {And the third. Here is the end.,
         And the third. Here is the end.}
```

It is often useful to call FindList on lists of files generated by functions such as FileNames.

FindList["!*command*", ...]	run an external command, and find text in its output

Finding text in the output from an external program.

| This runs the external Unix command date. | ```
In[7]:= !date
Wed Oct 17 12:03:45 CDT 1990
``` |
|---|---|
| This finds the time of day field in the date. | ```
In[7]:= FindList["!date", ":", RecordSeparators -> {" "}]
Out[7]= {12:03:46}
``` |

`OpenRead["file"]`	open a file for reading
`OpenRead["!command"]`	open a pipe for reading
`Find[stream, text]`	find the next occurrence of *text*
`Close[stream]`	close an input stream

Finding successive occurrences of text.

FindList works by making one pass through a particular file, looking for occurrences of the text you specify. Sometimes, however, you may want to search incrementally for successive occurrences of a piece of text. You can do this using Find.

In order to use Find, you first explicitly have to open an input stream using OpenRead. Then, every time you call Find on this stream, it will search for the text you specify, and make the current point in the file be just after the record it finds. As a result, you can call Find several times to find successive pieces of text.

| This opens an input stream for textfile. | ```
In[8]:= stext = OpenRead["textfile"]
Out[8]= InputStream[textfile, 8]
``` |
|---|---|
| This finds the first line containing And. | ```
In[9]:= Find[stext, "And"]
Out[9]= And the second.
``` |
| Calling Find again gives you the next line containing And. | ```
In[10]:= Find[stext, "And"]
Out[10]= And the third. Here is the end.
``` |
| This closes the input stream. | ```
In[11]:= Close[stext]
Out[11]= textfile
``` |

Once you have an input stream, you can mix calls to Find, Skip and Read. If you ever call FindList or ReadList, *Mathematica* will immediately read to the end of the input stream.

| This opens the input stream. | ```
In[12]:= stext = OpenRead["textfile"]
Out[12]= InputStream[textfile, 9]
``` |
|---|---|
| This finds the first line which contains second, and leaves the current point in the file at the beginning of the next line. | ```
In[13]:= Find[stext, "second"]
Out[13]= And the second.
``` |

Read can then read the word that appears at the beginning of the line.	*In[14]:=* **Read[stext, Word]**
	Out[14]= And
This skips over the next three words.	*In[15]:=* **Skip[stext, Word, 3]**
Mathematica finds is in the remaining text, and prints the entire record as output.	*In[16]:=* **Find[stext, "is"]**
	Out[16]= And the third. Here is the end.
This closes the input stream.	*In[17]:=* **Close[stext]**
	Out[17]= textfile

StreamPosition[*stream*]	find the position of the current point in an open stream
SetStreamPosition[*stream*, *n*]	set the position of the current point
SetStreamPosition[*stream*, 0]	set the current point to the beginning of a stream
SetStreamPosition[*stream*, Infinity]	
	set the current point to the end of a stream

Finding and setting the current point in a stream.

Functions like Read, Skip and Find usually operate on streams in an entirely sequential fashion. Each time one of the functions is called, the current point in the stream moves on.

Sometimes, you may need to know where the current point in a stream is, and be able to reset it. On most computer systems, StreamPosition returns the position of the current point as an integer giving the number of bytes from the beginning of the stream.

This opens the stream.	*In[18]:=* **stext = OpenRead["textfile"]**
	Out[18]= InputStream[textfile, 10]
When you first open the file, the current point is at the beginning, and StreamPosition returns 0.	*In[19]:=* **StreamPosition[stext]**
	Out[19]= 0
This reads the first line in the file.	*In[20]:=* **Read[stext, Record]**
	Out[20]= Here is the first line of text.
Now the current point has advanced.	*In[21]:=* **StreamPosition[stext]**
	Out[21]= 31
This sets the stream position back.	*In[22]:=* **SetStreamPosition[stext, 5]**
	Out[22]= 5
Now Read returns the remainder of the first line.	*In[23]:=* **Read[stext, Record]**
	Out[23]= is the first line of text.

This closes the stream.	In[24]:= **Close[stext]**
	Out[24]= textfile

■ 2.10.8 Searching and Reading Strings

Functions like Read and Find are most often used for processing text and data from external files. In some cases, however, you may find it convenient to use these same functions to process strings within *Mathematica*. You can do this by using the function StringToStream, which opens an input stream that takes characters not from an external file, but instead from a *Mathematica* string.

StringToStream["*string*"]	open an input stream for reading from a string
Close[*stream*]	close an input stream

Treating strings as input streams.

This opens an input stream for reading from the string.	In[1]:= **str = StringToStream["A string of words."]**
	Out[1]= InputStream[String, 3]
This reads the first "word" from the string.	In[2]:= **Read[str, Word]**
	Out[2]= A
This reads the remaining words from the string.	In[3]:= **ReadList[str, Word]**
	Out[3]= {string, of, words.}
This closes the input stream.	In[4]:= **Close[str]**
	Out[4]= String

Input streams associated with strings work just like those with files. At any given time, there is a current position in the stream, which advances when you use functions like Read. The current position is given as the number of bytes from the beginning of the string by the function StreamPosition[*stream*]. You can explicitly set the current position using SetStreamPosition[*stream*, *n*].

Here is an input stream associated with a string.	In[5]:= **str = StringToStream["123 456 789"]**
	Out[5]= InputStream[String, 4]
The current position is initially 0 bytes from the beginning of the string.	In[6]:= **StreamPosition[str]**
	Out[6]= 0
This reads a number from the stream.	In[7]:= **Read[str, Number]**
	Out[7]= 123
The current position is now 4 bytes from the beginning of the string.	In[8]:= **StreamPosition[str]**
	Out[8]= 4

This sets the current position to be 1 byte from the beginning of the string.

In[9]:= **SetStreamPosition[str, 1]**

Out[9]= 1

If you now read a number from the string, you get the 23 part of 123.

In[10]:= **Read[str, Number]**

Out[10]= 23

This sets the current position to the end of the string.

In[11]:= **SetStreamPosition[str, Infinity]**

Out[11]= 11

If you now try to read from the stream, you will always get EndOfFile.

In[12]:= **Read[str, Number]**

Out[12]= EndOfFile

This closes the stream.

In[13]:= **Close[str]**

Out[13]= String

Particularly when you are processing large volumes of textual data, it is common to read fairly long strings into *Mathematica,* then to use StringToStream to allow further processing of these strings within *Mathematica.* Once you have created an input stream using StringToStream, you can read and search the string using any of the functions discussed for files above.

This puts the whole contents of textfile into a string.

In[14]:= **s = First[ReadList["textfile", Record,**
                        RecordSeparators -> {}]]

Out[14]= Here is the first line of text.
          And the second.
          And the third. Here is the end.

This opens an input stream for the string.

In[15]:= **str = StringToStream[s]**

Out[15]= InputStream[String, 6]

This gives the lines of text in the string that contain is.

In[16]:= **FindList[str, "is"]**

Out[16]= {Here is the first line of text.,

  And the third. Here is the end.}

This resets the current position back to the beginning of the string.

In[17]:= **SetStreamPosition[str, 0]**

Out[17]= 0

This finds the first occurrence of the in the string, and leaves the current point just after it.

In[18]:= **Find[str, "the", RecordSeparators -> {" "}]**

Out[18]= the

This reads the "word" which appears immediately after the.

In[19]:= **Read[str, Word]**

Out[19]= first

This closes the input stream.

In[20]:= **Close[str]**

Out[20]= String

■ 2.10.9 Special Topic: Calling External Functions

Functions like RunThrough, discussed in Section 2.10.2, let you send input to external programs, and then get back output from the programs. Often, however, you do not want to send just one piece of input to a whole external program. Instead, you want to make many separate calls to individual functions inside the external program.

On most computer systems, you can do this using *MathLink*. The basic idea is to run the external program as a separate process alongside *Mathematica*, and then to send "requests" to the program every time you want to call a function inside it. The protocol for these requests is defined by the *MathLink* communication standard, as discussed in Section 1.10.8.

Most versions of *Mathematica* come with source code for *MathLink* routines which you can include in external programs. These routines set up what is necessary for the external programs to communicate with *Mathematica* via *MathLink*. If you want to use all the features of *MathLink*, you will need to call these routines directly. In simple cases, however, you can instead use *MathLink* template files to set up code to call the *MathLink* routines.

MathLink template files consist of sequences of directives specifying how functions in an external program can be called from *Mathematica*. The template files are preprocessed to produce code which must be included in the external program. This code makes the external program "*MathLink* compatible", and allows the functions in the program that you specified to be called from within *Mathematica*.

:BeginLink:	link specification follows
:Function: *f*	the source code name of the external function
:Pattern: *f*[*x_type*, *y_type*, ...]	
	the *Mathematica* pattern for which the external function is to be used
:Arguments: {*x*, *y*, ... }	*Mathematica* list of the arguments to be passed to the external function
:ArgumentTypes: {*mtype₁*, *mtype₂*, ... }	
	a list of the *MathLink* types to be used for arguments passed to the external function
:ReturnType: *mtype*	the *MathLink* type of the return value from the external function
:EndLink:	end of link specification
:Evaluate: *expr*	*Mathematica* input to be evaluated when the external program is started
:: *text*	a comment

Directives used in *MathLink* template files.

MathLink template files are used to set up a correspondence between functions defined in *Mathematica*, and functions defined in an external program. Doing this requires a correspondence between the data types used in *Mathematica* and in the external program. *MathLink* template files allow you to specify certain types for the arguments and return values of external functions. As described in Section 2.10.10 below, the full *MathLink* standard can handle any data type. To go beyond the types supported by *MathLink* template files, however, you need to call *MathLink* routines directly.

String	character string (`char *`, `int`)
Symbol	symbol name, represented as a character string (`char *`)
Integer	integer (`int`)
Real	floating-point number (`double`)
IntegerList, RealList	lists of numbers (`int *`, etc., `int`)
Null	null return type (`void`)
Manual	call *MathLink* routines directly to get or put data

MathLink type specifiers.

MathLink can in general be used with external programs written in practically any programming language. A common case, however, used for the examples here, is the C programming language.

```
:BeginLink:
:Function:        bitand
:Pattern:         BitAnd[x_Integer, y_Integer]
:Arguments:       {x, y}
:ArgumentTypes:   {Integer, Integer}
:ReturnType:      Integer
:EndLink:

:Evaluate:        BitAnd::usage = "BitAnd[x, y] gives the bitwise conjunction of
                          two integers x and y."
```

A *MathLink* template file for the external function `bitand`.

```
main()
{
        MMain( );
        /* Initialize and enter main loop. */
}

int
bitand(x, y)
int     x, y;
{
        return(x & y);
}
```

A C program for the function `bitand`.

In creating an external program which can communicate via *MathLink*, the first step is typically to make a *MathLink* template file. The next step is to process the template file to generate source code, typically using a preprocessor program called `mprep`. Next, you take the generated source code, and add it to the main source code for the external program. Then you compile all the source code to generate your external program.

The only special part of the main source code is that the program must be set up so that as soon as it starts, it calls a "main *MathLink* routine". This routine sends data to *Mathematica* via *MathLink*, telling *Mathematica* to define *Mathematica* functions which can call functions inside the external program. After this initialization, the routine goes into a state where it waits for requests from *Mathematica*. Whenever it receives a request, it calls the appropriate function in the external program, then returns the result via *MathLink* to *Mathematica*.

Install["*prog*"]	start an external program, set up *MathLink* communication with it, and install *Mathematica* function definitions
Uninstall[*link*]	terminate an external program, closing *MathLink* communication, and removing *Mathematica* function definitions

Controlling external programs from within *Mathematica*.

This starts the external program `bitprog`, obtained from the source code and *MathLink* template files above.	`In[1]:= bitprog = Install["bitprog"]` `Out[1]= LinkObject[bitprog, 1]`
When it was started, `bitprog` installed a *Mathematica* definition for `BitAnd`.	`In[2]:= ?BitAnd` `BitAnd[x, y]` gives the bitwise conjunction of two integers x and y.
When you use `BitAnd` with appropriate arguments, it is evaluated by calling the function `bitand` in the external program.	`In[3]:= BitAnd[65535, 2047]` `Out[3]= 2047`
You can call the functions in the external program as often as you want.	`In[4]:= BitAnd[65535, 2047 + 15]` `Out[4]= 2062`
This terminates the external program.	`In[5]:= Uninstall[bitprog]`

The details of how to call external functions via *MathLink* depend on the language in which your external functions are written, and on various features of the computer system you are using. For more complete information, see the Wolfram Research technical report, "The *MathLink* Communication Standard".

■ 2.10.10 Advanced Topic: The Structure of *MathLink*

The previous section discussed how *MathLink* can be used to call functions inside external programs. *MathLink* is however a general mechanism for communication between *Mathematica* and other programs, and it can be used in many different ways.

- Call functions in an external program from within *Mathematica*.

- Call *Mathematica* from within an external program.

- Implement your own front end for *Mathematica*.

- Exchange data between *Mathematica* and external programs.

- Exchange data between concurrent *Mathematica* processes.

Some typical applications of *MathLink*.

An important feature of *MathLink* is that it is essentially symmetrical: not only can you send "requests" from *Mathematica* to external programs, but external programs can also send requests to *Mathematica*. Thus, for example, an external program can send a request to *Mathematica* asking for *Mathematica* to evaluate a particular expression constructed by the external program, and to return the result of the evaluation to the external program.

In general, *MathLink* can be used with either *Mathematica* or the external program "in control". For example, *MathLink* can be used to allow an external program to call *Mathematica* essentially like a subroutine. In this case, *Mathematica* is typically started as a subsidiary process from within the external program, and is sent expressions to evaluate.

Front ends for *Mathematica* typically communicate with the *Mathematica* kernel via *MathLink* in this kind of way.

- *MathLink* is a standard for exchanging *Mathematica* expressions between programs.

The basic principle of *MathLink*.

Different applications of *MathLink* require it to handle different kinds of material. In all cases, however, *MathLink* represents the material in the form of *Mathematica* expressions.

There are standard *MathLink* routines which can be used in external programs for constructing and decoding *Mathematica* expressions. In typical cases, these routines "put" or "get" sequences of elements corresponding to *Mathematica* expressions. In many cases, the routines can be set up to work directly with data structures in the external program. Thus, for example, there are standard *MathLink* routines for converting between arrays in the external program and lists in *Mathematica*.

In most situations, the expressions sent or received through *MathLink* are wrapped in "packets", with heads that specify what the expressions are for. There are standard *MathLink* routines for decoding such packets, and setting up dispatch tables for determining what to do with them.

Packets are used for example to distinguish the different kinds of responses that can be produced when an external program sends an expression to *Mathematica* for evaluation. In the simplest case, the only response to such an evaluation request is the final result of the evaluation. This final result is typically sent as a "return packet" of the form `ReturnPacket[expr]`.

In general, however, an evaluation request can yield other kinds of responses. For example, if the evaluation involves a function like `Print`, *Mathematica* may generate additional output before giving the final result. Such output is typically given in a "text packet" of the form `TextPacket[string]`. Similarly, if during a computation, a message is generated, this is typically given in a packet of the form `MessagePacket[message]`.

When an external program sends an expression to *Mathematica* for evaluation, it is possible that *Mathematica* will require further input before it can complete the evaluation. This happens, for example, if the expression involves evaluation of a function such as `Input[ ]`. In such a case, *Mathematica* sends an `InputPacket` via *MathLink* to the external program. It is then the responsibility of the external program to supply the necessary input expression to *Mathematica* in order that it can continue with the computation.

There are further complications if the external program is allowed to interrupt calculations done by *Mathematica*. *MathLink* handles such interactions by sending special packets to the external program.

`LinkOpen[command]`	open a *MathLink* connection to an external program
`LinkClose[link]`	close a *MathLink* connection
`LinkInterrupt[link]`	send an interrupt to an external program via *MathLink*
`LinkWrite[link, expr]`	write an expression via *MathLink*
`LinkWriteHeld[link, expr]`	write an expression via *MathLink*, stripping any enclosing `Hold` or `HoldForm`
`LinkRead[link]`	read an expression via *MathLink*
`LinkReadHeld[link]`	read an expression via *MathLink*, wrapping the result with `Hold`

Typical low-level *MathLink* primitives in *Mathematica*.

At the lowest level, *MathLink* connections are typically implemented using standard interprocess communication mechanisms such as pipes. Note that these standard mechanisms usually allow communication not just within one computer, but in general between different computers connected via a network or serial line. Thus *MathLink* can often be used to communicate between programs running on different computers.

The standard *MathLink* routines nevertheless hide many of the details of how low-level *MathLink* communication is done. It is however possible to organize the basic *MathLink* interaction in many different ways. For example, using functions like `LinkWrite` and `LinkRead`, you can set up a special way for *Mathematica* to handle the requests it receives via a particular *MathLink* connection from an external program.

Details of both the *Mathematica* and external program sides of *MathLink* connections are described in the Wolfram Research technical report, "The *MathLink* Communication Standard".

2.11 Global Aspects of *Mathematica* Sessions

■ 2.11.1 The Main Loop

In any interactive session, *Mathematica* effectively operates in a loop. It waits for your input, processes the input, prints the result, then goes back to waiting for input again. As part of this "main loop", *Mathematica* maintains and uses various global objects. You will often find it useful to work with these objects.

You should realize, however, that if you use *Mathematica* through a special front end, your front end may set up its own main loop, and what is said in this section may not apply.

In[n]	the expression on the nth input line
InString[n]	the textual form of the nth input line
%n or Out[n]	the expression on the nth output line
Out[{n_1, n_2, ... }]	a list of output expressions
%%... % (n times) or Out[$-n$]	the expression on the nth previous output line
MessageList[n]	a list of messages produced while processing the nth line
$Line	the current line number

Input and output expressions.

In a standard interactive session, there is a sequence of input and output lines. *Mathematica* stores the values of the expressions on these lines in In[n] and Out[n].

As indicated by the usual In[n]:= prompt, the input expressions are stored with delayed assignments. This means that whenever you ask for In[n], the input expression will always be re-evaluated in your current environment.

This assigns a value to x.

```
In[1]:= x = 7
Out[1]= 7
```

Now the value for x is used.

```
In[2]:= x - x^2 + 5x - 1
Out[2]= -8
```

This removes the value assigned to x.

```
In[3]:= x =.
```

This is re-evaluated in your current environment, where there is no value assigned to x.

```
In[4]:= In[2]
              2
Out[4]= -1 + 6 x - x
```

This gives the textual form of the second input line, appropriate for editing or other textual manipulation.

```
In[5]:= InString[2] // InputForm

Out[5]//InputForm= "x - x^2 + 5x - 1"
```

In a standard session, *Mathematica* stores *all* your input and output lines for the duration of the session. In a very long session, this may take up a large amount of computer memory. You can nevertheless get rid of the input and output lines by explicitly clearing the values of In and Out, using Unprotect[In, Out], followed by Clear[In, Out].

An alternative strategy is to reset the line number counter $Line, so that new lines are numbered so as to overwrite previous ones.

$PreRead	a function applied to each input string before being fed to *Mathematica*
$Pre	a function applied to each input expression before evaluation
$Post	a function applied to each expression after evaluation
$PrePrint	a function applied after Out[*n*] is assigned, but before the result is printed
$SyntaxHandler	a function applied to any input line that yields a syntax error

Global functions used in the main loop.

Mathematica provides a variety of "hooks" that allow you to insert functions to be applied to expressions at various stages in the main loop. Thus, for example, any function you assign as the value of the global variable $Pre will automatically be applied before evaluation to any expression you give as input.

For a particular input line, the standard main loop begins by getting a text string of input. Particularly if you need to deal with special characters, you may want to modify this text string before it is further processed by *Mathematica*. You can do this by assigning a function as the value of the global variable $PreRead. This function will be applied to the text string, and the result will be used as the actual input string for the particular input line.

This tells *Mathematica* to replace <<... >> by {... } in every input string.

```
In[6]:= $PreRead = StringReplace[#, {"<<" -> "{", ">>" -> "}"}]&

Out[6]= StringReplace[#1, {<< -> {, >> -> }}] &
```

You can now enter braces as double angle brackets.

```
In[7]:= <<4, 5, 6>>

Out[7]= {4, 5, 6}
```

You can remove the value for $PreRead like this, at least so long as your definition for $PreRead does not modify this very input string.

In[8]:= **$PreRead =.**

Once any $PreRead processing on an input string is finished, the string is read by *Mathematica*. At this point, *Mathematica* may find that there is a syntax error in the string. If this happens, then *Mathematica* calls whatever function you have specified as the value of $SyntaxHandler. It supplies two arguments: the input string, and the character position at which the syntax error was detected. With $SyntaxHandler you can, for example, generate an analysis of the syntax error, or call an editor. If your function returns a string, then *Mathematica* will use this string as a new input string.

This specifies what *Mathematica* should do when it gets a syntax error.

In[9]:= **$SyntaxHandler =**
     (Print[StringForm["Error at char `1` in `2`",
                                    #2, #1]]; $Failed)&

Out[9]= (Print[Error at char #2 in #1]; $Failed) &

This input generates a syntax error.

In[10]:= **3 +/+ 5**

Syntax::sntxf: "3 +" cannot be followed by "/+ 5".

Error at char 3 in 3 +/+ 5

Once *Mathematica* has successfully read an input expression, it then evaluates this expression. Before doing the evaluation, *Mathematica* applies any function you have specified as the value of $Pre, and after the evaluation, it applies any function specified as the value of $Post. Note that unless the $Pre function holds its arguments unevaluated, the function will have exactly the same effect as $Post.

$Post allows you to specify arbitrary "post processing" to be done on results obtained from *Mathematica*. Thus, for example, to make *Mathematica* get a numerical approximation to every result it generates, all you need do is to set $Post = N.

This tells *Mathematica* to apply N to every result it generates.

In[10]:= **$Post = N**

Out[10]= N

Now *Mathematica* gets a numerical approximation to anything you type in.

In[11]:= **Sqrt[7]**

Out[11]= 2.64575

This removes the post-processing function you specified.

In[12]:= **$Post =.**

As soon as *Mathematica* has generated a result, and applied any $Post function you have specified, it takes the result, and assigns it as the value of Out[$Line]. The next step is for *Mathematica* to print the result. However, before doing this, it applies any function you have specified as the value of $PrePrint.

This tells *Mathematica* to shorten all output to two lines.

In[13]:= **$PrePrint = Short[#, 2]& ;**

Only a two-line version of the output is now shown.

$In[14]:=$ **Expand[(x + y)^40]**

$Out[14]=$ $x^{40} + 40 x^{39} y + 780 x^{38} y^2 + 9880 x^{37} y^3 + \langle\langle 35 \rangle\rangle +$
$40 x y^{39} + y^{40}$

This removes the value you assigned to $PrePrint.

$In[15]:=$ **$PrePrint =.**

Whenever *Mathematica* prints an output line, there are a number of other issues. First, if the last expression generated by *Mathematica* is the symbol Null, then no actual output line is printed. Nevertheless, if the Null was generated as the last segment of a compound expression such as $expr_1$; $expr_2$; ... ;, then *Mathematica* will take the last non-Null segment as the actual value of Out[$Line].

A second issue is that if the head of the output expression is an output form such as InputForm given in the list $OutputForms, then, as discussed on page 346, *Mathematica* will assign Out[$Line] to be the expression inside the output form, but will include the output form in the printed name of the output line.

Format[In] = *nameIn*	specify a format for input line names
Format[Out] = *nameOut*	specify a format for output line names

Modifying the format for input and output line names.

Beyond $PrePrint, *Mathematica* provides a variety of ways to modify the "look" of a standard interactive session. For example, you can assign a value to Format[In] to change the way that the names of your input lines are printed. You can use this as a way to distinguish different *Mathematica* sessions that you may have running on the same computer screen.

This changes the way names of your input and output lines are printed.

$In[16]:=$ **(Unprotect[In, Out] ; Format[In] = RemoteIn ;**
        Format[Out] = RemoteOut)

$RemoteOut[16]=$ RemoteOut

Now In and Out are printed differently, although their values are not affected.

$RemoteIn[17]:=$ **Out[11]**

$RemoteOut[17]=$ 2.64575

This restores the old form.

$RemoteIn[18]:=$ **(Format[In] =. ; Format[Out] =. ; Protect[In, Out])**

$Out[18]=$ {In, Out}

Mathematica uses the formats of various objects to determine the overall "look" of each piece of output it produces. By redefining the formats of these objects, you can change the look of *Mathematica* output.

Continuation[n]	given at the beginning of the nth line in a multi-line piece of output (default: ">" or "")
LineBreak[n]	given between the nth and n+1th line in a multi-line piece of output (default: a blank line)
Indent[d]	indentation for a depth d subexpression (default: d spaces)
StringBreak[n]	given at the end of the nth part of a string that is broken onto several lines (default: \)
Skeleton[n]	given in place of n omitted elements in Short or Shallow output (default: <<n>>)
StringSkeleton[n]	given in place of n omitted characters in a string in Short output (default: ..)
DialogIndent[d]	indentation for a depth d dialog (default: d spaces)

Objects that can be modified to affect the look of output.

This redefines the format for Continuation.

$In[1]:=$ **Format[Continuation[n_]] := StringForm["``> ", n]**

Now n> is printed at the beginning of the nth continuation line.

$In[2]:=$ **Expand[(1 + x)^15]**

$Out[2]=$ $1 + 15\ x + 105\ x^2 + 455\ x^3 + 1365\ x^4 + 3003\ x^5 +$

2> $5005\ x^6 + 6435\ x^7 + 6435\ x^8 + 5005\ x^9 + 3003\ x^{10} + 1365\ x^{11} +$

3> $455\ x^{12} + 105\ x^{13} + 15\ x^{14} + x^{15}$

This clears all definitions for Continuation.

$In[3]:=$ **Clear[Continuation]**

Mathematica is usually set up to leave a blank line between each line in a multiline piece of output. Sometimes, you may want to save space by omitting this blank line. You can do this by setting Format[LineBreak[_]] = "".

SetOptions[$Output, PageWidth -> n]	break output lines so they are at most n characters long
SetOptions[$Output, TotalWidth -> n]	use Short to make each complete piece of output at most n characters long

Setting global output parameters.

As discussed in Section 2.10.3, you can use `SetOptions` to specify various global options associated with output generated by *Mathematica*.

This puts a limit on the total length of each piece of output generated in your *Mathematica* session.	`In[4]:= SetOptions[$Output, TotalWidth -> 200] ;`

Now *Mathematica* uses `Short` to keep the output under 200 characters in length.

`In[5]:= Expand[(x + 1)^200]`

$$Out[5]= 1 + 200\ x + 19900\ x^2 + 1313400\ x^3 + 64684950\ x^4 +$$
$$2535650040\ x^5 + 82408626300\ x^6 + 2283896214600\ x^7 +$$
$$\ll189\gg + 1313400\ x^{197} + 19900\ x^{198} + 200\ x^{199} + x^{200}$$

This removes the output length restriction.	`In[6]:= SetOptions[$Output, TotalWidth -> Infinity] ;`

There are various kinds of output generated in a typical *Mathematica* session. In general, each kind of output is sent to a definite *output channel*, as discussed on page 486. Associated with each output channel, there is a global variable which gives a list of the output streams to be included in that output channel.

`$Output`	standard output and text generated by `Print`
`$Echo`	an echo of each input line (as stored in `InString[n]`)
`$Urgent`	input prompts and other urgent output
`$Messages`	standard messages and output generated by `Message`
`$Display`	graphics output generated by the default `$DisplayFunction`
`$SoundDisplay`	sound output generated by the default `$SoundDisplayFunction`

Output channels in a standard *Mathematica* session.

By modifying the list of streams in a given output channel, you can redirect or copy particular kinds of *Mathematica* output. Thus, for example, by opening an output stream to a file, and including that stream in the $Echo list, you can get each piece of input you give to *Mathematica* saved in a file.

Streams[ ]	list of all open streams
Streams["*name*"]	list of all open streams with the specified name
$Input	the name of the current input stream

Open streams in a *Mathematica* session.

The function `Streams` shows you all the input, output and other streams that are open at a particular point in a *Mathematica* session. The variable `$Input` gives the name of the current stream from which *Mathematica* input is being taken at a particular point. `$Input` is reset, for example, during the execution of a `Get` command.

$MessagePrePrint	a function to be applied to expressions that are given in messages
$Language	list of default languages to use for messages

Parameters for messages.

There are various global parameters which determine the form of messages generated by *Mathematica*.

As discussed in Section 2.8.8, typical messages include a sequence of expressions which are combined with the text of the message through `StringForm`. `$MessagePrePrint` gives a function to be applied to the expressions before they are printed. The default value of `$MessagePrePrint` is `Short`.

As discussed in Section 2.8.9, *Mathematica* allows you to specify the language in which you want messages to be produced. In a particular *Mathematica* session, you can assign a list of language names as the value of `$Language`.

Exit[ ] or Quit[ ]	terminate your *Mathematica* session
$Epilog	a global variable to be evaluated before termination

Terminating *Mathematica* sessions.

Mathematica will continue in its main loop until you explicitly tell it to exit. Most *Mathematica* interfaces provide special ways to do this. Nevertheless, you can always do it by explicitly calling `Exit` or `Quit`.

Mathematica allows you to give a value to the global variable `$Epilog` to specify operations to perform just before *Mathematica* actually exits. In this way, you can for example make *Mathematica* always save certain objects before exiting.

`$IgnoreEOF`	whether to ignore the end-of-file character

A global variable that determines the treatment of end-of-file characters.

As discussed in Section 2.8.2, *Mathematica* usually does not treat special characters in a special way. There is one potential exception, however. With the default setting `$IgnoreEOF = False`, *Mathematica* recognizes end-of-file characters. If *Mathematica* receives an end-of-file character as the only thing on a particular input line in a standard interactive *Mathematica* session, then it will exit the session.

Exactly how you enter an end-of-file character depends on the computer system you are using. Under Unix, for example, you typically press CONTROL-D.

Note that if you use *Mathematica* in a "batch mode", with all its input coming from a file, then it will automatically exit when it reaches the end of the file, regardless of the value of `$IgnoreEOF`.

■ 2.11.2 Dialogs

Within a standard interactive session, you can create "subsessions" or *dialogs* using the *Mathematica* command `Dialog`. Dialogs are often useful if you want to interact with *Mathematica* while it is in the middle of doing a calculation. As mentioned in Section 2.5.10, `TraceDialog` for example automatically calls `Dialog` at specified points in the evaluation of a particular expression. In addition, if you interrupt *Mathematica* during a computation, you can typically "inspect" its state using a dialog.

`Dialog[ ]`	initiate a *Mathematica* dialog
`Dialog[expr]`	initiate a dialog with *expr* as the current value of %
`Return[ ]`	return from a dialog, taking the current value of % as the return value
`Return[expr]`	return from a dialog, taking *expr* as the return value

Initiating and returning from dialogs.

This initiates a dialog.	`In[1]:= Dialog[ ]`
You can do computations in a dialog just as you would in any *Mathematica* session.	`In[2]:= 2^41` `Out[2]= 2199023255552`
You can use `Return` to exit from a dialog.	`In[3]:= Return[ ]` `Out[1]= 2199023255552`

When you exit a dialog, you can return a value for the dialog using Return[*expr*]. If you do not want to return a value, and you have set $IgnoreEOF = False, then you can also exit a dialog simply by giving an end-of-file character, at least on systems with text-based interfaces.

To evaluate this expression, *Mathematica* initiates a dialog.	*In[2]:=* **1 + Dialog[ ]^2**

The value **a + b** returned from the dialog is now inserted in the original expression.	*In[3]:=* **Return[a + b]**
	Out[2]= 1 + (a + b)^2

In starting a dialog, you will often find it useful to have some "initial expression". If you use Dialog[*expr*], then *Mathematica* will start a dialog, using *expr* as initial expression, accessible for example as the value of %.

This first starts a dialog with initial expression a^2.	*In[3]:=* **Map[Dialog, {a^2, b + c}]**
	Out[4]= a^2

% is the initial expression in the dialog.	*In[5]:=* **%^2 + 1**
	Out[5]= 1 + a^4

This returns a value from the first dialog, and starts the second dialog, with initial expression **b + c**.	*In[6]:=* **Return[%]**
	Out[4]= b + c

This returns a value from the second dialog. The final result is the original expression, with values from the two dialogs inserted.	*In[5]:=* **Return[444]**
	Out[3]= {1 + a^4, 444}

Dialog effectively works by running a subsidiary version of the standard *Mathematica* main loop. Each dialog you start effectively "inherits" various values from the overall main loop. Some of the values are, however, local to the dialog, so their original values are restored when you exit the dialog.

Thus, for example, dialogs inherit the current line number $Line when they start. This means that the lines in a dialog have numbers that follow the sequence used in the main loop. Nevertheless, the value of $Line is local to the dialog. As a result, when you exit the dialog, the value of $Line reverts to what it was in the main loop.

If you start a dialog on line 10 of your *Mathematica* session, then the first line of the dialog will be labeled *In[11]*. Successive lines of the dialog will be labeled *In[12]*, *In[13]* and so on. Then, when you exit the dialog, the next line in your main loop will be labeled *In[11]*. At this point, you can still refer to results generated within the dialog as *Out[11]*, *Out[12]* and so on. These results will be overwritten, however, when you reach lines *In[12]*, *In[13]*, and so on in the main loop.

In a standard *Mathematica* session, you can tell whether you are in a dialog by seeing whether your input and output lines are indented. If you call a dialog from within a dialog, you will get two levels of indentation. In general, the indentation you get inside *d* nested dialogs is determined by the output form of the object `DialogIndent[d]`. By defining the format for this object, you can specify how dialogs should be indicated in your *Mathematica* session.

`DialogSymbols :> {x, y, ... }`	symbols whose values should be treated as local to the dialog
`DialogSymbols :> {x = `x_0`, y = `y_0`, ... }`	symbols with initial values
`DialogProlog :> `*expr*	an expression to evaluate before starting the dialog

Options for `Dialog`.

Whatever setting you give for `DialogSymbols`, `Dialog` will always treat the values of `$Line`, `$Epilog` and `$MessageList` as local. Note that if you give a value for `$Epilog`, it will automatically be evaluated when you exit the dialog.

When you call `Dialog`, its first step is to localize the values of variables. Then it evaluates any expression you have set for the option `DialogProlog`. If you have given an explicit argument to the `Dialog` function, this is then evaluated next. Finally, the actual dialog is started.

When you exit the dialog, you can explicitly specify the return value using `Return[`*expr*`]`. If you do not do this, the return value will be taken to be the last value generated in the dialog.

■ 2.11.3 Interactive Input

The `Dialog` function discussed in the previous section allows you to initiate a complete subsidiary *Mathematica* session with a sequence of input and output lines. Sometimes, however, you may want to get *Mathematica* simply to ask for a single piece of input from the user. You can do this using the functions `Input` and `InputString`.

`Input[ ]`	read an expression as input
`InputString[ ]`	read a string as input
`Input["`*prompt*`"]`	issue a prompt, then read an expression
`InputString["`*prompt*`"]`	issue a prompt then read a string

Interactive input.

Exactly how `Input` and `InputString` work depends on the computer system and *Mathematica* interface you are using. With a text-based interface, they typically just wait for standard input, terminated with a newline. With a notebook interface, however, they typically get the front end to put a "dialog box", in which the user can enter input.

In general, `Input` is intended for reading complete *Mathematica* expressions. `InputString`, on the other hand, is for reading arbitrary strings.

■ 2.11.4 Date and Time Functions

`Date[ ]`	give the current local date and time in the form {*year, month, day, hour, minute, second*}
`Date[z]`	give the current date and time in time zone *z*
`TimeZone[ ]`	give the time zone assumed by your computer system

Finding the date and time.

This gives the current date and time.

```
In[1]:= Date[ ]
Out[1]= {1990, 10, 17, 12, 28, 53}
```

The *Mathematica* `Date` function returns whatever your computer system gives as the current date and time. It assumes that any corrections for daylight saving time and so on have already been done by your computer system. In addition, it assumes that your computer system has been set for the appropriate time zone.

The function `TimeZone[ ]` returns the current time zone assumed by your computer system. The time zone is given as the number of hours which must be added to Greenwich mean time (GMT) to obtain the correct local time. Thus, for example, U.S. eastern standard time (EST) corresponds to time zone -5. Note that daylight saving time corrections must be included in the time zone, so U.S. eastern daylight time (EDT) corresponds to time zone -4.

This gives the current time zone assumed by your computer system.

```
In[2]:= TimeZone[ ]
Out[2]= -5.
```

This gives the current date and time in time zone +9, the time zone for Japan.

```
In[3]:= Date[9]
Out[3]= {1990, 10, 18, 2, 28, 53}
```

AbsoluteTime[ ]	total number of seconds since the beginning of January 1, 1900
SessionTime[ ]	total number of seconds elapsed since the beginning of your current *Mathematica* session
TimeUsed[ ]	total number of seconds of CPU time used in your current *Mathematica* session
$TimeUnit	the minimum time interval recorded on your computer system

Time functions.

You should realize that on any computer system, there is a certain "granularity" in the times that can be measured. This granularity is given as the value of the global variable $TimeUnit. Typically it is about $\frac{1}{60}$ of a second.

Pause[*n*]	pause for at least *n* seconds

Pausing during a calculation.

This gives various time functions.

```
In[4]:= {AbsoluteTime[ ], SessionTime[ ], TimeUsed[ ]}

Out[4]= {2.8651733339 10 , 25.68, 0.9}
                         9
```

This pauses for 10 seconds, then re-evaluates the time functions. Note that TimeUsed[ ] is not affected by the pause.

```
In[5]:= Pause[10]; {AbsoluteTime[ ], SessionTime[ ],
                                         TimeUsed[ ]}

Out[5]= {2.8651733443 10 , 36.020001, 1.08333}
                         9
```

FromDate[*date*]	convert from date to absolute time
ToDate[*time*]	convert from absolute time to date

Converting between dates and absolute times.

This sets d to be the current date.

```
In[6]:= d = Date[ ]
Out[6]= {1990, 10, 17, 12, 29, 4}
```

This adds one month to the current date.

```
In[7]:= Date[ ] + {0, 1, 0, 0, 0, 0}
Out[7]= {1990, 11, 17, 12, 29, 5}
```

This gives the number of seconds in the additional month.

```
In[8]:= FromDate[%] - FromDate[d]
Out[8]= 2678401
```

Timing[*expr*]	evaluate *expr*, and return a list of the CPU time needed, together with the result obtained

Timing *Mathematica* operations.

Timing allows you to measure the CPU time, corresponding to the increase in TimeUsed, associated with the evaluation of a single *Mathematica* expression. Note that only CPU time associated with the actual evaluation of the expression within the *Mathematica* kernel is included. The time needed to format the expression for output, and any time associated with external programs, is not included.

You should realize that the time reported by Timing for a particular calculation depends on many factors.

First, the time depends in detail on the computer system you are using. It depends not only on instruction times, but also on memory caching, as well as on the details of the optimization done in compiling the parts of the internal code of *Mathematica* used in the calculation.

The time also depends on the precise state of your *Mathematica* session when the calculation was done. Many of the internal optimizations used by *Mathematica* depend on details of preceding calculations. For example, *Mathematica* often uses previous results it has obtained, and avoids unnecessarily re-evaluating expressions. In addition, some *Mathematica* functions build internal tables when they are first called in a particular way, so that if they are called in that way again, they run much faster. For all of these kinds of reasons, it is often the case that a particular calculation may not take the same amount of time if you run it at different points in the same *Mathematica* session.

This gives the CPU time needed for the calculation. The semicolon causes the result of the calculation to be given as Null.	*In[9]:=* **Timing[1000!;]** *Out[9]=* {1.95 Second, Null}
Now *Mathematica* has built internal tables for factorial functions, and the calculation takes much less time.	*In[10]:=* **Timing[1000!;]** *Out[10]=* {0.0166667 Second, Null}

Note that the results you get from Timing are only accurate to the timing granularity $TimeUnit of your computer system. Thus, for example, a timing reported as 0 could in fact be as much as $TimeUnit.

TimeConstrained[*expr*, *t*]	try to evaluate *expr*, aborting the calculation after *t* seconds
TimeConstrained[*expr*, *t*, *failexpr*]	
	return *failexpr* if the time constraint is not met

Time-constrained calculation.

When you use *Mathematica* interactively, it is quite common to try doing a calculation, but to abort the calculation if it seems to be taking too long. You can emulate this behavior inside a program by using TimeConstrained. TimeConstrained tries to evaluate a particular expression for a specified amount of time. If it does not succeed, then it aborts the evaluation, and returns either $Aborted, or an expression you specify.

You can use TimeConstrained, for example, to have *Mathematica* try a particular approach to a problem for a certain amount of time, and then to switch to another approach if the first one has not yet succeeded. You should realize however that TimeConstrained may overrun the time you specify if *Mathematica* cannot be interrupted during a particular part of a calculation. In addition, you should realize that because different computer systems run at different speeds, programs that use TimeConstrained will often give different results on different systems.

■ 2.11.5 Memory Management

MemoryInUse[ ]	number of bytes of memory currently being used by *Mathematica*
MaxMemoryUsed[ ]	maximum number of bytes of memory used by *Mathematica* in this session

Finding memory usage.

Particularly for symbolic computations, memory is usually the primary resource which limits the size of computations you can do. If a computation runs slowly, you can always potentially let it run longer. But if the computation generates intermediate expressions which simply cannot fit in the memory of your computer system, then you cannot proceed with the computation.

Mathematica is careful about the way it uses memory. Every time an intermediate expression you have generated is no longer needed, *Mathematica* immediately reclaims the memory allocated to it. This means that at any point in a session, *Mathematica* stores only those expressions that are actually needed; it does not keep unnecessary objects which have to be "garbage collected" later.

This gives the number of bytes of memory currently being used by *Mathematica*.

```
In[1]:= MemoryInUse[ ]
Out[1]= 2087572
```

This generates a 10000-element list.

```
In[2]:= Range[10000] // Short
Out[2]//Short=
    {1, 2, 3, 4, 5, 6, 7, 8, <<9988>>, 9997, 9998, 9999, 10000}
```

Additional memory is needed to store the list.

```
In[3]:= MemoryInUse[ ]
Out[3]= 2323692
```

This list is kept because it is the value of Out[2]. If you clear Out[2], the list is no longer needed.

In[4]:= **Unprotect[Out]; Out[2]=.**

The memory in use goes down again.

In[5]:= **MemoryInUse[ ]**

Out[5]= 2089528

This shows the maximum memory needed at any point in the session.

In[6]:= **MaxMemoryUsed[ ]**

Out[6]= 2404156

One issue that often comes up is exactly how much memory *Mathematica* can actually use on a particular computer system. Usually there is a certain amount of memory available for *all* processes running on the computer at a particular time. Sometimes this amount of memory is equal to the physical number of bytes of RAM in the computer. Often, it includes a certain amount of "virtual memory", obtained by swapping data on and off a mass storage device.

When *Mathematica* runs, it needs space both for data and for code. The complete code of *Mathematica* is typically a couple of megabytes in size. For any particular calculation, only a small fraction of this code is usually used. However, in trying to work out the total amount of space available for *Mathematica* data, you should not forget what is needed for *Mathematica* code. In addition, you must include the space that is taken up by other processes running in the computer. If there are fewer jobs running, you will usually find that your job can use more memory.

It is also worth realizing that the time needed to do a calculation can depend very greatly on how much physical memory you have. Although virtual memory allows you in principle to use large amounts of memory space, it is usually hundreds or even thousands of times slower to access than physical memory. As a result, if your calculation becomes so large that it needs to make use of virtual memory, it may run *much* more slowly.

MemoryConstrained[*expr*, *b*]	try to evaluate *expr*, aborting if more than *b* additional bytes of memory are requested
MemoryConstrained[*expr*, *b*, *failexpr*]	
	return *failexpr* if the memory constraint is not met

Memory-constrained computation.

MemoryConstrained works much like TimeConstrained. If more than the specified amount of memory is requested, MemoryConstrained attempts to abort your computation. As with TimeConstrained, there may be some overshoot in the actual amount of memory used before the computation is aborted.

ByteCount [*expr*]	the maximum number of bytes of memory needed to store *expr*
LeafCount [*expr*]	the number of terminal nodes in the expression tree for *expr*

Finding the size of expressions.

Although you may find ByteCount useful in estimating how large an expression of a particular kind you can handle, you should realize that the specific results given by ByteCount can differ substantially from one version of *Mathematica* to another.

Another important point is that ByteCount always gives you the *maximum* amount of memory needed to store a particular expression. Often *Mathematica* will actually use a much smaller amount of memory to store the expression. The main issue is how many of the subexpressions in the expression can be *shared*.

In an expression like f [1 + x, 1 + x], the two subexpressions 1 + x are identical, but they may or may not actually be stored in the same piece of computer memory. ByteCount gives you the number of bytes needed to store expressions with the assumption that no subexpressions are shared. You should realize that the sharing of subexpressions is often destroyed as soon as you use an operation like the / . operator.

Nevertheless, you can explicitly tell *Mathematica* to share subexpressions using the function Share. In this way, you can significantly reduce the actual amount of memory needed to store a particular expression.

Share [*expr*]	share common subexpressions in the storage of *expr*
Share [ ]	share common subexpressions throughout memory

Optimizing memory usage.

On most computer systems, the memory used by a running program is divided into two parts: memory explicitly allocated by the program, and "stack space". Every time an internal routine is called in the program, a certain amount of stack space is used to store parameters associated with the call. On many computer systems, the maximum amount of stack space that can be used by a program must be specified in advance. If the specified stack space limit is exceeded, the program usually just exits.

In *Mathematica*, one of the primary uses of stack space is in handling the calling of one *Mathematica* function by another. All such calls are explicitly recorded in the *Mathematica* Stack discussed in Section 2.5.11. You can control the size of this stack by setting the global parameter $RecursionLimit. You should be sure that this parameter is set small enough that you do not run out stack space on your particular computer system.

■ 2.11.6 Advanced Topic: System Parameters

The basic functionality of *Mathematica* is set up to be as independent as possible of the details of the computer environment in which it is run. However, particularly if you use *Mathematica* to communicate with external programs, you may need to be able to determine various aspects of your computer environment.

First, if you write a program, you may need to know how a user of that program is interacting with *Mathematica*. There are various global variables that are set to specify this.

$Linked	whether *Mathematica* is being run through *MathLink* (*e.g.*, from a front end)
$Notebooks	whether a notebook-based interface is being used
$BatchInput	whether input is being given in batch mode to the *Mathematica* kernel (*e.g.*, from a file)
$BatchOutput	whether output should be given in batch mode, without labeling, etc.
$CommandLine	the original command line or equivalent with which the *Mathematica* kernel was called

Global variables specifying mode of interaction.

The second major class of global variables consists of ones that reflect the version of *Mathematica* being used.

$Version	a string giving the complete version of *Mathematica* in use
$VersionNumber	the *Mathematica* kernel version number (*e.g.*, 2.0)
$ReleaseNumber	the release number for your version of the *Mathematica* kernel on your particular computer system
$CreationDate	the date, in Date format, on which your particular *Mathematica* release was created
$DumpDates	a list of all dates on which Dump was used in creating the *Mathematica* system you are using

Global variables specifying version of *Mathematica*.

Another class of global variables consists of those which characterize the type and identity of the computer system on which *Mathematica* is being run.

`$System`	a string specifying the complete type of computer system on which *Mathematica* is being run
`$OperatingSystem`	the operating system in use
`$MachineType`	the type of your computer
`$MachineName`	the "host name" or other identifying name of your particular computer
`$MachineID`	the ID of your computer, or your copy of *Mathematica*

Global variables specifying your computer system.

Versions of *Mathematica* on different computer systems can have slightly different capabilities. *Mathematica* provides some global variables which specify whether certain capabilities are available in a particular version of *Mathematica*.

`$LinkSupported`	whether *MathLink* is available
`$PipeSupported`	whether pipes are available
`$DumpSupported`	whether Dump is available

Global variables characterizing *Mathematica* capabilities.

If you have a variable such as x in one *Mathematica* session, you may or may not want that variable to be the same as an x in another *Mathematica* session. In order to make it possible to maintain distinct objects in different sessions, *Mathematica* supports the variable `$SessionID`, which is set up to be different for every *Mathematica* session, whether it is run on the same computer or a different one.

`$SessionID`	a number set up to be different for every *Mathematica* session

A unique number different for every *Mathematica* session.

■ 2.11.7 Special Topic: Saving the State of a *Mathematica* Session

On many computer systems, you can save the complete state of your *Mathematica* session, so you can start it up again exactly where you left off.

The basic mechanism for this is to save a "core image" file, and then to execute this core image when you want to start again.

Dump["*file*"]	write out the core image of a *Mathematica* session
Dump["*file*", *init*]	insert the expression *init* in the core image, so the expression is evaluated when the image starts up
Dump["*file*", *init*, "*code*"]	take the file *code*, rather than First[$CommandLine], to be the original *Mathematica* executable

Saving the state of a *Mathematica* session.

A common way to use Dump is in creating copies of *Mathematica* that have certain data "pre-loaded". If you want these copies to start up like a standard *Mathematica* session, you can use Dump["*file*", $Line=0; <<init.m].

You should realize that on most systems Dump creates a file that is several megabytes in size. If you want to save only some aspects of your *Mathematica* session, it is much more economical of storage space to save what you need in standard textual form using Save, rather than saving a complete core image using Dump.

If you have files open in *Mathematica* when you call Dump, these files will be closed. There would be no point in saving the file pointers in the core image, since there is no guarantee that the files will still exist, or be in the same place, when the core image is restarted.

Part 3.

Advanced Mathematics in *Mathematica*

3.1 Numbers

■ 3.1.1 Types of Numbers

Four types of numbers are built into *Mathematica*.

Integer	arbitrary-length exact integer
Rational	*integer/integer* in lowest terms
Real	approximate real number, with any specified precision
Complex	complex number of the form *number* + *number* I

Intrinsic types of numbers in *Mathematica*.

Rational numbers always consist of a ratio of two integers, reduced to lowest terms.	$In[1]:=$ **12344/2222** $$Out[1]= \frac{6172}{1111}$$
Approximate real numbers are distinguished by the presence of an explicit decimal point.	$In[2]:=$ **5456.** $Out[2]=$ 5456.
An approximate real number can have any number of digits.	$In[3]:=$ **4.545435234545435234534523452345234543** $Out[3]=$ 4.545435234545435234534523452345234543
Complex numbers can have integer or rational components.	$In[4]:=$ **4 + 7/8 I** $$Out[4]= 4 + \frac{7\,I}{8}$$
They can also have approximate real number components.	$In[5]:=$ **4 + 5.6 I** $Out[5]=$ 4. + 5.6 I

123	an exact integer
123.	an approximate real number
123.0000000000000	an approximate real number with a certain precision
123. + 0. I	a complex number with approximate real number components

Several versions of the number 123.

You can distinguish different types of numbers in *Mathematica* by looking at their heads. (Although numbers in *Mathematica* have heads like other expressions, they do not have explicit elements which you can extract.)

The object 123 is taken to be an exact integer, with head `Integer`.

```
In[6]:= Head[123]
Out[6]= Integer
```

The presence of an explicit decimal point makes *Mathematica* treat 123. as an approximate real number, with head `Real`.

```
In[7]:= Head[123.]
Out[7]= Real
```

NumberQ[x]	test whether x is any kind of number
IntegerQ[x]	test whether x is an integer
EvenQ[x]	test whether x is even
OddQ[x]	test whether x is odd
PrimeQ[x]	test whether x is a prime integer
Head[x]===*type*	test the type of a number

Tests for different types of numbers.

NumberQ[x] tests for any kind of number.

```
In[8]:= NumberQ[5.6]
Out[8]= True
```

5. is treated as a `Real`, so `IntegerQ` gives `False`.

```
In[9]:= IntegerQ[5.]
Out[9]= False
```

If you use complex numbers extensively, there is one subtlety you should be aware of. When you enter a number like 123., *Mathematica* treats it as an approximate real number, but assumes that its imaginary part is exactly zero. Sometimes you may want to enter approximate complex numbers with imaginary parts that are zero, but only to a certain precision.

When the imaginary part is the exact integer 0, *Mathematica* simplifies complex numbers to real ones.

```
In[10]:= Head[ 123 + 0 I ]
Out[10]= Integer
```

Here the imaginary part is only zero to a certain precision, so *Mathematica* retains the complex number form.

```
In[11]:= Head[ 123. + 0. I ]
Out[11]= Complex
```

The distinction between complex numbers whose imaginary parts are exactly zero, or are only zero to a certain precision, may seem like a pedantic one. However, when we discuss, for example, the interpretation of powers and roots of complex numbers in Section 3.2.7, the distinction will become significant.

One way to find out the type of a number in *Mathematica* is just to pick out its head using Head [*expr*]. For many purposes, however, it is better to use functions like IntegerQ which explicitly test for particular types. Functions like this are set up to return True if their argument is manifestly of the required type, and to return False otherwise. As a result, IntegerQ[x] will give False, unless you have assigned x an explicit integer value.

In doing symbolic computations, however, you may sometimes want to treat x as an integer, even though you have not assigned an explicit integer value to it. You can override the assumption that the symbol x is not an integer by explicitly making an assignment of the form x/: IntegerQ[x] = True. This assignment specifies that whenever you specifically test x with IntegerQ, it will give the result True. You should realize, however, that the assignment does not actually change the head of x, so that, for example, x will still not match n_Integer. *Mathematica* also does not automatically make inferences based on the assignment. Thus, for example, it cannot determine solely on the basis of this assignment that IntegerQ[x∧2] is also True.

x does not explicitly have head Integer, so IntegerQ returns False.	*In[12]:=* **IntegerQ[x]** *Out[12]=* False
This specifies that x is in fact an integer. The x/: specifies that the rule is associated with x, not IntegerQ.	*In[13]:=* **x/: IntegerQ[x] = True** *Out[13]=* True
The definition overrides the default assumption that x is not an integer.	*In[14]:=* **IntegerQ[x]** *Out[14]=* True

■ 3.1.2 Converting between Different Forms of Numbers

N[*x*, *n*]	convert *x* to an approximate real number with at most *n* digits of precision
Rationalize[*x*]	give a rational number approximation to *x*
Rationalize[*x*, *dx*]	give a rational number approximation to within tolerance *dx*

Functions that convert between different types of numbers.

This gives a 30-digit real number approximation to 3/7.	*In[1]:=* **N[3/7, 30]** *Out[1]=* 0.428571428571428571428571428571
This takes the 30-digit number you have just generated, and reduces it to 20-digit precision.	*In[2]:=* **N[%, 20]** *Out[2]=* 0.42857142857142857143

This converts the result back to a rational number.

In[3]:= **Rationalize[%]**

Out[3]= $\dfrac{3}{7}$

The numerical value of π is not "sufficiently close" to a rational number to be converted.

In[4]:= **Rationalize[N[Pi]]**

Out[4]= 3.14159

If you give a specific tolerance, Rationalize will give you a rational number approximation accurate to within that tolerance.

In[5]:= **Rationalize[N[Pi], 10^-5]**

Out[5]= $\dfrac{355}{113}$

With a tolerance of 0, Rationalize yields the best possible rational approximation given the precision of your input.

In[6]:= **Rationalize[N[Pi], 0]**

Out[6]= $\dfrac{245850922}{78256779}$

IntegerDigits[*n*]	a list of the decimal digits in the integer *n*
IntegerDigits[*n*, *b*]	the digits of *n* in base *b*
RealDigits[*x*]	a list of the decimal digits in the approximate real number *x*, together with the number of digits to the left of the decimal point
RealDigits[*x*, *b*]	the digits of *x* in base *b*

Extracting lists of digits.

Here is the list of base 16 digits for an integer.

In[7]:= **IntegerDigits[1234135634, 16]**

Out[7]= {4, 9, 8, 15, 6, 10, 5, 2}

This gives a list of digits, together with the number of digits that appear to the left of the decimal point.

In[8]:= **RealDigits[123.45678901234567890123456** **7]**

Out[8]= {{1, 2, 3, 4, 5, 6, 7, 8, 9, 0, 1, 2, 3, 4, 5, 6, 7, 8, 9, 0, 1, 2, 3, 4, 5, 7}, 3}

b^^*nnnn*	a number in base *b*
BaseForm[*x*, *b*]	print with *x* in base *b*

Numbers in other bases.

When the base is larger than 10, extra digits are represented by letters a–z.

The number 100101_2 in base 2 is 37 in base 10.

In[9]:= **2^^100101**

Out[9]= 37

This prints 37 in base 2.

In[10]:= `BaseForm[37, 2]`

Out[10]//BaseForm= 100101$_2$

Here is a number in base 16.

In[11]:= `16^^ffffaa00`

Out[11]= 4294945280

You can do computations with numbers in base 16. Here the result is given in base 10.

In[12]:= `16^^fffaa2 + 16^^ff - 1`

Out[12]= 16776096

This gives the result in base 16.

In[13]:= `BaseForm[%, 16]`

Out[13]//BaseForm= fffba0$_{16}$

You can give approximate real numbers, as well as integers, in other bases.

In[14]:= `2^^101.100101`

Out[14]= 5.578125

Here are the first few digits of $\sqrt{2}$ in octal.

In[15]:= `BaseForm[N[Sqrt[2], 30], 8]`

Out[15]//BaseForm= 1.32404746317716746220426276611546$7_8$

Section 2.7.5 describes how to print numbers in various formats. If you want to create your own formats, you will often need to use `MantissaExponent` to separate the pieces of approximate real numbers.

`MantissaExponent[x]`	give a list containing the mantissa and exponent of x

Separating the mantissa and exponent of numbers.

This gives a list in which the mantissa and exponent of the number are separated.

In[16]:= `MantissaExponent[3.45 10^125]`

Out[16]= {0.345, 126}

■ 3.1.3 Numerical Precision

As discussed in Section 1.1.2, *Mathematica* can handle approximate real numbers with any number of digits. In general, the *precision* of an approximate real number is the number of decimal digits in it which are treated as significant for computations. The *accuracy* of an approximate real number is the number of decimal digits which appear to the right of the decimal point. Precision is thus a measure of the relative error in a number, while accuracy is a measure of absolute error.

Precision[*x*]	the total number of significant decimal digits in *x*
Accuracy[*x*]	the number of significant decimal digits to the right of the decimal point in *x*

Precision and accuracy of real numbers.

Here is an approximate real number.	`In[1]:= xacc = 431.123145333555141444`
	
	`Out[1]= 431.123145333555141444`

This gives the total number of digits entered to specify the real number.	`In[2]:= Precision[xacc]`
	
	`Out[2]= 21`

This gives the number of digits which appear to the right of the decimal point.	`In[3]:= Accuracy[xacc]`
	
	`Out[3]= 18`

When you use N[*expr*, *n*], *Mathematica* evaluates the expression *expr* using numbers that have *n* digits of precision. As discussed below, however, the fact that such numbers are used does not necessarily mean that the results you get will have *n* digits of precision. In most cases, your results will have at least slightly fewer digits of precision.

This evaluates Pi^25 using numbers with 30 digits of precision.	`In[4]:= N[Pi^25, 30]` `Out[4]= 2.6837794143177645490099281244 10`^{12}

The result has 29 digits of precision.	`In[5]:= Precision[%]`
	
	`Out[5]= 29`

N[*expr*, *n*]	evaluate *expr* numerically using numbers with *n*-digit precision
N[*expr*]	evaluate *expr* numerically using machine-precision numbers

Numerical evaluation.

If you use N[*expr*], and do not explicitly specify the precision of numbers to use, *Mathematica* will use *machine-precision* numbers.

In general, *Mathematica* distinguishes two kinds of approximate real numbers: *arbitrary-precision* ones, and *machine-precision* ones. Arbitrary-precision numbers can contain any number of digits, and their precision is adjusted during computations. Machine-precision numbers, on the other hand, contain a fixed number of digits, and their precision remains unchanged throughout computations.

As discussed in more detail below, machine-precision numbers work by making direct use of the numerical capabilities of your underlying computer system. As a result, computations with them can be done quickly. However, machine-precision numbers are much less flexible than arbitrary-precision ones.

This evaluates Pi using machine precision.	In[6]:= **N[Pi]** Out[6]= 3.14159
On the computer system used to generate this example, the machine precision is 16 decimal digits.	In[7]:= **Precision[%]** Out[7]= 16
This gives the machine precision on the computer system.	In[8]:= **$MachinePrecision** Out[8]= 16

`$MachinePrecision`	the machine precision on your computer system
`MachineNumberQ[x]`	give True if x is a machine-precision number, and False otherwise

Machine-precision numbers.

When you enter an approximate real number, *Mathematica* has to decide whether to treat it as machine precision or arbitrary precision. In general, if you give less than $MachinePrecision digits, then *Mathematica* will treat the number as machine precision, and if you give more digits, it will treat the number as arbitrary precision. In the arbitrary-precision case, *Mathematica* assigns the number a precision equal to the number of digits you explicitly entered. In the machine-precision case, *Mathematica* effectively assumes that all decimal digits after the ones you explicitly entered are zero.

Here is a high-precision number. In standard *Mathematica* output form, the trailing zeros are not printed.	In[9]:= **3.00000000000000000000000000000** Out[9]= 3.
In input form, however, all the zeros you gave are printed explicitly.	In[10]:= **InputForm[%]** Out[10]//InputForm= 3.00000000000000000000000000000
The number has a precision equal to the total number of digits you gave.	In[11]:= **Precision[%]** Out[11]= 30
Mathematica treats 3. as a machine-precision number.	In[12]:= **Precision[3.]** Out[12]= 16
Giving anything less than $MachinePrecision digits yields a machine-precision number.	In[13]:= **Precision[3.00]** Out[13]= 16

In doing numerical computations, it is inevitable that you will sometimes end up with results that are less precise than you want. Particularly when you get numerical results that are very close to zero, you may well want to *assume* that the results should be exactly zero. The function Chop allows you to replace approximate real numbers that are close to zero by the exact integer 0.

Chop[*expr*]	replace all approximate real numbers in *expr* with magnitude less than 10^{-10} by 0
Chop[*expr*, *dx*]	replace numbers with magnitude less than *dx* by 0

Removing numbers close to zero.

This computation gives a small imaginary part.

```
In[14]:= Exp[ N[2 Pi I] ]
                         -16
Out[14]= 1. - 2.44921 10    I
```

You can get rid of the imaginary part using Chop.

```
In[15]:= Chop[%]
Out[15]= 1.
```

■ 3.1.4 Arbitrary-Precision Numbers

When you do calculations with arbitrary-precision numbers, *Mathematica* keeps track of precision at all points. In general, *Mathematica* tries to give you results which have the highest possible precision, given the precision of the input you provided.

Mathematica treats arbitrary-precision numbers as representing the values of quantities where a certain number of digits are known, and the rest are unknown. In general, an arbitrary-precision number x is taken to have Precision[x] digits which are known exactly, followed by an infinite number of digits which are completely unknown.

When you do a computation, *Mathematica* keeps track of which digits in your result could be affected by unknown digits in your input. It sets the precision of your result so that no affected digits are ever included. This procedure ensures that all digits returned by *Mathematica* are correct, whatever the values of the unknown digits may be.

This evaluates $\Gamma(1/7)$ using 30-digit-precision numbers.

```
In[1]:= N[Gamma[1/7], 30]
Out[1]= 6.54806294024782443771409334943
```

In this case, the result has a precision of exactly 30 digits.

```
In[2]:= Precision[%]
Out[2]= 30
```

If you give input only to a few digits of precision, *Mathematica* cannot give you such high-precision output.

```
In[3]:= N[Gamma[0.142], 30]
Out[3]= 6.589647294920399
```

If you want *Mathematica* to assume that 0.142 is *exactly* 142/1000, then you have to show this explicitly.

```
In[4]:= N[Gamma[142/1000], 30]
Out[4]= 6.58964729492039788328481917496
```

In many computations, the precision of the results you get progressively degrades as a result of "roundoff error". A typical case of this occurs if you subtract two numbers that are close together. The result you get depends on high-order digits in each number, and typically has far fewer digits of precision than either of the original numbers.

Both input numbers have a precision of 20 digits, but the result has a precision of only 3 digits.	`In[5]:= 1.11111111111111111111 -`
	`        1.11111111111111111000`
	
	`Out[5]= 1.11 10`$^{-18}$

Adding extra digits in one number but not the other is not sufficient to allow extra digits to be found in the result.	`In[6]:= 1.1111111111111111111345 -`
	`        1.11111111111111111000`
	
	`Out[6]= 1.11 10`$^{-18}$

The precision of the output from a function can depend in a complicated way on the precision of the input. Functions that vary rapidly typically give less precise output, since the variation of the output associated with uncertainties in the input is larger. Functions that are close to constants can actually give output that is more precise than their input.

Functions like Sin that vary rapidly typically give output that is less precise than their input.	`In[7]:= Sin[111111111.0000000000000000]` `Out[7]= -0.2975351033349432`

Here is e^{-40} evaluated using 20-digit precision.	`In[8]:= N[Exp[-40], 20]` `Out[8]= 4.248354255291589 10`$^{-18}$

The result you get by adding the exact integer 1 has a higher precision.	`In[9]:= 1 + %` `Out[9]= 1.000000000000000004248354255291589`

It is worth realizing that different ways of doing the same calculation can end up giving you results with very different precisions. Typically, if you once lose precision in a calculation, it is essentially impossible to regain it; in losing precision, you are effectively losing information about your result.

Here is a 40-digit number that is close to 1.	`In[10]:= x = N[1 - 10^-30, 40]` `Out[10]= 0.9999999999999999999999999999999`

Adding 1 to it gives another 40-digit number.	`In[11]:= 1 + x` `Out[11]= 1.9999999999999999999999999999999`

Most of the original precision has been maintained.	`In[12]:= Precision[%]` `Out[12]= 40`

This way of computing 1 + x loses precision.	`In[13]:= (x^2 - 1) / (x - 1)` `Out[13]= 2.`

The result obtained in this way has quite low precision.	`In[14]:= Precision[%]` `Out[14]= 10`

The internal algorithms that *Mathematica* uses to evaluate mathematical functions are set up to maintain as much precision as possible. In most cases, built-in *Mathematica* functions will give you results that have as much precision as can be justified on the basis of your input. In some cases, however, it is simply impractical to do this, and *Mathematica* will give you results that have lower precision. If you give higher-precision input, *Mathematica* will use higher precision in its internal calculations, and you will usually be able to get a higher-precision result.

The fact that different ways of doing the same calculation can give you different numerical answers means, among other things, that comparisons between approximate real numbers must be treated with care. In testing whether two real numbers are "equal", *Mathematica* effectively finds their difference, and tests whether the result is "consistent with zero" to the precision given.

These numbers are equal to the precision given.	`In[15]:= 3 == 3.000000000000000000`
	
	`Out[15]= True`

While many computations involve some loss of precision, most yield results in which many digits still survive. Sometimes, however, the loss of precision may be so severe that not a single reliable digit survives, so that the result has zero precision. *Mathematica* represents all such results by zero. The accuracy of the result specifies how large the deviation from zero in the true result may be. Negative accuracies correspond to deviations given by positive powers of ten.

The reduction of the argument to `Sin` cannot be done sufficiently precisely using 20-digit-precision numbers, so no reliable result can be found.	`In[16]:= N[Sin[10^30], 20]`
	
	`Out[16]= 0.`

The result is meaningless: it has zero precision, and negative accuracy.	`In[17]:= {Precision[%], Accuracy[%]}`
	
	`Out[17]= {0, -20}`

If 40-digit-precision numbers are used, a definite result is obtained.	`In[18]:= N[Sin[10^30], 40]`
	
	`Out[18]= -0.090116902`

When *Mathematica* works out the potential effect of unknown digits, it always assumes that these digits are completely independent in different numbers. While this assumption will never yield too high a precision in a result, it may lead to unnecessary loss of precision.

In particular, if two numbers are generated in the same way in a computation, some of their unknown digits may be equal. Then, when these numbers are, for example, subtracted, the unknown digits may cancel. By assuming that the unknown digits are always independent, however, *Mathematica* will miss such cancellations.

Here is a number computed to 20-digit precision.	`In[19]:= delta = N[3^-30, 20]`
	
	`Out[19]= 4.8569357496188611379 10^-15`

The quantity `1 + delta` has 35-digit precision.	`In[20]:= Precision[1 + delta]`
	
	`Out[20]= 35`

This quantity also has only 35-digit precision, since *Mathematica* assumes that the unknown digits in each number delta are independent.

```
In[21]:= Precision[(1 + delta) - delta]
Out[21]= 35
```

Numerical algorithms sometimes rely on cancellations between unknown digits in different numbers yielding results of higher precision. If you can be sure that certain unknown digits will eventually cancel, then you can explicitly introduce arbitrary digits in place of the unknown ones. You can carry these arbitrary digits through your computation, then let them cancel, and get a result of higher precision.

SetPrecision[x, n]	create a number with n decimal digits of precision, padding if necessary with binary zeros
SetAccuracy[x, n]	create a number with n decimal digits of accuracy

Functions for modifying precision and accuracy.

This adds 10 arbitrary digits to delta.

```
In[22]:= delta = SetPrecision[delta, 30]
Out[22]= 4.8569357496188611379062426651 10^-15
```

The digits that were added cancel out here.

```
In[23]:= (1 + delta) - delta
Out[23]= 1.
```

The precision of the result is now 45, rather than 35, digits.

```
In[24]:= Precision[%]
Out[24]= 45
```

SetPrecision works by adding digits which are zero in base 2. Sometimes, *Mathematica* stores slightly more digits in an arbitrary-precision number than it displays, and in such cases, SetPrecision will use these extra digits before introducing zeros.

This creates a number with a precision of 40 decimal digits. The extra digits correspond to zeros in base 2.

```
In[25]:= SetPrecision[0.300000000000000, 40]
Out[25]= 0.2999999999999999988897769753748434595763
```

■ 3.1.5 Machine-Precision Numbers

Whenever machine-precision numbers appear in a calculation, the whole calculation is typically done in machine precision. *Mathematica* will then give machine-precision numbers as the result.

Whenever the input contains any machine-precision numbers, *Mathematica* does the computation to machine precision.

```
In[1]:= 1.4444444444444444444 ^ 5.7
Out[1]= 8.13382
```

Zeta[5.6] yields a machine-precision result, so the N is irrelevant.

```
In[2]:= N[Zeta[5.6], 30]
Out[2]= 1.02337547922703
```

This gives a higher-precision result.

In[3]:= **N[Zeta[56/10], 30]**

Out[3]= 1.0233754792270299108604178810

When you do calculations with arbitrary-precision numbers, as discussed in the previous section, *Mathematica* always keeps track of the precision of your results, and gives only those digits which are known to be correct, given the precision of your input. When you do calculations with machine-precision numbers, however, *Mathematica* always gives you a machine-precision result, whether or not all the digits in the result can, in fact, be determined to be correct on the basis of your input.

This subtracts two machine-precision numbers.

In[4]:= **diff = 1.11111111 - 1.11111000**

Out[4]= 1.11 10^{-6}

The result is taken to have machine precision.

In[5]:= **Precision[diff]**

Out[5]= 16

Here are all the digits in the result.

In[6]:= **InputForm[diff]**

Out[6]//InputForm= 1.109999999915345*10^-6

The fact that you can get spurious digits in machine-precision numerical calculations with *Mathematica* is in many respects quite unsatisfactory. The ultimate reason, however, that *Mathematica* uses fixed precision for these calculations is a matter of computational efficiency.

Mathematica is usually set up to insulate you as much as possible from the details of the computer system you are using. In dealing with machine-precision numbers, you would lose too much, however, if *Mathematica* did not make use of some specific features of your computer.

The important point is that almost all computers have special hardware or microcode for doing floating-point calculations to a particular fixed precision. *Mathematica* makes use of these features when doing machine-precision numerical calculations.

The typical arrangement is that all machine-precision numbers in *Mathematica* are represented as "double-precision floating-point numbers" in the underlying computer system. On most current computers, such numbers contain a total of 64 binary bits, typically yielding 16 decimal digits of mantissa.

The main advantage of using the built-in floating-point capabilities of your computer is speed. Arbitrary-precision numerical calculations, which do not make such direct use of these capabilities, are usually many times slower than machine-precision calculations.

There are several disadvantages of using built-in floating-point capabilities. One already mentioned is that it forces all numbers to have a fixed precision, independent of what precision can be justified for them.

A second disadvantage is that the treatment of machine-precision numbers can vary slightly from one computer system to another. In working with machine-precision numbers, *Mathematica* is at the mercy of the floating-point arithmetic system of each particular computer. If floating-point arithmetic is done differently on two computers, you may get slightly different results for machine-precision *Mathematica* calculations on those computers.

`$MachinePrecision`	the number of decimal digits of precision
`$MachineEpsilon`	the minimum positive machine-precision number which can be added to 1.0 to give a result not equal to 1.0
`$MaxMachineNumber`	the maximum positive machine-precision number
`$MinMachineNumber`	the minimum positive machine-precision number

Properties of machine-precision numbers on a particular computer system.

Since machine-precision numbers on any particular computer system are represented by a definite number of binary bits, numbers which are too close together will have the same bit pattern, and so cannot be distinguished. The parameter `$MachineEpsilon` measures the smallest number which can be added to 1. to give a distinct result.

This gives the value of `$MachineEpsilon` for the computer system on which these examples are run.

```
In[7]:= $MachineEpsilon
```
$$Out[7]= 2.22045\ 10^{-16}$$

Although this prints as **1.**, *Mathematica* knows that the result is larger than one.

```
In[8]:= 1. + $MachineEpsilon
```
$$Out[8]= 1.$$

Subtracting 1 gives `$MachineEpsilon`.

```
In[9]:= % - 1.
```
$$Out[9]= 2.22045\ 10^{-16}$$

This again prints as **1.**

```
In[10]:= 1. + $MachineEpsilon/2
```
$$Out[10]= 1.$$

In this case, however, subtracting 1 yields 0, since 1 + `$MachineEpsilon`/2 is not distinguished from **1.** to machine precision.

```
In[11]:= % - 1.
```
$$Out[11]= 0.$$

Machine-precision numbers have not only limited precision, but also limited magnitude. If you generate a number which lies outside the range specified by `$MinMachineNumber` and `$MaxMachineNumber`, *Mathematica* will automatically convert the number to arbitrary-precision form.

This is the maximum machine-precision number which can be handled on the computer system used for this example.

```
In[12]:= $MaxMachineNumber
```
$$Out[12]= 1.79769\ 10^{308}$$

Mathematica automatically converts the result of this computation to arbitrary precision.

```
In[13]:= Exp[1000.]
```
$$Out[13]= 1.970071114017\ 10^{434}$$

■ 3.1.6 Advanced Topic: Indeterminate and Infinite Results

If you type in an expression like 0/0, *Mathematica* prints a message, and returns the result Indeterminate.

```
In[1]:= 0/0
```
$$\text{Power::infy: Infinite expression } \frac{1}{0} \text{ encountered.}$$

```
Infinity::indet:
     Indeterminate expression 0 ComplexInfinity encountered.
```

```
Out[1]= Indeterminate
```

An expression like 0/0 is an example of an *indeterminate numerical result*. If you type in 0/0, there is no way for *Mathematica* to know what answer you want. If you got 0/0 by taking the limit of x/x as $x \to 0$, then you might want the answer 1. On the other hand, if you got 0/0 instead as the limit of $2x/x$, then you probably want the answer 2. The expression 0/0 on its own does not contain enough information to choose between these and other cases. As a result, its value must be considered indeterminate.

Whenever an indeterminate result is produced in an arithmetic computation, *Mathematica* prints a warning message, and then returns Indeterminate as the result of the computation. If you ever try to use Indeterminate in an arithmetic computation, you always get the result Indeterminate. A single indeterminate expression effectively "poisons" any arithmetic computation. (The symbol Indeterminate plays a role in *Mathematica* similar to the "not a number" object in the IEEE Floating Point Standard.)

The usual laws of arithmetic simplification are suspended in the case of Indeterminate.

```
In[2]:= Indeterminate - Indeterminate
Out[2]= Indeterminate
```

Indeterminate "poisons" any arithmetic computation, and leads to an indeterminate result.

```
In[3]:= 2 Indeterminate - 7
Out[3]= Indeterminate
```

When you do arithmetic computations inside *Mathematica* programs, it is often important to be able to tell whether indeterminate results were generated in the computations. You can do this by using the function Check discussed on page 389 to test whether any warning messages associated with indeterminate results were produced.

You can use Check inside a program to test whether warning messages are generated in a computation.

```
In[4]:= Check[(7 - 7)/(8 - 8), meaningless]
```
$$\text{Power::infy: Infinite expression } \frac{1}{0} \text{ encountered.}$$

```
Infinity::indet:
     Indeterminate expression 0 ComplexInfinity encountered.
```

```
Out[4]= meaningless
```

Indeterminate	an indeterminate numerical result
Infinity	a positive infinite quantity
-Infinity	a negative infinite quantity (DirectedInfinity[-1])
DirectedInfinity[*r*]	an infinite quantity with complex direction *r*
ComplexInfinity	an infinite quantity with an undetermined direction
DirectedInfinity[ ]	equivalent to ComplexInfinity

Indeterminate and infinite quantities.

There are many situations where it is convenient to be able to do calculations with infinite quantities. The symbol Infinity in *Mathematica* represents a positive infinite quantity. You can use it to specify such things as limits of sums and integrals. You can also do some arithmetic calculations with it.

Here is an integral with an infinite limit.

```
In[5]:= Integrate[1/x^3, {x, 1, Infinity}]
```

$$Out[5]= \frac{1}{2}$$

Mathematica knows that $1/\infty = 0$.

```
In[6]:= 1/Infinity
Out[6]= 0
```

If you try to find the difference between two infinite quantities, you get an indeterminate result.

```
In[7]:= Infinity - Infinity
Infinity::indet:
     Indeterminate expression -Infinity + Infinity encountered.
Out[7]= Indeterminate
```

There are a number of subtle points that arise in handling infinite quantities. One of them concerns the "direction" of an infinite quantity. When you do an infinite integral, you typically think of performing the integration along a path in the complex plane that goes to infinity in some direction. In this case, it is important to distinguish different versions of infinity that correspond to different directions in the complex plane. $+\infty$ and $-\infty$ are two examples, but for some purposes one also needs $i\infty$ and so on.

In *Mathematica*, infinite quantities can have a "direction", specified by a complex number. When you type in the symbol Infinity, representing a positive infinite quantity, this is converted internally to the form DirectedInfinity[1], which represents an infinite quantity in the +1 direction. Similarly, -Infinity becomes DirectedInfinity[-1], and I Infinity becomes DirectedInfinity[I]. Although the DirectedInfinity form is always used internally, the standard output format for DirectedInfinity[*r*] is *r* Infinity.

Infinity is converted internally to DirectedInfinity[1].

```
In[8]:= Infinity // FullForm
Out[8]//FullForm= DirectedInfinity[1]
```

Although the notion of a "directed infinity" is often useful, it is not always available. If you type in 1/0, you get an infinite result, but there is no way to determine the "direction" of the infinity. *Mathe-*

matica represents the result of 1/0 as DirectedInfinity[ ]. In standard output form, this undirected infinity is printed out as ComplexInfinity.

1/0 gives an undirected form of infinity.	*In[9]:=* **1/0**

$$\text{Power::infy: Infinite expression } \frac{1}{0} \text{ encountered.}$$

Out[9]= ComplexInfinity

3.2 Mathematical Functions

■ 3.2.1 Naming Conventions

Mathematical functions in *Mathematica* are given names according to definite rules. As with most *Mathematica* functions, the names are usually complete English words, fully spelled out. For a few very common functions, *Mathematica* uses the traditional abbreviations. Thus the modulo function, for example, is Mod, not Modulo.

Mathematical functions that are usually referred to by a person's name have names in *Mathematica* of the form *PersonSymbol*. Thus, for example, the Legendre polynomials $P_n(x)$ are denoted LegendreP[n, x]. Although this convention does lead to longer function names, it avoids any ambiguity or confusion.

When the standard notation for a mathematical function involves both subscripts and superscripts, the subscripts are given *before* the superscripts in the *Mathematica* form. Thus, for example, the associated Legendre polynomials $P_n^m(x)$ are denoted LegendreP[n, m, x].

■ 3.2.2 Numerical Functions

Round[x]	integer $\langle x \rangle$ closest to x
Floor[x]	greatest integer $\lfloor x \rfloor$ not larger than x
Ceiling[x]	least integer $\lceil x \rceil$ not smaller than x
Sign[x]	1 for $x > 0$, -1 for $x < 0$
Abs[x]	absolute value $|x|$ of x
Max[x_1, x_2, ...] or Max[{x_1, x_2, ... }, ...]	the maximum of x_1, x_2, ...
Min[x_1, x_2, ...] or Min[{x_1, x_2, ... }, ...]	the minimum of x_1, x_2, ...

Some numerical functions of real variables.

x	Round$[x]$	Floor$[x]$	Ceiling$[x]$
2.4	2	2	3
2.5	2	2	3
2.6	3	2	3
−2.4	−2	−3	−2
−2.5	−2	−3	−2
−2.6	−3	−3	−2

Functions that convert to integers.

Round$[x]$, Floor$[x]$ and Ceiling$[x]$ can all be considered to give versions of the integer part of x. For positive numbers the fractional part is given by x − Floor$[x]$.

x + I y	the complex number $x + iy$
Re$[z]$	the real part Re z
Im$[z]$	the imaginary part Im z
Conjugate$[z]$	the complex conjugate z^* or $\overline{z}$
Abs$[z]$	the absolute value $|z|$
Arg$[z]$	the argument ϕ such that $z = |z|e^{i\phi}$

Numerical functions of complex variables.

■ 3.2.3 Pseudorandom Numbers

Random[ ]	a pseudorandom real between 0 and 1
Random[Real, *xmax*]	a pseudorandom real between 0 and *xmax*
Random[Real, {*xmin*, *xmax*}]	a pseudorandom real between *xmin* and *xmax*
Random[Complex]	a pseudorandom complex number in the unit square
Random[Complex, {*zmin*, *zmax*}]	
	a pseudorandom complex number in the rectangle defined by *zmin* and *zmax*
Random[*type*, *range*, *n*]	a pseudorandom number with *n*-digit precision
Random[Integer]	0 or 1 with probability $\frac{1}{2}$
Random[Integer, {*imin*, *imax*}]	a pseudorandom integer between *imin* and *imax*, inclusive
SeedRandom[ ]	reseed the pseudorandom generator, with the time of day
SeedRandom[*s*]	reseed with the integer *s*

Pseudorandom number generation.

This gives a list of 3 pseudorandom numbers.

```
In[1]:= Table[Random[ ], {3}]
Out[1]= {0.104826, 0.767415, 0.216417}
```

Here is a 30-digit pseudorandom real number in the range 0 to 1.

```
In[2]:= Random[Real, {0, 1}, 30]
Out[2]= 0.748823044099679773836330229338
```

This gives a list of 8 pseudorandom integers between 100 and 200 (inclusive).

```
In[3]:= Table[Random[Integer, {100, 200}], {8}]
Out[3]= {120, 108, 109, 147, 146, 189, 188, 187}
```

If you call Random[ ] repeatedly, you should get a "typical" sequence of numbers, with no particular pattern. There are many ways to use such numbers.

One common way to use pseudorandom numbers is in making numerical tests of hypotheses. For example, if you believe that two symbolic expressions are mathematically equal, you can test this by plugging in "typical" numerical values for symbolic parameters, and then comparing the numerical results. (If you do this, you should be careful about numerical accuracy problems and about functions of complex variables that may not have unique values.)

Here is a symbolic equation.

```
In[4]:= Sin[Cos[x]] == Cos[Sin[x]]
Out[4]= Sin[Cos[x]] == Cos[Sin[x]]
```

Substituting in a random numerical value shows that the equation is not always `True`.

```
In[5]:= % /. x -> Random[ ]
Out[5]= False
```

Other common uses of pseudorandom numbers include simulating probabilistic processes, and sampling large spaces of possibilities. The pseudorandom numbers that *Mathematica* generates are always uniformly distributed over the range you specify.

`Random` is unlike almost any other *Mathematica* function in that every time you call it, you potentially get a different result. If you use `Random` in a calculation, therefore, you may get different answers on different occasions.

The sequences that you get from `Random[ ]` are not in most senses "truly random", although they should be "random enough" for practical purposes. The sequences are in fact produced by applying a definite mathematical algorithm, starting from a particular "seed". If you give the same seed, then you get the same sequence.

When *Mathematica* starts up, it takes the time of day (measured in small fractions of a second) as the seed for the pseudorandom number generator. Two different *Mathematica* sessions will therefore almost always give different sequences of pseudorandom numbers.

If you want to make sure that you always get the same sequence of pseudorandom numbers, you can explicitly give a seed for the pseudorandom generator, using `SeedRandom`.

This reseeds the pseudorandom generator.

```
In[6]:= SeedRandom[143]
```

Here are three pseudorandom numbers.

```
In[7]:= Table[Random[ ], {3}]
Out[7]= {0.449809, 0.34676, 0.514834}
```

If you reseed the pseudorandom generator with the same seed, you get the same sequence of pseudorandom numbers.

```
In[8]:= SeedRandom[143]; Table[Random[ ], {3}]
Out[8]= {0.449809, 0.34676, 0.514834}
```

■ 3.2.4 Integer and Number-Theoretical Functions

`Mod[k, n]`	k modulo n (remainder from dividing k by n)
`Quotient[m, n]`	the quotient of m and n (integer part of m/n)
`GCD[n_1, n_2, ... ]`	the greatest common divisor of $n_1, n_2, ...$
`LCM[n_1, n_2, ... ]`	the least common multiple of $n_1, n_2, ...$
`IntegerDigits[n, b]`	the digits of n in base b

Some integer functions.

| The remainder on dividing 17 by 3. | $In[1]:=$ `Mod[17, 3]` |
| | $Out[1]=$ 2 |

| The integer part of 17/3. | $In[2]:=$ `Quotient[17, 3]` |
| | $Out[2]=$ 5 |

| Mod also works with real numbers. | $In[3]:=$ `Mod[5.6, 1.2]` |
| | $Out[3]=$ 0.8 |

| The result from Mod always has the same sign as the second argument. | $In[4]:=$ `Mod[-5.6, 1.2]` |
| | $Out[4]=$ 0.4 |

For any integers a and b, it is always true that b*Quotient$[a, b]$ + Mod$[a, b]$ is equal to a.

The **greatest common divisor** function GCD$[n_1, n_2, \ldots]$ gives the largest integer that divides all the n_i exactly. When you enter a ratio of two integers, *Mathematica* effectively uses GCD to cancel out common factors, and give a rational number in lowest terms.

The **least common multiple** function LCM$[n_1, n_2, \ldots]$ gives the smallest integer that contains all the factors of each of the n_i.

| The largest integer that divides both 24 and 15 is 3. | $In[5]:=$ `GCD[24, 15]` |
| | $Out[5]=$ 3 |

`FactorInteger[`n`]`	a list of the prime factors of n, and their exponents
`Divisors[`n`]`	a list of the integers that divide n
`Prime[`k`]`	the kth prime number
`PrimePi[`x`]`	the number of primes less than x
`PrimeQ[`n`]`	give True if n is a prime, and False otherwise
`FactorInteger[`n`, GaussianIntegers->True]`	
	a list of the Gaussian prime factors of the Gaussian integer n, and their exponents
`PrimeQ[`n`, GaussianIntegers->True]`	
	give True if n is a Gaussian prime, and False otherwise

Integer factoring and related functions.

| This gives the factors of 24 as 2^3, 3^1. The first element in each list is the factor; the second is its exponent. | $In[6]:=$ `FactorInteger[24]` |
| | $Out[6]=$ {{2, 3}, {3, 1}} |

Here are the factors of a larger integer. *In[7]:=* **FactorInteger[111111111111111111]**

Out[7]= {{3, 2}, {7, 1}, {11, 1}, {13, 1}, {19, 1}, {37, 1},

{52579, 1}, {333667, 1}}

You should realize that according to current mathematical thinking, integer factoring is a fundamentally difficult computational problem. As a result, you can easily type in an integer that *Mathematica* will not be able to factor in anything short of an astronomical length of time. As long as the integers you give are less than about 20 digits long, FactorInteger should have no trouble. Only in special cases, however, will it be able to deal with much longer integers. (You can make some factoring problems go faster by setting the option FactorComplete->False, so that FactorInteger[*n*] tries to pull out only one factor from *n*.)

Here is a rather special long integer. *In[8]:=* **30!**

Out[8]= 265252859812191058636308480000000

Mathematica can easily factor this special integer. *In[9]:=* **FactorInteger[%]**

Out[9]= {{2, 26}, {3, 14}, {5, 7}, {7, 4}, {11, 2}, {13, 2},

{17, 1}, {19, 1}, {23, 1}, {29, 1}}

Although *Mathematica* may not be able to factor a large integer, it can often still test whether or not the integer is a prime. In addition, *Mathematica* has a fast way of finding the kth prime number.

It is often much faster to test whether a number is prime than to factor it. *In[10]:=* **PrimeQ[234242423]**

Out[10]= False

Here is a plot of the first 100 primes. *In[11]:=* **ListPlot[Table[Prime[n], {n, 100}]]**

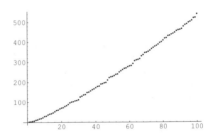

This is the millionth prime. *In[12]:=* **Prime[1000000]**

Out[12]= 15485863

Particularly in number theory, it is often more important to know the distribution of primes than their actual values. The function PrimePi[*x*] gives the number of primes $\pi(x)$ that are less than or equal to *x*.

This gives the number of primes less than a billion. *In[13]:=* **PrimePi[10^9]**

Out[13]= 50847534

By default, FactorInteger allows only real integers. But with the option setting GaussianIntegers -> True, it also handles **Gaussian integers**, which are complex numbers with integer real and imaginary parts. Just as it is possible to factor uniquely in terms of real primes, it is also possible to factor uniquely in terms of Gaussian primes. There is nevertheless some potential ambiguity in the choice of Gaussian primes. In *Mathematica*, they are always chosen to have positive real parts, and non-negative imaginary parts.

Over the Gaussian integers, 2 can be factored as $(-i)(1+i)^2$.	`In[14]:= FactorInteger[2, GaussianIntegers -> True]` `Out[14]= {{-I, 1}, {1 + I, 2}}`
Here are the factors of a Gaussian integer.	`In[15]:= FactorInteger[111 + 78 I, GaussianIntegers -> True]` `Out[15]= {{2 + I, 1}, {3, 1}, {20 + 3 I, 1}}`

PowerMod[a, b, n]	the power a^b modulo n
EulerPhi[n]	the Euler totient function $\phi(n)$
MoebiusMu[n]	the Möbius function $\mu(n)$
DivisorSigma[k, n]	the divisor function $\sigma_k(n)$
JacobiSymbol[n, m]	the Jacobi symbol $\left(\frac{n}{m}\right)$
ExtendedGCD[m, n]	the extended gcd of m and n
LatticeReduce[$\{v_1, v_2, \ldots\}$]	the reduced lattice basis for the set of integer vectors v_i

Some functions from number theory.

The **modular power function** PowerMod[a, b, n] gives exactly the same results as Mod[a^b, n]. PowerMod is much more efficient, however, because it avoids generating the full form of a^b.

You can use PowerMod not only to find positive modular powers, but also to find **modular inverses**. For negative b, PowerMod[a, b, n] gives, if possible, an integer k such that $ka^{-b} \equiv 1 \bmod n$. (Whenever such an integer exists, it is guaranteed to be unique modulo n.) If no such integer k exists, *Mathematica* leaves PowerMod unevaluated.

PowerMod is equivalent to using Power, then Mod, but is much more efficient.	`In[16]:= PowerMod[2, 13451, 3]` `Out[16]= 2`
This gives the modular inverse of 3 modulo 7.	`In[17]:= PowerMod[3, -1, 7]` `Out[17]= 5`
Multiplying the inverse by 3 modulo 7 gives 1, as expected.	`In[18]:= Mod[3 %, 7]` `Out[18]= 1`

The **Euler totient function** $\phi(n)$ gives the number of integers less than n that are relatively prime to n. An important relation (Fermat's Little Theorem) is that $a^{\phi(n)} \equiv 1 \bmod n$ for all a relatively prime to n.

The **Möbius function** $\mu(n)$ is defined to be $(-1)^k$ if n is a product of k distinct primes, and 0 if n contains a squared factor (other than 1). An important relation is the Möbius inversion formula, which states that if $g(n) = \sum_{d|n} f(d)$ for all n, then $f(n) = \sum_{d|n} \mu(d) g(n/d)$, where the sums are over all positive integers d that divide n.

The **divisor function** $\sigma_k(n)$ is the sum of the kth powers of the divisors of n. The function $\sigma_0(n)$ gives the total number of divisors of n, and is often denoted $d(n)$. The function $\sigma_1(n)$, equal to the sum of the divisors of n, is often denoted $\sigma(n)$.

For prime n, $\phi(n) = n - 1$.	*In[19]:=* **EulerPhi[17]**
	Out[19]= 16
The result is 1, as guaranteed by Fermat's Little Theorem.	*In[20]:=* **PowerMod[3, %, 17]**
	Out[20]= 1
This gives a list of all the divisors of 24.	*In[21]:=* **Divisors[24]**
	Out[21]= {1, 2, 3, 4, 6, 8, 12, 24}
$\sigma_0(n)$ gives the total number of distinct divisors of 24.	*In[22]:=* **DivisorSigma[0, 24]**
	Out[22]= 8

The **Jacobi symbol** JacobiSymbol[n, m] reduces to the **Legendre symbol** $\left(\frac{n}{m}\right)$ when m is an odd prime. The Legendre symbol is equal to zero if n is divisible by m, otherwise it is equal to 1 if n is a quadratic residue modulo the prime m, and to -1 if it is not. An integer n relatively prime to m is said to be a quadratic residue modulo m if there exists an integer k such that $k^2 \equiv n \bmod m$. The full Jacobi symbol is a product of the Legendre symbols $\left(\frac{n}{p_i}\right)$ for each of the prime factors p_i such that $m = \prod_i p_i$.

The **extended gcd** ExtendedGCD[m, n] gives a list $\{g, \{r, s\}\}$ where g is the greatest common divisor of m and n, and r and s are integers such that $g = rm + sn$. The extended gcd is important in finding integer solutions to linear (Diophantine) equations.

The first number in the list is the gcd of 105 and 196.	*In[23]:=* **ExtendedGCD[105, 196]**
	Out[23]= {7, {15, -8}}
The second pair of numbers satisfies $g = rm + sn$.	*In[24]:=* **15 105 - 8 196**
	Out[24]= 7

The lattice reduction function LatticeReduce[$\{v_1, v_2, \ldots\}$] is used in many modern number-theoretical and combinatorial algorithms. The basic idea is to think of the vectors v_k of integers as defining a mathematical *lattice*. The vector representing each point in the lattice can be written as a linear combination of the form $\sum c_k v_k$, where the c_k are integers. For a particular lattice, there are many possible choices of the "basis vectors" v_k. What LatticeReduce does is to find a reduced set of basis vectors $\bar{v}_k$ for the lattice, with certain special properties.

Three unit vectors along the three coordinate axes already form a reduced basis.	*In[25]:=* **LatticeReduce[{{1,0,0},{0,1,0},{0,0,1}}]**
	Out[25]= {{1, 0, 0}, {0, 1, 0}, {0, 0, 1}}

This gives the reduced basis for a lattice in four-dimensional space specified by three vectors.

```
In[26]:= LatticeReduce[{{1,0,0,12345}, {0,1,0,12435},
                        {0,0,1,12354}}]
Out[26]= {{-1, 0, 1, 9}, {9, 1, -10, 0}, {85, -143, 59, 6}}
```

Notice that in the last example, LatticeReduce replaces vectors that are nearly parallel by vectors that are more perpendicular. In the process, it finds some quite short basis vectors.

■ 3.2.5 Combinatorial Functions

$n!$	factorial $n(n-1)(n-2) \times ... \times 1$
$n!!$	double factorial $n(n-2)(n-4) \times ...$
Binomial[n, m]	binomial coefficient $\binom{n}{m} = \frac{n!}{m!(n-m)!}$
Multinomial[n_1, n_2, ...]	multinomial coefficient $\frac{(n_1+n_2+...)!}{n_1!n_2!...}$
BernoulliB[n]	Bernoulli number B_n
BernoulliB[n, x]	Bernoulli polynomial $B_n(x)$
EulerE[n]	Euler number E_n
EulerE[n, x]	Euler polynomial $E_n(x)$
StirlingS1[n, m]	Stirling number of the first kind $S_n^{(m)}$
StirlingS2[n, m]	Stirling number of the second kind $S_n^{(m)}$
PartitionsP[n]	the number $p(n)$ of unrestricted partitions of the integer n
PartitionsQ[n]	the number $q(n)$ of partitions of n into distinct parts
Signature[$\{i_1$, i_2, ... $\}$]	the signature of a permutation

Combinatorial functions.

The **factorial function** $n!$ gives the number of ways of ordering n objects. For non-integer n, the numerical value of $n!$ is obtained from the gamma function, discussed in Section 3.2.10.

The **binomial coefficient** Binomial[n, m] can be written as $\binom{n}{m} = \frac{n!}{m!(n-m)!}$. It gives the number of ways of choosing m objects from a collection of n objects, without regard to order. The **Catalan numbers**, which appear in various tree enumeration problems, are given in terms of binomial coefficients as $c_n = \frac{1}{n+1}\binom{2n}{n}$.

The **multinomial coefficient** Multinomial[n_1, n_2, ...], denoted $(N; n_1, n_2, ..., n_m) = \frac{N!}{n_1!n_2!..n_m!}$, gives the number of ways of partitioning N distinct objects into m sets of sizes n_i (with $N = \sum_{i=1}^{m} n_i$).

Mathematica gives the exact integer result for the factorial of an integer.	`In[1]:= 30!`
	
	`Out[1]= 265252859812191058636308480000000`

For non-integers, *Mathematica* evaluates factorials using the gamma function.	`In[2]:= 3.6!`
	
	`Out[2]= 13.3813`

Mathematica can give symbolic results for some binomial coefficients.	`In[3]:= Binomial[n, 2]` $Out[3]= \dfrac{(-1 + n)\ n}{2}$

This gives the number of ways of partitioning $6+5=11$ objects into sets containing 6 and 5 objects.	`In[4]:= Multinomial[6, 5]`
	
	`Out[4]= 462`

The result is the same as $\binom{11}{6}$.	`In[5]:= Binomial[11, 6]`
	
	`Out[5]= 462`

The **Bernoulli polynomials** BernoulliB[n, x] satisfy the generating function relation $\frac{te^{xt}}{e^t-1} = \sum_{n=0}^{\infty} B_n(x)\frac{t^n}{n!}$. The **Bernoulli numbers** BernoulliB[n] are given by $B_n = B_n(0)$. The B_n appear as the coefficients of the terms in the Euler-Maclaurin summation formula for approximating integrals.

Numerical values for Bernoulli numbers are needed in many numerical algorithms. You can always get these numerical values by first finding exact rational results using BernoulliB[n], and then applying N. The function NBernoulliB[n] gives the numerical value of B_n directly. NBernoulliB[n, p] gives the value to p-digit precision.

The **Euler polynomials** EulerE[n, x] have generating function $\frac{2e^{xt}}{e^t+1} = \sum_{n=0}^{\infty} E_n(x)\frac{t^n}{n!}$, and the **Euler numbers** EulerE[n] are given by $E_n = 2^n E_n(\frac{1}{2})$. The Euler numbers are related to the **Genocchi numbers** by $G_n = 2^{2-2n} n E_{2n-1}$.

This gives the second Bernoulli polynomial $B_2(x)$.	`In[6]:= BernoulliB[2, x]` $Out[6]= \dfrac{1}{6} - x + x^2$
You can also get Bernoulli polynomials by explicitly computing the power series for the generating function.	`In[7]:= Series[t Exp[x t]/(Exp[t] - 1), {t, 0, 4}]`

$$Out[7]= 1 + \left(-\left(\frac{1}{2}\right) + x\right) t + \left(\frac{1}{12} - \frac{x}{2} + \frac{x^2}{2}\right) t^2 +$$

$$\left(\frac{x}{12} - \frac{x^2}{4} + \frac{x^3}{6}\right) t^3 + \left(-\left(\frac{1}{720}\right) + \frac{x^2}{24} - \frac{x^3}{12} + \frac{x^4}{24}\right) t^4 + O[t]^5$$

BernoulliB[n] gives exact rational-number results for Bernoulli numbers.

In[8]:= **BernoulliB[20]**

Out[8]= $-(\dfrac{174611}{330})$

NBernoulliB[n] gives numerical values for the B_n directly.

In[9]:= **NBernoulliB[20]**

Out[9]= -529.124

Stirling numbers show up in many combinatorial enumeration problems. For **Stirling numbers of the first kind** StirlingS1[n, m], $(-1)^{n-m} S_n^{(m)}$ gives the number of permutations of n elements which contain exactly m cycles. These Stirling numbers satisfy the generating function relation $x(x-1)...(x-n+1) = \sum_{m=0}^{n} S_n^{(m)} x^m$. Note that some definitions of the $S_n^{(m)}$ differ by a factor $(-1)^{n-m}$ from what is used in *Mathematica*.

Stirling numbers of the second kind StirlingS2[n, m] give the number of ways of partitioning a set of n elements into m non-empty subsets. They satisfy the relation $x^n = \sum_{m=0}^{n} S_n^{(m)} x(x-1)...(x-m+1)$.

The **partition function** PartitionsP[n] gives the number of ways of writing the integer n as a sum of positive integers, without regard to order. PartitionsQ[n] gives the number of ways of writing n as a sum of positive integers, with the constraint that all the integers in each sum are distinct.

This gives a table of Stirling numbers of the first kind.

In[10]:= **Table[StirlingS1[5, i], {i, 5}]**

Out[10]= {24, -50, 35, -10, 1}

The Stirling numbers appear as coefficients in this product.

In[11]:= **Expand[Product[x - i, {i, 0, 4}]]**

Out[11]= $24 x - 50 x^2 + 35 x^3 - 10 x^4 + x^5$

This gives the number of partitions of 100, with and without the constraint that the terms should be distinct.

In[12]:= **{PartitionsQ[100], PartitionsP[100]}**

Out[12]= {444793, 190569292}

The partition function $p(n)$ increases asymptotically like $e^{\sqrt{n}}$. Note that you cannot simply use Plot to generate a plot of a function like PartitionsP because the function can only be evaluated with integer arguments.

In[13]:= **ListPlot[Table[**
            N[Log[PartitionsP[n]]], {n, 100}]]

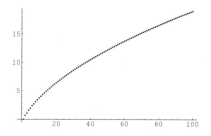

The functions in this section allow you to *enumerate* various kinds of combinatorial objects. Functions like Permutations, discussed in Section 1.8.13, allow you instead to *generate* lists of various combinations of elements.

The **signature function** `Signature[{`i_1`, `i_2`, ... }]` gives the signature of a permutation. It is equal to +1 for even permutations (composed of an even number of transpositions), and to –1 for odd permutations. The signature function can be thought of as a totally antisymmetric tensor, **Levi-Civita symbol** or **epsilon symbol**.

> `ClebschGordan[{`j_1`, `m_1`}, {`j_2`, `m_2`}, {`j`, `m`}]`
>
> Clebsch-Gordan coefficient
>
> `ThreeJSymbol[{`j_1`, `m_1`}, {`j_2`, `m_2`}, {`j_3`, `m_3`}]`
>
> Wigner 3-j symbol
>
> `SixJSymbol[{`j_1`, `j_2`, `j_3`}, {`j_4`, `j_5`, `j_6`}]`
>
> Racah 6-j symbol

Rotational coupling coefficients.

Clebsch-Gordan coefficients and n-j symbols arise in the study of angular momenta in quantum mechanics, and in other applications of the rotation group. The **Clebsch-Gordan coefficients** `ClebschGordan[{`j_1`, `m_1`}, {`j_2`, `m_2`}, {`j`, `m`}]` give the coefficients in the expansion of the quantum mechanical angular momentum state $|j, m\rangle$ in terms of products of states $|j_1, m_1\rangle |j_2, m_2\rangle$.

The **3-j symbols** or **Wigner coefficients** `ThreeJSymbol[{`j_1`, `m_1`}, {`j_2`, `m_2`}, {`j_3`, `m_3`}]` are a more symmetrical form of Clebsch-Gordan coefficients. In *Mathematica*, the Clebsch-Gordan coefficients are given in terms of 3-j symbols by $C_{m_1 m_2 m_3}^{j_1 j_2 j_3} = (-1)^{m_3+j_1-j_2} \sqrt{2j_3+1} \begin{pmatrix} j_1 & j_2 & j_3 \\ m_1 & m_2 & -m_3 \end{pmatrix}$.

The **6-j symbols** `SixJSymbol[{`j_1`, `j_2`, `j_3`}, {`j_4`, `j_5`, `j_6`}]` give the couplings of three quantum mechanical angular momentum states. The **Racah coefficients** are related by a phase to the 6-j symbols.

You can give symbolic parameters in 3-j symbols.

`In[14]:= ThreeJSymbol[{j, m}, {j+1/2, -m-1/2}, {1/2, 1/2}]`

$$Out[14]= \frac{(-1)^{-j+m}\,(j-m)\,\text{Sqrt}[1+j+m]}{\text{Sqrt}[1+2\,j]\,\text{Sqrt}[2+2\,j]\,(-j+m)}$$

■ 3.2.6 Elementary Transcendental Functions

Exp[z]	exponential function e^z
Log[z]	logarithm $\log_e(z)$
Log[b, z]	logarithm $\log_b(z)$ to base b
Sin[z], Cos[z], Tan[z], Csc[z], Sec[z], Cot[z]	
	trigonometric functions (with arguments in radians)
ArcSin[z], ArcCos[z], ArcTan[z], ArcCsc[z], ArcSec[z], ArcCot[z]	
	inverse trigonometric functions (giving results in radians)
ArcTan[x, y]	the argument of $x + iy$
Sinh[z], Cosh[z], Tanh[z], Csch[z], Sech[z], Coth[z]	
	hyperbolic functions
ArcSinh[z], ArcCosh[z], ArcTanh[z], ArcCsch[z], ArcSech[z], ArcCoth[z]	
	inverse hyperbolic functions

Elementary transcendental functions.

Mathematica gives exact results for logarithms whenever it can. Here is $\log_2 1024$.

```
In[1]:= Log[2, 1024]
Out[1]= 10
```

You can find the numerical values of mathematical functions to any precision.

```
In[2]:= N[Log[2], 40]
Out[2]= 0.6931471805599453094172321214581765680755
```

This gives a complex number result.

```
In[3]:= N[ Log[-2] ]
Out[3]= 0.693147 + 3.14159 I
```

Mathematica can evaluate logarithms with complex arguments.

```
In[4]:= N[ Log[2 + 8 I] ]
Out[4]= 2.10975 + 1.32582 I
```

The arguments of trigonometric functions are always given in radians.

```
In[5]:= Sin[Pi/2]
Out[5]= 1
```

You can convert from degrees by explicitly multiplying by the constant **Degree**.

```
In[6]:= N[ Sin[30 Degree] ]
Out[6]= 0.5
```

Here is a plot of the hyperbolic tangent function. It has a characteristic "sigmoidal" form.

$In[7]:=$ **Plot[Tanh[x], {x, -8, 8}]**

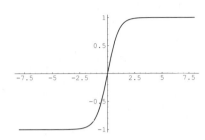

There are a number of additional trigonometric and hyperbolic functions that are sometimes used. The **versine** function is defined as $\mathrm{vers}(z) = 1 - \cos(z)$. The **haversine** is simply $\mathrm{hav}(z) = \frac{1}{2}\mathrm{vers}(z)$. The complex exponential e^{ix} is sometimes written as $\mathrm{cis}(x)$. The **gudermannian function** is defined as $\mathrm{gd}(z) = 2\tan^{-1}(e^z) - \frac{\pi}{2}$. The **inverse gudermannian** is $\mathrm{gd}^{-1}(z) = \log(\sec(z) + \tan(z))$. The gudermannian satisfies such relations as $\sinh(z) = \tan(\mathrm{gd}(x))$.

■ 3.2.7 Functions That Do Not Have Unique Values

When you ask for the square root s of a number a, you are effectively asking for the solution to the equation $s^2 = a$. This equation, however, in general has two different solutions. Both $s = 2$ and $s = -2$ are, for example, solutions to the equation $s^2 = 4$. When you evaluate the "function" $\sqrt{4}$, however, you usually want to get a single number, and so you have to choose one of these two solutions. A standard choice is that $\sqrt{x}$ should be positive for $x > 0$. This is what the *Mathematica* function Sqrt[x] does.

The need to make one choice from two solutions means that Sqrt[x] cannot be a true *inverse function* for x^2. Taking a number, squaring it, and then taking the square root can give you a different number than you started with.

$\sqrt{4}$ gives +2, not −2.

$In[1]:=$ **Sqrt[4]**

$Out[1]=$ 2

Squaring and taking the square root does not necessarily give you the number you started with.

$In[2]:=$ **Sqrt[(-2)^2]**

$Out[2]=$ 2

When you evaluate $\sqrt{-2i}$, there are again two possible answers: $-1 + i$ and $1 - i$. In this case, however, it is less clear which one to choose.

There is in fact no way to choose $\sqrt{z}$ so that it is continuous for all complex values of z. There has to be a "branch cut" – a line in the complex plane across which the function $\sqrt{z}$ is discontinuous. *Mathematica* adopts the usual convention of taking the branch cut for $\sqrt{z}$ to be along the negative real axis.

This gives $1 - i$, not $-1 + i$.

$In[3]:=$ **N[Sqrt[-2 I]]**

$Out[3]=$ 1. - 1. I

The branch cut in Sqrt along the negative real axis means that values of Sqrt[z] with z just above and below the axis are very different.

```
In[4]:= {Sqrt[-2 + 0.1 I], Sqrt[-2 - 0.1 I]}

Out[4]= {0.0353443 + 1.41466 I, 0.0353443 - 1.41466 I}
```

Their squares are nevertheless close.

```
In[5]:= %^2

Out[5]= {-2. + 0.1 I, -2. - 0.1 I}
```

The discontinuity along the negative real axis is quite clear in this three-dimensional picture of the imaginary part of the square root function.

```
In[6]:= Plot3D[ Im[Sqrt[x + I y]], {x, -4, 4}, {y, -4, 4} ]
```

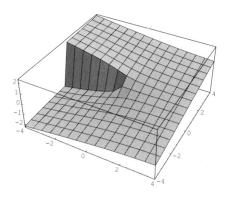

When you find an nth root using $z^{\frac{1}{n}}$, there are, in principle, n possible results. To get a single value, you have to choose a particular *principal root*. There is absolutely no guarantee that taking the nth root of an nth power will leave you with the same number.

This takes the tenth power of a complex number. The result is unique.

```
In[7]:= (2.5 + I)^10

Out[7]= -15781.2 - 12335.8 I
```

There are ten possible tenth roots. *Mathematica* chooses one of them. In this case it is not the number whose tenth power you took.

```
In[8]:= %^(1/10)

Out[8]= 2.61033 - 0.660446 I
```

There are many mathematical functions which, like roots, essentially give solutions to equations. The logarithm function, and inverse trigonometric functions, are examples. In almost all cases, there are many possible solutions to the equations. Unique "principal" values nevertheless have to be chosen for the functions. The choices cannot be made continuous over the whole complex plane. Instead, lines of discontinuity, or branch cuts, must occur. The positions of these branch cuts are often quite arbitrary. *Mathematica* makes the most standard mathematical choices for them.

Sqrt[z] and z^s	$(-\infty, 0)$ for $\mathrm{Re}\, s > 0$, $(-\infty, 0]$ for $\mathrm{Re}\, s \leq 0$ (s not an integer)	
Exp[z]	none	
Log[z]	$(-\infty, 0]$	
trigonometric functions	none	
ArcSin[z] and ArcCos[z]	$(-\infty, -1)$ and $(+1, +\infty)$	
ArcTan[z]	$(-i\infty, -i]$ and $[i, i\infty)$	
ArcCsc[z] and ArcSec[z]	$(-1, +1)$	
ArcCot[z]	$[-i, +i]$	
hyperbolic functions	none	
ArcSinh[z]	$(-i\infty, -i)$ and $(+i, +i\infty)$	
ArcCosh[z]	$(-\infty, +1)$	
ArcTanh[z]	$(-\infty, -1]$ and $[+1, +\infty)$	
ArcCsch[z]	$(-i, i)$	
ArcSech[z]	$(-\infty, 0]$ and $(+1, +\infty)$	
ArcCoth[z]	$[-1, +1]$	

Some branch-cut discontinuities in the complex plane.

ArcSin is a multiple-valued function, so there is no guarantee that it always gives the "inverse" of Sin.

```
In[9]:= ArcSin[Sin[4.5]]
Out[9]= -1.35841
```

Values of ArcSin[z] on opposite sides of the branch cut can be very different.

```
In[10]:= {ArcSin[2 + 0.1 I], ArcSin[2 - 0.1 I]}
Out[10]= {1.51316 + 1.31888 I, 1.51316 - 1.31888 I}
```

A three-dimensional picture, showing the two branch cuts for the function $\sin^{-1}(z)$.

$In[11]:=$ `Plot3D[ Im[ArcSin[x + I y]], {x, -4, 4}, {y, -4, 4}]`

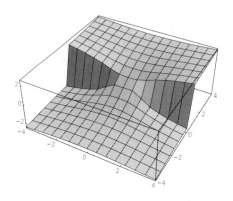

■ 3.2.8 Mathematical Constants

I	$i = \sqrt{-1}$
Infinity	∞
Pi	$\pi \simeq 3.14159$
Degree	$\pi/180$: degrees to radians conversion factor
GoldenRatio	$\phi = (1 + \sqrt{5})/2 \simeq 1.61803$
E	$e \simeq 2.71828$
EulerGamma	Euler's constant $\gamma \simeq 0.577216$
Catalan	Catalan's constant $\simeq 0.915966$

Mathematical constants.

Euler's constant EulerGamma is given by the limit $\gamma = \lim_{m\to\infty} \left(\sum_{k=1}^{m} \frac{1}{k} - \log m \right)$. It appears in many integrals, and asymptotic formulas. It is sometimes known as the **Euler-Mascheroni constant**, and denoted C.

   Catalan's constant Catalan is given by the sum $\sum_{k=0}^{\infty}(-1)^k(2k + 1)^{-2}$. It often appears in asymptotic estimates of combinatorial functions.

Mathematical constants can be evaluated to arbitrary precision.

$In[1]:=$ `N[EulerGamma, 40]`

$Out[1]=$ 0.5772156649015328606065120900824024310422

■ 3.2.9 Orthogonal Polynomials

LegendreP[*n*, *x*]	Legendre polynomials $P_n(x)$
LegendreP[*n*, *m*, *x*]	associated Legendre polynomials $P_n^m(x)$
SphericalHarmonicY[*l*, *m*, *theta*, *phi*]	
	spherical harmonics $Y_l^m(\theta, \phi)$
GegenbauerC[*n*, *m*, *x*]	Gegenbauer polynomials $C_n^m(x)$
ChebyshevT[*n*, *x*], ChebyshevU[*n*, *x*]	
	Chebyshev polynomials $T_n(x)$ and $U_n(x)$ of the first and second kinds
HermiteH[*n*, *x*]	Hermite polynomials $H_n(x)$
LaguerreL[*n*, *x*]	Laguerre polynomials $L_n(x)$
LaguerreL[*n*, *a*, *x*]	generalized Laguerre polynomials $L_n^a(x)$
JacobiP[*n*, *a*, *b*, *x*]	Jacobi polynomials $P_n^{(a,b)}(x)$

Orthogonal polynomials.

Legendre polynomials LegendreP[*n*, *x*] arise in studies of systems with three-dimensional spherical symmetry. They satisfy the differential equation $(1 - x^2)\frac{d^2y}{dx^2} - 2x\frac{dy}{dx} + n(n+1)y = 0$, and the orthogonality relation $\int_{-1}^{1} P_m(x)P_n(x)\,dx = 0$ for $m \neq n$.

The **associated Legendre polynomials** LegendreP[*n*, *m*, *x*] are obtained from derivatives of the Legendre polynomials according to $P_n^m(x) = (-1)^m(1 - x^2)^{m/2}\frac{d^m}{dx^m}P_n(x)$. Notice that for odd integers $m \le n$, the $P_n^m(x)$ contain powers of $\sqrt{1 - x^2}$, and are therefore not strictly polynomials. The $P_n^m(x)$ reduce to $P_n(x)$ when $m = 0$.

The **spherical harmonics** SphericalHarmonicY[*l*, *m*, *theta*, *phi*] are related to associated Legendre polynomials. They satisfy the orthogonality relation $\int Y_l^m(\theta, \phi)Y_{l'}^{m'}(\theta, \phi)\,d\Omega = 0$ for $l \neq l'$ or $m \neq m'$, where $d\Omega$ represents integration over the surface of the unit sphere.

This gives the algebraic form of the Legendre polynomial $P_6(x)$.

```
In[1]:= LegendreP[6, x]
```

$$Out[1]= \frac{-5 + 105\ x^2 - 315\ x^4 + 231\ x^6}{16}$$

The integral $\int_{-1}^{1} P_5(x)P_6(x)\,dx$ gives zero by virtue of the orthogonality of the Legendre polynomials.

```
In[2]:= Integrate[LegendreP[5,x] LegendreP[6,x], {x, -1, 1}]
Out[2]= 0
```

Integrating the square of a single Legendre polynomial gives a non-zero result.

$In[3]:=$ `Integrate[LegendreP[6, x]^2, {x, -1, 1}]`

$Out[3]= \dfrac{2}{13}$

High-degree Legendre polynomials oscillate rapidly.

$In[4]:=$ `Plot[LegendreP[10, x], {x, -1, 1}]`

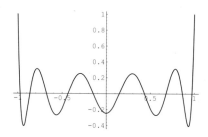

The associated Legendre "polynomials" contain pieces proportional to $\sqrt{1-x^2}$.

$In[5]:=$ `LegendreP[6, 3, x]`

$Out[5]= \dfrac{(1 - x^2)^{3/2} \ (945 \ x - 3465 \ x^3)}{2}$

Section 3.2.10 discusses the generalization of Legendre polynomials to Legendre functions, which can have non-integer degrees.

$In[6]:=$ `LegendreP[6.1, 0]`

$Out[6]= -0.306319$

Gegenbauer polynomials `GegenbauerC[n, m, x]` can be viewed as generalizations of the Legendre polynomials to systems with $(m + 2)$-dimensional spherical symmetry. They are sometimes known as **ultraspherical polynomials**.

Series of Chebyshev polynomials are often used in making numerical approximations to functions. The **Chebyshev polynomials of the first kind** `ChebyshevT[n, x]` are defined by $T_n(\cos \theta) = \cos(n \theta)$. They are normalized so that $T_n(1) = 1$. They satisfy the orthogonality relation $\int_{-1}^{1} T_m(x) T_n(x)(1-x^2)^{-\frac{1}{2}} \, dx = 0$ for $m \neq n$. The $T_n(x)$ also satisfy an orthogonality relation under summation at discrete points in x corresponding to the roots of $T_n(x)$.

The **Chebyshev polynomials of the second kind** `ChebyshevU[n, z]` are defined by $U_n(\cos \theta) = \frac{\sin(n+1)\theta}{\sin \theta}$. With this definition, $U_n(1) = n + 1$. The U_n satisfy the orthogonality relation $\int_{-1}^{1} U_m(x) U_n(x)(1 - x^2)^{\frac{1}{2}} \, dx = 0$ for $m \neq n$.

The name "Chebyshev" is a transliteration from the Cyrillic alphabet; several other English spellings, such as "Tschebyscheff", are sometimes used.

Hermite polynomials `HermiteH[n, x]` arise as the quantum-mechanical wave functions for a harmonic oscillator. They satisfy the differential equation $\frac{d^2y}{dx^2} - 2x\frac{dy}{dx} + 2ny = 0$, and the orthogonality relation $\int_{-\infty}^{\infty} H_m(x)H_n(x)e^{-x^2} \, dx = 0$ for $m \neq n$. An alternative form of Hermite polynomials sometimes used is $He_n(x) = H_n(\frac{x}{\sqrt{2}})$ (a different overall normalization of the $He_n(x)$ is also sometimes used).

The Hermite polynomials are related to the **parabolic cylinder functions** or **Weber functions** $D_n(x)$ by $D_n(x) = e^{-x^2/4}H_n(\frac{x}{\sqrt{2}})$.

This gives the density for an excited state of a quantum-mechanical harmonic oscillator. The average of the wiggles is roughly the classical physics result.

In[7]:= **Plot[(HermiteH[6, x] Exp[-x^2/2])^2, {x, -6, 6}]**

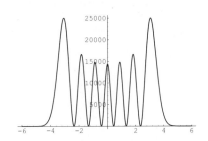

Generalized Laguerre polynomials LaguerreL[n, a, x] are related to hydrogen atom wave functions in quantum mechanics. They satisfy the differential equation $x\frac{d^2y}{dx^2} + (a+1-x)\frac{dy}{dx} + ny = 0$, and the orthogonality relation $\int_0^\infty L_m^a(x)L_n^a(x)x^a e^{-x}\,dx = 0$ for $m \neq n$. The **Laguerre polynomials** LaguerreL[n, x] correspond to the special case $a = 0$.

Jacobi polynomials JacobiP[n, a, b, x] occur in studies of the rotation group, particularly in quantum mechanics. They satisfy the orthogonality relation $\int_{-1}^1 P_m^{(a,b)}(x)P_n^{(a,b)}(x)(1-x)^a(1+x)^b\,dx = 0$ for $m \neq n$. Legendre, Gegenbauer and Chebyshev polynomials can all be viewed as special cases of Jacobi polynomials. The Jacobi polynomials are sometimes given in the alternative form $G_n(p, q, x) = \frac{n!\Gamma(n+p)}{\Gamma(2n+p)}P_n^{(p-q,q-1)}(2x-1)$.

You can get formulas for generalized Laguerre polynomials with arbitrary values of a.

In[8]:= **LaguerreL[2, a, x]**

$$Out[8]= \frac{2 + 3\,a + a^2 - 4\,x - 2\,a\,x + x^2}{2}$$

■ 3.2.10 Special Functions

AiryAi[z] and AiryBi[z]   Airy functions Ai(z) and Bi(z)

AiryAiPrime[z] and AiryBiPrime[z]

derivatives of Airy functions $Ai'(z)$ and $Bi'(z)$

BesselJ[n, z] and BesselY[n, z]

Bessel functions $J_n(z)$ and $Y_n(z)$

BesselI[n, z] and BesselK[n, z]

modified Bessel functions $I_n(z)$ and $K_n(z)$

Beta[a, b]   Euler beta function $B(a, b)$

Beta[z, a, b]   incomplete beta function $B_z(a, b)$

CosIntegral[z]   cosine integral function Ci(z)

Erf[z] and Erfc[z]   error function erf(z) and complementary error function erfc(z)

Erf[z_0, z_1]   generalized error function $erf(z_1) - erf(z_0)$

ExpIntegralE[n, z]   exponential integral $E_n(z)$

ExpIntegralEi[z]   exponential integral Ei(z)

Gamma[z]   Euler gamma function $\Gamma(z)$

Gamma[a, z]   incomplete gamma function $\Gamma(a, z)$

Gamma[a, z_0, z_1]   generalized incomplete gamma function $\Gamma(a, z_0) - \Gamma(a, z_1)$

Hypergeometric0F1[a, z]   hypergeometric function $_0F_1(; a; z)$

Hypergeometric1F1[a, b, z]   Kummer confluent hypergeometric function $_1F_1(a; b; z)$

HypergeometricU[a, b, z]   confluent hypergeometric function $U(a, b, z)$

Hypergeometric2F1[a, b, c, z]

hypergeometric function $_2F_1(a, b; c; z)$

LegendreP[n, z], LegendreQ[n, z]

Legendre functions $P_n(z)$ and $Q_n(z)$ of the first and second kinds

LegendreP[n, m, z], LegendreQ[n, m, z]

associated Legendre functions $P_n^m(z)$ and $Q_n^m(z)$

Special functions, part one.

LerchPhi[z, s, a]	Lerch's transcendent $\Phi(z, s, a)$
LogIntegral[z]	logarithmic integral li(z)
Pochhammer[a, n]	Pochhammer symbol $(a)_n$
PolyGamma[z]	digamma function $\psi(z)$
PolyGamma[n, z]	n^{th} derivative of the digamma function $\psi^{(n)}(z)$
PolyLog[n, z]	polylogarithm function Li$_n(z)$
RiemannSiegelTheta[t] and RiemannSiegelZ[t]	
	Riemann-Siegel functions $\vartheta(t)$ and $Z(t)$
SinIntegral[z]	sine integral function Si(z)
Zeta[s]	Riemann zeta function $\zeta(s)$
Zeta[s, a]	generalized Riemann zeta function $\zeta(s, a)$

Special functions, part two.

Mathematica includes all the common special functions of mathematical physics. We will discuss each of the functions in turn. You can find more extensive discussions in various handbooks, such as *Handbook of Mathematical Functions*, edited by M. Abramowitz and I. Stegun (Dover, 1965), *Formulas and Theorems for the Special Functions of Mathematical Physics*, by W. Magnus, F. Oberhettinger and R. P. Soni (Third edition, Springer-Verlag, 1966), or *Encyclopedic Dictionary of Mathematics*, Volume IV, edited by K. Itô (Second edition, MIT Press, 1987).

There are often several conflicting definitions of any particular special function in the literature. When you use a special function in *Mathematica*, you should look at the definition given below to make sure it is what you want.

Mathematica gives exact results for some values of special functions.

```
In[1]:= Gamma[15/2]
```
$$Out[1]= \frac{135135 \text{ Sqrt}[Pi]}{128}$$

No exact result is known here.

```
In[2]:= Gamma[15/7]
```
$$Out[2]= \text{Gamma}[\frac{15}{7}]$$

A numerical result, to arbitrary precision, can nevertheless be found.

```
In[3]:= N[%, 40]
```
```
Out[3]= 1.069071500448624397994137689702693267367
```

You can give complex arguments to special functions.

```
In[4]:= Gamma[3 + 4I] //N
```
```
Out[4]= 0.00522554 - 0.172547 I
```

Special functions automatically get applied to each element in a list.	$In[5]:=$ `Gamma[{3/2, 5/2, 7/2}]`

$$Out[5]= \{\frac{\text{Sqrt[Pi]}}{2}, \frac{3 \text{ Sqrt[Pi]}}{4}, \frac{15 \text{ Sqrt[Pi]}}{8}\}$$

Mathematica knows some analytical properties of special functions, such as derivatives.

$In[6]:=$ `D[Gamma[x], {x, 2}]`

$$Out[6]= \text{Gamma[x] PolyGamma[x]}^2 + \text{Gamma[x] PolyGamma[1, x]}$$

You can use `FindRoot` to find roots of special functions.

$In[7]:=$ `FindRoot[ BesselJ[0, x], {x, 1} ]`

$Out[7]=$ `{x -> 2.40483}`

Special functions in *Mathematica* can usually be evaluated for arbitrary complex values of their arguments. Often, however, the defining relations given below apply only for some special choices of arguments. In these cases, the full function corresponds to a suitable extension or "analytic continuation" of these defining relations. Thus, for example, integral representations of functions are valid only when the integral exists, but the functions themselves can usually be defined elsewhere by analytic continuation.

As a simple example of how the domain of a function can be extended, consider the function represented by the sum $\sum_{k=0}^{\infty} x^k$. This sum converges only when $|x| < 1$. Nevertheless, it is easy to show analytically that for any x, the complete function is equal to $\frac{1}{1-x}$. Using this form, you can easily find a value of the function for any x, at least so long as $x \neq 1$.

Gamma and Related Functions

The **Euler gamma function** `Gamma[z]` is defined by the integral $\Gamma(z) = \int_0^{\infty} t^{z-1} e^{-t} dt$. For positive integer n, $\Gamma(n) = (n-1)!$. $\Gamma(z)$ can be viewed as a generalization of the factorial function, valid for complex arguments z.

There are some computations, particularly in number theory, where the logarithm of the gamma function often appears. For positive real arguments, you can evaluate this simply as `Log[Gamma[z]]`. For complex arguments, however, this form yields spurious discontinuities. *Mathematica* therefore includes the separate function `LogGamma[z]`, which yields the **logarithm of the gamma function** with a single branch cut along the negative real axis.

The **Euler beta function** `Beta[a, b]` is $B(a, b) = \frac{\Gamma(a)\Gamma(b)}{\Gamma(a+b)} = \int_0^1 t^{a-1}(1-t)^{b-1} dt$.

The **Pochhammer symbol** or **rising factorial** `Pochhammer[a, n]` is $(a)_n = \frac{\Gamma(a+n)}{\Gamma(a)}$. It often appears in series expansions for hypergeometric functions. Note that the Pochhammer symbol has a definite value even when the gamma functions which appear in its definition are infinite.

The **incomplete gamma function** `Gamma[a, z]` is defined by the integral $\Gamma(a, z) = \int_z^{\infty} t^{a-1} e^{-t} dt$. *Mathematica* includes a generalized incomplete gamma function `Gamma[a, z_0, z_1]` defined as $\int_{z_0}^{z_1} t^{a-1} e^{-t} dt$. The alternative incomplete gamma function $\gamma(a, z)$ can therefore be obtained in *Mathematica* as `Gamma[a, 0, z]`.

The **incomplete beta function** Beta[z, a, b] is given by $B_z(a,b) = \int_0^z t^{a-1}(1-t)^{b-1}dt$. Notice that in the incomplete beta function, the parameter z is an *upper* limit of integration, and appears as the *first* argument of the function. In the incomplete gamma function, on the other hand, z is a *lower* limit of integration, and appears as the *second* argument of the function.

The incomplete beta and gamma functions, and their inverses, are common in statistics.

In certain cases, it is convenient not to compute the incomplete beta and gamma functions on their own, but instead to compute *regularized forms* in which these functions are divided by complete beta and gamma functions. *Mathematica* includes the **regularized incomplete beta function** BetaRegularized[z, a, b] defined for most arguments by $I(z,a,b) = B(z,a,b)/B(a,b)$, but taking into account singular cases. *Mathematica* also includes the **regularized incomplete gamma function** GammaRegularized[a, z] defined by $Q(a,z) = \Gamma(a,z)/\Gamma(a)$, with singular cases taken into account.

Derivatives of the gamma function often appear in summing rational series. The **digamma function** PolyGamma[z] is the logarithmic derivative of the gamma function, given by $\psi(z) = \frac{\Gamma'(z)}{\Gamma(z)}$. For integer arguments, the digamma function satisfies the relation $\psi(n) = -\gamma + \sum_{k=1}^{n-1} \frac{1}{k}$, where γ is Euler's constant (EulerGamma in *Mathematica*).

The **polygamma functions** PolyGamma[n, z] are given by $\psi^{(n)}(z) = \frac{d^n}{dz^n}\psi(z)$. Notice that the digamma function corresponds to $\psi^{(0)}(z)$: $\psi^{(n)}(z)$ is the $(n+1)^{th}$, not the nth, logarithmic derivative of the gamma function. The polygamma functions satisfy the relation $\psi^{(n)}(z) = (-1)^{n+1}n!\sum_{k=0}^{\infty} \frac{1}{(z+k)^{n+1}}$.

Many exact results for gamma and polygamma functions are built into *Mathematica*.

```
In[8]:= PolyGamma[6]

Out[8]= 137
        --- - EulerGamma
        60
```

Here is a contour plot of the gamma function in the complex plane.

```
In[9]:= ContourPlot[ Abs[Gamma[x + I y]], {x, -3, 3},
                {y, -2, 2}, PlotPoints->40 ]
```

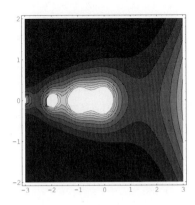

Zeta and Related Functions

The **Riemann zeta function** Zeta[s] is defined by the relation $\zeta(s) = \sum_{k=1}^{\infty} k^{-s}$ (for $s > 1$). Zeta functions with integer arguments arise in evaluating various sums and integrals. *Mathematica* gives exact results when possible for zeta functions with integer arguments.

There is an analytic continuation of $\zeta(s)$ for arbitrary complex $s \neq 1$. The zeta function for complex arguments is central to number-theoretical studies of the distribution of primes. Of particular importance are the values on the critical line $\operatorname{Re} s = \frac{1}{2}$.

In studying $\zeta(\frac{1}{2} + it)$, it is often convenient to define the two analytic **Riemann-Siegel functions** RiemannSiegelZ[t] and RiemannSiegelTheta[z] according to $Z(t) = e^{i\vartheta(t)}\zeta(\frac{1}{2}+it)$ and $\vartheta(t) = \operatorname{Im} \log \Gamma(\frac{1}{4} + i\frac{t}{2}) - t\frac{\log \pi}{2}$ (for t real). Note that the Riemann-Siegel functions are both real as long as t is real.

The **generalized Riemann zeta function** or **Hurwitz zeta function** Zeta[s, a] is given by $\zeta(s,a) = \sum_{k=0}^{\infty}(k+a)^{-s}$, where any term with $k + a = 0$ is excluded.

Mathematica gives exact results for $\zeta(2n)$.

```
In[10]:= Zeta[6]
```

$$Out[10] = \frac{Pi^6}{945}$$

Here is a three-dimensional picture of the Riemann zeta function in the complex plane.

```
In[11]:= Plot3D[ Abs[ Zeta[x + I y] ], {x, -3, 3},
            {y, 2, 35}, PlotPoints->30 ]
```

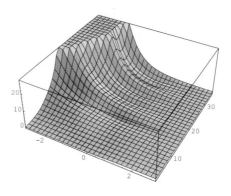

This is a plot of the absolute value of the Riemann zeta function on the critical line $\operatorname{Re} z = \frac{1}{2}$. You can see the first few zeros of the zeta function.

$In[12]:=$ **Plot[Abs[Zeta[1/2 + I y]], {y, 0, 40}]**

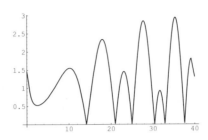

The **polylogarithm functions** PolyLog[n, z] are given by $\mathrm{Li}_n(z) = \sum_{k=1}^{\infty} \frac{z^k}{k^n}$. The **dilogarithm** PolyLog[2, z] satisfies $\mathrm{Li}_2(z) = \int_z^0 \frac{\log(1-t)}{t} dt$. $\mathrm{Li}_2(1-z)$ is sometimes known as **Spence's integral**. Polylogarithms crop up in Feynman diagram integrals in elementary particle physics. The polylogarithm function is sometimes known as **Jonquière's function**.

The **Lerch transcendent** LerchPhi[z, s, a] is a generalization of the zeta and polylogarithm functions, given by $\Phi(z,s,a) = \sum_{k=0}^{\infty} \frac{z^k}{(a+k)^s}$, where any term with $k+a=0$ is excluded. Many sums of reciprocal powers can be expressed in terms of the Lerch transcendent. For example, the **Catalan beta function** $\beta(s) = \sum_{k=0}^{\infty} (-1)^k (2k+1)^{-s}$ can be obtained as $2^{-s}\Phi(-1,s,\frac{1}{2})$.

The Lerch transcendent is related to integrals of the **Fermi-Dirac** distribution in statistical mechanics by $\int_0^{\infty} \frac{k^s}{e^{k-\mu}+1} dk = e^{\mu}\Gamma(s+1)\Phi(-e^{\mu},s+1,1)$.

The Lerch transcendent can also be used to evaluate **Dirichlet L series** which appear in number theory. The basic L series has the form $L(s,\chi) = \sum_{k=1}^{\infty} \chi(k)k^{-s}$, where the "character" $\chi(k)$ is an integer function with period m. L series of this kind can be written as sums of Lerch functions with z a power of $e^{2\pi i/m}$.

LerchPhi[z, s, a, DoublyInfinite->True] gives the doubly infinite sum $\sum_{k=-\infty}^{\infty} \frac{z^k}{(a+k)^s}$.

Exponential Integral and Related Functions

Mathematica has two forms of exponential integral: ExpIntegralE and ExpIntegralEi.

The **exponential integral function** ExpIntegralE[n, z] is defined by $E_n = \int_1^{\infty} \frac{e^{-zt}}{t^n} dt$.

The second **exponential integral function** ExpIntegralEi[z] is defined by $\mathrm{Ei}(z) = -\int_{-z}^{\infty} \frac{e^{-t}}{t} dt$ (for $z > 0$), where the principal value of the integral is taken.

The **logarithmic integral function** LogIntegral[z] is given by $\mathrm{li}(z) = \int_0^z \frac{dt}{\log t}$ (for $z > 1$), where the principal value of the integral is taken. $\mathrm{li}(z)$ is central to the study of the distribution of primes in number theory. The logarithmic integral function is sometimes also denoted by $\mathrm{Li}(z)$. In some number-theoretical applications, $\mathrm{li}(z)$ is defined as $\int_2^z \frac{dt}{\log t}$, with no principal value taken. This differs from the definition used in *Mathematica* by the constant $\mathrm{li}(2)$.

The **sine and cosine integral functions** SinIntegral[z] and CosIntegral[z] are defined by $\text{Si}(z) = \int_0^z \frac{\sin(t)}{t} dt$ and $\text{Ci}(z) = -\int_z^\infty \frac{\cos(t)}{t} dt$.

Error Function

The **error function** Erf[z] is the integral of the Gaussian distribution, given by $\text{erf}(z) = \frac{2}{\sqrt{\pi}} \int_0^z e^{-t^2} dt$. The **complementary error function** Erfc[z] is given simply by $\text{erfc}(z) = 1 - \text{erf}(z)$. The generalized error function Erf[z_0, z_1] is defined by the integral $\frac{2}{\sqrt{\pi}} \int_{z_0}^{z_1} e^{-t^2} dt$. The error function is central to many calculations in statistics.

Closely related to the error function are the **Fresnel integrals**, $C(z) = \int_0^z \cos\left(\frac{\pi t^2}{2}\right) dt$ and $S(z) = \int_0^z \sin\left(\frac{\pi t^2}{2}\right) dt$. These are given in terms of the error function by $C(z) + iS(z) = \frac{1+i}{2} \text{erf}(\frac{\sqrt{\pi}}{2}(1-i)z)$ (for z real). Fresnel integrals occur in diffraction theory.

Bessel Functions

The **Bessel functions** BesselJ[n, z] and BesselY[n, z] are linearly independent solutions to the differential equation $z^2 \frac{d^2 y}{dz^2} + z \frac{dy}{dz} + (z^2 - n^2)y = 0$. For integer n, the $J_n(z)$ are regular at $z = 0$, while the $Y_n(z)$ have a logarithmic divergence at $z = 0$.

Bessel functions arise in solving differential equations for systems with cylindrical symmetry.

$J_n(z)$ is often called the **Bessel function of the first kind**, or simply *the* Bessel function. $Y_n(z)$ is referred to as the **Bessel function of the second kind**, the **Weber function**, or the **Neumann function** (denoted $N_n(z)$).

The **Hankel functions** (or **Bessel functions of the third kind**) $H_n^{(1,2)}(z) = J_n(z) \pm iY_n(z)$ give an alternative pair of solutions to the Bessel differential equation.

In studying systems with spherical symmetry, **spherical Bessel functions** arise, defined by $f_n(z) = \sqrt{\frac{\pi}{2z}} F_{n+\frac{1}{2}}(z)$, where f and F can be j and J, y and Y, or h^i and H^i. For integer n, *Mathematica* gives exact algebraic formulas for spherical Bessel functions.

The **modified Bessel functions** BesselI[n, z] and BesselK[n, z] are solutions to the differential equation $z^2 \frac{d^2 y}{dz^2} + z \frac{dy}{dz} - (z^2 + n^2)y = 0$. For integer n, $I_n(z)$ is regular at $z = 0$; $K_n(z)$ always has a logarithmic divergence at $z = 0$. The $I_n(z)$ are sometimes known as **hyperbolic Bessel functions**.

Particularly in electrical engineering, one often defines the **Kelvin functions**, according to $\text{ber}_n(z) + i\,\text{bei}_n(z) = e^{n\pi i} J_n(ze^{-\pi i/4})$, $\text{ker}_n(z) + i\,\text{kei}_n(z) = e^{-n\pi i/2} K_n(ze^{\pi i/4})$.

The **Airy functions** AiryAi[z] and AiryBi[z] are the two independent solutions $\text{Ai}(z)$ and $\text{Bi}(z)$ to the differential equation $\frac{d^2 y}{dz^2} - zy = 0$. $\text{Ai}(z)$ tends to zero for large positive z, while $\text{Bi}(z)$ increases unboundedly. The Airy functions are related to modified Bessel functions with one-third-integer orders. The Airy functions often appear as the solutions to boundary value problems in electromagnetic theory and quantum mechanics. In many cases the **derivatives of the Airy functions** AiryAiPrime[z] and AiryBiPrime[z] also appear.

Here is a plot of $J_0(\sqrt{x})$. This is a curve that an idealized chain hanging from one end can form when you wiggle it.

In[13]:= Plot[BesselJ[0, Sqrt[x]], {x, 0, 50}]

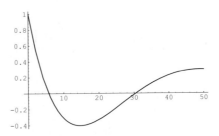

Mathematica generates explicit formulas for half-integer-order Bessel functions.

In[14]:= BesselK[3/2, x]

$$Out[14]= \frac{(1 + \frac{1}{x})\, \text{Sqrt}[\frac{Pi}{2\,x}]}{E^x}$$

The Airy function plotted here gives the quantum-mechanical amplitude for a particle in a potential that increases linearly from left to right. The amplitude is exponentially damped in the classically inaccessible region on the right.

In[15]:= Plot[AiryAi[x], {x, -10, 10}]

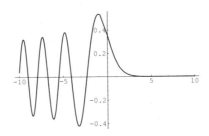

Legendre and Related Functions

The **Legendre functions** and **associated Legendre functions** satisfy the differential equation $(1 - z^2)\frac{d^2y}{dz^2} - 2z\frac{dy}{dz} + [(n(n + 1) - \frac{m^2}{1-z^2}]y = 0$. The Legendre functions of the first kind, LegendreP[n, z] and LegendreP[n, m, z], reduce to Legendre polynomials when n and m are integers. The **Legendre functions of the second kind** LegendreQ[n, z] and LegendreQ[n, m, z] give the second linearly independent solution to the differential equation. They have logarithmic singularities at $z = \pm 1$. The $P_n(z)$ and $Q_n(z)$ solve the differential equation with $m = 0$.

In general, both $P_n^m(z)$ and $Q_n^m(z)$ have a branch cut along the real axis running from $-\infty$ to $+1$. For integer n and even m, however, $P_n^m(z)$ is a Legendre polynomial, and has a unique value for all z.

It is often necessary to find values for Legendre functions with z a real number in the range $-1 < z < +1$. In this case, the different values from the two sides of the branch cut are conventionally combined to give a unique result using the formulas $P_n^m(x) = [e^{im\pi/2}P_n^m(x+i0) + e^{-im\pi/2}P_n^m(x-i0)]/2$ and $Q_n^m(x) = e^{-im\pi}[e^{-im\pi/2}Q_n^m(x+i0) + e^{im\pi/2}Q_n^m(x-i0)]/2$.

The two versions of Legendre functions are distinguished by settings for the option `LegendreType`. `LegendreType->Complex` gives Legendre functions with a branch cut from $-\infty$ to $+1$. The default setting `LegendreType->Real` combines values from the two sides of the branch cut to give functions with branch cuts from $-\infty$ to -1, and $+1$ to $+\infty$. These functions are continuous on the interval $(-1, 1)$.

The Legendre functions crop up in studies of quantum-mechanical scattering processes.

Toroidal functions or **ring functions**, which arise in studying systems with toroidal symmetry, can be expressed in terms of the Legendre functions $P_{\nu-\frac{1}{2}}^\mu(\cosh\eta)$ and $Q_{\nu-\frac{1}{2}}^\mu(\cosh\eta)$.

Conical functions can be expressed in terms of $P_{-\frac{1}{2}+ip}^\mu(\cos\theta)$ and $Q_{-\frac{1}{2}+ip}^\mu(\cos\theta)$.

When you use the function `LegendreP[n, x]` with an integer n, you get a Legendre polynomial. If you take n to be an arbitrary complex number, you get, in general, a Legendre function.

In the same way, you can use the functions `GegenbauerC` and so on with arbitrary complex indices to get **Gegenbauer functions, Chebyshev functions, Hermite functions, Jacobi functions** and **Laguerre functions**.

Confluent Hypergeometric Functions

Many of the special functions that we have discussed so far can be viewed as special cases of the **confluent hypergeometric function** `Hypergeometric1F1[a, b, z]`.

The confluent hypergeometric function can be obtained from the series expansion $_1F_1(a;b;z) = 1 + \frac{az}{b} + \frac{a(a+1)}{b(b+1)}\frac{z^2}{2!} + \dots = \sum_{k=0}^\infty \frac{(a)_k}{(b)_k}\frac{z^k}{k!}$. Some special results are obtained when a and b are both integers. If $a < 0$, and either $b > 0$ or $b < a$, the series yields a polynomial with a finite number of terms. If integer $b \leq 0$, $_1F_1(a;b;z)$ is undefined.

Among the functions that can be obtained from $_1F_1$ are the Bessel functions, error function, incomplete gamma function, and Hermite and Laguerre polynomials.

The function $_1F_1(a;b;z)$ is sometimes denoted $\Phi(a;b;z)$ or $M(a,b,z)$. It is often known as the **Kummer function**.

The $_1F_1$ function can be written in the integral representation $_1F_1(a;b;z) = \frac{\Gamma(b)}{\Gamma(b-a)\Gamma(a)}\int_0^1 e^{zt}t^{a-1}(1-t)^{b-a-1}\,dt$.

The $_1F_1$ confluent hypergeometric function is a solution to Kummer's differential equation $z\frac{d^2y}{dz^2} + (b-z)\frac{dy}{dz} - ay = 0$, with the boundary conditions $_1F_1(a;b;0) = 1$ and $\frac{\partial}{\partial z}{_1F_1}(a;b;z)|_{z=0} = \frac{a}{b}$.

The function `HypergeometricU[a, b, z]` gives a second linearly independent solution to Kummer's equation. This function behaves like z^{1-b} for small z. It has a branch cut along the negative real axis in the complex z plane.

The function $U(a,b,z)$ has the integral representation $U(a,b,z) = \frac{1}{\Gamma(a)}\int_0^\infty e^{-zt}t^{a-1}(1+t)^{b-a-1}\,dt$.

$U(a, b, z)$, like ${}_1F_1(a; b; z)$, is sometimes known as the **Kummer function**, and is sometimes denoted by Ψ.

The **Whittaker functions** give an alternative pair of solutions to Kummer's differential equation. The Whittaker function $M_{\kappa,\mu}$ is related to ${}_1F_1$ by $M_{\kappa,\mu}(z) = e^{-z/2} z^{\frac{1}{2}+\mu} {}_1F_1(\frac{1}{2} + \mu - \kappa; 1 + 2\mu; z)$. The second Whittaker function $W_{\kappa,\mu}$ obeys the same relation, with ${}_1F_1$ replaced by U.

The **parabolic cylinder functions** are related to Whittaker functions by $D_\nu(z) = 2^{\frac{1}{4}+\frac{\nu}{2}} z^{-\frac{1}{2}} W_{\frac{1}{4}+\frac{\nu}{2}, -\frac{1}{4}}(\frac{z^2}{2})$. For integer ν, the parabolic cylinder functions reduce to Hermite polynomials.

The **Coulomb wave functions** are also special cases of the confluent hypergeometric function. Coulomb wave functions give solutions to the radial Schrödinger equation in the Coulomb potential of a point nucleus. The regular Coulomb wave function is given by $F_L(\eta, \rho) = C_L(\eta) \rho^{L+1} e^{-i\rho} {}_1F_1(L + 1 - i\eta; 2L + 2; 2i\rho)$, where $C_L(\eta) = [2^L e^{-\pi\eta/2} | \Gamma(L + 1 + i\eta) |] / \Gamma(2L + 2)$.

Other special cases of the confluent hypergeometric function include the **Toronto functions** $T(m, n, r)$, **Poisson-Charlier polynomials** $\rho_n(\nu, x)$, **Cunningham functions** $\omega_{n,m}(x)$ and **Bateman functions** $k_\nu(x)$.

A limiting form of the confluent hypergeometric function which often appears is `HypergeometricOF1[a, z]`. This function is obtained as the limit ${}_0F_1(; a; z) = \lim_{q \to \infty} {}_1F_1(q; a; \frac{z}{q})$.

The ${}_0F_1$ function has the series expansion ${}_0F_1(; a; z) = \sum_{k=0}^{\infty} \frac{z^k}{(a)_k k!}$ and satisfies the differential equation $z \frac{d^2y}{dz^2} + a \frac{dy}{dz} - y = 0$.

Bessel functions of the first kind can be expressed in terms of the ${}_0F_1$ function.

Hypergeometric Functions

The **hypergeometric function** `Hypergeometric2F1[a, b, c, z]` has series expansion ${}_2F_1(a, b; c; z) = \sum_{k=0}^{\infty} \frac{(a)_k (b)_k}{(c)_k} \frac{z^k}{k!}$. The function is a solution of the hypergeometric differential equation $z(1 - z) \frac{d^2y}{dz^2} + [c - (a + b + 1)z] \frac{dy}{dz} - aby = 0$.

The hypergeometric function can also be written as an integral: ${}_2F_1(a, b; c; z) = \frac{\Gamma(c)}{\Gamma(b)\Gamma(c-b)} \int_0^1 t^{b-1}(1-t)^{c-b-1}(1 - tz)^{-a} \, dt$.

The hypergeometric function is also sometimes denoted by F, and is known as the **Gauss series** or the **Kummer series**.

The Legendre functions, and the functions which give generalizations of other orthogonal polynomials, can be expressed in terms of the hypergeometric function. Complete elliptic integrals can also be expressed in terms of the ${}_2F_1$ function.

The **Riemann P function**, which gives solutions to Riemann's differential equation, is also a ${}_2F_1$ function.

■3.2.11 Elliptic Integrals and Elliptic Functions

EllipticK[m]	complete elliptic integral of the first kind $K(m)$
EllipticF[phi, m]	elliptic integral of the first kind $F(\phi\|m)$
EllipticE[m]	complete elliptic integral of the second kind $E(m)$
EllipticE[phi, m]	elliptic integral of the second kind $E(\phi\|m)$
JacobiZeta[phi, m]	Jacobi zeta function $Z(\phi\|m)$
EllipticPi[n, m]	complete elliptic integral of the third kind $\Pi(n\|m)$
EllipticPi[n, phi, m]	elliptic integral of the third kind $\Pi(n;\phi\|m)$
JacobiAmplitude[u, m]	amplitude function $\mathrm{am}(u\|m)$
JacobiSN[u, m], JacobiCN[u, m], etc.	
	Jacobi elliptic functions $\mathrm{sn}(u\|m)$, etc.
InverseJacobiSN[v, m], InverseJacobiCN[v, m], etc.	
	inverse Jacobi elliptic functions $\mathrm{sn}^{-1}(v\|m)$, etc.
EllipticTheta[a, u, q]	elliptic theta functions $\theta_a(u\|q)$ ($a=1,...,4$)
EllipticLog[{x, y}, {a, b}]	generalized logarithm associated with the elliptic curve $y^2 = x^3 + ax^2 + bx$
EllipticExp[u, {a, b}]	generalized exponential associated with the elliptic curve $y^2 = x^3 + ax^2 + bx$
ArithmeticGeometricMean[a, b]	
	the arithmetic-geometric mean of a and b

Elliptic integrals and elliptic functions.

You should be very careful about the arguments you give to elliptic integrals and elliptic functions in *Mathematica*. There are several incompatible conventions in common mathematical use. You will often have to convert from a particular convention to the one that *Mathematica* uses.

In mathematical usage, the different argument conventions are sometimes distinguished by the use of separators other than commas between the arguments. Often, however, there is no clue about which notation is used, other than perhaps the specific names given to the arguments. In addition, in many cases, some arguments are not explicitly given.

- Amplitude ϕ (used by *Mathematica*, in radians)

- Delta amplitude $\Delta(\phi)$: $\Delta(\phi) = \sqrt{1 - m \sin^2(\phi)}$

- Coordinate x: $x = \sin(\phi)$

- Parameter m (used by *Mathematica*): preceded by |, as in $I(\phi|m)$

- Complementary parameter m_1: $m_1 = 1 - m$

- Modular angle α: preceded by \, as in $I(\phi \backslash \alpha)$; $m = \sin^2(\alpha)$

- Modulus k: preceded by comma, as in $I(\phi, k)$; $m = k^2$

- Nome q: preceded by comma in θ functions; $q = \exp(-\pi K(1-m)/K(m))$

- Characteristic n (used by *Mathematica* in elliptic integrals of the third kind)

- Argument u (used by *Mathematica*): related to the amplitude by $\phi = \text{am}(u)$

- Invariants g_2, g_3 (used by *Mathematica*)

- Periods ω, ω': $g_2 = 60 \sum_{r,s} \frac{1}{w^4}$, $g_3 = 140 \sum_{r,s} \frac{1}{w^6}$, where $w = 2r\omega + 2s\omega'$

- Parameters of curve a, b (used by *Mathematica*)

- Coordinate y (used by *Mathematica*): related by $y^2 = x^3 + ax^2 + bx$

Arguments and common notations for elliptic integrals and elliptic functions.

Elliptic Integrals

Integrals of the form $\int R(x, y) \, dx$, where R is a rational function, and y^2 is a cubic or quartic polynomial in x, are known as **elliptic integrals**. Any elliptic integral can be expressed in terms of the three standard kinds of **Legendre-Jacobi elliptic integrals**.

The **elliptic integral of the first kind** EllipticF[*phi*, *m*] is given by $F(\phi|m) = \int_0^\phi (1 - m \sin^2(\theta))^{-\frac{1}{2}} d\theta$ $= \int_0^{\sin(\phi)} [(1 - t^2)(1 - mt^2)]^{-\frac{1}{2}} dt$. This elliptic integral arises in solving the equations of motion for a simple pendulum. It is sometimes known as an **incomplete elliptic integral of the first kind**.

Note that the arguments of the elliptic integrals are sometimes given in the opposite order from what is used in *Mathematica*.

The **complete elliptic integral of the first kind** EllipticK[*m*] is given by $K(m) = F(\frac{\pi}{2}|m)$. Note that K is used to denote the *complete* elliptic integral of the first kind, while F is used for its incomplete form. In many applications, the parameter m is not given explicitly, and $K(m)$ is denoted simply by K. The **complementary complete elliptic integral of the first kind** $K'(m)$ is given by $K(1 - m)$. It is often denoted K'. K and iK' give the "real" and "imaginary" quarter-periods of the corresponding Jacobi elliptic functions discussed below. The **nome** q is given by $q(m) = \exp[-\pi K'(m)/K(m)]$.

The **elliptic integral of the second kind** `EllipticE[phi, m]` is given by $E(\phi|m) = \int_0^\phi (1 - m \sin^2(\theta))^{\frac{1}{2}} \, d\theta = \int_0^{\sin(\phi)} (1 - t^2)^{\frac{1}{2}} (1 - m t^2)^{-\frac{1}{2}} \, dt$.

The **complete elliptic integral of the second kind** `EllipticE[m]` is given by $E(m) = E(\frac{\pi}{2}|m)$. It is often denoted E. The complementary form is $E'(m) = E(1 - m)$.

The **Jacobi zeta function** `JacobiZeta[phi, m]` is given by $Z(\phi|m) = E(\phi|m) - E(m)F(\phi|m)/K(m)$.

The **Heuman lambda function** is given by $\Lambda_0(\phi|m) = F(\phi|1 - m)/K(1 - m) + \frac{2}{\pi}K(m)Z(\phi|1 - m)$.

The **elliptic integral of the third kind** `EllipticPi[n, phi, m]` is given by $\Pi(n; \phi|m) = \int_0^\phi (1 - n \sin^2(\theta))^{-1} [1 - m \sin^2(\theta)]^{-\frac{1}{2}} \, d\theta$.

The **complete elliptic integral of the third kind** `EllipticPi[n, m]` is given by $\Pi(n|m) = \Pi(n; \frac{\pi}{2}|m)$.

Here is a plot of the complete elliptic integral of the second kind $E(m)$.

```
In[1]:= Plot[EllipticE[m], {m, 0, 1}]
```

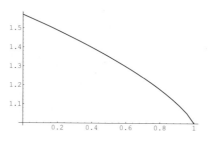

Here is $K(\alpha)$ with $\alpha = 30°$.

```
In[2]:= EllipticK[Sin[30 Degree]^2] // N

Out[2]= 1.68575
```

The elliptic integrals have a complicated structure in the complex plane.

```
In[3]:= Plot3D[ Im[EllipticF[px + I py, 2]],
                {px, 0.5, 2.5}, {py, -1, 1} ]
```

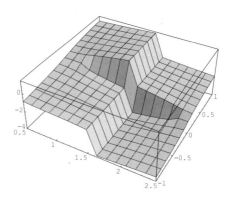

Elliptic Functions

Rational functions involving square roots of quadratic forms can be integrated in terms of inverse trigonometric functions. The trigonometric functions can thus be defined as inverses of the functions obtained from these integrals.

By analogy, **elliptic functions** are defined as inverses of the functions obtained from elliptic integrals.

The **amplitude** for Jacobi elliptic functions JacobiAmplitude[u, m] is the inverse of the elliptic integral of the first kind. If $u = F(\phi|m)$, then $\phi = \text{am}(u|m)$. In working with Jacobi elliptic functions, the argument m is often dropped, so $\text{am}(u|m)$ is written as $\text{am}(u)$.

The **Jacobi elliptic functions** JacobiSN[u, m] and JacobiCN[u, m] are given respectively by $\text{sn}(u) = \sin(\phi)$ and $\text{cn}(u) = \cos(\phi)$, where $\phi = \text{am}(u|m)$. In addition, JacobiDN[u, m] is given by $\text{dn}(u) = \sqrt{1 - m \sin^2(\phi)} = \Delta(\phi)$.

There are a total of twelve Jacobi elliptic functions JacobiPQ[u, m], with the letters P and Q chosen from the set S, C, D and N. Each Jacobi elliptic function JacobiPQ[u, m] satisfies the relation $\text{pq}(u) = \text{pn}(u)/\text{qn}(u)$, where for these purposes $\text{nn}(u) = 1$.

There are many relations between the Jacobi elliptic functions, somewhat analogous to those between trigonometric functions. In limiting cases, in fact, the Jacobi elliptic functions reduce to trigonometric functions. So, for example, $\text{sn}(u|0) = \sin(u)$, $\text{sn}(u|1) = \tanh(u)$, $\text{cn}(u|0) = \cos(u)$, $\text{cn}(u|1) = \text{sech}(u)$, $\text{dn}(u|0) = 1$ and $\text{dn}(u|1) = \text{sech}(u)$.

The notation Pq(u) is often used for the integrals $\int_0^u \text{pq}^2(t)\, dt$. These integrals can be expressed in terms of the Jacobi zeta function defined above.

One of the most important properties of elliptic functions is that they are *doubly periodic* in the complex values of their arguments. Ordinary trigonometric functions are singly periodic, in the sense that $f(z + s\omega) = f(z)$ for any integer s. The elliptic functions are doubly periodic, so that $f(z + r\omega + s\omega') = f(z)$ for any pair of integers r and s.

The Jacobi elliptic functions $\text{sn}(u|m)$, etc. are doubly periodic in the complex u plane. Their periods include $\omega = 4K(m)$ and $\omega' = 4iK(1 - m)$, where K is the complete elliptic integral of the first kind.

The choice of p and q in the notation pq($u|m$) for Jacobi elliptic functions can be understood in terms of the values of the functions at the quarter periods K and iK'.

This shows two complete periods in each direction of the absolute value of the Jacobi elliptic function $sn(u|\frac{1}{3})$.

```
In[4]:= ContourPlot[Abs[JacobiSN[ux + I uy, 1/3]],
            {ux, 0, 4 EllipticK[1/3]},
            {uy, 0, 4 EllipticK[2/3]},
            PlotPoints->40 ]
```

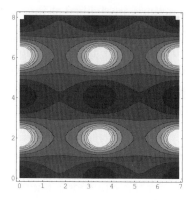

Also built into *Mathematica* are the **inverse Jacobi elliptic functions** InverseJacobiSN[v, m], InverseJacobiCN[v, m], etc. The inverse function $sn^{-1}(v|m)$, for example, gives the value of u for which $v = sn(u|m)$. The inverse Jacobi elliptic functions are related to elliptic integrals.

The four **elliptic theta functions** $\theta_a(u|m)$ are obtained from EllipticTheta[a, u, m] by taking a to be 1, 2, 3 or 4. The functions are defined by: $\theta_1(u,q) = 2q^{\frac{1}{4}}\sum_{n=0}^{\infty}(-1)^n q^{n(n+1)}\sin[(2n+1)u]$, $\theta_2(u,q) = 2q^{\frac{1}{4}}\sum_{n=0}^{\infty}q^{n(n+1)}\cos[(2n+1)u]$, $\theta_3(u,q) = 1+2\sum_{n=1}^{\infty}q^{n^2}\cos(2nu)$, $\theta_4(u,q) = 1+2\sum_{n=1}^{\infty}(-1)^n q^{n^2}\cos(2nu)$. The theta functions are sometimes given in the form $\theta(u|m)$, where m is related to q by $q = \exp(-\pi K(1-m)/K(m))$. In addition, q is sometimes replaced by τ, given by $q = e^{i\pi\tau}$. All the theta functions satisfy a diffusion-like differential equation $\frac{\partial^2\theta(u,\tau)}{\partial u^2} = 4\pi i \frac{\partial\theta(u,\tau)}{\partial\tau}$.

The Jacobi elliptic functions can be expressed as ratios of the theta functions.

An alternative notation for theta functions is $\Theta(u|m) = \theta_4(v|m)$, $\Theta_1(u|m) = \theta_3(v|m)$, $H(u|m) = \theta_1(v)$, $H_1(u|m) = \theta_2(v)$, where $v = \frac{\pi u}{2K(m)}$.

The **Neville theta functions** can be defined in terms of the theta functions as $\theta_s(u) = \frac{2K(m)\theta_1(v|m)}{\pi\theta_1'(0|m)}$, $\theta_c(u) = \frac{\theta_2(v|m)}{\theta_2(0|m)}$, $\theta_d(u) = \frac{\theta_3(v|m)}{\theta_3(0|m)}$, $\theta_n(u) = \frac{\theta_4(v|m)}{\theta_4(0|m)}$, where $v = \frac{\pi u}{2K(m)}$.

The **Weierstrass elliptic function** WeierstrassP[u, g_2, g_3] can be considered as the inverse of an elliptic integral. The Weierstrass function $\wp(u;g_2,g_3)$ gives the value of x for which $u = \int_{\infty}^{x}(4t^3 - g_2 t - g_3)^{-\frac{1}{2}} dt$. The function WeierstrassPPrime[u, g_2, g_3] is given by $\wp'(u;g_2,g_3) = \frac{\partial}{\partial u}\wp(u;g_2,g_3)$.

The Weierstrass functions are also sometimes written in terms of their *fundamental periods* ω and ω'.

Generalized Elliptic Integrals and Functions

The definitions for elliptic integrals and functions given above are based on traditional usage. For modern algebraic geometry, it is convenient to use slightly more general definitions.

The function `EllipticLog[{x, y}, {a, b}]` is defined as the value of the integral $\frac{1}{2} \int_\infty^x (t^3 + at^2 + bt)^{-\frac{1}{2}} dt$, where the sign of the square root is specified by giving the value of y such that $y = \sqrt{x^3 + ax^2 + bx}$. Integrals of the form $\int_\infty^x (t^2 + at)^{-\frac{1}{2}} dt$ can be expressed in terms of the ordinary logarithm (and inverse trigonometric functions). You can think of `EllipticLog` as giving a generalization of this, where the polynomial under the square root is now of degree three.

The function `EllipticExp[u, {a, b}]` is the inverse of `EllipticLog`. It returns the list $\{x, y\}$ that appears in `EllipticLog`. `EllipticExp` is an elliptic function, doubly periodic in the complex u plane.

`ArithmeticGeometricMean[a, b]` gives the **arithmetic-geometric mean** (**AGM**) of two numbers a and b. This quantity is central to many numerical algorithms for computing elliptic integrals and other functions. The AGM is obtained by starting with $a_0 = a$, $b_0 = b$, then iterating the transformation $a_{n+1} = \frac{1}{2}(a_n + b_n)$, $b_{n+1} = \sqrt{a_n b_n}$ until $a_n = b_n$ to the precision required.

■ 3.2.12 Statistical Distributions and Related Functions

There are standard *Mathematica* packages for evaluating functions related to common statistical distributions. *Mathematica* represents the statistical distributions themselves in the symbolic form *name*[*param*$_1$, *param*$_2$, ...], where the *param*$_i$ are parameters for the distributions. Functions such as `Mean`, which give properties of statistical distributions, take the symbolic representation of the distribution as an argument.

BetaDistribution[*alpha*, *beta*]   continuous beta distribution

   CauchyDistribution[*a*, *b*]   Cauchy distribution with location parameter *a* and scale parameter *b*

   ChiSquareDistribution[*n*]   chi-square distribution with *n* degrees of freedom

ExponentialDistribution[*lambda*]

                                  exponential distribution with scale parameter λ

ExtremeValueDistribution[*alpha*, *beta*]

                                    extreme value (Fisher-Tippett) distribution

 FRatioDistribution[n_1, n_2]   F-ratio distribution with n_1 numerator and n_2 denominator degrees of freedom

GammaDistribution[*alpha*, *lambda*]

                                    gamma distribution with shape parameter α and scale parameter λ

NormalDistribution[*mu*, *sigma*]

                                    normal (Gaussian) distribution with mean μ and standard deviation σ

LaplaceDistribution[*mu*, *beta*]

                                    Laplace (double exponential) distribution with mean μ and variance parameter β

LogNormalDistribution[*mu*, *sigma*]

                                    lognormal distribution with mean parameter μ and variance parameter σ

LogisticDistribution[*mu*, *beta*]

                                    logistic distribution with mean μ and variance parameter β

RayleighDistribution[*sigma*]   Rayleigh distribution

   StudentTDistribution[*n*]   Student *t* distribution with *n* degrees of freedom

UniformDistribution[*min*, *max*]

                                    uniform distribution on the interval {*min*, *max*}

WeibullDistribution[*alpha*, *beta*]

                                    Weibull distribution

Statistical distributions from the package `Statistics`ContinuousDistributions``.

Most of the continuous statistical distributions commonly used are derived from the **normal** or **Gaussian distribution** `NormalDistribution[`*mu*, *sigma*`]`. This distribution has probability density $\frac{1}{\sqrt{2\pi}\sigma}\exp(\frac{(x-\mu)^2}{2\sigma^2})$. If you take random variables that follow any distribution with bounded variance, then the Central Limit Theorem shows that the mean of a large number of these variables always follows a normal distribution.

The **logarithmic normal distribution** or **lognormal distribution** `LogNormalDistribution[`*mu*, *sigma*`]` is the distribution followed by the exponential of a normal-distributed random variable. This distribution arises when many independent random variables are combined in a multiplicative fashion.

The **chi-square distribution** `ChiSquareDistribution[`*n*`]` is the distribution of the quantity $\sum_{i=1}^{n} x_i^2$, where the x_i are random variables which follow a normal distribution with mean zero and unit variance. The chi-square distribution gives the distribution of variances of samples from a normal distribution.

The **Student t distribution** `StudentTDistribution[`*n*`]` is the distribution followed by the ratio of a variable that follows the normal distribution to one that follows the chi-square distribution with n degrees of freedom. The t distribution characterizes the uncertainty in a mean when both the mean and variance are obtained from data.

The **F-ratio distribution**, **F-distribution** or **variance ratio distribution** `FRatioDistribution[`*n₁*, *n₂*`]` is the distribution of the ratio of two chi-square variables with n_1 and n_2 degrees of freedom. The F-ratio distribution is used in the analysis of variance for comparing variances from different models.

The **extreme value distribution** `ExtremeValueDistribution[`*alpha*, *beta*`]` is the limiting distribution for the smallest or largest values in large samples drawn from a variety of distributions, including the normal distribution.

PDF[*dist*, *x*]	probability density function (frequency function) at *x*
CDF[*dist*, *x*]	cumulative distribution function at *x*
Quantile[*dist*, *q*]	q^{th} quantile
Mean[*dist*]	mean
Variance[*dist*]	variance
StandardDeviation[*dist*]	standard deviation
Skewness[*dist*]	coefficient of skewness
Kurtosis[*dist*]	coefficient of kurtosis
CharacteristicFunction[*dist*, *t*]	
	characteristic function $\phi(t)$
Random[*dist*]	pseudorandom number with specified distribution

Functions of statistical distributions.

The **cumulative distribution function** (cdf) CDF[*dist*, *x*] is given by the integral of the **probability density function** for the distribution up to the point *x*. For the normal distribution, the cdf is usually denoted $\Phi(x)$. Cumulative distribution functions are used in evaluating probabilities for statistical hypotheses. For discrete distributions, the cdf is given by the sum of the probabilities up to the point *x*. The cdf is sometimes called simply the **distribution function**. The cdf at a particular point *x* for a given distribution is often denoted $P(x|\theta_1, \theta_2, ...)$, where the θ_i are parameters of the distribution. The **upper tail area** is given in terms of the cdf by $Q(x|\theta_i) = 1 - P(x|\theta_i)$. Thus, for example, the upper tail area for a chi-square distribution with v degrees of freedom is denoted $Q(\chi^2|v)$ and is given by 1 - CDF[ChiSquareDistribution[*nu*], *chi2*].

The **quantile** Quantile[*dist*, *q*] is effectively the inverse of the cdf. It gives the value of *x* at which CDF[*dist*, *x*] reaches *q*. The median is given by Quantile[*dist*, 1/2]; quartiles, deciles and percentiles can also be expressed as quantiles. Quantiles are used in constructing confidence intervals for statistical parameter estimates.

The characteristic function CharacteristicFunction[*dist*, *t*] is given by $\phi(t) = \int p(x)\exp(itx)\,dx$, where $p(x)$ is the probability density for a distribution. The nth **central moment** of a distribution is given by the nth derivative $i^{-n}\phi^{(n)}(0)$.

Random[*dist*] gives pseudorandom numbers that follow the specified distribution. The numbers can be seeded as discussed in Section 3.2.3.

This loads the package which defines continuous statistical distributions.

In[1]:= **<<Statistics`ContinuousDistributions`**

This represents a normal distribution with mean zero and unit variance.	`In[2]:= ndist = NormalDistribution[0, 1]`
	`Out[2]= NormalDistribution[0, 1]`

Here is a symbolic result for the cumulative distribution function of the normal distribution.

`In[3]:= CDF[ndist, x]`

$$Out[3]= \frac{1 + \text{Erf}[\frac{x}{\text{Sqrt}[2]}]}{2}$$

This gives the value of x at which the cdf of the normal distribution reaches the value 0.9.

`In[4]:= Quantile[ndist, 0.9] // N`

`Out[4]= 1.28155`

Here is a list of five normal-distributed pseudorandom numbers.

`In[5]:= Table[ Random[ndist], {5} ]`

`Out[5]= {0.231933, -1.7368, -0.354474, -0.158884, 0.352565}`

`BernoulliDistribution[p]`	discrete Bernoulli distribution with mean p
`BinomialDistribution[n, p]`	binomial distribution for n trials with probability p
`DiscreteUniformDistribution[n]`	
	discrete uniform distribution with n states
`GeometricDistribution[p]`	discrete geometric distribution with mean $1/p$
`HypergeometricDistribution[n, `n_{succ}`, `n_{tot}`]`	
	hypergeometric distribution for n trials with n_{succ} successes in a population of size n_{tot}
`NegativeBinomialDistribution[r, p]`	
	negative binomial distribution for failure count r and probability p
`PoissonDistribution[mu]`	Poisson distribution with mean μ

Statistical distributions from the package `Statistics`DiscreteDistributions``.

Most of the common discrete statistical distributions can be derived by considering a sequence of "trials", each with two possible outcomes, say "success" and "failure".

The **Bernoulli distribution** `BernoulliDistribution[p]` is the probability distribution for a single trial in which success, corresponding to value 1, occurs with probability p, and failure, corresponding to value 0, occurs with probability $1 - p$.

The **binomial distribution** `BinomialDistribution[n, p]` is the distribution of the number of successes that occur in n independent trials when the probability for success in an individual trial is p. The distribution is given by $\binom{n}{k} p^k (1 - p)^{(n-k)}$.

The **negative binomial distribution** `NegativeBinomialDistribution[r, p]` gives the distribution of the number of failures that occur in a sequence of trials before r successes have occurred, given that the probability for success in each individual trial is p.

The **geometric distribution** `GeometricDistribution[p]` gives the distribution of the total number of trials before the first success occurs in a sequence of trials where the probability for success in each individual trial is p.

The **hypergeometric distribution** `HypergeometricDistribution[n, `n_{succ}`, `n_{tot}`]` is used in place of the binomial distribution for experiments in which the n trials correspond to sampling without replacement from a population of size n_{tot} with n_{succ} potential successes.

The **discrete uniform distribution** `DiscreteUniformDistribution[n]` represents an experiment with n outcomes that occur with equal probabilities.

3.3 Algebraic Manipulation

■ 3.3.1 Structural Operations on Polynomials

Expand[*poly*]	expand out products and powers
Factor[*poly*]	factor completely
FactorTerms[*poly*]	pull out any overall numerical factor
Collect[*poly*, *x*]	arrange a polynomial as a sum of powers of *x*
Collect[*poly*, {*x*, *y*, ... }]	arrange a polynomial as a sum of powers of *x*, *y*, ...

Structural operations on polynomials.

Here is a polynomial in one variable.

$In[1]:=$ `(2 + 4 x^2)^2 (x - 1)^3`

$Out[1]= (-1 + x)^3 (2 + 4 x^2)^2$

Expand expands out products and powers, writing the polynomial as a simple sum of terms.

$In[2]:=$ `t = Expand[ % ]`

$Out[2]= -4 + 12 x - 28 x^2 + 52 x^3 - 64 x^4 + 64 x^5 - 48 x^6 + 16 x^7$

Factor performs complete factoring of the polynomial.

$In[3]:=$ `Factor[ t ]`

$Out[3]= 4 (-1 + x)^3 (1 + 2 x^2)^2$

FactorTerms pulls out the overall numerical factor from t.

$In[4]:=$ `FactorTerms[ t ]`

$Out[4]= 4 (-1 + 3 x - 7 x^2 + 13 x^3 - 16 x^4 + 16 x^5 - 12 x^6 + 4 x^7)$

There are several ways to write any polynomial. The functions Expand, FactorTerms and Factor give three common ways. Expand writes a polynomial as a simple sum of terms, with all products expanded out. FactorTerms pulls out common factors from each term. Factor does complete factoring, writing the polynomial as a product of terms, each of as low degree as possible.

When you have a polynomial in more than one variable, you can put the polynomial in different forms by essentially choosing different variables to be "dominant". Collect[*poly*, *x*] takes a polynomial in several variables and rewrites it as a sum of terms containing different powers of the "dominant variable" *x*.

Here is a polynomial in two variables.

$In[5] :=$ **Expand[(1 + 2x + y)^3]**

$Out[5]= 1 + 6\ x + 12\ x^2 + 8\ x^3 + 3\ y + 12\ x\ y + 12\ x^2\ y +$
$3\ y^2 + 6\ x\ y^2 + y^3$

Collect reorganizes the polynomial so that x is the "dominant variable".

$In[6] :=$ **Collect[%, x]**

$Out[6]= 1 + 8\ x^3 + 3\ y + 3\ y^2 + y^3 + x^2\ (12 + 12\ y) +$
$x\ (6 + 12\ y + 6\ y^2)$

If you specify a list of variables, Collect will effectively write the expression as a polynomial in these variables.

$In[7] :=$ **Collect[Expand[(1 + x + 2y + 3z)^3], {x, y}]**

$Out[7]= 1 + x^3 + 8\ y^3 + 9\ z + 27\ z^2 + 27\ z^3 +$
$x^2\ (3 + 6\ y + 9\ z) + y^2\ (12 + 36\ z) + y\ (6 + 36\ z + 54\ z^2) +$
$x\ (3 + 12\ y^2 + 18\ z + 27\ z^2 + y\ (12 + 36\ z))$

Expand[*poly*, *patt*]	expand out *poly* avoiding those parts which do not contain terms matching *patt*

Controlling polynomial expansion.

This avoids expanding parts which do not contain x.

$In[8] :=$ **Expand[(x + 1)^2 (y + 1)^2, x]**

$Out[8]= (1 + y)^2 + 2\ x\ (1 + y)^2 + x^2\ (1 + y)^2$

This avoids expanding parts which do not contain objects matching b[_].

$In[9] :=$ **Expand[(a[1] + a[2] + 1)^2 (1 + b[1])^2, b[_]]**

$Out[9]= (1 + a[1] + a[2])^2 + 2\ (1 + a[1] + a[2])^2\ b[1] +$
$(1 + a[1] + a[2])^2\ b[1]^2$

PowerExpand[*expr*]	expand out $(ab)^c$ and $(a^b)^c$ in *expr*

Expanding powers.

    Mathematica does not automatically expand out expressions of the form $(a\ b)$^c except when c is an integer. In general it is only correct to do this expansion if a and b are positive reals. Nevertheless, the function PowerExpand does the expansion, effectively assuming that a and b are indeed positive reals.

Mathematica does not automatically expand out this expression.

$In[10] :=$ **(x y)^n**

$Out[10]= (x\ y)^n$

PowerExpand does the expansion, effectively assuming that x and y are positive reals.

In[11]:= **PowerExpand[%]**

Out[11]= $x^n \, y^n$

■ 3.3.2 Finding the Structure of a Polynomial

PolynomialQ[*expr*, *x*]	test whether *expr* is a polynomial in x
PolynomialQ[*expr*, {x_1, x_2, ... }]	
	test whether *expr* is a polynomial in the x_i
Variables[*poly*]	a list of the variables in *poly*
Length[*poly*]	the total number of terms in *poly*
Exponent[*poly*, *x*]	the maximum exponent with which x appears in *poly*
Coefficient[*poly*, *expr*]	the coefficient of *expr* in *poly*
Coefficient[*poly*, *expr*, *n*]	the coefficient of *expr*^*n* in *poly*
Coefficient[*poly*, *expr*, 0]	the term in *poly* independent of *expr*
CoefficientList[*poly*, {x_1, x_2, ... }]	
	generate an array of the coefficients of the x_i in *poly*

Finding the structure of polynomials written in expanded form.

Here is a polynomial in two variables, written in expanded form.

In[1]:= **t = Expand[(1 + x)^3 (1 - y - x)^2]**

Out[1]= $1 + x - 2 x^2 - 2 x^3 + x^4 + x^5 - 2 y - 4 x y + 4 x^3 y +$
$2 x^4 y + y^2 + 3 x y^2 + 3 x^2 y^2 + x^3 y^2$

PolynomialQ reports that t is a polynomial in x, with coefficients that depend on y.

In[2]:= **PolynomialQ[t, x]**

Out[2]= True

This expression, however, is not a polynomial in x.

In[3]:= **PolynomialQ[x + Sin[x], x]**

Out[3]= False

Variables gives a list of the variables in the polynomial t.

In[4]:= **Variables[t]**

Out[4]= {x, y}

The polynomial t has the form of a sum of terms. Length[t] gives the number of terms in this sum.

In[5]:= **Length[t]**

Out[5]= 14

This gives the maximum exponent with which x appears in the polynomial t. For a polynomial in one variable, Exponent gives the degree of the polynomial.

```
In[6]:= Exponent[t, x]
Out[6]= 5
```

Coefficient[*poly*, *expr*] gives the total coefficient with which *expr* appears in *poly*. In this case, the result is a sum of two terms.

```
In[7]:= Coefficient[t, x^2]
Out[7]= -2 + 3 y
             2
```

This is equivalent to Coefficient[t, x^2].

```
In[8]:= Coefficient[t, x, 2]
Out[8]= -2 + 3 y
             2
```

This picks out the coefficient of x^0 in t.

```
In[9]:= Coefficient[t, x, 0]
                       2
Out[9]= 1 - 2 y + y
```

CoefficientList gives a list of the coefficients of each power of x, starting with x^0.

```
In[10]:= CoefficientList[1 + 3x^2 + 4x^4, x]
Out[10]= {1, 0, 3, 0, 4}
```

For multivariate polynomials, CoefficientList gives an array of the coefficients for each power of each variable.

```
In[11]:= CoefficientList[t, {x, y}]
Out[11]= {{1, -2, 1}, {1, -4, 3}, {-2, 0, 3}, {-2, 4, 1},
          {1, 2, 0}, {1, 0, 0}}
```

It is important to realize that the functions in this section will work as shown above only on polynomials that are given in expanded form. If, for example, you apply Length to a factored polynomial, you will get the number of factors, rather than the number of terms in the expanded polynomial.

Many of the functions in this section also work on expressions that are not strictly polynomials.

Without giving specific integer values to a, b and c, this expression cannot strictly be considered a polynomial.

```
In[12]:= x^a + x^b + y^c
            a    b    c
Out[12]= x  + x  + y
```

Exponent[*expr*, x] still gives the maximum exponent of x in *expr*, but here has to write the result in symbolic form.

```
In[13]:= Exponent[%, x]
Out[13]= Max[0, a, b]
```

■ 3.3.3 Structural Operations on Rational Expressions

For ordinary polynomials, Factor and Expand give the most important forms. For rational expressions, there are many different forms that can be useful.

ExpandNumerator[*expr*]	expand numerators only
ExpandDenominator[*expr*]	expand denominators only
Expand[*expr*]	expand numerators, dividing the denominator into each term
ExpandAll[*expr*]	expand numerators and denominators completely

Different kinds of expansion for rational expressions.

Here is a rational expression.

$In[1]:=$ **t = (1 + x)^2 / (1 - x) + 3 x^2 / (1 + x)^2 + (2 - x)^2**

$$Out[1]= (2 - x)^2 + \frac{3 x^2}{(1 + x)^2} + \frac{(1 + x)^2}{1 - x}$$

ExpandNumerator writes the numerator of each term in expanded form.

$In[2]:=$ **ExpandNumerator[t]**

$$Out[2]= 4 - 4 x + x^2 + \frac{3 x^2}{(1 + x)^2} + \frac{1 + 2 x + x^2}{1 - x}$$

Expand expands the numerator of each term, and divides all the terms by the appropriate denominators.

$In[3]:=$ **Expand[t]**

$$Out[3]= 4 + \frac{1}{1 - x} - 4 x + \frac{2 x}{1 - x} + x^2 + \frac{x^2}{1 - x} + \frac{3 x^2}{(1 + x)^2}$$

ExpandDenominator expands out the denominator of each term.

$In[4]:=$ **ExpandDenominator[t]**

$$Out[4]= (2 - x)^2 + \frac{(1 + x)^2}{1 - x} + \frac{3 x^2}{1 + 2 x + x^2}$$

ExpandAll does all possible expansions in the numerator and denominator of each term.

$In[5]:=$ **ExpandAll[t]**

$$Out[5]= 4 + \frac{1}{1 - x} - 4 x + \frac{2 x}{1 - x} + x^2 + \frac{x^2}{1 - x} + \frac{3 x^2}{1 + 2 x + x^2}$$

ExpandAll[*expr*, *patt*], etc.	avoid expanding parts which contain no terms matching *patt*

Controlling expansion.

This avoids expanding the term which does not contain y.

$In[6]:=$ **ExpandAll[(x + 1)^2/y^2 + (y + 1)^2/y^2, y]**

$$Out[6]= 1 + y^{-2} + \frac{(1 + x)^2}{y^2} + \frac{2}{y}$$

Together[*expr*]	combine all terms over a common denominator
Apart[*expr*]	write an expression as a sum of terms with simple denominators
Cancel[*expr*]	cancel common factors between numerators and denominators
Factor[*expr*]	perform a complete factoring

Structural operations on rational expressions.

Here is a rational expression.

$In[7]:=$ **u = (-4x + x^2)/(-x + x^2) + (-4 + 3x + x^2)/(-1 + x^2)**

$$Out[7]= \frac{-4 x + x^2}{-x + x^2} + \frac{-4 + 3 x + x^2}{-1 + x^2}$$

Together puts all terms over a common denominator.

$In[8]:=$ **Together[u]**

$$Out[8]= \frac{-8 + 2 x^2}{(-1 + x)(1 + x)}$$

You can use **Factor** to factor the numerator and denominator of the resulting expression.

$In[9]:=$ **Factor[%]**

$$Out[9]= \frac{2 (-2 + x)(2 + x)}{(-1 + x)(1 + x)}$$

Apart writes the expression as a sum of terms, with each term having as simple a denominator as possible.

$In[10]:=$ **Apart[u]**

$$Out[10]= 2 - \frac{3}{-1 + x} + \frac{3}{1 + x}$$

Cancel cancels any common factors between numerators and denominators.

$In[11]:=$ **Cancel[u]**

$$Out[11]= \frac{-4 + x}{-1 + x} + \frac{4 + x}{1 + x}$$

Factor first puts all terms over a common denominator, then factors the result.

$In[12]:=$ **Factor[%]**

$$Out[12]= \frac{2 (-2 + x)(2 + x)}{(-1 + x)(1 + x)}$$

In mathematical terms, **Apart** decomposes a rational expression into "partial fractions".

In expressions with several variables, you can use Apart[*expr, var*] to do partial fraction decompositions with respect to different variables.

Here is a rational expression in two variables.

$$In[13]:= v = (x^2+y^2)/(x + x\ y)$$

$$Out[13]= \frac{x^2 + y^2}{x + x\ y}$$

This gives the partial fraction decomposition with respect to x.

$$In[14]:= \textbf{Apart[v, x]}$$

$$Out[14]= \frac{x}{1 + y} + \frac{y^2}{x\ (1 + y)}$$

Here is the partial fraction decomposition with respect to y.

$$In[15]:= \textbf{Apart[v, y]}$$

$$Out[15]= -(\frac{1}{x}) + \frac{y}{x} + \frac{1 + x^2}{x\ (1 + y)}$$

■ 3.3.4 Algebraic Operations on Polynomials

For many kinds of practical calculations, the only operations you will need to perform on polynomials are essentially the structural ones discussed in the preceding sections.

If you do more advanced algebra with polynomials, however, you will have to use the algebraic operations discussed in this section.

You should realize that most of the operations discussed in this section work only on ordinary polynomials, with integer exponents and rational-number coefficients for each term.

`PolynomialQuotient[`*poly₁*`, `*poly₂*`, `*x*`]`	
	find the result of dividing the polynomial *poly₁* in *x* by *poly₂*, dropping any remainder term
`PolynomialRemainder[`*poly₁*`, `*poly₂*`, `*x*`]`	
	find the remainder from dividing the polynomial *poly₁* in *x* by *poly₂*
`PolynomialGCD[`*poly₁*`, `*poly₂*`]`	find the greatest common divisor of two polynomials
`PolynomialLCM[`*poly₁*`, `*poly₂*`]`	find the least common multiple of two polynomials
`PolynomialMod[`*poly*`, `*m*`]`	reduce the polynomial *poly* modulo *m*
`PolynomialMod[`*poly*`, {`*m₁*`, `*m₂*`, ... }]`	
	reduce *poly* with respect to several moduli *mᵢ*
`Resultant[`*poly₁*`, `*poly₂*`, `*x*`]`	find the resultant of two polynomials
`Factor[`*poly*`]`	factor a polynomial
`FactorSquareFree[`*poly*`]`	write a polynomial as a product of powers of square-free factors
`FactorTerms[`*poly*`, `*x*`]`	factor out terms that do not depend on *x*
`FactorList[`*poly*`]`, `FactorSquareFreeList[`*poly*`]`, `FactorTermsList[`*poly*`]`	
	give results as lists of factors

Algebraic operations on polynomials.

Given two polynomials $p(x)$ and $q(x)$, one can always uniquely write $\frac{p(x)}{q(x)} = a(x) + \frac{b(x)}{q(x)}$, where the degree of $b(x)$ is less than the degree of $q(x)$. PolynomialQuotient gives the quotient $a(x)$, and PolynomialRemainder gives the remainder $b(x)$.

This gives the remainder from dividing x^2 by $1+x$.

```
In[1]:= PolynomialRemainder[x^2, x+1, x]
Out[1]= 1
```

Here is the quotient of x^2 and $x+1$, with the remainder dropped.

```
In[2]:= PolynomialQuotient[x^2, x+1, x]
Out[2]= -1 + x
```

This gives back the original expression.

```
In[3]:= Simplify[ (x+1) % + %% ]
        2
Out[3]= x
```

Here the result depends on whether the polynomials are considered to be in x or y.

```
In[4]:= {PolynomialRemainder[x+y, x-y, x],
                PolynomialRemainder[x+y, x-y, y]}
Out[4]= {2 y, 2 x}
```

PolynomialGCD[$poly_1$, $poly_2$] finds the highest degree polynomial that divides the $poly_i$ exactly. It gives the analog for polynomials of the integer function GCD.

PolynomialGCD gives the greatest common divisor of the two polynomials.

In[5]:= **PolynomialGCD[(1-x)^2 (1+x) (2+x), (1-x) (2+x) (3+x)]**

Out[5]= (1 - x) (2 + x)

PolynomialMod is essentially the analog for polynomials of the function Mod for integers. When the modulus m is an integer, PolynomialMod[$poly$, m] simply reduces each coefficient in $poly$ modulo the integer m. If m is a polynomial, then PolynomialMod[$poly$, m] effectively tries to get as low degree a polynomial as possible by subtracting from $poly$ appropriate multiples q m of m. The multiplier q can itself be a polynomial, but its degree is always less than the degree of $poly$. PolynomialMod yields a final polynomial whose degree is as small as possible, and whose leading coefficient is positive, but as small as possible.

This reduces x^2 modulo $x + 1$. The result is simply the remainder from dividing the polynomials.

In[6]:= **PolynomialMod[x^2, x+1]**

Out[6]= 1

In this case, PolynomialMod and PolynomialRemainder do not give the same result.

In[7]:= **{PolynomialMod[x^2, 2x+1],**

PolynomialRemainder[x^2, 2x+1, x]}

Out[7]= {x^2, $\frac{1}{4}$}

The main difference between PolynomialMod and PolynomialRemainder is that while the former works simply by multiplying and subtracting polynomials, the latter uses division in getting its results. In addition, PolynomialMod allows reduction by several moduli at the same time. A typical case is reduction modulo both a polynomial and an integer.

This reduces the polynomial $x^2 + 1$ modulo both $x + 1$ and 2.

In[8]:= **PolynomialMod[x^2 + 1, {x + 1, 2}]**

Out[8]= 0

The function Resultant[$poly_1$, $poly_2$, x] is needed in various algebraic algorithms. The resultant of two polynomials a and b, both with leading coefficient one, is given by the product of all the differences $a_i - b_j$ between the roots of the polynomials. It turns out that for any pair of polynomials, the resultant is also a polynomial. The resultant of two polynomials is zero if and only if the two polynomials have a common root, or if the leading coefficients simultaneously vanish.

Here is the resultant with respect to y of two polynomials in x and y. The original polynomials have a common root in y only for values of x at which the resultant vanishes.

In[9]:= **Resultant[(x-y)^2-2, y^2-3, y]**

Out[9]= 1 - 10 x^2 + x^4

The functions Factor, FactorTerms and FactorSquareFree perform various degrees of factoring on polynomials. Factor does full factoring over the integers. FactorTerms extracts the "content" of the polynomial. FactorSquareFree pulls out any factors that appear squared, and then writes the polynomial as a product of powers of square-free factors.

Here is a polynomial, in expanded form.

In[10]:= **t = Expand[2 (1 + x)∧2 (2 + x) (3 + x)]**

Out[10]= $12 + 34 x + 34 x^2 + 14 x^3 + 2 x^4$

FactorTerms only pulls out the factor of 2 that is common to all the terms.

In[11]:= **FactorTerms[t]**

Out[11]= $2 (6 + 17 x + 17 x^2 + 7 x^3 + x^4)$

FactorSquareFree factors out the term (1 + x)∧2, but leaves the rest unfactored.

In[12]:= **FactorSquareFree[t]**

Out[12]= $2 (1 + x)^2 (6 + 5 x + x^2)$

Factor does full factoring, recovering the original form.

In[13]:= **Factor[t]**

Out[13]= $2 (1 + x)^2 (2 + x) (3 + x)$

Particularly when you write programs that work with polynomials, you will often find it convenient to pick out pieces of polynomials in a standard form. The function FactorList gives a list of all the factors of a polynomial, together with their exponents. The first element of the list is always the over-all numerical factor for the polynomial.

The form that FactorList returns is the analog for polynomials of the form produced by FactorInteger for integers.

Here is a list of the factors of the polynomial in the previous set of examples. Each element of the list gives the factor, together with its exponent.

In[14]:= **FactorList[t]**

Out[14]= {{2, 1}, {1 + x, 2}, {2 + x, 1}, {3 + x, 1}}

Factor[*poly*, GaussianIntegers -> True]	
	factor a polynomial, allowing coefficients that are Gaussian integers

Factoring polynomials with complex coefficients.

Factor and related functions usually handle only polynomials with ordinary integer or rational-number coefficients. If you set the option GaussianIntegers -> True, however, then Factor will allow polynomials with coefficients that are complex numbers with rational real and imaginary parts. This often allows more extensive factorization to be performed.

This polynomial is irreducible when the coefficients are assumed to be ordinary integers.

In[15]:= **Factor[1 + x∧2]**

Out[15]= $1 + x^2$

When Gaussian integer coefficients are allowed, the polynomial factors.

In[16]:= **Factor[1 + x∧2, GaussianIntegers -> True]**

Out[16]= (-I + x) (I + x)

| Cyclotomic[*n*, *x*] | give the cyclotomic polynomial of order *n* in *x* |

Cyclotomic polynomials.

Cyclotomic polynomials arise as "elementary polynomials" in various algebraic algorithms. The cyclotomic polynomials are defined by $C_n(x) = \prod_k (x - e^{2\pi i k/n})$, where k runs over all positive integers less than n that are relatively prime to n.

This is the cyclotomic polynomial $C_6(x)$.	*In[17]:=* **Cyclotomic[6, x]**
	Out[17]= $1 - x + x^2$
$C_6(x)$ appears in the factors of $x^6 - 1$.	*In[18]:=* **Factor[x^6 - 1]**
	Out[18]= $(-1 + x)(1 + x)(1 - x + x^2)(1 + x + x^2)$

| Decompose[*poly*, *x*] | decompose *poly*, if possible, into a composition of a list of simpler polynomials |

Decomposing polynomials.

Factorization is one important way of breaking down polynomials into simpler parts. Another, quite different, way is *decomposition*. When one factors a polynomial $P(x)$, one writes it as a product $p_1(x)p_2(x)...$ of polynomials $p_i(x)$. Decomposing a polynomial $Q(x)$ consists of writing it as a *composition* of polynomials of the form $q_1(q_2(...(x)...))$.

Here is a simple example of Decompose. The original polynomial $x^4 + x^2 + 1$ can be written as the polynomial $\bar{x}^2 + \bar{x} + 1$, where $\bar{x}$ is the polynomial x^2.	*In[19]:=* **Decompose[x^4 + x^2 + 1, x]**
	Out[19]= $\{1 + x + x^2, x^2\}$
Here are two polynomial functions.	*In[20]:=* **(q1[x_] = 1 - 2x + x^4 ;**
	** q2[x_] = 5x + x^3 ;)**
This gives the composition of the two functions.	*In[21]:=* **Expand[q1[q2[x]]]**
	Out[21]= $1 - 10 x - 2 x^3 + 625 x^4 + 500 x^6 + 150 x^8 + 20 x^{10} + x^{12}$
Decompose recovers the original functions.	*In[22]:=* **Decompose[%, x]**
	Out[22]= $\{1 - 2 x + x^4, x(5 + x^2)\}$

Decompose[*poly*, *x*] is set up to give a list of polynomials in *x*, which, if composed, reproduce the original polynomial. The original polynomial can contain variables other than *x*, but the sequence of polynomials that Decompose produces are all intended to be considered as functions of *x*.

Unlike factoring, the decomposition of polynomials is not completely unique. For example, the two sets of polynomials q_i and q'_i, related by $q'_1(x) = q_1(x - a)$ and $q'_2(x) = q_2(x) + a$ give the same result on composition, so that $q_1(q_2(x)) = q'_1(q'_2(x))$. *Mathematica* follows the convention of absorbing any constant terms into the first polynomial in the list produced by Decompose.

InterpolatingPolynomial[{f_1, f_2, ... }, x]

        give a polynomial in x which is equal to f_i when x is the integer i

InterpolatingPolynomial[{{x_1, f_1}, {x_2, f_2}, ... }, x]

        give a polynomial in x which is equal to f_i when x is x_i

---

Generating interpolating polynomials.

This yields a quadratic polynomial which goes through the specified three points.

```
In[23]:= InterpolatingPolynomial[{{-1, 4}, {0, 2}, {1, 6}}, x]

Out[23]= 4 + (1 + x) (-2 + 3 x)
```

When x is 0, the polynomial has value 2.

```
In[24]:= % /. x -> 0

Out[24]= 2
```

■ 3.3.5 Polynomials Modulo Primes

Mathematica can work with polynomials whose coefficients are in the finite field Z_p of integers modulo a prime p.

    PolynomialMod[*poly*, *p*]   reduce the coefficients in a polynomial modulo p

    Factor[*poly*, Modulus->*p*]   factor *poly* modulo p

PolynomialGCD[*poly*$_1$, *poly*$_2$, Modulus->*p*]

        find the GCD of the *poly*$_i$ modulo p

Functions for manipulating polynomials over finite fields.

Here is an ordinary polynomial.

```
In[1]:= Expand[ (1 + x)^6 ]

              2       3       4      5    6
Out[1]= 1 + 6 x + 15 x + 20 x + 15 x + 6 x + x
```

This reduces the coefficients modulo 2.

```
In[2]:= PolynomialMod[%, 2]

             2    4    6
Out[2]= 1 + x + x + x
```

Here are the factors of the resulting polynomial over the integers.

```
In[3]:= Factor[%]
```

$$Out[3]= (1 + x^2) (1 + x^4)$$

If you work modulo 2, further factoring becomes possible.

```
In[4]:= Factor[%, Modulus->2]
```

$$Out[4]= (1 + x)^6$$

■ 3.3.6 Trigonometric Expressions

Trigonometric expressions like Sin[2x] are by default left unchanged by the algebraic manipulation functions discussed above. However, most of these functions allow you to set the option Trig -> True to manipulate trigonometric expressions.

Any trigonometric expression can be viewed as a rational function of exponentials. What the option setting Trig -> True effectively does is to use this form in performing algebraic manipulations you specify. With Trig -> True, *Mathematica* first converts all trigonometric functions to exponentials. Then it performs the algebraic operation you specify. Then it takes the exponentials in the result and attempts to combine them into trigonometric functions.

Without Trig -> True, Expand leaves trigonometric functions unchanged.

```
In[1]:= Expand[Sin[x]^2 + Sin[2x]^2]
```

$$Out[1]= Sin[x]^2 + Sin[2 x]^2$$

With Trig -> True, Expand transforms trigonometric functions.

```
In[2]:= Expand[%, Trig -> True]
```

$$Out[2]= 1 - \frac{Cos[2 x]}{2} - \frac{Cos[4 x]}{2}$$

Expand[*expr*, Trig -> True]	write $\sin(x)^2$ in terms of $\sin(2x)$, etc.
Factor[*expr*, Trig -> True]	write $\sin(2x)$ in terms of $\sin(x)^2$, etc.

Expanding and factoring trigonometric expressions.

Expand writes products and powers of trigonometric functions in terms of trigonometric functions with combined arguments.

```
In[3]:= Expand[Sin[a x] Cos[b x]^2, Trig -> True]
```

$$Out[3]= \frac{Sin[a x]}{2} + \frac{Sin[a x - 2 b x]}{4} + \frac{Sin[a x + 2 b x]}{4}$$

Factor writes trigonometric functions in terms of products and powers of trigonometric functions with simpler arguments.

```
In[4]:= Factor[%, Trig -> True]
```

$$Out[4]= Cos[b x]^2 Sin[a x]$$

■ 3.3.7 Expressions Involving Complex Variables

Mathematica usually pays no attention to whether variables like x stand for real or complex numbers. Sometimes, however, you may want to make transformations which are appropriate only if particular variables are assumed to be either real or complex.

The function ComplexExpand expands out algebraic and trigonometric expressions, making definite assumptions about the variables that appear.

ComplexExpand[*expr*]	expand *expr* assuming that all variables are real
ComplexExpand[*expr*, {*x₁*, *x₂*, ... }]	
	expand *expr* assuming that the x_i are complex

Expanding complex expressions.

This expands the expression, assuming that x and y are both real.

In[1]:= **ComplexExpand[Tan[x + I y]]**

$$Out[1]= \frac{\text{Sin}[2\ x]}{\text{Cos}[2\ x] + \text{Cosh}[2\ y]} + \frac{\text{I Sinh}[2\ y]}{\text{Cos}[2\ x] + \text{Cosh}[2\ y]}$$

In this case, a is assumed to be real, but x is assumed to be complex, and is broken into explicit real and imaginary parts.

In[2]:= **ComplexExpand[a + x^2, {x}]**

$$Out[2]= a - \text{Im}[x]^2 + 2\ \text{I Im}[x]\ \text{Re}[x] + \text{Re}[x]^2$$

With several complex variables, you quickly get quite complicated results.

In[3]:= **ComplexExpand[Sin[x]^2 Exp[y], {x, y}]**

$$Out[3]= -2\ \text{E}^{\text{Re}[y]}\ \text{Cos}[\text{Re}[x]]\ \text{Cosh}[\text{Im}[x]]\ \text{Sin}[\text{Im}[y]]\ \text{Sin}[\text{Re}[x]]$$

$$\text{Sinh}[\text{Im}[x]] + \text{E}^{\text{Re}[y]}\ \text{Cos}[\text{Im}[y]]$$

$$(\text{Cosh}[\text{Im}[x]]^2\ \text{Sin}[\text{Re}[x]]^2 - \text{Cos}[\text{Re}[x]]^2\ \text{Sinh}[\text{Im}[x]]^2) +$$

$$\text{I}\ (2\ \text{E}^{\text{Re}[y]}\ \text{Cos}[\text{Im}[y]]\ \text{Cos}[\text{Re}[x]]\ \text{Cosh}[\text{Im}[x]]\ \text{Sin}[\text{Re}[x]]$$

$$\text{Sinh}[\text{Im}[x]] + \text{E}^{\text{Re}[y]}\ \text{Sin}[\text{Im}[y]]$$

$$(\text{Cosh}[\text{Im}[x]]^2\ \text{Sin}[\text{Re}[x]]^2 - \text{Cos}[\text{Re}[x]]^2\ \text{Sinh}[\text{Im}[x]]^2))$$

There are several ways to write a complex variable *x* in terms of real parameters. As above, for example, *x* can be written in the "Cartesian form" Re[*x*] + I Im[*x*]. But it can equally well be written in the "polar form" Abs[*x*] Exp[I Arg[*x*]].

The option TargetFunctions in ComplexExpand allows you to specify how complex variables should be written. TargetFunctions can be set to a list of functions from the set {Re, Im, Abs, Arg, Conjugate, Sign}. ComplexExpand will try to give results in terms of whichever of these functions you request. The default is to give results in terms of Re and Im.

This gives an expansion in Cartesian form.

$In[4]:=$ **ComplexExpand[x^2, {x}]**

$Out[4]=$ $-Im[x]^2 + 2 I Im[x] Re[x] + Re[x]^2$

Here is an expansion in polar form.

$In[5]:=$ **ComplexExpand[x^2, {x},**
**   TargetFunctions -> {Abs, Arg}]**

$Out[5]=$ $Abs[x]^2 Cos[Arg[x]]^2 +$

$2 I Abs[x]^2 Cos[Arg[x]] Sin[Arg[x]] - Abs[x]^2 Sin[Arg[x]]^2$

Here is another form of expansion.

$In[6]:=$ **ComplexExpand[x^2, {x},**
**   TargetFunctions -> {Conjugate, Sign}]**

$Out[6]=$ $\dfrac{(x - Conjugate[x])^2}{4} +$

$\dfrac{(x - Conjugate[x]) (x + Conjugate[x])}{2} + \dfrac{(x + Conjugate[x])^2}{4}$

3.4 Manipulating Equations

■ 3.4.1 The Representation of Equations and Solutions

Mathematica treats equations as logical statements. If you type in an equation like x^2 + 3x == 2, *Mathematica* interprets this as a logical statement which asserts that x^2 + 3x is equal to 2. If you have assigned an explicit value to x, say x = 4, then *Mathematica* can explicitly determine that the logical statement x^2 + 3x == 2 is False.

If you have not assigned any explicit value to x, however, *Mathematica* cannot work out whether x^2 + 3x == 2 is True or False. As a result, it leaves the equation in the symbolic form x^2 + 3x == 2.

You can manipulate symbolic equations in *Mathematica* in many ways. One common goal is to rearrange the equations so as to "solve" for a particular set of variables.

Here is a symbolic equation.

$In[1]:=$ **x^2 + 3x == 2**

$$Out[1]= 3\ x + x^2 == 2$$

You can use the function Roots to rearrange the equation so as to give "solutions" for x. The result, like the original equation, can be viewed as a logical statement.

$In[2]:=$ **Roots[%, x]**

$$Out[2]= x == \frac{-3 + Sqrt[17]}{2}\ ||\ x == \frac{-3 - Sqrt[17]}{2}$$

The quadratic equation x^2 + 3x == 2 can be thought of as an implicit statement about the value of x. As shown in the example above, you can use the function Roots to get a more explicit statement about the value of x. The expression produced by Roots has the form x == r_1 || x == r_2. This expression is again a logical statement, which asserts that either x is equal to r_1, or x is equal to r_2. The values of x that are consistent with this statement are exactly the same as the ones that are consistent with the original quadratic equation. For many purposes, however, the form that Roots gives is much more useful than the original equation.

You can combine and manipulate equations just like other logical statements. You can use logical connectives such as || and && to specify alternative or simultaneous conditions. You can use functions like LogicalExpand to simplify collections of equations.

For many purposes, you will find it convenient to manipulate equations simply as logical statements. Sometimes, however, you will actually want to use explicit solutions to equations in other calculations. In such cases, it is convenient to convert equations that are stated in the form *lhs* == *rhs* into transformation rules of the form *lhs* -> *rhs*. Once you have the solutions to an equation in the form of explicit transformation rules, you can substitute the solutions into expressions by using the /. operator.

Roots produces a logical statement about the values of x corresponding to the roots of the quadratic equation.

$In[3]:=$ **Roots[x^2 + 3x == 2, x]**

$$Out[3]= x == \frac{-3 + Sqrt[17]}{2}\ ||\ x == \frac{-3 - Sqrt[17]}{2}$$

`ToRules` converts the logical statement into an explicit list of transformation rules.

```
In[4]:= {ToRules[ % ]}
```

$$Out[4]= \{\{x \to \frac{-3 + Sqrt[17]}{2}\}, \{x \to \frac{-3 - Sqrt[17]}{2}\}\}$$

You can now use the transformation rules to substitute the solutions for `x` into expressions involving `x`.

```
In[5]:= x^2 + a x /. %
```

$$Out[5]= \{\frac{(-3 + Sqrt[17])^2}{4} + \frac{(-3 + Sqrt[17]) \, a}{2},$$

$$\frac{(-3 - Sqrt[17])^2}{4} + \frac{(-3 - Sqrt[17]) \, a}{2}\}$$

The function `Solve` produces transformation rules for solutions directly.

```
In[6]:= Solve[ x^2 + 3x == 2, x ]
```

$$Out[6]= \{\{x \to \frac{-3 + Sqrt[17]}{2}\}, \{x \to \frac{-3 - Sqrt[17]}{2}\}\}$$

When `Solve` cannot find explicit solutions, it leaves the result in a symbolic form in terms of the functions `Roots` and `ToRules`.

```
In[7]:= Solve[ x^5 + 5x + 1 == 0, x ]
```

$$Out[7]= \{ToRules[Roots[5 \, x + x^5 == -1, x]]\}$$

If you apply `N`, `Roots` finds numerical roots, and `ToRules` converts the result into transformation rules.

```
In[8]:= N[ % ]
```

$$Out[8]= \{\{x \to -1.0045 - 1.06095 \, I\},$$

$$\{x \to -1.0045 + 1.06095 \, I\}, \{x \to -0.199936\},$$

$$\{x \to 1.10447 - 1.05983 \, I\}, \{x \to 1.10447 + 1.05983 \, I\}\}$$

■ 3.4.2 Equations in One Variable

The main equations that `Solve` and related *Mathematica* functions deal with are *polynomial equations*.

It is easy to solve a linear equation in `x`.

```
In[1]:= Solve[ a x + b == c , x ]
```

$$Out[1]= \{\{x \to -(\frac{b - c}{a})\}\}$$

One can also solve quadratic equations just by applying a simple formula.

```
In[2]:= Solve[ x^2 + a x + 2 == 0 , x ]
```

$$Out[2]= \{\{x \to \frac{-a + Sqrt[-8 + a^2]}{2}\}, \{x \to \frac{-a - Sqrt[-8 + a^2]}{2}\}\}$$

Mathematica can also find the exact solution to an arbitrary cubic equation. The results are however often very complicated. Here is the first solution to a comparatively simple cubic equation.

```
In[3]:= Solve[ x^3 + 34 x + 1 == 0 , x ] [[1]]
```

$$Out[3]= \{x \to$$

$$\frac{-34}{3 \, (-(-) + \frac{Sqrt[157243]^{1/3}}{6 \, Sqrt[3]})^{1}} + (-(-) + \frac{Sqrt[157243]^{1/3}}{6 \, Sqrt[3]})\}$$

Mathematica can always find exact solutions to polynomial equations of degree four or less. For cubic and quartic equations, however, the results can be extremely complicated. If the parameters in equations like these are symbolic, there can also be some subtlety in what the solutions mean. The result you get by substituting specific values for the symbolic parameters into the final solution may not be the same as what you would get by doing the substitutions in the original equation.

This generates the first solution to a cubic equation with symbolic parameters.

In[4]:= **Solve[x^3 + a x^2 + b x + 2 == 0 , x] [[1]] ;**

If you try substituting specific numerical values for the symbolic parameters, you end up dividing by zero, and getting a meaningless result.

In[5]:= **% /. {a->3, b->3}**

Power::infy: Infinite expression $0^{-(1/3)}$ encountered.

Infinity::indet:
    Indeterminate expression -(0 ComplexInfinity) encountered.

Out[5]= {x -> Indeterminate}

If you use specific values for the parameters in the original equation, then you get the correct result.

In[6]:= **Solve[x^3 + 3 x^2 + 3 x + 2 == 0 , x]**

Out[6]= $\{\{x \rightarrow -2\}, \{x \rightarrow \dfrac{-1 + \text{Sqrt}[-3]}{2}\}, \{x \rightarrow \dfrac{-1 - \text{Sqrt}[-3]}{2}\}\}$

In trying to solve polynomial equations with degrees higher than four, *Mathematica* runs into some fundamental mathematical difficulties.

The main mathematical result is that the solutions to an arbitrary polynomial equation of degree five or more cannot necessarily be written as algebraic expressions. More specifically, the solutions cannot be written as combinations of arithmetic functions and k^{th} roots. (It turns out that for equations with degree exactly five, the solutions can in principle be written in a complicated way in terms of elliptic functions; for higher-degree equations, even this is not possible.)

There are nevertheless two large classes of higher-degree equations which can be solved. The first are those in which the polynomial can be written using Factor as product of polynomials with low degrees. The second class are those where the polynomial can be written using Decompose as a composition of polynomials with low degrees. When you give a high-degree polynomial to Solve, it successively tries to use Factor and Decompose, together with some other tricks, to simplify the polynomial. As a result, Solve is able to give explicit algebraic solutions to many high-degree polynomial equations.

Here is a factorizable polynomial of degree 5.

In[7]:= **Expand[Product[x - i, {i, 5}]]**

Out[7]= $-120 + 274\ x - 225\ x^2 + 85\ x^3 - 15\ x^4 + x^5$

Mathematica solves the equation by factoring the polynomial.

In[8]:= **Solve[% == 0, x]**

Out[8]= {{x -> 5}, {x -> 4}, {x -> 3}, {x -> 2}, {x -> 1}}

Solve gives the solution to an equation like this in terms of complex numbers.

```
In[9]:= Solve[x^6 == 1, x]
                          I/3 Pi              (2 I)/3 Pi
Out[9]= {{x -> 1}, {x -> E      }, {x -> E            },
                   (4 I)/3 Pi           (5 I)/3 Pi
     {x -> -1}, {x -> E         }, {x -> E         }}
```

Here is an equation for which explicit algebraic solutions cannot be found. *Mathematica* leaves the result in a symbolic form.

```
In[10]:= Solve[x^5 - 1331 x + 11 == 0 , x]
                                  5
Out[10]= {ToRules[Roots[-1331 x + x  == -11, x]]}
```

Applying N gives the numerical result.

```
In[11]:= N[ % ]
Out[11]= {{x -> -6.04217}, {x -> -0.00206611 - 6.04011 I},
     {x -> -0.00206611 + 6.04011 I}, {x -> 0.00826446},
     {x -> 6.03804}}
```

Here is a complicated polynomial.

```
In[12]:= p = 3 + 3 x - 7 x^2 - x^3 + 2 x^4 +
                          3 x^7 - 3 x^8 - x^9 + x^10
                      2    3      4      7      8    9    10
Out[12]= 3 + 3 x - 7 x  - x  + 2 x  + 3 x  - 3 x  - x  + x
```

Mathematica finds some of the solutions, and leaves the rest in a symbolic form. Applying N would give the numerical solutions.

```
In[13]:= Solve[ % == 0 , x ]
Out[13]= {{x -> 1}, {x -> Sqrt[3]}, {x -> -Sqrt[3]},
                              7
     ToRules[Roots[1 + 2 x + x  == 0, x]]}
```

If you ultimately need only the numerical solution, it is usually a lot faster to use NSolve to ask for numerical results from the outset.

```
In[14]:= NSolve[ p == 0 , x ]
Out[14]= {{x -> -1.73205}, {x -> -0.868688 - 0.585282 I},
     {x -> -0.868688 + 0.585282 I}, {x -> -0.496292},
     {x -> 0.0763556 - 1.14095 I}, {x -> 0.0763556 + 1.14095 I},
     {x -> 1.}, {x -> 1.04048 - 0.56735 I},
     {x -> 1.04048 + 0.56735 I}, {x -> 1.73205}}
```

If there are approximate numbers in your original equation, Solve will immediately get a numerical solution.

```
In[15]:= Solve[x^3 + 7.8 x + 1 == 0, x]
Out[15]= {{x -> -0.127937}, {x -> 0.0639683 - 2.79504 I},
     {x -> 0.0639683 + 2.79504 I}}
```

If Solve cannot find an algebraic solution to a high-degree polynomial equation, then it is a good guess that no such solution exists. However, you should realize that one can construct complicated equations that have algebraic solutions which the procedures built into *Mathematica* do not find. The simplest example of such an equation that we know is $-23 - 36x + 27x^2 - 4x^3 - 9x^4 + x^6 = 0$, which has a solution $x = 2^{\frac{1}{3}} + 3^{\frac{1}{2}}$ that Solve does not find.

When *Mathematica* can find solutions to an nth-degree polynomial equation, it always gives exactly n solutions. The number of times that each root of the polynomial appears is equal to its multiplicity.

Solve gives two identical solutions to this equation.

$In[16]:=$ **Solve[(x-1)^2 == 0, x]**

$Out[16]=$ **{{x -> 1}, {x -> 1}}**

Mathematica knows how to solve some equations which are not explicitly in the form of polynomials.

Here is an equation that is not explicitly of polynomial form.

$In[17]:=$ **Solve[Sqrt[1-x] + Sqrt[1+x] == a, x]**

$Out[17]=$ **{{x -> Sqrt[$\dfrac{a^2 (4 - a^2)}{4}$]}, {x -> -Sqrt[$\dfrac{a^2 (4 - a^2)}{4}$]}}**

Mathematica can always give you numerical approximations to the solutions of a polynomial equation. For more general equations, involving say transcendental functions, there is often no systematic procedure even for finding numerical solutions. Section 3.9.6 discusses approaches to this problem in *Mathematica*.

This finds a numerical solution to the equation $x \sin(x) = \frac{1}{2}$, close to $x = 1$.

$In[18]:=$ **FindRoot[x Sin[x] - 1/2 == 0 , {x, 1}]**

$Out[18]=$ **{x -> 0.740841}**

Plotting a graph of $x \sin(x) - \frac{1}{2}$ makes it fairly clear that there are, in fact, an infinite number of solutions to the equation.

$In[19]:=$ **Plot[x Sin[x] - 1/2 , {x, 0, 30}]**

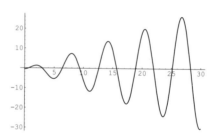

■ 3.4.3 Simultaneous Equations

You can give Solve a list of simultaneous equations to solve. Solve can find explicit solutions for a large class of simultaneous polynomial equations.

Here is a simple linear equation with two unknowns.

$In[1]:=$ **Solve[{ a x + b y == 1, x - y == 2 } , {x, y}]**

$Out[1]=$ **{{x -> -($\dfrac{1}{-a - b}$) - $\dfrac{2 b}{-a - b}$, y -> -($\dfrac{1}{-a - b}$) + $\dfrac{2 a}{-a - b}$}}**

Here is a more complicated example. The result is a list of solutions, with each solution consisting of a list of transformation rules for the variables.

$In[2] :=$ `Solve[{x^2 + y^2 == 1, x + y == a}, {x, y}]`

$$Out[2]= \left\{\left\{x \to \frac{2\,a - \text{Sqrt}[4\,a^2 - 8\,(-1 + a^2)]}{4}, \right.\right.$$

$$\left.y \to \frac{2\,a + \text{Sqrt}[4\,a^2 - 8\,(-1 + a^2)]}{4}\right\},$$

$$\left\{x \to \frac{2\,a + \text{Sqrt}[4\,a^2 - 8\,(-1 + a^2)]}{4}, \right.$$

$$\left.\left.y \to \frac{2\,a - \text{Sqrt}[4\,a^2 - 8\,(-1 + a^2)]}{4}\right\}\right\}$$

You can use the list of solutions with the `/.` operator.

$In[3] :=$ `x^3 + y^3 /. % /. a -> 0.7`

$Out[3]=$ `{0.8785, 0.8785}`

Even when `Solve` cannot find explicit solutions, it often can "unwind" simultaneous equations to produce a symbolic result in terms of nested `Roots` functions.

$In[4] :=$ `Solve[{x^3 + y^3 == x y, x + y + x y == 1},`
                                        `{x, y}]`

$Out[4]=$ `{ToRules[Roots[4 x == 3 - 3 y + y^2 - 2 y^3 - 2 y^4 - y^5,`

   `x, Using ->`

   `Roots[-4 y + 2 y^2 + y^3 + 4 y^4 + 3 y^5 + y^6 == -1, y]]]}`

You can then use N to get a numerical result.

$In[5] :=$ `N[ % ]`

$Out[5]=$ `{{x -> -1.74543 + 1.2018 I, y -> -1.74543 - 1.2018 I},`

   `{x -> -1.74543 - 1.2018 I, y -> -1.74543 + 1.2018 I},`

   `{x -> -0.17169 + 1.14626 I, y -> -0.17169 - 1.14626 I},`

   `{x -> -0.17169 - 1.14626 I, y -> -0.17169 + 1.14626 I},`

   `{x -> 0.507861, y -> 0.326382},`

   `{x -> 0.326382, y -> 0.507861}}`

The variables that you use in `Solve` do not need to be single symbols. Often when you set up large collections of simultaneous equations, you will want to use expressions like $a[i]$ as variables.

Here is a list of three equations for the $a[i]$.

$In[6] :=$ `Table[ 2 a[i] + a[i-1] == a[i+1], {i, 3} ]`

$Out[6]=$ `{a[0] + 2 a[1] == a[2], a[1] + 2 a[2] == a[3],`

   `a[2] + 2 a[3] == a[4]}`

This solves for some of the a[*i*].

$In[7]:=$ **Solve[% , {a[1], a[2], a[3]}]**

$Out[7]= \{\{a[1] \to \dfrac{-5\ a[0]}{12} + \dfrac{a[4]}{12},\ a[2] \to \dfrac{a[0]}{6} + \dfrac{a[4]}{6},$

$a[3] \to \dfrac{-a[0]}{12} + \dfrac{5\ a[4]}{12}\}\}$

Solve[*eqns*, {*x₁*, *x₂*, ... }]	solve *eqns* for the specific objects x_i
Solve[*eqns*]	try to solve *eqns* for all the objects that appear in them

Solving simultaneous equations.

If you do not explicitly specify objects to solve for, **Solve** will try to solve for all the variables.

$In[8]:=$ **Solve[{ x + y == 1, x - 3 y == 2 }]**

$Out[8]= \{\{x \to \dfrac{5}{4},\ y \to -(\dfrac{1}{4})\}\}$

- **Solve[{*lhs₁*==*rhs₁*, *lhs₂*==*rhs₂*, ... }, *vars*]**
- **Solve[*lhs₁*==*rhs₁* && *lhs₂*==*rhs₂* && ... , *vars*]**
- **Solve[{*lhs₁*, *lhs₂*, ... } == {*rhs₁*, *rhs₂*, ... }, *vars*]**

Ways to present simultaneous equations to **Solve**.

If you construct simultaneous equations from matrices, you typically get equations between lists of expressions.

$In[9]:=$ **{{3,1},{2,-5}}.{x,y}=={7,8}**

$Out[9]= \{3\ x + y,\ 2\ x - 5\ y\} == \{7, 8\}$

Solve converts equations involving lists to lists of equations.

$In[10]:=$ **Solve[%, {x, y}]**

$Out[10]= \{\{x \to \dfrac{43}{17},\ y \to -(\dfrac{10}{17})\}\}$

You can use **LogicalExpand** to do the conversion explicitly.

$In[11]:=$ **LogicalExpand[%%]**

$Out[11]= 3\ x + y == 7\ \&\&\ 2\ x - 5\ y == 8$

■ 3.4.4 Equations Involving Functions

Solve is primarily intended for solving algebraic equations. However, at least with the default option setting **InverseFunctions -> True**, **Solve** will attempt to solve some equations that involve other functions.

This solves a simple transcendental equation for **x**.

$In[1]:=$ **Solve[ArcSin[x] == a, x]**

$Out[1]= \{\{x \to Sin[a]\}\}$

In practice, very few equations involving transcendental functions can be solved exactly in symbolic form. And even in those cases where some solutions can be found, it is often impossible to get *all* the solutions.

Mathematica prints a warning indicating that solutions are lost in this case.

```
In[2]:= Solve[Sin[x] == a, x]

Solve::ifun:
    Warning: inverse functions are being used by Solve, so some
        solutions may not be found.

Out[2]= {{x -> ArcSin[a]}}
```

An equation like $\sin(x) = a$ in principle has an infinite number of solutions for x differing by multiples of 2π. However, even with the setting InverseFunctions -> True, Solve gives you only one of the possible solutions.

While all the solutions to this particular equation would be easy to parameterize, most such equations yield much more complicated sets of solutions. With simultaneous trigonometric equations, for example, it is common to end up needing solutions to arbitrary Diophantine equations, which cannot in general be found by any finite procedure.

The fact that *Mathematica* generates only some of the solutions to each equation means that if you try to solve several simultaneous equations, no solutions may be found, even though solutions do in fact exist.

With an unknown function f, *Mathematica* gives a formal solution in terms of the inverse function of f.

```
In[3]:= Solve[f[x] == a, x]

Solve::ifun:
    Warning: inverse functions are being used by Solve, so some
        solutions may not be found.

Out[3]= {{x -> f^(-1)[a]}}
```

This shows the structure of the inverse function.

```
In[4]:= InputForm[%]

Out[4]//InputForm= {{x -> InverseFunction[f, 1, 1][a]}}
```

If you ask *Mathematica* to solve an equation involving an unknown function, it will try to construct a formal solution to the equation in terms of inverse functions. In doing this, *Mathematica* effectively assumes that the function indeed has a unique inverse. If there are several possible inverses, as in the case of a function like Sin, *Mathematica* will inevitably lose solutions in such a case.

InverseFunction[*f*]	the inverse function of *f*
InverseFunction[*f*, *n*]	the inverse function of *f* with respect to its nth argument
InverseFunction[*f*, *n*, *tot*]	the inverse function of *f* when the total number of arguments is *tot*

Inverse functions.

Here is the inverse function of **f** evaluated with argument **a**.	`In[5]:= InverseFunction[f][a]` $Out[5]= f^{(-1)}[a]$

Applying **f** to the previous expression gives **a**.	`In[6]:= f[%]`
	
	`Out[6]= a`

■ 3.4.5 Getting Full Solutions

If you have an equation like 2 x == 0, it is perfectly clear that the only possible solution is x -> 0. However, if you have an equation like a x == 0, things are not so clear. If a is not equal to zero, then x -> 0 is again the only solution. However, if a is in fact equal to zero, then *any* value of x is a solution.

Solve implicitly assumes that the parameter **a** does not have the special value 0.	`In[1]:= Solve[ a x == 0 , x ]`
	
	`Out[1]= {{x -> 0}}`

Roots makes the same assumption.	`In[2]:= Roots[ a x == 0 , x ]`
	
	`Out[2]= x == 0`

Reduce, on the other hand, gives you all the possibilities, without assuming anything about the value of **a**.	`In[3]:= Reduce[ a x == 0 , x ]`
	
	`Out[3]= a != 0 && x == 0 || a == 0`

The results that Reduce gives are logical statements representing all possible solutions to an equation, allowing for special values of parameters.

A result like a != 0 && x == 0 || a == 0 is interpreted as follows. The && stands for AND; || stands for OR. Since in *Mathematica* the || operator has lower precedence than &&, the expression is equivalent to (a != 0 && x == 0) || (a == 0). The two pieces then represent alternative solutions. The first alternative is that a is not equal to 0, and x equals 0. This is the solution that Solve finds. The second alternative is that a is equal to 0, but there is no restriction on x.

lhs == *rhs*	an equation asserting that two quantities are equal
lhs != *rhs*	an inequation asserting that two quantities are unequal
eqn₁ && *eqn₂*	equations that must simultaneously be satisfied
eqn₁ || *eqn₂*	alternative equations, only one of which need be satisfied

Logical forms associated with equations.

This is the solution to an arbitrary linear equation given by Roots and Solve.	`In[4]:= Roots[a x + b == 0, x]` $Out[4]= x == -(\frac{b}{a})$

Reduce gives the full version, which includes the possibility a==b==0.

$In[5]:=$ **Reduce[a x + b == 0, x]**

$Out[5]=$ a != 0 && x == $-(\frac{b}{a})$ || a == 0 && b == 0

Here is the full solution to a general quadratic equation. There are three alternatives. If **a** is non-zero, then there are two solutions for **x**, given by the standard quadratic formula. If **a** is zero, however, the equation reduces to a linear one. Finally, if **a**, **b** and **c** are all zero, there is no restriction on **x**.

$In[6]:=$ **Reduce[a x^2 + b x + c == 0, x]**

$$Out[6]= a \text{ != } 0 \text{ \&\& } (x == \frac{-(\frac{b}{a}) + Sqrt[\frac{b^2}{a^2} - \frac{4 c}{a}]}{2} \text{ ||}$$

$$x == \frac{-(\frac{b}{a}) - Sqrt[\frac{b^2}{a^2} - \frac{4 c}{a}]}{2}) \text{ ||}$$

$$b \text{ != } 0 \text{ \&\& } a == 0 \text{ \&\& } x == -(\frac{c}{b}) \text{ || } a == 0 \text{ \&\& } b == 0 \text{ \&\& } c == 0$$

The most important difference between Reduce and Solve is that Reduce gives *all* the possible solutions to a set of equations, while Solve gives only the *generic* ones. Solutions are considered "generic" if they involve conditions only on the variables that you explicitly solve for, and not on other parameters in the equations. Reduce and Solve also differ in that Reduce always returns combinations of equations, while Solve gives results in the form of transformation rules.

Solve[*eqns*, *vars*]	find generic solutions to equations
Reduce[*eqns*, *vars*]	reduce equations, maintaining all solutions

Solving equations.

■ 3.4.6 Advanced Topic: Existence of Solutions

Using Reduce, you can find out under exactly what conditions a particular set of equations has solutions. Solve tells you whether any generic solutions exist.

There is no value of x which solves these simultaneous equations. Reduce thus simplifies the logical statement x==1 && x==2 to the explicit value False.

$In[1]:=$ **Reduce[x == 1 && x == 2 , x]**

$Out[1]=$ False

There is a solution to these equations, but only when **a** has the special value 1.

$In[2]:=$ **Reduce[x == 1 && x == a , x]**

$Out[2]=$ a == 1 && x == 1

The solution is not generic, and is rejected by Solve.

```
In[3]:= Solve[ x == 1 && x == a , x ]

Out[3]= {}
```

This equation is true for any value of x.

```
In[4]:= Reduce[ x == x , x ]

Out[4]= True
```

This is the kind of result Solve returns when you give an equation that is always true.

```
In[5]:= Solve[ x == x , x ]

Out[5]= {{}}
```

When you work with systems of linear equations, you can use Solve to get generic solutions, and Reduce to find out for what values of parameters solutions exist.

Here is a matrix whose i,j^{th} element is $i+j$.

```
In[6]:= m = Table[i + j, {i, 3}, {j, 3}]

Out[6]= {{2, 3, 4}, {3, 4, 5}, {4, 5, 6}}
```

The matrix has determinant zero.

```
In[7]:= Det[ m ]

Out[7]= 0
```

This makes a set of three simultaneous equations.

```
In[8]:= eqn = m . {x, y, z} == {a, b, c}

Out[8]= {2 x + 3 y + 4 z, 3 x + 4 y + 5 z, 4 x + 5 y + 6 z} ==

     {a, b, c}
```

Solve reports that there are no generic solutions.

```
In[9]:= Solve[eqn, {x, y, z}]

Out[9]= {}
```

Reduce, however, shows that there *would* be a solution if the parameters satisfied the special condition c == -a + 2b.

```
In[10]:= Reduce[eqn, {x, y, z}]

Out[10]= c == -a + 2 b && x == -4 a + 3 b + z &&

     y == 3 a - 2 b - 2 z
```

For non-linear equations, the conditions for the existence of solutions may be very complicated.

Here is a very simple pair of non-linear equations.

```
In[11]:= eqn = {x y == a, x^2 y^2 == b}

Out[11]= {x y == a, x  y  == b}
```

Solve shows that the equations have no generic solutions.

```
In[12]:= Solve[eqn, {x, y}]

Out[12]= {}
```

Reduce gives the complete conditions for a solution to exist.

```
In[13]:= Reduce[eqn, {x, y}]

                                      2              a
Out[13]= y != 0 && b == a  && x == -  ||
                                                      y

     a == 0 && b == 0 && y == 0
```

■ 3.4.7 Eliminating Variables

When you write down a set of simultaneous equations in *Mathematica*, you are specifying a collection of constraints between variables. When you use `Solve`, you are finding values for some of the variables in terms of others, subject to the constraints represented by the equations.

`Solve[eqns, vars, elims]`	find solutions for *vars*, eliminating the variables *elims*
`Eliminate[eqns, elims]`	rearrange equations to eliminate the variables *elims*

Eliminating variables.

Here are two equations involving x, y and the "parameter" a.

```
In[1]:= eqn = {x == 1 + 2 a, y == 9 + 2 x}

Out[1]= {x == 1 + 2 a, y == 9 + 2 x}
```

If you solve for both x and y, you get results in terms of a.

```
In[2]:= Solve[eqn, {x, y}]

Out[2]= {{x -> 1 + 2 a, y -> 9 - 2 (-1 - 2 a)}}
```

Similarly, if you solve for x and a, you get results in terms of y.

```
In[3]:= Solve[eqn, {x, a}]
```

$$Out[3]= \{\{x \to \frac{-9 + y}{2}, \ a \to -(\frac{1}{2}) + \frac{-9 + y}{4}\}\}$$

If you only want to solve for x, however, you have to specify whether you want to eliminate y or a. This eliminates y, and so gives the result in terms of a.

```
In[4]:= Solve[eqn, x, y]

Out[4]= {{x -> 1 + 2 a}}
```

If you eliminate a, then you get a result in terms of y.

```
In[5]:= Solve[eqn, x, a]
```

$$Out[5]= \{\{x \to \frac{-9 + y}{2}\}\}$$

In some cases, you may want to construct explicitly equations in which variables have been eliminated. You can do this using `Eliminate`.

This combines the two equations in the list eqn, by eliminating the variable a.

```
In[6]:= Eliminate[eqn, a]

Out[6]= y == 9 + 2 x
```

This is what you get if you eliminate y instead of a.

```
In[7]:= Eliminate[eqn, y]

Out[7]= 2 a == -1 + x
```

As a more sophisticated example of `Eliminate`, consider the problem of writing $x^5 + y^5$ in terms of the "symmetric polynomials" $x + y$ and xy.

To solve the problem, we simply have to write f in terms of a and b, eliminating the original variables x and y.

```
In[8]:= Eliminate[ {f == x^5 + y^5, a == x + y, b == x y},
                   {x, y} ]
```

$$Out[8]= -5 a^3 b + 5 a b^2 == -a^5 + f$$

■ 3.4.8 Solving Equations with Subsidiary Conditions

In doing calculations with equations, you will often find it convenient to think of a particular set of equations as the "main" ones you are working with, and to think of other equations as "subsidiary conditions" that must also be satisfied.

A typical thing to do is to assign a name to the list of subsidiary conditions, and then to include them by name in each list of equations you give to Solve.

sincos is defined to be the equation $\sin^2(x) + \cos^2(x) = 1$.

```
In[1]:= sincos =  Sin[x]^2 + Cos[x]^2 == 1
               2          2
Out[1]= Cos[x]  + Sin[x]  == 1
```

This solves the equation $\sin(x) + 2\cos(x) = 1$, with the "subsidiary condition" $\sin^2(x) + \cos^2(x) = 1$.

```
In[2]:= Solve[ { Sin[x] + 2 Cos[x] == 1, sincos } ,
                             { Sin[x], Cos[x] } ]
                         3             4
Out[2]= {{Sin[x] -> -(-), Cos[x] -> -},
                         5             5

        {Sin[x] -> 1, Cos[x] -> 0}}
```

Here is another equation, solved with the same "subsidiary condition".

```
In[3]:= Solve[ { Sin[x] == Cos[x], sincos } ,
                             { Sin[x], Cos[x] } ]
                          1                  1
Out[3]= {{Sin[x] ->  -------, Cos[x] ->  -------},
                       Sqrt[2]            Sqrt[2]

                          1                    1
        {Sin[x] -> -(-------), Cos[x] -> -(-------)}}}
                      Sqrt[2]              Sqrt[2]
```

Section 3.4.11 discusses another way to set up and use algebraic subsidiary conditions.

■ 3.4.9 Advanced Topic: Solving Logical Combinations of Equations

When you give a list of equations to Solve, it assumes that you want all the equations to be satisfied simultaneously. It is also possible to give Solve more complicated logical combinations of equations.

Solve assumes that the equations x + y == 1 and x - y == 2 are simultaneously valid.

```
In[1]:= Solve[{x + y == 1, x - y == 2}, {x, y}]
                     3        1
Out[1]= {{x -> -, y -> -(-)}}
                     2        2
```

Here is an alternative form, using the logical connective && explicitly.

```
In[2]:= Solve[ x + y == 1 && x - y == 2, {x, y}]
                     3        1
Out[2]= {{x -> -, y -> -(-)}}
                     2        2
```

This specifies that *either* x + y == 1 *or* x - y == 2. Solve gives two solutions for x, corresponding to these two possibilities.

```
In[3]:= Solve[ x + y == 1 || x - y == 2, x ]
Out[3]= {{x -> 1 - y}, {x -> 2 + y}}
```

Solve gives three solutions to this equation.

```
In[4]:= Solve[x^3 == x, x]
Out[4]= {{x -> 1}, {x -> -1}, {x -> 0}}
```

If you explicitly include the assertion that x != 0, one of the solutions is suppressed.

```
In[5]:= Solve[x^3 == x && x != 0, x]
Out[5]= {{x -> 1}, {x -> -1}}
```

Here is a slightly more complicated example. Note that the precedence of || is lower than the precedence of &&, so the equation is interpreted as (x^3 == x && x != 1) || x^2 == 2, not x^3 == x && (x != 1 || x^2 == 2).

```
In[6]:= Solve[x^3 == x && x != 1 || x^2 == 2 , x]
Out[6]= {{x -> -1}, {x -> 0}, {x -> Sqrt[2]}, {x -> -Sqrt[2]}}
```

When you use Solve, the final results you get are in the form of transformation rules. If you use Reduce or Eliminate, on the other hand, then your results are logical statements, which you can manipulate further.

This gives a logical statement representing the solutions of the equation x^2 == x.

```
In[7]:= Reduce[x^2 == x, x]
Out[7]= x == 1 || x == 0
```

This finds values of x which satisfy x^5 == x but do not satisfy the statement representing the solutions of x^2 == x.

```
In[8]:= Reduce[x^5 == x && !%, x]
Out[8]= x == -1 || x == I || x == -I
```

The logical statements produced by Reduce can be thought of as representations of the solution set for your equations. The logical connectives &&, || and so on then correspond to operations on these sets.

$eqns_1$ || $eqns_2$	union of solution sets
$eqns_1$ && $eqns_2$	intersection of solution sets
!$eqns$	complement of a solution set
Implies[$eqns_1$, $eqns_2$]	the part of $eqns_1$ that contains $eqns_2$

Operations on solution sets.

In dealing with sets of equations, it is common to consider some of the objects that appear as true "variables", and others as "parameters". In some cases, you may need to know for what values of parameters a particular relation between the variables is *always* satisfied.

SolveAlways[*eqns*, *vars*]	solve for the values of parameters for which the *eqns* are satisfied for all values of the *vars*

Solving for parameters that make relations always true.

This finds the values of a, b and c for which the relation x + y == 1 implies a x^2 + b x y + c y^2 == 1 for all x and y.

```
In[9]:= SolveAlways[
            Implies[ x + y == 1, a x^2 + b x y + c y^2 == 1 ] ,
                { x, y } ]
Out[9]= {{a -> 1, b -> 2, c -> 1}}
```

■ 3.4.10 Advanced Topic: Equations Modulo Integers

When you write an equation like *lhs* == *rhs*, you usually want to assert that the expressions *lhs* and *rhs* are exactly equal. For some purposes, however, it is convenient to use a weaker notion of equality, and to interpret *lhs* == *rhs* as meaning that two integer expressions are equal modulo some fixed integer. Solving equations that use this weaker notion of equality is important in many problems in number theory.

Solve[*eqns*, *vars*, ... , Mode->Modular]	
	solve equations with equality required only modulo an integer
Modulus == *p*	a special equation specifying the modulus used to determine equality

Solving equations modulo integers.

There are two ways to work with equations modulo integers. The first is explicitly to specify the modulus you want to use. The second is to let Solve find a modulus for which your equations are satisfied.

Mathematica cannot find a closed-form solution for this equation over complex numbers.

```
In[1]:= Solve[5 + 11x + 17x^2 + 7x^3 + 16x^4 + x^5==0, x]

Out[1]= {ToRules[Roots[11 x + 17 x   + 7 x   + 16 x   + x   == -5,
                                  2       3        4     5
          x]]}
```

The equation does, however, have simple solutions over integers modulo 19. Notice that if you include an equation for Modulus, you do not have to set Mode->Modular explicitly.

```
In[2]:= Solve[5 + 11x + 17x^2 + 7x^3 + 16x^4 + x^5==0 &&
                    Modulus==19, x]
Out[2]= {{Modulus -> 19, x -> -1}, {Modulus -> 19, x -> -7},
      {Modulus -> 19, x -> -12}, {Modulus -> 19, x -> -16},
      {Modulus -> 19, x -> -18}}
```

If you use `Mode->Modular`, but do not explicitly include an equation for the modulus you want to use, *Mathematica* will try to find a modulus for which your set of equations can be satisfied.

The result shows that these equations are satisfied modulo 2 when x is odd.

```
In[3]:= Solve[{x^2 + 1 == 0, x^3 + 1 == 0}, x, Mode->Modular]
Out[3]= {{Modulus -> 2, x -> -1}}
```

When you solve equations in the usual way over complex numbers, it takes n equations to determine the values of n complex variables. When you use `Mode->Modular` without specifying the modulus in advance, however, you can expect to get a finite number of solutions for n integer variables only by giving $n+1$ equations. You can think of the extra equation as being what is needed to determine the modulus.

Here is a polynomial of degree three.

```
In[4]:= f = x^3 + 4x + 17
                     3
Out[4]= 17 + 4 x + x
```

This finds the value of x and the modulus for which both f and its derivative vanish.

```
In[5]:= Solve[ f == D[f,x] == 0, x, Mode->Modular ]
Out[5]= {{Modulus -> 8059, x -> 1001}}
```

Here are the corresponding values of f and D[f,x].

```
In[6]:= {f, D[f,x]} /. %
Out[6]= {{1003007022, 3006007}}
```

They indeed do vanish modulo 8059.

```
In[7]:= Mod[%, 8059]
Out[7]= {{0, 0}}
```

Here is another example, based on a polynomial in two variables.

```
In[8]:= f = y^2 - y - x^3 + x^2
             2    3        2
Out[8]= x  - x  - y + y
```

In the language of arithmetic geometry, this shows that the curve defined by $f = 0$ has a singular point modulo the prime number 11.

```
In[9]:= Solve[ f == D[f,x] == D[f,y] == 0, {x, y},
                            Mode->Modular ]
Out[9]= {{Modulus -> 11, y -> -5, x -> -3}}
```

■ 3.4.11 Setting Up Algebraic Transformation Rules

Transformation rules in *Mathematica* are usually based on the *structure* of expressions, not their algebraic meaning. Using `Solve` and related functions, however, you can effectively carry out true algebraic transformations on expressions.

The transformation rule replaces the specific object x^2 by a. The rule says nothing about objects like x^4 that are algebraically related to x^2.

```
In[1]:= 1 + x^2 + x^4 /. x^2 -> a
                       4
Out[1]= 1 + a + x
```

By calling Solve with the equation x^2 == a, and asking it to eliminate x, you can effectively carry out a true algebraic transformation.

```
In[2]:= Solve[{ f == 1 + x^2 + x^4, x^2 == a } , f , x ]
                          2
Out[2]= {{f -> 1 + a + a }}
```

Often, you need to perform the same algebraic transformation several times. *Mathematica* therefore allows you to construct a set of *algebraic rules*, which embody the transformations you specify, and which you can apply simply by using the standard $/.$ operator.

`AlgebraicRules[eqns, vars]`	generate a set of algebraic rules which replace variables earlier in the list *vars* by ones later in the list, according to the equations *eqns*
expr $/.$ *algrules*	apply algebraic rules to a particular expression

Algebraic transformation rules.

This sets up algebraic transformation rules which try to replace x by a according to the equation x^2 == a.

$In[3]:=$ `ar = AlgebraicRules[x^2 == a, {x, a}]`

$Out[3]=$ $\{x^2 \to a\}$

You can apply the algebraic rules using the $/.$ operator.

$In[4]:=$ `1 + x^2 + x^4 /. ar`

$Out[4]=$ $1 + a + a^2$

The algebraic rules replace as many powers of x^2 as possible.

$In[5]:=$ `1 + x^3 + x^7 /. ar`

$Out[5]=$ $1 + a\,x + a^3\,x$

Algebraic rules in *Mathematica* are set up using mathematical objects known as *Gröbner bases*. Although the output from `AlgebraicRules` is usually displayed as a simple list of rules, it is in fact a representation of a Gröbner basis. You can construct the Gröbner basis explicitly using the function `GroebnerBasis`.

`GroebnerBasis[{poly₁, poly₂, ... }, {x₁, x₂, ... }]`	
	generate a Gröbner basis for the polynomials *polyᵢ*

Constructing Gröbner bases.

This constructs a Gröbner basis for a pair of polynomials.

$In[6]:=$ `GroebnerBasis[{x^2 - y^2, x^3 + y^3}, {x, y}]`

$Out[6]=$ $\{x\,y^2 + y^3, x^2 - y^2\}$

You can use `AlgebraicRules` to set up algebraic rules involving several variables.

This sets up algebraic rules which try to replace x and y by a and b using the equations given.

$In[7]:=$ `ar = AlgebraicRules[{a == x+y, b == x y},`
                          `{x, y, a, b}]`

$Out[7]=$ $\{-y^2 \to b - a\,y, -x \to -a + y\}$

By applying the algebraic rules `ar`, you can rewrite `x^3 + y^3` in terms of `a` and `b`.

```
In[8]:= x^3 + y^3 /. ar

Out[8]= a  - 3 a b
         3
```

You can apply the same rules to `x^4 + y^4`.

```
In[9]:= x^4 + y^4 /. ar

Out[9]= a  - 4 a  b + 2 b
         4      2        2
```

In this case, it is not possible to eliminate `x` and `y` entirely. Following the order of variables you specified in `AlgebraicRules`, *Mathematica* nevertheless tries to eliminate `x` in favor of `y`.

```
In[10]:= x^3 + y^4 /. ar

Out[10]= a  - 2 a b - a  b + b  - a  y + a  y + b y - 2 a b y
          3            2      2    2      3
```

3.5 Calculus

■ 3.5.1 Differentiation

$D[f, x]$	partial derivative $\frac{\partial}{\partial x}f$
$D[f, x_1, x_2, \ldots]$	multiple derivative $\frac{\partial}{\partial x_1}\frac{\partial}{\partial x_2}\ldots f$
$D[f, \{x, n\}]$	n^{th} derivative $\frac{\partial^n}{\partial x^n}f$
$D[f, x, \text{NonConstants} \rightarrow \{v_1, v_2, \ldots\}]$	
	$\frac{\partial}{\partial x}f$ with the v_i taken to depend on x

Partial differentiation operations.

This gives $\frac{\partial}{\partial x}x^n$.

```
In[1]:= D[x^n, x]
                -1 + n
Out[1]= n x
```

This gives the third derivative.

```
In[2]:= D[x^n, {x, 3}]
                              -3 + n
Out[2]= (-2 + n) (-1 + n) n x
```

You can differentiate with respect to any expression.

```
In[3]:= D[ x[1]^2 + x[2]^2, x[1] ]
Out[3]= 2 x[1]
```

D does *partial differentiation*. It assumes here that y is independent of x.

```
In[4]:= D[x^2 + y^2, x]
Out[4]= 2 x
```

If y does in fact depend on x, you can use the explicit functional form y[x]. Section 3.5.4 describes how objects like y'[x] work.

```
In[5]:= D[x^2 + y[x]^2, x]
Out[5]= 2 x + 2 y[x] y'[x]
```

Instead of giving an explicit function y[x], you can tell D that y *implicitly* depends on x.
D[y, x, NonConstants->{y}] then represents $\frac{\partial y}{\partial x}$, with y implicitly depending on x.

```
In[6]:= D[x^2 + y^2, x, NonConstants -> {y}]
Out[6]= 2 x + 2 y D[y, x, NonConstants -> {y}]
```

■ 3.5.2 Total Derivatives

$\text{Dt}[f]$	total differential df
$\text{Dt}[f, x]$	total derivative $\frac{df}{dx}$
$\text{Dt}[f, x_1, x_2, \ldots]$	multiple total derivative $\frac{d}{dx_1}\frac{d}{dx_2}\ldots f$
$\text{Dt}[f, x, \text{Constants} \rightarrow \{c_1, c_2, \ldots\}]$	
	total derivative with c_i constant (*i.e.*, $dc_i = 0$)
$y/: \text{Dt}[y, x] = 0$	set $\frac{dy}{dx} = 0$
$\text{SetAttributes}[c, \text{Constant}]$	define c to be a constant in all cases

Total differentiation operations.

When you find the derivative of some expression f with respect to x, you are effectively finding out how fast f changes as you vary x. Often f will depend not only on x, but also on other variables, say y and z. The results that you get then depend on how you assume that y and z vary as you change x.

There are two common cases. Either y and z are assumed to stay fixed when x changes, or they are allowed to vary with x. In a standard *partial derivative* $\frac{\partial f}{\partial x}$, all variables other than x are assumed fixed. On the other hand, in the *total derivative* $\frac{df}{dx}$, all variables are allowed to change with x.

In *Mathematica*, $\text{D}[f, x]$ gives a partial derivative, with all other variables assumed independent of x. $\text{Dt}[f, x]$ gives a total derivative, in which all variables are assumed to depend on x. In both cases, you can add an argument to give more information on dependencies.

This gives the *partial derivative* $\frac{\partial}{\partial x}(x^2 + y^2)$. y is assumed to be independent of x.	$In[1]:= \text{D[x\^2 + y\^2, x]}$ $Out[1]= 2\ x$
This gives the *total derivative* $\frac{d}{dx}(x^2 + y^2)$. Now y is assumed to depend on x.	$In[2]:= \text{Dt[x\^2 + y\^2, x]}$ $Out[2]= 2\ x + 2\ y\ \text{Dt[y, x]}$
You can make a replacement for $\frac{dy}{dx}$.	$In[3]:= \text{\% /. Dt[y, x] -> yx}$ $Out[3]= 2\ x + 2\ y\ yx$
You can also make an explicit definition for $\frac{dy}{dx}$. You need to use $y/:$ to make sure that the definition is associated with y.	$In[4]:= \text{y/: Dt[y, x] = 0}$ $Out[4]= 0$
With this definition made, Dt treats y as independent of x.	$In[5]:= \text{Dt[x\^2 + y\^2 + z\^2, x]}$ $Out[5]= 2\ x + 2\ z\ \text{Dt[z, x]}$
This removes your definition for the derivative of y.	$In[6]:= \text{Clear[y]}$

This takes the total derivative, with z held fixed.

```
In[7]:= Dt[x^2 + y^2 + z^2, x, Constants->{z}]
Out[7]= 2 x + 2 y Dt[y, x]
```

This specifies that c is a constant under differentiation.

```
In[8]:= SetAttributes[c, Constant]
```

The variable c is taken as a constant.

```
In[9]:= Dt[a^2 + c x^2, x]
Out[9]= 2 c x + 2 a Dt[a, x]
```

The *function* c is also assumed to be a constant.

```
In[10]:= Dt[a^2 + c[x] x^2, x]
Out[10]= 2 x c[x] + 2 a Dt[a, x]
```

This gives the total differential $d(x^2 + cy^2)$.

```
In[11]:= Dt[x^2 + c y^2]
Out[11]= 2 x Dt[x] + 2 c y Dt[y]
```

You can make replacements and assignments for total differentials.

```
In[12]:= % /. Dt[y] -> dy
Out[12]= 2 c dy y + 2 x Dt[x]
```

■ 3.5.3 Derivatives of Unknown Functions

Differentiating a known function gives an explicit result.

```
In[1]:= D[Log[x]^2, x]
```
$$Out[1]= \frac{2\ \text{Log}[x]}{x}$$

Differentiating an unknown function f gives a result in terms of f'.

```
In[2]:= D[f[x]^2, x]
Out[2]= 2 f[x] f'[x]
```

Mathematica applies the chain rule for differentiation, and leaves the result in terms of f'.

```
In[3]:= D[x f[x^2], x]
Out[3]= f[x^2] + 2 x^2 f'[x^2]
```

Differentiating again gives a result in terms of f, f' and f''.

```
In[4]:= D[%, x]
Out[4]= 6 x f'[x^2] + 4 x^3 f''[x^2]
```

When a function has more than one argument, superscripts are used to indicate how many times each argument is being differentiated.

```
In[5]:= D[g[x^2, y^2], x]
Out[5]= 2 x g^{(1,0)}[x^2, y^2]
```

This represents $\frac{\partial}{\partial x} \frac{\partial}{\partial x} \frac{\partial}{\partial y} g(x, y)$. *Mathematica* assumes that the order in which derivatives are taken with respect to different variables is irrelevant.

```
In[6]:= D[g[x, y], x, x, y]
Out[6]= g^{(2,1)}[x, y]
```

You can find the value of the derivative when $x = 0$ by replacing x with 0.

```
In[7]:= % /. x->0
Out[7]= g^{(2,1)}[0, y]
```

$f'[x]$ first derivative of a function of one variable

$f^{(n)}[x]$ n^{th} derivative of a function of one variable

$f^{(n_1, n_2, \ldots)}[x]$ derivative of a function of several variables, n_i times with respect to variable i

Output forms for derivatives of unknown functions.

■ 3.5.4 Advanced Topic: The Representation of Derivatives

Derivatives in *Mathematica* work essentially the same as in standard mathematics. The usual mathematical notation, however, often hides many details. To understand how derivatives are represented in *Mathematica*, we must look at these details.

The standard mathematical notation $f'(0)$ is really a shorthand for $\frac{d}{dt} f(t)\,|_{t=0}$, where t is a "dummy variable". Similarly, $f'(x^2)$ is a shorthand for $\frac{d}{dt} f(t)\,|_{t=x^2}$. As suggested by the notation f', the object $\frac{d}{dt} f(t)$ can in fact be viewed as a "pure function", to be evaluated with a particular choice of its parameter t. You can think of the operation of differentiation as acting on a *function f*, to give a new *function*, usually called f'.

With functions of more than one argument, the simple notation based on primes breaks down. You cannot tell for example whether $g'(0, 1)$ stands for $\frac{d}{dt} g(t, 1)\,|_{t=0}$ or $\frac{d}{dt} g(0, t)\,|_{t=1}$, and for almost any g, these will have totally different values. Once again, however, t is just a dummy variable, whose sole purpose is to show with respect to which "slot" g is to be differentiated.

In *Mathematica*, as in some branches of mathematics, it is convenient to think about a kind of differentiation that acts on *functions*, rather than expressions. We need an operation that takes the function f, and gives us the *derivative function f'*. Operations such as this that act on *functions*, rather than variables, are known in mathematics as *functionals*.

The object `f'` in *Mathematica* is the result of applying the differentiation functional to the function `f`. The full form of `f'` is in fact `Derivative[1][f]`. `Derivative[1]` is the *Mathematica* differentiation functional.

The arguments in the functional `Derivative[$n_1$, $n_2$, ... ]` specify how many times to differentiate with respect to each "slot" of the function on which it acts. By using functionals to represent differentiation, *Mathematica* avoids any need to introduce explicit "dummy variables".

This is the full form of the derivative of the function `f`.	`In[1]:= f' // FullForm` `Out[1]//FullForm= Derivative[1][f]`
Here an argument `x` is supplied.	`In[2]:= f'[x] // FullForm` `Out[2]//FullForm= Derivative[1][f][x]`

This is the second derivative.	`In[3]:= f''[x] // FullForm`
	
	`Out[3]//FullForm= Derivative[2][f][x]`

This gives a derivative of the function g with respect to its second "slot".	`In[4]:= D[g[x, y], y]`
	
	`Out[4]= g`$^{(0,1)}$`[x, y]`

Here is the full form.	`In[5]:= % // FullForm`
	
	`Out[5]//FullForm= Derivative[0, 1][g][x, y]`

Here is the second derivative with respect to the variable y, which appears in the second slot of g.	`In[6]:= D[g[x, y], {y, 2}] // FullForm`
	
	`Out[6]//FullForm= Derivative[0, 2][g][x, y]`

This is a mixed derivative.	`In[7]:= D[g[x, y], x, y, y] // FullForm`
	
	`Out[7]//FullForm= Derivative[1, 2][g][x, y]`

Since **Derivative** only specifies how many times to differentiate with respect to each slot, the order of the derivatives is irrelevant.	`In[8]:= D[g[x, y], y, y, x] // FullForm`
	
	`Out[8]//FullForm= Derivative[1, 2][g][x, y]`

Here is a more complicated case, in which both arguments of g depend on the differentiation variable.	`In[9]:= D[g[x, x], x]`
	
	`Out[9]= g`$^{(0,1)}$`[x, x] + g`$^{(1,0)}$`[x, x]`

This is the full form of the result.	`In[10]:= % // FullForm`
	
	`Out[10]//FullForm=`
	`Plus[Derivative[0, 1][g][x, x], Derivative[1, 0][g][x, x]]`

The object f' behaves essentially like any other function in *Mathematica*. You can evaluate the function with any argument, and you can use standard *Mathematica* /. operations to change the argument. (This would not be possible if explicit dummy variables had been introduced in the course of the differentiation.)

This is the *Mathematica* representation of the derivative of a function f, evaluated at the origin.	`In[11]:= f'[0] // FullForm`
	
	`Out[11]//FullForm= Derivative[1][f][0]`

The result of this derivative involves f' evaluated with the argument x^2.	`In[12]:= D[f[x^2], x]`
	
	`Out[12]= 2 x f'[x`^{2}`]`

You can evaluate the result at the point $x = 2$ by using the standard *Mathematica* replacement operation.	`In[13]:= % /. x->2`
	
	`Out[13]= 4 f'[4]`

There is some slight subtlety when you need to deduce the value of f' based on definitions for objects like f[x_].

Here is a definition for a function h.	*In[14]:=* **h[x_] := x^4**
When you take the derivative of h[x], *Mathematica* first evaluates h[x], then differentiates the result.	*In[15]:=* **D[h[x], x]** *Out[15]=* 4 x^3
You can get the same result by applying the function h' to the argument x.	*In[16]:=* **h'[x]** *Out[16]=* 4 x^3
Here is the function h' on its own.	*In[17]:=* **h'** *Out[17]=* 4 #1^3 &

The function f' is completely determined by the form of the function f. Definitions for objects like f[x_] do not immediately apply however to expressions like f'[x_]. The problem is that f'[x] has the full form Derivative[1][f][x], which nowhere contains anything that explicitly matches the pattern f[x_]. In addition, for many purposes it is convenient to have a representation of the function f' itself, without necessarily applying it to any arguments.

What *Mathematica* does is to try and find the explicit form of a *pure function* which represents the object f'. When *Mathematica* gets an expression like Derivative[1][f], it effectively converts it to the explicit form D[f[#], #]& and then tries to evaluate the derivative. In the explicit form, *Mathematica* can immediately use values that have been defined for objects like f[x_]. If *Mathematica* succeeds in doing the derivative, it returns the explicit pure-function result. If it does not succeed, it leaves the derivative in the original f' form.

This gives the derivative of Tan in pure-function form.	*In[18]:=* **Tan'** *Out[18]=* Sec[#1]^2 &
Here is the result of applying the pure function to the specific argument y.	*In[19]:=* **%[y]** *Out[19]=* Sec[y]^2

■ 3.5.5 Defining Derivatives

You can define the derivative in *Mathematica* of a function f of one argument simply by an assignment like f'[x_] = fp[x].

This defines the derivative of $f(x)$ to be $fp(x)$. In this case, you could have used = instead of :=.	*In[1]:=* **f'[x_] := fp[x]**
The rule for f'[x_] is used to evaluate this derivative.	*In[2]:=* **D[f[x^2], x]** *Out[2]=* 2 x fp[x^2]

Differentiating again gives derivatives of *fp*.

In[3]:= **D[%, x]**

Out[3]= $2 \text{ fp}[x^2] + 4 x^2 \text{ fp}'[x^2]$

This defines a value for the derivative of *g* at the origin.

In[4]:= **g'[0] = g0**

Out[4]= g0

The value for g'[0] is used.

In[5]:= **D[g[x]^2, x] /. x->0**

Out[5]= 2 g0 g[0]

This defines the second derivative of *g*, with any argument.

In[6]:= **g''[x_] = gpp[x]**

Out[6]= gpp[x]

The value defined for the second derivative is used.

In[7]:= **D[g[x]^2, {x, 2}]**

Out[7]= $2 \text{ g}[x] \text{ gpp}[x] + 2 \text{ g}'[x]^2$

To define derivatives of functions with several arguments, you have to use the general representation of derivatives in *Mathematica*.

$f'[x] := rhs$	define the first derivative of f
Derivative[n][f][x] := *rhs*	define the nth derivative of f
Derivative[n_1, n_2, ...][g][x_1, x_2, ...] := *rhs*	
	define derivatives of g with respect to various arguments

Defining derivatives.

This defines the second derivative of g with respect to its second argument.

In[8]:= **Derivative[0, 2][g][x_, y_] := g2p[x, y]**

■ 3.5.6 Indefinite Integrals

The *Mathematica* function Integrate[*f*, *x*] gives you the *indefinite integral* $\int f \, dx$. You can think of the process of indefinite integration as like an inverse of differentiation. If you take the result from Integrate[*f*, *x*], and then differentiate it, you always get a result that is mathematically equal to the original expression *f*.

In general, however, there is a whole family of results which have the property that their derivative is *f*. Integrate[*f*, *x*] gives you *an* expression whose derivative is *f*. You can get other expressions by adding an arbitrary constant of integration.

When you fill in explicit limits for your integral, any such constants of integration must cancel out. Even though the indefinite integral contains arbitrary constants, it is still often very convenient to manipulate it before filling in the limits.

Mathematica applies standard rules to
find indefinite integrals.

$In[1]:=$ **Integrate[x^2, x]**

$$Out[1]= \frac{x^3}{3}$$

You can add an arbitrary constant to the
indefinite integral, and still get the same
derivative. **Integrate** simply gives you
an expression with the required
derivative.

$In[2]:=$ **D[% + c , x]**

$$Out[2]= x^2$$

This gives the indefinite integral $\int \frac{dx}{x^2-1}$.

$In[3]:=$ **Integrate[1/(x^2 - 1), x]**

$$Out[3]= \frac{Log[-1 + x]}{2} - \frac{Log[1 + x]}{2}$$

Differentiating should give the original
function back again.

$In[4]:=$ **D[%, x]**

$$Out[4]= \frac{1}{2 (-1 + x)} - \frac{1}{2 (1 + x)}$$

You need to manipulate it to get it back
into the original form.

$In[5]:=$ **Simplify[%]**

$$Out[5]= \frac{1}{-1 + x^2}$$

The **Integrate** function assumes that any object that does not explicitly contain the integration variable is independent of it, and can be treated as a constant. As a result, **Integrate** is like an inverse of the *partial differentiation* function D.

The variable a is assumed to be
independent of x.

$In[6]:=$ **Integrate[a x^2, x]**

$$Out[6]= \frac{a x^3}{3}$$

The integration variable can be any
expression.

$In[7]:=$ **Integrate[x b[x]^2, b[x]]**

$$Out[7]= \frac{x b[x]^3}{3}$$

Another assumption that **Integrate** implicitly makes is that all the symbolic quantities in your integrand have "generic" values. Thus, for example, *Mathematica* will tell you that $\int x^n \, dx$ is $\frac{x^{n+1}}{n+1}$ even though this is not true in the special case $n = -1$.

Mathematica gives the standard result for
this integral, implicitly assuming that n
is not equal to −1.

$In[8]:=$ **Integrate[x^n, x]**

$$Out[8]= \frac{x^{1 + n}}{1 + n}$$

If you specifically give an exponent of −1, *Mathematica* produces a different result.

```
In[9]:= Integrate[x^-1, x]

Out[9]= Log[x]
```

The results you get by doing integrals can often be written in many different forms. *Mathematica* follows various principles in deciding which form to use in each particular case. One principle is that if your input does not contain complex numbers, then neither should your output. Thus, for example, *Mathematica* tries to choose between forms involving logarithms and arc tangents in such a way as to avoid unnecessary complex numbers.

Mathematica writes this integral in terms of logarithms.

```
In[10]:= Integrate[1/(x^2 - 8), x]

              -2 Sqrt[2] + x
          Log[--------------]
               2 Sqrt[2] + x
Out[10]= ------------------------
                4 Sqrt[2]
```

If you reverse the sign of the 8 in the denominator, *Mathematica* gives a result in terms of arc tangents.

```
In[11]:= Integrate[1/(x^2 + 8), x]

                      x
          ArcTan[-----------]
                  2 Sqrt[2]
Out[11]= ------------------------
                2 Sqrt[2]
```

If your integral involves symbolic parameters with unspecified signs, it is not so clear how to avoid complex numbers. In this case, *Mathematica* gives the result appropriate for positive a.

```
In[12]:= Integrate[1/(x^2 + a), x]

                    x
          ArcTan[-------]
                 Sqrt[a]
Out[12]= ------------------
               Sqrt[a]
```

In the course of evaluating the integral, *Mathematica* explicitly calls **Sign** to try and determine the sign of a. You can add your own definition for **Sign[a]**.

```
In[13]:= a/: Sign[a] = -1

Out[13]= -1
```

Now *Mathematica* will instead assume that a is negative, and will give the result in the appropriate form.

```
In[14]:= Integrate[1/(x^2 + a), x]

              -Sqrt[-a] + x
          Log[-------------]
               Sqrt[-a] + x
Out[14]= ------------------------
               2 Sqrt[-a]
```

◼ 3.5.7 Integrals That *Mathematica* Can and Cannot Do

Evaluating integrals is much more difficult than evaluating derivatives. For derivatives, there is a systematic procedure involving the chain and product rules that allows one to work out any derivative. For integrals, however, there is no such systematic procedure. There are some general principles, but there are many integrals that cannot be done using these principles.

Before going any further, one must address the important question of exactly what it means to "do" an integral. As an operational matter, the important issue is usually whether one can write down a definite formula for the integral, which one can then easily manipulate or evaluate. The most useful formulas are typically ones that involve only rather simple functions, such as logarithms and exponentials.

The class of integrals that can be done in terms of "simple functions" is an important one, albeit in many respects not a particularly large one. One of the main capabilities of the built-in *Mathematica* `Integrate` function is being able to take essentially any integrand that involves only a particular set of "simple functions", and find the integral if it can be expressed in terms of the same set of simple functions. The relevant set of "simple functions" includes rational functions, exponentials and logarithms, as well as trigonometric and inverse trigonometric functions.

Integrals of rational functions are usually quite easy to evaluate. The answers come out in terms of rational functions, together with logarithms and inverse trigonometric functions.

$$In[1]:= \text{Integrate}[x/((x - 1)(x + 2)), x]$$

$$Out[1]= \frac{\text{Log}[-1 + x]}{3} + \frac{2 \text{ Log}[2 + x]}{3}$$

If *Mathematica* cannot get explicit formulas for the roots of the denominator polynomial, however, it cannot give you an explicit formula for the integral.

$$In[2]:= \text{Integrate}[1/(1 + 3x + x\verb|^|5), x]$$

$$Out[2]= \text{Integrate}[\frac{1}{1 + 3 x + x^5}, x]$$

Integrals involving logarithms and powers can be done in terms of logarithms and powers.

$$In[3]:= \text{Integrate}[x\verb|^|4 \text{ Log}[x]\verb|^|2, x]$$

$$Out[3]= \frac{x^5 (2 - 10 \text{ Log}[x] + 25 \text{ Log}[x]^2)}{125}$$

Integrals of trigonometric functions usually come out in terms of other trigonometric functions.

$$In[4]:= \text{Integrate}[\text{Sin}[x]\verb|^|3 \text{ Cos}[x]\verb|^|2, x]$$

$$Out[4]= \frac{-\text{Cos}[x]}{8} - \frac{\text{Cos}[3 x]}{48} + \frac{\text{Cos}[5 x]}{80}$$

When you combine "simple functions", you sometimes get integrals that can be done.

$$In[5]:= \text{Integrate}[\text{Sin}[\text{Log}[x]], x]$$

$$Out[5]= \frac{-(x (\text{Cos}[\text{Log}[x]] - \text{Sin}[\text{Log}[x]]))}{2}$$

Often, however, you get integrals that cannot be done in terms of simple functions.

$$In[6]:= \text{Integrate}[\text{Sin}[\text{Sin}[x]], x]$$

$$Out[6]= \text{Integrate}[\text{Sin}[\text{Sin}[x]], x]$$

It is remarkable what simple integrands can lead to integrals that cannot be done, say in terms of "simple functions". In fact, if you were randomly to combine simple functions together, most of the integrals you would get could probably not be done in terms of simple functions.

In practical usage, however, there are certain integrals that occur much more often than others. These integrals can sometimes be expressed in terms of "special functions", which were often defined specifically as a way to represent the integrals. Most of the standard special functions are built into *Mathematica*, as discussed in Section 3.2. If you give an integral which can be done in terms of these special functions, *Mathematica* will often recognize it.

The integral $\int \frac{\log(1-x)}{x} dx$ comes out in terms of a special function known as the polylogarithm.

```
In[7]:= Integrate[Log[1-x]/x, x]

Out[7]= -PolyLog[2, x]
```

$\int \log(\log(x)) dx$ can be written in terms of the logarithmic integral function.

```
In[8]:= Integrate[Log[Log[x]], x]

Out[8]= x Log[Log[x]] - LogIntegral[x]
```

Although it may be entertaining to try and construct integrals which work out in particularly subtle ways, it is worth realizing that in practical applications, such integrals are usually quite rare. The integrals that crop up in practice can usually be divided into three classes:

- Simple integrals that can be done by simple methods.

- Integrals whose form is close to the definition of a particular special function.

- Integrals that cannot be done at all in terms of standard simple or special functions.

The algorithms that are built into *Mathematica* should allow you to do most of the *indefinite* integrals that are found in books of mathematical tables. Sometimes, however, you may want to add your own rules for certain kinds of integrals. Section 3.5.9 describes how to do this.

Mathematica could make the best use of rules that you add, if it could put all integrals into standard forms that it can recognize. The chain rule makes it possible to put all derivatives into standard forms, in terms of the *Mathematica* function Derivative, as discussed in Section 3.5.4. For integrals, however, there is no such systematic way to produce a standard form. Instead, *Mathematica* uses some simple transformations to try and produce easily recognizable forms.

Mathematica makes simple transformations to try and put integrals it cannot do into standard forms.

```
In[9]:= Integrate[4 Cos[Cos[x]], x]

Out[9]= 4 Integrate[Cos[Cos[x]], x]
```

Mathematica will sometimes do part of an integral, then leave the part it cannot do in a standard form.

```
In[10]:= Integrate[(1 + Log[x]^2)/(1 - Log[x]), x]

                          1
Out[10]= -2 Integrate[--------, x] - x Log[x]
                      -1 + Log[x]
```

There are some general transformations on integrals that *Mathematica* tries, regardless of the functions that the integrals involve.

Integrating $f'(x)$ for any f gives $f(x)$.

```
In[11]:= Integrate[f'[x], x]

Out[11]= f[x]
```

Mathematica can also deal with slightly more complicated cases.

```
In[12]:= Integrate[f'[x] f[x]^2, x]

              3
          f[x]
Out[12]= ------
            3
```

Here is a derivative.

```
In[13]:= D[Log[Log[Log[x]]], x]

                        1
Out[13]= ----------------------
         x Log[x] Log[Log[x]]
```

The general transformations that *Mathematica* applies often allow it to do integrals like this.

```
In[14]:= Integrate[%, x]

Out[14]= Log[Log[Log[x]]]
```

■ 3.5.8 Definite Integrals

Integrate[*f*, *x*]	the indefinite integral $\int f \, dx$
Integrate[*f*, {*x*, *xmin*, *xmax*}]	the definite integral $\int_{xmin}^{xmax} f \, dx$
Integrate[*f*, {*x*, *xmin*, *xmax*}, {*y*, *ymin*, *ymax*}]	the multiple integral $\int_{xmin}^{xmax} dx \int_{ymin}^{ymax} dy \, f$

Integration functions.

Here is the integral $\int_a^b x^2 \, dx$.

```
In[1]:= Integrate[x^2, {x, a, b}]

              3     3
            -a     b
Out[1]=    ---- + ----
             3     3
```

This gives the multiple integral $\int_0^a dx \int_0^b dy \, (x^2 + y^2)$.

```
In[2]:= Integrate[x^2 + y^2, {x, 0, a}, {y, 0, b}]

             3        3
           a  b     a b
Out[2]=   ------ + ------
             3        3
```

The y integral is done first. Its limits can depend on the value of x. This ordering is the same as is used in functions like Sum and Table.

```
In[3]:= Integrate[x^2 + y^2, {x, 0, a}, {y, 0, x}]

             4
           a
Out[3]=   ----
            3
```

You can often do a definite integral by first finding the indefinite one, and then explicitly substituting in the limits. You have to be careful, however, when the integration region contains a singularity. The integral $\int_{-1}^{1} x^{-2} \, dx$, for example, has an indefinite form which is finite at each end point. Nevertheless, the integrand has a double pole at $x = 0$, and the true integral is infinite.

■ 3.5.9 Defining Integrals

You can supplement the built-in integration functions of *Mathematica* by defining transformation rules for other integrals. You can, for example, enter some of the long lists of particular definite integrals that can be done.

The lack of a definite standard form for all integrals means that you sometimes have to give several different versions of the same integral: there is no guarantee that the appropriate changes of variable will automatically be done.

This integral cannot be done by the built-in *Mathematica* integration algorithm.

```
In[1]:= Integrate[Sin[Sin[x]], x]
Out[1]= Integrate[Sin[Sin[x]], x]
```

Before you add your own rules for integration, you have to remove write protection.

```
In[2]:= Unprotect[Integrate]
Out[2]= {Integrate}
```

You can, however, set up your own rule to define the integral to be, say, a "Jones" function.

```
In[3]:= Integrate[Sin[Sin[a_. + b_. x]], x] :=
                              Jones[a, x]/b
```

Now *Mathematica* can do integrals that give Jones functions.

```
In[4]:= Integrate[Sin[Sin[3x]], x]

          Jones[0, x]
Out[4]= -----------
              3
```

■ 3.5.10 Manipulating Integrals in Symbolic Form

When *Mathematica* cannot give you an explicit result for an integral, it leaves the integral in a symbolic form. It is often useful to manipulate this symbolic form.

Mathematica cannot give an explicit result for this integral, so it leaves the integral in symbolic form.

```
In[1]:= Integrate[x^2 f[x], x]
               2
Out[1]= Integrate[x  f[x], x]
```

Differentiating the symbolic form gives the integrand back again.

```
In[2]:= D[%, x]
          2
Out[2]= x  f[x]
```

Here is a definite integral which cannot be done explicitly.

```
In[3]:= Integrate[f[x], {x, a[x], b[x]}]
Out[3]= Integrate[f[x], {x, a[x], b[x]}]
```

This gives the derivative of the definite integral.

```
In[4]:= D[%, x]
Out[4]= -(f[a[x]] a'[x]) + f[b[x]] b'[x]
```

Here is a definite integral with end points that do not explicitly depend on x.

```
In[5]:= defint = Integrate[f[x], {x, a, b}]
Out[5]= Integrate[f[x], {x, a, b}]
```

The partial derivative of this with respect to x is zero.

```
In[6]:= D[defint, x]
Out[6]= 0
```

There is a non-trivial total derivative, however.

```
In[7]:= Dt[defint, x]
Out[7]= -(Dt[a, x] f[a]) + Dt[b, x] f[b]
```

■ 3.5.11 Differential Equations

As discussed in Section 1.5.8, you can use the *Mathematica* function DSolve to find symbolic solutions to ordinary differential equations.

Solving a differential equation consists essentially in finding the form of an unknown function. In *Mathematica*, unknown functions are represented by expressions like y[x]. The derivatives of such functions are represented by y'[x], y''[x] and so on.

The *Mathematica* function DSolve returns as its result a list of rules for functions. There is a question of how these functions are represented. If you ask DSolve to solve for y[x], then DSolve will indeed return a rule for y[x]. In some cases, this rule may be all you need. But this rule, on its own, does not give values for y'[x] or even y[0]. In many cases, therefore, it is better to ask DSolve to solve not for y[x], but instead for y itself. In this case, what DSolve will return is a rule which gives y as a pure function, in the sense discussed in Section 2.2.5.

If you ask DSolve to solve for y[x], it will give a rule specifically for y[x].	$In[1]:=$ **DSolve[y'[x] + y[x] == 1, y[x], x]** $Out[1]=$ $\{\{y[x] \rightarrow 1 + \dfrac{C[1]}{E^x}\}\}$
The rule applies only to y[x] itself, and not, for example, to objects like y[0] or y'[x].	$In[2]:=$ **y[x] + 2y'[x] + y[0] /. %** $Out[2]=$ $\{1 + \dfrac{C[1]}{E^x} + y[0] + 2\ y'[x]\}$
If you ask DSolve to solve for y, it gives a rule for the object y on its own as a pure function.	$In[3]:=$ **DSolve[y'[x] + y[x] == 1, y, x]** $Out[3]=$ $\{\{y \rightarrow (1 + \dfrac{C[1]}{E^{\#1}}\ \&\ )\}\}$
Now the rule applies to all occurrences of y.	$In[4]:=$ **y[x] + 2y'[x] + y[0] /. %** $Out[4]=$ $\{2 + C[1] - \dfrac{C[1]}{E^x}\}$

DSolve[*eqn*, $y[x]$, x]	solve a differential equation for $y[x]$
DSolve[*eqn*, y, x]	solve a differential equation for the function y

Getting solutions to differential equations in different forms.

In standard mathematical notation, one typically represents solutions to differential equations by explicitly introducing "dummy variables" to represent the arguments of the functions that appear. If all you need is a symbolic form for the solution, then introducing such dummy variables may be convenient. However, if you actually intend to use the solution in a variety of other computations, then you will usually find it better to get the solution in pure-function form, without dummy variables. Notice that this form, while easy to represent in *Mathematica*, has no direct analog in standard mathematical notation.

DSolve[{*eqn₁*, *eqn₂*, ... }, {*y₁*, *y₂*, ... }, {*x₁*, ... }]

        solve a list of differential equations

Solving simultaneous differential equations.

This solves two simultaneous differential equations.

```
In[5]:= DSolve[{y[x] == -z'[x], z[x] == -y'[x]}, {y, z}, x]
```

$$Out[5]= \{\{y \rightarrow (\frac{C[1] + E^{2\,\#1}\,C[1] + C[2] - E^{2\,\#1}\,C[2]}{2\,E^{\#1}}\ \&\ ),$$

$$z \rightarrow (\frac{C[1] - E^{2\,\#1}\,C[1] + C[2] + E^{2\,\#1}\,C[2]}{2\,E^{\#1}}\ \&\ )\}\}$$

Mathematica returns two distinct solutions for y in this case.

```
In[6]:= DSolve[y[x] y'[x] == 1, y, x]
Out[6]= {{y -> (Sqrt[2 (C[1] + #1)] & )},
        {y -> (-Sqrt[2 (C[1] + #1)] & )}}
```

You can add constraints and boundary conditions for differential equations by explicitly giving additional equations such as y[0] == 0.

This asks for a solution which satisfies the condition y[0] == 1.

```
In[7]:= DSolve[{y'[x] == a y[x], y[0] == 1}, y[x], x]
Out[7]= {{y[x] -> E^{a x}}}
```

Without sufficient constraints or boundary conditions, a particular differential equation typically has a whole family of possible solutions. These solutions typically differ in the values of certain undetermined "constants of integration". When necessary, *Mathematica* automatically generates objects to represent undetermined constants that occur in the solutions of differential equations.

The default is that these constants are named C[*n*], where the index *n* starts at 1 for each invocation of DSolve. You can override this choice, by explicitly giving a setting for the option DSolveConstants. Any function you give is applied to each successive index value *n* to get the constants to use for each invocation of DSolve.

3.6 Power Series, Limits and Residues

■ 3.6.1 Making Power Series Expansions

`Series[expr, {x, x₀, n}]`	find the power series expansion of *expr* about the point $x = x_0$ to order at most $(x - x_0)^n$
`Series[expr, {x, x₀, nₓ}, {y, y₀, n_y}]`	find series expansions with respect to *y* then *x*

Functions for creating power series.

Here is the power series expansion for $\exp(x)$ about the point $x = 0$ to order x^4.

$$In[1]:= \text{Series}[\ \text{Exp}[x],\ \{x,\ 0,\ 4\}\ ]$$

$$Out[1]= 1 + x + \frac{x^2}{2} + \frac{x^3}{6} + \frac{x^4}{24} + O[x]^5$$

Here is the series expansion of $\exp(x)$ about the point $x = 1$.

$$In[2]:= \text{Series}[\ \text{Exp}[x],\ \{x,\ 1,\ 4\}\ ]$$

$$Out[2]= E + E\ (-1 + x) + \frac{E\ (-1 + x)^2}{2} + \frac{E\ (-1 + x)^3}{6} +$$

$$\frac{E\ (-1 + x)^4}{24} + O[-1 + x]^5$$

If *Mathematica* does not know the series expansion of a particular function, it writes the result symbolically in terms of derivatives.

$$In[3]:= \text{Series}[\ f[x],\ \{x,\ 0,\ 3\}\ ]$$

$$Out[3]= f[0] + f'[0]\ x + \frac{f''[0]\ x^2}{2} + \frac{f^{(3)}[0]\ x^3}{6} + O[x]^4$$

In mathematical terms, `Series` can be viewed as a way of constructing Taylor series for functions.

The standard formula for the Taylor series expansion about the point $x = x_0$ of a function $g(x)$ with k^{th} derivative $g^{(k)}(x)$ is $g(x) = \sum_{k=0} g^{(k)}(x_0)\frac{(x-x_0)^k}{k!}$. Whenever this formula applies, it gives the same results as `Series`. (For common functions, `Series` nevertheless internally uses somewhat more efficient algorithms.)

`Series` can also generate some power series that involve fractional and negative powers, not directly covered by the standard Taylor series formula.

Here is a power series that contains negative powers of x.

$$In[4]:= \text{Series}[\ \text{Exp}[x]/x\wedge2,\ \{x,\ 0,\ 4\}\ ]$$

$$Out[4]= x^{-2} + \frac{1}{x} + \frac{1}{2} + \frac{x}{6} + \frac{x^2}{24} + \frac{x^3}{120} + \frac{x^4}{720} + O[x]^5$$

Here is a power series involving fractional powers of x.

$In[5]:=$ **Series[Exp[Sqrt[x]], {x, 0, 2}]**

$$Out[5]= 1 + Sqrt[x] + \frac{x}{2} + \frac{x^{3/2}}{6} + \frac{x^2}{24} + O[x]^{5/2}$$

Series can also handle series that involve logarithmic terms.

$In[6]:=$ **Series[Exp[2x] Log[x], {x, 0, 2}]**

$$Out[6]= Log[x] + 2 Log[x] x + 2 Log[x] x^2 + O[x]^3$$

There are, of course, mathematical functions for which no standard power series exist. *Mathematica* recognizes many such cases.

Series sees that $\exp(\frac{1}{x})$ has an essential singularity at $x = 0$, and does not produce a power series.

$In[7]:=$ **Series[Exp[1/x], {x, 0, 2}]**

Series::esss:

    Essential singularity encountered in $Exp[\frac{1}{x} + O[x]^3]$.

$$Out[7]= Series[E^{1/x}, \{x, 0, 2\}]$$

Series can nevertheless give you the power series for $\exp(\frac{1}{x})$ about the point $x = \infty$.

$In[8]:=$ **Series[Exp[1/x], {x, Infinity, 3}]**

$$Out[8]= 1 + \frac{1}{x} + \frac{1}{2 x^2} + \frac{1}{6 x^3} + O[\frac{1}{x}]^4$$

Especially when negative powers occur, there is some subtlety in exactly how many terms of a particular power series the function Series will generate.

One way to understand what happens is to think of the analogy between power series taken to a certain order, and real numbers taken to a certain precision. Power series are "approximate formulas" in much the same sense as finite-precision real numbers are approximate numbers.

The procedure that Series follows in constructing a power series is largely analogous to the procedure that N follows in constructing a real-number approximation. Both functions effectively start by replacing the smallest pieces of your expression by finite-order, or finite-precision, approximations, and then evaluating the resulting expression. If there are, for example, cancellations, this procedure may give a final result whose order or precision is less than the order or precision that you originally asked for. Unlike N, however, Series has some ability to retry its computations so as to get results to the order you ask for. In cases where it does not succeed, you can usually still get results to a particular order by asking for a higher order than you need.

Series compensates for cancellations in this computation, and succeeds in giving you a result to order x^3.

$In[9]:=$ **Series[Sin[x]/x^2, {x, 0, 3}]**

$$Out[9]= \frac{1}{x} - \frac{x}{6} + \frac{x^3}{120} + O[x]^4$$

When you make a power series expansion in a variable x, *Mathematica* assumes that all objects that do not explicitly contain x are in fact independent of x. Series thus does partial derivatives (effectively using D) to build up Taylor series.

Both a and n are assumed to be independent of x.

In[10]:= Series[(a + x)^n , {x, 0, 2}]

$$Out[10]= a^n + a^{-1 + n} \ n \ x + \frac{a^{-2 + n} \ (-1 + n) \ n \ x^2}{2} + O[x]^3$$

a[x] is now given as an explicit function of x.

In[11]:= Series[(a[x] + x)^n, {x, 0, 2}]

$$Out[11]= a[0]^n + n \ a[0]^{-1 + n} \ (1 + a'[0]) \ x +$$

$$(\frac{(-1 + n) \ n \ a[0]^{-2 + n} \ (1 + a'[0])^2}{2} + \frac{n \ a[0]^{-1 + n} \ a''[0]}{2})$$

$$x^2 + O[x]^3$$

You can use Series to generate power series in a sequence of different variables. Series works like Integrate, Sum and so on, and expands first with respect to the last variable you specify.

Series performs a series expansion successively with respect to each variable. The result in this case is a series in x, whose coefficients are series in y.

In[12]:= Series[Exp[x y], {x, 0, 3}, {y, 0, 3}]

$$Out[12]= 1 + (y + O[y]^4) \ x + (\frac{y^2}{2} + O[y]^4) \ x^2 +$$

$$(\frac{y^3}{6} + O[y]^4) \ x^3 + O[x]^4$$

■ 3.6.2 Advanced Topic: The Representation of Power Series

Power series are represented in *Mathematica* as SeriesData objects.

The power series is printed out as a sum of terms, ending with O[x] raised to a power.

In[1]:= Series[Cos[x], {x, 0, 4}]

$$Out[1]= 1 - \frac{x^2}{2} + \frac{x^4}{24} + O[x]^5$$

Internally, however, the series is stored as a SeriesData object.

In[2]:= InputForm[%]

Out[2]//InputForm=
        SeriesData[x, 0, {1, 0, -1/2, 0, 1/24}, 0, 5, 1]

By using SeriesData objects, rather than ordinary expressions, to represent power series, *Mathematica* can keep track of the order and expansion point, and do operations on the power series appropriately. You should not normally need to know the internal structure of SeriesData objects.

You can recognize a power series that is printed out in standard output form by the presence of an O[x] term. This term mimics the standard mathematical notation $O(x)$, and represents omitted terms of order x. For various reasons of consistency, *Mathematica* uses the notation O[x]^n for omitted terms of order x^n, corresponding to the mathematical notation $O(x)^n$, rather than the slightly more familiar, though equivalent, form $O(x^n)$.

Any time that an object like $O[x]$ appears in a sum of terms, *Mathematica* will in fact convert the whole sum into a power series.

<table>
<tr><td>The presence of $O[x]$ makes Mathematica convert the whole sum to a power series.</td><td>

$In[3]:=$ **a x + Exp[x] + O[x]^3**

$$Out[3]= 1 + (1 + a) \ x + \frac{x^2}{2} + O[x]^3$$
</td></tr>
</table>

■ 3.6.3 Operations on Power Series

Mathematica allows you to perform many operations on power series. In all cases, *Mathematica* gives results only to as many terms as can be justified from the accuracy of your input.

<table>
<tr><td>Here is a power series accurate to fourth order in x.</td><td>

$In[1]:=$ **Series[Exp[x], {x, 0, 4}]**

$$Out[1]= 1 + x + \frac{x^2}{2} + \frac{x^3}{6} + \frac{x^4}{24} + O[x]^5$$
</td></tr>
<tr><td>When you square the power series, you get another power series, also accurate to fourth order.</td><td>

$In[2]:=$ **%^2**

$$Out[2]= 1 + 2 \ x + 2 \ x^2 + \frac{4 \ x^3}{3} + \frac{2 \ x^4}{3} + O[x]^5$$
</td></tr>
<tr><td>Taking the logarithm gives you the result 2x, but only to order x^4.</td><td>

$In[3]:=$ **Log[%]**

$$Out[3]= 2 \ x + O[x]^5$$
</td></tr>
</table>

Mathematica keeps track of the orders of power series in much the same way as it keeps track of the precision of approximate real numbers. Just as with numerical calculations, there are operations on power series which can increase, or decrease, the precision (or order) of your results.

<table>
<tr><td>Here is a power series accurate to order x^4.</td><td>

$In[4]:=$ **Series[Exp[x], {x, 0, 4}]**

$$Out[4]= 1 + x + \frac{x^2}{2} + \frac{x^3}{6} + \frac{x^4}{24} + O[x]^5$$
</td></tr>
<tr><td>This gives a power series that is accurate only to order x^2.</td><td>

$In[5]:=$ **1 / (1 - %)**

$$Out[5]= -(\frac{1}{x}) + \frac{1}{2} - \frac{x}{12} + O[x]^3$$
</td></tr>
</table>

Mathematica also allows you to do calculus with power series.

<table>
<tr><td>Here is a power series for $\cos(x)$.</td><td>

$In[6]:=$ **Series[Cos[x], {x, 0, 6}]**

$$Out[6]= 1 - \frac{x^2}{2} + \frac{x^4}{24} - \frac{x^6}{720} + O[x]^7$$
</td></tr>
</table>

Here is its derivative with respect to x.	$In[7]:= $ **D[%, x]**

$$Out[7]= -x + \frac{x^3}{6} - \frac{x^5}{120} + O[x]^6$$

Integrating with respect to x gives back a power series with the same dependence on x as the original one, but with a different constant of integration.	$In[8]:= $ **Integrate[%, x]**

$$Out[8]= \frac{-x^2}{2} + \frac{x^4}{24} - \frac{x^6}{720} + O[x]^7$$

When you perform an operation that involves both a normal expression and a power series, *Mathematica* "absorbs" the normal expression into the power series whenever possible.

The 1 is automatically absorbed into the power series.	$In[9]:= $ **1 + Series[Exp[x], {x, 0, 4}]**

$$Out[9]= 2 + x + \frac{x^2}{2} + \frac{x^3}{6} + \frac{x^4}{24} + O[x]^5$$

The x^2 is also absorbed into the power series.	$In[10]:= $ **% + x^2**

$$Out[10]= 2 + x + \frac{3 x^2}{2} + \frac{x^3}{6} + \frac{x^4}{24} + O[x]^5$$

If you add Sin[x], *Mathematica* generates the appropriate power series for Sin[x], and combines it with the power series you have.	$In[11]:= $ **% + Sin[x]**

$$Out[11]= 2 + 2 x + \frac{3 x^2}{2} + \frac{x^4}{24} + O[x]^5$$

Mathematica also absorbs expressions that multiply power series. The symbol a is assumed to be independent of x.	$In[12]:= $ **(a + x) %^2**

$$Out[12]= 4 a + (4 + 8 a) x + (8 + 10 a) x^2 + (10 + 6 a) x^3 +$$
$$(6 + \frac{29 a}{12}) x^4 + O[x]^5$$

Mathematica knows how to apply a wide variety of functions to power series. However, if you apply an arbitrary function to a power series, it is impossible for *Mathematica* to give you anything but a symbolic result.

Mathematica does not apply the function f to a power series, so it just leaves the symbolic result.	$In[13]:= $ **f[Series[Exp[x], {x, 0, 3}]]**

$$Out[13]= f[1 + x + \frac{x^2}{2} + \frac{x^3}{6} + O[x]^4]$$

■ 3.6.4 Advanced Topic: Composition and Inversion of Power Series

When you manipulate power series, it is sometimes convenient to think of the series as representing *functions*, which you can, for example, compose or invert.

$series_1$ /. x->$series_2$	compose two power series
InverseSeries[*series*, x]	invert a power series

Composition and inversion of power series.

Here is the power series for $\sin(x)$ to order x^5.

In[1]:= **Series[Sin[x], {x, 0, 5}]**

$$Out[1]= x - \frac{x^3}{6} + \frac{x^5}{120} + O[x]^6$$

The variable in the original power series is now replaced by the power series for $\sin(x)$.

In[2]:= **% /. x -> Series[Sin[x], {x, 0, 5}]**

$$Out[2]= x - \frac{x^3}{3} + \frac{x^5}{10} + O[x]^6$$

The result is the power series for $\sin(\sin(x))$.

In[3]:= **Series[Sin[Sin[x]], {x, 0, 5}]**

$$Out[3]= x - \frac{x^3}{3} + \frac{x^5}{10} + O[x]^6$$

If you think of a power series in x as approximating a function $f(x)$, then substituting for x a power series for another function $g(y)$ gives a power series for the composed function $f(g(y))$. This power series can only be constructed if the first term in the power series for the inner function $g(y)$ involves a positive power of y.

If you have a power series for a function $f(y)$ where the first term is proportional to y, then it is possible to get a power series form of the solution for y in the equation $f(y) = x$. This power series effectively gives the inverse function $f^{-1}(x)$ such that $f(f^{-1}(x)) = x$. The operation of finding the power series for an inverse function is sometimes known as *reversion* of power series.

Here is the series for $\sin(y)$.

In[4]:= **Series[Sin[y], {y, 0, 5}]**

$$Out[4]= y - \frac{y^3}{6} + \frac{y^5}{120} + O[y]^6$$

Inverting the series gives the series for $\sin^{-1}(x)$.

In[5]:= **InverseSeries[%, x]**

$$Out[5]= x + \frac{x^3}{6} + \frac{3 x^5}{40} + O[x]^6$$

Composing the two series gives the identity function.

In[6]:= **% /. x -> %%**

$$Out[6]= y + O[y]^6$$

◼ 3.6.5 Converting Power Series to Normal Expressions

`Normal[expr]`	convert a power series to a normal expression

Converting power series to normal expressions.

As discussed above, power series in *Mathematica* are represented in a special internal form, which keeps track of such attributes as their expansion order.

For some purposes, you may want to convert power series to normal expressions. From a mathematical point of view, this corresponds to truncating the power series, and assuming that all higher-order terms are zero.

This generates a power series, with four terms.

$$In[1]:= \text{t = Series[ArcTan[x], \{x, 0, 8\}]}$$

$$Out[1]= x - \frac{x^3}{3} + \frac{x^5}{5} - \frac{x^7}{7} + O[x]^9$$

Squaring the power series gives you another power series, with the appropriate number of terms.

$$In[2]:= \text{t}^2$$

$$Out[2]= x^2 - \frac{2 x^4}{3} + \frac{23 x^6}{45} - \frac{44 x^8}{105} + O[x]^{10}$$

`Normal` truncates the power series, giving a normal expression.

$$In[3]:= \text{Normal[\%]}$$

$$Out[3]= x^2 - \frac{2 x^4}{3} + \frac{23 x^6}{45} - \frac{44 x^8}{105}$$

You can now apply standard algebraic operations.

$$In[4]:= \text{Factor[\%]}$$

$$Out[4]= \frac{x^2 \ (315 - 210 \ x^2 + 161 \ x^4 - 132 \ x^6)}{315}$$

◼ 3.6.6 Solving Equations Involving Power Series

`LogicalExpand[series₁ == series₂]`

give the equations obtained by equating corresponding coefficients in the power series

`Solve[series₁ == series₂, {a₁, a₂, ... }]`

solve for coefficients in power series

Solving equations involving power series.

Here is a power series.

$In[1]:=$ **y = 1 + Sum[a[i] x^i, {i, 3}] + O[x]^4**

$Out[1]=$ $1 + a[1] x + a[2] x^2 + a[3] x^3 + O[x]^4$

This gives an equation involving the power series.

$In[2]:=$ **D[y, x]^2 - y == x**

$Out[2]=$ $(-1 + a[1]^2) + (-a[1] + 4 a[1] a[2]) x +$

$(-a[2] + a[1]^2 (\dfrac{4 a[2]^2}{a[1]^2} + \dfrac{6 a[3]}{a[1]})) x^2 + O[x]^3 == x$

LogicalExpand generates a sequence of equations for each power of x.

$In[3]:=$ **LogicalExpand[%]**

$Out[3]=$ $-1 + a[1]^2 == 0$ && $-1 - a[1] + 4 a[1] a[2] == 0$ &&

$-a[2] + a[1]^2 (\dfrac{4 a[2]^2}{a[1]^2} + \dfrac{6 a[3]}{a[1]}) == 0$

This solves the equations for the coefficients a[*i*]. You can also feed equations involving power series directly to Solve.

$In[4]:=$ **Solve[%]**

$Out[4]=$ $\{\{a[3] \to -(\dfrac{1}{12}),\ a[2] \to \dfrac{1}{2},\ a[1] \to 1\},$

$\{a[3] \to 0,\ a[2] \to 0,\ a[1] \to -1\}\}$

Some equations involving power series can also be solved using the InverseSeries function discussed on page 644.

■ 3.6.7 Finding Limits

In doing many kinds of calculations, you need to evaluate expressions when variables take on particular values. In many cases, you can do this simply by applying transformation rules for the variables using the /. operator.

You can get the value of $\cos(x^2)$ at 0 just by explicitly replacing x with 0, and then evaluating the result.

$In[1]:=$ **Cos[x^2] /. x -> 0**

$Out[1]=$ 1

In some cases, however, you have to be more careful.

Consider, for example, finding the value of the expression $\frac{\sin(x)}{x}$ when $x = 0$. If you simply replace x by 0 in this expression, you get the indeterminate result $\frac{0}{0}$. To find the correct value of $\frac{\sin(x)}{x}$ when $x = 0$, you need to take the *limit*.

Limit[*expr*, $x \to x_0$]	find the limit of *expr* when x approaches x_0

Finding limits.

This gives the correct value for the limit of $\frac{\sin(x)}{x}$ as $x \to 0$.

```
In[2]:= Limit[ Sin[x]/x, x -> 0 ]
Out[2]= 1
```

No finite limit exists in this case.

```
In[3]:= Limit[ Sin[x]/x^2, x -> 0 ]
Out[3]= Infinity
```

Limit can find this limit, even though you cannot get an ordinary power series for $x \log(x)$ at $x = 0$.

```
In[4]:= Limit[ x Log[x], x -> 0 ]
Out[4]= 0
```

The same is true here.

```
In[5]:= Limit[ ( 1 + 2 x ) ^ (1/x), x -> 0 ]
         2
Out[5]= E
```

Not all functions have definite limits at particular points. For example, the function $\sin(1/x)$ oscillates infinitely often near $x = 0$, so it has no definite limit there. Nevertheless, at least so long as x remains real, the values of the function near $x = 0$ always lie between -1 and 1. Limit represents values with bounded variation using RealInterval objects. In general, RealInterval[{xmin, xmax}] represents an uncertain value which lies somewhere in the interval xmin to xmax.

Limit returns a RealInterval object, representing the range of possible values of $\sin(1/x)$ near its essential singularity at $x = 0$.

```
In[6]:= Limit[ Sin[1/x], x -> 0 ]
Out[6]= RealInterval[{-1, 1}]
```

Mathematica can do arithmetic with RealInterval objects.

```
In[7]:= (1 + %)^3
Out[7]= RealInterval[{0, 8}]
```

Mathematica represents this limit symbolically in terms of a RealInterval object.

```
In[8]:= Limit[ Exp[a Sin[x]], x -> Infinity ]
                              Max[-a, a]    Min[-a, a]
Out[8]= RealInterval[{Min[E          , E          ],
            Max[-a, a]    Min[-a, a]
       Max[E          , E          ]}]
```

Some functions may have different limits at particular points, depending on the direction from which you approach those points. You can use the Direction option for Limit to specify the direction you want.

Limit[*expr*, x -> x_0, Direction -> 1]

find the limit as x approaches x_0 from below

Limit[*expr*, x -> x_0, Direction -> -1]

find the limit as x approaches x_0 from above

Directional limits.

The function $1/x$ has a different limiting value at $x = 0$, depending on whether you approach from above or below.

In[9]:= `Plot[1/x, {x, -1, 1}]`

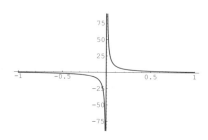

Approaching from below gives a limiting value of $-\infty$.

In[10]:= `Limit[ 1/x, x -> 0, Direction -> 1 ]`

Out[10]= `-Infinity`

Approaching from above gives a limiting value of ∞.

In[11]:= `Limit[ 1/x, x -> 0, Direction -> -1 ]`

Out[11]= `Infinity`

Limit makes no assumptions about functions like f [x] about which it does not have definite knowledge. As a result, Limit remains unevaluated in most cases involving symbolic functions.

Limit has no definite knowledge about f, so it leaves this limit unevaluated.

In[12]:= `Limit[ x f[x], x -> 0 ]`

Out[12]= `Limit[x f[x], x -> 0]`

■ 3.6.8 Residues

Limit [*expr*, $x \rightarrow x_0$] tells you what the value of *expr* is when x tends to x_0. When this value is infinite, it is often useful instead to know the *residue* of *expr* when x equals x_0. The residue is given by the coefficient of $(x - x_0)^{-1}$ in the power series expansion of *expr* about the point x_0.

`Residue[`*expr*`, {`*x*`, `*x₀*`}]`	the residue of *expr* when x equals x_0

Computing residues.

The residue here is equal to 1.

In[1]:= `Residue[1/x, {x, 0}]`

Out[1]= `1`

The residue here is zero.

In[2]:= `Residue[1/x^2, {x, 0}]`

Out[2]= `0`

3.7 Linear Algebra

■ 3.7.1 Constructing Matrices

Table[f, {i, m}, {j, n}]	build an $m \times n$ matrix where f is a function of i and j that gives the value of i, j^{th} entry
Array[f, {m, n}]	build an $m \times n$ matrix whose i, j^{th} entry is $f[i, j]$
DiagonalMatrix[$list$]	generate a diagonal matrix with the elements of $list$ on the diagonal
IdentityMatrix[n]	generate an $n \times n$ identity matrix

Functions for constructing matrices.

This generates a 2×2 matrix whose i, j^{th} entry is a[i, j].

```
In[1]:= Table[a[i, j], {i, 2}, {j, 2}]
Out[1]= {{a[1, 1], a[1, 2]}, {a[2, 1], a[2, 2]}}
```

Here is another way to produce the same matrix.

```
In[2]:= Array[a, {2, 2}]
Out[2]= {{a[1, 1], a[1, 2]}, {a[2, 1], a[2, 2]}}
```

DiagonalMatrix makes a matrix with zeros everywhere except on the leading diagonal.

```
In[3]:= DiagonalMatrix[{a, b, c}]
Out[3]= {{a, 0, 0}, {0, b, 0}, {0, 0, c}}
```

IdentityMatrix[n] produces an $n \times n$ identity matrix.

```
In[4]:= IdentityMatrix[3]
Out[4]= {{1, 0, 0}, {0, 1, 0}, {0, 0, 1}}
```

Of the functions for constructing matrices mentioned above, Table is the most general. You can use Table to produce many kinds of matrices.

`Table[0, {m}, {n}]`	a zero matrix
`Table[Random[ ], {m}, {n}]`	a matrix with random numerical entries
`Table[If[i >= j, 1, 0], {i, m}, {j, n}]`	
	a lower-triangular matrix
`Table[If[i <= j, 1, 0], {i, m}, {j, n}]`	
	an upper-triangular matrix
`Table[Switch[i-j,-1,a[[i]],0,b[[i]],1,c[[i-1]],_,0], {i, m}, {j, n}]`	
	a tridiagonal matrix

Some special types of matrices.

Table evaluates Random[ ] separately for each element, to give a different pseudorandom number in each case.

```
In[5]:= Table[Random[ ], {2}, {2}]
Out[5]= {{0.104826, 0.767415}, {0.216417, 0.519263}}
```

This gives a tridiagonal matrix.

```
In[6]:= Table[Switch[i-j, -1, a, 0, b, 1, c, _, 0],
                {i, 5}, {j, 5}]
Out[6]= {{b, a, 0, 0, 0}, {c, b, a, 0, 0}, {0, c, b, a, 0},
         {0, 0, c, b, a}, {0, 0, 0, c, b}}
```

MatrixForm prints the matrix in a two-dimensional array, and makes the structure in this case clearer.

```
In[7]:= MatrixForm[%]
                        b   a   0   0   0
                        c   b   a   0   0
                        0   c   b   a   0
                        0   0   c   b   a
Out[7]//MatrixForm=     0   0   0   c   b
```

■ 3.7.2 Getting Pieces of Matrices

$m[[i, j]]$ the i, j^{th} entry

$m[[i]]$ the ith row

`Transpose[`m`] [[`i`]]` or `Map[#[[`i`]]&,` m`]`

the ith column

$m[[\{i_1, \ldots, i_r\}, \{j_1, \ldots, j_s\}]]$

the $r \times s$ submatrix of m with elements having row indices i_k and column indices j_k

$m[[\text{Range}[i_0, i_1], \text{Range}[j_0, j_1]]]$

a submatrix with elements having row and column indices respectively in the ranges i_0 through i_1 and j_0 through j_1

Ways to get pieces of matrices.

Matrices in *Mathematica* are represented as lists of lists. You can use all the standard *Mathematica* list-manipulation operations on matrices.

Here is a sample 3×3 matrix.

```
In[1]:= t = Array[a, {3, 3}]
Out[1]= {{a[1, 1], a[1, 2], a[1, 3]},
   {a[2, 1], a[2, 2], a[2, 3]}, {a[3, 1], a[3, 2], a[3, 3]}}
```

This picks out the second row of the matrix.

```
In[2]:= t[[2]]
Out[2]= {a[2, 1], a[2, 2], a[2, 3]}
```

Here is the second column of the matrix.

```
In[3]:= Map[#[[2]]&, t]
Out[3]= {a[1, 2], a[2, 2], a[3, 2]}
```

This picks out a submatrix.

```
In[4]:= t[[ {1, 2}, {2, 3} ]]
Out[4]= {{a[1, 2], a[1, 3]}, {a[2, 2], a[2, 3]}}
```

Here is another way to specify the submatrix, convenient when you deal with bigger matrices.

```
In[5]:= t[[ Range[1,2], Range[2,3] ]]
Out[5]= {{a[1, 2], a[1, 3]}, {a[2, 2], a[2, 3]}}
```

■ 3.7.3 Scalars, Vectors and Matrices

Mathematica represents matrices and vectors using lists. Anything that is not a list *Mathematica* considers as a scalar.

A vector in *Mathematica* consists of a list of scalars. A matrix consists of a list of vectors, representing each of its rows. In order to be a valid matrix, all the rows must be the same length, so that the elements of the matrix effectively form a rectangular array.

VectorQ[*expr*]	give True if *expr* has the form of a vector, and False otherwise
MatrixQ[*expr*]	give True if *expr* has the form of a matrix, and False otherwise
Dimensions[*expr*]	a list of the dimensions of a vector or matrix

Functions for testing the structure of vectors and matrices.

The list {a, b, c} has the form of a vector.

```
In[1]:= VectorQ[ {a, b, c} ]
Out[1]= True
```

Anything that is not manifestly a list is treated as a scalar, so applying VectorQ gives False.

```
In[2]:= VectorQ[ x + y ]
Out[2]= False
```

This is a 2×3 matrix.

```
In[3]:= Dimensions[ {{a, b, c}, {ap, bp, cp}} ]
Out[3]= {2, 3}
```

For a vector, Dimensions gives a list with a single element equal to the result from Length.

```
In[4]:= Dimensions[ {a, b, c} ]
Out[4]= {3}
```

This object does not count as a matrix because its rows are of different lengths.

```
In[5]:= MatrixQ[ {{a, b, c}, {ap, bp}} ]
Out[5]= False
```

■ 3.7.4 Operations on Scalars, Vectors and Matrices

Most mathematical functions in *Mathematica* are set up to apply themselves separately to each element in a list. This is true in particular of all functions that carry the attribute Listable.

A consequence is that most mathematical functions are applied element by element to matrices and vectors.

The Log applies itself separately to each element in the vector.

```
In[1]:= Log[ {a, b, c} ]
Out[1]= {Log[a], Log[b], Log[c]}
```

The same is true for a matrix, or, for that matter, for any nested list.

```
In[2]:= Log[ {{a, b}, {c, d}} ]
Out[2]= {{Log[a], Log[b]}, {Log[c], Log[d]}}
```

The differentiation function D also applies separately to each element in a list.

In[3]:= **D[{x, x^2, x^3}, x]**

Out[3]= {1, 2 x, 3 x^2}

The sum of two vectors is carried out element by element.

In[4]:= **{a, b} + {ap, bp}**

Out[4]= {a + ap, b + bp}

If you try to add two vectors with different lengths, you get an error.

In[5]:= **{a, b, c} + {ap, bp}**

Thread::tdlen:
  Objects of unequal length in {a, b, c} + {ap, bp}
    cannot be combined.

Out[5]= {ap, bp} + {a, b, c}

This adds the scalar 1 to each element of the vector.

In[6]:= **1 + {a, b}**

Out[6]= {1 + a, 1 + b}

Any object that is not manifestly a list is treated as a scalar. Here c is treated as a scalar, and added separately to each element in the vector.

In[7]:= **{a, b} + c**

Out[7]= {a + c, b + c}

This multiplies each element in the vector by the scalar k.

In[8]:= **k {a, b}**

Out[8]= {a k, b k}

It is important to realize that *Mathematica* treats an object as a vector in a particular operation only if the object is explicitly a list at the time when the operation is done. If the object is not explicitly a list, *Mathematica* always treats it as a scalar. This means that you can get different results, depending on whether you assign a particular object to be a list before or after you do a particular operation.

The object p is treated as a scalar, and added separately to each element in the vector.

In[9]:= **{a, b} + p**

Out[9]= {a + p, b + p}

This is what happens if you now replace p by the list {c, d}.

In[10]:= **% /. p -> {c, d}**

Out[10]= {{a + c, a + d}, {b + c, b + d}}

You would have got a different result if you had replaced p by {c, d} before you did the first operation.

In[11]:= **{a, b} + {c, d}**

Out[11]= {a + c, b + d}

■ 3.7.5 Multiplying Vectors and Matrices

$c\ v$, $c\ m$, etc.	multiply each element by a scalar
$v.v$, $v.m$, $m.v$, $m.m$, etc.	vector and matrix multiplication
`Outer[Times, `t_1`, `t_2`, ... ]`	outer product

Different kinds of vector and matrix multiplication.

<table>
<tr><td>This multiplies each element of the vector by the scalar k.</td><td><code>In[1]:= k {a, b, c}</code>

<code>Out[1]= {a k, b k, c k}</code></td></tr>
<tr><td>The "dot" operator gives the scalar product of two vectors.</td><td><code>In[2]:= {a, b, c} . {ap, bp, cp}</code>

<code>Out[2]= a ap + b bp + c cp</code></td></tr>
<tr><td>You can also use dot to multiply a matrix by a vector.</td><td><code>In[3]:= {{a, b}, {c, d}} . {x, y}</code>

<code>Out[3]= {a x + b y, c x + d y}</code></td></tr>
<tr><td>Dot is also the notation for matrix multiplication in Mathematica.</td><td><code>In[4]:= {{a, b}, {c, d}} . {{1, 2}, {3, 4}}</code>

<code>Out[4]= {{a + 3 b, 2 a + 4 b}, {c + 3 d, 2 c + 4 d}}</code></td></tr>
</table>

It is important to realize that you can use "dot" for both left- and right-multiplication of vectors by matrices. *Mathematica* makes no distinction between "row" and "column" vectors. Dot carries out whatever operation is possible. (In formal terms, $a.b$ contracts the last index of the tensor a with the first index of b.)

<table>
<tr><td>Here are definitions for a matrix m and a vector v.</td><td><code>In[5]:= m = {{a, b}, {c, d}} ; v = {x, y}</code>

<code>Out[5]= {x, y}</code></td></tr>
<tr><td>This left-multiplies the vector v by m. The object v is effectively treated as a column vector in this case.</td><td><code>In[6]:= m . v</code>

<code>Out[6]= {a x + b y, c x + d y}</code></td></tr>
<tr><td>You can also use dot to right-multiply v by m. Now v is effectively treated as a row vector.</td><td><code>In[7]:= v . m</code>

<code>Out[7]= {a x + c y, b x + d y}</code></td></tr>
<tr><td>You can multiply m by v on both sides, to get a scalar.</td><td><code>In[8]:= v . m . v</code>

<code>Out[8]= x (a x + c y) + y (b x + d y)</code></td></tr>
</table>

For some purposes, you may need to represent vectors and matrices symbolically, without explicitly giving their elements. You can use dot to represent multiplication of such symbolic objects.

<table>
<tr><td>Dot effectively acts here as a non-commutative form of multiplication.</td><td><code>In[9]:= a . b . a</code>

<code>Out[9]= a . b . a</code></td></tr>
</table>

It is, nevertheless, associative.

$In[10]:=$ **(a . b) . (a . b)**

$Out[10]=$ a . b . a . b

Dot products of sums are not automatically expanded out.

$In[11]:=$ **(a + b) . c . (d + e)**

$Out[11]=$ (a + b) . c . (d + e)

You can apply the distributive law in this case using the function `Distribute`, as discussed on page 215.

$In[12]:=$ **Distribute[%]**

$Out[12]=$ a . c . d + a . c . e + b . c . d + b . c . e

The "dot" operator gives "inner products" of vectors, matrices, and so on. In more advanced calculations, you may also need to construct outer or Kronecker products of vectors and matrices. You can use the general function `Outer` to do this.

The outer product of two vectors is a matrix.

$In[13]:=$ **Outer[Times, {a, b}, {c, d}]**

$Out[13]=$ {{a c, a d}, {b c, b d}}

The outer product of a matrix and a vector is a rank three tensor.

$In[14]:=$ **Outer[Times, {{1, 2}, {3, 4}}, {x, y, z}]**

$Out[14]=$ {{{x, y, z}, {2 x, 2 y, 2 z}},

{{3 x, 3 y, 3 z}, {4 x, 4 y, 4 z}}}

Outer products will be discussed in more detail in Section 3.7.12 below.

■ 3.7.6 Matrix Inversion

Inverse[m]	find the inverse of a square matrix

Matrix inversion.

Here is a simple 2×2 matrix.

$In[1]:=$ **m = {{a, b}, {c, d}}**

$Out[1]=$ {{a, b}, {c, d}}

This gives the inverse of **m**. In producing this formula, *Mathematica* implicitly assumes that the determinant **a d - b c** is non-zero.

$In[2]:=$ **Inverse[m]**

$Out[2]=$ $\{\{\dfrac{d}{-(b\ c)\ +\ a\ d},\ -(\dfrac{b}{-(b\ c)\ +\ a\ d})\},$

$\{-(\dfrac{c}{-(b\ c)\ +\ a\ d}),\ \dfrac{a}{-(b\ c)\ +\ a\ d}\}\}$

Multiplying the inverse by the original matrix should give the identity matrix.

$In[3]:=$ **% . m**

$Out[3]=$ $\{\{-(\dfrac{b\ c}{-(b\ c)\ +\ a\ d})\ +\ \dfrac{a\ d}{-(b\ c)\ +\ a\ d},\ 0\},$

$\{0,\ -(\dfrac{b\ c}{-(b\ c)\ +\ a\ d})\ +\ \dfrac{a\ d}{-(b\ c)\ +\ a\ d}\}\}$

You have to use Together to clear the denominators, and get back a standard identity matrix.

```
In[4]:= Together[ % ]
Out[4]= {{1, 0}, {0, 1}}
```

Here is a matrix of rational numbers.

```
In[5]:= hb = Table[1/(i + j), {i, 4}, {j, 4}]
```

$$Out[5]= \{\{\frac{1}{2}, \frac{1}{3}, \frac{1}{4}, \frac{1}{5}\}, \{\frac{1}{3}, \frac{1}{4}, \frac{1}{5}, \frac{1}{6}\}, \{\frac{1}{4}, \frac{1}{5}, \frac{1}{6}, \frac{1}{7}\}, \{\frac{1}{5}, \frac{1}{6}, \frac{1}{7}, \frac{1}{8}\}\}$$

Mathematica finds the exact inverse of the matrix.

```
In[6]:= Inverse[hb]
Out[6]= {{200, -1200, 2100, -1120},
    {-1200, 8100, -15120, 8400}, {2100, -15120, 29400, -16800},
    {-1120, 8400, -16800, 9800}}
```

Multiplying by the original matrix gives the identity matrix.

```
In[7]:= % . hb
Out[7]= {{1, 0, 0, 0}, {0, 1, 0, 0}, {0, 0, 1, 0}, {0, 0, 0, 1}}
```

If you try to invert a singular matrix, *Mathematica* prints a warning message, and returns the inverse undone.

```
In[8]:= Inverse[ {{1, 2}, {1, 2}} ]
Inverse::sing: Matrix {{1, 2}, {1, 2}} is singular.
Out[8]= Inverse[{{1, 2}, {1, 2}}]
```

If you give a matrix with exact symbolic or numerical entries, *Mathematica* gives the exact inverse. If, on the other hand, some of the entries in your matrix are approximate real numbers, then *Mathematica* finds an approximate numerical result.

Here is a matrix containing approximate real numbers.

```
In[9]:= m = {{1.2, 5.7}, {4.2, 5.6}}
Out[9]= {{1.2, 5.7}, {4.2, 5.6}}
```

This finds the numerical inverse.

```
In[10]:= Inverse[ % ]
Out[10]= {{-0.325203, 0.33101}, {0.243902, -0.0696864}}
```

Multiplying by the original matrix gives you an identity matrix with small numerical errors.

```
In[11]:= % . m
```
$$Out[11]= \{\{1., -1.25442 \ 10^{-16}\}, \{1.00831 \ 10^{-17}, 1.\}\}$$

You can get rid of the small off-diagonal terms using Chop.

```
In[12]:= Chop[ % ]
Out[12]= {{1., 0}, {0, 1.}}
```

When you try to invert a matrix with exact numerical entries, *Mathematica* can always tell whether or not the matrix is singular. When you invert an approximate numerical matrix, *Mathematica* can never tell for certain whether or not the matrix is singular: all it can tell is for example that the determinant is small compared to the entries of the matrix. When *Mathematica* suspects that you are trying to invert a singular numerical matrix, it prints a warning.

Mathematica prints a warning if you invert a numerical matrix that it suspects is singular.

```
In[13]:= Inverse[ {{1., 2.}, {1., 2.}} ]
Inverse::sing: Matrix {{1., 2.}, {1., 2.}} is singular.
Out[13]= Inverse[{{1., 2.}, {1., 2.}}]
```

If you work with high-precision approximate numbers, *Mathematica* will keep track of the precision of matrix inverses that you generate.

This generates a 6×6 numerical matrix with entries of 50-digit precision.	`In[14]:= m = N [ Table[ Exp[i j], {i, 6}, {j, 6} ], 50 ] ;`
This takes the matrix, multiplies it by its inverse, and shows the first row of the result.	`In[15]:= (m . Inverse[m]) [[1]]` `Out[15]= {1., 0., 0., 0., 0., 0.}`
This gives the accuracy of the result. It is close to 50 digits.	`In[16]:= Accuracy[ % ]` `Out[16]= 48`
This generates a 50-digit numerical approximation to a 6×6 Hilbert matrix. Hilbert matrices are notoriously hard to invert numerically.	`In[17]:= m = N[Table[1/(i + j - 1), {i, 6}, {j, 6}], 50] ;`
The actual numbers given are again correct.	`In[18]:= (m . Inverse[m]) [[1]]` `Out[18]= {1., 0., 0., 0., 0., 0.}`
The accuracy of the result, however, is lower.	`In[19]:= Accuracy[ % ]` `Out[19]= 38`

`Inverse` works only on square matrices. Section 3.7.11 discusses the function `PseudoInverse`, which can also be used with non-square matrices.

■ 3.7.7 Basic Matrix Operations

`Transpose[m]`	transpose
`Inverse[m]`	matrix inverse
`Det[m]`	determinant
`Minors[m, k]`	a matrix of the $k \times k$ minors of m
`Sum[m[[i, i]], {i, Length[m]}]`	
	trace

Some basic matrix operations.

Transposing a matrix interchanges the rows and columns in the matrix. If you transpose an $m \times n$ matrix, you get an $n \times m$ matrix as the result.

Transposing a 2×3 matrix gives a 3×2 result.	`In[1]:= Transpose[ {{a, b, c}, {ap, bp, cp}} ]` `Out[1]= {{a, ap}, {b, bp}, {c, cp}}`

Det [*m*] gives the determinant of a square matrix *m*. Minors [*m*, *k*] gives a matrix of the determinants of all the *k*×*k* submatrices of *m*. You can apply Minors to rectangular, as well as square, matrices.

Here is the determinant of a simple 2×2 matrix.	`In[2]:= Det[ {{a, b}, {c, d}} ]`
	
	`Out[2]= -(b c) + a d`

This generates a 3×3 matrix, whose *i,j*th entry is a[*i*, *j*].

```
In[3]:= m = Array[a, {3, 3}]
Out[3]= {{a[1, 1], a[1, 2], a[1, 3]},
   {a[2, 1], a[2, 2], a[2, 3]}, {a[3, 1], a[3, 2], a[3, 3]}}
```

Here is the determinant of m.

```
In[4]:= Det[ m ]
Out[4]= -(a[1, 3] a[2, 2] a[3, 1]) + a[1, 2] a[2, 3] a[3, 1] +
   a[1, 3] a[2, 1] a[3, 2] - a[1, 1] a[2, 3] a[3, 2] -
   a[1, 2] a[2, 1] a[3, 3] + a[1, 1] a[2, 2] a[3, 3]
```

This gives the matrix of all 2×2 minors of m.

```
In[5]:= Minors[m, 2]
Out[5]= {{-(a[1, 2] a[2, 1]) + a[1, 1] a[2, 2],
   -(a[1, 3] a[2, 1]) + a[1, 1] a[2, 3],
   -(a[1, 3] a[2, 2]) + a[1, 2] a[2, 3]},
  {-(a[1, 2] a[3, 1]) + a[1, 1] a[3, 2],
   -(a[1, 3] a[3, 1]) + a[1, 1] a[3, 3],
   -(a[1, 3] a[3, 2]) + a[1, 2] a[3, 3]},
  {-(a[2, 2] a[3, 1]) + a[2, 1] a[3, 2],
   -(a[2, 3] a[3, 1]) + a[2, 1] a[3, 3],
   -(a[2, 3] a[3, 2]) + a[2, 2] a[3, 3]}}
```

You can use Det to find the characteristic polynomial for a matrix. Section 3.7.10 discusses ways to find eigenvalues and eigenvectors directly.

Here is a 3×3 matrix.

```
In[6]:= m = Table[ 1/(i + j), {i, 3}, {j, 3} ]
```
$$Out[6]= \{\{\frac{1}{2}, \frac{1}{3}, \frac{1}{4}\}, \{\frac{1}{3}, \frac{1}{4}, \frac{1}{5}\}, \{\frac{1}{4}, \frac{1}{5}, \frac{1}{6}\}\}$$

Following precisely the standard mathematical definition, this gives the characteristic polynomial for m.

```
In[7]:= Det[ m - x IdentityMatrix[3] ]
```
$$Out[7]= \frac{1}{43200} - \frac{131 \, x}{3600} + \frac{11 \, x^2}{12} - x^3$$

There are many other operations on matrices that can be built up from standard *Mathematica* functions. One example is the *trace* or *spur* of a matrix, given by the sum of the terms on the leading diagonal.

Here is a simple 2×2 matrix.

```
In[8]:= m = {{a, b}, {c, d}}
Out[8]= {{a, b}, {c, d}}
```

You can get the trace of the matrix by explicitly constructing a sum of the elements on its leading diagonal.	*In[9]:=* `Sum[ m[[i, i]], {i, 2} ]` *Out[9]=* `a + d`

`MatrixPower[`*m*`, `*n*`]`	n^{th} matrix power
`MatrixExp[`*m*`]`	matrix exponential

Powers and exponentials of matrices.

Here is a 2×2 matrix.	*In[10]:=* `m = {{0.4, 0.6}, {0.525, 0.475}}` *Out[10]=* `{{0.4, 0.6}, {0.525, 0.475}}`
This gives the third matrix power of m.	*In[11]:=* `MatrixPower[m, 3]` *Out[11]=* `{{0.465625, 0.534375}, {0.467578, 0.532422}}`
It is equivalent to multiplying three copies of the matrix.	*In[12]:=* `m . m . m` *Out[12]=* `{{0.465625, 0.534375}, {0.467578, 0.532422}}`
Here is the millionth matrix power.	*In[13]:=* `MatrixPower[m, 10^6]` *Out[13]=* `{{0.466667, 0.533333}, {0.466667, 0.533333}}`
This gives the matrix exponential of m.	*In[14]:=* `MatrixExp[m]` *Out[14]=* `{{1.7392, 0.979085}, {0.8567, 1.86158}}`
Here is an approximation to the exponential of m, based on a power series approximation.	*In[15]:=* `Sum[MatrixPower[m, i]/i!, {i, 0, 5}]` *Out[15]=* `{{1.73844, 0.978224}, {0.855946, 1.86072}}`

■ 3.7.8 Solving Linear Systems

Many calculations involve solving systems of linear equations. In many cases, you will find it convenient to write down the equations explicitly, and then solve them using `Solve`.

In some cases, however, you may prefer to convert the system of linear equations into a matrix equation, and then apply matrix manipulation operations to solve it. This approach is often useful when the system of equations arises as part of a general algorithm, and you do not know in advance how many variables will be involved.

A system of linear equations can be stated in matrix form as $\mathbf{m}.\mathbf{x} = \mathbf{b}$, where $\mathbf{x}$ is the vector of variables.

LinearSolve[*m*, *b*]	give a vector *x* which solves the matrix equation *m*.*x* == *b*
NullSpace[*m*]	a list of basis vectors whose linear combinations satisfy the matrix equation *m*.*x* == 0
RowReduce[*m*]	a simplified form of *m* obtained by making linear combinations of rows

Functions for solving linear systems.

Here is a 2×2 matrix.	`In[1]:= m = {{1, 5}, {2, 1}}` `Out[1]= {{1, 5}, {2, 1}}`
This gives two linear equations.	`In[2]:= m . {x, y} == {a, b}` `Out[2]= {x + 5 y, 2 x + y} == {a, b}`
You can use Solve directly to solve these equations.	`In[3]:= Solve[ %, {x, y} ]` $Out[3]= \{\{x \rightarrow \frac{-a}{9} + \frac{5\ b}{9}, y \rightarrow \frac{2\ a}{9} - \frac{b}{9}\}\}$
You can also get the vector of solutions by calling LinearSolve. The result is equivalent to the one you get from Solve.	`In[4]:= LinearSolve[m, {a, b}]` $Out[4]= \{-(\frac{a}{9} - \frac{5\ b}{9}), -(\frac{-2\ a}{9} + \frac{b}{9})\}$
Another way to solve the equations is to invert the matrix m, and then multiply {a, b} by the inverse. This is not as efficient as using LinearSolve.	`In[5]:= Inverse[m] . {a, b}` $Out[5]= \{\frac{-a}{9} + \frac{5\ b}{9}, \frac{2\ a}{9} - \frac{b}{9}\}$

Particularly when you have large, sparse, matrices, LinearSolve is the most efficient method to use.

If you have a square matrix **m** with a non-zero determinant, then you can always find a unique solution to the matrix equation **m**.**x** = **b** for any **b**. If, however, the matrix **m** has determinant zero, then there may be either no vector, or an infinite number of vectors **x** which satisfy **m**.**x** = **b** for a particular **b**. This occurs when the linear equations embodied in **m** are not independent.

When **m** has determinant zero, it is nevertheless always possible to find non-zero vectors **x** that satisfy **m**.**x** = **0**. The set of vectors **x** satisfying this equation form the *null space* or *kernel* of the matrix **m**. Any of these vectors can be expressed as a linear combination of a particular set of basis vectors, which can be obtained using NullSpace[*m*].

Here is a simple matrix, corresponding to two identical linear equations.	`In[6]:= m = {{1, 2}, {1, 2}}` `Out[6]= {{1, 2}, {1, 2}}`
The matrix has determinant zero.	`In[7]:= Det[ m ]` `Out[7]= 0`

LinearSolve cannot find a solution to the equation **m.x = b** in this case.	`In[8]:= LinearSolve[m, {a, b}]`
	
	`LinearSolve::nosol:`
	`    Linear equation encountered which has no solution.`
	
	`Out[8]= LinearSolve[{{1, 2}, {1, 2}}, {a, b}]`

There is a single basis vector for the null space of m.	`In[9]:= NullSpace[ m ]`
	
	`Out[9]= {{-2, 1}}`

Multiplying the basis vector for the null space by m gives the zero vector.	`In[10]:= m . %[[1]]`
	
	`Out[10]= {0, 0}`

Here is a simple symbolic matrix with determinant zero.	`In[11]:= m = {{a, b, c}, {2 a, 2 b, 2 c}, {3 a, 3 b, 3 c}}`
	
	`Out[11]= {{a, b, c}, {2 a, 2 b, 2 c}, {3 a, 3 b, 3 c}}`

The basis for the null space of m contains two vectors. Any linear combination of these vectors gives zero when multiplied by m.	`In[12]:= NullSpace[ m ]` $Out[12]= \{\{-(\frac{b}{a}), 1, 0\}, \{-(\frac{c}{a}), 0, 1\}\}$

An important feature of `LinearSolve` and `NullSpace` is that they work with *rectangular*, as well as *square*, matrices.

When you represent a system of linear equations by a matrix equation of the form **m.x = b**, the number of columns in **m** gives the number of variables, and the number of rows give the number of equations. There are a number of cases.

Underdetermined	number of independent equations less than the number of variables; no solutions or many solutions may exist
Overdetermined	number of equations more than the number of variables; solutions may or may not exist
Nonsingular	number of independent equations equal to the number of variables, and determinant non-zero; a unique solution exists
Consistent	at least one solution exists
Inconsistent	no solutions exist

Classes of linear systems represented by rectangular matrices.

This asks for the solution to the inconsistent set of equations $x = 1$ and $x = 0$.	`In[13]:= LinearSolve[{{1}, {1}}, {1, 0}]`
	
	`LinearSolve::nosol:`
	`    Linear equation encountered which has no solution.`
	
	`Out[13]= LinearSolve[{{1}, {1}}, {1, 0}]`

This matrix represents two equations, for three variables.

```
In[14]:= m = {{1, 3, 4}, {2, 1, 3}}
Out[14]= {{1, 3, 4}, {2, 1, 3}}
```

LinearSolve gives one of the possible solutions to this underdetermined set of equations.

```
In[15]:= v = LinearSolve[m, {1, 1}]
              2   1
Out[15]= {-, -, 0}
              5   5
```

When a matrix represents an underdetermined system of equations, the matrix has a non-trivial null space. In this case, the null space is spanned by a single vector.

```
In[16]:= NullSpace[m]
Out[16]= {{-1, -1, 1}}
```

If you take the solution you get from LinearSolve, and add any linear combination of the basis vectors for the null space, you still get a solution.

```
In[17]:= m . (v + 4 %[[1]])
Out[17]= {1, 1}
```

You can find out the number of redundant equations corresponding to a particular matrix by evaluating Length[NullSpace[m]]. Subtracting this quantity from the number of columns in m gives the *rank* of the matrix m.

■ 3.7.9 Advanced Topic: Generalized Linear Algebra

Many of the matrix operations discussed in the preceding sections work by trying to find combinations of matrix elements which give zero. By default, a simple test of the form Together[e] == 0 is applied to each combination that is generated to see if it is in fact zero.

Sometimes, however, you may want to apply more complicated tests. The option ZeroTest for Inverse, LinearSolve, NullSpace and RowReduce allows you to specify a function which is applied to each combination of matrix elements generated to determine whether the combination should be considered to be zero.

Inverse[m, ZeroTest -> f], etc.	apply f to determine whether combinations of matrix elements are zero

Generalized linear algebra.

The ZeroTest option is particularly useful in handling complicated symbolic matrices. The results you get from functions like NullSpace depend on whether particular combinations of matrix elements are zero. But determining this may require extensive algebraic manipulation. You can use ZeroTest to specify the algebraic manipulation to perform in a particular case.

Here is a matrix of trigonometric expressions.

```
In[1]:= m = {{Sin[t]^2, Cos[t]^2}, {Sin[t]^2, 1 - Sin[t]^2}}

Out[1]= {{Sin[t]^2, Cos[t]^2}, {Sin[t]^2, 1 - Sin[t]^2}}
```

With the default `ZeroTest`, `NullSpace` does not take account of relations between the trigonometric expressions.

```
In[2]:= NullSpace[m]

Out[2]= {}
```

With this setting for `ZeroTest`, the relations between the trigonometric expressions are used, and `NullSpace` returns a different result.

```
In[3]:= NullSpace[m, ZeroTest -> (Simplify[#] == 0 &)]

Out[3]= {{-Cot[t]^2, 1}}
```

`Inverse[`*m*`, Modulus -> `*p*`]`, etc.	require combinations of matrix elements to be zero only modulo *p*

Linear algebra over finite fields.

Here is a 2×2 matrix of integers.

```
In[4]:= m = {{2, 4}, {3, 7}}

Out[4]= {{2, 4}, {3, 7}}
```

This gives the inverse of the matrix computed using rational numbers.

```
In[5]:= Inverse[m]

Out[5]= {{7/2, -2}, {-(3/2), 1}}
```

Here is the inverse computed over the field of integers modulo 11.

```
In[6]:= Inverse[m, Modulus -> 11]

Out[6]= {{9, 9}, {4, 1}}
```

Multiplying this result by the original matrix does not immediately give the identity matrix.

```
In[7]:= m . %

Out[7]= {{34, 22}, {55, 34}}
```

Reducing modulo 11 does however give the identity matrix.

```
In[8]:= Mod[%, 11]

Out[8]= {{1, 0}, {0, 1}}
```

■ 3.7.10 Eigenvalues and Eigenvectors

Eigenvalues[*m*]	a list of the eigenvalues of *m*
Eigenvectors[*m*]	a list of the eigenvectors of *m*
Eigensystem[*m*]	a list of the form *{eigenvalues, eigenvectors}*
Eigenvalues[N[*m*]], etc.	numerical eigenvalues
Eigenvalues[N[*m, k*]], etc.	numerical eigenvalues, starting with *k*-digit precision

Eigenvalues and eigenvectors.

The eigenvalues of a matrix **m** are the values λ_i for which one can find non-zero vectors x_i such that $m.x_i = \lambda_i x_i$. The eigenvectors are the vectors x_i.

Finding the eigenvalues of an $n \times n$ matrix in principle involves solving an nth degree polynomial equation. Since for $n \geq 5$ explicit algebraic solutions cannot in general be found, it is impossible to give explicit algebraic results for the eigenvalues and eigenvectors of all but the simplest or sparsest matrices.

Even for a matrix as simple as this, the explicit form of the eigenvalues is quite complicated.

```
In[1]:= Eigenvalues[ {{a, b}, {-b, 2a}} ]
```
$$Out[1]= \{\frac{3\,a + Sqrt[9\,a^2 - 4\,(2\,a^2 + b^2)]}{2},$$
$$\frac{3\,a - Sqrt[9\,a^2 - 4\,(2\,a^2 + b^2)]}{2}\}$$

If you give a matrix of approximate real numbers, *Mathematica* will find the approximate numerical eigenvalues and eigenvectors.

Here is a 2×2 numerical matrix.

```
In[2]:= m = {{2.3, 4.5}, {6.7, -1.2}}
Out[2]= {{2.3, 4.5}, {6.7, -1.2}}
```

The matrix has two eigenvalues, in this case both real.

```
In[3]:= Eigenvalues[ m ]
Out[3]= {6.31303, -5.21303}
```

Here are the two eigenvectors of m.

```
In[4]:= Eigenvectors[ m ]
Out[4]= {{0.746335, 0.66557}, {-0.523116, 0.873374}}
```

Eigensystem computes the eigenvalues and eigenvectors at the same time. The assignment sets vals to the list of eigenvalues, and vecs to the list of eigenvectors.

```
In[5]:= {vals, vecs} = Eigensystem[m]
Out[5]= {{6.31303, -5.21303},
    {{0.746335, 0.66557}, {-0.523116, 0.873374}}}
```

This verifies that the first eigenvalue and eigenvector satisfy the appropriate condition.

```
In[6]:= m . vecs[[1]] == vals[[1]] vecs[[1]]
Out[6]= True
```

This finds the eigenvalues of a random 4×4 matrix. For non-symmetric matrices, the eigenvalues can have imaginary parts.

```
In[7]:= Eigenvalues[ Table[Random[ ],{i,4},{j,4}] ]
Out[7]= {1.70302, -0.727791, 0.423923, -0.0481403}
```

The function `Eigenvalues` always gives you a list of n eigenvalues for an $n \times n$ matrix. The eigenvalues correspond to the roots of the characteristic polynomial for the matrix, and may not necessarily be distinct. `Eigenvectors`, on the other hand, gives a list of eigenvectors which are guaranteed to be independent. If the number of such eigenvectors is less than n, then `Eigenvectors` appends zero vectors to the list it returns, so that the total length of the list is always n.

Here is a 3×3 matrix.

```
In[8]:= mz = {{0, 1, 0}, {0, 0, 1}, {0, 0, 0}}
Out[8]= {{0, 1, 0}, {0, 0, 1}, {0, 0, 0}}
```

The matrix has three eigenvalues, all equal to zero.

```
In[9]:= Eigenvalues[mz]
Out[9]= {0, 0, 0}
```

There is, however, only one independent eigenvector for the matrix. `Eigenvectors` appends two zero vectors to give a total of three vectors in this case.

```
In[10]:= Eigenvectors[mz]
Out[10]= {{1, 0, 0}, {0, 0, 0}, {0, 0, 0}}
```

■ 3.7.11 Advanced Topic: Matrix Decompositions

`SingularValues[`m`]`	find the singular value decomposition of a numerical matrix
`PseudoInverse[`m`]`	compute the pseudoinverse of a numerical matrix

Singular value decomposition and pseudoinverse.

Singular value decomposition is an important element of many numerical matrix algorithms. The basic idea is to write any matrix $\mathbf{m}$ in the form $\mathbf{u}^T \mathbf{m}_D \mathbf{v}$, where $\mathbf{m}_D$ is a diagonal matrix, and $\mathbf{u}$ and $\mathbf{v}$ are row orthonormal matrices. The function `SingularValues[`m`]` returns a list containing the matrix $\mathbf{u}$, the list of diagonal elements of $\mathbf{m}_D$, and the matrix $\mathbf{v}$.

The diagonal elements of $\mathbf{m}_D$ are known as the *singular values* of the matrix $\mathbf{m}$. One interpretation of the singular values is as follows. If you take a unit sphere in n-dimensional space, and multiply each vector in it by an $m \times n$ matrix $\mathbf{m}$, you will get an ellipsoid in m-dimensional space. The singular values give the lengths of the principal axes of the ellipsoid. If the matrix $\mathbf{m}$ is singular in some way, this will be reflected in the shape of the ellipsoid. In fact, the ratio of the largest singular value of a matrix to the smallest one gives the *condition number* of the matrix, which determines, for example, the accuracy of numerical matrix inverses.

In general, very small singular values are numerically meaningless. `SingularValues` removes any singular values that are smaller than a certain *tolerance* multiplied by the largest singular value. The option `Tolerance` specifies the tolerance to use.

Here is the singular value decomposition for a non-singular 2×2 matrix.	`In[1]:= SingularValues[N[{{1, 3}, {-4, 3}}]]`
	
	`Out[1]= {{{-0.957092, 0.289784}, {-0.289784, -0.957092}},`
	
	`{2.91309, 5.14916}, {{-0.726454, -0.687215},`
	
	`{0.687215, -0.726454}}}`

Here is a convenient way to pick out the pieces of the result.	`In[2]:= {u, md, v} = %`
	
	`Out[2]= {{{-0.957092, 0.289784}, {-0.289784, -0.957092}},`
	
	`{2.91309, 5.14916}, {{-0.726454, -0.687215},`
	
	`{0.687215, -0.726454}}}`

This gives something close to the original matrix.	`In[3]:= Transpose[u] . DiagonalMatrix[md] . v`
	
	`Out[3]= {{1., 3.}, {-4., 3.}}`

Here is the singular value decomposition of a singular matrix. Only one singular value is given.	`In[4]:= SingularValues[N[{{1, 2}, {1, 2}}]]`
	
	`Out[4]= {{{0.707107, 0.707107}}, {3.16228},`
	
	`{{0.447214, 0.894427}}}`

The standard definition for the inverse of a matrix fails if the matrix is not square. Using singular value decomposition, however, it is possible to define a *pseudoinverse* even for non-square matrices, or for singular square ones. The pseudoinverse is defined in terms of the objects $\mathbf{u}$, $\mathbf{m}_D$ and $\mathbf{v}$ as $\mathbf{m}^{(-1)} = \mathbf{v}^T \mathbf{m}_D^{-1} \mathbf{u}$. The pseudoinverse has the property that the sum of the squares of all the entries in $\mathbf{m}.\mathbf{m}^{(-1)} - \mathbf{I}$, where $\mathbf{I}$ is an identity matrix, is minimized. The pseudoinverse found in this way is important, for example, in carrying out fits to numerical data. The pseudoinverse is sometimes known as the generalized inverse, or the Moore-Penrose inverse.

`QRDecomposition[`*m*`]`	find the QR decomposition of a numerical matrix
`SchurDecomposition[`*m*`]`	find the Schur decomposition of a numerical matrix

QR and Schur decomposition.

Singular value decomposition writes any matrix as a product of a diagonal matrix with row and column orthonormal matrices. In some algorithms, it is also important to be able to decompose matrices as products involving *triangular matrices*.

QR decomposition writes any matrix $\mathbf{m}$ as a product $\mathbf{q}^\dagger \mathbf{r}$, where $\mathbf{q}$ is an orthonormal matrix, † denotes Hermitian conjugate, and $\mathbf{r}$ is a triangular matrix, in which all entries below the leading diagonal are zero. The function `QRDecomposition[`*m*`]` returns a list containing the matrices $\mathbf{q}$ and $\mathbf{r}$. QR decomposition is often used in solving least-squares fitting problems, and is typically faster than singular value decomposition.

This computes the QR decomposition of a 2×2 matrix, then extracts the matrices **q** and **r**.	`In[5]:= {q, r} = QRDecomposition[ N[{{1, 5}, {-7, 3}}] ]`
	
	`Out[5]= {{{-0.141421, 0.989949}, {-0.989949, -0.141421}},`
	
	   `{{-7.07107, 2.26274}, {0, -5.37401}}}`

Since **q** is orthogonal, this gives the identity matrix.	`In[6]:= Transpose[q] . q // Chop`
	
	`Out[6]= {{1., 0}, {0, 1.}}`

This gives the original matrix.	`In[7]:= Transpose[q] . r`
	
	`Out[7]= {{1., 5.}, {-7., 3.}}`

Schur decomposition writes any matrix **m** in the form $\mathbf{q}\mathbf{t}\mathbf{q}^t$, where **q** is an orthogonal matrix, and **t** is block-upper triangular. The function `SchurDecomposition[`*m*`]` returns a list containing the matrices **q** and **t**. Schur decomposition is often used in evaluating functions of matrices.

The stability of numerical matrix algorithms is sometimes improved by "pivoting" or "balancing", in which the rows and columns of the matrix **m** are permuted and perhaps rescaled before QR or Schur decomposition is done. Setting the option `Pivoting -> True` tells *Mathematica* to perform such pivoting or balancing, and to give the matrix required as the last element of the list returned.

■ 3.7.12 Advanced Topic: Tensors

Tensors are mathematical objects that give generalizations of vectors and matrices. In *Mathematica*, a tensor is represented as a set of lists, nested to a certain number of levels. The nesting level is the *rank* of the tensor.

rank 0	scalar
rank 1	vector
rank 2	matrix
rank k	rank k tensor

Interpretations of nested lists.

A tensor of rank k is essentially a k-dimensional table of values. To be a true rank k tensor, it must be possible to arrange the elements in the table in a k-dimensional cuboidal array. There can be no holes or protrusions in the cuboid.

The *indices* that specify a particular element in the tensor correspond to the coordinates in the cuboid. The *dimensions* of the tensor correspond to the side lengths of the cuboid.

One simple way that a rank k tensor can arise is in giving a table of values for a function of k variables. In physics, the tensors that occur typically have indices which run over the possible directions in space or spacetime. Notice, however, that there is no built-in notion of covariant and contravariant tensor indices in *Mathematica*: you have to set these up explicitly using metric tensors.

`Table[f, {i₁, n₁}, {i₂, n₂}, ... , {i_k, n_k}]`	
	create an $n_1 \times n_2 \times ... \times n_k$ tensor whose elements are the values of f
`Array[a, {n₁, n₂, ... , n_k}]`	create an $n_1 \times n_2 \times ... \times n_k$ tensor with elements given by applying a to each set of indices
`Dimensions[t]`	give a list of the dimensions of a tensor
`TensorRank[t]`	find the rank of a tensor
`MatrixForm[t]`	print with the elements of t arranged in a two-dimensional array

Functions for creating and testing the structure of tensors.

Here is a $2 \times 3 \times 2$ tensor.

```
In[1]:= t = Table[i1+i2 i3, {i1, 2}, {i2, 3}, {i3, 2}]

Out[1]= {{{2, 3}, {3, 5}, {4, 7}}, {{3, 4}, {4, 6}, {5, 8}}}
```

This is another way to produce the same tensor.

```
In[2]:= Array[(#1 + #2 #3)&, {2, 3, 2}]

Out[2]= {{{2, 3}, {3, 5}, {4, 7}}, {{3, 4}, {4, 6}, {5, 8}}}
```

MatrixForm displays the elements of the tensor in a two-dimensional array. You can think of the array as consisting of two 3×2 matrices arranged side by side.

```
In[3]:= MatrixForm[ t ]

                         2  3    3  4
                         3  5    4  6
Out[3]//MatrixForm= 4  7    5  8
```

Dimensions gives the dimensions of the tensor.

```
In[4]:= Dimensions[ t ]

Out[4]= {2, 3, 2}
```

Here is the 111 element of the tensor.

```
In[5]:= t[[1, 1, 1]]

Out[5]= 2
```

TensorRank gives the rank of the tensor.

```
In[6]:= TensorRank[ t ]

Out[6]= 3
```

The rank of a tensor is equal to the number of indices needed to specify each element. You can pick out subtensors by using a smaller number of indices.

`Transpose[t]`	transpose the first two indices in a tensor
`Transpose[t, {`p_1`, `p_2`, ... }]`	transpose the indices in a tensor so that the kth becomes the p_k^{th}
`Outer[f, `t_1`, `t_2`, ... ]`	form the generalized outer product of the tensors t_i with "multiplication operator" f
t_1 `.` t_2	form the dot product of t_1 and t_2 (last index of t_1 contracted with first index of t_2)
`Inner[f, `t_1`, `t_2`, `g`]`	form the generalized inner product, with "multiplication operator" f and "addition operator" g

Tensor manipulation operations.

You can think of a rank k tensor as having k "slots" into which you insert indices. Applying `Transpose` is effectively a way of reordering these slots. If you think of the elements of a tensor as forming a k-dimensional cuboid, you can view `Transpose` as effectively rotating (and possibly reflecting) the cuboid.

In the most general case, `Transpose` allows you to specify an arbitrary reordering to apply to the indices of a tensor. The function `Transpose[`T`, {`p_1`, `p_2`, ... , `p_k`}]`, gives you a new tensor T' such that the value of $T'_{i_1 i_2 \ldots i_k}$ is given by $T_{i_{p_1} i_{p_2} \ldots i_{p_k}}$.

If you originally had an $n_{p_1} \times n_{p_2} \times \ldots \times n_{p_k}$ tensor, then by applying `Transpose`, you will get an $n_1 \times n_2 \times \ldots \times n_k$ tensor.

Here is a matrix that you can also think of as a 2×3 tensor.

```
In[7]:= m = {{a, b, c}, {ap, bp, cp}}

Out[7]= {{a, b, c}, {ap, bp, cp}}
```

Applying `Transpose` gives you a 3×2 tensor. `Transpose` effectively interchanges the two "slots" for tensor indices.

```
In[8]:= mt = Transpose[m]

Out[8]= {{a, ap}, {b, bp}, {c, cp}}
```

The element `m[[2, 3]]` in the original tensor becomes the element `m[[3, 2]]` in the transposed tensor.

```
In[9]:= { m[[2, 3]], mt[[3, 2]] }

Out[9]= {cp, cp}
```

This produces a $2 \times 3 \times 1 \times 2$ tensor.

```
In[10]:= t = Array[a, {2, 3, 1, 2}]

Out[10]= {{{{a[1, 1, 1, 1], a[1, 1, 1, 2]}},
    {{a[1, 2, 1, 1], a[1, 2, 1, 2]}},
    {{a[1, 3, 1, 1], a[1, 3, 1, 2]}}},
   {{{a[2, 1, 1, 1], a[2, 1, 1, 2]}},
    {{a[2, 2, 1, 1], a[2, 2, 1, 2]}},
    {{a[2, 3, 1, 1], a[2, 3, 1, 2]}}}}
```

This transposes the first two levels of t.

In[11]:= **tt1 = Transpose[t]**

Out[11]= {{{{a[1, 1, 1, 1], a[1, 1, 1, 2]}},

{{a[2, 1, 1, 1], a[2, 1, 1, 2]}}},

{{{a[1, 2, 1, 1], a[1, 2, 1, 2]}},

{{a[2, 2, 1, 1], a[2, 2, 1, 2]}}},

{{{a[1, 3, 1, 1], a[1, 3, 1, 2]}},

{{a[2, 3, 1, 1], a[2, 3, 1, 2]}}}}

The result is a $3 \times 2 \times 1 \times 2$ tensor.

In[12]:= **Dimensions[tt1]**

Out[12]= {3, 2, 1, 2}

Outer products, and their generalizations, are a way of building higher-rank tensors from lower-rank ones. Outer products are also sometimes known as direct, tensor or Kronecker products.

From a structural point of view, the tensor you get from Outer[*f*, *t*, *u*] has a copy of the structure of *u* inserted at the "position" of each element in *t*. The elements in the resulting structure are obtained by combining elements of *t* and *u* using the function *f*.

This gives the "outer f" of two vectors. The result is a matrix.

In[13]:= **Outer[f, {a, b}, {ap, bp}]**

Out[13]= {{f[a, ap], f[a, bp]}, {f[b, ap], f[b, bp]}}

If you take the "outer f" of a length 3 vector with a length 2 vector, you get a 3×2 matrix.

In[14]:= **Outer[f, {a, b, c}, {ap, bp}]**

Out[14]= {{f[a, ap], f[a, bp]}, {f[b, ap], f[b, bp]},

{f[c, ap], f[c, bp]}}

The result of taking the "outer f" of a 2×2 matrix and a length 3 vector is a $2 \times 2 \times 3$ tensor.

In[15]:= **Outer[f, {{m11, m12}, {m21, m22}}, {a, b, c}]**

Out[15]= {{{f[m11, a], f[m11, b], f[m11, c]},

{f[m12, a], f[m12, b], f[m12, c]}},

{{f[m21, a], f[m21, b], f[m21, c]},

{f[m22, a], f[m22, b], f[m22, c]}}}

Here are the dimensions of the tensor.

In[16]:= **Dimensions[%]**

Out[16]= {2, 2, 3}

If you take the generalized outer product of an $m_1 \times m_2 \times ... \times m_r$ tensor and an $n_1 \times n_2 \times ... \times n_s$ tensor, you get an $m_1 \times ... \times m_r \times n_1 \times ... \times n_s$ tensor. If the original tensors have ranks r and s, your result will be a rank $r + s$ tensor.

In terms of indices, the result of applying Outer to two tensors $T_{i_1 i_2 ... i_r}$ and $U_{j_1 j_2 ... j_s}$ is the tensor $V_{i_1 i_2 ... i_r j_1 j_2 ... j_s}$ with elements f$[T_{i_1 i_2 ... i_r}, U_{j_1 j_2 ... j_s}]$.

In doing standard tensor calculations, the most common function f to use in Outer is Times, corresponding to the standard outer product.

Particularly in doing combinatorial calculations, however, it is often convenient to take f to be `List`. Using `Outer`, you can then get combinations of all possible elements in one tensor, with all possible elements in the other.

In constructing `Outer[f, t, u]` you effectively insert a copy of u at every point in t. To form `Inner[f, t, u]`, you effectively combine and collapse the last dimension of t and the first dimension of u. The idea is to take an $m_1 \times m_2 \times ... \times m_r$ tensor and an $n_1 \times n_2 \times ... \times n_s$ tensor, with $m_r = n_1$, and get an $m_1 \times m_2 \times ... \times m_{r-1} \times n_2 \times ... \times n_s$ tensor as the result.

The simplest examples are with vectors. If you apply `Inner` to two vectors of equal length, you get a scalar. `Inner[f, v_1, v_2, g]` gives a generalization of the usual scalar product, with f playing the role of multiplication, and g playing the role of addition.

This gives a generalization of the standard scalar product of two vectors.	`In[17]:= Inner[f, {a, b, c}, {ap, bp, cp}, g]` `Out[17]= g[f[a, ap], f[b, bp], f[c, cp]]`

This gives a generalization of a matrix product.	`In[18]:= Inner[f, {{1, 2}, {3, 4}}, {{a, b}, {c, d}}, g]`
	`Out[18]= {{g[f[1, a], f[2, c]], g[f[1, b], f[2, d]]},`
	`  {g[f[3, a], f[4, c]], g[f[3, b], f[4, d]]}}`

Here is a $3 \times 2 \times 2$ tensor.	`In[19]:= a = Array[1&, {3, 2, 2}]` `Out[19]= {{{1, 1}, {1, 1}}, {{1, 1}, {1, 1}}, {{1, 1}, {1, 1}}}`
Here is a $2 \times 3 \times 1$ tensor.	`In[20]:= b = Array[2&, {2, 3, 1}]` `Out[20]= {{{2}, {2}, {2}}, {{2}, {2}, {2}}}`

This gives a $3 \times 2 \times 3 \times 1$ tensor.	`In[21]:= a . b`
	`Out[21]= {{{{4}, {4}, {4}}, {{4}, {4}, {4}}},`
	`  {{{4}, {4}, {4}}, {{4}, {4}, {4}}},`
	`  {{{4}, {4}, {4}}, {{4}, {4}, {4}}}}`

Here are the dimensions of the result.	`In[22]:= Dimensions[ % ]` `Out[22]= {3, 2, 3, 1}`

You can think of `Inner` as performing a "contraction" of the last index of one tensor with the first index of another. If you want to perform contractions across other pairs of indices, you can do so by first transposing the appropriate indices into the first or last position, then applying `Inner`, and then transposing the result back.

In many applications of tensors, you need to insert signs to implement antisymmetry. The function `Signature[{i_1, i_2, ... }]`, which gives the signature of a permutation, is often useful for this purpose.

3.8 Numerical Operations on Data

■ 3.8.1 Curve Fitting

Built into *Mathematica* are various facilities for finding least-squares fits to data. The basic idea of the fits is to take a list of functions that you specify, and try to find a linear combination of them which approximates your data as well as possible. The goodness of fit is measured by the quantity $\chi^2 = \sum_i |F_i - f_i|^2$, where F_i is the value of your i^{th} data point, and f_i is the value obtained from the fit. The best fit is the one which minimizes χ^2.

`Fit[data, funs, vars]`	fit a list of data points using the functions *funs* of variables *vars*

The basic form of the `Fit` function.

`Fit[{f_1, f_2, ... }, {1, x}, x]`	linear fit
`Fit[{f_1, f_2, ... }, {1, x, x^2}, x]`	quadratic fit
`Fit[data, Table[x^i, {i, 0, n}], x]`	n^{th}-degree polynomial fit
`Exp[ Fit[Log[data], {1, x}, x] ]`	fit to e^{a+bx}

Some fits to lists of data.

Here is a table of the first 20 primes.

```
In[1]:= fp = Table[Prime[x], {x, 20}]

Out[1]= {2, 3, 5, 7, 11, 13, 17, 19, 23, 29, 31, 37, 41, 43,
   47, 53, 59, 61, 67, 71}
```

Here is a plot of this "data".

```
In[2]:= gp = ListPlot[ fp ]
```

This gives a linear fit to the list of primes. The result is the best linear combination of the functions 1 and x.

In[3]:= **Fit[fp, {1, x}, x]**

Out[3]= -7.67368 + 3.77368 x

Here is a plot of the fit.

In[4]:= **Plot[%, {x, 0, 20}]**

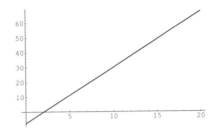

Here is the fit superimposed on the original data.

In[5]:= **Show[%, gp]**

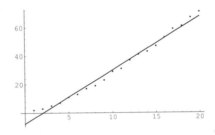

This gives a quadratic fit to the data.

In[6]:= **Fit[fp, {1, x, x^2}, x]**

Out[6]= $-1.92368 + 2.2055 x + 0.0746753 x^2$

Here is a plot of the quadratic fit.

In[7]:= **Plot[%, {x, 0, 20}]**

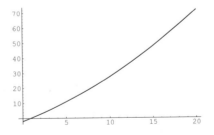

This shows the fit superimposed on the original data. The quadratic fit is better than the linear one.

$In[8]:=$ **Show[%, gp]**

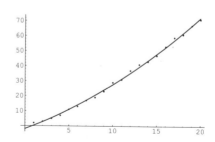

Polynomial fits are the most common kind to use. However, if you have a reason to believe that your data follows some other functional form, you can include the appropriate functions in the list you give to Fit.

This gives a table of the values of $1 + 2e^{-\frac{x}{3}}$ for x from 1 to 10 in steps of 1.

$In[9]:=$ **ft = Table[N[1 + 2 Exp[-x/3]] , {x, 10}]**

$Out[9]=$ {2.43306, 2.02683, 1.73576, 1.52719, 1.37775, 1.27067,

1.19394, 1.13897, 1.09957, 1.07135}

This fit recovers the original functional form.

$In[10]:=$ **Fit[ft, {1, Exp[-x/3]}, x]**

$Out[10]=$ $1. + \dfrac{2.}{E^{x/3}}$

If you include other functions in the list, Fit determines that they occur with small coefficients.

$In[11]:=$ **Fit[ft, {1, Sin[x], Exp[-x/3], Exp[-x]}, x]**

$Out[11]=$ $1. - \dfrac{9.91806\ 10^{-15}}{E^{x}} + \dfrac{2.}{E^{x/3}} + 5.77338\ 10^{-17}\ Sin[x]$

You can use Chop to get rid of the terms with small coefficients.

$In[12]:=$ **Chop[%]**

$Out[12]=$ $1. + \dfrac{2.}{E^{x/3}}$

There are several common reasons for doing fits.

If you have a particular model for some data, you can do a fit to try and determine the parameters of the model.

Another common use of fits is in finding approximate formulas to describe a particular set of data. You can use the form you get from a Fit as a summary of your actual data.

In the examples of Fit so far, the data points you give are assumed to correspond to the results of evaluating a function of one variable when the variable successively takes on values 1, 2, ... You can also specify data that depends on several variables, each given an arbitrary sequence of values, not necessarily arranged in any kind of regular array.

$\{f_1,\ f_2,\ \dots\ \}$	data points obtained when a single coordinate takes on values 1, 2, ...
$\{\{x_1,\ y_1,\ \dots\ ,\ f_1\},\ \{x_2,\ y_2,\ \dots\ ,\ f_2\},\ \dots\ \}$	data points obtained with values $x_i,\ y_i,\ \dots$ of a sequence of coordinates

Ways of specifying data in **Fit**.

This gives a table of the values of x, y and $1+5x-xy$. You need to use **Flatten** to get it in the right form for **Fit**.

```
In[13]:= Flatten[ Table[ {x, y, 1 + 5x - x y},
                      {x, 0, 1, 0.4}, {y, 0, 1, 0.4} ], 1]
Out[13]= {{0, 0, 1}, {0, 0.4, 1}, {0, 0.8, 1}, {0.4, 0, 3.},
        {0.4, 0.4, 2.84}, {0.4, 0.8, 2.68}, {0.8, 0, 5.},
        {0.8, 0.4, 4.68}, {0.8, 0.8, 4.36}}
```

This produces a fit to a function of two variables.

```
In[14]:= Fit[ % , {1, x, y, x y}, {x, y} ]
                              -16
Out[14]= 1. + 5. x + 1.66479 10    y - 1. x y
```

Fit takes the list of functions you give, and finds the best fit to your data, according to the least-squares criterion, using these functions. There is absolutely no guarantee that the fit you get will in fact accurately reproduce your data. To find out whether it can, you should use statistical testing functions, such as those in the statistics section of the *Mathematica* library.

`InterpolatingPolynomial[`$\{f_1,\ f_2,\ \dots\ ,\ f_n\}$, x`]`	find a polynomial in x which fits the values f_i exactly
`InterpolatingPolynomial[`$\{\{x_1,\ f_1\},\ \{x_2,\ f_2\},\ \dots\ \}$, x`]`	find a polynomial which fits the points $\{x_i,\ f_i\}$ exactly
`InterpolatingPolynomial[`$\{\{x_1,\ \{f_1,\ df_1,\ ddf_1,\ \dots\ \}\},\ \dots\ \}$`]`	find a polynomial which fits the specified values and derivatives exactly

Finding exact fits.

If you have sufficiently few data points, then by including sufficiently many terms, you can construct a polynomial which fits your data exactly. In general, if you have n data points, you may need a polynomial of degree up to $n-1$. The function `InterpolatingPolynomial` gives you such a polynomial. Such polynomials can in fact be useful not only in fitting numerical data, but also in various algebraic algorithms.

This gives a degree 4 polynomial which fits the data given exactly.

$In[15]:=$ **efit = InterpolatingPolynomial[{1, 2, 6, 24, 120}, x]**

$Out[15]=$ $1 + (1 + (\frac{3}{2} + (\frac{11}{6} + \frac{53\ (-4 + x)}{24})\ (-3 + x))\ (-2 + x))$

$(-1 + x)$

When $x = 4$, the polynomial reproduces the fourth data point exactly.

$In[16]:=$ **efit /. x -> 4**

$Out[16]=$ 24

This uses the polynomial fit to extrapolate the data.

$In[17]:=$ **efit /. x -> 7.5**

$Out[17]=$ 1599.49

■ 3.8.2 Approximate Functions and Interpolation

In many kinds of numerical computations, it is convenient to introduce *approximate functions*. Approximate functions can be thought of as generalizations of ordinary approximate real numbers. While an approximate real number gives the value to a certain precision of a single numerical quantity, an approximate function gives the value to a certain precision of a quantity which depends on one or more parameters. *Mathematica* uses approximate functions, for example, to represent numerical solutions to differential equations obtained with NDSolve, as discussed in Section 1.6.4.

Approximate functions in *Mathematica* are represented by InterpolatingFunction objects. These objects work like the pure functions discussed in Section 2.2.5. The basic idea is that when given a particular argument, an InterpolatingFunction object finds the approximate function value that corresponds to that argument.

The InterpolatingFunction object contains a representation of the approximate function based on interpolation. Typically it contains values and possibly derivatives at a sequence of points. It effectively assumes that the function varies smoothly between these points. As a result, when you ask for the value of the function with a particular argument, the InterpolatingFunction object can interpolate to find an approximation to the value you want.

Interpolation[{f_1, f_2, ... }]	construct an approximate function with values f_i at successive integers
Interpolation[{{x_1, f_1}, {x_2, f_2}, ... }]	construct an approximate function with values f_i at points x_i

Constructing approximate functions.

Here is a table of the values of the sine function.

$In[1]:=$ **Table[{x, Sin[x]}, {x, 0, 2, 0.25}]**

$Out[1]=$ $\{\{0, 0\}, \{0.25, 0.247404\}, \{0.5, 0.479426\},$
$\{0.75, 0.681639\}, \{1., 0.841471\}, \{1.25, 0.948985\},$
$\{1.5, 0.997495\}, \{1.75, 0.983986\}, \{2., 0.909297\}\}$

This constructs an approximate function which represents these values.

```
In[2]:= sin = Interpolation[%]
Out[2]= InterpolatingFunction[{0, 2.}, <>]
```

The approximate function reproduces each of the values in the original table.

```
In[3]:= sin[0.25]
Out[3]= 0.247404
```

It also allows you to get approximate values at other points.

```
In[4]:= sin[0.3]
Out[4]= 0.2955
```

In this case the interpolation is a fairly good approximation to the true sine function.

```
In[5]:= Sin[0.3]
Out[5]= 0.29552
```

You can work with approximate functions much as you would with any other *Mathematica* functions. You can plot approximate functions, or perform numerical operations such as integration or root finding.

If you give a non-numerical argument, the approximate function is left in symbolic form.

```
In[6]:= sin[x]
Out[6]= InterpolatingFunction[{0, 2.}, <>][x]
```

Here is a numerical integral of the approximate function.

```
In[7]:= NIntegrate[sin[x]^2, {x, 0, Pi/2}]
Out[7]= 0.78531
```

Here is the same numerical integral for the true sine function.

```
In[8]:= NIntegrate[Sin[x]^2, {x, 0, Pi/2}]
Out[8]= 0.785398
```

A plot of the approximate function is essentially indistinguishable from the true sine function.

```
In[9]:= Plot[sin[x], {x, 0, 2}]
```

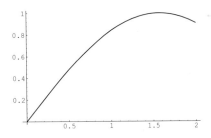

InterpolatingFunction objects contain all the information *Mathematica* needs about approximate functions. In standard *Mathematica* output format, however, only the first element of each InterpolationFunction object is printed explicitly. This element gives the range of arguments for which values of the approximate function can be found. The later elements of the InterpolatingFunction object give actual values of the approximate function, its derivatives, and so on.

In standard output format, only the first element of InterpolatingFunction objects is printed explicitly.

```
In[10]:= sin
Out[10]= InterpolatingFunction[{0, 2.}, <>]
```

Mathematica will not compute values for approximate functions outside the range of arguments specified by the first element.	`In[11]:= sin[3]`
	
	`InterpolatingFunction::dmval:`
	    `Input value lies outside domain of interpolating function.`
	
	`Out[11]= InterpolatingFunction[{0, 2.}, <>][3]`

Subsequent elements contain information on the approximate function.	`In[12]:= Short[ InputForm[sin], 2 ]`
	
	`Out[12]//Short=`
	  `InterpolatingFunction[{0, 2.},`
	    `{{0, 0, {0, 0}, {0}}, <<7>>,`
	      `{2., 1.75, {<<4>>}, {0., 0.25, 0.5}}}]`

The more information you give about the function you are trying to approximate, the better the approximation *Mathematica* constructs can be. You can, for example, specify not only values of the function at a sequence of points, but also derivatives.

`Interpolation[{{`x_1`, {`f_1`, `df_1`, `ddf_1`, ... }}, ... }]`
          construct an approximate function with specified
          derivatives at points x_i

Constructing approximate functions with specified derivatives.

`Interpolation` works by fitting polynomial curves between the points you specify. You can use the option `InterpolationOrder` to specify the degree of these polynomial curves. The default setting is `InterpolationOrder -> 3`, yielding cubic curves.

This makes a table of values of the cosine function.	`In[13]:= tab = Table[{x, Cos[x]}, {x, 0, 6}] ;`

This creates an approximate function using linear interpolation between the values in the table.	`In[14]:= Interpolation[tab, InterpolationOrder -> 1]`
	
	`Out[14]= InterpolatingFunction[{0, 6}, <>]`

The approximate function consists of a collection of straight-line segments.	`In[15]:= Plot[%[x], {x, 0, 6}]`

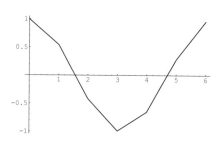

With the default setting
`InterpolationOrder -> 3`, cubic
curves are used, and the function looks
smooth.

In[16]:= `Plot[Evaluate[Interpolation[tab]][x], {x, 0, 6}]`

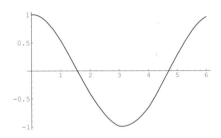

Increasing the setting for `InterpolationOrder` typically leads to smoother approximate functions. However, if you increase the setting too much, spurious wiggles may develop.

`Interpolation[{{x₁, y₁, ... , f₁}, ... }]`	
	specify function values on a grid of points
`Interpolation[{{x₁, y₁, ... , {f₁, {dxf₁, dyf₁, ... }}}, ... }]`	
	specify function values and derivatives on a grid of points

Multi-dimensional approximate functions.

Mathematica can handle approximate functions with more than one argument. You can specify such functions by giving values on a grid of points in several dimensions.

■ 3.8.3 Fourier Transforms

A common operation in analyzing various kinds of data is to find the Fourier transform, or spectrum, of a list of values. The idea is typically to pick out components of the data with particular frequencies, or ranges of frequencies.

`Fourier[{a₀, a₁, ... }]`	Fourier transform
`InverseFourier[{b₀, b₁, ... }]`	inverse Fourier transform

Fourier transforms.

There are several conventions that can be used in defining Fourier transforms. In *Mathematica*, the Fourier transform b_s of a list a_r of length n is taken to be $\frac{1}{\sqrt{n}} \sum_{r=1}^{n} a_r e^{2\pi i (r-1)(s-1)/n}$. Notice that the zero frequency term appears at position 1 in the resulting list.

Note that the convention for defining the Fourier transform used in *Mathematica* is the one common in the physical sciences. In electrical engineering, the sign of the exponent is typically reversed, leading to a list of values which is reversed.

The Fourier transform takes you from a time series of data to the frequency components of the data. You can use the inverse Fourier transform to get back to the time series. The inverse Fourier transform a_r of a list b_s of length n is defined to be $\frac{1}{\sqrt{n}} \sum_{s=1}^{n} b_s e^{-2\pi i (r-1)(s-1)/n}$.

Here is some data, corresponding to a square pulse.	`In[1]:= {-1, -1, -1, -1, 1, 1, 1, 1}` `Out[1]= {-1, -1, -1, -1, 1, 1, 1, 1}`

Here is the Fourier transform of the data. It involves complex numbers.

```
In[2]:= Fourier[%]
Out[2]= {0., -0.707107 - 1.70711 I, 0., -0.707107 - 0.292893 I,
         0., -0.707107 + 0.292893 I, 0., -0.707107 + 1.70711 I}
```

Here is the inverse Fourier transform.

```
In[3]:= InverseFourier[%]
                          -17                      -16
Out[3]= {-1. + 7.85046 10    I, -1. - 1.1101 10      I,

                 -16                     -16
  -1. + 2.7477 10    I, -1. + 1.43555 10    I,

                 -17                    -16
  1. - 7.85046 10    I, 1. + 1.1101 10     I,

                -16                    -16
  1. - 2.7477 10    I, 1. - 1.43555 10    I}
```

After using Chop, this gives back exactly your original data.

```
In[4]:= Chop[%]
Out[4]= {-1., -1., -1., -1., 1., 1., 1., 1.}
```

Fourier works whether or not your list of data has a length which is a power of two. It is, however, significantly more efficient when the length is a power of two.

```
In[5]:= Fourier[{1, -1, 1}]
Out[5]= {0.57735, 0.57735 - 1. I, 0.57735 + 1. I}
```

This generates a length-256 list containing a periodic signal with random noise added.

```
In[6]:= data = Table[ N[Sin[30 2 Pi n/256] + (Random[ ] - 1/2)],
                      {n, 256} ] ;
```

The data looks fairly random if you plot it directly.

```
In[7]:= ListPlot[ data, PlotJoined -> True ]
```

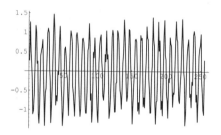

The Fourier transform, however, shows a very strong peak at 30, the frequency of the original periodic signal. There is a second peak at $256 - 30$, which is essentially a consequence of aliasing.

In[8]:= **ListPlot[Abs[Fourier[data]], PlotJoined -> True, PlotRange -> All]**

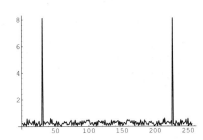

A common and important application of Fourier transforms is doing *convolutions*. The basic idea is that integrals of the form $\bar{f}(x) = \int f(y)k(y - x)dy$ can be evaluated simply by multiplying the Fourier transforms of f and k. Convolutions are used extensively, for example, in smoothing data.

This generates some "data".

In[9]:= **data = Table[N[BesselJ[1, 10 n/256] + 0.2 (Random[ ] - 1/2)], {n, 256}] ;**

Here is a plot of the data.

In[10]:= **ListPlot[data]**

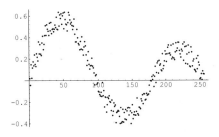

This generates a typical convolution kernel suitable for smoothing data.

In[11]:= **kern = Table[N[Exp[-200 (n/256)^2]], {n, 256}] ;**

Here is a plot of the convolution kernel.

In[12]:= **ListPlot[kern, PlotRange -> All]**

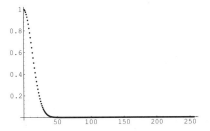

The convolution is done by multiplying the Fourier transform of the data by the Fourier transform of the kernel, then taking the inverse Fourier transform of the result.

In[13]:= **conv = InverseFourier[Fourier[data] Fourier[kern]] ;**

This plots the result. The **Chop** removes small imaginary parts that are generated in the Fourier transforms. The final plot is a smoothed version of the original data.

In[14]:= **ListPlot[Chop[conv]]**

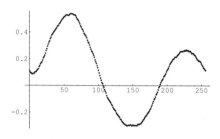

Fourier[{{a_{00}, a_{01}, ... }, {a_{10}, a_{11}, ... }, ... }]
two-dimensional Fourier transform

Two-dimensional Fourier transform.

Mathematica can find Fourier transforms for data in any number of dimensions. In n dimensions, the data is specified by a list nested n levels deep. Two-dimensional Fourier transforms are often used in image processing.

3.9 Numerical Operations on Functions

■ 3.9.1 Numerical Mathematics in *Mathematica*

One of the most important features of *Mathematica* is its ability to give you exact, symbolic, results for computations. There are, however, computations where it is just mathematically impossible to get exact "closed form" results. In such cases, you can still often get approximate numerical results.

There is no "closed form" result for $\int_0^1 \sin(\exp(x))\,dx$. *Mathematica* returns the integral in its original symbolic form.

```
In[1]:= Integrate[Sin[Exp[x]], {x, 0, 1}]

Out[1]= Integrate[Sin[E ], {x, 0, 1}]
                         x
```

You can now take the symbolic form of the integral, and ask for its approximate numerical value.

```
In[2]:= N[%]

Out[2]= 0.874957
```

When *Mathematica* cannot find an explicit result for something like a definite integral, it returns a symbolic form. You can take this symbolic form, and try to get an approximate numerical value by applying N.

By giving a second argument to N, you can specify the numerical precision to use.

```
In[3]:= N[ Integrate[Sin[Exp[x]], {x, 0, 1}], 40 ]

Out[3]= 0.8749571987803840302385072720 26
```

If you want to evaluate an integral numerically in *Mathematica*, then using Integrate and applying N to the result is not the most efficient way to do it. It is better instead to use the function NIntegrate, which immediately gives a numerical answer, without first trying to get an exact, symbolic, result. You should realize that even when Integrate does not in the end manage to give you an exact result, it may spend a lot of time trying to do so.

NIntegrate evaluates numerical integrals directly, without first trying to get a symbolic result.

```
In[4]:= NIntegrate[ Sin[Exp[x]], {x, 0, 1} ]

Out[4]= 0.874957
```

Integrate	NIntegrate	definite integrals
Sum	NSum	sums
Product	NProduct	products
Solve	NSolve	solutions of algebraic equations
DSolve	NDSolve	solutions of differential equations

Symbolic and numerical versions of some *Mathematica* functions.

■ 3.9.2 The Uncertainties of Numerical Mathematics

Mathematica does operations like numerical integration very differently from the way it does their symbolic counterparts.

When you do a symbolic integral, *Mathematica* takes the functional form of the integrand you have given, and applies a sequence of exact symbolic transformation rules to it, to try and evaluate the integral.

When you do a numerical integral, however, *Mathematica* does not look directly at the functional form of the integrand you have given. Instead, it simply finds a sequence of numerical values of the integrand at particular points, then takes these values and tries to deduce from them a good approximation to the integral.

An important point to realize is that when *Mathematica* does a numerical integral, the *only* information it has about your integrand is a sequence of numerical values for it. To get a definite result for the integral, *Mathematica* then effectively has to make certain assumptions about the smoothness and other properties of your integrand. If you give a sufficiently pathological integrand, these assumptions may not be valid, and as a result, *Mathematica* may simply give you the wrong answer for the integral.

This problem may occur, for example, if you try to integrate numerically a function which has a very thin spike at a particular position. *Mathematica* samples your function at a number of points, and then assumes that the function varies smoothly between these points. As a result, if none of the sample points come close to the spike, then the spike will go undetected, and its contribution to the numerical integral will not be correctly included.

Here is a plot of the function $\exp(-x^2)$.   *In[1]:=* **Plot[Exp[-x^2], {x, -10, 10}, PlotRange->All]**

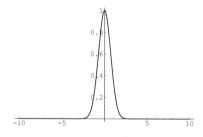

NIntegrate gives the correct answer for the numerical integral of this function from -10 to +10.

In[2]:= **NIntegrate[Exp[-x^2], {x, -10, 10}]**

Out[2]= 1.77245

If, however, you ask for the integral from -1000 to 1000, NIntegrate will miss the peak near $x = 0$, and give the wrong answer.

In[3]:= **NIntegrate[Exp[-x^2], {x, -1000, 1000}]**

Out[3]= $1.34946 \, 10^{-26}$

Although `NIntegrate` follows the principle of looking only at the numerical values of your integrand, it nevertheless tries to make the best possible use of the information that it can get. Thus, for example, if `NIntegrate` notices that the estimated error in the integral in a particular region is large, it will take more samples in that region. In this way, `NIntegrate` tries to "adapt" its operation to the particular integrand you have given.

The kind of adaptive procedure that `NIntegrate` uses is similar, at least in spirit, to what `Plot` does in trying to draw smooth curves for functions. In both cases, *Mathematica* tries to go on taking more samples in a particular region until it has effectively found a smooth approximation to the function in that region.

The kinds of problems that can appear in numerical integration can also arise in doing other numerical operations on functions.

For example, if you ask for a numerical approximation to the sum of an infinite series, *Mathematica* samples a certain number of terms in the series, and then does an extrapolation to estimate the contributions of other terms. If you insert large terms far out in the series, they may not be detected when the extrapolation is done, and the result you get for the sum may be incorrect.

A similar problem arises when you try to find a numerical approximation to the minimum of a function. *Mathematica* samples only a finite number of values, then effectively assumes that the actual function interpolates smoothly between these values. If in fact the function has a sharp dip in a particular region, then *Mathematica* may miss this dip, and you may get the wrong answer for the minimum.

If you work only with numerical values of functions, there is simply no way to avoid the kinds of problems we have been discussing. Exact symbolic computation, of course, allows you to get around these problems.

In many calculations, it is therefore worthwhile to go as far as you can symbolically, and then resort to numerical methods only at the very end. This gives you the best chance of avoiding the problems that can arise in purely numerical computations.

One might imagine that you could use symbolic methods to check for any features, say in the integrand of a numerical integral, that would give rise to problems in numerical computation. As soon as your integrand contains conditionals, control structures or nested function calls, there can be no general procedure, however, to do the tests that are needed. Nevertheless, for specific classes of integrands, it may be possible to perform some such tests. You can always implement these tests by defining special rules for `NIntegrate` in certain cases.

■ 3.9.3 Numerical Integration

`N[Integrate[`*expr*`, {`*x*`, `*xmin*`, `*xmax*`}]]`

        try to perform an integral exactly, then find numerical approximations to the parts that remain

`NIntegrate[`*expr*`, {`*x*`, `*xmin*`, `*xmax*`}]`

        find a numerical approximation to an integral

`NIntegrate[`*expr*`, {`*x*`, `*xmin*`, `*xmax*`}, {`*y*`, `*ymin*`, `*ymax*`}, ... ]`

        multidimensional numerical integral $\int_{xmin}^{xmax} dx \int_{ymin}^{ymax} dy \ldots expr$

`NIntegrate[`*expr*`, {`*x*`, `*xmin*`, `*x₁*`, `*x₂*`, ... , `*xmax*`}]`

        do a numerical integral along a line, starting at *xmin*, going through the points x_i, and ending at *xmax*

Numerical integration functions.

This finds a numerical approximation to the integral $\int_0^\infty e^{-x^3}\,dx$.	`In[1]:= NIntegrate[Exp[-x^3], {x, 0, Infinity}]` `Out[1]= 0.89298`
Here is the numerical value of the double integral $\int_{-1}^1 dx \int_{-1}^1 dy\,(x^2 + y^2)$.	`In[2]:= NIntegrate[x^2 + y^2, {x, -1, 1}, {y, -1, 1}]` `Out[2]= 2.66667`

An important feature of `NIntegrate` is its ability to deal with functions that "blow up" at known points. `NIntegrate` automatically checks for such problems at the end points of the integration region.

The function $1/\sqrt{x}$ blows up at $x = 0$, but `NIntegrate` still succeeds in getting the correct value for the integral.	`In[3]:= NIntegrate[1/Sqrt[x], {x, 0, 1}]` `Out[3]= 2.`
Mathematica can find the integral of $1/\sqrt{x}$ exactly.	`In[4]:= Integrate[1/Sqrt[x], {x, 0, 1}]` `Out[4]= 2`

`NIntegrate` detects that the singularity in $\frac{1}{x}$ at $x = 0$ is not integrable.

```
In[5]:= NIntegrate[1/x, {x, 0, 1}]

NIntegrate::slwcon:
    Numerical integration converging too slowly; suspect one of
        the following: singularity, oscillatory integrand, or
        insufficient WorkingPrecision.

NIntegrate::ncvb:
    NIntegrate failed to converge to prescribed accuracy after 7
                                                              -57
        recursive bisections in x near x == 4.36999 10    .

Out[5]= 23953.1
```

`NIntegrate` does not automatically look for singularities except at the end points of your integration region. When other singularities are present, `NIntegrate` may not give you the right answer for the integral. Nevertheless, in following its adaptive procedure, NIntegrate will often detect the presence of potentially singular behavior, and will warn you about it.

NIntegrate does not handle the singularity in $1/\sqrt{|x|}$ in the middle of the integration region. However, it warns you of a possible problem. In this case, the final result is numerically quite close to the correct answer.

```
In[6]:= NIntegrate[1/Sqrt[Abs[x]], {x, -1, 2}]

NIntegrate::slwcon:
    Numerical integration converging too slowly; suspect one of
       the following: singularity, oscillatory integrand, or
       insufficient WorkingPrecision.

NIntegrate::ncvb:
    NIntegrate failed to converge to prescribed accuracy after 7
       recursive bisections in x near x == -0.00390625.

Out[6]= 4.79343
```

If you know that your integrand has singularities at particular points, you can explicitly tell NIntegrate to deal with them. NIntegrate[*expr*, {*x*, *xmin*, x_1, x_2, ... , *xmax*}] integrates *expr* from *xmin* to *xmax*, looking for possible singularities at each of the intermediate points x_i.

This again gives the integral $\int_{-1}^{1} \frac{1}{\sqrt{|x|}}\,dx$, but now explicitly deals with the singularity at $x = 0$.

```
In[7]:= NIntegrate[1/Sqrt[Abs[x]], {x, -1, 0, 2}]

Out[7]= 4.82843
```

You can also use the list of intermediate points x_i in NIntegrate to specify an integration contour to follow in the complex plane. The contour is taken to consist of a sequence of line segments, starting at *xmin*, going through each of the x_i, and ending at *xmax*.

This integrates $\frac{1}{x}$ around a closed contour in the complex plane, going from -1, through the points $-i$, 1 and i, then back to -1.

```
In[8]:= NIntegrate[1/x, {x, -1, -I, 1, I, -1}]

Out[8]= 1.11022 10^{-16} + 6.28319 I
```

The integral gives $2\pi i$, as expected from Cauchy's theorem.

```
In[9]:= N[ 2 Pi I ]

Out[9]= 6.28319 I
```

There are a number of ways you can control the operation of NIntegrate. First, you may want to specify the accuracy of the answers you are trying to get. If you use Integrate, and then apply N to get numerical results, then the second argument you give to N specifies the precision to use in the internal computations used to do the numerical integral. You can also specify this precision using the option WorkingPrecision -> *n* for NIntegrate.

You should realize, however, that the option WorkingPrecision specifies only the precision to use for internal computations done by NIntegrate. The final answer that NIntegrate gives will almost always have a lower precision. You can nevertheless use NIntegrate to try and get an answer with a particular precision or accuracy by setting the options PrecisionGoal or AccuracyGoal. The default setting PrecisionGoal -> Automatic attempts to get answers with a precision equal to WorkingPrecision minus 10 digits. In general, NIntegrate continues until it achieves either of the goals specified by PrecisionGoal or AccuracyGoal.

This evaluates $\int_1^2 \frac{1}{x}\,dx$ using 40-digit precision for internal computations. The precision goal in this case is automatically set to 30 digits.

In[10]:= **NIntegrate[1/x, {x, 1, 2}, WorkingPrecision->40]**

Out[10]= 0.6931471805599453094172321214581766

The difference from the exact result is given as 0.

In[11]:= **% - N[Log[2], 40]**

Out[11]= 0.

In fact, the result was correct to about 33 digits.

In[12]:= **Accuracy[%]**

Out[12]= 33

option name	*default value*	
AccuracyGoal	Infinity	number of digits of accuracy to try and get in the final answer
PrecisionGoal	Automatic	number of digits of precision to try and get in the final answer
MinRecursion	0	minimum number of recursive subdivisions of the integration region
MaxRecursion	6	maximum number of recursive subdivisions of the integration region
SingularityDepth	4	number of recursive subdivisions to use before doing a change of variables at the endpoints
GaussPoints	Automatic	number of sample points to use at first
WorkingPrecision	$MachinePrecision	number of digits to use in internal computations
Compiled	True	whether the integrand should be compiled

Options for NIntegrate.

When NIntegrate tries to evaluate a numerical integral, it samples the integrand at a sequence of points. If it finds that the integrand changes rapidly in a particular region, then it recursively takes more sample points in that region. The parameters MinRecursion and MaxRecursion specify the minimum and maximum number of levels of recursive subdivision to use. Increasing the value of MinRecursion guarantees that NIntegrate will use a larger number of sample points. MaxRecursion limits the number of sample points which NIntegrate will ever try to use. Increasing MinRecursion or MaxRecursion will make NIntegrate work more slowly. For one-dimensional integrals, the option

GaussPoints specifies how many sample points NIntegrate should use before it starts recursive subdivision. SingularityDepth specifies how many levels of recursive subdivision NIntegrate should try before it concludes that the integrand is "blowing up" at one of the endpoints, and does a change of variables.

With the default settings for all options, NIntegrate misses the peak in $\exp(-x^2)$ near $x = 0$, and gives the wrong answer for the integral.

```
In[13]:= NIntegrate[Exp[-x^2], {x, -1000, 1000}]

            -26
Out[13]= 1.34946 10
```

With the option MinRecursion->3, NIntegrate samples enough points that it notices the peak around $x = 0$. With the default setting of MaxRecursion, however, NIntegrate cannot use enough sample points to be able to expect an accurate answer.

```
In[14]:= NIntegrate[Exp[-x^2], {x, -1000, 1000},
                                    MinRecursion->3]

NIntegrate::ncvb:
    NIntegrate failed to converge to prescribed accuracy after 7
        recursive bisections in x near x == 7.8125.

Out[14]= 0.99187
```

With this setting of MaxRecursion, NIntegrate can get an accurate answer for the integral.

```
In[15]:= NIntegrate[Exp[-x^2], {x, -1000, 1000},
                          MinRecursion->3, MaxRecursion->10]

Out[15]= 1.77245
```

Another way to solve the problem is to make NIntegrate break the integration region into several pieces, with a small piece that explicitly covers the neighborhood of the peak.

```
In[16]:= NIntegrate[Exp[-x^2], {x, -1000, -10, 10, 1000}]

Out[16]= 1.77245
```

■ 3.9.4 Numerical Evaluation of Sums and Products

NSum[f, {i, $imin$, $imax$}]	find a numerical approximation to the sum $\sum_{i=imin}^{imax} f$
NSum[f, {i, $imin$, $imax$, di}]	use step di in the sum
NProduct[f, {i, $imin$, $imax$}]	find a numerical approximation to the product $\prod_{i=imin}^{imax} f$

Numerical sums and products.

This gives a numerical approximation to $\sum_{i=1}^{\infty} \frac{1}{i^3}$.

```
In[1]:= NSum[1/i^3, {i, 1, Infinity}]

Out[1]= 1.20206
```

Mathematica does not know the exact result for this sum, so leaves it in symbolic form.

```
In[2]:= Sum[1/i^3, {i, 1, Infinity}]
                -3
Out[2]= Sum[i  , {i, 1, Infinity}]
```

You can apply N explicitly to get a numerical result.

```
In[3]:= N[%]

Out[3]= 1.20206
```

The way NSum works is to include a certain number of terms explicitly, and then to try and estimate the contribution of the remaining ones. There are two approaches to estimating this contribution. The first uses the Euler-Maclaurin method, and is based on approximating the sum by an integral. The second method, known as the Wynn epsilon method, samples a number of additional terms in the sum, and then tries to fit them to a polynomial multiplied by a decaying exponential.

option name	*default value*	
AccuracyGoal	Infinity	number of digits of accuracy to try and get in the Euler-Maclaurin method
PrecisionGoal	Automatic	number of digits of precision to try and get in the Euler-Maclaurin method
WorkingPrecision	$MachinePrecision	number of digits of precision to use in internal computations
Method	Automatic	Integrate (Euler-Maclaurin method) or Fit (Wynn epsilon method)
NSumTerms	15	number of terms to include explicitly
NSumExtraTerms	12	number of terms to use for extrapolation in the Wynn epsilon method
Compiled	True	whether to compile the summand

Options for NSum.

If you do not explicitly specify the method to use, NSum will try to choose between the methods it knows. In any case, some implicit assumptions about the functions you are summing have to be made. If these assumptions are not correct, you may get inaccurate answers.

The most common place to use NSum is in evaluating sums with infinite limits. You can, however, also use it for sums with finite limits. By making implicit assumptions about the objects you are evaluating, NSum can often avoid doing as many function evaluations as an explicit Sum computation would require.

This finds the numerical value of $\sum_{n=0}^{100} e^{-n}$ by extrapolation techniques.

```
In[4]:= NSum[Exp[-n], {n, 0, 100}]
Out[4]= 1.58198
```

You can also get the result, albeit much less efficiently, by constructing the symbolic form of the sum, then evaluating it numerically.

```
In[5]:= Sum[Exp[-n], {n, 0, 100}] //N
Out[5]= 1.58198
```

NProduct works in essentially the same way as NSum, with analogous options.

■ 3.9.5 Numerical Solution of Polynomial Equations

When Solve cannot find explicit solutions to polynomial equations, it returns a symbolic form of the result.

In[1]:= `Solve[x^5 + 7x + 1 == 0, x]`

Out[1]= $\{ToRules[Roots[7\ x + x^5 == -1, x]]\}$

You can get numerical solutions by applying N.

In[2]:= `N[%]`

Out[2]= {{x -> -1.11308 - 1.15173 I},
  {x -> -1.11308 + 1.15173 I}, {x -> -0.142849},
  {x -> 1.1845 - 1.15139 I}, {x -> 1.1845 + 1.15139 I}}

This gives the numerical solutions to 25-digit precision.

In[3]:= `N[%%, 25]`

Out[3]= {{x ->
    -1.113077976547710735600398 - 1.15173436215167430504677 I},
  {x -> -1.113077976547710735600398 +
    1.15173436215167430504677 I},
  {x -> -0.142848645525004434134116},
  {x -> 1.184502299310212952657104 -
    1.151390075408837074699147 I},
  {x -> 1.184502299310212952657104 +
    1.151390075408837074699147 I}}

You can use NSolve to get numerical solutions to polynomial equations directly, without first trying to find exact results.

In[4]:= `NSolve[x^7 + x + 1 == 0, x]`

Out[4]= {{x -> -0.796544}, {x -> -0.705298 - 0.637624 I},
  {x -> -0.705298 + 0.637624 I}, {x -> 0.123762 - 1.05665 I},
  {x -> 0.123762 + 1.05665 I}, {x -> 0.979808 - 0.516677 I},
  {x -> 0.979808 + 0.516677 I}}

NSolve[*poly*==0, *x*]	get approximate numerical solutions to a polynomial equation
NSolve[*poly*==0, *x*, *n*]	get solutions to *n*-digit precision

Numerical solution of polynomial equations.

NSolve will always give you the complete set of numerical solutions to any polynomial equation in one variable.

You can also get numerical solutions to sets of simultaneous polynomial equations. You can use Solve to "unwind" the simultaneous equations, and then apply N to get numerical results.

Solve writes these equations as a composition of simpler equations.

```
In[5]:= Solve[{x^2 + y^2 == 1, x^3 + y^3 == 2}, {x, y}]

Out[5]= {ToRules[Roots[3 x == y (-3 - 6 y - y^2 + 4 y^3 + 2 y^4),

          x, Using -> Roots[3 y^2 - 4 y^3 - 3 y^4 + 2 y^6 == -3, y]]]}
```

You can apply N to get a numerical result.

```
In[6]:= N[%]

Out[6]= {{x -> -1.09791 + 0.839887 I,

         y -> -1.09791 - 0.839887 I},

        {x -> -1.09791 - 0.839887 I, y -> -1.09791 + 0.839887 I},

        {x -> 1.22333 - 0.0729987 I, y -> -0.125423 - 0.712005 I},

        {x -> 1.22333 + 0.0729987 I, y -> -0.125423 + 0.712005 I},

        {x -> -0.125423 - 0.712005 I, y -> 1.22333 - 0.0729987 I},

        {x -> -0.125423 + 0.712005 I, y -> 1.22333 + 0.0729987 I}}
```

■ 3.9.6 Numerical Root Finding

NSolve gives you a general way to find numerical approximations to the solutions of polynomial equations. Finding numerical solutions to more general equations, however, can be much more difficult, as discussed in Section 3.4.2. FindRoot gives you a way to search for a numerical solution to an arbitrary equation, or set of equations.

FindRoot[*lhs*==*rhs*, {x, x_0}]	search for a numerical solution to the equation *lhs*==*rhs*, starting with x=x_0
FindRoot[*lhs*==*rhs*, {x, {x_0, x_1}}]	search for a solution using x_0 and x_1 as the first two values of x (this form must be used if symbolic derivatives of the equation cannot be found)
FindRoot[*lhs*==*rhs*, {x, *xstart*, *xmin*, *xmax*}]	search for a solution, stopping the search if x ever gets outside the range *xmin* to *xmax*
FindRoot[{*eqn*$_1$, *eqn*$_2$, ... }, {x, x_0}, {y, y_0}, ...]	search for a numerical solution to the simultaneous equations *eqn*$_i$

Numerical root finding.

The curves for cos(*x*) and *x* intersect at one point.

`In[1]:= Plot[{Cos[x], x}, {x, -1, 1}]`

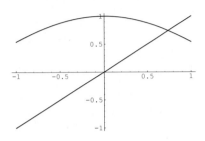

This finds a numerical approximation to the value of *x* at which the intersection occurs. The 0 tells FindRoot what value of *x* to try first.

`In[2]:= FindRoot[Cos[x] == x, {x, 0}]`

`Out[2]= {x -> 0.739085}`

In trying to find a solution to your equation, FindRoot starts at the point you specify, and then progressively tries to get closer and closer to a solution. Even if your equations have several solutions, FindRoot always returns the first solution it finds. Which solution this is will depend on what starting point you chose. So long as you start sufficiently close to a particular solution, FindRoot will always return that solution.

The equation sin(*x*) = 0 has an infinite number of solutions of the form $x = n\pi$. If you start sufficiently close to a particular solution, FindRoot will give you that solution.

`In[3]:= FindRoot[Sin[x] == 0, {x, 3}]`

`Out[3]= {x -> 3.14159}`

If you start with *x* = 6, you get a numerical approximation to the solution $x = 2\pi$.

`In[4]:= FindRoot[Sin[x] == 0, {x, 6}]`

`Out[4]= {x -> 6.28319}`

This is what happens if FindRoot cannot find a solution to your equation.

`In[5]:= FindRoot[Sin[x] == 2, {x, 1}]`

```
FindRoot::cvnwt:
    Newton's method failed to converge to the prescribed accuracy
        after 15 iterations.
```

`Out[5]= {x -> 2.06095}`

If you want FindRoot to search for complex solutions to this equation, then you have to give a complex starting value.

`In[6]:= FindRoot[Sin[x] == 2, {x, I}]`

`Out[6]= {x -> 1.5708 + 1.31696 I}`

You can give FindRoot bounds on the region in which you want it to look for solutions.

This tells FindRoot to try values of x starting at 1, but never going outside the region 0.5 to 1.5. In this case, FindRoot finds no solutions in the region you specified.

`In[7]:= FindRoot[Sin[x] == 0, {x, 1, 0.5, 1.5}]`

```
FindRoot::regex:
    Reached the point {-0.557408} which is outside the region
        {{0.5, 1.5}}.
```

`Out[7]= FindRoot[Sin[x] == 0, {x, 1, 0.5, 1.5}]`

Picking good starting points is crucial in getting useful answers from FindRoot. To know how to pick good starting points, you need to understand a little about how FindRoot actually works.

In the simplest case, FindRoot uses *Newton's method*. To find a solution to an equation of the form $f(x) = 0$, the method starts at x_0, then uses knowledge of the derivative f' to take a sequence of steps toward a solution. Each new point x_n that it tries is found from the previous point x_{n-1} by the formula $x_n = x_{n-1} - f(x_{n-1})/f'(x_{n-1})$.

One important limitation of Newton's method is that it "gets stuck" if it ever gets to a point where the derivative of the function vanishes. You can usually avoid this problem by choosing starting points that have no special properties with respect to the equations you are trying to solve.

The derivative of $x^2 - 1$ is zero at the starting point $x = 0$. As a result FindRoot cannot decide whether to take its first step in the positive or the negative direction.

```
In[8]:= FindRoot[x^2 - 1 == 0, {x, 0}]

FindRoot::jsing:
     Encountered a singular Jacobian at the point {x} = {0.}
        . Try perturbing the initial point(s).
                  2
Out[8]= FindRoot[x  - 1 == 0, {x, 0}]
```

If you start at a random point, however, FindRoot will usually succeed in finding a solution.

```
In[9]:= FindRoot[x^2 - 1 == 0, {x, Random[ ]}]

Out[9]= {x -> 1.}
```

FindRoot uses versions of Newton's method in many cases. Especially when there are several variables, the precise set of starting points which lead to a particular solution can become extremely complicated. The best policy is to try and start as close to the solution as possible, and to avoid any "special points".

This finds a solution to a set of simultaneous equations. It is a good idea to avoid taking the starting values for x and y to be equal, or in any other way "special".

```
In[10]:= FindRoot[{Sin[x] == Cos[y], x + y == 1},
                      {x, .1}, {y, .2}]

Out[10]= {x -> 1.2854, y -> -0.285398}
```

If the functions that appear in your equations are sufficiently simple, then *Mathematica* will be able to find their derivatives symbolically. In all the examples of FindRoot that we have used so far, this is possible. As a result, FindRoot can use the formula for Newton's method directly.

If, on the other hand, FindRoot has to estimate the derivative of your functions numerically, then it must take another approach. In simple cases, the approach it uses is based on the "secant method". One feature of this method is that to get it started, you have to specify not just the first value to try, but rather the first *two* values.

This specifies the first two values of x to try.

```
In[11]:= FindRoot[Cos[x] == x, {x, {0, 1}}]

Out[11]= {x -> 0.739085}
```

If *Mathematica* cannot get an explicit formula for the function that appears in your equation, you *have to* specify the first two values to try. Here FindRoot finds a zero of the Riemann zeta function.

```
In[12]:= FindRoot[Zeta[1/2 + I t] == 0, {t, {12, 13}}]
```
$$Out[12]= \{t \rightarrow 14.1347 - 4.42626 \; 10^{-7} \; I\}$$

If you are finding a root of a function of one variable, and the first two points you tell FindRoot to try give values of the function with opposite signs, then FindRoot is guaranteed to find a root. (This is true so long as your function is real and satisfies some basic continuity conditions.)

option name	default value	
AccuracyGoal	Automatic	the accuracy with which functions must be zero in order to be accepted as a solution
WorkingPrecision	$MachinePrecision	the number of digits of precision to keep in internal computations
MaxIterations	15	the maximum number of steps to take in trying to find a solution
Compiled	True	whether to compile the function

Options for FindRoot.

There are several options you can use to control the operation of FindRoot. First, you can set MaxIterations to specify the maximum number of steps that FindRoot should use in attempting to find a solution. Even if FindRoot does not successfully find a solution in the number of steps you specify, it returns the most recent values it has tried. If you want to continue the search, you can then give these values as starting points.

To work out whether it has found an acceptable root, FindRoot evaluates your function and sees whether the result is zero to within the accuracy specified by the option AccuracyGoal. FindRoot will always print a warning message if it does not find a solution to within the specified accuracy. In doing internal computations, FindRoot uses the precision specified by the option WorkingPrecision. The default AccuracyGoal is 10 digits less than WorkingPrecision.

This specifies that the zeta function needs to be zero to 10-digit accuracy at the solution. The Riemann hypothesis asserts that the imaginary part of t should be exactly zero at a root.

```
In[13]:= FindRoot[Zeta[1/2 + I t] == 0, {t, {12, 13}},
                    AccuracyGoal -> 10]
```
$$Out[13]= \{t \rightarrow 14.1347 - 4.43745 \; 10^{-13} \; I\}$$

■ 3.9.7 Numerical Solution of Differential Equations

The function `NDSolve` discussed in Section 1.6.4 allows you to find numerical solutions to differential equations. `NDSolve` handles both single differential equations, and sets of simultaneous differential equations. It has the restriction, however, that all the differential equations must be *ordinary differential equations*, not *partial differential equations*. This means that while the differential equations you give can involve any number of unknown functions y_i, all of these functions must depend on a single "independent variable" x, which is the same for each function.

`NDSolve[{eqn₁, eqn₂, ... }, y, {x, xmin, xmax}]`
find a numerical solution for the function y with x in the range *xmin* to *xmax*
`NDSolve[{eqn₁, eqn₂, ... }, {y₁, y₂, ... }, {x, xmin, xmax}]`
find numerical solutions for several functions y_i

Finding numerical solutions to differential equations.

`NDSolve` represents solutions for the functions y_i as `InterpolatingFunction` objects. The `InterpolatingFunction` objects provide approximations to the y_i over the range of values *xmin* to *xmax* for the independent variable x.

`NDSolve` finds solutions iteratively. It starts at a particular value of x, then takes a sequence of steps, trying eventually to cover the whole range *xmin* to *xmax*.

In order to get started, `NDSolve` has to be given appropriate "initial conditions" for the y_i and their derivatives. Initial conditions specify values for $y_i[x]$, and perhaps derivatives $y_i'[x]$, at particular values of x. In general, the initial conditions you give can be at any value of x: `NDSolve` will automatically start stepping from that value to cover the range *xmin* to *xmax*.

This finds a solution for y with x in the range 0 to 2, using an initial condition for y[0].	`In[1]:= NDSolve[{y'[x] == y[x], y[0] == 1}, y, {x, 0, 2}]`
	
	`Out[1]= {{y -> InterpolatingFunction[{0., 2.}, <>]}}`

This still finds a solution with x in the range 0 to 2, but now the initial condition is for y[3].	`In[2]:= NDSolve[{y'[x] == y[x], y[3] == 1}, y, {x, 0, 2}]`
	
	`Out[2]= {{y -> InterpolatingFunction[{0., 3.}, <>]}}`

When you use `NDSolve`, the initial conditions you give must be sufficient to determine the solutions for the y_i completely. When you use `DSolve` to find symbolic solutions to differential equations, you can get away with specifying fewer initial conditions. The reason is that `DSolve` automatically inserts arbitrary constants `C[i]` to represent degrees of freedom associated with initial conditions that you have not specified explicitly. Since `NDSolve` must give a numerical solution, it cannot represent these kinds of additional degrees of freedom. As a result, you must explicitly give all the initial conditions that are needed to determine the solution.

In a typical case, if you have differential equations with up to n^{th} derivatives, then you need to specify initial conditions for up to $(n - 1)^{th}$ derivatives.

With a third-order equation, you need to give initial conditions for up to second derivatives.

```
In[3]:= NDSolve[
            { y'''[x] + 8 y''[x] + 17 y'[x] + 10 y[x] == 0,
               y[0] == 6, y'[0] == -20, y''[0] == 84},
                y, {x, 0, 1} ]
Out[3]= {{y -> InterpolatingFunction[{0., 1.}, <>]}}
```

This plots the solution obtained.

```
In[4]:= Plot[Evaluate[ y[x] /. % ], {x, 0, 1}]
```

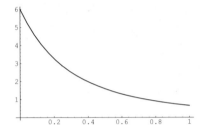

In most cases, all the initial conditions you give must involve the same value of x, say x_0. As a result, you can avoid giving both *xmin* and *xmax* explicitly. If you specify your range of x as $\{x, x_1\}$, then *Mathematica* will automatically generate a solution over the range x_0 to x_1.

This generates a solution over the range 0 to 2.

```
In[5]:= NDSolve[{y'[x] == y[x], y[0] == 1}, y, {x, 2}]
Out[5]= {{y -> InterpolatingFunction[{0., 2.}, <>]}}
```

You can give initial conditions as equations of any kind. In some cases, these equations may have multiple solutions. In such cases, NDSolve will correspondingly generate multiple solutions.

The initial conditions in this case lead to multiple solutions.

```
In[6]:= NDSolve[{y'[x]^2 - y[x]^2 == 0, y[0]^2 == 4},
                    y[x], {x, 1}]
Out[6]= {{y[x] -> InterpolatingFunction[{0., 1.}, <>][x]},
          {y[x] -> InterpolatingFunction[{0., 1.}, <>][x]},
          {y[x] -> InterpolatingFunction[{0., 1.}, <>][x]},
          {y[x] -> InterpolatingFunction[{0., 1.}, <>][x]}}
```

Here is a plot of all the solutions.   *In[7]:=* **Plot[Evaluate[y[x] /. %], {x, 0, 1}]**

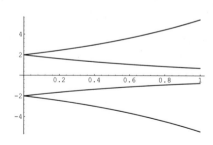

You can use NDSolve to solve systems of coupled differential equations.

This finds a numerical solution to a pair   *In[8]:=* **sol = NDSolve[**
of coupled equations.   **{x'[t] == -y[t] - x[t]^2, y'[t] == 2 x[t] - y[t],**
                                                                               x[0] == y[0] == 1}, {x, y}, {t, 10}]

Out[8]= **{{x -> InterpolatingFunction[{0., 10.}, <>],**
               y -> InterpolatingFunction[{0., 10.}, <>]}}

This plots the solution for y from these   *In[9]:=* **Plot[Evaluate[y[t] /. sol], {t, 0, 10}]**
equations.

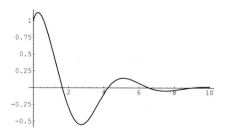

This generates a parametric plot using   *In[10]:=* **ParametricPlot[Evaluate[{x[t], y[t]} /. sol],**
both x and y.   **{t, 0, 10}, PlotRange -> All]**

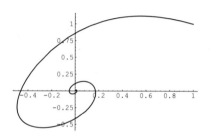

Unknown functions in differential equations do not necessarily have to be represented by single symbols. If you have a large number of unknown functions, you will often find it more convenient, for example, to give the functions names like $y[i]$.

This constructs a set of five coupled differential equations and initial conditions.

```
In[11]:= eqns = Join[
           Table[ y[i]'[x] == y[i-1][x] - y[i][x], {i, 2, 4} ],
           {y[1]'[x] == -y[1][x], y[5]'[x] == y[4][x],
                                              y[1][0] == 1},
           Table[ y[i][0] == 0, {i, 2, 5}]
           ]
Out[11]= {(y[2])'[x] == y[1][x] - y[2][x],
   (y[3])'[x] == y[2][x] - y[3][x],
   (y[4])'[x] == y[3][x] - y[4][x], (y[1])'[x] == -y[1][x],
   (y[5])'[x] == y[4][x], y[1][0] == 1, y[2][0] == 0,
   y[3][0] == 0, y[4][0] == 0, y[5][0] == 0}
```

This solves the equations.

```
In[12]:= NDSolve[eqns, Table[y[i], {i, 5}], {x, 10}]
Out[12]= {{y[1] -> InterpolatingFunction[{0., 10.}, <>],
   y[2] -> InterpolatingFunction[{0., 10.}, <>],
   y[3] -> InterpolatingFunction[{0., 10.}, <>],
   y[4] -> InterpolatingFunction[{0., 10.}, <>],
   y[5] -> InterpolatingFunction[{0., 10.}, <>]}}
```

Here is a plot of the solutions.

```
In[13]:= Plot[ Evaluate[Table[y[i][x], {i, 5}] /. %],
                                           {x, 0, 10} ]
```

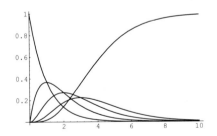

option name	default value	
AccuracyGoal	Automatic	number of digits of accuracy to try and get in the solution
PrecisionGoal	Automatic	number of digits of precision to try and get in the solution
WorkingPrecision	$MachinePrecision	number of digits to use in internal computations
MaxSteps	500	maximum number of steps in x to take
StartingStepSize	Automatic	starting size of step in x to use
Compiled	True	whether to compile the equations

Options for `NDSolve`.

NDSolve allows you to specify the precision or accuracy of result you want. In general, NDSolve makes the steps it takes smaller and smaller until the solution it gets satisfies either the AccuracyGoal *or* the PrecisionGoal you give. The setting for AccuracyGoal effectively determines the absolute error to allow in the solution, while the setting for PrecisionGoal determines the relative error. If you need to track a solution whose value comes close to zero, then you will typically need to increase the setting for AccuracyGoal. By setting AccuracyGoal -> Infinity, you tell NDSolve to use PrecisionGoal only.

NDSolve uses the setting you give for WorkingPrecision to determine the total number of digits to use in its internal computations. If you specify large values for AccuracyGoal or PrecisionGoal, then you typically need to give a somewhat larger value for WorkingPrecision. With the default setting of Automatic, AccuracyGoal and PrecisionGoal are both equal to the setting for WorkingPrecision minus 10 digits.

This generates a high-precision solution to a complex differential equation.

```
In[14]:= NDSolve[{y'[x] == I/4 y[x], y[0] == 1}, y, {x, 1},
                    AccuracyGoal -> 20, PrecisionGoal -> 20,
                                WorkingPrecision -> 25]

Out[14]= {{y -> InterpolatingFunction[{0., 1}, <>]}}
```

Here is an approximation to $e^{i/4}$ found from the solution.

```
In[15]:= y[1] /. %
Out[15]= {0.9689124217106447841185519 +
          0.2474039592545229296234111 I}
```

As mentioned above, NDSolve works by taking a sequence of steps in the independent variable x. NDSolve uses an adaptive procedure to determine the size of these steps. In general, if the solution appears to be varying rapidly in a particular region, then NDSolve will reduce the step size so as to be able to track the solution better.

This solves a differential equation in which the derivative has a discontinuity.

```
In[16]:= NDSolve[
            {y'[x] == If[x < 0, 1/(x-1), 1/(x+1)],
             y[-5] == 5},
            y, {x, -5, 5}]
Out[16]= {{y -> InterpolatingFunction[{-5., 5.}, <>]}}
```

NDSolve reduced the step size around $x = 0$ so as to reproduce the kink accurately.

```
In[17]:= Plot[Evaluate[y[x] /. %], {x, -5, 5}]
```

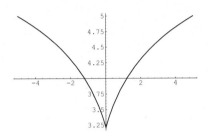

Through its adaptive procedure, NDSolve is able to solve "stiff" differential equations in which there are several components which vary with x at very different rates.

In these equations, y varies much more rapidly than z.

```
In[18]:= sol = NDSolve[
            {y'[x] == -40 y[x], z'[x] == -z[x]/10,
                              y[0] == z[0] == 1},
            {y, z}, {x, 0, 1}]
Out[18]= {{y -> InterpolatingFunction[{0., 1.}, <>],
          z -> InterpolatingFunction[{0., 1.}, <>]}}
```

NDSolve nevertheless tracks both components successfully.

```
In[19]:= Plot[Evaluate[{y[x], z[x]} /. sol], {x, 0, 1},
                              PlotRange -> All]
```

NDSolve follows the general procedure of reducing step size until it tracks solutions accurately. There is a problem, however, when the true solution has a singularity. In this case, NDSolve might go on reducing the step size forever, and never terminate. To avoid this problem, the option MaxSteps specifies the maximum number of steps that NDSolve will ever take in attempting to find a solution. The default setting is MaxSteps -> 500.

NDSolve stops after taking 500 steps.

```
In[20]:= NDSolve[{y'[x] == -1/(x - 2)^2, y[0] == -1/2},
                                            y, {x, 0, 3}]
NDSolve::mxst: Maximum number of steps reached at the point 2..
Out[20]= {{y -> InterpolatingFunction[{0., 2.}, <>]}}
```

There is in fact a singularity in the solution at $x = 2$.

```
In[21]:= Plot[Evaluate[y[x] /. %], {x, 0, 2}]
```

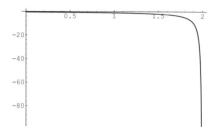

The default setting MaxSteps -> 500 should be sufficient for most equations with smooth solutions. When solutions have a complicated structure, however, you may sometimes have to choose larger settings for MaxSteps. With the setting MaxSteps -> Infinity there is no upper limit on the number of steps used.

To reproduce the full structure of the solution to the Lorenz equations, you need to give a larger setting for MaxSteps.

```
In[22]:= NDSolve[ {x'[t] == -3 (x[t] - y[t]),
                   y'[t] == -x[t] z[t] + 26.5 x[t] - y[t],
                   z'[t] == x[t] y[t] - z[t],
                   x[0] == z[0] == 0, y[0] == 1},
                  {x, y, z}, {t, 0, 20}, MaxSteps->3000 ]
Out[22]= {{x -> InterpolatingFunction[{0., 20.}, <>],
           y -> InterpolatingFunction[{0., 20.}, <>],
           z -> InterpolatingFunction[{0., 20.}, <>]}}
```

Here is a parametric plot of the solution in three dimensions.

In[23]:= `ParametricPlot3D[Evaluate[{x[t], y[t], z[t]} /. %],`
`                           {t, 0, 20}, PlotPoints -> 1000]`

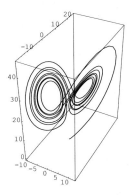

When `NDSolve` solves a particular set of differential equations, it always tries to choose a step size appropriate for those equations. In some cases, the very first step that `NDSolve` makes may be too large, and it may miss an important feature in the solution. To avoid this problem, you can explicitly set the option `StartingStepSize` to specify the size to use for the first step.

■ 3.9.8 Numerical Minimization

`FindRoot` gives you a way to find points at which a particular function is equal to zero. It is also often important to be able to find points at which a function has its minimum value. In principle, you could do this by applying `FindRoot` to the derivative of the function. In practice, however, there are much more efficient approaches.

`FindMinimum` gives you a way to find a minimum value for a function. As in `FindRoot`, you specify the first one or two points to try, and then `FindMinimum` tries to get progressively more accurate approximations to a minimum. If `FindMinimum` returns a definite result, then the result is guaranteed to correspond to at least a local minimum of your function. However, it is important to understand that the result may not be the global minimum point.

You can understand something about how `FindMinimum` works by thinking of the values of your function as defining the height of a surface. What `FindMinimum` does is essentially to start at the points you specify, then follow the path of steepest descent on the surface. Except in pathological cases, this path always leads to at least a local minimum on the surface. In many cases, however, the minimum will not be a global one. As a simple analogy which illustrates this point, consider a physical mountain. Any water that falls on the mountain takes the path of steepest descent down the side of the mountain. Yet not all the water ends up at the bottom of the valleys; much of it gets stuck in mountain lakes which correspond to local minima of the mountain height function.

You should also realize that because `FindMinimum` does not take truly infinitesimal steps, it is still possible for it to overshoot even a local minimum.

This finds the value of x which minimizes $\Gamma(x)$, starting from $x = 2$.	`In[1]:= FindMinimum[Gamma[x], {x, 2}]`
	
	`Out[1]= {0.885603, {x -> 1.46163}}`

Here is a function with many local minima.	`In[2]:= Plot[Sin[x] + x/5, {x, -10, 10}]`

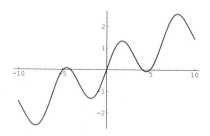

`FindMinimum` finds the local minimum closest to $x = 1$. This is not the global minimum for the function.	`In[3]:= FindMinimum[Sin[x] + x/5, {x, 1}]`
	
	`Out[3]= {-1.33423, {x -> -1.77215}}`

This finds the local minimum of a function of two variables. As in `FindRoot`, it is a good idea to choose starting values that are not too "special".	`In[4]:= FindMinimum[x^4 + 3 x^2 y + 5 y^2 + x + y,`
	`                {x, 0.1}, {y, 0.2}]`
	
	`Out[4]= {-0.832579, {x -> -0.886326, y -> -0.335672}}`

`FindMinimum[f, {x, x₀}]`	search for a local minimum in the function f, starting from the point $x=x_0$
`FindMinimum[f, {x, {x₀, x₁}}]`	search for a local minimum using x_0 and x_1 as the first two values of x (this form must be used if symbolic derivatives of f cannot be found)
`FindMinimum[f, {x, xstart, xmin, xmax}]`	
	search for a local minimum, stopping the search if x ever gets outside the range *xmin* to *xmax*
`FindMinimum[f, {x, x₀}, {y, y₀}, ... ]`	
	search for a local minimum in a function of several variables

Numerical minimization.

■ 3.9.9 Linear Programming

FindMinimum can find local minima for arbitrary functions. In solving optimization problems, it is however often important to be able to find *global* maxima and minima.

Linear programming provides a way to do this for linear functions. In general, linear programming allows you to find the global minimum or maximum of any linear function subject to a set of constraints defined by linear inequalities.

For a function of n variables, the constraints effectively define a region in n-dimensional space. Each linear inequality gives a plane in n-dimensional space which forms one of the sides of the region.

ConstrainedMax[f, {*inequalities*}, {x, y, ... }] find the global maximum of f in the region specified by the inequalities
ConstrainedMin[f, {*inequalities*}, {x, y, ... }] find the global minimum of f in the region specified by the inequalities

Solving linear optimization problems.

The functions ConstrainedMax and ConstrainedMin allow you to specify an "objective function" to maximize or minimize, together with a set of linear constraints on variables. *Mathematica* assumes in all cases that the variables are constrained to have non-negative values.

The maximum value of $x + y$ in this case is attained when $x = 1$ and $y = 2$.

```
In[1]:= ConstrainedMax[x + y, {x < 1, y < 2}, {x, y}]
Out[1]= {3, {x -> 1, y -> 2}}
```

Mathematica assumes that x and y are constrained to be non-negative.

```
In[2]:= ConstrainedMin[x + y, {x < 1, y < 2}, {x, y}]
Out[2]= {0, {x -> 0, y -> 0}}
```

Here is a slightly more complicated linear programming problem.

```
In[3]:= ConstrainedMax[17x - 20y + 18z,
                {x - y + z < 10, x < 5, x + z > 20}, {x, y, z}]
Out[3]= {160, {x -> 0, y -> 10, z -> 20}}
```

You can give both exact and approximate numbers as coefficients in linear programming problems. When the numbers you give are exact, *Mathematica* will always generate results in terms of exact rational numbers.

If the coefficients in your input are exact, *Mathematica* will give exact rational numbers in the output.

```
In[4]:= ConstrainedMin[x + 3 y + 7 z,
                {x - 3 y < 7, 2 x + 3 z >= 5, x + y + z < 10},
                                                {x, y, z}]
```

$$Out[4]= \{\frac{5}{2}, \{x \to \frac{5}{2}, y \to 0, z \to 0\}\}$$

Mathematica allows you to use both strict inequalities of the form $a < b$ and non-strict inequalities of the form $a <= b$ in specifying linear programming problems. If you work with approximate numbers, then these types of inequalities cannot be distinguished. However, if you work with exact numbers, then these types of inequalities could in principle yield different results.

It turns out that the solution to any linear programming problem always corresponds to a point which lies at the boundary of the region defined for that problem. With non-strict inequalities, the solution point lies actually *on* the boundary. With strict inequalities, however, the solution point in principle lies infinitesimally within the boundary. *Mathematica* ignores this issue when giving exact results for linear programming problems. Thus *Mathematica* may yield a result like x -> 1 when in fact x must in principle be infinitesimally smaller than 1.

As a result of this phenomenon, exact results you get from functions like `ConstrainedMax` may have the property that they do not satisfy strict inequalities that appear in the constraints you specify. The results would however satisfy non-strict versions of the same inequalities.

The result x -> 1 satisfies x <= 1 but not x < 1.

```
In[5]:= ConstrainedMax[x, {x < 1}, {x}]

Out[5]= {1, {x -> 1}}
```

`ConstrainedMax` and `ConstrainedMin` allow you to give an arbitrary list of inequalities, as well as equations, to specify constraints between variables. In some cases, these constraints may turn out to be inconsistent. In such cases, `ConstrainedMax` and `ConstrainedMin` return unevaluated.

The constraints given here are inconsistent.

```
In[6]:= ConstrainedMax[x, {x < 1, x > 2}, {x}]

ConstrainedMax::nsat:
    Specified constraints cannot be satisfied.

Out[6]= ConstrainedMax[x, {x < 1, x > 2}, {x}]
```

In most practical linear optimization problems, the region corresponding to the constraints you specify is finite in all directions. It is however possible to give inequalities which specify infinite regions. In such cases, there may be no bound on the objective function, and *Mathematica* will return infinite or indeterminate results.

The region specified in this case is unbounded.

```
In[7]:= ConstrainedMax[x, {x > 1}, {x}]

ConstrainedMax::nbdd:
    Specified domain appears unbounded.

Out[7]= {Infinity, {x -> Indeterminate}}
```

In `ConstrainedMax` and `ConstrainedMin` the objective functions and constraints are specified in symbolic form. Sometimes, however, it is more convenient to handle linear programming problems simply by setting up vectors and matrices which represent the appropriate coefficients of the linear functions that appear. You can do this using `LinearProgramming`.

`LinearProgramming[c, m, b]`	find the vector **x** which minimizes **c.x** subject to the constraints **m.x** ≥ **b** and **x** ≥ 0

Linear programming in matrix form.

Here is a linear programming problem given in symbolic form.

```
In[8]:= ConstrainedMin[2x - 3y,
                {x + y < 10, x - y > 2, x > 1}, {x, y}]

Out[8]= {0, {x -> 6, y -> 4}}
```

Here is the same problem given in matrix form.

```
In[9]:= LinearProgramming[{2, -3},
                {{-1, -1}, {1, -1}, {1, 0}}, {-10, 2, 1}]

Out[9]= {6, 4}
```

Appendix.

Mathematica Reference Guide

A.1 Basic Objects

■ A.1.1 Expressions

Expressions are the main type of data in *Mathematica*.

Expressions can be written in the form $h[e_1, e_2, \ldots]$. The object h is known generically as the *head* of the expression. The e_i are termed the *elements* of the expression. Both the head and the elements may themselves be expressions.

The *parts* of an expression can be referred to by numerical indices. The head has index 0; element e_i has index i. Part[*expr*, *i*] or *expr*[[*i*]] gives the part of *expr* with index i. Negative indices count from the end.

Part[*expr*, i_1, i_2, $\ldots$] or *expr*[[i_1, i_2, $\ldots$]] gives the piece of *expr* found by successively extracting parts of subexpressions with indices $i_1, i_2, \ldots$. If you think of expressions as trees, the indices specify which branch to take at each node as you descend from the root.

The pieces of an expression that are specified by giving a sequence of exactly n indices are defined to be at *level* n in the expression. You can use levels to determine the domain of application of functions like Map. Level 0 corresponds to the whole expression.

The *depth* of an expression is defined to be the maximum number of indices needed to specify any part of the expression, plus one. A negative level number $-n$ refers to all parts of an expression that have depth n.

■ A.1.2 Symbols

Symbols are the basic named objects in *Mathematica*.

The name of a symbol can be any sequence of letters and digits, not starting with a digit. Symbol names can also contain the character $. Upper- and lower-case letters are always distinguished in *Mathematica*. Symbol names may also contain any 8- or 16-bit characters that are not part of the standard printable ASCII character set.

aaaaa	user-defined symbol
Aaaaa	system-defined symbol
$Aaaa	global or internal system-defined symbol
aaaa$	symbol renamed in a scoping construct
aa$nn	unique local symbol generated in a module

Symbol naming conventions.

The convention is usually that the names of system-defined symbols consist of one or more complete English words. The first letter of each word is capitalized, and the words are run together.

Once created, an ordinary symbol in *Mathematica* continues to exist unless it is explicitly removed using `Remove`. However, symbols created automatically in scoping constructs such as `Module` carry the attribute `Temporary` which specifies that they should automatically be removed as soon as they no longer appear in any expression.

When a new symbol is to be created, *Mathematica* first applies any value that has been assigned to `$NewSymbol` to strings giving the name of the symbol, and the context in which the symbol would be created.

If the message `General::newsym` is switched on, then *Mathematica* reports new symbols that are created. This message is switched off by default. Symbols created automatically in scoping constructs are not reported.

If the message `General::spell` is switched on, then *Mathematica* prints a warning if the name of a new symbol is close to the names of one or more existing symbols.

■ A.1.3 Contexts

The full name of any symbol in *Mathematica* consists of two parts: a *context*, and a *short name*. The full name is written in the form *context*`*name*. The context *context*` can contain the same characters as the short name. It may also contain any number of context mark characters `, and must end with a context mark.

At any point in a *Mathematica* session, there is a *current context* `$Context` and a *context search path* `$ContextPath` consisting of a list of contexts. Symbols in the current context, or in contexts on the context search path can be specified by giving only their short names.

name	search `$Context`, then `$ContextPath`; create in `$Context` if necessary
`*name*	search `$Context` only; create there if necessary
context`*name*	search *context* only; create there if necessary
`*context*`*name*	search `$Context`*context* only; create there if necessary

Contexts used for various specifications of symbols.

With *Mathematica* packages, it is conventional to associate contexts whose names correspond to the names of the packages. Packages typically use `BeginPackage` and `EndPackage` to define objects in the appropriate context, and to add the context to the global `$ContextPath`. `EndPackage` prints a warning about any symbols that were created in a package but which are "shadowed" by existing symbols on the context search path.

The context is included in the printed form of a symbol only if it would be needed to specify the symbol *at the time of printing*.

■ A.1.4 Special Objects

There are a number of types of special objects, which form the indivisible elements of expressions in *Mathematica*.

These objects have heads which are symbols that can be thought of as "tagging" their types. The objects contain "raw data", which can usually be accessed only by functions specific to the particular type of object. You can extract the head of a special object using Head, but you cannot explicitly extract any of its other parts.

Symbol	symbol
String	character string "*cccc*"
Integer, Real, Rational and Complex	numbers

Special objects.

Most special objects are input and output in special forms.

As an optimization for some special kinds of computations, the raw data in *Mathematica* special objects can be given explicitly using Raw[*head*, "*hexstring*"]. The data is specified as a string of hexadecimal digits, corresponding to an array of bytes. When no special output form exists, InputForm prints special objects using Raw. *The behavior of* Raw *differs from one implementation of Mathematica to another; its general use is strongly discouraged.*

■ A.1.5 Numbers

Integer	integer *nnnn*
Real	approximate real number *nnn.nnn*
Rational	rational number *nnn/nnn*
Complex	complex number *nnn* + *nnn* I

Basic types of numbers.

All numbers in *Mathematica* can contain any number of digits. *Mathematica* does exact computations when possible with integers and rational numbers, and with complex numbers whose real and imaginary parts are integers or rational numbers.

There are two types of approximate real numbers in *Mathematica*: *arbitrary precision* and *machine precision*. In manipulating arbitrary-precision numbers, *Mathematica* always tries to modify the precision so as to ensure that all digits actually given are correct.

With machine-precision numbers, all computations are done to the same fixed precision, so some digits given may not be correct.

Unless otherwise specified, *Mathematica* treats as machine-precision numbers all approximate real numbers that lie between $MinMachineNumber and $MaxMachineNumber and that are input with less than $MachinePrecision digits.

In InputForm, *Mathematica* prints machine-precision numbers with $MachinePrecision digits, except when trailing digits are zero.

When the precision of a arbitrary-precision number is zero, *Mathematica* prints the whole number as 0.

Numbers can be entered in any base from 2 to 36, using the notation *base*^^*digits*. *base* is given in decimal. For bases larger than 10, additional digits are chosen from the letters a–z or A–Z. Upper- and lower-case letters are equivalent for these purposes. Floating-point numbers can be specified by including . in the *digits* sequence.

There is a limit on the range of magnitudes for any number in *Mathematica*. Numbers outside this range are represented by Underflow[ ] and Overflow[ ].

■ A.1.6 Character Strings

Character strings in *Mathematica* can contain any sequence of characters. Character strings are input in the form "*ccccc*".

The individual characters can be printable ASCII, or in general any 8- or 16-bit characters.

All 8-bit characters can be entered directly. If 16-bit characters are entered directly, either each character must explicitly be prefaced with \!, or every sequence of 16-bit characters must be prefaced by \+, and terminated with a double null byte.

Within a character string, \" stands for ".

Special characters in strings may be input using the sequences specified in Section A.2.1.

Null bytes can appear at any point within *Mathematica* strings.

A.2 Input Syntax

■ A.2.1 Characters

Mathematica handles both 8-bit and 16-bit characters. All 8-bit characters can be entered directly. They can also be entered using various sequences of printable ASCII characters.

\\	single backslash (decimal code 92)
\b	backspace or CONTROL-H (decimal code 8)
\t	tab or CONTROL-I (decimal code 9)
\n	newline or CONTROL-J (decimal code 10)
\f	form feed or CONTROL-L (decimal code 12)
\r	carriage return or CONTROL-M (decimal code 13)
\∧A through \∧Z or \∧a through \∧z	CONTROL-A (decimal code 1) through CONTROL-Z (decimal code 26)
\0	null byte (code 0)
nnn	an 8-bit character with octal code *nnn*
\.*nn*	an 8-bit character with hexadecimal code *nn*

Sequences for entering 8-bit characters.

Even when they are entered directly, 16-bit characters must be prefaced by specific printable ASCII sequences.

\:*nnnn*	a 16-bit character with hexadecimal code *nnnn*
\!*c*	a 16-bit character *c*
\+*ccccc*	a sequence of 16-bit characters, terminated by a double null byte

Sequences for entering 16-bit characters.

The operators used in the *Mathematica* language involve only printable ASCII characters (decimal codes 32 through 126).

Other 8- and 16-bit characters can be used in character strings, symbol names, comments and file names.

Integer codes for characters correspond to the bit patterns which represent those characters.

Decimal code 0	\0
Decimal codes 1 through 26	\^A through \^Z
Decimal codes 27 through 31	\033 through 037
Decimal codes 32 through 126	standard characters
Decimal codes 127 through 255	\177 to \377
Decimal codes 256 through 65535	\:0100 through \:ffff
Decimal codes 65536 through 65791	
	\:0000 through \:00ff

Integer codes for characters.

■ A.2.2 Bracketed Objects

(*expr*)	parenthesization: grouping of input
$h[e_1, e_2, \ldots]$	standard expression
$e[[i_1, i_2, \ldots]]$	Part$[e, i_1, i_2, \ldots]$
$\{e_1, e_2, \ldots\}$	List$[e_1, e_2, \ldots]$
(* *any text* *)	comment

Bracketed objects.

$h[\ ]$ is an expression with zero elements. {} is List[ ]. Throughout this book the notation ... is used to stand for any sequence of expressions.

Comments can be nested, and may continue for any number of lines. Comments can contain both 8- and 16-bit characters.

■ A.2.3 Special Input Forms

special input form	full form	grouping
digits . *digits*	(approximate number)	
n∧∧*digits*	(base *n* integer)	
n∧∧*digits* . *digits*	(base *n* approximate number)	
expr : : *string*	MessageName[*expr*, "*string*"]	
expr : : *string*$_1$: : *string*$_2$	MessageName[*expr*, "*string*$_1$", "*string*$_2$"]	
forms containing #	(see below)	
forms containing %	(see below)	
forms containing _	(see below)	
<< *filename*	Get["*filename*"]	
expr$_1$?*expr*$_2$	PatternTest[*expr*$_1$,*expr*$_2$]	
expr$_1$ [*expr*$_2$, ...]	*expr*$_1$ [*expr*$_2$, ...]	(e[e])[e]
expr$_1$ [[*expr*$_2$, ...]]	Part[*expr*$_1$, *expr*$_2$, ...]	(e[[e]])[[e]]
expr++	Increment[*expr*]	
expr--	Decrement[*expr*]	
++*expr*	PreIncrement[*expr*]	
--*expr*	PreDecrement[*expr*]	
expr$_1$ @ *expr*$_2$	*expr*$_1$ [*expr*$_2$]	e @ (e @ e)
expr$_1$ ~ *expr*$_2$ ~ *expr*$_3$	*expr*$_2$ [*expr*$_1$,*expr*$_3$]	(e ~ e ~ e) ~ e ~ e
expr$_1$ /@ *expr*$_2$	Map[*expr*$_1$,*expr*$_2$]	e /@ (e /@ e)
expr$_1$ //@ *expr*$_2$	MapAll[*expr*$_1$,*expr*$_2$]	e //@ (e //@ e)
expr$_1$ @@ *expr*$_2$	Apply[*expr*$_1$,*expr*$_2$]	e @@ (e @@ e)
expr!	Factorial[*expr*]	
expr!!	Factorial2[*expr*]	
expr'	Derivative[1][*expr*]	
expr$_1$ <> *expr*$_2$ <> *expr*$_3$	StringJoin[*expr*$_1$,*expr*$_2$,*expr*$_3$]	e <> e <> e
expr$_1$ ** *expr*$_2$ ** *expr*$_3$	NonCommutativeMultiply[*expr*$_1$,*expr*$_2$,*expr*$_3$]	
		e ** e ** e
expr$_1$. *expr*$_2$. *expr*$_3$	Dot[*expr*$_1$,*expr*$_2$,*expr*$_3$]	e . e . e

Special input forms, in order of decreasing precedence, part one.

special input form	full form	grouping
$expr_1$ ^$expr_2$	`Power[`$expr_1$`,`$expr_2$`]`	e^$(e$^$e)$
$-expr$	`Times[-1,`$expr$`]`	
$+expr$	$expr$	
$expr_1$`/`$expr_2$	$expr_1$ `(`$expr_2$`)^-1`	$(e$ `/` $e)$ `/` e
$expr_1$ $expr_2$ $expr_3$	`Times[`$expr_1$`,`$expr_2$`,`$expr_3$`]`	e e e
$expr_1$ `*` $expr_2$ `*` $expr_3$	`Times[`$expr_1$`,`$expr_2$`,`$expr_3$`]`	e `*` e `*` e
$expr_1$ `+` $expr_2$ `+` $expr_3$	`Plus[`$expr_1$`,`$expr_2$`,`$expr_3$`]`	e `+` e `+` e
$expr_1$ `-` $expr_2$	$expr_1$ `+ (-1` $expr_2$`)`	$(e - e) - e$
$expr_1$ `==` $expr_2$	`Equal[`$expr_1$`,`$expr_2$`]`	e `==` e `==` e
$expr_1$ `!=` $expr_2$	`Unequal[`$expr_1$`,`$expr_2$`]`	e `!=` e `!=` e
$expr_1$ `>` $expr_2$	`Greater[`$expr_1$`,`$expr_2$`]`	e `>` e `>` e
$expr_1$ `>=` $expr_2$	`GreaterEqual[`$expr_1$`,`$expr_2$`]`	e `>=` e `>=` e
$expr_1$ `<` $expr_2$	`Less[`$expr_1$`,`$expr_2$`]`	e `<` e `<` e
$expr_1$ `<=` $expr_2$	`LessEqual[`$expr_1$`,`$expr_2$`]`	e `<=` e `<=` e
$expr_1$ `===` $expr_2$	`SameQ[`$expr_1$`,`$expr_2$`]`	e `===` e `===` e
$expr_1$ `=!=` $expr_2$	`UnsameQ[`$expr_1$`,`$expr_2$`]`	e `=!=` e `=!=` e
`!`$expr$	`Not[`$expr$`]`	`!(!`e`)`
$expr_1$ `&&` $expr_2$ `&&` $expr_3$	`And[`$expr_1$`,`$expr_2$`,`$expr_3$`]`	e `&&` e `&&` e
$expr_1$ `||` $expr_2$ `||` $expr_3$	`Or[`$expr_1$`,`$expr_2$`,`$expr_3$`]`	e `||` e `||` e
$expr$`..`	`Repeated[`$expr$`]`	
$expr$`...`	`RepeatedNull[`$expr$`]`	
$expr_1$ `|` $expr_2$	`Alternatives[`$expr_1$`,`$expr_2$`]`	e `|` e `|` e
$symb$`:`$expr$	`Pattern[`$symb$`,`$expr$`]`	
$expr_1$ `/;` $expr_2$	`Condition[`$expr_1$`,`$expr_2$`]`	$(e$`/;`$e)$`/;`e
$expr_1$ `->` $expr_2$	`Rule[`$expr_1$`,`$expr_2$`]`	e`->(`e`->`$e)$
$expr_1$ `:>` $expr_2$	`RuleDelayed[`$expr_1$`,`$expr_2$`]`	e`:>(`e`:>`$e)$
$expr_1$ `/.` $expr_2$	`ReplaceAll[`$expr_1$`,`$expr_2$`]`	$(e$`/.`$e)$`/.`e
$expr_1$ `//.` $expr_2$	`ReplaceRepeated[`$expr_1$`,`$expr_2$`]`	$(e$`//.`$e)$`//.`e
$expr_1$ `+=` $expr_2$	`AddTo[`$expr_1$`,`$expr_2$`]`	
$expr_1$ `-=` $expr_2$	`SubtractFrom[`$expr_1$`,`$expr_2$`]`	
$expr_1$ `*=` $expr_2$	`TimesBy[`$expr_1$`,`$expr_2$`]`	
$expr_1$ `/=` $expr_2$	`DivideBy[`$expr_1$`,`$expr_2$`]`	
$expr$ `&`	`Function[`$expr$`]`	
$expr_1$ `//` $expr_2$	$expr_2$ `[`$expr_1$`]`	$(e$`//`$e)$`//`e

Special input forms, in order of decreasing precedence, part two.

input form	full form	grouping
$expr_1$ = $expr_2$	Set[$expr_1$,$expr_2$]	$e = (e = e)$
$expr_1$:= $expr_2$	SetDelayed[$expr_1$,$expr_2$]	
$expr_1$ ^= $expr_2$	UpSet[$expr_1$,$expr_2$]	
$expr_1$ ^:= $expr_2$	UpSetDelayed[$expr_1$,$expr_2$]	
$symb$/: $expr_1$ = $expr_2$	TagSet[$symb$,$expr_1$,$expr_2$]	
$symb$/: $expr_1$:= $expr_2$	TagSetDelayed[$symb$,$expr_1$,$expr_2$]	
$expr$ =.	Unset[$expr$]	
$symb$/: $expr$ =.	TagUnset[$symb$,$expr$]	
$expr$ >> $filename$	Put[$expr$,"$filename$"]	
$expr$ >>> $filename$	PutAppend[$expr$,"$filename$"]	
$expr_1$;$expr_2$;$expr_3$	CompoundExpression[$expr_1$,$expr_2$,$expr_3$]	
$expr_1$;$expr_2$;	CompoundExpression[$expr_1$,$expr_2$,Null]	

Special input forms, in order of decreasing precedence, part three.

expr and *expr*$_i$	any expression
symb	any symbol
n	a non-negative integer
string and *string*$_i$	"*cccc*" or a sequence of letters, digits and special characters
filename	like *string*, but can include additional characters described below
digits	a sequence of digits (including letters when *base* is above 10)

Objects used in the tables of special input forms.

special input form	*full form*
#	Slot[1]
#*n*	Slot[*n*]
##	SlotSequence[1]
##*n*	SlotSequence[*n*]
%	Out[ ]
%%	Out[-2]
%%... % (*n* times)	Out[-*n*]
%*n*	Out[*n*]
_	Blank[ ]
_*expr*	Blank[*expr*]
__	BlankSequence[ ]
__*expr*	BlankSequence[*expr*]
___	BlankNullSequence[ ]
___*expr*	BlankNullSequence[*expr*]
_.	Optional[Blank[ ]]
*symb*_	Pattern[*symb*,Blank[ ]]
*symb*_*expr*	Pattern[*symb*,Blank[*expr*]]
*symb*__	Pattern[*symb*,BlankSequence[ ]]
*symb*__*expr*	Pattern[*symb*,BlankSequence[*expr*]]
*symb*___	Pattern[*symb*,BlankNullSequence[ ]]
*symb*___*expr*	Pattern[*symb*,BlankNullSequence[*expr*]]
*symb*_.	Optional[Pattern[*symb*,Blank[ ]]]

Additional special input forms.

Precedence and the Ordering of Input Forms

The tables of input forms are arranged in decreasing order of precedence. Input forms in the same box have the same precedence. As discussed in Section 2.1.3, precedence determines how *Mathematica* groups terms in input expressions. The general rule is that if $\otimes$ has higher precedence than $\oplus$, then $a \oplus b \otimes c$ is interpreted as $a \oplus (b \otimes c)$, and $a \otimes b \oplus c$ is interpreted as $(a \otimes b) \oplus c$.

Grouping of Input Forms

The third columns in the tables show how multiple occurrences of a single input form, or of several input forms with the same precedence, are grouped. For example, a/b/c is grouped as (a/b)/c ("left associative"), while a∧b∧c is grouped as a∧(b∧c) ("right associative"). No grouping is needed in an expression like a + b + c, since Plus can take any number of arguments.

Where the third column of the table is left blank, the input forms cannot be grouped: you always have to insert explicit parentheses.

Spaces and Multiplication

Spaces in *Mathematica* denote multiplication, just as they do in standard mathematical notation. In addition, *Mathematica* takes complete expressions that are adjacent, not necessarily separated by spaces, to be multiplied together.

- x y z ⟶ x*y*z
- 2x ⟶ 2*x
- 2(x+1) ⟶ 2*(x+1)
- c(x+1) ⟶ c*(x+1)
- (x+1)(y+2) ⟶ (x+1)*(y+2)
- x! y ⟶ x!*y
- x!y ⟶ x!*y

Alternative forms for multiplication.

An expression like x!y could potentially mean either (x!)*y or x*(!y). The first interpretation is chosen because Factorial has higher precedence than Not.

Spaces within single input forms are ignored. Thus, for example, a + b is equivalent to a+b. You will often want to insert spaces around lower precedence operators to improve readability.

You can give a "coefficient" for a symbol by preceding it with any sequence of digits. When you use numbers in bases larger than 10, the digits can include letters. (In bases other than 10, there must be a space between the end of the coefficient, and the beginning of the symbol name.)

- x∧2y, like x∧2 y, means (x∧2) y
- x/2y, like x/2 y, means (x/2) y
- xy is a single symbol, not x*y

Some cases to be careful about.

Spaces to Avoid

You should avoid inserting any spaces between the different characters in composite operators such as /., =. and >=. Although in some cases such spaces are allowed, they are liable to lead to confusion.

Another case where spaces must be avoided is between the characters of the pattern object x_. If you type x _, *Mathematica* will interpret this as x*_, rather than the single named pattern object x_.

Similarly, you should not insert any spaces inside pattern objects like *x*:*value*.

Relational Operators

Relational operators can be mixed. An expression like a > b >= c is converted to Inequality[a, Greater, b, GreaterEqual, c], which effectively evaluates as (a > b) && (b >= c). (The reason for the intermediate Inequality form is that it prevents objects from being evaluated twice when something like a > b >= c is processed.)

File Names

Any file name can be given in quotes after <<, >> and >>>. File names can also be given without quotes if they contain only alphanumeric characters, special characters and the characters `, /, ., \, !, -, _, :, $, *, ~ and ?, together with matched pairs of square brackets enclosing any characters other than spaces, tabs and newlines. Note that file names given without quotes can be followed only by spaces, tabs or newlines, or by the characters),], } as well as semicolon and comma.

■ A.2.4 Input Control

Mathematica expressions can continue for several lines. Newlines (line feeds or returns) are equivalent to spaces.

With many front ends, *Mathematica* tests to see whether your input is finished every time you get to the end of a line. This means that you can open a bracket on one line, then type several lines of input. *Mathematica* will assume that you have not finished giving your input until you type a matching close bracket.

If the presence of unmatched brackets, or some other input structure, does not already indicate it, you can always show that your input continues for several lines by typing \ at the end of the line.

Note that if one line ends with a \, then any spaces that appear at the beginning of the next line are ignored. This means, for example, that indentation is allowed in a number which is broken across several lines.

■ A.2.5 Formatting Conventions

Good formatting conventions are essential in making *Mathematica* code easy to read. Here are a few suggestions.

- Insert spaces around operators like + that have comparatively low precedence.

- Leave spaces after commas and semicolons.

- Break lines so as to keep logically connected units on the same line.

- Use a separate line for different transformation rules, or different steps in a program.

- Try to use temporary variables to avoid deep nesting of functions.

- Leave spaces in expressions like f[g[h[x]]] to emphasize outer brackets.

- Use Part[*expr*, *n*] instead of *expr*[[*n*]] when there are many brackets present.

- Indent blocks of code in programs.

- Insert comments when you need to label arguments of functions, such as f[e, (*variable=*)x].

■ A.2.6 Special Input

?*symbol*	get information
??*symbol*	get more information
?s_1 s_2 ...	get information on several objects
!*command*	execute an external command
!!*file*	display the contents of an external file

Special input lines.

In most implementations of *Mathematica*, you can give a line of special input anywhere in your input. The only constraint is that the special input must start at the beginning of a line.

Some implementations of *Mathematica* may not allow you to execute external commands using !*command*.

A.3 Some General Notations and Conventions

■ A.3.1 Function Names

The names of built-in functions follow some general guidelines.

- The name consists of complete English words, or standard mathematical abbreviations. American spelling is used.

- The first letter of each word is capitalized.

- Functions whose names end with Q usually "ask a question", and return either `True` or `False`.

- Mathematical functions that are named after people usually have names in *Mathematica* of the form *PersonSymbol*.

■ A.3.2 Function Arguments

The main expression or object on which a built-in function acts is usually given as the first argument to the function. Subsidiary parameters appear as subsequent arguments.

The following are exceptions:

- In functions like `Map` and `Apply`, the function to apply comes before the expression it is to be applied to.

- In scoping constructs such as `Module` and `Function`, local variables and parameter names come before bodies.

- In functions like `Write` and `Display`, the name of the file is given before the objects to be written to it.

For mathematical functions, arguments that are written as subscripts in standard mathematical notation are given before those that are written as superscripts.

■ A.3.3 Options

Some built-in functions can take *options*. Each option has a name, represented as a symbol. Options are set by giving rules of the form *name->value*. Such rules must appear after all the other arguments in a function. Rules for different options can be given in any order. If you do not explicitly give a rule for a particular option, a default setting for that option is used.

Options[*f*]	give the default rules for all options associated with *f*
Options[*expr*]	give the options set in a particular expression
Options[*expr*, *name*]	give the setting for the option *name* in an expression
FullOptions[*expr*, *name*]	give the full setting for *name*, even if its actual setting is Automatic
SetOptions[*f*, *name*->*value*, ...]	
	set default rules for options associated with *f*

Operations on options.

■ A.3.4 Part Numbering

n	element *n* (starting at 1)
-*n*	element *n* from the end
0	head
{*n₁*, *n₂*, ... }	a list of parts *nᵢ*

Numbering of parts.

■ A.3.5 Sequence Specifications

n	elements 1 through *n*
-*n*	last *n* elements
{*n*}	element *n* only
{*m*, *n*}	elements *m* through *n* (inclusive).

Specifications for sequences of parts.

Sequence specifications are used in the functions Drop, StringDrop, StringTake, Subscripted, Take and Thread.

■ A.3.6 Level Specifications

n	levels 1 through n
Infinity	all levels
{n}	level n only
{n_1, n_2}	levels n_1 through n_2
Heads -> True	include heads of expressions
Heads -> False	do not include heads of expressions

Level specifications.

The level in an expression corresponding to a non-negative integer n is defined to consist of parts specified by n indices. A negative level number $-n$ represents all parts of an expression that have depth n. The depth of an expression, Depth[*expr*], is the maximum number of indices needed to specify any part, plus one. Levels *do not* include heads of expressions, except with the option setting Heads -> True. Level 0 is the whole expression. Level -1 contains all symbols and other objects that have no subparts.

Ranges of levels specified by {n_1, n_2} contain all parts that are neither above level n_1, nor below level n_2 in the tree. The n_i need not have the same sign. Thus, for example, {2, -2} specifies subexpressions which occur anywhere below the top level, but above the leaves, of the expression tree.

Level specifications are used by functions such as Apply, Cases, Count, FreeQ, Level, Map, MapIndexed, Position, and Scan. Note, however, that the default level specifications are not the same for all of these functions.

Functions with level specifications visit different subexpressions in an order that corresponds to depth-first traversal of the expression tree, with leaves visited before roots. The subexpressions visited have part specifications which occur in an order which is lexicographic, except that longer sequences appear before shorter ones.

■ A.3.7 Iterators

{*imax*}	iterate *imax* times
{*i*, *imax*}	*i* goes from *1* to *imax* in steps of *1*
{*i*, *imin*, *imax*}	*i* goes from *imin* to *imax* in steps of *1*
{*i*, *imin*, *imax*, *di*}	*i* goes from *imin* to *imax* in steps of *di*
{*i*, *imin*, *imax*}, {*j*, *jmin*, *jmax*}, ...	
	i goes from *imin* to *imax*, and for each value of *i*, *j* goes from *jmin* to *jmax*, etc.

Iterator notation.

Iterators are used in such functions as Sum, Table, Do and Range.

The iteration parameters *imin*, *imax* and *di* do not need to be integers. The variable *i* is given a sequence of values starting at *imin*, and increasing in steps of *di*, stopping when the next value of *i* would be greater than *imax*. The iteration parameters can be arbitrary symbolic expressions, so long as (*imax*−*imin*)/*di* is a number.

When several iteration variables are used, the limits for the later ones can depend on the values of earlier ones.

The variable *i* can be any symbolic expression; it need not be a single symbol. The value of *i* is automatically set up to be local to the iteration function. This is effectively done by wrapping a Block construct containing *i* around the iteration function.

The procedure for evaluating iteration functions is described on page 730.

■ A.3.8 Scoping Constructs

Function[{*x*, ... }, *body*]	local parameters
lhs -> *rhs* and *lhs* :> *rhs*	local pattern names
lhs = *rhs* and *lhs* := *rhs*	local pattern names
With[{*x* = x_0, ... }, *body*]	local constants
Module[{*x*, ... }, *body*]	local variables

Scoping constructs in *Mathematica*.

Scoping constructs allow the names of certain symbols to be local.

When nested scoping constructs are evaluated, new symbols are automatically generated in the inner scoping constructs so as to avoid name conflicts with symbols in outer scoping constructs.

In general, symbols with names of the form *xxx* are renamed *xxx*$.

When a transformation rule or definition is used, `ReplaceAll` (`/.`) is effectively used to replace the pattern names that appear on the right-hand side, even if they are local symbols in scoping constructs. Nevertheless, other local symbols in these scoping constructs are renamed when necessary.

Each time it is evaluated, `Module` generates symbols with unique names of the form *xxx*$*nnn* as replacements for all local variables that appear in its body.

■ A.3.9 Mathematical Functions

The mathematical functions such as `Log[`*x*`]` and `BesselJ[`*n*, *x*`]` that are built into *Mathematica* have a number of features in common.

- They carry the attribute `Listable`, so that they are automatically "threaded" over any lists that appear as arguments.

- They give exact results in terms of integers, rational numbers and algebraic expressions in special cases.

- Except for functions whose arguments are always integers, mathematical functions in *Mathematica* can be evaluated to any numerical precision, with any complex numbers as arguments. If a function is undefined for a particular set of arguments, it is returned in symbolic form in this case.

- Numerical evaluation leads to results of a precision no higher than can be justified on the basis of the precision of the arguments. Thus `N[Gamma[27/10], 100]` yields a high-precision result, but `N[Gamma[2.7], 100]` cannot.

- When possible, symbolic derivatives, integrals and series expansions of built-in mathematical functions are evaluated in terms of other built-in functions.

■ A.3.10 Mathematical Constants

Mathematical constants such as `E` and `Pi` that are built into *Mathematica* have the following properties:

- They do not have values as such.

- They have numerical values that can be found to any precision.

- They carry the attribute `Constant`, and so are treated as constants in derivatives.

■ A.3.11 Protection

Mathematica allows you to make assignments that override the standard operation and meaning of built-in *Mathematica* objects.

To make it difficult to make such assignments by mistake, most built-in *Mathematica* objects have the attribute `Protected`. If you want to make an assignment for a built-in object, you must first remove this attribute. You can do this by calling the function `Unprotect`.

There are a few fundamental *Mathematica* objects to which you absolutely cannot assign your own values. These objects carry the attribute `Locked`, as well as `Protected`. The `Locked` attribute prevents you from changing any of the attributes, and thus from removing the `Protected` attribute.

■ A.3.12 String Patterns

Functions such as `StringMatchQ`, `Names` and `Remove` allow you to give *string patterns*. String patterns can contain *metacharacters*, which can stand for sequences of ordinary characters.

*	zero or more characters
@	zero or more characters excluding upper-case letters
* etc.	literal *, etc.

Metacharacters used in string patterns.

A.4 Evaluation

■ A.4.1 The Standard Evaluation Sequence

The following is the sequence of steps that *Mathematica* follows in evaluating an expression like $h[e_1, e_2, \ldots]$. Every time the expression changes, *Mathematica* effectively starts the evaluation sequence over again.

- ■ If the expression is a raw object (*e.g.*, `Integer`, `String`, etc.), leave it unchanged.

- ■ Evaluate the head h of the expression.

- ■ Evaluate each element e_i of the expression in turn. If h is a symbol with attributes `HoldFirst`, `HoldRest` or `HoldAll`, then skip evaluation of certain elements.

- ■ If h has attribute `Flat`, then flatten out all nested expressions with head h.

- ■ If h has attribute `Listable`, then thread through any e_i that are lists.

- ■ If h has attribute `Orderless`, then sort the e_i into order.

- ■ Use any applicable transformation rules associated with f that you have defined for objects of the form $h[\ f[e_1, \ldots], \ldots\ ]$.

- ■ Use any built-in transformation rules associated with f for objects of the form $h[\ f[e_1, \ldots], \ldots\ ]$.

- ■ Use any applicable transformation rules that you have defined for $h[e_1, e_2, \ldots]$ or for $h[\ \ldots\ ][\ \ldots\ ]$.

- ■ Use any built-in transformation rules for $h[e_1, e_2, \ldots]$ or for $h[\ \ldots\ ][\ \ldots\ ]$.

■ A.4.2 Non-Standard Argument Evaluation

There are a number of built-in *Mathematica* functions that evaluate their arguments in special ways. The control structure `While` is an example. The symbol `While` has the attribute `HoldAll`. As a result, the arguments of `While` are not evaluated as part of the standard evaluation process. Instead, the internal code for `While` evaluates the arguments in a special way. In the case of `While`, the code evaluates the arguments repeatedly, so as to implement a loop.

Control structures	arguments evaluated in a sequence determined by control flow (*e.g.*, CompoundExpression)
Conditionals	arguments evaluated only when they correspond to branches that are taken (*e.g.*, If, Which)
Logical operations	arguments evaluated only when they are needed in determining the logical result (*e.g.*, And, Or)
Iteration functions	first argument evaluated for each step in the iteration (*e.g.*, Do, Sum, Plot)
Tracing functions	form never evaluated (*e.g.*, Trace)
Assignments	first argument only partially evaluated (*e.g.*, Set, AddTo)
Pure functions	function body not evaluated (*e.g.*, Function)
Scoping constructs	variable specifications not evaluated (*e.g.*, Module, Block)
Holding functions	argument maintained in unevaluated form (*e.g.*, Hold, Literal)

Built-in functions that evaluate their arguments in special ways.

Logical Operations

In an expression of the form e_1 && e_2 && e_3 the e_i are evaluated in order. As soon as any e_i is found to be False, evaluation is stopped, and the result False is returned. This means that you can use the e_i to represent different "branches" in a program, with a particular branch being evaluated only if certain conditions are met.

The Or function works much like And; it returns True as soon as it finds any argument that is True. Xor, on the other hand, always evaluates *all* its arguments.

Iteration Functions

An iteration function such as Do[*f*, {*i*, *imin*, *imax*}] is evaluated as follows:

- The iteration specification is evaluated. If it is not found to be of the form {*i*, *imin*, *imax*}, the evaluation stops.

- The value of the iteration variable *i* is made local, effectively using Block.

- *imin* and *imax* are used to determine the sequence of values to be assigned to the iteration variable *i*.

- The iteration variable is successively set to each value, and *f* is evaluated in each case.

- The local values assigned to *i* are cleared.

    If there are several iteration variables, the same procedure is followed for each variable in turn.

    Unless otherwise specified, *f* is not evaluated until a specific value has been assigned to *i*, and is then evaluated for each value of *i* chosen. You can use Evaluate[*f*] to make *f* be evaluated immediately, rather than only after a specific value has been assigned to *i*.

Assignments

The left-hand sides of assignments are only partially evaluated.

- If the left-hand side is a symbol, no evaluation is performed.

- If the left-hand side is a function, the arguments of the function are evaluated, but the function itself is not evaluated.

    The right-hand side is evaluated for immediate (=), but not for delayed (:=), assignments.

    Any subexpression of the form Literal[*expr*] that appears on the left-hand side of an assignment is not evaluated, but is replaced by the unevaluated form of *expr* before the assignment is done.

■ A.4.3 Overriding Non-Standard Argument Evaluation

f[*expr*$_1$, ... , Evaluate[*expr*$_n$], ...] evaluates the argument *expr*$_n$, whether or not the attributes of *f* specify that it should be held

Overriding holding of arguments.

By using Evaluate, you can get any argument of a function evaluated immediately, even if the argument would usually be evaluated later under the control of the function.

■ A.4.4 Preventing Evaluation

Mathematica provides various functions which act as "wrappers" to prevent the expressions they contain from being evaluated.

Hold[*expr*]	treated as Hold[*expr*] in all cases
HoldForm[*expr*]	treated as *expr* for printing
Literal[*expr*]	treated as *expr* in rules, definitions and patterns
Unevaluated[*expr*]	treated as *expr* when arguments are passed to a function

Wrappers that prevent expressions from being evaluated.

■ A.4.5 Global Control of Evaluation

In the evaluation procedure described above, two basic kinds of steps are involved:

- Iteration: evaluate a particular expression until it no longer changes.
- Recursion: evaluate subsidiary expressions needed to find the value of a particular expression.

Iteration leads to evaluation chains in which successive expressions are obtained by the application of various transformation rules.

Trace shows evaluation chains as lists, and shows subsidiary evaluations corresponding to recursion in sublists.

The expressions associated with the sequence of subsidiary evaluations which lead to an expression currently being evaluated are given in the list returned by Stack[ ].

| $RecursionLimit | maximum recursion depth |
| $IterationLimit | maximum number of iterations |

Global variables controlling the evaluation of expressions.

■ A.4.6 Aborts

You can ask *Mathematica* to abort at any point in a computation, either by calling the function Abort[ ], or by typing appropriate interrupt keys.

When asked to abort, *Mathematica* will terminate the computation as quickly as possible. If the answer obtained would be incorrect or incomplete, then *Mathematica* returns $Aborted instead of giving that answer.

Aborts can be caught using CheckAbort, and can be postponed using AbortProtected.

A.5 Patterns and Transformation Rules

■ A.5.1 Patterns

Patterns stand for classes of expressions. They contain *pattern objects* which represent sets of possible expressions.

_	any expression
*x*_	any expression, given the name *x*
x:*pattern*	a pattern, given the name *x*
pattern ? *test*	a pattern that yields True when *test* is applied to its value
_*h*	any expression with head *h*
*x*_*h*	any expression with head *h*, given the name *x*
__	any sequence of one or more expressions
___	any sequence of zero or more expressions
*x*__ and *x*___	sequences of expressions, given the name *x*
__*h* and ___*h*	sequences of expressions, each with head *h*
*x*__*h* and *x*___*h*	sequences of expressions with head *h*, given the name *x*
*x*_:*v*	an expression with default value *v*
*x*_*h*:*v*	an expression with head *h* and default value *v*
*x*_.	an expression with a globally defined default value
Optional[*x*_*h*]	an expression that must have head *h*, and has a globally defined default value
pattern..	a pattern repeated one or more times
pattern...	a pattern repeated zero or more times
pattern₁ | *pattern₂* | ...	a pattern which matches at least one of the *patternᵢ*
pattern /; *cond*	a pattern for which *cond* evaluates to True

Pattern objects.

When several pattern objects with the same name occur in a single pattern, all the objects must stand for the same expression. Thus f[x_, x_] can stand for f[2, 2] but not f[2, 3].

In a pattern object such as _h, the head *h* can be any expression, but cannot itself be a pattern.

A pattern object such as x__ stands for a *sequence* of expressions. So, for example, f[x__] can stand for f[a, b, c], with x being the *sequence* (a, b, c). If you use x, say in the result of a transformation rule, the sequence will be spliced into the function in which x appears. Thus g[u, x, u] would become g[u, a, b, c, u].

When the pattern objects x_:v and x_. appear as arguments of functions, they represent arguments which may be omitted. When the argument corresponding to x_:v is omitted, x is taken to have value *v*. When the argument corresponding to x_. is omitted, x is taken to have a *default value* that is associated with the function in which it appears. You can specify this default value by making assignments for Default[*f*] and so on.

Default[*f*]	default value for *x_.* when it appears as any argument of the function *f*
Default[*f*, *n*]	default value for *x_.* when it appears as the *n*th argument (negative *n* count from the end)
Default[*f*, *n*, *tot*]	default value for the nth argument when there are a total of *tot* arguments

Default values.

A pattern like f[x__, y__, z__] can match an expression like f[a, b, c, d, e] with several different choices of x, y and z. The choices with x and y of minimum length are tried first. In general, when there are multiple __ or ___ in a single function, the case that is tried first takes all the __ and ___ to stand for sequences of minimum length, except the last one, which stands for "the rest" of the arguments.

When x_:v or x_. are present, the case that is tried first is the one in which none of them correspond to omitted arguments. Cases in which later arguments are dropped are tried next.

Orderless	$f[x, y]$ and $f[y, x]$ are equivalent
Flat	$f[f[x], y]$ and $f[x, y]$ are equivalent
OneIdentity	$f[x]$ and x are equivalent

Attributes used in matching patterns.

Pattern objects like *x_* can represent any sequence of arguments in a function *f* with attribute Flat. The value of *x* in this case is *f* applied to the sequence of arguments. If *f* has the attribute OneIdentity, then *e* is used instead of $f[e]$ when *x* corresponds to a sequence of just one argument.

■ A.5.2 Assignments

lhs = *rhs*	immediate assignment: *rhs* is evaluated at the time of assignment
lhs := *rhs*	delayed assignment: *rhs* is evaluated when the value of *lhs* is requested

The two basic types of assignment in *Mathematica*.

Assignments in *Mathematica* specify transformation rules for expressions. Every assignment that you make must be associated with a particular *Mathematica* symbol.

f[*args*] = *rhs*	assignment is associated with *f* (downvalue)
t/: *f*[*args*] = *rhs*	assignment is associated with *t* (upvalue)
f[*g*[*args*]] ^= *rhs*	assignment is associated with *g* (upvalue)

Assignments associated with different symbols.

In the case of an assignment like *f*[*args*] = *rhs*, *Mathematica* looks at *f*, then the head of *f*, then the head of that, and so on, until it finds a symbol with which to associate the assignment.

When you make an assignment like *lhs* ^= *rhs*, *Mathematica* will set up transformation rules associated with each distinct symbol that occurs either as an argument of *lhs*, or as the head of an argument of *lhs*.

The transformation rules associated with a particular symbol *s* are always stored in a definite order, and are tested in that order when they are used. Each time you make an assignment, the corresponding transformation rule is inserted at the end of the list of transformation rules associated with *s*, except in the following cases:

■ The left-hand side of the transformation rule is identical to a transformation rule that has already been stored, and any /; conditions on the right-hand side are also identical. In this case, the new transformation rule is inserted in place of the old one.

■ *Mathematica* determines that the new transformation rule is more specific than a rule already present, and would never be used if it were placed after this rule. In this case, the new rule is placed before the old one. Note that in many cases it is not possible to determine whether one rule is more specific than another; in such cases, the new rule is always inserted at the end.

■ A.5.3 Types of Values

Attributes[*f*]	attributes of *f*
DefaultValues[*f*]	default values for arguments of *f*
DownValues[*f*]	values for *f*[...], *f*[...] [...], etc.
FormatValues[*f*]	print forms associated with *f*
Messages[*f*]	messages associated with *f*
NValues[*f*]	numerical values associated with *f*
Options[*f*]	defaults for options associated with *f*
OwnValues[*f*]	values for *f* itself
UpValues[*f*]	values for ... [... , *f*[...], ...]

Types of values associated with symbols.

■ A.5.4 Clearing and Removing Objects

expr =.	clear a value defined for *expr*
f /: *expr* =.	clear a value associated with *f* defined for *expr*
Clear[*s₁*, *s₂*, ...]	clear all values for the symbols *s_i*, except for attributes, messages and defaults
ClearAll[*s₁*, *s₂*, ...]	clear all values for the *s_i*, including attributes, messages and defaults
Remove[*s₁*, *s₂*, ...]	clear all values, and then remove the names of the *s_i*

Ways to clear and remove objects.

Clear, ClearAll and Remove can all take string patterns as arguments, to specify action on all symbols whose names match the string pattern.

Clear, ClearAll and Remove do nothing to symbols with the attribute Protected.

■ A.5.5 Transformation Rules

lhs -> *rhs*	immediate rule: *rhs* is evaluated when the rule is first given
lhs :> *rhs*	delayed rule: *rhs* is evaluated when the rule is used

The two basic types of transformation rules in *Mathematica*.

Replacements for pattern variables that appear in transformation rules are effectively done using `ReplaceAll` (the `/.` operator).

A.6 Input and Output

■ A.6.1 Streams

InputStream["*name*", *n*]	input from a file or pipe
OutputStream["*name*", *n*]	output to a file or pipe

Types of streams.

option name	default value	
FormatType	InputForm	default format for expressions
PageWidth	78	number of characters per line
StringConversion	None	function applied to convert strings containing special characters
TotalWidth	Infinity	maximum number of characters in a single expression

Options for output streams.

You can reset options for an output stream using SetOptions.

■ A.6.2 File Names

When you refer to a file, *Mathematica* tries to resolve its name as follows:

- If the name starts with !, *Mathematica* treats the remainder of the name as an external command, and uses a pipe to this command.

- If the name contains metacharacters used by your operating system, then *Mathematica* passes the name directly to the operating system for interpretation.

- Unless the file is to be used for input, no further processing on the name is done.

- Unless the name given is an absolute file name under your operating system, *Mathematica* will search each of the directories specified in $Path for a file with the name you specified.

- Names that end with ` are translated using ContextToFilename.

■ A.6.3 Format Types

CForm[*expr*]	C language form
FortranForm[*expr*]	Fortran language form
InputForm[*expr*]	*Mathematica* input form
OutputForm[*expr*]	standard output form
TeXForm[*expr*]	TEX input form
TextForm[*expr*]	textual output form

Basic format types.

■ A.6.4 Graphics Output

%!	standard PostScript file beginning
%%BoundingBox: *xmin ymin xmax ymax*	
	coordinates of corners of the bounding box
%%Creator: Mathematica	standard PostScript convention
prolog	PostScript definitions to be inserted
%%AspectRatio: *r*	suggested ratio of height to width for the final image
MathPictureStart	initialization of *Mathematica* graphics
graphics	*Mathematica* graphics
MathPictureEnd	termination of *Mathematica* graphics

Typical sequence of PostScript generated by *Mathematica*.

The PostScript output generated directly by the *Mathematica* kernel uses a number of special PostScript procedures. Most *Mathematica* front ends automatically interpret these special procedures. However, if you want to send PostScript from *Mathematica* to a generic PostScript output device, you have to include the definitions of these procedures, written in PostScript. On most systems, the external program psfix creates the necessary procedures, and prepends them to PostScript files generated by *Mathematica*.

`-epsf`	generate Encapsulated PostScript Form
`-height` *n*	specify the height of the page in inches (default: 11 inches)
`-width` *n*	specify the width of the page in inches (default: 8.5 inches)
`-lmarg` *n*	specify the left margin in inches (default: 1 inch)
`-rmarg` *n*	specify the right margin in inches (default: 1 inch)
`-bmarg` *n*	specify the bottom margin in inches (default: 1 inch)
`-tmarg` *n*	specify the top margin in inches (default: 1 inch)
`-land`	produce landscape-mode rotated output
`-stretch`	stretch the graphics, ignoring the suggested aspect ratio
`-stringfix`	stretch proportionally spaced text
`-dashfix`	combine multiple dashes in text into underlines

Some typical options for `psfix`.

Mathematica inserts font names you specify using `DefaultFont` and `FontForm` directly into the PostScript output. It assumes that you have suitably loaded into your PostScript device any fonts that are needed for a particular piece of graphics.

The PostScript generated by *Mathematica* tests to see whether PostScript functions like `colorimage` and `setcmykcolor` are already defined in your PostScript system. If they are not, it gives its own definitions.

Sound output in *Mathematica* is specified by the function `sampledsound`. If this function is not supported in your PostScript system, it is defined to ignore the data that is supplied to it.

A.7 *Mathematica* Sessions and Global Objects

■ A.7.1 System Parameters

`$CreationDate`	the date on which the version of *Mathematica* you are running was originally created
`$DumpSupported`	whether Dump is available
`$DumpDates`	a list of dates on which Dump was used to create the *Mathematica* system you are running
`$Linked`	whether the *Mathematica* kernel is being run through *MathLink*
`$LinkSupported`	whether *MathLink* is available
`$MachineEpsilon`	the numerical uncertainty associated with the machine number 1.0 on your computer
`$MachineID`	the ID of your computer or your copy of *Mathematica*
`$MachineName`	the host name or other identifying name of your computer
`$MachinePrecision`	the precision for machine numbers on your computer
`$MachineType`	the type of your computer
`$MaxMachineNumber`	the largest machine number on your computer
`$MinMachineNumber`	the smallest machine number on your computer
`$OperatingSystem`	the operating system on your computer
`$PipeSupported`	whether pipes are available
`$ReleaseNumber`	the release number for the *Mathematica* you are running
`$System`	full specification of your computer system
`$TimeUnit`	the granularity of time measurements on your computer system
`$Version`	full specification of the version of *Mathematica* you are running
`$VersionNumber`	the number of the *Mathematica* version you are running

Read-only parameters characterizing a *Mathematica* system.

■ A.7.2 Global Objects and Variables

$BatchInput	whether input is being given in batch mode
$BatchOutput	whether output should be given in batch mode
$CommandLine	the text of original command line used to invoke *Mathematica*
$Notebooks	whether a notebook-based interface is being used
$SessionID	a unique integer characterizing the current *Mathematica* session

Parameters characterizing a particular *Mathematica* session.

$Display	list of default streams to use for graphics output
$DisplayFunction	default function to use for graphics output
$Echo	streams to echo each line of input to
$Messages	streams to send messages to
$Output	streams to send standard output to
$SoundDisplayFunction	default function to use for sound output
$Urgent	streams to send urgent output to

Global variables for output.

`AbsoluteTime[ ]`	the total number of seconds since the beginning of January 1, 1900
`Date[ ]`	a list giving the current date and time
`Environment["var"]`	the value of an operating system variable
`In[n]`	the expression on the nth input line
`InString[n]`	the text of the nth input line
`MaxMemoryUsed[ ]`	the maximum number of bytes of memory used in the current *Mathematica* session
`MemoryInUse[ ]`	the number of bytes of memory in use
`MessageList[n]`	the messages generated for the nth output line
`Out[n]` or `%n`	the expression on the nth output line
`SessionTime[ ]`	the total number of seconds elapsed since the beginning of the current *Mathematica* session
`Stack[ ]`	the current *Mathematica* evaluation stack
`Streams[ ]`	a list of the streams that are currently open
`TimeUsed[ ]`	the total number of seconds of CPU time used in the current *Mathematica* session
`TimeZone[ ]`	the time zone set for your computer system
`$Input`	the name of the stream currently used for input
`$Line`	the current line number
`$MessageList`	the messages generated during processing of the current input line
`$ModuleNumber`	the current module number

Global objects in *Mathematica* sessions.

`$Inspector`	function to be applied to inspect the state of *Mathematica* during an interrupt
`$MessagePrePrint`	a function to apply to expressions to be printed in messages
`$NewMessage`	function to be applied to the symbol name and message tag of messages that are requested but have not yet been defined
`$NewSymbol`	function to be applied to names and contexts of new symbols that are created
`$Pre`	a function to apply to each input expression before evaluation
`$PrePrint`	a function to apply to each output expression after assignment to `Out[n]`, but before printing
`$PreRead`	a function to apply to every input string
`$Post`	a function to apply to every output expression
`$StringConversion`	a function to apply before printing strings containing special characters
`$SyntaxHandler`	a function applied to any input line that yields a syntax error

Global functions in *Mathematica* sessions.

$Context	the current context
$ContextPath	the current context search path
$DefaultFont	the default font to use for text in graphics
$Epilog	an expression to be executed when you exit a session or subsession
$IgnoreEOF	whether to ignore end-of-file in this session or subsession
$IterationLimit	the maximum number of iterations to use in evaluating an expression
$Language	a list of languages to use for messages
$Letters	a list specifying characters to be treated as letters
$Packages	a list of the context of all packages that have been loaded
$Path	the current list of directories to search for files
$RecursionLimit	the maximum number of levels of recursion to use in evaluating an expression
$StringOrder	a list specifying the canonical ordering of characters

Global variables in *Mathematica* sessions.

■ A.7.3 The Main Loop

- Read in input.

- Apply $PreRead function, if defined, to the input string.

- Print syntax warnings if necessary.

- Apply $SyntaxHandler function if there is a syntax error.

- Assign InString[n].

- Apply $Pre function, if defined, to the input expression.

- Assign In[n].

- Evaluate expression.

- Apply $Post function, if defined.

- Assign Out[n].

- Apply $PrePrint function, if defined.

- Assign MessageList[*n*] and clear $MessageList.

- Print expression, if it is not Null.

- Increment $Line.

- Clear any pending aborts.

An important point is that when the value of Out[*n*] (and thus %) is assigned, certain formatting functions are stripped off. In addition to the format types OutputForm, InputForm, CForm, etc., the following formatting functions are removed: Shallow, Short, TreeForm, MatrixForm and TableForm. As a result, when In[*n*] is Short[*expr*], the value assigned to the corresponding Out[*n*] will still be the evaluated form of *expr*.

If your input consists of a compound expression ending with a semicolon, then Null will be returned, and no output will be printed. The value of Out[*n*] will nevertheless be assigned to be the last element in the compound expression.

■ A.7.4 Messages

Messages can be generated by built-in functions, or by explicit calls to Message.

f::*name*::*lang*	a message in a specific language
f::*name*	a message in a default language
General::*name*	a general message with a given name

Message names.

If no language is specified for a particular message, text for the message is sought in each of the languages specified by $Language. If *f*::*name* is not defined, a definition for General::*name* is sought. If still no message is found, any value defined for $NewMessage is applied to *f* and "*name*".

Off[*message*] prevents a specified message from ever being printed. Check allows you to determine whether particular messages were generated during the evaluation of an expression. $MessageList and MessageList[*n*] record all the messages that were generated during the evaluation of a particular line in a *Mathematica* session.

Messages are specified as strings to be used as the first argument of StringForm. $MessagePrePrint is applied to each expression to be spliced into the string.

■ A.7.5 Initialization

`init.m`	file to read when *Mathematica* starts

Conventional *Mathematica* initialization file.

The details of how *Mathematica* starts up differ from one computer system to another. However, on all systems, unless you specify otherwise, *Mathematica* will try to read the file `init.m` when it starts up. It searches for this file in all directories that are given in the list `$Path`.

On most systems, there is a "script" for running *Mathematica* which is created at the time when you originally install *Mathematica* on your computer. This script typically sets up appropriate operating system parameters and defines the values of *Mathematica* variables such as `$Path`. On systems with text-based interfaces, the script can usually pass various command-line options through to *Mathematica*.

`-batchinput`	use batch input mode (set `$BatchInput = True`)
`-batchoutput`	use batch output mode (set `$BatchOutput = True`)
`-mathlink`	communicate via *MathLink*
`-mathpass` *file*	read *Mathematica* passwords from the specified file
`-noinit`	inhibit the reading of `init.m`
`-run` *command*	run the specified *Mathematica* commands
`-x` *file*	set up the state of the session from the specified dump file

Some typical command-line options for *Mathematica*.

■ A.7.6 Termination

`Exit[ ]` or `Quit[ ]`	terminate *Mathematica*
`$Epilog`	symbol to evaluate before *Mathematica* exits
`$IgnoreEOF`	whether to exit an interactive *Mathematica* session when an end-of-file character is received
`end.m`	file to read when *Mathematica* terminates

Mathematica termination.

There are several ways to end a *Mathematica* session. If you are using *Mathematica* interactively, typing Exit[ ] or Quit[ ] on an input line will always terminate *Mathematica*.

If you are taking input for *Mathematica* from a file, *Mathematica* will exit when it reaches the end of the file. If you are using *Mathematica* interactively, it will still exit if it receives an end-of-file character (typically CONTROL-D). You can stop *Mathematica* from doing this by setting $IgnoreEOF=True.

A.8 Listing of Built-in *Mathematica* Objects

■ A.8.1 Introduction

This section gives an alphabetical list of all the built-in objects which are supported in *Mathematica* Version 2.0. The list does not include objects that are defined in *Mathematica* packages, even those distributed as a standard part of the *Mathematica* system. Note also that options which appear only in a single built-in *Mathematica* function are sometimes not given as separate entries in the list.

Objects that were not present in *Mathematica* Version 1.0 are indicated by ■.

A few objects in the list, mostly ones related to external operations, are not available on some computer systems.

Note that in a typical version of *Mathematica*, there are some additional objects present, which are not included in this list. You should avoid using such objects. Some may be provided for compatibility with older *Mathematica* systems; others may be preliminary or experimental. In general, however, the specifications of such objects can be expected to change.

In many versions of *Mathematica*, you can access the text given in this section directly. Typing ?*F*, for example, will typically give you the main description of the object *F* from this section.

■ A.8.2 Conventions in This Listing

`text in this style`	literal *Mathematica* input that you type in as it is printed (*e.g.*, function names)
text in this style	expressions that you fill in (*e.g.*, function arguments)
object$_1$, *object$_2$* , …	a sequence of any number of expressions

Conventions used in the list of built-in objects.

◪ Abort

Abort[ ] generates an interrupt to abort a computation.

You can call **Abort** anywhere within a computation. It has the same effect as an interactive interrupt in which you select the abort option. ▪ You can use **Abort** as an "emergency stop" in a computation. ▪ Once **Abort** has been called, *Mathematica* functions currently being evaluated return as quickly as possible. ▪ In an interactive session, the final result from an aborted computation is **$Aborted**. ▪ You can use **CheckAbort** to "catch" returns from an abort. ▪ See page 311. ▪ See also: **Throw, TimeConstrained, MemoryConstrained**.

◪ AbortProtect

AbortProtect[*expr*] evaluates *expr*, saving any aborts until the evaluation is complete.

Aborts that are generated during an **AbortProtect** take effect as soon as the execution of the **AbortProtect** is over. ▪ **CheckAbort** can be used inside **AbortProtect** to catch and absorb any aborts that occur. ▪ **AbortProtect** also protects against aborts generated by **TimeConstrained** and **MemoryConstrained**. ▪ See page 311.

■ Abs

Abs[*z*] gives the absolute value of the real or complex number *z*.

For complex numbers *z*, **Abs[*z*]** gives the modulus $|z|$. ▪ **Abs[*z*]** is left unevaluated if *expr* is not a number. ▪ See pages 550 and 551. ▪ See also: **Re, Im, Arg, Mod, ComplexExpand**.

◪ AbsoluteDashing

AbsoluteDashing[{*d₁*, *d₂*, ... }] is a graphics directive which specifies that lines which follow are to be drawn dashed, with successive segments having absolute lengths $d_1, d_2, ...$ (repeated cyclically).

The absolute lengths are measured in units of printer's points, approximately equal to $\frac{1}{72}$ of an inch. ▪ **AbsoluteDashing[{ }]** specifies that lines should be solid. ▪ **AbsoluteDashing** can be used in both two- and three-dimensional graphics. ▪ See page 409. ▪ See also: **AbsoluteThickness, Thickness, GrayLevel, Hue, RGBColor**.

◪ AbsolutePointSize

AbsolutePointSize[*d*] is a graphics directive which specifies that points which follow are to be shown if possible as circular regions with absolute radius *d*.

The absolute radius is measured in units of printer's points, approximately equal to $\frac{1}{72}$ of an inch. ▪ **AbsolutePointSize** can be used in both two- and three-dimensional graphics. ▪ See page 408. ▪ See also: **PointSize, Thickness**.

◪ AbsoluteThickness

AbsoluteThickness[*d*] is a graphics directive which specifies that lines which follow are to be drawn with absolute thickness *d*.

The absolute thickness is measured in units of printer's points, approximately equal to $\frac{1}{72}$ of an inch. ▪ **AbsoluteThickness** can be used in both two- and three-dimensional graphics. ▪ See page 409. ▪ See also: **AbsoluteDashing, PointSize, Dashing**.

■ **AbsoluteTime**

AbsoluteTime[ ] gives the total number of seconds since the beginning of January 1, 1900, in your time zone.

AbsoluteTime[ ] uses whatever date and time have been set on your computer system. It performs no corrections for time zones, daylight saving time, etc. ■ AbsoluteTime[z] gives the date in time zone z. This is inferred by knowing your local date and time, and local time zone. The time zone is given as the number of hours to be added to Greenwich mean time to obtain local time. ■ AbsoluteTime[ ] is accurate only down to a granularity of at least $TimeUnit seconds. ■ There are 2208988800 seconds from the beginning of January 1, 1900 to the beginning of January 1, 1970 and 2840140800 seconds to the beginning of January 1, 1990. ■ See page 524. ■ See also: Date, SessionTime, TimeUsed, Timing, TimeZone, ToDate, FromDate.

■ **AccountingForm**

AccountingForm[*expr*] prints with all numbers in *expr* given in standard accounting notation.

AccountingForm never uses scientific notation. ■ AccountingForm uses parentheses to indicate negative numbers. ■ AccountingForm takes the same options as NumberForm, but uses a different default function for ExponentFunction, and a different default for NumberSigns. ■ AccountingForm acts as a "wrapper", which affects printing, but not evaluation. ■ See page 350. ■ See also: PaddedForm, NumberForm.

■ **Accuracy**

Accuracy[*x*] gives the number of digits to the right of the decimal point in the number *x*.

If *x* is not a number, Accuracy[*x*] gives the minimum value of Accuracy for all the numbers that appear in *x*. ■ Accuracy gives Infinity when applied to exact numbers, such as integers. ■ Accuracy assumes a precision of $MachinePrecision when applied to machine precision numbers. ■ Accuracy can yield a negative result when applied to zero precision numbers. ■ See page 539. ■ See also: Precision, N, Chop, SetAccuracy.

■ **AccuracyGoal**

AccuracyGoal is an option for various numerical operations which specifies how many digits of accuracy should be sought in the final result.

AccuracyGoal is an option for such functions as NIntegrate, NDSolve and FindRoot. ■ AccuracyGoal -> Automatic yields an accuracy goal equal to 10 digits less than the setting for WorkingPrecision. ■ AccuracyGoal -> Infinity specifies that accuracy should not be used as the criterion for terminating the numerical procedure. PrecisionGoal is typically used in this case. ■ Even though you may specify AccuracyGoal->*n*, the results you get may have much less than *n*-digit accuracy. ■ In most cases, you must set WorkingPrecision to be at least as large as AccuracyGoal. ■ AccuracyGoal effectively specifies the absolute error allowed in a numerical procedure. ■ See page 687. ■ See also: PrecisionGoal, WorkingPrecision.

■ **AddTo**

x += *dx* adds *dx* to *x* and returns the new value of *x*.

AddTo has the attribute HoldFirst. ■ *x* += *dx* is equivalent to *x* = *x* + *dx*. ■ See page 248. ■ See also: Increment, PreIncrement, Set, PrependTo.

■ **AiryAi**

AiryAi[z] gives the Airy function Ai(*z*).

Mathematical function (see Section A.3.9). ■ The Airy function Ai(*z*) is a solution to the differential equation $\frac{d^2y}{dx^2} - xy = 0$. ■ Ai(*z*) tends to zero as $z \to \infty$. ■ See page 570.

AiryAiPrime

AiryAiPrime[z] gives the derivative of the Airy function Ai′(z).

Mathematical function (see Section A.3.9). ▪ See notes for **AiryAi**. ▪ See page 570.

AiryBi

AiryBi[z] gives the Airy function Bi(z).

Mathematical function (see Section A.3.9). ▪ The Airy function Bi(z) is a solution to the differential equation $\frac{d^2y}{dx^2} - xy = 0$. ▪ Bi($z$) increases exponentially as $z \to \infty$. ▪ See page 570.

AiryBiPrime

AiryBiPrime[z] gives the derivative of the Airy function Bi′(z).

Mathematical function (see Section A.3.9). ▪ See notes for **AiryBi**. ▪ See page 570.

AlgebraicRules

AlgebraicRules[*eqns*, {x_1, x_2, ... }] generates a set of algebraic rules which replace variables earlier in the list of x_i with ones later in the list, according to the equation or equations *eqns*.

You can use **AlgebraicRules** to set up algebraic transformations which you need to apply many times. ▪ The argument *eqns* can be a single equation of the form *lhs*==*rhs*, or a list of equations {lhs_1==rhs_1, lhs_2==rhs_2, ... }. ▪ **AlgebraicRules** generates an **AlgebraicRulesData** object, which contains a representation of the Gröbner basis for the equations *eqns*. In standard **OutputForm**, the output from **AlgebraicRules** is printed like a list of replacements. ▪ You can use *expr/.arules* to apply a set of algebraic rules to a particular expression. ▪ See page 622. ▪ See also: **Eliminate**, **Replace**.

All

All is a setting used for certain options.

For example, **PlotRange -> All** specifies that all points are to be included in a plot. ▪ See page 141.

Alternatives

p_1 | p_2 | ... is a pattern object which represents any of the patterns p_i.

Example: _Integer | _Real represents an object with head either **Integer** or **Real**. ▪ Unless the same set of pattern names appears in all of the p_i, you cannot use these pattern names on the right-hand side of transformation rules for the pattern. Thus, for example, you can use x in a[x_] | b[x_], but you can use neither x nor y in a[x_] | b[y_]. ▪ See page 229. ▪ See also: **Optional**.

AmbientLight

AmbientLight is an option to Graphics3D and related functions that gives the level of simulated ambient illumination in a three-dimensional picture.

The setting for **AmbientLight** must be a **GrayLevel**, **Hue** or **RGBColor** directive. ▪ See page 455. ▪ See also: **Lighting**, **LightSources**, **SurfaceColor**.

AnchoredSearch

AnchoredSearch is an option for Find and FindList which specifies whether the text searched for must be at the beginning of a record.

With the default setting **RecordSeparators -> {"\n"}**, **AnchoredSearch -> True** specifies that the text must appear at the beginning of a line. ▪ See page 501.

■ And

e_1 && e_2 && ... is the logical AND function. It evaluates its arguments in order, giving False immediately if any of them are False, and True if they are all True.

And evaluates its arguments in a non-standard way (see page 730). ■ And gives symbolic results when necessary. It applies no simplification rules, except removing initial arguments that are True. ■ See page 94. ■ See also: LogicalExpand.

■ Apart

Apart[*expr*] rewrites a rational expression as a sum of terms with minimal denominators.

Apart[*expr*, *var*] treats all variables other than *var* as constants.

Example: Apart[(x^2+1)/(x-1)] $\longrightarrow$ $1 + \dfrac{2}{-1 + x} + x$. ■ Apart gives the partial fraction decomposition of a rational expression. ■ Apart[*expr*, *var*] writes *expr* as a polynomial in *var* together with a sum of ratios of polynomials, where the degree in *var* of each numerator polynomial is less than that of the corresponding denominator polynomial. ■ Apart[(x + y)/(x - y), x] $\longrightarrow$ $1 + \dfrac{2 y}{x - y}$. ■ Apart[(x + y)/(x - y), y] $\longrightarrow$ $-1 - \dfrac{2 x}{-x + y}$. ■ Apart[*expr*, Trig -> True] treats trigonometric functions as rational functions of exponentials, and manipulates them accordingly. ■ See page 596. ■ See also: Together, Cancel, PolynomialQuotient.

■ Append

Append[*expr*, *elem*] gives *expr* with *elem* appended.

Examples: Append[{a,b}, c] $\longrightarrow$ {a, b, c}; Append[f[a], b+c] $\longrightarrow$ f[a, b + c]. ■ See page 128. ■ See also: Prepend, Insert, AppendTo.

■ AppendTo

AppendTo[*s*, *elem*] appends *elem* to the value of *s*, and resets *s* to the result.

AppendTo[*s*, *elem*] is equivalent to *s* = Append[*s*, *elem*]. ■ AppendTo[*s*, *elem*] does not evaluate *s*. ■ You can use AppendTo repeatedly to build up a list. ■ An alternative and often more efficient way to build up a list is to use a sequence of assignments of the form *s* = {*s*, *elem*}, and then to call Flatten on the resulting structure. ■ See page 249. ■ See also: PrependTo.

■ Apply

Apply[*f*, *expr*] or *f* @@ *expr* replaces the head of *expr* by *f*.

Apply[*f*, *expr*, *levelspec*] replaces heads in parts of *expr* specified by *levelspec*.

Examples: Apply[f, {a, b, c}] $\longrightarrow$ f[a, b, c]; Apply[Plus, g[a, b]] $\longrightarrow$ a + b. ■ Level specifications are described on page 725. ■ The default value for *levelspec* in Apply is {0}. ■ Examples: Apply[f, {{a,b},{c,d}}] $\longrightarrow$ f[{a, b}, {c, d}]. ■ Apply[f, {{a,b},{c,d}}, {1}] $\longrightarrow$ {f[a, b], f[c, d]}. ■ Apply[f, {{{{a}}}}, -2] $\longrightarrow$ {f[f[f[a]]]}. ■ See page 203. ■ See also: Map, Scan, Level, Operate, MapThread.

■ ArcCos

ArcCos[z] gives the arc cosine $\cos^{-1}(z)$ of the complex number *z*.

Mathematical function (see Section A.3.9). ■ All results are given in radians. ■ For real *z* between −1 and 1, the results are always in the range 0 to π. ■ See page 562.

■ **ArcCosh**

ArcCosh[z] gives the inverse hyperbolic cosine $\cosh^{-1}(z)$ of the complex number z.

Mathematical function (see Section A.3.9). ▪ See page 562. ▪ See also: ArcSech.

■ **ArcCot**

ArcCot[z] gives the arc cotangent $\cot^{-1}(z)$ of the complex number z.

Mathematical function (see Section A.3.9). ▪ All results are given in radians. ▪ For real z, the results are always in the range $-\pi/2$ to $\pi/2$, excluding 0. ▪ See page 562.

■ **ArcCoth**

ArcCoth[z] gives the inverse hyperbolic cotangent $\coth^{-1}(z)$ of the complex number z.

Mathematical function (see Section A.3.9). ▪ See page 562.

■ **ArcCsc**

ArcCsc[z] gives the arc cosecant $\csc^{-1}(z)$ of the complex number z.

Mathematical function (see Section A.3.9). ▪ All results are given in radians. ▪ For real z outside the interval -1 to 1, the results are always in the range $-\pi/2$ to $\pi/2$, excluding 0. ▪ See page 562.

■ **ArcCsch**

ArcCsch[z] gives the inverse hyperbolic cosecant $\operatorname{csch}^{-1}(z)$ of the complex number z.

Mathematical function (see Section A.3.9). ▪ See page 562.

■ **ArcSec**

ArcSec[z] gives the arc secant $\sec^{-1}(z)$ of the complex number z.

Mathematical function (see Section A.3.9). ▪ All results are given in radians. ▪ For real z outside the interval -1 to 1, the results are always in the range 0 to π, excluding $\pi/2$. ▪ See page 562.

■ **ArcSech**

ArcSech[z] gives the inverse hyperbolic secant $\operatorname{sech}^{-1}(z)$ of the complex number z.

Mathematical function (see Section A.3.9). ▪ See page 562.

■ **ArcSin**

ArcSin[z] gives the arc sine $\sin^{-1}(z)$ of the complex number z.

Mathematical function (see Section A.3.9). ▪ All results are given in radians. ▪ For real z between -1 and 1, the results are always in the range $-\pi/2$ to $\pi/2$. ▪ See page 562.

■ **ArcSinh**

ArcSinh[z] gives the inverse hyperbolic sine $\sinh^{-1}(z)$ of the complex number z.

Mathematical function (see Section A.3.9). ▪ See page 562. ▪ See also: ArcCsch.

■ **ArcTan**

ArcTan[z] gives the arc tangent $\tan^{-1}(z)$ of the complex number z.

ArcTan[x, y] gives the arc tangent of $\frac{y}{x}$, taking into account which quadrant the point (x, y) is in.

Mathematical function (see Section A.3.9). ■ All results are given in radians. ■ For real z, the results are always in the range $-\pi/2$ to $\pi/2$. ■ If x or y is complex, then ArcTan[x, y] gives $-i \log\left(\frac{x + i\, y}{\sqrt{x^2 + y^2}}\right)$. When $x^2 + y^2 = 1$, ArcTan[x, y] gives the number ϕ such that $x = \cos\phi$ and $y = \sin\phi$. ■ See page 562. ■ See also: Arg.

■ **ArcTanh**

ArcTanh[z] gives the hyperbolic arc tangent $\tanh^{-1}(z)$ of the complex number z.

Mathematical function (see Section A.3.9). ■ See page 562. ■ See also: ArcCoth.

■ **Arg**

Arg[z] gives the argument of the complex number z.

Mathematical function (see Section A.3.9). ■ Arg[z] gives the phase angle of z in radians. ■ The result from Arg[z] is always between $-\pi$ and $+\pi$. ■ See page 551. ■ See also: ArcTan, Sign.

■ **ArithmeticGeometricMean**

ArithmeticGeometricMean[a, b] gives the arithmetic-geometric mean of a and b.

See page 580.

■ **Array**

Array[f, n] generates a list of length n, with elements $f[i]$.

Array[f, {n_1, n_2, ... }] generates an $n_1 \times n_2 \times$... array of nested lists, with elements $f[i_1, i_2, ...]$.

Array[f, dims, origin] generates a list using the specified index origin (default 1).

Array[f, dims, origin, h] uses head h, rather than List, for each level of the array.

Example: Array[f, 3] ⟶ {f[1], f[2], f[3]}.
■ Array[f, {2, 3}] ⟶ {{f[1, 1], f[1, 2], f[1, 3]}, {f[2, 1], f[2, 2], f[2, 3]}} generates a 2×3 matrix. ■ Array[#1^#2 &, {2, 2}] ⟶ {{1, 1}, {2, 4}}. ■ Array[f, 3, 0] ⟶ {f[0], f[1], f[2]} generates an array with index origin 0. ■ Array[f, 3, 1, Plus] ⟶ f[1] + f[2] + f[3]. ■ Note that the dimensions given to Array are *not* in standard *Mathematica* iterator notation. ■ See page 210. ■ See also: Table.

■ **AspectRatio**

AspectRatio is an option for Show and related functions which specifies the ratio of height to width for a plot.

AspectRatio determines the scaling for the final image shape. ■ AspectRatio -> Automatic determines the ratio of height to width from the actual coordinate values in the plot. ■ The default value AspectRatio -> 1/GoldenRatio is used for two-dimensional plots. AspectRatio -> Automatic is used for three-dimensional plots. ■ See page 416. ■ See also: BoxRatios, PlotRegion.

■ **AtomQ**

> AtomQ [*expr*] yields True if *expr* is an expression which cannot be divided into subexpressions, and yields False otherwise.

> You can use AtomQ in a recursive procedure to tell when you have reached the bottom of the tree corresponding to an expression. ■ AtomQ gives True for symbols, numbers, strings and other raw objects. ■ AtomQ gives True on any object whose subparts cannot be accessed using functions like Map. ■ See page 228. ■ See also: NumberQ, Head, LeafCount, Length.

■ **Attributes**

> Attributes [*symbol*] gives the list of attributes for a symbol.

> The attributes of a symbol can be set by assigning a value to Attributes [*s*]. If a single attribute is assigned, it need not be in a list. ■ Attributes [*s*] = {} clears all attributes of a symbol. ■ Attributes [{s_1, s_2, ... }] gives a list of the attributes for each of the s_i. ■ Attributes ["*str*"] gives a list of the attributes for all symbols which match the string pattern *str*. ■ Attributes [Literal [*s*]] is treated as equivalent to Attributes [*s*]. ■ Attributes for functions must be set before any definitions that involve the functions are given. ■ The complete list of possible attributes for a symbol *f* is:

Constant	all derivatives of *f* are zero
Flat	*f* is associative
HoldAll	all the arguments of *f* are not evaluated
HoldFirst	the first argument of *f* is not evaluated
HoldRest	all but the first argument of *f* are not evaluated
Listable	*f* is automatically "threaded" over lists
Locked	attributes of *f* cannot be changed
OneIdentity	*f*[*a*], *f*[*f*[*a*]], etc. are equivalent to *a* in pattern matching
Orderless	*f* is commutative
Protected	values of *f* cannot be changed
ReadProtected	values of *f* cannot be read
Stub	Needs is automatically called if the symbol is ever input
Temporary	*f* is a local variable, removed when no longer used

> ■ See page 271. ■ See also: SetAttributes, ClearAttributes.

■ **Automatic**

> Automatic represents an option value that is to be chosen automatically by a built-in function.

> See page 141.

■ **Axes**

> Axes is an option for graphics functions that specifies whether axes should be drawn.

> Axes -> True draws all axes. ■ Axes -> False draws no axes. ■ Axes -> {False, True} draws a *y* axis but no *x* axis in two dimensions. ■ In two dimensions, axes are drawn to cross at the position specified by the option AxesOrigin. ■ In three dimensions, axes are drawn on the edges of the bounding box specified by the option AxesEdge. ■ See pages 418 and 459. ■ See also: AxesLabel, Frame, GridLines, Boxed.

◪ AxesEdge

AxesEdge is an option for 3D graphics functions that specifies on which edges of the bounding box axes should be drawn.

AxesEdge->{{dir_y, dir_z**}, {**dir_x, dir_z**}, {**dir_x, dir_y**}}** specifies on which three edges of the bounding box axes are drawn. The dir_i must be either **+1** or **-1**, and specify whether axes are drawn on the edge of the box with a larger or smaller value of coordinate *i*, respectively. ■ The default setting **AxesEdge->Automatic** chooses automatically on which exposed box edges axes should be drawn. ■ Any pair **{**dir_i, dir_j**}** in the setting for **AxesEdge** can be replaced by **Automatic** to specify that the position of the corresponding axis is to be chosen automatically. ■ Any pair **{**dir_i, dir_j**}** can be replaced by **None**, in which case the corresponding axis will not be drawn. ■ If you explicitly specify on which edge to draw an axis, the axis will be drawn on that edge, whether or not the edge is exposed with the view point you have chosen. ■ See page 461.

■ AxesLabel

AxesLabel is an option for graphics functions that specifies labels for axes.

AxesLabel -> None specifies that no labels should be given. ■ **AxesLabel ->** *label* specifies a label for the *y* axis of a two-dimensional plot, and the *z* axis of a three-dimensional plot. ■ **AxesLabel -> {**$xlabel$, $ylabel$, ... **}** specifies labels for different axes. ■ By default, axes labels in two-dimensional graphics are placed at the ends of the axes. In three-dimensional graphics, they are aligned with the middles of the axes. ■ Any expression can be specified as a label. It will be given in **OutputForm**. Arbitrary strings of text can be given as "*text*". ■ See pages 419 and 462. ■ See also: **PlotLabel**, **FrameLabel**.

◪ AxesOrigin

AxesOrigin is an option for two-dimensional graphics functions which specifies where any axes drawn should cross.

AxesOrigin -> {x, y**}** specifies that the axes should cross at the point **{**x, y**}**. ■ **AxesOrigin -> Automatic** uses an internal algorithm to determine where the axes should cross. If the point **{0, 0}** is within, or close to, the plotting region, then it is usually chosen as the axis origin. ■ In contour and density plots, **AxesOrigin -> Automatic** puts axes outside the plotting area. ■ See page 419.

◪ AxesStyle

AxesStyle is an option for graphics functions which specifies how axes should be rendered.

AxesStyle can be used in both two- and three-dimensional graphics. ■ **AxesStyle ->** *style* specifies that all axes are to be generated with the specified graphics directive, or list of graphics directives. ■ **AxesStyle -> {{**$xstyle$**}, {**$ystyle$**}, ... }** specifies that axes should use graphics directives *xstyle*, ... The styles must be enclosed in lists, perhaps of length one. ■ Styles can be specified using graphics directives such as **Dashing**, **Hue** and **Thickness**. ■ The default color of axes is specified by the option **DefaultColor**. ■ See pages 419 and 461. ■ See also: **Prolog**, **Epilog**, **PlotStyle**, **FrameStyle**.

◪ Background

Background is an option for graphics functions which specifies the background color to use.

The setting for **Background** must be a **CMYKColor**, **GrayLevel**, **Hue** or **RGBColor** directive. ■ The default setting is **Background->Automatic**, which produces a white background on most output devices. ■ See page 412. ■ See also: **Prolog**, **DefaultColor**, **PlotRegion**.

■ **BaseForm**

BaseForm[*expr*, *n*] prints with the numbers in *expr* given in base *n*.

The maximum allowed base is 36. For bases larger than 10, additional digits are chosen from the letters a–z. ▪ You can enter a number in an arbitrary base using *base*∧∧*digits*. ▪ When a number in an arbitrary base is given in scientific notation, the exponent is still given in base 10. ▪ You can mix BaseForm with NumberForm and related functions. ▪ BaseForm acts as a "wrapper", which affects printing, but not evaluation. ▪ See pages 353 and 537. ▪ See also: IntegerDigits, RealDigits.

■ **Begin**

Begin["*context*`"] resets the current context.

Begin resets the value of $Context. ▪ The interpretation of symbol names depends on context. Begin thus affects the parsing of input expressions. ▪ See page 339. ▪ See also: BeginPackage, End, $ContextPath.

■ **BeginPackage**

BeginPackage["*context*`"] makes *context*` and System` the only active contexts.

BeginPackage["*context*`", {"*need₁*`", "*need₂*`", ... }] calls Needs on the *needᵢ*.

BeginPackage is typically used at the beginning of a *Mathematica* package. ▪ BeginPackage resets the values of both $Context and $ContextPath. ▪ The interpretation of symbol names depends on context. BeginPackage thus affects the parsing of input expressions. ▪ See page 339. ▪ See also: EndPackage.

■ **BernoulliB**

BernoulliB[*n*] gives the Bernoulli number B_n.

BernoulliB[*n*, *x*] gives the Bernoulli polynomial $B_n(x)$.

Mathematical function (see Section A.3.9). ▪ The Bernoulli polynomials satisfy the generating function relation $\frac{te^{xt}}{e^t - 1} = \sum_{n=0}^{\infty} B_n(x) \frac{t^n}{n!}$. ▪ The Bernoulli numbers are given by $B_n = B_n(0)$. ▪ See page 558. ▪ See also: NBernoulliB.

■ **BesselI**

BesselI[*n*, *z*] gives the modified Bessel function of the first kind $I_n(z)$.

Mathematical function (see Section A.3.9). ▪ $I_n(z)$ satisfies the differential equation $z^2 \frac{d^2y}{dz^2} + z \frac{dy}{dz} - (z^2 + n^2)y = 0$. ▪ See page 570.

■ **BesselJ**

BesselJ[*n*, *z*] gives the Bessel function of the first kind $J_n(z)$.

Mathematical function (see Section A.3.9). ▪ $J_n(z)$ satisfies the differential equation $z^2 \frac{d^2y}{dz^2} + z \frac{dy}{dz} + (z^2 - n^2)y = 0$. ▪ See page 570.

■ **BesselK**

BesselK[*n*, *z*] gives the modified Bessel function of the second kind $K_n(z)$.

Mathematical function (see Section A.3.9). ▪ $K_n(z)$ satisfies the differential equation $z^2 \frac{d^2y}{dz^2} + z \frac{dy}{dz} - (z^2 + n^2)y = 0$. ▪ See page 570.

■ **BesselY**

`BesselY[n, z]` gives the Bessel function of the second kind $Y_n(z)$.

Mathematical function (see Section A.3.9). ■ $Y_n(z)$ satisfies the differential equation $z^2 \frac{d^2 y}{dz^2} + z \frac{dy}{dz} + (z^2 - n^2)y = 0$. ■ See page 570.

■ **Beta**

`Beta[a, b]` gives the Euler beta function $B(a, b)$.

`Beta[z, a, b]` gives the incomplete beta function $B_z(a, b)$.

Mathematical function (see Section A.3.9). ■ $B(a,b) = \frac{\Gamma(a)\Gamma(b)}{\Gamma(a+b)} = \int_0^1 t^{a-1}(1-t)^{b-1}dt$. ■ $B_z(a,b) = \int_0^z t^{a-1}(1-t)^{b-1}dt$.
■ `Beta[`z_0`, `z_1`, a, b]` gives the generalized incomplete beta function $\int_{z_0}^{z_1} t^{a-1}(1-t)^{b-1}dt$. ■ See page 570.

■ **BetaRegularized**

`BetaRegularized[z, a, b]` gives the regularized incomplete beta function $I_z(a,b)$.

Mathematical function (see Section A.3.9). ■ For non-singular cases, $I(z,a,b) = B(z,a,b)/B(a,b)$.
■ `BetaRegularized[`z_0`, `z_1`, a, b]` gives the generalized regularized incomplete beta function defined in non-singular cases as `Beta[`z_0`, `z_1`, a, b]/Beta[a, b]`. ■ See page 573.

■ **Binomial**

`Binomial[n, m]` gives the binomial coefficient $\binom{n}{m}$.

Integer mathematical function (see Section A.3.9). ■ `Binomial` is evaluated whenever n and m differ by an integer.
■ Example: `Binomial[x+2, x]` $\longrightarrow \dfrac{(1 + x)\,(2 + x)}{2}$. ■ See page 558. ■ See also: `Multinomial`, `Pochhammer`.

■ **Blank**

`_` or `Blank[ ]` is a pattern object that can stand for any *Mathematica* expression.

`_h` or `Blank[h]` can stand for any expression with head h.

The head h in `_h` cannot itself contain pattern objects. ■ See page 219. ■ See also: `Pattern`, `Optional`.

■ **BlankNullSequence**

`___` (three `_` characters) or `BlankNullSequence[ ]` is a pattern object that can stand for any sequence of zero or more *Mathematica* expressions.

`___h` or `BlankNullSequence[h]` can stand for any sequence of expressions, all of which have head h.

Blank sequences work slightly differently depending on whether or not the head of the expression in which they appear is a symbol with the attribute `Flat`. ■ Consider matching the pattern $f[a_1, a_2, \ldots, \_\_\_, c_1, \ldots]$ against the expression $f[a_1, a_2, \ldots, b_1, \ldots, c_1, \ldots]$. If f is a symbol with attribute `Flat`, then the `___` will be taken to stand for the expression $f[b_1, \ldots]$. If f is not a symbol with attribute `Flat`, then `___` will be taken to stand for the sequence of expressions $b_1, \ldots$. With a named pattern, such as $x\_\_\_$, x can be used only as an element in an expression. The sequence of expressions $b_1, \ldots$ is "spliced in" to replace x, thereby usually increasing the length of the expression.
■ See pages 232 and 719. ■ See also: `Pattern`.

■ **BlankSequence**

__ (two _ characters) or `BlankSequence[ ]` is a pattern object that can stand for any sequence of one or more *Mathematica* expressions.

__*h* or `BlankSequence[h]` can stand for any sequence of one or more expressions, all of which have head *h*.

See notes for `BlankNullSequence`. ■ See pages 232 and 719.

■ **Block**

`Block[{x, y, ... }, expr]` specifies that *expr* is to be evaluated with local values for the symbols *x*, *y*, ...

`Block[{x = x₀, ... }, expr]` defines initial local values for *x*, ...

Block allows you to set up an environment in which the values of variables can temporarily be changed. ■ When you execute a block, values assigned to *x*, *y*, ... are cleared. When the execution of the block is finished, the original values of these symbols are restored. ■ Block affects only the *values* of symbols, not their names. ■ Initial values specified for *x*, *y*, ... are evaluated before *x*, *y*, ... are cleared. ■ You can use `Block[{vars}, body /; cond]` as the right-hand side of a transformation rule with a condition attached. ■ Block has attribute `HoldAll`. ■ Block implements dynamic scoping of variables. ■ Block is automatically used to localize values of iterators in iteration constructs such as Do, Sum and Table. ■ See page 329. ■ See also: `Module`, `With`, `CompoundExpression`.

■ **Boxed**

Boxed is an option for `Graphics3D` which specifies whether to draw the edges of the bounding box in a three-dimensional picture.

`Boxed -> True` draws the box; `Boxed -> False` does not. ■ See pages 156 and 459.

■ **BoxRatios**

BoxRatios is an option for `Graphics3D` and `SurfaceGraphics` which gives the ratios of side lengths for the bounding box of the three-dimensional picture.

`BoxRatios -> {sₓ, s_y, s_z}` gives the side-length ratios. ■ See page 441.

■ **BoxStyle**

BoxStyle is an option for three-dimensional graphics functions which specifies how the bounding box should be rendered.

BoxStyle can be set to a list of graphics directives such as `Dashing`, `Thickness`, `GrayLevel` and `RGBColor`. ■ See pages 411 and 461. ■ See also: `AxesStyle`, `Prolog`, `Epilog`, `DisplayFunction`.

■ **Break**

`Break[ ]` exits the nearest enclosing Do, For or While.

Break is effective only if it is generated as the value of a segment in a compound expression, or as the body of a control structure. ■ The value Null is returned from the enclosing control structure. ■ See page 293. ■ See also: `Continue`, `Return`.

■ **Byte**

Byte represents a single byte of data in Read.

See page 495.

■ **ByteCount**

ByteCount [*expr*] gives the number of bytes used internally by *Mathematica* to store *expr*.

ByteCount does not take account of any sharing of subexpressions. The results it gives assume that every part of the expression is stored separately. ByteCount will therefore often give an overestimate of the amount of memory currently needed to store a particular expression. When you manipulate the expression, however, subexpressions will often stop being shared, and the amount of memory needed will be close to the value returned by ByteCount. ▪ See page 528. ▪ See also: LeafCount, MemoryInUse, MaxMemoryUsed, StringByteCount.

■ **C**

C[*i*] is the default form for the ith constant of integration produced in solving a differential equation with DSolve.

The indices *i* are chosen to be successive integers, starting at 1 every time DSolve is called. ▪ The function applied to the index *i* to produce the ith constant of integration is determined by the setting for the option DSolveConstants in DSolve. The default is DSolveConstants->C. ▪ See pages 99 and 638. ▪ See also: Unique.

■ **Cancel**

Cancel [*expr*] cancels out common factors in the numerator and denominator of *expr*.

Example: Cancel[(x^2-1)/(x-1)] ⟶ 1 + x. ▪ Cancel is Listable. ▪ Cancel cancels out the greatest common divisor of the numerator and denominator. ▪ Cancel[*expr*, Trig -> True] treats trigonometric functions as rational functions of exponentials, and manipulates them accordingly. ▪ See page 596. ▪ See also: Apart, GCD.

■ **Cases**

Cases [{*e₁*, *e₂*, ... }, *pattern*] gives a list of the e_i that match the pattern.

Cases [{*e₁*, ... }, *pattern* -> *rhs*] gives a list of the values of *rhs* corresponding to the e_i that match the pattern.

Cases [*expr*, *pattern*, *levspec*] gives a list of all parts of *expr* on levels specified by *levspec* which match the pattern.

Cases [*expr*, *pattern* -> *rhs*, *levspec*] gives the values of *rhs* which match the pattern.

Example: Cases[{2, x, 4}, _Integer] ⟶ {2, 4}. ▪ The first argument to Cases need not have head List. ▪ Cases[*expr*, *pattern*, *levspec*, *n*] gives the first *n* parts in *expr* which match the pattern. ▪ Level specifications are described on page 725. ▪ See page 221. ▪ See also: Select, Position.

■ **Catalan**

Catalan is Catalan's constant, with numerical value ≈ 0.915966.

Catalan's constant is given by the sum $\sum_{k=0}^{\infty}(-1)^k(2k+1)^{-2}$. ▪ See page 566.

■ **Catch**

Catch [*expr*] returns the argument of the first Throw generated in the evaluation of *expr*.

Catch [*expr*] returns the value of *expr* if no Throw was generated during the evaluation. ▪ Throw and Catch can be used to implement non-local returns and jumps in procedural programs. ▪ See page 293.

■ **Ceiling**

> Ceiling[*x*] gives the smallest integer greater than or equal to *x*.

Mathematical function (see Section A.3.9). ■ Examples: Ceiling[2.4] ⟶ 3; Ceiling[2.6] ⟶ 3; Ceiling[-2.4] ⟶ -2; Ceiling[-2.6] ⟶ -2. ■ See page 550. ■ See also: Floor, Round, Chop.

■ **CForm**

> CForm[*expr*] prints as a C language version of *expr*.

Standard arithmetic functions and certain control structures are translated. ■ No declarations are generated. ■ CForm acts as a "wrapper", which affects printing, but not evaluation. ■ See pages 182 and 344. ■ See also: FortranForm.

■ **Character**

> Character represents a single character in Read.

See page 495.

■ **Characters**

> Characters["*string*"] gives a list of the characters in a string.

Each character is given as a length one string. ■ The characters may be 8- or 16-bit. ■ See page 366. ■ See also: StringJoin, StringLength, ToCharacterCode, StringByteCount, StringToStream.

■ **ChebyshevT**

> ChebyshevT[*n*, *x*] gives the Chebyshev polynomial of the first kind $T_n(x)$.

Mathematical function (see Section A.3.9). ■ Explicit polynomials are given for integer *n*. ■ $T_n(\cos\theta) = \cos(n\theta)$. ■ See page 567.

■ **ChebyshevU**

> ChebyshevU[*n*, *x*] gives the Chebyshev polynomial of the second kind $U_n(x)$.

Mathematical function (see Section A.3.9). ■ Explicit polynomials are given for integer *n*. ■ $U_n(\cos\theta) = \frac{\sin(n+1)\theta}{\sin\theta}$. ■ See page 567.

■ **Check**

> Check[*expr*, *failexpr*] evaluates *expr*, and returns the result, unless messages were generated, in which case it evaluates and returns *failexpr*.
>
> Check[*expr*, *failexpr*, s_1::t_1, s_2::t_2, ...] checks only for the specified messages.

Check has attribute HoldAll. ■ Check tests only for messages that are actually output. It does not test for messages that have been suppressed using Off. ■ See page 389. ■ See also: MessageList, $MessageList, Message, Indeterminate, TimeConstrained, CheckAbort.

■ **CheckAbort**

> CheckAbort[*expr*, *failexpr*] evaluates *expr*, returning *failexpr* if an abort occurs.

CheckAbort absorbs any aborts it handles, and does not propagate them further. ■ CheckAbort works inside AbortProtect. ■ CheckAbort has attribute HoldAll. ■ See page 311. ■ See also: Catch.

■ **Chop**

Chop[*expr*] replaces approximate real numbers in *expr* that are close to zero by the exact integer 0.

Chop[*expr*, *delta*] replaces numbers smaller in absolute magnitude than *delta* by 0. ■ Chop uses a default tolerance of 10^{-10}. ■ Chop works on both Real and Complex numbers. ■ See page 541. ■ See also: Rationalize, Round.

■ **Circle**

Circle[{*x*, *y*}, *r*] is a two-dimensional graphics primitive that represents a circle of radius *r* centered at the point *x*, *y*.

Circle[{*x*, *y*}, {r_x, r_y}] yields an ellipse with semi-axes r_x and r_y.

Circle[{*x*, *y*}, *r*, {*theta₁*, *theta₂*}] represents a circular arc.

Angles are measured in radians counter-clockwise from the positive *x* direction. ■ Scaled[{dr_x, dr_y}] or Scaled[{dr_x, dr_y}, {r_x, r_y}] can be used in the radius specification. The dr_i are in scaled coordinates, and the r_i are in absolute coordinates. ■ The thickness of the circle can be specified using the Thickness primitive. ■ See page 404. ■ See also: Disk.

■ **Clear**

Clear[*symbol₁*, *symbol₂*, ...] clears values and definitions for the *symbolᵢ*.

Clear["*form₁*", "*form₂*", ...] clears values and definitions for all symbols whose names match any of the string patterns *formᵢ*.

Clear does not clear attributes, messages, or defaults associated with symbols. ■ Clear["*form*"] allows metacharacters such as *, as specified on page 728. ■ Clear["*context*`*"] clears all symbols in a particular context. ■ Clear is HoldAll. ■ Clear does not affect symbols with the attribute Protected. ■ See pages 113, 247 and 736. ■ See also: Remove.

■ **ClearAll**

ClearAll[*symb₁*, *symb₂*, ...] clears all values, definitions, attributes, messages and defaults associated with symbols.

ClearAll["*form₁*", "*form₂*", ...] clears all symbols whose names textually match any of the *formᵢ*.

See notes for Clear. ■ See pages 273 and 736. ■ See also: Remove.

■ **ClearAttributes**

ClearAttributes[*s*, *attr*] removes *attr* from the list of attributes of the symbol *s*.

ClearAttributes modifies Attributes[*s*]. ■ ClearAttributes[*s*, {*attr₁*, *attr₂*, ... }] removes several attributes at a time. ■ ClearAttributes[{*s₁*, *s₂*, ... }, *attrs*] removes attributes from several symbols at a time. ■ ClearAttributes is HoldFirst. ■ ClearAttributes does not affect symbols with the attribute Locked. ■ See also: SetAttributes, Unprotect. ■ See page 271.

■ **ClebschGordan**

ClebschGordan[{j_1, m_1}, {j_2, m_2}, {*j*, *m*}] gives the Clebsch-Gordan coefficient for the decomposition of $|j, m\rangle$ in terms of $|j_1, m_1\rangle |j_2, m_2\rangle$.

The Clebsch-Gordan coefficients vanish except when $m = m_1 + m_2$ and the j_i satisfy a triangle inequality. ■ The parameters of ClebschGordan can be integers, half-integers or symbolic expressions. ■ *Mathematica* uses the standard conventions of Edmonds for the phase of the Clebsch-Gordan coefficients. ■ See page 561. ■ See also: ThreeJSymbol, SixJSymbol, SphericalHarmonicY.

■ ClipFill

ClipFill is an option for SurfaceGraphics that specifies how clipped parts of the surface are to be drawn.

ClipFill specifies what is to be shown in places where the surface would extend beyond the bounding box. ■ The possible settings are:

Automatic	show clipped areas like the rest of the surface
None	make holes in the surface where it would be clipped
color	show clipped areas with a particular color
{*bottom*, *top*}	use different specifications for bottom and top clipped areas

■ The colors for clipped areas can be specified by GrayLevel, Hue or RGBColor directives, or SurfaceColor objects.
■ See page 450.

■ Close

Close[*stream*] closes a stream.

The argument to Close can be an InputStream or OutputStream object. ■ If there is only one stream with a particular name, the argument to close can be "*name*". ■ See page 485. ■ See also: OpenAppend, SetOptions, Streams.

■ CMYKColor

CMYKColor[*cyan*, *magenta*, *yellow*, *black*] is a graphics directive which specifies that graphical objects which follow are to be displayed in the color given.

Color levels outside the range 0 to 1 will be clipped. ■ CMYKColor can be used to specify colors for color printing. ■ CMYKColor specifications are automatically converted to RGBColor when simulated lighting calculations are done. ■ See page 472. ■ See also: RGBColor, ColorOutput.

■ Coefficient

Coefficient[*expr*, *form*] gives the coefficient of *form* in the polynomial *expr*.

Coefficient[*expr*, *form*, *n*] gives the coefficient of *form*^*n* in *expr*.

Coefficient picks only terms that contain the particular form specified. x^2 is not considered part of x^3. ■ *form* can be a product of powers. ■ Coefficient[*expr*, *form*, 0] picks out terms that are not proportional to *form*. ■ See page 593. ■ See also: Exponent.

■ CoefficientList

CoefficientList[*poly*, *var*] gives a list of coefficients of powers of *var* in *poly*, starting with power 0.

CoefficientList[*poly*, {*var*$_1$, *var*$_2$, ... }] gives a matrix of coefficients of the *var*$_i$.

Example: CoefficientList[x^2 + 2 x y - y, {x, y}] ⟶ {{0, -1}, {0, 2}, {1, 0}}. ■ The dimensions of the matrix returned by CoefficientList are determined by the values of the Exponent[*poly*, *var*$_i$]. ■ Terms that do not contain positive integer powers of a particular variable are included in the first element of the list for that variable. ■ CoefficientList always returns a rectangular matrix. Combinations of powers that do not appear in *poly* give zeros in the matrix. ■ See page 593. ■ See also: Series, Collect, FactorList.

■ **Collect**

Collect[*expr*, *x*] collects together terms involving the same power of *x*.

Collect[*expr*, {*x₁*, *x₂*, ... }] collects together terms that involve the same powers of x_1, x_2, ...

Collect[*expr*, *x*] effectively writes *expr* as a polynomial in *x*. ■ Examples:
Collect[x + n x + m, x] ⟶ m + (1 + n) x;
Collect[Expand[(1+x+y)^3], x] ⟶ $1 + x^3 + 3 y + 3 y^2 + y^3 + x^2 (3 + 3 y) + x (3 + 6 y + 3 y^2)$.
■ The "variables" x_i can themselves be products. ■ Collect[*expr*, Trig -> True] treats trigonometric functions as rational functions of exponentials, and manipulates them accordingly. ■ See page 591. ■ See also: Series, CoefficientList, Together.

■ **ColorFunction**

ColorFunction is an option for various graphics functions which specifies a function to apply to *z* values to determine the color to use for a particular *x*, *y* region.

ColorFunction is an option for Plot3D, ListPlot3D, DensityPlot, ContourPlot, Raster and related functions.
■ The arguments provided for the function specified by ColorFunction are always in the range 0 to 1. ■ For three-dimensional, density and contour plots, the arguments correspond to scaled *z* values. ■ The function specified by ColorFunction must return a CMYKColor, GrayLevel, Hue or RGBColor directive. ■ ColorFunction -> Automatic yields a range of gray levels. ■ ColorFunction -> Hue yields a range of colors. ■ In three-dimensional graphics, ColorFunction is used only with the option setting Lighting -> False. ■ See page 406. ■ See also: Lighting, ColorOutput.

■ **ColorOutput**

ColorOutput is an option for graphics functions which specifies the type of color output to produce.

Possible settings are:

Automatic	use whatever color directives are given
CMYKColor	convert to CMYKColor
GrayLevel	convert to GrayLevel
RGBColor	convert to RGBColor
f	convert using the function *f*

■ *Mathematica* performs color conversions using approximations to typical primary display and printing colors. ■ See page 473.

■ **ColumnForm**

ColumnForm[{e_1, e_2, ... }] prints as a column with e_1 above e_2, etc.

ColumnForm[*list*, *horiz*] specifies the horizontal alignment of each element.

ColumnForm[*list*, *horiz*, *vert*] also specifies the vertical alignment of the whole column.

Possible horizontal alignments are:

Center	centered
Left	left justified (default case)
Right	right justified

■ Possible vertical alignments are:

Above	the bottom element of the column is aligned with the baseline
Below	the top element is aligned with the baseline (default case)
Center	the column is centered on the baseline

■ The first argument of ColumnForm can have any head, not necessarily List. ■ ColumnForm acts as a "wrapper", which affects printing, but not evaluation. ■ See page 361. ■ See also: TableForm, MatrixForm, Subscripted, SequenceForm.

■ **Compile**

Compile[{x_1, x_2, ... }, *expr*] creates a compiled function which evaluates *expr* assuming numerical values of the x_i.

Compile[{{x_1, t_1}, ... }, *expr*] assumes that x_i is of a type which matches t_i.

Compile[*vars*, *expr*, {{p_1, pt_1}, ... }] assumes that subexpressions in *expr* which match p_i are of types which match pt_i.

The types handled by Compile are:

_Integer	machine-size integer
_Real	machine-precision approximate real number (default)
_Complex	machine-precision approximate complex number
True | False	logical variable

■ Compile generates a CompiledFunction object. ■ Compiled code does not handle numerical precision and local variables in the same way as ordinary *Mathematica* code. ■ If a compiled function cannot be evaluated with particular arguments using compiled code, ordinary *Mathematica* code is used instead. ■ Ordinary *Mathematica* code can be called from within compiled code. Results obtained from the *Mathematica* code are assumed to be approximate real numbers, unless specified otherwise by the third argument of Compile. ■ Compile generates compiled code for arithmetic and logical operations, elementary transcendental functions, and basic control structures. ■ The number of times and the order in which objects are evaluated by Compile may be different from ordinary *Mathematica* code. ■ Compile has attribute HoldAll. ■ See page 312. ■ See also: Dispatch, Function, InterpolatingFunction.

■ **Compiled**

Compiled is an option for various numerical and plotting functions which specifies whether the expressions they work with should automatically be compiled.

Compiled -> True automatically creates compiled functions. ■ You should set Compiled -> False if you need to use high-precision numbers. ■ See page 313.

◪ CompiledFunction

CompiledFunction[*args*, *nregs*, *instr*, *func*] represents compiled code for evaluating a compiled function.

args is a list giving a pattern for the type of each argument to the function. The types are specified as in Compile. ▪ *nregs* is a list giving the number of integer, real, complex and logical registers required to evaluate the compiled code. ▪ *instr* is a list of actual compiled code instructions. ▪ *func* is a *Mathematica* pure function to be used if no result can be obtained from the compiled code for any reason. ▪ Compile generates a CompiledFunction object which can be executed by applying it to appropriate arguments. ▪ CompiledFunction objects that are constructed explicitly can also be executed. Basic consistency checks are done when such objects are first evaluated by *Mathematica*. ▪ The code in a CompiledFunction object is based on an idealized register machine. ▪ See page 316.

■ Complement

Complement[*eall*, e_1, e_2, ...] gives the elements in *eall* which are not in any of the e_i.

The list returned by Complement is sorted into standard order. ▪ Example:
Complement[{a,b,c,d,e}, {a,c}, {d}] ⟶ {b, e}. ▪ See page 129. ▪ See also: Intersection, Union.

■ Complex

Complex is the head used for complex numbers.

You can enter a complex number in the form x + I y. ▪ _Complex can be used to stand for a complex number in a pattern. ▪ You have to use Re and Im to extract parts of Complex numbers. ▪ Only the real part is printed in complex numbers of the form x + 0. I. ▪ See page 534. ▪ See also: Real, Re, Im.

◪ ComplexExpand

ComplexExpand[*expr*] expands *expr* assuming that all variables are real.

ComplexExpand[*expr*, {x_1, x_2, ... }] expands *expr* assuming that variables matching any of the x_i are complex.

Example: ComplexExpand[Sin[x + I y]] ⟶ Cosh[y] Sin[x] + I Cos[x] Sinh[y]. ▪ The variables given in the second argument of ComplexExpand can be patterns. ▪ Example:
ComplexExpand[Sin[x], x] ⟶ Cosh[Im[x]] Sin[Re[x]] + I Cos[Re[x]] Sinh[Im[x]]. ▪ The option TargetFunctions can be given as a list of functions from the set {Re, Im, Abs, Arg, Conjugate, Sign}. ComplexExpand will try to give results in terms of functions specified.
▪ ComplexExpand[*expr*, *vars*, TargetFunctions -> {Abs, Arg}] converts to polar coordinates. ▪ See page 604.
▪ See also: GaussianIntegers.

■ ComplexInfinity

ComplexInfinity represents a quantity with infinite magnitude, but undetermined complex phase.

ComplexInfinity is converted to DirectedInfinity[ ]. ▪ In OutputForm, DirectedInfinity[ ] is printed as ComplexInfinity. ▪ See page 548. ▪ See also: Infinity, Indeterminate.

◪ ComposeList

ComposeList[{f_1, f_2, ... }, x] generates a list of the form {x, f_1[x], f_2[f_1[x]], ... }.

Example: ComposeList[{a, b, c}, x] ⟶ {x, a[x], b[a[x]], c[b[a[x]]]}. ▪ See page 210. ▪ See also: NestList, FoldList.

◪ Composition

Composition[f_1, f_2, f_3, ...] represents a composition of the functions $f_1, f_2, f_3, \ldots$.

Composition allows you to build up compositions of functions which can later be applied to specific arguments. ▪ Example: Composition[a, b, c][x] ⟶ a[b[c[x]]]. ▪ Composition objects containing Identity or InverseFunction[*f*] are automatically simplified when possible. ▪ Composition has the attributes Flat and OneIdentity. ▪ *a* @ *b* @ *c* gives *a*[*b*[*c*]]. ▪ *a* // *b* // *c* gives *c*[*b*[*a*]]. ▪ See page 213. ▪ See also: Nest, Function.

■ CompoundExpression

$expr_1$; $expr_2$; ... evaluates the $expr_i$ in turn, giving the last one as the result.

CompoundExpression evaluates its arguments in a sequence corresponding to the control flow. ▪ The returned value can be the result of Return[*expr*]. ▪ The evaluation of the $expr_i$ can be affected by Return, Throw and Goto. ▪ $expr_1$; $expr_2$; returns value Null. If it is given as input, the resulting output will not be printed. Out[*n*] will nevertheless be assigned to be the value of $expr_2$. ▪ See pages 59 and 718. ▪ See also: Block.

■ Condition

patt /; *test* is a pattern which matches only if the evaluation of *test* yields True.

lhs :> *rhs* /; *test* represents a rule which applies only if the evaluation of *test* yields True.

lhs := *rhs* /; *test* is a definition to be used only if *test* yields True.

Example: The pattern x_ /; x > 0 represents an expression which must be positive. ▪ All pattern variables used in *test* must also appear in *patt*. ▪ Example: f[x_] := fp[x] /; x > 1 defines a function in the case when x > 1. ▪ *lhs* := Module[{*vars*}, *rhs* /; *test*] allows local variables to be shared between *test* and *rhs*. You can use the same construction with Block and With. ▪ See pages 224 and 287. ▪ See also: If, Switch, Which, PatternTest.

■ Conjugate

Conjugate[z] gives the complex conjugate z^* of the complex number z.

Mathematical function (see Section A.3.9). ▪ See page 551.

■ Constant

Constant is an attribute which indicates zero derivative of a symbol with respect to all parameters.

Constant is used by Dt. ▪ Functions *f*[...] are taken to have zero total derivative if *f* has attribute Constant. ▪ Mathematical constants such as Pi have attribute Constant. ▪ See pages 272 and 625.

■ Constants

Constants is an option for Dt which gives a list of objects to be taken as constants.

If *f* appears in the list of Constants, then both Dt[*f*] and Dt[*f*[...]] are taken to be zero. ▪ See page 625. ▪ See also: D.

◨ ConstrainedMax

`ConstrainedMax[f, {inequalities}, {x, y, ... }]` finds the global maximum of f in the domain specified by the inequalities. The variables $x, y, ...$ are all assumed to be non-negative.

`ConstrainedMax` returns a list of the form $\{f_{max}, \{x\text{->}x_{max}, y\text{->}y_{max}, ... \}\}$, where f_{max} is the maximum value of f in the specified domain, and $x_{max}, y_{max}, ...$ give the point at which the maximum is attained. ▪ `ConstrainedMax` implements linear programming. It can always get a result so long as f and the inequalities you specify depend only linearly on the variables $x, y, ...$. The inequalities can contain no parameters other than the explicit variables you specify. The inequalities cannot involve complex numbers. ▪ `ConstrainedMax` returns unevaluated if the inequalities are inconsistent. ▪ `ConstrainedMax` returns an infinite result if the value of f is unbounded in the domain specified by the inequalities. ▪ `ConstrainedMax` yields exact rational number results if f and the inequalities are specified exactly. ▪ `ConstrainedMax` accepts both strict inequalities of the form *lhs* `<` *rhs*, and non-strict ones of the form *lhs* `<=` *rhs*. It also accepts equalities of the form *lhs* `==` *rhs*. ▪ When `ConstrainedMax` returns rational number results, it assumes that all inequalities are not strict. Thus, for example, `ConstrainedMax` may return `x->1/2`, even though strict inequalities allow only $\frac{1}{2} - \epsilon$. ▪ `ConstrainedMax` finds approximate numerical results if its input contains approximate numbers. The option `Tolerance` specifies the tolerance to be used for internal comparisons. The default is `Tolerance->Automatic`, which does exact comparisons for exact numbers, and uses tolerance 10^{-6} for approximate numbers. ▪ See page 705. ▪ See also: `LinearProgramming`, `FindMinimum`.

◨ ConstrainedMin

`ConstrainedMin[f, {inequalities}, {x, y, ... }]` finds the global minimum of f in the domain specified by the inequalities. The variables $x, y, ...$ are all assumed to be non-negative.

See notes for `ConstrainedMax`. ▪ See page 705.

◼ Context

`Context[ ]` gives the current context.

`Context[symbol]` gives the context in which a symbol appears.

The current context is the value of `$Context`. ▪ See page 334. ▪ See also: `Begin`, `$ContextPath`, `Remove`.

◨ Contexts

`Contexts[ ]` gives a list of all contexts.

`Contexts["string"]` gives a list of the contexts which match the string.

The string can contain metacharacters such as `*` and `@`, as described on page 728. ▪ See pages 334 and 385. ▪ See also: `$Packages`, `$ContextPath`.

◨ ContextToFilename

`ContextToFilename["context`"]` gives the string specifying the file name that is by convention associated with a particular context.

`Needs` uses `ContextToFilename` to determine the name of the file to get in order to define objects in the specified context. ▪ The built-in action of `ContextToFilename` differs from one computer type to another, reflecting differences in file naming mechanisms. ▪ On Unix systems, `ContextToFilename["aaa`bbb`"]` is usually set up to give the file name *aaa/bbb*.m. ▪ You can define rules for `ContextToFilename` in order to specify different translations for particular contexts. ▪ See page 492.

◼ Continuation

`Continuation[n]` is output at the beginning of the nth line in a multiline printed expression.

Redefining `Format[Continuation[n_]]` changes the way continuation lines are printed. ▪ See page 517. ▪ See also: `StringBreak`, `LineBreak`, `Indent`.

■ **Continue**

Continue[ ] exits to the nearest enclosing Do, For or While in a procedural program.

Continue is effective only if it is generated as the value of a segment in a semicolon-delimited compound expression, or as the body of a control structure. ■ See page 293. ■ See also: Break.

■ **ContourGraphics**

ContourGraphics[*array*] is a representation of a contour plot.

array must be a rectangular array of real numbers, representing *z* values. ■ The following options can be given:

AspectRatio	1	ratio of height to width
Axes	False	whether to draw axes
AxesLabel	None	axes labels
AxesOrigin	Automatic	where axes should cross
AxesStyle	{}	graphics directives to specify the style for axes
Background	Automatic	background color for the plot
ColorFunction	Automatic	function specifying the color of regions between contour lines
ColorOutput	Automatic	type of color output to produce
ContourLines	True	whether to draw explicit contour lines
Contours	10	what contours to use
ContourShading	True	whether to shade the regions between contours
ContourSmoothing	None	how to smooth contour lines
ContourStyle	Automatic	the style for contour lines
DefaultColor	Automatic	the default color for plot elements
DefaultFont	$DefaultFont	the default font for text
DisplayFunction	$DisplayFunction	function for generating output
Epilog	{}	graphics primitives to be rendered after the main plot
Frame	True	whether to put a frame around the plot
FrameLabel	None	frame labels
FrameStyle	Automatic	graphics directives giving the style for the frame
FrameTicks	Automatic	frame tick marks
MeshRange	Automatic	ranges of *x* and *y* coordinates
PlotLabel	None	a label for the plot
PlotRange	Automatic	range of *z* values to include
PlotRegion	Automatic	the final display region to be filled
Prolog	{}	graphics primitives to be rendered before the main plot
RotateLabel	True	whether to rotate *y* labels on the frame
Ticks	Automatic	tick marks

■ ContourGraphics[*g*] converts DensityGraphics and SurfaceGraphics objects to ContourGraphics. The resulting graphics can be rendered using Show. ■ ContourGraphics is generated by ContourPlot and ListContourPlot. ■ See page 425. ■ See also: ListContourPlot, DensityGraphics.

◪ **ContourLines**

ContourLines is an option for contour plots which specifies whether to draw explicit contour lines.

ContourLines -> True draws contour lines. ContourLines -> False does not. ■ See page 427. ■ See also: ContourStyle, Contours, ContourSmoothing.

■ ContourPlot

ContourPlot[*f*, {*x*, *xmin*, *xmax*}, {*y*, *ymin*, *ymax*}] generates a contour plot of *f* as a function of *x* and *y*.

ContourPlot evaluates its arguments in a non-standard way (see page 730). You should use Evaluate to evaluate the function to be plotted if this can safely be done before specific numerical values are supplied. ■ ContourPlot has the same options as ContourGraphics, with the following additions:

| Compiled | True | whether to compile the function to plot |
| PlotPoints | 15 | the number of points in each direction at which to sample the function |

■ ContourPlot has the default option setting Frame -> True. ■ ContourPlot returns a ContourGraphics object, with the MeshRange option set. ■ See page 151. ■ See also: DensityPlot.

■ Contours

Contours is an option for ContourGraphics specifying the contours to use.

Contours -> *n* chooses *n* equally spaced contours between the minimum and maximum *z* values. ■ Contours -> {z_1, z_2, ... } specifies the explicit *z* values of contours to use. ■ See pages 152 and 427.

■ ContourShading

ContourShading is an option for contour plots which specifies whether the regions between contour lines should be shaded.

With ContourShading -> False, regions between contour lines are left blank. ■ With ContourShading -> True, regions are colored based on the setting for the option ColorFunction. The default is to color the regions with gray levels running from black to white with increasing height. ■ The value given as the argument for the ColorFunction function is the average of the values of the contour lines bounding a particular region, scaled so that it lies between 0 and 1. ■ See page 427.

■ ContourSmoothing

ContourSmoothing is an option for contour plots which specifies how contour lines should be smoothed.

ContourSmoothing -> None specifies that no smoothing should be done, and each contour line should consist of straight segments between successive grid lines. ■ ContourSmoothing -> *n* specifies that contour lines should be found by dividing each grid square *n* times in each direction. ■ The amount of PostScript code generated from a particular contour plot increases rapidly as the setting for ContourSmoothing increases. ■ ContourSmoothing -> Automatic is equivalent to ContourSmoothing -> 4. ■ See pages 427 and 429.

■ ContourStyle

ContourStyle is an option for contour plots that specifies the style in which contour lines should be drawn.

ContourStyle -> *style* specifies that all contour lines are to be generated with the specified graphics directive, or list of graphics directives. ■ ContourStyle -> {{$style_1$}, {$style_2$}, ... } specifies that successive contour lines should use graphics directives $style_1$, ... The styles must be enclosed in lists, perhaps of length one. ■ The $style_i$ are used cyclically. ■ Styles can be specified using graphics directives such as Dashing, Hue and Thickness. ■ See page 427. ■ See also: PlotStyle.

◪ CopyDirectory

CopyDirectory["*dir₁*", "*dir₂*"] copies the directory *dir₁* to *dir₂*.

dir₁ must already exist; *dir₂* must not. ■ CopyDirectory copies all the files in *dir₁* to *dir₂*. ■ CopyDirectory sets the modification dates for *dir₂* and for all the files in it to be the same as those for *dir₁*. ■ CopyDirectory returns the full name of the directory it copies to, and $Failed if it cannot complete the copy. ■ See page 493. ■ See also: RenameDirectory, CreateDirectory, DeleteDirectory.

◪ CopyFile

CopyFile["*file₁*", "*file₂*"] copies *file₁* to *file₂*.

file₁ must already exist; *file₂* must not. ■ CopyFile sets the modification date for *file₂* to be the same as for *file₁*. ■ CopyFile returns the full name of the file it copies to, and $Failed if it cannot do the copy. ■ See page 492. ■ See also: RenameFile, DeleteFile, CopyDirectory.

■ Cos

Cos[z] gives the cosine of *z*.

Mathematical function (see Section A.3.9). ■ The argument of Cos is assumed to be in radians. (Multiply by Degree to convert from degrees.) ■ See page 562. ■ See also: ArcCos, Sec.

■ Cosh

Cosh[z] gives the hyperbolic cosine of *z*.

Mathematical function (see Section A.3.9). ■ $\cosh(z) = \frac{1}{2}(e^z + e^{-z})$. ■ See page 562. ■ See also: ArcCosh, Sech.

◪ CosIntegral

CosIntegral[z] gives the cosine integral function Ci(*z*).

Mathematical function (see Section A.3.9). ■ $\text{Ci}(z) = -\int_z^\infty \frac{\cos(t)}{t}\,dt$. ■ See page 570. ■ See also: SinIntegral, ExpIntegralE, ExpIntegralEi.

■ Cot

Cot[z] gives the cotangent of *z*.

Mathematical function (see Section A.3.9). ■ The argument of Cot is assumed to be in radians. (Multiply by Degree to convert from degrees.) ■ $\cot(z) = \frac{1}{\tan(z)}$. ■ See page 562. ■ See also: ArcCot.

■ Coth

Coth[z] gives the hyperbolic cotangent of *z*.

Mathematical function (see Section A.3.9). ■ See page 562. ■ See also: ArcCoth.

■ Count

Count[*list*, *pattern*] gives the number of elements in *list* that match *pattern*.

Count[*expr*, *pattern*, *levelspec*] gives the total number of subexpressions matching *pattern* that appear at the levels in *expr* specified by *levelspec*.

Level specifications are described on page 725. ■ See page 221. ■ See also: FreeQ, MemberQ, Cases, Select, Position.

▰ CreateDirectory

CreateDirectory["*dir*"] creates a directory.

CreateDirectory creates a subdirectory of your current working directory. ▪ The directory created by CreateDirectory is initially empty. ▪ CreateDirectory returns the full name of the directory it creates, and $Failed if it cannot create the directory. ▪ See page 493. ▪ See also: DeleteDirectory, RenameDirectory, CopyDirectory.

▪ Csc

Csc[*z*] gives the cosecant of *z*.

Mathematical function (see Section A.3.9). ▪ The argument of Csc is assumed to be in radians. (Multiply by Degree to convert from degrees.) ▪ $\csc(z) = \frac{1}{\sin(z)}$. ▪ See page 562. ▪ See also: ArcCsc.

▪ Csch

Csch[*z*] gives the hyperbolic cosecant of *z*.

Mathematical function (see Section A.3.9). ▪ $\operatorname{csch}(z) = \frac{1}{\sinh(z)}$. ▪ See page 562. ▪ See also: ArcCsch.

▪ Cubics

Cubics is an option for Roots and related functions which specifies whether explicit solutions should be generated for irreducible cubic equations.

Cubics->False causes irreducible cubics to be left unsolved in their original symbolic form. Numerical solutions can be found by applying N. ▪ Setting Cubics->True causes explicit solutions to be generated. These solutions are usually very complicated. ▪ See also: Quartics, NSolve.

▰ Cuboid

Cuboid[{*xmin*, *ymin*, *zmin*}] is a three-dimensional graphics primitive that represents a unit cuboid, oriented parallel to the axes.

Cuboid[{*xmin*, *ymin*, *zmin*}, {*xmax*, *ymax*, *zmax*}] specifies a cuboid by giving the coordinates of opposite corners.

Each face of the cuboid (rectangular parallelepiped) is effectively a Polygon object. ▪ You can specify how the faces and edges of the cuboid should be rendered using the same graphics directives as for polygons. ▪ The coordinates of the corners of the cuboid can be given using Scaled. ▪ See page 430. ▪ See also: Polygon, Rectangle.

▪ Cyclotomic

Cyclotomic[*n*, *x*] gives the cyclotomic polynomial of order *n* in *x*.

The cyclotomic polynomial $C_n(x)$ of order n is defined to be $\prod_k (x - e^{2\pi i k/n})$, where the product runs over integers k less than n that are relatively prime to n. ▪ See page 601. ▪ See also: Factor.

■ D

$D[f, x]$ gives the partial derivative $\frac{\partial}{\partial x}f$.

$D[f, \{x, n\}]$ gives the multiple derivative $\frac{\partial^n}{\partial x^n}f$.

$D[f, x_1, x_2, \ldots]$ gives $\frac{\partial}{\partial x_1}\frac{\partial}{\partial x_2}\ldots f$.

All quantities that do not explicitly depend on the x_i are taken to have zero partial derivative.
■ $D[f, x_1, \ldots, \text{NonConstants} \rightarrow \{v_1, \ldots\}]$ specifies that the v_i implicitly depend on the x_i, so that they do not have zero partial derivative. ■ The derivatives of built-in mathematical functions are evaluated when possible in terms of other built-in mathematical functions. ■ D uses the chain rule to simplify derivatives of unknown functions. ■ See page 624. ■ See also: Dt, Derivative.

■ Dashing

$\text{Dashing}[\{r_1, r_2, \ldots\}]$ is a two-dimensional graphics directive which specifies that lines which follow are to be drawn dashed, with successive segments of lengths $r_1, r_2, \ldots$ (repeated cyclically). The r_i is given as a fraction of the total width of the graph.

Dashing can be used in both two- and three-dimensional graphics. ■ Dashing[{ }] specifies that lines should be solid. ■ See page 409. ■ See also: AbsoluteDashing, Thickness, GrayLevel, Hue, RGBColor.

◪ Date

Date[ ] gives the current local date and time in the form
{*year*, *month*, *day*, *hour*, *minute*, *second*}.

Date[ ] uses whatever date and time have been set on your computer system. It performs no corrections for time zones, daylight saving time, etc. ■ Date[z] gives the date in time zone z. This is inferred by knowing your local date and time, and local time zone. The time zone is given as the number of hours to be added to Greenwich mean time to obtain local time. ■ All values returned by Date[ ] are integers, except the number of seconds. The number of seconds is never more accurate than $TimeUnit. ■ You can compare two lists returned by Date using Order. ■ See page 523.
■ See also: AbsoluteTime, TimeZone, SessionTime, TimeUsed, ToDate, FromDate, FileDate, $CreationDate.

◪ DeclarePackage

DeclarePackage["*context*`", {"*name*₁", "*name*₂", … }] declares that Needs["*context*`"] should automatically be executed if a symbol with any of the specified names is ever used.

You can use DeclarePackage to tell *Mathematica* automatically to load a particular package when any of the symbols defined in it are used. ■ DeclarePackage creates symbols with the attribute Stub in the specified context.
■ DeclarePackage prepends *context*` to $ContextPath. ■ See page 342. ■ See also: Needs, $NewSymbol.

■ Decompose

Decompose[*poly*, x] decomposes a polynomial, if possible, into a composition of simpler polynomials.

Decompose gives a list of the polynomials P_i which can be composed as $P_1(P_2(\ldots(x)\ldots))$ to give the original polynomial.
■ The set of polynomials P_i is not necessarily unique. ■ Decomposition is an operation which is independent of polynomial factorization. ■ See page 601. ■ See also: FactorList, Solve.

■ Decrement

x-- decreases the value of x by 1, returning the old value of x.

Decrement has attribute HoldFirst. ■ See page 248. ■ See also: PreDecrement, SubtractFrom, Set.

■ Default

Default[*f*], if defined, gives the default value for arguments of the function *f* obtained with a _. pattern object.

Default[*f*, *i*] gives the default value to use when _. appears as the *i*th argument of *f*.

Default[*f*, *i*, *n*] gives the default value for the *i*th argument out of a total of *n* arguments.

_. represents an optional argument to a function, with a default value specified by Default. ■ The necessary values for Default[*f*] must always be defined before _. is used as an argument of *f*. ■ Values defined for Default[*f*] are stored with the Options values of *f*. ■ See page 734. ■ See also: Options.

■ DefaultColor

DefaultColor is an option for graphics functions which specifies the default color to use for lines, points, etc.

The setting for DefaultColor must be a CMYKColor, GrayLevel, Hue or RGBColor directive. ■ The default setting is DefaultColor->Automatic, which gives a default color complementary to the background specified. ■ See page 412. ■ See also: Prolog, Background.

■ DefaultFont

DefaultFont is an option for graphics functions which specifies the default font to use for text.

DefaultFont -> {"*font*", *size*} specifies the name and size of the font to use. ■ The font is used by default for all text, including labels and tick marks. ■ See notes for FontForm. ■ The default setting is DefaultFont :> $DefaultFont. ■ See page 467.

■ Definition

Definition[*s₁*, *s₂*, ...] prints as the definitions given for the symbols *sᵢ*.

Definition has attribute HoldAll. ■ Definition[*s₁*, ...] prints as all values and attributes defined for the symbols *sᵢ*. ■ ?*s* uses Definition. ■ See page 479. ■ See also: FullDefinition, Information.

■ Degree

Degree gives the number of radians in one degree. It has a numerical value of $\frac{\pi}{180}$.

You can multiply by Degree to convert from degrees to radians. ■ Example: 30 Degree represents 30°. ■ See page 566.

■ Delete

Delete[*expr*, *n*] deletes the element at position *n* in *expr*. If *n* is negative, the position is counted from the end.

Delete[*expr*, {*i*, *j*, ... }] deletes the part at position {*i*, *j*, ... }.

Delete[*expr*, {{*i₁*, *j₁*, ... }, {*i₂*, *j₂*, ... }, ... }] deletes parts at several positions.

Example: Delete[{a, b, c, d}, 3] ⟶ {a, b, d}. ■ Delete[{a, b, c, d}, {{1}, {3}}] ⟶ {b, d}. ■ Deleting the head of a particular element in an expression is equivalent to applying FlattenAt to the expression at that point. ■ Example: Delete[{a, {b}, c}, {2, 0}] ⟶ {a, b, c}. ■ See page 128. ■ See also: Insert, MapAt, ReplacePart, FlattenAt, DeleteCases.

◪ DeleteCases

DeleteCases[*expr*, *pattern*] removes all elements of *expr* which match *pattern*.

DeleteCases[*expr*, *pattern*, *levspec*] removes all parts of *expr* on levels specified by *levspec* which match *pattern*.

Example: DeleteCases[{1, a, 2, b}, _Integer] ⟶ {a, b}. ▪ With the option Heads -> True, you can delete heads with DeleteCases. Deleting the head of a particular element in an expression is equivalent to applying FlattenAt to the expression at that point. ▪ Example: DeleteCases[{1, f[2, 3], 4}, f, {2}, Heads -> True] ⟶ {1, 2, 3, 4}. ▪ Level specifications are described on page 725. ▪ See page 222. ▪ See also: Cases, ReplaceAll, Delete.

◪ DeleteDirectory

DeleteDirectory["*dir*"] deletes the specified directory.

DeleteDirectory["*dir*", DeleteContents -> True] deletes *dir* and all files and directories that it contains. ▪ DeleteDirectory["*dir*"] deletes the directory *dir* only if it contains no files. ▪ DeleteDirectory returns Null if it succeeds in deleting a directory, and $Failed if it fails. ▪ See page 493. ▪ See also: CreateDirectory, DeleteFile.

◪ DeleteFile

DeleteFile["*file*"] deletes a file.

DeleteFile[{"*file$_1$*", "*file$_2$*", ... }] deletes a list of files.

DeleteFile returns Null if it succeeds in deleting files, and $Failed if it fails. ▪ See page 492. ▪ See also: RenameFile, DeleteDirectory.

◼ Denominator

Denominator[*expr*] gives the denominator of *expr*.

Denominator picks out terms which have superficially negative exponents. Numerator picks out all remaining terms. ▪ An exponent is "superficially negative" if it has a negative number as a factor. ▪ The standard representation of rational expressions as products of powers means that you cannot simply use Part to extract denominators. ▪ Denominator can be used on rational numbers. ▪ See page 82. ▪ See also: ExpandDenominator.

■ **DensityGraphics**

DensityGraphics[*array*] is a representation of a density plot.

array must be a rectangular array of real numbers, representing z values. ■ The following options can be given:

AspectRatio	1	ratio of height to width
Axes	False	whether to draw axes
AxesLabel	None	axes labels
AxesOrigin	Automatic	where axes should cross
AxesStyle	Automatic	graphics directives to specify the style for axes
Background	Automatic	background color for the plot
ColorFunction	Automatic	function specifying the color for each cell
ColorOutput	Automatic	type of color output to produce
DefaultColor	Automatic	the default color for plot elements
DefaultFont	$DefaultFont	the default font for text
DisplayFunction	$DisplayFunction	function for generating output
Epilog	{}	graphics primitives to be rendered after the main plot
Frame	True	whether to put a frame around the plot
FrameLabel	None	frame labels
FrameStyle	Automatic	graphics directives giving the style for the frame
FrameTicks	Automatic	frame tick marks
Mesh	True	whether to draw a mesh
MeshRange	Automatic	ranges of x and y coordinates
MeshStyle	Automatic	graphics directives to specify the style for mesh lines
PlotLabel	None	a label for the plot
PlotRange	Automatic	range of z values to include
PlotRegion	Automatic	the final display region to be filled
Prolog	{}	graphics primitives to be rendered before the main plot
RotateLabel	True	whether to rotate y labels on the frame
Ticks	Automatic	tick marks

■ DensityGraphics can be displayed using Show. ■ DensityGraphics is generated by DensityPlot and ListDensityPlot. ■ DensityGraphics[*g*] converts ContourGraphics and SurfaceGraphics objects to DensityGraphics. The resulting graphics can be rendered using Show. ■ See page 425. ■ See also: ListDensityPlot, ContourGraphics, Raster, RasterArray.

■ **DensityPlot**

DensityPlot[*f*, {*x*, *xmin*, *xmax*}, {*y*, *ymin*, *ymax*}] makes a density plot of *f* as a function of *x* and *y*.

DensityPlot evaluates its arguments in a non-standard way (see page 730). You should use Evaluate to evaluate the function to be plotted if this can safely be done before specific numerical values are supplied. ■ DensityPlot has the same options as DensityGraphics, with the following additions:

Compiled	True	whether to compile the function to plot
PlotPoints	15	the number of points in each direction at which to sample the function

■ DensityPlot has the default option setting Frame -> True. ■ DensityPlot returns a DensityGraphics object, with the MeshRange option set. ■ See page 151. ■ See also: ContourPlot.

■ **Depth**

Depth[*expr*] gives the maximum number of indices needed to specify any part of *expr*, plus one.

Raw objects have depth 1. ■ The computation of Depth does not include heads of expressions. ■ See page 199. ■ See also: TensorRank, Level, LeafCount, Length, Nest.

■ **Derivative**

f′ represents the derivative of a function *f* of one argument.

Derivative[n_1, n_2, ...][*f*] is the general form, representing a function obtained from *f* by differentiating n_1 times with respect to the first argument, n_2 times with respect to the second argument, and so on.

f′ is equivalent to Derivative[1][*f*]. ■ *f′′* evaluates to Derivative[2][*f*]. ■ You can think of Derivative as a *functional operator* which acts on functions to give derivative functions. ■ Derivative is generated when you apply D to functions whose derivatives *Mathematica* does not know. ■ *Mathematica* attempts to convert Derivative[*n*][*f*] and so on to pure functions. Whenever Derivative[*n*][*f*] is generated, *Mathematica* rewrites it as D[*f*[#]&, {#, *n*}]. If *Mathematica* finds an explicit value for this derivative, it returns this value. Otherwise, it returns the original Derivative form. ■ Example: Cos′ ⟶ -Sin[#1] &. ■ See page 627. ■ See also: D, Dt.

■ **Det**

Det[*m*] gives the determinant of the square matrix *m*.

Det[*m*, Modulus->*p*] computes the determinant modulo *p*. ■ See page 657. ■ See also: Minors, RowReduce, NullSpace.

■ **DiagonalMatrix**

DiagonalMatrix[*list*] gives a matrix with the elements of *list* on the leading diagonal, and 0 elsewhere.

See page 649. ■ See also: IdentityMatrix.

◪ **Dialog**

Dialog[ ] initiates a dialog.

Dialog[*expr*] initiates a dialog with *expr* as the current value of %.

Dialog creates a dialog which consists of a sequence of input and output lines. ■ You can exit a dialog using Return. ■ With the global setting $IgnoreEOF = False, you can also exit a dialog by entering an end-of-file character. ■ If you exit with Return[*expr*], then *expr* is the value returned by the Dialog function. Otherwise, the value returned is the expression on the last output line in the dialog. ■ Dialog automatically localizes the values of $Line, $MessageList and $Epilog. ■ Dialog initially sets the local value of $Line to be equal to its global value. This means that the numbering of input and output lines in the dialog follows the sequence outside the dialog. When the dialog is exited, however, the numbering reverts to the sequence that would be followed if there had been no dialog. ■ Within a dialog, input and output lines are indented by printing the output form of DialogIndent[*d*] before each In[*n*] or Out[*n*]. *d* is the nesting level of the dialog. ■ Any local value assigned to $Epilog is evaluated when the dialog is exited. ■ The main loop within a dialog uses global variables such as $Pre and $Post. ■ The option DialogSymbols :> {*x*, *y*, ... } sets up local values for variables within the dialog. DialogSymbols :> {*x* = x_0, ... } defines initial values for the variables. ■ The option DialogProlog :> *expr* specifies an expression to evaluate before starting the dialog. ■ Dialog first localizes variables, then evaluates any expression specified by DialogProlog, then evaluates any argument you have given for Dialog. ■ See page 520. ■ See also: TraceDialog, Input, $Inspector.

■ **DialogIndent**

DialogIndent [*d*] is printed as the indentation for input and output lines in a depth *d* dialog.

You can redefine DialogIndent [*d*] to change indentation in dialogs. ▪ See page 517. ▪ See also: Indent.

■ **DialogProlog**

DialogProlog is an option for Dialog which can give an expression to evaluate before the dialog starts.

You must use a delayed rule of the form DialogProlog :> *expr* to prevent *expr* from evaluating prematurely. ▪ Expressions given by DialogProlog are evaluated after symbol values are localized, and before any expression given as the argument of Dialog is evaluated. ▪ See page 522. ▪ See also: $Epilog.

■ **DialogSymbols**

DialogSymbols is an option for Dialog which gives a list of symbols whose values should be localized in the dialog.

DialogSymbols :> {*x*, *y*, ... } specifies that *x*, *y*, ... should have local values for the duration of the dialog. ▪ DialogSymbols :> {*x* = x_0, ... } defines initial values for variables. ▪ In addition to any symbols you specify, Dialog always uses local values for $Epilog, $Line and $MessageList. ▪ The DialogSymbols option sets up local values in a dialog in the same way that a Block enclosing the dialog would. ▪ See page 522.

■ **DigitBlock**

DigitBlock is an option for NumberForm and related functions which specifies the maximum length of blocks of digits between breaks.

The default setting is DigitBlock -> Infinity, which specifies that no breaks should be inserted. ▪ DigitBlock -> *n* inserts a break every *n* digits. ▪ DigitBlock -> {*nleft*, *nright*} inserts a break every *nleft* digits to the left of the decimal point, and every *nright* digits to the right of the decimal point. ▪ The setting for NumberSeparator determines what string should be used at each break. ▪ See page 351.

■ **DigitQ**

DigitQ [*string*] yields True if all the characters in the string are digits in the range 0 through 9, and yields False otherwise.

See page 378. ▪ See also: LetterQ, Number.

■ **Dimensions**

Dimensions [*expr*] gives a list of the dimensions of *expr*.

Dimensions [*expr*, *n*] gives a list of the dimensions of *expr* down to level *n*.

expr must be a *full array*, with all the pieces of *expr* at a particular level having the same length. (The elements of *expr* can then be thought of as filling up a hyper-rectangular region.) ▪ Each successive level in *expr* sampled by Dimensions must have the same head. ▪ Example: Dimensions[{{a,b,c},{d,e,f}}] ⟶ {2, 3}. ▪ See page 652. ▪ See also: TensorRank, VectorQ, MatrixQ.

■ **DirectedInfinity**

> DirectedInfinity[ ] represents an infinite numerical quantity whose direction in the complex plane is unknown.
>
> DirectedInfinity[z] represents an infinite numerical quantity that is a positive real multiple of the complex number z.
>
> You can think of DirectedInfinity[z] as representing a point in the complex plane reached by starting at the origin and going an infinite distance in the direction of the point z. ▪ The following conversions are made:
>
> Infinity   DirectedInfinity[1]
> -Infinity   DirectedInfinity[-1]
> ComplexInfinity   DirectedInfinity[ ]
>
> ▪ Certain arithmetic operations are performed on DirectedInfinity quantities. ▪ In OutputForm, DirectedInfinity[z] is printed in terms of Infinity, and DirectedInfinity[ ] is printed as ComplexInfinity. ▪ See page 548. ▪ See also: Indeterminate.

■ **Directory**

> Directory[ ] gives the current working directory.
>
> Directory returns the full name of the directory as a string. ▪ See page 489. ▪ See also: $Path, SetDirectory, ResetDirectory, ParentDirectory, HomeDirectory, FileNames.

■ **DirectoryStack**

> DirectoryStack[ ] gives the directory stack which represents the sequence of current directories used.
>
> DirectoryStack[ ] returns a list of full names of directories. ▪ Each call to SetDirectory appends one element to the directory stack; each call to ResetDirectory removes one. ▪ See page 489.

■ **Disk**

> Disk[{x, y}, r] is a two-dimensional graphics primitive that represents a filled disk of radius r centered at the point x, y.
>
> Disk[{x, y}, {r_x, r_y}] yields an elliptical disk with semi-axes r_x and r_y.
>
> Disk[{x, y}, r, {$theta_1$, $theta_2$}] represents a segment of a disk.
>
> Angles are measured in radians counter-clockwise from the positive x direction. ▪ Scaled can be used in the radius specification (see notes for Circle). ▪ See page 404. ▪ See also: Circle, Polygon.

■ **Dispatch**

> Dispatch[{lhs_1 ->rhs_1, lhs_2 ->rhs_2, ... }] generates an optimized dispatch table representation of a list of rules. The object produced by Dispatch can be used to give the rules in *expr* /. *rules*.
>
> The use of Dispatch will never affect results that are obtained, but may make the application of long lists of rules much faster. ▪ Lists of rules are usually scanned sequentially when you evaluate an expression like *expr* /. *rules*. Rules such as a[1]->a1 and a[2]->a2, which cannot simultaneously apply, need not both be scanned explicitly. Dispatch generates a dispatch table which uses hash codes to specify which sets of rules need actually be scanned for a particular input expression. ▪ Lists of rules produced by assignments made with = and := are automatically optimized with dispatch tables when appropriate. ▪ See page 246. ▪ See also: ReplaceAll, Compile.

■ **Display**

Display[*channel*, *graphics*] writes graphics or sound to the specified output channel.

The output channel can be a single file or pipe, or a list of them. ■ Display writes graphics in PostScript form. ■ The *graphics* in Display can be Graphics, Graphics3D, SurfaceGraphics, ContourGraphics, DensityGraphics or GraphicsArray. ■ The *graphics* can also include Sound. ■ The PostScript produced by Display does not include initialization or termination commands, nor does it include text font definitions. ■ $DisplayFunction is usually given in terms of Display. ■ If any of the specified files or pipes in *channel* are not open, Display uses OpenWrite to open them, then closes these particular files or pipes when it has finished. ■ The option StringConversion can be given to specify a function used to convert strings containing special characters that appear in Text objects. ■ See page 465. ■ See also: Write, Show.

■ **DisplayFunction**

DisplayFunction is an option for graphics and sound functions that specifies the function to apply to graphics and sound primitives in order to display them.

The default setting for DisplayFunction in graphics functions is $DisplayFunction, and in sound functions is $SoundDisplayFunction. ■ A typical setting is DisplayFunction->Display[*channel*, #]&. ■ Setting DisplayFunction->Identity will cause the primitives to be returned, but no display to be generated. ■ See page 464. ■ See also: Show.

■ **Distribute**

Distribute[*f*[x_1, x_2, ...]] distributes *f* over Plus appearing in any of the x_i.

Distribute[*expr*, *g*] distributes over *g*.

Distribute[*expr*, *g*, *f*] performs the distribution only if the head of *expr* is *f*.

Distribute effectively implements the distributive law for operators *f* and *g*. ■ Distribute explicitly constructs the complete result of a distribution; Expand, on the other hand, builds up results iteratively, simplifying at each stage. ■ Example: Distribute[f[a+b,c+d]] ⟶ f[a, c] + f[a, d] + f[b, c] + f[b, d]. ■ Distribute[f[a+b,g[x,y],c], g] ⟶ g[f[a + b, x, c], f[a + b, y, c]]. ■ Distribute[*expr*, *g*, *f*, *gp*, *fp*] gives *gp* and *fp* in place of *g* and *f* respectively in the result of the distribution. ■ See page 216. ■ See also: Expand, Thread.

■ **Divide**

x/*y* or Divide[*x*, *y*] is equivalent to *x* *y*∧-1.

x/*y* is converted to *x* *y*∧-1 on input. ■ See page 47.

■ **DivideBy**

x /= *c* divides *x* by *c* and returns the new value of *x*.

DivideBy has the attribute HoldFirst. ■ *x* /= *c* is equivalent to *x* = *x*/*c*. ■ See page 248. ■ See also: TimesBy, SubtractFrom, Set.

■ **Divisors**

Divisors[*n*] gives a list of the integers that divide *n*.

Example: Divisors[12] ⟶ {1, 2, 3, 4, 6, 12}. ■ Divisors[*n*, GaussianIntegers -> True] includes divisors that are Gaussian integers. ■ See page 554. ■ See also: FactorInteger.

■ DivisorSigma

DivisorSigma[k, n] gives the divisor function $\sigma_k(n)$.

Integer mathematical function (see Section A.3.9). ■ $\sigma_k(n)$ is the sum of the kth powers of the divisors of n. ■ DivisorSigma[k, n, GaussianIntegers -> True] includes divisors that are Gaussian integers. ■ See page 556. ■ See also: EulerPhi.

■ Do

Do[*expr*, {*imax*}] evaluates *expr imax* times.

Do[*expr*, {*i*, *imax*}] evaluates *expr* with the variable *i* successively taking on the values 1 through *imax* (in steps of 1).

Do[*expr*, {*i*, *imin*, *imax*}] starts with *i* = *imin*. Do[*expr*, {*i*, *imin*, *imax*, *di*}] uses steps *di*.

Do[*expr*, {*i*, *imin*, *imax*}, {*j*, *jmin*, *jmax*}, ...] evaluates *expr* looping over different values of *j*, etc. for each *i*.

Do uses the standard *Mathematica* iteration specification. ■ Do evaluates its arguments in a non-standard way (see page 730). ■ You can use Return, Break, Continue and Throw inside Do. ■ Unless an explicit Return is used, the value returned by Do is Null. ■ See page 290. ■ See also: For, While, Table, Nest, Fold.

■ Dot

a.b.c or Dot[a, b, c] gives products of vectors, matrices and tensors.

a.b gives an explicit result when a and b are lists with appropriate dimensions. It contracts the last direction in a with the first direction in b. ■ Various applications of Dot:

$\{a_1, a_2\}$. $\{b_1, b_2\}$	scalar product of vectors
$\{a_1, a_2\}$. $\{\{m_{11}, m_{12}\}, \{m_{21}, m_{22}\}\}$	product of a vector and a matrix
$\{\{m_{11}, m_{12}\}, \{m_{21}, m_{22}\}\}$. $\{a_1, a_2\}$	product of a matrix and a vector
$\{\{m_{11}, m_{12}\}, \{m_{21}, m_{22}\}\}$. $\{\{n_{11}, n_{12}\}, \{n_{21}, n_{22}\}\}$	product of two matrices

■ Examples: {a, b} . {c, d} $\longrightarrow$ a c + b d. ■ {{a, b}, {c, d}} . {x, y} $\longrightarrow$ {a x + b y, c x + d y}. ■ The result of applying Dot to two tensors $T_{i_1 i_2 \cdots i_n}$ and $U_{j_1 j_2 \cdots j_m}$ is the tensor $\sum_k T_{i_1 i_2 \cdots i_{n-1} k} U_{k j_2 \cdots j_m}$. Dot effectively contracts the last index of the first tensor with the first index of the second tensor. Applying Dot to a rank n tensor and a rank m tensor gives a rank $n + m - 2$ tensor. ■ When its arguments are not lists, Dot remains unevaluated. It has the attribute Flat. ■ See pages 121 and 654. ■ See also: Inner, Outer, NonCommutativeMultiply.

■ DownValues

DownValues[f] gives a list of transformation rules corresponding to all downvalues defined for the symbol f.

You can specify the downvalues for f by making an assignment of the form DownValues[f] = *list*. ■ The list returned by DownValues has elements of the form Literal[*lhs*] :> *rhs*. ■ See page 266. ■ See also: Set, UpValues.

■ Drop

Drop[*list*, n] gives *list* with its first n elements dropped.

Drop[*list*, $-n$] gives *list* with its last n elements dropped.

Drop[*list*, {n}] gives *list* with its nth element dropped.

Drop[*list*, {m, n}] gives *list* with elements m through n dropped.

Drop uses the standard *sequence specification* (see page 724). ■ Example: Drop[{a,b,c,d,e}, 2] $\longrightarrow$ {c, d, e}. ■ Drop[{a,b,c,d,e}, -3] $\longrightarrow$ {a, b}. ■ Drop can be used on an object with any head, not necessarily List. ■ See page 125. ■ See also: Rest, StringDrop, Take, Cases.

◪ DSolve

DSolve[*eqn*, $y[x]$, x] solves a differential equation for the functions $y[x]$, with independent variable x.

DSolve[{*eqn₁*, *eqn₂*, ... }, {$y_1[x_1,$ ...], ... }, {$x_1,$ ... }] solves a list of differential equations.

Examples: DSolve[y'[x] == 2 a x, y[x], x] ⟶ {{y[x] -> a x² + C[1]}}. ■ Differential equations must be stated in terms of derivatives such as $y'[x]$, obtained with D, not total derivatives obtained with Dt. ■ DSolve generates constants of integration indexed by successive integers. The option DSolveConstants specifies the function to apply to each index. The default is DSolveConstants->C, which yields constants of integration C[1], C[2], ... ■ DSolveConstants->(Module[{C}, C]&) guarantees that the constants of integration are unique, even across different invocations of DSolve. ■ Boundary conditions can be specified by giving equations such as y'[0] == b. ■ See page 637. ■ See also: NDSolve, Solve.

■ Dt

Dt[*f*, x] gives the total derivative $\frac{d}{dx} f$.

Dt[*f*] gives the total differential df.

Dt[*f*, {x, n}] gives the multiple derivative $\frac{d^n}{dx^n} f$.

Dt[*f*, x_1, x_2, ...] gives $\frac{d}{dx_1} \frac{d}{dx_2} \ldots f$.

Dt[*f*, x_1, ... , Constants -> {c_1, ... }] specifies that the c_i are constants, which have zero total derivative. ■ Symbols with attribute Constant are taken to be constants, with zero total derivative. ■ If an object is specified to be a constant, then all functions with that object as a head are also taken to be constants. ■ All quantities not explicitly specified as constants are assumed to depend on the x_i. ■ Example: Dt[x y] ⟶ y Dt[x] + x Dt[y]. ■ Dt[x y, Constants -> {x}] ⟶ x Dt[y]. ■ You can specify total derivatives by assigning values to Dt[*f*], etc. ■ See page 625. ■ See also: D, Derivative.

■ Dump

Dump["*filename*"] writes a complete image of the current state of your *Mathematica* session to a file.

Dump["*filename*", *startup*] includes the *Mathematica* expression *startup*, to be run when the image is executed.

Dump["*filename*", *startup*, "*code*"] uses the executable binary in the file "*code*". The default for "*code*" is First[$CommandLine].

$DumpSupported specifies whether Dump is available on a particular computer system. ■ The files produced by Dump may be very large. ■ No files are assumed to be open in the image created by Dump. (Files could have been changed by the time the image is restarted.) ■ When available, the option DataOnly -> True can be used to specify that only data and not *Mathematica* program text should be included in the dump file. ■ *Mathematica* is typically started from a dump file using the operating system command math -x *filename*. ■ See page 531. ■ See also: Save, $DumpSupported.

■ E

E is the exponential constant e (base of natural logarithms), with numerical value $\simeq 2.71828$.

Mathematical constant (see Section A.3.10). ■ See page 566. ■ See also: Exp.

■ **EdgeForm**

EdgeForm[*g*] is a three-dimensional graphics directive which specifies that edges of polygons are to be drawn using the graphics directive or list of graphics directives *g*.

EdgeForm[ ] draws no edges of polygons. ▪ The directives RGBColor, CMYKColor, GrayLevel, Hue and Thickness can be used in EdgeForm. ▪ EdgeForm does not affect the rendering of Line objects. ▪ See page 437. ▪ See also: FaceForm, Line.

■ **Eigensystem**

Eigensystem[*m*] gives a list {*values*, *vectors*} of the eigenvalues and eigenvectors of the square matrix *m*.

Eigensystem finds numerical eigenvalues and eigenvectors if *m* contains approximate real numbers. ▪ The elements of *m* can be complex. ▪ All the nonzero eigenvectors given are independent. If the number of eigenvectors is equal to the number of non-zero eigenvalues, then corresponding eigenvalues and eigenvectors are given in corresponding positions in their respective lists. ▪ If there are more eigenvalues than independent eigenvectors, then each extra eigenvalue is paired with a vector of zeros. ▪ The eigenvalues and eigenvectors satisfy the matrix equation m.Transpose[*vectors*] == Transpose[*vectors*].DiagonalMatrix[*values*]. ▪ See page 664. ▪ See also: NullSpace.

■ **Eigenvalues**

Eigenvalues[*m*] gives a list of the eigenvalues of the square matrix *m*.

Eigenvalues finds numerical eigenvalues if *m* contains approximate real numbers. ▪ Repeated eigenvalues appear with their appropriate multiplicity. ▪ An $n \times n$ matrix gives a list of exactly n eigenvalues, not necessarily distinct. ▪ See page 664. ▪ See also: Det.

■ **Eigenvectors**

Eigenvectors[*m*] gives a list of the eigenvectors of the square matrix *m*.

Eigenvectors finds numerical eigenvectors if *m* contains approximate real numbers. ▪ Eigenvectors corresponding to degenerate eigenvalues are chosen to be linearly independent. ▪ Eigenvectors are not normalized. ▪ For an $n \times n$ matrix, Eigenvectors always returns a list of length n. The list contains each of the independent eigenvectors of the matrix, followed if necessary by an appropriate number of vectors of zeros. ▪ Eigenvectors[*m*, ZeroTest -> *test*] applies *test* to determine whether expressions should be assumed to be zero. ▪ See page 664. ▪ See also: NullSpace.

■ **Eliminate**

Eliminate[*eqns*, *vars*] eliminates variables between a set of simultaneous equations.

Equations are given in the form *lhs* == *rhs*. ▪ Simultaneous equations can be combined either in a list or with &&. ▪ A single variable or a list of variables can be specified. ▪ Example: Eliminate[{x == 2 + y, y == z}, y] ⟶ z == -2 + x. ▪ Variables can be any expressions. ▪ Eliminate works primarily with linear and polynomial equations. ▪ Additional options to Eliminate can be specified, as in MainSolve. ▪ See page 617. ▪ See also: Reduce, SolveAlways, Solve, MainSolve, AlgebraicRules.

■ **EllipticE**

EllipticE[*m*] gives the complete elliptic integral $E(m)$.

EllipticE[*phi*, *m*] gives the elliptic integral of the second kind $E(\phi|m)$.

Mathematical function (see Section A.3.9). ▪ $E(\phi|m) = \int_0^{\phi} (1 - m \sin^2(\theta))^{\frac{1}{2}} \, d\theta$. ▪ $E(m) = E(\frac{\pi}{2}|m)$. ▪ Argument conventions for elliptic integrals are discussed on page 580. ▪ See page 580. ▪ See also: JacobiZeta.

■ **EllipticExp**

EllipticExp[u, {a, b}] gives the generalized exponential associated with the elliptic curve $y^2 = x^3 + ax^2 + bx$.

EllipticExp is the inverse function for EllipticLog. ■ EllipticExp is the basis for all elliptic functions in *Mathematica*. ■ See page 580.

■ **EllipticF**

EllipticF[phi, m] gives the elliptic integral of the first kind $F(\phi|m)$.

Mathematical function (see Section A.3.9). ■ $F(\phi|m) = \int_0^\phi (1 - m \sin^2(\theta))^{-\frac{1}{2}} d\theta$. ■ The complete elliptic integral associated with EllipticF is EllipticK. ■ Argument conventions for elliptic integrals are discussed on page 580. ■ See page 580. ■ See also: JacobiZeta.

■ **EllipticK**

EllipticK[k] gives the complete elliptic integral of the first kind $K(m)$.

Mathematical function (see Section A.3.9). ■ EllipticK is given in terms of the incomplete elliptic integral of the first kind by $K(m) = F(\frac{\pi}{2}|m)$. ■ Argument conventions for elliptic integrals are discussed on page 580. ■ See page 580. ■ See also: JacobiZeta.

■ **EllipticLog**

EllipticLog[{x, y}, {a, b}] gives the generalized logarithm associated with the elliptic curve $y^2 = x^3 + ax^2 + bx$.

EllipticLog[{x, y}, {a, b}] is defined as the value of the integral $\frac{1}{2} \int_\infty^x (t^3 + at^2 + bt)^{-\frac{1}{2}} dt$, where the sign of the square root is specified by giving the value of y such that $y = \sqrt{x^3 + ax^2 + bx}$. ■ EllipticLog is the basis for all elliptic integrals in *Mathematica*. ■ See page 580. ■ See also: EllipticExp.

■ **EllipticPi**

EllipticPi[n, m] gives the complete elliptic integral of the third kind $\Pi(n|m)$.

EllipticPi[n, phi, m] gives the incomplete elliptic integral $\Pi(n; \phi|m)$.

Mathematical function (see Section A.3.9). ■ $\Pi(n; \phi|m) = \int_0^\phi (1 - n \sin^2(\theta))^{-1} [1 - m \sin^2(\theta)]^{-\frac{1}{2}} d\theta$. ■ $\Pi(n|m) = \Pi(n; \frac{\pi}{2}|m)$. ■ See page 580.

■ **EllipticTheta**

EllipticTheta[a, u, q] gives the elliptic theta function $\theta_a(u|q)$ ($a = 1, ..., 4$).

Mathematical function (see Section A.3.9). ■ $\theta_1(u, q) = 2q^{\frac{1}{4}} \sum_{n=0}^\infty (-1)^n q^{n(n+1)} \sin((2n + 1)u)$, $\theta_2(u, q) = 2q^{\frac{1}{4}} \sum_{n=0}^\infty q^{n(n+1)} \cos((2n + 1)u)$, $\theta_3(u, q) = 1 + 2 \sum_{n=1}^\infty q^{n^2} \cos(2nu)$, $\theta_4(u, q) = 1 + 2 \sum_{n=1}^\infty (-1)^n q^{n^2} \cos(2nu)$. ■ See page 580.

◪ Encode

Encode["*source*", "*dest*"] writes an encoded version of the file *source* to the file *dest*.

<<*dest* decodes the file before reading its contents.

Encode["*source*", "*dest*", "*key*"] produces an encoded file which must be read in using Get["*dest*", "*key*"].

Encoded files contain only printable ASCII characters. They begin with a special sequence which is recognized by Get. ▪ On certain computer systems Encode["*source*", "*dest*", MachineID->"*ID*"] can be used to generate an encoded file which can only be read in on a computer with a particular $MachineID. ▪ See page 480. ▪ See also: ReadProtected, $MachineID.

■ End

End[ ] returns the present context, and reverts to the previous one.

Every call to End must be balanced by an earlier call to Begin. ▪ End[ ] resets the value of $Context. ▪ End[ ] returns the present context name as a string of the form "*context*`". ▪ End[ ] does not modify $ContextPath. ▪ See page 339.

■ EndOfFile

EndOfFile is a symbol returned by Read when it reaches the end of a file.

Subsequent calls to Read will also give EndOfFile. ▪ See page 498.

■ EndPackage

EndPackage[ ] restores $Context and $ContextPath to their values before the preceding BeginPackage, and prepends the current context to the list $ContextPath.

Every call to EndPackage must be balanced by an earlier call to BeginPackage. ▪ EndPackage is typically used at the end of a *Mathematica* package. ▪ EndPackage returns the name of context it ends. ▪ EndPackage resets the values of both $Context and $ContextPath. ▪ See page 339.

■ EngineeringForm

EngineeringForm[*expr*] prints with all real numbers in *expr* given in engineering notation.

In "engineering notation" the exponent is always arranged to be a multiple of 3. ▪ EngineeringForm takes the same options as NumberForm, but uses a different default function for ExponentFunction. ▪ You can mix EngineeringForm and BaseForm. ▪ EngineeringForm acts as a "wrapper", which affects printing, but not evaluation. ▪ See page 350. ▪ See also: EngineeringForm, NumberForm.

■ Environment

Environment["*var*"] gives the value of an operating system environment variable.

The values of environment values are returned by Environment as strings. ▪ Environment returns $Failed if it cannot find a value for the operating system variable you requested. ▪ The behavior of Environment depends on the computer system you are using. ▪ See page 743. ▪ See also: Run, $CommandLine, $System.

◪ Epilog

Epilog is an option for graphics functions which gives a list of graphics primitives to be rendered after the main part of the graphics is rendered.

In three-dimensional graphics, two-dimensional graphics primitives can be specified by the Epilog option. The graphics primitives are rendered in a 0,1 coordinate system. ▪ See page 412. ▪ See also: Prolog, AxesStyle, PlotStyle, DisplayFunction.

■ **Equal**

lhs == *rhs* returns True if *lhs* and *rhs* are identical.

lhs == *rhs* is used to represent a symbolic equation, to be manipulated using functions like Solve. ▪ *lhs* == *rhs* returns True if *lhs* and *rhs* are identical expressions. ▪ *lhs* == *rhs* returns False if *lhs* and *rhs* are determined to be unequal by comparisons between numbers or other raw data, such as strings. ▪ Approximate numbers are considered equal if they differ in at most their last two decimal digits. ▪ 2 == 2. gives True. ▪ e_1 == e_2 == e_3 gives True if all the e_i are equal. ▪ Equal[e] gives True. ▪ See page 94. ▪ See also: SameQ, Unequal, Order.

■ **Erf**

Erf[z] gives the error function erf(z).

Erf[z_0, z_1] gives the generalized error function erf(z_1) − erf(z_0).

Mathematical function (see Section A.3.9). ▪ Erf[z] is the integral of the Gaussian distribution, given by erf(z) = $\frac{2}{\sqrt{\pi}} \int_0^z e^{-t^2} dt$. ▪ Erf[$z_0$, z_1] is given by $\frac{2}{\sqrt{\pi}} \int_{z_0}^{z_1} e^{-t^2} dt$. ▪ See page 570. ▪ See also: ExpIntegralE, ExpIntegralEi.

■ **Erfc**

Erfc[z] gives the complementary error function erfc(z).

Erfc[z] is given by erfc(z) = 1 − erf(z). ▪ See notes for Erf. ▪ See page 570.

■ **EulerE**

EulerE[n] gives the Euler number E_n.

EulerE[n, x] gives the Euler polynomial $E_n(x)$.

Mathematical function (see Section A.3.9). ▪ The Euler polynomials satisfy the generating function relation $\frac{2e^{xt}}{e^t+1} = \sum_{n=0}^{\infty} E_n(x)\frac{t^n}{n!}$. ▪ The Euler numbers are given by $E_n = 2^n E_n(\frac{1}{2})$. ▪ See page 558.

■ **EulerGamma**

EulerGamma is Euler's constant γ, with numerical value ≈ 0.577216.

Mathematical constant (see Section A.3.10). ▪ See page 566. ▪ See also: PolyGamma.

■ **EulerPhi**

EulerPhi[n] gives the Euler totient function $\phi(n)$.

Integer mathematical function (see Section A.3.9). ▪ $\phi(n)$ gives the number of positive integers less than n which are relatively prime to n. ▪ See page 556. ▪ See also: FactorInteger, Divisors, MoebiusMu.

■ **Evaluate**

Evaluate[*expr*] causes *expr* to be evaluated, even if it appears as the argument of a function whose attributes specify that it should be held unevaluated.

Example: Hold[Evaluate[1 + 1]] ⟶ Hold[2]. ▪ You can use Evaluate to override HoldFirst, etc. attributes of built-in functions. ▪ See page 280. ▪ See also: ReleaseHold.

■ **EvenQ**

EvenQ[*expr*] gives True if *expr* is an even integer, and False otherwise.

EvenQ[*expr*] returns False unless *expr* is manifestly an even integer (*i.e.*, has head Integer, and is even). ▪ You can use EvenQ[x] = True to override the normal operation of EvenQ, and effectively define x to be an even integer. ▪ See pages 227 and 535. ▪ See also: IntegerQ, OddQ, TrueQ.

▪ Exit

Exit[ ] terminates a *Mathematica* session.

Exit is a synonym for Quit. ▪ Exit terminates the session even if called from within Dialog. ▪ On some computer systems, Exit[*n*] can be used to pass the integer exit code *n* to the operating system. ▪ See pages 519 and 747. ▪ See also: Return, $IgnoreEOF.

▪ Exp

Exp[z] is the exponential function.

Mathematical function (see Section A.3.9). ▪ Exp[z] is converted to E^z. ▪ See page 562. ▪ See also: Power, E.

▪ Expand

Expand[*expr*] expands out products and positive integer powers in *expr*.

Expand[*expr*, *patt*] avoids expanding elements of *expr* which do not contain terms matching the pattern *patt*.

Expand works only on positive integer powers. ▪ Expand applies only to the top level in *expr*. ▪ Expand[*expr*, Trig -> True] treats trigonometric functions as rational functions of exponentials, and expands them accordingly. ▪ Example: Expand[2 Sin[x]^2, Trig -> True] ⟶ 1 - Cos[2 x]. ▪ See page 591. ▪ See also: Distribute, Apart, Series, Factor, LogicalExpand, PowerExpand.

▪ ExpandAll

ExpandAll[*expr*] expands out all products and integer powers in any part of *expr*.

ExpandAll[*expr*, *patt*] avoids expanding parts of *expr* which do not contain terms matching the pattern *patt*.

ExpandAll[*expr*] effectively maps Expand and ExpandDenominator onto every part of *expr*. ▪ ExpandAll[*expr*, Trig -> True] treats trigonometric functions as rational functions of exponentials, and expands them accordingly. ▪ See page 595.

▪ ExpandDenominator

ExpandDenominator[*expr*] expands out products and powers that appear as denominators in *expr*.

ExpandDenominator works only on negative integer powers. ▪ ExpandDenominator applies only to the top level in *expr*. ▪ See page 595. ▪ See also: Together.

▪ ExpandNumerator

ExpandNumerator[*expr*] expands out products and powers that appear in the numerator of *expr*.

ExpandNumerator works on terms that have positive integer exponents. ▪ ExpandNumerator applies only to the top level in *expr*. ▪ See page 595.

▪ ExpIntegralE

ExpIntegralE[*n*, *z*] gives the exponential integral function $E_n(z)$.

Mathematical function (see Section A.3.9). ▪ $E_n(z) = \int_1^\infty \frac{e^{-zt}}{t^n} dt$. ▪ See page 570. ▪ See also: Erf, LogIntegral, SinIntegral, CosIntegral.

- **ExpIntegralEi**

    ExpIntegralEi[*z*] gives the exponential integral function Ei(*z*).

    Mathematical function (see Section A.3.9). ▪ $Ei(z) = - \int_{-z}^{\infty} \frac{e^{-t}}{t} dt$, where the principal value of the integral is taken. ▪ See page 570. ▪ See also: Erf, LogIntegral, SinIntegral, CosIntegral.

- **Exponent**

    Exponent[*expr*, *form*] gives the maximum power with which *form* appears in *expr*.

    Exponent[*expr*, *form*, *h*] applies *h* to the set of exponents with which *form* appears in *expr*.

    expr is assumed to be a single term, or a sum of terms. Exponent applies only to the top level in *expr*. ▪ Example: Exponent[x^2 + a x^3, x] ⟶ 3. ▪ The default taken for *h* is Max. ▪ Example: Exponent[x^2 + a x^3, x, List] ⟶ {2, 0, 3}. ▪ *form* can be a product of terms. ▪ See page 593. ▪ See also: Coefficient, Cases.

- **ExponentFunction**

    ExponentFunction is an option for NumberForm and related functions which determines the exponent to use in printing approximate real numbers.

    Functions like NumberForm first find the exponent that would make exactly one digit appear to the left of the decimal point when the number is printed in scientific notation. Then they take this exponent and apply the function specified by ExponentFunction to it. If the value obtained from this function is an integer, it is used as the exponent of the number. If it is Null, then the number is printed not in scientific notation. ▪ The argument provided for the function specified by ExponentFunction is always an integer. ▪ In NumberForm, the default setting for ExponentFunction never modifies the exponent, but returns Null for machine numbers with exponents between -5 and 5, and for high-precision numbers where insignificant zeros would have to be inserted if the number were not printed in scientific notation. ▪ In ScientificForm, the default setting for ExponentFunction never returns Null. ▪ In EngineeringForm, the default setting for ExponentFunction returns an exponent that is a multiple of 3. ▪ In AccountingForm, the default setting for ExponentFunction always returns Null. ▪ See page 351. ▪ See also: NumberFormat.

- **Expression**

    Expression is a symbol that represents an ordinary *Mathematica* expression in Read and related functions.

    See page 495. ▪ See also: ToExpression.

- **ExtendedGCD**

    ExtendedGCD[*n*, *m*] gives the extended greatest common divisor of the integers *n* and *m*.

    Integer mathematical function (see Section A.3.9). ▪ ExtendedGCD[*n*, *m*] returns the list {*g*, {*r*, *s*}}, where *g* is GCD[*n*, *m*], and *r* and *s* satisfy the relation $g = nr + ms$. ▪ See page 556. ▪ See also: GCD.

- **FaceForm**

    FaceForm[*gf*, *gb*] is a three-dimensional graphics directive which specifies that the front faces of polygons are to be drawn with the graphics primitive *gf*, and the back faces with *gb*.

    The graphics specifications *gf* and *gb* must be CMYKColor, GrayLevel, Hue or RGBColor directives, or SurfaceColor objects. ▪ Specifications given outside of FaceForm will apply both to the front and back faces of polygons. ▪ The front face of a polygon is defined to be the one for which the corners as you specify them are in counter-clockwise order (right-hand rule). ▪ See page 438. ▪ See also: EdgeForm.

◤ FaceGrids

FaceGrids is an option for three-dimensional graphics functions that specifies grid lines to draw on the faces of the bounding box.

The following settings can be given for **FaceGrids**:

None	no grid lines drawn
All	grid lines drawn on all faces
{*face₁*, *face₂*, ... }	grid lines drawn on the specified faces
{{*face₁*, {*xgrid₁*, *ygrid₁*}}, ... }	details of grid lines specified

- Faces are specified as {dir_x, dir_y, dir_z}, where two of the dir_i must be 0, and the third one must be +1 or -1. ■ Example: the *x*-*y* face with smallest *z* value is specified as {0, 0, -1}. ■ For each face, specifications {*xgrid_i*, *ygrid_i*} can be given to determine the arrangement of grid lines. These specifications have the form described in the notes for **GridLines**. ■ See page 463. ■ See also: **Ticks**.

■ Factor

Factor[*poly*] factors a polynomial over the integers.

Factor[*poly*, Modulus->*p*] factors a polynomial modulo a prime *p*.

Factor applies only to the top level in an expression. You may have to use **Map**, or apply **Factor** again, to reach other levels. ■ **Factor** works only with exact **Integer** or **Rational** coefficients, not with **Real** numbers. ■ **Factor[*poly*, GaussianIntegers->True]** factors allowing Gaussian integer coefficients. ■ If any coefficients in *poly* are complex numbers, factoring is done allowing Gaussian integer coefficients. ■ The exponents of variables need not be positive integers. **Factor** can deal with exponents that are linear combinations of symbolic expressions. ■ **Factor[*poly*, Variables->{x_1, x_2, ... }]** allows you to specify an ordering on the variables in *poly*. The time needed to do the factorization may depend on the ordering you specify. ■ **Factor[*expr*, Trig -> True]** treats trigonometric functions as rational functions of exponentials, and factors them accordingly. ■ Example: **Factor[Sin[2x], Trig -> True]** ⟶ 2 Cos[x] Sin[x]. ■ See page 591. ■ See also: **FactorTerms**, **Solve**, **Expand**, **Simplify**, **FactorInteger**.

■ FactorComplete

FactorComplete is an option for **FactorInteger** which specifies whether complete factorization is to be performed.

FactorComplete->False causes at most one factor to be extracted. ■ See page 555.

■ Factorial

n! gives the factorial of *n*.

Mathematical function (see Section A.3.9). ■ For non-integer *n*, the numerical value of *n*! is given by **Gamma[1 + *n*]**. ■ See page 558. ■ See also: **Gamma**, **Binomial**.

■ Factorial2

n!! gives the double factorial of *n*.

Mathematical function (see Section A.3.9). ■ $n!! = n(n-2)(n-4) \times ...$. ■ *n*!! is a product of even numbers for *n* even, and odd numbers for *n* odd. ■ See page 558. ■ See also: **Gamma**.

■ **FactorInteger**

FactorInteger[*n*] gives a list of the prime factors of the integer *n*, together with their exponents.

Example: FactorInteger[2434500] ⟶ {{2, 2}, {3, 2}, {5, 3}, {541, 1}}. ■ For negative integers, the unit {-1, 1} is included in the list of factors. ■ FactorInteger[*n*, *pmax*] factors only over primes up to size *pmax*. Any unfactored part of *n* is left as an element of the returned list. ■ FactorInteger[*n*, FactorComplete->False] finds only the first factor of *n*. ■ FactorInteger[*n*, GaussianIntegers->True] factors over Gaussian integers. ■ When necessary, a unit of the form {I, 1} or {-I, 1} is included in the list of factors. ■ See page 554. ■ See also: Prime, PrimeQ, Divisors.

■ **FactorList**

FactorList[*poly*] gives a list of the factors of a polynomial, together with their exponents.

The first element of the list is always the overall numerical factor. It is {1, 1} if there is no overall numerical factor. ■ Example: FactorList[3 (1+x)^2 (1-x)] ⟶ {{3, 1}, {1 - x, 1}, {1 + x, 2}}. ■ FactorList[*poly*, Modulus->*p*] factors modulo a prime *p*. ■ FactorList[*poly*, GaussianIntegers->True] allows Gaussian integer coefficients. ■ See page 598. ■ See also: CoefficientList.

■ **FactorSquareFree**

FactorSquareFree[*poly*] pulls out any squared factors in a polynomial.

FactorSquareFree[*poly*, Modulus->*p*] pulls out squared factors modulo a prime *p*. ■ See page 598.

■ **FactorSquareFreeList**

FactorSquareFreeList[*poly*] gives a list of square-free factors of a polynomial, together with their exponents.

See page 598.

■ **FactorTerms**

FactorTerms[*poly*] pulls out any overall numerical factor in *poly*.

FactorTerms[*poly*, *x*] pulls out factors in *poly* that do not depend on *x*.

FactorTerms[*poly*, {x_1, x_2, ... }] successively pulls out factors in *poly* that do not depend on each of the x_i.

Example: FactorTerms[3 - 3x^2] ⟶ -3 (-1 + x^2). ■ FactorTerms[*poly*, *x*] extracts the content of *poly* with respect to *x*. ■ See notes for Factor. ■ See page 591.

■ **FactorTermsList**

FactorTermsList[*poly*, {x_1, x_2, ... }] gives a list of factors of *poly*. The first element in the list is the overall numerical factor. The second element is a factor that does not depend on any of the x_i. Subsequent elements are factors which depend on progressively more of the x_i.

See notes for FactorTerms. ■ See page 598.

■ **False**

False is the symbol for the Boolean value false.

See page 93. ■ See also: TrueQ, True.

■ **FileByteCount**

FileByteCount ["*file*"] gives the number of bytes in a file.

If a particular file is moved from one computer system to another, the number of bytes in the file as reported by FileByteCount may change. ▪ See page 492. ▪ See also: StringByteCount, FileType.

■ **FileDate**

FileDate ["*file*"] gives the date and time at which a file was last modified.

FileDate returns the date and time in the format used by Date. ▪ See page 492. ▪ See also: SetFileDate, FromDate.

■ **FileNames**

FileNames [ ] lists all files in the current working directory.

FileNames ["*form*"] lists all files in the current working directory whose names match the string pattern *form*.

FileNames [{"*form₁*", "*form₂*", ... }] lists all files whose names match any of the *form_i*.

FileNames [*forms*, {"*dir₁*", "*dir₂*", ... }] lists files with names matching *forms* in any of the directories *dir_i*.

FileNames [*forms*, *dirs*, *n*] includes files that are in subdirectories up to *n* levels down.

The string pattern "*form*" can contain the metacharacters specified on page 728. ▪ FileNames ["*"] is equivalent to FileNames [ ]. ▪ FileNames [*forms*, *dirs*, Infinity] looks for files in all subdirectories of the *dirs*. ▪ The list of files returned by FileNames is sorted in the order generated by the function Sort. ▪ FileNames [*forms*, *dirs*, *n*] includes names of directories only if they appear exactly at level *n*. ▪ The *forms* must be names of files only, not including any directory information. Thus, for example, FileNames ["../*"] will not work. Instead FileNames ["*", ".."] is the appropriate form. ▪ Setting the option IgnoreCase -> True makes FileNames treat lower- and upper-case letters in file names as equivalent. ▪ On operating systems such as MS-DOS, FileNames always treats lower- and upper-case letters in file names as equivalent. ▪ See page 491. ▪ See also: Directory, FileType.

■ **FileType**

FileType ["*file*"] gives the type of a file, typically File, Directory or None.

FileType returns None if the file specified does not exist. ▪ See page 492. ▪ See also: FileNames, FileByteCount.

■ **Find**

Find[*stream*, "*text*"] finds the first line in an input stream that contains the specified string.

Find[*stream*, {"*text₁*", "*text₂*", ... }] finds the first line that contains any of the specified strings.

Find breaks the input stream into records, delimited by record separators, and scans each record for the strings you specify. ■ Find returns as a string the first record which contains the specified text. ■ If Find does not find any record which contains the specified text before it reaches the end of the file, it it returns EndOfFile. ■ The following options can be given:

AnchoredSearch	False	whether to require the text searched for to be at the beginning of a record
IgnoreCase	False	whether to treat lower- and upper-case as equivalent
RecordSeparators	{"\n"}	separators for records
WordSearch	False	whether to require that the text searched for appear as a word
WordSeparators	{" ", "\t"}	separators for words

■ The first argument to Find can be InputStream["*name*", *n*], or simply "*name*" if there is only one open input stream with the specified name. ■ You can open a file or pipe to get an InputStream object using OpenRead. ■ Find does not close streams after it finishes reading from them. ■ See page 502. ■ See also: Read, Skip, StreamPosition, StringToStream.

■ **FindList**

FindList["*file*", "*text*"] gives a list of lines in the file that contain the specified string.

FindList["*file*", {"*text₁*", "*text₂*", ... }] gives a list of all lines that contain any of the specified strings.

FindList[{"*file₁*", ... }, ...] gives a list of lines containing the specified strings in any of the *fileᵢ*.

FindList[*files*, *text*, *n*] includes only the first *n* lines found.

FindList returns {} if it fails to find any record which contains the specified text. ■ If FindList opens a file or pipe, it closes it again when it has finished. ■ See notes for Find. ■ See page 500. ■ See also: ReadList.

■ FindMinimum

FindMinimum[f, {x, x_0}] searches for a local minimum in f, starting from the point $x=x_0$.

FindMinimum returns a list of the form {f_{min}, {x->x_{min}}}, where f_{min} is the minimum value of f found, and x_{min} is the value of x for which it is found. ■ FindMinimum[f, {x, {x_0, x_1}}] searches for a local minimum in f using x_0 and x_1 as the first two values of x. This form must be used if symbolic derivatives of f cannot be found. ■ FindMinimum[f, {x, *xstart*, *xmin*, *xmax*}] searches for a local minimum, stopping the search if x ever gets outside the range *xmin* to *xmax*. ■ FindMinimum[f, {x, x_0}, {y, y_0}, ...] searches for a local minimum in a function of several variables. ■ FindMinimum has attribute HoldAll. ■ FindMinimum works by following the path of steepest descent from each point that it reaches. The minima it finds are local, but not necessarily global, ones. ■ The following options can be given:

AccuracyGoal	Automatic	the accuracy sought in the value of the function at the minimum
Compiled	True	whether the function should be compiled
Gradient	Automatic	the list of gradient functions {D[f, x], D[f, y], ... }
MaxIterations	30	maximum number of iterations used
PrecisionGoal	Automatic	the precision sought in the value of the function at the minimum
WorkingPrecision	Precision[1.]	the number of digits used in internal computations

■ The default settings for AccuracyGoal and PrecisionGoal are 10 digits less than WorkingPrecision. ■ FindMinimum continues until either of the goals specified by AccuracyGoal or PrecisionGoal is achieved. ■ See page 703. ■ See also: ConstrainedMin, LinearProgramming, D, Fit.

■ FindRoot

FindRoot[*lhs==rhs*, {x, x_0}] searches for a numerical solution to the equation *lhs==rhs*, starting with $x=x_0$.

FindRoot[*lhs==rhs*, {x, {x_0, x_1}}] searches for a solution using x_0 and x_1 as the first two values of x. This form must be used if symbolic derivatives of the equation cannot be found.
■ FindRoot[*lhs==rhs*, {x, *xstart*, *xmin*, *xmax*}] searches for a solution, stopping the search if x ever gets outside the range *xmin* to *xmax*. ■ FindRoot[{eqn_1, eqn_2, ... }, {x, x_0}, {y, y_0}, ...] searches for a numerical solution to the simultaneous equations eqn_i. ■ FindRoot returns a list of replacements for x, y, ... , in the same form as obtained from Solve. ■ FindRoot has attribute HoldAll. ■ If you specify only one starting value of x, FindRoot searches for a solution using Newton's method. If you specify two starting values, FindRoot uses a variant of the secant method.
■ The following options can be given:

AccuracyGoal	Automatic	the accuracy sought in the value of the function at the root
Compiled	True	whether the function should be compiled
DampingFactor	1	damping factor in Newton's method
Jacobian	Automatic	the Jacobian of the system
MaxIterations	15	maximum number of iterations used
WorkingPrecision	$MachinePrecision	the number of digits used in internal computations

■ The default setting for AccuracyGoal is 10 digits less than WorkingPrecision. ■ If FindRoot does not succeed in finding a solution to the accuracy you specify within MaxIterations steps, it returns the most recent approximation to a solution that it found. You can then apply FindRoot again, with this approximation as a starting point. ■ The size of each step taken in Newton's method is multiplied by the setting given for DampingFactor. ■ See page 692. ■ See also: NSolve, Solve, FindMinimum.

■ First

First[*expr*] gives the first element in *expr*.

First[*expr*] is equivalent to *expr*[[1]]. ■ See page 125. ■ See also: Part, Last, Rest, Take, Select.

■ Fit

Fit[*data*, *funs*, *vars*] finds a least-squares fit to a list of data as a linear combination of the functions *funs* of variables *vars*.

The data can have the form $\{\{x_1, y_1, \ldots, f_1\}, \{x_2, y_2, \ldots, f_2\}, \ldots\}$, where the number of coordinates $x, y, \ldots$ is equal to the number of variables in the list *vars*.

The data can also be of the form $\{f_1, f_2, \ldots\}$, with a single coordinate assumed to take values 1, 2, … .

The argument *funs* can be any list of functions that depend only on the objects *vars*.

Fit[$\{f_1, f_2, \ldots\}$, {1, x, x^2}, x] gives a quadratic fit to a sequence of values f_i. The result is of the form $a_0 + a_1$ x $+ a_2$ x^2, where the a_i are real numbers. The successive values of x needed to obtain the f_i are assumed to be 1, 2, … . ■ Fit[$\{\{x_1, f_1\}, \{x_2, f_2\}, \ldots\}$, {1, x, x^2}, x] does a quadratic fit, assuming a sequence of x values x_i. ■ Fit[$\{\{x_1, y_1, f_1\}, \ldots\}$, {1, x, y}, {x, y}] finds a fit of the form $a_0 + a_1$ x $+ a_2$ y. ■ Fit always finds the linear combination of the functions in the list *forms* that minimizes the sum of the squares of deviations from the values f_i. ■ Exact numbers given as input to Fit are converted to approximate numbers with machine precision. ■ See page 672. ■ See also: Interpolation, InterpolatingPolynomial, Solve, PseudoInverse, QRDecomposition, FindMinimum.

■ FixedPoint

FixedPoint[*f*, *expr*] starts with *expr*, then applies *f* repeatedly until the result no longer changes.

FixedPoint[*f*, *expr*, *n*] stops after at most *n* steps. ■ FixedPoint always returns the last result it gets. ■ The option SameTest -> *comp* allows you to specify a comparison function to apply to successive pairs of results to determine whether a fixed point has been reached. The default is SameTest -> Equal. ■ FixedPoint takes the option MaxIterations, which specifies the maximum number of times it will try to apply the rules you give. The default setting is MaxIterations -> 65536. With MaxIterations -> Infinity there is no limit. ■ See page 201. ■ See also: FixedPointList, Nest, ReplaceRepeated.

■ FixedPointList

FixedPointList[*f*, *expr*] generates a list giving the results of applying *f* repeatedly, starting with *expr*, until the results no longer change.

See notes for FixedPoint. ■ FixedPointList[*f*, *expr*] gives *expr* as the first element of the list it produces. ■ See page 201. ■ See also: NestList, ComposeList.

■ Flat

Flat is an attribute that can be assigned to a symbol *f* to indicate that all expressions involving nested functions *f* should be flattened out. This property is accounted for in pattern matching.

Flat corresponds to the mathematical property of associativity. ■ For a symbol *f* with attribute Flat, *f*[*f*[a, b], *f*[c]] is automatically reduced to *f*[a, b, c]. ■ Functions like Plus, Times and Dot are Flat. ■ For a Flat function *f*, the variables x and y in the pattern *f*[x_, y_] can correspond to any sequence of arguments. ■ The Flat attribute must be assigned before defining any values for a Flat function. ■ See page 272. ■ See also: Orderless, OneIdentity.

■ **Flatten**

Flatten[*list*] flattens out nested lists.

Flatten[*list*, *n*] flattens to level *n*.

Flatten[*list*, *n*, *h*] flattens subexpressions with head *h*.

Example: Flatten[{a,{b,c},{d}}] ⟶ {a, b, c, d}. ■ Flatten "unravels" lists, effectively just deleting inner braces. ■ Flatten[*list*, *n*] effectively flattens the top level in *list* *n* times. ■ Flatten[*f*[*e*, …]] flattens out subexpressions with head *f*. ■ See pages 132 and 215. ■ See also: Partition.

■ **FlattenAt**

FlattenAt[*list*, *n*] flattens out a sublist that appears as the nth element of *list*. If *n* is negative, the position is counted from the end.

FlattenAt[*expr*, {*i*, *j*, … }] flattens out the part of *expr* at position {*i*, *j*, … }.

FlattenAt[*expr*, {{i_1, j_1, … }, {i_2, j_2, … }, … }] flattens out parts of *expr* at several positions.

Example: FlattenAt[{a, {b, c}, {d, e}}, 2] ⟶ {a, b, c, {d, e}}. ■ See pages 132 and 215. ■ See also: DeleteCases, Flatten.

■ **Floor**

Floor[*x*] gives the greatest integer less than or equal to *x*.

Mathematical function (see Section A.3.9). ■ Examples: Floor[2.4] ⟶ 2; Floor[2.6] ⟶ 2; Floor[-2.4] ⟶ -3; Floor[-2.6] ⟶ -3. ■ See page 550. ■ See also: Ceiling, Round, Chop.

■ **Fold**

Fold[*f*, *x*, *list*] gives the last element of FoldList[*f*, *x*, *list*].

Example: Fold[f, x, {a, b, c}] ⟶ f[f[f[x, a], b], c]. ■ See notes for FoldList. ■ See page 202. ■ See also: Nest.

■ **FoldList**

FoldList[*f*, *x*, {*a*, *b*, … }] gives {*x*, *f*[*x*, *a*], *f*[*f*[*x*, *a*], *b*], … }.

Example: FoldList[f, x, {a, b, c}] ⟶ {x, f[x, a], f[f[x, a], b], f[f[f[x, a], b], c]}. ■ FoldList[Plus, 0, *list*] generates cumulative sums of the elements in *list*. ■ Example: FoldList[Plus, 0, {a, b, c}] ⟶ {0, a, a + b, a + b + c}. ■ With a length *n* list, FoldList generates a list of length *n* +1. ■ The head of *list* in FoldList[*f*, *x*, *list*] need not be List. ■ See page 202. ■ See also: NestList, ComposeList, Partition, MapIndexed.

■ **FontForm**

FontForm[*expr*, {"*font*", *size*}] specifies that *expr* should be printed in the specified font and size.

FontForm is used primarily for text included in graphics. ■ The font size is specified in units of printer's points, approximately $\frac{1}{72}$ of an inch. ■ The font name in FontForm is used in the PostScript form of *expr*. Most PostScript rendering systems translate the specifications into ones appropriate for the particular output device being used. ■ Typical font names are "Courier", "Helvetica" and "Times", together with "*Name*-Bold", "*Name*-Oblique" and "*Name*-BoldOblique" (with Italic replacing Oblique in the case of Times). ■ See page 468. ■ See also: Text, DefaultFont, PlotLabel.

■ For

For[*start*, *test*, *incr*, *body*] executes *start*, then repeatedly evaluates *body* and *incr* until *test* fails to give True.

For evaluates its arguments in a non-standard way. ■ For[*start*, *test*, *incr*] does the loop with a null body. ■ The sequence of evaluation is *test*, *body*, *incr*. The For exits as soon as *test* fails. ■ If Break[ ] is generated in the evaluation of *body*, the For loop exits. ■ Continue[ ] exits the evaluation of *body*, and continues the loop by evaluating *incr*. ■ Unless Return[ ] or Throw[ ] are generated, the final value returned by For is Null. ■ Example: For[tot=0; i=0, i < 3, i++, tot += f[i]]. Note that the roles of semicolon and comma are *reversed* relative to the C programming language. ■ See page 292. ■ See also: Do, While.

■ Format

Format[*expr*] prints as the formatted form of *expr*.

Assigning values to Format[*expr*] defines print forms for expressions.

Format[*expr*, *type*] gives a format of the specified type.

Standard format types are:

CForm	C language input form
FortranForm	Fortran input form
InputForm	one-dimensional form suitable for input to *Mathematica*
OutputForm	two-dimensional mathematical form
TeXForm	TEX input form
TextForm	textual form

■ You can add your own format types. ■ Example: Format[*s*] := *form* defines a special print form for a symbol *s*. ■ Format[*f*[...]] := *form* defines a print form for a function *f*. ■ Definitions for Format are stored in the PrintValue of a symbol. ■ See pages 358 and 359. ■ See also: ToString, Short.

■ FormatType

FormatType is an option for output streams which specifies the default format type used when printing expressions.

Standard values for FormatType are given in the notes for Format. ■ SetOptions[*stream*, FormatType -> *type*] resets the format type for an open stream. ■ See page 487.

■ FortranForm

FortranForm[*expr*] prints as a Fortran language version of *expr*.

Standard arithmetic functions and certain control structures are translated. ■ FortranForm acts as a "wrapper", which affects printing, but not evaluation. ■ The width of output lines must be set explicitly by giving the option PageWidth -> *n* for the relevant output stream. ■ SetOptions[$Output, PageWidth -> 72] uses a line width of 72 characters for standard *Mathematica* output. ■ No declarations are generated. ■ See pages 182 and 344. ■ See also: CForm.

■ Fourier

Fourier[*list*] finds the discrete Fourier transform of a list of complex numbers.

The Fourier transform b_s of a list a_r of length n is defined to be $\frac{1}{\sqrt{n}} \sum_{r=1}^{n} a_r e^{2\pi i (r-1)(s-1)/n}$. ■ Note that the zero frequency term appears at position 1 in the resulting list. ■ The definition of the Fourier transform used is the one common in the physical sciences. The sign of the exponent must be reversed to obtain the definition common in electrical engineering. ■ The list of data need not have a length equal to a power of two. ■ The *list* given in Fourier[*list*] can be nested to represent an array of data in any number of dimensions. ■ The array of data must be rectangular. ■ See page 679. ■ See also: InverseFourier, Fit.

◪ Frame

Frame is an option for two-dimensional graphics functions which specifies whether a frame should be drawn around the plot.

Frame -> True by default draws a frame with tick marks. If Ticks -> Automatic, setting Frame -> True suppresses tick marks on axes. ▪ See pages 418 and 422. ▪ See also: Boxed.

◪ FrameLabel

FrameLabel is an option for two-dimensional graphics functions that specifies labels to be placed on the edges of a frame around a plot.

FrameLabel -> None specifies that no labels should be given. ▪ FrameLabel -> {*xmlabel*, *ymlabel*} specifies labels for the bottom and left-hand edges of the frame. ▪ FrameLabel -> {*xmlabel*, *ymlabel*, *xplabel*, *yplabel*} specifies labels for each of the edges of the frame, ordered clockwise starting from the bottom edge. ▪ Any expression can be specified as a label. It will be given in OutputForm. Arbitrary strings of text can be given as "*text*". ▪ Labels for the vertical edges of the frame are by default written vertically. RotateLabel -> False specifies that they should be horizontal. ▪ See page 422. ▪ See also: AxesLabel, PlotLabel.

◪ FrameStyle

FrameStyle is an option for two-dimensional graphics functions that specifies how the edges of a frame should be rendered.

FrameStyle -> *style* specifies that all edges of the frame are to be generated with the specified graphics directive, or list of graphics directives. ▪ FrameStyle -> {{*xmstyle*}, {*ymstyle*}, … } specifies that different edges of the frame should be generated with different styles. The edges are ordered clockwise starting from the bottom edge. All styles must be enclosed in lists, perhaps of length one. ▪ Styles can be specified using graphics directives such as Dashing, Hue and Thickness. ▪ The default color of frame edges is specified by the option DefaultColor. ▪ See page 422. ▪ See also: Prolog, Epilog, AxesStyle.

◪ FrameTicks

FrameTicks is an option for two-dimensional graphics functions that specifies tick marks for the edges of a frame.

The following settings can be given for FrameTicks:

None	no tick marks drawn
Automatic	tick marks placed automatically
{*xmticks*, *ymticks*, … }	tick mark options specified separately for each edge

▪ When tick mark specifications are given separately for each edge, the edges are ordered clockwise starting from the bottom of the frame. ▪ With the Automatic setting, tick marks are usually placed at points whose coordinates have the minimum number of digits in their decimal representation. ▪ For each edge, tick marks can be specified as described in the notes for Ticks. ▪ See page 422. ▪ See also: Ticks, GridLines, FaceGrids.

■ FreeQ

FreeQ[*expr*, *form*] yields True if no subexpression in *expr* matches *form*, and yields False otherwise.

FreeQ[*expr*, *form*, *levelspec*] tests only those parts of *expr* on levels specified by *levelspec*.

form can be a pattern. ▪ Example: FreeQ[f[x^2] + y^2, x^_] $\longrightarrow$ False. ▪ FreeQ looks at the heads of raw expressions, testing whether those heads match *form*. ▪ See page 228. ▪ See also: MemberQ, Count.

◾ FromCharacterCode

FromCharacterCode[*n*] gives a string consisting of the character with integer code *n*.

FromCharacterCode[{n_1, n_2, ... }] gives a string consisting of the sequence of characters with codes n_i.

The integer *n* must be non-negative. ▪ If *n* is less than 256, then FromCharacterCode[*n*] yields an 8-bit character. ▪ If *n* is between 256 and 65791, FromCharacterCode[*n*] yields a 16-bit character. ▪ See page 366. ▪ See also: ToCharacterCode.

◾ FromDate

FromDate[*date*] converts a date of the form {y, m, d, h, m, s} to an absolute number of seconds since the beginning of January 1, 1900.

FromDate converts between the forms returned by Date and AbsoluteTime. ▪ FromDate assumes that both the date and the absolute time are to be given in the same time zone. ▪ See page 524. ▪ See also: ToDate.

■ FullDefinition

FullDefinition[s_1, s_2, ...] prints as the definitions given for the symbols s_i, and all symbols on which these depend.

FullDefinition has attribute HoldAll. ▪ FullDefinition[s_1, ...] recursively prints as all definitions for the symbols s_i, and for the symbols that appear in these definitions. ▪ FullDefinition does not look at rules or attributes of symbols that have the attribute Protected. ▪ See page 479. ▪ See also: Definition, Save, Information.

■ FullForm

FullForm[*expr*] prints as the full form of *expr*, with no special syntax.

Example: FullForm[a + b∧2] ⟶ Plus[a, Power[b, 2]]. ▪ FullForm acts as a "wrapper", which affects printing, but not evaluation. ▪ See page 344. ▪ See also: InputForm, TreeForm.

◾ FullGraphics

FullGraphics[*g*] takes a graphics object, and generates a new one in which objects specified by graphics options are given as explicit lists of graphics primitives.

FullGraphics generates explicit graphics primitives for objects specified by options such as Axes, Ticks, etc. ▪ See page 398. ▪ See also: FullOptions.

◾ FullOptions

FullOptions[*expr*] gives the full settings of options explicitly specified in an expression such as a graphics object.

FullOptions[*expr*, *name*] gives the full setting for the option *name*.

FullOptions[*expr*, {$name_1$, $name_2$, ... }] gives a list of the full settings for the options $name_i$.

FullOptions gives the actual settings for options used internally by *Mathematica* when the setting given is Automatic or All. ▪ You can use FullOptions on graphics options such as PlotRange and Ticks. ▪ See pages 150 and 398. ▪ See also: Options, FullGraphics.

■ Function

Function[*body*] or *body*& is a pure function. The formal parameters are # (or #1), #2, etc.

Function[*x*, *body*] is a pure function with a single formal parameter *x*.

Function[{x_1, x_2, ... }, *body*] is a pure function with a list of formal parameters.

Example: (# + 1)&[x] $\longrightarrow$ 1 + x. ■ Map[(# + 1)&, {x, y, z}] $\longrightarrow$ {1 + x, 1 + y, 1 + z}. ■ When Function[*body*] or *body*& is applied to a set of arguments, # (or #1) is replaced by the first argument, #2 by the second, and so on. #0 is replaced by the function itself. ■ If there are more arguments supplied than #*i* in the function, the remaining arguments are ignored. ■ ## stands for the sequence of all arguments supplied. ■ ##*n* stands for arguments from number *n* on. ■ f[##, ##2]& [x, y, z] $\longrightarrow$ f[x, y, z, y, z]. ■ Function is analogous to λ in LISP or formal logic. ■ Function has attribute HoldAll. The function body is evaluated only after the formal parameters have been replaced by arguments. ■ The named formal parameters x_i in Function[{x_1, ... }, *body*] are treated as local, and are renamed x_i\$ when necessary to avoid confusion with actual arguments supplied to the function. ■ Function is treated as a scoping construct (see Section A.3.8).
■ Function[*params*, *body*, {$attr_1$, $attr_2$, ... }] represents a pure function that is to be treated as having attributes $attr_i$ for the purpose of evaluation. ■ See page 207. ■ See also: Apply, CompiledFunction.

■ Gamma

Gamma[*z*] is the Euler gamma function $\Gamma(z)$.

Gamma[*a*, *z*] is the incomplete gamma function $\Gamma(a, z)$.

Gamma[*a*, z_0, z_1] is the generalized incomplete gamma function $\Gamma(a, z_0) - \Gamma(a, z_1)$.

Mathematical function (see Section A.3.9). ■ The gamma function satisfies $\Gamma(z) = \int_0^\infty t^{z-1} e^{-t} dt$. ■ The incomplete gamma function satisfies $\Gamma(a, z) = \int_z^\infty t^{a-1} e^{-t} dt$. ■ The generalized incomplete gamma function is given by the integral $\int_{z_0}^{z_1} t^{a-1} e^{-t} dt$. ■ See page 570. ■ See also: Factorial, LogGamma, PolyGamma, RiemannSiegelTheta.

▶ GammaRegularized

GammaRegularized[*a*, *z*] is the regularized incomplete gamma function $Q(a, z)$.

Mathematical function (see Section A.3.9). ■ In non-singular cases, $Q(a, z) = \Gamma(a, z)/\Gamma(a)$.
■ GammaRegularized[*a*, z_0, z_1] is the generalized regularized incomplete gamma function, defined in non-singular cases as Gamma[*a*, z_0, z_1]/Gamma[*a*]. ■ See page 573.

▶ GaussianIntegers

GaussianIntegers is an option for FactorInteger, PrimeQ, Factor and related functions which specifies whether factorization should be done over Gaussian integers.

With GaussianIntegers -> False, factorization is done over the ordinary ring of integers **Z**. ■ With GaussianIntegers -> True, factorization is done over the ring of integers with *i* adjoined **Z**[*i*]. ■ Example: FactorInteger[13, GaussianIntegers -> True] $\longrightarrow$ {{-I, 1}, {2 + 3 I, 1}, {3 + 2 I, 1}}. ■ The Gaussian primes used when GaussianIntegers -> True are chosen to have both real and imaginary parts positive. ■ The first entry in the list given by FactorInteger with GaussianIntegers -> True may be -1 or -I. ■ See page 556. ■ See also: ComplexExpand.

■ GCD

GCD[n_1, n_2, ...] gives the greatest common divisor of the integers n_i.

Integer mathematical function (see Section A.3.9). ■ GCD[n_1, ...] gives the integer factors common to all the n_i.
■ See page 553. ■ See also: PolynomialGCD, Rational, LCM, ExtendedGCD.

■ GegenbauerC

GegenbauerC[n, m, x] gives the Gegenbauer polynomial $C_n^m(x)$.

Mathematical function (see Section A.3.9). ■ Explicit polynomials are given for integer n and m. ■ The Gegenbauer polynomials are orthogonal with weight function $(1 - x^2)^{m-1/2}$, corresponding to integration over a unit hypersphere. ■ See page 567. ■ See also: LegendreP, ChebyshevT.

■ General

General is a symbol to which general system messages are attached.

When you refer to a message with name s::*tag* in On or Off, the text of the message is obtained from General::*tag* if no specific message named s::*tag* exists. ■ See page 388.

■ Get

<<*name* reads in a file, evaluating each expression in it, and returning the last one.

On systems with advanced graphical interfaces, there will usually be graphical tools for reading in files. ■ If *name* is the name of a *Mathematica* context, ending with a ` context mark character, then Get calls ContextToFilename to find the name of the file to read. ■ For files, any .m extension must be included explicitly. ■ Get is for reading in files that contain *Mathematica* input only. ■ The list of directories $Path is searched for a file with the specified name. ■ <<"*name*" is equivalent to <<*name*. The double quotes can be omitted if the name is of the form specified on page 721. ■ Syntax errors in files are reported in the standard form: *filename*: *line*: syntax error in *expr*. Get continues attempting to read a file even after a syntax error has been detected. However, if an error is detected, $Context and $ContextPath are reset to the values they had when Get was called. ■ During the execution of Get, the global variable $Input is set to the name of the file being read. ■ Get["*file*", "*key*"] reads a file which has been encoded using Encode["*source*", "*file*", "*key*"]. ■ See page 477. ■ See also: Read, Install, RunThrough, Put, Splice, FileNames.

■ GoldenRatio

GoldenRatio is the golden ratio $\phi = (1 + \sqrt{5})/2$, with numerical value $\simeq 1.61803$.

Mathematical constant (see Section A.3.10). ■ See page 566.

■ Goto

Goto[*tag*] scans the current compound expression for Label[*tag*], and transfers control to that point.

See pages 293 and 295.

■ **Graphics**

Graphics[*primitives*, *options*] represents a two-dimensional graphical image.

Graphics is displayed using Show. ■ The following graphics primitives can be used:

Circle[{x, y}, r]	circle
Disk[{x, y}, r]	filled disk
Line[{{x_1, y_1}, ... }]	line
Point[{x, y}]	point
Polygon[{{x_1, y_1}, ... }]	filled polygon
PostScript["*string*"]	PostScript code to include verbatim
Raster[*array*]	array of gray levels
RasterArray[*garray*]	array of colored cells
Rectangle[{*xmin*, *ymin*}, {*xmax*, *ymax*}]	filled rectangle
Text[*expr*, {x, y}]	text

■ The sound primitives SampledSoundList and SampledSoundFunction can also be included. ■ The following graphics directives can be used:

AbsoluteDashing[{d_1, ... }]	absolute line dashing specification
AbsolutePointSize[d]	absolute point size specification
AbsoluteThickness[d]	absolute line thickness specification
CMYKColor[c, m, y, k]	color specification
Dashing[{r_1, ... }]	line dashing specification
GrayLevel[i]	intensity specification
Hue[h]	hue specification
RGBColor[r, g, b]	color specification
PointSize[r]	point size specification
Thickness[r]	line thickness specification

■ The following options can be given:

AspectRatio	1/GoldenRatio	ratio of height to width
Axes	False	whether to draw axes
AxesLabel	None	axes labels
AxesOrigin	Automatic	where axes should cross
AxesStyle	Automatic	graphics directives to specify the style for axes
Background	Automatic	background color for the plot
ColorOutput	Automatic	type of color output to produce
DefaultColor	Automatic	the default color for plot elements
DefaultFont	$DefaultFont	the default font for text
DisplayFunction	$DisplayFunction	function for generating output
Epilog	{}	graphics primitives to be rendered after the main plot
Frame	False	whether to put a frame around the plot
FrameLabel	None	frame labels
FrameStyle	Automatic	graphics directives giving the style for the frame
FrameTicks	Automatic	frame tick marks
GridLines	None	grid lines to draw
PlotLabel	None	a label for the plot
PlotRange	Automatic	range of values to include
PlotRegion	Automatic	the final display region to be filled
Prolog	{}	graphics primitives to be rendered before the main plot
RotateLabel	True	whether to rotate y labels on the frame
Ticks	Automatic	tick marks

(continued)

■ Graphics *(continued)*

Nested lists of graphics primitives can be given. Specifications such as `GrayLevel` remain in effect only until the end of the list which contains them. ■ The standard print form for `Graphics[...]` is `-Graphics-`. `InputForm` prints the explicit list of primitives. ■ See page 395. ■ See also: `Plot`, `ListPlot`, `ParametricPlot`.

■ Graphics3D

`Graphics3D[primitives, options]` represents a three-dimensional graphical image.

`Graphics3D` is displayed using `Show`. ■ The following graphics primitives can be used:

`Cuboid[{xmin, ymin, zmin}, ... ]`	cuboid
`Line[{{x_1, y_1, z_1}, ... }]`	line
`Point[{x, y, z}]`	point
`Polygon[{{x_1, y_1, z_1}, ... }]`	polygon
`Text[expr, {x, y, z}]`	text

■ The sound primitives `SampledSoundList` and `SampledSoundFunction` can also be included. ■ The following graphics directives can be used:

`AbsoluteDashing[{d_1, ... }]`	absolute line dashing specification
`AbsolutePointSize[d]`	absolute point size specification
`AbsoluteThickness[d]`	absolute line thickness specification
`CMYKColor[c, m, y, k]`	color specification
`Dashing[{r_1, ... }]`	line dashing specification
`EdgeForm[spec]`	polygon edge specification
`FaceForm[spec]`	polygon face specification
`GrayLevel[i]`	gray-level specification
`Hue[h]`	hue specification
`PointSize[r]`	point size specification
`RGBColor[r, g, b]`	color specification
`SurfaceColor[spec]`	surface properties specification
`Thickness[r]`	line thickness specification

■ The following options can be given:

`AmbientLight`	`GrayLevel[0.]`	ambient illumination level
`AspectRatio`	`Automatic`	ratio of height to width
`Axes`	`False`	whether to draw axes
`AxesEdge`	`Automatic`	on which edges to put axes
`AxesLabel`	`None`	axes labels
`AxesStyle`	`Automatic`	graphics directives to specify the style for axes
`Background`	`Automatic`	background color for the plot
`Boxed`	`True`	whether to draw the bounding box
`BoxRatios`	`Automatic`	bounding 3D box ratios
`BoxStyle`	`Automatic`	graphics directives to specify the style for the box
`ColorOutput`	`Automatic`	type of color output to produce
`DefaultColor`	`Automatic`	the default color for plot elements
`DefaultFont`	`$DefaultFont`	the default font for text
`DisplayFunction`	`$DisplayFunction`	function for generating output

(continued)

■ Graphics3D *(continued)*

Epilog	{}	2D graphics primitives to be rendered after the main plot
FaceGrids	None	grid lines to draw on the bounding box
Lighting	True	whether to use simulated illumination
LightSources	(see below)	positions and colors of light sources
PlotLabel	None	a label for the plot
PlotRange	Automatic	range of values to include
PlotRegion	Automatic	the final display region to be filled
PolygonIntersections	True	whether to leave intersecting polygons unchanged
Prolog	{}	2D graphics primitives to be rendered before the main plot
RenderAll	True	whether to render all polygons
Shading	True	whether to shade polygons
SphericalRegion	False	whether to make the circumscribing sphere fit in the final display area
Ticks	Automatic	tick marks
ViewCenter	Automatic	point to put at the center of final display area
ViewPoint	{1.3, -2.4, 2.}	viewing position
ViewVertical	{0, 0, 1}	direction to make vertical

■ Nested lists of graphics primitives can be given. Specifications such as GrayLevel remain in effect only until the end of the list which contains them. ■ The standard print form for Graphics3D[...] is -Graphics3D-. InputForm prints the explicit list of primitives. ■ The default light sources used are
{{{1,0,1}, RGBColor[1,0,0]}, {{1,1,1}, RGBColor[0,1,0]}, {{0,1,1}, RGBColor[0,0,1]}}
■ Graphics3D[SurfaceGraphics[...]] can be used to convert a SurfaceGraphics object into Graphics3D representation. ■ See page 395. ■ See also: Plot3D, SurfaceGraphics, ParametricPlot3D.

▨ GraphicsArray

GraphicsArray[{g_1, g_2, ... }] represents a row of graphics objects.

GraphicsArray[{{g_{11}, g_{12}, ... }, ... }] represents a two-dimensional array of graphics objects.

You can display a GraphicsArray object using Show. ■ GraphicsArray sets up identical rectangular display areas for each of the graphics objects it contains. ■ GraphicsArray takes the same options as Graphics, with the defaults for Ticks and FrameTicks changed to None. ■ GraphicsArray takes the additional option GraphicsSpacing, which specifies the spacing between the rectangular areas containing each graphics object. The default setting is GraphicsSpacing -> 0.1. ■ The options DisplayFunction, ColorOutput and StringConversion are ignored for graphics objects given inside GraphicsArray. ■ See pages 144 and 395. ■ See also: Rectangle, RasterArray, TableForm.

▨ GraphicsSpacing

GraphicsSpacing is an option for GraphicsArray which specifies the spacing between elements in the array.

GraphicsSpacing -> 0 inserts no horizontal or vertical spacing, so that all adjacent rectangular areas in the array are shown abutting. ■ GraphicsSpacing -> {h, v} specifies horizontal and vertical spacing to use.
■ GraphicsSpacing -> s is equivalent to GraphicsSpacing -> {s, s}. ■ The spacing is given in scaled coordinates, relative to each rectangular area in the array. ■ Example: a horizontal spacing of 0.1 yields an array in which the rectangular areas are separated horizontally by distances equal to 0.1 of their widths. ■ See page 146. ■ See also: TableSpacing.

■ **GrayLevel**

GrayLevel[*level*] is a graphics directive which specifies the gray-level intensity with which graphical objects that follow should be displayed.

The gray level must be a number between 0 and 1. ■ 0 represents black; 1 represents white. ■ On display devices with no native gray-level capability, dither patterns are typically used, as generated by the PostScript interpreter. ■ Page 40 shows examples of gray levels generated with various GrayLevel specifications. ■ See page 407. ■ See also: RGBColor, Hue, Raster.

■ **Greater**

$x > y$ yields True if x is determined to be greater than y.

$x_1 > x_2 > x_3$ yields True if the x_i form a strictly decreasing sequence.

Greater gives True or False when its arguments are real numbers. ■ Greater does some simplification when its arguments are not numbers. ■ See page 94. ■ See also: Less, Positive.

■ **GreaterEqual**

$x >= y$ yields True if x is determined to be greater than or equal to y.

$x_1 >= x_2 >= x_3$ yields True if the x_i form a non-increasing sequence.

GreaterEqual gives True or False when its arguments are real numbers. ■ GreaterEqual does some simplification when its arguments are not numbers. ■ See page 94.

■ **GridLines**

GridLines is an option for two-dimensional graphics functions that specifies grid lines.

The following settings can be given for GridLines:

None	no grid lines drawn
Automatic	grid lines placed automatically
{*xgrid*, *ygrid*}	grid lines specified separately in each direction

■ With the Automatic setting, grid lines are usually placed at points whose coordinates have the minimum number of digits in their decimal representation. ■ For each direction, the following grid line options can be given:

None	no grid lines drawn
Automatic	grid line positions chosen automatically
{x_1, x_2, ... }	grid lines drawn at the specified positions
{{x_1, *style_i*}, ... }	grid lines with specified styles
func	a function to be applied to *xmin*, *xmax* to get the grid line option

■ Grid line styles can involve graphics directives such as RGBColor and Thickness. ■ Grid lines are by default colored light blue. ■ The grid line function *func*[*xmin*, *xmax*] may return any other grid line option. ■ FullOptions gives the explicit form of GridLines specifications when Automatic settings are used. ■ See pages 418 and 423. ■ See also: Ticks, FrameTicks, FaceGrids.

■ **GroebnerBasis**

GroebnerBasis[{*poly_1*, *poly_2*, ... }, {x_1, x_2, ... }] gives a list of polynomials which form a Gröbner basis for the ideal generated by the *poly_i*.

Gröbner bases are not in general unique. The Gröbner basis obtained from GroebnerBasis may depend on the order in which the variables x_i are specified. ■ See page 622. ■ See also: AlgebraicRules, Solve.

■ Head

Head[*expr*] gives the head of *expr*.

Examples: Head[f[x]] ⟶ f; Head[a + b] ⟶ Plus; Head[4] ⟶ Integer; Head[x] ⟶ Symbol. ■ See page 191.

◪ Heads

Heads is an option for functions which use level specifications that specifies whether heads of expressions should be included.

Heads -> True treats heads just like other elements of expressions for the purpose of levels. ■ Heads -> False never includes heads as part of any level of an expression. ■ Most functions which use level specifications have the default setting Heads -> False. One exception is Position, for which the default is Heads -> True. ■ See page 198. ■ See also: Level.

◪ HeldPart

HeldPart[*expr*, *pos*] extracts the part or parts specified by *pos*, and wraps each of them in Hold.

See notes for Part. ■ Example: HeldPart[Hold[{1 + 1, 2 + 2}], 1, 2] ⟶ Hold[2 + 2]. ■ See page 282. ■ See also: ReplaceHeldPart, ReleaseHold.

■ HermiteH

HermiteH[*n*, *x*] gives the Hermite polynomial $H_n(x)$.

Mathematical function (see Section A.3.9). ■ Explicit polynomials are given for integer *n*. ■ The Hermite polynomials satisfy the differential equation $\frac{d^2y}{dx^2} - 2x\frac{dy}{dx} + 2ny = 0$. ■ They are orthogonal polynomials with weight function e^{-x^2}. ■ See page 567.

■ HiddenSurface

HiddenSurface is an option for SurfaceGraphics which specifies whether hidden surfaces are to be eliminated.

HiddenSurface -> True eliminates hidden surfaces. ■ See page 156. ■ See also: Shading.

■ Hold

Hold[*expr*] maintains *expr* in an unevaluated form.

Hold has attribute HoldAll, and performs no operation on its arguments. ■ Example: Hold[1+1] ⟶ Hold[1 + 1]. ■ Hold is removed by ReleaseHold. ■ Hold[e_1, e_2, ...] maintains a sequence of unevaluated expressions to which a function can be applied using Apply. ■ See page 281. ■ See also: Literal, HoldForm, Unevaluated.

■ HoldAll

HoldAll is an attribute which specifies that all arguments to a function are to be maintained in an unevaluated form.

You can use Evaluate to evaluate the arguments of a HoldAll function in a controlled way. ■ See pages 272 and 279. ■ See also: Unevaluated.

■ HoldFirst

HoldFirst is an attribute which specifies that the first argument to a function is to be maintained in an unevaluated form.

See pages 272 and 279.

■ **HoldForm**

HoldForm[*expr*] prints as the expression *expr*, with *expr* maintained in an unevaluated form.

HoldForm allows you to see the output form of an expression without evaluating the expression. ■ HoldForm has attribute HoldAll. ■ HoldForm is removed by ReleaseHold. ■ See pages 281 and 349. ■ See also: ToString, WriteString.

■ **HoldRest**

HoldRest is an attribute which specifies that all but the first argument to a function are to be maintained in an unevaluated form.

See page 279.

■ **HomeDirectory**

HomeDirectory[ ] gives your "home" directory.

HomeDirectory returns the full name of the directory as a string. ■ On multi-user operating systems, HomeDirectory gives the main directory for the current user. ■ See page 490. ■ See also: Directory, ParentDirectory.

■ **Hue**

Hue[*h*] is a graphics directive which specifies that graphical objects which follow are to be displayed, if possible, in a color corresponding to hue *h*.

Hue[*h*, *s*, *b*] specifies colors in terms of hue, saturation and brightness.

The parameters h, s and b must all be between 0 and 1. Values of s and b outside this range are clipped. Values of h outside this range are treated cyclically. ■ As h varies from 0 to 1, the color corresponding to Hue[*h*] runs through red, yellow, green, cyan, blue, magenta, and back to red again. ■ Hue[*h*] is equivalent to Hue[*h*, 1, 1]. ■ On monochrome displays, a gray level based on the brightness value is used. ■ Page 40 shows examples of colors generated with various Hue specifications. ■ See page 407. ■ See also: RGBColor, GrayLevel, CMYKColor.

■ **Hypergeometric0F1**

Hypergeometric0F1[*a*, *z*] is the hypergeometric function $_0F_1(;a;z)$.

Mathematical function (see Section A.3.9). ■ The $_0F_1$ function has the series expansion $_0F_1(;a;z) = \sum_{k=0}^{\infty} \frac{z^k}{(a)_k k!}$. ■ See page 570. ■ See also: Pochhammer.

■ **Hypergeometric1F1**

Hypergeometric1F1[*a*, *b*, *z*] is the Kummer confluent hypergeometric function $_1F_1(a;b;z)$.

Mathematical function (see Section A.3.9). ■ The $_1F_1$ function has the series expansion $_1F_1(a;b;z) = \sum_{k=0}^{\infty} \frac{(a)_k}{(b)_k} \frac{z^k}{k!}$. ■ See page 570.

■ **Hypergeometric2F1**

Hypergeometric2F1[*a*, *b*, *c*, *z*] is the hypergeometric function $_2F_1(a, b; c; z)$.

Mathematical function (see Section A.3.9). ■ The $_2F_1$ function has the series expansion $_2F_1(a, b; c; z) = \sum_{k=0}^{\infty} \frac{(a)_k (b)_k}{(c)_k} \frac{z^k}{k!}$. ■ See page 570.

■ **HypergeometricU**

HypergeometricU[*a*, *b*, *z*] is the confluent hypergeometric function $U(a, b, z)$.

Mathematical function (see Section A.3.9). ■ The function $U(a, b, z)$ has the integral representation $U(a, b, z) = \frac{1}{\Gamma(a)} \int_0^{\infty} e^{-zt} t^{a-1} (1+t)^{b-a-1} \, dt$. ■ See page 570.

■ **I**

I represents the imaginary unit $\sqrt{-1}$.

Numbers containing I are converted to the type Complex. ■ See page 566. ■ See also: Re, Im, ComplexExpand, GaussianIntegers.

■ **Identity**

Identity[*expr*] gives *expr* (the identity operation).

See page 213. ■ See also: Composition, Through, InverseFunction.

■ **IdentityMatrix**

IdentityMatrix[*n*] gives the $n \times n$ identity matrix.

See page 649. ■ See also: DiagonalMatrix, Table.

■ **If**

If[*condition*, *t*, *f*] gives *t* if *condition* evaluates to True, and *f* if it evaluates to False.

If[*condition*, *t*, *f*, *u*] gives *u* if *condition* evaluates to neither True nor False.

If evaluates only the argument determined by the value of the condition. ■ If[*condition*, *t*, *f*] is left unevaluated if *condition* evaluates to neither True nor False. ■ If[*condition*, *t*] gives Null if *condition* evaluates to False. ■ See page 287. ■ See also: Switch, Which, Condition.

■ **IgnoreCase**

IgnoreCase is an option for string manipulation and searching functions which specifies whether lower- and upper-case letters should be treated as equivalent.

With the default setting IgnoreCase -> False, lower- and upper-case letters are treated as totally different. ■ With the setting IgnoreCase -> True, lower- and upper-case letters are treated as equivalent. ■ IgnoreCase is an option for StringPosition, StringReplace, Find and FindList. ■ IgnoreCase uses $Letters to determine letter equivalences. ■ IgnoreCase in no way affects the parsing of *Mathematica* expressions. ■ See page 379. ■ See also: ToUpperCase, ToLowerCase, SpellingCorrection.

■ **Im**

Im[*z*] gives the imaginary part of the complex number *z*.

Im[*expr*] is left unevaluated if *expr* is not a number. ■ See page 551. ■ See also: Re, Abs, Arg, ComplexExpand.

■ **Implies**

Implies[*p*, *q*] represents the logical implication $p \Rightarrow q$.

Implies[*p*, *q*] is equivalent to !*p* || *q*. ■ See page 619. ■ See also: LogicalExpand, If.

■ **In**

In[*n*] is a global object that is assigned to have a delayed value of the nth input line.

Typing In[*n*] causes the nth input line to be re-evaluated. ■ In[ ] gives the last input line. ■ In[-*k*] gives the input *k* lines back. ■ See pages 62 and 513. ■ See also: InString, Out, $Line.

■ **Increment**

x++ increases the value of *x* by 1, returning the old value of *x*.

Increment has attribute HoldFirst. ■ See page 248. ■ See also: PreIncrement, AddTo, Set.

■ **Indent**

> `Indent[d]` is printed as the indentation for a depth d subexpression.

> You can redefine `Indent[d]` to change the indentation in the printed forms of expressions. ■ See page 517. ■ See also: `LineBreak`, `Continuation`, `StringBreak`, `DialogIndent`.

■ **Indeterminate**

> `Indeterminate` is a symbol that represents a numerical quantity whose magnitude cannot be determined.

> Computations like 0/0 generate `Indeterminate`. ■ A message is produced whenever an operation first yields `Indeterminate` as a result. ■ See page 547. ■ See also: `DirectedInfinity`, `Check`.

■ **Infinity**

> `Infinity` is a symbol that represents a positive infinite quantity.

> `Infinity` is converted to `DirectedInfinity[1]`. ■ Certain arithmetic operations work with `Infinity`. ■ Example: `1/Infinity` $\longrightarrow$ 0. ■ See pages 548 and 566. ■ See also: `ComplexInfinity`, `Indeterminate`.

■ **Infix**

> `Infix[f[e₁, e₂, ... ]]` prints with $f[e_1, e_2, ...]$ given in default infix form:
> $e_1 \sim f \sim e_2 \sim f \sim e_3 ... $.

> `Infix[expr, h]` prints with arguments separated by h: e_1 h e_2 h e_3 ... .

> `Infix[expr, h, precedence, grouping]` can be used to specify how the output form should be parenthesized. ■ Precedence levels are specified by integers. In `OutputForm`, some precedence levels are:

> | | |
> |---|---|
> | x . y . z | 210 |
> | x y z | 150 |
> | $x + y + z$ | 140 |
> | $x == y$ | 130 |
> | $x = y$ | 60 |

> ■ Possible grouping (associativity) specifications are:

> | | |
> |---|---|
> | `NonAssociative` | not associative – always parenthesized |
> | `None` | always associative – never parenthesized |
> | `Left` | left associative (*e.g.*, $(a/b)/c$) |
> | `Right` | right associative (*e.g.*, $a \wedge (b \wedge c)$) |

> ■ See page 362. ■ See also: `Postfix`, `Prefix`, `PrecedenceForm`.

■ **Information**

> `Information[symbol]` prints information about a symbol.

> `Information[symbol]` prints the same information as the input escape `??symbol` would give. ■ `Information` has attribute `HoldAll`. ■ See pages 69 and 722. ■ See also: `Definition`, `Names`, `ValueQ`, `DownValues`, `UpValues`.

■ Inner

Inner[f, *list₁*, *list₂*, g] is a generalization of Dot in which f plays the role of multiplication and g of addition.

Example: Inner[f,{a,b},{x,y},g] ⟶ g[f[a, x], f[b, y]]. ■ Inner[f,{{a,b},{c,d}},{x,y},g] ⟶ {g[f[a, x], f[b, y]], g[f[c, x], f[d, y]]}. ■ Like Dot, Inner effectively contracts the last index of the first tensor with the first index of the second tensor. Applying Inner to a rank r tensor and a rank s tensor gives a rank $r + s - 2$ tensor. ■ Inner[f, *list₁*, *list₂*] uses Plus for g. ■ Inner[f, *list₁*, *list₂*, g, n] contracts index n of the first tensor with the first index of the second tensor. ■ The heads of *list₁* and *list₂* must be the same, but need not necessarily be List. ■ See page 669. ■ See also: Outer, Thread, MapThread.

■ Input

Input[ ] interactively reads in one *Mathematica* expression.

Input["*prompt*"] requests input, using the specified string as a prompt.

Input returns the expression it read. ■ The operation of Input may vary from one computer system to another. When a *Mathematica* front end is used, Input may work through a dialog box. ■ When no front end is used, Input reads from standard input. ■ If the standard input is a file, then Input returns EndOfFile if you try to read past the end of the file. ■ On most systems, Input[ ] uses ? as a prompt. ■ When Input is evaluated, *Mathematica* stops until the input has been read. ■ See page 522. ■ See also: InputString, Read, Get, Dialog.

■ InputForm

InputForm[*expr*] prints as a version of *expr* suitable for input to *Mathematica*.

Example: InputForm[x∧2 + 1/a] ⟶ a∧(-1) + x∧2. ■ InputForm always produces one-dimensional output, suitable to be typed as lines of *Mathematica* input. ■ InputForm acts as a "wrapper", which affects printing, but not evaluation. ■ Put (>>) produces InputForm by default. ■ Short[InputForm[*expr*]] can be used, but may generate skeleton objects which cannot be given as *Mathematica* input. ■ See page 343. ■ See also: OutputForm, FullForm.

■ InputStream

InputStream["*name*", n] is an object that represents an input stream for functions such as Read and Find.

OpenRead returns an InputStream object. ■ The serial number n is unique across all streams, regardless of their name. ■ StringToStream returns an object of the form InputStream[String, n]. ■ See page 484. ■ See also: $Input, Streams, OutputStream.

■ InputString

InputString[ ] interactively reads in a character string.

InputString["*prompt*"] requests input, using the specified string as a prompt.

See notes for Input. ■ See page 522.

■ **Insert**

Insert [*list*, *elem*, *n*] inserts *elem* at position *n* in *list*. If *n* is negative, the position is counted from the end.

Insert [*expr*, *elem*, {*i*, *j*, ... }] inserts *elem* at position {*i*, *j*, ... } in *expr*.

Insert [*expr*, *elem*, {{*i₁*, *j₁*, ... }, {*i₂*, *j₂*, ... }, ... }] inserts *elem* at several positions.

Examples: Insert [{a, b, c}, x, 2] ⟶ {a, x, b, c}.
■ Insert [{a, b, c}, x, {{1}, {-1}}] ⟶ {x, a, b, c, x}.
■ Insert [{{a, b}, {c, d}}, x, {2, 1}] ⟶ {{a, b}, {x, c, d}}. ■ *list* can have any head, not necessarily List. ■ See page 128. ■ See also: Prepend, Append, StringInsert, Take, Drop, Delete, ReplacePart, FlattenAt, Position.

▨ **Install**

Install ["*command*"] starts an external program and installs *Mathematica* definitions to call functions in it.

The *Mathematica* definitions set up by Install are typically specified in the *MathLink* template file used to create the source code for the external program. ■ Install returns an object representing a *MathLink* link. ■ LinkPatterns [*link*] gives a list of the patterns defined when the specified link was set up. ■ You can remove these definitions, and terminate the execution of the external program by calling Uninstall [*link*]. ■ If you call Install ["*command*"] multiple times with the same *command*, the later calls will overwrite definitions set up by earlier ones, unless the definitions depend on the values of global variables which have changed. ■ See page 509. ■ See also: Get, Run, RunThrough, Uninstall.

▨ **InString**

InString [*n*] is a global object that is assigned to be the text of the nth input line.

InString [*n*] gives the string that *Mathematica* read for the nth input line. The string includes all intermediate newlines in the input, but not the newline at the end. ■ The value of InString [*n*] is assigned after the input is verified to be syntactically correct, and after any function given as the value of $PreRead has been applied. ■ InString [ ] gives the text of the last input line. ■ InString [-k] gives the text of the input *k* lines back. ■ See pages 62 and 513. ■ See also: In, $SyntaxHandler.

■ **Integer**

Integer is the head used for integers.

_Integer can be used to stand for an integer in a pattern. ■ Integers can be of any length. ■ You can enter an integer in base *b* using *b*^^*digits*. The base must be less than 36. The letters are used in sequence to standard for digits 10 through 35. ■ See page 534. ■ See also: IntegerDigits, BaseForm.

▨ **IntegerDigits**

IntegerDigits [*n*] gives a list of the decimal digits in the integer *n*.

IntegerDigits [*n*, *b*] gives a list of the base-*b* digits in the integer *n*.

Examples: IntegerDigits [5810] ⟶ {5, 8, 1, 0}; IntegerDigits [5810, 16] ⟶ {1, 6, 11, 2}. ■ See page 537. ■ See also: RealDigits, BaseForm.

■ **IntegerQ**

IntegerQ [*expr*] gives True if *expr* is an integer, and False otherwise.

IntegerQ [*expr*] returns False unless *expr* is manifestly an integer (*i.e.*, has head Integer). ■ You can use IntegerQ [*x*] = True to override the normal operation of IntegerQ, and effectively define *x* to be an integer. ■ See pages 227 and 535. ■ See also: EvenQ, OddQ, NumberQ, TrueQ.

■ Integrate

Integrate [f, x] gives the indefinite integral $\int f\,dx$.

Integrate [f, {x, $xmin$, $xmax$}] gives the definite integral $\int_{xmin}^{xmax} f\,dx$.

Integrate [f, {x, $xmin$, $xmax$}, {y, $ymin$, $ymax$}] gives the multiple integral $\int_{xmin}^{xmax} dx \int_{ymin}^{ymax} dy\, f$.

Multiple integrals use a variant of the standard iterator notation. The first variable given corresponds to the outermost integral, and is done last. ■ **Integrate** can evaluate integrals of rational functions. It can also evaluate integrals that involve exponential, logarithmic, trigonometric and inverse trigonometric functions, so long as the result comes out in terms of the same set of functions. ■ **Integrate** can give results in terms of functions such as **LogIntegral**, **Erf** and **PolyLog**. ■ **Integrate** carries out some simplifications on integrals it cannot explicitly do. ■ You can get a numerical result by applying **N** to a definite integral. ■ You can assign values to patterns involving **Integrate** to give results for new classes of integrals. ■ The integration variable can be any expression. However, **Integrate** uses only its literal form. The object $d(x^n)$, for example, is not converted to $nx^{n-1}dx$. ■ **Integrate** evaluates expressions of the form **Sign** [arg] to determine whether to give results in terms of **Log** [arg], **ArcTan** [arg] or **ArcTanh** [arg]. ■ **Integrate** can evaluate definite integrals whenever the correct result can be found by taking limits of the indefinite form at the endpoints. ■ See page 630. ■ See also: **NIntegrate**, **DSolve**.

■ InterpolatingFunction

InterpolatingFunction [$range$, $table$] represents an approximate function whose values are found by interpolation.

InterpolatingFunction works like **Function**. ■ **InterpolatingFunction** [...] [x] finds the value of an approximate function with a particular argument x. ■ In standard output format, only the first element of an **InterpolatingFunction** object is printed explicitly. The remaining elements are indicated by <>. ■ The first element specifies the range of parameter values over which the approximate function is defined. ■ If you supply arguments outside of the range, a warning is generated, and the **InterpolatingFunction** object is returned unevaluated. ■ **InterpolatingFunction** objects that take any number of real arguments may be constructed. ■ **InterpolatingFunction** [...] is listable. ■ **NDSolve** returns its results in terms of **InterpolatingFunction** objects. ■ See page 676. ■ See also: **CompiledFunction**.

■ InterpolatingPolynomial

InterpolatingPolynomial [$data$, var] gives a polynomial in the variable *var* which provides an exact fit to a list of data.

The data can have the forms {{x_1, f_1}, {x_2, f_2}, ... } or {f_1, f_2, ... }, where in the second case, the x_i are taken to have values 1, 2, ...

The f_i can be replaced by {f_i, df_i, ddf_i, ... }, specifying derivatives at the points x_i.

With a list of data of length n, **InterpolatingPolynomial** gives a polynomial of degree $n-1$. ■ Example: **InterpolatingPolynomial** [{4, 5, 8}, x] $\longrightarrow$ 4 + (-1 + x)^2. ■ **InterpolatingPolynomial** gives the interpolating polynomial in Newton form, suitable for numerical evaluation. ■ See pages 602 and 675. ■ See also: **Fit**.

◪ Interpolation

Interpolation[*data***]** constructs an **InterpolatingFunction** object which represents an approximate function that interpolates the data.

The data can have the forms $\{\{x_1, f_1\}, \{x_2, f_2\}, \dots \}$ or $\{f_1, f_2, \dots \}$, where in the second case, the x_i are taken to have values 1, 2, ...

Data can be given in the form $\{\{x_1, \{f_1, df_1, ddf_1, \dots \}\}, \dots \}$ to specify derivatives as well as values of the function at the points x_i. You can specify different numbers of derivatives at different points. ■ Function values and derivatives may be either real or complex numbers. The x_i must be real. ■ Multi-dimensional data can be given in the form $\{\{x_1, y_1, \dots, f_1\}, \dots \}$. Derivatives in this case can be given by replacing f_1 and so on by $\{f_1, \{dxf_1, dyf_1, \dots \}\}$. ■ **Interpolation** works by fitting polynomial curves between successive data points. ■ The degree of the polynomial curves is specified by the option **InterpolationOrder**. ■ The default setting is **InterpolationOrder -> 3**. ■ You can do linear interpolation by using the setting **InterpolationOrder -> 1**. ■ See page 676. ■ See also: **InterpolatingPolynomial, Fit**.

◪ Interrupt

Interrupt[ ] generates an interrupt.

You can call **Interrupt** anywhere within a computation. It has the same effect as an interactive interrupt at that point. ■ See page 311. ■ See also: **Abort, TimeConstrained, MemoryConstrained, $Inspector**.

■ Intersection

Intersection[*list_1, list_2, ...***]** gives a sorted list of the elements common to all the *list_i*.

If the *list_i* are considered as sets, **Intersection** gives their intersection. ■ The *list_i* must have the same head, but it need not be **List**. ■ See page 129. ■ See also: **Union, Complement**.

■ Inverse

Inverse[*m***]** gives the inverse of a square matrix *m*.

Inverse works on both symbolic and numerical matrices. ■ For matrices with approximate real or complex numbers, the inverse is generated to the maximum possible precision given the input. A warning is given for ill-conditioned matrices. ■ **Inverse[***m***, Modulus->***p***]** evaluates the inverse modulo *p*. ■ **Inverse[***m***, ZeroTest -> ***test***]** evaluates *test*[*m*[[*i*, *j*]]] to determine whether matrix elements are zero. The default setting is **ZeroTest -> (Together[#] == 0)&**. ■ See page 655. ■ See also: **PseudoInverse, LinearSolve, NullSpace**.

■ InverseFourier

InverseFourier[*list***]** finds the discrete inverse Fourier transform of a list of complex numbers.

The inverse Fourier transform a_r of a list b_s of length n is defined to be $\frac{1}{\sqrt{n}} \sum_{s=1}^{n} b_s e^{-2\pi i (r-1)(s-1)/n}$. ■ Note that the zero frequency term must appear at position 1 in the input list. ■ The definition of the Fourier transform used is the one common in the physical sciences. The sign of the exponent must be reversed to obtain the definition common in electrical engineering. ■ The list of data need not have a length equal to a power of two. ■ The *list* given in **InverseFourier[***list***]** can be nested to represent an array of data in any number of dimensions. ■ The array of data must be rectangular. ■ See page 679. ■ See also: **Fourier**.

◪ InverseFunction

InverseFunction[*f*] represents the inverse of the function *f*, defined so that InverseFunction[*f*] [*y*] gives the value of *x* for which *f*[*x*] is equal to *y*.

For a function with several arguments, InverseFunction[*f*] represents the inverse with respect to the first argument. InverseFunction[*f*, *n*] represents the inverse with respect to the *n*[th] argument. InverseFunction[*f*, *n*, *tot*] represents the inverse with respect to the *n*[th] argument when there are *tot* arguments in all.

In OutputForm, InverseFunction[*f*] is printed as $f^{(-1)}$. ▪ As discussed in Section 3.2.7, many mathematical functions do not have unique inverses. In such cases, InverseFunction[*f*] can represent only one of the possible inverses for *f*. ▪ Example: InverseFunction[Sin] ⟶ ArcSin. ▪ InverseFunction is generated by Solve when the option InverseFunctions is set to Automatic or True. ▪ See pages 213 and 613. ▪ See also: Solve, InverseSeries, Composition, Derivative.

◪ InverseFunctions

InverseFunctions is an option to Solve and related functions which specifies whether inverse functions should be used.

Settings for InverseFunctions are:

True	always use inverse functions
Automatic	use inverse functions, printing a warning message (default)
False	never use inverse functions

▪ Example: Solve[f[x] == a, x, InverseFunctions->True] ⟶ {{x -> f$^{(-1)}$[a]}}. ▪ Inverse functions provide a way to get some, but not in general all, solutions to equations that involve functions which are more complicated than polynomials. ▪ Solve[Sin[x] == a, x, InverseFunctions->True] ⟶ {{x -> ArcSin[a]}} gives a single solution in terms of ArcSin. In fact, there is an infinite number of solutions to the equation, differing by arbitrary multiples of 2π. Solve gives only one of these solutions. ▪ When there are several simultaneous equations to be solved in terms of inverse functions, Solve may fail to find any solutions, even when one exists. ▪ When inverse functions are allowed, Solve solves for *f*[*expr*] first, then applies InverseFunction[*f*] to the result, equates it to *expr*, and continues trying to solve for the remainder of the variables. ▪ See page 612. ▪ See also: FindRoot.

◼ InverseJacobiSN

InverseJacobiSN[*v*, *m*], InverseJacobiCN[*v*, *m*], etc. give the inverse Jacobi elliptic functions $sn^{-1}(v|m)$ etc.

There are a total of twelve functions, with names of the form InverseJacobi*PQ*, where *P* and *Q* can be any distinct pair of the letters S, C, D and N.

Mathematical functions (see Section A.3.9). ▪ $sn^{-1}(v|m)$ gives the value of *u* for which $v = sn(u|m)$. ▪ The inverse Jacobi elliptic functions are related to elliptic integrals. ▪ See page 580.

◼ InverseSeries

InverseSeries[*s*, *x*] takes the series *s* generated by Series, and gives a series for the inverse of the function represented by *s*.

InverseSeries performs "reversion" of series. ▪ Given a series *s*(*y*), InverseSeries[*s*, *x*] gives a series for *y* such that *s*(*y*) = *x*. ▪ See page 644. ▪ See also: Solve, InverseFunction.

■ **JacobiAmplitude**

JacobiAmplitude[*u*, *m*] gives the amplitude $am(u|m)$ for Jacobi elliptic functions.

JacobiAmplitude is the inverse of the elliptic integral of the first kind. If $u = F(\phi|m)$, then $\phi = am(u|m)$. ■ See page 580.

■ **JacobiP**

JacobiP[*n*, *a*, *b*, *x*] gives the Jacobi polynomial $P_n^{(a,b)}(x)$.

Mathematical function (see Section A.3.9). ■ Explicit polynomials are given when possible. ■ The Jacobi polynomials are orthogonal with weight function $(1-x)^a(1+x)^b$. ■ See page 567.

■ **JacobiSN**

JacobiSN[*u*, *m*], JacobiCN[*u*, *m*], etc. give the Jacobi elliptic functions $sn(u|m)$, $cn(u|m)$, etc.

There are a total of twelve functions, with the names of the form Jacobi*PQ*, where *P* and *Q* can be any distinct pair of the letters S, C, D and N.

Mathematical functions (see Section A.3.9). ■ $sn(u) = \sin(\phi)$, $cn(u) = \cos(\phi)$ and $dn(u) = \sqrt{1 - m\sin^2(\phi)}$, where $\phi = am(u|m)$. ■ Other Jacobi elliptic functions can be found from the relation $pq(u) = pr(u)/qr(u)$, where for these purposes $pp(u) = 1$. ■ See page 580. ■ See also: InverseJacobiSN.

■ **JacobiSymbol**

JacobiSymbol[*n*, *m*] gives the Jacobi symbol $\left(\frac{n}{m}\right)$.

Integer mathematical function (see Section A.3.9). ■ For prime *m*, the Jacobi symbol reduces to the Legendre symbol. The Legendre symbol is equal to ±1 depending on whether *n* is a quadratic residue modulo *m*. ■ See page 556.

■ **JacobiZeta**

JacobiZeta[*phi*, *m*] gives the Jacobi zeta function $Z(\phi|m)$.

Mathematical function (see Section A.3.9). ■ The Jacobi zeta function is given in terms of elliptic integrals by $Z(\phi|m) = E(\phi|m) - E(m)F(\phi|m)/K(m)$. ■ Argument conventions for elliptic integrals are discussed on page 580. ■ See page 580. ■ See also: EllipticE, EllipticF, EllipticK.

■ **Join**

Join[*list_1*, *list_2*, ...] concatenates lists together. Join can be used on any set of expressions that have the same head.

See page 129. ■ See also: Union, StringJoin, Append, Prepend.

■ **Label**

Label[*tag*] represents a point in a compound expression to which control can be transferred using Goto.

Label must appear as an explicit element of a CompoundExpression object. ■ Label has attribute HoldFirst. ■ See page 295.

■ **LaguerreL**

LaguerreL[*n*, *a*, *x*] gives the Laguerre polynomial $L_n^a(x)$.

Mathematical function (see Section A.3.9). ■ Explicit polynomials are given when possible. ■ The Laguerre polynomials are orthogonal with weight function $x^a e^{-x}$. ■ They satisfy the differential equation $x\frac{d^2y}{dx^2} + (a+1-x)\frac{dy}{dx} + ny = 0$. ■ See page 567.

■ **Last**

Last [*expr*] gives the last element in *expr*.

Last [*expr*] is equivalent to *expr*[[-1]]. ■ See page 125. ■ See also: Part, First, Take.

■ **LatticeReduce**

LatticeReduce [{v_1, v_2, ... }] gives a reduced basis for the set of integer vectors v_i.

LatticeReduce uses the Lenstra-Lenstra-Lovasz lattice reduction algorithm. ■ See page 556. ■ See also: RowReduce, Rationalize.

■ **LCM**

LCM [n_1, n_2, ...] gives the least common multiple of the integers n_i.

Integer mathematical function (see Section A.3.9). ■ See page 553. ■ See also: GCD.

■ **LeafCount**

LeafCount [*expr*] gives the total number of indivisible subexpressions in *expr*.

LeafCount gives a measure of the total "size" of an expression. ■ LeafCount counts the number of subexpressions in *expr* which correspond to "leaves" on the expression tree. ■ Example: LeafCount [1 + a + b∧2] ⟶ 6. ■ See page 528. ■ See also: ByteCount, Length, Depth, AtomQ.

■ **LegendreP**

LegendreP [n, x] gives the Legendre polynomial $P_n(x)$.

LegendreP [n, m, x] gives the associated Legendre polynomial $P_n^m(x)$.

Mathematical function (see Section A.3.9). ■ Explicit polynomials are given for integer n and m. ■ The Legendre polynomials satisfy the differential equation $(1-x^2)\frac{d^2y}{dx^2} - 2x\frac{dy}{dx} + n(n+1)y = 0$. ■ The Legendre polynomials are orthogonal with unit weight function. ■ The associated Legendre polynomials are defined by $P_n^m(x) = (-1)^m(1-x^2)^{m/2}\frac{d^m}{dx^m}P_n(x)$. ■ For arbitrary complex values of n, m and z, LegendreP [n, z] and LegendreP [n, m, z] give Legendre functions of the first kind. ■ The option LegendreType determines the choice of branch cuts used. The default is LegendreType -> Real. ■ See pages 567 and 570. ■ See also: SphericalHarmonicY.

■ **LegendreQ**

LegendreQ [n, z] gives the Legendre function of the second kind $Q_n(z)$.

LegendreQ [n, m, z] gives the associated Legendre function of the second kind $Q_n^m(z)$.

Mathematical function (see Section A.3.9). ■ For integer n and m, explicit formulas are generated. ■ The Legendre functions satisfy the differential equation $(1-z^2)\frac{d^2y}{dz^2} - 2z\frac{dy}{dz} + [(n(n+1) - \frac{m^2}{1-z^2}]y = 0$. ■ The option LegendreType determines the choice of branch cuts used. The default is LegendreType -> Real. ■ See page 570.

■ **LegendreType**

LegendreType is an option for LegendreP and LegendreQ which specifies choices of branch cuts for Legendre functions in the complex plane.

The possible settings for LegendreType are Real and Complex. ■ With LegendreType->Complex, there is a branch cut from −∞ to +1. With LegendreType->Real, there are branch cuts from −∞ to −1 and +1 to +∞. ■ See page 578.

■ **Length**

Length [*expr*] gives the number of elements in *expr*.

See page 196. ■ Length [*expr*] returns 0 whenever AtomQ [\#expr] is True. ■ See also: LeafCount, ByteCount, Depth.

■ **LerchPhi**

LerchPhi[z, s, a] gives the Lerch transcendent $\Phi(z, s, a)$.

Mathematical function (see Section A.3.9). ■ $\Phi(z, s, a) = \sum_{k=0}^{\infty} \frac{z^k}{(a+k)^s}$, where any term with $k + a = 0$ is excluded.
■ LerchPhi[z, s, a, DoublyInfinite->True] gives the sum $\sum_{k=-\infty}^{\infty} \frac{z^k}{(a+k)^s}$. ■ LerchPhi is a generalization of Zeta and PolyLog. ■ See page 571.

■ **Less**

x < y yields True if x is determined to be less than y.

x_1 < x_2 < x_3 yields True if the x_i form a strictly increasing sequence.

Less gives True or False when its arguments are real numbers. ■ Less does some simplification when its arguments are not numbers. ■ See page 94. ■ See also: Greater, Positive.

■ **LessEqual**

x <= y yields True if x is determined to be less than or equal to y.

x_1 <= x_2 <= x_3 yields True if the x_i form a non-decreasing sequence.

LessEqual gives True or False when its arguments are real numbers. ■ LessEqual does some simplification when its arguments are not numbers. ■ See page 94.

■ **LetterQ**

LetterQ[*string*] yields True if all the characters in the string are letters, and yields False otherwise.

LetterQ[*string*] by default gives False if *string* contains any space or punctuation characters. ■ LetterQ takes only the characters which appear in the list $Letters to be letters. ■ See page 378. ■ See also: DigitQ, UpperCaseQ, LowerCaseQ.

■ **Level**

Level[*expr*, *levelspec*] gives a list of all subexpressions of *expr* on levels specified by *levelspec*.

Level[*expr*, *levelspec*, *f*] applies *f* to the list of subexpressions.

Level uses the standard level specification described on page 725. ■ Level[*expr*, {-1}] gives a list of all "atomic" objects in *expr*. ■ Level traverses expressions in depth-first order, so that the subexpressions in the final list are ordered lexicographically by their indices. ■ See page 199. ■ See also: Apply, Map, Scan.

■ **Lighting**

Lighting is an option to Graphics3D and related functions that specifies whether to use simulated illumination in three-dimensional pictures.

Lighting -> True uses simulated illumination. The ambient light level is specified by the option AmbientLight. The option LightSources gives the positions and intensities of point light sources. ■ Lighting -> False uses no simulated illumination. In SurfaceGraphics, polygons are then shaded according to their height, or according to the ColorFunction option that is given. ■ See pages 436 and 455. ■ See also: Shading, ColorFunction, SurfaceColor.

■ **LightSources**

LightSources is an option to Graphics3D and related functions that specifies the properties of point light sources for simulated illumination.

The basic form is LightSources -> {s_1, s_2, ... }, where the s_i are the specifications for each light source. Each s_i has the form {*direction*, *color*}. The direction is specified as {x, y, z}, where the components are with respect to the final display area. The x and y are horizontal and vertical in the plane of the display; z is orthogonal to the display. Positive z is in front. Only the relative magnitude of the components is relevant; the overall normalization of the vector is ignored. The color can be specified by GrayLevel, Hue or RGBColor. ■ Simulated illumination determines the shading of polygons in three-dimensional pictures. ■ The shading of a particular polygon is computed as a sum of contributions from point light sources, plus a contribution from ambient light. ■ Surface properties of polygons are specified by SurfaceColor directives. ■ Light reflection properties assumed for polygons are described in the notes for SurfaceColor. ■ See page 455. ■ See also: AmbientLight.

■ **Limit**

Limit[*expr*, x->x_0] finds the limiting value of *expr* when x approaches x_0.

Example: Limit[Sin[x]/x, x->0] ⟶ 1. ■ Limit[*expr*, x->x_0, Direction -> 1] computes the limit as x approaches x_0 from below. Limit[*expr*, x->x_0, Direction -> -1] computes the limit as x approaches x_0 from above. ■ Limit returns objects of the form RealInterval[{*xmin*, *xmax*}] to represent ranges of possible values, for example at essential singularities. ■ Limit returns unevaluated when it encounters functions about which it has no specific information. Limit therefore makes no explicit assumptions about symbolic functions. ■ See page 646. ■ See also: Series, Residue.

■ **Line**

Line[{pt_1, pt_2, ... }] is a graphics primitive which represents a line joining a sequence of points.

Line can be used in both Graphics and Graphics3D (two- and three-dimensional graphics). ■ The positions of points can be specified either in absolute coordinates, as {x, y} or {x, y, z}, or in scaled coordinates as Scaled[{x, y}] or Scaled[{x, y, z}]. ■ The line consists of a sequence of straight segments joining the specified points. ■ Line thickness can be specified using Thickness or AbsoluteThickness. ■ Line dashing can be specified using Dashing or AbsoluteDashing. ■ Line shading or coloring can be specified using CMYKColor, GrayLevel, Hue or RGBColor. ■ In three dimensions, the properties of lines that appear at intersections between polygons can be specified using EdgeForm. ■ See pages 400 and 430. ■ See also: Polygon, PlotJoined.

■ **LinearProgramming**

LinearProgramming[c, m, b] finds the vector **x** which minimizes the quantity **c.x** subject to the constraints **m.x** $\geq$ **b** and **x** ≥ 0.

All entries in the vectors c and b and the matrix m must be numbers. ■ LinearProgramming gives exact rational number results if its input is exact. ■ LinearProgramming accepts the same Tolerance option as ConstrainedMax. ■ See page 707. ■ See also: ConstrainedMin.

■ **LinearSolve**

LinearSolve[m, b] gives the vector x which solves the matrix equation $m.x==b$.

LinearSolve works on both numerical and symbolic matrices. ■ The matrix m can be square or rectangular.
■ LinearSolve[m, b, Modulus -> p] takes the matrix equation to be modulo the prime p.
■ LinearSolve[m, b, ZeroTest -> *test*] evaluates *test*[m[[i, j]]] to determine whether matrix elements are zero. The default setting is ZeroTest -> (Together[#] == 0 &). ■ See page 660. ■ See also: Inverse, PseudoInverse, Solve, NullSpace.

■ **LineBreak**

LineBreak[n] is output between the nth and $(n+1)^{th}$ lines in a multiline printed expression.

Redefining Format[LineBreak[n_]] changes the way spaces are printed between lines. ■ Setting Format[LineBreak[_]] = "" specifies that a zero-size object is to be used between lines, and causes successive lines to be printed with no intervening blank lines. ■ Additional blank lines can be inserted by setting Format[LineBreak[_]] to be an object that is several lines high. ■ See page 517. ■ See also: Continuation, StringBreak, Indent.

■ **List**

{e_1, e_2, ... } is a list of elements.

Lists are very general objects that represent collections of expressions. ■ Functions with attribute Listable are automatically "threaded" over lists, so that they act separately on each list element. Most built-in mathematical functions are Listable. ■ {a, b, c} represents a vector. ■ {{a, b}, {c, d}} represents a matrix. ■ Nested lists can be used to represent tensors. ■ See page 118.

■ **Listable**

Listable is an attribute that can be assigned to a symbol f to indicate that the function f should automatically be threaded over lists that appear as its arguments.

Listable functions are effectively applied separately to each element in a list, or to corresponding elements in each list if there is more than one list. ■ Most built-in mathematical functions are Listable. ■ Example: Log is Listable. Log[{a,b,c}] $\longrightarrow$ {Log[a], Log[b], Log[c]}. ■ All the arguments which are lists in a Listable function must be of the same length. ■ Arguments that are not lists are copied as many times as there are elements in the lists. ■ Example: Plus is Listable. {a, b, c} + x $\longrightarrow$ {a + x, b + x, c + x}. ■ See page 272. ■ See also: Thread, Map.

■ **ListContourPlot**

ListContourPlot[*array*] generates a contour plot from an array of height values.

ListContourPlot returns a ContourGraphics object. ■ ListContourPlot has the same options as ContourGraphics. ■ See notes for ContourGraphics. ■ See page 164.

■ **ListDensityPlot**

ListDensityPlot[*array*] generates a density plot from an array of height values.

ListDensityPlot returns a DensityGraphics object. ■ ListDensityPlot has the same options as DensityGraphics. ■ See notes for DensityGraphics. ■ See page 164.

◪ ListPlay

ListPlay[{a_1, a_2, ... }] plays a sound whose amplitude is given by the sequence of levels a_i.

ListPlay returns a Sound object. ■ The following options can be given:

DisplayFunction	$SoundDisplayFunction	function for generating output
Epilog	{}	sound or graphics to be used as an epilog
PlayRange	Automatic	the range of amplitude levels to include
Prolog	{}	sound or graphics to be used as a prolog
SampleDepth	8	how many bits to use to represent each amplitude level
SampleRate	8192	how many times per second amplitude samples should be generated

■ ListPlay[{*list_1*, *list_2*}] generates stereo sound. The left-hand channel is given first.
■ ListPlay[{*list_1*, *list_2*, ... }] generates sound on any number of channels. If the lists are of different lengths, silence is inserted at the ends of the shorter lists. ■ See page 177. ■ See also: Play, SampledSoundList, Show.

■ ListPlot

ListPlot[{y_1, y_2, ... }] plots a list of values. The x coordinates for each point are taken to be 1, 2, ...

ListPlot[{{x_1, y_1}, {x_2, y_2}, ... }] plots a list of values with specified x and y coordinates.

ListPlot returns a Graphics object. ■ ListPlot has the same options as Graphics, with the following additions:

PlotJoined	False	whether to draw a line joining the points
PlotStyle	Automatic	graphics directives to determine the style of the points or line

■ Setting PlotJoined -> True gives a line joining the points. ■ ListPlot has the default option setting Axes -> True. ■ See page 164. ■ See also: Plot, Fit.

■ ListPlot3D

ListPlot3D[*array*] generates a three-dimensional plot of a surface representing an array of height values.

ListPlot3D[*array*, *shades*] generates a plot with each element of the surface shaded according to the specification in *shades*.

ListPlot3D returns a SurfaceGraphics object. ■ ListPlot3D has the same options as SurfaceGraphics.
■ ListPlot3D has the default option setting Axes -> True. ■ *array* should be a rectangular array of real numbers, representing z values. There will be holes in the surface corresponding to any array elements that are not real numbers.
■ If *array* has dimensions $m \times n$, then *shades* must have dimensions $(m-1) \times (n-1)$. ■ The elements of *shades* must be either GrayLevel, Hue or RGBColor, or SurfaceColor objects. ■ See page 164. ■ See also: Plot3D.

■ Literal

Literal[*expr*] is equivalent to *expr* for pattern matching, but maintains *expr* in an unevaluated form.

Literal has attribute HoldAll. ■ The left-hand sides of rules are usually evaluated, as are parts of the left-hand sides of assignments. You can use Literal to stop any part from being evaluated. ■ Example:
expr /. Literal[Integrate[y_, x_]] -> *rhs* transforms any subexpression of the form Integrate[y_, x_] in *expr*. Without the Literal, the Integrate[y_, x_] in the rule would immediately be evaluated to give x_ y_, and the replacement would not work. ■ Example: f[Literal[Integrate[y_, x_]]] := *value* can be used to make an assignment for expressions of the form f[Integrate[y_, x_]]. Without Literal, the Integrate function would be evaluated at the time of assignment. ■ See pages 283 and 732. ■ See also: Hold.

■ **Locked**

Locked is an attribute which, once assigned, prevents modification of any attributes of a symbol.

See page 272. ■ See also: Protected, ReadProtected.

■ **Log**

Log[z] gives the natural logarithm of z (logarithm to base e).

Log[b, z] gives the logarithm to base b.

Mathematical function (see Section A.3.9). ■ Log gives exact rational number results when possible. ■ See page 562. ■ See also: Exp, Power.

■ **LogGamma**

LogGamma[z] gives the logarithm of the gamma function log Γ(z).

Mathematical function (see Section A.3.9). ■ Unlike Log[Gamma[z]], LogGamma[z] is analytic throughout the complex plane, except for a branch cut along the negative real axis. ■ See page 572.

■ **LogicalExpand**

LogicalExpand[*expr*] expands out expressions containing logical connectives such as && and ||.

LogicalExpand applies distributive laws for logical operations. ■ Example: LogicalExpand[p && !(q || r)] ⟶ p && !q && !r. ■ See page 94. ■ See also: Expand.

■ **LogIntegral**

LogIntegral[z] is the logarithmic integral function li(z).

Mathematical function (see Section A.3.9). ■ The logarithmic integral function is defined by $\text{li}(z) = \int_0^z \frac{dt}{\log t}$, where the principal value of the integral is taken. ■ See page 571. ■ See also: ExpIntegralE.

■ **LowerCaseQ**

LowerCaseQ[*string*] yields True if all the characters in the string are lower-case letters, and yields False otherwise.

LowerCaseQ determines which characters should be considered lower-case letters from the list $Letters. ■ See page 378. ■ See also: UpperCaseQ, LetterQ, ToLowerCase, ToCharacterCode.

■ **MachineNumberQ**

MachineNumberQ[*expr*] returns True if *expr* is a machine-precision real number, and returns False otherwise.

See page 540. ■ See also: Precision, NumberQ.

■ **MainSolve**

MainSolve [*eqns*] is the underlying function for transforming systems of equations. Solve and Eliminate call it.

The equations must be of the form *lhs* == *rhs*. They can be combined using && and ||.

MainSolve returns False if no solutions to the equations exist, and True if all values of variables are solutions.

MainSolve rearranges the equations using certain directives.

MainSolve [*eqns*, *vars*, *elim*, *rest*] attempts to rearrange the equations *eqns* so as to solve for the variables *vars*, and eliminate the variables *elim*. The list *rest* can be included to specify the elimination order for any remaining variables.

MainSolve is essentially an internal routine. The functions Solve and Eliminate should be used for most practical purposes. ■ MainSolve works by creating a Gröbner basis from the equations. ■ The following options can be given:

Mode -> Generic	rational numbers and denominators depending on parameters can be introduced
Mode -> Integer	solutions must be over the integers; rational numbers cannot be introduced
Mode -> Modular	equality is required only modulo an integer
Mode -> Rational	rational numbers can be introduced (default)
Method -> 1	do one pass of elimination of variables only
Method -> 2	generate a disjunction of two equations to account for cases in which an expression can be zero
Method -> 3	solve the final equations for their roots

■ See also: Solve, Eliminate, Reduce, SolveAlways.

■ **MantissaExponent**

MantissaExponent [*x*] gives a list containing the mantissa and exponent of an approximate real number *x*.

The mantissa is always a number between -1 and +1. In absolute magnitude, the mantissa always lies between 1/10 and 1. ■ Example: MantissaExponent [3.4 10∧25] ⟶ {0.34, 26}. ■ MantissaExponent [*x*, *b*] gives the base-*b* mantissa and exponent. Its absolute magnitude is between 1/*b* and 1. ■ See page 538. ■ See also: Log, RealDigits.

■ **Map**

Map [*f*, *expr*] or *f* /@ *expr* applies *f* to each element on the first level in *expr*.

Map [*f*, *expr*, *levelspec*] applies *f* to parts of *expr* specified by *levelspec*.

Examples: Map[f, {a, b, c}] ⟶ {f[a], f[b], f[c]}; Map[f, a + b + c] ⟶ f[a] + f[b] + f[c]. ■ Level specifications are described on page 725. ■ The default value for *levelspec* in Map is {1}. ■ Examples: Map[f, {{a,b},{c,d}}] ⟶ {f[{a, b}], f[{c, d}]}; Map[f, {{a,b},{c,d}}, 2] ⟶ {f[{f[a], f[b]}], f[{f[c], f[d]}]}; Map[f, {{a,b},{c,d}}, -1] ⟶ {f[{f[a], f[b]}], f[{f[c], f[d]}]}. ■ See page 204. ■ See also: Apply, Scan, Level, Operate, MapThread.

■ **MapAll**

MapAll [*f*, *expr*] or *f* //@ *expr* applies *f* to every subexpression in *expr*.

Example: MapAll[f, {{a,b},{c,d}}] ⟶ f[{f[{f[{f[a], f[b]}], f[{f[c], f[d]}]}]}]. ■ MapAll [*f*, *expr*] is equivalent to Map [*f*, *expr*, {0, Infinity}]. ■ MapAll [*f*, *expr*, Heads -> True] applies *f* inside the heads of the parts of *expr*. ■ See page 204. ■ See also: ExpandAll, ReplaceAll.

■ **MapAt**

MapAt[*f*, *expr*, *n*] applies *f* to the element at position *n* in *expr*. If *n* is negative, the position is counted from the end.

MapAt[*f*, *expr*, {*i*, *j*, ... }] applies *f* to the part of *expr* at position {*i*, *j*, ... }.

MapAt[*f*, *expr*, {{i_1, j_1, ... }, {i_2, j_2, ... }, ... }] applies *f* to parts of *expr* at several positions.

Example: MapAt[f, {a, b, c}, 2] ⟶ {a, f[b], c}.
■ MapAt[f, {a, b, c, d}, {{1}, {4}}] ⟶ {f[a], b, c, f[d]}. ■ MapAt[*f*, *expr*, {*i*, *j*, ... }] or MapAt[*f*, *expr*, {{*i*, *j*, ... }}] applies *f* to the part *expr*[[*i*, *j*, ...]].
■ MapAt[*f*, *expr*, {{i_1, j_1, ... }, {i_2, j_2, ... }, ... }] applies *f* to parts *expr*[[i_1, j_1, ...]], *expr*[[i_2, j_2, ...]], ... ■ The list of positions used by MapAt is in the same form as is returned by the function Position. ■ MapAt applies *f* repeatedly to a particular part if that part is mentioned more than once in the list of positions. ■ Example: MapAt[f, {a, b, c}, {{1}, {3}, {1}}] ⟶ {f[f[a]], b, f[c]}. ■ See page 205. ■ See also: ReplacePart, Delete, FlattenAt.

■ **MapIndexed**

MapIndexed[*f*, *expr*] applies *f* to the elements of *expr*, giving the part specification of each element as a second argument to *f*.

MapIndexed[*f*, *expr*, *levspec*] applies *f* to all parts of *expr* on levels specified by *levspec*.

Example: MapIndexed[f, {a, b, c}] ⟶ {f[a, {1}], f[b, {2}], f[c, {3}]}. ■ Level specifications are described on page 725. ■ The default value for *levelspec* in MapIndexed is {1}. ■ Example: MapIndexed[f, {{a, b}, {c, d}}, Infinity] ⟶ {f[{f[a, {1, 1}], f[b, {1, 2}]}, {1}], f[{f[c, {2, 1}], f[d, {2, 2}]}, {2}]}. ■ See page 206. ■ See also: MapAt.

■ **MapThread**

MapThread[*f*, {{a_1, a_2, ... }, {b_1, b_2, ... }, ... }] gives {*f*[a_1, b_1, ...], *f*[a_2, b_2, ...], ... }.

MapThread[*f*, {$expr_1$, $expr_2$, ... }, *levspec*] applies *f* to the parts of the $expr_i$ specified by *levspec*.

Example: MapThread[f, {{a1, a2}, {b1, b2}}] ⟶ {f[a1, b1], f[a2, b2]}.
■ MapThread[f, {{{a1, a2}}, {{b1, b2}}}] ⟶ {f[{a1, a2}, {b1, b2}]}.
■ MapThread[f, {{{a1, a2}}, {{b1, b2}}}, 2] ⟶ {{f[a1, b1], f[a2, b2]}}. ■ Level specifications are described on page 725. ■ See page 206. ■ See also: Map, Thread, Inner.

■ **MatchLocalNames**

MatchLocalNames is an option for Trace and related functions which specifies whether symbols such as *x* should match symbols with local names of the form *x*$*nnn*.

The default setting is MatchLocalNames -> True. ■ With the default setting, Trace[*expr*, *x* = *rhs*] will show assignments to local variables whose names are of the form *x*$*nnn*.
■ Trace[*expr*, *x* = *rhs*, MatchLocalNames->False] shows assignments only for the global symbol *x*. ■ See page 304.

■ **MatchQ**

MatchQ[*expr*, *form*] returns True if the pattern *form* matches *expr*, and returns False otherwise.

See page 228. ■ See also: StringMatchQ.

▮ MatrixExp

MatrixExp[*mat*] gives the matrix exponential of *mat*.

MatrixExp[*mat*] effectively evaluates the power series for the exponential function, with ordinary powers replaced by matrix powers. ■ MatrixExp works only on square matrices. ■ See page 659. ■ See also: MatrixPower, Dot.

■ MatrixForm

MatrixForm[*list*] prints with the elements of *list* arranged in a regular array.

MatrixForm prints with every element in the array effectively enclosed in a square cell of the same size. ■ MatrixForm prints a single-level list in a column. It prints a two-level list in standard matrix form. More deeply nested lists are by default printed with successive dimensions alternating between rows and columns. ■ MatrixForm takes the same set of options as TableForm. ■ MatrixForm acts as a "wrapper", which affects printing, but not evaluation. ■ See page 354. ■ See also: TableForm, ColumnForm, GraphicsArray.

▮ MatrixPower

MatrixPower[*mat*, *n*] gives the nth matrix power of *mat*.

MatrixPower[*mat*, *n*] effectively evaluates the product of a matrix with itself *n* times. ■ When *n* is negative, MatrixPower finds powers of the inverse of *mat*. ■ MatrixPower works only on square matrices. ■ See page 659. ■ See also: Dot, MatrixExp.

■ MatrixQ

MatrixQ[*expr*] gives True if *expr* is a list of lists that can represent a matrix, and gives False otherwise.

MatrixQ[*expr*, *test*] gives True only if *test* yields True when applied to each of the matrix elements in *expr*.

MatrixQ[*expr*] gives True only if *expr* is a list, and each of its elements are lists of equal length, containing no elements that are themselves lists. ■ MatrixQ[*expr*, NumberQ] tests whether *expr* is a numerical matrix. ■ See pages 227 and 652. ■ See also: VectorQ, TensorRank.

■ Max

Max[x_1, x_2, ...] yields the numerically largest of the x_i.

Max[{x_1, x_2, ... }, {y_1, ... }, ...] yields the largest element of any of the lists.

Max yields a definite result if all its arguments are real numbers. ■ In other cases, Max carries out some simplifications. ■ Max[ ] gives -Infinity. ■ See page 550. ■ See also: Min, Order.

■ MaxBend

MaxBend is an option for Plot which measures the maximum bend angle between successive line segments on a curve.

Plot uses an adaptive algorithm to try and include enough sample points that there are no bends larger than MaxBend between successive segments of the plot. ■ Plot will not, however, subdivide by a factor of more than PlotDivision. ■ Smaller settings for MaxBend will lead to smoother curves, based on more sample points. ■ See page 143.

■ MaxMemoryUsed

MaxMemoryUsed[ ] gives the maximum number of bytes used to store all data for the current *Mathematica* session.

On most computer systems, MaxMemoryUsed[ ] will give results close to those obtained from external process status requests. ■ See page 526. ■ See also: MemoryInUse, ByteCount.

■ **MemberQ**

MemberQ[*list*, *form*] returns True if an element of *list* matches *form*, and False otherwise.

MemberQ[*list*, *form*, *levelspec*] tests all parts of *list* specified by *levelspec*.

form can be a pattern. ■ Example: MemberQ[{x^2, y^2}, x^_] ⟶ True. ■ The first argument of MemberQ can have any head, not necessarily List. ■ See page 228. ■ See also: FreeQ, Count, Cases.

■ **MemoryConstrained**

MemoryConstrained[*expr*, *b*] evaluates *expr*, stopping if more than *b* bytes of memory are requested.

MemoryConstrained[*expr*, *b*, *failexpr*] returns *failexpr* if the memory constraint is not met.

MemoryConstrained generates an interrupt to stop the evaluation of *expr* if the amount of additional memory requested during the evaluation of *expr* exceeds *b* bytes. ■ MemoryConstrained returns $Aborted if the evaluation is aborted and no *failexpr* is specified. ■ MemoryConstrained has attribute HoldFirst. ■ Aborts generated by TimeConstrained are treated just like those generated by Abort, and can thus be overruled by AbortProtect. ■ See page 527. ■ See also: TimeConstrained, MaxMemoryUsed, $RecursionLimit.

■ **MemoryInUse**

MemoryInUse[ ] gives the number of bytes currently being used to store all data in the current *Mathematica* session.

See page 526. ■ See also: MaxMemoryUsed, ByteCount.

■ **Mesh**

Mesh is an option for SurfaceGraphics and DensityGraphics that specifies whether an explicit *x*–*y* mesh should be drawn.

See page 449. ■ See also: FaceGrids, Boxed.

■ **MeshRange**

MeshRange is an option for ListPlot3D, SurfaceGraphics, ListContourPlot, ListDensityPlot and related functions which specifies the range of *x* and *y* coordinates that correspond to the array of *z* values given.

MeshRange->{{*xmin*, *xmax*}, {*ymin*, *ymax*}} specifies ranges in *x* and *y*. Mesh lines are taken to be equally spaced. ■ MeshRange->Automatic takes *x* and *y* to be a grid of integers determined by indices in the array. ■ Settings for MeshRange are produced automatically by Plot3D, etc. for insertion into SurfaceGraphics etc. ■ MeshRange is used to determine tick values for surface, contour and density plots. ■ See page 449. ■ See also: PlotRange, PlotPoints.

■ **MeshStyle**

MeshStyle is an option for Plot3D, ContourPlot, DensityPlot and related functions which specifies how mesh lines should be rendered.

MeshStyle can be set to a list of graphics directives including Dashing, Thickness, GrayLevel, Hue and RGBColor. ■ See page 411. ■ See also: Mesh, AxesStyle, Prolog, Epilog, DisplayFunction.

■ Message

Message[*symbol*::*tag*] prints the message *symbol*::*tag* unless it has been switched off.

Message[*symbol*::*tag*, e_1, e_2, ...] prints a message, inserting the values of the e_i as needed.

Message generates output on the channel $Messages. ■ You can switch off a message using Off[*symbol*::*tag*]. You can switch on a message using On[*symbol*::*tag*]. ■ Between any two successive input lines, *Mathematica* prints a message with a particular name at most three times. On the last occurrence, it prints the message General::stop. ■ During the evaluation of a particular input line, names of messages associated with that input line are appended to the list $MessageList, wrapped with HoldForm. At the end of the evaluation of the nth input line, the value of $MessageList is assigned to MessageList[*n*]. ■ Message[*mname*, e_1, e_2, ...] is printed as StringForm[*mess*, e_1, e_2, ...] where *mess* is the value of the message *mname*. Entries of the form '*i*' in the string *mess* are replaced by the corresponding e_i. ■ Given a message specified as *symbol*::*tag*, Message first searches for messages *symbol*::*tag*::*lang_i* for each of the languages in the list $Language. If it finds none of these, it then searches for the actual message *symbol*::*tag*. If it does not find this, it then performs the same search procedure for General::*tag*. If it still finds no message, it applies any value given for the global variable $NewMessage to *symbol* and "*tag*". ■ If you specify a message as *symbol*::*tag*::*lang*, then Message will search only for messages with the particular language *lang*. ■ See page 390. ■ See also: Print, Write, On, Off, Check, MessageList.

■ MessageList

MessageList[*n*] is a global object assigned to be a list of the names of messages generated during the processing of the nth input line.

Only messages that are actually output are included in the list MessageList[*n*]. ■ The message names in the list are wrapped with HoldForm. ■ MessageList[*n*] includes messages generated both by built-in functions and by explicit invocations of Message. ■ See pages 389 and 513. ■ See also: $MessageList.

■ MessageName

symbol::*tag* is a name for a message.

You can specify messages by defining values for *symbol*::*tag*. ■ *symbol*::*tag* is converted to MessageName[*symbol*, "*tag*"]. *tag* can contain any characters that can appear in symbol names. *symbol*::"*tag*" can also be used. ■ Assignments for *s*::*tag* are stored in the Messages value of the symbol *s*. ■ The following messages for functions are often defined:

f::usage   how to use the function
f::example   examples of the function
f::notes   notes on the function

■ ?*f* prints out the message *f*::usage. ■ When ?*form* finds more than one function, only the names of each function are printed. ■ You can switch on and off messages using On[*s*::*tag*] and Off[*s*::*tag*]. ■ MessageName[*symbol*, "*tag*", "*lang*"] or *symbol*::*tag*::*lang* represents a message in a particular language. ■ See page 387. ■ See also: Message, MessageList, $MessageList.

■ Messages

Messages[*symbol*] gives all the messages assigned to a particular symbol.

Messages that have been switched off using Off are enclosed in $Off. ■ See page 387.

■ Min

Min[x_1, x_2, ...] yields the numerically smallest of the x_i.

Min[{x_1, x_2, ... }, {y_1, ... }, ...] yields the smallest element of any of the lists.

Min yields a definite result if all its arguments are real numbers. ■ In other cases, Min carries out some simplifications. ■ Min[ ] gives Infinity. ■ See page 550. ■ See also: Max, Order.

■ **Minors**

Minors[*m*, *k*] gives a matrix consisting of the determinants of all $k \times k$ submatrices of *m*.

The results for different submatrices are given in lexicographic order. ■ See page 657. ■ See also: Det.

■ **Minus**

−*x* is the arithmetic negation of *x*.

−*x* is converted to Times[-1, *x*] on input. ■ See page 47. ■ See also: Subtract.

■ **Mod**

Mod[*m*, *n*] gives the remainder on division of *m* by *n*.

The sign of Mod[*m*, *n*] is always the same as the sign of *n*. ■ Mod[*m*, *n*] is equivalent to *m* − *n* Quotient[*m*, *n*]. ■ Mod[*x*, *y*] can have Rational and Real as well as Integer arguments. ■ See page 553. ■ See also: Quotient, PolynomialMod, PolynomialRemainder.

■ **Modular**

Modular is a setting for the option Mode in Solve and related functions, which specifies that equations need be satisfied only modulo an integer.

An explicit equation Modulus==*p* can be given to specify a particular modulus to use. If no such equation is given, Solve attempts to solve for possible moduli. ■ See page 620. ■ See also: Modulus.

◪ **Module**

Module[{*x*, *y*, ... }, *expr*] specifies that occurrences of the symbols *x*, *y*, ... in *expr* should be treated as local.

Module[{*x* = x_0, ... }, *expr*] defines initial values for *x*, ...

Module allows you to set up local variables with names that are local to the module. ■ Module creates new symbols to represent each of its local variables every time it is called. ■ Module creates a symbol with name *xxx*$*nnn* to represent a local variable with name *xxx*. The number *nnn* is the current value of $ModuleNumber. ■ The value of $ModuleNumber is incremented every time any module is used. ■ Before evaluating *expr*, Module substitutes new symbols for each of the local variables that appear anywhere in *expr* except as local variables in scoping constructs. ■ Symbols created by Module carry the attribute Temporary. ■ Symbols created by Module can be returned from modules. ■ You can use Module[{*vars*}, *body* /; *cond*] as the right-hand side of a transformation rule with a condition attached. ■ Module has attribute HoldAll. ■ Module is a scoping construct (see Section A.3.8). ■ Module constructs can be nested in any way. ■ Module implements lexical scoping. ■ See page 318. ■ See also: With, Block, Unique.

■ **Modulus**

Modulus->*n* is an option that can be given in certain algebraic functions to specify that integers should be treated modulo *n*.

Equations for Modulus can be given in Solve and related functions.

Modulus appears as an option in Factor, PolynomialGCD and PolynomialLCM, as well as in linear algebra functions such as Inverse, LinearSolve and Det. ■ Arithmetic is usually done over the full ring **Z** of integers; setting the option Modulus specifies that arithmetic should instead be done in the finite ring $\mathbf{Z}_n$. ■ The setting Modulus -> 0 specifies the full ring **Z** of integers. ■ Some functions require that Modulus be set to a prime, or a power of a prime. $\mathbf{Z}_n$ is a finite field when *n* is prime. ■ See pages 602 and 620. ■ See also: Modular.

■ **MoebiusMu**

MoebiusMu[*n*] gives the Möbius function $\mu(n)$.

Integer mathematical function (see Section A.3.9). ■ $\mu(n)$ is 1 if *n* is a product of an even number of distinct primes, −1 if it is a product of an odd number of primes, and 0 if it has a multiple prime factor. ■ See page 556. ■ See also: FactorInteger.

■ **Multinomial**

Multinomial[n_1, n_2, ...] gives the multinomial coefficient $\frac{(n_1+n_2+...)!}{n_1!n_2!...}$.

Integer mathematical function (see Section A.3.9). ■ The multinomial coefficient Multinomial[n_1, n_2, ...], denoted $(N; n_1, n_2, ..., n_m)$, gives the number of ways of partitioning N distinct objects into m sets, each of size n_i (with $N = \sum_{i=1}^{m} n_i$). ■ See page 558. ■ See also: Binomial.

■ **N**

N[*expr*] gives the numerical value of *expr*.

N[*expr*, *n*] does computations to *n*-digit precision.

N[*expr*, *n*] performs computations with *n*-digit precision numbers. Often the results will have fewer than *n* digits of precision. ■ N[*expr*] does computations with machine precision numbers. ■ N converts all numbers to Real form. ■ You can define numerical values of functions using *f*/: N[*f*[*args*]] := *value* and *f*/: N[*f*[*args*], *n*] := *value*. ■ See pages 48, 51 and 539. ■ See also: Chop, CompiledFunction, Rationalize, $MachinePrecision.

■ **NameQ**

NameQ["*string*"] yields True if there are any symbols whose names match the string pattern given, and yields False otherwise.

You can test for classes of symbol names using string patterns with metacharacters such as *, as specified on page 728. ■ See page 385. ■ See also: Names.

■ **Names**

Names["*string*"] gives a list of the names of symbols which match the string.

Names["*string*", SpellingCorrection->True] includes names which match after spelling correction.

Names["*string*"] gives the same list of names as ?*string*. ■ Names returns a list of strings corresponding to the names of symbols. ■ The string can be a string pattern, with metacharacters such as * and @, as described on page 728. ■ Names["*context*`*"] lists all symbols in the specified context. ■ With SpellingCorrection -> True, Names includes names which differ in a small fraction of their characters from those specifically requested. ■ With IgnoreCase -> True or SpellingCorrection -> True, Names treats lower- and upper-case letters as equivalent when matching names. ■ Names[ ] lists all names in all contexts. ■ See page 385. ■ See also: Information, Contexts, Unique, ValueQ, FileNames, NameQ.

■ **NBernoulliB**

NBernoulliB[*n*] gives the numerical value of the Bernoulli number B_n.

NBernoulliB[*n*, *d*] gives B_n to *d*-digit precision.

NBernoulliB[*n*] gives the same results as N[BernoulliB[*n*]], but is considerably faster. ■ See notes for BernoulliB. ■ See page 559.

◪ NDSolve

NDSolve[*eqns*, *y*, {*x*, *xmin*, *xmax*}] finds a numerical solution to the differential equations *eqns* for the function *y* with the independent variable *x* in the range *xmin* to *xmax*.

NDSolve[*eqns*, {y_1, y_2, ... }, {*x*, *xmin*, *xmax*}] finds numerical solutions for the functions y_i.

NDSolve gives results in terms of InterpolatingFunction objects. ▪ NDSolve[*eqns*, *y*[*x*], {*x*, *xmin*, *xmax*}] gives solutions for *y*[*x*] rather than for the function *y* itself. ▪ Differential equations must be stated in terms of derivatives such as *y*′[*x*], obtained with D, not total derivatives obtained with Dt. ▪ NDSolve solves ordinary differential equations, but not partial differential equations. ▪ All the functions y_i must depend only on the single variable *x*. ▪ The differential equations must contain enough initial conditions to determine the solutions for the y_i completely. ▪ Initial conditions are typically stated in form $y[x_0]$ == c_0, $y′[x_0]$ == dc_0, etc., but may consist of more complicated equations. ▪ The point x_0 that appears in the initial conditions need not lie in the range *xmin* to *xmax* over which the solution is sought. ▪ In most cases, all initial conditions given must involve the same value x_0 of the independent variable. If the third argument to NDSolve is given as {*x*, x_1}, then the range of the independent variable in such cases will be taken as x_0 to x_1. ▪ The differential equations in NDSolve can involve complex numbers. ▪ The following options can be given:

AccuracyGoal	Automatic	digits of absolute accuracy sought
MaxSteps	500	maximum number of steps to take
PrecisionGoal	Automatic	digits of precision sought
StartingStepSize	Automatic	initial step size used
WorkingPrecision	$MachinePrecision	the number of digits used in internal computations

▪ NDSolve stops when either the AccuracyGoal or the PrecisionGoal specified is met. ▪ The default setting of Automatic for AccuracyGoal and PrecisionGoal yields goals equal to the setting for WorkingPrecision minus 10 digits. ▪ AccuracyGoal effectively specifies the absolute error allowed in solutions, while PrecisionGoal specifies the relative error. ▪ If solutions must be followed accurately when their values are close to zero, AccuracyGoal should be set larger, or to Infinity. ▪ See page 696. ▪ See also: DSolve, NIntegrate.

■ Needs

Needs["*context*`"] loads an appropriate file if the specified context is not already in $Packages.

Needs["*context*`", "*file*"] loads *file* if the specified context is not already in $Packages.

Needs["*context*`"] loads the file specified by ContextToFilename["*context*`"]. By convention, this file is the one which contains a package that defines *context*`. ▪ Example: Needs["Collatz`"] typically reads in a file named Collatz.m. ▪ See page 340. ▪ See also: Get, DeclarePackage, ContextToFilename, FileNames.

■ Negative

Negative[*x*] gives True if *x* is a negative number.

Negative[*x*] gives False if *x* is manifestly a non-negative number. Otherwise, it remains unevaluated. ▪ A definition like Negative[*x*] = True effectively specifies that *x* is a negative number. ▪ Definitions for Sign are tested in determining whether linear combinations of expressions are negative. ▪ See also: NonNegative, Positive, Sign.

■ Nest

Nest[*f*, *expr*, *n*] gives an expression with *f* applied *n* times to *expr*.

Example: Nest[f, x, 3] ⟶ f[f[f[x]]]. ▪ See page 201. ▪ See also: Fold, Function, FixedPoint, Do.

■ **NestList**

NestList[*f*, *expr*, *n*] gives a list of the results of applying *f* to *expr* 0 through *n* times.

Example: NestList[f, x, 3] $\longrightarrow$ {x, f[x], f[f[x]], f[f[f[x]]]}. ▪ NestList[*f*, *expr*, *n*] gives a list of length *n* + 1. ▪ See page 201. ▪ See also: FoldList, ComposeList.

■ **NIntegrate**

NIntegrate[*f*, {*x*, *xmin*, *xmax*}] gives a numerical approximation to the integral $\int_{xmin}^{xmax} f \, dx$.

Multidimensional integrals can be specified, as in Integrate. ▪ NIntegrate tests for singularities at the end points of the integration range. ▪ NIntegrate[*f*, {*x*, x_0, x_1, ... , x_k}] tests for singularities at each of the intermediate points x_i. If there are no singularities, the result is equivalent to an integral from x_0 to x_k. You can use complex numbers x_i to specify an integration contour in the complex plane. ▪ The following options can be given:

AccuracyGoal	Infinity	digits of absolute accuracy sought
Compiled	True	whether the integrand should be compiled
GaussPoints	Automatic	initial number of sample points
MaxRecursion	6	maximum number of recursive subdivisions
MinRecursion	0	minimum number of recursive subdivisions
PrecisionGoal	Automatic	digits of precision sought
SingularityDepth	4	number of recursive subdivisions before changing variables
WorkingPrecision	$MachinePrecision	the number of digits used in internal computations

▪ NIntegrate uses an adaptive algorithm, which recursively subdivides the integration region as needed. In one dimension, GaussPoints specifies the number of initial points to choose. The default setting for GaussPoints is Floor[WorkingPrecision/3]. In any number of dimensions, MinRecursion specifies the minimum number of recursive subdivisions to try. MaxRecursion gives the maximum number. ▪ NIntegrate continues doing subdivisions until the error estimate it gets implies that final result achieves either the AccuracyGoal or the PrecisionGoal specified. ▪ The default setting for PrecisionGoal is equal to the setting for WorkingPrecision minus 10 digits. ▪ You should realize that with sufficiently pathological functions, the algorithms used by NIntegrate can give wrong answers. In most cases, you can test the answer by looking at its sensitivity to changes in the setting of options for NIntegrate. ▪ N[Integrate[...]] calls NIntegrate. ▪ NIntegrate has attribute HoldAll. ▪ See page 686. ▪ See also: NDSolve, NSum.

■ **NonCommutativeMultiply**

a ** *b* ** *c* is a general associative, but non-commutative, form of multiplication.

NonCommutativeMultiply has attribute Flat. ▪ Instances of NonCommutativeMultiply are automatically flattened, but no other simplification is performed. ▪ You can use NonCommutativeMultiply as a generalization of ordinary multiplication for special mathematical objects. ▪ See page 716. ▪ See also: Dot, Times.

■ **NonConstants**

NonConstants is an option for D which gives a list of objects to be taken to depend implicitly on the differentiation variables.

If *c* does not appear in the list of NonConstants, then D[*c*, *x*] is taken to be 0 unless *c* and *x* are identical expressions. ▪ See page 624. ▪ See also: Dt.

■ **None**

None is a setting used for certain options.

■ NonNegative

NonNegative[*x*] gives True if *x* is a non-negative number.

NonNegative[*x*] gives False if *x* is manifestly a negative number. Otherwise, it remains unevaluated. ■ A definition like NonNegative[*x*] = True effectively specifies that *x* is a non-negative number. ■ Definitions for Sign are tested in determining whether linear combinations of expressions are non-negative. ■ See also: Negative, Positive, Sign.

■ Normal

Normal[*expr*] converts *expr* to a normal expression, from a variety of special forms.

Normal[*expr*] converts a power series to a normal expression by truncating higher-order terms. ■ When additional "data types" are introduced, Normal should be defined to convert them, when possible, to normal expressions. ■ See page 645.

■ Not

!*expr* is the logical NOT function. It gives False if *expr* is True, and True if it is False.

Not gives symbolic results when necessary, and applies various simplification rules to them. ■ You cannot use the notation !*expr* for Not[*expr*] if it appears at the very beginning of a line. In this case, !*expr* is interpreted as a shell escape. ■ See page 94. ■ See also: LogicalExpand.

■ NProduct

NProduct[*f*, {*i*, *imin*, *imax*}] gives a numerical approximation to the product $\prod_{i=imin}^{imax} f$.

NProduct[*f*, {*i*, *imin*, *imax*, *di*}] uses a step *di* in the product.

See notes for NSum. The options NSumExtraTerms and NSumTerms are replaced by NProductExtraFactors and NProductFactors. ■ See page 689.

■ NSolve

NSolve[*lhs*==*rhs*, *var*] gives a list of numerical approximations to the roots of a polynomial equation.

NSolve[*eqn*, *var*, *n*] gives results to *n*-digit precision. ■ NSolve[*eqn*, *var*] gives the same final result as N[Solve[*eqn*, *var*]], apart from issues of numerical precision. ■ See pages 609 and 691. ■ See also: Solve, FindRoot, NDSolve.

■ **NSum**

NSum[f, {i, *imin*, *imax*}] gives a numerical approximation to the sum $\sum_{i=imin}^{imax} f$.
NSum[f, {i, *imin*, *imax*, *di*}] uses a step *di* in the sum.

NSum can be used for sums with both finite and infinite limits. ■ NSum[f, {i, ... }, {j, ... }, ...] can be used to evaluate multidimensional sums. ■ The following options can be given:

AccuracyGoal	Infinity	number of digits of final accuracy to try and get
Compiled	True	whether to compile the summand
Method	Automatic	method to use: Integrate or Fit
NSumExtraTerms	12	maximum number of terms to use in extrapolation
NSumTerms	15	number of terms to use before extrapolation
PrecisionGoal	Automatic	number of digits of final precision to try and get
VerifyConvergence	True	whether to explicitly test for convergence
WorkingPrecision	$MachinePrecision	the number of digits used in internal computations

■ NSum uses either the Euler-Maclaurin (Integrate) or Wynn epsilon (Fit) method. ■ With the Euler-Maclaurin method, the options AccuracyGoal and PrecisionGoal can be used to specify the accuracy and precision to try and get in the final answer. NSum stops when the error estimates it gets imply that either the accuracy or precision sought has been reached. ■ You should realize that with sufficiently pathological summands, the algorithms used by NSum can give wrong answers. In most cases, you can test the answer by looking at its sensitivity to changes in the setting of options for NSum. ■ VerifyConvergence is only used for sums with infinite limits. ■ N[Sum[...]] calls NSum. ■ NSum has attribute HoldAll. ■ See page 689. ■ See also: NProduct.

■ **Null**

Null is a symbol used to indicate the absence of an expression or a result. When it appears as an output expression, no output is printed.

e_1 ; e_2 ; ... ; e_k ; returns Null, and prints no output. ■ Expressions like $f[e_1 , ,e2]$ are interpreted to have Null between each pair of adjacent commas. ■ See pages 516 and 746.

■ **NullRecords**

NullRecords is an option for Read and related functions which specifies whether null records should be taken to exist between repeated record separators.

With the default setting NullRecords -> False, repeated record separators are treated like single record separators. ■ See page 496. ■ See also: WordSeparators.

■ **NullSpace**

NullSpace[m] gives a list of vectors that forms a basis for the null space of the matrix m.

NullSpace works on both numerical and symbolic matrices. ■ NullSpace[m, Modulus->p] finds null spaces for integer matrices modulo p. ■ NullSpace[m, ZeroTest -> *test*] evaluates *test*[$m[[i, j]]$] to determine whether matrix elements are zero. The default setting is ZeroTest -> (# == 0)&. ■ See page 660. ■ See also: RowReduce, LinearSolve.

■ **NullWords**

NullWords is an option for Read and related functions which specifies whether null words should be taken to exist between repeated word separators.

With the default setting NullWords -> False, repeated word separators are treated like single word separators. ■ See page 496. ■ See also: TokenWords, RecordSeparators.

■ Number

Number represents an exact integer or an approximate real number in Read.

An integer is returned if no explicit decimal point is present. ■ Approximate real numbers can be given in C or Fortran forms, such as 2.4E5 or -3.4e-4. ■ See pages 181 and 495. ■ See also: Real, DigitQ.

■ NumberForm

NumberForm[*expr*, *n*] prints with approximate real numbers in *expr* given to *n*-digit precision.

NumberForm[*expr*, {*n*, *f*}] prints with approximate real numbers having *n* digits, with *f* digits to the right of the decimal point. ■ NumberForm works on integers as well as approximate real numbers. ■ The following options can be given:

DigitBlock	Infinity	number of digits between breaks
ExponentFunction	Automatic	function to apply to exponents
NumberFormat	Automatic	function used to assemble mantissa, base, exponent
NumberPadding	{"", ""}	strings to use for left and right padding
NumberPoint	"."	decimal point string
NumberSeparator	","	string to insert at breaks between blocks
NumberSigns	{"-", "+"}	strings to use for signs of negative and positive numbers
SignPadding	False	whether to insert padding after the sign

■ All options except ExponentFunction apply to integers as well as approximate real numbers. ■ You can mix NumberForm and BaseForm. ■ NumberForm acts as a "wrapper", which affects printing, but not evaluation. ■ See page 350. ■ See also: ScientificForm, EngineeringForm, AccountingForm, BaseForm, PaddedForm, N.

■ NumberFormat

NumberFormat is an option for NumberForm and related functions which specifies how the mantissa, base and exponent should be assembled into a final print form.

With the setting NumberFormat -> *f*, the function *f* is supplied with three arguments: the mantissa, base and exponent of each number to be printed. ■ The arguments are all given as strings. ■ When no exponent is to be printed, the third argument is given as "". ■ The function *f* must return the final format for the number. ■ See page 351. ■ See also: ExponentFunction.

■ NumberPadding

NumberPadding is an option for NumberForm and related functions which gives strings to use as padding on the left- and right-hand sides of numbers.

NumberPadding -> {"*sleft*", "*sright*"} specifies strings to use for padding on the left and right. ■ In NumberForm, the default setting is NumberPadding -> {"", ""}. ■ In PaddedForm, the default setting is NumberPadding -> {" ", "0"}. ■ The strings specified as padding are inserted in place of digits. ■ See page 351. ■ See also: SignPadding.

■ NumberPoint

NumberPoint is an option for NumberForm and related functions which gives the string to use as a decimal point.

The default is NumberPoint -> ".". ■ See page 351.

■ NumberQ

NumberQ[*expr*] gives True if *expr* is a number, and False otherwise.

NumberQ[*expr*] returns False unless *expr* is manifestly a number (*i.e.*, has head Complex, Integer, Rational or Real). ■ You can use NumberQ[*x*] = True to override the normal operation of NumberQ, and effectively define *x* to be a number. ■ See pages 227 and 535. ■ See also: IntegerQ, TrueQ.

■ NumberSeparator

NumberSeparator is an option for NumberForm and related functions which gives the string to insert at breaks between digits.

NumberSeparator -> "*s*" specifies that the string *s* should be inserted at every break between digits specified by DigitBlock. ■ NumberSeparator -> {"*sleft*", "*sright*"} specifies different strings to be used on the left and right of the decimal point. ■ The default setting is NumberSeparator -> ",". ■ See page 351.

■ NumberSigns

NumberSigns is an option for NumberForm and related functions which gives strings to use as signs for negative and positive numbers.

NumberSigns -> {"*sneg*", "*spos*"} specifies that "*sneg*" should be given as the sign for negative numbers, and "*spos*" for positive numbers. ■ The default setting is NumberSigns -> {"-", ""}. ■ NumberSigns -> {{"*snleft*", "*snright*"}, {"*spleft*", "*spright*"}} specifies strings to put both on the left and right of numbers to specify their signs. ■ In AccountingForm, the default setting is NumberSigns -> {{"(", ")"}, ""}. ■ See page 351. ■ See also: SignPadding.

■ Numerator

Numerator[*expr*] gives the numerator of *expr*.

Numerator picks out terms which do not have superficially negative exponents. Denominator picks out the remaining terms. ■ An exponent is "superficially negative" if it has a negative number as a factor. ■ The standard representation of rational expressions as products of powers means that you cannot simply use Part to extract numerators. ■ Numerator can be used on rational numbers. ■ See page 82. ■ See also: ExpandNumerator.

■ O

O[*x*]^*n* represents a term of order x^n.

O[*x*]^*n* is generated to represent omitted higher-order terms in power series.

O[*x*, x_0]^*n* represents a term of order $(x - x_0)^n$.

Normal can be used to truncate power series, and remove O terms. ■ See page 641. ■ See also: Series, SeriesData.

■ OddQ

OddQ[*expr*] gives True if *expr* is an odd integer, and False otherwise.

OddQ[*expr*] returns False unless *expr* is manifestly an odd integer (*i.e.*, has head Integer, and is odd). ■ You can use OddQ[*x*] = True to override the normal operation of OddQ, and effectively define *x* to be an odd integer. ■ See pages 227 and 535. ■ See also: IntegerQ, EvenQ, TrueQ.

■ **Off**

Off [*symbol*::*tag*] switches off a message, so that it is no longer printed.

Off [*s*] switches off tracing messages associated with the symbol *s*.

Off [*m₁* , *m₂* , ...] switches off several messages.

Off [ ] switches off all tracing messages.

The *value* of *symbol*::*tag* is not affected by Off. ■ Off [*s*] is equivalent to Off [*s*::trace]. ■ Off [ ] is equivalent to Off [*s*::trace] for all symbols. ■ Switching off the printing of a message does not affect its detection by Check. ■ See pages 70 and 387. ■ See also: Message, Check.

■ **On**

On [*symbol*::*tag*] switches on a message, so that it can be printed.

On [*s*] switches on tracing for the symbol *s*.

On [*m₁* , *m₂* , ...] switches on several messages.

On [ ] switches on tracing for all symbols.

When tracing is switched on, each evaluation of a symbol, on its own, or as a function, is printed, together with the result. ■ Note that the tracing information is printed when a function *returns*. As a result, traces of recursive functions appear in the opposite order from their calls. ■ On [*s*] is equivalent to On [*s*::trace]. ■ On [ ] is equivalent to On [*s*::trace] for all symbols. ■ See pages 70 and 387.

■ **OneIdentity**

OneIdentity is an attribute that can be assigned to a symbol *f* to indicate that $f[x]$, $f[f[x]]$, etc. are all equivalent to *x* for the purpose of pattern matching.

Functions like Plus and Times have the attribute OneIdentity. ■ The fact that Times has attribute OneIdentity allows a pattern like n_. x_ to match x. ■ See pages 230 and 272. ■ See also: Flat, Nest.

■ **OpenAppend**

OpenAppend ["*file*"] opens a file to append output to it, and returns an OutputStream object.

The following options can be given:

FormatType	InputForm	default format for printing expressions
NameConversion	None	function for converting symbol names with special characters
PageHeight	22	number of lines per page
PageWidth	78	number of character widths per line
StringConversion	None	function for converting strings with special characters
TotalHeight	Infinity	maximum number of lines for a single expression
TotalWidth	Infinity	maximum number of character widths for a single expression

■ On computer systems that support pipes, OpenAppend ["!*command*"] runs the external program specified by *command*, and opens a pipe to send input to it. ■ If OpenRead does not succeed in opening a particular file or pipe, it generates a message, and returns $Failed. ■ OpenAppend resolves file names according to the procedure described in Section A.6.2. ■ OpenAppend returns OutputStream ["*name*", *n*], where *name* is the full name of a file or command, and *n* is a serial number that is unique across all streams opened in the current *Mathematica* session. ■ SetOptions can be used to change the properties of an output stream, after it is already open. ■ Functions like Put and Write automatically open the files or pipes they need, if they are not already open. ■ See page 485. ■ See also: Close, Put, Streams.

■ **OpenRead**

OpenRead["*file*"] opens a file to read data from, and returns an InputStream object.

OpenRead prepares to read from a file, starting at the beginning of the file. ■ On systems that support pipes, OpenRead["!*command*"] runs the external program specified by *command*, and opens a pipe to get input from it. ■ If OpenRead does not succeed in opening a particular file or pipe, it generates a message, and returns $Failed. ■ OpenRead resolves file names according to the procedure described in Section A.6.2. ■ The function ReadList automatically opens files or pipes that it needs. ■ OpenRead returns InputStream["*name*", *n*], where *name* is the full name of a file or command, and *n* is a serial number that is unique across all streams opened in the current *Mathematica* session. ■ See page 499. ■ See also: Close, Read, ReadList, Streams.

■ **OpenTemporary**

OpenTemporary[ ] opens a temporary file to which output can be written, and returns an OutputStream object.

OpenTemporary is often used in conjunction with Put and Get as a way of preparing data that is exchanged between *Mathematica* and external programs. ■ OpenTemporary always creates a new file, that does not already exist. ■ On Unix systems, OpenTemporary typically creates a file in the /tmp directory. ■ The global variable $TemporaryPrefix gives the base of the file name used by OpenTemporary. ■ See page 482. ■ See also: Close, Run.

■ **OpenWrite**

OpenWrite["*file*"] opens a file to write output to it, and returns an OutputStream object.

OpenWrite deletes any existing contents in a file, and prepares to write output starting at the beginning of the file. ■ For output to pipes, OpenWrite and OpenAppend are equivalent. ■ See notes for OpenAppend. ■ See page 485.

■ **Operate**

Operate[*p*, *f*[*x*, *y*]] gives *p*[*f*][*x*, *y*].

Operate[*p*, *expr*, *n*] applies *p* at level *n* in the head of *expr*.

Examples: Operate[p, f[x,y]] ⟶ p[f][x, y]; Operate[p, f[x][y][z], 1] ⟶ p[f[x][y]][z]; Operate[p, f[x][y][z], 2] ⟶ p[f[x]][y][z]. ■ Operate[*p*, *f*[*x*]] effectively applies the functional operator *p* to the function *f*. ■ Operate is essentially a generalization of Apply, which allows you to apply an operator to the head of an expression, rather than simply to replace the head. ■ See page 214. ■ See also: Through, Apply, Heads.

■ **Optional**

p:*v* is a pattern object which represents an expression of the form *p*, which, if omitted, should be replaced by *v*.

Optional is used to specify "optional arguments" in functions represented by patterns. The pattern object *p* gives the form the argument should have, if it is present. The expression *v* gives the "default value" to use if the argument is absent. ■ Example: the pattern f[x_, y_:1] is matched by f[a], with x taking the value a, and y taking the value 1. It can also be matched by f[a, b], with y taking the value b. ■ The form *s*_:*v* is equivalent to Optional[*s*_, *v*]. This form is also equivalent to *s*:_:*v*. There is no syntactic ambiguity since *s* must be a symbol in this case. ■ The special form *s*_. is equivalent to Optional[*s*_] and can be used to represent function arguments which, if omitted, should be replaced by default values globally specified for the functions in which they occur. ■ Values for Default[*f*, ...] specify default values to be used when _. appears as an argument of *f*. Any assignments for Default[*f*, ...] must be made *before* _. first appears as an argument of *f*. ■ Optional[*s_h*] represents a function which can be omitted, but which, if present, must have head *h*. There is no simpler syntactic form for this case. ■ Functions with built-in default values include Plus, Times and Power. ■ See pages 234 and 719. ■ See also: Alternatives.

■ Options

Options [*symbol*] gives the list of default options assigned to a symbol.

Options [*expr*] gives the options explicitly specified in a particular expression such as a graphics object.

Options [*stream*] or Options ["*sname*"] gives options associated with a particular stream.

Options [*expr*, *name*] gives the setting for the option *name* in an expression.

Options [*expr*, {*name₁*, *name₂*, ... }] gives a list of the settings for the options *name_i*.

Many built-in functions allow you to give additional arguments that specify options with rules of the form *name* -> *value*. ■ Options [*f*] gives the list of rules to be used for the options associated with a function *f* if no explicit rules are given when the function is called. ■ Options always returns a list of transformation rules for option names. ■ You can assign a value to Options [*symbol*] to redefine all the default option settings for a function. ■ SetOptions [*symbol*, *name* -> *value*] can be used to specify individual default options. ■ You can use Options on InputStream and OutputStream objects. If there is only one stream with a particular name, you can give the name as a string as the argument of Options. ■ See pages 149 and 724. ■ See also: FullOptions.

■ Or

e₁ || *e₂* || ... is the logical OR function. It evaluates its arguments in order, giving True immediately if any of them are True, and False if they are all False.

Or evaluates its arguments in a non-standard way (see page 730). ■ Or gives symbolic results when necessary. It applies no simplification rules, except removing initial arguments that are False. ■ See page 94. ■ See also: Xor, LogicalExpand.

■ Order

Order [*expr₁*, *expr₂*] gives 1 if *expr₁* is before *expr₂* in canonical order, and −1 if *expr₁* is after *expr₂* in canonical order. It gives 0 if *expr₁* is identical to *expr₂*.

Examples: Order[a, b] ⟶ 1; Order[b, a] ⟶ −1. ■ Order uses canonical order as described in the notes for Sort. ■ See page 215. ■ See also: Equal, SameQ, Sort, $StringOrder.

■ OrderedQ

OrderedQ [*h*[*e₁*, *e₂*, ...]] gives True if the *e_i* are in canonical order, and False otherwise.

See notes for Order. ■ OrderedQ[{*e*, *e*}] gives True. ■ By default, OrderedQ uses canonical order as described in the notes for Sort. ■ OrderedQ [*list*, *p*] uses the function *p* to determine whether each pair of elements in *list* is in order. ■ See pages 133 and 228. ■ See also: Signature, Sort, $StringOrder.

■ Orderless

Orderless is an attribute that can be assigned to a symbol *f* to indicate that the elements *e_i* in expressions of the form *f*[*e₁*, *e₂*, ...] should automatically be sorted into canonical order. This property is accounted for in pattern matching.

The Orderless attribute for a function corresponds to the mathematical property of commutativity. ■ Functions with the Orderless attribute use canonical order as described in the notes for Sort. The canonical order can be changed by modifying the value of $StringOrder. ■ For an object that represents a matrix or a tensor, the Orderless attribute represents symmetry among indices. ■ Functions like Plus and Times are Orderless. ■ In matching patterns with Orderless functions, all possible orders of arguments are tried. ■ The Orderless attribute must be assigned before defining any values for an Orderless function. ■ See page 272. ■ See also: Sort, Flat, OneIdentity, $StringOrder.

■ **Out**

> %*n* or Out [*n*] is a global object that is assigned to be the value produced on the nth output line. % gives the last result generated.
>
> %% gives the result before last. %%... % (*k* times) gives the kth previous result.
>
> Out[ ] is equivalent to %. ■ Out [-*k*] is equivalent to %%... % (*k* times). ■ See page 513. ■ See also: In, $Line, MessageList.

■ **Outer**

> Outer[*f*, *list₁*, *list₂*, ...] gives the generalized outer product of the *listᵢ*.
>
> Example: Outer[f,{a,b},{x,y}] ⟶ {{f[a, x], f[a, y]}, {f[b, x], f[b, y]}}.
> ■ Outer[Times, *list₁*, *list₂*, ...] gives an outer product. ■ The result of applying Outer to two tensors $T_{i_1 i_2 \cdots i_r}$ and $U_{j_1 j_2 \cdots j_s}$ is the tensor $V_{i_1 i_2 \cdots i_r j_1 j_2 \cdots j_s}$ with elements $f[T_{i_1 i_2 \cdots i_r}, U_{j_1 j_2 \cdots j_s}]$. Applying Outer to two tensors of ranks *r* and *s* gives a tensor of rank $r+s$. ■ The heads of all the *listᵢ* must be the same, but need not necessarily be List. ■ The *listᵢ* need not necessarily be cuboidal arrays. ■ See page 669. ■ See also: Inner, Distribute.

■ **OutputForm**

> OutputForm[*expr*] prints as the standard *Mathematica* output form for *expr*.
>
> OutputForm imitates standard two-dimensional mathematical notation. ■ The OutputForm of many kinds of expressions is quite different from their internal representation. ■ OutputForm acts as a "wrapper", which affects printing, but not evaluation. ■ See page 343. ■ See also: InputForm, TeXForm, Short, FullForm.

■ **OutputStream**

> OutputStream["*name*", *n*] is an object that represents an output stream for functions such as Write.
>
> OpenWrite and OpenAppend return OutputStream objects. ■ The serial number *n* is unique across all streams, regardless of their name. ■ See page 484. ■ See also: Streams, InputStream.

■ **PaddedForm**

> PaddedForm[*expr*, *n*] prints with all numbers in *expr* padded to leave room for a total of *n* digits.
>
> PaddedForm[*expr*, {*n*, *f*}] prints with approximate real numbers having exactly *f* digits to the right of the decimal point.
>
> By default, PaddedForm pads with spaces on the left to leave room for *n* digits. ■ PaddedForm pads with zeros on the right in approximate real numbers. ■ The length *n* specified in PaddedForm counts only digits, and not signs, breaks between digits, and so on. ■ PaddedForm takes the same options as NumberForm, but with some defaults different. ■ You can use PaddedForm to align columns of numbers. ■ PaddedForm acts as a "wrapper", which affects printing, but not evaluation. ■ See page 352. ■ See also: ColumnForm, TableForm.

■ **PageHeight**

> PageHeight is an option for output streams which specifies how many lines of text should be printed between page breaks.
>
> PageHeight -> Infinity specifies that there should be no page breaks. ■ See also: TotalHeight.

■ **PageWidth**

> **PageWidth** is an option which can be set for output streams to specify how wide each line of printed text should be.
>
> **PageWidth -> Infinity** specifies that individual lines can be arbitrarily long.
> ■ **SetOptions**[*stream*, **PageWidth -> *n***] resets the line width allowed for an open stream. ■ See page 487. ■ See also: **TotalWidth**.

■ **ParametricPlot**

> **ParametricPlot**[{f_x, f_y}, {t, *tmin*, *tmax*}] produces a parametric plot with x and y coordinates f_x and f_y generated as a function of t.
>
> **ParametricPlot**[{{f_x, f_y}, {g_x, g_y}, ... }, {t, *tmin*, *tmax*}] plots several parametric curves.
>
> **ParametricPlot** evaluates its arguments in a non-standard way (see page 730). You should use **Evaluate** to evaluate the function to be plotted if this can safely be done before specific numerical values are supplied. ■ The options that can be given for **ParametricPlot** are the same as for **Plot**. ■ **ParametricPlot** has the default option setting **Axes -> True**. ■ **ParametricPlot** returns a **Graphics** object. ■ See page 167.

■ **ParametricPlot3D**

> **ParametricPlot3D**[{f_x, f_y, f_z}, {t, *tmin*, *tmax*}] produces a three-dimensional space curve parameterized by a variable t which runs from *tmin* to *tmax*.
>
> **ParametricPlot3D**[{f_x, f_y, f_z}, {t, *tmin*, *tmax*}, {u, *umin*, *umax*}] produces a three-dimensional surface parametrized by t and u.
>
> **ParametricPlot3D**[{f_x, f_y, f_z, s}, ...] shades the plot according to the color specification s.
>
> **ParametricPlot3D**[{{f_x, f_y, f_z}, {g_x, g_y, g_z}, ... }, ...] plots several objects together.
>
> **ParametricPlot3D** evaluates its arguments in a non-standard way (see page 730). You should use **Evaluate** to evaluate the function to be plotted if this can safely be done before specific numerical values are supplied.
> ■ **ParametricPlot3D** has the same options as **Graphics3D**, with the following additions:

Compiled	True	whether to compile the function to plot
PlotPoints	Automatic	the number of sample points for each parameter

> ■ **ParametricPlot3D** has the default option setting **Axes -> True**. ■ With the default setting **PlotPoints -> Automatic**, **ParametricPlot3D** uses **PlotPoints -> 75** for curves and **PlotPoints -> {15, 15}** for surfaces. ■ **ParametricPlot3D** returns a **Graphics3D** object. ■ See page 168.

■ **ParentDirectory**

> **ParentDirectory**[ ] gives the parent of the current working directory.
>
> **ParentDirectory**["*dir*"] gives the parent of the directory *dir*.
>
> **ParentDirectory** returns the full name of the directory as a string. ■ **ParentDirectory** works only under operating systems which support hierarchical file systems. ■ See page 490. ■ See also: **Directory**, **HomeDirectory**.

■ **Part**

expr[[*i*]] or Part[*expr*, *i*] gives the ith part of *expr*.

expr[[-*i*]] counts from the end.

expr[[0]] gives the head of *expr*.

expr[[*i*, *j*, ...]] or Part[*expr*, *i*, *j*, ...] is equivalent to *expr*[[*i*]] [[*j*]] ... .

expr[[{i_1, i_2, ... }]] gives a list of the parts i_1, i_2, ... of *expr*.

You can make an assignment like *t*[[*i*]] = *value* to modify part of an expression. ▪ When *expr* is a list, *expr*[[{i_1, i_2, ... }]] gives a list of parts. In general, the head of *expr* is applied to the list of parts. ▪ You can get a nested listing of parts from *expr*[[*list*₁, *list*₂, ...]]. Each part has one index from each list. ▪ Notice that lists are used differently in Part than in functions like MapAt and Position. ▪ *expr*[[Range[*i*, *j*]]] can be used to extract sequences of parts. ▪ See page 195. ▪ See also: First, Head, Last, HeldPart, Position, ReplacePart, MapAt, Take.

■ **Partition**

Partition[*list*, *n*] partitions *list* into non-overlapping sublists of length *n*.

Partition[*list*, *n*, *d*] generates sublists with offset *d*.

Partition[*list*, {n_1, n_2, ... }, {d_1, d_2, ... }] partitions successive levels in *list* into length n_i sublists with offsets d_i.

Example: Partition[{a,b,c,d,e,f}, 2] ⟶ {{a, b}, {c, d}, {e, f}}. ▪ All the sublists generated by Partition[*list*, *n*, *d*] are of length *n*. As a result, some elements at the end of *list* may not appear in any sublist. ▪ The element e in Partition[{a,b,c,d,e}, 2] ⟶ {{a, b}, {c, d}} is dropped. ▪ Partition[{a,b,c,d,e}, 3, 1] ⟶ {{a, b, c}, {b, c, d}, {c, d, e}} generates sublists with offset 1. ▪ If *d* is greater than *n* in Partition[*list*, *n*, *d*], then elements in the middle of *list* are skipped. ▪ The object *list* need not have head List. ▪ Partition[f[a,b,c,d], 2] ⟶ f[f[a, b], f[c, d]]. ▪ If *list* has length *N*, then Partition[*list*, *n*, *d*] yields Max[0, Floor[(*N* + *d* - *n*)/*d*]] sublists. ▪ Partition[*list*, {n_1, n_2, ... }, *d*] uses offset *d* at each level. ▪ See page 131. ▪ See also: Flatten, RotateLeft.

■ **PartitionsP**

PartitionsP[*n*] gives the number $p(n)$ of unrestricted partitions of the integer *n*.

Integer mathematical function (see Section A.3.9). ▪ See page 558.

■ **PartitionsQ**

PartitionsQ[*n*] gives the number $q(n)$ of partitions of the integer *n* into distinct parts.

Integer mathematical function (see Section A.3.9). ▪ See page 558.

■ **Pattern**

s:*obj* represents the pattern object *obj*, assigned the name *s*.

The name *s* must be a symbol. ▪ The object *obj* can be any pattern object. ▪ When a transformation rule is used, any occurrence of *s* on the right-hand side is replaced by whatever expression it matched on the left-hand side. ▪ The operator : has a comparatively low precedence. The expression x:_+_ is thus interpreted as x:(_+_), not (x:_)+_. ▪ The form *s*_ is equivalent to *s*:_. Similarly, *s*_*h* is equivalent to *s*:_*h*, *s*__ to *s*:__, and so on. ▪ See pages 223 and 719.

■ PatternTest

p?test is a pattern object that stands for any expression which matches *p*, and on which the application of *test* gives True.

Any result for *test*[*pval*] other than True is taken to signify failure. ■ Example: _?NumberQ represents a number of any type. The _ matches any expression, and ?NumberQ restricts to any expression which gives True on application of the number test NumberQ. ■ The operator ? has a high precedence. Thus _^_?t is _^(_?t) not (_^_)?t. ■ See pages 228 and 716. ■ See also: Condition.

■ Pause

Pause[*n*] pauses for at least *n* seconds.

Pause is accurate only down to a granularity of at least $TimeUnit seconds. ■ The time elapsed during the execution of Pause is counted in SessionTime, but not in TimeUsed, Timing or TimeConstrained. ■ Under multitasking operating systems, there may be a delay of significantly more than *n* seconds when you execute Pause[*n*]. ■ See page 524.

■ Permutations

Permutations[*list*] generates a list of all possible permutations of the elements in *list*.

Example:
Permutations[{a,b,c}] ⟶ {{a, b, c}, {a, c, b}, {b, a, c}, {b, c, a}, {c, a, b}, {c, b, a}}.
■ There are *n*! permutations of a list of *n* elements. ■ Each element of the original list is treated as distinct. ■ The object *list* need not have head List. ■ See page 133. ■ See also: Sort, Signature, Reverse, RotateLeft.

■ Pi

Pi is π, with numerical value $\simeq 3.14159$.

Mathematical constant (see Section A.3.10). ■ See page 566. ■ See also: Degree.

■ Play

Play[*f*, {*t*, *tmin*, *tmax*}] plays a sound whose amplitude is given by *f* as a function of time *t* in seconds between *tmin* and *tmax*.

Play evaluates its arguments in a non-standard way (see page 730). ■ Play[{f_1, f_2}, {*t*, *tmin*, *tmax*}] produces stereo sound. The left-hand channel is given first. ■ Play[{f_1, f_2, ... }, ...] generates sound output on any number of channels. ■ The following options can be given:

Compiled	True	whether to compile *f* for evaluation
DisplayFunction	$SoundDisplayFunction	function for generating output
Epilog	{}	sound or graphics to be used as a epilog
PlayRange	Automatic	the range of amplitude levels to include
Prolog	{}	sound or graphics to be used as a prolog
SampleDepth	8	how many bits to use to represent each amplitude level
SampleRate	8192	how many times per second amplitude samples should be generated

■ Play returns a Sound object. ■ See page 176. ■ See also: ListPlay, SampledSoundFunction, Show.

◪ PlayRange

PlayRange is an option for **Play** and related functions which specifies what range of sound amplitude levels should be included.

All amplitudes are scaled so that the amplitude levels to be included lie within the range that can be output. ▪ Amplitude levels outside the range specified are clipped. ▪ The possible settings for **PlayRange** are:

All	include all amplitude levels
Automatic	outlying levels are dropped
{*amin*, *amax*}	explicit amplitude limits

▪ See page 177. ▪ See also: **SampleDepth**.

■ Plot

Plot[*f*, {*x*, *xmin*, *xmax*}] generates a plot of *f* as a function of *x* from *xmin* to *xmax*.

Plot[{f_1, f_2, ... }, {*x*, *xmin*, *xmax*}] plots several functions f_i.

Plot evaluates its arguments in a non-standard way (see page 730). You should use **Evaluate** to evaluate the function to be plotted if this can safely be done before specific numerical values are supplied. ▪ **Plot** has the same options as **Graphics**, with the following additions:

Compiled	True	whether to compile the function to plot
MaxBend	10.	maximum bend between segments
PlotDivision	20.	maximum subdivision factor in sampling
PlotPoints	25	initial number of sample points
PlotStyle	Automatic	graphics directives to specify the style for each curve

▪ **Plot** uses the default setting **Axes -> True**. ▪ **Plot** initially evaluates *f* at a number of equally spaced sample points specified by **PlotPoints**. Then it uses an adaptive algorithm to choose additional sample points, attempting to produce a curve in which the bend between successive segments is less than **MaxBend**. It subdivides a given interval by a factor of at most **PlotDivision**. ▪ You should realize that with the finite number of sample points used, it is possible for **Plot** to miss features in your function. To check your results, you should increase the setting for **PlotPoints**. ▪ **Plot** returns a **Graphics** object. ▪ See page 134. ▪ See also: **ListPlot**, **Graphics**.

■ Plot3D

Plot3D[*f*, {*x*, *xmin*, *xmax*}, {*y*, *ymin*, *ymax*}] generates a three-dimensional plot of *f* as a function of *x* and *y*.

Plot3D[{*f*, *s*}, {*x*, *xmin*, *xmax*}, {*y*, *ymin*, *ymax*}] generates a three-dimensional plot in which the height of the surface is specified by *f*, and the shading is specified by *s*.

Plot3D evaluates its arguments in a non-standard way (see page 730). You should use **Evaluate** to evaluate the function to be plotted if this can safely be done before specific numerical values are supplied. ▪ **Plot3D** has the same options as **SurfaceGraphics**, with the following additions:

Compiled	True	whether to compile the function to plot
PlotPoints	15	the number of sample points in each direction

▪ **Plot3D** has the default option setting **Axes -> True**. ▪ **Plot3D** returns a **SurfaceGraphics** object. ▪ The function *f* should give a real number for all values of *x* and *y* at which it is evaluated. There will be holes in the final surface at any values of *x* and *y* for which *f* does not yield a real number value. ▪ If **Lighting->False** and no shading function *s* is specified, the surface is shaded according to height. The shading is determined by the option **ColorFunction**; the default is gray levels. ▪ The shading function *s* must yield **GrayLevel**, **Hue** or **RGBColor** directives, or **SurfaceColor** objects. ▪ **Plot3D** includes a setting for the **MeshRange** option in the **SurfaceGraphics** object it returns. ▪ See page 154. ▪ See also: **ListPlot3D**, **ContourPlot**, **DensityPlot**, **Graphics3D**.

■ **PlotDivision**

PlotDivision is an option for Plot which specifies the maximum amount of subdivision to be used in attempting to generate a smooth curve.

Plot initially uses PlotPoints equally spaced sample points. In attempting to generate curves with no bends larger than MaxBend, Plot subdivides by at most a factor of PlotDivision. ■ The finest resolution in Plot is of order 1/(PlotPoints PlotDivision). ■ See page 143. ■ See also: MaxBend.

■ **PlotJoined**

PlotJoined is an option for ListPlot that specifies whether the points plotted should be joined by a line.

The style of the line can be specified using the option PlotStyle. ■ See page 164. ■ See also: Line.

■ **PlotLabel**

PlotLabel is an option for graphics functions that specifies an overall label for a plot.

PlotLabel -> None specifies that no label should be given. ■ PlotLabel -> *label* specifies a label to give. ■ Any expression can be used as a label. It will be given in OutputForm. Arbitrary strings of text can be given as "*text*". ■ See page 418. ■ See also: AxesLabel.

■ **PlotPoints**

PlotPoints is an option for plotting functions that specifies how many sample points to use.

The sample points are equally spaced. ■ In Plot, an adaptive procedure is used to choose more sample points. ■ With a single variable, PlotPoints -> *n* specifies the total number of sample points to use. ■ With two variables, PlotPoints -> *n* specifies that *n* points should be used in both *x* and *y* directions. ■ PlotPoints -> $\{n_x, n_y\}$ specifies different numbers of sample points for the *x* and *y* directions. ■ See page 143. ■ See also: PlotDivision.

■ **PlotRange**

PlotRange is an option for graphics functions that specifies what points to include in a plot.

PlotRange can be used for both two- and three-dimensional graphics. ■ The following settings can be used:

All	all points are included
Automatic	outlying points are dropped
{*min*, *max*}	explicit limits for *y* (2D) or *z* (3D)
{{*xmin*, *xmax*}, … }	explicit limits

■ When no explicit limits are given for a particular coordinate, a setting of Automatic is assumed. ■ With the Automatic setting, the distribution of coordinate values is found, and any points sufficiently far out in the distribution are dropped. Such points are often produced as a result of singularities in functions being plotted. ■ A setting of the form {*min*, Automatic} specifies a particular minimum value for a coordinate, and a maximum value to be determined automatically. ■ FullOptions gives the explicit form of PlotRange specifications when Automatic settings are given. ■ See page 142. ■ See also: PlotRegion, AspectRatio, FullOptions.

◪ **PlotRegion**

PlotRegion is an option for graphics functions that specifies what region of the final display area a plot should fill.

PlotRegion -> {{*sxmin*, *sxmax*}, {*symin*, *symax*}} specifies the region in scaled coordinates that the plot should fill in the final display area. ■ The scaled coordinates run from 0 to 1 in each direction. ■ The default setting PlotRegion -> {{0, 1}, {0, 1}} specifies that the plot should fill the whole display area. ■ When the plot does not fill the whole display area, the remainder of the area is rendered according to the setting for the option Background. ■ See page 414. ■ See also: PlotRange, AspectRatio, Scaled, SphericalRegion.

■ PlotStyle

PlotStyle is an option for Plot and ListPlot that specifies the style of lines or points to be plotted.

PlotStyle -> *style* specifies that all lines or points are to be generated with the specified graphics directive, or list of graphics directives. ■ PlotStyle -> {{*style₁*}, {*style₂*}, ... } specifies that successive lines generated should use graphics directives *style₁*, ... The styles must be enclosed in lists, perhaps of length one. ■ The *styleᵢ* are used cyclically. ■ Styles can be specified using graphics directives such as Dashing, Hue and Thickness. ■ See pages 143 and 411. ■ See also: Graphics.

■ Plus

$x + y + z$ represents a sum of terms.

Plus has attributes Flat, Orderless and OneIdentity. ■ The default value for arguments of Plus, as used in x_. patterns, is 0. ■ Plus[ ] is taken to be 0. ■ Plus[x] is x. ■ $x + 0$ evaluates to x, but $x + 0.0$ is left unchanged. ■ See page 47. ■ See also: Minus, Subtract, AddTo, Increment.

■ Pochhammer

Pochhammer[*a*, *n*] gives the Pochhammer symbol $(a)_n$.

Mathematical function (see Section A.3.9). ■ $(a)_n = \frac{\Gamma(a+n)}{\Gamma(a)}$. ■ See page 571. ■ See also: Beta, Binomial, Gamma, Factorial, Hypergeometric0F1, Hypergeometric1F1, Hypergeometric2F1.

■ Point

Point[*coords*] is a graphics primitive that represents a point.

The coordinates can be given either in the absolute form {*x*, *y*} or {*x*, *y*, *z*} or in scaled form Scaled[{*x*, *y*}] or Scaled[{*x*, *y*, *z*}]. ■ Points are rendered if possible as circular regions. Their radii can be specified using the graphics primitive PointSize. ■ Point radii are not accounted for in hidden surface elimination for three-dimensional graphics. ■ Shading and coloring of points can be specified using CMYKColor, GrayLevel, Hue or RGBColor. ■ See pages 400 and 430. ■ See also: Text.

■ PointSize

PointSize[*r*] is a graphics directive which specifies that points which follow are to be shown if possible as circular regions with radius *r*. The radius *r* is given as a fraction of the total width of the graph.

PointSize can be used in both two- and three-dimensional graphics. ■ The initial default is PointSize[0.008] for two-dimensional graphics, and PointSize[0.01] for three-dimensional graphics. ■ See page 408. ■ See also: AbsolutePointSize, Thickness.

■ PolyGamma

PolyGamma[*z*] gives the digamma function $\psi(z)$.

PolyGamma[*n*, *z*] gives n^{th} derivative of the digamma function $\psi^{(n)}(z)$.

PolyGamma[*z*] is the logarithmic derivative of the gamma function, given by $\psi(z) = \frac{\Gamma'(z)}{\Gamma(z)}$. ■ PolyGamma[*n*, *z*] is given by $\psi^{(n)}(z) = \frac{d^n}{dz^n}\psi(z)$. ■ The digamma function is $\psi(z) = \psi^{(0)}(z)$; $\psi^{(n)}(z)$ is the $(n+1)^{th}$ logarithmic derivative of the gamma function. ■ See page 571. ■ See also: Gamma, LogGamma, EulerGamma.

■ **Polygon**

Polygon[{pt_1, pt_2, ... }] is a graphics primitive that represents a filled polygon.

Polygon can be used in both Graphics and Graphics3D (two- and three-dimensional graphics). ■ The positions of points can be specified either in absolute coordinates as {x, y} or {x, y, z}, or in scaled coordinates as Scaled[{x, y}] or Scaled[{x, y, z}]. ■ The boundary of the polygon is formed by joining the last point you specify to the first one. ■ In two dimensions, self-intersecting polygons are allowed. ■ In three dimensions, planar polygons that do not intersect themselves will be drawn exactly as you specify them. Other polygons will be broken into triangles. ■ You can use graphics directives such as GrayLevel and RGBColor to specify how polygons should be filled. ■ In three dimensions, the shading can be produced from simulated illumination. ■ In three-dimensional graphics, polygons are considered to have both a front and a back face. The sense of a polygon is defined in terms of its first three vertices. When taken in order, these vertices go in a *counter-clockwise* direction when viewed from the *front*. (The frontward normal is thus obtained from a *right-hand* rule.) ■ You can use FaceForm to specify colors for the front and back faces of polygons. ■ In three-dimensional graphics, intersections between polygons are shown as lines, with forms specified by the graphics directive EdgeForm. ■ See pages 400 and 430. ■ See also: Raster, Rectangle, Cuboid, SurfaceColor.

■ **PolygonIntersections**

PolygonIntersections is an option for Graphics3D which specifies whether intersecting polygons should be left unchanged.

With the default setting PolygonIntersections -> True, Graphics3D objects are returned unchanged whether or not they contain intersecting polygons. ■ With the setting PolygonIntersections -> False, Graphics3D objects are modified by breaking polygons into smaller pieces which do not intersect each other.
■ PolygonIntersections -> False is useful in creating graphics objects which can be sent to certain external three-dimensional rendering programs. ■ See page 467. ■ See also: RenderAll.

■ **PolyLog**

PolyLog[n, z] gives the polylogarithm function $\mathrm{Li}_n(z)$.

Mathematical function (see Section A.3.9). ■ $\mathrm{Li}_n(z) = \sum_{k=1}^{\infty} \frac{z^k}{k^n}$. ■ See page 571. ■ See also: Zeta, PolyGamma, LerchPhi.

■ **PolynomialGCD**

PolynomialGCD[$poly_1$, $poly_2$] gives the greatest common divisor of the polynomials $poly_1$ and $poly_2$.

PolynomialGCD[$poly_1$, $poly_2$, Modulus->n] evaluates the GCD modulo the integer n.

Example: PolynomialGCD[1 + x y, x + x^2 y] ⟶ 1 + x y. ■ In PolynomialGCD[$poly_1$, $poly_2$], all symbolic parameters are treated as variables, and no division by them is allowed. ■ See page 598. ■ See also: PolynomialLCM, PolynomialQuotient, GCD, Cancel, PolynomialMod.

■ **PolynomialLCM**

PolynomialLCM[$poly_1$, $poly_2$] gives the least common multiple of the polynomials $poly_1$ and $poly_2$.

PolynomialLCM[$poly_1$, $poly_2$, Modulus->n] evaluates the LCM modulo the integer n.

Example: PolynomialLCM[1 + x y, x + x^2 y] ⟶ $x + x^2 y$. ■ See page 598. ■ See also: PolynomialGCD, LCM.

▨ PolynomialMod

PolynomialMod[*poly*, *m*] gives the polynomial *poly* reduced modulo *m*.

PolynomialMod[*poly*, {*m₁*, *m₂*, ... }] reduces modulo all of the m_i.

PolynomialMod[*poly*, *m*] for integer *m* gives a polynomial in which all coefficients are reduced modulo *m*.

■ Example: PolynomialMod[3x^2 + 2x + 1, 2] ⟶ $1 + x^2$ ■ When *m* is a polynomial, PolynomialMod[*poly*, *m*] reduces *poly* by subtracting polynomial multiplies of *m*, to give a result with minimal degree and leading coefficient. ■ PolynomialMod gives results according to a definite convention; other conventions could yield results differing by multiples of *m*. ■ Unlike PolynomialRemainder, PolynomialMod never performs divisions in generating its results. ■ See page 598. ■ See also: PolynomialGCD, Mod, PolynomialRemainder.

■ PolynomialQ

PolynomialQ[*expr*, *var*] yields True if *expr* is a polynomial in *var*, and yields False otherwise.

PolynomialQ[*expr*, {*var₁*, ... }] tests whether *expr* is a polynomial in the var_i.

The var_i need not be symbols; PolynomialQ[f[a] + f[a]^2, f[a]] ⟶ True. ■ PolynomialQ[*expr*] tests whether *expr* can be considered as a polynomial in any set of variables. It fails, for example, if *expr* contains approximate real numbers. ■ See page 593. ■ See also: Collect, Series.

■ PolynomialQuotient

PolynomialQuotient[*p*, *q*, *x*] gives the result of dividing *p* by *q*, treated as polynomials in *x*, with any remainder dropped.

See page 598. ■ See also: PolynomialGCD, Apart, Cancel, Quotient.

■ PolynomialRemainder

PolynomialRemainder[*p*, *q*, *x*] gives the remainder from dividing *p* by *q*, treated as polynomials in *x*.

The degree of the result in *x* is guaranteed to be smaller than the degree of *q*. ■ Unlike PolynomialMod, PolynomialRemainder performs divisions in generating its results. ■ See page 598. ■ See also: Apart, Cancel, PolynomialMod, Mod.

■ Position

Position[*expr*, *pattern*] gives a list of the positions at which objects matching *pattern* appear in *expr*.

Position[*expr*, *pattern*, *levspec*] finds only objects that appear on levels specified by *levspec*.

Example: Position[{1+x^2, 5, x^4}, x^_] ⟶ {{1, 2}, {3}}. ■ Position[*expr*, *pattern*] tests all the subparts of *expr* in turn to try and find ones that match *pattern*. ■ Position returns a list of positions in a form suitable for use in MapAt. ■ The default level specification for Position is Infinity, with Heads -> True. ■ Position[*list*, *pattern*, {1}, Heads -> False] finds positions only of objects that appear as complete elements of *list*. ■ Level specifications are described on page 725. ■ Position[*expr*, *pattern*, *levspec*, *n*] gives the positions of the first *n* parts of *expr* which match the pattern. ■ See page 221. ■ See also: Cases, Count, StringPosition, Insert, Delete.

■ Positive

Positive[*x*] gives True if *x* is a positive number.

Positive[*x*] gives False if *x* is manifestly a negative number, or zero. Otherwise, it remains unevaluated. ■ A definition like Positive[*x*] = True effectively specifies that *x* is a positive number. ■ Definitions for Sign are tested in determining whether linear combinations of expressions are positive. ■ See also: Negative, NonNegative, Sign.

■ Postfix

`Postfix[f[expr]]` prints with *f[expr]* given in default postfix form: *expr // f*.

`Postfix[f[expr], h]` prints as *exprh*.

`Postfix[expr, h, precedence, grouping]` can be used to specify how the output form should be parenthesized. ■ See the notes for `Infix` about precedence and grouping. ■ See page 362. ■ See also: `Infix`, `Prefix`.

◪ PostScript

`PostScript["string_1", "string_2", ... ]` is a graphics primitive which specifies PostScript code to include verbatim in graphics output.

The coordinate system for the PostScript runs from 0 to 1 across the plot in the horizontal direction, and from 0 to the aspect ratio in the vertical direction. ■ After execution of PostScript code included by the `PostScript` command, all PostScript stacks must be restored to their original states. ■ The utility of the `PostScript` command depends on your PostScript interpreter's ability to process the PostScript commands you specify. ■ See page 465. ■ See also: `RGBColor`, `Dashing`, `Thickness`, `PointSize`.

■ Power

x^y gives *x* to the power *y*.

Mathematical function (see Section A.3.9). ■ Exact rational number results are given when possible for roots of the form $n^{\frac{1}{m}}$. ■ For complex numbers *x* and *y*, `Power` gives the principal value of $e^{y \log(x)}$. ■ *(a b)^c* is automatically converted to *a^c b^c* only if *c* is an integer. ■ *(a^b)^c* is automatically converted to *a^(b c)* only if *c* is an integer. ■ See page 47. ■ See also: `Sqrt`, `Exp`, `PowerExpand`, `PowerMod`, `Log`.

◪ PowerExpand

`PowerExpand[expr]` expands all powers of products and powers.

Example: `PowerExpand[Sqrt[x y]]` $\longrightarrow$ `Sqrt[x] Sqrt[y]`. ■ `PowerExpand` converts *(a b)^c* to *a^c b^c*, whatever the form of *c* is. ■ `PowerExpand` also converts *(a^b)^c* to *a^(b c)*, whatever the form of *c* is. ■ The transformations made by `PowerExpand` are correct in general only if *c* is an integer or *a* and *b* are positive real numbers. ■ See page 592. ■ See also: `Expand`, `Distribute`.

■ PowerMod

`PowerMod[a, b, n]` gives a^b mod *n*.

For negative *b*, `PowerMod[a, b, n]` gives modular inverses.

Integer mathematical function (see Section A.3.9). ■ For positive *b*, `PowerMod[a, b, n]` gives the same answers as `Mod[a^b, n]` but is much more efficient. ■ For negative *b*, `PowerMod[a, b, n]` gives the integer *k* such that $ka^{-b} \equiv 1$ mod *n*. If no such integer exists, `PowerMod` returns unevaluated. ■ See page 556.

■ PrecedenceForm

`PrecedenceForm[expr, prec]` prints with *expr* parenthesized as it would be if it contained an operator with precedence *prec*.

prec must be an integer. See notes for `Infix`. ■ Example: `a + PrecedenceForm[b c, 10]` $\longrightarrow$ `a + (b c)`. ■ `PrecedenceForm` acts as a "wrapper", which affects printing, but not evaluation. ■ See page 362.

■ **Precision**

Precision[*x*] gives the number of digits of precision in the number *x*.

If *x* is not a number, Precision[*x*] gives the minimum value of Precision for all the numbers that appear in *x*.
■ Precision gives Infinity when applied to exact numbers, such as integers. ■ Precision gives $MachinePrecision for machine-precision numbers. ■ See page 539. ■ See also: Accuracy, N, Chop, SetPrecision, MachineNumberQ.

■ **PrecisionGoal**

PrecisionGoal is an option for various numerical operations which specifies how many digits of precision should be sought in the final result.

PrecisionGoal is an option for such functions as NIntegrate and NDSolve. ■ PrecisionGoal -> Automatic yields a precision goal equal to 10 digits less than the setting for WorkingPrecision.
■ PrecisionGoal -> Infinity specifies that precision should not be used as the criterion for terminating the numerical procedure. AccuracyGoal is typically used in this case. ■ Even though you may specify PrecisionGoal->*n*, the results you get may have much less than *n*-digit precision. ■ In most cases, you must set WorkingPrecision to be at least as large as PrecisionGoal. ■ PrecisionGoal effectively specifies the relative error allowed in a numerical procedure. ■ See page 688. ■ See also: PrecisionGoal, WorkingPrecision.

■ **PreDecrement**

--*x* decreases the value of *x* by 1, returning the new value of *x*.

PreDecrement has attribute HoldFirst. ■ --*x* is equivalent to *x*=*x*-1. ■ See page 248. ■ See also: Decrement, SubtractFrom, Set.

■ **Prefix**

Prefix[*f*[*expr*]] prints with *f*[*expr*] given in default prefix form: *f* @ *expr*.

Prefix[*f*[*expr*], *h*] prints as *h*expr.

Prefix[*expr*, *h*, *precedence*, *grouping*] can be used to specify how the output form should be parenthesized. ■ See the notes for Infix about precedence and grouping. ■ See page 362. ■ See also: Infix, Postfix.

■ **PreIncrement**

++*x* increases the value of *x* by 1, returning the new value of *x*.

PreIncrement has attribute HoldFirst. ■ ++*x* is equivalent to *x*=*x*+1. ■ See page 248. ■ See also: Increment, AddTo, Set.

■ **Prepend**

Prepend[*expr*, *elem*] gives *expr* with *elem* prepended.

Examples: Prepend[{a,b}, x] ⟶ {x, a, b}; Prepend[f[a], x+y] ⟶ f[x + y, a]. ■ See page 128. ■ See also: Append, Insert.

■ **PrependTo**

PrependTo[*s*, *elem*] prepends *elem* to the value of *s*, and resets *s* to the result.

PrependTo[*s*, *elem*] is equivalent to *s* = Prepend[*s*, *elem*]. ■ PrependTo[*s*, *elem*] does not evaluate *s*. ■ You can use PrependTo repeatedly to build up a list. ■ See page 249. ■ See also: AppendTo.

■ **Prime**

Prime[*n*] gives the nth prime number.

Prime[1] is 2. ■ On most computer systems, Prime[*n*] for *n* up to 10^8 can be obtained quite quickly. ■ See page 554. ■ See also: FactorInteger, PrimeQ, PrimePi.

■ **PrimePi**

PrimePi[*x*] gives the number of primes $\pi(x)$ less than or equal to *x*.

The argument of PrimePi can be any positive real number. ■ PrimePi[1] gives 0. ■ See page 554. ■ See also: Prime, Zeta.

■ **PrimeQ**

PrimeQ[*expr*] yields True if *expr* is a prime number, and yields False otherwise.

PrimeQ[1] gives False. ■ PrimeQ[-*n*], where *n* is prime, gives True. ■ PrimeQ[*n*, GaussianIntegers->True] determines whether *n* is a Gaussian prime. ■ In *Mathematica* Version 2.0, PrimeQ[*n*] uses the Rabin strong pseudoprime test and the Lucas test. This procedure has been proved correct for all $n < 2.5 \times 10^{10}$. As of 1990, however, the procedure has not been proved correct for larger *n*, and it is conceivable that it could claim that a composite number was prime (though not vice-versa). Nevertheless, as of 1990, no example of such behavior is known. ■ In *Mathematica* Version 2.0, the package NumberTheory`PrimeQ` contains a much slower PrimeQ based on a procedure which been proved correct for all numbers. ■ See page 554. ■ See also: FactorInteger.

■ **Print**

Print[*expr*$_1$, *expr*$_2$, ...] prints the *expr*$_i$, followed by a newline (line feed).

Print sends its output to the channel $Output. ■ Print uses OutputForm as the default format type. ■ Print concatenates the output from each *expr*$_i$ together, effectively using SequenceForm. ■ You can arrange to have expressions on several lines by using ColumnForm. ■ See page 363. ■ See also: Message, Put, Write.

■ **PrintForm**

PrintForm[*expr*] prints as the internal printform representation of *expr*.

The printform consists of a nested collection of the primitives:

String	raw character string
HorizontalForm	horizontal array of print objects
VerticalForm	vertical array of print objects

■ See page 344. ■ See also: FullForm, TreeForm.

■ **Product**

Product[*f*, {*i*, *imax*}] evaluates the product $\prod_{i=1}^{imax} f$.

Product[*f*, {*i*, *imin*, *imax*}] starts with *i* = *imin*. Product[*f*, {*i*, *imin*, *imax*, *di*}] uses steps *di*.

Product[*f*, {*i*, *imin*, *imax*}, {*j*, *jmin*, *jmax*}, ...] evaluates the multiple product $\prod_{i=imin}^{imax} \prod_{j=jmin}^{jmax} \cdots f$.

Product evaluates its arguments in a non-standard way (see page 730). ■ Product uses the standard *Mathematica* iteration specification. ■ The iteration variable *i* is treated as local. ■ In multiple products, the range of the outermost variable is given first. ■ See page 90. ■ See also: Do, Sum, Table, NProduct.

◪ Prolog

Prolog is an option for graphics functions which gives a list of graphics primitives to be rendered before the main part of the graphics is rendered.

Graphics primitives specified by Prolog are rendered after axes, boxes and frames are rendered. ■ In three-dimensional graphics, two-dimensional graphics primitives can be specified by the Prolog option. The graphics primitives are rendered in a 0,1 coordinate system. ■ See page 412. ■ See also: Background, DefaultColor, Epilog, AxesStyle, PlotStyle, DisplayFunction.

■ Protect

Protect[s_1, s_2, ...] sets the attribute Protected for the symbols s_i.

Protect["*form$_1$*", "*form$_2$*", ...] protects all symbols whose names match any of the string patterns *form$_i$*.

Protect["*form*"] allows metacharacters such as *, as specified on page 728. ■ Protect["*context*`*"] protects all symbols in a particular context. ■ See pages 264 and 728. ■ See also: Unprotect.

■ Protected

Protected is an attribute which prevents any values associated with a symbol from being modified.

Many built-in *Mathematica* functions have the attribute Protected. ■ See page 272. ■ See also: Locked, ReadProtected.

■ PseudoInverse

PseudoInverse[m] finds the pseudoinverse of a rectangular matrix.

PseudoInverse works on both symbolic and numerical matrices. ■ For numerical matrices, PseudoInverse[m, Tolerance -> t] specifies that singular values smaller than t times the maximum singular value are to be removed. ■ The default setting Tolerance -> Automatic takes t to be $10^{(-p+4)}$ where p is the numerical precision of the input. ■ For non-singular square matrices **M**, the pseudoinverse $\mathbf{M}^{(-1)}$ is equivalent to the standard inverse. ■ See page 665. ■ See also: Inverse, SingularValues, Fit.

■ Put

expr >> *filename* writes *expr* to a file.

Put[*expr$_1$*, *expr$_2$*, ... , "*filename*"] writes a sequence of expressions *expr$_i$* to a file.

On systems with advanced graphical interfaces, there will usually be graphical tools for saving expressions in files. ■ Put uses the format type InputForm by default. ■ Put starts writing output at the beginning of the file. It deletes whatever was previously in the file. ■ Put inserts a newline (line feed) at the end of its output. ■ *expr* >> *filename* is equivalent to *expr* >> "*filename*". The double quotes can be omitted if the file name is of the form specified on page 721. ■ It is conventional to use names that end with .m for files containing *Mathematica* input. ■ See page 478. ■ See also: Save, Definition, Dump, Get.

■ PutAppend

expr >>> *filename* appends *expr* to a file.

Put[*expr$_1$*, *expr$_2$*, ... , "*filename*"] appends a sequence of expressions *expr$_i$* to a file.

PutAppend works the same as Put, except that it adds output to the end of file, rather than replacing the complete contents of the file. ■ See page 478. ■ See also: Write.

◪ QRDecomposition

QRDecomposition[*m*] yields the QR decomposition for a numerical matrix *m*. The result is a list {*q*, *r*}, where *q* is an orthogonal matrix and *r* is an upper triangular matrix.

The original matrix *m* is equal to Conjugate[Transpose[*q*]] . *r*. ■ For non-square matrices, *q* is row orthonormal. ■ The matrix *r* has zeros for all entries below the leading diagonal. ■ QRDecomposition[*m*, Pivoting -> True] yields a list {*q*, *r*, *p*} where *p* is a permutation matrix such that *m* . *p* is equal to Conjugate[Transpose[*q*]] . *r*. ■ See page 666. ■ See also: SchurDecomposition, SingularValues.

■ Quartics

Quartics is an option for Roots and related functions which specifies whether explicit solutions should be generated for irreducible quartic equations.

Quartics->False causes irreducible fourth-degree equations to be left unsolved in their original symbolic form. Numerical solutions can be found by applying N. ■ Setting Quartics->True causes explicit solutions to be generated. These solutions are usually very complicated. ■ See also: Cubics, NSolve.

■ Quit

Quit[ ] terminates a *Mathematica* session.

All definitions that you have not explicitly saved in files are lost when the *Mathematica* session terminates. ■ Before terminating a session, *Mathematica* executes any delayed value that has been assigned to the global variable $Epilog. Conventionally, this attempts to read in a file end.m of commands to be executed before termination. ■ On most computer systems, Quit[*n*] terminates *Mathematica*, passing the integer *n* as an exit code to the operating system. ■ Exit is a synonym for Quit. ■ See pages 519 and 747. ■ See also: Return, $IgnoreEOF.

■ Quotient

Quotient[*n*, *m*] gives the integer quotient of n and m.

Integer mathematical function (see Section A.3.9). ■ Quotient[*n*, *m*] is equivalent to Floor[*n*/*m*] for integers *n* and *m*. ■ See page 553. ■ See also: Mod, PolynomialQuotient.

■ Random

Random[ ] gives a uniformly distributed pseudorandom Real in the range 0 to 1.

Random[*type*, *range*] gives a pseudorandom number of the specified *type*, lying in the specified range. Possible types are: Integer, Real and Complex. The default range is 0 to 1. You can give the range {*min*, *max*} explicitly; a range specification of *max* is equivalent to {0, *max*}.

Random[Integer] gives 0 or 1 with probability $\frac{1}{2}$. ■ Random[Complex, {*zmin*, *zmax*}] gives a pseudorandom complex number in the rectangle defined by *zmin* and *zmax*. ■ Random[Real, *range*, *n*] generates a pseudorandom real number with a precision of *n* digits. ■ Random gives a different sequence of pseudorandom numbers whenever you run *Mathematica*. You can start Random with a particular seed using SeedRandom. ■ See page 552.

■ Range

Range[*imax*] generates the list {1, 2, ... , *imax*}.

Range[*imin*, *imax*] generates the list {*imin*, ... , *imax*}. Range[*imin*, *imax*, *di*] uses step *di*.

Example: Range[4] ⟶ {1, 2, 3, 4}. ■ The arguments to Range need not be integers. ■ Range starts from *imin*, and successively adds increments of *di* until the result is greater than *imax*. ■ Range[0, 1, .3] ⟶ {0, 0.3, 0.6, 0.9}. ■ Range[x, x+2] ⟶ {x, 1 + x, 2 + x}. ■ Range uses the standard *Mathematica* iteration specification, as applied to a single variable. ■ See page 122. ■ See also: Table.

■ Raster

Raster[{{a_{11}, a_{12}, ... }, ... }] is a two-dimensional graphics primitive which represents a rectangular array of gray cells.

Raster[*array*, ColorFunction -> *f*] specifies that each cell should be rendered using the graphics directives obtained by applying the function *f* to the cell value a_{ij}. ■ Raster[*array*, ColorFunction -> Hue] generates an array in which cell values are specified by hues. ■ If *array* has dimensions {m, n}, then Raster[*array*] is assumed to occupy the rectangle Rectangle[{0, 0}, {m, n}]. ■ Raster[*array*, {{*xmin*, *ymin*}, {*xmax*, *ymax*}}] specifies that the raster should be taken instead to fill the rectangle Rectangle[{*xmin*, *ymin*}, {*xmax*, *ymax*}]. ■ Scaled coordinates can be used to specify the rectangle. ■ Raster[*array*, *rect*, {*zmin*, *zmax*}] specifies that cell values should be scaled so that *zmin* corresponds to 0 and *zmax* corresponds to 1. Cell values outside this range are clipped. ■ See page 405. ■ See also: RasterArray, DensityGraphics, GraphicsArray.

■ RasterArray

RasterArray[{{g_{11}, g_{12}, ... }, ... }] is a two-dimensional graphics primitive which represents a rectangular array of cells colored according to the graphics directives g_{ij}.

Each of the g_{ij} must be GrayLevel, RGBColor or Hue. ■ If *array* has dimensions {m, n}, then RasterArray[*array*] is assumed to occupy the rectangle Rectangle[{0, 0}, {m, n}]. ■ RasterArray[*array*, {{*xmin*, *ymin*}, {*xmax*, *ymax*}}] specifies that the raster should be taken instead to fill the rectangle Rectangle[{*xmin*, *ymin*}, {*xmax*, *ymax*}]. ■ Scaled coordinates can be used to specify the rectangle. ■ See page 405. ■ See also: Raster, GraphicsArray.

■ Rational

Rational is the head used for rational numbers.

You can enter a rational number in the form *n/m*. ■ The pattern object _Rational can be used to stand for a rational number. It cannot stand for a single integer. ■ You have to use Numerator and Denominator to extract parts of Rational numbers. ■ See page 534. ■ See also: Integer, Numerator, Denominator.

■ Rationalize

Rationalize[*x*] takes Real numbers in *x* that are close to rationals, and converts them to exact Rational numbers.

Rationalize[*x*, *dx*] performs the conversion whenever the error made is smaller in magnitude than *dx*.

Example: Rationalize[3.78] $\longrightarrow \dfrac{189}{50}$. ■ Rationalize[N[Pi]] $\longrightarrow$ 3.14159 does not give a rational number, since there is none "sufficiently close" to N[Pi]. ■ A rational number p/q is considered "sufficiently close" to a Real x if $|p/q - x| < c/q^2$, where c is chosen to be 10^{-4}. ■ Rationalize[*x*, 0] converts any *x* to rational form. ■ See page 536. ■ See also: Chop, Round, LatticeReduce.

■ Raw

Raw[*h*, "*hexstring*"] constructs a raw data object with head *h*, and with contents corresponding to the binary bit pattern represented by the string *hexstring*, interpreted as a hexadecimal number.

Raw should be used only under very special circumstances. ■ It is possible to crash *Mathematica* by creating a fundamental *Mathematica* data object with Raw, and specifying illegal internal data for it. If you create an object with head Real, but with internal data incompatible with *Mathematica* Real numbers, you may end up crashing your whole *Mathematica* session. ■ Raw encodes data so that two hexadecimal digits represent one byte. Identical *hexstring* may lead to different internal data on different computer systems. ■ You cannot necessarily transport raw arrays of bytes from one type of computer to another without encountering byte swap incompatibilities. ■ See page 712. ■ See also: Run.

■ **Re**

Re[*z*] gives the real part of the complex number *z*.

Re[*expr*] is left unevaluated if *expr* is not a number. ■ See page 551. ■ See also: Im, Abs, Arg, ComplexExpand.

■ **Read**

Read[*stream*] reads one expression from an input stream, and returns the expression.

Read[*stream*, *type*] reads one object of the specified type.

Read[*stream*, {*type₁*, *type₂*, ... }] reads a sequence of objects of the specified types.

Possible types to read are:

Byte	single byte, returned as an integer code
Character	single character, returned as a one-character string
Expression	complete *Mathematica* expression
Number	integer or an approximate number, given in "E" format
Real	approximate number, given in "E" format
Record	sequence of characters delimited by record separators
String	string terminated by a newline
Word	sequence of characters delimited by word separators

■ Objects of type Real can be given in the scientific notation format used by languages such as C and Fortran. A form like 2.e5 or 2E5 can be used to represent the number 2×10^5. Objects read as type Real are always returned as approximate numbers. Objects read as type Number are returned as integers if they contain no explicit decimal points. ■ The following options can be given:

NullRecords	False	whether to assume a null record between repeated record separators
NullWords	False	whether to assume a null word between repeated word separators
RecordSeparators	{"\n"}	separators allowed between records
TokenWords	{}	words taken as delimiters
WordSeparators	{" ", "\t"}	separators allowed between words

■ Objects of type String must be terminated by newlines ("\n" characters). ■ You can specify any nested list of types for Read to look for. Each successive object read will be placed in the next position in the list structure. A depth-first traversal of the list structure is used. ■ Example: Read[*stream*, {Number, Number}] reads a pair of numbers from an input stream, and gives the result as a two-element list. ■ Read[*stream*, {{Number, Number}, {Number, Number}}] reads a 2×2 matrix, going through each column, then each row. ■ You can use Read to get objects to insert into any expression structure, not necessarily a list. Example: Read[*stream*, Hold[Expression]] gets an expression and places it inside Hold. ■ The first argument to Read can be InputStream["*name*", *n*], or simply "*name*" if there is only one open input stream with the specified name. ■ You can open a file or pipe to get an InputStream object using OpenRead. ■ There is always a "current point" maintained for any stream. When you read an object from a stream, the current point is left after the input you read. Successive calls to Read can therefore be used to read successive objects in a stream such as a file. ■ Read returns EndOfFile for each object you try to read after you have reached the end of a file. ■ Read returns $Failed if it cannot read an object of the type you requested. ■ If there is a syntax error in a *Mathematica* expression that you try to read, then Read leaves the current point at the position of the error, and returns $Failed. ■ See page 499. ■ See also: Input, Get, Skip, Find, StringToStream.

■ ReadList

ReadList["*file*"] reads all the remaining expressions in a file, and returns a list of them.

ReadList["*file*", *type*] reads objects of the specified type from a file, until the end of the file is reached. The list of objects read is returned.

ReadList["*file*", {*type₁*, *type₂*, ... }] reads objects with a sequence of types, until the end of the file is reached.

ReadList["*file*", *types*, *n*] reads only the first *n* objects of the specified types.

The option setting RecordLists -> True makes ReadList create separate sublists for objects that appear in separate records. ■ With the default setting RecordSeparators -> {"\n"}, RecordLists -> True puts objects on separate lines into separate sublists. ■ The option RecordSeparators gives a list of strings which are taken to delimit records. ■ ReadList takes the same options as Read, with the addition of RecordLists. ■ If *file* is not already open for reading, ReadList opens it, then closes it when it is finished. If the file is already open, ReadList does not close it at the end. ■ ReadList prints a message if any of the objects remaining in the file are not of the specified types. ■ ReadList["*file*", {*type₁*, ... }] looks for the sequence of *typeᵢ* in order. If the end of file is reached while part way through the sequence of *typeᵢ*, EndOfFile is returned in place of the elements in the sequence that have not yet been read. ■ ReadList[*stream*] reads from an open input stream, as returned by OpenRead. ■ See notes for Read. ■ See pages 181 and 493. ■ See also: FindList.

■ ReadProtected

ReadProtected is an attribute which prevents values associated with a symbol from being seen.

Individual values associated with read-protected symbols can be used during evaluation. ■ Definition[*f*], ?*f*, and related functions give only the attributes for read-protected symbols *f*. ■ See page 272. ■ See also: Locked, Protected.

■ Real

Real is the head used for real (floating-point) numbers.

_Real can be used to stand for a real number in a pattern. ■ You can enter a floating-point number of any length. ■ You can enter a number in scientific notation by explicitly giving the form *mantissa* 10^*exponent*. ■ You can enter a floating-point number in base *b* using *b*^^*digits*. The base must be less than 36. The letters a–z or A–Z are used in sequence to stand for digits 10 through 35. ■ Real is also used to indicate an approximate real number in Read. ■ See page 534. ■ See also: RealDigits, BaseForm, Number.

■ RealDigits

RealDigits[*x*] gives a list of the digits in the approximate real number *x*, together with the number of digits that appear to the left of the decimal point in scientific notation.

RealDigits[*x*, *b*] gives a list of base-*b* digits in *x*.

RealDigits[*x*] returns a list of digits whose length is equal to Precision[*x*]. ■ The base *b* in RealDigits[*x*, *b*] need not be an integer. For any real *b* such that $b > 1$, RealDigits[*x*, *b*] successively finds the largest integer multiples of powers of *b* that can be removed while leaving a non-negative remainder. ■ See page 537. ■ See also: MantissaExponent, IntegerDigits, BaseForm.

■ Record

Record represents a record in Read, Find and related functions.

The record is delimited by strings in the list given as the setting for RecordSeparators. ■ See page 495. ■ See also: Word.

◪ RecordLists

RecordLists is an option for ReadList which specifies whether objects from separate records should be returned in separate sublists.

With the default setting RecordSeparators -> {"\n"}, setting RecordLists -> True makes RecordLists return objects that appear on different lines in different sublists. ▪ With RecordLists -> False, ReadList returns a single list of all objects it reads. ▪ With RecordLists -> True, ReadList returns a list containing a sublist for each record. ▪ See page 494.

◪ RecordSeparators

RecordSeparators is an option for Read, Find and related functions which specifies the list of strings to be taken as delimiters for records.

The default setting is RecordSeparators -> {"\n"}. With this setting, each complete line of input is considered as a record. ▪ Strings used as record separators may contain several characters. ▪ The characters may be either 8- or 16-bit. ▪ With the option setting NullRecords -> False, any number of record separators may appear between any two successive records. ▪ RecordSeparators -> { } specifies that everything is to be included in a single record. ▪ RecordSeparators -> {{$lsep_1$, ... }, {$rsep_1$, ... }} specifies different left and right separators for records. When there are nested left and right separators, records are taken to be delimited by the innermost balanced pairs of separators. ▪ Example: with RecordSeparators -> {{"<"}, {">"}}, the records aaa and bbb are extracted from <x<aaa>yyy<<bbb>>>. ▪ Text that does not appear between left and right separators is discarded. ▪ See page 496. ▪ See also: WordSeparators.

■ Rectangle

Rectangle[{$xmin$, $ymin$}, {$xmax$, $ymax$}] is a two-dimensional graphics primitive that represents a filled rectangle, oriented parallel to the axes.

Rectangle[{$xmin$, $ymin$}, {$xmax$, $ymax$}, $graphics$] gives a rectangle filled with the specified graphics.

Rectangle[Scaled[{$xmin$, $ymin$}], Scaled[{$xmax$, $ymax$}]] can also be used.
▪ Rectangle[{$xmin$, $ymin$}, {$xmax$, $ymax$}] is equivalent to a suitable Polygon with four corners. ▪ You can use graphics directives such as GrayLevel and RGBColor to specify how Rectangle[{$xmin$, $ymin$}, {$xmax$, $ymax$}] should be filled. ▪ In Rectangle[{$xmin$, $ymin$}, {$xmax$, $ymax$}, $graphics$], $graphics$ can be any graphics object. ▪ The rectangle is taken as the complete display area in which the graphics object is rendered. ▪ When rectangles overlap, their backgrounds are effectively taken to be transparent. ▪ Fonts and absolute size specifications are not affected by the size of the rectangle in which the graphics are rendered. ▪ The options DisplayFunction, ColorOutput and StringConversion are ignored for graphics objects given inside Rectangle. ▪ See page 400. ▪ See also: Polygon, Raster, RasterArray, Cuboid, GraphicsArray.

■ Reduce

Reduce[$eqns$, $vars$] simplifies the equations $eqns$, attempting to solve for the variables $vars$. The equations generated by Reduce are equivalent to $eqns$, and contain all the possible solutions.

Reduce[$eqns$, $vars$, $elims$] simplifies the equations, trying to eliminate the variables $elims$.

The equations given to Reduce are in the form lhs == rhs. Simultaneous equations can either be given in a list, or combined with &&. ▪ Example: Reduce[a x + b == 0, x] $\longrightarrow$ a != 0 && x == -$(\frac{b}{a})$ || a == 0 && b == 0.
▪ Reduce generates equations (==) and nonequalities (!=), combined with && and ||. ▪ Reduce primarily deals with polynomial equations. ▪ You can give options to Reduce, as described in the notes on MainSolve. ▪ See page 614.
▪ See also: Solve, Eliminate, LogicalExpand, ToRules.

■ ReleaseHold

ReleaseHold[*expr*] removes Hold and HoldForm in *expr*.

Example: ReleaseHold[{2, Hold[1 + 1]}] ⟶ {2, 2}. ■ ReleaseHold removes only one layer of Hold or HoldForm; it does not remove inner occurrences in nested Hold or HoldForm functions. ■ See page 282. ■ See also: Evaluate.

■ Remove

Remove[*symbol$_1$*, ...] removes symbols completely, so that their names are no longer recognized by *Mathematica*.

Remove["*form$_1$*", "*form$_2$*", ...] removes all symbols whose names match any of the string patterns *form$_i$*.

You can use Remove to get rid of symbols that you do not need, and which may shadow symbols in contexts later on your context path. ■ Remove["*form*"] allows metacharacters such as *, as specified on page 728. ■ Remove["*context*`*"] removes all symbols in a particular context. ■ Remove does not affect symbols with the attribute Protected. ■ Once you have removed a symbol, you will never be able to refer to it again, unless you recreate it. ■ If you have an expression that contains a symbol which you remove, the removed symbol will be printed as Removed["*name*"], where its name is given in a string. ■ See pages 335 and 736. ■ See also: Clear.

■ RenameDirectory

RenameDirectory["*dir$_1$*", "*dir$_2$*"] renames the directory *dir$_1$* to *dir$_2$*.

dir$_1$ must already exist; *dir$_2$* must not. ■ RenameDirectory sets the modification date for *dir$_2$* to be the same as for *dir$_1$*. ■ RenameDirectory returns the full new directory name, or $Failed if the directory cannot be renamed. ■ See page 493. ■ See also: CopyDirectory, CreateDirectory, DeleteDirectory.

■ RenameFile

RenameFile["*file$_1$*", "*file$_2$*"] renames *file$_1$* to *file$_2$*.

file$_1$ must already exist; *file$_2$* must not. ■ RenameFile sets the modification date for *file$_2$* to be the same as for *file$_1$*. ■ RenameFile returns the full new file name, or $Failed if the file cannot be renamed. ■ See page 492. ■ See also: CopyFile, DeleteFile, RenameDirectory.

■ RenderAll

RenderAll is an option to Graphics3D which specifies whether or not PostScript should be generated for *all* polygons.

When RenderAll->False, PostScript will be generated only for those polygons or parts of polygons which are visible in the final picture. ■ If RenderAll->True, PostScript is generated for *all* polygons. The PostScript for polygons that are further back is given before the PostScript for those in front. If the PostScript is displayed incrementally, you can see the object being drawn from the back. ■ Setting RenderAll->False will usually lead to a smaller amount of PostScript code, but may take longer to run. ■ There may be slight differences in the images obtained with different settings for RenderAll, primarily as a result of different numerical roundoff in the PostScript code, and the rendering system. ■ See page 466. ■ See also: PolygonIntersections.

■ Repeated

p.. is a pattern object which represents a sequence of one or more expressions, each matching *p*.

p.. can appear as an argument of any function. It represents any sequence of arguments. ■ All the objects in the sequence represented by *p*.. must match *p*, but the objects need not be identical. ■ The expression *p* may, but need not, itself be a pattern object. ■ See pages 237 and 717. ■ See also: BlankSequence.

■ **`RepeatedNull`**

> *p*`...` is a pattern object which represents a sequence of zero or more expressions, each matching *p*.
>
> See notes for `Repeated`. ■ See pages 237 and 717.

■ **`Replace`**

> `Replace[`*expr*, *rules*`]` applies a rule or list of rules in an attempt to transform the entire expression *expr*.
>
> Example: `Replace[x^2, x^2 -> a]` ⟶ `a`. ■ `Replace[x + 1, x -> a]` ⟶ `1 + x`. ■ The rules must be of the form *lhs* `->` *rhs* or *lhs* `:>` *rhs*. ■ A list of rules can be given. The rules are tried in order. The result of the first one that applies is returned. If none of the rules apply, the original *expr* is returned. ■ If the rules are given in nested lists, `Replace` is effectively mapped onto the inner lists. Thus `Replace[`*expr*, `{{`r_{11}, r_{12}`}`, `{`r_{21}, `... }`, `... }]` is equivalent to `{Replace[`*expr*, `{`r_{11}, r_{12}`}]`, `Replace[`*expr*, `{`r_{21}, `... }]`, `... }`. ■ Delayed rules defined with `:>` can contain `/;` conditions. ■ `Replace[`*expr*, *rules*`]` applies rules only to the complete expression *expr*. You can use `ReplaceAll` to apply rules separately to each part of an expression. ■ See page 245. ■ See also: `Rule`, `Set`, `ReplacePart`, `AlgebraicRules`, `StringReplace`.

■ **`ReplaceAll`**

> *expr* `/.` *rules* applies a rule or list of rules in an attempt to transform each subpart of an expression *expr*.
>
> Example: `x + 2 /. x -> a` ⟶ `2 + a`. ■ `ReplaceAll[`*expr*, *rules*`]` is equivalent to `MapAll[Replace[#, `*rules*`]&, `*expr*`]`. ■ `ReplaceAll` looks at each part of *expr*, tries all the *rules* on it, and then goes on to the next part of *expr*. The first rule that applies to a particular part is used; no further rules are tried on that part, or on any of its subparts. ■ `ReplaceAll` applies a particular rule only once to an expression. ■ Example: `x /. x -> x + 1` ⟶ `1 + x`. ■ See the notes on `Replace` for a description of how rules are applied to each part of *expr*. ■ *expr* `/.` *rules* returns *expr* if none of the rules apply. ■ See page 243. ■ See also: `Rule`, `Set`.

■ **`ReplaceHeldPart`**

> `ReplaceHeldPart[`*expr*, `Hold[`*new*`]`, *n*`]` yields an expression in which the nth part of *expr* is replaced by *new*.
>
> `ReplaceHeldPart[`*expr*, `Hold[`*new*`]`, `{`*i*, *j*, `... }]` replaces the part at position `{`*i*, *j*, `... }`.
>
> `ReplaceHeldPart[`*expr*, `Hold[`*new*`]`, `{{`i_1, j_1, `... }`, `{`i_2, j_2, `... }`, `... }]` replaces parts at several positions by *new*.
>
> See notes for `ReplacePart`. ■ `ReplaceHeldPart` is useful for replacing objects inside functions that do not evaluate their arguments. ■ `ReplaceHeldPart` allows both `Hold` and `HoldForm` wrappers for the expression to be inserted. ■ See page 282. ■ See also: `HeldPart`, `Unevaluated`.

■ **`ReplacePart`**

> `ReplacePart[`*expr*, *new*, *n*`]` yields an expression in which the nth part of *expr* is replaced by *new*.
>
> `ReplacePart[`*expr*, *new*, `{`*i*, *j*, `... }]` replaces the part at position `{`*i*, *j*, `... }`.
>
> `ReplacePart[`*expr*, *new*, `{{`i_1, j_1, `... }`, `{`i_2, j_2, `... }`, `... }]` replaces parts at several positions by *new*.
>
> Example: `ReplacePart[{a, b, c, d}, x, 3]` ⟶ `{a, b, x, d}`. ■ See pages 128 and 195. ■ See also: `Part`, `MapAt`, `FlattenAt`, `Insert`, `Delete`.

■ **ReplaceRepeated**

expr //. *rules* repeatedly performs replacements until *expr* no longer changes.

expr //. *rules* effectively applies /. repeatedly, until the results it gets no longer change. ■ It performs one complete pass over the expression using /., then carries out the next pass. ■ You should be very careful to avoid infinite loops when you use the //. operator. The command x //. x -> x + 1 will, for example, lead to an infinite loop. ■ ReplaceRepeated takes the option MaxIterations, which specifies the maximum number of times it will try to apply the rules you give. The default setting is MaxIterations -> 65536. With MaxIterations -> Infinity there is no limit. ■ See page 244. ■ See also: Rule, Set, FixedPoint.

■ **ResetDirectory**

ResetDirectory[ ] resets the current working directory to its previous value.

Successive calls to ResetDirectory yield earlier and earlier current directories. ■ ResetDirectory uses the directory stack given by DirectoryStack[ ]. ■ ResetDirectory removes the last element from the directory stack, and makes the second-to-last element current. ■ See pages 489 and 490. ■ See also: SetDirectory, Directory, $Path.

■ **Residue**

Residue[*expr*, {*x*, x_0}] finds the residue of *expr* at the point $x = x_0$.

The residue is defined as the coefficient of $(x - x_0)$^-1 in the Laurent expansion of *expr*. ■ *Mathematica* can usually find residues at a point only when it can evaluate power series at that point. ■ See page 648. ■ See also: Series, Limit.

■ **Rest**

Rest[*expr*] gives *expr* with the first element removed.

Example: Rest[{a, b, c}] ⟶ {b, c}. ■ Rest[*expr*] is equivalent to Drop[*expr*, 1]. ■ See page 125. ■ See also: Drop, First, Part, Take.

■ **Resultant**

Resultant[$poly_1$, $poly_2$, *var*] computes the resultant of the polynomials $poly_1$ and $poly_2$ with respect to the variable *var*.

Resultant[$poly_1$, $poly_2$, *var*, Modulus->*p*] computes the resultant modulo the prime *p*.

The resultant of two polynomials *a* and *b*, both with leading coefficient one, is the product of all the differences $a_i - b_j$ between roots of the polynomials. The resultant is always a number or a polynomial. ■ See page 598. ■ See also: PolynomialGCD, Eliminate.

■ **Return**

Return[*expr*] returns the value *expr* from a function.

Return[ ] returns the value Null.

Return[*expr*] exits control structures within the definition of a function, and gives the value *expr* for the whole function. ■ Return is effective only if it is generated as the value of a segment in a compound expression, or as the body of a control structure. Return also works in Scan. ■ See page 293. ■ See also: Break, Throw.

■ **Reverse**

Reverse[*expr*] reverses the order of the elements in *expr*.

Example: Reverse[{a, b, c}] ⟶ {c, b, a}. ■ See page 130. ■ See also: Permutations, RotateLeft, RotateRight, StringReverse.

■ **RGBColor**

RGBColor[*red*, *green*, *blue*] is a graphics directive which specifies that graphical objects which follow are to be displayed, if possible, in the color given.

Red, green and blue color intensities outside the range 0 to 1 will be clipped. ■ On monochrome displays, a gray level based on the average of the color intensities is used. ■ Page 40 shows examples of colors generated with various RGBColor specifications. ■ See page 407. ■ See also: Hue, GrayLevel, CMYKColor, ColorOutput.

■ **RiemannSiegelTheta**

RiemannSiegelTheta[*t*] gives the Riemann-Siegel function $\vartheta(t)$.

Mathematical function (see Section A.3.9). ■ $\vartheta(t) = \Im \log \Gamma(\frac{1}{4} + i\frac{t}{2}) - t\frac{\log \pi}{2}$ for real t. ■ $\vartheta(t)$ arises in the study of the Riemann zeta function on the critical line. It is closely related to the number of zeros of $\zeta(\frac{1}{2} + iu)$ for $0 < u < t$. ■ $\vartheta(t)$ is an analytic function of t except for branch cuts on the imaginary axis running from $\pm\frac{i}{2}$ to $\pm i\infty$. ■ See page 571. ■ See also: Zeta.

■ **RiemannSiegelZ**

RiemannSiegelZ[*t*] gives the Riemann-Siegel function $Z(t)$.

Mathematical function (see Section A.3.9). ■ $Z(t) = e^{i\vartheta(t)}\zeta(\frac{1}{2} + it)$, where ϑ is the Riemann-Siegel theta function, and ζ is the Riemann zeta function. ■ $|Z(t)| = |\zeta(\frac{1}{2} + it)|$ for real t. ■ $Z(t)$ is an analytic function of t except for branch cuts on the imaginary axis running from $\pm\frac{i}{2}$ to $\pm i\infty$. ■ See page 571. ■ See also: Zeta.

■ **Roots**

Roots[*lhs==rhs*, *var*] yields a disjunction of equations which represent the roots of a polynomial equation.

Roots uses Factor and Decompose in trying to find roots. ■ You can find numerical values of the roots by applying N. ■ Roots can take the following options:

Cubics	True	whether to generate explicit solutions for cubics
EquatedTo	Null	expression to which the variable solved for should be equated
Modulus	Infinity	integer modulus
Multiplicity	1	multiplicity in final list of solutions
Quartics	True	whether to generate explicit solutions for quartics
Using	True	subsidiary equations to be solved

■ Roots is generated when Solve and related functions cannot produce explicit solutions. Options are often given in such cases. ■ Roots gives several identical equations when roots with multiplicity greater than one occur. ■ See page 606. ■ See also: Solve, NSolve, FindRoot, ToRules.

■ **RotateLabel**

RotateLabel is an option for two-dimensional graphics functions which specifies whether labels on vertical frame axes should be rotated to be vertical.

For frame labels, the default is RotateLabel -> True. ■ With RotateLabel -> True, vertical frame axes labels read from bottom to top. ■ See page 422. ■ See also: Text.

■ **RotateLeft**

RotateLeft[*expr*, *n*] cycles the elements in *expr* *n* positions to the left.

RotateLeft[*expr*] cycles one position to the left.

RotateLeft[*expr*, {n_1, n_2, ... }] cycles elements at successive levels n_i positions to the left.

Example: RotateLeft[{a, b, c}, 1] $\longrightarrow$ {b, c, a}. ■ RotateLeft[*expr*, −*n*] rotates *n* positions to the right. ■ See page 130. ■ See also: Reverse.

■ **RotateRight**

RotateRight[*expr*, *n*] cycles the elements in *expr* *n* positions to the right.

RotateRight[*expr*] cycles one position to the right.

RotateRight[*expr*, {n_1, n_2, ... }] cycles elements at successive levels n_i positions to the right.

Example: RotateRight[{a, b, c}, 1] $\longrightarrow$ {c, a, b}. ■ RotateRight[*expr*, −*n*] rotates *n* positions to the left. ■ See page 130. ■ See also: Reverse.

■ **Round**

Round[*x*] gives the integer closest to *x*.

Mathematical function (see Section A.3.9). ■ Examples: Round[2.4] $\longrightarrow$ 2; Round[2.6] $\longrightarrow$ 3; Round[−2.4] $\longrightarrow$ −2; Round[−2.6] $\longrightarrow$ −3. ■ Round rounds numbers of the form *x*.5 towards 0. ■ See page 550. ■ See also: Floor, Ceiling, Chop.

■ **RowReduce**

RowReduce[*m*] gives the row-reduced form of the matrix *m*.

RowReduce adds multiples of rows together, producing zero elements when possible. The final matrix is in reduced row echelon form. ■ RowReduce works on both numerical and symbolic matrices. ■ RowReduce[*m*, Modulus -> *p*] performs row reduction modulo the prime *p*. ■ RowReduce[*m*, ZeroTest -> *test*] evaluates *test*[*m*[[*i*, *j*]]] to determine whether matrix elements are zero. The default setting is ZeroTest -> (Together[#] == 0)&. ■ See page 660. ■ See also: NullSpace, LatticeReduce.

■ **Rule**

lhs -> *rhs* represents a rule that transforms *lhs* to *rhs*.

lhs -> *rhs* evaluates *rhs* immediately. ■ You can apply rules using Replace. ■ The assignment *lhs* = *rhs* specifies that the rule *lhs* -> *rhs* should be used whenever it applies. ■ Rule is a scoping construct (see Section A.3.8). ■ Symbols that occur as pattern names in *lhs* are treated as local to the rule. This is true when the symbols appear on the right-hand side of /; conditions in *lhs*, and when the symbols appear anywhere in *rhs*, even inside other scoping constructs. ■ See pages 243 and 737. ■ See also: Replace, Set, AlgebraicRules, RuleDelayed.

■ **RuleDelayed**

lhs :> *rhs* represents a rule that transforms *lhs* to *rhs*, evaluating *rhs* only when the rule is used.

RuleDelayed has the attribute HoldRest. ■ You can apply rules using Replace. ■ The assignment *lhs* := *rhs* specifies that the rule *lhs* :> *rhs* should be used whenever it applies. ■ You can use Condition to specify when a particular rule applies. ■ See notes for Rule. ■ See pages 243 and 737. ■ See also: Replace, SetDelayed, Rule.

■ Run

Run[$expr_1$, $expr_2$, ...] generates the printed form of the expressions $expr_i$, separated by spaces, and runs it as an external, operating system, command.

Run is not available on all computer systems. ▪ Run prints the $expr_i$ in InputForm format. ▪ Run returns an integer which corresponds, when possible, to the exit code for the command returned by the operating system. ▪ The command executed by Run cannot usually require interactive input. On most computer systems, it can, however, generate textual output. ▪ You can enter the input line !*command* to execute an external command. ▪ See page 482. ▪ See also: Put, Splice.

■ RunThrough

RunThrough["*command*", *expr*] executes an external command, giving the printed form of *expr* as input, and taking the output, reading it as *Mathematica* input, and returning the result.

RunThrough is not available on all computer systems. ▪ RunThrough writes the InputForm of *expr* on the standard input for *command*, then reads its standard output, and feeds it into *Mathematica*. ▪ RunThrough starts *command*, then gives input to *command*, then terminates the input. ▪ See page 483. ▪ See also: Install, Put, Get, Splice.

■ SameQ

lhs === *rhs* yields True if the expression *lhs* is identical to *rhs*, and yields False otherwise.

SameQ requires exact correspondence between expressions, except that it considers Real numbers equal if their difference is less than the uncertainty of either of them. ▪ 2 === 2. gives False. ▪ e_1 === e_2 === $e3$ gives True if all the e_i are identical. ▪ See page 228. ▪ See also: UnsameQ, Equal, Order.

■ SameTest

SameTest is an option for functions like FixedPoint that specifies the comparison function to apply to pairs of results to determine whether they should be considered the same.

The default is usually SameTest -> Equal. ▪ Settings for SameTest must be functions that take two arguments, and return True or False. ▪ See page 201. ▪ See also: ZeroTest.

■ SampleDepth

SampleDepth is an option for sound primitives which specifies how many bits should be used to encode sound amplitude levels.

The default setting is SampleDepth -> 8. ▪ With the default setting, 256 distinct sound amplitudes are allowed. ▪ See page 475. ▪ See also: PlayRange, SampleRate.

■ SampledSoundFunction

SampledSoundFunction[f, n, r] is a sound primitive, which represents a sound whose amplitude sampled r times a second is generated by applying the function f to successive integers from 1 to n.

SampledSoundFunction[{f_1, f_2, ... }, n, r] yields sound on several channels. ▪ SampledSoundFunction is generated by Play. ▪ SampledSoundFunction primitives can appear inside Sound, Graphics and Graphics3D objects. ▪ See page 475.

■ **SampledSoundList**

SampledSoundList[{a_1, a_2, ... }, r] is a sound primitive, which represents a sound whose amplitude has levels a_i sampled r times a second.

SampledSoundList[{$list_1$, $list_2$, ... }, r] yields sound on several channels. If the lists are of different lengths, silence is inserted at the ends of shorter lists. ■ SampledSoundList is generated by ListPlay. ■ SampledSoundList primitives can appear inside Sound, Graphics and Graphics3D objects. ■ See page 475.

■ **SampleRate**

SampleRate is an option for sound primitives which specifies the number of samples per second to generate for sounds.

The default setting is SampleRate -> 8192. ■ The highest frequency in Hertz that can be present in a particular sound is equal to half the setting for SampleRate. ■ See page 176. ■ See also: SampleDepth.

■ **Save**

Save["*filename*", $symb_1$, $symb_2$, ...] appends the definitions of the symbols $symb_i$ to a file.

Save uses FullDefinition to include subsidiary definitions. ■ Save writes out definitions in InputForm. ■ See pages 178 and 479. ■ See also: PutAppend, Get, Dump.

■ **Scaled**

Scaled[{x, y, ... }] gives the position of a graphical object in terms of coordinates scaled to run from 0 to 1 across the whole plot in each direction.

Scaled[{dx, dy, ... }, {x_0, y_0, ... }] gives a position obtained by starting at absolute coordinates {x_0, y_0, ... }, then moving by a scaled offset {dx, dy, ... }.

Scaled can be used to specify scaled coordinates in any two- or three-dimensional graphics primitive. ■ You can use Scaled to represent objects that occupy a fixed region in a plot, independent of the specific range of coordinates in the plot. ■ See pages 413 and 440. ■ See also: PlotRange.

■ **Scan**

Scan[f, $expr$] evaluates f applied to each element of $expr$ in turn.

Scan[f, $expr$, $levelspec$] applies f to parts of $expr$ specified by $levelspec$.

Scan[f, $expr$] discards the results of applying f to the subexpressions in $expr$. Unlike Map, Scan does not build up a new expression to return. ■ You can use Return to exit from Scan. Return[ret] causes the final value of Scan to be ret. If no explicit return values are specified, the final result from Scan is Null. ■ Scan is useful in carrying out an operation on parts of expressions where the operation has a "side effect", such as making an assignment. ■ Level specifications are described on page 725. ■ The default value for $levelspec$ in Scan is {1}. ■ See page 207. ■ See also: Apply, Map, Level.

■ **SchurDecomposition**

SchurDecomposition[m] yields the Schur decomposition for a numerical matrix m. The result is a list {q, t} where q is an orthogonal matrix and t is a block upper triangular matrix.

The original matrix m is equal to q . t . Conjugate[Transpose[q]].
■ SchurDecomposition[m, Pivoting -> True] yields a list {q, t, d} where d is a permuted diagonal matrix such that m . d is equal to d . q . t . Conjugate[Transpose[q]]. ■ See page 666. ■ See also: QRDecomposition, SingularValues.

■ **ScientificForm**

ScientificForm[*expr*] prints with all real numbers in *expr* given in scientific notation.

ScientificForm takes the same options as NumberForm, but uses a different default function for ExponentFunction. ▪ You can mix ScientificForm and BaseForm. ▪ ScientificForm acts as a "wrapper", which affects printing, but not evaluation. ▪ See page 350. ▪ See also: EngineeringForm, NumberForm.

■ **Sec**

Sec[*z*] gives the secant of *z*.

Mathematical function (see Section A.3.9). ▪ The argument of Sec is assumed to be in radians. (Multiply by Degree to convert from degrees.) ▪ $\sec(z) = \frac{1}{\cos(z)}$. ▪ See page 562. ▪ See also: ArcSec.

■ **Sech**

Sech[*z*] gives the hyperbolic secant of *z*.

Mathematical function (see Section A.3.9). ▪ $\operatorname{sech}(z) = \frac{1}{\cosh(z)}$. ▪ See page 562. ▪ See also: ArcSech.

■ **SeedRandom**

SeedRandom[*n*] resets the pseudorandom number generator, using the integer *n* as a seed.

SeedRandom[ ] resets the generator, using as a seed the time of day.

You can use SeedRandom[*n*] to make sure you get the same sequence of pseudorandom numbers on different occasions. ▪ You can also use SeedRandom["*string*"], although the seed set in this way may be different on different computer systems. ▪ See page 552. ▪ See also: Random.

■ **Select**

Select[*list*, *crit*] picks out all elements e_i of *list* for which *crit*[e_i] is True.

Select[*list*, *crit*, *n*] picks out the first *n* elements for which *crit*[e_i] is True.

Example: Select[{1,4,2,7,6}, EvenQ] $\longrightarrow$ {4, 2, 6}. ▪ The object *list* can have any head, not necessarily List. ▪ See page 211. ▪ See also: Cases, Take, Drop.

■ **SequenceForm**

SequenceForm[$expr_1$, $expr_2$, ...] prints as the textual concatenation of the printed forms of the $expr_i$.

Expressions printed by SequenceForm have their baselines aligned. ▪ SequenceForm acts as a "wrapper", which affects printing, but not evaluation. ▪ See pages 349 and 361. ▪ See also: ColumnForm, TableForm.

■ **Series**

Series[*f*, {*x*, x_0, *n*}] generates a power series expansion for *f* about the point $x = x_0$ to order $(x - x_0)^n$.

Series[*f*, {*x*, x_0, n_x}, {*y*, y_0, n_y}] successively finds series expansions with respect to *y*, then *x*.

Series can construct standard Taylor series, as well as certain expansions involving negative powers, fractional powers and logarithms. ▪ Series detects certain essential singularities. ▪ Series can expand about the point $x = \infty$. ▪ Series[*f*, {*x*, 0, *n*}] constructs Taylor series for any function *f* according to the formula $f(0) + f'(0)x + f''(0)x^2/2 + ... f^{(n)}(0)x^n/n!$. ▪ Series effectively evaluates partial derivatives using D. It assumes that different variables are independent. ▪ The result of Series is a SeriesData object, which you can manipulate with other functions. ▪ See page 639. ▪ See also: InverseSeries, Limit, Normal.

■ SeriesData

SeriesData[x, x_0, {a_0, a_1, ... }, $nmin$, $nmax$, den] represents a power series in the variable x about the point x_0. The a_i are the coefficients in the power series. The powers of $(x-x_0)$ that appear are $nmin/den$, $(nmin+1)/den$, ... , $nmax/den$.

SeriesData objects are generated by Series. ■ SeriesData objects are printed as sums of the coefficients a_i, multiplied by powers of $x - x_0$. A SeriesData object representing a power series is printed with $O[x - x_0]{\wedge}p$ added, to represent omitted higher-order terms. ■ When you apply certain mathematical operations to SeriesData objects, new SeriesData objects truncated to the appropriate order are produced. ■ The operations you can perform on SeriesData objects include arithmetic ones, mathematical functions with built-in derivatives, and integration and differentiation. ■ Normal[$expr$] converts a SeriesData object into a normal expression, truncating omitted higher-order terms. ■ If the variable in a SeriesData object is itself a SeriesData object, then the composition of the SeriesData objects is computed. Substituting one series into another series with the same expansion parameter therefore automatically leads to composition of the series. Composition is only possible if the first term of the inner series involves a positive power of the variable. ■ InverseSeries can be applied to SeriesData objects to give series for inverse functions. ■ See page 641.

■ SessionTime

SessionTime[ ] gives the total number of seconds of real time that have elapsed since the beginning of your *Mathematica* session.

SessionTime starts counting time as soon as your operating system considers your *Mathematica* process to be executing. ■ TimeUsed is accurate only down to a granularity of at least $TimeUnit seconds. ■ See page 524. ■ See also: TimeUsed, AbsoluteTime, Date.

■ Set

lhs = *rhs* evaluates *rhs* and assigns the result to be the value of *lhs*. From then on, *lhs* is replaced by *rhs* whenever it appears.

{l_1, l_2, ... } = {r_1, r_2, ... } evaluates the r_i, and assigns the results to be the values of the corresponding l_i.

lhs can be any expression, including a pattern. ■ f[x_] = x∧2 is a typical assignment for a pattern. Notice the presence of _ on the left-hand side, but not the right-hand side. ■ An assignment of the form *f*[*args*] = *rhs* sets up a transformation rule associated with the symbol *f*. ■ Different rules associated with a particular symbol are usually placed in the order that you give them. If a new rule that you give is determined to be *more specific* than existing rules, it is, however, placed before them. When the rules are used, they are tested in order. ■ New assignments with identical *lhs* overwrite old ones. ■ You can see all the assignments associated with a symbol *f* using ?*f* or Definition[*f*]. ■ If you make assignments for functions that have attributes like Flat and Orderless, you must make sure to set these attributes before you make assignments for the functions. ■ Set has attribute HoldFirst. ■ If *lhs* is of the form *f*[*args*], then *args* are evaluated. ■ There are some special functions for which an assignment to *s*[*f*[*args*]] is automatically associated with *f* rather than *s*. These functions include: Attributes, Default, Format, MessageName, Messages, N and Options. ■ When it appears in symbolic form, Set is treated as a scoping construct (see Section A.3.8). ■ *lhs* = *rhs* returns *rhs* even if for some reason the assignment specified cannot be performed. ■ Some global variables such as $RecursionLimit can only be assigned a certain range or class of values. ■ See pages 255 and 735. ■ See also: TagSet, Unset, Clear, Literal, DownValues.

◪ SetAccuracy

SetAccuracy[*expr*, *n*] yields a version of *expr* in which all numbers have been set to have an accuracy of *n* digits.

When SetAccuracy is used to increase the accuracy of a number, the number is padded with zeros. The zeros are taken to be in base 2. In base 10, the additional digits are usually not zero. ▪ Example: SetAccuracy[0.4, 25] ⟶ 0.4000000000000002220446. ▪ SetAccuracy always returns an arbitrary-precision number, even if the precision requested is less than $MachinePrecision. ▪ SetAccuracy[*expr*, *n*] does not modify *expr* itself. ▪ See page 544. ▪ See also: N, Accuracy, SetPrecision.

◪ SetAttributes

SetAttributes[*s*, *attr*] adds *attr* to the list of attributes of the symbol *s*.

SetAttributes modifies Attributes[*s*]. ▪ SetAttributes[*s*, {*attr₁*, *attr₂*, ... }] sets several attributes at a time. ▪ SetAttributes[{*s₁*, *s₂*, ... }, *attrs*] sets attributes of several symbols at a time. ▪ SetAttributes has the attribute HoldFirst. ▪ See also: ClearAttributes, Protect. ▪ See page 271.

◪ SetDelayed

lhs := *rhs* assigns *rhs* to be the delayed value of *lhs*. *rhs* is maintained in an unevaluated form. When *lhs* appears, it is replaced by *rhs*, evaluated afresh each time.

See notes for Set. ▪ SetDelayed has attribute HoldAll, rather than HoldFirst. ▪ You can make assignments of the form *lhs* := *rhs* /; *test*, where *test* gives conditions for the applicability of each transformation rule. You can make several assignments with the same *lhs* but different forms of *test*. ▪ *lhs* := *rhs* returns Null if the assignment specified can be performed, and returns $Failed otherwise. ▪ See pages 255 and 735. ▪ See also: TagSetDelayed, Unset, Clear.

◪ SetDirectory

SetDirectory["*dir*"] sets the current working directory.

SetDirectory sets the current working directory, then returns its full name. ▪ SetDirectory appends the current working directory to the directory stack given by DirectoryStack[ ]. ▪ See page 489. ▪ See also: ResetDirectory, Directory, $Path.

◪ SetFileDate

SetFileDate["*file*"] sets the modification date for a file to be the current date.

SetFileDate["*file*", *date*] sets the modification date to be the specified date. ▪ The date must be given in the {*year*, *month*, *day*, *hour*, *minute*, *second*} format used by Date. ▪ See page 492. ▪ See also: FileDate.

◪ SetOptions

SetOptions[*s*, *name₁*->*value₁*, *name₂*->*value₂*, ...] sets the specified default options for a symbol *s*.

SetOptions[*stream*, ...] or SetOptions["*name*", ...] sets options associated with a particular stream.

SetOptions is equivalent to an assignment which redefines certain elements of the list Options[*s*] of default options. ▪ SetOptions can be used on Protected symbols. ▪ SetOptions returns the new form of Options[*s*]. ▪ You can use SetOptions on InputStream and OutputStream objects. If there is only one stream with a particular name, you can give the name as a string as the argument of Options. ▪ SetOptions can be used on a list of streams, such as the value of $Output. ▪ See pages 149 and 724.

■ **SetPrecision**

SetPrecision[*expr*, *n*] yields a version of *expr* in which all numbers have been set to have a precision of *n* digits.

When SetPrecision is used to increase the precision of a number, the number is padded with zeros. The zeros are taken to be in base 2. In base 10, the additional digits are usually not zero. ▪ Example: SetPrecision[0.4, 25] ⟶ 0.400000000000000022044605. ▪ SetPrecision always returns an arbitrary-precision number, even if the precision requested is less than $MachinePrecision. ▪ SetPrecision[*expr*, *n*] does not modify *expr* itself. ▪ See page 544. ▪ See also: N, Precision, Chop, SetAccuracy.

■ **SetStreamPosition**

SetStreamPosition[*stream*, *n*] sets the current point in an open stream.

The integer *n* given to SetStreamPosition should usually be a value obtained from StreamPosition. ▪ SetStreamPosition[*stream*, 0] sets the current point to the beginning of a stream. ▪ SetStreamPosition[*stream*, Infinity] sets the current point to the end of a stream. ▪ See page 503.

■ **Shading**

Shading is an option for SurfaceGraphics that specifies whether the surfaces should be shaded.

With Shading -> False, the surface will be white all over. So long as Mesh -> True, however, mesh lines will still be drawn. ▪ When Shading -> True, the actual shading used can either be determined by the height, or, when Lighting -> True, from simulated illumination. ▪ See page 156. ▪ See also: HiddenSurface, ClipFill.

■ **Shallow**

Shallow[*expr*] prints as a shallow form of *expr*.

Shallow[*expr*, *depth*] prints with all parts of *expr* below the specified depth given in skeleton form.

Shallow[*expr*, {*depth*, *length*}] also gives parts whose lengths are above the specified limit in skeleton form.

Shallow[*expr*, {*depth*, *length*}, *form*] uses skeleton form for any parts which match the pattern *form*.

Omitted sequences of elements are given as Skeleton objects, which print in the form <<*k*>>. ▪ Depth and length can be specified as Infinity. ▪ By default, Shallow uses the value 4 for both depth and length cutoffs. ▪ Shallow acts as a "wrapper", which affects printing, but not evaluation. ▪ See page 346. ▪ See also: Short.

■ **Share**

Share[*expr*] changes the way *expr* is stored internally, to try and minimize the amount of memory used.

Share[ ] tries to minimize the memory used to store all expressions.

Share works by sharing the storage of common subexpressions between different parts of an expression, or different expressions. ▪ Using Share will never affect the results you get from *Mathematica*. It may, however, reduce the amount of memory used, and in many cases also the amount of time taken. ▪ See page 528. ▪ See also: MemoryInUse, ByteCount.

■ Short

Short[*expr*] prints as a short form of *expr*, less than about one line long.

Short[*expr*, *n*] prints as a form of *expr* about *n* lines long.

Short[*expr*] gives a "skeleton form" of *expr*, with omitted sequences of *k* elements indicated by <<*k*>>. ■ Omitted sequences of elements are printed as Skeleton objects. ■ Short prints long strings in skeleton form, using StringSkeleton objects. ■ The number of lines specified need not be an integer. ■ Short can be used with InputForm and other formats as well as OutputForm. ■ Short acts as a "wrapper", which affects printing, but not evaluation. ■ See page 346. ■ See also: Shallow, Format.

■ Show

Show[*graphics*, *options*] displays two- and three-dimensional graphics, using the options specified.

Show[g_1, g_2, ...] shows several plots combined.

Show can be used with Graphics, Graphics3D, SurfaceGraphics, ContourGraphics, DensityGraphics and GraphicsArray. ■ Options explicitly specified in Show override those included in the graphics expression. ■ When plots are combined, their lists of non-default options are concatenated. ■ Show is effectively the analog of Print for graphics. The option DisplayFunction determines the actual output mechanism used. ■ Functions like Plot automatically apply Show to the graphics expressions they generate. ■ See pages 144 and 395. ■ See also: Plot, etc., and Display.

■ Sign

Sign[*x*] gives −1, 0 or 1 depending on whether *x* is negative, zero, or positive.

For non-zero complex numbers *z*, Sign[*z*] is defined as *z*/Abs[*z*]. ■ Sign tries simple transformations in trying to determine the sign of symbolic expressions. ■ You can define values for Sign[*expr*] which are used when *expr*, and linear combinations involving it, appear in Sign, as well as functions like Positive and Negative. ■ See page 550. ■ See also: Abs, Positive, Negative, NonNegative.

■ Signature

Signature[*list*] gives the signature of the permutation needed to place the elements of *list* in canonical order.

Examples: Signature[{a,b,c}] ⟶ 1; Signature[{a,c,b}] ⟶ −1. ■ The signature of the permutation is $(-1)^n$, where *n* is the number of transpositions of pairs of elements that must be composed to build up the permutation. ■ If any two elements of *list* are the same, Signature[*list*] gives 0. ■ See pages 558 and 671. ■ See also: Order, Sort.

■ SignPadding

SignPadding is an option for NumberForm and related functions which specifies whether padding should be inserted after signs.

SignPadding -> True specifies that any padding that is needed should be inserted between the sign and the digits in a number. ■ SignPadding -> False specifies that the padding should be inserted before the sign. ■ See page 351. ■ See also: NumberPadding.

■ **Simplify**

Simplify[*expr*] performs a sequence of algebraic transformations on *expr*, and returns the simplest form it finds.

Simplify[*expr*] returns the form of *expr* that it finds which has the smallest LeafCount. ■ Simplify tries expanding and factoring parts of expressions, keeping track of which transformations make the parts simplest. ■ Simplify[*expr*, Trig -> False] does not use trigonometric identities. ■ See page 77. ■ See also: Factor, Expand.

■ **Sin**

Sin[*z*] gives the sine of *z*.

Mathematical function (see Section A.3.9). ■ The argument of Sin is assumed to be in radians. (Multiply by Degree to convert from degrees.) ■ See page 562. ■ See also: ArcSin, Csc.

■ **SingularValues**

SingularValues[*m*] gives the singular value decomposition for a numerical matrix *m*. The result is a list {*u*, *w*, *v*}, where *w* is the list of non-zero singular values, and *m* can be written as Transpose[*u*].DiagonalMatrix[*w*].*v*.

SingularValues[*m*, Tolerance -> *t*] specifies that singular values smaller than *t* times the maximum singular value are to be removed. ■ The default setting Tolerance -> Automatic takes *t* to be $10^{(-p+4)}$ where *p* is the numerical precision of the input. ■ *u* and *v* are row orthonormal matrices, which can be considered as lists of orthonormal vectors. ■ See page 665. ■ See also: PseudoInverse, QRDecomposition, SchurDecomposition.

■ **Sinh**

Sinh[*z*] gives the hyperbolic sine of *z*.

Mathematical function (see Section A.3.9). ■ See page 562. ■ See also: ArcSinh, Csch.

■ **SinIntegral**

SinIntegral[*z*] gives the sine integral function Si(*z*).

Mathematical function (see Section A.3.9). ■ Si(*z*) = $\int_0^z \frac{\sin(t)}{t} dt$. ■ See page 571. ■ See also: CosIntegral, ExpIntegralE, ExpIntegralEi.

■ **SixJSymbol**

SixJSymbol[{j_1, j_2, j_3}, {j_4, j_5, j_6}] gives the values of the Racah 6-j symbol.

The 6-j symbols vanish except when certain triples of the j_i satisfy triangle inequalities. ■ The parameters of SixJSymbol can be integers, half-integers or symbolic expressions. ■ See page 561. ■ See also: ThreeJSymbol, ClebschGordan.

■ **Skeleton**

Skeleton[*n*] represents a sequence of *n* omitted elements in an expression printed with Short. The standard print form for Skeleton is <<*n*>>.

You can reset the print form of Skeleton. ■ See page 517. ■ See also: Short, StringSkeleton, TotalWidth.

■ Skip

Skip[*stream*, *type*] skips one object of the specified type in an input stream.

Skip[*stream*, *type*, *n*] skips *n* objects of the specified type.

Skip behaves like Read, except that it returns Null when it succeeds in skipping the specified objects, and $Failed otherwise. ■ See notes for Read. ■ See page 499. ■ See also: SetStreamPosition, Find.

■ Slot

represents the first argument supplied to a pure function.

#*n* represents the nth argument.

is used to represent arguments or formal parameters in pure functions of the form *body*& or Function[*body*]. ■ # is equivalent to Slot[ ] or Slot[1]. ■ #*n* is equivalent to Slot[*n*]. *n* must be a non-negative integer. ■ #0 gives the head of the function, *i.e.*, the pure function itself. ■ See page 208.

■ SlotSequence

represents the sequence of arguments supplied to a pure function.

##*n* represents the sequence of arguments supplied to a pure function, starting with the nth argument.

is used to represent sequences of arguments in pure functions of the form *body*& or Function[*body*]. ■ ## is equivalent to SlotSequence[ ] or SlotSequence[1]. ■ ##*n* is equivalent to SlotSequence[*n*]. *n* must be a positive integer. ■ A sequence of arguments supplied to a pure function is "spliced" into the body of the function wherever ## and so on appear. ■ See page 208.

■ Solve

Solve[*eqns*, *vars*] attempts to solve an equation or set of equations for the variables *vars*.

Solve[*eqns*, *vars*, *elims*] attempts to solve the equations for *vars*, eliminating the variables *elims*.

Equations are given in the form *lhs* == *rhs*. ■ Simultaneous equations can be combined either in a list or with &&. ■ A single variable or a list of variables can be specified. ■ Solve[*eqns*] tries to solve for all variables in *eqns*. ■ Example: Solve[3 x + 9 == 0, x]. ■ Solve gives explicit solutions as rules of the form *x* -> *sol*. ■ When there are several variables, the solution is given as a list of rules: {*x* -> s_x, *y* -> s_y, ... }. ■ When there are several solutions, Solve gives a list of them. ■ When a particular root has multiplicity greater than one, Solve gives several copies of the corresponding solution. ■ Solve deals primarily with linear and polynomial equations. ■ The option InverseFunctions specifies whether Solve should use inverse functions to try and find solutions to more general equations. The default is InverseFunctions->Automatic. In this case, Solve can use inverse functions, but prints a warning message. See notes on InverseFunctions. ■ Solve gives generic solutions only. It discards solutions that are valid only when the parameters satisfy special conditions. Reduce gives the complete set of solutions. ■ Solve will not always be able to get explicit solutions to equations. It will give the explicit solutions it can, then give a symbolic representation of the remaining solutions, in terms of the function Roots. If there are sufficiently few symbolic parameters, you can then use N to get numerical approximations to the solutions. ■ Solve gives {} if there are no possible solutions to the equations. ■ Solve[*eqns*, ... , Mode->Modular] solves equations with equality required only modulo an integer. You can specify a particular modulus to use by including the equation Modulus==*p*. If you do not include such an equation, Solve will attempt to solve for the possible moduli. ■ See page 612. ■ See also: Reduce, Eliminate, Roots, NSolve, FindRoot, LinearSolve, DSolve.

■ SolveAlways

SolveAlways[*eqns*, *vars*] gives the values of parameters that make the equations *eqns* valid for all values of the variables *vars*.

Equations are given in the form *lhs* == *rhs*. ■ Simultaneous equations can be combined either in a list or with &&. ■ A single variable or a list of variables can be specified. ■ Example: SolveAlways[a x + b == 0, x] ⟶ {{b -> 0, a -> 0}}. ■ SolveAlways works primarily with linear and polynomial equations. ■ SolveAlways produces relations between parameters that appear in *eqns*, but are not in the list of variables *vars*. ■ SolveAlways[*eqns*, *vars*] is equivalent to Solve[!Eliminate[!*eqns*, *vars*]]. ■ See page 620. ■ See also: Eliminate, Solve, Reduce, AlgebraicRules.

■ Sort

Sort[*list*] sorts the elements of *list* into canonical order.

Sort[*list*, *p*] sorts using the ordering function *p*.

Example: Sort[{b, c, a}] ⟶ {a, b, c}. ■ The canonical order for strings is determined by the character ordering in $StringOrder. ■ Symbols are ordered according to their textual names. ■ Integers, rational and approximate real numbers are ordered by their numerical values. ■ Expressions are ordered by comparing their parts in a depth-first manner. Shorter expressions come first. ■ Sort[*list*, *p*] applies the function *p* to pairs of elements in *list* to determine whether they are in order. The default function *p* is OrderedQ[{#1, #2}]&. ■ Example: Sort[{4, 1, 3}, Greater] ⟶ {4, 3, 1}. ■ Sort can be used on expressions with any head, not only List. ■ See pages 130 and 214. ■ See also: Order, OrderedQ, Orderless, $StringOrder.

◨ Sound

Sound[*primitives*] represents a sound.

Any number of sound primitives or lists of sound primitives can be given. They are played in sequence. ■ Sound can be played using Show. ■ The following primitives can be used:

SampledSoundFunction[*f*, *n*, *r*]   amplitude levels generated by a function
SampledSoundList[{a_1, a_2, ... }, *r*]   amplitude levels given in a list

■ The standard print form for Sound[...] is -Sound-. InputForm prints the explicit list of primitives. ■ See page 474.

◨ SpellingCorrection

SpellingCorrection is an option for StringMatchQ, Names and related functions which specifies whether strings should be considered to match even when a small fraction of the characters in them are different.

The default setting SpellingCorrection -> False requires exact matching. ■ ?*name* effectively uses SpellingCorrection -> True when it cannot find an exact match for *name*. ■ See page 384. ■ See also: IgnoreCase.

■ SphericalHarmonicY

SphericalHarmonicY[*l*, *m*, *theta*, *phi*] gives the spherical harmonic $Y_l^m(\theta, \phi)$.

Mathematical function (see Section A.3.9). ■ The spherical harmonics are orthogonal with respect to integration over the surface of the unit sphere. ■ See page 567. ■ See also: LegendreP, ClebschGordan.

▰ SphericalRegion

SphericalRegion is an option for three-dimensional graphics functions which specifies whether the final image should be scaled so that a sphere drawn around the three-dimensional bounding box would fit in the display area specified.

SphericalRegion -> False scales three-dimensional images to be as large as possible, given the display area specified. ▪ SphericalRegion -> True scales three-dimensional images so that a sphere drawn around the three-dimensional bounding box always fits in the display area specified. ▪ The center of the sphere is taken to be at the center of the bounding box. The radius of the sphere is chosen so that the bounding box just fits within the sphere. ▪ With SphericalRegion -> True, the image of a particular object remains consistent in size, regardless of the orientation of the object. ▪ SphericalRegion -> True overrides any setting given for ViewCenter. ▪ See page 446. ▪ See also: PlotRegion, ViewPoint.

■ Splice

Splice["*file*"] splices *Mathematica* output into an external file. It takes text enclosed between <* and *> in the file, evaluates the text as *Mathematica* input, and replaces the text with the resulting *Mathematica* output.

Splice["*infile*", "*outfile*"] processes text from the file *infile*, and writes output into *outfile*. ▪ Splice["*file*"] takes files with names of the form *name*.mx and writes output in files with names *name*.x. ▪ Text in the input file not enclosed between <* and *> is copied without change to the output file. ▪ The default format for *Mathematica* output is determined by the extension of the input file name:

name.mc	CForm
name.mf	FortranForm
name.mtex	TeXForm

▪ The following options for Splice can be used:

Delimiters	{"<*", "*>"}	delimiters to search for
FormatType	Automatic	default format for *Mathematica* output
PageWidth	78	number of character widths per output line

▪ You can use pipes instead of files for input and output to Splice. ▪ See page 184. ▪ See also: RunThrough.

■ Sqrt

Sqrt[*z*] gives the square root of *z*.

Mathematical function (see Section A.3.9). ▪ Sqrt[*z*] is converted to z^(1/2). ▪ Sqrt[*z*^2] is not automatically converted to *z*. ▪ Sqrt[*a b*] is not automatically converted to Sqrt[*a*] Sqrt[*b*]. ▪ These conversions can be done using PowerExpand. ▪ See page 49. ▪ See also: Power, PowerExpand.

▰ Stack

Stack[ ] shows the current evaluation stack, giving a list of the tags associated with evaluations that are currently being done.

Stack[*pattern*] gives a list of expressions currently being evaluated which match the pattern.

Stack[_] shows all expressions currently being evaluated. ▪ You can call Stack from inside a dialog to see how the dialog was reached. ▪ In the list returned by Stack[*pattern*], each expression is wrapped with HoldForm. ▪ The maximum length of Stack[ ] is limited by $RecursionLimit. ▪ Stack has attribute HoldFirst. ▪ See page 306. ▪ See also: Trace.

◪ StackBegin

StackBegin[*expr*] evaluates *expr*, starting a fresh evaluation stack.

You can use StackBegin to prevent "outer" evaluations from appearing in the evaluation stack when you call Stack. ▪ StackBegin has attribute HoldFirst. ▪ A StackBegin is automatically done when the evaluation of each input line begins in an interactive *Mathematica* session. ▪ See page 308. ▪ See also: StackInhibit.

◪ StackComplete

StackComplete[*expr*] evaluates *expr* with intermediate expressions in evaluation chains included on the stack.

Mathematica normally includes only the latest expression on each evaluation chain involved in the evaluation of a particular expression. Inside StackComplete, however, all preceding expressions on the evaluation chains are included. ▪ StackComplete typically increases significantly the number of expressions kept on the evaluation stack. ▪ See page 308. ▪ See also: TraceBackwards, TraceAbove.

◪ StackInhibit

StackInhibit[*expr*] evaluates *expr* without modifying the evaluation stack.

You can use StackInhibit to prevent "innermost" evaluations from appearing in the evaluation stack when you look at it with Stack. ▪ StackInhibit has attribute HoldFirst. ▪ See page 307. ▪ See also: StackBegin.

◼ StirlingS1

StirlingS1[*n*, *m*] gives the Stirling number of the first kind $S_n^{(m)}$.

Integer mathematical function (see Section A.3.9). ▪ $(-1)^{n-m} S_n^{(m)}$ gives the number of permutations of *n* elements which contain exactly *m* cycles. ▪ See page 558.

◼ StirlingS2

StirlingS2[*n*, *m*] gives the Stirling number of the second kind $S_n^{(m)}$.

Integer mathematical function (see Section A.3.9). ▪ $S_n^{(m)}$ gives the number of ways of partitioning a set of *n* elements into *m* non-empty subsets. ▪ See page 558.

◪ StreamPosition

StreamPosition[*stream*] returns an integer which specifies the position of the current point in an open stream.

On most computer systems, the integer returned by StreamPosition gives the position counting from the beginning of the file in bytes. ▪ See page 503. ▪ See also: SetStreamPosition.

◪ Streams

Streams[ ] gives a list of all streams that are currently open.

Streams["*name*"] lists only streams with the specified name.

The list returned by Streams can contain InputStream and OutputStream objects. ▪ See page 519. ▪ See also: OpenRead, OpenWrite, $Input, Options, SetOptions.

■ String

String is the head of a character string "*text*".

Strings can contain any sequence of 8- or 16-bit characters. Sequences for entering special characters are given on page 714. ■ *x*_String can be used as a pattern that represents a string. ■ String is used as a tag to indicate strings in Read, terminated by RecordSeparators characters. ■ Output conversion for strings containing special characters is specified by the option StringConversion. ■ See page 365. ■ See also: ToExpression, ToString, SyntaxQ, Characters.

■ StringBreak

StringBreak[*n*] is output at the end of the *n*th line where a string is broken.

StringBreak is used when symbol names, strings and numbers are broken. ■ You can think of StringBreak as being like a "hyphenation character". ■ The default setting for Format[StringBreak[_]] is "\". ■ You can specify what is printed when a string is broken by defining a new value for Format[StringBreak[n_]]. ■ See page 517. ■ See also: Continuation, LineBreak, Indent.

■ StringByteCount

StringByteCount["*string*"] gives the total number of bytes used to store the characters in a string.

If a string contains only 8-bit characters, StringByteCount gives the same result as StringLength. ■ You can find out whether a particular character in a string uses 16 bits by seeing whether its integer code is larger than 255. ■ See page 374. ■ See also: Characters, ToCharacterCode, ByteCount, FileByteCount.

■ StringConversion

StringConversion is an option for output functions which specifies how strings containing special characters should be output.

StringConversion -> None specifies that all special characters should be output without modification. ■ StringConversion -> Automatic specifies that all special characters should be output using the \ sequences given on page 714. ■ StringConversion -> *f* specifies that the function *f* should be applied to convert all strings containing special characters. The function must always return a string. ■ The default setting is StringConversion :> $StringConversion. ■ StringConversion affects the output of all strings of characters, including symbol names and comments. ■ StringConversion also affects strings that appear in Text graphics primitives. ■ See pages 469 and 487. ■ See also: StringReplace.

■ StringDrop

StringDrop["*string*", *n*] gives "*string*" with its first *n* characters dropped.

StringDrop["*string*", −*n*] gives "*string*" with its last *n* characters dropped.

StringDrop["*string*", {*n*}] gives "*string*" with its *n*th character dropped.

StringDrop["*string*", {*m*, *n*}] gives "*string*" with characters *m* through *n* dropped.

StringDrop uses the standard *sequence specification* (see page 724). ■ Example:
StringDrop["abcdefgh", 2] ⟶ cdefgh. ■ StringDrop handles both 8- and 16-bit characters. ■ See page 376. ■ See also: Drop, StringTake, StringPosition.

■ **StringForm**

StringForm["*controlstring*", *expr*$_1$, ...] prints as the text of the *controlstring*, with the printed forms of the *expr*$_i$ embedded.

`` `i` `` in the control string indicates a point at which to print *expr*$_i$. ■ `` `` `` includes the next *expr*$_i$ not yet printed.  ■ `` \` ``  prints a raw `` ` `` in the output string. ■ StringForm acts as a "wrapper", which affects printing, but not evaluation. ■ You can use StringForm to set up "formatted output". ■ Messages given as values for objects of the form *s*::*t* are used as control strings for StringForm. ■ See page 348. ■ See also: SequenceForm, ToString, Message.

■ **StringInsert**

StringInsert["*string*", "*snew*", *n*] yields a string with "*snew*" inserted starting at position *n* in "*string*".

StringInsert["*string*", "*snew*", -*n*] inserts at position *n* from the end of "*string*".

Example: StringInsert["abcdefg", "XYZ", 2] ⟶ aXYZbcdefg. ■ StringInsert["*string*", "*snew*", *n*] makes the first character of *snew* the nth character in the new string. ■ StringInsert["*string*", "*snew*", -*n*] makes the last character of *snew* the nth character from the end of the new string. ■ StringInsert handles both 8- and 16-bit characters. ■ See page 376. ■ See also: Insert.

■ **StringJoin**

"*s*$_1$" <> "*s*$_2$" <> ... , StringJoin["*s*$_1$", "*s*$_2$", ...] or StringJoin[{"*s*$_1$", "*s*$_2$", ... }] yields a string consisting of a concatenation of the *s*$_i$.

Example: "the" <> " " <> "cat" ⟶ the cat. ■ StringJoin has attribute Flat. ■ When arguments are not strings, StringJoin is left in symbolic form. ■ See page 376. ■ See also: Join, Characters.

■ **StringLength**

StringLength["*string*"] gives the number of characters in a string.

Example: StringLength["tiger"] ⟶ 5. ■ Each character in a string can be either 8- or 16-bit. ■ See page 376. ■ See also: StringByteCount, Length, Characters.

■ **StringMatchQ**

StringMatchQ["*string*", "*pattern*"] yields True if *string* matches the specified string pattern, and yields False otherwise.

The pattern string can contain literal characters, together with the metacharacters * and @ specified on page 728. ■ Example: StringMatchQ["apppbb", "a*b"] ⟶ True. ■ Setting the option IgnoreCase -> True makes StringMatchQ treat lower- and upper-case letters as equivalent. ■ Setting the option SpellingCorrection -> True makes StringMatchQ allow strings to match even if a small fraction of their characters are different. ■ See page 383. ■ See also: StringPosition, Equal, Names, MatchQ.

■ StringPosition

`StringPosition["`*string*`", "`*sub*`"]` gives a list of the starting and ending character positions at which `"`*sub*`"` appears as a substring of `"`*string*`"`.

`StringPosition["`*string*`", "`*sub*`", `*k*`]` includes only the first *k* occurrences of `"`*sub*`"`.

`StringPosition["`*string*`", {"`*sub₁*`", "`*sub₂*`", ... }]` gives positions of all the `"`*subᵢ*`"`.

Example: `StringPosition["abbaabbaa", "bb"]` ⟶ `{{2, 3}, {6, 7}}`. ■ With the default option setting `Overlaps -> True`, `StringPosition` includes substrings that overlap. With the setting `Overlaps -> False` such substrings are excluded. ■ Setting the option `IgnoreCase -> True` makes `StringPosition` treat lower- and upper-case letters as equivalent. ■ Example: `StringPosition["abAB", "a", IgnoreCase -> True]` ⟶ `{{1, 1}, {3, 3}}`. ■ `StringPosition` handles both 8- and 16-bit characters. ■ `StringPosition` returns sequence specifications in the form used by `StringTake` and `StringDrop`. ■ See page 376. ■ See also: `Position`, `Characters`, `FindList`.

■ StringReplace

`StringReplace["`*string*`", "`*s₁*`" -> "`*sp₁*`"]` or
`StringReplace["`*string*`", {"`*s₁*`" -> "`*sp₁*`", "`*s₂*`" -> "`*sp₂*`", ... }]` replaces the `"`*sᵢ*`"` by `"`*spᵢ*`"` whenever they appear as substrings of `"`*string*`"`.

`StringReplace` goes through a string, testing substrings that start at each successive character position. On each substring, it tries in turn each of the transformation rules you have specified. If any of the rules apply, it replaces the substring, then continues to go through the string, starting at the character position after the end of the substring. ■ Setting the option `IgnoreCase -> True` makes `StringReplace` treat lower- and upper-case letters as equivalent. ■ `StringReplace` handles both 8- and 16-bit characters. ■ See page 376. ■ See also: `Replace`, `StringPosition`, `ToLowerCase`, `ToUpperCase`.

■ StringReverse

`StringReverse["`*string*`"]` reverses the order of the characters in `"`*string*`"`.

Example: `StringReverse["abcde"]` ⟶ `edcba`. ■ `StringReverse` handles both 8- and 16-bit characters. ■ See page 376. ■ See also: `Reverse`.

■ StringSkeleton

`StringSkeleton[`*n*`]` represents a sequence of *n* omitted characters in a string printed with `Short`.

The standard print form for `StringSkeleton` is an ellipsis.

You can reset the print form of `StringSkeleton`. ■ See page 517. ■ See also: `Short`, `Skeleton`, `TotalWidth`.

■ StringTake

`StringTake["`*string*`", `*n*`]` gives a string containing the first *n* characters in `"`*string*`"`.

`StringTake["`*string*`", -`*n*`]` gives the last *n* characters in `"`*string*`"`.

`StringTake["`*string*`", {`*n*`}]` gives the *n*th character in `"`*string*`"`.

`StringTake["`*string*`", {`*m*`, `*n*`}]` gives characters *m* through *n* in `"`*string*`"`.

`StringTake` uses the standard *sequence specification* (see page 724). ■ Example: `StringTake["abcdefg", 3]` ⟶ `abc`. ■ `StringTake` handles both 8- and 16-bit characters. ■ See page 376. ■ See also: `Take`, `StringDrop`, `StringPosition`.

◪ StringToStream

StringToStream["*string*"] opens an input stream for reading from a string.

StringToStream yields a stream of the form InputStream[String, *n*]. ▪ Operations like Read and Find work on streams returned by StringToStream. ▪ You must use Close to close streams created by StringToStream. ▪ See pages 382 and 504. ▪ See also: Characters.

◪ Stub

Stub is an attribute which specifies that if a symbol is ever used, Needs should automatically be called on the context of the symbol.

Symbols with the Stub attribute are created by DeclarePackage. ▪ A symbol is considered "used" if its name appears explicitly, not in the form of a string. ▪ Names["*nameform*"] and Attributes["*nameform*"] do not constitute "uses" of a symbol. ▪ See pages 272 and 342.

■ Subscript

Subscript[*expr*] prints *expr* as a subscript.

Subscript[*expr*] prints with the top of *expr* below the baseline. ▪ Example: f[Subscript[x], y] $\longrightarrow$ f[$_x$, y].

▪ See page 361. ▪ See also: Superscript, ColumnForm.

■ Subscripted

Subscripted[*f*[arg_1, arg_2, ...]] prints with the arg_i given as subscripts of *f*.

Subscripted[*expr*, *sub*, *sup*] prints with the arguments specified by *sub* as subscripts, and the arguments specified by *sup* as superscripts. Arguments not included either in *sub* or *sup* are printed in standard functional form.

The specification *n* takes the first *n* arguments. −*n* takes the last *n* arguments. {*m*, *n*} takes arguments *m* through *n*.

Example: Subscripted[f[a,b]] $\longrightarrow$ f$_{a,b}$. ▪ Subscripted takes standard sequence specifications, as used by Take and Drop. ▪ Example: Subscripted[f[a,b,c], 1] $\longrightarrow$ f$_a$[b,c]. ▪ Subscripted[*expr*, {}, *sup*] can be used to specify superscripts only. ▪ Subscripted does not allow subscript and superscript specifications that overlap. ▪ See page 360. ▪ See also: ColumnForm.

■ Subtract

$x - y$ is equivalent to $x + (-1 * y)$.

$x - y$ is converted to $x + (-1 * y)$ on input. ▪ See page 47. ▪ See also: Minus, Decrement.

■ SubtractFrom

x -= dx subtracts dx from x and returns the new value of x.

SubtractFrom has the attribute HoldFirst. ▪ x -= dx is equivalent to $x = x - dx$. ▪ See page 248. ▪ See also: Decrement, PreDecrement, Set.

■ **Sum**

Sum[*f*, {*i*, *imax*}] evaluates the sum $\sum_{i=1}^{imax} f$.

Sum[*f*, {*i*, *imin*, *imax*}] starts with *i* = *imin*. Sum[*f*, {*i*, *imin*, *imax*, *di*}] uses steps *di*.

Sum[*f*, {*i*, *imin*, *imax*}, {*j*, *jmin*, *jmax*}, ...] evaluates the multiple sum $\sum_{i=imin}^{imax} \sum_{j=jmin}^{jmax} \dots f$.

Sum evaluates its arguments in a non-standard way (see page 730). ■ Sum uses the standard *Mathematica* iteration specification. ■ The iteration variable *i* is treated as local. ■ In multiple sums, the range of the outermost variable is given first. ■ See page 90. ■ See also: Do, Product, Table, NSum.

■ **Superscript**

Superscript[*expr*] prints *expr* as a superscript.

Superscript[*expr*] prints with the bottom of *expr* one character height above the baseline. ■ Example: f[Superscript[x], y] $\longrightarrow$ f[^{x}, y]. ■ See page 361. ■ See also: Subscript, Subscripted, ColumnForm.

■ **SurfaceColor**

SurfaceColor[*dcol*] is a three-dimensional graphics directive which specifies that the polygons which follow should act as diffuse reflectors of light with a color given by *dcol*.

SurfaceColor[*dcol*, *scol*] specifies that a specular reflection component should be included, with a color given by *scol*.

SurfaceColor[*dcol*, *scol*, *n*] specifies that the reflection should occur with specular exponent *n*.

SurfaceColor directives give surface properties which determine the effect of simulated illumination on polygons. ■ SurfaceColor directives can appear inside FaceForm directives. ■ If no SurfaceColor directive is given, polygons are assumed to be white diffuse reflectors of light, obeying Lambert's law of reflection, so that the intensity of reflected light is cos(α) times the intensity of incident light, where α is the angle between the direction of the incident light and the polygon normal. When $\alpha > 90°$, there is no reflected light. ■ SurfaceColor[GrayLevel[*a*]] specifies that polygons should act as diffuse reflectors, but with albedo *a*. The intensity of reflected light is therefore *a* times the intensity of the incident light, multiplied by cos(α), and is of the same color. ■ SurfaceColor[RGBColor[*r*, *g*, *b*]] specifies that the red, green and blue components of the reflected light are respectively *r*, *g* and *b* times those of the incident light, multiplied by cos(α). ■ The second element in SurfaceColor[*dcol*, *scol*] specifies a specular reflection component. *scol* must be a GrayLevel, Hue or RGBColor specification. The color components of *scol* give the fractions of each color component in the incident intensity which are reflected in a specular way by the surface. ■ The parameter *n* gives the specular exponent. The intensity of specularly reflected light at angle θ from the mirror-reflection direction falls off like cos(θ)^n as θ increases. It is zero when $\theta > 90°$. ■ For real materials, *n* is typically between about 1 and a few hundred. With a coarse polygonal mesh, however, values of *n* below 10 are usually most appropriate. The default value for *n* is 1. ■ *Mathematica* implements a version of the Phong lighting model, in which the intensity of reflected light is given schematically by $I_{in}(d \cos(\alpha) + s \cos(\theta)^n)$. ■ The intensity of light from diffuse and specular reflection is added linearly for each color component. The final color shown for a particular polygon is the sum of contributions from each light source, and from ambient light. ■ See page 457. ■ See also: Lighting, LightSources, AmbientLight.

■ SurfaceGraphics

SurfaceGraphics[*array*] is a representation of a three-dimensional plot of a surface, with heights of each point on a grid specified by values in *array*.

SurfaceGraphics[*array*, *shades*] represents a surface, whose parts are shaded according to the array *shades*.

SurfaceGraphics can be displayed using Show. ■ SurfaceGraphics has the same options as Graphics3D, with the following additions:

ClipFill	Automatic	how to draw clipped parts of the surface
ColorFunction	Automatic	function to determine color based on z value
HiddenSurface	True	whether to eliminate hidden surfaces
Mesh	True	whether to draw a mesh on the surface
MeshStyle	Automatic	graphics directives to specify the style for a mesh
MeshRange	Automatic	the original range of x, y coordinates for the plot

■ SurfaceGraphics does not support the options PolygonIntersections and RenderAll available for Graphics3D. ■ For SurfaceGraphics, the default setting for BoxRatios is BoxRatios -> {1, 1, 0.4}. ■ *array* should be a rectangular array of real numbers, representing z values. There will be holes in the surface corresponding to any array elements that are not real numbers. ■ If *array* has dimensions $m \times n$, then *shades* must have dimensions $(m-1) \times (n-1)$. ■ The elements of *shades* must be GrayLevel, Hue or RGBColor directives, or SurfaceColor objects. ■ Graphics3D[SurfaceGraphics[...]] can be used to convert a SurfaceGraphics object into the more general Graphics3D representation. ■ SurfaceGraphics is generated by Plot3D and ListPlot3D. ■ See page 447. ■ See also: ListPlot3D, Plot3D, ContourGraphics, DensityGraphics.

■ Switch

Switch[*expr*, *form₁*, *value₁*, *form₂*, *value₂*, ...] evaluates *expr*, then compares it with each of the $form_i$ in turn, evaluating and returning the $value_i$ corresponding to the first match found.

Only the $value_i$ corresponding to the first $form_i$ that matches *expr* is evaluated. Each $form_i$ is evaluated only when the match is tried. ■ If the last $form_i$ is the pattern _, then the corresponding $value_i$ is always returned if this case is reached. ■ If none of the $form_i$ match *expr*, the Switch is returned unevaluated. ■ You can use Break, Return and Throw in Switch. ■ See page 287. ■ See also: If, Condition, Which.

■ Symbol

Symbol is the head associated with a symbol.

Example: Head[x] ⟶ Symbol. ■ x_Symbol can be used as a pattern that represents a symbol. ■ See page 712.

◧ SyntaxLength

SyntaxLength["*string*"] finds the number of characters starting at the beginning of a string that correspond to syntactically correct input for a single *Mathematica* expression.

SyntaxLength effectively returns the position of a syntax error, if one exists. ■ If SyntaxLength returns a position past the end of the string, it indicates that the string is syntactically correct as far as it goes, but needs to be continued in order to correspond to input for a complete *Mathematica* expression. ■ See page 381. ■ See also: $SyntaxHandler.

◧ SyntaxQ

SyntaxQ["*string*"] returns True if the string corresponds to syntactically correct input for a single *Mathematica* expression, and returns False otherwise.

If SyntaxQ returns False, you can find the position of a syntax error using SyntaxLength. ■ See page 381. ■ See also: ToExpression, ToHeldExpression, $SyntaxHandler.

■ **Table**

Table[*expr*, {*imax*}] generates a list of *imax* copies of *expr*.

Table[*expr*, {*i*, *imax*}] generates a list of the values of *expr* when *i* runs from 1 to *imax*.

Table[*expr*, {*i*, *imin*, *imax*}] starts with *i* = *imin*.

Table[*expr*, {*i*, *imin*, *imax*, *di*}] uses steps *di*.

Table[*expr*, {*i*, *imin*, *imax*}, {*j*, *jmin*, *jmax*}, ...] gives a nested list. The list associated with *i* is outermost.

Table evaluates its arguments in a non-standard way (see page 730). ■ Example: Table[f[i], {i, 4}] ⟶ {f[1], f[2], f[3], f[4]}. ■ Table uses the standard *Mathematica* iteration specification. ■ Example: Table[i-j, {i, 2}, {j, 2}] ⟶ {{0, -1}, {1, 0}}. ■ You can use Table to build up vectors, matrices and tensors. ■ See page 118. ■ See also: Range, DiagonalMatrix, IdentityMatrix, Array, Do, Sum, Product.

■ **TableAlignments**

TableAlignments is an option for TableForm and MatrixForm which specifies how entries in each dimension should be aligned.

TableAlignments -> {a_1, a_2, ... } specifies alignments for successive dimensions. ■ For dimensions that are given as columns, possible alignments are Left, Center and Right. For dimensions that are given as rows, possible alignments are Bottom, Center and Top. ■ The default setting TableAlignments -> Automatic uses Left for column alignment, and Bottom for row alignment. ■ See page 357. ■ See also: TableDirections.

■ **TableDepth**

TableDepth is an option for TableForm and MatrixForm which specifies the maximum number of levels to be printed in tabular or matrix format.

TableForm[*list*, TableDepth -> *n*] prints elements in *list* below level *n* as ordinary lists, rather than arranging them in tabular form. ■ With the default setting TableDepth -> Infinity, as many levels as possible are printed in tabular form. In TableForm, the levels printed need not consist of elements with the same list structure. In MatrixForm, they must. ■ See page 357. ■ See also: TensorRank.

■ **TableDirections**

TableDirections is an option for TableForm and MatrixForm which specifies whether successive dimensions should be arranged as rows or columns.

TableDirections -> Column specifies that successive dimensions should be arranged alternately as columns and rows, with the first dimension arranged as columns. ■ TableDirections -> Row takes the first dimension to be arranged as rows. ■ TableDirections -> {dir_1, dir_2, ... } specifies explicitly whether each dimension should be arranged with Column or Row. ■ See page 356. ■ See also: TableSpacing.

■ **TableForm**

TableForm[*list*] prints with the elements of *list* arranged in an array of rectangular cells.

The height of each row and the width of each column are determined by the maximum size of an element in the row or column. ■ Unlike `MatrixForm`, `TableForm` does not require all cells in the table to be the same size. ■ `TableForm` prints a single-level list in a column. It prints a two-level list as a two-dimensional table. More deeply nested lists are by default printed with successive dimensions alternating between rows and columns. ■ The following options can be given:

TableAlignments	Automatic	how to align entries in each dimension
TableDepth	Infinity	maximum number of levels to include
TableDirections	Automatic	whether to arrange dimensions as rows or columns
TableHeadings	None	how to label table entries
TableSpacing	Automatic	how many spaces to put between entries in each dimension

■ `TableForm` acts as a "wrapper", which affects printing, but not evaluation. ■ See page 354. ■ See also: `ColumnForm`, `MatrixForm`, `GraphicsArray`.

■ **TableHeadings**

TableHeadings is an option for `TableForm` and `MatrixForm` which gives the labels to be printed for entries in each dimension of a table or matrix.

`TableHeadings -> None` gives no labels in any dimension. ■ `TableHeadings -> Automatic` gives successive integer labels for each entry in each dimension. ■ `TableHeadings -> {{lab_{11}, lab_{12}, ... }, ... }` gives explicit labels for each entry. ■ The labels can be strings or other *Mathematica* expressions. ■ The labels are placed as headings for rows or columns. ■ See page 357.

■ **TableSpacing**

TableSpacing is an option for `TableForm` and `MatrixForm` which specifies how many spaces should be left between each successive row or column.

`TableSpacing -> {s_1, s_2, ... }` specifies that s_i spaces should be left in dimension *i*. ■ For columns, the spaces are rendered as space characters. For rows, the spaces are rendered as blank lines. ■ For `TableForm`, `TableSpacing -> Automatic` yields spacings {1, 3, 0, 1, 0, 1, ... }. ■ See page 357. ■ See also: `GraphicsSpacing`.

■ **TagSet**

f/: *lhs* = *rhs* assigns *rhs* to be the value of *lhs*, and associates the assignment with the symbol *f*.

TagSet defines upvalues or downvalues as appropriate. ■ The symbol *f* in *f*/: *lhs* = *rhs* must appear in *lhs* as the head of *lhs*, the head of the head, one of the elements of *lhs*, or the head of one of the elements. ■ A common case is *f*: h[*f*[*args*]] = *rhs*. ■ You can see all the rules associated with a particular symbol by typing ?*symbol*. ■ If *f* appears several times in *lhs*, then *f*/: *lhs* = *rhs* associates the assignment with each occurrence. ■ When it appears in symbolic form, `TagSet` is treated as a scoping construct (see Section A.3.8). ■ See pages 262 and 735. ■ See also: `Set`, `UpSet`.

■ **TagSetDelayed**

f/: *lhs* := *rhs* assigns *rhs* to be the delayed value of *lhs*, and associates the assignment with the symbol *f*.

See notes for `TagSet` and `SetDelayed`. ■ See page 262.

■ **TagUnset**

f /: *lhs* =. removes any rules defined for *lhs*, associated with the symbol *f*.

Rules are removed only when their left-hand side is identical to *lhs*, and the tests in Condition given on the right-hand side are also identical. ■ See pages 718 and 736. ■ See also: Clear, Unset.

■ **Take**

Take [*list*, *n*] gives the first *n* elements of *list*.

Take [*list*, -*n*] gives the last *n* elements of *list*.

Take [*list*, {*m*, *n*}] elements *m* through *n* of *list*.

Take uses the standard *sequence specification* (see page 724). ■ Example: Take[{a,b,c,d,e}, 3] ⟶ {a, b, c}. ■ Take[{a,b,c,d,e}, -2] ⟶ {d, e}. ■ Take can be used on an object with any head, not necessarily List. ■ See page 125. ■ See also: Part, Drop, StringTake, Select, Cases.

■ **Tan**

Tan [*z*] gives the tangent of *z*.

Mathematical function (see Section A.3.9). ■ The argument of Tan is assumed to be in radians. (Multiply by Degree to convert from degrees.) ■ See page 562. ■ See also: ArcTan, Cot.

■ **Tanh**

Tanh [*z*] gives the hyperbolic tangent of *z*.

Mathematical function (see Section A.3.9). ■ See page 562. ■ See also: ArcTanh, Coth.

■ **Temporary**

Temporary is an attribute assigned to symbols which are created as local variables by Module.

Symbols with attribute Temporary are automatically removed when they are no longer needed. ■ Symbols with attribute Temporary conventionally have names of the form *aaa*$*nnn*. ■ See pages 272 and 323. ■ See also: Module, Unique.

■ **TensorRank**

TensorRank [*expr*] gives the depth to which *expr* is a full array, with all the parts at a particular level being lists of the same length.

TensorRank [*list*] is equivalent to Length [Dimensions [*list*]]. ■ Examples: TensorRank[{a,b}] ⟶ 1; TensorRank[{a,{b}}] ⟶ 1. ■ TensorRank [*expr*, *n*] tests only down to level *n*. ■ See page 668. ■ See also: Dimensions, Depth, VectorQ, MatrixQ.

■ **TeXForm**

TeXForm [*expr*] prints as a TeX language version of *expr*.

TeXForm produces plain TeX. Its output should be suitable for both LaTeX and AMSTeX. ■ TeXForm acts as a "wrapper", which affects printing, but not evaluation. ■ TeXForm translates standard mathematical functions and operations. ■ Symbols with names like alpha and ALPHA that correspond to TeX symbols are translated into their corresponding TeX symbols. ■ Following standard mathematical conventions, single-character symbol names are given in italic font, while multiple character names are given in Roman font. ■ Print forms such as ColumnForm, MatrixForm and Subscripted are translated by TeXForm. ■ See pages 183 and 344.

■ Text

Text[*expr*, *coords*] is a graphics primitive that represents text corresponding to the printed form of *expr*, centered at the point specified by *coords*.

The *text* is printed by default in OutputForm. ■ Text can be used in both two- and three-dimensional graphics. ■ The coordinates can be specified either as {*x*, *y*, ... } or as Scaled[{*x*, *y*, ... }]. ■ Text[*expr*, *coords*, *offset*] specifies an offset for the block of text relative to the coordinates given. Giving an offset {*sdx*, *sdy*} specifies that the point {*x*, *y*} should lie at relative coordinates {*sdx*, *sdy*} within the bounding rectangle that encloses the text. Each relative coordinate runs from −1 to +1 across the bounding rectangle. ■ The offsets specified need not be in the range -1 to +1. ■ Here are sample offsets to use in two-dimensional graphics:

{0, 0}	text centered at {*x*, *y*}
{-1, 0}	left-hand end at {*x*, *y*}
{1, 0}	right-hand end at {*x*, *y*}
{0, -1}	centered above {*x*, *y*}
{0, 1}	centered below {*x*, *y*}

■ Text[*expr*, *coords*, *offset*, *dir*] specifies the orientation of the text is given by the direction vector *dir*. Possible values of *dir* are:

{1, 0}	ordinary horizontal text
{0, 1}	vertical text reading from bottom to top
{0, -1}	vertical text reading from top to bottom
{-1, 0}	horizontal upside-down text

■ Text in three-dimensional graphics is placed at a position that corresponds to the projection of the point {*x*, *y*, *z*} specified. Text is drawn in front of all other objects. ■ The font for text can be specified using FontForm. If no FontForm specification is given, the font is determined from the option DefaultFont, which is by default set to the global variable $DefaultFont. ■ You can specify the color of text using CMYKColor, GrayLevel, Hue and RGBColor directives. ■ The option StringConversion for Display can be used to specify a function to be applied to strings generated from Text which contain special characters. ■ See pages 400 and 469. ■ See also: PlotLabel, AxesLabel.

■ TextForm

TextForm[*expr*] prints as a textual form of *expr*.

TextForm prints standard expressions in OutputForm. ■ TextForm prints strings in a way that corresponds to standard text. It breaks lines only at word boundaries, and does not put blank lines between lines of text. ■ See page 739.

■ Thickness

Thickness[*r*] is a graphics directive which specifies that lines which follow are to be drawn with a thickness *r*. The thickness *r* is given as a fraction of the total width of the graph.

Thickness can be used in both two- and three-dimensional graphics. ■ The initial default is Thickness[0.004] for two-dimensional graphics, and Thickness[0.001] for three-dimensional graphics ■ See page 409. ■ See also: AbsoluteThickness, PointSize, Dashing.

■ **Thread**

Thread[*f*[*args*]] "threads" *f* over any lists that appear in *args*.

Thread[*f*[*args*], *h*] threads *f* over any objects with head *h* that appear in *args*.

Thread[*f*[*args*], *h*, *n*] threads *f* over objects with head *h* that appear in the first *n* args.

Thread[*f*[*args*], *h*, -*n*] threads over the last *n* args.

Thread[*f*[*args*], *h*, {*m*, *n*}] threads over arguments *m* through *n*.

Example: Thread[f[{a,b}, c, {d,e}]] ⟶ {f[a, c, d], f[b, c, e]}. ▪ Functions with attribute Listable are automatically threaded over lists. ▪ All the elements in the specified *args* whose heads are *h* must be of the same length. ▪ Arguments that do not have head *h* are copied as many times as there are elements in the arguments that do have head *h*. ▪ **Thread** uses the standard *sequence specification* (see page 724). ▪ See page 216. ▪ See also: Distribute, Map, Inner, MapThread.

■ **ThreeJSymbol**

ThreeJSymbol[{j_1, m_1}, {j_2, m_2}, {j_3, m_3}] gives the values of the Wigner 3-j symbol.

The 3-j symbols vanish except when $m_1 + m_2 + m_3 = 0$ and the j_i satisfy a triangle inequality. ▪ The parameters of **ThreeJSymbol** can be integers, half-integers or symbolic expressions. ▪ The Clebsch-Gordan coefficients and 3-j symbols in *Mathematica* satisfy the relation $C_{m_1 m_2 m_3}^{j_1 j_2 j_3} = (-1)^{m_3 + j_1 - j_2} \sqrt{2j_3 + 1} \begin{pmatrix} j_1 & j_2 & j_3 \\ m_1 & m_2 & -m_3 \end{pmatrix}$. ▪ See page 561. ▪ See also: ClebschGordan, SixJSymbol, SphericalHarmonicY.

■ **Through**

Through[*p*[f_1, f_2][*x*]] gives *p*[f_1[*x*], f_2[*x*]].

Through[*expr*, *h*] performs the transformation wherever *h* occurs in the head of *expr*.

Example: Through[(f + g)[x, y]] ⟶ f[x, y] + g[x, y]. ▪ Through distributes operators that appear inside the heads of expressions. ▪ See page 214. ▪ See also: Operate.

■ **Throw**

Throw[*expr*] exits from nested control structures, returning the value *expr* to the nearest enclosing Catch.

You can use **Throw** and **Catch** to implement non-local returns. ▪ See page 293. ▪ See also: Return, Goto.

■ Ticks

Ticks is an option for graphics functions that specifies tick marks for axes.

The following settings can be given for Ticks:

None	no tick marks drawn
Automatic	tick marks placed automatically
{*xticks*, *yticks*, ... }	tick mark options specified separately for each axis

■ With the Automatic setting, tick marks are usually placed at points whose coordinates have the minimum number of digits in their decimal representation. ■ For each axis, the following tick mark options can be given:

None	no tick marks drawn
Automatic	tick mark positions and labels chosen automatically
$\{x_1, x_2, ... \}$	tick marks drawn at the specified positions
$\{\{x_1, label_1\}, \{x_2, label_2\}, ... \}$	tick marks drawn with the specified labels
$\{\{x_1, label_1, len_1\},... \}$	tick marks with specified scaled length
$\{\{x_1, label_1, \{plen_1, mlen_1\}\}, ... \}$	ticks marks with specified lengths in the positive and negative directions
$\{\{x_1, label_1, len_1, style_1\}, ... \}$	ticks marks with specified styles
func	a function to be applied to *xmin*, *xmax* to get the tick mark option

■ If no explicit labels are given, the tick mark labels are given as the numerical values of the tick mark positions. ■ Any expression can be given as a tick mark label. The expressions are formatted in OutputForm. ■ Tick mark lengths are given as a fraction of the distance across the whole plot. ■ Tick mark styles can involve graphics directives such as RGBColor and Thickness. ■ The tick mark function *func*[*xmin*, *xmax*] may return any other tick mark option. ■ Ticks can be used in both two- and three-dimensional graphics. ■ FullOptions gives the explicit form of Ticks specifications when Automatic settings are given. ■ See pages 420 and 463. ■ See also: Axes, AxesLabel, FrameTicks, GridLines, MeshRange.

■ TimeConstrained

TimeConstrained[*expr*, *t*] evaluates *expr*, stopping after *t* seconds.

TimeConstrained[*expr*, *t*, *failexpr*] returns *failexpr* if the time constraint is not met.

TimeConstrained generates an interrupt to abort the evaluation of *expr* if the evaluation is not completed within the specified time. ■ TimeConstrained returns $Aborted if the evaluation is aborted and no *failexpr* is specified. ■ TimeConstrained has attribute HoldFirst. ■ TimeConstrained is accurate only down to a granularity of at least $TimeUnit seconds. ■ Aborts generated by TimeConstrained are treated just like those generated by Abort, and can thus be overruled by AbortProtect. ■ See page 525. ■ See also: MemoryConstrained, Timing, $IterationLimit, $RecursionLimit, Pause.

■ Times

$x*y*z$ or $x\ y\ z$ represents a product of terms.

Times has attributes Flat, Orderless and OneIdentity. ■ The default value for arguments of Times, as used in x_. patterns, is 1. ■ Times[ ] is taken to be 1. ■ Times[x] is x. ■ 0 x evaluates to 0, but 0.0 x is left unchanged. ■ See page 47. ■ See also: Divide, NonCommutativeMultiply, Dot.

■ TimesBy

x *= c multiplies x by c and returns the new value of x.

TimesBy has the attribute HoldFirst. ■ x *= c is equivalent to $x = x*c$. ■ See page 248. ■ See also: DivideBy, AddTo, Set.

▩ TimeUsed

TimeUsed[ ] gives the total number of seconds of CPU time used so far in the current *Mathematica* session.

TimeUsed records only CPU time actually used by the *Mathematica* kernel. It does not include time used by external processes called by the kernel. It also does not include time during pauses produced by Pause. ▪ TimeUsed is accurate only down to a granularity of at least $TimeUnit seconds. ▪ See page 524. ▪ See also: Timing, SessionTime.

▩ TimeZone

TimeZone[ ] gives the time zone set for your computer system.

The time zone gives the number of hours which must be added to Greenwich mean time (GMT) to obtain local time. ▪ U.S. eastern standard time (EST) corresponds to time zone -5. ▪ Daylight saving time corrections must be included in the time zone, so U.S. eastern daylight time (EDT) corresponds to time zone -4. ▪ See page 523. ▪ See also: Date, AbsoluteTime.

▪ Timing

Timing[*expr*] evaluates *expr*, and returns a list of time used, together with the result obtained.

Timing has attribute HoldAll. ▪ Timing[*expr*;] will give {*timing*, Null}. ▪ TimeUsed is accurate only down to a granularity of at least $TimeUnit seconds. ▪ See page 525. ▪ See also: TimeUsed, TimeConstrained, SessionTime, AbsoluteTime.

▩ ToCharacterCode

ToCharacterCode["*string*"] gives a list of the integer codes corresponding to the characters in a string.

Characters can be either 8- or 16-bit. ▪ See page 366. ▪ See also: FromCharacterCode, Characters, DigitQ, LetterQ.

▩ ToDate

ToDate[*time*] converts an absolute time in seconds since the beginning of January 1, 1900 to a date of the form {*y*, *m*, *d*, *h*, *m*, *s*}.

ToDate converts between the forms returned by AbsoluteTime and Date. ▪ ToDate assumes that both the absolute time and the date are to be given in the same time zone. ▪ See page 524. ▪ See also: FromDate.

▪ ToExpression

ToExpression["*string*"] gives the expression obtained by taking *string* as *Mathematica* input.

Example: ToExpression["1 + 1"] ⟶ 2. ▪ ToExpression[{"s_1", "s_2", ... }] takes the concatenation of the strings s_i as *Mathematica* input. ▪ ToExpression prints a message and returns $Failed if it finds a syntax error. ToExpression does not call $SyntaxHandler. ▪ The strings given in ToExpression must correspond to a single *Mathematica* expression. If they do not, ToExpression returns $Failed. ▪ See page 380. ▪ See also: ToHeldExpression, SyntaxQ, SyntaxLength, ToString, Read.

■ Together

Together [*expr*] puts terms in a sum over a common denominator, and cancels factors in the result.

Example: Together[1/x + 1/(1-x)] $\longrightarrow \dfrac{1}{(1 - x)\ x}$. ■ Together makes a sum of terms into a single rational function. ■ The denominator of the result of Together is the lowest common multiple of the denominators of each of the terms in the sum. ■ Together avoids expanding out denominators unless it is necessary. ■ Together is effectively the inverse of Apart. ■ Together[*expr*, Trig -> True] treats trigonometric functions as rational functions of exponentials, and manipulates them accordingly. ■ See page 596. ■ See also: Collect, Cancel, Factor.

■ ToHeldExpression

ToHeldExpression ["*string*"] gives the expression obtained by taking *string* as *Mathematica* input, enclosed in Hold.

Example: ToHeldExpression["1 + 1"] $\longrightarrow$ Hold[1 + 1]. ■ See notes for ToExpression. ■ See page 381.

■ TokenWords

TokenWords is an option for Read and related functions which gives a list of token words to be used to delimit words.

The setting for TokenWords is a list of strings which are used as delimiters for words to be read. ■ The delimiters specified by TokenWords are themselves returned as words. ■ See page 496. ■ See also: WordSeparators.

■ ToLowerCase

ToLowerCase [*string*] yields a string in which all letters have been converted to lower case.

ToLowerCase determines the correspondence between upper- and lower-case letters from the list $Letters. ■ See page 378. ■ See also: LowerCaseQ, ToUpperCase, StringReplace, IgnoreCase.

■ ToRules

ToRules [*eqns*] takes logical combinations of equations, in the form generated by Roots and Reduce, and converts them to lists of rules, of the form produced by Solve.

Example: {ToRules[x==1 || x==2]} $\longrightarrow$ {{x -> 1}, {x -> 2}}. ■ ToRules discards nonequalities (!=), and thus gives only "generic" solutions. ■ See page 607.

■ ToString

ToString [*expr*] gives a string corresponding to the printed form of *expr*.

ToString uses OutputForm by default. ■ You can use ToString[InputForm[*expr*]] to generate a string giving the input form of *expr*. ■ ToString supports the same set of options as OpenAppend, with default settings FormatType -> OutputForm, PageWidth -> Infinity, TotalWidth -> Infinity. ■ See page 380. ■ See also: ToExpression, HoldForm, WriteString.

■ TotalHeight

TotalHeight is an option for output streams which specifies the maximum number of lines of text that should be printed for each output expression. Short forms of expressions are given if the number of lines needed to print the whole expression is too large.

TotalHeight bounds the actual numbers of lines generated. ■ TotalHeight -> Infinity allows expressions of any length to be printed. ■ SetOptions[*stream*, TotalHeight -> *n*] resets the total height allowed for an open stream. ■ See also: Short, Skeleton, PageHeight.

■ **TotalWidth**

> **TotalWidth** is an option which can be set for output streams to specify the maximum total number of characters of text that should be printed for each output expression. Short forms of expressions are given if the number of characters needed to print the whole expression is too large.
>
> TotalWidth bounds the actual numbers of characters generated. Line breaks are not counted. ▪ TotalWidth -> Infinity allows expressions of any length to be printed. ▪ SetOptions[*stream*, TotalWidth -> *n*] resets the total width allowed for an open stream. ▪ See page 517. ▪ See also: Short, Skeleton, PageWidth.

◪ **ToUpperCase**

> **ToUpperCase**[*string*] yields a string in which all letters have been converted to upper case.
>
> ToUpperCase determines the correspondence between upper- and lower-case letters from the list $Letters. ▪ See page 378. ▪ See also: UpperCaseQ, ToLowerCase, StringReplace, IgnoreCase.

◪ **Trace**

> **Trace**[*expr*] generates a list of all expressions used in the evaluation of *expr*.
>
> **Trace**[*expr*, *form*] includes only those expressions which match *form*.
>
> **Trace**[*expr*, *s*] includes all evaluations which use transformation rules associated with the symbol *s*.
>
> In general, *form* in Trace[*expr*, *form*] is compared both with each complete expression that is evaluated, and with the tag associated with any transformation rule used in the evaluation. ▪ Trace[*expr*, *lhs* -> *rhs*] picks out expressions which match *lhs*, then replaces them with *rhs* in the list returned. ▪ All expressions in the list returned by Trace are wrapped in HoldForm. ▪ Trace returns a set of nested lists. Each individual list corresponds to a single evaluation chain, which contains the sequence of forms found for a particular expression. The list has sublists which give the histories of subsidiary evaluations. ▪ Example: Trace[2 3 + 4] ⟶ {{2 3, 6}, 6 + 4, 4 + 6, 10}. ▪ The following options can be given:

MatchLocalNames	True	whether to allow x to stand for $x\$nnn$
TraceAbove	False	whether to show evaluation chains which contain the chain containing *form*
TraceBackward	False	whether to show expressions preceding *form* in the evaluation chain
TraceDepth	Infinity	how many levels of nested evaluations to include
TraceForward	False	whether to show expressions following *form* in the evaluation chain
TraceOff	None	forms within which to switch off tracing
TraceOn	_	forms within which to switch on tracing
TraceOriginal	False	whether to look at expressions before their heads and arguments are evaluated

> ▪ During the execution of Trace, the settings for the *form* argument, and for the options TraceOn and TraceOff, can be modified by resetting the values of the global variables $TracePattern, $TraceOn and $TraceOff, respectively. ▪ See page 295. ▪ See also: TraceDialog, TracePrint, TraceScan.

◪ **TraceAbove**

> **TraceAbove** is an option for Trace and related functions which specifies whether to include evaluation chains which contain the evaluation chain containing the pattern *form* sought.
>
> TraceAbove -> True includes the first and last expressions in all evaluation chains within which the evaluation chain containing *form* occurs. ▪ TraceAbove -> All includes all expressions in these evaluation chains. ▪ TraceAbove -> {*backward*, *forward*} allows you to specify separately which expressions to include in the backward and forward directions. ▪ Using TraceAbove, you can see the complete paths by which expressions matching *form* arose during an evaluation. ▪ See page 302. ▪ See also: StackComplete.

◢ TraceBackward

TraceBackward is an option for Trace and related functions which specifies whether to include preceding expressions on the evaluation chain that contains the pattern *form* sought.

TraceBackward -> True includes the first expression on the evaluation chain that contains *form*.
- TraceBackward -> All includes all expressions before *form* on the evaluation chain that contains *form*.
- TraceBackward allows you to see the previous forms that an expression had during an evaluation. ▪ See page 302.
- See also: StackComplete.

◢ TraceDepth

TraceDepth is an option for Trace and related functions which specifies the maximum nesting of evaluation chains that are to be included.

Setting TraceDepth -> *n* keeps only parts down to level *n* in nested lists generated by Trace. ▪ By setting TraceDepth, you can make Trace and related functions skip over "inner" parts of a computation, making their operation more efficient. ▪ See page 301. ▪ See also: TraceOff.

◢ TraceDialog

TraceDialog[*expr*] initiates a dialog for every expression used in the evaluation of *expr*.

TraceDialog[*expr*, *form*] initiates a dialog only for expressions which match *form*.

TraceDialog[*expr*, *s*] initiates dialogs only for expressions whose evaluations use transformation rules associated with the symbol *s*.

See notes for Trace. ▪ The expression to be evaluated when a dialog is called is given as Out[$Line] of the dialog, wrapped in HoldForm. The expression can be seen by asking for % when the dialog is first started. ▪ Any value returned from the dialog is discarded. ▪ TraceDialog[*expr*] returns the result of evaluating *expr*. ▪ See page 305.

◢ TraceForward

TraceForward is an option for Trace and related functions which specifies whether to include later expressions on the evaluation chain that contains the pattern *form* sought.

TraceForward -> True includes the final expression on the evaluation chain that contains *form*.
- TraceForward -> All includes all expressions after *form* on the evaluation chain that contains *form*.
- TraceForward allows you to see the transformations performed on an expression generated during an evaluation.
- See page 302.

◢ TraceOff

TraceOff is an option for Trace and related functions which specifies forms inside which tracing should be switched off.

The setting for TraceOff gives a pattern which is compared with expressions to be evaluated. If the pattern matches the expression, then tracing will be switched off while that expression is being evaluated. The pattern is also tested against tags associated with the evaluation. ▪ You can use TraceOff to avoid tracing inner parts of a computation. ▪ The default setting TraceOff -> None never switches off tracing. ▪ TraceOn will not work inside TraceOff. ▪ During the execution of Trace, the settings for TraceOn and TraceOff can be modified by resetting the values of the global variables $TraceOn and $TraceOff. ▪ See page 300. ▪ See also: TraceDepth, TraceOn.

◪ TraceOn

TraceOn is an option for `Trace` and related functions which specifies when tracing should be switched on.

With the setting `TraceOn -> `*patt*, `Trace` and related functions do not start tracing until they encounter expressions to evaluate which match the pattern *patt*. This pattern is also tested against tags associated with the evaluation. ▪ `TraceOff` can be used within tracing switched on by `TraceOn`. ▪ Once tracing has been switched off by `TraceOff`, however, `TraceOn` will not switch it on again. ▪ During the execution of `Trace`, the settings for `TraceOn` and `TraceOff` can be modified by resetting the values of the global variables `$TraceOn` and `$TraceOff`. ▪ See page 300. ▪ See also: `TraceOff`.

◪ TraceOriginal

TraceOriginal is an option for `Trace` and related functions which specifies whether to test the form of each expression before its head and arguments are evaluated.

With the default `TraceOriginal -> False`, the forms of expressions generated during an evaluation are tested only after their head and arguments have been evaluated. In addition, evaluation chains for expressions which do not change under evaluation are not included. ▪ With `TraceOriginal -> True`, the forms before evaluation of the head and arguments are also tested, and evaluation chains for expressions which do not change under evaluation are included. ▪ See page 303.

◪ TracePrint

TracePrint[*expr*] prints all expressions used in the evaluation of *expr*.

TracePrint[*expr*, *form*] includes only those expressions which match *form*.

TracePrint[*expr*, *s*] includes all evaluations which use transformation rules associated with the symbol *s*.

See notes for `Trace`. ▪ `TracePrint` indents its output in correspondence with the nesting levels for lists generated by `Trace`. ▪ The indentation is done using the print form defined for the object `Indent[`*d*`]`. ▪ `TracePrint` prints the forms of expressions before any of their elements are evaluated. ▪ `TracePrint` does not support the `TraceBackward` option of `Trace`. ▪ `TracePrint` yields only the forward part of the output specified by the option setting `TraceAbove -> All`. ▪ `TracePrint[`*expr*`]` returns the result of evaluating *expr*. ▪ See page 305.

◪ TraceScan

TraceScan[*f*, *expr*] applies *f* to all expressions used in the evaluation of *expr*.

TraceScan[*f*, *expr*, *form*] includes only those expressions which match *form*.

TraceScan[*f*, *expr*, *s*] includes all evaluations which use transformation rules associated with the symbol *s*.

TraceScan[*f*, *expr*, *form*, *fp*] applies *f* before evaluation and *fp* after evaluation to expressions used in the evaluation of *expr*.

See notes for `Trace`. ▪ All expressions are wrapped in `HoldForm` to prevent evaluation before *f* or *fp* are applied to them. ▪ The function *fp* is given as arguments both the form before evaluation and the form after evaluation. ▪ `TraceScan[`*f*, *expr*`]` returns the result of evaluating *expr*. ▪ See page 305.

■ **Transpose**

Transpose[*list*] transposes the first two levels in *list*.

Transpose[*list*, {n_1, n_2, ... }] transposes *list* so that the kth level in *list* is the $n_k{}^{\text{th}}$ level in the result.

Example: Transpose[{{a,b},{c,d}}] $\longrightarrow$ {{a, c}, {b, d}}. ■ Transpose gives the usual transpose of a matrix. ■ Acting on a tensor $T_{i_1 i_2 i_3...}$ Transpose gives the tensor $T_{i_2 i_1 i_3...}$. ■ See page 657. ■ See also: Flatten.

■ **TreeForm**

TreeForm[*expr*] prints with different levels in *expr* shown at different depths.

See pages 197 and 344. ■ See also: FullForm, MatrixForm.

■ **Trig**

Trig is an option for algebraic manipulation functions which specifies whether trigonometric functions should be treated as rational functions of exponentials.

With the setting Trig -> False, which is the default for all functions other than Simplify, trigonometric functions are treated as indivisible objects for the purposes of algebraic manipulation. ■ With the setting Trig -> True, trigonometric functions are treated as rational functions of exponentials for the purposes of algebraic manipulation. ■ Examples: Expand[2 Cos[x]^2, Trig->True] $\longrightarrow$ 1 + Cos[2 x]; Factor[Sin[2 x], Trig->True] $\longrightarrow$ 2 Cos[x] Sin[x]. ■ Trig works with both circular and hyperbolic trigonometric functions. ■ See page 603. ■ See also: ComplexExpand.

■ **True**

True is the symbol for the Boolean value true.

See page 93. ■ See also: True, TrueQ.

■ **TrueQ**

TrueQ[*expr*] yields True if *expr* is True, and yields False otherwise.

Example: TrueQ[x==y] $\longrightarrow$ False. ■ You can use TrueQ to "assume" that a test fails when its outcome is not clear. ■ TrueQ[*expr*] is equivalent to If[*expr*, True, False, False]. ■ See page 288. ■ See also: If, Condition, SameQ.

■ **Unequal**

lhs != *rhs* returns False if *lhs* and *rhs* are identical.

lhs != *rhs* returns True if *lhs* and *rhs* are determined to be unequal by comparisons between numbers or other raw data, such as strings. ■ Approximate numbers are considered unequal if they differ beyond their last two decimal digits. ■ e_1 != e_2 != e_3 != ... gives True only if none of the e_i are equal. 2 != 3 != 2 $\longrightarrow$ False. ■ *lhs* != *rhs* represents a symbolic condition that can be generated and manipulated by functions like Reduce and LogicalExpand. ■ Unequal[*e*] gives True. ■ See page 94. ■ See also: Equal, UnsameQ, Order.

■ **Unevaluated**

Unevaluated[*expr*] represents the unevaluated form of *expr* when it appears as the argument to a function.

f[Unevaluated[*expr*]] effectively works by temporarily setting attributes so that *f* holds its argument unevaluated, then evaluating *f*[*expr*]. ■ Example: Length[Unevaluated[1 + 1]] $\longrightarrow$ 2. ■ See page 282. ■ See also: Hold, HoldFirst, ReplaceHeldPart.

■ **Uninstall**

Uninstall[*link*] terminates an external program started by Install, and removes *Mathematica* definitions set up by it.

The argument of Uninstall is an object representing a *MathLink* link as returned by Install. ■ Uninstall calls Unset to remove definitions set up by Install. ■ See page 509. ■ See also: Install, Close.

■ **Union**

Union[*list₁*, *list₂*, ...] gives a sorted list of all the distinct elements that appear in any of the *listᵢ*.

Union[*list*] gives a sorted version of a list, in which all duplicated elements have been dropped.

If the *listᵢ* are considered as sets, Union gives their union. ■ The *listᵢ* must have the same head, but it need not be List. ■ See page 129. ■ See also: Join, Intersection, Complement.

■ **Unique**

Unique[ ] generates a new symbol, whose name is of the form $\$nnn$.

Unique[*x*] generates a new symbol, with a name of the form $x\$nnn$.

Unique[{*x*, *y*, ... }] generates a list of new symbols.

Unique["*xxx*"] generates a new symbol, with a name of the form *xxxnnn*.

Unique[*x*] numbers the symbols it creates using $ModuleNumber, and increments $ModuleNumber every time it is called. ■ Unique["*xxx*"] numbers the symbols it creates sequentially, starting at 1 for each string *xxx*. ■ Unique[*name*, {*attr₁*, *attr₂*, ... }] generates a symbol which has the attributes *attrᵢ*. ■ See page 323. ■ See also: ToExpression, Names, C, Module.

■ **Unprotect**

Unprotect[*s₁*, *s₂*, ...] removes the attribute Protected for the symbols *sᵢ*.

Unprotect["*form₁*", "*form₂*", ...] unprotects all symbols whose names textually match any of the *formᵢ*.

A typical sequence in adding your own rules for built-in functions is Unprotect[*f*] ; *definition*; Protect[*f*]. ■ See notes for Protect. ■ See pages 264 and 728. ■ See also: Protect, Locked, SetOptions.

■ **UnsameQ**

lhs =!= *rhs* yields True if the expression *lhs* is not identical to *rhs*, and yields False otherwise.

See notes for SameQ. ■ *e₁* =!= *e₂* =!= *e3* gives True if no two of the *eᵢ* are identical. ■ See page 228. ■ See also: Equal, Order.

■ **Unset**

lhs =. removes any rules defined for *lhs*.

Rules are removed only when their left-hand sides are identical to *lhs*, and the tests in Condition given on the right-hand side are also identical. ■ See pages 247 and 736. ■ See also: Clear, TagUnset.

■ Update

Update[*symbol*] tells *Mathematica* that hidden changes have been made which could affect values associated with a symbol.

Update[ ] specifies that the value of any symbol could be affected.

Update manipulates internal optimization features of *Mathematica*. It should not need to be called except under special circumstances that rarely occur in practice. ■ One special circumstance is that changes in the value of one symbol can affect the value of another symbol by changing the outcome of Condition tests. In such cases, you may need to use Update on the symbol you think may be affected. ■ Using Update will never give you incorrect results, although it will slow down the operation of the system. ■ See page 310.

■ UpperCaseQ

UpperCaseQ[*string*] yields True if all the characters in the string are upper-case letters, and yields False otherwise.

UpperCaseQ determines which characters should be considered upper-case letters from the list $Letters. ■ See page 378. ■ See also: LowerCaseQ, LetterQ, ToUpperCase, ToCharacterCode.

■ UpSet

lhs^=*rhs* assigns *rhs* to be the value of *lhs*, and associates the assignment with symbols that occur at level one in *lhs*.

f[*g*[*x*]]=*value* makes an assignment associated with *f*. *f*[*g*[*x*]]^=*value* makes an assignment associated instead with *g*. ■ UpSet associates an assignment with *all* the distinct symbols that occur either directly as arguments of *lhs*, or as the heads of arguments of *lhs*. ■ See pages 261 and 735. ■ See also: TagSet, UpValues.

■ UpSetDelayed

lhs^:=*rhs* assigns *rhs* to be the delayed value of *lhs*, and associates the assignment with symbols that occur at level one in *lhs*.

See notes for UpSet and SetDelayed. ■ See pages 260 and 261.

■ UpValues

UpValues[*f*] gives a list of transformation rules corresponding to all upvalues defined for the symbol *f*.

You can specify the upvalues for *f* by making an assignment of the form UpValues[*f*] = *list*. ■ The list returned by UpValues has elements of the form Literal[*lhs*] :> *rhs*. ■ See page 266. ■ See also: Set, DownValues.

■ ValueQ

ValueQ[*expr*] gives True if a value has been defined for *expr*, and gives False otherwise.

ValueQ has attribute HoldFirst. ■ ValueQ gives False only if *expr* would not change if it were to be entered as *Mathematica* input. ■ See page 228. ■ See also: Information.

■ Variables

Variables[*poly*] gives a list of all independent variables in a polynomial.

See page 593. ■ See also: Coefficient.

■ **VectorQ**

VectorQ[*expr*] gives True if *expr* is a list, none of whose elements are themselves lists, and gives False otherwise.

VectorQ[*expr*, *test*] gives True only if *test* yields True when applied to each of the elements in *expr*.

VectorQ[*expr*, NumberQ] tests whether *expr* is a vector of numbers.   ■ See pages 227 and 652.   ■ See also: MatrixQ, TensorRank.

■ **ViewCenter**

ViewCenter is an option for Graphics3D and SurfaceGraphics which gives the scaled coordinates of the point which appears at the center of the display area in the final plot.

With the default setting ViewCenter -> Automatic, the whole bounding box is centered in the final image area. ■ With the setting ViewCenter -> {1/2, 1/2, 1/2}, the center of the three-dimensional bounding box will be placed at the center of the final display area. ■ The setting for ViewCenter is given in scaled coordinates, which run from 0 to 1 across each dimension of the bounding box. ■ With SphericalRegion -> True, the circumscribing sphere is always centered, regardless of the setting for ViewCenter. ■ See page 443.

■ **ViewPoint**

ViewPoint is an option for Graphics3D and SurfaceGraphics which gives the point in space from which the objects plotted are to be viewed.

ViewPoint -> {*x*, *y*, *z*} gives the position of the view point relative to the center of the three-dimensional box that contains the object being plotted. ■ The view point is given in a special scaled coordinate system in which the longest side of the bounding box has length 1. The center of the bounding box is taken to have coordinates {0, 0, 0}. ■ Common settings for ViewPoint are:

{1.3, -2.4, 2}	default setting
{0, -2, 0}	directly in front
{0, -2, 2}	in front and up
{0, -2, -2}	in front and down
{-2, -2, 0}	left-hand corner
{2, -2, 0}	right-hand corner
{0, 0, 2}	directly above

■ Choosing ViewPoint further away from the object reduces the distortion associated with perspective. ■ The view point must lie outside the bounding box. ■ The coordinates of the corners of the bounding box in the special coordinate system used for ViewPoint are determined by the setting for the BoxRatios option. ■ See page 442. ■ See also: ViewCenter, ViewVertical, SphericalRegion.

■ **ViewVertical**

ViewVertical is an option for Graphics3D and SurfaceGraphics which specifies what direction in scaled coordinates should be vertical in the final image.

The default setting is ViewVertical -> {0, 0, 1}, which specifies that the *z* axis in your original coordinate system should end up vertical in the final image. ■ The setting for ViewVertical is given in scaled coordinates, which run from 0 to 1 across each dimension of the bounding box. ■ Only the direction of the vector specified by ViewVertical is important; its magnitude is irrelevant. ■ See page 443.

■ **WeierstrassP**

WeierstrassP[*u*, *g2*, *g3*] gives the Weierstrass elliptic function $\wp(u; g_2, g_3)$.

$\wp(u; g_2, g_3)$ gives the value of x for which $u = \int_\infty^x (4t^3 - g_2 t - g_3)^{-\frac{1}{2}} dt$. ■ See page 584.

■ **WeierstrassPPrime**

WeierstrassPPrime[*u*, *g2*, *g3*] gives the derivative of the Weierstrass elliptic function $\wp'(u; g_2, g_3)$.

$\wp'(u; g_2, g_3) = \frac{\partial}{\partial u} \wp(u; g_2, g_3)$. ■ See page 584.

■ **Which**

Which[*test₁*, *value₁*, *test₂*, *value₂*, ...] evaluates each of the *test$_i$* in turn, returning the value of the *value$_i$* corresponding to the first one that yields True.

Example: Which[1==2, x, 1==1, y] ⟶ y. ■ Which has attribute HoldAll. ■ If any of the *test$_i$* evaluated by Which give neither True nor False, then the whole Which object is returned unevaluated. ■ You can make Which return a "default value" by taking the last *test$_i$* to be True. ■ If all the *test$_i$* evaluate to False, Which returns Null. ■ See page 287. ■ See also: Switch.

■ **While**

While[*test*, *body*] evaluates *test*, then *body*, repetitively, until *test* first fails to give True.

While[*test*] does the loop with a null body. ■ If Break[ ] is generated in the evaluation of *body*, the While loop exits. ■ Continue[ ] exits the evaluation of *body*, and continues the loop. ■ Unless Return[ ] or Throw[ ] are generated, the final value returned by While is Null. ■ Example: i=0; While[i < 0, tot += f[i]; i++]. Note that the roles of ; and , are *reversed* relative to the C programming language. ■ See page 292. ■ See also: Do, For, Nest, Fold, Select.

■ **With**

With[{*x* = *x₀*, *y* = *y₀*, ... }, *expr*] specifies that in *expr* occurrences of the symbols *x*, *y*, ... should be replaced by *x₀*, *y₀*, ...

With allows you to define local constants. ■ With replaces symbols in *expr* only when they do not occur as local variables inside scoping constructs. ■ You can use With[{*vars*}, *body* /; *cond*] as the right-hand side of a transformation rule with a condition attached. ■ With has attribute HoldAll. ■ With is a scoping construct (see Section A.3.8). ■ With constructs can be nested in any way. ■ With implements read-only lexical variables. ■ See page 320. ■ See also: Module, Block, ReplaceAll.

■ **Word**

Word represents a word in Read, Find and related functions.

Words are defined to be sequences of characters that lie between separators. The separators are strings given as the settings for WordSeparators and RecordSeparators. ■ The default is for words to be delimited by "white space" consisting of spaces, tabs and newlines. ■ See page 495. ■ See also: Record.

■ **WordSearch**

WordSearch is an option for Find and FindList which specifies whether the text searched for must appear as a word.

With the setting WordSearch -> True, the text must appear as a word, delimited by word or record separators, as specified by WordSeparators or RecordSeparators. ■ See page 501. ■ See also: AnchoredSearch.

◪ WordSeparators

WordSeparators is an option for Read, Find and related functions which specifies the list of strings to be taken as delimiters for words.

The default setting is WordSeparators -> {" ", "\t"}. ▪ Strings used as word separators may contain several characters. ▪ The characters may be either 8- or 16-bit. ▪ With the option setting NullWords -> False, any number of word separators may appear between any two successive words.
▪ WordSeparators -> {{$lsep_1$, ... }, {$rsep_1$, ... }} specifies different left and right separators for words. Words must have a left separator at the beginning, and a right separator at the end, and cannot contain any separators.
▪ Strings given as record separators are automatically taken as word separators. ▪ See page 495. ▪ See also: RecordSeparators, TokenWords.

■ WorkingPrecision

WorkingPrecision is an option for various numerical operations which specifies how many digits of precision should be maintained in internal computations.

WorkingPrecision is an option for such functions as NIntegrate and FindRoot. ▪ Setting WorkingPrecision->n causes all internal computations to be done to at most n-digit precision. ▪ Even if internal computations are done to n-digit precision, the final results you get may have much lower precision. ▪ See page 687. ▪ See also: AccuracyGoal, Precision, Accuracy, N.

■ Write

Write[*channel*, *expr_1*, *expr_2*, ...] writes the expressions *expr_i* in sequence, followed by a newline, to the specified output channel.

The output channel can be a single file or pipe, or list of them, each specified by a string giving their name, or by an OutputStream object. ▪ Write is the basic *Mathematica* output function. Print and Message are defined in terms of it. ▪ If any of the specified files or pipes are not already open, Write calls OpenWrite to open them. ▪ Write does not close files and pipes after it finishes writing to them. ▪ By default, Write generates output in the form specified by the setting of the FormatType option for the output stream used. ▪ See page 485. ▪ See also: Print, Display, Message, Read.

■ WriteString

WriteString[*channel*, *expr_1*, *expr_2*, ...] converts the *expr_i* to strings, and then writes them in sequence to the specified output channel.

WriteString uses the InputForm of the *expr_i*. ▪ WriteString allows you to create files which are effectively just streams of bytes. ▪ WriteString does not put a newline at the end of the output it generates. ▪ See notes for Write.
▪ See page 485.

■ Xor

Xor[e_1, e_2, ...] is the logical XOR (exclusive OR) function.

It gives True if an odd number of the e_i are True, and the rest are False. It gives False if an even number of the e_i are True, and the rest are False.

Xor gives symbolic results when necessary, and applies various simplification rules to them. ▪ Unlike And and Or, Xor is not a control structure, and does not have attribute HoldAll. ▪ See page 94. ▪ See also: LogicalExpand.

■ ZeroTest

ZeroTest is an option for LinearSolve and other linear algebra functions, which gives a function to be applied to combinations of matrix elements to determine whether or not they should be considered equal to zero.

The default setting is typically ZeroTest -> (Together[#]==0 &). ■ For matrices with symbolic entries, ZeroTest->(Expand[#]==0 &) is often appropriate. ■ See page 662. ■ See also: Modulus, SameTest.

■ Zeta

Zeta[s] gives the Riemann zeta function $\zeta(s)$.

Zeta[s, a] gives the generalized Riemann zeta function $\zeta(s, a)$.

Mathematical function (see Section A.3.9). ■ $\zeta(s) = \sum_{k=1}^{\infty} k^{-s}$. ■ $\zeta(s, a) = \sum_{k=0}^{\infty} (k + a)^{-s}$, where any term with $k + a = 0$ is excluded. ■ See page 571. ■ See also: PolyLog, LerchPhi, RiemannSiegelZ, PrimePi.

■ $Aborted

$Aborted is a special symbol that is returned as the result from a calculation that has been aborted.

See page 311. ■ See also: Abort, Interrupt.

■ $BatchInput

$BatchInput is True if input in the current session is being fed directly to the *Mathematica* kernel in batch mode.

$BatchInput is True if input is being taken from a file. ■ $BatchInput can be reset during a *Mathematica* session. ■ When $BatchInput is True, *Mathematica* terminates if it ever receives an interrupt, does not discard input when blank lines are given, and terminates when it receives end-of-file. ■ See page 529. ■ See also: $IgnoreEOF, $BatchOutput, $Linked, $Notebooks.

■ $BatchOutput

$BatchOutput is True if output in the current session is being sent in batch mode, suitable for reading by other programs.

The initial value of $BatchOutput is typically determined by a command-line option when the *Mathematica* session is started. ■ $BatchOutput can be reset during a *Mathematica* session. ■ When $BatchOutput is set to True, *Mathematica* generates all output in InputForm, with the PageWidth option effectively set to Infinity, does not give In and Out labels, and does not give any banner when it starts up. ■ See page 529. ■ See also: $BatchInput, $Linked, $CommandLine.

■ $CommandLine

$CommandLine is a list of strings giving the elements of the original operating system command line with which *Mathematica* was invoked.

See page 529. ■ See also: Environment, $BatchInput, $BatchOutput, $Linked, In.

■ $Context

$Context is a global variable that gives the current context.

Contexts are specified by strings of the form "*name*`". ■ $Context is modified by Begin, BeginPackage, End and EndPackage. ■ $Context is a rough analog for *Mathematica* symbols of the current working directory for files in many operating systems. ■ See page 333. ■ See also: Context.

■ **$ContextPath**

$ContextPath is a global variable that gives a list of contexts, after $Context, to search in trying to find a symbol that has been entered.

Each context is specified by a string of the form "*name*`". ■ The elements of $ContextPath are tested in order to try and find a context containing a particular symbol. ■ $ContextPath is modified by Begin, BeginPackage, End and EndPackage. ■ $ContextPath is a rough analog for *Mathematica* symbols of the "search path" for files in many operating systems. ■ See page 334.

◪ **$CreationDate**

$CreationDate gives the date and time at which the particular release of the *Mathematica* kernel you are running was created.

$CreationDate is in the form {*year*, *month*, *day*, *hour*, *minute*, *second*} returned by Date. ■ See page 529. ■ See also: $DumpDates, $VersionNumber, $ReleaseNumber, FileDate.

◪ **$DefaultFont**

$DefaultFont gives the default font to use for text in graphics.

The value of $DefaultFont must be of the form {"*font*", *size*}, where *font* gives the name of the font to use, and *size* gives its size in printer's points. ■ $DefaultFont is the default setting for the option DefaultFont. ■ The initial value for $DefaultFont is typically {"Courier", 10}. ■ See notes for FontForm. ■ See page 467.

■ **$Display**

$Display gives a list of files and pipes to be used with the default $DisplayFunction.

The initial setting of $Display is {}. ■ See pages 518 and 742.

■ **$DisplayFunction**

$DisplayFunction gives the default setting for the option DisplayFunction in graphics functions.

The initial setting of $DisplayFunction is Display[$Display, #]&. ■ $DisplayFunction is typically set to a procedure which performs the following: (1) open an output channel; (2) send a PostScript prolog to the output channel; (3) use Display to send PostScript graphics; (4) send PostScript epilog; (5) close the output channel and execute the external commands needed to produce actual display. ■ See pages 399 and 742. ■ See also: Display, Put, Run, $SoundDisplayFunction.

◪ **$DumpDates**

$DumpDates gives the list of all dates and times at which Dump was used in creating the *Mathematica* system you are running.

The elements of $DumpDates are given in the form {*year*, *month*, *day*, *hour*, *minute*, *second*} returned by Date. ■ On systems that do not Dump, $DumpDates is always {}. On such systems, $DumpSupported is False. ■ When you run a *Mathematica* system created with Dump, the last element of $DumpDates gives the time at which Dump was called to create that system. ■ See page 529. ■ See also: $CreationDate, $VersionNumber, $ReleaseNumber, FileDate.

◪ **$DumpSupported**

$DumpSupported is True if Dump can be used in the version of *Mathematica* you are running, and is False otherwise.

$DumpSupported is True on most systems that support virtual memory. ■ See page 530. ■ See also: Dump.

■ **$Echo**

$Echo gives a list of files and pipes to which all input is echoed.

You can use $Echo to keep a file of all your input commands. ■ See pages 518 and 742.

■ **$Epilog**

$Epilog is a symbol whose value, if any, is evaluated when a dialog or a *Mathematica* session is terminated.

For *Mathematica* sessions, $Epilog is conventionally defined to read in a file named end.m. ■ See page 519. ■ See also: Exit, Quit, Dialog.

◪ **$Failed**

$Failed is a special symbol returned by certain functions when they cannot do what they were asked to do.

Get returns $Failed when it cannot find the file or other object that was specified. ■ See page 477.

■ **$IgnoreEOF**

$IgnoreEOF specifies whether *Mathematica* should terminate when it receives an end-of-file character as input.

$IgnoreEOF defaults to False. ■ $IgnoreEOF is assumed to be False if the input to *Mathematica* comes from a file, rather than an interactive device. ■ See pages 520 and 748. ■ See also: Exit, Quit, $BatchInput.

◪ **$Input**

$Input is a global variable whose value is the name of the stream from which input to *Mathematica* is currently being sought.

During the execution of <<*file*, $Input is set to "*file*". ■ During interactive input, $Input is "". ■ See page 519. ■ See also: Get, Streams, $BatchInput.

◪ **$Inspector**

$Inspector is a global variable which gives a function to apply when the inspector is invoked from an interrupt menu.

The argument supplied is the number of nested invocations of the inspector that are in use. ■ The default value of $Inspector is Dialog[ ]&. ■ See page 744. ■ See also: Interrupt.

◪ **$IterationLimit**

$IterationLimit gives the maximum length of evaluation chain used in trying to evaluate any expression.

$IterationLimit limits the number of times *Mathematica* tries to re-evaluate a particular expression.
■ $IterationLimit gives an upper limit on the length of any list that can be generated by Trace. ■ See page 309.
■ See also: $RecursionLimit.

◩ $Language

$Language is a list of strings which give the names of languages to use for messages.

All language names are conventionally given in English, and are capitalized, as in "French". ▪ When a message with a name s::tag is requested either internally or through the Message function, *Mathematica* searches for messages with names s::tag::$lang_i$ corresponding to the entries "$lang_i$" in the list $Language. Only if it fails to find any of these messages will it use the message with the actual name s::tag. ▪ See pages 391 and 519. ▪ See also: MessageName.

◩ $Letters

$Letters is a list containing characters which are to be treated as letters.

The lower- and upper-case forms of a particular letter can be given in a sublist.

The default value for $Letters is {{"a", "A"}, {"b", "B"}, ... , {"z", "Z"}}. ▪ Letters that do not have lower- and upper-case forms are given directly in the list $Letters, rather than in sublists. ▪ The value of $Letters is used by functions such as LetterQ and ToUpperCase. ▪ The order of elements in $Letters is not significant. ▪ See page 379. ▪ See also: $StringOrder.

■ $Line

$Line is a global variable that specifies the number of the current input line.

You can reset $Line. ▪ See page 513. ▪ See also: In, Out.

◩ $Linked

$Linked is True if the *Mathematica* kernel is being run through *MathLink*.

$Linked is True when *Mathematica* is being run with a front end. ▪ $Linked is typically False when *Mathematica* is being run with a text-based interface. ▪ See page 529. ▪ See also: $CommandLine, $BatchInput, $BatchOutput, $Notebooks.

◩ $LinkSupported

$LinkSupported is True if *MathLink* can be used in the version of *Mathematica* you are running, and is False otherwise.

$LinkSupported is True on all Unix-based systems, and on most systems that support multitasking. ▪ See page 530. ▪ See also: $PipeSupported.

◩ $MachineEpsilon

$MachineEpsilon gives the smallest machine-precision number which can be added to 1.0 to give a result not equal to 1.0.

$MachineEpsilon is typically 2^{-n+1}, where n is the number of binary bits used in the internal representation of machine-precision floating-point numbers. ▪ $MachineEpsilon measures the granularity of machine-precision numbers. ▪ See page 546. ▪ See also: $MachinePrecision, $MinMachineNumber, $MaxMachineNumber.

◩ $MachineID

$MachineID is a string which gives, if possible, a unique identification code for the computer being used.

On many computers, $MachineID is the "mathid" string printed by the external program mathinfo. ▪ See page 530. ▪ See also: $System, $MachineName.

◢ $MachineName

$MachineName is a string which gives the assigned name of the computer being used, if such a name is defined.

For many classes of computers, $MachineName is the network host name. ▪ $MachineName is "" if no name is defined. ▪ See page 530. ▪ See also: $System, $MachineID.

◢ $MachinePrecision

$MachinePrecision gives the number of decimal digits of precision used for machine-precision numbers.

A typical value of $MachinePrecision is 16. ▪ $MachinePrecision gives the default precision assumed for approximate real numbers where few explicit digits are entered. ▪ $MachinePrecision is the default precision used by N and other numerical functions. ▪ See pages 540 and 546. ▪ See also: $MachineEpsilon, $MinMachineNumber, $MaxMachineNumber.

◢ $MachineType

$MachineType is a string giving the general type of computer on which *Mathematica* is being run.

$MachineType is intended to reflect general machine architecture, rather than particular manufacturers or models. ▪ Typical values are "Macintosh", "IBM PC", "SPARC", "VAX". ▪ See page 530. ▪ See also: $OperatingSystem, $System.

◢ $MaxMachineNumber

$MaxMachineNumber is the largest machine-precision number that can be used on a particular computer system.

Numbers larger than $MaxMachineNumber are represented in arbitrary-precision form. ▪ $MaxMachineNumber is typically 2^n, where n is the maximum exponent that can be used in the internal representation of machine-precision numbers. ▪ See page 546. ▪ See also: $MinMachineNumber, $MachineEpsilon, $MachinePrecision.

◢ $MessageList

$MessageList is a global variable that gives a list of the names of messages generated during the evaluation of the current input line.

Whenever a message is output, its name, wrapped with HoldForm is appended to $MessageList. ▪ With the standard *Mathematica* main loop, $MessageList is reset to {} when the processing of a particular input line is complete. ▪ You can reset $MessageList during a computation. ▪ See page 389. ▪ See also: MessageList, Check.

◢ $MessagePrePrint

$MessagePrePrint is a global variable whose value, if set, is applied to expressions before they are included in the text of messages.

The default value of $MessagePrePrint is Short. ▪ $MessagePrePrint is applied after each expression is wrapped with HoldForm. ▪ See pages 388 and 519. ▪ See also: $PrePrint.

◼ $Messages

$Messages gives the list of files and pipes to which message output is sent.

Output from Message is always given on the $Messages channel. ▪ See pages 518 and 742.

◼ **$MinMachineNumber**

$MinMachineNumber is the smallest positive machine-precision number that can be used on a particular computer system.

See notes for $MaxMachineNumber. ▪ See page 546.

◼ **$ModuleNumber**

$ModuleNumber gives the current serial number to be used for local variables that are created.

$ModuleNumber is incremented every time Module or Unique is called. ▪ Every *Mathematica* session starts with $ModuleNumber set to 1. ▪ You can reset $ModuleNumber to any positive integer, but if you do so, you run the risk of creating naming conflicts. ▪ See page 322. ▪ See also: $SessionID, Temporary.

◼ **$NewMessage**

$NewMessage is a global variable which, if set, is applied to the symbol name and tag of messages that are requested but have not yet been defined.

$NewMessage is applied to the symbol name, tag and language of a message if an explicit language is specified. ▪ *Mathematica* looks for the value of *name*::*tag* or *name*::*tag*::*lang* after $NewMessage has been applied. ▪ You can set up $NewMessage to read the text of messages from files when they are first needed. ▪ A typical value for $NewMessage might be Function[ToExpression[FindList[*files*, ToString[MessageName[#1, #2]]]]]. ▪ See page 390. ▪ See also: $NewSymbol.

◼ **$NewSymbol**

$NewSymbol is a global variable which, if set, is applied to the name and context of each new symbol that *Mathematica* creates.

The name and context of the symbol are given as strings. ▪ $NewSymbol is applied before the symbol is actually created. If the action of $NewSymbol causes the symbol to be created, perhaps in a different context, then the symbol as created will be the one used. ▪ $NewSymbol is applied even if a symbol has already been created with a Stub attribute by DeclarePackage. ▪ $NewSymbol is not applied to symbols automatically created by scoping constructs such as Module. ▪ See page 386. ▪ See also: DeclarePackage, $NewMessage.

◼ **$Notebooks**

$Notebooks is True if *Mathematica* is being used with a notebook-based front end.

$Notebooks is automatically set by the front end when it starts the *Mathematica* kernel. ▪ See page 529. ▪ See also: $Linked, $BatchInput.

◼ **$OperatingSystem**

$OperatingSystem is a string giving the type of operating system under which *Mathematica* is being run.

Typical values for $OperatingSystem are "Unix", "MS-DOS", "MacOS" and "VMS". ▪ $OperatingSystem typically has the same value for different versions or variants of a particular operating system. ▪ See page 530. ▪ See also: $MachineType, $System.

◼ **$Output**

$Output gives the list of files and pipes to which standard output from *Mathematica* is sent.

Output from Print is always given on the $Output channel. ▪ See pages 518 and 742. ▪ See also: Streams.

◪ $Packages

$Packages gives a list of the contexts corresponding to all packages which have been loaded in your current *Mathematica* session.

$Packages is updated when EndPackage is executed. ▪ $Packages is used by Needs to determine whether a particular package needs to be loaded explicitly. ▪ See page 338. ▪ See also: Contexts, $ContextPath, DeclarePackage.

■ $Path

$Path gives a list of directories to search in attempting to find an external file.

$Path is used by Get. ▪ The structure of directory and file names may differ from one computer system to another. ▪ The directory names are specified by strings. The full file names tested are of the form *directory*/*name*, where the separator / is taken to be the appropriate one for the computer system used. ▪ On most computer systems, the following special characters can be used in directory names:

.   the current directory
..   the directory one level up in the hierarchy
~   the user's home directory

▪ See page 490. ▪ See also: Directory, SetDirectory.

◪ $PipeSupported

$PipeSupported is True if pipes can be used in the version of *Mathematica* you are running, and is False otherwise.

$PipeSupported is True on all Unix-based systems, and on most systems that support multitasking. ▪ See page 530. ▪ See also: $LinkSupported.

■ $Post

$Post is a global variable whose value, if set, is applied to every output expression.

See page 514. ▪ See also: $Pre, $PrePrint.

■ $Pre

$Pre is a global variable whose value, if set, is applied to every input expression.

Unless $Pre is assigned to be a function which holds its arguments unevaluated, input expressions will be evaluated before $Pre is applied, so the effect of $Pre will be the same as $Post. ▪ $Pre is applied to expressions, while $PreRead is applied to strings which have not yet been parsed into expressions. ▪ See page 514. ▪ See also: $Post.

■ $PrePrint

$PrePrint is a global variable whose value, if set, is applied to every expression before it is printed.

$PrePrint is applied after Out[*n*] is assigned, but before the output result is printed. ▪ See page 514. ▪ See also: $Post, $MessagePrePrint.

◪ $PreRead

$PreRead is a global variable whose value, if set, is applied to the text of every input expression before it is fed to *Mathematica*.

$PreRead is always applied to each complete input string that will be fed to *Mathematica*. ■ In multiline input with a text-based interface, **$PreRead** is typically applied to the input so far whenever each line is terminated. ■ **$PreRead** is applied to all strings returned by a **$SyntaxHandler** function. ■ **$PreRead** is applied before **InString**[*n*] is assigned. ■ See page 514. ■ See also: **StringReplace**, **ToExpression**.

■ $RecursionLimit

$RecursionLimit gives the current limit on the number of levels of recursion that *Mathematica* can use.

$RecursionLimit=*n* sets the limit on the number of recursion levels that *Mathematica* can use to be *n*. ■ **$RecursionLimit=Infinity** removes any limit on the number of recursion levels. ■ **$RecursionLimit** gives the maximum length of the stack returned by **Stack[ ]**. ■ Each time the evaluation of a function requires the nested evaluation of the same or another function, one recursion level is used up. ■ On most computers, each level of recursion uses a certain amount of stack space. **$RecursionLimit** allows you to control the amount of stack space that *Mathematica* can use from within *Mathematica*. On some computer systems, your whole *Mathematica* session may crash if you allow it to use more stack space than the computer system allows. ■ **MemoryInUse** and related functions do not count stack space. ■ See pages 308 and 309. ■ See also: **$IterationLimit**, **MemoryConstrained**.

◪ $ReleaseNumber

$ReleaseNumber is an integer which gives the current *Mathematica* kernel release number, and increases in successive releases.

Each released revision of the *Mathematica* kernel for any particular computer system is assigned a new release number. ■ The same source code may yield releases with different numbers on different computer systems. ■ See page 529. ■ See also: **$VersionNumber**.

◪ $SessionID

$SessionID is a number set up to be unique to a particular *Mathematica* session.

$SessionID should be different for different *Mathematica* sessions run either on the same computer or on different computers. ■ The value of **$SessionID** is based on **$MachineID**, as well as **AbsoluteTime[ ]** and operating system parameters such as the *Mathematica* process ID. ■ See pages 324 and 530. ■ See also: **$ModuleNumber**.

◪ $SoundDisplayFunction

$SoundDisplayFunction gives the default setting for the option **DisplayFunction** in sound functions.

The initial setting of **$SoundDisplayFunction** is **Display[$SoundDisplay, #]&**. ■ See page 476. ■ See also: **Play**, **ListPlay**, **Show**, **$DisplayFunction**.

◪ $StringConversion

$StringConversion gives the default setting for the option **StringConversion** in output functions.

The initial setting of **$StringConversion** is **None**, which specifies that no conversion should be done on strings containing special characters. ■ Resetting the value of **$StringConversion** during a *Mathematica* session has an immediate effect on standard *Mathematica* output. ■ See notes for **StringConversion**. ■ See page 371. ■ See also: **$DisplayFunction**.

▨ $StringOrder

$StringOrder gives the ordering of characters to be used in sorting strings and symbol names.

The default value of **$StringOrder** is {{"a", "A"}, {"b", "B"}, ... , {"z", "Z"}, "0", "1", ... , "9"}. ▪ In comparing two strings, *Mathematica* first ignores any characters that do not appear anywhere in **$StringOrder**, and treats characters which appear in the same sublist in **$StringOrder** as equivalent. If two strings are equivalent according to this procedure, *Mathematica* then takes account of the ordering of characters in the sublists of **$StringOrder**. If two strings are still equivalent, *Mathematica* then compares characters which are not in **$StringOrder**. It takes shorter sequences of such characters to be before longer ones, and it sorts the characters themselves according to their integer character codes. ▪ The default value of **$StringOrder** yields essentially the standard order used for English-language indices. ▪ Setting **$StringOrder = {}** causes all ordering to be done according to character codes. ▪ The value of **$StringOrder** determines the canonical ordering of strings and symbol names used by orderless functions, as well as by **Sort**, **OrderedQ** and **Order**. ▪ See page 379. ▪ See also: **$LetterQ**.

▨ $SyntaxHandler

$SyntaxHandler is a global variable which, if set, is applied to any input string that is found to contain a syntax error.

The arguments given to **$SyntaxHandler** are the complete input string and an integer specifying the character position at which the syntax error was detected. ▪ The first character in the string is taken to have position 1. ▪ Any string returned by **$SyntaxHandler** is used as a new version of the input string, and is fed to *Mathematica*. ▪ If **$SyntaxHandler** returns **$Failed**, input to *Mathematica* is abandoned if possible. ▪ Input is not assigned to **InString[*n*]** until after **$SyntaxHandler** is applied. ▪ **$SyntaxHandler** is not called for input from files obtained using **Get**. ▪ See page 514. ▪ See also: **SyntaxLength**, **SyntaxQ**.

▧ $System

$System is a string specifying the type of computer system used.

Computer systems with the same values of **$System** should be binary compatible, so that the same compiled external programs can run on them. ▪ See page 530. ▪ See also: **$Version**, **$MachineType**, **$OperatingSystem**.

▨ $TimeUnit

$TimeUnit gives the minimum time interval in seconds recorded on your computer system.

On many systems **$TimeUnit** is equal to 1/60. ▪ **$TimeUnit** determines the minimum granularity of measurement in functions like **Timing** and **Date**. ▪ In some functions the actual time granularity may be larger than **$TimeUnit**. ▪ See page 524.

▧ $Urgent

$Urgent gives the list of files and pipes to which urgent output from *Mathematica* is sent.

Urgent output includes input prompts, and results from ?*name* information requests. ▪ See pages 518 and 742.

▧ $Version

$Version is a string that represents the version of *Mathematica* you are running.

See page 529. ▪ See also: **$System**.

◪ $VersionNumber

$VersionNumber is a real number which gives the current *Mathematica* kernel version number, and increases in successive versions.

To find out if you are running under Version 2.0 or above, you can use the test `TrueQ[$VersionNumber >= 2.0]`. ■ A version with a particular number is typically derived from the same source code on all computer systems. ■ See page 529. ■ See also: **$ReleaseNumber**.

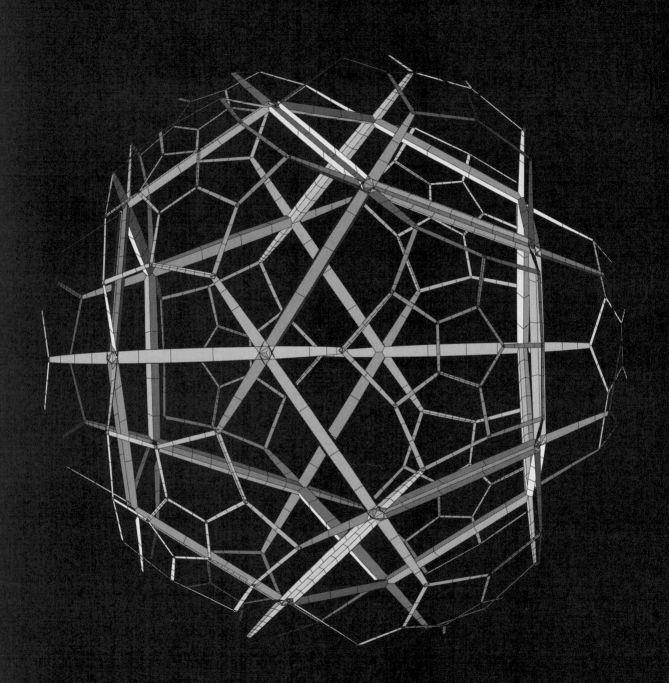

Index